1980-81 EDITION

ARTHUR FROMMER'S

DOLLARWI$E
GUIDE TO
Canada

By
John Godwin
Tom Brosnahan
Marilyn Wood

Sponsored by

CP Air
Canadian Pacific

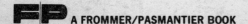

F/P A FROMMER/PASMANTIER BOOK

Excerpts from "The Spell of The Yukon" by Robert W. Service from *The Collected Poems of Robert Service* reprinted by permission of McGraw-Hill Ryerson Limited, Canada; Dodd, Mead & Company, U.S.A.; and Ernest Benn Limited, England.

Published by Frommer/Pasmantier Publishers
A Simon & Schuster Division of
Gulf & Western Corporation
380 Madison Avenue
New York, NY 10017

ISBN 0-671-25179-1

Manufactured in the United States of America

Cover photo by Eric Carle/Shostal Associates

*Although every effort was made to ensure the accuracy
of price information appearing in this book,
it should be kept in mind that prices
can and do fluctuate in the course of time.*

CONTENTS

MAPS

Publisher's Note

Canada is a *big* country, too big for one person to research adequately alone. And for this reason we asked three seasoned travel writers—all professionals—to divide up this huge area, each taking a section. The result is this edition of *A Dollarwise Guide to Canada.*

Part One, "Atlantic Canada," covering the provinces of Nova Scotia, New Brunswick, Prince Edward Island, Newfoundland and Labrador, and Québec, was prepared by Tom Brosnahan. "Central Canada," Part Two, written by Marilyn Wood, covers the heartland, the provinces of Ontario (including the capital, Ottawa), Manitoba, and Saskatchewan. John Godwin prepared the overall introductory chapters, and wrote Part Three, "Western Canada," covering the provinces of Alberta and British Columbia, and the Northwest and Yukon Territories. Each author has a distinct style of writing, and although the book was edited to provide a sense of unity and continuity, each of the three parts retains its own special flavor.

Inflation Alert!

The authors of this book have spent laborious hours attempting to ensure the accuracy of the information and prices appearing in this book. As we go to press, we believe we have obtained the most reliable data possible. Nonetheless, in the lifetime of this edition—particularly in its second year (1981)—the wise traveler will add at least 10% to 15% to the prices quoted in these pages.

Currency Note: Unless otherwise stated, *prices are quoted in Canadian dollars* throughout this guidebook.

A DOLLARWISE GUIDE TO CANADA

1. A Capsule History
2. The Original Canadians
3. Fauna and Fish

FOR AN AMERICAN, a trip to Canada is like going abroad and staying home at the same time. Therein lies the peculiar charm of the U.S.'s big, amiable neighbor in the north.

The surface features of the country evoke instant familiarity. Her currency and traffic regulations, slang terms and fashion styles, supermarkets, fast-food chains, and TV commercials, plus a thousand other home touches can give you the impression that you've strayed into a vast elongation of your own backyard. Yet Canada is also uniquely *different,* and exploring those differences will be the most fascinating aspect of your trip.

For a start, she is so much roomier that the sheer amount of elbow space makes you dizzy. Measuring 3.8 million square miles, (200,000 more than the U.S.A.), Canada ranks second in size after Russia. This colossal expanse, however, contains only 23 million people—barely 3 million more than California. What's more, the overwhelming majority of them cluster in a relatively narrow southern belt that boasts all of the nation's large cities and nearly all of her industries. As you head north, the landscape becomes emptier and emptier, until you reach an endless majestic wilderness almost devoid of human habitation.

The big metropolitan centers of the south—chic Montréal, dynamic Toronto, panoramic Vancouver—resemble somewhat better scrubbed and considerably safer counterparts of major U.S. cities. The silent north of the Yukon and Northwest Territories—where 51,000 people dot 1½ million square miles —remains a pioneer frontier, a mysterious vastness stretching to the Arctic shores, embracing thousands of lakes no one has ever charted, counted, or named.

Canada's people are even more diverse than her scenery. In the eastern province of Québec live six million French Canadians, whose motto *Je me souviens*—"I remember"—has kept them "more French than France" through two centuries of Anglo domination. They have transformed Canada into a bilingual country where everything official—including parking tickets and airline passes—comes in two tongues.

The English-speaking majority of the populace is a mosaic rather than a block. Two massive waves of immigration—one before 1914, the other between 1945 and 1972—poured 6½ million assorted Europeans and Americans into the country, providing muscles and skills as well as a kaleidoscope of cultures. Thus Nova Scotia is as Scottish as haggis and kilts, Vancouver has a Germanic core alongside a Chinatown, the plains of Manitoba are sprinkled with the onion-shaped domes of Ukrainian churches, and Ontario offers Italian street markets and a Shakespeare Festival at—yes, Stratford, Ontario.

You can join an Indian tribal pow-wow, a Chinese New Year dragon parade, an Eskimo spring celebration, a German bierfest, a Highland gathering, or a Slavic folk dance. There are group settlements on the prairies where the working parlance is Danish or Czech or Hungarian, and entire villages that speak Icelandic. For Canada has not been a "melting pot" in our sense, but sought "unity through diversity" as a national ideal.

The important thing is that you'll be made welcome everywhere—regardless whether the locals say *bienvenue, kalosoresate, bitaemo,* or *wilkommen!*

Officially, Canada is a member of the British Commonwealth of Nations, but her ties with the Old Country are sentimental and historical rather than political. Britain's Queen Elizabeth II is also Queen of Canada, which makes the country—theoretically—a monarchy. In practice, executive power rests with the prime minister and Parliament. Canada today is as independent as any member of the United Nations.

Yet the bonds of tradition remain: some quaint, some beautiful, some very useful indeed. They become visible in towns like Victoria, as regally English as Big Ben, in the scarlet coats and bearskins of the soldiers "trooping the colour" at Government House in Ottawa, in the profusion of British merchandise in the stores and Olde English shingles and inn signs all over the country. Less visible but most pervasive is the British style of law enforcement, which keeps Canada's streets safe and her ratio of criminality minuscule by U.S. standards.

Canada's traditional hospitality, however—which can be overwhelming—has nothing to do with any particular ethnic background. It is the essence of a pioneering people not yet far removed from an age when hospitality could mean the difference between death and survival. The stranger you fed and sheltered today might do the same for you tomorrow. It's an almost legendary characteristic of Newfoundland, Canada's youngest province, affectionately known as "Newfie." There, a quest for directions often leads to an invitation to a meal of the local specialty, salt beef and bannock. Or more likely, an offer of a noggin of "screech," an absolutely fiendish rum concoction guaranteed to straighten curly hair and keep drowning fishermen afloat in a North Atlantic gale.

1. A Capsule History

The Vikings landed in Canada over 1000 years ago, but it was the French who got the first toehold on the country. In 1608, Samuel de Champlain established a settlement on the cliffs overlooking the St. Lawrence River—today's Québec City. This was exactly a year after the Virginia Company founded Jamestown. Hundreds of miles of unexplored wilderness lay between the embryo colonies, but they were inexorably headed on a collision course.

The early stages of the struggle for the new continent were explorations, and there the French outdid the English. Their *coureurs de bois*—adventurous fur traders—their navigators, soldiers, and missionaries opened up not only Canada but most of the U.S. At least 35 of the 50 United States were either discovered, mapped, or settled by Frenchmen, who left behind some 4000 place names to prove it, among them Detroit, St. Louis, New Orleans, Duluth, and Des Moines.

Gradually they staked out an immense colonial empire which, in patches and minus recognized borders, stretched from Hudson's Bay in the Arctic to the Gulf of Mexico. Christened New France, it was run on an ancient seignorial system, whereby settlers were granted land by the Crown in return for military service.

The military part was essential, for the colony knew hardly a moment of peace during its existence. New France blocked the path of western expansion by England's seaboard colonies with a string of forts that lined the Ohio-Mississippi Valley. The Anglo-Americans were determined to break through, and so the frontier clashes crackled and flared, with the Indian tribes participating ferociously. These miniature wars were nightmares of savagery, waged with knives and tomahawks as much as with muskets and cannon, with raids and counterraids, burning villages, and massacred women and children. According to some historians, the English introduced scalping to America by offering a cash bounty for each French scalp the Indian braves brought in!

The French retaliated in kind. They converted the Abenaki tribe to Christianity and encouraged them to raid deep into New England territory where, in 1704, they totally destroyed the town of Deerfield, Massachusetts. The Americans answered with a punitive blitz expedition by the famous greenclad Roger's Rangers, who wiped out the Abenaki head village and slaughtered half its population.

By far the most dreaded of the redskins were the Iroquois, who played the same role in the Canadian east as the Sioux (another French label) played in the American west. Although unspeakably cruel (their torture techniques can't be described here), the Iroquois were also astute politicians who learned how to play off the English against the French and vice versa, lending their scalping knives now to one side, then to the other. It took more than a century before they finally succumbed to the white man's smallpox, firewater, and gunpowder . . . in that order.

In this border warfare a young Virginian officer named George Washington learned his profession—including how to take a licking. In 1754 the French defeated his unit in Ohio and took him prisoner.

THE FALL OF QUÉBEC: There were only about 65,000 Frenchmen in the colony, but they more than held their own against the million Anglo-Americans. First, because they were natural forest fighters—one Canadian trapper could stalemate six redcoats in the woods. Mainly, however, because they made friends with the Indians instead of robbing them. Thus the majority of tribes sided with the French and made the English pay a terrible price for their blindness.

When the final round began in 1756, it opened with a series of shattering English debacles. The French had a brilliant commander, the Marquis de Montcalm, exactly the kind of unorthodox tactician needed for the fluid semiguerrilla warfare of the American wilderness.

Britain's proud General Braddock rode into a French-Indian ambush that killed him and scattered his army. Montcalm led an expedition against Fort Oswego that wiped out the stronghold and turned Lake Ontario into a French waterway. The following summer he repeated the feat with Fort William Henry, at the head of Lake George, which fell amid ghastly scenes of Indian massacres, later immortalized by James Fenimore Cooper in *The Last of the*

Mohicans. Middle New York now lay wide open to raids, and England's hold on America seemed to be slipping.

Then, like a cornered boxer bouncing from the ropes, the British came back with a devastating right-left-right that not only saved their colonies but won them the entire continent.

The first punches were against Fort Duquesne, in Pennsylvania, and against the Fortress Louisbourg, on Cape Breton, both of which they took after bloody sieges. Then, where least expected, came the ultimate haymaker, aimed straight at the enemy's solar plexus—Québec.

In June 1759, a British fleet nosed its way from the Atlantic Ocean down the St. Lawrence River. In charge of the troops on board was the youngest general in her army, 32-year-old James Wolfe, whose military record was remarkable and whose behavior was so eccentric that he had the reputation of being "mad as a march hare." When King George II—who, whatever his other failings, did not lack wit—heard the rumors, he snorted: "Mad, is he, what? Then, by Jove, I wish he would bite some of my sane generals!"

The struggle for Québec dragged on until September, when Wolfe, near desperation, played his final card. He couldn't storm those gallantly defended fortress walls, although the British guns had shelled the town to rubble. Wolfe therefore loaded 5000 men into boats and rowed upriver to a cove *behind* the city. Then they silently climbed the towering cliff face in the darkness, and when morning came Wolfe had his army squarely astride Montcalm's supply lines. Now the French had to come out of their stronghold and give battle in the open.

The British formed their famous "thin red line" across the bush-studded Plains of Abraham, just west of the city. Montcalm advanced upon them with five regiments, all in step, and in the next quarter of an hour the fate of Canada was decided. The redcoats stood like statues as the French drew closer—100 yards, 60 yards, 40 yards. . . . Then a command rang out, and—in such perfect unison that it sounded like a single thunderclap—the English muskets crashed. The redcoats advanced four measured paces, halted, fired, advanced another four paces with robot precision—halted, fired again. Then it was all over.

The plain was covered with fallen Frenchmen. Montcalm lay mortally wounded, the rest of his troops were fleeing helter-skelter. But among the British casualties was Wolfe himself. With two bullets through his body, he lived just long enough to hear that he had won. Montcalm died a few hours after him.

Today, overlooking the boardwalk of Québec, you'll find a unique memorial to both these outstanding men—the only statue in the world commemorating both victor and vanquished of the same battle!

THE U.S. INVASION: The capture of Québec determined the war and left Britain master of all North America down to the Mexican border. Yet, oddly enough, it was this victory that generated Britain's worst defeat. For if the French had held Canada, the British government would certainly have been more careful in its treatment of the American colonists.

As it was, the British felt cocksure and decided to make the colonists themselves pay for the outrageous costs of the French and Indian Wars. Hence the taxes slapped on all imports—especially tea—that infuriated the colonists to the point of open rebellion against the Crown. You could, at a stretch, say that the British triumph at Québec led directly to her disaster at Yorktown and the creation of the United States.

But if the British misjudged the temper of the colonists, the Americans were equally wrong about the mood of the Canadians. Washington felt sure that the French in the north would join the Revolution, or at least not resist her soldiers. He was terribly mistaken on both counts.

The French had little love for either of the English-speaking antagonists. But they were staunch Royalists and devout Catholics, with no sympathy for the "godless" republicans from the south. Only a handful changed sides, and most French Canadians fought grimly shoulder to shoulder with their erstwhile enemies.

So Washington's three fighting-est generals came to grief over French resistance. The daredevil Vermonter Ethan Allen and his Green Mountain Boys were taken prisoner at Montréal. Montgomery fell before Québec, while the ambitious Benedict Arnold was driven back with defeat on his record and the first seeds of treason ripening in his heart.

Thirty-eight years later, in the War of 1812, another U.S. army marched up the banks of the Richelieu River where it flows from Lake Champlain to the St. Lawrence. And once again the French Canadians stuck by the British and flung back the invaders. The war ended in a draw, but had surprisingly happy results. Britain and the young United States agreed to demilitarize the Great Lakes and to extend their mutual border along the 49th Parallel to the Rockies.

LOYALISTS AND IMMIGRANTS: One of the side effects of the American Revolution was an influx of English-speaking newcomers for Canada. About 50,000 Americans who had remained faithful to King George, the United Empire Loyalists, migrated to Canada because they were given a very rough time in the U.S. They settled mostly in Nova Scotia and began to populate the almost empty shores of what is now New Brunswick.

After the Napoleonic wars, a regular tide of immigrants came from England, which was going through the early and cruelest stages of the so-called Industrial Revolution. They were fleeing from the new and hideously bleak factory towns, from work houses, starvation wages, and impoverished Scottish farms. Even the unknown perils of the New World seemed preferable to these blessings of the Dickens era.

By 1850 more than half a million immigrants had arrived, pushing Canada's population above two million. And now the population centers shifted westward, away from the old seaboard colonies in the east, opening up the territories now called Ontario, Manitoba, and Saskatchewan.

With increased population came the demand for union, largely because the various colony borders hampered trade. Britain complied fairly promptly. In 1867 the British Parliament passed an act creating a federal union out of the colonies of Upper and Lower Canada, Nova Scotia, and New Brunswick. British Columbia hesitated whether to remain separate, join the United States, or merge with Canada, but finally voted herself in. Remote Newfoundland hesitated longest of all. She remained a distinct colony until 1949, when she became Canada's tenth province.

THE REVOLT OF THE HALF-BREEDS: Geographically, Canada stretched from the Atlantic to the Pacific Oceans, but in reality most of the immense region in between lay beyond the rule of Ottawa, the nation's capital. The endless prairies and forest lands of the west and northwest were inhabited by about 40,000 people, over half of them nomadic Indians. They lived by hunting, fishing, and trapping, depending largely on the buffalo for food, clothing, and shelter. As the once-enormous herds began to dwindle, life grew increasingly hard for the nomads. Adding to their troubles were whiskey traders peddling poisonous rotgut for furs, and packs of outlaws who took what they wanted at gunpoint.

Ordinary law officers were nearly useless in this environment. In 1873 the federal government therefore created a quite extraordinary force: the North West Mounted Police, now called the Royal Canadian Mounted Police (and rarely mounted). The scarlet-coated Mounties earned a legendary reputation for toughness, fairness, and the ability to hunt down wrongdoers. And unlike their American counterparts, they usually brought in prisoners alive.

The Mounties proceeded to tame the west, and did so with astonishingly little manpower. One trooper would clean up a settlement, throw out the liquor traders, and clap the armed thugs in irons. When Chief Sitting Bull's tribe of Sioux drifted into Canada after the battle of the Little Big Horn, the government sent *five* Mounties to escort them to a reservation. Custer had tried it with 400 U.S. Cavalry and died in the attempt. The Mounties accomplished the feat without ever drawing their guns, evoking Sitting Bull's comment: "Now I know why the queen needs so few men to uphold her peace."

But even the Mounties couldn't handle the desperate uprising that shook western Saskatchewan in 1885. As the railroad relentlessly pushed across the prairies and the buffalo vanished, the people known as Métis felt they had to fight for their existence. The Métis were half-breeds, offspring of French trappers and Indian women, superb hunters and trackers, but with few "civilized" skills.

The march of civilization had driven them from Manitoba to the banks of the Saskatchewan River, where some 6000 of them now made their last stand against iron rails and wooden farmhouses. They had a charismatic leader in Louis Riel, a man educated enough to teach school and mad enough to think that God wanted him to found a new religion.

With Riel's rebels rose their natural allies, the Indians, under their chiefs Poundmaker and Big Bear. Together they were a formidable force. The Métis attacked the Mounted Police at Duck Lake, cut the telegraph wires, and proclaimed an independent republic. The Indians stormed the town of Battleford, then captured and burned Fort Pitt.

The alarmed administration in Ottawa sent an army marching westward under General Middleton, equipped with artillery and Gatling machine guns. The Métis checked them briefly at Fish Creek, but had to fall back on their main village of Batoche. There the last battle of the west took place—long lines of redcoats charging with fixed bayonets, the half-breeds fighting from house to house, from rifle pits and crude trenches, so short of ammunition that they had to shoot lead buttons instead of bullets.

Batoche fell (you can still see the bullet marks on the houses there) and the Indians quit the warpath shortly afterward. Louis Riel was tried for treason and murder. Although any modern court would have found him insane, the Canadian authorities duly hanged him.

RAILROADS, WHEAT, AND WAR: The reason why the army could crush Riel's rebellion so quickly was also the reason for its outbreak: the Canadian Pacific Railway. The railroad was more than a marvel of engineering—it formed a steel band holding the country together, enabling Canada to live up to her motto, *A Mari Usque ad Mare*—"From Sea to Sea."

Much as the free-roaming prairie people hated the Iron Horse, railroads were vital to Canada's survival as a nation. They had to be pushed through, against all opposition, if the isolated provinces were not to drift into the orbit of the United States and the Dominion cease to exist. As one journalist of the time put it: "The whistle of a locomotive is the true cradle song and anthem of our country."

If Canada had adopted a national color, it would have been yellow—for wheat. As the country's transportation system developed, the central provinces emerged as one of the world's biggest bread baskets. In one decade wheat production zoomed from 56 million bushels to over 200 million, which put her on a par with the U.S. and Russia as a granary.

And despite the bitterness engendered by the execution of Riel, the following year Canada elected her first prime minister of French heritage. Sir Wilfrid Laurier had one foot in each ethnic camp and proved a superlative statesman— according to some, the best his country ever produced. His terms of office, from 1896 to 1911, were golden years in which Canada flexed her muscles like a young giant and looked forward to unlimited growth and a century of peaceful prosperity—just like her equally optimistic American neighbor in the south.

Came 1914 and World War I. The Dominion went to war together with the Mother Country and, like her, tried to fight it on a volunteer basis. It didn't work. The tall, health-brimming Canadians, together with the Australians, formed the shock troops of the British Empire and earned that honor with torrents of blood. The entire Western Front in France was littered with Canadian bones. The flow of volunteers became a trickle, and in 1917 the Dominion was forced to introduce conscription. The measure ran into violent opposition from the French-speaking minority, who saw conscription as a device to thin out their numbers.

The draft law went through, but it strained the nation's unity almost to the breaking point. And the results were ghastly. Some 60,000 Canadians fell in battle, a terrible bloodletting for a country of 7¼ million inhabitants. (In World War II, by contrast, Canada lost 40,000 killed from a population of 11½ million.)

The one benefit Canada reaped from the slaughter was an acceleration of industrial development and an enormous boost to mining activity. In the post-war years Canada emerged not merely as an agricultural exporter, but as a budding power in the mineral and manufacturing fields.

TOWARD WORLD POWER: Between the wars the fortunes of Canada more or less reflected those of the United States, except that Canada was never foolish enough to join the "noble experiment" of Prohibition. Some of her citizens, in fact, waxed rich on the lucrative bootlegging trade across the border.

But the Depression, coupled with disastrous droughts in the western provinces, hit her all the harder. There was no equivalent of Roosevelt's New Deal in the Dominion. The country staggered along from one financial crisis to the next until the outbreak of the Second World War totally transformed the situation. The war provided the boost Canada needed to join the ranks of the major industrial nations. And the surge of postwar immigration gave her the manpower required to work the newly developed industries. From 1941 to 1974 Canada doubled her population and increased her gross national product (GNP) nearly tenfold.

With the discovery of huge uranium deposits in Ontario and Saskatchewan, Canada was in the position to add nuclear energy to her power resources.

And with the opening of the St. Lawrence Seaway, she turned Toronto—which lies more than 1000 miles from the nearest ocean—into a major seaport. The project, incidentally, did the same for Chicago, Buffalo, and Detroit on the U.S. side. When Queen Elizabeth and President Eisenhower jointly opened the colossal seaway in 1959, it represented the biggest technical undertaking ever completed by two countries working in partnership.

All these achievements propelled Canada into her present position: the sixth-ranking manufacturing and trading nation on the globe, with a standard of living roughly equal to that of the U.S.A. But, simultaneously, old and never-banished ghosts were raising their heads again.

TROUBLE IN QUÉBEC: As an ethnic enclave the French Canadians had won their battle for survival with flying colors. From their original 65,000 settlers they had grown to over six million, and had done so without receiving reinforcements from overseas, for the French are not a migrating people and can rarely be induced to leave their homeland for new pastures.

The French Canadians had preserved and increased their presence by means of large families, rigid cultural cohesion, and the unifying influence of their Catholic faith. But they had fallen way behind the English-speaking majority economically and politically. Few of them held top positions in industry or finance, and although they ran the province of Québec, they enjoyed relatively little say in national matters.

What rankled most with them was that Canada never recognized French as a second *national* language, the way Switzerland does. In other words, the French were expected to be bilingual if they wanted a good career, but the Anglos got along nicely with just their own tongue. On a general cultural basis, too, the country overwhelmingly reflected Anglo-Saxon attitudes rather than an Anglo-French mixture.

By the early 1960s this discontent led to a dramatic radicalization of Québec politics. A new separatist movement arose that regarded Québec not as simply one of ten provinces, but as *l'état du Québec,* a distinct state and people that might—if it chose—break away from the country. The most extreme faction of the movement, the Front de Libération du Québec (FLQ), was frankly revolutionary and terroristic. It backed its demands with bombs, arson, and murder, culminating with the kidnap-killing of Cabinet Minister Pierre Laporte in October 1970.

The Ottawa government, under Prime Minister Pierre Trudeau, imposed the War Measures Act and moved 10,000 troops into the province. The police used their exceptional powers under the act to break up civil disorders, arrested hundreds of suspects, and caught the murderers of Laporte. And in the provincial elections of 1973, the separatists were badly defeated, winning only 6 seats from a total of 110.

The crisis calmed down. In some ways its effects may have been beneficial. The federal government redoubled its efforts to remove the worst grievances of the French Canadians. Federal funds flowed to French schools outside Québec (nearly half of the schoolchildren of New Brunswick, for example, are French speaking). French Canadians were appointed to senior positions. Most important, all provinces were asked to make French an official language, which entailed bilingual signposts, government forms, and transport schedules. Civil servants had to bone up on French to pass their examinations and the business world began to stipulate bilinguality for men aiming at executives' desks. All these measures, it should be noted, were already afoot before the turmoil began, but there is no doubt that bloodshed helped to accelerate them.

THE NEW VISION: Biculturalism is nothing new for Europe, but for Americans it still has a distinctly exotic flavor. For Canada it may make the difference between continued national unity and a fractured country. For Québec, secession could well mean economic disaster. Most of Canada's industrial muscle is located in the English-speaking provinces, as is most of her money power. An independent Québec would very likely be a poor one.

But if the two national entities can achieve the vision of a true and harmonious blending, a symbiosis of Anglo-Saxon and Latin traits, the entire American continent will be the richer.

2. The Original Canadians

INDIANS: There are actually more Indians living in Canada today than existed at the time of the first white settlements. Anthropologists have estimated that the original number of Indians was about 200,000. The native population began to decline with the arrival of the Europeans. By the early 20th century it was down to almost half, and common belief labeled the Indians a dying race. But the patient recovered and began to regain strength. At the last census the total number of Indians had reached 282,000, which definitely placed them off the danger list.

Ethnically Canada's Indians are the same as those in the U.S. Some tribes, like the Cree, Sioux, and Blackfoot, can be found on both sides of the border. In Canada they belong to ten distinct linguistic groups, subdivided into widely differing local dialects. Their customs, religion, and methods of hunting and warfare were very similar to those of their brethren in the United States. The treatment they received, however, was rather different.

In the 1870s—before the bulk of white settlers reached the west—the Canadian government began to negotiate a series of treaties with the prairie tribes. By the end of the decade most of the western Indians had agreed to treaties in which they surrendered their lands in return for guaranteed reservations, small cash payments for each individual member, supplies of seeds and tools, and assistance in changing over to farming for a livelihood. By and large, with a few inglorious exceptions, those treaties were kept.

The Canadian government wielded much greater control over the white settlers than its counterpart in Washington. It was thus able to prevent the continual incursions by gold prospectors, buffalo hunters, railroad companies, and squatters that sparked most of the Indian wars south of the border. The Mounties, as distinct from the U.S. Cavalry, actually protected Indians. As the Blackfoot chief Crowfoot said: "The police have shielded us from bad men as the feathers of birds protect them from the winter frosts. If the police had not come, very few of us would have been left today."

The decline of the Indian population was mainly due to sickness brought in by the white man, combined with the tremendous difficulties of exchanging one lifestyle for another—trying to accomplish in a few decades what had taken Europeans several thousand years. Tens of thousands of erstwhile nomadic hunters simply couldn't bear a life tied to one patch of soil; they died from sheer discouragement, unwilling to continue an existence that appeared joyless and stale.

People can die when they lose all pleasure in living—it happened to the Australian Aborigines and to many of the nomadic hunters of Siberia. The switch from wandering and tracking to sowing and harvesting, from settling disputes by warfare to going through incomprehensible court procedures, is one of the most traumatic human beings can undergo.

The fact that the Indians succeeded proves their amazing flexibility. Or perhaps not so amazing—after all, they learned to breed and utilize horses within a century of the Europeans' bringing them to America. It also proves the amount of goodwill the Canadians devoted to the transformation.

Today the country has 574 separate Indian communities, known as "bands." A few—a very few—of them still roam the northern regions. The others share among them 2110 reserves, although less than two-thirds actually live on reservations. Indians today are successful farmers, nurses, builders, secretaries, doctors, teachers, clergymen, salesmen, and industrial workers, both on and off the reserves. In 1973 the government accepted a proposal by the National Indian Brotherhood by which increasing numbers of bands now manage their own schools. Instead of trying to blot out their past, the new school curricula study it and include Indian language courses for those children who had almost forgotten their native tongues.

Which is only fair, since the very name "Canada" derives from the Huron word *kanata,* meaning a settlement.

INUIT: The word means "people," and that is what the Canadian Eskimos call themselves. So remote was their native habitat, so completely isolated from the rest of the world, that they were unaware that any men except themselves existed. Inuit, in fact, meant human beings—the only ones.

The Eskimos are a unique people, the Canadian branch even more so than the others. There are only around 80,000 Eskimos in the entire world, forming part of four nations: Russia, the United States, Canada, and Denmark (in Greenland, which is a Danish possession). This makes the Eskimos the only natives of the same ethnic group to live in both Asia and America.

Some 22,000 Inuit live in Canada today, and we have no idea how many there might have been originally. They inhabited the far north, the very last portion of the country to be explored, much later than the other Arctic lands of the globe. While their cousins elsewhere were trading with the white men, the Inuit hardly knew there was such a creature as a paleface.

The Eskimos were traditionally coastal people, fishermen and hunters of seals, whales, and polar bears. These animals supplied their food, clothing, light, and heat (in the form of blubber lamps and stoves), and were utilized to the last shred of skin. Their earliest outside contacts, therefore, were whalers, frequently with tragic results. The Inuit were gentle people, intensely hospitable and so averse to violence that theirs was a language that had no term for "war." Life was such a struggle against a harsh environment that they couldn't conceive of the idea of humans wasting precious strength in fighting each other.

When the first British and American whaling ships touched Baffin Bay in the 1820s, they found that the Eskimos had no conception of private property, of food and clothing that was *not* shared with whoever needed it. The Inuit marveled at the white mens' wooden whaleboats, firearms, iron tools, and glass bottles—none of which they had ever seen. They had no idea of the dangers associated with these wonders.

Murder and rape were the least of them. Liquor was far more destructive, but worst of all were the diseases the whalers introduced. For all its harshness, the Arctic was a healthy region, free of bacteria. Eskimos might starve and freeze to death, but they rarely succumbed to illness. Which meant that their bodies had no resistance against the measles, smallpox, and tuberculosis the white men brought in along with their rum and gadgetry.

The Inuit—particularly their children—died like flies. The only doctors available to them were a handful of missionaries, usually with very limited medical supplies. The present breed of Inuit, therefore, are a race of survivors, the strain that somehow battled through a century that killed uncounted numbers of their kind.

It was not until the 1950s that the Canadian government took serious steps to assure the Eskimos' rightful place in their Arctic homeland. As air transport and radio communications broke down the isolation of the far north, the government introduced improved educational, health, and welfare services. Eskimos are now full citizens in every respect—not in name only—electing members of the Territorial Council of the Northwest Territories and running their own communities.

They have ceased to be nomads and have moved into permanent settlements. But unlike the Indians, the Inuit are still basically hunters, although nowadays they use rifles instead of the traditional harpoons. But don't compare their hunting with the white man's weekend sport. Eskimos hunt in order to eat, and no one has more ecological consciousness than they. Everything in their prey is used—a walrus represents a miniature supermarket to an Eskimo —and they kill nothing for pleasure and not one animal more than absolutely necessary.

The Inuit Tapirisat (Eskimo Brotherhood) is their nonpolitical organization dedicated to preserving the Eskimo language and culture and to helping them achieve full participation in Canada's society. This would include legal rights to some of the enormous lands the Inuit once roamed and utilized, but without establishing fixed borders for their domain. Some of these areas have been found to contain valuable deposits of oil, natural gas, and minerals, which made the question of ownership more than merely academic.

If you want a glimpse of the Inuit soul, look at their art, which you'll find in stores all over Canada. Their craftsmanship shouldn't surprise you: Eskimo women are perhaps the greatest needle (fishbone) experts in the world, and their completely waterproof sealskin kayak canoe is possibly the best designed and finished vehicle in marine history.

But Eskimo carvings of man and animals have a quality all their own. They are imbued with a sense of movement, a feeling for anatomy, almost a smell. Their expressions are so hauntingly lifelike, yet so curiously abstract, that they give you an eerie notion of having seen them before in some strange dream.

3. Fauna and Fish

Canada has the same animals as the northern United States, but she has them in larger quantities and spread over wider areas. You still come across brown bears and grizzlies in British Columbia and the Laurentians of Québec; buffalo in Alberta; elks and moose in Saskatchewan; deer, skunks, raccoons, and beavers in most of the provinces.

The fewer the people, the richer the animal life, which is why the Northwest Territories, the Yukon, and the northern regions of Québec boast the most numerous fauna—huge white polar bears lumbering over ice floes, musk-oxen and caribou grazing on the tundras, seals, walruses, and penguins waddling along the shorelines, occasional packs of wolves prowling the forests.

Most of these animals are now protected (although in the case of seals and polar bears, not protected enough). But Canada is an absolute paradise for sports fishermen, some say the greatest fishing hole in the world. Hundreds of thousands of lakes, rivers, and streams teem with all the major freshwater species, while the Atlantic and Pacific coasts harbor striped bass, bluefin tuna, sharks, and the entire gamut of deep-sea fish.

Each region has one or several favorite species: rainbow trout (called kamloops) in British Columbia, Atlantic salmon in Labrador, bluefin tuna in Prince Edward Island, brook trout in Nova Scotia, northern pike and walleye (pickerel) in Québec, smallmouth bass in Manitoba, Arctic grayling and char in the Yukon and Northwest Territories.

As a rough rule of thumb, the further north you go, the more fabulous the fishing—and the shorter the season for it. In the Yukon and Northwest Territories, open-water fishing extends from June to late September and is at its best just after the ice is gone from streams and lakes—the latter half of June through the first half of July. Since the water in these Arctic regions is very cold, game fish fight harder than they do in the south, an added attraction for sportsmen.

Some of the finest fishing in Canada is a fly-in proposition: the fishing camps and lodges can only be reached by aircraft. We'll describe some of the package plans available when we deal with the provinces concerned. A week-long fishing excursion—including flights, meals, and guides—varies as much as $400 to $850 per person, according to the time of year and the location of the camps.

Each province and territory has its own licensing regulations, simple in some parts of the country, complicated in others. Fishing permits are readily available, but if you go for Atlantic salmon in New Brunswick, for instance, the rule is that nonresident anglers must hire guides in required numbers: one guide per angler in a boat, but only one guide per three wading anglers. Don't ask us why.

The cost of fishing licenses varies considerably. In the Northwest Territories you can get a three-day permit for $3.50; in Saskatchewan, it costs $10; in Alberta, $4. The Tourist Information offices in each province will give you booklets listing all the red tape wrapped around the rods in their particular realm.

Chapter I

CANADA: A TOURIST SURVEY

WE STRONGLY RECOMMEND that you read this chapter *before* you set out on your trip. It could save you money, luggage space, time, and possibly aggravation. It contains capsulated tourist know-how: when to come, what to bring, the documentation you'll need, where to go, where to stay, where to make inquiries, what to eat and drink—as well as a few things to avoid.

It's all very basic stuff, but you'd be surprised how a little foreknowledge can spell the difference between a smooth and a bumpy excursion. Or maybe you wouldn't be surprised—if you've been over the bumps before. Anyway, the purpose of this chapter is to package the information you need so you can concentrate henceforth solely on the business of enjoying yourself. And I can't think of a worthier cause.

Since this book is deliberately money-oriented, we'll start with finance—which, surprisingly, is good news.

THE CURRENCY: Canada figures in dollars and cents, but with a very pleasing balance: the Canadian dollar is worth around 87¢ in U.S. money, give or take a couple of points daily variation. Which means that your American travelers checks get you about 13% more the moment you change them for local currency. That makes quite a difference in your budget—$130 in every thousand, to be exact. And since prices are roughly on a par with the U.S., the difference is real, not imaginary. You can bring in or take out any amount of money, but if you are importing or exporting sums of $5000 or more you must file a report of the transaction with the U.S. Customs. Most tourist establishments in Canada will take U.S. cash, but for your own advantage you should change your funds into Canadian currency.

TRAVEL DOCUMENTS: More good news: you need the barest minimum. U.S. citizens or permanent residents of the United States require neither passports nor visas. You should, however, carry some identifying papers such as birth, baptismal, or voter's certificate to show your citizenship. Permanent U.S. residents who are not citizens *must* have their Alien Registration Cards.

Customs regulations are very generous in most respects, but get pretty complicated when it comes to firearms, plants, meats, and pet animals. Fishing tackle poses no problems, but the bearer must possess a nonresident license for the province or territory where he plans to use it. You can bring in free of duty up to 50 cigars, 200 cigarettes, and two pounds of tobacco, providing you're over 16 years of age. You are also allowed 40 ounces of liquor or wine.

For more detailed information concerning customs regulations, write to: Customs and Excise, Connaught Building, Sussex Drive, Ottawa, ON K1A 0L5.

POSTAL SERVICE: Canadian postal rates vary from those in the U.S., and all mail posted in Canada must have Canadian stamps. And as you may note from the above sample, Canadian ZIP Codes are a ghastly melange of numbers and letters, but absolutely essential for delivery.

U.S. CONSULATES: In the rather unlikely event that you require assistance from a U.S. consul, here are their addresses in the Canadian capital cities:

Nova Scotia: Cogswell Tower, Suite 910, Scotia Square, Halifax, NS B3J 3K1 (tel. 902/429-2480).
Québec: P.O. Box 939, 1 rue Geneviève, Québec City, PQ G1R 4T9 (tel. 418/692-2095).
Ontario: 360 University Ave., Toronto, ON M5G 1S4 (tel. 416/595-1700).
Manitoba: Room 100, 6 Donald St., Winnipeg, MB R3L 0K7 (tel. 204/475-3344).
Alberta: Room 1050, 615 Macleod Trail SE, Calgary, AB T2G 4T8 (tel. 403/266-8962).
British Columbia: Columbia Centre IV, 1199 W. Hastings St., Vancouver, BC V6E 2Y4 (tel. 604/685-4311).

CLIMATE—WHEN TO COME: Canada has a more equitable climate than the U.S., since it contains neither tropical nor desert regions. In the southern and central portions the weather is the same as in the northern United States. As you head north the climate becomes Arctic, meaning long and extremely cold winters, brief and surprisingly warm summers (with lots of flies), and absolutely magical springs.

Using a rough rule of thumb, you can say that the spring season runs from mid-March to mid-May, summer from mid-May to mid-September, fall from mid-September to mid-November, and winter from mid-November to mid-March. So pick the season best suited to your tastes and temperament, but remember that your car should be winterized through March and that snow sometimes falls as late as April. September and October are best, in fact fantastic, for color photography.

Evenings tend to be cool everywhere, particularly on or near water. In late spring and early summer you'll definitely need a supply of insect repellent if you're planning bush travel.

To give you an idea of temperature variations, I'll list some of the summer and winter extremes in various spots:

Location	Summer	Winter
Québec City	77°	5°
Nova Scotia	74°	21°
Ontario	81°	−2°
Manitoba	80°	−12°
Alberta	76°	−1°
British Columbia	74°	31°
Yukon	67°	−4°
Northwest Territories	69°	−26°

With the huge size of some provinces and territories, you naturally get considerable climate variations inside their borders. Québec, for instance, sprawls all the way from the moderate south to the Arctic, and the weather varies accordingly. British Columbia shows the slightest changes: it rarely goes above the 70s in summer or drops below the 30s in winter.

What to Pack

The wearables in your luggage naturally depend on the time of year you come and whether you're out to ski or to swim. But there are a few items we recommend taking along in all of our travel books—the result of wisdom acquired in many years of solid globetrotting:

(1) A travel alarm clock, which renders you independent of hotel wake-up calls. (2) A washcloth in a plastic bag—although nearly all Canadian hotels supply them for their guests, a few do not. (3) One pair of light wooden (not plastic) shoe trees. Sightseeing is rough on your footwear and feet, and plastic does not absorb the moisture in your shoes. (4) A small flashlight, particularly if you're driving. (5) A very small screwdriver. (6) A magnifying glass to read the tiny print on maps. (7) And if you intend to go to Québec, an Anglo-French dictionary.

As far as **clothing** is concerned, include at least one warm sweater, a warm coat, and a light overcoat, even in summer. Canada is prone to cold snaps. Canadians tend to be casual in their apparel—although not as casual as, say, Californians. Therefore it's wise for men to bring along a tie (an ascot will also do) in case you run into one of the few restaurants that still refuse to serve you without one. And, vitally important, at least one pair of sturdy, no-nonsense walking shoes for both sexes. A lot of holidays have been ruined because every pair packed either hurt or fell to pieces.

Since Canada hums on the same current and uses the same plugs as the U.S., you can take any electrical gadget you wish. But do yourself a favor and don't take too many. They weigh too much and take up more luggage space than their use justifies. Do, however, pack one of those small travel umbrellas. Canada gets plenty of rain, even in summer.

A final on packing in general—*travel light.* Never bring more luggage than you yourself can carry without assistance. Porters aren't always available at air terminals and rail stations, and those handy luggage carts have a habit of vanishing just when you need one. The ideal tourist kit consists of one suitcase and a shoulderbag. In that respect, those who follow this book are more fortunate than those who wrote it. They don't have to lug any typewriters.

Matters Metric

Canada "went metric" a few years back, but in a somewhat half-baked manner. Thus while distances now come in kilometers (km) and gas by liters, weights are still reckoned in pounds and ounces, at least as far as shopkeepers are concerned. In order not to confuse you further, we've generally stuck to miles when indicating distances, although most Canadian maps show km.

But if you're driving, and particularly driving a car without a metric speedometer, the following figures are of vital importance:

30 km/h equals 20 mph, and is the speed for school zones.
50 km/h equals 30 mph, and is the speed limit in most city areas.
80 km/h equals 50 mph, and is the speed limit on most rural two-lane roadways.

100 km/h equals 60 mph, and is the maximum speed limit on most freeways.

3.8 m equals 11′ 6″, and is the height of a bridge or overpass that will let a large truck go underneath.

The little conversion table below is easily memorized:

$$1 \text{ inch} = 2.54 \text{ cm (centimeters)}$$
$$1 \text{ foot} = 0.305 \text{ m (meters)}$$
$$1 \text{ mile} = 1.61 \text{ km (kilometers)}$$

Unfortunately, things become complicated with the gallon-liter conversion because Canada uses (or used) the so-called Imperial gallon, which is larger than the U.S. gallon. The new equivalents are 4.6 liters in the Imperial gallon to 3.78 liters in the U.S. gallon. This makes one U.S. quart equal to 0.94 liters, but one old Canadian quart equals 1.14 liters.

Regarding weather information, Canada is nice enough to give most thermometer readings in both the new Celsius and the old Fahrenheit degrees. In places where they don't, this conversion table will tell you whether you're supposed to feel hot or cold:

Celsius		Fahrenheit
0	=	32
5	=	41
10	=	50
20	=	68
30	=	86
35	=	95

THE $15-A-DAY TRAVEL CLUB: Before plunging into our exploration of the best values in Canada let me tell you about a program that can help you save money on all your travels, the $15-a-Day Travel Club, now in its 16th year of operation. The Club was formed at the urging of numerous readers of the $$$-a-Day and Dollarwise Guides, who felt that such an organization could provide continuing travel information and a sense of community to value-minded travelers in all parts of the world. And so it does!

In keeping with the budget concept, the membership fee is low and is immediately exceeded by the value of your benefits. Upon receipt of $10 (U.S. residents), $12 (Canadian and Mexican residents), or $14 (other foreign residents) in U.S. currency to cover one year's membership, we will send all new members, by return mail (book rate), the following items:

(1) The latest edition of *any two* of the following books (please designate in your letter which two you wish to receive):

Europe on $15 a Day
Australia on $20 a Day
England and Scotland on $20 a Day
Greece and Yugoslavia on $15 & $20 a Day
Hawaii on $25 a Day
Ireland on $15 a Day
Israel on $15 & $20 a Day
Mexico and Guatemala on $10 and $15 a Day

New Zealand on $15 & $20 a Day
Scandinavia on $20 a Day
South America on $15 a Day
Spain and Morocco (plus the Canary Is.) on $10 & $15 a Day
Turkey on $10 & $15 a Day
Washington, D.C. on $25 a Day

Dollarwise Guide to the Caribbean (including Bermuda and the Bahamas)
Dollarwise Guide to Canada
Dollarwise Guide to Egypt
Dollarwise Guide to England and Scotland
Dollarwise Guide to France
Dollarwise Guide to Germany
Dollarwise Guide to Italy
Dollarwise Guide to Portugal (plus Madeira and the Azores)
Dollarwise Guide to California and Las Vegas
Dollarwise Guide to New England
Dollarwise Guide to the Southeast and New Orleans
(Dollarwise Guides discuss accommodations and facilities in all price ranges, with emphasis on the medium-priced).

The Caribbean Bargain Book
(A one-of-a-kind guide to the "off-season" Caribbean—mid-April to mid-December—and the fabulous resorts that slash their rates from 20% to 60%; includes almost every island group in the Caribbean, and the Bahamas too.)

Where to Stay USA
(By the Council on International Educational Exchange, this extraordinary guide is the first to list accommodations in all 50 states that cost anywhere from $3 to $20 a night.)

(2) A copy of **Arthur Frommer's Guide to New York,** a newly revised pocket-size guide to hotels, restaurants, night spots, and sightseeing attractions in all price ranges throughout the New York area.

(3) A one-year subscription to the quarterly Club newsletter—**The Wonderful World of Budget Travel** (about which more below)—which keeps members up-to-date on fast-breaking developments in low-cost travel to all areas of the world.

(4) A voucher entitling you to a $5 discount on any Arthur Frommer International, Inc. tour booked by you through travel agents in the United States and Canada.

(5) Your personal membership card, which, once received, entitles you to purchase through the Club all Arthur Frommer Publications for a third to a half off their regular retail prices during the term of your membership.

Those are the immediate and definite benefits which we can assure to members of the Club at this time. Further benefits, which it has been our continuing aim to achieve for members, are announced to members in *The Wonderful World of Budget Travel (WWBT)*. An eight-page, full-size newspaper, *WWBT* carries such continuing features as "The Traveler's Directory" (a list of members all over the world who are willing to provide hospitality to other members as they pass through their home cities) and "Share-a-Trip" (offers and requests from members for travel companions who can share costs); worldwide travel news and feature stories by our acclaimed expert travel writers; plus tips and articles on specific plans and methods for travel savings.

If you would like to join this hardy band of international budgeteers and participate in its exchange of travel information and hospitality, simply send your name and address, together with your membership fee of $10 (U.S. residents), $12 (Canadian and Mexican residents), or $14 (other foreign residents) in U.S. currency to: $15-a-Day Travel Club, Inc., 380 Madison Avenue, New York, NY 10017. Remember to specify which *two* of the books in section (1) above you wish to receive in your initial package of members' benefits. Or, if you prefer, use the last page of this book, simply checking off the two books you want and enclosing $10, $12, or $14 in U.S. currency.

THE FUTURE OF THIS BOOK: Like all the books in this series, *Dollarwise Guide to Canada* hopes to maintain a continuing dialogue between its authors and its readers. All of us share a common aim—to travel as widely and as well as possible, at the lowest possible cost—and in achieving that goal, your comments and suggestions can be of tremendous aid to other readers. Therefore, if you come across a particularly appealing hotel, restaurant, shop, or bargain, please don't keep it to yourself. We'll send free copies of the next edition of this book to readers whose suggestions are used. And this applies to any comments you may have about the existing listings. The fact that a hotel or restaurant is recommended in this edition doesn't mean that it will necessarily appear in future editions if readers report that its service has slipped or that its prices have risen too drastically. Send your comments or finds to the individual authors, c/o Arthur Frommer, Inc., 380 Madison Avenue, New York, NY 10017.

WHERE TO STAY: Tourist accommodation in Canada closely parallels that of the United States—meaning it gets tight at just the time and in just those places most people want to travel in and to. Resort areas and "fun" cities bulge at the seams during holiday periods.

Consequently, hostelries in such areas charge seasonal rates, considerably higher during whatever is their peak season. Unless indicated, all rates quoted in this book are peak-season rates. You can figure on a large saving if you travel out of season. But don't forget that *all prices are given in Canadian money,* so you must deduct 13% to get the correct U.S. equivalent. Given this automatic rebate, even luxury establishments become quite reasonable by comparison.

Motels

Although the types of establishments will be familiar, there are a few differences that should be noted. Because the country is so huge and thinly populated, the number of motels in outlying areas is much smaller than you're accustomed to find. In the northern regions they become very sparse indeed, so it's wise to book ahead, particularly if you're traveling with a family. Don't drive off into the blue and expect a motel to materialize by the roadside when you're feeling tired. There may be no motel or, if it does appear, it may be filled to the rafters.

Hotels

In Canada the term "hotel" also has slightly different connotations. These are hangovers from the old British liquor laws which, when applied to the tourist industry, were an infernal nuisance for all concerned (although no more infernal than the regulations still enforced in certain dry states and counties in the U.S.). A Canadian *hotel* can actually be three different types of establishments:

The majority, including most of the large ones, cater mainly to house guests and run their bars and restaurants as adjuncts. A second group, sometimes called "private hotels," operate without a liquor license and may not even have a restaurant on the premises. A third category, mostly smallish, consists of a bar first and bedrooms as a kind of afterthought. These places have the advantage of usually being on the cheap side, since their profits come almost entirely from the bar trade. They *may* have the drawback of not caring very much about house guests and therefore not doing much for them. In this book, however, we have eliminated that type as far as possible.

Few Canadian hotels offer complimentary breakfasts of the kind known in the U.S. as "continental"—and bearing no resemblance whatever to a European morning meal. A great many, however, provide coffee-making facilities of sorts, mostly instant. And in their services—particularly maid service—they do rather better than their U.S. colleagues. You get far less of that terrible sausage-machine effect that afflicts so many of our mass hostelries.

Bathrooms, as a whole, are excellent; a surprising number come equipped with heat lamps, and the towel and soap supplies are usually ample. You can take room telephones for granted in all but the cheapest establishments. The same goes for TV sets. There is, however, a distinct shortage of shoe-cleaning equipment. You'd do well to bring your own kit along.

Rates are pretty much what you pay in the U.S., ranging from around $45 per night for a single room in a deluxe establishment to $8 or less in the economy class. Except that the exchange rate is in your favor.

Some hotels offer special deals known as American Plan (AP) or Modified American Plan (MAP). The former stands for bed, breakfast, lunch, and dinner; the latter, for bed, breakfast, and dinner only. These plans can save you quite a slice of money, particularly if you're traveling with a family. But they have the obvious drawback of tying you to your hotel for mealtimes, which interferes with your sightseeing and excursions. They'll also prevent you from trying the budget eateries thoughtfully included in this book.

The Ys

Both the YMCA and YWCA have establishments scattered throughout Canada. You'll find descriptions of them in the appropriate chapters. Generally the Ys are both good and economical, ranging around $15 for a single room with a shared bath. They are also a bit confusing, since some now take in both sexes while others still stick to their original *M* and *W* definitions and exclude the opposite gender. In Vancouver, for instance, the YMCA takes only men while the YWCA accepts both, which gives the males an unfair edge in this type of accommodation.

Youth Hostels

Canada has a total of 58 youth hostels, charging between $1 and $3.50 per night. All of them contain separate sleeping quarters for men and women, a recreation room, and a communal kitchen where hostellers can prepare their own meals. All of them provide blankets, pillows, and cooking utensils, although patrons are expected to bring their own food and sleeping bags. (A few hostels rent out sleeping bags by the night, but don't bank on it.) They *may* also ask you to help a little with the housework.

Serviced Apartments

For couples, groups, and families, these can be the greatest vacation bargains of all. Such apartments consist of one to three rooms, plus bathrooms and kitchens. They come fully equipped with cooking and eating utensils, refrigerators, bed linen, etc., and enable you to set up house for weeks or months. Your food bills go down amazingly when you cook for yourself.

Canada is proportionally much better supplied with these apartments than the U.S., especially in resort areas. They can be located in buildings containing nothing else, in apartment hotels, or occasionally in motels. Sometimes the management supplies breakfast (as an extra), but as a rule the only meals available on the premises are those you make. Tariffs are given either as a daily rate for one or two persons, or as a weekly rate for the whole apartment, which applies for the maximum number of people it will accommodate.

All feature maid service, the main difference being that in the more expensive types the maid will wash your dishes; in others, she won't. The vast majority have TV, telephones, and laundry facilities. The quality of the fittings and furnishings, of course, varies with the price—all the way from sumptuous to basic.

It's difficult to give an average rate for this category (see the listings in the chapters that follow). Tariffs depend entirely on *where* the apartment is located and *when* you intend to use it, as well as for how long. Weekly rates for couples in peak season hover around the $120 to $140 vicinity.

Colleges

A number of university colleges will accept both students and nonstudents as residents during vacation periods, although bona fide students usually get priority. These accommodations are excellent, if you can get them: comfortable, congenial, and relaxed, as well as cheap. Single rooms for adults go at between $11 and $14 per day, and the facilities frequently include swimming pools, golf courses, tennis courts, etc.—the trappings of a resort hotel at economy prices. You'll find examples listed in the city chapters.

Camping Grounds

Canada—at least the tourist areas—is chock-a-block with campgrounds and trailer parks of all shapes, sizes, and degrees of comfort. The more scenic the territory, the more numerous the camping facilities. A standard sample would be open from May through September and offer power and water hookups, a sanitary block, hot showers, flush toilets, a laundromat, a general store, and a childrens' playground. A caravan site costs $4 to $6, with an additional dollar or so for electricity.

Some campgrounds also rent out house trailers at reasonable rates. But these are only practicable if you have your own wheels, since most camps are located way out of town and public transport to and from may be sparse or nonexistent. Get a list of campsites from the provincial tourist office and pinpoint their locations on a map before you consider renting a trailer.

Farm Vacations

These can be memorable if your tastes are truly rustic and the bright lights mean naught to you. You're a paying guest on a working farm, but the accent is usually on the word "guest." This is perhaps the best way to get to know Canadians, because you visit, eat, relax, and—if you want—work with your farm hosts. The food is solid, rich country fare; and you can ride, swim, boat, fish, or try your hand at milking a cow or a goat. And head home cityward feeling you've really unwound. We'll give you further details on this mode of vacation in the provincial chapters.

Indian Camps

This is no doubt the most excitingly *different* type of accommodation in our listing, but not everybody's holiday brew. These facilities are offered by Canada's Indian tribes, and they range from family recreation areas to remote fishing and hunting lodges. The more remote, the more fascinating—but also the more expensive. Those lying in the real wilderness can only be reached by charter aircraft. And in order to enjoy the unexcelled hunting and fishing they offer, you need Indian guides, considerable equipment, and a certain amount of physical stamina.

The samples below will give you an idea of the variety of camps available. But they can't convey the sheer fascination of hitting the trail with an Indian companion, a man linked to the country by bonds of blood and heritage and willing to impart some of his knowledge to you:

Burnt Church Reserve: This is the fishing reserve of the Burnt Church Indians in northern New Brunswick. It has campgrounds, trailer parks, and motel facilities, and fishing from lobster boats. Write to: Chief Frank Paul, Burnt Church Indian Reserve, Burnt Church, N.B.

Big Trout Lake Indian Reserve: Here's a log cabin and an adjacent cookhouse in Ontario, with fishing for lake trout and northern pike; hunting for moose, bear, grouse, and woodland caribou. Access is by aircraft. Write to: Mr. Aglias Chapman, Big Trout Lake, Ontario, via Central Patricia.

Silvester Jack: This is a big-game hunting camp in the Yukon Territory, with black bear, grizzly, moose, caribou, and superb fishing for trout and grayling. Hunters reach the base camp by boat; dogs are used for packing out to spike camps. Write to: Mr. Silvester Jack, Atlin, B.C.

Point-Bleue Reserve: This tourist camp with gas station and stores is in central Québec, with hunting for moose and grouse, and fishing for lake trout, Atlantic salmon, and whitefish. It features Indian dances, canoe races, and sports competitions. Rail and bus transportation are from Québec City. Write to: Chief Harry Kurtness, Point-Bleue, Québec.

EATING AND DRINKING:
You can, if that's your notion, eat your way around Canada on a strict U.S. diet. Every place you visit will offer hamburgers, hot dogs, soggy-greasy french fries, chemical fizz drinks, and whatever else passes as the great American cuisine. The standard Canadian hotel breakfast is every inch as awful as the U.S. version: the eggs as leathery, the toast as limp, the coffee as watery. Only the milk is usually fresher and the butter doesn't taste as if it had been squeezed from a test tube.

But if you want to please your palate as well as your other senses, you'll seek out the hostelries that serve the country's regional specialties, which rank among the finest devised by human ingenuity. Canada's native cuisine is a mouth-watering blend of traditional French, Scottish, and Irish recipes modified by local raw materials. Not to speak of the influence of German, Russian, Ukrainian, Italian, and Chinese imports.

Regional cooking is one of Canada's contributions to the sum total of human happiness. You can't always get it, but it's worth hunting down those hostelries that provide it.

The Atlantic provinces are famous for their fish dishes, but since Canada houses nearly one-third of all the fresh water on the globe, freshwater fish count among her specialties. All in all it's a marine gastronome's paradise, as anyone who has tasted Lac La Ronge trout, Boundary Bay crab, Malpeque oysters, Digby scallops, Arctic char, Selkirk whitefish, or B.C. salmon will testify. Don't shy away from dishes that may sound rather too exotic for your sensibilities. In Newfoundland, where there is little soil for raising meat or vegetables, they've developed delicacies such as baked cod's tongues and seal flippers pie (served with black currant jelly) that will amply repay a bit of culinary courage.

Québec, of course, reigns supreme among the provincial kitchens. There you'll find French genius modified by native raw materials. Some of the French-Canadian recipes date back 300 years and are still being served—which you'll rarely see in France. On no account should you miss tasting Habitant pea soup, the magnificent pork pies called tourtières, the local pâté de foie gras (made with chicken livers instead of goose livers), and the cretons (served on rye bread) we still dream about.

While not in Québec's class, the other provinces boast their own table highlights. In Ontario, it's Haliburton pheasant and Niagara apple-cheese Betty. In British Columbia, black cod with lemon butter, Saltspring lamb, or apple dumplings. In Alberta, chuck wagon stew and a very special mincemeat containing cider, molasses, and ground cinnamon. In Nova Scotia, with its curious blend of Scottish, French, and German cooking, it's fish chowder, Lunenburg sausage with sauerkraut, and baked scallops. In Manitoba, it's Lake Winnipegosis wild duck and jellied cucumber salad. And so on . . . right through the ten provinces.

The prairie provinces, which form one of the world's greatest breadbaskets, also produce some of the world's finest beef. The unforgettable flavor of western beef is because the calves are milk-fed longer than anywhere else. If you're a steak lover, then Canada is your country.

Looking at restaurant menus, the prices *seem* to be roughly on a par with the United States. Actually they're considerably cheaper. First, because of the advantageous exchange rate. Second, because some provinces have no sales tax, which removes quite a slug from your bill. If you subtract first 13%, then the percentage of whatever tax would be added at home, you'll find that you're eating very economically indeed.

A breakfast of juice, bacon and eggs, hash browns, coffee, and toast will set you back around $3.30 in Canadian cash. (You'll have a tough time getting unsugared fruit juice anywhere. But the bacon makes up for that—it's superb.) A good standard three-course restaurant dinner runs to about $6.40, providing you don't have steak, which would mean another two dollars or so.

The country's drinking situation is somewhat complicated because of (a) the antiquated liquor laws, and (b) the over-the-counter sale of alcoholic beverages is a government monopoly. Meaning that you can purchase bottles only in official liquor stores, which are not very conspicuous and rather thin on the ground. Liquor also carries a Social Service tax. That does not mean it's expensive. A bottle of Canadian whiskey costs $6.50, local gin $3.15, while Canadian table wines come in two-liter jugs costing $3.50 to $4.90.

You may be surprised to hear that Canada produces wine, but there's quite a lot of the wonderful stuff in Ontario's southwestern "sun parlor," which also grows soya beans and even tobacco. Her light table wines are almost as good as the Californian vintages, and have the advantage of being considerably cheaper. In a restaurant, a quarter-liter carafe of "house wine" costs in the vicinity of $2.

The hours in which you may drink it, however, are rather restricted. Bars (called lounges hereabouts) close at different times in the various provinces, but nowhere do they remain open later than 1 a.m. All of them close on Sundays. The only place you can get a drink on that day is in a restaurant, and then only if you order a meal.

The term "fully licensed" behind a restaurant's name denotes that it has a permit to dispense spirits as well as beer and wine. Some of the older hotel lounges still retain separate drinking sections for "ladies" and "gentlemen," another hangover from Old Britain which everybody ignores.

But unless you order imported vintage imbibements in fancy dineries, drink prices won't tear a hole in your travelers checks. Canadian beer (which is excellent) comes at around $1 a pint. A bottle of sauterne is in the vicinity of $3. Cinzano is around $1 per 3-ounce glass, and cocktails range from $1.75 to $2.80, depending on the concoction and where you have it.

This, in very rough strokes, is the gastronomic scene in Canada. There are thousands of nuances and surprises you will discover for yourself as you move around the country—such as the native passion for bran muffins, the remarkably good drinking water, the omnipresence of Cockney-style fish and chips, the tart and refreshing local ciders, the amazing ethnic variety of smorgasbords (they come in Chinese, Indian, American, and several other variations), the superlative tang of Montréal Jewish hot smoked beef—and so on, so forth, et cetera. So I close this section by wishing you good luck as well as *bon appétit!*

WHAT TO BUY: While Canada is by no means a bargain hunter's stomping ground, the exchange rate does offer a chance of getting some items cheaper than you would at home. Let me point out, however, that the U.S. Customs only allows you $100 worth of merchandise for your personal use free of duty, providing you have remained in Canada more than 48 hours.

All-around Canadian merchandise represents a mirror image of what's for sale in the U.S.A., but with a considerably greater presence of imported British goods. This is particularly noticeable in mens' clothing, books, and certain lines of hardware. To get something uniquely Canadian, you'll have to look for arts and handicrafts.

Every city has stores retailing magnificent Indian and Eskimo statuary, paintings, weaving products, carvings, along with piles of imitation junk. It's up to you to distinguish between them, but just as a tip, let me tell you that the real stuff is rather expensive. A tiny Inuit figurine usually sells at around $15 to $25. If it's much cheaper than that, you'd better look for the "Made in Hong Kong" imprint on the bottom.

You'll find the stores selling these and other local specialties, such as Indian sports shirts and moccasins, mentioned in the individual chapters. But if you're seeking replicas of red-coated Mounties, mass-produced mountain scapes, or a "flowing" Niagara Falls on lampshades, you won't have to consult this book. They're *everywhere.*

WHAT TO DO: Canadians are every inch as sports crazy as their U.S. brethren, except that ice hockey beats every other game in terms of arousing fan fanaticism. We all know that **Les Canadiens** are the world's greatest with the puck, and if you get to Montréal don't miss your chance of seeing them in action.

Nearly all of the annual provincial events, such as the **Calgary Stampede,** the **Québec Winter Carnival,** the Nova Scotia **Highland Games,** the Newfoundland **Regatta,** have a sports element to them. In winter vast portions of the country virtually seem to revolve around skiing (downhill and trail), ice skating, sledding, and curling.

Canadians also get the maximum mileage out of their summers. City parks abound with sporting facilities. In several towns you get the feeling that the recreation grounds were built first, and the houses around them as an afterthought. Bicycling has caught on in Canada to a much greater extent than in the U.S.—and minus the stimulus of a gas shortage. Virtually every park boasts bike trails, and there's no better way of exploring them than pedaling. Bike rentals cost between $1.50 and $2.50 an hour, depending on whether you get an ordinary steed or a ten-speed marvel.

Otherwise there's a profusion of sights, museums, exhibitions, shopping malls and centers, outdoor performances, and spectacles to keep you busy. Many of them are free, some unique and astounding. We guarantee you'll never forget a stroll around the cannon-bristling ramparts of old Québec City, the only walled town in America, or a visit to the fabulous Heritage Court of Victoria, B.C., one of the most imaginative museums anywhere.

The main attractions, though, are the cities themselves. They vary so tremendously that any kind of generalization about them would be self-defeating. There is no common denominator that embraces the dynamic newness of Calgary, the Gallic flair of Montréal, the Olde English quaintness of Victoria, the dazzling panoramas of Vancouver, the stateliness of Ottawa. It would be like trying to stuff Chicago and New Orleans into one all-American grab bag.

The point is that they have enough diversity and individualism to keep you interested (and footsore) through all the daylight hours of your trip. Regardless of whether your taste leans toward the ultra-contemporary or the relics of the past, Canada has both—sometimes so intermingled that you seem to be strolling through two different centuries simultaneously.

Evening Activities

Canada's live theater is very much so, and has the added advantage of being bilingual. Québec province alone has more than 30 stage companies, and there are several hundred in the country. If your French can stand the pace, attend a production of the excellent **Théâtre Expérimental de Montréal,** which features some of the finest performances in North America . . . as well as the most controversial. But the majority of plays are in English, giving you a choice between imported, well-tried Broadway successes, and the work of native playwrights, which is frequently as good, if not better. This could be your opportunity of getting acquainted with Canadian authors like Sharon Pollock and Timothy Findlay—both nationally famous—and with some of the more obscure but quite delightful groups like the Mummers of Newfoundland, who use their remarkable miming skills to dramatize local history and current social problems.

Ballet, fortunately, knows no language limitations, so you can enjoy an evening with the **Entre-Six** of Montréal just as much as with the Toronto Dance Theatre. The **Royal Winnipeg Ballet,** incidentally, gave its première performance of Araiz's *Rite of Spring* in Washington in honor of the U.S. Bicentennial. And the **National Ballet of Canada,** which celebrated its 25th anniversary in 1976, is considered one of the world's leading dance troupes. You will find the performances of these and other groups listed in the evening newspapers of whichever city you're in.

Finding Canadian films is not so easy. To be sure, there are plenty of them around, but you'll have a difficult time learning from the ads that they're *Canadian.* You have to turn to the reviews for that.

One reason for this is that Canadian moviemakers tend to go in for co-productions—with Britain, France, the U.S., Mexico, and so on—and the Canadian origins are apt to get lost in the shuffle. Which is a pity, for film production happens to be one of Canada's greatest accomplishments. They do extremely well at international film festivals, winning two awards in one year at Cannes, but at home they seem to get drowned in the flood of Hollywood imports. If you can catch titles like *Ragtime Summer, The Disappearance,* or *Leopard in the Snow* during your trip, you'll see what I mean by quality.

Talking about quality—the consistently finest native movies are turned out, strangely enough, by a government department. The **National Film Board,** an agency of the federal government, was created in 1939 and cut its teeth on wartime propaganda efforts of such outstanding merit that Nazi Germany's Dr. Goebbels paid them the compliment of demanding that his staff copy their technique. After the war, the board ventured into an entirely different field—animated cartoons—and produced a series of all-time classic abstracts with titles like *Dots and Dashes* and *Fiddle-de-Dee* which are still being played to rapt audiences at cartoon festivals.

Cartoons are still the board's pièce de résistance, and occasionally you come across one accompanying the main feature. It invariably has audiences laughing their heads off, most of them without realizing they're watching a product of the NFB. But today the board turns out around 100 new films annually in English and French, including TV specials, documentaries, dramatizations, and a vast variety of educational strips. If you hear of one playing anywhere, don't miss it.

Nightlife

Canada's nightlife has become almost synonymous with disco dancing. Observing the seething mass of discos in any of her large cities, you might think the craze started *here* instead of Paris. They've taken over so thoroughly that every other brand of after-dark carousery runs a very poor fourth.

The great thing in writing about discos is that once you've described one, you have virtually pictured the lot from ocean to ocean. They're all so dark that you can't tell who you're dancing with, so noisy that you can't hear what your partner is saying, and so crowded that you don't actually need a partner at all. Every one features flickering epileptic lights, music in the decibel range of a battleship broadside, and tables jammed so closely together that when you reach for your wallet you unbutton your neighbor's shirt. The salient difference is that in some the din is produced by live performers, while others rely on DJs spinning equally loud discs.

The number available is legion, the distinction between them virtually zero. Some charge admission ranging from $1 to $3.50; a few have truly elegant decor (which you can't see, anyway). But they're still springing up like mushrooms. In this book we've made a valiant effort to list a selection of the major ones. Don't blame us if we seem to have omitted the most "in" among them. At the time of writing it may not even have been built.

In terms of quantity, the next-biggest segment of nightlife takes place in hotel or tavern lounges. Here the variety is immense, ranging from sophisticated piano bars to sing-along organists, rock, country-western, folk, and jazz groups, standup comics, and ethnic entertainment giving forth French, Irish, Scots, German, or Russian vibes. Some of them are in the top-quality bracket, and few are expensive. The majority have no cover charge; you merely pay for what you drink. The number of actual jazz clubs has unfortunately diminished. They were swept away by the disco deluge.

Deluxe nightlife is mostly confined to a few swank hotels or svelte restaurants. This is liable to run into money—say, $25 a head, not counting wine or tips. But this is where you get star-class performers, some local, others imported from Las Vegas, New York, or Paris. And these spots, naturally, are confined to the largest cities, plus a handful of fashionable resort spots.

MEETING CANADIANS: No need to waste words on this subject. Canadians are among the most meetable people on the face of the earth—any time, any place, any occasion. Their friendliness to strangers is almost proverbial and formal introductions are quite redundant. As one newspaper columnist phrased it: "Canadians have terminal *nice.*"

Chapter II

GETTING THERE

1. Getting to Canada
2. Getting Around Canada

GETTING TO CANADA is a snap in this day and age. You can choose to fly from anywhere in the world to her major international airports or, if you are headed from the U. S., then you can choose to ride the rails, the buses, or in your own car. In what follows we'll first outline the various ways of getting to the country and then explain how to get around it.

1. By Air, Rail, Bus, and Car

BY AIR: Canada is served by almost all the international air carriers. The major international airports in the east are Toronto and Montreal; in the west it's Winnipeg, Edmonton, Calgary, and Vancouver.

From the U. S.
Direct flights to Canada leave from the following major U. S. cities: Chicago, Cleveland, Dallas, Houston, Los Angeles, Miami, New York and San Francisco. Just to give you some idea of prices, which are of course *very* subject to change, here are one or two sample roundtrip economy airfares: Los Angeles-Vancouver $259.50; Los Angeles-Toronto $462.96; New York-Montreal $132.16; New York-Vancouver $503.64; Chicago-Calgary $361.08. You can realize substantial savings on these fares by purchasing one of the many special excursion fares available, for example, CP Air's Circle Fare which allows you to fly from Los Angeles-Vancouver-Toronto-Los Angeles for only $347. Many of these special excursion fares (which usually feature minimum-maximum stays and advance purchase requirements) offer a 40% discount on regular economy fares. So be sure to check with the airlines and try to take advantage of these opportunities.

Fares from Outside the U. S.
Currently your cheapest direct flight options fall into three categories. The APEX Fare (Advance Purchase Excursion) which is usually valid from seven to 60 days and must be purchased at least 21 days in advance. These requirements do vary (minimally though), not only from airline to airline but also from one part of the world to the other. The second category is the GIT Fare (Group Inclusive Tour) which requires a minimum of five persons traveling together

on a complete air and land itinerary. Tours using these fares must include your hotel and sightseeing and may be purchased from your travel agent or airline. You must stay abroad a minimum of seven and a maximum of 21 days. Tickets must be issued and land arrangements paid for more than seven days before departure. Again the rules vary somewhat depending on the airline and the geographic area. The third option, the Excursion Fare, usually requires a minimum stay of seven days and maximum of 60. The ticket allows one stopover in each direction at $25 additional. There are no advance purchase requirements on this one. These, then, are your least expensive options.

CP Air, the aviation arm of the worldwide transportation and resources company, Canadian Pacific Ltd., provides great scope in getting to Canada from the far-flung corners of the globe. She operates twice weekly flights from Sydney and flies four or five times weekly from Tokyo to Vancouver. From South America there's a weekly service from Buenos Aires, Santiago, and Lima, to both Vancouver and Toronto. In 1955 CP Air pioneered the polar route to Europe and still flies the route to Amsterdam (her principal European gateway), Milan, Rome, Athens, and Lisbon.

Just to give you some ballpark figures to help you calculate (very roughly) your transportation costs here are several of CP Air's fares from various parts of the world. The fares are correct as we go to press but with the current energy problems and worldwide inflation we must stress their liability to change and their use as mere guidelines.

	Regular	Excursion	APEX
Tokyo-Vancouver	$1340	$1298	$874
Sydney, Australia-Vancouver	1654		648
Amsterdam-Vancouver	1542	1005	753
Amsterdam-Toronto	1210	832	547
Athens-Montreal	1276	715	
Lisbon-Montreal	746	501	398
Lisbon-Toronto	810	527	425
Rome-Montreal	972	689	644
Buenos Aires-Vancouver	1616	1423	
Lima-Toronto	914	843	

BY RAIL: Amtrak has two main routes into Canada. On the West Coast the *Pacific International* plies daily between Portland and Vancouver, stopping at Seattle. The East Coast is served by the *Montrealer,* an overnight train originating in Washington D.C. and stopping at New York's Pennsylvania Station, and the *Adirondack* which starts at Grand Central Station, New York. This is a daylight train which travels via Albany and upstate New York to Montreal. Both these trains run daily.

From Buffalo's Exchange St. Station you can make the trip to Toronto on the Toronto/Hamilton/Buffalo Railway (THB) which is a two-car "bud" train. In Toronto you can make connections to Montreal, Ottawa, and so on.

Connecting services are available from other major cities along the border in addition to these direct routes. Call Amtrak, toll-free, for further information, and to check the fares given below which are, of course, subject to change.

Sample Rail Fares

	Coach Fare One-way	Roomette (bed) and One-way Fare	Round-trip Excursion
New York to Montreal	$38	$36.50	$45

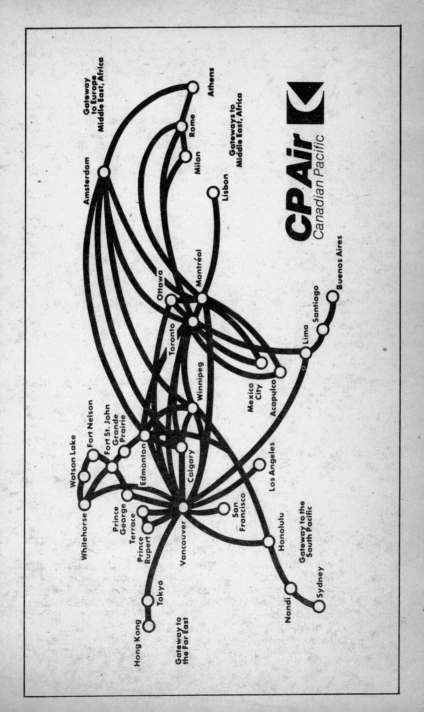

Seattle to			
Vancouver	$12.75	-	$18
Buffalo to			
Toronto	$7.75	-	-

Remember that meals are *not* included in these prices; you must pay for meals on the train when you receive them, or carry your own food.

BY BUS: Greyhound is the only bus company that crosses the border into Canada from the U.S. Its routes are so extensive that you should be able to travel from almost anywhere in the U.S. to any destination in Canada, perhaps making a few changes along the way. In many cases the bus can be faster than the train, a little cheaper, and routes are flexible if you want to stop off on the way. On the other hand they are more cramped, meals are at rest-stops, and you may find yourself stopping at 20 cities or more on trans-continental routes.

Sample Bus Fares

From New York to: *One-way Fare*

Halifax	$98.55	
Québec City	$50.85	
Montréal	$36.75	
Toronto	$52.70	
Winnipeg (via Toronto)	$98.20	(via Chicago) $133.70
Saskatoon (via Toronto)	$110.05	(via Chicago) $165.05
Calgary (via Toronto)	$127.25	(via Chicago) $189.20
Edmonton (via Toronto)	$126.25	(via Chicago) $189.20
Vancouver (via Toronto)	$141.35	(via Chicago) $212.45

From Los Angeles to:

Vancouver	$87.05
Edmonton	$142.80
Toronto	$188.45

These rates are subject to change so check with your local Greyhound office. You should also look into discount fares and their special unlimited-travel passes. Rates vary from season to season, but sometimes the discounts are incredible.

BY CAR: Hopping across the border by car is no problem as the U. S. Highway System leads directly into Canada at 13 points. Once across the border you can link up with the Trans Canada Highway which runs from St. John's, Newfoundland, to Victoria, British Columbia—a total distance of 5000 miles.

2. Getting Around Canada

As we've stated several times before, and will undoubtedly mention again, Canada is a land of immense distances. Which means that transportation from point A to point B forms a prime item in your travel budget as well as your timetable. To give you some idea of the mileage you're dealing with, here are some sample distances (in miles) between major cities, as the crow flies or the jet jets: Montréal to Vancouver, 3041; Vancouver to Halifax, 3897; Toronto to Victoria, 2911; Winnipeg to St. John's, 3159; Calgary to Montréal, 2299; St. John's to Vancouver, 4723; Ottawa to Victoria, 2979.

With this hunk of territory to cover, it isn't surprising that Canadians rank high among pioneers of air travel and that the country's airline network is extensive.

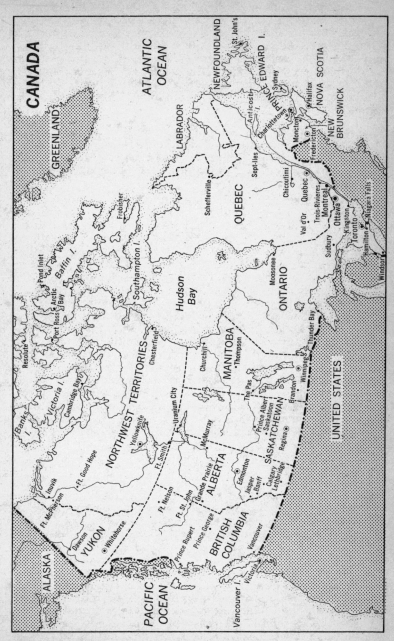

Map Courtesy of The Minister of Supply and Services, Canada

BY AIR: Canada has two major transcontinental airlines, **CP Air** and the government-owned **Air Canada.** There are also five regional airlines plus numerous little local companies handling commuter and specialized traffic, but these will only concern us when we get into their particular regions.

In offering the sampling of typical air fares inside Canada below, I must also add that these (and all other fares quoted) are in force *at the time of writing.* As we all know, rates these days have a tendency to bounce upward at the drop of a hat or the click of a typewriter key. However, they will give you a notion of the price range to expect for air transportation. All rates given are one-way economy class: Toronto–Montréal, $54; Montréal–Vancouver, $206; Ottawa–Winnipeg, $112; Calgary–Toronto, $160; Regina–Ottawa, $138; Toronto–Ottawa, $45; Vancouver–Halifax, $243.

Apart from these bald point-to-point rates you can also get some very attractive package deals, wrapped mostly by the smaller; i.e., nongovernment, companies.

Some of the best and most budget oriented are offered by **Canadian Pacific Airlines** (CP Air), which one aviation writer dubbed "a lovable and aggressive David among the airline Goliaths." Well, lovable and aggressive she is, but the David simile is only correct when you apply standards of international bigness. CP Air, once a backwoods outfit, is now a global carrier of pretty weighty dimensions. Radiating from Vancouver, her routes now extend to San Francisco and Los Angeles in the U.S., to Latin America and Europe, as well as to Australia, Japan, Hong Kong, Fiji, and Hawaii. "David" hasn't done so badly with his slingshot.

How did this little David grow so big? By the only method available to smallish airlines: spoiling their customers. Which is why we have always preferred the midgets to the giants when it comes to international air travel. With CP Air, the spoiling starts the moment you dial the phone to book your flight. The reservation clerk answers within 20 seconds or so—a real rarity these days. It continues through your check-in and culminates in your meals which feature fresh ingredients rather than the canned variety. CP Air serves some of the best in-flight meals we know of, and we've eaten more of those than we care to remember. It's an accumulation of little touches: a bit of extra attention, meals served on china with silverware, a smidgeon of additional courtesy, an added ounce of thoughtfulness, all emanating from the motto laid down by headquarters back in the early and tiny days of the company: "Please the customer, *superlatively* if possible."

The sum total of these touches gives you an understanding of why this particular David was able to make it among the Goliaths.

The airline's most recent innovation is its transcontinental SkyBus service which offers no frills non-stop service linking Toronto with Calgary, Edmonton, and Winnipeg and Vancouver with Winnipeg and Montréal. Fares are approximately half the regular economy rate. Tickets are sold *only* in Canada and must be purchased in person from a travel agent or from a CP Air ticket office. To ensure a seat you should get your ticket as much in advance as possible, but you must plan your itinerary carefully to avoid a no-show penalty.

Besides regular flight service, CP Air's 13 special fly-drive-coach packages, known collectively as **Canadian Routes,** can add another dimension to your view of the country within a remarkably short space of time. (Some of these routes include a camper or motor home as part of the package price.) A few samples will suffice:

Tour 1. Fly to one of eight cities of your choice (from within Canada). Drive a Budget rental car for seven full days. The tour price also includes three nights of deluxe accommodation, plus your return flight. Peak-season price for two persons ranges from $291 to $525, according to the city chosen.

Tour 2. A nine-day scenic jaunt through the Rocky Mountains by air, motorcoach, ferry, and rail. Fly to Victoria or Calgary, motor to Banff, view the Rockies from a train, tour Vancouver, ferry to Victoria, and fly back to your Canadian city base. Price includes accommodation for eight nights. In peak season for two persons sharing, the package costs from $539 to $683, depending on your point of origin.

Tour 8. A 14-day circle route by air, cruise ship, and motor coach. Fly to Victoria, motor to Campbell River, take a cruise liner to Prince Rupert, motor through Banff and Jasper National Parks in the Rockies, drive through the Okanagan Valley, ride the famous Hell's Gate airtram, then motor to Vancouver. Price includes accommodation for 14 nights. Peak-season rate for a double sharing is $972 to $1116.

For further details on these and the other package routes, contact the CP Air office in your hometown or write to CP Air, Vancouver International Airport, BC V7B 1V1.

Pacific Western Transair is certainly no midget. In fact, it's Canada's third-largest airline and the country's biggest regional carrier. But except for its cargo fleet, Pacific Western operates almost solely within Canada and has developed some extremely handy and economical hops you can utilize. The company started back in 1946 with one rented biplane, flown by its founder Russ Baker. From this gnat beginning—delivering men and material to the remote mining and logging camps in northern British Columbia—the enterprise grew into a network covering all of northwestern Canada, plus Seattle in the U.S.

Its handiest service, perhaps, is the remarkable AirBus flitting between Calgary and Edmonton in Alberta (of which more in the appropriate section).

But here is the place to tell you about Pacific Western's package bundles embracing most of western Canada. They hinge on your stopping over one Saturday night in a town of your choice and save you up to 35% on the airfare and up to 25% on hotel rooms and rental cars. There are conditions, of course (aren't there always?), such as booking your ticket at least seven days in advance. The savings, however, also include free coupons on a variety of sights, rides, and attractions at your destination that add up to quite a tidy amount.

For detailed information on these packages, write for the *Economizer Plus Book* to Pacific Western Airlines Ltd., #700, 700 Second St. SW, Calgary, AB T2P 2W1.

BY RAIL: Canada has several privately owned railroads (Canadians say rail-*way,* in the British fashion), but virtually all passenger traffic is carried by a Crown Corporation called **VIA Rail Canada.** For those readers who have experienced the U.S. equivalent of a government-run railroad, let's state quite clearly that there are not even coincidental similarities between them. VIA trains not only run on time, but they run frequently, comfortably, even luxuriously. You might take at least one train journey in Canada, if only to convince yourself that a railroad can actually charm passengers instead of perpetually trying to get rid of them.

You can book tickets by phone and talk to a human voice instead of Amtrak's permanent "busy" bleep; dining cars offer good-quality meals instead of prepacked blotting paper sandwiches; the coaches are clean and the vista-domes on the more scenic routes (sometimes two per train) can make this the most memorable part of your trip.

VIA shares one weakness with its U.S. parallel: baggage handling. A big and busy station rarely has more than half a dozen redcaps to cope with avalanches of luggage. And those handy trollies are never available at the spots where they're needed. Hence our advice at the start of this book of not taking more bags than *you* can carry yourself.

Rail travel is relatively cheap, as the sample fares below will show. All fare prices mentioned are economy class in day coaches: Vancouver–Halifax, $139; Montréal–Edmonton, $81; Ottawa–Montréal, $7; Toronto–Ottawa, $15; Winnipeg–Toronto, $55; Edmonton–Toronto, $79.

One of the most spectacular journeys you can choose is the trip from Vancouver to Calgary. This leads you through the Canadian Rockies, past views that literally take your breath away. You simply can't click your camera fast enough to capture the monumental kaleidoscope of soaring white-capped peaks, immense chasms, roaring mountain streams, and spiderweb bridges spanning them. This is the kind of scenery for which dome coaches were invented, and you'll find it hard to tear yourself away long enough to go to the dining car.

VIA, too, has a vast choice of package tours, many of them combining train with air and bus travel. Some of the most economical are the "Invitation" (midweek) and "Rapido Weekend" deals to about 20 of Canada's larger cities. A Rapido Weekend to Montréal, for instance, includes the return fare, one to three nights' hotel accommodation, and a meal coupon for each night for $60. These package tours go up all the way to two full weeks on the "National Parks Discoverer," costing $825 from Toronto. You can get all the details of these trips from the brochure *VIA Tours Canada* at most travel agents and rail stations.

You might also consider the **Canrailpass,** a travel card offering unlimited transportation on VIA trains at fixed cost within a designated region. They work out differently on season and off and for the specified territories, but an example would be the on-season, Winnipeg and East, 15-day coupon, which costs $180.

BY BUS: There are seven main bus lines operating in Canada, including the familiar Greyhounds. Bus travel is the cheapest form of transportation available (if you exclude your thumb), and the coaches have the same degree of comfort you'll find in the U.S. The bus stations, incidentally, are almost equally as drab, except that they're somewhat better swept and considerably safer. Again, a few sample fares: Winnipeg–Halifax, $112; Ottawa–Montréal, $6; Vancouver–Toronto, $95; Calgary–Regina, $22.

We'll deal with the sightseeing and excursion tours offered by various bus lines in the appropriate chapters.

BY CAR: Let us preface this section by stating that while we're writing this—in the summer of 1979—there's *no* gas shortage in Canada. How the situation will be by the time you read it remains in the lap of Allah, the files of the oil cartels, and the mood of the OPEC powers.

At this stage, Canada—especially Alberta—is wallowing in the liquid gold; the gas stations are actually making efforts to sell more of it! While in the U.S. self-service stations are rapidly dwindling in number, in Canada they have a clear majority. In fact, you may occasionally have difficulties finding one where the service isn't self. The pumps keep open on weekends, just as they used to at home, and the gas prices may give you an attack of nostalgia.

Gas sells by the liter, and pumps at *around* 22.4¢ per liter. This means that the old Imperial gallon costs $1.02. Since the Canadian gallon is one-fifth larger than the U.S. version, and furthermore since you are paying in Canadian money, thus the hypothetical price per U.S. gallon is considerably below the $1 (U.S.) mark. Unfortunately so many Americans are currently driving across the border and filling up that there may be some restrictions in force by the time this book is published. It is unlikely, however, that these will seriously affect driving *within* Canada.

Canada's highway system is excellent, although conditions within the various cities differ sharply. This is due partly to the temperament of the locals, partly to urban renewal processes. Calgary, for instance, has hellish driving conditions because half the downtown area is in the process of reconstruction. To make up for this, it has the politest and most patient motorists in the entire country. In Montréal, on the other hand, they drive with maniacal Gallic panache—meaning very badly—and you'd better use whatever you know of defensive motoring, because the others sure don't.

Car Rentals

The biggest and most thoroughly Canadian car rental company is Tilden, which has come a long way since 1925 when it was started with three cars and a small rented garage. Now Tilden has 350 locations across Canada, is represented at every major airport and also has worldwide affiliates, including National Car Rental, Europcar, and Godfrey Davis. Service, efficiency and competitive rates account for much of this success. Their five reservation offices, located in Montréal, Ottawa, Toronto, Calgary, and Vancouver are equipped with a super sophisticated reservations system that can have a car waiting for you almost anywhere you travel. Their fleet of GM vehicles is kept up to date every year and the company offers several special discount plans to suit different kinds of travelers.

Rental-car rates are, to put it mildly, in a state of flux. So much so that companies have ceased printing rate sheets because the prices are apt to change before the print is dry. This may be confusing to renters, but it's positively agonizing for travel writers trying to give their readers a notion of what may have to be forked out six months hence! The rates below, therefore, should be treated merely as guidelines, rather like the way you treat weather reports or stock market predictions:

Tilden: Daily rates are (as of this writing): subcompacts, $17.95; compacts, $21.95; intermediates, $22.95; regular, $23.95; luxury, $26.95; station wagons, $27.95.

With all makes you get 200 free kilometers (km), then pay 10¢ per additional km. Tilden also offers special three-day weekend rates, with sub-compacts costing $39.91 for the three days.

Budget: Charges the following per day: subcompacts, $19.95; compacts, $23.95; intermediates, $25.95; full size, $28.95; luxury, $30.95.

Unlimited mileage with all types. Budget has a special weekend rate, Friday noon to Monday noon, in which the daily rate for a compact is $19.95.

Avis: Daily charges are: compacts, $19; intermediates, $23; full size, $26; luxury, $28 to $31; station wagons, $26 to $30.

Daily rates include 200 free km, then charges of 10¢ to 13¢ per additional km.

Hertz: Has daily rates for subcompacts of $19.95; compacts, $21.95; intermediates, $22.95; full size, $25.95.

These daily rates include 100 free km, then 10¢ to 15¢ per additional km.

Part One

ATLANTIC CANADA

by Tom Brosnahan

NOVA SCOTIA

NOVA SCOTIA WEARS its Scottish allegiance as proudly as any Highlander wears his kilt. From town names like Inverness, Iona, and New Glasgow, to the musical Scots dialect of the province's oldtimers, Scottish culture and traditions are remembered and revered.

But Nova Scotia is not completely Scottish in tradition. The MicMac Indians were here long before the first European settlers came—and the first European settlers were French. A Scottish colony established a few years after Samuel de Champlain's first (1605) did not survive. The French did, and soon their colonists filled the valley of the Annapolis Basin. And Halifax, named for a Yorkshire town, has more of London about it than it has of Edinburgh.

Toasting the Queen in Halifax, watching the Highland Games in Antigonish, visiting the Acadian memorials at Grand Pré, learning of MicMac history and lore—all these take second place to the beauty of the land itself. The rugged coastlines scooped with rows of small coves, the dramatic mountain scenery of Cape Breton's highlands, the lush, fertile fields lining the Fundy shores—these are the real Nova Scotia, beautiful and hospitable to all who come here.

Assuming that most visitors coming by land will cross from New Brunswick on the Trans Canada Hwy., this chapter is arranged to start at Amherst, coming south to Halifax, and then touring the peninsula on the motor routes mapped out by the provincial tourist authorities. Then it's off to Cape Breton Island, Nova Scotia's most exciting tourist destination.

For toll-free information about Nova Scotia, call these numbers: in Ontario, 800/565-7140; in Québec and Newfoundland, 800/565-7180; in the State of Maine, 800/492-0643; in the rest of the continental United States, 800/341-6096.

When you get to Nova Scotia, any travel bureau or information center operated by the provincial authorities will help you find a room through the **Check-Inns** system. While a good number of Nova Scotia hostelries participate in the system, not all do; often the ones that don't are the less expensive ones. But it's good to know that assistance is available. You can even reserve a room from New Brunswick or Prince Edward Island by dialing the same number as

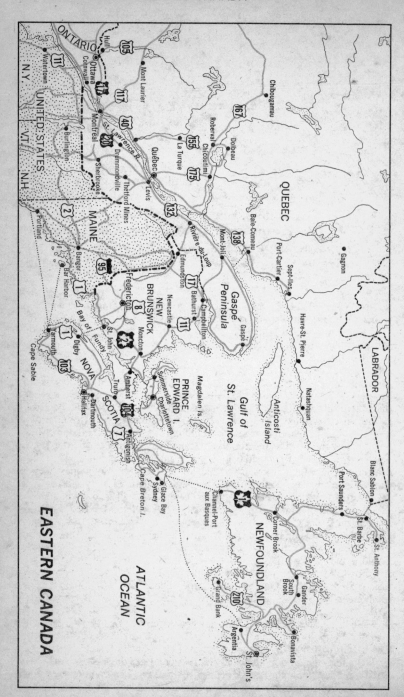

you would in Nova Scotia: 800/565-7105 (from Newfoundland, dial 800/565-7180).

Meals over $3 and all hotel accommodations in Nova Scotia are subject to an 8% provincial tax—remember when toting up your bill.

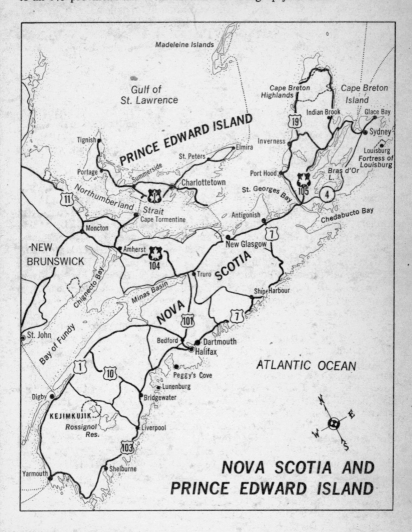

NOVA SCOTIA AND PRINCE EDWARD ISLAND

GETTING THERE: Nova Scotia is accessible by car, by bus, by rail, by car ferry, and easily by air.

By Car and Ferry

Coming overland by car, one enters Nova Scotia from New Brunswick, most probably along the Trans Canada Hwy., entering at Amherst. Then there are the ferry connections: with Prince Edward Island (Wood Islands) at Caribou, N.S.; with Newfoundland (Port aux Basques) at North Sydney, N.S.; with New Brunswick (Saint John) at Digby, N.S.; and with Maine, U.S.A. (Bar Harbor and Portland), at Yarmouth, N.S. Ferries to other Atlantic provinces are covered in the chapters dealing with the provinces they serve. The ones from Maine are popular, convenient, and fun. Here are details:

From Portland, Maine, two services connect with Yarmouth, at the southwestern tip of Nova Scotia. **Prince of Fundy Cruises** operates the M/S *Caribe,* and **CN Marine** runs similar vessels, on daily voyages during the busy summer months.

The M/S *Caribe* departs Portland late in the evening almost every day in season, arriving in Yarmouth at breakfast time after a ten-hour and 15-minute cruise. Departure from Yarmouth is about midmorning, arriving in Portland late in the evening. One-way fares are $30 for adults, $15 for children ages 5 to 14 accompanied by an adult. Vehicle fares depend on the season; the charge in high summer is $50 per car, $45 in the "shoulder" season of mid-May to late June and early September to late October. Cabins on the night trip from Portland cost anywhere from $27 for an inside two-berth cabin to $68 for an outside four-berth one; the choicest two-berth cabins cost $34 to $37. On the day trip from Yarmouth, day cabins cost $16, or $48 for one of the roomy, deluxe ones. (Note that all of these prices are in U.S. dollars.) Prince of Fundy Cruises sponsors all sorts of money-saving package deals, including round-trip specials, "mini-cruises" which give you bargain-priced round-trip tickets, cabin and meals (but no car passage), and tours which include ferry passage for car and passengers, and then rooms in hotels and motels on a predetermined route. A travel agent can fill you in on details, or contact Prince of Fundy Cruises, International Terminal, Portland, ME 04101 (tel. 207/775-5616; toll free in Maine, tel. 800/482-0955; toll free in New England and south to Washington and west to Ohio, tel. 800/341-7540; in Yarmouth, tel. 902/742-3411). Needless to say, reservations are a must during the busy summer months.

CN Marine's ferries operate between Portland and Yarmouth all year long, departing Portland in the evening on Mondays, Wednesdays, and Fridays, and departing Yarmouth in late morning or early afternoon on Sundays, Tuesdays, and Thursdays. Passenger fares are $30 one way, $15 for children ages 5 through 12; cars cost $50 from late June to early September, $45 other times of the year. Cabins can be had at $12 per berth, $24 per cabin on night trips, and $9 per berth, $18 per cabin on day trips. All these fares are payable in Canadian dollars at Yarmouth, in U.S. dollars at Portland. Sailing time is about 11 hours. You will need reservations for sure in high summer: contact the Terminal Supervisor, CN Marine, P.O. Box 4098, Station A, Portland, ME 04101, (tel. 207/775-6581; in Maine, call toll free 800/492-0622; in New England and south to Washington and west to Ohio, tel. 800/341-0222); in Yarmouth, write the Terminal Supervisor, CN Marine, Yarmouth, NS B5A 1K9 (tel. 902/742-3513).

Between Bar Harbor, Maine, and Yarmouth, N.S., sailings are aboard the CN Marine's M/V *Bluenose,* which operates on the six-hour run from mid-May until mid-October. Up to mid-June and after late September, the *Bluenose* departs Bar Harbor in the morning on Tuesdays, Thursdays, and Saturdays, and departs Yarmouth on Mondays, Wednesdays, and Fridays, also in the morning. But in high season departures are daily, from Bar Harbor in the morning, from Yarmouth in late afternoon. In high season, fares are $15 per adult, $35 per car; off-season, fares are $9 per adult, $27 per car. Children 5 through 12 pay half fare. Cabin prices are $10, $13, and $15 year round; the cheapest cabins have no private toilets, medium-priced cabins are with toilets, on the mezzanine deck; highest priced cabins are on the promenade deck, and come equipped with toilet. Fares are payable in U.S. dollars in Bar Harbor, in Canadian dollars in Yarmouth. For reservations, call the toll-free numbers listed above for the Portland–Yarmouth CN Marine ferry, or call Bar Harbor at 207/288-3395.

Greyhound and Trailways buses can take you to Portland and Bar Harbor from Washington, New York, and Boston; some buses even stop right at Portland's International Terminal. When you reach Yarmouth, fast VIA Rail "Dayliner" railcar service is available to and from Halifax (see below). Bus service, outlined below, can also get you around Nova Scotia.

On these ferry cruises between Maine and Nova Scotia, restaurants and bars are on each ship, along with slot machines, gambling tables, and duty-free shops—this is considered a voyage on the high seas.

By Air

Halifax is the air hub of the Atlantic provinces, although many long-distance flights come via Montréal. **Eastern Provincial Airways** is the regional carrier which connects Halifax and Sydney with the rest of Atlantic Canada. Call them in Halifax at 902/861-3860; in Sydney at 902/564-4545.

By Rail

VIA Rail operates diesel railcars called "Dayliners" on the route between Yarmouth and Halifax, stopping at Kentville, Annapolis Royal, Digby, and most other stations along the line. Dayliners carry no meal facilities, but you can bring your own snacks or grab one during the stop at Kentville. In summer, two trains make the trip in each direction, usually with one running in the morning, the other in the evening. In October there may be one or two trains per day, depending on the day.

Two supertrains connect Halifax with the rest of Canada. The *Scotian* and the *Ocean* operate daily between Halifax and Montréal on the route from Montréal to Levis (Québec City), Rivière du Loup, Matapedia, Campbellton, Bathurst, Newcastle, Moncton, Sackville, Amherst, Truro, and Halifax, making stops at numerous other stations along the way. Both haul restaurant and sleeping cars. The *Ocean* leaves Montréal at the end of the business day, the *Scotian* late in the evening; on the return trip, the *Ocean* leaves Halifax about noon, the *Scotian* at the end of the business day. The trip, by either train, takes about 23 hours.

Sydney and Halifax are connected by daily train service on the route from Sydney to North Sydney, Antigonish, New Glasgow, Truro, and Halifax. A diesel railcar with snack service leaves Sydney very early, soon after sunrise, and another leaves Halifax just after dinner, on the 7½-hour run between these two cities. Another train, with "Dayniter" reclining seats, restaurant, snack, and beverage service, departs Sydney daily before lunch, Halifax at a similar hour, on an express run stopping only at major stations. This trip stops fewer times, but takes longer—10 or 11 hours—although one travels in greater comfort.

By Bus

Two companies handle most of Nova Scotia's bus traffic. **Acadian Lines** has routes connecting Halifax with Amherst (and buses from New Brunswick), Sydney, and Yarmouth. The Halifax–Yarmouth buses connect with the ferries to Bar Harbor and Portland, Maine. Acadian also has daily service between Halifax and Charlottetown, P.E.I., via the Caribou–Wood Islands ferry boat.

On Cape Breton Island, Acadian will take you to points from which you can connect with other lines to Inverness and Baddeck. In Halifax, call Acadian at 454-9321; in Yarmouth, at 742-5131; in Sydney, at 564-8123; in New Glasgow, at 752-7141.

MacKenzie Bus Line Ltd. runs coaches along the southern shore between Halifax and Yarmouth via Bridgewater, Liverpool, Shelburne, and Barrington. For information, call MacKenzie's head office in Bridgewater, N.S. (tel. 902/543-2491).

Car Rentals

Tilden Car Rentals has offices throughout Nova Scotia, but major ones are in Halifax at 1130 Hollis St. (tel. 902/422-4439); in Sydney at 265 Prince St. (tel. 902/564-6417); and in Yarmouth at the Esso station, 70 Starr's Rd. (tel. 902/742-4611). You should reserve your rental car in advance during the busy summer months, particularly if you plan to arrive in Yarmouth by ferry and then rent a car to continue your travels—lots of people want to do this, and cars are limited. Note also that you may have to pay a stiff return charge if you drop the car at a city other than that in which you rented it, so plan to make your way back to Halifax, Sydney, or Yarmouth. You can reserve a Tilden car through any National Car Rental office in the U.S.

1. Amherst to Halifax

AMHERST: Coming from New Brunswick, the first town across the Nova Scotia border is Amherst, lying right at the edge of the Tantramar marshes. Through the marshes surge the waters of a tidal bore—a strong inland current generated by the high Fundy tides.

Staying the night in Amherst is no problem. Just after crossing the border from New Brunswick, look for the LaPlanche St. exit. This is the one to take for Amherst's roadside motels.

Letcher's Motel (tel. 902/667-3881) has a small heated swimming pool for guests' use, and a breakfast room. The 32 units all have color TV, radio, and telephone, and cost $22 to $26 single, $26 to $28 double. Rates drop after mid-September, until the end of May.

The nearby **Tantramar Motel** (tel. 902/667-3838) has very reasonably priced rooms done in Early American style; all 16 rooms have the standard conveniences, including color TV. Rates are $16 to $22 single, $22 to $24 double, with discounts in order from September through mid-June, and for senior citizens anytime.

On Hwy. 6, two miles from the center of Amherst going toward Pugwash, stands the big white house which is **D'Orsay Lodge** (tel. 902/667-7702). Set well back from the road in a swath of lawn, D'Orsay Lodge has five rooms which share a bathroom, and the lowest rates in town: $10 single, $12 double, $2 for an extra person sharing a room. Breakfast is available.

The "Sunrise Trail," outlined by Nova Scotia's Department of Tourism, starts in Amherst on Hwy. 6, heading southeast. Driving along the coast, past little inlets, beaches, and villages, will eventually bring you to Tatamagouche and the **Balmoral Motel** (tel. 902/657-2000). A favorite with Nova Scotians passing through town, the Balmoral has ten cozy units with color TV, radio, telephone, and private bath for $22 single, $25 double. There's a private beach you can use near the motel. The **Mill Dining Room** is open only during the busy season, but when it's serving you can have breakfast, lunch, or dinner (7 a.m. to 9 p.m.). Sandwiches and fish and chips are prominent on the menu, but there's always a "Dinner of the Day" which is a real bargain. The last I had was made up of chicken noodle soup, roast beef, vegetables, and coffee for $5.25. Liquor is served.

TRURO: Once called by its Indian name of Cobequid, Truro is a communications center. Rail lines and the Trans Canada Hwy. pass through this town of 13,000 people, and its location at junctions makes it the perfect location for the Nova Scotia Provincial Exhibition, an agricultural and amusement fair held each August. The perfect location for the fair in town is its marvelous **Victoria Park**, one of the most dramatically beautiful city parks to be seen anywhere. A deep gorge cuts through the park, filled by a clear stream which cascades from level to level among the rocks—you must see it. The best way is with a picnic lunch or a glass of wine in the evening. It's only a 700-foot stroll to Howe Falls from the parking area.

Truro is also known for the **tidal bore** which rushes up the Salmon River from the Bay of Fundy via Cobequid Bay. The bore, a rushing current which can develop into a wall of water several feet high in peak season, needs planning to be appreciated. Check with the locals to see what the current status is, and at what hour the bore is at its most dramatic. Usually, the days of the full moon in August or later in autumn bring the bore in like a torrent.

Most of Truro's recommendable hostelries are out of town by the highway, overlooking the tidal bore. With any luck, you won't even have to move from the comfort of your room to see it. At the **Tideview Motel** (tel. 902/893-8951), for instance, the marshy estuary of the Salmon River is all around you, and the tidal bore is visible from the bridge right next to the motel's Palliser Restaurant. Some of the motel's 42 units have baths, others have showers, all have TVs of one sort or another; one unit has a kitchenette. Prices are moderate: $18 to $22 for one, $22 to $30 for two. These are the rates for July, August, and September, with other months subject to reductions.

The **Palliser Restaurant** is well known among local people for its pine-paneled dining room, decorated with colorful plates high along the walls, and a large coat-of-arms. Windows look onto the Salmon River, just in case the tide rises during your mealtime. Breakfast is on from 8 to 10:30 a.m., lunch from 11:30 to 2:30, dinner from 5 to an early 8:30 p.m.—mid-May to mid-October only. Food at the Palliser is solid and tasty rather than exotic, and a full dinner can easily be put together for less than $10. Wine, beer, and drinks are served. The Palliser and its companion Tideview Motel are at the end of a drive near Exit 14 from the Trans Canada Hwy.

Also at Exit 14 is the **Tidal Bore Inn** (tel. 902/895-9241), up on the hillside above the Salmon River marshes. It's a new, two-story motel, dark and handsome, with 24 modern units, color TV equipped and moderately priced. Single rooms cost $21, doubles are $24, and an additional person pays $3.

Should you choose to stay downtown in Truro, the **Glengarry Motel** (tel. 902/895-5388), 138 Willow St., is not very far from the Victorian brick-and-stone public buildings which mark the center of town. Big and newish, the Glengarry's two-floor motel building stands beside and behind Glengarry House, a beautiful old mansion converted to be the motel's restaurant. The 47 motel units have color TVs and all the conveniences, and cost $26 to $28 single, $28 to $32 double in one bed, $32 to $36 double in twin beds. The motel has a heated outdoor pool. In the **Glengarry House** restaurant, breakfast is served from 7 to 11:30 a.m., lunch from noon to 5, dinner from 5 to 9 p.m. (till 10 in summer), all year round. Food is familiar and good; prices are moderate. At dinner, for instance, only a few steaks cost over $8, and the Glengarry House always provides a table d'hôte dinner—everything from soup to coffee—for $6 (plus tax and tip).

Shubenacadie Wildlife Park

Twenty-four miles (38 km) south of Truro along Hwy. 102, at Exit 10, is Shubenacadie Wildlife Park. It's a free provincial park established and operated by Nova Scotia's Department of Land and Forests to give visitors and Nova Scotians alike a close look at the animals that inhabit this province, so full of natural beauties. Shubenacadie is truly a park, too—it's not a zoo. Animals are kept in large enclosures rather than in cages. Most of the birds aren't restrained at all; they come just because the park is so hospitable. Ducks and swans, foxes, caribou, and white-tail deer are only some of the species you'll see. Hours are from 8:30 a.m. to 9:30 p.m., mid-May to mid-October, and there's no admission charge.

2. Halifax

Halifax is the British heart of Atlantic Canada. Maritime metropolis, capital of Nova Scotia, it feels the pulse of eastern Canadian life. And yet in the depths of its romantic soul, Halifax dreams of England and of things English.

A quick look at history explains why Halifax is unabashedly Anglophile. Nova Scotia was explored by the English, but settled by the French, Irish, and Scots—all except for Halifax, which was founded under the benevolent and watchful eye of George Montague Dunk, Earl of Halifax. The earl was president of England's Board of Trade and Plantations in 1749, when the town was founded under the auspices of that board. Halifax was fortunate in many things, but above all in that it could derive its name from the earl's bailiwick—the Yorkshire city of Halifax—rather than from the Earl's family name. (Imagine if the city were named "Dunk"!) Founded by this English body, Halifax's role in the New World was to be Britain's commercial center and naval stronghold, two duties which Halifax performs to this day. For this purpose, the board recruited settlers from England rather than from other British lands.

The location picked for the city was superb, on a hilly peninsula surrounded by one of the world's great natural harbors. Fortresses crowned the hills in early times, and pastures surrounded them. A few of the grand fortresses survive, and the pastures have been turned into parks: Halifax is one of the greenest cities you'll visit. But location, green space, and water views don't account totally for Halifax's charm. Although this city shoulders the responsibilities of a regional as well as a provincial capital, of a major port, business, and communications center, it's not gigantic. With a population of 122,000, Halifax has all the vibrant activity and cultural opportunities of a much larger city, but none of the crowding and sprawl found in Montréal, New York, and Mexico City.

Keep in mind, then, that when you get to Halifax you'll be walking up and down its hillside a lot, and that the sun will play hide-and-seek with the fog. And don't be surprised to see a color photograph of Her Majesty Queen Elizabeth II gracing a wall in every shop and office. And also, as in London, remember that pedestrians have the right of way and crosswalks are sacrosanct: in Halifax, *stop your car* whenever you approach a crosswalk if a pedestrian has stepped off the curb to cross. Otherwise, you'll set yourself up for a scolding (or a citation) from a policeman in a veddy British-style uniform with a very Canadian way of getting his message across.

ORIENTATION AND INFORMATION: Halifax occupies a peninsula. The heart of the old town was between Bedford Row, on the water, and the Citadel, a star-shaped fortress occupying the hilltop behind the town. Today this same area is the heart of downtown Halifax, filled with shiny office towers and shopping streets, but retaining several blocks of historic buildings which have been restored beautifully to their appearance of colonial days. **Historic Properties** is the first goal of every tourist, and the constant haunt of many Haligonians. At the wharf in Historic Properties is where *Bluenose II,* a replica of Canada's famous schooner, has her home berth (look on the reverse of any 1937 Canadian dime—that's *Bluenose*).

Across the harbor from Halifax is her sister city of Dartmouth, with residential and business quarters of her own.

There's a **Nova Scotia Travel Information Centre** at Halifax International Airport on Hwy. 102. The City of Halifax maintains **information booths** in Historic Properties, in the Old Red Store on Lower Water St.; in the huge office-hotel-shopping complex of Scotia Square, in the Fountain Court of the Lower Mall; and in the Lord Nelson Hotel, the Hotel Nova Scotian, and the Holiday Inn.

WHERE TO STAY: Luxurious and expensive hotel rooms are easy to find in downtown Halifax, and the city center even provides a surprising number of beds at rock-bottom prices. But good, clean, moderately priced hostelries are not easy to come by. As in most cities in North America, the best-value-for-money rooms are in suburban motels, built out where real estate is cheaper and highway signs can attract customers. Luckily, Halifax's little neighbor Bedford, on the northern shores of the harbor known as Bedford Basin, has a good selection of motels. City bus routes pass by all of the highway establishments recommended below, so you needn't fight traffic to enter Halifax for the day's sightseeing. But first, some notes on Halifax's downtown hostelries:

The majority of Halifax's downtown hotel rooms are in the half-dozen giant places which can boast all the luxuries—and prices to match. But the center of the city does harbor a few exceptional, middle-range hotels and motels. At the bottom of the price scale are the Ys and Youth Hostels, which are incredible bargains: right downtown, rock-bottom prices, clean and respectable. Here they all are, arranged by price category.

The Top Hotels

Although it's not Halifax's largest hotel, the **Citadel Inn** (tel. 902/422-1391), a cross between a hotel and a motel, has many things to recommend it: a heated outdoor swimming pool, free parking, a dining room called King Arthur's Court, and a good location just opposite the Scotia Square complex. The 200 guest rooms are luxurious, and some have fine views of the city and the harbor, as well as all the modern conveniences. When I last visited, the Citadel was in the midst of expansion, adding a wing of super-luxurious rooms, which will rent for $39.50 single, $46.50 double or twin; the standard rooms cost less, at $34.50 to $37.50 single, $41.50 to $44.50 double. An extra person in a room pays $5, except for children 12 years and under, who can stay with their parents for free. The Citadel Inn is at 1960 Brunswick St., at the corner of Cogswell.

Halifax's mammoth new downtown luxury hotel is the **Château Halifax** (tel. 902/425-6700), a CP Hotel built right into the new Scotia Square complex. The Château is virtually a city-within-a-city, as Scotia Square houses all the shops, restaurants, bars, and nightclubs anyone can handle—in addition to the hotel's own rooftop aerie, the Night Watch Restaurant. Edward and Julie's, another of the Château's restaurants, specializes in fondues, and Dick Turpin's Pub is the place with live entertainment. The hotel staff is fully trained to do your laundry, rent you a car, babysit your children, take dictation, and serve meals in your room. And the rooms—all 305 of them—can boast the latest in luxury, and city views to match. Regular rates are $40 single, $47 double, $7 for an extra person. But as with all such large hotels, special offers are frequently made for weekend stays. Of course, the Château Halifax has its own enclosed pool on the indoor-outdoor model, open year round.

Right next to Halifax's rail terminus is the **Hotel Nova Scotian** (tel. 902/423-7231), a CN hotel (right next to a CN station) that offers some outstanding money-saving opportunities to stay in comfort. Although the main hotel building was constructed some time ago, a new addition of luxury rooms can satisfy the finicky traveler. All rooms, of course, have color cable TV and private baths; the newer rooms have air conditioning as well. If you want all the services of a grand hotel, yet at a discount price, ask for one of the older rooms, renting for $35 single, $41 double; the newer ones cost $41 single, $49 double. On weekends, an incredible bargain rate of $28, single or double, is offered, provided you check in Friday or Saturday and stay two nights at least. Children of any age can stay free with their parents, even at this special weekend rate. The Nova Scotian has no less than three drinking places and two licensed restaurants, one of which is the Evangeline Room (described below). The hotel's location, at 1181 Hollis St., corner of Morris, is a few blocks from the center of town, but a free hotel shuttle bus makes regular runs, to save you the walk (no service on Sundays, or after 8 p.m.). If you're planning a three-night stay in Halifax, make it Friday, Saturday, and Sunday nights at the Nova Scotian—no better bargain exists.

For Edwardian grandeur, no hotel in Halifax outdoes the **Lord Nelson** (tel. 902/423-6331), 1515 So. Park St., corner of Spring Garden, facing Halifax's lovely Public Gardens. A sense of gentility and quiet pervades the baronial halls and streetside veranda of the hotel, lent force by a number of dignified elderly types who reside here. Rooms are quite comfortable, all with color TV, private bath or shower, and telephone. Rates depend on the size of the room and whether one has a park view, besides the obvious bath or shower option. The best cost $38 single, $46 double; standard rooms are $35 single, $43 double. The lowest priced rooms, at $27 single, $35 double, offer good value for money. Children 13 and under can share their parents' room for free; over this age, the extra-person charge of $6 applies. The Lord Nelson is sedate and well located, near the Citadel, parks, and many of the city's better restaurants.

A final note about a hotel which doesn't exist yet: the **Barrington Place Inn,** at the corner of Duke and Granville Sts. right down near Historic Properties, is abuilding as this book goes to press. It's located in a group of buildings called the Prince of Wales Block, currently under renovation. The original facade is being preserved, while completely new and modern structures are being erected behind. Prices and facilities will no doubt be comparable to Halifax's best. The inn is a project of Delta Hotels, and will be worth a look.

Middle-Range Hotels

The best all-round moderately priced hostelry in central Halifax is undoubtedly the **Dresden Arms Motor Hotel** (tel. 902/422-1625), 5530 Artillery Pl. When you head out in search of the hotel, note that Artillery Pl. is a little one-block-long street which runs between Dresden Row and Birmingham St., between Spring Garden and the Citadel. This location puts you in a quiet neighborhood near the Citadel and Public Gardens, but only a few minutes' walk from the center of town. The Dresden Arms is new, very modern, and supremely comfortable, with such big-hotel luxuries as an indoor swimming pool, sauna, whirlpool bath, nightclub, and restaurant, but moderate room prices. A single person pays $28 to $30, two pay $32 to $36, and an additional person pays $4. The 94 rooms all have color cable TV, radio, telephone, private baths with shower, large windows, and air conditioning. Good location, good prices, fine rooms—a winner.

Without doubt, Halifax's coziest and most charming place to stay is the **Queen's Street Inn** (tel. 902/422-9828), 1266 Queen St. at Morris, near Halifax Infirmary. Here, a fine old town house has been converted to a small and very personal hotel, with absolutely spotless rooms tastefully decorated in antiques and old pieces. The inn is a delightful change from the sameness of modern hotels, and while you won't have color TV (although black-and-white sets are available if you want one) or swimming pools or nightclubs, you'll have a unique room with quiet dignity and a good, new bed (Alfred Saulnier, the owner, boasts that his beds cost him $600 apiece). The inn's six rooms are all different, and rent for $20 to $25 per room. There's no other place in Halifax like the Queen's Street Inn—reserve in advance to be sure you get a place.

Young people who want to stay right at the center of the action will want to take a look at the **Carleton Hotel** (tel. 902/423-7111), at the corner of Argyle and Prince Sts., right downtown. Although the lobby is covered in dark-wood paneling and has otherwise been refurbished, the guest rooms are largely unredeemed, left from an earlier era. New bedspreads and similar touches brighten them up, but beds may be spongy—by all means, inspect the room before you register. But the hotel's location is excellent, and the prices are very good: $19 single, $23 double in one bed, $27 in twin beds, plus that 8% provincial tax. All the rooms have baths, color TVs, radios, and telephones. If you triple up, the extra person pays $5. The Carleton's rooms need fixing up—but if renovation comes, these low prices will be gone from downtown for ever. By the way, the pub downstairs is one of the liveliest gathering places in town.

The Ys and Hostels

The **YMCA Halifax** (tel. 902/422-6437), 1565 So. Park St., has an excellent location near the Public Gardens and the expensive Lord Nelson Hotel, and yet single rooms without bath cost only $12, plus tax. Men can reserve rooms in advance. Women are welcome at the YM, as are couples, but neither may reserve rooms in advance. Only two rooms are suitable for couples out of the 66 in the residence: the one with a double bed costs $15.50, with twin beds $16.50.

Halifax's **YWCA** (tel. 902/423-6162) accepts women only. Singles are a bargain $11 plus tax; double rooms are $15 for two. Several single rooms with private toilet cost the same as a double room. The YW's health club, swimming pool, gymnasium, tennis courts, and other services are open to visitors.

The local **Youth Hostel** is in the basement of the Halifax YMCA (see above; tel. 902/429-7853), and is open from June through August only. You can check your bags after 1 p.m., but the hostel doesn't open until 5 p.m.; it closes at 8:30 a.m. Youth hostel members pay $2.25 for one of the 100 beds, others pay $3.50. As at the YM, the location is worth $40 a day, although the comforts are minimal.

Motels on the Outskirts

The **Bedford Hwy.** (Hwys. 1 and 2) skirts the western shore of Bedford Basin, starting a few miles north of Halifax. A dozen motels, from budget priced to luxury, from simple to housekeeping, stand along Bedford Hwy. City buses nos. 80 and 85 serve the Bedford Hwy., making convenient stops only a short distance from each motel drive.

The **Chebucto Inn** (tel. 902/453-4330), 6151 Lady Hammond Rd., is on the outskirts of Halifax just before coming to the Bedford Hwy. The same buses go by the Chebucto as the Bedford Hwy. motels, but the Chebucto is just that much closer into town. The dark, rustic-looking two-story motel could be called "modern alpine," an attractive style which fits right into the residential area the Chebucto shares. Full bath and shower, color TV, radio, telephone, and air conditioning are in all 32 rooms, which rent for $23 to $26, single or double, depending on whether you have one bed in the room, or two. Children under 5 stay free; all other extra people in a room pay $3 apiece. You can get breakfast here from 7 to 10 a.m. As the Chebucto Inn is the closest moderately priced motel to downtown Halifax, it fills early. Get your reservation several days in advance.

Next along the road, at 374 Bedford Hwy., is the **Wedgewood Motel** (tel. 902/443-1576). Nearby Wedgewood Park lends its name to the motel, but the Wedgwood ware of England has inspired the decor: behind the stone pillars on the two-story facade, colors are white and that classic Wedgwood blue. The 40 rooms have color cable TV, air conditioning, radio, phone, and private bath, and go for a single price in season: $29. Off-season discounts are in effect October through May. In summer, you can get a light breakfast at the Wedgewood. Well-kept, attractive, convenient—a good choice.

The **Prince's Lodge Motel** (tel. 902/835-3558), next hostelry north along Bedford Hwy. at 554, (P.O. Box 133, Bedford, N.S.), is up on the hill overlooking the road and the Bedford Basin. It's a supremely quiet location, and although you can enjoy the fine view from the parking lot, the motel's orientation means the rooms don't have that same view. No matter, as the Prince's small, comfy rooms are a real bargain. Each of the ten units has a black-and-white TV, a shower, and a radio. Prices are low: $22 single, $24 for two in a double bed, $26 for two in twin beds. Note that Prince's Lodge is open only June through September.

The **Sea King Motel** (tel. 902/835-8367), right next to Prince's Lodge, at 560 Bedford Hwy. (Halifax, N.S.), may take its name from Bedford Basin, right across the road, or from its own little indoor swimming pool. In any case, it's a modern motel surrounded by trees, with very competitive rates. The 33 units have luxury accoutrements without the luxury price: $22 single, $26 double, for a room with bath, color TV, radio, and phone. Breakfast is served from 7 to 11 a.m. The pool and the extra-comfortable rooms make this one of the best bargains on the Bedford Hwy. Off-season reductions are in effect October through May.

The **Bluenose Motel** (tel. 902/835-3388) is as trim and tidy as the schooner from which it takes its name. Single-story brick buildings are laid out perpendicular to the highway to keep the noise level low; shrubs and bushes are dotted here and there. Of the 34 rooms, all have color TV, phone, and private bath, two have kitchenettes, and four are air-conditioned. Rates are competitive: $24 single, $27 double in a double bed, $29 double in twin beds. An additional person pays $3. These rates drop between the beginning of November and mid-May. Breakfast is available at the Bluenose between 7 and 11 a.m.

The swimming pool and the rather lavish, attractive layout at the **Motel Esquire** (tel. 902/835-3367), P.O. Box 610, Halifax, account for the prices, which are slightly higher than at some other motels nearby. Rooms are especially large and spacious, and all 28 are equipped with the luxuries, including color cable TV. There are even two suites, and the motel has a restaurant just on the other side of Bedford Hwy. Rates are $29 to $31 for one or two persons; the suites cost $45. At the Esquire, the off-season period is from mid-October through May. The Motel Esquire is part of the Quality Inn chain, which means you can call 800/268-8990 (in Toronto, 416/485-2600) for toll-free reservations from anywhere in Canada.

Right next door to the Motel Esquire is the **Travellers Motel** (tel. 902/835-3394), a hybrid establishment with 25 very comfortable and well-equipped motel units, plus ten cottages which hold 20 bedrooms; the cottages, although not as luxurious as the motel units, offer a bargain in terms of price. With black-and-white TV and a shower, a double bedroom in a cottage costs only $20 to $22. Motel units have full baths and color cable TVs, and cost $28 to $31, single or double. The Travellers Motel has some nice touches: hanging plants and flower beds here and there, a small swimming pool, and the cottages have the further advantage of being up the hillside a short distance, away from the road noise.

WHERE TO DINE: Halifax offers many good opportunities to dine, and while the variety of restaurants can't approach such gustatorily cosmopolitan cities as London or New York, you will still find good Italian, Chinese, Indian, French, and French-Canadian, as well as English and Canadian-American menus. Starting with the special and fairly expensive places where you might want to go for a celebration or for a romantic last-night-in-Halifax, the list below continues through moderately priced places, with quick lunch, snack, and sandwich eateries covered at the end.

Elegant Dining

The Hotel Nova Scotian's elegant dining room is named **L'Evangeline** (tel. 423-7231) and, as in many other cities with CN Hotels, it is generally regarded as the most dignified place to dine. Service is gracious and soft-spoken, the decor is elegant in an old-fashioned way—understated and unobtrusive. A piano adds a musical charm, drifting into the dining room from the adjoining lounge. As for the menu, it's short (as menus go) but laden with sumptuous dishes: smoked cod liver on toast ($1.75) for an appetizer, or smoked salmon, or lobster cocktail in cognac (both more expensive). As a main course, you can order any one of several seafood items, or fowl, or veal Esquire (veal fried in butter with a cream sauce, $10.75). But it's difficult not to order the Carpet Bag steak: tenderloin stuffed with oysters and herbs, for $13.75. Desserts and cheeses come on the trolley, for about $1.75 a portion. The wine list is fairly short but well chosen, with selections evenly spread in price from $6.50 to $28, not expensive for this class of restaurant. Plan to spend about $40 to $50 for two with wine, tax, and tip included. L'Evangeline is small, and reservations are a must. Dinner is served Monday through Saturday.

Fat Frank's (tel. 423-6618), despite its plebian name, has acquired a reputation for elegant dining in an Edwardian atmosphere. It's built into a renovated Edwardian town house at 5411 Spring Garden Rd., only a short distance from the corner of Brunswick. The lushness of Edwardian England, when the country rebounded from the wise but ponderous reign of Victoria, is all around. Antiques from the period add visual interest, and a wine bar brings in an extra dose of conviviality. Lunch is served on business days from 11:30 to 2, dinner is from 6 to 10:30 p.m. seven days a week. Although the chef prides himself on his oyster-and-spinach bisque and his bouillabaisse (a south-of-France fish stew), the vichyssoise ($1.85) might be better on a hot summer day. Atlantic salmon, if it's in season (June and July), is a must; otherwise there's veal Cordon Bleu ($5.50 at lunch), or tournedos, which at Fat Frank's means strips of filet steak in a red currant and port wine sauce ($13.50 for two, at lunch). The salade niçoise, a favorite light-lunch item, is $3.50. At dinnertime, the menu is fuller, the portions heftier, the prices higher—plan to spend $45 for two, with wine, tax, and tip included in this figure.

The **Henry House** (tel. 423-1309), 1222 Barrington St., corner of South St., is actually two dining rooms in one. Upstairs in the restored colonial town house is the main dining room, high ceilinged, with elegantly laid tables and quiet, friendly service. Downstairs is the Little Stone Jug, fraught with colonial atmosphere, surrounded by deep-red brick, rough wood beams, and period collectibles. The same menu reigns in both places, and diners choose the upstairs room because they like light, elegance, and smoke-free air, or the downstairs because they like a cozy, quaint, and dusky rendezvous spot. At lunchtime you can dine for $3 (plus tax, tip, and beverage), as that's the price of the daily special which might be a haddock steak or a quiche Lorraine with soup and coffee. Omelets, shrimp cocktail, oysters, or an hors d'oeuvres plate are all good luncheon choices, and all priced from $2.50 to $3.50. The dinner menu is long with a good mix of familiar items and novelties. Fifteen different soups and appetizers, from seafood chowder to gazpacho, cost 50¢ to $5.25; seafood main courses are around $8, although the interesting fish kebab (scallops, lobster, shrimp, and vegetables, flamed in brandy and served on rice) is a bit more at $10. Beef prices start at $8.50 and rise to $12, more for the chateaubriand bouquetière. A delicious English trifle ($1.75) was my choice for dessert as it's so difficult to find in restaurants. A half-liter carafe (slightly less than a bottle) of the imported house wine was $4.25. The Henry House, which takes its name from one-time owner Hon. William A. Henry, one of the Fathers of Confederation, is open for lunch Monday through Friday, for dinner every day of the week.

Clipper Cay (tel. 423-6818) is the place to dine if you're out for an elegant meal in Historic Properties. Located at Privateers' Wharf, it serves lunch every day but Sunday, dinner seven days a week. The restored warehouse has had the most charming antique features well preserved, and lots of plants have been added. The view of the harbor is as good as can be. The menu is a long and varied one, but well within the moderate price range. I had an expensive ($3.25) appetizer of melon and prosciutto, then bluefish with herbs ($7), dessert, and coffee, and the bill still only came to $15—not bad for such a place in such a location. Most dinner main courses are priced under $10. By the way, a before-dinner cocktail will cost $1.50 to $3, a bottle of wine with your meal $8 to $18. The Barnacle, an indoor/outdoor eatery in the same building, is under the same management as Clipper Cay.

Seafood

Halifax has it, and a great deal of it is served up in style at the **Five Fishermen** (tel. 423-1678), at the corner of Argyle and George Sts. In fact, seafood is almost the only thing on the menu: oyster stew, big plates of steamed clams, coquilles St-Jacques ($2.25 to $3.85) start things off. Main courses run the underwater gamut, but many have a special appeal, such as the sole homardine—no plain sole here, but rather a filet stuffed with lobster (*homard* in French) and bathed in a savory sauce ($32 for two). The halibut is "soused," laced with vermouth, for $7.75. The salad bar has beans as well as greens. Desserts include pies and cakes, but also a real maple log ($3.50 a portion). The Five Fishermen is a pretty place, in an old schoolhouse that's been redone with handsome etched-glass doors, authentic Tiffany lamps, antique coat racks, and exposed stonework. The lounge is downstairs, as is a small dining room good for lunch; the main dining room is upstairs. Wines, by the way, range from $10 to $110, with most being fairly expensive. Reservations, after 7 p.m., are a good idea.

International Fare

Of the city's Italian restaurants, **La Scala** (tel. 425-6087), on Dresden Row, is the best for a spirited Italian-style night out. Besides the rich decor— lots of red in the flocked wallpaper, chairs, and carpets—La Scala boasts glittering chandeliers and a small dance floor, with a live band every night for no extra charge. The staff is ready to give you a warm welcome, and to serve up Italian classics such as scampi (shrimp) for $13, or less expensive veal scallopine ($9) or chicken alla Caruso ($8.50). Wines are moderately priced at $12 to $14, and drinks cost about $2.25. Go all the way, and drinks, dinner with wine, and dancing for two could cost $55, but there's no need to spend that much. La Scala is open for lunch on weekdays, for dinner Monday through Saturday from 5 to 11:30 p.m. Reservations are a good idea, especially on Friday and Saturday nights.

La Gondola (tel. 423-8719), a half-block from the Hotel Nova Scotian at 5175 South St., near Hollis, is where the young and the adventurous gather for Italian-style lunches and dinners. The several small dining rooms and the bar laden with artful Italian wine bottles remind one immediately of a little trat- toria-made-good, but the glassed-in sunporch overlooking the park is the place to get a table—if you can. The long and very Italian menu has an interesting feature: someone, in a fit of Mediterranean realism, arranged all the items according to *price,* starting with the cheapest spaghetti (with meat sauce, $3.75), working through eight other varieties of spaghetti (to $6), and baked cheese macaroni ($4.50) to medallions of tenderloin for $11. Some steak and seafood items squeeze into the long list, but basically all is Italian. For dessert? Spumone and zabaglione, of course. In the Velvet Room, a small band plays for dancing on Friday and Saturday evenings. La Gondola has been around for a long time, and looks it in places, but the chipped paint becomes part of the ambience. It's open from 11 to 2 and from 5 to midnight (1 a.m. on Fridays and Saturdays) every day but Sunday.

For some curious reason, Greek food in Greek restaurants in Greece often leaves a lot to be desired, while Greek restaurants outside Greece prepare some of the most delicious food in the world. Perhaps all the best chefs have emigrat- ed, and if so, there's no doubt that one of the best has set up shop in Halifax, at **Old Man Morias** (tel. 422-7960). The name comes from the affectionate Greek nickname of hero George Kolokotronis. Dinner is served in the small parlor and dining room of an old town house with quaint fireplaces and Greek touches such as heavily worked stucco walls and ceiling. A cheerful matron in the requisite black dress will seat you and immediately make you feel comfortable. For devotees of Greek food (of which I am one) the menu is a dream come true: octopus tidbits, zatzicki (the hot garlic-and-yogurt dip), mousakka, and even bourekia ala Smirni (stuffed, fried dough pastry, Smyrna style) make choosing difficult. The specialty is al fresco lamb, cut from the whole spit-roasted animal ($8.50). Steaks, seafood, Greek-style pork, Greek salads—it's easy to "overeat with your eyes" here. Dinner of an appetizer, main course, baklava, and cafe ellenikon (Greek—or Turkish—coffee), will be about $16, tax and tip included. Add a few dollars more for retsina or a glass or two of a Cambas vintage. Dinner, the only meal served, is on Monday through Saturday from 6 to 11 p.m. (11:30 Thursday through Saturday). You should have reservations as this is a small restaurant. To get there, go to 1150 Barrington St., where Barrington curves (at an Esso station) before intersecting Hollis. It's tricky—persevere.

Those who know Swiss food tend to take every chance possible to have it. **L'Hermitage** (tel. 423-7638) is a very fine, elegant Swiss restaurant somewhat out of the center of town at 1030 So. Park St., corner of Inglis, on the ground floor of the huge Somerset Building. The dining room is dark, rich, and air-conditioned, with some Swiss rustic touches but a formal "feel" to it. The cuisine is not peasant inspired, but rather the haute cuisine taught in world-famous Swiss hotel schools. National specialties like zürcher geschnetzeltes (veal strips with mushrooms in a creamed white wine sauce, with rösti) and fondue vaudoise cost $4.20 to $8.20; meats and local seafoods done with Swiss touches are $7 to $11. But the best times to visit L'Hermitage are at lunch, when special offerings make a delicious meal possible for $5 to $6; or on the nights restaurateurs hate—Tuesday and Wednesday. On those nights, eight-course table d'hôte gourmet dinners are served up for a set price of $12. On Mondays, the dish to attract customers is suckling pig, again served for a set price with a whole dinner. L'Hermitage is worth going out of the way to try. Lunch is served Monday through Friday, 11:30 a.m. to 2:30 p.m.; dinner, 7 to 11 p.m. every night of the week. Reserve for dinner.

The **Newsroom,** in the Carleton Hotel at Argyle and Prince Sts., is the upbeat, moderately priced restaurant where Halifax's young and upwardly mobile set congregates. Of the three dining rooms, two are dark and woody, with paisley coverings on seats and booths, and the third is a garden patio, glassed in with a large skylight. Apple-green placemats, light bentwood chairs, and plants everywhere make this the cheeriest place to dine. Whether you have meat (sirloin strips, $9.45) or fish (baked stuffed sole, $7), a trip to the well-stocked salad bar is included in the price. At lunchtime, sandwiches and cold-cuts platters cost $2 to $6. Wine is inexpensive ($3) by the carafe, moderate ($8 to $12 and up) by the bottle. Visit the Newsroom from noon to 2:30, or 5 to 11 p.m. (till midnight on Friday and Saturday, till 10 on Sunday). No reservations accepted.

Halifax has a delightful, and delightfully inexpensive, East Indian restaurant named the **Guru** (tel. 422-6347), 1665 Argyle St., right downtown. The tiny dining room has exactly 14 seats, with Indian paintings on the walls and ragas twanging quietly as background music. Beef, chicken, lamb, shrimp, and vegetable curries fill a long menu, with the specialties being bhoonas and tandoori chicken (order a day in advance). In hotness, the curries cover all the ground from savory fruit-and-nut korma to fiery vindaloo and phal. All are priced from $3 to $4.65. A vindaloo fire extinguisher of dahi (homemade yogurt) is 60¢; pappadoms and chutneys are 50¢ apiece. A complete dinner for $7 is simple to put together; at lunch, the daily specials let you do it for $2.75.

No liquor served. Hours are 11:30 to 2 for lunch on weekdays, 4 to 10 p.m. Monday through Saturday for dinner. By the way, all the Guru's meals can be put up to take out.

For Chinese food, try the **Palms,** at Prince and Grafton—look for the green facade with red windows. The dauntingly long menu lists lots of Cantonese dishes, with a sprinkling from other regions as well. The combination plates priced at $2.45 to $3.75 offer good value, although few things cost more, except for the Palms' special chicken, shrimp, and barbecued pork plate with salad of the season ($5.45). The decor is contemporary Chinese lunchroom. Continuous service makes this a good choice outside normal mealtimes: hours are 11 a.m. to 9 p.m. Monday through Thursday, 11 a.m. to 11 p.m. on Friday, 4 to 11 p.m. on Saturday, 4 to 9 p.m. on Sunday.

Lobster Suppers

In summertime, a blue-and-white canvas pavilion is raised down on the waterfront, next to Historic Properties at the water's edge of the parking lot. Beneath the big top are picnic tables belonging to an enterprise called the **Lobster Caper,** which specializes in Atlantic-style lobster dinners. For a set price you get a Nova Scotia lobster, potato salad, cole slaw, rolls, butter, pie, and tea or coffee; a cold-cuts plate can take the place of lobster if you're allergic. Price varies with the cost of lobster, but should be about $12 to $13. Drop by and ask when the "seatings" take place.

Sandwich Snacks and Health Foods

For sandwich lovers, **As You Like It** (tel. 422-4347) is a piece of paradise. Set in a redeemed gas station at 1581 Argyle St. not far from the corner with Prince, it includes a cheery outdoor cafe as well as a "creative sandwich bar." Make yourself a cream cheese and asparagus sandwich ($1.75) or a lettuce, cucumber, and sour cream salad ($1.50), order one of the cafe's delicious health-juice drinks, and lunch need cost only $2.25 to $3.

Speaking of health foods, you can supply yourself with beans, shoots, nutritious bread, and any of hundreds of herbs (for cooking or curing) at the **Bean Sprout,** 1588 Barrington between Sackville and Salter. They have the best selection of herbs I've ever seen.

THE SIGHTS OF HALIFAX: Halifax is scenic as well as historic, and walks around the city, through its parks, and along its waterfront are enjoyable whether one delves into the city's history or not. But history is everywhere, and bits of Halifax's romantic past will stick in your mind without any effort. For a general overview, take a guided tour, or follow the walking tour outlined below.

Guided Tours

Halifax's own **Metro Transit** bus system (tel. 426-6600) runs regular two-hour city tours for the low price of $4 per adult, with children under 12 riding with a parent for free. In high summer, three tours are operated each day from Historic Properties; buses will pick you up from your hotel or motel on Bedford Hwy. before the tour. Buses are laid on as required, so you need no reservations; buy your ticket from your hotel or motel desk clerk or bell captain, or right from the driver on the bus.

The famous, ubiquitous **Gray Line** (tel. 454-9321), operating through the Acadian Lines bus company, has city tours lasting 2½ hours. Tickets are $4 per adult, $2 for children 6 to 12, free for children under 6 who don't occupy a seat "to the exclusion of a fare-paying passenger." Gray Line will pick you up from major downtown hotels, or along Bedford Hwy. as well.

The most exciting tour of Halifax is the one you take in the harbor aboard **Bluenose II,** replica of Canada's trophy-winning schooner. *Bluenose* is moored at Privateers' Wharf in Historic Properties, and while she does hoist sail and leave Halifax a few times in summer, most days she's available for harbor tours. Places are on a first-come, first-served basis for the three daily sailings; pick up your tickets at the Bluenose Store on Privateers' Wharf. Cost for adults is $9; for seniors, $4.50; for children, $4 (12 and under). The cruise lasts two hours.

A modern alternative to *Bluenose II* is **Halifax Water Tours** (tel. 423-7783 or 425-7414) which will welcome you aboard a modern 194-passenger vessel with canteen, bar, washrooms, an open-air upper deck, and a fully enclosed lower deck. From late May to mid-June and in most of September two daily tours are offered; from mid-June through early September you can book on any of four tours. There is a daily run during the first week in October. Adults pay $5.50 for the two-hour cruise, children 13 to 18 pay $3.75, and those 5 to 12 pay $2.25. Boats leave from Privateers' Wharf in Historic Properties.

The cheapest water tour of all costs only 25¢, and begins at the foot of George St., off Water St., in Historic Properties. It's the **Halifax–Dartmouth ferryboat,** which has been plying the waters of the harbor since 1752 in one form or another. Boats powered by horses turning a windlass on deck have been replaced by many-horsepowered engines, but the "mini-cruise" is as enjoyable as ever—especially for the price.

Walking Tours

In high summer, the local tourist bureaus in the Old Red Store, Privateers' Wharf, Historic Properties, sponsor free walking tours of the city. In recent years the schedule has been one of 50-minute tours leaving every hour, on the hour, from 9 a.m. to 6 p.m. The 2 p.m. tour is an especially detailed, two-hour excursion through the city's history. Drop in at the Old Red Store and pick up the latest schedule.

Historic Properties

Start your Halifax stroll in the heart of the city's successful restoration and redevelopment effort. Although the streets of Historic Properties now harbor shops, offices, restaurants, and bars, this was the original settlement of Halifax. The waterfront area was where privateers ("legal" pirates) brought the booty seized from the merchantmen of other countries. Warehouses, ships' chandlers, pubs, and counting houses filled the ironstone buildings of the city's naval and commercial heart.

In summer, Historic Properties is the scene of free open-air concerts and shows, some put on as part of the International Atlantic Summer Festival, others hosted by city agencies or by Historic Properties itself. The Halifax Visitors' and Convention Bureau, in the Old Red Store on Privateers' Wharf, has the latest schedules of events.

The Big Bang

Everything in Halifax was affected, in one manner or another, by the Great Halifax Explosion of December 6, 1917. A munitions ship, the *Mont Blanc,* was laden with eight million pounds of TNT when she collided with another ship, the *Imo.* Two thousand Haligonians were killed outright or later died of their wounds, and many thousands of others survived with injuries. Half the city was flattened by the blast, or by the fires which broke out immediately afterward. Damage was in the tens of millions of dollars, even at 1917 prices. For a look at a memento of the catastrophe, examine the sculpture in front of the Halifax North Memorial Library: it is made partially with metal from the ill-fated *Mont Blanc.*

Downtown Landmarks

Scattered through the downtown section are buildings famous in Halifax history. **Province House,** on Hollis St. near the corner of Prince, is the seat of the Nova Scotia Legislative Assembly. A handsome Georgian mansion of weathered stone, Province House was finished in 1819, and the Assembly has occupied it ever since. You can tour Province House with a guide anytime Monday through Friday from 9 to 5, and visit the chamber of the Legislative Assembly. The Red Chamber, a sumptuous room with fine, large oil paintings, was the seat of Nova Scotia's Legislative Council until it was disbanded.

Counterpart to Province House is **Government House,** the official residence of the lieutenant-governor of Nova Scotia. Before Province House was built, the provincial governor and his wife lived in a wooden house on the same site. The wooden house was, according to Lady Frances Wentworth, Gov. Sir John Wentworth's wife, about to collapse into its own cellar by the year 1805. The provincial assembly agreeably voted to build a nice stone mansion for the gubernatorial couple, but the price of construction—when all of Lady Frances's preferences were met—grew to three times the original estimate. After two years abuilding, Government House was ready for Sir John and Lady Frances to move in, which they did, as has every lieutenant-governor and family since 1807. Although Government House is not open to visitors, you can pass its imposing original entrance on Hollis St. near the corner of Bishop; then go around to the other side, on Barrington St., and compare the more mundane entrance used today.

The Citadel

When Cornwallis and his band of settlers founded Halifax in 1749, they knew the town was to be a military and naval defense point as well as a commercial center. One of the first projects they undertook was to build a crude fortress atop the hill behind the docks, and then to link it to other forts in a line of defense. British forces drove their French rivals from Louisbourg (on Cape Breton) and Québec in the next decade.

The American Revolution and the wars with France at the end of the 1700s inspired Halifax's defenders to rebuild and expand the fortress defenses, but the temporary structures all fell to ruins shortly afterward. In 1825 it was decided to build a long-lasting Citadel of masonry.

The Citadel you'll visit today is a fascinating place, not simply because of its size and might, but because of its cost effectiveness. Modern taxpayers grumble about the immense outlays their governments must make for defense, but things were no different a century and a half ago. Begun in 1825 at an estimated cost of £116,000, the Citadel was not completed until 1861, at a cost of £233,882, a "cost overrun" of more than 200%. By 1870—less than a decade later—the Citadel was obsolescent: artillery had become powerful enough to damage its three- to six-foot-thick walls. But perhaps the lesson is in the Citadel's battles, of which there were none. Enemy commanders must certainly have thought twice about attacking such a formidable fortress. No doubt the citizens of Halifax looked upon £233,882 as a small price to pay for peace!

Today the Citadel is a National Historic Park, and within its mighty walls are the **Centennial Art Gallery,** which shows traveling exhibits of works by Canada's best modern painters and sculptors. The **Army Museum** is in the mighty casemates meant to house officers and storerooms; and the **Nova Scotia Museum's** Human History and Marine History collections are in the barracks built to house over 300 soldiers of the Citadel's garrison.

Wander around within the fortress, peering down into the wells (one could hold almost 19,000 gallons of water), marveling at the seemingly impregnable powder magazines, taking in the panoramic views of the city and its harbor. You can have a guide take you around for free if you ask at the information center, on your left as you enter. The Citadel is one of Canada's most visited historic sites, open June through September from 9 a.m. to 8 p.m., October through May from 9 a.m. to 5 p.m. Admission is free. Be sure to stop in and see the excellent free films on the fortress and on the city of Halifax, which run continuously every day.

While you're up here on top of the hill, inspect the **Old Town Clock,** designed by the Duke of Kent while he was commander of the Citadel (1794–1800), built in London, and erected here in 1803. The duke valued punctuality in his soldiers and in the townfolk, and he liked tinkering with things mechanical. Designing the clock made him happy on both points.

Northern Downtown

In the northern part of downtown, near the corner of George and Argyle Sts., is the **Grand Parade,** once the drilling ground for Halifax's militia. Up by Duke St. stands the **Old City Hall,** built in 1890, and graced with the largest wooden flagpole made of one piece of timber in the world. You won't believe it when you see it. **St. Paul's Church,** on Barrington St. by the Grand Parade, is Canada's oldest Anglican church, dating from 1750. It's English in more ways than one: the building was fabricated in England, shipped over, and erected here with the help of a royal endowment from King George II. The simple white interior has fine stained-glass windows, and dozens of little memorial plaques put up in honor of past parishioners. The church has an interesting—and mysterious—attraction: in the Great Explosion of 1917, a piece of flying debris smashed through the third window on the right (Argyle St.) side, and embedded itself in the left wall of the narthex. The hole it made in the window looks distinctly like the silhouette of a man, and oldtimers say it closely resembles the head of the church's rector, killed in the blast.

The Parks

First park to visit is Halifax's fine old **Public Gardens,** bounded by Sackville, So. Park, Spring Garden, and Summer Sts. Tended with loving care, the gardens are formal and very English. Ducks and swans cruise across the glassy surfaces of ponds, fountains play, and the sweet fragrance of flowers comes to you as soon as you enter. The 18-acre gardens have been soothing the souls of Haligonians for over a century, since the time of Queen Victoria. Watch for a schedule of band concerts, performed in the red-topped gazebo.

Point Pleasant Park, at the southern tip of Halifax peninsula, is a marvelous 186-acre forest laced with walking trails and dotted with picnic spots and viewpoints. You can park your car in the lot near the end of Young Ave. (that's the southern extension of So. Park St.), but that's as far as cars are allowed—after that, it's all on foot. Point Pleasant Park holds an old Martello Tower, one of the cylindrical defense towers erected throughout the British Isles and eastern Canada in the 19th century.

The Nova Scotia Museum

Strictly speaking, the Nova Scotia Museum (tel. 429-4610) is spread throughout Nova Scotia in 18 different locations. Historically significant houses, farms, and old industrial sites have all been incorporated into this grand museum plan, but the headquarters is at 1747 Summer St., near the corner of Bell Rd., west of the Citadel. Exhibits of Nova Scotia's natural history, wildlife and peoples, industries, marine life, and famous men fill the museum's modern galleries. Changing exhibits keep the museum current, and guarantee that there is always something new to see here. Admission is free, and summer hours are from 9 a.m. to 9 p.m. weekdays, 9 a.m. to 5 p.m. weekends and holidays (mid-June to Labour Day). At other times, hours are 9 to 5, with a late closing at 9 p.m. on Wednesdays.

SHOPPING: Halifax has two downtown shopping complexes well worth exploring, no matter whether you're out to buy or just out to window-shop. **Scotia Square,** a tremendous development complex bounded by Barrington, Duke, Market, and Cogswell Sts., has over 100 various shops and services from barbers and hairdressers to fine crystal and china. Restaurants and snack stands, cinemas, tailors, travel bureaus, opticians, and cigar stores make Scotia Square a Halifax in microcosm. An Information Centre in the Lower Mall can provide you with a map of the complex's two levels, but even with this aid, expect to get lost a few times. Scotia Square is open Monday, Tuesday, Wednesday, and Saturday from 9:30 a.m. to 6 p.m.; on Thursday and Friday from 9:30 a.m. to 9:30 p.m.; closed Sunday.

Maritime Mall, a less ambitious commercial development, is in the Maritime Centre at 1505 Barrington St., near the corner with Spring Garden. Almost 30 shops are gathered here in an indoor environment complete with trees and flower boxes. Although smaller than Scotia Square, Maritime Mall has the advantage of being less confusing as well.

NIGHTLIFE: All of Halifax's larger hotels have clubs and lounges with live entertainment, and in summer **Historic Properties** hosts a series of free concerts and shows right in its stone-paved streets. Across the harbor in neighboring Dartmouth the city fathers also sponsor summer shows, which often take place right at the Dartmouth ferry landing, called **Wharf Park.** Catch the ferry (25¢, one way) at the foot of George St., off Water St.

Cinemas

There's one in Scotia Square's Upper Mall, two on Granville between Sackville and Prince, yet another, the Wormwood, at 1572 Barrington St. The first seems to concentrate on big-time general-audience films, the next two on this and that, the last on intellectual stuff.

The **National Film Board,** on Barrington St. not far from Spring Garden, has daily showings of films—for free—in its own cinema. Drop by and see what's offered.

Theater

The **Neptune Theatre,** at 5216 Sackville and Argyle, is small and unprepossessing, but offers some of the city's liveliest drama and comedy.

Grander productions can be staged at **Dalhousie University Arts Centre,** University Ave. and Seymour St. Watch for newspaper listings of current events.

Concerts

Halifax's outspokenly modern **Metro Centre** has drawn both praise and complaints from Haligonians. The praise is usually voiced at sports events, especially hockey matches; the complaints come when Victor Borge, Nathalie Cole, or a rock band puts on a concert—the Centre's acoustics prove to be less than adequate. Steps are afoot to solve the problems of ricochet sound, and Metro Centre will remain the focal point for traveling extravaganzas. Buy tickets at the Centre, on Brunswick near George St., or at the Metro ticket office in Scotia Square Mall's Upper Mall.

Clubs

A lot of local and national talent flows through Halifax's clubs and lounges. Newspaper listings and free entertainment sheets can keep you up-to-date on who's playing where. Here are some nightspots which never fail to draw good crowds:

Privateers' Warehouse, in Historic Properties, is several clubs and restaurants in one. The Upper Loft serves lunch and dinner, and charges $1.50 cover in the evenings. Most people come here for an elegant dinner with entertainment afterward. On the Middle Deck, one flight below, a guitarist or jazz group holds forth from 9 p.m. to 1 a.m. on Thursday, Friday, and Saturday evenings, with the same $1.50 cover in force. The Lower Deck, at street level, is far removed from the elegance of the Upper Loft. The Lower Deck's stone walls resound most evenings with rousing folk songs from the maritime coasts, led by a songster and roared by several hundred happy listeners. The long wooden tables are filled with beer mugs, bowls of clam chowder, and plates of sausage and sauerkraut (served 11:30 a.m. to 7:30 p.m.). The beer costs $1.20 for Canadian, $1.75 for imported brews.

For jazz, **Whiskers** is a regular Halifax spot, on Argyle St. near the corner of George St. The setting is sumptuous, with velvet easy chairs and loveseats, dim lights, and a stainless-steel dance floor.

The hottest disco in Halifax as of this writing is on the ground floor of Pepe's restaurant, at 5680 Spring Garden Rd. The **5680 Disco** has hot lights and cool music, two bars, and a cover charge of $1.50 which is waived if you dine upstairs in Pepe's before you hit the dance floor. Expect crowds on weekends.

ON THE OUTSKIRTS—PEGGY'S COVE: Peggy's Cove is a small fishing village on Hwy. 333 due west of Halifax, 43 km (27 miles) away. It's a pretty spot, with old clapboard houses, fishnets drying, lobster traps crowding the wharves, and a winking lighthouse atop the smooth, sea-washed coastal rocks.

The village is like many another Nova Scotia fishing village, only more perfectly picturesque, and very close to Halifax. For these reasons it's acquired a reputation almost like that of the Cabot Trail, or the Annapolis Valley: guidebooks and tourist bureau personnel steer armies of visitors toward the one narrow dead-end street in the village, and the result is that what most tourists see in Peggy's Cove is other tourists.

Should you bother to go? Yes, under certain conditions. First, don't bother going on a foggy day. The village would be picturesque in the fog if one were alone there, but you won't be. Second, go off-season if you can, in early June or mid-September, and get there as early in the morning as possible. Park in the public lot at the entrance to the village—it's well-marked by signs—and don't take your car down the narrow street to tangle with the tour buses. Remember, there's nothing wrong with the village itself. It's beautiful, and it is now protected from commercial development by the government of Nova Scotia. There's nothing wrong with the tourist traffic either, except when too many people come at the same time. While you're in the village, you can have a meal at its only restaurant, the Sou'Wester, or post a letter or card from the tiny post office located in the lighthouse.

3. The Lighthouse Route to Yarmouth

Nova Scotia's "Lighthouse Route" follows the southwestern coast along Hwy. 103 from Halifax to Yarmouth, passing through or near dozens of quaint coastal villages and several interesting small cities. The first of these, Lunenburg, requires a short detour off 103 via Hwy. 3, but the detour is well worth the time spent. Besides being a charming town with several exceptional places to stay and to dine, Lunenburg is home for the Lunenburg Fisheries Museum and Aquarium of Native Fish, a Nova Scotia "must see."

LUNENBURG: Coming into Lunenburg from the highway, you'll pass the town green, then over the railroad tracks into the business center. Go up the hill on Lincoln St., follow it to the end at Blockhouse Hill Rd., and you'll be near the **Lunenburg Tourist Bureau,** in a lighthouse at the top of the hill. The bureau is open from 9 a.m. to 9 p.m. daily in high summer. They have good maps of the town, and can answer any questions. While you're there, pick up the guide to the *Walking Tour to Distinctive Old Lunenburg Houses* (25¢). And don't neglect to take in the view—best in town.

Where to Stay and Eat

Stopping in Lunenburg would be worth the trouble just to stay and dine at **Boscawen Manor** (tel. 902/634-8149), on Cumberland St. at the corner of Prince, up on the hillside. First off, your eye will be drawn to the gorgeous stained-glass windows (which are even more spectacular from inside). This old mansion has been restored and stuffed with period pieces, and the guest rooms are all different. No. 2 is the choicest, with a canopy bed, fireplace, private bath, all this in a circular "tower" room with fine views, for $35 to $40 double. Plainer rooms in the "new" wing are much less expensive, at $16 to $20 without bath; or with private bath, $20 to $25. All the bathrooms have tubs; a few rooms don't have private bath.

Downstairs, the parlor and dining room have been filled with small tables for dining, and one might imagine a Victorian-era hostess setting it up just this way for a large party. Dining here is the most elegant in Lunenburg. The table d'hôte menu at dinner costs $12.50 per person, plus tax, tip, and wine (if you order it), and you'll have several choices for each course. Other meals are served as well, and if you can't stay at Boscawen Manor, go for breakfast—just to see the place.

Another old Lunenburg house which has been refurbished to receive guests is the **Bluenose Lodge** (tel. 902/634-8851), 10 Falkland St., right downtown in the commercial center by the railroad tracks. The Bluenose built its solid reputation on the good food served in the dining room, but it has six spotless guest rooms with bath renting for $14 to $16 single, $16 to $18 double, $2 for an extra person in a room.

Now for those well-reputed repasts: the Bluenose's dining room is open for breakfast from 8 to 9:30 a.m., for lunch from noon to 2, and for dinner from 5:30 to 8:30 p.m. Seafood is the strong item in this fisheries town, with most full meals based on fish or scallops costing $6.50 to $9.50—that's with appetizer or soup and dessert. The fisherman's platter has portions of lobster, scallops, clams, haddock, and french fries, and including soup and dessert it costs $10.25. There are other treats as well: pork sausage, ham, chicken, and steak are good for a change from fish. When you head out to find the Bluenose Lodge, look for the big white Victorian house with blue trim, not far from Lunenburg's railroad station.

For motel lovers, Lunenburg has the **Belroy Motel** (tel. 902/634-8867), next to the high school and the exhibition grounds (coming into town from the highway, bear right at the town green). Appropriately blue and white for this nautical town, the trim 15-unit motel has a color TV, radio, and phone in each room. Singles cost $20, doubles are $24, and you can get a light breakfast right at the motel.

The **Braeco Motel** (tel. 902/634-8234), 167 Victoria Rd., is set back from the road into town a good quarter mile to be away from any noise. The 11 units have black-and-white TVs, one double and one single bed in each room, and private baths. The Braeco is open April to mid-October only, and charges $18 single, $22 double (slightly less in April and May). The motel's own outdoor games, picnic tables, and barbecues are available to guests.

What to See

Located at the foot of Duke St., below Montague, the **Lunenburg Fisheries Museum** consists of a quaint but large wharfside building, the wharf itself, and the three vessels tied up at the wharf: the salt-bank schooner *Theresa E. Connor,* the trawler *Cape North,* and the rumrunner *Reo II.* The museum is open May through September from 9 a.m. to 8 p.m. daily; adult admission price is $1.50, only 25¢ for children, and a family ticket costs $3.50. Inside, exhibits explain the various sorts of nets and traps used in times past, and those used today. Maps show where different kinds of fish are caught, and other displays follow the fish from the catch through the commercial processing plant to stores and consumers. Perhaps the most exciting exhibit of all, apart from the ships outside, is the well-done 25-minute film, a mini-course in marine life and its harvesting. When you enter the museum, ask when the next film screening will take place and then time your visit to the ships and the indoor exhibits with that in mind.

Lunenburg is home for the largest fish-processing plant in North America, with a staff of 1000. It's located at Battery Point, southeast of downtown. Owned by **National Sea Products,** the plant produces commercial seafood under the Hi-Liner label.

Before leaving Lunenburg, take a walk or a drive through the older part of town, up on the hill. Right by the Town Hall at Duke and Cumberland Sts.

is St. John's Church, a lovely old clapboard building painted white with dramatic black trim. St. Andrews, a block away at King and Townsend is also very fine. The grand old houses all around beg to be inspected, as does the bold half-timbered Lunenburg Academy building, at the western end of Lawrence St., on the edge of the hill.

ON THE ROAD: Bridgewater (pop. 6000) is aptly named, as you'll discover if you pass through the town instead of bypassing it on Hwy. 103. The bridge over the LaHave River gives you a view of the railroad sidings which in past years brought Bridgewater its prosperity. Today a tire-manufacturing plant is the main commercial concern.

Up the hill from the center of town on Aberdeen Rd. (no. 324), is the **Mariner Motel** (tel. 902/543-2447), a neat 30-unit motel with a small pool in front, color TV, radio, and phone in each room, and 20 of the 30 units are equipped for housekeeping as well. Singles here are $22, doubles are $24 to $30, and each extra person pays $5; these rates are less expensive than the local branch of the Wandlyn chain, not far away. Breakfast and dinner are served in the motel's dining room.

The next large town along the Lighthouse Route is Liverpool, near which there's a turnoff for **Kejimkujik National Park,** 67 km (42 miles) to the north. Kejimkujik is filled with glacial lakes and streams, stands of pine and spruce, and bogs. Boating and canoeing are among the foremost activities here, but hiking is also good as the terrain is mostly level. The principal campground is at Jeremy's Bay, just off Hwy. 8.

SHELBURNE: "A Loyalist Town" like many others in the Fundy region, Shelburne was settled by families loyal to the Crown who disagreed with the American Revolution. Four hundred families came to Shelburne in the 1780s, increasing its population so much that the tiny village of Port Roseway (Shelburne's former name) was unrecognizable.

Many old Loyalist houses still stand in Shelburne, and the **tourist bureau** (tel. 902/875-4547) at the foot of King St., right on the water, will provide you with a walking tour guide for the town.

Where to Stay and Eat

Shelburne's Motels are west of the center of town on Hwy. 3. The **Cape Cod Colony Motel** (tel. 902/875-3411), on Water St. (Hwy. 3), is the handsomest of the Shelburne motels, with 22 fully equipped rooms, a breakfast room (open 7:30 to 9:30 a.m.), and even wheelchair ramps. Rates are surprisingly moderate: $20 for one, $22 to $24 for two people.

Rates for rooms are very similar to the Colony's at the nearby **Wildwood Motel** (tel. 902/875-2964). Twenty rooms here, again with all the conveniences, including color TV and a breakfast room.

MacKenzie's Motel and Cottages (tel. 902/875-2842), also west of the town center on Water St. (Hwy. 3) has six motel units and four housekeeping cottages—the cottages hold a total of seven bedrooms. Color TV throughout. One person pays $17 here, two pay $18 to $20, with an extra charge of $3 if you use one of the cottage kitchenettes. These rates apply from May to mid-October, after which off-season reductions are in order.

Right downtown in Shelburne is the **Loyalist Inn** (tel. 902/875-2343), on Water St. near the corner of King. Rooms are simple and modern, with color TV, private bath or shower, and the best prices in town: $14 single, $18 double.

Downstairs in the inn is a snackbar and a licensed dining room, both air-conditioned.

The **Hamilton House,** also on Water St. near the intersection with King, is one of Shelburne's most popular places for lunch or dinner. Open from 11 a.m. to 10:30 p.m. daily, the lunch menu always bears a selection of sandwiches which, with a cup of the house's hearty seafood chowder, can make a filling meal for under $4. Luncheon specials are the best bargains if you're ravenous, though: a grilled ham steak, cole slaw, vegetable, potato, dessert, and coffee was offered last time we were there at a mere $5.25, plus tax and tip. Prices are higher at dinnertime, but portions are bigger and platters made of heartier fare such as T-bone steak ($9) or fresh scallops ($6.50). Drinks are $2 once you add in the tax; a liter of red table wine, a moderate $6.50.

A visit to Shelburne would be worthwhile even if one just visited the **Tea Cup** (tel. 875-4590) for luncheon or afternoon tea. Located in a fine old house on King St. only steps from the Tourist Bureau, the Tea Cup specializes in authentic English afternoon teas. Authentic means having any of 12 varieties of tea, plus delights such as Devonshire splits (biscuits spread with *real* Devonshire cream and homemade preserves), or delicious oatcakes, for $1.50 to $1.75. The teas are a valuable discovery for those who enjoy this satisfying English custom, but the luncheons here are tasty as well. Soup and a salmon sandwich, or a cheese salad bowl, will come to about $4. Don't miss the Tea Cup—I guarantee you won't forget your visit for a long time. Lunch is served from 11:30 a.m. to 1:30 p.m., tea from 3 to 5 p.m., weekdays only. By the way, in the **Annex** next door, Norma Worden (who runs the Tea Cup) has assembled some of the region's finest handicraft items, all of which are for sale.

What to See

With your walking tour map from the tourist bureau, track down the **Ross-Thomson House,** a thriving store during the boomtime of Shelburne at the end of the 1700s. It's open daily for free, courtesy of the Nova Scotia Museum and the Shelburne Historical Society. The house has been restored to its condition of the 1780s, and fitted out as a store of the time would have been. Visit the front store, with its long counter, stacks of hides and barrels of provisions, the clerk's room, the sitting room, two bedrooms upstairs, and the kitchen in the basement (enter from the back of the house).

Nearby on the shore is a working cooperage firm, still making barrels the old-fashioned way, carving the staves from blocks of wood. Stacks of staves set out to dry fill a field across the road from the coopers' workshop.

A special attraction in Shelburne is the presence of **Maritime Canoe Outfitters** (tel. 902/875-3055 or 875-3649), an innovative firm which will lend you all the equipment you need for an adventuresome canoe trip along the Roseway River for only $16 per person per day, plus 8% tax, two-day minimum (that's a minimum of $64 for an overnight, two-day trip for two in a canoe, including everything you'll need—meals, too). It's the easiest canoeing opportunity for those without equipment that I've ever come across. Maritime Canoe Outfitters will even come to Yarmouth and pick you up (for a taxi charge), and drop you off at the head of the river and pick you up at the end of your tour, downstream. Six-day guided nature-study trips through Nova Scotia's wild interior cost $325 per person, everything (except tax) included. The best thing to do is plan ahead: write to them at R.R. 1, Shelburne, NS B0T 1W0 for information.

HEADING WEST: If you're still deep into the 1700s as you leave Shelburne, continue your antique explorations at **Barrington,** west of Shelburne on Hwy. 3. The Barrington Woolen Mill, on the highway, was begun in 1884 as the town's fishing fortunes began to dwindle. Through the turn of the century, World War I, and even as late as 1962, the mill was turning out pure-wool yarns and blankets, using water power. Although the mill no longer produces cloth, much of the machinery is still in place, and to tour it is to discover how cloth was made before the modern age of automated looms. Admission is free.

YARMOUTH: "The Gateway to Nova Scotia," Yarmouth is the terminus for ferryboats from Bar Harbor and Portland, Maine. Hotels and motels provide a lot of the town's income. Yarmouth has lots of hotels and motels, but in the busy weeks between mid-July and the end of August most of them are booked solid. If you can't get a reservation at one of the places listed below, consider staying in Digby (if you're coming from the north) or Shelburne (if you're coming from the south).

For tourist information, Yarmouth has a huge, bold provincial visitors' center right down by the ferry docks—you can't miss it as you come off the boat. For more detailed local information, check with the **Yarmouth County Tourist Bureau** (tel. 902/742-5355), open June through September, at 404 Main St. in Frost Park, opposite the Court House. Frost Park is within walking distance of the ferry docks.

Where to Stay and Eat

A few Yarmouth motels are within a block of the ferry docks; others are within a mile or so—walking distance if your bags are light. Still others are on the outskirts of town, and for these last ones you'll need a car or a cab.

The **Capri Motel** (tel. 902/742-7168), 8 Herbert St. behind 577 Main, is one of Yarmouth's most popular places to stay not merely because of its clean, modern rooms, but also because it is close to Captain Kelley's Restaurant. Actually, the people who oerate Captain Kelley's also run the Capri, and the Mermaid Motel (tel. 902/742-7821) at 545 Main St.

At the Capri, 36 motel rooms have all the comforts, including color cable TV, for $21.50 to $38, double or single. The lower prices are for rooms in the older "Annex," built behind Captain Kelley's Restaurant. All these Annex rooms have shower and color TV, and solid-color sheets (more expensive rooms have little luxuries such as patterned sheets), and for $21.50 double, they can't be beat. In the new motel building the bathrooms have tub and shower, but these rooms cost $36 to $38 double.

The **Mermaid Motel** has its own swimming pool, and 45 rooms on two floors, all with the latest conveniences, five with kitchenettes. Two people pay $26 to $39, depending on the size and accoutrements of the room. Continental breakfast is served at the hotel, and a coin laundry is here for guests' use.

The third establishment in the trio, **Captain Kelley's Restaurant,** is located in the big white mansion at 577 Main St. (tel. 742-9191), a walk from the ferry docks only if you have no bags (the walk takes about 20 minutes). Captain Kelley's is one of the most popular dining places in Yarmouth, open long hours from 7 a.m. to 10 p.m., seven days a week. Rooms both downstairs and upstairs in the old house have been converted for dining, using some old pieces and antique-style touches to achieve a half-modern, half-oldtime decor. Prices at dinner are moderate, with a plate of Digby scallops cooked in white wine for $8.25, roast beef and Yorkshire pudding for a bit more ($9.50). Most of the menu is devoted to seafood, but several steaks provide land-locked variety. The wine list is short, good, and rather expensive. After dinner, the person at the cash register will be glad to sell you a luxury difficult to find in the U.S. these days: real Cuban cigars. If you come for dinner on the weekends, have reservations.

The **Colony Motor Inn** (tel. 902/742-9194) is perched on the hillside right atop the ferry terminal in Yarmouth. Rates at this fully modern and extremely comfortable motel are high, but for what you pay, you get a lot: it's Yarmouth's newest motel, with large rooms, most of which overlook the busy ferry terminal, all with color cable TV, radio, telephone, bath and shower. There's a sauna, free coffee, a game room with Ping-Pong and billiards, and children under 16 can share a room with their parents at no extra charge. The rates, then, are $24 to $36 double, with the higher price going for a room with the ferry view and two double beds. The Colony has its own licensed lounge and restaurant in the same building.

Equally near the ferry docks is the **Ferry Inn** (tel. 902/742-5092), at 216 Main St., which offers a good selection of accommodations in a wide range of prices. The simplest, most essential rooms are in the hotel, and of the 14, only half have private baths; the other half have washbasins, and share two public bathrooms. Prices for these are $12 double without bath, $16 double with bath; in the motel unit, rooms cost $20 double, $25 if you take one of the five efficiency units. Motel rooms all have private baths and black-and-white TV sets. Off-season rates, from September through June, are even lower.

Yarmouth has a large and modern hotel, called the **Grand Hotel** (tel. 902/742-2446), 4 Grand St. (off Main by Frost Park). Popular with tour groups and those who want complete luxury, the Grand has 138 rooms on its seven floors, priced at $36 single, $40 double, $6 for an extra person. All rooms are fully equipped, and in the lobby you'll find a tour desk, car-rental desk, and other big-hotel services. The hotel's licensed restaurant serves all three meals.

On the way out of town along Lakeside Dr. (Hwy. 1, heading for Digby), is the hilltop motel named **El Rancho** (tel. 902/742-4363). Although the 16 rooms have little Spanish about them, most have fine views of Lake Milo (an extension of Yarmouth Harbour), private baths, and color TV/radio sets. Two people pay $17 to $24; an extra person pays $3. These rates go down anytime but in July and August.

Yarmouth's **Manor Inn** (tel. 902/742-7841) is actually in Hebron, five miles from the ferry terminal along Hwy. 1, heading north. Set on its own large estate, the Manor House was once the country seat of Commodore H. H. Raymond, president of several shipping companies and friend of the great and famous (including two U.S. presidents, Hoover and Harding). The opulent, colonial-style mansion is surrounded by swaths of lawn and shady trees. In the main house are six hotel rooms done in grand style and rented at grand prices: $40 to $45 for a room with two double beds, $30 to $35 for one with twin beds, $24 for a room with one double bed. The remainder of the Manor Inn's 28 rooms are in motel-style buildings called the Coach House ($26 for a room with two double beds), and the Lakeside ($28 for a room with two double beds). All of the rooms have private bath and TV, plus a telephone.

In the downstairs dining rooms of the Manor Inn, prime rib of beef is the house specialty ($13), but live lobster (in season) is actually cheaper at $11. Seafood dishes cost about $8 to $10. Although the dining rooms are rather formal, the dress code is "come as you are"—within reason, of course. Besides the elegant dining rooms, the Manor Inn can boast two cozy lounges, one an English bar, the other in the commodore's basement wine cellar. There's live entertainment most nights.

Another popular place to dine is **Harris's Seafood** (tel. 742-5420), three miles from the center of town going east/north on Hwy. 1. The restaurant is off the main road, down by the shore, and the parking lot always seems to be crowded with diners coming for lunch or dinner (noon to 11 p.m.). The one large dining room is adorned with fishnets and bits of nautical paraphernalia, and is usually pretty full in high summer season. And with offerings like the following, it's to be expected: a plate of Digby scallops, with potato, vegetable, and a trip to the salad bar, costs $8.50; the seafood casserole is even cheaper, the fresh swordfish (when they have it) a bit more. Some steak dishes are always on the menu for those who'd rather not have seafood. With a bowl of soup (90¢ to $1.30) to start, and dessert and coffee, a meal at Harris's need come to no more than $12, plus tax and tip.

For hot homemade breakfast rolls from 7 a.m. onward, and for quick and tasty seafood snacks and light meals the rest of the day, drop by the **Harris's Quick and Tasty,** right on Hwy. 1 by the turnoff to the seafood restaurant. It's a day tripper's version of the aforementioned seaside dining room.

What to See

Waiting for the ferryboat to arrive or depart? Wander up Collins St., off Main between the ferry terminal and Frost Park, to no. 22 and the **Yarmouth County Museum.** Exhibits are heavily nautical, as one might expect, with ship models and paintings, rooms decorated authentically to date from various periods in Yarmouth's history, and artifacts illuminating the way Yarmouthians have earned their livings in times past. In July and August, the museum is open Monday through Saturday from 9 to 5, (Sunday, 1 to 5); Wednesday, Thursday, and Friday evenings there are extra open hours between 7 and 9 p.m. From mid-June to the end of June and in September, hours are 9 to 5, Monday through Saturday.

4. The Evangeline Trail and Annapolis Valley

In 1605, Samuel de Champlain founded the first European settlement in Canada, other than the short-lived camps of the Vikings. Champlain's foothold was near Annapolis Royal, on Nova Scotia's Annapolis River near a fine natural harbor. In the century to come, Champlain's career would see him become governor of Canada and lieutenant-general of New France, and French fortunes throughout the lush farmlands and forests of Nova Scotia would thrive. The land not yet called "Nova Scotia" would be dotted with French settlements.

Although these early settlers of "Acadie" (or Acadia, the French name for Nova Scotia) came from the same homeland as those who settled in what is now Québec, their history was to take a very different course. Before French and English interests in the New World came to the point of armed struggle in the Seven Years' War (1756–1763), the British had largely taken control of Acadia. They knew there would be war, and they believed that Acadia's French-speaking inhabitants would secretly struggle for French victory. The British governors decided on a bold and ruthless plan of military necessity: all Acadians who would not openly pledge allegiance to the British sovereign must be deported from the land. The deportation order came in 1755, and French-speaking families throughout the province were forcibly moved from their homes, many resettling in the French territory of Louisiana where their "Cajun" (Acadian) language and culture are still alive today.

To replace the Acadians, shiploads of Scottish and Irish settlers arrived from the British Isles, and the province soon acquired the name Nova Scotia, the New Scotland.

But the Acadian people, a hardy lot before and after the deportation, began to return to the land their ancestors had first settled after the hostilities ended. Canada was firmly under British rule, and Acadian farmers were no longer seen to be a "fifth column." Many French-speaking people returned to the rich Annapolis Valley, to cultivate farms and fishing grounds in peace, on good terms with their British and Indian neighbors as they had been before the deportation. They are here to this day.

The Evangeline Trail, named for Longfellow's romantic poem which recounts the fictitious but true-to-life story of one Acadian woman's struggles, will lead you through the original land of the Acadians. Tidy towns and villages, each with its church of wood or stone, its shops filled with traditional crafts and farm products, line Hwy. 1, alternating with stately towns built in colonial British style.

DIGBY: Leaving Yarmouth on Hwy. 1, the first city of size along the Evangeline Trail is Digby, famous for its scallops gathered from the Bay of Fundy, and for "Digby chicken" (locally cured smoked herring). Digby is the southern terminus of CN Marine's M/V *Princess of Acadia,* a car ferryboat connecting the town with Saint John, New Brunswick. (For details on ferry crossings, see the section on Saint John.)

Where to Stay and Eat

Digby itself has several motels and restaurants, but many others are scattered in the outskirts, especially in the resort hamlet of Smith's Cove, a few miles east along Hwy. 1.

One of Nova Scotia's three plush resort hotels operated by the provincial government is in Digby, right on the road to the CN ferry dock. The **Pines Resort Hotel** (tel. 902/245-2511) is a mammoth mansion in French Norman style, surrounded by 30 cottages and set on a 300-acre tract of forests, lawns, and spectacular views of the Annapolis Basin. An 18-hole golf course, tennis courts, shuffleboard, croquet, boating, deep-sea fishing, and a huge glass-enclosed heated swimming pool make the Pines a complete summer resort. A supervised playground will delight children, and will also keep them conveniently occupied most of the day. As with most resorts, the Pines charges for room and two meals: in the hotel rooms, all with private baths, two people pay $44 to $80, and an extra person pays $10 to $16. Prices are similar for the cottages, which come with living room and fireplace, veranda, and bedrooms to hold from one to eight people—the exact price depends on how many people occupy a cabin. Remember to add that 8% tax. The Pines stays open only during the summer season, from June through September.

The **Admiral Digby Inn** (tel. 902/245-2531), a half mile from the CN Marine ferry dock, is without doubt the closest hostelry to the boats, and therefore full up most of the time—get reservations well in advance. The 40 rooms on two floors have color TVs, private baths, and radios, and those in the front of the inn have very fine views of the water. The indoor, heated swimming pool is handy on days when the sun can't cut through the fog (plenty of these days), and the licensed dining room provides sustinence during the "season," which starts in April and lasts through October. Rate reductions come into effect April 15 to June 15, and after September 15, but in the warmer months two people pay $29 to $31 for a room, and an extra person pays $3. Get reservations: the inn's "Sorry, Full Crew" sign stays on most of the time.

Downtown in Digby, not far from the tourist bureau, is the **Siesta Motel** (tel. 902/245-2568), a modest 15-room hostelry with nice, color-TV–equipped rooms going for $20 to $26, double or single. Reductions in price come October through May.

In Smith's Cove, my favorite is the **Hedley House Motor Hotel and Restaurant** (tel. 902/245-2585), off Hwy. 1 about five miles (eight kilometers) east of Digby. The 14 rooms are nice, set back from the road, all with TV and radio, six with kitchenettes, but the grounds are even nicer. Spacious lawns spread right down to the water's edge, and flower beds and boxes are everywhere. Nicest of all is the staff, some of the friendliest and most accommodating I've encountered. Room prices are moderate: $22 to $28 for two, with an additional charge of $5 per day for use of the kitchenette facilities.

The **Hedley House dining room,** in the big converted house by the road, has a liquor license and serves breakfast between 8 and 10 a.m., dinner from 5:45 to 8 p.m. For dinner on my last visit, I started—patriotically—with Digby marinated herring ($1.50), then went on to a cold crabmeat and salmon salad plate ($8.35), which came with a glass of dry white wine. Chicken with herbs ($6.25) was an alternative. The choice for dessert (as far as I was concerned) was between fresh blueberry pie ($1) or Hedley House's renowned pecan pie—a difficult choice, for sure. The total bill, with tax, tip, and coffee, was $13.50. By the way, Hedley House has its own very original list of cocktails, priced between $2 and $3.

For a snack or a meal downtown in Digby, try the **Fundy Restaurant** at 30 Water St., on the town's main thoroughfare. It's open long hours (7 a.m. to 11 p.m.), and has fine views of the water from windows at the back of the dining room. A breakfast of two eggs, juice, toast, and coffee is a low $2.15, luncheon sandwiches not much more. At dinner, a good Digby-style repast at a very acceptable price is the seafood casserole of lobster, clams, haddock, scallops, and melted cheese for $7.25—and that's the price for the complete dinner, from soup to coffee.

ON THE ROAD: East of Digby on Hwy. 1 heading for Annapolis Royal, you'll pass a good place to spend the night, well off the road in a cool, shady location. It's **Brydon's Motel** (tel. 902/638-8806), in Deep Brook, N.S., a mile west of Cornwallis. The cheery white motel building and house look onto pretty lawns, and the location near the shore allows you to go out clam digging to pass any extra time you have. For a double room with bath, color TV, and radio, two people pay $20 if they share a double bed, $22 if they have separate beds. Breakfast is served from 8 to 10 a.m., but 8 of the 16 units have their own little kitchens (for $4 extra per night) in which you can whip up your own meals if you wish.

The Annapolis Valley is verdant with farms and forests. From the road you'll have sweeping vistas across the Annapolis Basin and River. As the highway turns corners, small villages, each with a neat little church, come into view. Around one corner is a town with no less than four steeples poking through the trees, up to the sky.

At Cornwallis, the highway goes through a huge Canadian Forces base before heading on again toward the "capital" of the region, Annapolis Royal.

ANNAPOLIS ROYAL: Samuel de Champlain built his original "Habitation" at a place distant from the modern town of Annapolis Royal. The fortified enclosure put up by these earliest of French settlers had long since passed into ruin when a modern reconstruction effort was begun. The new-old Habitation is now a national historic park.

The town changed locations in the area over the years as the French and English battled for control of the narrow mouth of the Annapolis River, where it empties into the Annapolis Basin. In 1710 the English won decisively, setting up a garrison at the French town of Port Royal and changing its name (to honor Queen Anne) to Annapolis Royal. Until the deportation of the Acadians, Annapolis Royal was an English enclave in a region of French-speaking people.

Past animosities long forgotten, Annapolis Royal's citizens take pride in their pretty and historic town, and well they should—you'll see as you walk around.

Where to Stay

Annapolis Royal's quaint colonial spirit is best captured if you stay not in a modern motel, but in an old house converted to accept overnight guests. The best one in town, and one of the finest such places in Canada, is **Bread and Roses** (tel. 902/532-5727), 82 Victoria St. The beautiful old red brick Victorian mansion, topped by a slate roof, is filled with fine woodwork, tiled fireplaces, and similar luxuries. John and Barbara Taylor, its owners, have put months of work and quantities of love into restoring the house—and it shows. The seven rooms (five with private bath) are done with thoughtfulness and affection, and many period pieces from the 1880s, when the house was built. One person staying here pays $14, two pay $18, an additional person pays $3. Breakfasts are big and plentiful, and cost $1 to $2.50 extra. Bread and Roses is open from June 1 to October 15; other times by special arrangement.

Across the river from Annapolis Royal in the town of Granville Ferry is **The Moorings** (tel. 902/532-2146), a guest house with three bedrooms, two bathrooms, and two lounges (one lounge has a fireplace, library, and color TV). A single person pays $12, two pay $14, an additional person pays $2. Like Bread and Roses, the Moorings is a restored 19th-century house with all the grace and beauty the times could give a home. It's only about a mile from Annapolis Royal, over the bridge; open June through September.

What to See

Right in the center of Annapolis Royal is **Fort Anne National Historic Park,** commemorating the fortress built by the French at the beginning of the 1700s. Actually, the fort was never completed, although it saw a lot of action in the fierce sieges and battles which raged around the site. Today the powder magazines and the largely rebuilt officers' quarters buildings are still standing, where artifacts discovered on the site have been arranged to outline the turbulent history of the town and the fortress. The fort is open daily, for free. Take a stroll through the nearby cemetery, too, for a look at the ancient headstones.

Annapolis Royal's 19th-century history comes alive on **Lower St. George St.,** an area undergoing restoration to return it to the way it looked in 1878. The **O'Dell Inn and Tavern,** a Victorian stagecoach inn, has been fully restored and is open to the public from June to mid-September, 9 a.m. to 5:30 p.m., for $1 admission. The inn's downstairs rooms are filled with odd Victoriana set up to show aspects of life a century ago: a wedding room is complete with bride, the mourning room holds such strange items as coffin plaques, memorial pictures, and wreathes of hair from the Dear Departed. A dollhouse with furnishings adds a much lighter note to a visit here.

To view **Champlain's Habitation,** the first permanent settlement by Europeans north of St. Augustine, Florida, cross the Annapolis River and head west. Several miles along is Port Royal, and Port Royal National Historic Park. Archeological digs here had uncovered some of the foundations of Champlain's Habitation when the Canadian government decided to restore the early settlement in 1938–39. What you'll see when you visit is quaint and rustic, yes, but also thrilling. As you walk through the bunkrooms, chapel, kitchens, storerooms, and the governor's lodgings, imagine what it meant to these men to be here, thousands of sea miles from France, with unknown people and perils around them, and pirates liable to approach on any day. It's no wonder the "Habitants" founded the "Order of Good Cheer," the fraternal body dedicated to making each evening's meal a happy and memorable banquet, and to dispelling gloomy thoughts of fear and loneliness. They survived, as did Canada, which in a real sense began right at this spot.

ON TO GRAND PRÉ:
Bridgetown and Lawrencetown, on Hwy. 1, are fine old towns with lots of graceful Victorian houses and lofty shade trees.

In **Bridgetown,** the main street, called Granville St. (which is also the highway), passes the **Bridgetown Motor Hotel** (tel. 902/665-4491), with 33 modern motel rooms arranged in two floors around an open-air swimming pool. After a swim, the hotel's sauna is perfect for relaxing. All rooms have color TV, and rent for $22 single, $26 to $29 double; children under 14 can stay with their parents free of charge. The Bridgetown's dining room, lounge, and coffeeshop provide well for all meals.

If you pass through **Lawrencetown** in mid-August, plan to spend a few hours touring the region's largest agricultural fair, the Annapolis County Exhibition. The highway goes right past the exhibition grounds.

Past **Kingston,** you have a choice of roads: old Hwy. 1 continues on its meandering course through the countryside, while newer, faster Hwy. 101 will speed you toward Grand Pré and Halifax. Take Exit 10 for Grand Pré National Historic Park.

GRAND PRÉ NATIONAL HISTORIC PARK:
Acadian history's saddest times began at Grand Pré, which was the center of Acadian civilization in the early 1700s. The fierce French-British struggles for the rich lands of Nova Scotia caught these early French-speaking settlers right in the middle. Unwilling to give up their cultural connections with France, unable to bring themselves to be British, they were deported swiftly and in great numbers. The deportations began in 1755, urged on by British governors and generals whose forces were locked in a life-and-death struggle with French forces. The prize was Nova Scotia. Some 14,000 Acadians were ejected from their homes, families were sundered, and many were to die searching for new lands which would accept them.

Grand Pré National Historic Park is a memorial to the Acadians who suffered through the deportation, to those who returned, and also to those who have always lived in the province—and still do today. The memorial church, built in the 1920s in traditional Acadian style, has never been consecrated as a house of worship. Rather, it has always been a memorial, and inside it holds exhibits detailing the history of the Acadian people. Parks and gardens surround the church—a fitting place to ponder the great and terrible machinations of history.

If you need to stay the night, Grand Pré's **Evangeline Motel** (tel. 902/542-2703) stands right at the intersection of the highway and the road into Grand Pré National Historic Park. The wood-fronted motel units are up the hillside, away from the intersection. Three rooms with private bath are rented in the house right down by the road, for $18 double, but the motel rooms, which are slightly larger and quieter, cost $24, all with TVs. The motel has a pool, and a small restaurant good for a light lunch or dinner whether you stay overnight or not. The same lady who operates the Evangeline Motel is also in charge of the **Evangeline Beach Motel** (same phone), a nine-room building down the road toward the beach.

WINDSOR: Although few visitors realize it at first, Windsor was the birthplace of many of the English language's most colorful turns of phrase. "Quick as a wink," "city slicker," and countless other expressions first saw the light in the writings of Judge Thomas Chandler ("T.C.") Haliburton, creator of a character named Sam Slick. Sam was perhaps the first and foremost character in early North American humor, and while Judge Haliburton's Mark Twain–style stories are not read much anymore, the bon mots which made the stories lively are part of every North American English-speaker's fund of language.

T. C. Haliburton's grand house in Windsor is now part of the **Nova Scotia Museum,** open to visits from mid-May to mid-October, 9:30 a.m. to 5:30 p.m. for free. The huge house, filled with antiques and Judge Haliburton's possessions, sits in its own ten-acre estate of lawns, gardens, and copses of trees on one of Windsor's graceful old streets. For a map of the town, stop at the tourist bureau at the southeastern end of the causeway over the Avon River, in Windsor. They'll sell you a copy of Haliburton's collection of Sam Slick tales, too.

In Windsor, the **Hampshire Court Motel** (tel. 902/798-3133) has a superb location in the midst of gorgeous mansions and graceful shade trees at 1081 King St. This has got to be one of the most unusual and elegant places for a motel anywhere in Canada. The rooms are not grand but quite adequate, with private baths and TV sets. Four cottages (with seven bedrooms in all) and four rooms in the house next to the motel make a total of 22 rooms which rent for $12 to $19 single, $16 to $22 double, $3 for an extra person. Not to be outdone by its magnificent neighbors, the Hampshire Court Motel has its own private tennis court. The motel is open only May to mid-October.

5. Marine Drive, New Glasgow, Antigonish

East of Halifax, the jagged southeastern coast of Nova Scotia stretches as far as Cape Canso. Rivers and streams descend from the hills to enter the sea—the highway seems to cross a river every few miles. Much more sparsely settled than the southwest coast or the Annapolis Valley, it is that much more picturesque.

MARINE DRIVE: Leave Halifax by Hwy. 107, the new, fast road, which soon joins the older Hwy. 7. Winding along the coast, Hwy. 7 is the Nova Scotia Tourism Department's Marine Drive. At the northern end of Hwy. 7 is Antigonish, on the road to the Cape Breton highlands.

Every little village along the way seems to have something unique about it, if you take the time to explore. At **Tangier,** for instance, a weathered sign points to a side road announcing that at the end of it can be found J. Willi Krauch, a maker of smoked salmon, herring, mackerel, and similar delicacies. Smoked salmon, a delicacy often reserved for the rich and the royal, is much cheaper if you buy it right from J. Willi's smokehouse, a modern operation with a clerk on duty during business hours. On the smokehouse wall is a letter from Buckingham Palace, thanking Mr. Krauch for his gift to Her Majesty of a Nova Scotia smoked salmon.

In **Port Dufferin,** the road winds around Beaver Harbour and past the **Marquis of Dufferin Motel** (tel. 902/654-2696), a small 14-room motel in which over half of the rooms have TVs, but all have such a splendid view of the harbor that the TVs are hardly ever turned on. A single room costs $16 to $20, or $18 to $25 for two. Breakfast and dinner are served April through October.

Of the three resorts operated by the Nova Scotia government, the most rustic one is located on the Marine Drive, at **Liscomb Mills. Liscombe Lodge** (tel. 902/779-2307) is a complex of small chalets and deluxe cottages clustered around a main lodge surrounded by trees and fronting on the seashore. The chalets have fireplaces and little porches for sitting, electric heat, and private baths; cottages are more elaborate, with four bedrooms each, plus a common living room with a fireplace, and verandas. Every bedroom has its own private tub-shower bath facilities. One person pays $30 for a bedroom, two pay $33, and an extra person in a bedroom pays $5; children under 12 but over 3 who share a room with their parents pay only $3. The main lodge's dining room is open to guests and passersby alike from 7 a.m. to 9:30 p.m. People staying at Liscombe Lodge have the option of buying breakfast and dinner each day for one set price of $13 per person per day (half price for kids 3 to 12). Relaxing, walking the nature trails, boating, canoeing, and paddle boating fill one's days at Liscombe Lodge, and the days pass all too quickly.

The major attraction along Marine Drive is at Sherbrooke, up the St. Mary's River as Hwy. 7 heads northeast. **Sherbrooke Village,** unlike other "living museums" you may visit, is not an old town or colony assembled from various buildings brought to the site or reconstructed. Rather, it is a small town which changed very little between its gold-rush days (yes, there was a gold rush here) in the 1860s and the middle of the present century. Restoration work consisted of putting the town in order and opening it to the public. Sherbrooke Village is low key, with the townspeople dressed in costumes from the 19th century and going about their daily business. Churches, craft workshops, the town schoolhouse, a pharmacy and print shop, and over a dozen other buildings are open and working, with the citizens moving in rhythm to the schedule tolled by the town bell. Sherbrooke Village is off Hwy. 7 a short distance—signs clearly point the way—and is open from 9:30 a.m. to 5:30 p.m. daily in summer. Admission costs $1.50 for adults, 25¢ for children 6 to 16; a family pays a maximum of $3.50 for all members.

Right at the corner in Sherbrooke where the side road goes off to Sherbrooke Village is **Bright House** (tel. 902/522-2691), a fine old house restored in the spirit of Sherbrooke Village and opened as a restaurant. A garden next to the house supplies the vegetables, and the couple who own the house do the cooking and serving. Food and service, then, have an exceptionally personal touch, and prices are eminently reasonable. For lunch, you'll do well to order the daily special priced for about $3.25. In the evening, start with French onion soup or a cup of clam chowder (95¢), and perhaps they'll have roast beef and Yorkshire pudding for a main course, or a seafood casserole made up of lobster, scallops, and sole. Either dish will cost only $6.50. Everything about Bright House is charming, from the wood floors and hanging plants to the hooked rugs and the friendly service, and as it's the best restaurant on Marine Drive, it can be very busy Saturday and Sunday evenings. Call for reservations, just to be sure. Bright House is open from 11:30 a.m. to 9 p.m. every day in the warm months.

Should you need to stay the night in Sherbrooke, try the **Marine Motel** (tel. 902/522-2235), on Hwy. 7 west of town. Every room of the 12 has a full bath and shower, a radio, and a TV, and the cost is only $15 single, $16 to $20 double. They serve breakfast and dinner.

North of Sherbrooke the highway follows the St. Mary's River through lush farmland. Herds of dairy cattle graze slowly in the rich pastures, and now and then you'll see a sign inviting you to "pick your own" strawberries—farms along the road specialize in them. Finally, the highway enters Antigonish.

NEW GLASGOW: Fresh off the ferryboat from Prince Edward Island at Caribou, N.S., the first large town you'll encounter inland is New Glasgow, a steel and manufacturing town with plenty of places to put up for the night.

Where to Stay

New Glasgow's fanciest transient address is the modern, full-service **Heather Motor Hotel** (tel. 902/752-8401), on Hwy. 104 at the interchange with Foord St. and Stellarton Rd. The Heather is actually within the town limits of Stellarton, although it seems closer to New Glasgow. A large dining room, a lounge with live entertainment, and 76 fully equipped up-to-date rooms keep people coming to the Heather. For one, the charge is $24 to $30; for two, $28 to $36. The dining room serves three meals a day, and doesn't close between 7 a.m. and 11 p.m.

Much more basic, with modest rates to match, is the **Tara Motel** (tel. 902/752-8458), on E. River Rd. (Hwy. 389), on the way into New Glasgow from the Trans Canada Hwy. (Hwy. 104). Double rooms here cost only $27 for two sharing a double bed, $30 for two in two separate beds. TV, radio, telephone, and wall-to-wall carpeting are in each of the 32 rooms; some of the TV sets are color ones. It's quiet, the neighbors can't disturb you; breakfast is served year round.

New Glasgow's prettiest and most interesting place to stay—and, happily, its least expensive—is the **Wynward Inn** (tel. 902/755-5316 or 752-4527), 71 Stellarton Rd., near the junction of Abercrombie, George, and Stellarton. Go slowly and keep an eye out for the small Wynward sign (I missed it easily the first time I visited the inn). The inn's high-ceilinged downstairs rooms, filled with fine woodwork, stained glass, and other elegant touches, serve as lounge and breakfast nook. Guest rooms (there are six) upstairs are homey, each with a radio, some with washbasins, although all the rooms share two bathrooms. One person pays $10, two pay $14 in one bed, $16 in two beds, and that includes a self-served light breakfast of toast and coffee, made whenever you feel like it in the downstairs kitchen. Mrs. Walsh, the proprietor, will see that you enjoy your stay.

ANTIGONISH: Halfway between Halifax and Sydney, Antigonish (pronounced "anna-go-*nish*") has become a way station on the drive to Cape Breton Island for Nova Scotians and outside visitors alike. But other things draw people to this pretty town located at the junction of several major roads. Prime among these are the annual **Highland Games,** held in mid-July and attended by devotees of Scottish sports, pipe bands, and dances from North America and from Scotland itself. **St. Francis Xavier University's** lovely campus has been a beautiful and significant part of the Antigonish town scene since the university's founding in 1855. **St. Ninian's Cathedral** (built 1867) is the seat of the Roman Catholic bishop of Antigonish.

Where to Stay and Eat

Should you be coming for the Highland Games, have reservations well in advance as the town's inns and motels fill up quickly with visiting fans and sportsmen. If everything's full, get a reservation on the far side of Antigonish (in whichever direction you're headed) and plan to visit the games for the day.

The **Dingle Motel** (tel. 902/863-3730), on the Trans Canada Hwy., 4½ miles east of town, has several things to recommend it. The location is not bad, housekeeping standards are first rate, and the selection of rooms in several price ranges makes it a good place to inquire no matter what you can spend. The Dingle has 35 motel rooms in all, 11 of which are new, modern, and equipped with color TVs; these are the most expensive, at $26 single, $34 double. But around at the back are older, quite presentable rooms which are quieter than the new ones in front, and priced at only $20 single, $22 double. All have TVs and private baths. Rooms in the Dingle's lodge rent at these low prices as well. Fifteen small cabins in the back are cozy, and good for families.

The **Oasis Motel** (tel. 902/863-3557) is two miles east of town on the Trans Canada Hwy., with 13 modern and moderately priced motel rooms, and a bonus for families with young children: a play area with swings, slides, and seesaws. Rooms have tub-shower baths, radios, and TVs, and cost $20 to $28 double, May through October; reduced rates are offered other times of the year.

Right downtown in Antigonish is the gracious old **Bonnie Brae Inn** (tel. 902/863-1184), 95 College St., not far from the corner with Main St. Of the 28 rooms in this fine old wooden inn, 12 have private baths and cost $20 single, $24 double; the others have washbasins only, for a cost of $14 single, $18 double; an extra person pays $3 in either sort of room. The Bonnie Brae's rooms are basic and simple, without all the modern paraphernalia, but well located.

An extra bonus is the **Bonnie Brae Restaurant** (tel. 863-5818) on the main floor, open from 8 a.m. to 10 p.m. daily. Under an old-fashioned embossed metal ceiling (such things are now bona fide antiques), the large, wood-wainscotted dining rooms have an informally elegant air like you'd find in a well-established Victorian summer resort. Meals at the Bonnie Brae fall into the higher reaches of the moderate price category, but the food is well prepared and the service very efficient and friendly. Daily table d'hôte meals offer good value. During the Highland Games held as part of the Second International Gathering of the Clans, I dropped in and had the set-price dinner of fresh trout, salad, potatoes, fresh bread baked in the Bonnie Brae's ovens, and strawberry shortcake for $11; with tax and tip, the total came to $13. Cocktails ($2.50 to $3.50), wine, and beer are available with meals. By the way, as you approach the Bonnie Brae along College St., the "main" entrance leads to the dining room. The smaller entrance down the side of the building to the left leads to the inn lobby and the guest rooms.

For seafood, the **Lobster Treat** (tel. 863-5465) is the town favorite. It's on the Trans Canada Hwy. just west of the town, open 7 a.m. to 11 p.m. in summer (11 a.m. to 11 p.m. in winter). You wouldn't look twice at the restaurant's rickety lobster-red exterior were it not for a parking lot always filled with the cars of loyal customers come to chow down on delicious chowder ($1.25 a cupful), lobster salad plates with vegetables ($5.25 at lunch, $8.25 at dinner), or the real thing: boiled live lobster. These are sold by weight, and usually work out to about $13.50. Cocktails, wine, and beer are served. The two wood-paneled dining rooms, paved in the regulation tartan carpeting, are always busy.

Something less expensive? Try the **Venice Pizzaria Restaurant,** 76 College St., near the intersection with Main St. Two small dining rooms here have recently been renovated and furnished with red-and-white tablecloths on small, cozy tables. Pizza is the specialty, and price depends on size: a 10-inch cheese pizza is $2.65, a larger 16-inch one costs $5, and there are two sizes in between. Add extra pennies for extra toppings of meat, eggs, etc. Despite the restaurant's Italian name, the chef is Greek, and so with your Italian sub sandwich you can have a Greek salad with feta cheese and black olives ($2.75). The Venice is fully licensed, and stays open from 11 a.m. to 1 a.m.

The Highland Games

Stop by the tourist bureau at the western entrance to town off the Trans Canada Hwy., and then proceed down Main St. to Columbus Field, by Right's River, where the games are held. You pay one admission price to enter the grounds for the day (they ink-stamp your hand so you can come and go), and then Antigonish's incredible, lavish display of Highland lore, art, strength, and skill is yours to enjoy.

At one end of the field are the Highland dancers, at the other brawny athletes are throwing the hammer, broad-jumping, and "tossing the caber," while pipe bands march and skirl in between. Highlights of the day are the dance finals, the massed pipe bands—hundreds of bagpipers marching and playing together—and the caber toss. The latter event is a marvel. The caber, a log peeled of its bark, about 26 feet long and six inches in diameter, is lifted and tossed end-over-end by any of the thick-muscled athletes who can handle it. It takes immense strength and skill to get the mammoth tree trunk into the air, then straight up like a flagpole as it goes over, and few can do it.

But not even the caber toss can compete with the massed pipe bands for sheer emotional thrill. After competing for points in playing, marching, uniforms, and bearing all day, the bands come together in an unforgettable display of Scottish color, glitter, and ceremony. The bands alone are worth taking the trouble to schedule your Nova Scotia visit so as to catch the Highland Games at Antigonish.

6. Cape Breton Island

Cape Breton Island, the wild and beautiful eastern end of Nova Scotia, is actually several islands surrounding the great Bras d'Or Lake. The mountain-ous country of Cape Breton kept it from being heavily settled, although it was just this remoteness which appealed to hardy Scots settlers who founded small towns back in the mountains. They named the towns for familiar places in Scotland, with the occasional MicMac Indian name being left in place.

Cape Breton is still very much a land of rugged highlands, dramatic mountains and valleys, rocky coasts, and tranquil lakes. Except for Sydney and Glace Bay, twin industrial giants in the southeastern reaches of the island, Cape Breton towns are small, perhaps with no more than a dozen houses, a general store, and a post office.

Driving your own car is the best way to see Cape Breton. The time-honored drive is along the **Cabot Trail** through the northern tip of the island in Cape Breton Highlands National Park. North Sydney, suburb of Nova Scotia's second-largest city, is the departure point for ferries to Newfoundland.

The Fortress of Louisbourg, south of Sydney, is undoubtedly Cape Breton's most impressive and exciting historical place. For tranquil relaxation, the island has tiny resort hamlets on the shores of Bras d'Or Lake.

The explorations of Cape Breton which follow make a start at Canso Causeway—the only road to Cape Breton from the mainland—then head north to the national park. From there, roads go south to North Sydney and Louisbourg, and then west to the shores of Bras d'Or before returning to Canso Causeway.

But before setting out, you should know about Cape Breton's unique bed-and-breakfast program. Motels and inns are sprinkled along Cape Breton's roads, but they fill quickly in summer. To encourage tourism at modest prices, local authorities have organized lists of Cape Breton residents with spare rooms to rent. You'll see the distinctive "Bed and Breakfast" signs frequently along the road. A house may have only one, or several, rooms for rent, but the cost will always be about $14 for one, $16 for two sharing a bed, breakfast included. The tourist bureau can provide you with a leaflet listing the participants in the program.

OVER CANSO CAUSEWAY: Canso Causeway, connecting Cape Breton with the mainland, is the deepest in the world. You pay a toll to cross going east; the return west is toll free.

Just across the causeway is a large and ever-busy **tourist bureau,** and a cluster of motels set to catch those who cross at nightfall.

At the eastern end of the causeway, Hwy. 105, the Trans Canada, intersects Hwy. 19. Drive north on 19, heading into the highland foothills past the tiny hamlets along the way. The first big town is Inverness, with banks, stores, gas stations, a beach, and a large campground and vacation center.

Margaree Harbour and Margaree Forks can boast several fine places to stay. At Margaree Forks, the **Margaree Lodge** (tel. 902/248-2193), on the hill above the road, has 46 motel units with baths, radios, and TVs, for $24 to $26 double. The views are very fine, the swimming pool is heated, and the lodge even has its own small golf course. The licensed dining room is open for breakfast from 7:30 to 9:30 a.m., for dinner from 5:30 to 10 p.m.

At Margaree Harbour, it's the **Duck Cove Inn** (tel. 902/235-2658), overlooking the mouth of the Margaree River from its perch on the hillside above the highway. Rooms with the enchanting water view also have little balconies so you can get closer to nature. For these, two pay $28 to $30; older rooms, with a view but not quite so fine, cost $26 double. If you don't have the panorama right out your room window, at least you can enjoy it from the inn's modern restaurant, which has a wall of glass to let nature in. Dining hours are 7:30 to 11:30 a.m., noon to 1:30, and 6 to 8 p.m.

CHETICAMP: The center of Acadian life on Cape Breton's north shore is in Cheticamp, a large French-speaking fishing town famous for its handicrafts shops.

First place to stop in Cheticamp is at the **Musée Acadien,** also called the **Co-operative Artisanale de Cheticamp** (the Handicrafts Cooperative). Both establishments are in the same building on the main street. Upstairs, fine-quality hooked rugs and other craft items are on sale. In the basement is a small collection of artifacts from Acadian traditional life, and best of all, a small cafe. Behind the counter, smiling Acadian ladies dish up light lunches and suppers, from a simple piece of hot gingerbread with hot syrup (80¢, with coffee) to a complete codfish dinner ($3.50), or just a serving of potato pancakes ($1.85). It's the only true "home-cooking" I've found so far, as these ladies just do it part time to help out, and they really do cook as they would at home. The museum and crafts cooperative, and the cafe, are open from 8 a.m. to 9 p.m. daily from mid-May to mid-October.

Other craft stores abound, their quality craft items intermingled with many standard souvenir items. Mrs. Freddy Deveau, proprietress of the **Foyer du Souvenir,** on the main street, has a good collection, conveniently located.

Should you want to stay the night here, **Albert's Motel** (tel. 902/224-2077) is a tiny but comely place, with only four units, all fixed up with TV, bath and shower, and coffee service. Albert's charges $14 for one, $16 for two, and has the great advantage of being an easy walk from the shops and stores of the town. The rooms at the south end of the motel building have views of the sea. Open late May to late October.

Laurie's Motel and Dining Room (tel. 902/224-2400) is an old Cheticamp standby, with 21 rooms and a famous restaurant. The rooms: all with bath, radio and TV, some with color TVs and telephones, go for $24 single, $26 to $28 double. The restaurant: specializing in seafood, Laurie's has built a good reputation in a town where the seafood is bound to be fresh since it comes in right off the boats. As always, a few choice steak and chicken items squeeze onto the menu, but for most people the attraction is a full dinner of soup, vegetable, salad, dessert, and coffee based on a main-course dish such as fresh fish steak ($8), lobster ($10), or seafood casserole ($9.50). Dining room hours are 7:30 to 10 a.m., 11:30 a.m. to 2 p.m., and 5 to 8 p.m.

Northward out of town, the road passes the tidy little cabins, very French, each with a large picture window, of **Cabines Leblanc** (tel. 902/224-2822), just a mile before coming to the national park entrance. The six cabins have baths and TV, and three have kitchenettes. They cost only $16 per night for one or two persons, a mere $2 more per night for each extra person.

The **Park View Motel** (tel. 902/224-3232) has just that: a view of the entrance to Cape Breton Highlands National Park, a short stroll away. You pay a bit more here as you're so near the park entrance, and as there is a swimming pool on the grounds. Seventeen rooms with baths, radios, and TVs rent for $22 single, $26 double. The Park View's licensed dining room is open for all three meals each day.

CAPE BRETON HIGHLANDS NATIONAL PARK: It's one of Canada's most spectacular—and that's saying a lot, as so many are so exceptionally beautiful. The **Cabot Trail** begins at Margaree Forks, heads to Cheticamp, and then enters the national park to wind up into the dramatic scenery of the mountains. Camping areas, picnic sites, and scenic lookouts are spaced at good intervals along the trail. The drive from Cheticamp to Ingonish, the town on the eastern shore with many tourist services, can easily be done in a day, or even a half day. But take a picnic and enjoy a leisurely drive, or plan to stop—when the road loops outside the park boundaries for several miles—at the Black Whale.

Right by the side of the road at Pleasant Bay, the **Black Whale Restaurant** has a good selection of native seafood dishes at good prices. When I stopped for lunch, salmon steaks were only $5, whole baby flounder even less. Prices rise at dinnertime, but portions get larger as well. The Black Whale, a rustic-style place which does little to disturb the forest scenery, has lots of windows so you needn't be far from the spectacular views. Fully licensed, children's portions, hamburgers for the landlubbers—just the thing.

THE INGONISHES: At the southeastern entrance to Cape Breton Highlands National Park are the villages of Ingonish, Ingonish Centre, and Ingonish Beach. Most of the national park recreational facilities—golf, tennis, boating, and sailing, not to mention the fine sandy beaches in both Ingonish and Ingonish Beach—are right in this area, as are the park's administrative headquarters.

Where to Stay and Eat

If your budget will allow it, the only place to stay is at the breathtaking **Keltic Lodge** (tel. 902/285-2880), a simply palatial place on a vast estate, all run by the Nova Scotia government. Rooms are rented in the baronial Main Lodge, the nearby modern White Birch Inn, and in two- and four-bedroom cottages. Rates vary with accommodations: in the lodge, single rooms cost $34; doubles, $43. White Birch rooms, larger and more modern, are a few dollars more at $41 single, $50 double. In the cottages, one pays $50 for a bedroom, two pay $66, and if they want a two-bedroom cottage to themselves, the cost is $100 a day. An extra person pays $10 in a room at the lodge, $16 in the inn or cabins. For another $17 per day per person you can have breakfast and dinner in the Main Lodge's grand dining room.

Swimming possibilities encompass a big pool, a freshwater lake, and a mile-long ocean beach; for golfers, there's a full 18-hole course. Even if you can't stay at this fabulous place, you should drive up for a look around, perhaps staying for the table d'hôte breakfast ($4), lunch ($8), or dinner ($12), all subject to that 8% tax, and tip.

More modest accommodations, but positively charming ones, are yours at the **Driftwood Lodge** (tel. 902/285-2558), in Ingonish, run by the ever-smiling and cheerful Mrs. Susan Kulig. The rooms are either in the new, natural-wood lodge or in the older red house next door. None has private bath, but some have balconies with a marvelous sea view. In fact, each room at the Driftwood is unique, so it's a good idea to ask about what is currently available. A small double in the older building can cost as little as $12; in the new buildings, doubles are $16 to $22, depending on size, view, and location.

Breakfast at the Driftwood is served to overnight guests only (8 to 9:30 a.m.), but anyone can come for lunch (noon to 2 p.m.) or dinner (5 to 9 p.m.). And what meals! Mrs. Kulig puts her central European heritage to work and produces wienerschnitzel, veal goulash, Polish sausages with potatoes, sauerkraut, rye bread and mustard—even borscht and blintzes. Seafood is always on the menu as well, but you will probably want to take the opportunity to have different fare. Prices are moderate: at lunch a meal will be about $6, at dinner about $10 to $11.

The **Ingonish Motel** (tel. 902/285-2888) is right near the shore and just off the highway in Ingonish, set in a copse of trees. The motel is fairly new, and certainly comfortable with each of the 32 rooms having two double beds. The dual-bed arrangement makes it perfect for families with small children, as kids under 10 can stay with their folks for free. Rooms cost $31, plus tax, a dollar extra if you want to have a black-and-white TV set.

In the motel dining room, breakfast is served from 7:30 to 9:30 a.m.; dinner from 6 to 9 p.m. (no lunch). The dinner menu is short but sweet, with lobster, T-bone steak ($8.75), and less expensive dishes like baked breast of chicken ($5.50). Drinks are served. The season for the Ingonish Motel is from June through October.

In Ingonish Centre, the **Amber Gate Motel** (tel. 902/285-2525) prides itself on its own sandy beach and a number of housekeeping cottages scattered among the trees near the beach. Motel rooms come with radios, private baths, and TVs (by special request), and cost $24 to $28; there are two single, two double, and two family (three-room) cottages, all with private bath, radio, and TV, for $12 single, $28 double, $45 for three in a family cottage. The Amber Gate is open from June to Canadian Thanksgiving; off-season rates apply before mid-June and after mid-September.

The **Tartan Terrace Inn** (tel. 902/285-2404) in Ingonish Beach has recently been renovated from top to bottom. You'll recognize it as a big white house very near the entrance to the national park and the driveway to the Keltic Lodge. Every room in the inn is different: some have private baths, some do not; some have twin beds, others have double beds. One person pays $17 and up to stay; two pay $20 to $23 without private bath, $26 to $27 with private bath. The inn's small dining room serves simple and inexpensive fare. Luncheon sandwiches, for instance, are all priced about $2.

SOUTH TO BADDECK: The Cabot Trail heads southwest from the Ingonishes to rejoin the Trans Canada Hwy. at South Gut St. Ann's. Before meeting the highway, though, it passes by the tiny hamlet of St. Ann's (marked as Goose Cove on some maps) where you'll see the **Tartan Village Restaurant** (tel. 929-2820), a good place for breakfast, lunch, or dinner. In the morning, a ham-and-cheese omelet is a good starter ($2.50); at lunch or dinner, meat dishes with vegetable, potato, and a hot, freshly made biscuit cost $5. Daily special meals are always featured for $5 to $6, but the Tartan Village's forte is fish: salmon, scallops, lobster ($7 to $9), and whatever else is in season. Food and service are fine, but if you're the sort who enjoys a glass of white wine with seafood, you may despair when you examine the wine list. The closest you'll get to a dry white is the Château-Gai sauterne, called a demi-sec, but in fact it has a rather nice dryness—not like a sauterne at all. The Tartan Village is neat and attractive, with wood-paneled walls and oak chairs to remind you that you're in Cape Breton, and plaques with the most prominent family tartans ("plaids") hung on the walls.

When you reach the Trans Canada Hwy. (105), you have the choice of going left (east) to Bras d'Or, North Sydney, and Louisbourg, or right (west) to Baddeck, Whycocomagh, and back to the Canso Causeway. Both routes are outlined below, beginning with Baddeck and Whycocomagh.

BADDECK: Baddeck is one of Cape Breton's most delightful old resort towns, famed for its tranquil beauty and fine views of St. Patrick's Channel. Surprisingly, this small town also has a place in aviation history, being the spot where one J. A. D. McCurdy made the first heavier-than-air flight in the British Empire, on February 23, 1909.

But Baddeck's scientific claim to fame is that Alexander Graham Bell came to spend his summers here, and Baddeck is now the site of the Alexander Graham Bell National Historic Park, with exhibits devoted to Bell's life and work.

Where to Stay and Eat

Baddeck is a lazy summer resort, a highway rest stop, and a historic tourist destination, and its lodging and dining establishments reflect this diversity.

The **Inverary Inn** (tel. 902/295-2674), on Hwy. 205, "Shore Rd.," has that lazy summer resort feeling about it, with wicker chairs on the vine-covered veranda and piles of magazines and paperbacks in the comfy living room. Set back from the road deep in its own grounds, flowers are everywhere. There's a private beach, pool, and children's playground. All in all, the Inverary has 64 rooms in the main lodge, in seven cottages, and in a motel-type building. Rates are $18 to $35 single, $20 to $45 double, $3 for an extra person; you can have breakfast and dinner each day on a specially priced meal plan. The air-conditioned dining room is open to the public as well as inn guests for breakfast (8 to 9:30 a.m.) and dinner (5:45 to 8 p.m.). At dinnertime when last I visited, the menu listed oysters or shrimp cocktail ($3.50) as appetizers, seafood chowder for soup, then beef stew ($6.70) or seafood casserole ($9). My bill, with the soup, seafood casserole, dessert, and coffee, tax, and tip, was $15.

Telegraph House (tel. 902/295-9988), right in the center of Baddeck on Chebucto St., is best described as a country inn, even though it's right in town. On all but the warmest days a fire crackles in the living room fireplace, and the dining room is filled with good smells. The rooms in the house itself are preferable, in my opinion, to the modern motel rooms in an annex next door, for the house rooms have character as well as private baths (in 12 out of 15) and TV sets. House rooms cost $22 to $24 single, $24 to $27 double; in the motel, rooms cost $28 to $32 single, $30 to $32 double. An extra person is charged $3, or $2 for a child under 12.

The dining room in Telegraph House is open 7:30 to 10 a.m., noon to 2 p.m., and 5:30 to 8 p.m. daily, and menus tend to be European style, with one soup offering, juices, a half dozen main courses to choose from, and several desserts. Grilled Margaree trout with lemon ($7) or steamed scallops on the half shell, topped with a cheese sauce ($8.25) are typical of the fresh seafood offerings, although you will always find a beef dish, and perhaps ham or chicken, too.

The **Motel Gisele** (tel. 902/295-2849), P.O. Box 132, is on the hillside along Shore Rd. Some tables in the pretty dining room have a fine view over the lawns, and the tables are topped with blue tiles—a distinctive touch. If you're just dropping in to dine, hours are 7:30 to 9:30 a.m., noon to 2 p.m., and 5:30 to 10 p.m. At dinner you may be surprised by some of the original and intriguing dishes served: fresh stuffed Bras d'Or trout, cooked in butter and bourbon whiskey ($8.70) was the surprise last time I dined here. Scallops, salmon, and steaks are almost always served up, at prices of $9 to $12 for the main course and a vegetable.

Want to stay the night? The Gisele's rooms are good looking and thoroughly modern, with color TVs and spotless baths. Prices for two people are $30 to $32, $4 for an extra person. The Gisele is open from mid-May through mid-November.

Alexander Graham Bell National Historic Park

The inventor of the telephone was not a single-track inventor by any means. Bell put his lively intelligence to work in the solution of medical and surgical problems, and to probe the mysteries of flight, besides his widely known experiments with electricity and speech devices.

Bell was a Scot, born in the Old Country in 1847, later moving to Canada and then the U.S. Baddeck was his choice of locations for a summer house, called "Beinn Bhreagh" and still owned by the Bell family. Although you can't visit his house, you can visit the great, modern museum filled with exhibits detailing his life and work, particularly his experiments with the *Silver Dart,* an early airplane, and the HD-4, an early type of seaplane. Once done with the exhibits, go up to the museum's roof for the fine view of Baddeck Bay and Bras d'Or Lake.

The museum is open from late May to mid-October, 9 a.m. to 9 p.m. every single day; and in the colder months from 9 to 5 every day except holidays. Admission is free.

WHYCOCOMAGH: A tiny village of less than 400 souls, Whycocomagh is near a MicMac Indian reservation and a provincial park, and is right on the northwestern bay of Bras d'Or Lake. Should you want a break from your travels or a place to stay the night, turn off the Trans Canada Hwy. and make your way to the **Village Inn** (tel. 902/756-2002), P.O. Box 22, on the town's main street. The inn has eight rooms, and another six bedrooms are in five cabins nearby. Rates are low: $10 to $14 single, $12 to $16 double, depending on the room and the facilities (a few rooms have private baths, others have washbasins, some use baths and washrooms down the hall). The quaint little dining room has a table set in a windowed alcove, with other tables around the walls. Breakfast (7 to 9:30 a.m.), lunch (noon to 1:30 p.m.) and dinner (5 to 8 p.m.) are served. At lunchtime, I had clam chowder ($1.50), a very filling bowlful, followed by pork chops ($6), a slice of homemade pie ($1), and coffee for $11, tax and tip included. Fresh biscuits, two vegetables plus potato, and the most delicious oatcakes I'd ever tasted were included (I found I could buy a neatly typed copy of the oatcake recipe for $1). Service is friendly, as you'd expect in a small, hometown place—almost the same as being a distant cousin who's dropped by for a meal.

BRAS D'OR AND NORTH SYDNEY: The city of Sydney is Nova Scotia's second largest, a pulp-and-paper manufacturing town, a rail terminus, and the commercial center of Cape Breton. But most tourists who approach the urban conglomeration are going to the suburb of North Sydney to catch the New-foundland ferry; or they're headed around Sydney for the Fortress of Louis-bourg, due south. If you must stay overnight in the area, motels and tourist lodges in North Sydney and nearby Little Bras d'Or (on the western side of the bridge over the Little Bras d'Or River) offer the most convenience. They're the nearest ones to the ferry docks, and don't involve dealing with the complexities of city streets and traffic. You can also use these places as a convenient base for trips to Louisbourg.

Where to Stay

Of the motels north of North Sydney, my favorite is the neat and trim little **MacNeil's Motel** (tel. 902/736-9106), ten rooms in white buildings with eye-catching black roofs and yellow accents. It's on the Trans Canada Hwy., on the right-hand side as you head east, three miles before the CN Marine ferry docks. The ten rooms have private baths and TVs, and cost $19 to $21 single, $22 to $24 double. Off-season reductions are in effect November through May.

The **Clansman Motel** (tel. 902/794-7226), is on Hwy. 125, the bypass road around Sydney, at the Peppett St. exit (mail address: P.O. Box 216, North Sydney, NS B2A 3M3). Rooms in both the older and newer sections of the motel cost the same, $24 to $28 single, $26 to $32 double. Picnic tables, swings, and a small swimming pool are good diversions for families, and if you haven't brought a picnic you can dine in their small restaurant. Off-season rates are in effect for all months except July and August.

The **Kawaja Tourist Lodge** (tel. 902/794-4876) is at 88 Queen St. in North Sydney (Queen St. is the continuation of Commercial St. southwest of the center of town, along the waterfront). The lodge is exactly a mile from the ferry docks, which is as close a lodging place as you'll find. Of the six rooms in this large old white house, four have washbasins; they all share 3½ bathrooms. Mrs. Shebib will provide you with a television set if you feel you want one, and the same goes for breakfast. One person pays $12 to $14, two pay $16 to $18, the higher price being for a room with two beds. The Kawaja stays open year round.

The Fortress of Louisbourg

The great Fortress of Louisbourg is a historical curiosity. Construction was begun shortly after the Treaty of Utrecht (1713) took away the French bases in Newfoundland, and Cape Breton, another French possession, became the country's major base for cod fishing in the Grand Banks. A prosperous commercial town grew up within the massive fortified enclosure, and while the fortifications looked impregnable and daunting to the untrained eye, bad positioning of the fort by its military designers virtually predestined it to capture. When the battle came and the English laid siege to the place in 1749, the design flaws were immediately apparent and the fortress fell in less than two months. The vagaries of the peace treaty handed the defeated stronghold right back to its French defenders, but by 1758 Louisbourg was under siege by the English once again. This time it was lost for good.

Proven to be of limited usefulness, the great fortifications and the French town were abandoned, which condemned them to slow obliteration. But it also meant no city would grow up to engulf the ruins, and when Cape Breton's coal mines were shut down in the 1960s, freeing a large and hearty force of workmen, it was possible to begin resurrecting the fort and town just as they had been two centuries before.

Since 1961 the Canadian government's reconstruction project has achieved amazing results, and visitors to the Fortress of Louisbourg National Historic Park can easily picture themselves in the prosperous French base. Streets, houses, kitchen gardens, workshops, and storerooms are filled with the people (in period dress) and things they held long ago. Bread is baked daily in the old ovens, chickens and geese waddle here and there, and the inns and taverns serve meals and refreshments of the kind popular when Louisbourg flourished. Louisbourg is Canada's best time machine.

When you approach the park, zooming down Hwy. 22 from Sydney, park at the Visitors' Centre, buy your tickets ($2 per adult, free for seniors, 50¢ per child, $4 for a family pass), and take the time to view the short slide shows on the ramp to the lower level. Then board the free bus which will take you the mile or two to the site.

Maps, booklets, and the people of Louisbourg themselves will fill you in on everything, from the colony's history to the crafts they are pursuing. You can easily spend three or four hours opening doors and exploring buildings, buying fresh whole-wheat bread at the bakery, having a meal in one of two historical inns, and buttonholing guards in the "Bastion du Roi" (the central part of the fortress) with questions about where soldiers slept, what they ate, why they couldn't marry, what they had to do to get tossed in the guardhouse.

To enjoy your visit you must plan ahead: don't come late in the day; wear shoes which will be comfortable on rough, cobbled streets; without fail, bring an extra sweater or windbreaker, and preferably some waterproof garment—fog and drizzle can sweep in unexpectedly (I didn't know this, and I suffered badly from the chill on my first visit).

The park is open in June daily from 10 to 6, in July and August daily from 9 a.m. to 8 p.m. (but most of the townspeople in Louisbourg go home between

5 and 6 p.m., and you'll get only a skeleton tour then); after Labour Day, hours revert to those of June. A sign on Hwy. 22 well north of Louisbourg warns you of current closing times, but the best way to avoid disappointment is to come in the morning, or at least right after lunch.

HEADING BACK: From the eastern reaches of Cape Breton, including North Sydney and Louisbourg, two routes go back to Canso Causeway and the mainland.

Highway 223 follows the shore of St. Andrew's Channel to Grand Narrows, where a small ferryboat chugs you and your car across the Barra Strait to the village of Iona. Continue east on 223 and soon you'll see signs for the **Highland Heights Inn** (tel. 902/622-2360), a modern motel perched on the hillside above the road, with fabulous views of the Bras d'Or Lake from its two floors of rooms. All 16 rooms have private baths and color TVs, and cost $24 to $26 single, $28 to $35 double. In the dining room, a dramatic sloping ceiling rises high above your head, letting in lots of light from tall windows—a favorite place for passersby to stop (and therefore a good place to make reservations before coming to dinner). The menu is simple and short, but good, with perhaps soup of the day or a half-dozen oysters on the half shell to start, then a salmon or halibut steak ($8), or T-bone ($9), served with vegetable and potato. Afterward, you can choose from three or four desserts. Wine and beer, or cocktails, are all served. From the Highland Heights Inn, it's only 13 miles (21 km) to Hwy. 105, the Trans Canada.

The other route west from North Sydney is Hwy. 4 south and west to St. Peters, a historic town on St. Peters Bay. St. Peters has several places to stay and to dine. The one right in town is the **Country Inn** (tel. 902/535-2997), right behind the Irving station; it was once known as the MacDonald Hotel. All 13 rooms here are simple, and have running water. Four public bathrooms provide for the guest rooms; there is a TV in the lounge. Prices are eminently reasonable: $12 to $14 single, $17 double. The licensed dining room does a booming trade with both travelers and townspeople as it's open for all three meals (7:30 to 10 a.m., noon to 2:30, and 5 to 9 p.m., with snacks and sandwiches served outside mealtimes). The big drawing card at dinner is the double-whammy surf-and-turf for $15.50, with which one gets *two* lobster tails as well as the steak, and vegetables and potato. Other steaks and fish dishes cost $6.50 to $9. Liquor is served.

Outside of St. Peters, west on Hwy. 4, is the **Motel Richmond** (tel. 902/535-3304)—official address R.R. 1, River Bourgeois, N.S. All logs and unabashed rusticity, the Motel Richmond's facade seems constantly to be covered in flowers. The rooms echo these preoccupations, except that the conveniences are modern and each of the eight rooms has a TV set. One person pays $16; two pay $20. In the restaurant, Italian specialties predominate, as you will discover if you go for breakfast (7 to 11 a.m.), lunch (11:30 a.m. to 2:30 p.m.) or dinner (5 to 10 p.m.). By the way, the Motel Richmond is open all year, and off-season prices are in effect from October through May.

From St. Peters, Hwy. 4 goes east to Port Hawkesbury and Port Hastings, where it joins the Trans Canada (Hwy. 105) to cross Canso Causeway, back to the mainland. The Nova Scotian mainland is filled with great beauty, but everyone leaving Cape Breton feels a pang when they reach the causeway and leave the island.

NEW BRUNSWICK

VITAL STATISTICS about New Brunswick are impressive: 1400 miles of coastline, 88% of the province covered in forest. Along its shores are some of the oldest cities and towns in Canada, founded by Loyalist refugees from the American Revolution and made rich by shipbuilding and timber wealth. In recent years, with competition from other sources cutting into New Brunswick's timber business, unemployment has been a problem.

But these figures and facts have little meaning in the lovely old summer resort town of St. Andrews, or the genteel reaches of FDR's beloved Campobello Island. In these and other cities and towns on the Bay of Fundy, the future looks bright with a light to be made from harnessing the Fundy tides, highest in the world.

Daily life along the Fundy coast concerns itself with fog and weather predictions, with the price of live lobster, salmon, scallops, and other treasures from the bay's chilly waters.

The seafood is as plentiful, and the beaches much warmer, along New Brunswick's Northumberland Strait shores. Special conditions make the salt water here—as you'll hear local people boast—"the warmest waters north of Virginia, U.S.A."

Along New Brunswick's northern shores are small Acadian French towns and villages. Once driven from their traditional homes, the Acadians have returned to cling to their ancestral lands. French-speakers make up almost 40% of New Brunswick's population, and the province is officially bilingual—the only province officially bilingual in Canada since Québec declared French its only official language.

Some details: whether you enter New Brunswick from the State of Maine or from Québec, remember that this province and all the other Atlantic provinces except Newfoundland and Labrador operate on Atlantic Time, which is one hour ahead of Eastern Time. Set your watch ahead one hour as you cross

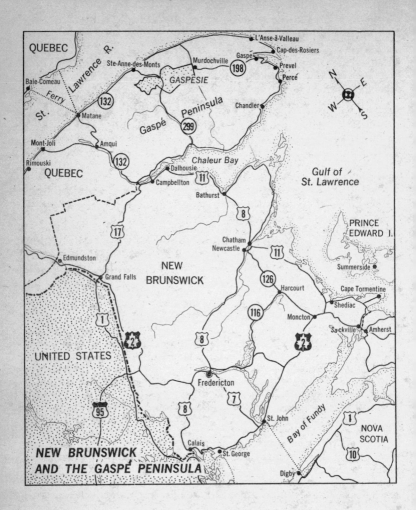

NEW BRUNSWICK AND THE GASPÉ PENINSULA

the border, summer or winter.

For **tourist information** anytime, toll free, dial 800/561-0123 to get the New Brunswick tourist authorities. In addition, it's good to know that provincial tourist bureaus will assist you in finding accommodations through their "Dial-a-Night" hotel reservation service, available at any bureau.

GETTING THERE: New Brunswick, the "gateway to Atlantic Canada," is the crossroads linking the rest of Canada to Prince Edward Island, Nova Scotia, Newfoundland, and Labrador. Transport is a snap.

By Car

From Maine, the best way to come to New Brunswick (in this writer's opinion) is via U.S. 1 to Maine 189 to Lubec. Cross from Lubec to Campobello Island, take the little ferry to Deer Island, and then the free government ferry from Deer Island to the mainland. It's scenic, historic, and adventurous. Full details appear a bit farther on in this book.

Entering via St. Stephen, take I-95 to Maine 9, to Calais, Maine, from whence two bridges lead across the St. Croix River into St. Stephen, New Brunswick.

Those headed straight for New Brunswick's capital city of Fredericton may want to take I-95 to Maine 6 to Vanceboro—on the New Brunswick side it's McAdam—although it's a shame not to see the delightful shores of the Bay of Fundy.

From Québec City and the south shore of the St. Lawrence, the Trans Canada Hwy. crosses the wilds of Québec and northwestern New Brunswick to enter the St. John River Valley, and thence to Fredericton.

You've just come all the way around Gaspé? Then cross via the ferry at Miguasha to Dalhousie, and head south on Hwy. 11. Full details on the ferry appear at the end of the chapter dealing with the Gaspé.

By Bus

New Brunswick's province-wide bus network is served by the **SMT company,** with headquarters in Saint John (tel. 506/693-6500). SMT buses connect with the daily Greyhound coaches which come direct from Washington via New York, Boston, and Portland. The daily bus which originates in Boston arrives at St. Stephen in the evening, and if you ride this one, you'd better plan to stay overnight. From St. Stephen you can catch a bus to Moncton, or Amherst, Nova Scotia, or any point along that route, including St. Andrews, St. George, Blacks Harbour (for Grand Manan Island), or Saint John. In Saint John you'll change buses for points farther along: Moncton, Fredericton, points in Nova Scotia, or points in Québec.

Traveling from Québec, **Voyageur buses** to Rivière-du-Loup tie in with buses to Edmundston, N.B., where SMT buses take over on the run down to Fredericton and Saint John. Another such route is Rimouski to Mont Joli to Campbellton (via Voyageur), then to Dalhousie, Bathurst, and south via SMT.

Buses to Newcastle depart from the SMT terminal in Fredericton; at Newcastle there are connections with Blanchard bus lines to Tracadie.

Coming from or going to Nova Scotia, the change point is Moncton. Through buses operate on a route between Halifax, Truro, Amherst (Acadian Bus Lines), and Moncton.

For up-to-date information on schedules and fares, call these local numbers: in St. Stephen, tel. 506/466-1368; in Fredericton, tel. 506/455-3303; in Moncton, tel. 506/855-2280; in Campbellton, tel. 506/753-4244.

By Rail

VIA Rail Canada will carry you by rail between Rivière-du-Loup, Québec, via Matapedia, Campbellton, Bathurst, Newcastle, Moncton, and Sackville to Amherst, Nova Scotia, and other points east and south. The trains are the *Scotian* and the *Ocean,* both of which depart daily on their runs from Rivière-du-Loup all the way to Halifax, Nova Scotia. There are sleeping cars as the trip from Rivière-du-Loup to Moncton takes about 10½ hours.

Daily railcars speed between Québec (Ste.-Foy) and Edmundston, N.B., where you must lay over for the night before boarding another railcar for Fredericton and Moncton.

Within New Brunswick, railcars make the 87-mile (141-km) trip between Moncton and Saint John twice daily in less than two hours.

VIA Rail's international express, the *Atlantic,* speeds between Saint John and Montréal daily, picking up and setting down passengers at Fredericton Junction (take a bus there from Fredericton), McAdam, and several towns in Maine. Having passed through Maine, it stops in Sherbrooke, Magog, and other Eastern Townships points before chugging into Montréal. The *Atlantic* hauls sleeping cars and has full dining facilities. The trip between Montréal and Saint John (or vice versa) takes almost 12 hours, which is the perfect amount of time for a night-train trip.

By Air

Air Canada provides most of the long-distance service to Saint John and Fredericton, with **CP Air** and **Delta** flying into Chatham/Newcastle from points outside Atlantic Canada.

Within New Brunswick and the Atlantic provinces, the local carrier is **Eastern Provincial Airways,** with flights to the major cities of New Brunswick from points throughout the region. For reservations and information, call: in Fredericton, tel. 506/454-4089; in Saint John, tel. 506/657-3860; in Moncton, tel. 506/389-9181; in other areas, dial toll free 800/332-3950.

Rental Cars

Available from **Tilden Car Rentals** in St. Stephen (tel. 506/466-3460), in Saint John (tel. 506/657-4757), in Fredericton (tel. 506/454-5818), or in Moncton (tel. 506/382-6644). Call Tilden direct at these stations, or reserve your car through any Tilden office (in Canada), or any National Car Rental office in the U.S.

Most visitors to New Brunswick enter the province from Maine. If you're among these, the road leads directly to one of the province's loveliest spots: Campobello.

1. Campobello Island and St. Stephen

CAMPOBELLO ISLAND: A Canadian island with an Italian-sounding name on which an American president spent his summers: these little mysteries are not at all as difficult to conceive as one might at first suppose. Campobello is indeed part of Canada, even though the major access road comes from Lubec, Maine. And the "Italian" name is nothing more than the name of a former Nova Scotian governor—William Campbell—with two "o's" added for exotic flavor. When the island was granted to Capt. William Owen by Governor Campbell in 1767, it was still part of Nova Scotia. (The province of New Brunswick was not formed until 1784, when large numbers of United Empire Loyalists fled New England to live in King George III's still-loyal dominions to the north.)

Franklin Delano Roosevelt's father, James, bought some land on the island in 1883, at a time when lots of important city people were building summer "cottages" at Bar Harbor, Passamaquoddy Bay, and other northern coastal locations. Young Franklin—to solve that last little mystery—came here long before he was president of the United States, and spent many a teenaged summer rowing, paddling, and sailing on the waters and hiking through the woods.

In 1920, FDR ran for the vice-presidency—and lost. Taking on a banking job instead, he looked forward to a relaxing summer at Campobello in 1921. On August 10 of that year the first signs of sickness showed, and two weeks later the doctors diagnosed the crippling disease as polio. When he left the island in September, he had no way of knowing that the few more times he would see the summer cottage and his Campobello friends would be brief weekend visits—as president of the United States.

The day-to-day lives of the great and powerful are fascinating to explore in detail, and a visit to the Roosevelt house on Campobello gives one a peek at the early years of this incredibly courageous man who went on to become governor of New York and president of the United States after having been crippled by polio. It is no less intriguing to see how a well-to-do family spent its summers at the turn of the century, with long and leisurely days filled by sports, games, and family fun. Servants saw to the chores, and even they must have enjoyed getting away from the city to such a beautiful spot.

The Roosevelt Cottage is now part of the **Roosevelt Campobello International Park,** a joint Canadian-American preservation effort open to everyone from late May to mid-October, 9 a.m. to 4 p.m. Eastern Time (10 a.m. to 5 p.m. Atlantic Time). Guides at the reception center will point out the path to the Roosevelt Cottage, and will show you movies about the island, and map out the various walks and drives you can take to get to know this beautiful spot.

New Brunswick has a pretty provincial park at Herring Cove, with a camping area, golf course, and fine sandy beach.

Where to Stay and Eat

On Friar's Bay not far from the international park is the **Friar's Bay Restaurant and Motor Lodge** (tel. 506/752-2056), officially located in Welshpool. The ten-room motel unit is on the inland side of the road; rooms come with private baths and TVs, and cost $26 to $30 double. On the beach side of the road is the restaurant, made of rough wood boards inside and out to preserve Campobello's woodsy feeling, but with modern bay windows so you can take in the marvelous sea view. Gull-topped posts and fishing weirs appear and disappear in the morning mist as you start the day with a brace of eggs, toast, coffee, and bacon or ham for $3.25. Griddle cakes with ham and a cheese omelet both cost even less. At lunch or dinnertime, equally economical repasts are served up, and can be accompanied by beer, wine, or a cocktail. For instance, smoked mackerel, pollock, or haddock—local delicacies—and most other fish dinners cost $7.25 and $8.50, including soup, cole slaw, potato, dessert, and coffee. If you prefer, have only the main course for about $1.50 less.

The Deer Island Ferry

As long as the weather's not too stormy, a tiny ferryboat operates between Campobello and Deer Islands. Signs direct motorists to the ferry docks, where the boat leaves about every 1½ hours—seven trips a day in each direction, lasting about 45 minutes. Don't be surprised when you see the ferry—a small fishing boat with a car-carrying barge (capacity: nine full-sized cars) casually attached to the side. Fees to or from Campobello are $4.50 per car and driver, and 50¢ for each additional passenger up to a maximum charge of $6 per car.

When you get to the ferry dock (whether on Campobello or Deer Island), don't be surprised if you're all alone. That's a good sign, meaning you'll be first in line. If the ferry's not running that day, there will be a sign posted to tell you so. Ferries normally operate from 9:15 a.m. (first trip from Deer Island) and 10 a.m. (first trip from Campobello) to 6:15 p.m. and 7 p.m. (last trips, respectively); the season is from the last weekend in June until (Canadian) Labour Day. Nonscheduled trips can be arranged, although you'll have to dicker over the fare. By the way, those lining up at Deer Island dock for the ferry to Campobello should make sure they're in the proper waiting lane. The ferry to Eastport departs this dock as well.

Between Deer Island and the mainland there's a free-of-charge ferry service run by the government, in operation continuously from 7 a.m. to 9 p.m. or longer every day during the busy summer months.

ST. STEPHEN: Residents of Maine and New Brunswick, while the best of friends, cling to memories of their ancestors' fervent support for, respectively, George Washington and George III. With the success of the American Revolution, United Empire Loyalists flocked across the frontier into Canada so as not to be disloyal to the monarch. "Loyalist" and "Revolutionary" towns preserve this good-natured rivalry.

But things are different in St. Stephen and its sister city, Calais, Maine. Folks in these two towns, cheek-by-jowl on the St. Croix River, make a point of telling visitors how they ignored the affinities of *both* sides during the War of 1812, and St. Stephen even supplied powder-poor Calais with gunpowder for its Fourth of July celebrations! In fact, by the time the war came, families in the twin towns were so closely intermarried that no one wanted to take the time to sort out who should be loyal to whom.

These days residents celebrate this unique plague-on-both-their-houses philosophy with an International Festival in the first week of August. The two bridges over the river between the two towns are thronged with merry-makers moving back and forth—through the watchful but benevolent eye of Customs, certainly—and Canadian and American flags fly everywhere.

Besides a number of attractive Victorian-era mansions, St. Stephen harbors a railroad station-turned-library, a former post office which is now an arts center, and a collection of recommendable hotels and restaurants.

Where to Stay and Eat

Crossing from the United States, follow the signs for New Brunswick Hwy. 1 to reach the tourist information office on King St. Right next door is the new and modern **Wandlyn Inn** (tel. 506/466-1814), 90 King St., the first of many motels in this Canadian chain which you will meet in your travels. This inn has an attractive gabled roof above its second story, making the whole building look something like a quaint bungalow that just goes on and on. All 64 rooms here are luxurious, with color cable TV, showers and bathtubs, and—in a few rooms—kitchenettes. But you pay for what you get: singles cost $30; doubles, $35 to $40 per night.

The Wandlyn's dining room, called the **Chowder Room,** is not elegant by any means, but friendly and informal. Fish is the specialty, with portions of trout, scallops, halibut, haddock, or whatever's fresh going for $4 to $6, very large and filling bowls of fish or seafood chowder for $3 to $4, pies made in their own kitchen for $1 the slice. Fiddleheads, those delicate spring fern tops so beloved by New Brunswickers, cost $1.50 a portion when they're available. The Chowder Room has a liquor license.

At the **Fundy Line Motel** (tel. 506/466-2130), the rooms cost only $23 single, $26 to $28 double, the higher prices being for two beds. About half of the 41 units come with air conditioning; all have private baths and color cable TVs, and there's a little cafe for your morning pick-me-up. The Fundy Line is at 198 King St. (Hwy. 1).

Rooms at the small (ten-room) **Hi-Way Motel** (tel. 506/466-2195) are clustered together cozily. Services are similar to those offered by neighboring establishments, but prices are lower: $21 single, $23 to $26 double, $34 for a family of four—but you should note that the Hi-Way is open during the tourist season only.

Even cheaper? **Mitchell's Tourist Home** (tel. 506/466-3936) is a big white house with a barn out back, right near the cluster of motels on Hwy. 1 (official address: 189 King St.). The six rooms here are plainish but very homey, with shared baths in the hallways. Prices are St. Stephen's best: $8 for one, $10 for two if they share a bed, $20 for the big room with two beds.

St. Stephen has a restaurant called the **Lobster House,** on Hwy. 1 east of town about 1½ miles. Modern in decor, the Lobster House concentrates on seafood first of all, but gives almost equal importance to meat and fowl. Prices for seafood plates hover in the range of $5.50 to $8, although meat and chicken dishes are a good deal less. The pie is only 90¢ a portion. Licensed.

Having set foot in St. Stephen, and thus in New Brunswick, the province is all ahead of you to be explored. Head east on Hwy. 1, turning south on Hwy. 127 to reach what may just be the most delightful town in all New Brunswick.

2. St. Andrews

The story of St. Andrews's founding is as romantic as the pretty town's seaside location. Loyalists in disagreement with the American Revolution moved north out of American towns to the safe harbor of British-controlled land at Fort George (later Castine, Maine). Now, Castine is a breathtakingly beautiful spot, and when these same Loyalists found that the new British-American boundary was to be the St. Croix River (at St. Stephen) and not the Penobscot (at Bucksport, Maine), they were at a loss. But they found a way. Pushing and shoving their newly built wood-frame houses onto ships, they *sailed* the entire town northward until they were again in British lands. The place they picked for their new—and final—settlement was at the tip of a peninsula in Passamaquoddy Bay: St. Andrews.

Luckily, the hardy and enterprising St. Andrians were not disturbed again, even during the War of 1812. The town had some blockhouses built for defense, but the war never reached Passamaquoddy. Prosperity came after the war with the shipbuilding trade, but as the century wore on and iron ships replaced wooden ones, St. Andrews felt the weight of stagnation. Just in time it found a new industry: tourism.

The great Canadian Pacific Railway Company owned the line which ran from Québec to the southern New Brunswick coast, and they put up a grand hotel in St. Andrews. Company directors and managers built sumptuous summer "cottages" in the vicinity, and today St. Andrews tells its history in its houses: many of the 90 or so houses brought from Castine or erected about that time are still standing proudly, along with those raised by magnates in the 19th-century lumber and shipbuilding boom. Turn-of-the-century cottages and the sumptuous, continually modernized Hotel Algonquin lend St. Andrews an air of gentility rare to the coast.

Today it's a summer visitors' haven, with not much to do but relax, shop, dine, stroll, play golf, swim, or take boat tours of Passamaquoddy Bay—in short, you'll love it.

WHERE TO STAY AND EAT: Although it started life as a resort for the rich and powerful, St. Andrews today has accommodations and dining places to suit all budgets. Chief among its hostelries is, of course, the splendid **Hotel Algonquin** (tel. 506/529-8823), an Elizabethan-inspired castle of white stucco, dark timbers, and a red tile roof set in the midst of its own park and surrounded by its things to do: golf, swimming, tennis, cycling, shuffleboard, and even croquet on the lawn. CP Hotels still operates the Algonquin as it has for the better part of the century, with top-flight food, service, and personal attention. The 200 rooms and suites are modern despite the hotel's age, and are priced at $38 to $43 single, $47 to $52 double, and $58 for two in a bed-sitting room. Suites start at $73 for two. Your children 14 and under can stay in your room for free, and if you need a roll-away bed (for children or adults) the charge is a mere $5. For about $16 per person per day more, you can have breakfast and dinner at the hotel, table d'hôte.

Once installed in your room, get your bearings by checking out the *two* golf courses—one's 9, the other's 18 holes—and the heated swimming pool. The hotel may be out of your range, but don't write off the **Passamaquoddy Room** for lunch or dinner. In this almost baronial setting, or in the adjoining glassed-in terrace dining room overlooking the sprawl of emerald lawns, you can have the daily buffet lunch for a mere $5 (although 15% service and 8% tax will bring the total, without beverage, to $6.15). Dinner, à la carte, is more expensive, but certainly not outrageous, coming to less than $20 all in. After dinner, wander down to **Dick Turpin's Pub** in the basement, where there's live entertainment every night (except Sunday, when the pub's closed). The lounge off the lobby has entertainment daily except Mondays, and it's open every day. Drinks at either place cost about $2, or $1.50 for beer.

The Algonquin is a summer hotel, its season running from late May to the end of September. Those flying in can get limousine transport from the Saint John airport, 70 miles away, by prior arrangement with the hotel. The cost is a moderate $10 one way, per person.

The **Shiretown Inn** (tel. 506/529-8877), P.O. Box 145, St. Andrews, is right downtown on the main street. A nice old summer hotel (although it stays open all year round), the Shiretown's rooms all come furnished with this and that. There's always a clean-and-shiny bathroom, and perhaps even a marble fireplace (nonworking, alas) or other quaint and graceful Victorian touch. Priced at $24 double, plus the 8% New Brunswick sales tax, the rooms are St. Andrews's best moderate-range bargains.

On the Shiretown's front-porch terrace, take in the passing parade of strollers and sightseers while you dine from a long and varied menu which covers all bases, from breakfast to boiled live lobster. Breakfasttime is anytime from 7:30 a.m. onward. At lunch, the $4 buffet constitutes the best bargain. For dinner, a portion of the soup du jour (75¢) can be followed by a fish filet of your choice ($5.25), an Atlantic salmon steak ($8), or a prime sirloin for the same price, and that includes vegetable, salad, homemade bread, and coffee or tea. Your bill may be as little as $7.40. And that price includes not only food, service, and tax, but also the charming feeling of having dined in St. Andrews's oldest hotel, built in 1881 on the site of an even older hostelry which dated from the early days of that century.

The **Gleason Arms** (tel. 506/529-3532), 159 Water St., is a fine old St. Andrews house with a few rooms to rent, with all the advantages that small scale and a friendly host and hostess can afford, not to mention the most reasonable of prices. Two people sleeping in one bed pay $15, $20 if you use two beds. You'll have your own toilet, and in the hallway there's a kitchenette good for cooking breakfast or other light meals. Randal and Eileen Gleason will see that you're well taken care of, but for this one you should definitely telephone ahead for reservations. Lots of satisfied guests return year after year to the Gleason Arms.

The **Seaside Inn** (tel. 506/529-3224), 340 Water St., is a delight, a huge, rambling Victorian summer "cottage" with much of the antique decor and all of the ambience intact from that graceful age: embossed wallpaper, carved wood furniture in the downstairs front parlor, grand old porches and verandas for sitting and rocking—or just sitting. All this and quiet, too, as the Seaside is at the southeastern reaches of Water St., away from the bustle—such as it is—of downtown. Rooms at the Seaside have running water, but share baths, and cost $20 for one bed (single or double), $25 to $30 for twin beds, depending on the size, location, and view of the room in question.

St. Andrews has motels, and they're well-adapted to the genteel mood and carefully preserved beauty of the town. The **Picket Fence Motel** (tel. 506/529-8985), P.O. Box 144, is on Reed Ave. on the way into town and not far from the Algonquin. It is most easily recognized by—you guessed it—the tidy picket fence enclosing the lawn in front. The standard, streamlined motel comforts and conveniences are embodied in its rooms: TV (black and white), tub-shower baths, etc. But each room in the blue-roofed structure has a bright-yellow door and a window box brimming with flowers; marigolds march through the garden plots scattered in the lawn. For all this you pay $24 single, $26 to $28 double. The Algonquin's golf courses are just across the street.

Downtown dining is best at the **Gables Inn and Dining Rooms** (tel. 506/529-3073), 143 Water St. Although the inn has four nice rooms for rent at $18 single, $20 to $24 double, they're often booked solid in August. But the dining rooms are yours to enjoy with a reservation. All *four* British meals are served in style here, from a full breakfast for $3.40 (7:15 to 10 a.m.), through lunch and afternoon tea to dinner. The luncheon menu of soups, chowders, sandwiches, and desserts is served from 11 a.m. to 10 p.m., but if you come between 2:30 and 4 p.m. you'd do well to order the set-price "tea." For $3 you'll get a pot of tea, a plate of mixed sandwiches, a cup of sherbet, and sweets for dessert. Dinner is served from 5 to 9:30 p.m., and for one price you receive a full meal of appetizer, salad, main course, dessert, and coffee. If you choose scallops as your main course, the tab will be about $7.35; or $8 for tenderloin, $10.50 for filet mignon. Fish of several kinds is always listed. Wine, beer, and cocktails are served. The Gables Inn bears remembering whenever you're hungry in St. Andrews: cheerful, gracious period dining rooms, interesting menus, moderate prices, long hours.

Acknowledged favorite eating place for St. Andrians in an informal mood is the **Sea Breeze,** in the center of town on Water St., licensed to sell drinks and open from 7 a.m. to 9 p.m. Enter and find your way to the rear, up the steps to the wood-lined back room, where there's less come-and-go traffic. Sandwiches in these bare but friendly surroundings cost $1 to $2, but for $2.25 you can have a big plate of fish and chips. Other plates run the gamut of tastes and cuisines up to a T-bone steak ($7), and platters all come with soup, rolls, potatoes, and coffee or tea. Good, fast, inexpensive, and friendly.

Summer visitors to St. Andrews like the **Smugglers' Wharf Restaurant,** on Water St., because it has a fine view of the bay. Light lunches based on hamburgers with various garnishings cost $2.50 to $2.75; seafood platters with vegetables, salad, and coffee are about $7 to $8; but you should note that Smugglers' Wharf adds a 12½% service charge in place of tipping, and with the ubiquitous 8% sales tax, all these prices will jump 20½%. During normal mealtime hours, minimum purchase rules apply.

The **Rossmount Inn** (tel. 506/529-3351), three miles north of St. Andrews on the way to St. George via Hwy. 127, looks at first glance like a great Swiss chalet. Dominating the road from a perch at the top of a sloping expanse of lawn, the Rossmount commands a fine view of the bay and ragged coastline. The 18 rooms at the Rossmount are nice, with private baths and color TVs ($25 single, $32 to $35 double), but the real attraction is the kitchen, from which issue multiple platters of seafood and steak capable of pleasing even the most finicky of appetites and palates. From a drink in the congenial lounge, through appetizer or soup, salad, salmon, dessert, coffee, and wine, one can easily part with $25 to $30 per person, and go away pleased. But to sample the Rossmount's cuisine you must have a car, and you must call host-owner G. E. Brewin and make reservations.

WHAT TO DO: Take it easy. That's what a St. Andrews summer is all about. But for diversion, stroll past **Greenock Church,** a graceful and comely colonial structure completed by Capt. Christopher Scott, a leader of the Presbyterian congregation, in 1824. The **St. Andrews Blockhouse National Historic Site,** at the northwest end of Water St., is the sole surviving (reconstructed) wood fortress of the several which were built for St. Andrews's defense in the War of 1812. Visits are allowed from mid-May to mid-September from 9 a.m. to 5 p.m. (9 to 8 in high summer).

The **aquarium at Huntsman Marine Laboratories,** northwest of town on Brandy Cove Rd., takes you into the fascinating world of marine biological research as it's carried out here, in St. Andrews's largest industry—after tourism. From the end of May to mid-September the aquarium and the lab's museum are open between 10 a.m. and 4:30 p.m. (until 8 p.m. in high summer) for $1 per adult, 50¢ per child.

If the weather's cool, **swimming** is available in the Algonquin's heated pool—at a small charge. If the weather's warm, though, desert the pool for the salty tang of a splash in the waters of **Katy's Cove.** While the cove, east of town, opens onto Passamaquoddy Bay, the small cove inlet keeps the cold tides from rushing in and chilling the water as one might expect. Other good beaches— these open to the surf—are at the two provincial parks near St. Andrews. **Oak Bay Provincial Park** is on Hwy. 1 to the west, and **New River Beach** is to the east on the same road, past the town of St. George.

Twice a day, the M/V *Fundy Isles* (tel. 506/529-3688) putts out of St. Andrews on a **tour of the bay** and the islands, passing the rugged coasts and graceful fishing weirs, and sometimes braving the rolling mists. Departures are at 10 a.m. and 2 p.m. from St. Andrews harbor, costing $4.50 for adults, $2.50 for children 4 to 14. Tots sail free.

Touring Passamaquoddy Bay is an adventurous experience. Sandbars loll in the waters here and there, little evergreen-cloaked islets seem to float on the calm morning sea, and clouds of morning mist glide slowly along the shore. The frequent fogs bring a thrilling sense of mystery and romance, but they also bring a thrilling chill—sometimes just the thing to cool off a week of hot summer weather.

Passamaquoddy Bay, like the Bay of Fundy, is subject to the world's highest tides. The steepness of the shoreline, the narrowness, and the orientation of Fundy all contribute to the twice-daily rushing in and out of immense volumes of water. Fundy is just the place for future engineers to try their theories of producing electricity from tidal power.

Whether you take a boat tour or just drive along the shore, you're sure to come across one of the graceful **fishing weirs** used to trap schools of herring in these waters. The weirs, circles of long poles stuck into the seabed and projecting above the waterline, form frames for the netting which encloses the circle. A funnel-shaped entrance leads into the circle of the weir. As the fish encounter the weir, the funnel of the entrance leads them toward the circle's narrow entrance. Once in the weir's circle, few fish find their way out before fishermen come and lift the nets, catching tons at a time. Weirs have been used not for centuries but for millennia to catch great quantities of fish, but today efficient trawlers, able to follow the schools of fish, have put many New Brunswick weirs in the category of being picturesque antiques.

Traveling east from St. Andrews on Hwy. 1, the next place of note is St. George, a tiny town with a paper mill, the oldest Presbyterian church in Canada (1790), and the beautiful cascade of Magaguadavic Falls which plummet 100 feet. Turn off on Hwy. 778 and 776 to go south to Blacks Harbour, jumping-off point on a cruise to Passamaquoddy's most feather-filled bird sanctuary, Grand Manan Island.

3. Grand Manan Island

There is something special about islands which makes them the best of all places for a relaxing vacation, and Grand Manan Island in the Bay of Fundy might be the perfect example of this. Anchored far out in Fundy's waters like a mammoth aircraft carrier, it is visited daily by almost 250 different kinds of "aircraft," which find it the perfect spot to touch down. It was the famous John James Audubon who first discovered the exceptional variety of bird life on Grand Manan in 1831, and lesser but equally enthusiastic ornithologists have been coming here to peek at puffins, Arctic terns, and even the occasional bald eagle ever since.

Another characteristic to draw scientists is Grand Manan's geology, split between fantastically ancient six-billion-year-old formations and much, much younger volcanic deposits. But most people come just to relax, to take walks through the rocky countryside or along the rugged, cove-indented shores, to sample the salt-bitterness of dulse (edible seaweed gathered here), and to feel that island feeling of comfortable security and remoteness from the worries of the world.

GETTING THERE: One reason for Grand Manan's remote feeling is that it takes some getting-to. The ferry from Blacks Harbour (tel. 506/657-3306 or 466-1139) departs only three times a day in each direction, and in the busy summer months the line of cars waiting to board the ferry can be long enough so that some people don't make it on, and will have to wait for the next sailing. My advice, then, is to plan lots of time to get there and to return, and a good amount of time to stay. Put your car in the waiting line as soon as you arrive or—to avoid the disappointment of not making the boat—leave your car in Blacks Harbour and just sail over as a passenger. You can go for the day, taking the first morning ferry and returning by the late-afternoon one, but this can be a lot of sailing for one day as the voyage takes between 1½ and 2 hours, one way. Fares are $9 per car, $3 per adult, $1.50 per child, each way.

WHAT TO DO: Once arrived on Grand Manan, make your way to its prime hostelry, the two-century-old **Marathon Inn** (tel. 506/662-8144), in North Head where the ferry docks. A graceful reminder of a graceful era, the Marathon has 36 guest rooms with ocean views, a restaurant, and a heated swimming pool. Rooms come with running water or showers, black-and-white or color TV sets, and quaint period furnishings for $35 single, $60 double, with breakfast and dinner included. In the restaurant, seafood is the thing of prime importance, although meat and fowl come daily from the mainland. They'll whip up a box lunch if you plan to be out exploring at lunchtime.

And exploring is the thing to do. Grand Manan is about 15 miles long by 5 miles wide, a walker's paradise as far as size is concerned. The Red Trail to the **Hole-in-the-Wall** rock formation (30 minutes away) starts from the Marathon and takes you to **Whale Cove,** where novelist Willa Cather spent her summers. Another walk takes you to **Swallowtail Light,** a picturesque lighthouse of the sort which always appears in tourist brochures and seems unreal—until you see it towering above the rugged seashore, winking in the night.

Farther afield, **Dark Harbour** is the island's dulse-gathering and drying center. This edible seaweed makes a good flavoring in soups, but first-time tasters might be well advised to approach it gingerly. Exotic, yes. For low-sodium diets, no.

Anywhere you see men in boats, you can check out the possibilities of setting out in the morning with the herring fishermen on their daily catch. When it comes home with you, follow the fish's progress from net to weir to smokehouse. Smoked mackerel, herring, and salmon are among the finest delicacies produced by this seafood-rich island.

Grand Manan has its own museum in Grand Harbour. The **Grand Manan Museum** has—of course—a collection of the many varieties of birds which visit the island, plus displays explaining the island's unique geology. Artifacts from the island's Loyalist past are here, too. From mid-June to Labour Day you can visit between 2 and 5 each afternoon, and Thursday evenings from 7 to 9:30 p.m.

Whatever you do, whether bird life fascinates you or not, don't leave Grand Manan without getting a glimpse of the playful puffins, the big-beaked birds resembling toy-sized penguins which are the island's mascots. Puffins' fishing abilities are simply amazing, and in the clear Fundy waters they dip beneath the surface and swim swiftly like seals to catch their small-fry prey. A puffin's wings—amazingly—are as effective deep in the water as they are high in the air.

4. Saint John

People in Saint John are proud of their city and proud of its name. While they call it the Loyalist City because it was incorporated by settlers from the revolutionary United States, it was actually "founded" by Samuel de Champlain on St. John the Baptist's Day in 1604. It took a while after Champlain's visit for the French to set up a fort here for trade with the friendly Indians and defense against the unfriendly English, and after that first fort was built (1631), it changed hands frequently. The English were well established by 1783, when thousands of Loyalists flocked to the shelter of the British Crown in Canada.

"Loyalist City" is actually the oldest incorporated city in Canada, for these early settlers established their town on a legal basis way back in 1785.

And about that name: nowhere, except in publications written by "foreigners," will you see "St. John" rather than "Saint John." As Pittsburgh and Edinburgh must have that final "h," Saint John must be spelled out—or there will be trouble. As for "St. John's," that's the capital of Newfoundland—no relation.

The Loyalists who founded Saint John were hard-working and industrious types who soon turned their city into one of the World's greatest shipbuilding ports. When the wooden ship was replaced by the iron one, Saint John's builders followed suit, and the city has never lost its close connection with ships and the sea. Vessels flying every flag enter her port to unload or take on cargo, for repairs, or for supplies. You can see this great variety of ships down in the harbor—if you can see at all, that is. Saint John may be a sailor's delight, but it's a vegetable-grower's sorrow as fog blankets the town more often than not.

Local citizens don't seem to mind the fog, and in the back of their minds there may lurk the idea that fog, being veddy English, is in fact patriotic, the best possible weather for Loyalist City. Besides, when landlubbers in Fredericton and Moncton are sweltering in summer's sticky heat, in Saint John it's cool, even on those days when the sun appears.

But unquestionably the biggest tourist draw to this ancient and honorable town is the bewildering phenomenon of the St. John River's "Reversing Falls," a Fundy high-tide trick worthy of seeing, and begging for explanation.

FOR INFORMATION: Saint John has two tourism bureaus: one is at Reversing Falls Bridge over the St. John River on Hwy. 100 (tel. 506/672-6990); the other is right on the town's central park—King Square—at 24 Sydney St. (tel. 506/658-2855). Either place will be happy to supply you with city maps and tide tables so you won't miss the action at Reversing Falls Rapids.

Should you come to Saint John in the third week of July, be sure to ask about the city's Loyalist Days celebration, when everybody dresses up in colonial costumes for a reenactment of the Loyalists' landing of 1784. Special programs and concerts, parades, and pageants fill the festival week.

WHERE TO STAY: By far the largest concentration of lodging places in the city is the collection of motels along Manawagonish Rd., parallel to Hwy. 100 in Saint John West. But there is a good place to stay right downtown, and if you're traveling by plane, train, or bus, this is the place to try first.

The **Admiral Beatty Hotel** (tel. 506/652-1212), taken over and refurbished by the Wandlyn hotel and motel chain, has Saint John's finest lodging location: it's right on King Square, the city center's most charming park. Although newer and fancier hostelries have taken away its title as the most luxurious hotel in town, the Admiral Beatty possesses an ambience of dignified tradition, not to mention 196 completely satisfactory and comfortable guest rooms with private bath-shower, color TV, and reasonable prices: $27 single, $31 to $35 double, $6 per extra person in the room. The hotel's Loyalist Dining Room (see below) and Library Lounge are favorite gathering places for city business people.

Keddy's Motor Inn (tel. 506/657-7320), 10 Portland St., corner of Main St., is an all-new and luxurious in-town motel with a hilltop location not far from the center of town. One of your first actions if you stay here (and if the fog lifts) should be to take the elevator to the top floor and have a drink or a meal in the motor inn's Top of the Walk Restaurant, overlooking Saint John Harbour and the city center. The latest up-to-date comforts are built into the 137 rooms: color cable TV, air conditioning, tub-shower combination bathrooms, and from some rooms that marvelous city view. For all this, prices are actually moderate, and lower than the less-well-located Holiday Inn. Keddy rooms cost $29 single, $32 double in one bed, $36 for two people in two beds, and only $5 for an extra person in a roll-away bed. Although you'll probably want to take a bus or taxi to the center of town, you're not all that far from Reversing Falls. And at the end of the day, you've got an indoor swimming pool in which to refresh yourself.

Apart from these in-town places to stay, most other motels are a short drive from the city center. The drive translates directly into cash savings, however, as some of these edge-of-town motels offer rooms at very moderate, even budget, prices.

The **Balmoral Court Motel** (tel. 506/672-3019), 1284 Manawagonish Rd. in Saint John West is truly a "court," as the 13 motel units and 11 cabins form a quiet little courtyard. Should you want to use Saint John West as a base for explorations of New Brunswick, you should ask for one of the Balmoral's housekeeping rooms, of which there are eight. But whether you get a kitchenette or not, you'll have a clean, presentable room in one of the little white buildings, with private bath and TV set (specify color if you must have it). Prices are delightfully low: $18 for a room with one double bed (whether one person uses it or two), $22 for a room with two beds, $30 for four people in a room with two double beds. Add $2 to these prices if you wish to use the housekeeping equipment.

Rooms at the nearby **Seacoast Motel** (tel. 506/672-6442) are "modern in every way" (as the management proudly says), down to the color cable TVs in all ten rooms. At first glance, prices are surprisingly high—$25 single, $27 to $30 double—but when you see a room, you'll see why. The Seacoast, built on the side of the hill, has a fine view of the rolling hills and forests across the highway.

The handsomest motel along Manawagonish Rd. is also the most expensive. The **White House Lodge** (tel. 506/672-1000) has 34 modern motel rooms, all fitted with two double beds and cable color TV, and all going for the same price: $34. A bonus here is that the motel's restaurant serves all three meals a day, and is licensed to serve drinks. Special note: The White House is a seasonal operation, open in the warmer months only.

WHERE TO EAT: Sightseeing in the center of Saint John can be tiring, but if you remember to dress in something fancier than dungarees, you'll qualify to join in the buffet lunch served in the **Loyalist Dining Room** of the Admiral Beatty Motor Hotel on King Square. "Buffet" is a genteel way of saying "all you can eat," and in this case the hot and cold offerings are yours to tuck away as you will for $6, plus tax and tip. Sandwiches and snacks can be ordered too, if the sight of the lavish buffet tables proves daunting.

At dinnertime, the Loyalist Dining Room's elegant tables are also the scene of Saint John's best priced meal. Although you can dine richly from the à la carte menu, the kitchen always prepares two full-course daily special dinners, one of which is priced at $6, the other about $8 or so, and that low figure pays for salad, main course, vegetables, dessert, and coffee. Otherwise, most main courses alone cost $7 to $8, with steak and lobster reaching the delicious-but-pricey reaches of $12 to $14 per portion.

Alternative to the Admiral Beatty is Saint John's steakhouse-in-the-sky, the **Top of the Walk** at Keddy's Motor Inn, Portland and Main Sts. Pick a clear evening, and start with a drink or a cocktail ($1.75 to $2.50) before your soup or appetizer course. For entree, escargots are fine and buttery ($5); the rainbow trout and chicken chasseur are both moderately priced at $7, but the specialty of the house is over twice that price—and worth it. When the chef prepares Keddy's steak Diana, it's flamed right at your table.

Among Saint John's serviceable and moderately priced downtown dining places, the **Riviera,** 91 Charlotte St. on King Square, is the most popular. Service in the tasteful, modern dining room is quiet but efficient, and a full meal of soup, baked ham or roast chicken, french fries, rolls, and coffee can cost only $4.75, plus tax and tip, if that is the special of the day. The à la carte menu is long and varied, and although prices can't equal the bargain daily specials, a plate of fresh salmon in egg sauce, with soup, potato, vegetable, and coffee, will come to only $8.50. Steaks and lobsters cost more, for sure.

Calling the **Chapel Restaurant** unorthodox is to get into a terrible tangle of terms, for in one way it's as orthodox as can be: the restaurant is located in a desanctified church. But it's just this feature which is unorthodox for a restaurant, not to mention that it shares the now-mundane structure with the local karate studio. The Chapel is at the corner of Peel and Carleton Sts., a short walk from City Hall or King Square. Pews from the old church serve as restaurant benches drawn up to long tables at which a convivial crowd starts the day with breakfast, or tucks into a lunch of seafood chowder ($2), or barbecued spare ribs ($3.50) or chicken ($3). As of this writing, the Chapel has applied for a liquor license, and when it comes through, the present hours from 7:30 a.m. to 3 p.m. should be extended well into the evening.

WHAT TO SEE: Reversing Falls, without a doubt! But before you set off in search of the swirling waters, you should know that **Saint John Tours and Sightseeing Ltd.,** Chesley Pl., 400 Main St. (tel. 506/674-1932) conducts guided tours twice daily, each tour lasting 2¼ hours and costing $4 for adults, $3 for seniors, $2 for students 7 to 16 (free for children 6 and under). The tour bus will pick you up at Reversing Falls, Keddy's, the tourist bureau on Sydney St. (on King Square), the Holiday Inn, or the Rockwood Park Campground.

Reversing Falls

Many Saint John citizens are careful nowadays to boast of "Reversing Falls Rapids" rather than "Reversing Falls"—the difference in names is important. Don't expect to see a waterfall with tides leaping 100 feet up the rocks, a phenomenon which the name "Reversing Falls" might be expected to conjure up in the imagination. But what you'll see is equally amazing in natural terms, although not visually as spectacular.

At the bridge over the St. John River on Hwy. 100 is a small building housing the **Reversing Falls tourist bureau,** a restaurant, and viewing point. Short films shown here collapse the action-time of the tides and explain the amazing process whereby the St. John River empties into the Bay of Fundy at low tide, rippling swiftly under the bridge as any good river should. But as the tide rises, a "slack" period is reached when no water moves and the river's surface is as still and calm as any trout pond's. Then, slowly, the flow of water reverses, and soon a swift current is speeding under the bridge and *up* the St. John River as the powerful Fundy tide rolls in. At high tide another slack time is reached, the water is calm again, but not for long. Soon the tide begins to recede, beginning the process all over again.

High tide comes twice a day, and tide tables are handed out everywhere so visitors can be on the spot to watch the river reverse its flow. If the observation booth is too crowded, watch from the little grassy park nearby, or from riverside Falls View Park which is on the east side of the bridge, to the north, more or less behind the New Brunswick Museum.

The Loyalist Trail

Saint John's Loyalist Trail takes you on a walking tour of Loyalist City's historical landmarks. The **tourist bureau** on King Square will be able to supply you with a map. The trail starts at the old **County Courthouse,** with its unsupported spiral staircase, an architectural marvel. Then it's out through King Square to **Trinity Church,** built in 1880 to replace an earlier church destroyed by Saint John's Great Fire of 1877. Over the west door are emblazoned the British royal arms, which in itself is not remarkable, except that this particular replica of the coat-of-arms was taken by Loyalist immigrants from the rebellious town of Boston and brought to Saint John.

Farther along the trail, at the corner of Union and Germain Sts., is **Loyalist House,** Saint John's oldest unchanged building, dating from 1817. A well-to-do Loyalist family from New York, headed by David Daniel Merritt, had the house built in typically Georgian style and furnished with the elegant furniture of the time. Guides from the New Brunswick Historical Society will gladly point out the house's charming details, but you must come between 10 a.m. and 5 p.m. on weekdays in July and August (1 to 5 on Sunday), or from 10 to 5 on weekdays in June and September (closed weekends). Admission price is $1 for adults, 25¢ for kids.

St. John's **Stone Church,** on Carleton St. at the end of Wellington, is the city's oldest stone church (1825), made completely from stone brought as ballast in ships from England. Two blocks away is the **Old City Market,** one of several such quaint old structures which once acted as the center of Saint John's commerce, although the others haven't survived. Look inside at the heavy roof beams and the art and craft of the city's wooden shipbuilding carpenters is immediately apparent. On Fridays and Saturdays the colorful produce market takes over, but you can visit any day of the week provided you come during business hours. The market is closed and locked in the evening.

Loyalist Burial Ground, east of King Square, has tombstones dating back to 1784. Just across the street from the Burial Ground is one of Saint John's most absorbing attractions. In **Barbour's General Store** on King St. East, you'll be transported a century backward in time to an amazingly faithful replica of the kind of store our grandparents and great-grandparents thought of as modern and up-to-date. From the cracker barrel to the spice cupboard, from the salt cod to the spats, from whiskey to molasses, everything is in its place—although, alas, it's no longer for sale. Three Saint John ladies, so I'm told, scoured the city and surrounding towns for all of the authentic products and packages which now fill the store's shelves. While you can't buy the ancient pharmaceuticals, you can get a free snack of dulse, New Brunswick's edible seaweed. Barbour's General Store is open from mid-May through September from 9 a.m. to 9 p.m. every day but Sunday, when the hours are 1 to 9 p.m.

Other Sights

Before leaving downtown Saint John, wander down to the corner of Prince William and Princess Sts. There, on the northwest corner of the intersection, is the **Chubb Building,** erected in the latter part of the 19th century by a George Chubb—who you'll see on the facade in the guise of a grinning gargoyle. Chubb had all of his children and half the city's political leaders immortalized on the facade in little rosettes as well, and there they still are today.

A block away, at the center of modern Saint John, is the bold tower of the new **City Hall.** From an observation deck on its top floor there's a fine view (on a clear day) of the city and the harbor. Next to City Hall, the sleek and ultramodern bulk of a shopping-hotel-parking-office complex named **Brunswick Square** will catch your eye. Wander in for a look around at the wave of the future.

How dense is the fog today? If it's very dense, or if there's rain, the perfect place to go is the **New Brunswick Museum,** 277 Douglas Ave. not far from Reversing Falls (coming from downtown, make a sharp right turn just before the Reversing Falls Bridge, and the museum is a few blocks up on the left). Paintings and displays of sailing vessels outline Saint John's maritime past, and cases holding colonial uniforms and weapons, furniture, and other memorabilia help one to imagine what life was like in the New Brunswick of two centuries ago. But old things don't fill the museum: there is an entire section devoted to New Brunswick's modern artists and craftsmen as well. Natural science exhibits—even an aquarium—will fascinate the kids. Museum hours are 10 a.m. to 9 p.m. daily from June through September, and from 2 to 5 p.m. at other times. Admission is 50¢ for adults, 25¢ for children, to a maximum family charge of $2.

If that fog's not so dense, cross the bridge over Reversing Falls and look for the sign which points the way to the left up the hill to Saint John's **Carleton Martello Tower.** From 10 a.m. to 5 p.m. in the first part of June and in all of September, and from 9 a.m. to 8 p.m. from mid-June through August, the tower is open to visitors, with guides on hand. Martello Towers, grand cylindrical stone defense fortifications, were built throughout England and Ireland in the early years of the 19th century, and over a dozen were put up in North America as well, of which this is one.

Another clear-day activity is a visit to the **Cherry Brook Zoo,** in the northern reaches of Rockwood Park, which itself is north of the city a few miles. No doubt it would be strange to have one's first encounter with a Siberian tiger, or a wallaby, or a South American llama in Saint John, New Brunswick—but that's exactly what the zoo holds in store.

THE FERRY TO DIGBY, N.S.: CN Marine's M/V *Princess of Acadia* plies the Bay of Fundy between Saint John, N.B., and Digby, N.S., all year round, making the crossing in 2½ hours. In the peak summer period from mid-June through September, the ship carries her load of 159 cars and 650 passengers three times a day (two times on Sundays) in each direction. In "shoulder" season, single daily crossings are the rule, with two supplemental trips on Saturdays (making a total of three trips), and one on Sunday (for two trips in all); this schedule holds from mid-May to mid-June and during October. In winter, rough conditions lengthen the trip time to three hours, and the *Princess* travels once a day in each direction. Adults pay $5.75 one way, $10 round trip; children 5 to 12 pay $2.90 one way, $5 round trip. Charge for a car is $24, and for an extra $7 to $9.75 you can even rent a cabin and make the several-hour trip a mini-cruise. You should have reservations: call, in Saint John, 506/672-

9270; in Digby, 902/245-2116; or toll free anywhere in central and eastern Canada, 800/565-9411. From Maine, the number is 800/432-7344; from other points in the northeastern U.S., it's 800/341-7981.

ON THE ROAD TO FREDERICTON: Two roads lead from Saint John to Fredericton. Highway 7 is fast, but pretty dull. Highway 102 follows the sinuous banks of the St. John River north through little riverside communities to Gagetown, site of a tremendous Canadian Forces base, and then heads west up the river to Fredericton.

If you decide to take the scenic route, you can stop in Evandale at the **Eveleigh Hotel** (tel. 506/425-9993), right next to the ferry landing on the riverbank. This "last of the riverboat hotels" has clean and simple guest rooms for $12 to $15 double (in one bed) in the hotel, motel, or cabins, but chances are that you'll want to stop for a meal as well. The cheerful, homey dining room and lounge are decorated with oil paintings and bric-a-brac, enough to provide visual interest all through breakfast, lunch, or dinner. The food is good, inexpensive, and prepared to order. A sandwich or snack costs $1.25 to $2; luncheon or dinner platters, $4 to $5. Note these hours carefully: on weekdays, breakfast starts at 9 a.m., lunch at 11:30 a.m.; dinner is served from 5 to 7 p.m. On weekends, breakfast starts at 9, and the full dinner menu is served between noon and 8 p.m.

5. Fredericton

New Brunswick's capital city on the banks of the St. John River is older than the province itself. Three hundred years ago, the St. John River, named Woolastook by the MicMac and Maliseet Indians, was a good place to fish, and Indian settlements dotted its shores. By the end of the 1600s, the French had built a fort here where the St. John and Nashwaak Rivers meet, and soon afterward a civilian settlement was established, and named for St. Anne.

When the British took control of French North America in the mid-1700s, they took over the site of St. Anne's, but it was really the influx of Loyalists fleeing the American Revolution who shaped the city—and the province. At first part of Nova Scotia, New Brunswick was declared a separate province when the flood of Loyalists brought a population boom. The new province's first chief executive, Gov. Thomas Carleton, put his finger on the map at St. Anne's, marking it as the capital city and renaming it in honor of King George III's second son Frederick, bishop of Osnabruck.

If Saint John is New Brunswick's hard-working, masculine town, Fredericton is the genteel lady, proud of her high society which includes the province's lieutenant-governor, the legislature, and all the dons at the dignified University of New Brunswick. New Brunswick's most famous native son, Lord Beaverbrook, had a special affection for the city, casting largesse in the form of a fine arts gallery and other projects. And only Fredericton, named for a bishop and royal scion, would be the proper place for an Anglican bishopric—and so it is.

FOR INFORMATION: Main source of maps and information in the city is right inside the door of the Victorian red brick Fredericton City Hall (tel. 506/455-9426), at the corner of Queen and York Sts. right down by the river. The **City Hall Visitors' Information Centre** is open from 8:30 to 5, Monday through Friday, year round.

The **Fredericton Jaycees** operate a booth on the Trans Canada Hwy. near the Hanwell Rd. exit, no. 289 (tel. 506/455-3092), which is open every day during the summer tourist season from 9 to 5, later in the busiest weeks.

When you drop into one of these offices, ask for a free "Tourist Parking Pass," which allows you to park for free at meters and in town lots.

WHERE TO STAY: Although there are lots of motels along the Trans Canada Hwy. which runs around the town, Fredericton also has several very good places to stay right downtown.

Hotels and Rooms

Named for Fredericton's benefactor and Britain's powerful press baron, the **Lord Beaverbrook Hotel** (tel. 506/455-3371), corner of Queen and Saint John Sts., is Fredericton's most convenient and prestigious place to put up for the night. The location couldn't be better: only steps from the SMT bus station, across the street from the Playhouse, and very near the Legislative Assembly Building. The hotel has two sections, an older one with rooms that are smaller but well maintained, and a new wing with more modern and luxurious units. All 212 rooms are air-conditioned and color-cable-TV–equipped, and no matter where you stay you have use of the new wing's swimming pool and sauna. Prices for the older rooms are $26 single, $30 to $33 double; for the newer rooms, $30 single, $36 to $38 double. A money-saving tip: check into one of the older rooms, and if you decide you really need the extra dose of luxury, move up to a new-wing room the next night.

Of the other downtown hostelries, one is a budget-priced hotel, the other a tourist home. The first will appeal more to younger travelers, while the tourist home provides the quiet and simplicity that older travelers favor.

The **Colonial Inn** (tel. 506/455-3343), 72 Regent St. near the corner with Queen St., is a budget traveler's dream come true, a very centrally located, reasonably priced older hotel. Rooms have been refurbished to keep the decor up-to-date, and even such luxuries as air conditioning, TV, telephone, and tub-shower are in every one. Three rooms even have kitchenettes. And the price is right: $12 single, $16 to $18 double, $20 for four people sharing a room with two beds.

At the **Elms Tourist Home** (tel. 506/454-3410), 269 Saunders St. between Northumberland and Westmorland Sts., the loudest sound you'll hear is the ticking of your own alarm clock. It's a fine, big old house on a residential street, presided over by Mrs. J. T. Irvine, who will rent you one of her six various bathless rooms for only $12 single, $13 to $15 double. Comfy and homey, the Elms allows you to stay in the midst of Fredericton gentility rather than in a this-could-be-anywhere motel unit.

Want to stay, cheaply, on the lovely **University of New Brunswick** campus? During the summer months the university rents some of its **dormitory rooms,** usually about 50 of them, to visitors, and you can find out what's available by calling 506/453-4835. Singles are $11.50 and doubles are $17, but that includes use of the UNB's indoor athletic swimming pool.

Motels

Of the city's motels, one is in a quiet, garden location adjacent to Wilmot Park and a choice residential area. It's the **Diplomat Motor Hotel** (tel. 506/454-5584), 225 Woodstock Rd., a ten-minute walk to the west of the center of town, or a few minutes by the no. 4 "Silverwood" bus. Overlooking the river, the Diplomat's 80 rooms have all the comforts of air conditioning, color cable TV, and sparkling-clean bathrooms. There's a heated outdoor pool and a convenient Pool Bar, plus a Patio Restaurant and coffeeshop which specializes —in the midst of all this Western luxury—in Chinese cuisine (see below). For all this, the rates are reasonable: $28 single, $30 to $34 double, $6 for an extra person. The Diplomat's your best motel choice: quiet, extremely comfortable, and more convenient than other city motels.

Rates at the modern **Sequoia Motel** (tel. 506/455-9900), 1216 Regent St. (at the Trans Canada Hwy.), are reasonable indeed considering what you get for your money: an indoor heated swimming pool, a licensed restaurant and bar, and 56 brand-new, air-conditioned rooms with, naturally, color cable TV, modern baths, and floor-to-ceiling windows. The building is well insulated against both noise and extreme temperatures and drafts, so the proximity of the Trans Canada Hwy.—it runs right next door—is more an asset than a liability. One person pays $26; two pay $29 to $32. Central Fredericton is only a few minutes' drive from the Sequoia, or you can hop a no. 10 bus to downtown from Fredericton Mall, just across Regent St. from the motel.

Another moderately priced highway motel is the local representative of a Canadian chain. **Keddy's Motor Inn** (tel. 506/454-4461), a two-story building among the trees at the south end of the Princess Margaret Bridge, has two rate lists to correspond to its two motel sections. One section is three years newer than the other, and the rooms here cost $1 more than the "older" rooms, but in fact all the rooms are comfortable and recommendable. All 120 rooms have color cable TV and air conditioning, and cost $26 single, $30 to $34 double, $5 for an extra person. Keddy's has an indoor pool and a sauna, plus a licensed dining room, a lounge, and a coffeeshop. Just don't miss the exit, no. 295 "Forest Hill," as you approach the south end of Princess Margaret Bridge. You can go between Keddy's and downtown by bus, but it's a rather lengthy journey involving a change from a no. 9 to a no. 10 at Regent Mall.

WHERE TO DINE: Being the province's capital and chief university town, Fredericton has a good assortment of restuarants, from the elegant and pricey through the exotic to the familiar, informal, and rock-bottom low-priced eateries.

The Lord Beaverbrook Hotel's **Terrace Room Restaurant** gets high marks for elegance of setting and finesse of service. Tremendous windows overlook the river, and even in cold or rainy weather the plant-bedecked "arbor" inside the dining room helps one to conjure up images of sunny springtime. Service is from 7 a.m. to 10 p.m., with the bargain luncheon buffet ($4.50, plus tax and tip) being served between 11:30 and 2, Monday through Friday. At dinnertime you can choose your own lobster from the Terrace Room's tank, have it weighed, and pay by the pound—ask what the per-pound rate is first, though, and then request the size of lobster you'd like to pay for. Lobster may be a luxury, but other seafood main courses are not, being only $7 to $9 for most. Steaks, however, cost several dollars more.

On the subject of steaks, the Lord Beaverbrook has a steakhouse called the **Maverick Room** in its basement, with a congenial bar. Dinner and late-night suppers only are served, from 6 p.m. to 12 midnight (Sundays they open at 5 p.m.). The steaks range in price from $10 to $34, the latter being chateaubriand for two. Spare ribs are less. Yet another Beaverbrook eatery, the **River Room,** has the ambience of a plush Old Englishy private club, popular with the business set who come for the luncheon buffet (11:30 to 2 on weekdays) costing $4.85, for Happy Hour on weekdays from 5 to 7, or for the live entertainment which begins each evening at 9 and goes on till 1 a.m. Drinks in the evening cost $1.70 to $2; cocktails are a bit more expensive at $2.50 to $3.

Fredericton's newest and most ambitious seafood restaurant is **Le Martinique** (tel. 506/455-0655), 151 Westmorland at the corner of Brunswick. You'll notice right as you enter that Le Martinique was once an Oriental restaurant—the pleasant bamboo decor has been kept, streamlined with decorator lamps and other simple, modern touches. Lunch (11:30 to 2, Monday through Friday) and dinner (6 to 11 p.m. daily, to 10 p.m. on Sundays) are the meals served, and lunch can be something as simple and delicious as seafood spaghetti ($3) or as fancy as seafood crêpes ($4.50), but you can easily dine for $6 or less if you like. For dinner, most main courses like coquilles St-Jacques, poached rainbow trout, or the various fish steaks are priced from $8 to $9; lobsters are not unreasonable at about $10 to $11, depending on season. The wine list is short, well chosen, and priced so that you'll want to order a bottle with dinner. Bottles start at $6 and rise to about $14 (many choices) before soaring into the loftier ranges.

Although the Chinese restaurant has moved from the premises of Le Martinique, you can fill your craving for Oriental treats at the **Diplomat Motor Hotel's dining room,** which serves Cantonese specialties in a simple, modern lunchroom decor. While the menu lists familiar Canadian-American items as well, go for the sweet-and-sour combination platter ($7), the Chinese seafood platter ($11.50), or the house's most extravagant treat: Cantonese lobster, stuffed with pork and black bean sauce ($14).

The capital's young professionals crowd into the **Cosmo Dining Room** to see and be seen, dine and be wined and dined, to dance and disco. Actually, the rustic-looking building at 546 King St. houses the restaurant, the Club Cosmo, and the eating place named Once Upon a Stove. Except for the latter, where a Grandma's Kitchen decor prevails, the Cosmo possesses more barnboards and weathered wood, more overmortared bricks and dim yellow lamps than have ever existed in one location previously. It all makes for a cozy, relaxed meal, and the service is surpassingly friendly. The menu is eclectic, with soups (85¢ to $2.50), quiches, sandwiches, burgers, and plates of spaghetti ($2.50 to $5.50), with prices slightly lower than these at lunchtime. In the evening, and especially on weekends, the "club" aspect of the Cosmo comes to the fore. The city's most eligible singles and most dashing couples crowd in. As a visitor, you'll only be refused when the press of the crowd is overwhelming and the doorman has to resort to a members-only policy.

For a taste of Central Europe, visit **Martha's Kitchen,** 625 King St., corner of Regent. Although Martha's is not fancy, it's not a kitchen or lunchroom either, and the tables all have cloths and carefully laid settings. For lunch a special is always offered. Last time I was there, I had soup, roast pork, vegetable, potato, dessert, and coffee for $5; with tip and tax, and the total came to $6. If you don't order the daily special you can indulge in stuffed cabbage or wienerschnitzel ($7 to $8), or throw caution, budget, and diet to the winds with Martha's Special Plate-for-Two: breaded liver, wienerschnitzel, breaded pork parisienne, filet mignon, cauliflower, potatoes, red cabbage, lettuce, and tomato—all for two people and all for $17.

For snacks, sandwiches and burgers, and old-fashioned barbecued chicken to eat in or take out, drop by **Big Al's,** 74 Regent St. between King and Queen Sts. Big Al's red-and-white-checked tablecloths are laden with big breakfasts ($3), lunches, and dinners from 7 a.m. to 7 p.m. Sunday through Thursday, 7 a.m. to 2:30 a.m. the rest of the week. Buy your barbecued chicken by the part or the whole, for $3 to $8.25. Daily dinner specials are the best bargains of all, with large portions of, say, fish and chips ($3) or steak ($7). Beer and wine are served, and everything can be wrapped up to take out.

Those staying in the Sequoia Motel out by the Trans Canada Hwy. will want to have at least one meal in the **Coffee Mill,** a Fredericton institution, located in Fredericton Mall. Shopping mall eateries are almost always a disappointment, but the Coffee Mill is an exception—in fact, it may be the city's most popular restaurant of all, and at these prices, why not: lobster (1¼ lb.) dinner, $9; New York pepper steak, $10; spare ribs in honey-and-garlic sauce $7. The daily luncheon special last time I visited was liver and onions, soup, and vegetable, for the price of a sandwich elsewhere: $2.50. One side of the restaurant is licensed; the other serves nothing stronger than coffee. Open Monday through Saturday from 11:30 a.m. to 10 p.m.

Newest of Fredericton eateries is **The Deli,** 56 Regent St. very near Queen. It's a family operation with the purpose of bringing to Fredericton a Montréal-style deli complete with Ben's smoked meat. A smoked-meat sandwich built into a soul and appetite-pleasing meal with cheese, pickles, and the like, will cost $1.50 to $2.50, depending on contents. A meat and cheese retail counter allows you to construct your own sandwiches at home, if you prefer. The Deli is open Monday through Saturday from 9 a.m. to 6 p.m., later on Thursday and Friday evenings. It's closed Sunday.

WHAT TO SEE: Starting point for any Fredericton tour should be **Officers' Square** on Queen St. between Carleton and Regent. Get there at 10 a.m., Tuesday through Saturday from mid-July to the third week in August, and you'll catch the Changing of the Guard ceremony: brilliant uniforms, brisk commands, the works. At 2 p.m. the troops return for a mini-tattoo, complete with a rifle salute.

Officers' Square is the site of free summer band concerts on Tuesday evenings at 7:30 p.m. Pipe bands, marching and military bands from the city and the region provide the music; you provide your own blanket, cushion, or chair. If it rains, come on Thursday instead.

Lord Beaverbrook, New Brunswick's famous native son, is immortalized in a statue which stands in Officers' Square. Nearby is Fredericton's memorial to America's fallen chief executive, John F. Kennedy.

The square—actually a fine downtown park today—was once the city's military parade ground, and the barracks which housed officers of the British garrison are still here, on the western side of the square. Built between 1839 and 1851, the barracks now house the **York-Sunbury Historical Society Museum,** open in July and August from 10 a.m. to 6 p.m. Monday through Saturday, 2 to 6 on Sunday; admission for adults is only 75¢, and 25¢ for children. Army uniforms and weapons, a restored Loyalist-period sitting room, MicMac and Maliseet Indian furnishings, a children's room, and other displays recount Fredericton's history-filled past. At the top of the stairway to the second floor, be sure not to miss—are you ready?—a taxidermically preserved 42-pound frog. Fredericton's legendary Coleman frog was the pet of one Fred Coleman, a local innkeeper who adopted it as a youngster and nurtured it to record-breaking size. With such a formula for nutritive success, it's a wonder Coleman's inn was not the prototype for a world-girdling chain—but maybe his recipes were strictly frog-fattening.

For a look at where the soldiers (not the officers) lived, walk down to Carleton St., turn toward the river, and enter the **Military Compound.** The Soldiers' Barracks (1827), completely restored a few years ago, has a room set up as it would have been when 19 infantrymen occupied it over 100 years ago.

In the same compound stands the Guard House (1828), the lock-up where men who disobeyed orders or regulations were held. It's now a museum of military memorabilia, and, like the Soldiers' Barracks, is open free of charge between late May and Labour Day.

East of Officers' Square, a short walk along Queen St. brings you to the **Playhouse,** one of Lord Beaverbrook's gifts to the city and the province, built in 1964. Call 455-3080 for the latest information on plays staged by Theatre New Brunswick, the resident company.

Next along Queen St. is the impressive bulk of the **New Brunswick Legislative Assembly Building** (1882), with its crimson-carpeted Assembly Chamber and Speaker's Chair. The Speaker's Chair is just that when the Speaker of the House presides over a session of the Assembly; but when the queen's representative, New Brunswick's lieutenant-governor, attends a session of the Assembly, the chair becomes the throne, symbol of the monarch's reign. Guides are on hand to take you around the Legislative Assembly Building from mid-June through mid-September, Monday through Friday between 8 a.m. and 9 p.m.; Saturday, Sunday, and holidays, from 10 a.m. to 9 p.m. In winter, times are 8 a.m. to 12:30 p.m. and 2 p.m. to 4:30 p.m., Monday through Friday. Be sure to see the handsome spiral staircase, at the end of the main hallway.

The center of Fredericton's artistic life is the **Beaverbrook Art Gallery,** across Queen St. from the Legislative Assembly Building. Lord Beaverbrook gave this fine modern gallery to the people of New Brunswick too, and you should not miss its impressive collection of British paintings (Reynolds, Gainsborough, Constable, Turner, and other greats), Canadian and provincial works, and Salvador Dali's *Santiago el Grande.* Summer hours in June, July, and August are 10 a.m. to 9 p.m. Tuesday through Saturday, noon to 9 p.m. on Sunday, closed Monday. At other times of the year the gallery opens at the same hours on the same days, but closes earlier, at 5 p.m.

Past the Art Gallery, the **Green** stretches along the bank of the St. John River, and if you stroll far enough in this pretty setting, you'll reach an old Loyalist cemetery, with tombstones dating back to 1783.

On your way back to the center of twon, pass the intersection of Brunswick and Church Sts. for a look at **Christ Church Cathedral,** built as the seat of Fredericton's Anglican bishop between 1845 and 1853. From mid-June to Labour Day, free tours of the church are given daily: on weekdays between 8:30 a.m. and 8 p.m.; on Saturdays from 8:30 a.m. to 5 p.m.; on Sundays after church, from 12:30 p.m. to 6:30 p.m.

WHAT TO DO: Stop in to see what's on at the **National Exhibition Centre** (tel. 506/453-3747), corner of Queen and Carleton Sts. It might be anything from a collection of Japanese kites or Canadian photographers' works, to a display of the latest in computer technology. Hours are 10 a.m. to 5 p.m. Monday to Thursday and Saturday, 10 a.m. to 9 p.m. on Friday, 1 to 5 p.m. on Sunday.

The **University of New Brunswick's Art Centre** hosts summer exhibits in Memorial Hall on the UNB campus, open weekdays from 10 to 5, Sundays from 2 to 4.

Don't leave town without at least a quick auto tour of the lovely hillside campus which harbors two universities: the **University of New Brunswick** (founded 1785), and **Saint Thomas University** (1910). For free campus tours, call 453-4793.

On Saturdays, the **Boyce Farmers' Market** is a delight to explore, with over 100 stalls selling not only fresh fruits and vegetables, but all sorts of homemade edible goodies and craft items as well. The market, on George St. between Regent and St. John'Sts., is the home of Fredericton's most informal "restaurant," an assemblage of tables and chairs known as **Goofy Roofy's.** "Roofy" is the redoubtable Ruth Chappell, who presides over the preparation and cooking of a very appetizing selection of fresh market goodies.

Outside Fredericton

Not far from the capital are opportunities to do and to see things you won't find elsewhere in New Brunswick. **Mactaquac Provincial Park,** 15 miles west of Fredericton off the Trans Canada Hwy., is the province's largest and most elaborate. A spinoff of the Mactaquac Power Development, the park spreads along the shores of the dam's 65-mile-long "headpond," in which park visitors can swim, fish, sail, row, waterski, or all of the above. Nearly 300 campsites are set up in the park, and at the 18-hole golf course you don't even have to bring your own clubs; rental sets, lessons, and electric carts are all yours for a reasonable fee. In Mactaquac Lodge, the "19th hole," you will find a licensed lounge and restaurant for golfers and anyone else who's worked up an appetite.

Woolastook Wildlife Park is only a few miles west of Mactaquac Park, off the Trans Canada Hwy.: follow the bear-shaped signs. For a living lesson in Canadian fauna, Woolastook can't be beat as the grounds harbor deer, caribou, moose, seals, cougars, even coyotes and skunks. Open 9 a.m. to sunset daily.

If Mactaquac is your introduction to New Brunswick's flora, and Woolastook to fauna, **King's Landing Historical Settlement** will immerse you in New Brunswick's quaint past. A few miles west of the intersection with Hwy. 3 on the Trans Canada Hwy., King's Landing (tel. 506/363-3081) is a full-fledged community based on many actual old buildings. The King's Head Inn, for instance, was an inn for much of its history, serving up grub and grog to the hardy types who traveled along the St. John River a century or more ago. It still serves food and drink today, but you must get a table early before lunch or dinner in the high summer months. Don't despair if they're all taken, as the Visitor Reception Centre has a cafeteria, and a few other eating places are found here and there in the settlement.

Every facet of life in pioneer New Brunswick, before the age of gasoline and electricity, finds a place in King's Landing, from sheep shearing to spinning and weaving. The smell of freshly baked bread mixes with the smell of horses and livestock, and the sound of the blacksmith's hammer alternates with that of the church's bell. "Interpreters" in every house, shop, and workplace will tell you all about how things were done and life was lived—although you'll learn most of what you want to know just by watching them at work and play. The summer season for King's Landing is from the last Saturday in May through Labour Day, from 10 a.m. to 6 p.m. daily. Adult tickets cost $3; youth (6 to 16) and senior tickets are $1.50; a family pass good for two adults and three children is a bargain at $7.

Fundy National Park

Traveling east from Fredericton or Saint John, the Trans Canada Hwy. meets Hwy. 114, the road to Fundy National Park. Get an early start on the road, and there will be plenty of time to take the detour through the park on 114, which eventually will lead to Moncton.

The park area was chosen—as are all the Canadian national parks—to preserve and make available various unique features of Canadian terrain.

Fundy National Park harbors examples of forest and bog resembling those found much farther north, in Newfoundland, not to mention the world-record Fundy tides (at low tide there's good beachcombing, and little marine creatures are everywhere). Besides 80 km of hiking trails, Fundy Park has a number of "auto trails," one-lane dirt roads kept in good condition for auto-bound explorers.

Civilized amusements compete with the call of the wild: a crafts school, heated saltwater swimming pool, tennis courts, lawn bowling green, and a nine-hole golf course are all here, in addition to the five campgrounds.

6. Moncton

To New Brunswickers, Moncton is the brash young lad from the Atlantic coast, without the sense of history found in Saint John or the gentility of Fredericton, but with business savvy and eyes on the future. Coming into the city, the city's Telephone Tower spikes to the sky like some technological minaret, a symbol of the city's promise.

Moncton was built on communications, as the region's rail and road networks met here. With this important start, Monctonians have built on their advantage to make their city the fast-growing commercial capital of Atlantic New Brunswick.

Although the city's name was given to honor Lt. Robert Monckton, commander of the British force which took nearby Fort Beauséjour in 1795, it was actually some legal clerk who gave the city its name. By inadvertently leaving out the "k," he blessed the town with a unique moniker.

But Moncton's fame comes not from its commerce or its name, rather from a freak of nature known as Magnetic Hill—but more of that later.

FOR INFORMATION: Magnetic Hill, at the intersection of Hwy. 2 (the Trans Canada) and Hwy. 126, has its own tourism information bureau, open from 9 a.m. to 8 p.m. daily, mid-May to early September. Another is in **Centennial Park,** on St. George St. west of the center of town. The Community Services Department of the **Downtown Civic Centre,** 100 Westmorland St., will answer your questions and hand out free maps from 9 to 5, Monday through Friday.

WHERE TO STAY AND EAT: Moncton's showplace is the giant new **Hotel Beauséjour** (tel. 506/854-4344), a CN hotel which dominates the downtown shopping area at 750 Main St. The hotel was built very recently as part of a new City Hall government-shopping-hotel complex. Over 300 ultramodern guest rooms all have radio and color TV, for prices ranging from $33 to $40 single, $41 to $48 double; suites cost more. On weekends, a 20% discount is usually in order—if you ask. Included in the rates are parking in the hotel's lot, use of the outdoor pool and sundeck, and easy access to Moncton's prime disco and some of its best restaurants.

The Beauséjour's Canadian-French restaurant, called **L'Auberge,** has a long and moderately priced menu of delights which include lots of cream soups, and coq au vin ($5), tourtière ($5.50), and plenty of seafood dishes prepared from the produce of nearby Shediac ($5.50 to $8). Each main course comes with a vegetable. For lunch at L'Auberge, plan to spend $5 to $7; for dinner, with wine, tax, and tip, between $12 and $15. The **Windjammer,** next door to L'Auberge in the Hotel Beauséjour, demands more generous budgeting but less agonizing menu choosing. Choices at the Windjammer are fewer, although perhaps more select: roast beef with Yorkshire pudding comes teamed up with coquilles St-Jacques, for instance, an elegant and quintessentially New Brunswick variation on the familiar "surf and turf." Served with fiddleheads and other garnishes, it costs $13.50. Rock Cornish game hen, a mouth-watering alternative to the beef and seafood, costs a good deal less, at $7.50.

In the evening, the Hotel Beauséjour's Cloud 9 Disco opens at 8:30 and rocks until 2 in the morning every day but Sunday. Live entertainment shares the stage with records, and a dazzling light show provides the visual excitement. The cover charge is $1.75 if you're not a hotel guest (free if you are). Drinks, after that, cost from $2 to $3.50.

A motel alternative to the Beauséjour, and much less pricey, is the **Colonial Inn** (tel. 506/382-3395), 42 Highfield St., not far from the intersection with Main St. and the Highfield Square Mall. While smaller than the Beauséjour, the Colonial's 57 rooms have the same color TVs and air conditioning. You won't find a swimming pool here—but neither will you pay for it. The location is still good, as virtually everything is within walking distance, and the prices are even better: $29 single, $30 to $33 double, $5 for an extra person in the room.

Just across the street from the Colonial Inn, at 35 Highfield St., is Moncton's charming old **YWCA** (tel. 506/855-4349). Through the tower-topped front entrance lies a genteel old Moncton mansion, converted to accept guests (women only, however) for $8 per night in bathless rooms. The YWCA also serves inexpensive, simple meals: $1.25 for breakfast, $2 for lunch or supper, $2.75 for a full-fledged dinner.

Another mansion, this one accepting all comers, is the **Hotel Canadiana** (tel. 506/382-1054), at 46 Archibald St., corner of Queen, just a short stroll from the YWCA. Here, another fine old Moncton mansion has been converted to a hotel of 20 rooms, all cheerful and simple, and all surpassingly quiet. Special family rates apply for those with children, but base rates are $20 for a double room with shared bath, $30 for a similar room with private bath.

Moncton's **Youth Hostel** ("Auberge de Jeunesse"; tel. 506/388-4793) is in the grand old mansion at 141 King St., very near the Moncton Museum. The 46-bed hostel, part of the Canadian Hostelling Association, accepts men and women, and charges only $3.50 per bed for those with hostel organization membership cards, $4 for those without.

For dining out, Moncton's classic seafood place is **Cy's,** 170 E. Main St., just before the big shopping mall. Although Cy's is not on the ocean, it does have a choice riverbank location on the Petitcodiac River (the seafood comes from Shediac, in any case). Scallops, halibut, salmon, lobster—whatever's fresh and in season shows up on Cy's tables, along with steaks for the landlubbers. Liquor is served, and an evening meal when you're feeling only moderately extravagant should not cost more than $14 per person, all in all.

Budget-minded readers loose in business-minded Moncton can save themselves from expense-account meals by seeking out **Vito's Pizza,** 726 Mountain Rd. More than a pizza oven, Vito's is a Moncton institution which serves up—or ships out—pizzas measuring 9 or 12 inches, and also spaghetti and pasta dishes priced to leave both you and your billfold full. From simple cheese pizza to what Vito calls, simply, "the works," 9-inch pizzas cost $2.45 to $4; 12-inches are $3.50 to $5.50. Plates of spaghetti, lasagne, cannelloni, etc., come regular or large size, for $2.60 to $4.25. Chicken cacciatore costs a little more.

WHAT TO SEE: Moncton's claim to fame, more than its two museums or the Petitcodiac's tidal bore, is unquestionably **Magnetic Hill.** Drive out Hwy.

126 to the intersection with Hwy. 2, the Trans Canada, and Magnetic Hill signs will guide you the short distance to the site. Bus tours of the city include not only Magnetic Hill, but the other attractions as well, for $3 per adults, $1 per child—call 388-2883 or drop in and sign up at the tour desk in the Hotel Beauséjour.

Magnetic Hill is fun—but it's also confusing, and to enjoy the sensation of "coasting uphill," you must follow directions. (If you're not in a car, you can't really get the feel of the hill.) As you approach the hill, signs will instruct you to drive down the slope. At the bottom, cross to the *left* side of the roadway and stop your car by the white post. Put it in neutral, let off the brakes, and voila!—back you go up the gentle slope to the top where you started. How?

Well, if you've followed these directions and haven't turned your car around at the bottom of the hill, and haven't gone to the top of the slope past the white post, you'll still be baffled. It really does seem like your car's gliding smoothly up the gentle slope. But now that you've had the fun, drive or walk to the top of the hill *past* the white post, near the turn-around area for cars with trailers, and all will come clear. Although anyone would swear that Magnetic Hill slopes upward from the white post, from any spot higher up it's evident that the slope is *downward*. What could cause so baffling an optical illusion? That's still a mystery to me.

While Magnetic Hill is Moncton's great tourist attraction, the city has more serious and cultural diversions. The **Moncton Museum** (tel. 506/854-1001), 20 Mountain Rd. near the corner of Belleview, charges no admission, and houses lots of Moncton memorabilia as well as paintings and sculpture. You'll be into the realm of Old Moncton even before you enter the museum building: the door through which one enters was in the facade of Moncton's old City Hall—when it was razed, its front was preserved and reerected as part of the facade of the modern museum.

Inside Moncton Museum, a fully furnished Victorian parlor might be set up when you visit, or there might be a display of old radio gear donated by a local aficionado of the airwaves. For sure, a top-class traveling exhibition will be hung in the attractive, modern galleries, and for the price, this is Moncton's most worthwhile attraction. Summer hours for the museum are weekdays from 10 a.m. to 8 p.m., Sundays and holidays from 2 to 8 p.m.; in winter, the museum is open from 2 to 5 daily, but note that it is closed on Saturdays all year round.

Right next to the museum, have a glance at Moncton's **Free Meeting House,** built in 1821. At the confluence of King St. and Mountain Rd. is the **Dunlap Mansion,** another Moncton landmark, dating from about 1870.

In the center of town off Main St. is **Bore View Park,** best spot for watching the rippling waters of the **tidal bore** (or current) rush up the Petitcodiac River from the Bay of Fundy. A large signboard lists the times for the action. Sometimes it's impressive, sometimes it's not.

Moncton is a university town, and the sprawling campus of the French-language **Université de Moncton** occupies a large area north of the center of town. Drive out for a look, and drop in at the Bibliothèque Champlain (the library) to see the 6000 artifacts and relics which form the collection of the **Musée Acadien** (Acadian Museum). New Brunswick absorbed large numbers of the Acadian settlers driven from Nova Scotia by British troops, and the Acadian Museum's collection chronicles almost every phase of daily life for this displaced people. Hours are liberal: 10 a.m. to 9 p.m. weekdays, 1 to 5 p.m. weekends; free admission.

7. Shediac and Sackville

SHEDIAC: This port town for fishing craft is a summer resort for Monctonians, the location of an annual Lobster Festival (around the middle of July). But more important, Shediac is the town nearest New Brunswick's balmy, warm Northumberland Strait beaches. Special conditions—low sand bars and shallow waters—allow the sun to warm up the chilly waters of the strait almost to bath temperatures. **Parlee Beach,** east of Shediac, is the most popular (and the most crowded during high season), but other beaches north and east of Shediac are almost as warm and less intensely used. On your beach search, get off Hwy. 15, which is too fast and too far inland, and wander the shorefront roads; 133, 134, 950, and 530.

Lunch or dinner in Shediac is for seafood lovers, especially during the Lobster Festival when the delicious denizens of New Brunswick's waters are offered in quantity and at lower prices than normal.

Paturel Shore House (tel. 506/532-4774) is the quintessential seafood restaurant, located right on the shore with a fine ocean view, and right next to a fish-packing plant. Take Hwy. 15 east from Shediac, and watch for signs to Paturel about five miles along your way. As you come down to the water, the National Sea Products' Shediac Division plant will be on your right, the Paturel on your left, in a colony of summer beach houses. Dining hours for the Paturel are 11 a.m. to 11 p.m. Sunday through Friday and 11 a.m. to 1 a.m. on Saturday; it would be good to call ahead for reservations on weekends in high summer. Reservation made, enter the large plain-ish dining room, where the main feature of the decor is the ocean view. Go with a good appetite, and start with the hearty lobster stew ($4.30), followed by the mammoth seafood platter ($10), a mini-recreation of the myriad products put up by the plant next door. If all this is too much to eat, a fish steak or seafood casserole is more manageable, and moderately priced at $7 to $8.

Fisherman's Paradise (tel. 506/532-6811) is in the commercial strip which forms the eastern reaches of Shediac's Main St., not far from the intersection with Hwy. 15. Nets, shells, and nautical paraphernalia put you in the mood, and their fisherman's platter will put you in the heavyweight seafood eater's class: half a lobster, fried clams, scallops, stuffed shrimp, and several kinds of fish are the usual ingredients, for $12.50. The lobster or seafood chowder costs $4.50; lobster dishes in general, from live boiled to the fancier stuffed and salad items, are $10 to $12. Drinks are served, and there is a limited wine list. Service is slow but friendly, and beach picnickers should note that they'll put up most of their orders to go: we took the savory lobster stew with us last time.

SACKVILLE–FORT BEAUSÉJOUR: Southeast of Moncton on the road to Nova Scotia, the rolling farmland contains some culinary surprises and a historical site worthy of a visit.

The small, attractive town of Sackville has a famous old New Brunswick inn called the **Marshlands Inn,** after the Tantramar marshes nearby. The Marshlands (tel. 506/536-0170) has one of Canada's most renowned dining rooms, not only for the freshness and delicacy of its food but also for the elegance of its table settings and decor. Before you go to Sackville in search of the big white mansion at 73 Bridge St., however, get a reservation: breakfast is served from 7 to 9:30 a.m. Monday through Friday, 8 to 11 a.m. on weekends; lunch comes on weekdays only, from 12 noon to 2 p.m.; dinner is in two sittings, at 6 p.m. and 8 p.m. (it's for dinner that you really need reservations).

As the inn's owners and chefs pride themselves on the freshness of ingredients, the menu depends on the season and its produce. Appetizers and soups are priced about $1 to $2; Atlantic salmon, poached or grilled ($10), shares the menu with halibut (a bit cheaper) in summer, but the list is not restricted to seafood by any means. Pork chops, liver and onions, and hearty steak-and-kidney pie all have a place on it. The wine list is well chosen, with prices about 225% of store prices. Egri Bikaver, the inexpensive Hungarian red, is $8; Prince Blanc (B&G), the cheapest decent white wine, is $12; prices rise from there.

As with dinner at the Marshlands, you should reserve in advance for rooms. The 16 rooms are very comfortable indeed, with air conditioners, color television, and shower-bath facilities. The Marshlands rents its rooms year round for $28 to $32 double.

Although the name is similar, the **Marshlands Motor Inn** (tel. 506/536-1327) is no relation to the aforementioned inn. The Motor Inn is in fact a modern roadside motel set in a spacious lawn, back from the Trans Canada Hwy. right by the easternmost turnoff for Sackville at Hwys. 6 and 104. The 20 units all have color TV and radio, air conditioning, and bathtubs with showers; breakfast is served in the little coffeeshop, and the use of coin laundry machines is open to guests. All rooms are doubles, costing $28 for two in one double bed, $32 for two in two beds.

Just down the road from Sackville almost at the Nova Scotia border is **Fort Beauséjour National Historic Park,** near the little town of Aulac. The French built Fort Beauséjour (1751–55), commanding the sprawling Tantramar marshes and the road between New Brunswick and Nova Scotia, in an attempt to stop the British takeover of Atlantic Canada. The British troops proved unstoppable, however, and even before the fortress was completed it had been captured (June 1755) by young Colonel Monckton, who renamed it Fort Cumberland. Admission to the impressive earthworks—a favorite picnic site—is free, and park staff are on hand to explain the great fort and its history. Go between 10 a.m. and 5 p.m. off-season, 9 a.m. to 8 p.m. between mid-June and Labour Day.

If you haven't brought a picnic to Fort Beauséjour, don't despair, for one of the region's best restaurants is right next door. The **Drury Lane Steak House** (tel. 506/536-1252 has, it would seem, little to do with Drury Lane; neither is it strictly a steakhouse, as the seafood is as good or better. The rough wood beams and pine boards in the dining room give it a rustic quality, accentuated by the collection of handmade quilts and knitted craft items displayed (and on sale) near the cash register. Prices at the Drury Lane are high, but portions tend to be big—compensate if you're not ravenously hungry. The large bowl of seafood chowder ($5) might fill you up, especially if combined with a huge bucketful of steamed clams, enough for two people ($7). Seafood as a main course runs $9 to $12, steaks a bit more, but this price includes salad or vegetable and hot rolls. As for the steaks, don't overeat in your imagination. Can you really handle the "King Cut" of 18 ounces? Or even the "Queen Cut," a full pound?

The Drury Lane is open daily between April 15 and October 31 from noon to 10 p.m., on Sundays from noon to 9 p.m. The more expensive dinner menu comes into force at 4 p.m.

8. Chatham and Newcastle

The chilly waters of the Northumberland Strait are warmed by the New Brunswick coast from Shediac all the way to Miramichi Bay. Highway 11 north from Shediac is the direct route, but the smaller coastal roads—530, 535, 475, 505—are the ones with the sights.

At **Cocagne,** the big yearly event is the Hydroplane Regatta, which usually takes place on the second weekend in August. Dozens of the swift, powerful boats compete for the trophies in various classes, with exciting action and top speeds of 120 miles per hour, or more.

Buctouche, the next town to the north, is famous for the tastiness of its oysters and the warm waters of its beaches. More beaches await you at Richibucto and near Rexton—the latter being the birthplace of Andrew Bonar Law, the only man born outside Great Britain to become that country's prime minister.

Kouchibouguac National Park, one of Canada's newest, has a daunting name but inviting beaches. At Kellys Beach, lifeguards are on duty to watch children and adults; other beaches—by far the less crowded ones—have no lifeguards but lots more elbow room. Dig your own clams, wherever you go. The water all along the coast is incredibly warm, but the beaches also tend to be shallow—can't have everything! Hiking trails interlace the park. Canoe rentals and lessons can be had at the rental center (call 876-2320, or ask any ranger). Although the number of campsites in Kouchibouguac Park is large and growing, the number of campers who vie for them in July and August—particularly on weekends—is even larger, and growing even faster. Get there early.

CHATHAM: In Chatham, a son of the world-famous shipbuilding Cunard family, Joseph Cunard, once built an empire of wooden lumber-carrying ships. His fleet was the vehicle for exploitation of New Brunswick's vast timber resources, and the town and the region boomed as long as wooden ships commanded the seas.

But with the coming of steel ships, Joseph Cunard, his company, and his ships became things of the past. The Miramichi River's timber wealth is still there, however, and these days it is floated down to neighboring Newcastle.

Chatham has a museum that should be on any trivia lover's list: old costumes, one of Canada's first typewriters, a deer fetus, and some of the town's old books and records all find a place here. Visit any day, mid-June through August, from 9 a.m. to 5:30 p.m.

NEWCASTLE: Besides being the site of a tremendous (and "fragrant") paper-pulp mill, Newcastle is famous as the birthplace of Max Aitken. Aitken was a local boy who grew up here, studied law in neighboring Chatham, and went on to become one of the most powerful "press barons" Britain had ever seen. A statesman and philanthropist as well as a newspaper publisher, William Maxwell Aitken (1879–1964) became Baron Beaverbrook—an appropriate title, as he sprang from the shores of the Miramichi.

Lord Beaverbrook lavished tribute on his hometown and on his native province, and many places are in his debt for public parks and buildings. Here in Newcastle, the 17th-century English benches, the Italian gazebo, and other furnishings in the main square were among his gifts to the city. The town said "thanks" with a monument, and after Lord Beaverbrook's death his ashes were buried beneath it.

Another Beaverbrook gift to Newcastle was **The Enclosure,** a beautiful forest park now combined with a provincial park, south of the town off Hwy. 8. The spot was the site of a very early Protestant church, and its graveyard of ancient tombstones was spruced up by His Lordship. Tell the park guard you're just going to the Enclosure, and you won't have to pay the park entrance fee.

If Beaverbrook lore intrigues you, drop in at his father's house—Max's boyhood home—at 255 Mary St. Called the Old Manse, it's now a library.

Staying overnight in Newcastle is a pleasure if you make your way to the brand-new **Wharf Inn** (tel. 506/622-0302), 1 Jane St. right on the water just beneath the west end of Morrissey Bridge. As it's a favorite with traveling businessmen, the 50 up-to-date air-conditioned rooms are a bit higher in price than you might expect, but still not unreasonable: single rooms cost $27, doubles are $30 (on the entrance side) and $36 (on the riverview side). Rooms on the river side have two double beds, those on the landward or entrance side have one double bed. A color cable TV set is in every room.

9. Northern New Brunswick

North of Chatham and Newcastle lie the dense forests and trout-filled rivers which draw hunters to this mostly wild province. Along the coast, between the Gulf of St. Lawrence and the Baie des Chaleurs, Acadian settlers, forced from their homelands farther south, have lived for centuries. Fishing, farming, and the production of peat and peat moss are the region's main occupations, with lumbering also prominent.

Caraquet, right on Hwy. 11, is famous for its new **Village Historique Acadien** (tel. 506/732-5350), a "living museum" of 17 buildings in which "interpreters" in period costumes work at the trades, the daily chores, and the traditional games which made up the fabric of town and home life in Acadia 100 or 200 years ago. In summer, you can visit the village seven days a week from 10 a.m. to 6 p.m.

Bathurst, with a pretty situation on the Bathurst Basin, is an industrial town of 17,000 souls, many of whom make their living at the city's large pulp paper mill. In recent years, other industries have moved nearby, and when important strikes of minerals and metals were discovered in the region, the result was a mining boom.

For travelers heading north to the Gaspé Peninsula, **Danny's Motel and Restaurant** (tel. 506/546-6621), north of Bathurst on Hwy. 134, is the perfect oasis at which to make an overnight stop. Laid out like a resort motel on its own large estate, Danny's can boast 50 modern, air-conditioned, and color-TV–equipped guest rooms, priced at $21 to $28 double, $30 for four persons in one room. There is even a tennis court, Ping-Pong tables, and shuffleboard. The dining facilities cover all meals: in the coffeeshop, you'll have breakfast at a table next to local businessmen who've dropped in for the same purpose. Lunch and dinner in the dining room are more fancy, but never formal. Danny's is licensed, and has a cocktail lounge.

ONWARD AND UPWARD: From Bathurst, Hwy. 11 skirts the shore of the Baie des Chaleurs to Dalhousie and Campbellton. Past Campbellton is the city of Matapedia, Québec, on the road across the Gaspé to Mont Joli. A much more scenic route, however, is around the tip of the peninsula. For this, you can save a considerable number of miles (or kilometers) by taking the ferryboat which operates between Dalhousie, N.B., and Miguasha, Québec. For full information on the ferry, see the end of the chapter dealing with Québec City and the Gaspé Peninsula.

PRINCE EDWARD ISLAND

ATLANTIC CANADA'S "million-acre farm" in the Gulf of St. Lawrence can be described in two words: simply beautiful. The pastoral beauty and rural simplicity are carefully preserved by an island people proud of their land and their traditions. Each summer season, visitors come from all over North America to share the island's beauties: country roads bordered by swaths of wildflower color; tidy farms raising potatoes (the island's principal crop), broccoli, tomatoes, strawberries, grains, or dairy cattle; and thousands of kilometers of sinuous coastline bordered by beaches of red or white sand. Offshore waters teem with lobster, giant tuna, clams, and scallops. Malpeque Bay oysters are world-famous. And island streams and lakes yield trout and salmon.

Harvesting the island's natural wealth is the prime industry here, but tourism is a close second. The two are very carefully matched to one another: a large number of island farms supplement their incomes by renting rooms to visitors. In fact, there are many more tourist homes, housekeeping cottages, and farmhouse rooms than there are hotels and motels. Most people who come to Prince Edward Island are looking for a week or two of peace and quiet, simple living, pretty scenery, and excellent beaches.

For all its beauty, Prince Edward Island is still Canada's smallest and most densely populated province, which fact may surprise you when you see the miles of rolling farmland and the small-scale cities and towns. But P.E.I. has no vast northern expanse as does, say, Québec or Ontario. In fact, the island province is a mere 145 miles from end to end, and only about 40 miles wide at its widest point. Although the population grows markedly during the warm summer months, year-round islanders number fewer than 120,000.

P.E.I.'S MULTINATIONAL HERITAGE: Of the European empire-building nations, it was the French who first laid claim to the island, doing so in 1523 even before Jacques Cartier had sailed up the St. Lawrence. When Cartier came across the island in 1534, he was enchanted by it and wrote glowing reports to Paris. Samuel de Champlain, the great French colonizer who founded Québec City, named the island after St. John, and the name Île St-Jean stuck for almost two centuries.

Frenchmen came here to settle in 1663, with larger groups coming a half century later. The great French fortress of Louisbourg on Cape Breton Island fell to British troops in 1758, and many French colonists fled to the Île St-Jean to escape British domination. It did them little good, for the island was in British hands soon after the fall of Louisbourg, called St. John's Island by its new British owners. Some French settlers managed to remain on the island, although settlers whose loyalty to the British Crown was in question were being deported throughout British North America.

In 1763 the island was part of Nova Scotia, but in 1769 it was named a colony in its own right, with Charlottetown as its capital, named after King George III's wife. Loyalists from the rebellious American colonies escaped the strife by coming to the island, and 1803 saw the beginning of a large influx of impoverished Scottish settlers seeking a better life in the New World, led by Lord Selkirk. In 1798, the island was renamed for Queen Victoria's father, Edward, Duke of Kent. Prince Edward Island was well on its way to possessing the rich national mix it enjoys today: MicMac Indians, Acadian French settlers, Scots, and English.

By 1851 the island colony was self-governing, and in 1864 it had the honor of hosting the famous talks which would lead to Canada's confederation. Throughout its history, the fertile red soil has provided richly for anyone willing to till and plant it, and the fantastic abundance of the "Garden of the Gulf" and its offshore waters attracts visitors from thousands of miles away.

GETTING TO P.E.I.: For an island, the "Garden of the Gulf" is surprisingly accessible.

By Air

Air Canada (tel. toll free 800/561-3933 in Charlottetown) has daily flights between Charlottetown, P.E.I., and Boston, Calgary/Banff, Edmonton, Halifax/Dartmouth, Montréal, Ottawa/Hull, St. John's (Newfoundland), Toronto, Vancouver, and Winnipeg. Except for the flights from Montréal, you'll make a stopover in Halifax, Ottawa, or Toronto. **Eastern Provincial Airways** (tel. 892-3581 in Charlottetown) flies to the island's capital from Halifax and Montréal—flights from other points in eastern Canada all stop in one or the other of those two cities.

Once you reach the Charlottetown Airport (which serves the entire island), you can catch the airport limousine to get to any downtown hotel or motel for $2.50 a person. Taxis will run you to other points on the island, the fare varying with distance traveled.

By Car

Most people come to P.E.I. by car ferry from either Cape Tormentine, New Brunswick, or Caribou, Nova Scotia.

From Cape Tormentine, N.B., CN Marine operates huge, two-level car ferries to Borden, P.E.I. Boats leave every hour on the hour in summer between 6 a.m. and 10 p.m., with extra night sailings at 11:30 p.m. and 1 a.m. Extra sailings are made at peak times during midday busy hours, but in high season (July and August) there are sometimes long lines nonetheless. You can avoid them by planning to take a ferry before 10 a.m. or after 6 p.m., when the boats often go half or three-quarters full. The ferry is a very efficient operation: you drive through a turnpike-style tollbooth and pay your fare: 90¢ for adults, 45¢ for children (5 to 13), $3.40 for a car. Then you drive down the wharf and right onto the boat. You can't make reservations—indeed, none are necessary—but if you want to know how they're running, call 506/538-7654 in Cape Tormentine, N.B.; or 902/855-2030 in Borden, P.E.I. The trip takes about 45 minutes.

From Caribou, N.S., the ferryboats are operated by Northumberland Ferries Ltd. Between June 22 and September 3, boats sail from both Caribou and Woods Island (P.E.I.) at 6, 7:30, and 9:05 a.m., and about every 50 minutes thereafter until 8:15 p.m. Then there are boats at 9, 9:30, and 11:15 p.m. At other times in June and September there are ten sailings a day. The crossing takes about 1¼ hours, and costs $1.45 per adult, 75¢ per child (5 to 12), $5.25 per car. The Caribou–Woods Island ferry is more subject to crowding and waiting lines than the shorter, less expensive one between Cape Tormentine and Borden. It's even more important to get to the docks early in the morning or late at night, rather than during the midday rush. You can contact the company for information at these numbers: Charlottetown (head office), 902/894-3473; Woods Island, P.E.I., 902/962-2016; Caribou, N.S., 902/485-6580. Often local radio stations will broadcast bulletins on ferry operations after news broadcasts.

Finally, there is car-ferry service between Souris, P.E.I., and Magdalen Islands, Québec: see below under "Souris" in the section on King's Byway for schedules and details.

By Rail/Bus

Believe it or not, you can get to Charlottetown by train—well, sort of. Take a train on Canada's VIA Rail network to Amherst, Nova Scotia. From Amherst, two buses a day make the run to Cape Tormentine for the ferry crossing, then continue on to Charlottetown. The Amherst–Charlottetown trip takes three hours. Current times for departure are: from Amherst, 12:15 p.m. and 7:10 p.m.; from Charlottetown, 7:10 a.m. and 10 a.m.

ORIENTATION: The beaches and the quiet country life are what visitors search for here. The best beaches are those warmed by the Gulf Stream on the northern side of the island between New London Bay and Tracadie Bay. Each summer the towns and villages along Rte. 6 between New London and Mill Cove are busy with visitors looking for lodgings or on their way to the beaches of Prince Edward Island National Park. Beaches along the rest of the island's coast are pleasantly uncrowded, being in general farther from the concentrations of hotels and tourist homes, and also a few degrees cooler.

The quiet country life is everywhere: west, central, and east on the island. Although most people stay in one of the three major lodging centers—Charlottetown, Summerside, or near the northern beaches—a trip or two by car through less thickly settled regions lets you see the "Garden of the Gulf" at its most beautiful. The Department of Tourism has mapped out three scenic drives and marked the highways with signs which are easy to follow. **Lady Slipper Drive** circles the western reaches of the island, sparsely populated and unspoiled. **Blue Heron Drive** circles the central portion of the island, through Charlottetown, past Summerside, and along the northern beach route. **King's Byway** completes the map by winding along the sinuous coasts of the eastern portion.

The recommendations below cover Charlottetown, the northern beaches near Cavendish, and Summerside in that order, and then detail the things to see, places to stay, and recommendable restaurants along each of the scenic drives.

ISLAND TRANSPORTATION: The island province is really a place where one needs a car as a bus system would be economically unfeasible. **Abegweit Sightseeing Tours** (tel. 902/894-9966) will provide a limousine with driver-guide, and if you have a family or small group it may turn out to be affordable. Otherwise, you'll need to rent a car.

Charlottetown has several car-rental offices, among them **Budget,** 115 St. Peter's Rd. (tel. 892-8333); and **Holiday,** 47A St. Peter's Rd. (tel. 892-3414). To rent a small car for a week with unlimited mileage should cost about $130; you pay for gas.

Charlottetown and Summerside have **Tilden Car Rental** stations, the cars rented in Summerside being the less expensive ones. Contact Tilden at Charlottetown Airport (tel. 902/894-8311), or at 311 Market St. in Summerside (tel. 902/436-2157). Reservations for a car can be made at any Tilden office in Canada, or National Car Rental office in the U.S.

P.E.I. ACCOMMODATIONS: Tourist homes, farmhouses, and housekeeping cottages make up a large part of Prince Edward Island's stock of accommodations, preserving the scenic beauty from overdevelopment with hotels and motels. The few hotels and motels on the island may be filled by tour groups—which depend on such standard, uniform accommodations—on any given night during the high season in July and August. It's a good idea to call in advance for reservations no matter where you plan to stay: farmhouse, cottage, or motel. But if you do arrive on the island without a reservation, go to any **P.E.I. Tourist Information Center** and they'll be happy to help you find a room. Since many tourist homes and farmhouses have only a few rooms—or even just one room—to rent, the tourism people are in a better position to locate the vacant ones than you are.

The somewhat tight rooms situation during the peak time of late July to early August stems from the fact that the island is a summer destination. Few lodging places remain open all year. Any lodging place must fill its rooms during the months of July and August to make a go of it.

DINING ON P.E.I.: Tourism is strictly a seasonal business on Prince Edward Island, and as most island residents live on farms, city-style restaurants are few and are concentrated in major tourist areas such as Charlottetown and Cavendish. The question of where to eat is answered automatically for the many summer visitors who rent housekeeping cottages: you cook and eat at "home." But even if city streets and country roads are not lined with places to eat, you won't go hungry. The best places for a good meal are indicated in this guide. In high season and at festival times, churches and civic groups sponsor "lobster suppers," held in church basements, Lions' Clubs, and recreational centers—the only buildings on the island large enough to accommodate the hundreds of hungry, lobster-hunting tourists. In a very real sense, the year-round residents of P.E.I. open their doors to summer visitors to provide hospitality. Don't be surprised if you find the best restaurant in town to be a church or Lions' Club!

1. Charlottetown

The capital of Prince Edward Island is a lovely old town of 20,000 citizens, with many fine colonial and Victorian buildings and the brand-new ultramodern Confederation Centre of the Arts. "Confederation" is a word much bruited about in Charlottetown since it was here, in P.E.I.'s Province House, that the first discussions on the subject of Canada's confederation were held in 1864. At first it seems odd that the island province did not join the confederation until 1873, but the delay was entirely reasonable. Islanders had nothing against joining—they simply wanted the details to be worked out first, particularly those dealing with communications between P.E.I. and the rest of Canada. No doubt the marvelously easy access to the island today is the result of that prudence of a century ago.

It's virtually impossible to get lost for long in Charlottetown's small downtown section. Most of the best hotels and restaurants are very near the center, easily reached on foot.

TOURIST INFORMATION AND RESERVATIONS: The local Tourism Information Centre is on University Ave. at Summer St., which is also Hwy. 1, the Trans Canada Hwy. If you come into town from the Borden ferry dock or from Kensington on Hwy. 1, you'll pass it on your right, in a shopping center. If you arrive after hours, or out of season, telephone 892-2457 for help, 24 hours a day.

GUIDED TOURS: Abegweit Sightseeing Tours, 157 Nassau St. (tel. 902/894-9966), will take you on a one-hour tour of Charlottetown for $2.50 per adult, $1 per child. You'll ride in a double-decker London Transport bus which departs from Confederation Centre and the Charlottetown Hotel six times a day in season—buy your tickets at either boarding point.

Abegweit offers two other services as well. For $9.75 per adult ($5 per child) they'll take you on a tour of the North Shore and its tourist attractions: beaches, Woodleigh Replicas, Jewell's Country Gardens, and the Acadian village of North Rustico. The bus leaves the Charlottetown Hotel at 10:30 a.m. daily, returning in late afternoon. But if you'd rather bypass the attractions and just go to the beach, then hop on the bus, pay $6 per adult ($3 per child), hop off at the beach, and they'll swing by to retrieve you in late afternoon for the trip back to Charlottetown. By the way, Abegweit will pick you up from your hotel or wherever you're staying and drive you to the Charlottetown Hotel to catch a tour, free of charge. Just give them plenty of time—at least an hour or more—to get there, or call the night before and set it up.

WHERE TO STAY AND EAT: You won't find it difficult to locate the lodging or meal of your choice in Charlottetown. The small downtown area holds most of them. A few others are located just over the city line in the neighboring community of West Royalty, on Hwy. 1, the Trans Canada.

Several of the capital's prime hostelries are located just off Rochford Square, the city's finest downtown park, bounded by Pownal, Kent, Rochford, and Fitzroy Sts.

Primest of the prime is the elegant old hotel called the **Charlottetown** (tel. 902/894-7371; toll-free reservations through Air Canada, Eastern Provincial Airways, or American Express), at the corner of Kent and Pownal Sts. Although the hotel was built some decades ago, the rooms are kept up to the latest standards of style and decoration. There are 110 rooms in all, boasting modern bath-shower combinations and color TVs in each, plus air conditioning throughout. An indoor pool and saunas provide for off-hour enjoyment.

You may want to have a jacket and tie or after-five dress for an evening in the Charlottetown's rather elegant dining room, the **Georgian.** The menu is based on the plan whereby you select your main course, and with it comes soup, dessert, and coffee. The short but easily satisfying selection of fish, meat, and fowl dishes is quite adequate, as is the wine list. Most complete dinners are priced around $10, but add more for wine, tax, and tip. If you don't wish to dress up or to dine amid cream-white walls and gilt accents, the hotel's coffee-shop has equally good fare at lower prices in less daunting—but still pretty elegant—surroundings.

Just across the street from the Charlottetown is a modern two-floor motel called the **Islander Motor Lodge** (tel. 902/892-1217), official address at 146-148 Pownal St. All but three of the Islander's 49 rooms are for overnight guests, the other three being housekeeping apartments. The rooms are all modern motel style, which means they have both bathtubs and showers, and color televisions. The Islander's breakfast room is right off the lobby-reception area; the dining room is licensed—alcoholic drinks are served. Room rates are $22 to $25 single, $27 to $31 double, plus the 8% tax. You'll be offered lower rates off-season, as the motor lodge is open year-round. But as for summer, call for reservations: buses sometimes fill the place up.

Without the bulky, weighty grandeur of the Charlottetown or the spic-and-span modernity of the Islander, the **Dundee Arms Motel and Inn** (tel. 902/892-2496) has what neither of the two aforementioned places has—charm. If you choose to stay in the original inn at 200 Pownal St., behind the Charlotte-town, you can have a double room on the third floor with private bath, black-and-white TV, and brass bed for only $27; or a similar, larger room on the second floor with the bonus of color cable TV for $33—brass bed included. There's also a suite good for families priced at $45. The Dundee has a block of motel-style rooms next to the original inn, all with bath-shower combinations and color cable television sets, for $36 per room in high season. In another building at 22 Richmond St. are several housekeeping rooms which go for $33 per night without use of the kitchen, $37 with use. Bus tours often fill the Dundee as well, so have reservations.

Besides its rooms, the Dundee is famous as one of Charlottetown's best places to have a cocktail or a fine dinner. The pine-paneled **Hearth and Cricket Room** has a huge fireplace, antiques and old guns hung here and there, and a clientele of the town's young professional set. It's open from noon to 1 a.m. Monday through Saturday, 4 p.m. to 1 a.m. on Saturday, closed Sunday. Across the hall from the Hearth and Cricket is the **Griffin Room,** done in colonial style with several old benches along the walls and a china cabinet stocked with antique pieces. The fare is the best, although not cheap: a dinner of Malpeque oysters ($4.50), or rollmops of Atlantic herring ($2.25), followed by baked salmon cooked in butter and tarragon and covered with a hollandaise sauce ($10), and strawberries Romanoff ($1.50), with wine, tax, and tip, will easily come to something like $20 to $23 per person. If you come at lunchtime, the prices will be only half the amounts quoted, of course. The Griffin Room opens at 11:30 a.m. every day in summer, and closes up at 10 p.m. In winter it's closed Mondays, but open from noon to 2:30 and 6 to 9:30 p.m. other days.

The **Inn on the Hill** (tel. 902/894-8572) is a short walk from the very center of town, but not enough to inconvenience you. It's at 150 Euston St., and you won't miss noticing its posh, modern facade. The inn bills itself as "the most luxurious motor inn in Charlottetown," which it probably is: all rooms are undeniably and outspokenly modern, with the standard luxuries of tub-shower bathrooms, color cable TVs, and telephones. As the inn is five stories high, an elevator serves the rooms. Singles cost $30, doubles are $38 to $40, depending on whether or not you want air conditioning (15 of the 48 rooms have it).

The inn has a cocktail lounge with the daunting name of the Gallows, and a dining room which offers very good value for money: on our last visit, the daily special of soup, salad, filet mignon wrapped in bacon, vegetable, potato, a glass of red wine, and a cup of coffee cost only $8, plus tax and tip. The special is served nightly from 5 to 8:30 p.m.

MacLauchlan's Motel (tel. 902/892-2461) greets you with a Gaelic *ciad mile failte* ("100,000 welcomes") and tartan patterns in prominent places. Prices match the Scottish decor: for the modern motel rooms just a few blocks from Rochford Square you pay only $29, single or double, and this includes tub-shower bathrooms, color cable TV, air conditioning, an indoor pool, and a sauna. Of the 82 rooms, 30 are housekeeping units for which you must pay $35 to $48, single or double. There's a restaurant, and even a beauty parlor all in the same building at 238 Grafton St., corner of Hillsborough. Like other places in town, however, bus tours may take many of the rooms, and rather than have to pay extra for a housekeeping unit, reserve in advance.

If you're willing to travel a mile from the center of town, the **Garden Province Motel** (tel. 902/892-3411), on Hwy. 1 (Trans Canada) just north of the Charlottetown city limits, is a cozy and tidy place to stay. The 12 units are all perfectly kept and fully equipped: tub-shower, color cable TV, and two double beds in each. Prices match the comfort, at $32 single, $35 double, $3 for each extra person. The motel prides itself on its quiet situation and its quiet clientele. It's open year round.

Should you still be hunting for a motel room, you may find it at the **Kirkwood Motor Hotel** (tel. 902/892-4206), 455 University Ave. (which is the Trans Canada, Hwy. 1) in Charlottetown. The Kirkwood has 69 motel rooms with tub-shower and color TV, plus a pool, and while its situation in a shopping area is not exactly bucolic, it does put you within walking distance of shops, services, and the Charlottetown Tourist Information Center. The Kirkwood is open all year, and charges $34 to $42 for its rooms, single or double. It has its own licensed restaurant, and there are others nearby. Here, you're a bit less than a mile—a 15- or 20-minute walk—from downtown Charlottetown.

Charlottetown has a very good selection of tourist homes, but like the motels in the capital, they tend to be filled by people who have made reservations in advance. For location, you can't beat the **Caroma Lodge** (tel. 902/894-9039), a big white house at the corner of Grafton and West Sts., a mere block from Rochford Square and an even shorter distance from the Government House. The nine rooms come with a variety of services and bed configurations, from one double bed through twin beds to a suite which can sleep six and has its own bath-shower. Depending on what you need—private bath or common bath, TV or no TV—you pay $10 to $30 single, $16 to $30 double. Contact them well ahead of time, however, especially for space during August.

Minnie's (tel. 894-7232), at 130 St. Peter's Rd. not far from the airport, is in an inconspicuous brick building which looks little like a restaurant. But park in the lot behind it and you'll come face to face with a rather grand doorway leading to simple but attractive dining rooms. The cuisine is good and somewhat fancy, but always well prepared. Luncheon specials ($3 to $5) are a real bargain, and for that price you might have soup or juice, baked ham or a small cut of sirloin, and coffee. That will satisfy midday cravings, but at dinnertime the menu expands to include steamed mussels ($2) and escargots bourguignons (snails, $3.25), to mention only two of the appetizers. Minnie's goes in strongly for seafood, of course, with sole Marguery (served with a shrimp-and-mushroom sauce) costing $9; it may also be the only place on the island in which you can order chicken Kiev (boned chicken leg rewrapped with cubes of butter and chicken meat, breaded and cooked, $7.85). Chocolate layer cake ($1) is there if you have room. Cocktails cost $1.50 to $2.50, and wines are $9 to $18 for most bottles, although house wines en carafe cost less—about $3.75 to $4.75 for a half liter. Minnie's is open for lunch on weekdays from noon to 2:30 p.m., weekdays and Saturdays for dinner from 5:30 to 10:30 p.m., closed Sundays.

Charlottetown's most convivial gathering place is the **Dispensary** (tel. ·892-5195), 99 Grafton St. near Confederation Plaza. Despite its medical moniker it has nothing to do with first aid, unless it's of the culinary kind served in the popular stone-and-wood lounge: sandwiches, crêpes, and desserts for $2 to $2.50 each. For dinner, though, you'll want to tuck into something more substantial such as tournedos Rossini ($8) or a giant three-pound lobster ($20, serves two). A helping of steamed clams ($3) can start your meal, and peach Melba can finish it off. Wednesday and Saturday nights are the most popular ones at the Dispensary, because that's when the live entertainment comes on. Saturday night, it's fiddlers. But heed a warning: have reservations. The Dispensary lounge is open from 11 a.m. to midnight daily; the dining room stays open an hour later, until 1 a.m.

For Chinese food, try **Chan's** (tel. 894-5444), 51 Grafton at the corner of Pownal. A simple, one-room garden-variety place, Chan's carries on the tradition of offering the lowest priced full meals possible. Here, $4.75 will get you wonton soup, sweet-and-sour spare ribs, chicken chow mein, pork fried rice, a cookie for dessert, and tea. The menu, as is the Chinese custom, goes on forever, but the set dinners offer the best bargain.

WHAT TO SEE: Charlottetown has been going through a period of revitalization, ever since construction of the huge **Confederation Centre of the Arts** beginning in 1960. The Centre, at the corner of Grafton and Queen St., houses a library, theater, museum, and gift shop. The museum and its art gallery are located on the ground floor—enter from the side which faces the old Province House. Entrance is free; hours are 9 a.m. to 8 p.m. daily in July and August; 9 to 5 on every day but Monday the rest of the year.

As you enter the Arts Centre, heading for the attractive gallery, the foyer holds a very handsome chrome-and-crystal sculpture emblazoned with the arms of each Canadian province and territory, a gift from the United States commemorating the centennial anniversary of Canada's confederation in 1967. In the gallery of three floors are notable works by modern Canadian artists. One room is dedicated to the works of Robert Harris, one of Canada's most renowned painters from the turn of the century. Be sure to see also the fine soapstone sculpture of a mother and child by Inukpuk, perhaps Canada's reigning master of this Inuit (Eskimo) art.

Confederation Centre is the focus of the annual **Charlottetown Festival** held from mid-June to mid-September. Guest performers, special shows, and a list of dramatic performances are highlights, and a musical based on Prince Edward Island's own *Anne of Green Gables* is always part of the showbill. Schedules and tickets are at the box office near the corner of Queen and Grafton Sts., or in the foyer of the gallery. For reservations, call 902/892-1267, or stop for tickets between noon and 5:30 p.m. Monday through Saturday.

Next door to Confederation Centre to the east is **Province House,** the "birthplace of Canada." The three-story sandstone building was put up in 1843 as the courthouse and archives, and with a market, office, and post office buildings, it framed Queen's Square Gardens. The other buildings were torn down in 1962 to make way for the Confederation Centre, but you can get a good idea of what it must have been like when the eight delegates walked up Queen St. to sign the confederation papers by visiting the exhibit on Province House's second floor. The garden, with its circular drive and manicured lawns, must have been a delightful place. Province House is the seat of P.E.I.'s legislature, but visitors are welcome free of charge from 9 a.m. to 8 p.m. daily during June through September, 9 to 5 other times of year.

On the first floor to the right as you enter is the room where Canada's confederate life began in 1864. Upstairs, exhibits of photographs and documents bring those momentous days to life. On the third floor are the legislative chambers, also open to visitors. When the house is in session you'll get to see the Speaker in his ceremonial black robes, and the formally clad pages, as well as the attending members.

East of Province House on Church St. is the red sandstone landmark of **St. Paul's Anglican Church,** dating from 1747. St. Paul's is the oldest Protestant church on the island.

South of Province House at the corner of Great George and Richmond Sts. is **St. Dunstan's,** a Roman Catholic church in Gothic style which boasts an elaborate interior. The nave and altar have handsome Italianate carved work, and above the altar is a magnificent medallion stained-glass window.

The street north of and parallel to Grafton St. is Kent St. Walk west on Kent to get a feel for the Victorian soul of Charlottetown, with gabled houses from that era, and spacious parks and gardens. Three blocks from the corner of Queen St. along Kent will bring you to **Beaconsfield,** a marvelous Victorian mansion designed by William Harris, brother of the painter Robert Harris whose work hangs in Confederation Centre. The house dates from 1877, and today is the home of the Prince Edward Island Heritage Foundation. Go in anytime between 9 a.m. and 4 p.m. Monday through Friday for a look at the lovely house, and to see exhibits outlining the history of the capital city. Entrance is free.

Just west of Beaconsfield on the opposite side of Kent is **Victoria Park** and the white mansion of **Government House,** since 1835 the official residence of the lieutenant-governor for Prince Edward Island. The house is not open to visits, although you're free to stroll through the grounds and the park.

Charlottetown is the major center in the east-central part of the island. In the west-central part, activity is focused in and around Summerside.

2. Summerside

Summerside is the commercial center for western P.E.I., and with 10,000 people living here, it's the province's second-largest city. Besides being on the "summer side of the island" to which Charlottetown residents used to move in good weather, the town is famous for its annual **Lobster Festival** which occupies everyone in town for a whole week in mid-July. Lobster feasts are held nightly in the civic stadium, while baseball games, fiddling contests, and other good-time events fill the days and nights.

While you're here, drop in at the new exhibition center called **EPTEK,** near the shopping center on the waterfront. The small gallery has traveling shows of works by Canadian artists, and there's a Sports Hall of Fame as well. Admission to EPTEK is free, and it's open from 1 to 5 p.m. daily except Monday.

WHERE TO STAY AND EAT: Summerside, as the island's western commercial and industrial center, has a good variety of places to stay. In general, prices are well below those of Charlottetown, and here the pleasures of the northern beaches and of Lady Slipper Drive are only a short auto trip away.

First among Summerside's motels is the **Quality Inn—Garden of the Gulf** (tel. 902/436-2295; or toll free in Canada, 800/261-6222; in the U.S., 800/323-5151), 618 Water St. East (Hwy. 1A) right downtown in Summerside. Obviously the poshest place on this side of the island, its 60 rooms all have tub-showers and TVs (20 of which are color), and rent for a reasonable $32, double or single, whether you have one double bed or two. An extra person in a room pays $4. With your room you get these extras: an outdoor heated pool, a beach down on the bay, shuffleboard, a dining room, disco, and poolside lounge for drinks. There's even a nine-hole golf course out back.

Right next door to the Garden of the Gulf, and part of the same operation, is the much-advertised **Brothers Two Restaurant** (tel. 436-9654), run by the same people who operate the T.G.I. Friday's restaurants in various places. Done in eye-catching red and gold, the restaurant offers particularly good prices at lunchtime: seafood chowder for $1.50, a roast beef or club sandwich for $3.25, spaghetti for only a bit more, fish and chips for $4. House wines come by the liter or half liter ($3.25 to $5.90), and there's a children's menu. Double these prices and you'll have the average dinner prices. In Captain Grady's Pub—part of the Brothers Two—there's Irish entertainment from 9 p.m. to 1 a.m., as well as food and drink. As if these two eateries weren't enough, Brothers Two has yet another twist, called the **Governor's Feast.** This dinner-and-a-show requires reservations and costs $13, but for that price you get a set dinner of steamed clams, Malpeque oysters, seafood chowder, lobster, scallops, filet of sole, salad, and bread; dinner is served by a staff dressed in period costumes from 1842 and rehearsed in the songs and dances of the period. Dinner and the show are one and the same, and it all starts at 6:30 each evening during the summer. Call 436-7674 for reservations and ticket information.

For years the most comfortable hostelry in Summerside has been the **Linkletter Motel** (tel. 902/436-2157), 311 Market St., right in the heart of town. The management boasts of a historical connection with earlier Summerside hospitality, for the site of the motel was first the site of an inn called Summerside House, built in 1839 and operated by one Joseph Green. The town took its name from the inn; the motel took its name from one of the families prominent in the area. But history aside, the Linkletter's rooms are all of the modern motel type, and fully appointed: each has color cable TV and bath with tub-shower. There are 55 rooms in all, renting for $25 to $35 single, $28 to $35 double; within this range, you'll probably be charged $28 for a double room with one bed, $31 for a double with two beds—except if you come during the Lobster Carnival in the middle of July. Rates may be a few dollars per room higher at that time.

Downstairs in the **Coach Room** (open 11:30 a.m. to 10 p.m.), you can sit at circular tables in a room with vaguely English decor and dine on salmon ($6) or sirloin ($7), served with vegetable, potato, and salad. Drinks cost about $1.50 to $2, depending on what you have.

East of Summerside on Hwy. 1A are some very reasonably priced accommodations acceptable to any but the most luxury-crazed traveler. The **Sunny Isle Motel** (tel. 902/436-5665), 720 Water St., is on the highway just a mile from the center of town. The motel is surrounded by fine lawns with plots for flowers here and there. All 21 rooms have radio, color TV, and tub-shower bathrooms, but if you get a room numbered from 8 to 22, you'll have a quieter place to stay and also a view of the lawns all the way down to the bay shore.

Prices are super-reasonable: $19 for a single, or for a double room with one bed; $21 for a double with two beds. Highly recommended.

Just across the highway from the Sunny Isle is the equally presentable **Cairns Motel** (tel. 902/436-5841), 721 Water St. Run by a very hospitable couple, the Cairns Motel has rooms and prices virtually identical with those at the Sunny Isle: $19 for a single, or a double with one bed; $21 for two beds; $23 for three people in a room; $25 for four—making this an unbeatable bargain for families.

The **Summerside Motel and Cottages** (tel. 902/436-3865) is slightly farther east of Summerside, and is actually in the suburb of Read's Corner, a mile and a half from the center of Summerside on Hwy. 1A. Besides being able to choose among several sorts of accommodations, at the Summerside you can also find the cheapest double rooms in the area: $12 for two in a tiny cabin with shower (but no TV). Other cabins have two or three bedrooms and cost from $16 to $24 per night. In the more modern motel units, there are ten luxury rooms with bath-shower combinations, black-and-white TV sets, and twin double beds, priced at $24 double per night. Weekly rates are even more reasonable, and you can actually house a family of six in a three-bedroom cabin for as little as $24 per night.

Summerside is not particularly noted as a gastronomic mecca, although the mid-July Lobster Carnival changes this state of affairs somewhat. If you need fast services, good prices, and pleasant surroundings, you might as well drop in at the **Villager Restaurant** in the shopping center known as Summerside Mall. A breakfast special boasts two eggs, bacon, and toast for a mere $1.09; lunch specials might be pepper steak with vegetable and french fries for $2.49, or fish and chips for the same price.

Want to make your own lunch? Start by dropping by the supermarket in Summerside Mall, then head out of town going west on Hwy. 1A. As you leave the commercial district behind and head into residential Summerside, the sea will appear on your left, and **Theresa's bakery** on your right. Theresa makes a fantastic loaf of jogger's bread, a heavy bread of oats, wheat germ, dates, and flour, for 90¢ the (small) loaf. A small loaf goes a long way, but if you need more, try one of her meat pies, with pastries or doughnuts for dessert.

3. Cavendish and the Northern Beaches

It seems that everyone coming to the island is doing so, at least in part, for the beaches. The very best are on the north coast in Prince Edward Island National Park, and, appropriately, there are lots of lodging places right near the beaches. Only one is in the national park proper, but others are a mere kilometer or so away. As many summer visitors come for extended stays, many northern beach hostelries have housekeeping units or cabins which they prefer to rent by the week. Even if you plan to stay for less than a week it's worth giving them a call, as there may be gaps of several days between week-long reservations.

WHERE TO STAY AND EAT: The very best place to stay in Cavendish, in my opinion, is at the **Ingleside Lodge** (tel. 902/963-2431), which is literally a stone's throw from the National Park Visitors' Centre—go through the Cavendish intersection headed for the national park beaches and it'll be on your right. The Ingleside is the best place not just because of its location (within a short stroll of the beaches), but also because of the accommodations and the very pleasant owners. All 19 units are for housekeeping, and some cabins have fireplaces in addition to the kitchenettes. Each has a shower in the bathroom. Prices for a week are $165, $175 (that's with a fireplace), or $185 for one or two people. Some cabins can sleep four or five people, bringing the prices to $215, $240, or $250 for the week. If you're lucky enough to find a cabin free for a day or two, two people will pay $27 to $36 for it, depending on amenities. Reserve as far in advance as possible for these choice rooms. By the way, the day-use vehicle fee ($1) charged for those to drive to the beach doesn't apply to you, as you can walk into the park and to the beach from the Ingleside. Highly recommended.

The **Green Gables Bungalow Court** (tel. 902/963-2722) has it all: a location right next to Green Gables Golf Course (part of the national park), only a short walk to the beaches, and attractive housekeeping units set well back from the road and shaded by trees. The cottages have one, two, or three bedrooms, each with a shower in the bathroom, and prices of $23 to $40 per night, depending on the cabin and the number in the party. The largest cabins can sleep up to eight. No TVs, but you can rent them from a private agency—the management will give you full details. To find the Green Gables if you're coming up Hwy. 13 from Charlottetown, turn left (west) at the Cavendish intersection, and the cabins will be on the left-hand side, only a few dozen yards past the golf course, on Hwy. 6.

Also along this stretch of Hwy. 6 west of the Cavendish intersection is the **Lakeview Lodge and Cottages** (tel. 902/963-2436), 32 attractive housekeeping units of one or two bedrooms with shower (some with tub as well), priced from $25 to $49 per day, $175 to $343 per week. Near the golf course, tennis courts, and not all that far from the beaches, the Lakeview is among the most pleasant and attractive hostelries in the area.

The **Links Inn** (tel. 902/963-2434), bordering on the Green Gables Golf Course (as its name implies), has nine housekeeping cottages, but also 14 overnight rooms. Housekeeping units have showers only, but if you stay in an overnight cabin you get a tub-shower and a black-and-white TV for $28, single or double. In the lodge, overnight rooms come mostly with showers only (although a few have tubs), and without TVs, and cost $20 to $28 single, $24 to $28 double. The inn is on Hwy. 6, just west of the Cavendish intersection.

Other establishments in Cavendish have housekeeping cabins as well, and most are only a few minutes' drive from the national park entrance. The **Anne Shirley Motel and Cabins** (tel. 902/963-2224) takes its name from P.E.I.'s most famous fictional character. On Hwy. 13 just a short distance southwest of the Cavendish intersection, it's within walking distance of the beaches and right next door to the town's Tourist Information Centre. Although it's in a busy spot, it's set well back from the highway. The motel has 18 overnight rooms and 20 housekeeping units, most with tub-shower and black-and-white TV. On a daily basis, two people sharing the same room and the same bed pay $22, or $35 if they want separate double beds; in a housekeeping cabin, a double costs $28 per night. Weekly rates depend on which unit you choose (some are newer and more modern than others) and how many people occupy it, and the cost can be anywhere from $108 to $335 per week.

If it's a motel you're looking for, my favorite is the **Bay Vista Motor Inn** (tel. 902/675-2225), on Hwy. 6 several miles west of the Cavendish intersection. While it's not immediately convenient to the beaches, the drive is still a short one, and out where the Bay Vista is located one gets away from the traffic and activity of Cavendish. Peaceful, rolling farm country, marsh, and a pond or two make the motel's setting. The 38 units are predominantly for overnight guests, although ten have kitchenettes as well. Rooms have the standard motel comforts and conveniences, including tub-showers and TV sets, and some not-so-standard views of the pretty farmlands, woods, and water. The staff is friendly and the prices are reasonable: $28 for two in a double bed, $32 for two in two double beds, up to a top price of $46 for four people in a housekeeping unit. One of Cavendish's best restaurants, **Fiddles 'n' Vittles**, is right next to the motel. You'll meet the staff from the one place if you visit the other. Recommended.

You will see the **Cavendish Motel** (tel. 902/963-2244) dominating the intersection of Hwys. 13 and 6 in Cavendish. It's a modern place with the comforts of a luxury motel: color TV sets, tub-showers, and a heated outdoor swimming pool. Most rooms have two double beds, and with a roll-away, families of five can be set up very nicely. The national park beaches are an easy five-minute walk. But the location is the most frenetic in all P.E.I., and prices for the luxury accommodations are the most expensive in the area: $31 to $45 per unit (taking from two to five people).

Cavendish proper harbors some tourist homes, but the most beautiful ones are scattered through the lovely scenery west of the Cavendish intersection, along Hwy. 6. The **Sunny Acres Tourist Home** (tel. 902/963-2721) has an exceptionally pretty setting, well off the road on a farm. The five rooms rent to overnight guests for $7 to $10; all the rooms share one bathroom.

Continuing west along Hwy. 6, the stretch of road between New London and Kensington has an exceptionally rich concentration of nice tourist homes, all renting rooms with double beds for about $10 per room (shared bath, of course). Two of my favorites are the **Stone House Farm** (tel. 902/886-2651), only five miles from Kensington; and **Whitehead's Tourist Home,** near Margate, with four rooms for rent. If these are full, drive along this section of Hwy. 6 for a look at many other possibilities.

One of the north beach's best all-around restaurants, serving seafood, meats, and poultry, and with a liquor license, is the **Idle Oars Restaurant** (tel. 963-2534), in North Rustico. Breakfast, lunch, and dinner are all served here (a rarity) as the Idle Oars opens at 9:30 a.m. and closes at 11 p.m. You dine in bright and modern surroundings in a large room with lots of windows overlooking the farming country which surrounds the place. Prices are moderate: a lobster dinner, with juice and dessert, is $11, but you can have fish and chips for $3.60, or the fabulous fisherman's platter of lobster, scallops, clams, halibut, and smelts for $7.80. Hamburgers, sandwiches, and other light-lunch fare are priced from $1 to $2. There is a special children's menu. The Idle Oars is open only during the summer season, of course.

In 1895, a graceful mansion rose on the north shore of Prince Edward Island. Its owner was Alexander MacDonald, a partner with John D. Rockefeller in the Standard Oil Company. As you can imagine, no expense was spared in building Mr. MacDonald's magnificent "summer cottage." You can enjoy the lavish place today, because it is operated as a hotel by the national park. **Dalvay-by-the-Sea Hotel** (tel. 902/672-2048; in winter, 902/892-0488) is off Rte. 25 in the national park grounds just before you come to Dalvay Beach. Rooms in the mansion are rented by the week with all three meals included; all have private bath. With twin beds, a double room costs $68 to $76 per day for the week; a room with double bed is $66 for two, per day for the week. Single rooms cost $40 per day for the week. Two cottages are attached to the hotel's operation. The "Governor General's Cottage" costs $35 to $37 per person and the "Lake Cottage" costs $72 to $144, depending on how many occupants rent it—capacity, two to five. A third person in a double room pays $18; special rates apply on children sharing their parents' room. Besides grandeur, good food, and Dalvay Beach, the mansion offers lovely grounds, two tennis courts, a bowling green, a children's playground, a driving range, Ping-Pong, canoeing, and boating. Dalvay-by-the-Sea has only 26 bedrooms, and demand for this northern Shangri-La is intense, so reserve as far in advance as possible; and remember, you must rent a room for a week or more.

Brackley Beach has a gracious old resort hotel and cottages tucked away down a long drive. It's **Shaw's Hotel** (tel. 902/672-2022), a small old Victorian hotel kept immaculately, its white-and-red exterior looking like the day it was built. The public rooms and guest rooms have been modernized to make them comfortable, but not enough to remove their charm. Shaw's is a resort in that the beach is only a five-minute walk away, and rooms rent with breakfast and dinner included in the rates. The cottages, which hold ten rooms, do not have housekeeping facilities as occupants dine in the hotel dining room. All cottages have bathrooms, with tub-shower combinations. Nine of the hotel rooms have similar facilities. A single person pays $27.50 per day for room and two meals; couples pay from $55 to $70 in the hotel, $40 in the cottages. An extra person pays $15 to $25 in the hotel, $20 in the cabins. The dining room is licensed. Shaw's is open only for the tourist season, from June 15 to September 10. To get there, look for the signs on Rte. 15 near Brackley Beach.

LOBSTER SUPPERS AND OTHER FARE: Prince Edward Island is famous for its lobster suppers, and this is not so much because of what is eaten—lots of places throughout Atlantic Canada and New England serve lobster—but because of how it's eaten. No doubt the idea began as a fundraising plan for the local church, when members of the congregation were invited to bring a covered dish of something to be shared, and the church would provide the lobsters. Everyone would pay a nominal amount, the church would make some money for charitable causes, and all would go home well fed.

Things have changed a bit from this original plan, but not much. Diners have their lobster supper in the church hall or basement, each gets a lobster and other fixings such as potato salad, tossed salad, rolls, corn on the cob, steamed clams, vegetables, cole slaw, french fries or baked potato, dessert, etc. For spouses, children, and relatives who don't like lobster, roast beef (hot or cold) is often served as a second choice. The atmosphere is simple but very convivial, and the food is plenteous and good. Prices these days run about $10 for the entire evening, with variations up to a dollar more or less. Churches, social clubs, and other organizations host the suppers occasionally, or even on a regular basis during the tourist-thronged summer months, and trade is always brisk. In fact, in July and August it's not unusual to wait for an hour or more in line to get a seat (no reservations accepted), and that's where the recommendations below come in. You can save a lot of time and frustration by knowing the situation before setting out for dinner.

Several institutions serve the dinners every night, and have become famous for them, with picture postcards of the groaning board in motel lobbies, and large advertisements in local newspapers. There are important differences, though, which you should know about:

New Glasgow Lobster Suppers (tel. 964-2870) is perhaps the most famous. Service is in the basement of the town recreation center, and music from a Hammond organ accompanies your dinner. Two points you should note: at New Glasgow, the lobster is hot, but virtually everything else from the roast beef alternative to the vegetables is in a cold format; and the waiting lines to get into the New Glasgow suppers can be an hour or even longer. Tour buses abound. If you go, go early. The suppers are served in the tiny town of New Glasgow on Rte. 224 from mid-June to the beginning of October, with July and

August the very busy months. Dinner is served from 4 to 8:30 p.m. No wine, beer, or liquor is served.

St. Ann's Church Suppers (tel. 964-2351 or 964-2385) is not far from New Glasgow at Hope River on Rte. 224. It has advantages of being licensed (wine and beer are served), and for those who don't want lobster the alternative is a steak. St. Ann's is also very popular and crowded in July and August. Dinners are served from 4 to 9 p.m. from late June to early September.

At the **New London Lions' Club** (tel. 886-2599), you dine in the cozy hall of the club, and you can have a drink in the lounge beforehand if you wish. Late June to early September is the season; 4 to 8:30 p.m. is the time. The Lions' Club is on Rte. 6 not far from the center of New London. Special note: the Lions' Club also has a fantastic buffet luncheon where you can eat all you want (no lobsters, though) at a very reasonable price.

Brackley Beach Lobsters Suppers (tel. 672-2352 or 672-2997) are held in Howe's Hall, about two miles from the center of Brackley Beach, on Rte. 15. You can have breakfast here from 8:30 to 11 a.m., or the lobster supper from 4 to 8:30 p.m.; take-out service is also available should there be too large a sit-down crowd.

Arrangements, times, season, and price are all virtually the same at the **Borden Kinsmen Lobster Suppers** (tel. 855-2477) in Borden. Crowds tend not to be so great as Borden is some distance from the northern beaches resort area.

RESTAURANT LOBSTER SUPPERS: As lobster suppers proved so popular and people were waiting in long lines to get in, several local restaurants decided to get into the act serving similar fare at similar prices, and usually without the same long waiting lines.

Fiddles 'n' Vittles (tel. 963-2225) is right next to the Bay Vista Motor Inn, several miles west of the Cavendish intersection on Hwy. 6. It's a plain-looking place from the outside, but the inside is cozy and attractive, with a raised level surrounding a square-dance floor—at one time fiddlers played for Saturday dancing here, but now the floor is crowded with more dining tables. The staff is made up of local young people who are super-friendly and anxious to please, and the background music is usually of country-style violins. The lobster dinner includes various vegetables, potato salad or cole slaw, rolls and lots of butter, plus a lobster, and is priced at $10—for what you get it's almost the same as in the famous "lobster supper" places. You can start with Malpeque oysters for $2.85. The wine list is short but decently priced for P.E.I., and you may pay from $9 to $15 for a bottle to accompany your dinner. Beer (local) is $1.25; whiskey and such drinks are $2 to $2.50. Fiddles 'n' Vittles is open daily from late June through early September from 4:30 to 9 p.m. Their busiest season is the last three weeks in July and the first two in August. Seafood lovers will find they can come back to Fiddles 'n' Vittles and try the other items such as scallops, fried clams, and fish, while meat eaters can always get chicken, steak, or chops.

The **Stanhope Beach Lodge-Motel** (tel. 902/672-2047) adds a different twist to the "lobster supper" theme. Here the evening repast is a lobster smorgasbord—as much as you can eat for $12.50 per person ($6.50 for children), plus tax and tip. At this price it's essential to have a reservation; make yours as far ahead as possible. You'll dine in the lodge's attractive dining room, which is fully licensed. Stanhope Beach Lodge is on Rte. 25 in Covehead, 14 miles from Charlottetown, and only a short distance from the grounds of the national park.

The guest rooms at Stanhope Beach Lodge are almost as popular as the lobster smorgasbords. Modern motel-style rooms in a separate building have shower-bath combinations and television sets, and rent for $32 to $35 per night. These are in hot demand, so reserve ahead. But the real bargain here are the older rooms in the lodge proper, which are in the style of turn-of-the-century resort hotel rooms without private bath or television. These cost $25 to $27 double, and are well worth it when you consider that the Stanhope Beach Lodge has its own tennis courts, sailboats, and rowboats, and a beach nearby. The lodge has 31 rooms; the motel annex, 17. The setting, on rolling green lawns near the water, is very fine.

4. Lady Slipper Drive

Like most of Prince Edward Island, the region along Lady Slipper Drive is agricultural. The farms are meticulously cared for, with neat and sometimes surprisingly bright-colored farmhouses. You'll pass field after field of potatoes, the green-leafed plants topping long mounds, a few white flowers at the top of each plant. Tomatoes, tobacco, wheat, corn, and other crops grow well on the island too, but this is predominantly spud country.

Expanses of tilled fields end at patches of clover, or hills covered in wildflowers, or down in cattail-lined bottoms. Here and there you'll spot a herd of the Holsteins which provide the basis of the island's dairy-farming and beef industry. And nearby, always a handsome weathered-shingle barn or a steep-gabled farmhouse. Western Prince Edward Island contains some of the prettiest farm country in all North America.

Following Rte. 1A from Summerside, go to St. Eleanors, and then follow Rte. 2 west to Miscouche. Right on the highway in Miscouche is the **Acadian Museum,** in a small log cabin—look for the antique carriage out front, being pulled by a cut-out horse. Sisters in the Notre Dame Convent, next door to the museum, founded the little collection in 1964 and have been improving it since that time. The two small rooms hold farming tools, kitchen utensils, a four-poster feather bed, and a fascinating handmade high chair which easily converts into a rocking chair or stroller for the baby. Photographs and memorabilia of the early Acadian settlers provide a candid look at life in the old days. The serious-minded faces in the photos of the old families—Arsenaults, Gallants, Gaudets, Dorions—show them to have been hard-working, peace-loving homebodies. The Acadians lived in friendship with the MicMac Indians, as shown by traces of intermarriage in the photos, although other settlers battled with the Indians constantly. The 17,000 Acadians still on P.E.I. today are often the ones who operate the tidy farms in this western region; about 6000 still speak French as their first language. Don't miss the three portraits on the right wall as you enter, of couples who have identical features even down to the facial lines, which seems to prove conclusively that couples do indeed start to resemble one another if they live together long enough.

The Acadian Museum is open every day during July and August from 10 a.m. to 6 p.m. (Sundays, 1 to 6); $1 for adults, 50¢ for children. By the way, the flag which flies in front of the museum is the Acadian flag, designed here at the second national Acadian convention in 1884 to symbolize the cultural unity of the Acadian people. The flag combines the French tricolor with a yellow "star of the sea," and is used throughout eastern Canada wherever Acadians have settled.

From Miscouche, take Rte. 12 northwest toward Grand River, a bucolic village highlighted by its pale yellow church with white trim. North of Grand River the road follows the curve of Malpeque Bay, famed for its delicate-tasting oysters. At Port Hill, stop to see **Green Park Provincial Historic Park,** centered on the elegant old home of 19th-century shipbuilding magnate James Yeo, Jr. Besides the fine mansion furnished with period pieces and peopled with guides in period costume, the park has a modern exhibit building with displays outlining the history of shipbuilding in P.E.I., and the ruins of Mr. Yeo's shipyard down by the water.

Buy your tickets, good for all the sights in the park, at the modern building next to the parking lot ($1 per person, children under 12 free). The house was built in 1865, and you can wander as you like through its three floors, even clambering up to the widow's walk for the panoramic view. Look for such oddities as the green glass "lusters" on the mantelpiece in one room, the old foot bath, the marble occasional tables, the four-poster beds, and the intriguing gadgets in the kitchen, laundryroom, and pantry. Green Park, besides being a historical park, is a provincial park with areas for camping, picnicking, and swimming in Malpeque Bay.

Back on Rte. 12, you have a chance to sample the famous Malpeque oysters close to the source at **The Wayton** (tel. 831-2431), a small restaurant very near the intersection of Rtes. 12 and 133, in the tiny settlement of Ellerslie Bideford. The oysters here—and they don't serve them if they're not absolutely fresh—cost $3.25 the half dozen. Daily platters are very reasonably priced, and a brace of pork chops with apple sauce ($4.90), or a hamburger steak with juice, roll, dessert, and coffee ($4), will set you up for the rest of the drive. The Wayton is open from 9 a.m. to 9 p.m. Monday through Saturday, from 11 a.m. to 8 p.m. on Sunday.

Continuing along Rte. 12 brings you to the junction with Rte. 163, the turnoff for the **MicMac Indian Reservation** on Lennox Island. In the settlement is a small museum outlining the history of the tribe (it's right across the street from the church). Nearby is an Indian craft shop operated by Ray Sark, a MicMac whose father and grandfather were both chiefs of the island tribe. Ray is an extremely pleasant and helpful man—typical of most P.E.I. residents—devoted to the promotion of craftwork. His shop is stuffed with all types of beadwork, woodcarving, leather items, and curiosities such as porcupine-quill boxes. The crafts represent many tribes in Canada, not just the MicMacs, and his whole stock is of genuine Canadian handmade pieces.

Rte. 12 continues along to Alberton, where the **Alberton Museum** holds a collection of antiques, mementos, and furnishings used by the pioneers of P.E.I. It's in an old barn in the center of town, open in July and August from 10 a.m. to 5 p.m. daily, closed Sunday; adults pay 80¢ to get in, and children under 12 are admitted for free.

If you still have plenty of time left in your day, you can circle the North Cape on Rtes. 12 and 14, stopping at Tignish, a town rich in Acadian heritage. But if the day is wearing on, take Rte. 2 south and east for an express trip back to Summerside. Just after the road crosses Grand River, turn right onto Rte. 124 for a detour to Mount Carmel at the southern tip of Prince County and **Le Village des Pionniers Acadiens,** near the junction of Rtes. 124 and 11. The village, a faithful reproduction of a settlement from the early days of Acadian life here in the beginning of the 1800s, has a school, a store, a church, and all the other necessities of civilized town life. The journey back into the Acadian past can be made any day between 10 a.m. and 7 p.m. for $1 per adult, 50¢ per child.

5. Blue Heron Drive

The most popular attraction of this drive around the central portion of Prince Edward Island is the long, glittering stretch of sandy beach washed by the warm Gulf Stream waters of the north coast. All the best beaches are within **Prince Edward Island National Park,** and a fee of $1 per day, $2 for four days, per automobile is charged for entrance. If you're on foot, you don't have to pay. Once into the national park, you can go to Cavendish, Brackley, Stanhope, or Dalvay Beaches, use the changing rooms and showers, eat at the picnic areas, and walk through the lawns and woods at no extra fee.

From Charlottetown, Rte. 15 goes northwest to join Rte. 6., which skirts the northern shore passing through small summer-resort towns, and past many of the various tourist attractions and amusement parks on the island: the Royal Atlantic Wax Museum, Rainbow Valley, the Enchanted Castle, and other sites. The places which draw the most interest are those associated with P.E.I.'s own famous author Lucy Maud Montgomery, and with her storybook heroine named Anne Shirley, of Green Gables. One mile west of Cavendish on Rte. 6 is **Green Gables House,** the farmhouse where Anne Shirley, an orphan girl, was taken in by Matthew and Marilla Cuthbert. The house is open for visits from mid-May to mid-October from 9 a.m. to 8 p.m., at other times of the year from 9 a.m. to 5 p.m. Entrance is free as the house is part of the national park. Picnic areas and recreation facilities nearby are free, and part of the park as well.

If you continue east on Rte. 6, you'll come to a **stable** offering trail rides of three miles, 45 minutes, for $6 per person. The mounts are docile, but if you want to bring a child less than 7 years of age, you'll have to convince the ride leader about his or her riding ability. Kids love just being around the horses, and here you can do just that until 7:30 in the evening any summer night.

Rainbow Valley, a 30-acre amusement area east of Cavendish on Rte. 6, has pretty landscaped grounds, a pond for boating, a barn full of things for the kids to look at, and a gift shop in the shape of a flying saucer. Although the gifts may not be out of this world, your young children will think the park is just that. Open June through September from 9 a.m. to dusk (Sundays, from 1 p.m. to dusk), entrance to the park costs $2 for adults, $1.50 for kids 5 to 15, free for preschoolers.

Another location rich in Anne Shirley lore is the **Anne of Green Gables Museum** at Park Corner on Rte. 20, less than five miles north of the intersection with Rte. 6. The house, built in 1872 by John Campbell, was the home of John and his wife Annie Laura MacNeill. Annie was Lucy Maud Montgomery's aunt, and young Lucy spent a good deal of time here collecting, as it turned out, material for stories she was later to write. Lucy had her wedding here in 1911, and visitors today can see the organ on which the wedding music was played, as well as the author's childhood room. Young girls who have read the "Anne" books will be thrilled to see so many objects and places which became parts of the romantic stories. The museum is open from 8 a.m. to 10 p.m. daily, for $1.25 per adult, 50¢ per child.

Along the southern parts of the Blue Heron Trail are several provincial parks with beaches, campgrounds and picnic areas, and the turnoff for Borden, departure point for car ferries to Cape Tormentine, New Brunswick. The trail eventually joins the Trans Canada Hwy. to reenter Charlottetown.

6. King's Byway

If western P.E.I. is traditionally Acadian French, the island's eastern reaches are still predominantly peopled by the descendants of early Scottish settlers, as a quick look at place names on the map will show. Farming and fishing are the prime occupations here, with tourism adding a healthy boost to the local economy. King's Byway begins in Charlottetown, and then wanders west and south along the coast past numerous beaches and pretty provincial parks, most notable of which is Lord Selkirk Provincial Park, named for the man who brought a large group of Scottish settlers to the island in 1803. At Wood Islands you'll pass near the car-ferry dock to Caribou, Nova Scotia.

Nearest hostelry to the Wood Islands car-ferry dock is the **Meadow Lodge Motel** (tel. 902/962-2022), only a mile from the dock and the beaches on the Trans Canada Hwy. Of the 20 motel units here grouped in a U shape around a grassy lawn and flagpole, 18 have bath-shower combinations, and two have only showers. All have black-and-white TV sets; one room has kitchen facilities. Room rates are the same whether one or two persons use a room; an extra person costs $3. Prices go from $22 to $36, depending on the number of beds and bedrooms (some units have two bedrooms) and whether or not you want the one unit with kitchen facilities. The motel's restaurant is not on the grounds, but down by the ferry docks.

Not far from Murray River, your kids may want to make a detour to **Fantasyland Provincial Park,** an outdoor amusement area for children and their parents established and operated by the provincial government. Statues of fairytale characters people the wooded grounds, picnic tables provide just the place for an outdoor lunch, and a nearby beach is just right for a cooling dip. Entrance to the park is free.

North of Murray River, King's Byway follows Rte. 17 north and east, although many people turn left onto Rte. 4 instead, not to miss **Buffaloland** and its small herd of American bison. Just a few miles' drive north, and you're at **Moore's Migratory Bird Sanctuary.** Bird lover Harvey Moore founded the sanctuary years ago, and his benevolent attitude allowed dozens of different species of waterfowl to thrive here, as they still do. Stop for a look at the Canadian geese—often the tiny goslings will be here, too—and perhaps a blue goose plus various types of ducks. Free pamphlets will guide you on a nature trail in the sanctuary. Several years ago the provincial authorities bought the land from Mr. Moore's widow, and founded the Harvey Moore Wildlife Management Area (as the sanctuary is now called), open free to the public.

Only a few miles from the Moore sanctuary is the town of Montague.

Montague

Montague is the commercial center for the eastern coast of P.E.I., and while it's not at all a large town, it has several very recommendable places to stay and eat.

A popular, modern motel near Montague is the **Kingsway Motel** (tel. 902/838-2112), at Poole's Corner, which is the intersection of Rtes. 3 and 4, three miles from Montague. Some of the units here have big picture windows, all have flower boxes on the front and comfy furnishings within, including TVs (in most cases, color sets). You pay $20 to $26 single, $24 to $30 double per night, and an extra person in the room pays a mere $2. Ten of the 28 rooms have housekeeping facilities for preparing your own meals, or you can dine in the motel's lobby restaurant. The licensed lounge has live entertainment on weekends in season, and is open from 11 a.m. to midnight.

If you'd rather have a little cottage all to yourself, you can't do better than one at **Lane's Tourist Court** (tel. 902/838-2433), in Montague down a side street: just follow the signs. John and Barb Morse have recently acquired the little white cottages, and they're out to please. Each cottage has a shower, good views of the water and the forest, and six out of ten have housekeeping facilities. You can walk to everything in Montague from here, but the location is very peaceful. The overnight cottages rent for $15 double, the housekeeping ones for $20 double—a bargain for sure.

At **Fraser's Cottages** (tel. 902/838-2453) the cottages are bright red and extra-large, with either two or three bedrooms, and fully equipped with housekeeping facilities. You have to follow the signs to find Fraser's as it's down a dirt road outside of Montague, on the north side of the Montague River. There are ten cottages in all, going for $22 double, $26 for four people, $30 for six people. Although you're not far from Montague here, you're certainly in a quiet, bucolic hideaway far from anything which could be called frantic.

The **Lobster Shanty North** (tel. 902/838-2463), on Main St. (Rte. 17) just outside Montague, attracts a young crowd of guests who come to stay in the mod-rustic rooms ($23.50 to $29.50), or to dine in the rough-wood dining room. Seafood takes predominance on the menu, of course, with a P.E.I. Sampler ($9.50) having a prominent place: it's the Lobster Shanty's assorted seafood platter, including half a lobster. For big eaters, the surf 'n' turf costs $15.

An Island Resort

Certainly not all accommodations on Prince Edward Island are in hotels, motels, or tourist homes. For instance, on King's Byway, Rte. 3 not far from Georgetown, is **Brudenell** (tel. 902/652-2332; in winter, 902/893-8527). Operated by a provincial authority, Brudenell is a modern resort complex which includes a heated swimming pool, tennis, shuffleboard, an 18-hole golf course, lawn bowling, canoe and bicycle rentals, outdoor games, and a day camp and babysitting service for children. The layout is spacious, with over 1400 acres of lawns, beaches, and woodlands on Cardigan Bay. Guests stay in 50 one-room chalets, and use the lodge (a modernized P.E.I. farmhouse) for dining, snacks, its bar facilities, and for other indoor activities like movies, Bingo, and nature talks.

The chalets all have two double beds, and rent for $30 per day, $200 per week for two people; an additional person pays $4 per day, $25 per week. Children under 12 can stay for free with their parents (cribs and cots cost a few dollars). These rates apply during the "season," mid-June to the first week in September. In early June and in the balance of September until the resort closes, off-season rates about 12% lower apply.

Remember to bring your whites for tennis and lawn bowling. Another activity, in nearby Georgetown, is the **King's Theatre** which hosts summer stock productions in high season. Brudenell is beautiful, reasonably priced, and very popular, and you should have reservations well in advance, although it doesn't hurt to call and ask if there have been cancellations should you arrive without them.

North of Brudenell resort, King's Byway follows the sinuous coastline past beaches and through fishing areas up to Souris.

Souris

You can stay overnight in Souris, should that fit in with your tour of the King's Byway. The **Lord Rollo Motel** (tel. 902/687-2339) is in Souris West on the Lower Rollo Bay Rd., about 1½ miles before coming to Souris proper. Open during July and August only, the Lord Rollo's modern rooms mostly have showers, although a few have baths as well; two of the 17 units have kitchen facilities. A single person pays $14; two persons pay $16 to $26, the high price being for the housekeeping units, of course.

More modest accommodations at very attractive prices are yours at the **Souris West Motel and Cottages** (tel. 902/687-2676), on Rte. 2 just west of Souris, on the north side of the highway, half hidden by trees and bushes. Seven motel rooms and three housekeeping cottages all have bathtubs and black-and-white televisions, and rent for $14 single, $16 double for the rooms, $20 for the cottages.

From Souris, you can double back and cut due west across to St. Peter's on Rte. 2 if time is short, or you can continue north on King's Byway. Take a detour by turning left at South Lake onto Rte. 16A to reach the tiny hamlet of **Elmira**, the terminus of P.E.I.'s railroad line. Passenger trains are a thing of the past on the island, although a certain amount of freight is still carried. But the Elmira station has been turned into a railroad buff's museum, where memorabilia of the great age of steam revive the days of chuffing locomotives and happy excursionists.

North Lake Harbour, a short distance north of Elmira, is a center for deep-sea tuna fishing, one of P.E.I.'s most famous sports. While hauling in one of the tremendous denizens after an exhausting fight of an hour or more is the thrill of a lifetime, not every boat that goes out comes back with a tuna. Boats put out at breakfasttime with amateur fishermen aboard, all equipped by the captain for a fee of $25 to $40 per person. Note especially that if you hook a tuna—it may weigh up to half a ton!—you only carry away with you the memory of the struggle, because the captain of the boat legally owns the fish no matter who catches it. He'll probably sell it to an outfit who will ship it to Japan, where lax laws on mercury content allow the giant fish to be cut up and sold as a delicacy.

Like the southern stretch of King's Byway, the northern portion winds its way along the coast past provincial parks and beaches, and ultimately brings you to Tracadie Cross, where you can turn right to get to the northern beaches and the P.E.I. National Park, or left to return to Charlottetown.

7. Magdalen Islands (Îles de la Madeleine)

Although they're nearer than predominantly English-speaking Atlantic provinces, the Magdalen Islands are an outpost of Québec far out in the Gulf of St. Lawrence. The several islands are joined to one another by long sand spits which make marvelous beaches, as hordes of young Québecois have discovered. Accommodations and services are very limited, and demand usually outstrips supply.

Québecair and **Eastern Provincial Airways** fly to Havre-aux-Maisons, and the **Cooperative de Transport Maritime** (C.T.M.A.) operates a weekly boat from Montréal via Québec City to Cap-aux-Meules, called *Le Madeleine*. It carries only 12 passengers, who pay $250 each for a one-week cruise to the islands from Montréal or Québec, and return. More frequent and commodious service is operated out of Souris by the M/V *Lucy Maud Montgomery*, capable of taking 70 cars and 330 passengers on the five-hour trip to the islands. Passengers pay $13 each way; cars pay $24 (driver not included). Ship space is limited, and one cannot reserve space from Souris (for cars), although reservations can be made for the return trip from the islands at Cap-aux-Meules or by calling 418/986-4624. During the busy summer months, the *Lucy* makes about ten trips per week, leaving Souris at 2 p.m.

Chapter VI

NEWFOUNDLAND AND LABRADOR

1. Port aux Basques and Corner Brook
2. The Great Northern Peninsula
3. From Deer Lake to Gander
4. Onward to Avalon
5. St. John's
6. Labrador

DRAMATIC SCENERY and a sense of adventure fill any journey to Newfoundland. Although the island was one of the first European landfalls in the New World (John Cabot touched here in 1497, the Vikings even earlier), Newfoundland is still sparsely populated. Labrador is even more so.

All of this land, with few people, makes the province perfect for outdoor adventures. The glacial lakes and streams are full of fish from trout to salmon; moose, caribou, and smaller game roam freely over the vast forests and bogs; and seabirds flock along the rugged coasts. Those interested in **hunting and fishing** in the province should get a copy of the booklet entitled *Newfoundland Labrador Fishing and Hunting Guide,* published annually and distributed free by the Tourist Services Division of the Department of Tourism and Recreation, Confederation Building, St. John's, Newfoundland. Sometimes you will find the brochure at tourism information offices.

Whether you're out for sport or just to watch birds, examine wild orchids, and admire the breathtaking scenery, you'll enjoy your trip more if you have a car. While transport does exist between the major towns, you'll need a car to strike out on your own into the country. Rental agencies can be found in St. John's and Corner Brook. (For Labrador, forget the car—you need a seaplane.)

Until 1949, Newfoundland was a separate British colony, unrelated to Canada except by friendly neighborliness. In that year the natives decided that union with Canada was in their interests—the busy time of World War II, with important Allied airbases providing a vital link between North America and Europe, was over. Stagnation had begun to set in, but confederation with Canada brought a shot of new vigor. As a reminder of its long and colorful colonial period, Newfoundland retained the British Union Jack as its provincial flag.

The English first set foot on the island at the end of the 1400s, interested in the incredible marine wealth of the Grand Banks. Other European nations were not long in discovering the seemingly inexhaustible supplies of nourishing codfish to be had from the Grand Banks, and soon Newfoundland was hotly disputed by the English, French, and Dutch as the base for Grand Banks fishing. Challenged in their ownership for centuries, the British finally gained undisputed control of the island with the victory of Col. William Amherst in St. John's, in 1762. Pirates—Americans and others—raided thereafter, but rule of the island was never in doubt.

Remote from the mainlands of Europe and North America, Newfoundland developed a lively and colorful folk life of its own, based on life in the interior wilds and fishing along the coasts. "Newfie" talk was—and sometimes still is—salted with quaint expressions and hilarious turns of phrase, and not a small dose of folk wisdom. Odd place names given by early explorers continue to delight anyone who pores over a map of the island: Blow Me Down, Tickle Cove, Little Heart's Ease, Sitdown Pond, Joe Batts Arm (that's the name of a town)—hours of driving pass like minutes if someone in the car searches for the delightful names, and reads them off. Speaking of names, "Newfoundland" is officially pronounced "new-found-*land*," to sound like "un-der-*stand*."

Share in the folklore by doing what Newfies do. The favorite sport is "cod-jigging." Just take a length of fishing line, a hook, and a bit of bait, and plop it into the sea. Before you know it, you've got a cod on the line. The cod can serve as the basis for the island's folk delicacies: cod tongues, fried in batter, are a treat once you get past certain anatomical associations. Then there's "fish and brewis" (that's "brooze"): codfish soaked overnight to get out the brine, cooked with boiled hardtack (thick unleavened bread—today stale bread is often used), and topped with fried bits of pork, called "scrunchions." Some Newfies can even do without the brewis, in which case the dish is "cod and scrunchions." For dessert you've got to get some bake-apple berries, a locally found cousin of the raspberry which, with some sugar, tastes amazingly like baked apples. If all this is too exotic, fall back on other, more familiar, Newfie treats: fresh brook trout, Atlantic salmon, herring, or halibut.

Before you plunge into your Newfoundland adventure, note: Newfoundland and Labrador are on "Newfoundland Time," a half hour ahead of Atlantic Time. When you board the ferryboat at North Sydney, or the plane at Halifax, set your watch ahead 30 minutes. Also, be aware that rooms in the province are subject to a whopping 11% tax.

Some final figures: the province of Newfoundland and Labrador has a population of close to 600,000 people, almost a quarter of whom live in or near St. John's. The island has 6000 miles of roads, and almost 11,000 miles of coastline. Temperatures along the east coast are moderate all year round due to the warm Gulf Stream currents—but when this flow meets the chilly Arctic Stream coming from the north, there's bound to be fog.

GETTING THERE: The Trans Canada Hwy. reaches across the sea from North Sydney, Nova Scotia, to Port aux Basques, Newfoundland—on paper at least. By the terms of the 1949 agreement whereby Newfoundland became part of Canada, the ferry across the Cabot Strait is legally part of the highway. In fact, the ferry operation is so big, it is indeed almost like a highway across the water. Details:

By Ferry

Two ways exist to get to Newfoundland: by air, or by ferryboat, the latter being the continuation of any car, bus, or rail trip. The terminal for ferries to Port aux Basques (6 hours away) and Argentia (18 hours away) is at North Sydney, Nova Scotia. CN Marine's mammoth ocean-going ferries depart North Sydney three or four times daily in high summer, twice daily September through early June, with a similar number of boats making the return run. Between North Sydney and Argentia, ferries operate only from mid-June to mid-September, departing North Sydney on Mondays, Wednesdays, and Fridays; and departing Argentia on Tuesdays, Thursdays, and Saturdays in late June and early September. In July and August, however, boats leave North Sydney Sunday through Friday, and Argentia Monday through Saturday.

Fares are surprisingly reasonable: North Sydney to Port aux Basques is $6 per adult, $2.50 per child 5 through 12, slightly more on summer weekends. One-way car transport costs $18 normally, $25 on summer weekends. Between North Sydney and Argentia fares are higher, of course, and you may want to rent a cabin for the overnight voyage, or at least a comfy reclining seat. The simple passage fare is $15 per adult, $7.50 per child 5 through 12; cars cost $40; cabins cost $9 per berth, $16 per berth in deluxe cabins with two single beds, shower, and toilet. A "Daynighter" reclining chair costs $4.50. For my wife and I, with our car and a normal, two-berth cabin, plus dinner and breakfast in the ship's cafeteria, the total cost came to $104, one way. Cabin and car space on the North Sydney–Argentia run is always heavily booked well in advance, which brings me to the topic of reservations.

CN Marine recommends that *all* passengers on its two Newfoundland ferry runs make advance reservations. For one thing, it helps them arrange the flow of traffic. But this is not always easy. In summer, the toll-free numbers are often busy for long periods, and if you run into this problem, spend the money to make a regular call to one of the local numbers listed. Call toll free: in central and eastern Canada, 800/565-9411; in the northeastern U.S., 800/341-7981; in Maine, 800/432-7344. Or call these local numbers (paying normal long-distance charges): in North Sydney, N.S., 902/794-7203; in Port aux Basques, Nfld., 709/695-2124; in Argentia, Nfld., 709/227-2311.

If you don't succeed in getting through and you arrive without a car or cabin reservation, here's what you should do: from North Sydney to Port aux Basques, if you're on foot, don't worry as there will be plenty of space. If you're in a car, however, you should try very hard to arrive the night before the day you want to sail; get your tickets, get a waiting-line number, and park your car in line. You can sleep in your car, using the facilities (open 24 hours a day) of the terminal waiting room. If you can't get there the night before, get to the docks as early as possible in the morning—5 or 6 a.m. is not necessarily too early. If you're in line the night before, in almost every case you will be able to get on the first boat in the morning; even if that fails you'll get over, as you will have priority on the second boat of the day.

The waiting line procedure for Argentia is similar, although here there is the problem of cabins. Buy your tickets, put your car in line, and ask for a cabin waiting-list number (if you have no car, you still must get to the docks early in the morning and get that cabin waiting-list number). Shortly after the ship arrives in port, the cabins freed by cancellations will be given to those on the waiting list, but you must be in the waiting room when your number is called. When you hear your number, run up and pay for the cabin, then rush out to your car (if you've got one) as the line may already be moving aboard. Sound hectic? It's not, really. All goes quite smoothly, and just about everyone who gets to the docks very early in the morning gets a place for their car and a cabin for themselves on that day's boat. It seems there are always lots of canceled car and cabin reservations. The simplest method of all is to have your iron-clad reservations for car and/or cabin well in advance, and then to arrive at the dock *at least* two hours before scheduled sailing time to retrieve them and buy your tickets.

One last note: if you get reservations and later decide not to use them, call and cancel, or send a card to CN Marine Reservations Bureau, P.O. Box 250, North Sydney, NS B2A 3M3. Think of all those people waiting in line—give 'em a chance.

All of this dauntingly detailed inside information will speed your trip, but don't get the idea that a ferry trip to Newfoundland is difficult or exhausting: it's not. It's just that running that Trans Canada Hwy. across the Cabot Strait takes a bit of organization.

By Air

Although flying to Newfoundland is a simple matter, one loses the sense of nautical adventure which comes from a sea voyage. Actually, Newfoundland's place in aviation history is almost as thrilling as its Viking past. The early transatlantic air routes all passed through Gander, and during World War II it was the western jumping-off point for the transports which ran a virtual airborne pipeline of supplies to the Allied armies in Europe.

In most cases, visitors coming from far away will have to change planes in Montréal, Toronto, or Halifax before continuing to one of Newfoundland's airports at St. John's, Gander, Deer Lake/Corner Brook, or Stephenville/Corner Brook. **Eastern Provincial Airways,** the major regional carrier in the Atlantic provinces, handles most of the flights. Call them in St. John's at 709/722-0222; in Gander at 709/256-4801; in Deer Lake at 709/635-2004; in Corner Brook at 709/639-9262; in Stephenville at 709/643-4671.

Getting Around in Newfoundland

Once off the ferry in Port aux Basques, a **Canadian National Roadcruiser bus** will be waiting to trundle you onward. One or two buses a day make the run between Port aux Basques and St. John's, taking about 14 hours for the entire trip along the Trans Canada Hwy. Stops are made at all important towns and crossroads along the 562-mile (904-km) route.

From the ferry terminal in Argentia, there is usually a simple bus link to St. John's. If it's not running, though, you'll have to call a taxi. Find others to share the cost, then call 726-4400—**Bugden's Taxi** in St. John's.

Rental Cars

You can rent a car to see Newfoundland if you haven't brought your own, but be sure to reserve the car you want well in advance. Although there are **Tilden Car Rentals** stations in most Newfoundland and Labrador cities of any size, cars go quickly because public transportation in Newfoundland is so limited. Reserve your car by calling any Tilden office in Canada, or National Car Rentals in the U.S. Or call these offices direct: in Port aux Basques, tel. 709/695-3689; in Corner Brook, tel. 709/634-5111; in Deer Lake, tel. 709/635-3282; in Gander, tel. 709/256-4934; in St. John's, tel. 709/722-4307.

Basic charges for a Tilden car vary from $24 per day for a Vega or Chevette to $27 for a Chevelle; with insurance, 10% provincial tax, gas, and incidental charges, a week's car rental in Newfoundland might cost approximately $250. But note: if you plan to drive one way across Newfoundland, picking up the car at one end and dropping it at the other, you'll probably have to pay a hefty return charge—up to $60, say, if you pick up a car at St. John's and leave it at Port aux Basques, or vice versa. But in fact the return charge works out to be cheaper than driving the car all the way back yourself, when you add up the gas, hotel, meal, and daily rental charges involved.

GETTING TO LABRADOR: Labrador is not the sort of place one "travels to"; rather, one penetrates this almost-uncharted wilderness, usually on business or on safari. Distances, both to Labrador and within Labrador, are vast, and tickets to get there are relatively expensive. Goose Bay, Churchill Falls, and Wabush have airports served by daily flights from outside Labrador, most originating in Newfoundland.

CN Marine operates a weekly coastal freight-and-passenger service from Lewisporte, Nfld., to various points on the northern Newfoundland and Labrador coasts, although it's not a practical means of transport for the short-term visitor. Another CN Marine boat crosses from St. Barbe, far up the Great Northern Peninsula of Newfoundland, to the other side of the Strait of Belle Isle at Blanc-Sablon, Québec. The boat can carry 40 cars and 100 passengers, but once landed in Québec, the road across the border into Labrador and up the coast to Red Bay is rough, and only 20 miles long. If you're game, go: the boat makes three trips a day. For current information and reservations, contact the Passenger Service Supervisor, CN Marine, P.O. Box 520, Port aux Basques, NF A0M 1C0, or call tollfree, Zenith 07081.

1. Port aux Basques and Corner Brook

PORT AUX BASQUES: Cruising into Port aux Basques aboard the ferry, one's first impression is of rocks. Under a gray sky, the rocky coast is topped by treeless hills covered by a thick carpet of brilliant green grass, ferns, and moss. No large plants or tall buildings hide anything in the town. It's stark, but not barren.

Port aux Basques (pop. 8000) makes its living working on the CN ferry and railroad freight terminus, and in a fish-packing plant. It's a hometown of the old sort, where everyone knows everyone else, and close-knit community spirit prevails.

As touchdown point in Newfoundland, Port aux Basques has several good motels. On Hwy. 1 (the Trans Canada) just out of town on the way to St. John's (turn right out of the ferry dock area), you'll come to the **Hotel Port aux Basques** (tel. 709/695-2171), P.O. Box 400. The simple but efficient building is much more luxurious inside than out, all 50 rooms being furnished in modern motel style with color TV, telephones, private bath and shower. Charges for a room come to $23 to $25 single, $30 to $32 double, plus 11% tax. This is Port aux Basques' most luxurious place to put up for the night.

In the hotel's dining room, "Newfie" seafood is the hottest thing going. An appetite-smothering assorted seafood platter costs only $6.25, but chicken is even less at $4.25, spaghetti with meat sauce even less again. Fish and chips is always available, and with a beer can make a hearty lunch, Newfie style, for only $5.60, tax and tip included.

Turn left just before the Hotel Port aux Basques, go to the top of the hill, and turn right onto Grand Bay Rd. Down at the dead-end of the road is the **Grand Bay Motel** (tel. 709/695-2105). Wild rose bushes in front add a welcome dash of color to the motel's white facade. Inside, all is spick-and-span paneling, and all 24 rooms plus two suites have color TV, radio, telephone, and private bath. Some of the rooms have very fine views of the bay—ask for one of these. Rates are reasonable: singles cost $19 to $21; doubles are $25 to $27; extra adults in a room pay $4; extra children over 12 pay $2. Try to reserve your room here at least 24 hours in advance, but if you forget, don't fret—call and see if there's a vacancy (most times there is). The Grand Bay is walking distance from Port aux Basques' modern shopping center and cinema.

For cheaper accommodations right in the town itself, search out **Collier's Hospitality Home** (tel. 709/695-3311), just off the main street on Collier Rd.—as you come into town from the ferry dock, watch for a sign on the left-hand side of the main street. Collier's rents simple, bathless rooms for the very low price of $10 double per day.

Not far from Collier's is Port aux Basques' **Youth Hostel**—the only way to direct you is to tell you to look for signs. Men and women are both accepted here; $3.50 per bed for hostel association members, $4 for others.

Port aux Basques was named in honor of early Basque fishermen-explorers who are thought to have set foot on these shores even before the intrepid Vikings. For the first-time visitor to Newfoundland setting out on the road north, the sense of adventure is almost as intense as what those early explorers must have felt.

The dramatic scenery of Newfoundland rolls out before you as you drive: volcanic cones, blankets of mist and fog, copses of evergreen trees. The rushing streams have got to be full of salmon—they just look that way. Near the shore, sea chimneys jut upward from the chilly waters.

If you haven't chosen to stay the night in Port aux Basques, a good alternative is the tidy **Starlite Lodge** (tel. 709/955-2760), right beside the highway at the settlement named Doyles. White with eye-catching black trim, the Starlite's facade hides eight equally tidy rooms with bath, TV, and telephone. Per days $20 rents a room for one person, $25 pays for two. A restaurant is in the same building.

CORNER BROOK: The first city along the Trans Canada Hwy. north is Newfoundland's second largest (pop. 30,000): Corner Brook. Once a one-industry town with all business life centered on the huge Bowater pulp-and-paper mill, Corner Brook now can boast a thriving herring fishing industry, a cement plant, and a factory for producing gypsum.

For services and stores in western Newfoundland, Corner Brook is the place to look. You can stay overnight very comfortably as well, as Corner Brook's hotels and motels are aimed at the business trade. The **Holiday Inn** (tel. 709/634-5381), on West St. between Todd and Chestnut, is a tree-shaded hostelry which is brand new and laden with comforts: coffeeshop, licensed lounge, and dining room, plus 103 ultramodern rooms with all the conveniences. Prices, for what you get, are moderate at $28 to $30 single, $33 to $36 double, $5 for an extra person—plus that enormous 11% tax.

Not far from the Holiday Inn is the smaller and cozier **Mamateek Motor Inn** (tel. 709/639-8901), P.O. Box 787, at the corner of West and Central Sts. The motel's several units, scattered among shady trees, house 55 rooms with bath and shower, color TV, radio, telephone—in short, all the comforts for business or pleasure. A licensed dining room and lounge will see to sustenance, which, by the way, you can have brought to you by room service. Daily rates are $27.50 to $31.50 single, $34.50 to $38.50 double, and $4 per extra person.

2. The Great Northern Peninsula

DEER LAKE: Northeast of Corner Brook, the Trans Canada Hwy. skirts the eastern shore of Deer Lake. At the northern end of the lake stands the little town of Deer Lake, at the junction of the Trans Canada and Hwy. 430, the road to Gros Morne National Park and the Great Northern Peninsula.

Deer Lake (pop. 4500) is dominated by the Bowater Power Company's hydroelectric generating plant, which supplies the current needed at the Corner Brook pulp-and-paper mill. The **Hotel St. George** (tel. 709/635-2188), near the intersection of Main St. and Nicholsville Rd., is the town's best moderately priced place to stay and dine. The wooden facade gives a rough-and-ready first impression, but inside modernity reigns. There are 24 guest rooms, all with private bath, color TV, radio, and telephone, costing $18 to $20 single, $24 to $27 double, plus 11% tax. The hotel is just a short walk from the CN station. From the Trans Canada, turn at the Esso station (next to the tourist information kiosk) onto Nicholsville Rd.

The dining room of the Hotel St. George is the first place I ever dined on cods' tongues—a local delicacy. A portion of the deep-fried tongues came with potatoes, peas and carrots, roll, and coffee or tea for $4.75. The tongues have a flavor and texture somewhere between scallops and fried clams. If prepared well, as they are at the St. George, they're simply delicious. If you're not ready for cods' tongues, try the salmon ($6), which may be the ouananiche—the variety which is caught in this area. The flavor is a blend of salmon and halibut, the flesh white or pinkish.

Besides its dining room, the Hotel St. George has a licensed lounge and, in the basement, Deer Lake's hottest disco.

Alternative to the Hotel St. George is the **Deer Lake Motel** (tel. 709/635-2108), P.O. Box 820, with 39 rooms easily spotted from the Trans Canada Hwy. An oasis of city-style services in the small town of Deer Lake, the motel can boast a car-rental agency, room service, a food take-out service (for those zooming through town), a licensed dining room and lounge, a coffeeshop, and modern motel units. Equipped with color TV, radio, telephone, and private bath, the rooms cost $23 to $27 single, $27 to $33 double, plus tax.

Campers and those who've been on the road for a while will want to know that Deer Lake has its own coin-operated laundromat, at the far end of Main St.

GROS MORNE NATIONAL PARK: Canada's collection of national parks includes many with breathtaking scenery, and Gros Morne has got to be in the first rank of these. Eons ago, glaciers gouged and ground out the Long Range mountains, and left fjords and lakes scattered among them. The vistas, rock and land formations, and waterways are spectacular.

As you come to Wiltondale on Hwy. 430, watch for the park sign which points the way to a small wooden box marked "Information." Grab a brochure from the box before continuing your drive into the park. Two roads leave Wiltondale to enter the park: 430 goes along the northern shore of Bonne Bay, while 431 goes south to the small fishing villages of Lomond, Glenburnie, Woody Point, and Trout River. You may want to poke around in these picturesque little communities first, then take the short ferry trip from Woody Point to Norris Point. From Norris Point, the road heads north to the park Visitor Centre, on Hwy. 430. On your return trip, take Hwy. 430 as it passes through some of the park's most beautiful formations.

Stop in at the **Visitors' Centre** for any information you might want, and stay to see the 15-minute film entitled *A Matter of Time.* It's well worth seeing, and gives one a good outline of the park's geological history, flora, and fauna.

West and north of the Visitors Centre, Hwy. 430 passes near the majority of Gros Morne's campgrounds before reaching the village of Sally's Cove. Ask at the tiny store in Sally's Cove to find out if the boatmen are in attendance at **Western Brook Pond,** farther north along Hwy. 430. If the answer is yes, drive north to the trailhead for the pond, and park. The walk in to Western Brook Pond takes about an hour (four miles), through forests and along boardwalks over the bog. Tiny wild orchids can be spotted along the trail, and in the bogs you're sure to see the insect-eating pitcher plant, Newfoundland's provincial flower. At the pond end of the trail is a small cabin where boatmen wait to ferry visitors down the fjord-like "pond," past towering rock cliffs over 2000 feet high. It's simply spectacular, a "must see" for anyone in Gros Morne—but only if the weather is good. Sudden storms can rush down the lake in a fury, drenching boat and passengers and even endangering lives. Standard rate for the boat trip, which lasts slightly over two hours, is about $40. Team up with aquaintances met on the trail or at the boat cabin and split the fee—the boatmen won't mind—as the boat can carry six or seven passengers. The $40 fee pays for up to four people; extra adults above this number pay $6 and extra children pay $3. Dress very warmly. Plastic sheets in the boat will keep you dry if the bow throws up spray.

HEADING NORTH If you're game, head north up the western shore of the Great Northern Peninsula. It's 443 km (284 miles) from Deer Lake to the tip of the peninsula at St. Anthony's. Tourist services and motels along the way can provide for your needs.

At **Port aux Choix** is a national historic park on the site of excavations into Newfoundland's aboriginal past. Artifacts dating from the time of the Maritime Archaic people, over 4000 years ago, have been found aplenty at Port aux Choix, along with much later remains from the Dorset Eskimo culture.

At the very tip of the Great Northern Peninsula is **L'Anse aux Meadows National Historic Park,** harboring one of the most thrilling archeological discoveries in modern times. Guided by the verses of the 12th century *Green-landers' Saga,* Norwegian explorer Helge Ingstad and an international team of archeologists discovered unmistakable evidence of a Viking settlement at L'Anse aux Meadows, dating from A.D. 1000.

The **St. Anthony Motel** (tel. 709/454-2722) is the perfect place to rest from your long journey. Twenty-three modern rooms here have color TV, bath and shower, and telephones. The licensed restaurant is open for breakfast, lunch, and dinner, and room service will even bring sustenance right to your door. Single rooms cost $22 to $24; doubles are $26 to $28.

3. From Deer Lake to Gander

ON THE TRANS CANADA HWY.: The Trans Canada Hwy. weaves its way westward through the glacial lakes and rivers which fill the Newfoundland interior. Having stayed the night at Deer Lake, it may be time to take a break for lunch, or fuel, or a snack by the time you reach the junction of Hwys. 390/391 and the Trans Canada. A few miles along 390 from the Trans Canada lies **Springdale,** and in Springdale the top-flight place to stay is the **Pelley Inn** (tel. 709/673-3931), P.O. Box 10, right on the main road before you come to the center of town. Businessmen prefer the Pelley's 24 comfortable, modern rooms to any others in town, and are willing to pay $25 single, $30 double to stay in them. Color TV, radio, and telephone are in each room, and a lounge, dining room, and coffeeshop are on the main (which is not exactly the "ground") floor—you'll see what I mean.

Marie's Motel and Restaurant (tel. 709/673-3831), has moderately priced rooms and moderately priced meals. The rooms, all nine with color TV, telephone, and private bath, cost $18 single, $20 double. The meals in the restaurant (actually a cafe) all seem to cost under $5; a turkey dinner and pork chops both cost $3.90; roast beef is $4.50. Waitresses in the restaurant will be glad to provide room service, bringing your choice of meals from the kitchen back to the motel unit which, for the sake of quiet, is set well away from the road.

The twin towns of **Grand Falls** (pop. 7000) and **Windsor** (pop. 9000) lie astride the Trans Canada Hwy. 73 miles (113 km) from Springdale. This is paper-making country, first exploited by Lord Northcliffe and Lord Rother-mere as a source of newsprint for their publishing enterprises in Britain. Grand Falls is the home of the **Mary March Museum,** on Cromer Ave. (which intersects with the Trans Canada), dedicated to the memory and study of the Beothuck (bee-*oh*-thuk) Indians. The Beothucks inhabited the region of Grand

Falls, and much of Newfoundland's interior, when the first European settlers of the 1600s came ashore. Early contacts were friendly, but misunderstandings arose and led to bloodshed. Continued settlement of the island by outsiders—mostly Nova Scotians and MicMac Indians from Cape Breton—kept the Beothucks from living according to their centuries-old annual rhythm. In winter they retired inland, built teepee-shaped shelters called "mamateeks," and hunted caribou. In spring they would migrate to the coast to live on birds' eggs, seals, and whales.

Mary March, a Beothuck whose Indian name was Desmaduit, was the last of the unassimilated Beothucks. Her knowledge of Beothuck lore was the foundation of the museum. She and "Nancy" (or Shanawdithit), another Beothuck survivor, gave researchers the clues which allowed them to identify the Beothuck language with others in the Algonkian group. Both Mary and Nancy lived in the early 1800s.

Whether the Beothucks were descendants of the Maritime Archaic people, Newfoundland's earliest known inhabitants, is not known, although some anthropologists believe they were. In any case, the sad story of the Beothucks' extinction is an important—and touching—part of Newfoundland's long, deep history.

Staying in Grand Falls is easy, as two comfortable motels exist on either side of the Trans Canada near where Lincoln Rd.'s eastern end joins the highway.

The **Mt. Peyton Motel** (tel. 709/489-2251) is new, large, and luxurious, with 99 rooms, 22 of which are air-conditioned. All rooms have private baths, color cable TV, radio, and telephone, and all are served by room service from the motel's **Peyton Corral Steak House,** and lounge. Single rooms are $26 to $28 per night, doubles are $32 to $34, and twin-bedded rooms cost $33 to $35.

On the north side of the highway is the **Clover Leaf Motel** (tel. 709/489-2116), a 32-room establishment with similar if less ambitious services, and prices a few dollars cheaper than the aforementioned Mt. Peyton Motel.

GANDER: From Grand Falls and Windsor it's 60 miles (94 km) to Gander (pop. 12,000), Newfoundland's most famous town after St. John's. In the 1930s, the men establishing the first regular transatlantic flights chose Gander as the western station on the Atlantic hop. It was almost the closest point to the British Isles, and it was noted for being fog free. Little did these early planners know how important Gander would become during World War II, when literally thousands of aircraft flew to Gander from all parts of Canada and the United States, and from Gander made the leap to Europe. The air link was crucial to the Allied victory.

Gander's primacy survived the war, but not the commercial jet's invention. When long-range cargo and passenger jets took over command of the airways, Gander lost some of its importance since these big planes could fly directly from New York, Montréal, or even Chicago to European cities. But Gander, still as fog free as ever, continues to be an important touchdown point, particularly for world-girdling flights.

Visit Gander's center of attraction, its **airport,** and inspect the **War Memorial** (a propeller-driven plane such as flew the ocean during the war), the museum, and the trememdous mural in the waiting area. It'll give you a thrill—a taste of 20th-century heroism and adventure.

Where to Stay and Eat

As a town with international connections, Gander can boast a good number of hotels and motels, most of them lined up along the Trans Canada Hwy.

The **Albatross Motel** (tel. 709/256-3956), P.O. Box 450, on the Trans Canada, is noted not just for the comfort of its rooms, but even more for the popularity of its dining room. All the rooms, over 100 of them, have color TV, private baths, radio, and telephone, for $28 to $29 single, $34 to $35 double, plus 11% tax. You'll recognize the Albatross by the two-story lobby structure which, from the outside, looks a bit like an airport control tower. (It's actually functional: on the deck above the entry breezeway is a sun and picnic deck.)

The Albatross's dining room is almost always crowded with regulars and those passing through town who stop for an entire salmon dinner for $8.75—if that's the daily special. Filet of flounder ($6) and pork chops ($7.25) are even less costly, and they still include a full dinner of soup, main course, two vegetables, potato, dessert, and coffee. The wine list is long, as is the list of cocktails.

Gander has a **Holiday Inn** (tel. 709/256-3981), with 64 modern rooms in the Holiday Inn style, and all the comforts. Rates are a bit high for Gander, but not unreasonable: $27 to $32 single, $35 to $40 double. The Holiday Inn's restaurant is open long hours, from 7 a.m. to 11 p.m. At lunch, an omelet is $4, but for $6.25 you can have half a broiled chicken, and the price includes soup, vegetable, dessert, and coffee. In the evening, main-course prices stay about the same ($6 to $8), but you don't get the extras such as soup and dessert.

The **Hotel Gander** (tel. 709/256-3931) is the Holiday Inn's main competition, and therefore prices at this locally owned and operated place are lower. A few rooms, the cheaper ones, will have black-and-white TV sets instead of color. But compare the prices: singles at the Hotel Gander are $23 to $26 daily; doubles are $32 to $38. Gander gets lots of single travelers—pilots, businessmen, stewardesses, etc.—and thus the single-room rates are quite reasonable.

Run by the same people as the Hotel Gander, the **Airport Inn** (tel. 709/256-3535) has much cheaper rates, as it should. Although the 62 rooms at the Airport Inn are presentable, they're not luxurious. All have carefully kept and shiny-clean private baths, plus new black-and-white TVs. Furnishings are bright and colorful, but you must be careful of the beds—some are fine, others have seen an awful lot of wear. But look at these prices: $14 to $16 single, $18 to $20 double, plus tax of course. Restaurant facilities consist of a coin-operated soft-drink machine, but this doesn't matter as all the dining rooms of the previously mentioned motels are within a few minutes' walk of the Airport Inn.

Gander has a number of restaurants in the city center. For fast service with moderate prices and good food, try one of the Chinese restaurants (there are three) in the shopping centers at the corner of Elizabeth Dr. and Fraser Rd. The **Highlight Restaurant,** on the right as you approach Fraser Rd. driving along Elizabeth, can scoop any other place in town. An Oriental combination plate consisting of egg roll, sweet-and-sour chicken, fried rice, and soup, is a mere $3.25. It's not elegant—furnishings are lunchroom modern and seating is at the familiar booths—but for budget travelers it's a find.

An even rarer discovery, however, is a shop called the **Bread Man,** on Fraser Dr. just east of Bennett Dr., in a row of shops. The Bread Man's assortment of freshly baked breads, rolls, pastries, and buns is truly astounding: whole-wheat, whole-wheat/rye/buckwheat, pumpernickel, white, raisin—the list goes to well over a dozen types of bread alone, not to mention all the other good things. It's all made fresh, right here in the bakery, and the shop door never seems to stop opening and closing as Gander residents drop in to pick up the day's crisp products. For inveterate picnic makers, the Bread Man's shop is a find worth celebrating.

TERRA NOVA NATIONAL PARK: Not long after you depart Gander, the Trans Canada Hwy. will bring you to Terra Nova National Park. The highway runs right through the middle of the vast reserve, bringing drivers conveniently close to the beaches, boat ramp, camping areas, and trailheads in the park. At Sandy Pond, the beach is supervised. Although Terra Nova is the national park nearest to St. John's, campgrounds are sufficiently large to handle the volume of summer traffic. You may find one or two of the campgrounds full if you arrive late in the afternoon, but unless you come in very late indeed, you should be able to find a place.

ST-PIERRE AND MIQUELON: South of Clarenville on the Trans Canada Hwy. is the intersection with Hwy. 210, the route to the Burin Peninsula. It's 145 miles from Clarenville to Grand Bank, near the tip of the peninsula, but once you've driven that distance, you'll be surprisingly close to France. France?

The boot-shaped Burin Peninsula, seen on a map, seems about to punt three small islands, named Great Miquelon, Little Miquelon, and St-Pierre. Believe it or not, these three bits of turf belong to—and are looked upon as an integral part of—the French Republic. Gendarmes, French wines and perfumes, those long loaves of bread—they're all here, in the chilly waters off Fortune Bay.

Jacques Cartier, on one of his cruises of exploration in the 1500s, routinely touched at St-Pierre and Miquelon and claimed them for the king of France. The king is long gone, but the islands are still French.

The town and island of St-Pierre, named for the patron saint of fishermen, can boast 6000 citizens and over 20 miles of roads, a museum, and shops in which to buy French goods. Besides tourism, St-Pierre is engaged in supplying fishing and cargo boats which touch port here; some of the people have small farms.

Want to go? The daily ferry departs from the town of Fortune, a few miles southwest of Grand Bank, on the 12-mile voyage to St-Pierre.

4. Onward to Avalon

Leaving Terra Nova National Park, the Trans Canada Hwy. heads due south to the isthmus which joins the main part of Newfoundland to the Avalon Peninsula. Framed by Trinity Bay to the north and Placentia Bay to the south, the isthmus has unusual weather conditions. While Gander, not all that far away, remains virtually fogless year round, the isthmus always seems to be fogged in. Highway signs will warn you of this, but you hardly need them: the dense white clouds rushing dramatically over the roadway speak for themselves.

Once off the isthmus and into Avalon, watch for the junction of the Trans Canada and Hwy. 100. South along 100 takes you to Argentia, terminus for CN Marine's car ferry. (See "Getting There," earlier in this chapter, for details about ferries to North Sydney, N.S.) Just south of Argentia is Placentia, today a small town, but the capital city of French Newfoundland in the 1600s. In August 1941, Winston Churchill and Franklin D. Roosevelt hammered out the agreement called the Atlantic Charter while moored on a warship in Placentia Bay. The shape of the world was changed here, as the charter dealt with what was to happen when the Allied armies were victorious. In 1941 that was an optimistic thing to be doing, as the Allied armies at that time were in quite a fix, but history ultimately vindicated these long-range planners.

Deep into the Avalon Peninsula on the Trans Canada Hwy., Hwy. 90 leaves the main road to go south along the Salmonier River. Seven miles (12 km) from the main road along Hwy. 90 is one of Newfoundland's most fascinating attractions, a "must see" for any visitor interested in the province's natural beauties. Whoever conceived of the **Salmonier Nature Park** should be heartily applauded, for this zoo-with-a-difference gives visitors and Newfoundlanders the best possible introduction to the many species of wildlife which also live in the island province. Open between 11 a.m. and 7 p.m. daily from early June to Labour Day, Salmonier Nature Park has moose, snowy owls, beavers, red foxes, caribou, ducks and geese, hawks and eagles, all living in natural mini-environments rather than cages. Roomy enclosures keep the animals and some of the birds from roaming outside the park without cramping them as cages would do. Visitors circulate among the enclosures on a self-explanatory nature trail through the forest and bog. The trail walk can take anywhere between one and two hours to complete, depending how long you want to linger, watching the moose suckle its young, or the red fox dart about its habitat, or the beavers slap the pond's surface with their broad tails. Entrance fees are minimal: 50¢ per adult, 25¢ per child, seniors free.

As the Trans Canada Hwy. turns northeast in the direction of St. John's, a sign will come into view marking the entrance to **Butter Pot Provincial Park,** one of the province's nicest—and certainly its most crowded.

Along the highway you may notice cars parked here and there. Many of the occupants will be fishing, but others will be circulating through the fields and hills on either side of the road, bending down to gather bake-apple berries (*Rubus chamaemorus,* also called cloudberries). The plants flower in June, and by late July the amber-colored fruit is ready to pick. Bake-apple berries are related to raspberries, and they look it, but the taste—with a spoonful of sugar—is distinctly and surprisingly like baked apples! If you see one of the enthusiastic berrypickers holding up a few jars of the reddish fruit as you speed by, that's an invitation to buy. Take them up on it if you're at all curious, as bake-apple berries are more of a home-bound delicacy, rarely appearing on restaurant menus.

5. St. John's

No place in Newfoundland has a more fascinating and romantic history than St. John's. Its location as the North American point closest to Europe was the prime factor in shaping its history; second came its beautiful, safe, rock-bound natural harbor. No wonder the earliest Renaissance explorers from Europe chose to put in here.

First of these swashbuckling commodores was John Cabot, who is said to have sailed into the harbor on St. John's Day in 1497. Documents show for certain that Capt. John Rut, aboard the *Mary of Guildford,* came to the harbor 30 years later. He wrote home to his sovereign, Henry VIII, to recommend that a permanent settlement be established here, no doubt for the benefit of the cod fishermen as much as for military purposes. A year later, in 1528, this was done, and St. John's citizens today take this date for the city's founding.

From its founding, St. John's went on to a series of attacks, defenses, pirate raids, celebrations, great fires, and great feasts unmatched in North America. Today, quaint little town houses with their brightly colored facades line the streets in St. John's old downtown section, while modern suburbs sprawl on the outskirts. You can't miss St. John's connection with the sea: flags from any nation may be flying from the ships in port, sailors stroll through the town, and reminders of a nautical past are everywhere.

WHERE TO STAY: Although St. John's has lots of good places to stay, they all seem to be in the upper part of the moderate price range, designed to please visiting businessmen who can charge the room bill to an expense account. However, my search through St. John's did turn up one hostelry—a highway motel—which is truly a bargain for the price. But as it's outside the city center, I'll begin my recommendations with the hotels that are within walking distance of things to see and do in Newfoundland's capital city.

Downtown

CN Hotels' **Hotel Newfoundland** (tel. 709/726-4980) is the city's Old Faithful, a large and weathered brick structure which is kept scrupulously contemporary and up-to-date inside. It rises seven stories above Cavendish Square, at the eastern end of Duckworth St. where it meets King's Bridge Rd. The services of a large, centrally located hotel are here: airport limousine, car-rental agencies, barber and beauty shops, newsstand, airline and travel offices. The 134 guest rooms have color TV, radio, and private bath, and cost $34 to $40 single, $42 to $48 double or twin; children sharing their parents' room do so at no charge, but an extra adult in a room costs $8. As with other large hotels with a business clientele, weekend discounts and special rates are offered from time to time—ask when you reserve, or even when you check in.

When it comes to views of the harbor and the city, no place can top the helicopter-like panoramas which are yours if you stay at the **Battery Inn** (tel. 709/722-0040), atop Signal Hill. Popular with businessmen visiting St. John's, the Battery even has six single rooms ($26 to $33), as well as the 89 standard double rooms ($31 to $38), all with color TV, radio, telephone, and private bath. Higher prices are for the rooms with the view of course, and my advice would be to spend the extra money—the view is fantastic. The Battery has a lounge and coffeeshop, and a restaurant that shares the marvelous view (see below). The Battery's got an indoor swimming pool as well.

Farther Out

Newest, shiniest hostelry in St. John is the **Holiday Inn** (tel. 709/722-0506), at the intersection of Portugal Cove Rd. and MacDonald Dr., about 1½ miles from the center of town. Known for their comfort and luxury, Holiday Inn rooms have all the modern conveniences; these cost $32 to $36 single, $38 to $42 double. A restaurant, lounge, and coffeeshop, plus room service, see to your dining needs.

The **Airport Inn** (tel. 709/753-3500) is, as its name suggests, very close to St. John's Torbay Airport. Coming from St. John's, follow Portugal Cove Rd. (Hwy. 40), cross Prince Philip Dr., and take a right onto Airport Rd. The motel is about two miles from the city's center and only a short walk from the air terminal. All 103 rooms at the motel have color TV, radio, telephone, and bright spreads and curtains. Rates are moderate: $26 to $28 single, $30 to $32 double. The Airport Inn's Wine Cellar Dining Room and Silver Knight Lounge are popular local dining and drinking places, and you may just encounter an engagement party, wedding reception, or graduation celebration. Dining room prices are moderate: a full meal in the evening need cost only $10 or less.

On the Trans Canada Hwy.

Now for St. John's biggest overnight bargain:. the **Skyline Motel** (tel. 709/722-5400), on Kenmount Rd. (the Trans Canada Hwy.), has 31 neat and clean motel units which, although not fancy, are very comfortable. Color TVs, phones, and private baths are in all units. The prices are the best part of all, as singles cost only $21 to $23, doubles only $25 to $30, plus tax. The motel is just at the beginning of the commercial strip as the highway enters St. John's, but as the units are built perpendicular to the road, noise is not a problem.

In the same commercial strip stands the **Hotel St. John's** (tel. 709/722-9330), 102-108 Kenmount Rd., with 80 fully modern units. In the same building is a restaurant with Chinese and Canadian food, and St. John's large post office building is right next door. All of the units here are set up for housekeeping, and thus the prices of $28 single, $33 double, are not at all unreasonable.

WHERE TO DINE: For its size, St. John's could be expected to have a good selection of dining places—and it does. Whether your taste goes to hamburgers or tournedos Rossini, or to native Newfie "fish and brewis," you'll find it easily in the capital city.

You would not be surprised to find a restaurant such as **Upstairs Downstairs** (tel. 709/753-2901) in Boston or San Francisco or Montréal, and it is a real joy to have it in St. John's. The "Downstairs" of the name refers to the kitchenware shop at 4-6 Bates' Hill, which carries antiques and locally made craft items as well as exotic culinary utensils. "Upstairs," the utensils are wielded with a passion, producing, each morning after 10, croissants and coffee cake; at lunch, soups, salads, quiches, and desserts; until 5 p.m., English cream tea. The evening meal is served from 6 to 10 p.m., and the menu (which changes daily) always lists three or four appetizers, the same number of main courses, and desserts. We had the homemade pâté ($2.50) and a serving of vichyssoise ($1.50), followed by coquilles St-Jacques (scallops baked with cheese, $7.50) and bracciole (Italian stuffed beef rolls, $9); then on to the fresh fruit cheese-cake ($1.75) and a slice of Portuguese almond cake ($1.50). Without wine (we couldn't reconcile the coquilles and the bracciole), the total price for two, tax and tip included, was $29. With careful choosing (but still delicious dining), this could have been as low as $18 for two. Obviously, Upstairs Downstairs is good. Just as obviously, early reservations are a must at dinner (no reservations accepted at lunch). By the way, the street called Bates' Hill is between Queen's Rd. and Duckworth St., two blocks east of City Hall.

St. John's newest and best restaurant for seafood is, appropriately, **The Aquarium** (tel. 709/754-1392), recently reestablished at 325 Duckworth St. Light-wood tables without cloths offset the heaviness of red drapes on the Aquarium's huge windows. Clients are mostly youngish, fish-loving, and by no means wealthy, and the Aquarium's menu and prices are out to please this bunch. The assorted Atlantic seafood plate, called Neptune's Platter, costs only $6.50, as would a portion of trout almondine. The tasty squid is even cheaper. In season, something elegant such as lobster or salmon is featured as the special of the day, keeping the price of these luxuries down too. The Aquarium's wine list is short but good, at reasonable prices. On Friday and Saturday evenings you should have reservations. Dinner is from 6 to 10 p.m. And yes, there is an aquarium at the Aquarium.

St. John's top-class restaurant list must include **Act III** (tel. 709/754-0790), in the Arts and Culture Centre at the intersection of Prince Philip Dr. and Allandale Rd. Act III is open weekdays noon to 2:30 and 6 to 10 p.m., Saturdays 6 to 10:30 p.m., serving the crowds who tour the galleries during the day and come for theater in the evening. Lunch is a table d'hôte meal with appetizer, vegetables, dessert, and coffee included in the price of the main course, which may be anything from a Spanish omelet ($4.50) to a steak sandwich ($6). Dinner might start with cod tongues as a genuine Newfie appetizer ($3.10), then go on to steaks ($8.25 to $13) or fish ($6.25 to $12.75); a specialty, steak Diane, comes flavored with onions and garlic, and flamed in sherry, brandy, and cream ($12.50). Wines cost $8.50 to $14 per bottle, and up. Have reservations on those busy theater nights.

Undoubtedly, the tables with the best views of St. John's are at the **Battery,** in their Harbour View dining room. Gleaming wine glasses, shining flatware, and pristine tablecloths set the mood for an elegant dinner, and the view brings in the romance. It's a perfect setting for chateaubriand bouquetière ($27.50 for two), although the prime rib of beef au jus is a good choice at $9.50. Other main courses cost a bit less; the price of the main course includes starter, vegetables, and salad as well. Lunch is good here too, but the city lights at night make dinner the more exciting repast.

Similar elegance exists at the **Starboard Quarter** (tel. 709/753-9510), in the Royal Trust building at the corner of Prescott and Water Sts. The restaurant takes its decor, as well as its name, from St. John's nautical past, and the main dining room is fitted out to resemble an elegant turn-of-the-century cruise vessel, with lots of polished brass fittings, fringed curtains, and large windows through which to get a view of the harbor. Catering to the successful business set, the Starboard Quarter bears a sign which says "Jacket and Tie Appreciated." Having passed muster, you can enter and enjoy a soup or appetizer (to $3.50), and perhaps the Oceanus casserole (of seafood, $8.75), although curried chicken costs the same. Steaks at the Starboard are priced at $11 to $13. On weekend evenings it's not a bad idea to have a reservation. Service is from noon to 2:30 and 5:30 to 10 p.m. (11 on Saturdays).

A popular hangout for St. John's University set is the **Galley** (tel. 709/753-7360) and its Anchor Pub, on Harbour Dr. right down by the docks. Informality is the rule, hearty meals the aim: a plate of spare ribs ($6.75) is a good choice, but the filet mignon costs just over a dollar more. Good Newfie cod 'n' scrunchions (fried bits of pork) costs the same as the spare ribs, and all these main courses come with rights to the salad bar. Wines can be had for about $8 to $9 the bottle. Have reservations; if you don't, try arriving after 9 o'clock in the evening. There will no doubt be room then, and the Galley stays open until 11 p.m.

Upstairs in the **Anchor Pub,** you have your choice of snacking and drinking seated on an open-air deck, or in the Victoriana-filled inside room. Entertainment is offered Monday through Saturday evenings, with Monday being country music night; on Sundays it's disco. No cover charge, beer $1.10 (Canadian).

Talk of the town in recent years is a place called **Gary's** (tel. 709/364-4666), 510 Topsail Rd. just after you pass the K-Mart Shopping Plaza (on your right) coming from downtown. Gary's is a brand-new restaurant all made of natural-finish wood with lots of hanging plants and big windows to yield a delightful greenhouse effect. The mood is not formal, but neither is it folksy. It seems to me that Gary must have sat down one day and asked himself, "What do people want?" The answer he found was barbecued spare ribs, chicken, and steaks, served in attractive, modern surroundings—and that's exactly what he delivers. A full rack of ribs costs $9 (a half rack is $6; a quarter rack, $4), chicken is $4 to $5, and steaks are $8 to $11. Garnishes are available, and drinks and beer are on sale, too. Open Sunday through Thursday 11:30 a.m. to 1 a.m., on Friday and Saturday till 3 a.m. Have reservations on weekends.

Best for Least

Finnegan's Pub (tel. 709/753-1750) sounds as though it should be a dark-ish auld country bar with plenty of old salts up against their Guinness. Well, there is hearty Irish atmosphere alright, but this attractive pub has begun to offer a buffet on Friday and Saturday evenings that can't be beat. Baked ham, Irish stew, crabmeat salad, fresh fruit salad, and literally a dozen other cold dishes from spring rice salad to deviled eggs are laid out, and patrons tuck in. The charge is $6 per person, which, with a glass of beer, tax, and tip, comes to $8.50. The food is good and there is as much as you can handle. Even when the buffet's not on, you can have a weighty sandwich at Finnegan's, for $2.50 to $3.50, and cod au gratin or sirloin for similarly moderate prices. Every night after 9:30 there's free folk, country, or Irish music. Finnegan's is at 51-53 Harvey Rd. Don't let its drab exterior drive you away—it's nice inside.

Most popular sailors' pub in Newfoundland, where you're liable to hear Greek, Bulgarian, Finnish, and Italian all at once, is the **Ship Inn,** 265 Duck-worth St. Actually, the pub is entered by descending either of the sets of stairs which bracket no. 265-269 Duckworth. Open every day, the bar is cozy, the sailors interesting, the local people (often young) friendly. Sandwiches are $1.75 to $2; beer is $1.05 Canadian, $1.40 imported.

WHAT TO SEE: Except for the downtown section of St. John's, it's good to have a car for sightseeing. If you are car-less, call **Bugden's Taxi** (tel. 726-4400), and they'll be glad to arrange a cab tour for you. Along Marine Dr. (described below) to Torbay should cost $15; to Flat Rock, $25; to Cape Spear and Petty Harbour, $30 (round trip, of course).

A less expensive alternative to a taxi tour is a bus tour with **Tours by Overland Ltd.** (tel. 722-6990 during business hours; after hours and on week-ends, tel. 726-6565). The full-fledged three-hour city tour costs $7.50 for adults, $5 for kids 12 and under. Other tours are of Marine Dr. (three hours; $7.50 for adults, $5 for kids); of Cape Spear and Petty Harbour (same time, same prices); or a junket all the way to Conception Bay (eight hours; $15 per adult, $10 per child, meals not included). Call and reserve tour places in advance.

The city sponsors daily **walking tours** of interesting points during the season from mid-June to mid-September, departing the modern City Hall at 10:30 a.m., and 2 and 7 p.m. Check with the tourism information office in City Hall on New Gower St., or call 722-7080.

Touring the City

St. John's grew up around its harbor, so the first thing to do is take a walk along Harbour Dr. for a look at the ships. They fly flags from all over the world, and any one ship might have sailors of half a dozen different nationalities.

Water St., a block north of Harbour Dr., is said to be "the oldest main street on the continent" because it served as a pathway for the earliest explorers here, and later for the settlers. Go east on Water St. to the **War Memorial,** for men of Newfoundland fallen in World War I. The War Memorial stands on the spot where, in 1583, Sir Humphrey Gilbert proclaimed that Newfoundland was a territory under the British Crown.

Up the stairs by the War Memorial brings you to Duckworth St. Turn left on Duckworth and walk five blocks to the corner of Duckworth and Prescott, where you'll find the **Newfoundland Museum.** As of this writing, the museum is closed for restoration and remodeling, but it should be open by the time you arrive: hours will be from 10 a.m. to 7 p.m. daily, mid-June to mid-September (you can call 737-2460 to check if the museum's open). If it is, wander in for a look at Newfoundland's past: exhibits will explain the culture and history of the Beothucks, the explorations and settlements of the Vikings, the architectural history of St. John's.

Next door to the museum is the **Courthouse,** built in 1904 of brick and locally quarried stone. Five blocks to the east is the new and modern concrete **City Hall,** in front of which stands a sign marking the beginning of the Trans Canada Hwy.—the longest national artery in the world, it ends in Victoria, B.C., 7775 km (4976 miles) away.

Start from the Newfoundland Museum, at Duckworth and Prescott, to see a few of the city's impressive churches. Up the hill from the museum along Prescott is Gower St.; turn left and walk to the Anglican **Cathedral of St. John the Baptist** (enter on the north side, not by the main door). The cathedral is immense, and always seems to be under restoration (as one local wag put it, "They just move the scaffolding from one side to the other, then back again"). Built in 1816 under the supervision of Sir Gilbert Scott, the cathedral was damaged by fire several times, but restoration work done in 1905 has given it the look it has today. The Gothic nave, stained-glass windows, and carved-wood pews are very handsome indeed. Inside the entry is a schedule (which changes frequently) of when the church is open. You can always have a look on Sundays, of course.

Continue north on Church Hill (that's the name of the street) to Queen's Rd. Turn right, then left, and keep walking uphill, on Garrison Hill. At the top of the hill is a yellow fire station, built on the site of the old Fort Townsend, which once commanded the harbor. To your right, on Military Rd., is the impressive **Roman Catholic basilica,** with a large granite entrance gate and two towers which dominate the city. Inside, the marble foyer opens into a nave of clean lines. The ceiling has a gilded relief of scrolls and leaves, which is very appealing. Around the basilica are the Academy of Our Lady of Mercy, and the Mercy Convent; St. Patrick's Hall; and St. Bonaventure College.

Walking east from the basilica along Military Rd., glance down the steep streets for a look at the colorful old row houses and their clapboards sporting pastel hues and some bold colors. If you've got the time, explore some of these side streets, and Gower St.'s eastern portion as well.

A few blocks east of the basilica on Military Rd., is **Bannerman Park,** a delightful place to rest your feet and your spirit.

Just past Bannerman Park, still on Military Rd., is the **Colonial Building,** built in 1850 from stone brought in ships as ballast from County Cork, in Ireland. Until 1958 this was Newfoundland's House of Assembly as well, but in that year the Assembly moved to newer and roomier quarters in the Confederation Building, to the north in the newer part of town. Colonial House is open for your inspection, free, in summer, Monday through Friday from 9 a.m. to 5 p.m.

Across Bannerman Rd., is **Government House,** the official residence of Newfoundland's lieutenant-governor. The elegant mansion is not open to the public. One block farther along Military Rd. is **St. Thomas Church,** which opened its doors to worshippers in 1836, making it today the oldest place of worship, still standing, in the province. St. Thomas's was the garrison church for the British forces until they were withdrawn in the late 1800s.

At the intersection of Military Rd. and King's Bridge Rd. is **Cavendish Square,** one-time site of Fort William, but now occupied by the Hotel Newfoundland. Fort William, and Fort Townsend to the west, were linked by Military Rd. even in early times, forming the city's line of defense from harbor attack.

Turn left onto King's Bridge Rd., and a few steps up that street on the left is the entrance to **Commissariat House.** A beautiful Georgian house recently restored, it's the best possible spot for getting the feeling of what life was like when Newfoundland was a vital link in the defense chain of the young British Empire. The Canadian government and the Newfoundland Historical Society lovingly restored the house and grounds: the process of restoration is described through displays in the carriage house, on your right as you enter. England was scoured for furnishings with which to redo Commissariat House, and what the searchers came up with were beautiful Brussels carpets, English china, silver, lace, and fine paintings. The first floor of the house, which dates from 1818, was for offices, archives, and messengers of Commissary business. On the second floor were the officers' private quarters. The military stores were kept in Forts Townsend and William. When the British forces withdrew in 1870, Commissariat House was used as the rectory for St. Thomas Church, and later as a children's hospital, until 1969 when it was acquired for the restoration.

Signal Hill

On the eastern heights above the Narrows (entrance to St. John's Harbour) is **Signal Hill National Historic Park.** The view from the hill is magnificent, and the breezes are cool even on the hottest day in summer. City buses don't run to Signal Hill, but you can walk, taxi, or drive by following Duckworth St. east to Signal Hill Rd.

Midway up the slope is the park's **Visitors' Centre,** with attractive exhibits explaining the history and importance of Signal Hill and the harbor and town it protected. Drop in and ask for the booklets which describe three walks you can take in the park: to Gibbett Hill, Queen's Battery, and Ladies Lookout. If it's not a sweltering day, you can park at the Centre and walk to the top of the hill; if it is very hot, drive, and park right by fort-like Cabot Tower.

About two-thirds of the way uphill from the Visitors' Centre is **Queen's Battery,** established in the late 1700s by the British and enlarged during the War of 1812. Originally an elaborate complex of barracks, blockhouses, and furnaces for hotshots, the battery was left to deteriorate by the elements until 1969, when restoration began. Several of the great old cannons are still at the battery, mounted on carriages with small wheels which ran on a semicircular track for ease of aiming. Hotshots, by the way, were cannonballs heated until they glowed, then stuffed into the guns and shot at enemy ships. If a hotshot hit the water, rather than sink it would skip along the surface as the water it contacted would instantly turn to steam, "exploding" under the hotshot and keeping it from sinking. This skipping gave the shot more distance, allowing it to damage ships even beyond normal range. If ships were within cannon range, a hotshot might easily set fire to an enemy vessel's sails, rigging, or wooden decks.

Across the Narrows from Queen's Battery is **Fort Amherst,** named for Col. William Amherst who captured St. John's from the French in 1762. The lighthouse on the point was built in 1813. Together with a chain which stretched across the Narrows, Queen's Battery and Fort Amherst were very effective in closing the harbor of St. John's to enemy attack until larger guns and ironclad vessels rendered such defenses obsolete. By the way, past Fort Amherst, to the south, you should be able to see Cape Shear jutting into the Atlantic—that's the most easterly point in North America.

Atop Signal Hill, **Cabot Tower** was begun in 1897 in commemoration of John Cabot's landing on Newfoundland's shores in 1497, four centuries previous. The tower was opened in 1900, and served as a lookout and signal tower until 1958. It was from this tower that Guglielmo Marconi received the first transatlantic wireless broadcast from a village in Cornwall, England, in 1901. The broadcast consisted of the Morse Code letter "S" (· · ·), three short signals which made communications history. Cabot Tower maintains communications with the world through the branch post office on its ground floor; upstairs is a gallery with displays which recount the early experiments of Sir Home Popham and the great Marconi in electromagnetic wave transmission. On the tower's top level is an observation deck with the finest of panoramic views. Guides are on hand to answer all your questions, and the tower is open daily, mid-June to mid-September, from 9 a.m. to 5 p.m., for free.

Quidi Vidi Lake and Battery

Pronounced "Kitty Vitty," this odd Latinate name refers to the pretty lake east of downtown, and to the battery which protected its narrow entrance channel, known as "The Gut." You can walk to Quidi Vidi Battery in about 20 minutes from Signal Hill if you choose: go down the hill from Cabot Tower toward the Visitors' Centre. Just beyond George's Pond is a kiosk dated "1916," and a road off to the right, nicknamed "Burma Road" by the American servicemen who once occupied the large base near Quidi Vidi. Burma Rd. leads to a path which ends in the parking lot for Quidi Vidi Battery. If you're driving from Signal Hill, descend from the hill, turn right onto Temperance (which becomes Quidi Vidi Rd.), then right again onto Forest Rd. Quidi Vidi Lake will be on your left. At the eastern end of the lake, turn right onto McDonnell Rd., which leads into Cuckhold's Rd., which leads to the Battery parking lot.

Quidi Vidi Battery, a provincial historic site, is a lovely spot overlooking the fishing village of Quidi Vidi. The battery was constructed in 1762 by the French troops who held St. John's for a short period that year. Within three months of its construction the battery was in British hands. The American Revolution caused the British to reinforce this strongpoint against American privateers, and again in 1812 it was spruced up for action. Totally restored in 1967 as a Canada centennial project, the battery's little building houses a small museum explaining the era of its activity. Quidi Vidi's open free of charge daily, 9 a.m. to 5 p.m. mid-June to mid-September.

If you have time, stroll through Quidi Vidi, a truly picturesque spot. The lake nearby is the scene, on the first Wednesday in August of each year, of the St. John's Regatta, a contest held annually since 1826.

On the Outskirts

Gallery fans take note: St. John's has a marvelous new **Arts and Culture Centre** (1966) at the corner of Allandale Rd. and Prince Philip Dr., a mile or so from downtown (go west on Military Rd., which becomes Harvey Rd. and then Freshwater Rd., and turn right onto Mayor Ave., which eventually becomes Allandale Rd.). In the Centre is the Gallery, open Tuesday through Sunday from noon to 10 p.m., free of charge. Traveling collections fill the gallery's rooms and provide a look at the best of modern Canadian painting and sculpture. Terrarium windows in the gallery are inhabited by tremendous banana plants, giving a splash of green to the white walls and lending an air of the tropical to this northern climate. Also in the Arts and Culture Centre are a library, card and gift shop, restaurant (Act III, noted above), and the theater (for information or ticket reservations, call 737-3900).

The **Confederation Building**, seat of Newfoundland and Labrador's provincial government, rises above Prince Philip Dr. east of the Arts and Culture

Centre. You can visit the building, and a small military museum, free of charge during weekday business hours.

Take Hwy. 10 west (Waterford Bridge Rd.) from downtown to reach **Bowring Park,** the city's favorite green spot a few miles from the center. Given to the city by the Bowring family, the park was opened by the Duke of Connaught in 1914. Look for the statues: *The Fighting Newfoundlander, Peter Pan* (a copy of the one in London's Kensington Park), and the Caribou, a military memorial.

North and South of St. John's

No visitor to St. John's should leave that city without having taken the ride along **Marine Dr.,** north of the city. Past Logy Bay to Outer Cove and Torbay is some of the area's prettiest scenery, not to mention one of the best spots for watching puffins and whales. On my first visit to Torbay I was captivated by the sight of a single whale rolling through the sea, and then an oldtimer sunning nearby pointed out an entire school of the monster denizens rolling and spouting farther out to sea. Right near the base of the cliffs, puffins dove and swam deep below the surface to catch the little fish they live on.

Marine Dr. goes all the way through Flat Rock to Pouch ("pooch") Cove. Past this quaint town the paved road ends, but a road of dirt and crushed stone climbs into the hills, past even more marvelous views, to a lighthouse at Cape St. Francis.

South of St. John's along the shore are the favorite haunts of many species of sea birds, at **Cape Spear** and **Witless Bay.** At Witless Bay are several islands protected as sanctuaries for the birds. You'll have to strike a bargain with local fishermen to get out to Gull Island, Green Island, or Great Island (best time to go is in June and July).

At **Ferryland,** farther south, is some strikingly beautiful country, and a very photogenic lighthouse.

6. Labrador

Not exactly what one could call a tourist mecca, Labrador is a forbidding land almost three times the size of its provincial sister Newfoundland. Until a few decades ago, Labrador was inhabited by a handful of people in tiny fishing villages along its rugged shore, with a few more people at the Goose Bay military base. But recently the incredible wealth of Labrador has come under the beginnings of development: mines at Labrador City and Wabush produce almost half of Canada's iron ore, and at Churchill Falls a mammoth hydroelectric project puts out power equivalent to seven million horsepower.

Most people who aren't among Labrador's original Inuit (Eskimo) inhabitants go there to mine, to man the military base, or to hunt and fish. Combatting the great swarms of black flies and mosquitoes is a minor matter for sportsmen who see the chance to bag a caribou, or dozens of succulent fish from Labrador's chilly waters. Virtually the only way to explore the country's interior is by seaplane and tent camp, which makes hunting and fishing trips pretty expensive.

Labrador's geology, at the edge of the fantastically old Laurentian Shield, has apparently remained unchanged since long before the beginning of animal life on this planet. It's possible that Labrador is the only such spot in the world, and that alone might make it worth a visit: to look upon the world as it was when life began. Details on getting to Labrador are given at the beginning of this chapter.

Chapter VII

MONTRÉAL

1. Where to Stay
2. Montréal's Restaurants
3. The Sights of Montréal
4. Montréal Shopping
5. Montréal's Nightlife

BOLD AND ADVENTUROUS, Montréal pursues its unique destiny every day. Laced with expressways, dominated by New York–style skyscrapers, this island city 50 miles from the U.S. border may look at first like other cities you've visited, but after just one day here you'll know otherwise. Only Montréal can claim to be the largest city in Canada, and the second-largest French-speaking city in the world. Only in Montréal can you stroll through a North American version of Paris's Latin Quarter, streets lined with sidewalk cafes and little bistros, and later wander among some of the oldest and quaintest buildings in North America; or do business in an office tower with a staff of 100% bilingual people, then hike up a mountain which is a city park right in the center of town. Only Montréal has an Underground City, a vast maze of corridors, shopping concourses, subway tunnels, and sunken plazas in which you can literally travel for miles without retracing your steps, going to movies, relaxing in bars and nightclubs, buying everything imaginable, strolling through flower shows, attending concerts—all without ever getting your feet wet.

Montréal's flags give a clue to its character. The blue-and-white flag of Québec bears the royal French fleur-de-lis, from the time when Montréal was founded by the intrepid French explorer Maisonneuve, in 1642. The city's white-and-red flag displays the English rose, the Irish shamrock, the Scottish thistle, and the French fluer-de-lis, one symbol for each of the major ethnic groups which built Montréal in the 18th and 19th centuries. And the Canadian maple-leaf flag encompasses all these groups and more, hinting at the city's present ethnic diversity.

Headlines may shout about linguistic battles, but every Montréaler knows that speaking *both* languages is the best solution. It's the exciting blend of French and English cultures that gives Montréal its special spirit. Elegance in dress, finesse in cuisine, and perfection of service are more important here than perhaps anywhere else in North America. But students at the city's half dozen major universities offer a laid-back alternative to the chic haute couture stylishness of downtown, and yet another clue to the fascinating diversity of this scintillating metropolis. Summer or winter, day or night, Montréal is a mini-universe of pleasures and peoples just waiting to be enjoyed.

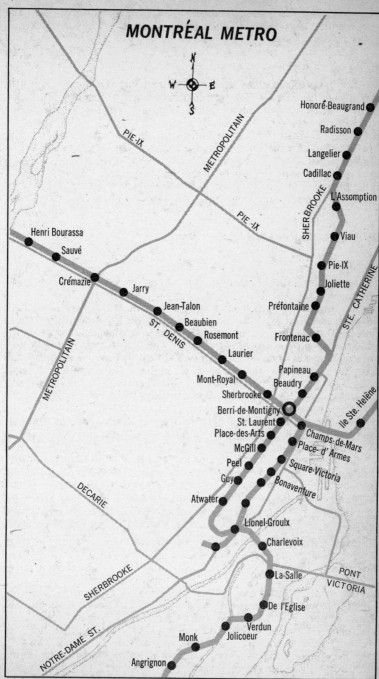

MONTRÉAL METRO

Honoré-Beaugrand
Radisson
Langelier
Cadillac
L'Assomption
Viau
Pie-IX
Joliette
Préfontaine
Frontenac

Henri Bourassa
Sauvé
Crémazie
Jarry
Jean-Talon
Beaubien
Rosemont
Laurier
Mont-Royal
Sherbrooke
Berri-de-Montigny
St. Laurent
Place-des-Arts
McGill
Peel
Guy
Atwater

Papineau
Beaudry

Champs-de-Mars
Place-d'Armes
Square-Victoria
Bonaventure

Lionel-Groulx
Charlevoix
La-Salle
De l'Eglise
Verdun
Jolicoeur
Monk
Angrignon

PIE-IX
METROPOLITAIN
PIE-IX
SHERBROOKE
STE. CATHERINE
Ile Ste. Hélène
ST. DENIS
METROPOLITAIN
DECARIE
SHERBROOKE
NOTRE-DAME ST.
PONT VICTORIA

Map Courtesy of Tourisme Québec

GETTING THERE: Served by superhighways, transcontinental trains and buses, and the largest airport in the world, Montréal is easily accessible, no matter how you travel.

By Car

The Trans Canada Hwy. runs right through the city, connecting it with both ends of the country. Interstate 87 runs due north from New York City to link up with Canada's Hwy. 15 at the border, and the entire 400-mile journey is thus on expressways. Likewise from Boston, I-93 north joins I-89 just south of Concord, N.H. At White River Junction you have the choice of continuing on I-89 to Lake Champlain, crossing the lake by various smaller roads to join I-87 and Canada Hwy. 15 north; or, joining I-91 at White River Junction to go due north toward Sherbrooke, P.Q. At the border I-91 becomes Canada Hwy. 55, and joins Canada Hwy. 10 ("Autoroute des Cantons de l'Est," or Autoroute of the Eastern Townships), a toll road to Montréal. From Boston to Montréal is about 320 miles, from Toronto it's 540 km (350 miles), from Ottawa it's 190 km (120 miles). Remember, highway distances and speed limits are given in kilometers and kilometers per hour in Canada.

By Bus

Montréal's main bus terminal is the **Terminus Voyageur,** 505 Blvd. de Maisonneuve Est (tel. 514/842-2281). The Voyageur company operates buses between here and all parts of Québec, with frequent runs through the Eastern Townships to Sherbrooke, to the various villages in the Laurentians, and to Québec City. Morning, noon, early afternoon, and midnight buses cover the distance between Toronto and Montréal in about seven hours. From Boston, **Vermont Transit** (tel. 617/423-5810) runs three daily buses to Montréal, with extra service in the busy summer months. The journey takes about seven hours and costs $30.90. From New York City, **Greyhound** (tel. 212/594-2000) operates eight buses daily in each direction on the eight-hour journey; tickets cost $31.55 one way, $59.95 round trip.

In summer, Greyhound Lines also operates services daily on the route from Montréal to Burlington, Vt., North Conway, N.H., Old Orchard Beach, Me., Boston, Mass.

Once you've arrived at the Terminus Voyageur in Montréal, you're virtually right on top of the **Berri-de-Montigny Métro station,** the junction of all lines and the starting point for a quick trip to any quarter of the city. If you'd rather take a taxi, there will be one waiting just outside the terminal building.

By Air

Montréal's two international airports are served by most of the world's major airlines. By far the greatest number of visitors come by way of North American carriers: Air Canada, CP Air, Delta, and the closer-to-home regional airlines such as Eastern Provincial Airways and Québecair.

Montréal's **Mirabel Airport,** 35 miles northwest of the city, is the world's largest in terms of surface area. It handles most flights from other continents. **Dorval Airport,** 13 miles southwest of the center of town on Montréal Island, handles intra-Canadian flights and those coming from the United States and Mexico. To travel between airports, take the **Aéroservice bus** (tel. 849-4761; $5), which connects the two airports and also downtown Montréal (the terminal is in the Place Bonaventure parking garage building, next to the Queen Elizabeth and Bonaventure hotels, at the corner of University and Lagauchetière Sts.). **Murray Hill Bus Company** runs airport buses to and from Dorval Airport, stopping at the major downtown hotels. First stop downtown is the Queen Elizabeth. Trips run every 20 minutes. If you're staying at a smaller hotel, to catch the bus out to the airport (Dorval) take the Métro to the Bonaventure station, follow signs for Central Station and the Queen Elizabeth Hotel, and wait at the hotel's Mansfield St. entrance.

Canada's major car-rental firm, **Tilden Car Rentals,** has service desks at both airports, and in the city. You can reserve a Tilden car ahead of time through any Tilden office in Canada, or through any National Car Rental office in the U.S. or call the reservation office in Montréal (tel. 514/842-9445). At Dorval, the number is 514/636-9030; at Mirabel, 514/476-3460; the rental office in Montréal is at 514/878-2771.

By Rail

Montréal is a major terminus on Canada's **VIA Rail** network, and is served by daily trains from Halifax, Sydney, Gaspé, Saint John, Chicoutimi, Senneterre, Québec City, Sherbrooke, Ottawa/Hull, Mont-Laurier, Toronto, Vancouver, and Winnipeg. From the U.S., Amtrak operates two trains to Montréal. The *Montrealer* is a night train operating between Washington via New York to Montréal; the *Adirondack* is a day train between New York and Montréal. The trip between New York and Montréal takes slightly over nine hours.

There are two principal train stations in the center of Montréal. **Windsor Station** (tel. 395-5151), Peel and Lagauchetière Sts., is right next to the Place du Canada, and is connected to the Bonaventure Métro station by an underground walkway. Windsor is the terminus for Canadian Pacific trains. **Central Station,** (tel. 861-7311), Canadian National's terminus, is right beneath the Queen Elizabeth Hotel at Mansfield and Dorchester, also connected to the Bonaventure Métro station by an underground passage. The two stations, Windsor and Central, are only about four blocks apart.

ORIENTATION: When Jacques Cartier sailed up the St. Lawrence in 1535,

he came to a large island dominated by a hill and inhabited by at least a thousand people. The "Indians" called the place Hochelaga; Cartier christened it Mont Réal ("Royal Mountain"), perhaps in honor of his patron, the king of France. **Mount Royal** is now a park right in the center of Montréal, and you can drive, walk, or take a horse-drawn calèche to the top for a view of the city, the island, and the St. Lawrence.

You can get a marvelous view of the city without even hiking up Mount Royal, though. The Canadian Imperial Bank of Commerce building at the southwest corner of Dominion Square (corner of Dorchester and Peel Sts.) has a rooftop observatory open 10 a.m. to 10 p.m. daily, at 75¢ admission for adults, 25¢ for children. For a nighttime view, rocket to the 36th floor of the Château Champlain hotel just half a block away from the bank and gaze at the glittering lights through the floor-to-ceiling semicircular windows of L'Escapade bar and supper club. A quick look around will cost you nothing; a drink at the bar with a window-side seat runs about $3 to $4. If you come here at lunch, the all-you-can-eat buffet costs $7.50, plus tax, service, and tip. There's a similar buffet special offered in Place Ville-Marie's cross-shaped skyscraper. Enter the Royal Bank Building and take the elevator to Altitude 737 on the 45th floor. The buffet lunch ($9.75) is served daily from noon to 3, a buffet dinner ($18.75) from 6 to 9 p.m. Call 861-3511 for reservations.

The heart of Montréal is just south of Mount Royal. In the 19th century the western portion of the center of town—roughly from University St. west—was English-speaking, and the eastern portion was French-speaking. Although this neat division is long gone, vestiges of English "West" Montréal and French "East" Montréal remain. For instance, the largely English-controlled business district is in the west, centered on Dominion Square; the French-speaking Université de Montréal is in eastern Montréal around the Berri-de-Montigny Métro station and rue St-Denis. **Old Montréal,** the historic heart of the city, is south of the East-West Autoroute and down by the seaport. Long neglected as a waterfront district, today it is booming as a protected architectural-historic area, although businesses, warehouses, and shipping companies still occupy many of the buildings.

If the wealthy English-speaking Montrealers lived in the plush stone houses of Westmount, and French-speaking Montrealers filled the eastern parts, immigrants from Europe tended to settle in between, along **St. Lawrence Blvd.** (nicknamed "The Main") and rue St-Urbain. Today the area is still one of delightful cultural diversity. The Chinese, however, settled in a mini-**Chinatown** south of Dorchester Blvd. and north of Old Montréal, centered on Lagauchetière and Clark Sts. Dozens of Chinese groceries, import shops, restaurants, laundries, churches, and businesses—even pagoda-topped telephone booths—still crowd these narrow streets.

On the northern side of Mount Royal, and south across the St. Lawrence in **Longueuil,** the city's residential districts expanded to form one great urban conglomeration connected by bridges, expressways, and Montréal's marvelously modern and efficient Métro subway system—which brings us to the subject of transportation.

GETTING AROUND: About the nicest way to get around in Montréal is to walk: at street level in summer, in the underground city during winter. But for speed and economy, nothing beats Montréal's fabulous **Métro** system. Long, modern, speedy trains whisk you through an ever-expanding network of underground tunnels for 50¢ a ride; if you buy a book of 13 tickets for $5, the price per ride goes down to 38½¢. Buy your ticket book (*carnet de tickets*) at the ticket window of any station, and then slip a ticket into the slot in the turnstile to enter the system. (If you pay cash, drop two quarters down the little plastic chute in the ticket-seller's booth; if you need change, he'll give you the full amount, and *then* you drop the 50¢ down the chute.) Take a transfer from the machine (*correspondances*) just inside the turnstiles of every station, and this allows you to catch a bus at *any other* Métro station for no extra fare. But remember to take your transfer at the station where you enter the system. The Métro runs from about 5:30 a.m. to 1:30 a.m. By the way, if you're starting your trip by bus and you plan to continue on the Métro, ask the bus driver for a transfer when you board, and the Métro portion is yours at no extra cost. Buses cost the same as Métro trains, but the fare must be paid in exact change; and Métro tickets are good on buses, too. Most transfers from one Métro line to another can be made at the Berri-de-Montigny and Lionel Groulx stations.

Otherwise, there are the **taxis:** large American-style cars of various makes run by a variety of private companies and charging 70¢ drop-rate, about 70¢ per kilometer thereafter. Tip about 15%, as in the U.S. Your hotel can help you call a cab, or you can walk to any large hotel or transport terminal.

Finally, there are Montréal's romantic calèches (warm weather only), horse-drawn open carriages which wait at Dominion Square downtown, and at Place Jacques-Cartier in Old Montréal, to take visitors clip-clopping through the city's sights. In winter, the drivers hitch their steeds to old-fashioned sleighs for the ride to the top of Mount Royal, the horses puffing steam, the passengers bundled in sleigh rugs. A ride is simply unforgettable. Prices are open to haggling, but start about $15 to $20 per hour for the carriage or sleigh, which can seat four comfortably, five if one sits with the driver.

Guided Tours

Dominion Square is the center for guided tours. Many **taxi drivers** will be happy to take you on a tour of the city for the calèche rate of $15 to $20 per hour.

From time to time **free walking tours** of the city are offered. You can get the latest up-to-date information on itineraries and schedules by calling the Tourism Information Office of the city's Public Relations Department at 872-3561 on weekdays, 872-3455 on weekends; or try the Québec Tourism Information Office at 873-2015.

Commercial guided tours in air-conditioned buses are offered by the **Gray Line** (Metropolitan Provincial), 1241 Peel St. (tel. 866-4641): and by the **Murray Hill Company,** 1380 rue Barre (tel. 937-5311). Prices and tour itineraries are similar for both companies. The basic city tour takes 2½ hours and costs $6.50 for adults, $3.25 for children. For an extra $2 per adult, $1 per child, you can sign up for the deluxe city tour which includes a trailer-train ride through Mount Royal Park (tour buses are forbidden there, hence the open-sided trailer-train) and an hour-long stop at St. Joseph's Oratory. Other tours take you to St. Helen's Island, the St. Lawrence Seaway, the Laurentians, and even for a cruise on the river; but speaking of cruises, you can sign up for a cruise directly with the boat company and save yourself some money: read on.

River Cruises

Montréal Harbor Cruises, P.O. Box 217, Brossard, P.Q. (tel. 676-2966), operates several boats which ply the waters of Montréal harbor and the St. Lawrence, giving voyagers a unique skyline view of the city from the water. The M/V *Miss Olympia* sails on two tours daily, 1½ hours in length, departing at 2 and 4 p.m. from mid-May to mid-June and during the last three weeks of September. In high summer, *Miss Olympia* sets out on a 4 p.m. cruise (1½ hours), an 8 p.m. "sunset cruise," (one hour), and a 9 p.m. evening cruise (two hours). You save money if you take the sunset cruise—$4.50 per adult, $2 per child—but you also meet up with the tour-group people, who are encouraged to take this sailing. At other times, the fare is $5 for adults, $2.50 for kids.

The same company operates the M/V *Concordia,* with four daily cruises lasting two hours (at night, three hours) priced at $6 for adults, $3 for kids. Both boats have toilets and bars, and the *Concordia* has a dance floor as well for that three-hour evening cruise.

Departure for both boats is from Victoria Pier at the foot of rue Berri in Old Montréal. You can park free at the dock, or take the Métro to the Champ-de-Mars station and walk the six blocks to the dock.

1. Where to Stay

Luckily for visitors, Montréal has a full range of accommodations, with suitable rooms in all price categories from $10 a night to $100 a night and up. The bulk of the city's rooms are concentrated in the moderate to high price brackets, but with careful shopping following the suggestions outlined below, you'll be able to savor this fabulous city's delights at a very reasonable cost.

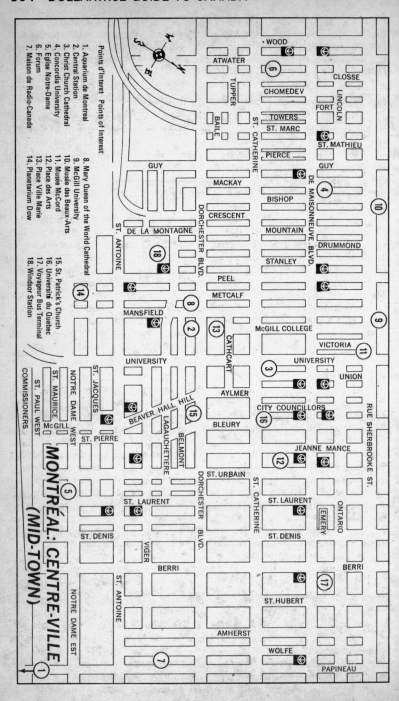

Points d'interet Points of Interest

1. Aquarium de Montreal
2. Central Station
3. Christ Church Cathedral
4. Concordia University
5. Eglise Notre-Dame
6. Forum
7. Maison de Radio-Canada

8. Mary Queen of the World Cathedral
9. McGill University
10. Musée des Beaux-Arts
11. Musée McCord
12. Place des Arts
13. Place Ville Marie
14. Planetarium Dow

15. St. Patrick's Church
16. Université du Quebec
17. Voyageur Bus Terminal
18. Windsor Station

MONTRÉAL: CENTRE-VILLE (MID-TOWN)

English and French are spoken in every place recommended here. To encourage the tourist trade, the provincial government withdrew its room tax, and so you will have no tax added to your bill, although in the more expensive places there may be a service charge.

Read carefully now, for these tips could save you tens or even hundreds of dollars. First of all, plan at least part of your visit in Montréal for Friday, Saturday, and Sunday nights, for those are the nights when virtually all luxury hotels and many moderately priced hotels offer special weekend rates, sometimes as much as 50% lower than normal Monday through Thursday night rates. You must stay a minimum of two nights; sometimes bonuses such as a continental breakfast, a welcome cocktail, or a free city tour are thrown in. The special rates might look like this: if a double room costs $50 to $66 Monday through Thursday, you may pay only $28 to $30 per night on Friday through Sunday for the same double room (if you're traveling alone, you end up paying the same $28 to $30 double rate). After the weekend rate is past you may want to move to a more modest establishment, but for three nights you will have had all the luxuries of a grand hotel—swimming pool, sauna, perhaps even tennis courts and health club, not to mention luxury accommodations—all for just a few dollars over the price of a well-run pension or tourist home. It's best to call and reserve your room in advance at the special rate. In mid-July and August it's conceivable that some hotels might be full and not offer the special rates, but Montréal's hotel industry is presently suffering from overcapacity (too many rooms) and more often than not there are lots of rooms available on weekends, when the business clientele is not in town.

Next, a family almost always gets to occupy a room paying only the normal double-room price, that is, kids stay for free; you may have to take one of the hotel's better and slightly higher priced rooms (usually with two double beds) to qualify for the kids-free deal. Age limits vary from up to 12 years to up to 18 or even 19 years old. If you do need two rooms to house your large family, normally you will be charged only the *single*-person price for each room—if you know to ask for it, of course. In addition, every large hotel has roll-away beds for a small charge (usually only $2 to $6), and so even if your adult son or daughter (or aunt, uncle, friend, etc.) doesn't qualify for kids-free, you pay only marginally more.

Senior citizens who are members of a recognized senior-citizens' organization can often get discounts in large hotels merely by showing their ID card and asking. In fact, very few people staying in a large moderately priced or high-priced hotel pay the so-called rack rates (the prices charged someone who just walks in off the street and asks for a room). Salesmen, honeymooners, military personnel, "scouts" for conventions, conventioneers themselves, sports fans on a trip to a match, etc., all get special rates. Most times they've been reserved in advance, but in any case, on any rationale, it's worthwhile asking about discounts if you plan to stay at a big place Monday through Thursday. Even a little good-natured haggling is liable to produce dollar-saving results, particularly during off-season times. Try it, and then go to dinner on the substantial savings.

Here, then, are Montréal's best places to stay. They've been chosen for their good locations, presentability, value for money, and for such things as good views, quiet locations, and interesting histories. First some of the city's very finest (and very expensive) establishments, then the many moderately priced hotels, and finally some selected small hotels and tourist homes, plus "Ys" and a Youth Hostel.

BONJOUR MONTRÉAL: Montréal had its best tourism year ever in 1976, when the XXI Olympiad drew hundreds of thousands of visitors from all over the world. Recent years have hardly approached that level, and so the city's Chamber of Commerce, the national transportation ministry, and the provincial government have gotten together to offer special package deals on hotel rooms, meals, rental cars, public transportation, and tickets to concerts and special events. Called "Bonjour Montréal," the program will be aimed first at European travelers, and later at the North American market. As of this writing, "Bonjour Montréal" is expected to swing into action at the beginning of the 1980 tourism season. Under the plan, if you pay for two nights at a participating hotel (most of these are first class or deluxe), you'll get the third night for free, and also a host of other cut-rate deals. Look for advertisements, ask at the Tourism Information Offices, or drop by Central Station beneath the Queen Elizabeth Hotel and see if "Bonjour Montréal" has its information booth set up by the time you arrive.

THE TOP HOTELS (Doubles for $50 and up): Remember—it's worth repeating—that the prices quoted below are the normal man-off-the-street rates, and that most people staying in these luxury places do so with the benefit of discounts and special deals: be sure to ask about ways of bringing the price down.

In 1912 the **Ritz-Carlton** (tel. 514/842-4212; toll-free reservations through Inter-Continental Hotels) opened its doors to the carriage trade, and over the years the clientele has remained faithful. Carriages gave way to Pierce-Arrows, and those in turn gave way to Rollses and Lamborghinis. You'll always see a few of these (or at *least* a Cadillac limo or custom-built Lincoln) parked in readiness near the front door at 1228 Sherbrooke West, corner of Drummond, Montréal, PQ H3G 1H6.

Svelte beauties and silver-haired tycoons move easily through the classic elegance of gilt trim and crystal-and-brass sconces, the Palm Court reminiscent of Victoria's reign, and in fine weather, in the gardens complete with duck pond. Although the Ritz is only a few blocks from the boutiques of Crescent St., the antique shops on Mountain St. and Sherbrooke, and the big department stores of downtown, the hotel has its own branch of Holt Renfrew so that guests can shop for Paris haute couture and Savile Row–style tailoring right "at home." The Ritz's Café de Paris (see restaurants, below) is one of Montréal's finest, and the wine cellar has been building its stock for three-quarters of a century.

Rooms are priced the same here, whether occupied by one person or two. There are 247 of them, priced at $44 to $53 single, $54 to $62 double. Not that it matters much to faithful clients of the Ritz, but you should know that like several other long-established downtown hotels, this one has no swimming pool.

The **Hyatt Regency Montréal** (tel. 514/879-1370; for toll-free reservations in the U.S., call 800/288-9000; in Canada, 800/361-6172) keeps to the tradition established by earlier Hyatt hotels for breathtaking design and the height of modern luxury. All of the familiar Hyatt trademarks are found in the Montréal hotel: glass-walled elevators, a revolving rooftop restaurant, a lofty "atrium" reception hall, an indoor pool with a view of the city, and no fewer than nine bars and restaurants. The 763 rooms are outspokenly modern in decor and amenities, and predictably high in price: $58 to $66 single, $65 to $73 double. But the special weekend offer makes the Hyatt a good place to stay Friday through Sunday nights, and two people can usually stay for less than

$20 per person per night—ultimate luxury for a moderate price. You'll find the futuristic Hôtel Régence Hyatt Montréal (that's its name in French) at Place Victoria (Métro: Victoria), 777 University St., Montréal, PQ H3C 3Z7.

Of all the striking ultramodern architecture in this city of great new buildings, the Complexe Desjardins has got to be the most awe-inspiring. Air France's Montréal hostelry, the **Hôtel Méridien,** (tel. 514/285-1450; toll-free reservations through Air France) is an integral part of the complex, and from its "foyer" (lobby) or coffeeshop you can gaze down on the complex's plaza, always bustling with activity. Service is of a high standard, decor is bold but harmonious, and convenience is unsurpassed. A glass-enclosed elevator glides from the foyer down to the various levels of the complex while others whiz up and down the dozen floors which hold 600 guest rooms.

One could easily spend a week's vacation at the Méridien and never tire of attractions that are all within the same complex, one of the foremost attractions being the most alluring hotel swimming-pool-cum-sundeck in all Montréal. But for diversion, the Place des Arts is right across the street (or right under the street if you use the underground walkway); the Place des Arts Métro station connects you with the rest of Montréal's underground world. The downtown shopping district, Old Montréal, and the ethnic neighborhoods are each about a 15-minute walk away. The haunts of Montréal's Chinatown are in the next block.

As the Méridien is an Air France hotel, and located in a predominantly French-speaking part of town, the staff takes special delight—and patience—with guests who make an effort to resurrect their sometimes long-neglected French; but no worry if you've never spoken a word, for the staff all speak English, and will be glad to do so if you want them to.

Rooms are priced at $50 to $60 single, $56 to $66 double. Parking in the complex garage is $4 a day, which is fairly inexpensive by city standards. Even if you don't stay here, come for a look and perhaps a spot of breakfast in Le Vieux Marché coffeeshop, overlooking the plaza of Complexe Desjardins.

Perhaps the best words to describe the **Queen Elizabeth** (tel. 514/861-3511; toll-free reservations through Hilton Reservation Service) are "solid comfort." The substantial 1200-room building at 900 Dorchester Blvd. West (corner of Manchester), Montréal, PQ H3B 4A5, has been providing well-heeled travelers with luxury accommodations and dependable service for several decades. Besides a prime location for downtown sightseeing, the Queen is the first stop on the route of the Murray Hill bus from Dorval Airport. Canadian National's Central Station is as close as can be: the hotel is built right on top of it! Place Ville-Marie is right across the street; Place Bonaventure, Place du Canada, the Métro, and Canadian Pacific's Windsor Station are all accessible by underground arcades. In short, you're right at the center of everything here, and satisfaction is a sure thing.

Room rates go from $40 to $49 single, $49 to $58 double, with roll-away beds priced at $8. Various discounts, weekend and excursion packages bring down these prices, as does the hotel's unusual family plan whereby children not only stay free with their parents, but if the family's large and needs two rooms, both rooms are priced at the *single* rate, which works out to a discount of almost 25% from the comparable rate for two double rooms. One of Montréal's best restaurants, the Beaver Club, is just off the lobby. Hilton runs the whole show. If you want to be at the very heart of Montréal, this is the place to stay.

Les Quatre Saisons ("The Four Seasons," tel. 514/284-1110; for toll-free reservations, call Four Seasons Hotels) is a fabulous sybarites' hostelry very near the business and shopping center of Montréal, at 1050 Sherbrooke West, near the intersection of Peel. The whole idea here is to get away from the normal "business meeting and/or convention" mentality, concentrating instead on pleasure: the 320 rooms are particularly large and stylishly furnished, and if you're going all out you can hire one of 32 suites or even a split-level penthouse. Saunas, whirlpool baths, indoor pool, valet parking, and 24-hour room service are laid on to keep guests happy, even euphoric. Restaurants and discos abound, naturally, and the pastimes and pleasures of Crescent St. are a short four-block walk away. McGill University is right next door.

To stay here, whatever the season, one person pays $59 to $74; two persons pay $70 to $84. As for those split-level penthouses, there are only two of them, and if you have to ask the price, well. . . . Nearest Métro station is Peel.

The bold and comely architecture of the **Château Champlain** (tel. 514/878-1688; or call LRI Reservations) has given rise to many compliments despite wisecracks about "a 36-story, 614-room cheese grater"—when you see the hotel, towering above the Place du Canada (Montréal, PQ H3B 4C9), you can judge for yourself. The semicircular plate-glass windows may lend the hotel its resemblance to a kitchen utensil, but they also provide dramatic views of the city; from the Penthouse L'Escapade on the top floor, the views carry past the city limits, and are simply breathtaking. From the hotel, just south of Dominion Square, you can walk easily to the shops on rue Ste-Catherine, or take the Métro from beneath the hotel to anywhere in town. Windsor Station is right next door. Room rates start at $50 single, $60 double.

In the realm of luxury accommodations, Loew's **Hôtel La Cité** (tel. 514/288-6666; toll-free reservations through Loew's Representation International) offers top-class luxury rooms and service for a surprisingly moderate price. The reason is that the hotel is part of a beautiful shopping-cinema-apartment development slightly out of the mainstream of downtown life, being four blocks from the Place des Arts, and about ten blocks from the central downtown focus of Dominion Square. But its position at 3625 Ave. du Parc (at Prince Arthur; Montréal, PQ H2X 3P8), is certainly not what one would call inconvenient. And for the low prices of $40, $44, $48, $52, or $56 single, $50, $54, $58, $62, or $66 double, you get public and guest rooms of a bold modern design and supreme comfort, plus the facilities of the La Cité complex: indoor and outdoor pools, squash and tennis courts, saunas, massage, and inhalation, even a gymnasium. And of course a disco, cinemas, and shops are all within the same structure. Parking is free here, making it a particularly good hotel for those with private cars. Weekend special deals can bring the price of a double room down to as low as $28 per day (if you stay at least two days). Nearest Métro station is at Place des Arts.

THE UPPER BRACKET (Doubles for $30 to $50): In this price range, weekend and special-deal discounts are also a prominent feature which may bring the $30 to $50 figure down to something like $24 to $40. Remember also that rooms with only one double bed and with not-so-choice views are offered at a nicely lower price than their more deluxe neighboring chambers.

For many years the **Sheraton Mount Royal Hotel** (tel. 514/842-7777; toll-free reservations through Sheraton) has been Old Faithful to tens of thousands of Montréal visitors. With over 1000 guest rooms, the hotel can host the largest groups and still have a few rooms left over. Old-fashioned and graceful public rooms echo the hotel's long tradition of hospitality, while cheery and up-to-date guest rooms provide every comfort. "Rack rates" (the prices charged the traveler who just walks in and asks for a room) are fairly reasonable at $38 to $46 single, $45 to $55 double, and the ebb and flow of trade should provide many opportunities for reductions. Weekend deals are a natural, and with a bit of good-natured haggling one should be able to make a deal on a stay of several days at an attractive reduced rate. Remember, an empty hotel room is lost money to a hotelier. The Shertaon's location is excellent, at 1455 Peel St., between rues Ste-Catherine and Maisonneuve; it sits right on top of the Peel Métro station.

The **Hotel Constellation** (tel. 514/845-1231; toll-free reservations through KLM) is the Royal Dutch airline's contribution to Montréal hospitality. Comfortable and modern without being ostentatious, its 162 rooms all come with color TVs, and many have city views worthy of even more expensive hotels. Its location at 3407 Peel St., Montréal, PQ H3A 1W7, is a bit misleading as it actually towers over Sherbrooke, although the front door is in fact on Peel. The location has its advantages: nothing downtown is more than about four blocks away, and the slopes of Mount Royal are even closer. McGill University is virtually next door. Besides 200 modern rooms, the Constellation has several restaurants, its own disco, a piano bar, and a glassed-in sidewalk cafe looking onto busy Sherbrooke. Room prices are especially good if you're traveling alone: singles cost $38 to $46; doubles are $46 to $54. Children under 16 stay free. If you're going by Métro, get off at Peel and walk one block north to the hotel. No pool here, by the way.

The handsome tower standing at 505 Sherbrooke East (at Berri) is the luxurious **Hotel Howard Johnson Richelieu** (tel. 514/842-8581; toll-free reservations through Howard Johnson's), Montréal, PQ H2L 1K2. Hojo's hostelry here, unlike the highway motor lodges, is quite deluxe and can boast an enclosed and heated swimming pool, a sauna, and its own (free) covered parking garage in addition to 330 deluxe guest rooms, all with color TV. The location is not bad, being right next to the Sherbrooke Métro station, only a block or so from Place St-Louis, and a short stroll from the French-language university quarter. Special weekend package deals are offered virtually all the time, and the family plan allows kids under 18 to stay with their parents for free (unless they need a roll-away, which costs $6; cribs are free in any case). Basic rates, then, are $34 to $46 for a single room, $42 to $54 double. Because most rooms have two double beds, the Howard Johnson Richelieu is an especially good place for families to stay.

The Holiday Inn chain has no less than seven hotels in and around Montréal, but besides the Holiday Inn Downtown, only one other is convenient to the heart of the city. It's the **Holiday Inn Place Dupuis** (tel. 514/842-4881; toll-free reservations through any Holiday Inn), 1415 rue St-Hubert, at Ste-Catherine. The 357 rooms are priced at $39 to $41 single, $45 to $49 double, the higher price in each case being for a room with two double beds. An extra person pays $4, and a roll-away bed is $2. The two-double-bed price, as always at Holiday Inns, is the super-bargain for families, as teenage children stay free. The Holiday Inn Place Dupuis has an indoor, year-round swimming pool and a sauna. As for location, here you're in the heart of traditionally Gallic eastern Montréal, recently completely redeveloped. The Voyageur bus terminal is a block away, and the mammoth Berri-de-Montigny Métro station, where all tracks meet, is only a few steps from the hotel's door. Free parking.

The trio of modern high-rise hotels at the corner of Sherbrooke St. West and Ave. due Parc is led by the huge 500-room **Holiday Inn Downtown** (tel. 514/842-6111; for toll-free reservations contact any Holiday Inn; official address: 420 Sherbrooke St. West, Montréal, PQ H3A 2L9). Behind that incredible metal-sculpture facade are the various accoutrements of an up-to-date modern and ultra-comfortable hotel: indoor pool and sauna, a newsstand which carries U.S. as well as Canadian newspapers, free indoor parking, restaurants, a lounge with live entertainment, and rooms with color TV. Single rooms cost

$39 to $41 and double rooms are $45 to $49, the higher price being for a room with two double beds (this higher price is the one you must pay to have your teenage children stay free with you in the same room). Kids under 12 are free with their parents in any room; if you need a roll-away, the cost is only $2. Each extra person (not a child) pays $4. At this price, two couples could occupy a room with two double beds for $57 per night, or only $14.25 per person. Nearest Métro station is Place des Arts, one block south.

Also at the intersection of Sherbrooke St. West and Ave. du Parc is the towering **Quality Inn Montréal** (tel. 514/844-8851; toll-free reservation through Quality Inns), 410 Sherbrooke St. West (between Durocher and Hutcheson) Montréal, PQ H3A 1B9. Accommodations here are virtually the same as at the Holiday Inn nearby, even to the sauna and indoor pool, although a few rooms have kitchenette units. Rates are about the same, too: single rooms cost $34 to $38 and doubles are $40 to $48; an extra person in a room pays $5. Kids under 16 stay free, and senior citizens who hold eligible ID cards can get a 10% discount. Note that the Quality Inn prices are a bit lower than Holiday Inn's because the Quality Inn has no private parking facilities.

Last of the triad of hotels at Sherbrooke and Ave. du Parc is the least expensive of all. It's the modern 200-room **Hôtel Le Sherbourg** (tel. 514/842-3961; toll-free reservations in the U.S., 800/228-2000; in Canada, Zenith 06040), 475 Sherbrooke St. West, Montréal, PQ H3A 2L9. A member of the Rodeway Inns group, Le Sherbourg has several bonuses to set it apart from its neighbors. Besides indoor parking, sauna, indoor swimming pool, restaurants, and the like, Le Sherbourg has a kitchenette unit in each room, and a flair for rock-bottom weekend specials. In recent years the price for a two-night weekend stay starting Friday or Saturday has been $24.50 per night, double or single; another deal throws in a bunch of roses for her, a Cuban cigar for him, at a price of $28 per night. Both these special rates apply to a two-room suite. Normal weekday rates, then, are $32 single, $36 double—still very reasonable. If you arrive by Métro, get off at Place des Arts.

Now for one of Montréal's greatest lodging bargains, in terms of value for money. There's a hotel overlooking Dominion Square, equidistant from the Peel and Bonaventure Métro stations, surrounded by restaurants, department stores, and the business world; its guest ledger reads like a "Who's Who Among the Great and Powerful" during the time when the British Empire was at its height. This is the **Windsor Hotel** (tel. 514/866-9611), 1170 Peel St., Montréal, PQ H3B 2T4.

As you climb its front stairs and enter the reception area paneled in dark wood, you begin to realize that the Windsor is a well-preserved "period piece," kept much the same as in its heyday. Past the reception area is an antechamber, and then a long promenade glittering with crystal chandeliers and lined with serene old oil paintings. Mirrored double doors along the promenade open onto immense ballrooms, now used mostly for business meetings. At the end of the promenade up a short flight of stairs is a baronial fireplace and a baby grand piano.

The Windsor is the sort of place which might have been gutted and completely rebuilt inside at fantastic expense if the owners had wanted to "go modern." Instead, they wisely sought to preserve its character, adding modern conveniences and carefully maintaining—rather than reconstructing—the guest rooms. This is how they kept prices to such reasonable levels: single rooms with a double bed are $30 to $34, with twin beds $32 to $36; double rooms are $35 to $42 with a double bed, $38 to $44 with twin beds. Family rooms cost $58 to $69; an extra cot is only $6. Two children up to 14 years old can stay in the same room with their parents for no extra charge. Special weekend packages are offered for the deluxe suites. There's no swimming pool, and some of the room TVs might be black and white, but the ambience is unmatchable: if potentates were in the habit of scribbling graffiti, some rooms in the Windsor would bear scrawls saying "Winston Churchill Slept Here."

Montréal's **Hôtel Château Versailles** (tel. 514/933-3611), 1659 Sherbrooke St. West (at Côte-des-Neiges), Montréal, PQ H3H 1E3, has a unique reputation among the city's fine hostelries. For many years it has been the place to stay for visitors who wanted elegant, dignified accommodations and service at rates just at the top of the moderate price scale. Although its owners began the establishment as a European-style pension in the late 1950s, it has grown and absorbed four fine old stone houses holding a total of 70 guest rooms. For its owners, it's a dream come true: a family-run hostelry of comfort and distinction to serve as an alternative to the convention-filled towers downtown. Rates are $32 to $40 single, $36 to $48 double, with an extra person paying $6 (ask about special family rates—but reserve in advance for these). For this price you get the usual high-class hotel services: bellhop, color TV, air conditioning, private baths—without the usual anonymous treatment.

The Château Versailles is one-of-a-kind in Montréal, and so you should make reservations as far as possible in advance. From Québec, Ontario, and the Atlantic provinces you can even call toll free: 800/361-7169. The nearest Métro station is Guy, 2½ blocks away. By the way, if you visit Montréal during the winter months, you may be able to benefit from the special weekend rates offered by the Château Versailles, something like $48 to $55 for two persons for two nights.

At the corner of Dorchester and Guy is the **Hôtel Maritime** (tel. 514/932-1411; toll-free reservations in Canada, 800/661-1061), one of the smaller but modern hotels which are sort of hard to find in Montréal. Big-name hotel facilities are all yours here, right down to the indoor pool, sauna, exercise room, individually controlled room air conditioning, and color TV. But prices are moderate, and offer particularly good bargains during the off-season period from November through April. Single rooms are $34 to $40 and double rooms are $40 to $46 in summer's high season, dropping about $6 per room in wintertime. An extra person pays $6, but children up to 16 years old can stay with their parents for no extra charge. Free indoor parking. When you're out searching for the Hôtel Maritime, you'll spot it easily by the circular restaurant perched on a concrete pillar right at the corner of Dorchester and Guy—official address: 1155 Guy St., Montréal, PQ H3H 2K5. Get off the Métro at either Laurent L'Allier or Guy. Here you're only about three blocks from downtown and the frenetic action on Crescent St.

A half-block from the Hôtel Maritime is **Ramada Inn Montréal Downtown** (tel. 514/866-4611; toll-free reservations through Ramada Inn), a slightly more luxurious place to stay with about the same services and facilities. Prices are $37 single, $45 double, for the 200 rooms in the modern seven-story structure.

THE MODERATE-PRICE BARGAINS (Doubles for $17 to $36):

Several hotels offer exceptional value, giving full hotel service and comfort even though prices are at the very bottom of the moderate range. Location may not be as central as the more expensive establishments, but a book of Métro tickets ($5) shortens the distance, and one book should last you for the entire stay.

One of Montreal's most sensible places to stay is the modern and attractive **Hôtel Royal Roussillon** (tel. 514/849-3214), just steps from the Voyageur bus terminal and the "Latin Quarter" of rue St-Denis. The small, neat, and tidy building actually holds a surprisingly large number of guest rooms, 107 in all, plus a restaurant and bar. Emphasis is on good, cheerful, up-to-date guest rooms for a surprisingly moderate price, rather than on pools, sauna baths, tennis courts, and conventions. Thus two people can pay as little as $17 for a room with double bed, sink, radio, and TV, or $20 for a similar room with shower. More deluxe rooms come with combination tub-shower, air conditioning, radio, and TV, and cost $25 for a double bed, $27 for twin beds. Room prices are the same whether one or two people occupy the room; an extra person pays $5. The Royal Roussillon has two entrances, the main one being at 1610 rue St-Hubert, Montréal, PQ H2L 3Z3, only a few steps from the Métro station of Berri-de-Montigny. Free parking.

Now for one of Montréal's most fantastic lodging bargains. Because of the importance of tourism in Québec, the provincial government has set up an Institute of Tourism and Hotel Management for expert training of tourism personnel. Part of the institute's headquarters building at 3535 rue St-Denis (corner of Rigaud), Montréal, PQ H2X 3P1, is an honest-to-goodness no-nonsense hotel complete with reception desk, tremendous lobby, bar and lounge, and dining room. The **Hôtel de l'Institut** (tel. 514/873-4163) has 40 luxurious rooms and two suites, all serviced by students of the institute who are out to do their best. The rooms are top-rate, with the cheerful but tasteful decor and color TV you'd expect, but the service is even better because these young men and women really *care*. Prices for the relatively small number of rooms are incredibly low for what you get: $26 for a room with one large bed, $34 for a room with two large beds, for one or two people. An extra person pays $6; kids 12 and under stay free with their folks. The two sybaritic suites, by the way, cost $43, single or double.

When the institute was built a few years ago on the west side of lovely, traditional place St-Louis there was much grumbling by local residents who didn't want the intrusion of a large, modern structure. Now it's become part of the landscape, however, and offers budget-wise visitors a very special opportunity. A block-and-a-half walk will take you to the sidewalk cafes of rue St-Denis; the same stroll gets you to colorful St. Lawrence Blvd. Place St-Louis is right out the front door, and the Sherbrooke Métro station is literally right underneath the institute. Unbeatable!

The **Hôtel de La Salle** (tel. 514/866-6492), 1240 Drummond St. (at Ste-Catherine), Montréal, PQ H3G 1V7, is one of the city's older hotels. Much favored by young businessmen in town for work, the La Salle has all the conveniences in its 185 rooms, including air conditioning, TV sets, and private bathrooms. While it's not stylish, it's a comfortable place to stay, and certainly well located as the bustle of rue Ste-Catherine is a mere half block away. Summer rates are $30 to $32 single, $36 to $40 double, $46 triple; children 12 and under stay free in their parents' room. From November through April discount off-season rates are in effect, bringing these prices down $6 to $10 per room. The hotel has a disco, and the Irish pub in the basement draws a heavily local crowd. Parking is available at an extra fee.

Apartment Hotels

You can save money by preparing some of your own meals if you book a room at the **Crescent Apartment Hotel** (tel. 514/878-2711), 1214 Crescent St. Montréal, PQ H3G 2A9, because each room in this 14-story modern structure comes with a kitchenette fully equipped with pots, pans, plates, and utensils, plus a *grille-pain* (that's a toaster). AM-FM radio and color TV, air conditioning, and telephone are all here, and each room has a little balcony.

There's no pool or even lobby to speak of, and so prices are moderate, even for this choice downtown location. By the day, the price is $22 to $28 single, $26 to $33 double; by the week, handsome reductions are in order. Nearest Métro: Peel or Guy.

If the Crescent is full, have a look at **Bosquet Apartments** (tel. 514/585-0256), 1425 rue Beaubien Est, Montréal, PQ H2G 3C9, a smallish four-story modern building with furnished 2½-room apartments renting for $80 per week, $140 for two weeks. The only disadvantage here is that Bosquet Apartments is a good distance from downtown. Take the Métro to the Beaubien station and walk east along Beaubien to the corner of Garnier, and the Bosquet Apartments are right there.

THE BUDGET LINE-UP (Doubles for $10 to $20): By far the most economical place to stay in Montréal is at a tourist home, the YMCA, a small hotel in Old Montréal, or the Youth Hostel. The city has a very large number of tourist homes—something like 100—but the number of eligible places drops dramatically when the noisy ones, the ones a long way from the center of town, the ones filled with long-term occupants, and the substandard ones are excluded. Those that are left have been included here. Because low-cost lodgings are so scarce in this metropolis, it's good to have reservations in advance if you can manage it.

On the Place Jacques-Cartier

Believe it or not, there are two budget-priced hotels right on the colorful Place Jacques-Cartier, the very heart of Old Montréal. Although they're both quite suitable I hasten to add that they're not for everyone. But if you're (a) young, and (b) traveling on a restricted budget, and (c) unconcerned about such luxuries as air conditioning other than an open window, or TVs in rooms, or even baths in rooms; if you (d) like rock music, and (e) antique, crafts, and imports shops, and (f) historical buildings, outdoor cafes, and a lively atmosphere, then you're the perfect candidate to be a guest at either the Hotel Iroquois or the Hotel Nelson.

The **Hotel Iroquois** (tel. 514/861-5416), 446 Place Jacques-Cartier, is on the west side of the square, with 99 rooms priced at $11 to $13 single, $22 to $26 double. Rooms are quite simple, and only the more expensive have bathrooms; others have washbasins, though. The **Hotel Nelson** (tel. 514/861-5731), 425 Place Jacques-Cartier, is even plainer than the Iroquois; rooms here are priced at $8 to $12 single, $13 to $20 double. If the hotel isn't very busy, chances are good you will be able to haggle over the price a bit, or perhaps pay bathless-room price for a room with bath. Virtually everyone staying here will be in their 20s, and most won't mind the rock music which throbs heavily in each hotel's street-level club (especially heavily Thursdays through Saturdays). If noise bothers you, be sure to get a room on one of the upper floors. Needless to say, it's a good idea to check out the room before you put your money down.

Montréal's "Ys"

Montréal has a number of YMCA and YWCA branches, but the two right downtown rent reasonably priced and respectable rooms, besides providing the traditional services such as swimming pool, athletic, and classroom facilities. The **YWCA Residence**, 1355 Dorchester West, Montréal, PQ H3G 1T3 (tel. 514/866-9941), is at the corner of Dorchester and Crescent, and thus very near the center of all the action. The closest Métro station is Laurent L'Allier. The residence has 120 rooms, but a portion of these are taken up by long-term residents. Make advance reservations by phone or letter to be sure of a room at these prices: singles for $10, $15, or $16; doubles for $18, $22, or $24. Dormitory beds cost only $6. The cheapest rooms have only running water; those next up in price have running water and are located very near a bathroom; the most expensive have private baths in the rooms. During the months from October through March, if you stay at the YW and pay for six nights, the seventh night is thrown in for free. There's a budget-priced cafeteria in the building, open from 8 a.m. to 7 p.m. *Note:* The YWCA accepts only women guests.

At the **YMCA,** 1441 Drummond St., Montréal, PQ H3G 1W5 (tel. 514/849-5331), both men and women are accepted as guests, and the location is even more central than that of the sister institution. Rooms start at $12.25 single ($10.25 if you're under 21 years of age), and progress to $27.50 for a double room with shower, toilet, washbasin, and color TV. In between are rooms with washbasins and TVs costing $16.75 to $20.25 single, $25.50 double. If your room has a telephone, it'll cost you an extra 50¢ per day. Although there are almost 500 rooms, it's still a good idea to call or write for rooms in advance. Métro: Peel.

Tourist Homes

Among the sturdy old stone row houses which line quiet Stanley St. is an attractive and very well-kept tourist lodge with the imposing dual-language name, **Le Foyer des Voyageurs Ambrose Travel Lodge** (tel. 514/844-0342 or 288-6922), 3422 Stanley St. (between McGregor and Sherbrooke), Montréal, PQ H3A 1R8. Situated only half a block north of Sherbrooke on the slopes of Mount Royal, it's a little over a block from the Peel Métro station, and barely three blocks from Dominion Square, the center of downtown Montréal. Behind the Ambrose's sturdy old oak doors and shingled gables painted bright blue is a selection of 22 guest rooms, varying in comfort and services, and priced from $14 to $18 single, $18 to $28 double, with a few suites costing as much as $35 per night. The lowest priced rooms share a bathroom; suites are good as family accommodations as they have private baths. Rooms are good, prices are right, and the location couldn't be better.

The **Bishop Guest House** (tel. 514/879-0500) at 1242 Bishop St., half a block south of rue Ste-Catherine, has only ten rooms, but all are equipped with bathrooms, air conditioning, and black-and-white television sets, plus comfortable beds. You may see a bit of chipped paint here and there, but housekeeping standards are in fact quite good, and while prices are officially $20 single, $30 double, substantial reductions are in order whenever the midsummer jam of crowds disappears. Good location, free parking.

Among the inexpensive and homey tourist lodges in Montréal's Latin Quarter, the **Castel St-Denis** (tel. 514/842-9719) is among the best. At 2099 Blvd. St-Denis, it's midway between Place St-Louis and the cafe-filled lower reaches of the boulevard, and not more than three blocks from the Voyageur bus terminal. The few rooms overlooking the busy street may be a bit noisy until midnight, but most of the 14 rooms are quiet all day and all night. Prices are right: singles cost $12 to $15 and doubles are $16 to $20, the more expensive rooms being slightly more deluxe and larger, with such services as private shower and TV set. Cheery, colorful, and clean. Although you're in the heart of French-speaking Montréal here, the man at the desk speaks both languages. The Castel St-Denis is just about equidistant from the Berri-de-Montigny and Sherbrooke Métro stations, but if you get off at Sherbrooke you will be walking downhill to get to the Castel—an important consideration if your bags are heavy.

Want a cozy guest house right near the bus station? **Le Breton Tourist Rooms** (tel. 514/524-7273) is at 1609 rue St-Hubert, so near that even the heaviest bags will not bog you down. Go out the main doors of the Voyageur terminal and turn left; St-Hubert is the next street over. Le Breton is in a row of fine old town houses once much the worse for wear, but now being refurbished and polished to a Beacon Hill sheen. Rooms at Le Breton are very comfortable and comely, not at all stark or basic, and cost $18 to $19 double without private bath, $22 with private bath. In any time but the hectic summer months these prices are open to dickering, and will no doubt be reduced a few dollars.

The **Armstrong Tourist Lodge** (tel. 514/845-6336) is the place to stay if you want plain but supremely convenient accommodations at a low price for a day or two. At 2028 Metcalfe St., Montréal, PQ H3A 1X8, the Armstrong is one of the few old houses left on a block which has seen a great deal of urban renewal. The nine rooms are old-fashioned, furnished with this and that, and may accommodate from one to four people (depending on which room) for anything from $10 to $14 single, to $16 for a small room with one double bed for two, or $18 for a larger double-bedded room with private shower. The Armstrong is on Metcalfe between Maisonneuve and Sherbrooke; nearest Métro station is Peel.

The Youth Hostel

Montréal's quaint **Youth Hostel** ("Auberge de Jeunesse" in French) is right next to the McGill campus at 3541 Aylmer St., between Milton and Prince Arthur, Montréal, PQ H2X 2B9 (tel. 514/843-3317). Clean and ship-shape, it draws a fascinating international crowd who come for the fellowship and the cheapest beds in town: $4.25 per person if you have a Youth Hostel card, $5.25 if you don't. The location's good, on a quiet street, but bed space is limited, and in the heavy summer season it may be good to call in advance.

Sometimes during the summer months it's possible to find a place to sleep in college dormitories or other large buildings converted to dormitories. The place to check for cheap beds in the central office for youth hostel activities. It's called the **Fédération Québecoise de l'Ajisme,** 1324 Sherbrooke St. West, Montréal, PQ H3G 1H9 (tel. 514/842-9048). "Ajisme" comes from the abbreviation "A.J." for Auberge de Jeunesse.

In fact, check with the Fédération for all the information you need on budget-priced youth and student travel, as they're plugged into the International Federation of Youth Travel Organizations, the outfit that knows all about student train, bus, and air discounts and special tours.

2. Montréal's Restaurants

No one's done an exact count, but Montréal is generally thought to have at least 5000 restaurants, large and small. Not only that, but Montréal's citizens of French, English, or immigrant background use them all heavily, all the time. Newspapers and even TV stations carry reportage on the latest new places to dine out. It all comes of a tradition born of the French passion for good dining, nurtured by the wealth of a New World colony, and later diversified by the immigrant flood from across the seas which brought diversity and exuberance along with many exotic recipes.

Finding your way through this culinary wonderland on a first visit can be dazzling, bewildering, and exhausting (not to mention fattening), and so I'll attempt to chart a course by recommending some of the best and most interesting places, grouped into convenient categories. This is by no means a complete or even inclusive list; many fine places had to be excluded because of space limitations; others were left out because they were inconvenient or confusing to find if you're a first-time visitor. You shouldn't go wrong at any establishment mentioned here. If you find an establishment to be otherwise than I've described it, please let me know at once. Also, if you come across a restaurant, cafe, or brasserie which seems exceptionally appealing, drop me a line and your suggestion may be printed as a "Reader's Selection" in the next edition of this guide.

MONTRÉAL'S TOP RESTAURANTS: French cuisine is not just an adman's or menu-writer's folly in Montréal, but a living tradition born in the days when France ruled this part of Canada. Chefs from France, Belgium, and Switzerland have come here to open their own restaurants in recent years, and the influx has helped to preserve the high standards of French cuisine à la Montréalaise. But cuisses de grenouille (frog legs) and onion soup are not the only things served in Montréal's top restaurants, for the sweeping plains of the prairie provinces provide a dependable supply of choice beef, and the northern wilderness yields such exotic things as moose, bear, venison, and elk. Whatever your preference, be it a hearty steak, succulent lobster, or delicate soufflé, you won't find better than in the following restaurants.

Important Note: Play it safe and call for reservations in any of these top places, and then keep the appointment. It's looked upon as very bad form to come late or not to come at all. If you can't make it, call and cancel. Proper dress is required in all of these establishments, even at lunchtime.

In a city with so much good cooking, it's almost impossible to choose one establishment to rank as "the best restaurant in Montréal." But a very large number of gourmets, if polled, would cast their votes for **Chez Bardet** (tel. 381-1777), 591 Blvd. Henri-Bourassa Est, open for lunch and dinner every day except Sunday. The restaurant is simple but elegant in the modern style, with reproductions of famous paintings on the walls and a magnificent tapestry as focal point. A small lounge near the bar accommodates diners waiting for their table. Service is supremely quiet, dignified, and attentive, and the food is the best.

The daily menu gastronomique might read like this: petite marmite or terrine de canard à l'Armagnac as first course (that's a duck pâté flavored with Armagnac brandy), followed by a fish course such as quenelles de brochet au Pernod (wonderfully light dumplings made of pike and flavored with Pernod, the anise liqueur) or perhaps delicate filets of sole and salmon. For a main course there is always a choice of, say, breast of capon or filet mignon; and dessert is a miracle of lightness: a soufflé Grand Marnier or poire bavaroise au Kümmel (pears Bavarian style, flavored with caraway). With coffee, service, and tip (but not including wine), the set price per person for such a memorable repast comes to about $34. Add $12 to $15 for a decent bottle of wine, and dinner for two can easily mount to $85. Full dinners ordered à la carte will cost more.

Call for reservations, and ask what the day's menu gastronomique is at the same time. Then take the Métro to the distant Henri-Bourassa station, northern end of the line. Take the escalator up and turn left at the top, following signs for "Boul. Henri-Bourassa Nord." When you emerge at street level, turn left and Chez Bardet is right there, in the building next door to the Métro exit.

The Hotel Ritz-Carlton, 1226 Sherbrooke St. West, corner of Drummond, has a long tradition to uphold when it comes to good dining. The Ritz's wine cellar has been abuilding for decades, and the hotel's **Café de Paris** (tel. 842-4212) is the place to go for a taste of the vintages and a superb lunch or dinner, at a suitably lofty price. The Café's dining room has a classic decor meant to harmonize with a delicious repast, and further harmony is provided by a pianist or trio. If you order from the Café's short but well-chosen menu, you might begin with iced melon au porto ($3), go on to tomatoes stuffed with shrimps ($10) or a chef's salad ($9); main courses can be light or hearty as you choose. There's curry ($9), sirloin steaks (priced from $8.50 to $14.50), to calf liver and bacon ($10). The wine list is much longer than the menu, and prices for well-chosen bottles begin at $10, hover at $16 to $20, and then shoot ever upward. Two can easily spend $60 to $75 for dinner here, with wine, a bit less at lunchtime, but the chef's daily suggestions are sure to be excellently prepared and much more moderately priced. A $25 lunch for two, with wine, is a possibility. The Café de Paris is open daily for lunch from noon to 3 p.m. and for dinner from 6 to 11 p.m.

After a morning or afternoon of shopping in the boutiques of Crescent St. or the antique stores along Sherbrooke, escape to the simple elegance of **Le Vert Galant** (tel. 844-4155), 1423/25 Crescent St. A headwaiter in tuxedo (naturally) will welcome you into several small rooms decorated with an old-fashioned and elegant simplicity, nothing being allowed to distract from the food itself. Lunch is quite a bargain, considering the standards of preparation and service, and you may have something like filet de doré amandine (a filet of Canada's supremely delicious walleyed pike/perch, sauteed with almonds), plus soup, vegetables, and dessert, for about $6 to $7. But dinner is the main performance, and whereas lunch is served only on weekdays, dinner is served seven days a week starting at 6 p.m. Appetizers range in price from oysters Rockefeller ($4) to Volga caviar (the real thing—and it should be, at $20 the portion!). As a main course, try perhaps the ris de veau au chanterelles (veal sweetbreads prepared with rare horn-shaped wild mushrooms, $16.50). Most meat entrees cost about the same; the rack of lamb (for two people) is $28. Seafood dishes are priced at $10 to $20. Convenient, dignified, delicious.

Say you're sightseeing in Old Montréal and you want to relax in a cozy little French restaurant for a superb lunch, only the best and price is no object. **Au Vieux Montréal** (tel. 861-5337), 361 rue St-Paul Est, is the perfect place, only a short stroll from Place Jacques-Cartier (St-Paul is the street at the south side of the square) and across the street from the Marché Bonsecours. Lunch is no businessman's special here, but a fine table d'hôte repast made only with the best ingredients. A typical menu, priced at $15, might read like this: lobster bisque or cream of asparagus soup for a start, followed by pears in vinaigrette dressing. For main courses you'd choose from succulent morsels of veal braised with mushrooms, or lobster grilled with garlic butter, or filet mignon flavored with fresh spices. Vegetables and potatoes or rice come as garnishes. Black Forest cake and mocca coffee close out the meal, and by this time two or three absolutely delightful hours have slipped past. Dinners are equally delectable, with main courses priced at $10 to $13, full meals for about $25 per person, but lunch here is a real treat. It's served weekdays only, although you can come for dinner any night. Reservations are a good idea.

After you've spent a day or two in Montréal and are high on the beauty and excitement of this vibrant city, and you want a quiet, intimate restaurant full of charm and a sense of history for a romantic dinner à deux, call for reservations at **Le Saint-Amable** (tel. 866-3471). The front door is at 188 rue Saint-Amable, but the front windows are on the west side of Place Jacques-Cartier in the heart of Old Montréal. The cuisine is classic French, the service is impeccable, the decor restrained. It's a small, cozy restaurant, full of quiet dignity without snobbery. Luncheon prices are very reasonable: a three-course meal based on an omelet main course costs about $5; on cold salmon, about $8 (without wine). But go here for dinner, for that's when the chef is trying his hardest and when the romance of the place is at its height. The duckling in Calvados (that's French apple brandy) is delectable at $12; lobster tail in Pernod (a French anise-flavored brandy) costs $15; but one bite and the price seems not to matter. But romantic togetherness comes to a height with the pheasant marinated in port, served with truffles and foie gras, served for two people ($28). Summer or winter, Le Saint-Amable never loses its charm. It's open for lunch Monday through Friday, for dinner every day.

It's easy to get a taste of Paris in this predominantly French-speaking city, but **Les Halles** (tel. 844-2328), 1450 Crescent St., carries the similarity past cuisine with a tasteful decor reminiscent of the bistros which once surrounded Paris's downtown central market. Paris-style street signs on the walls read "rue des Halles" and "rue Bâtard," legends and slogans are painted here and there, but there's not a trace of sawdust on the floor, and the clientele is drawn from nearby offices at lunchtime and Montréal's legion of gourmets at night—no market workers here. Les Halles is a good place for a fine and not-so-expensive lunch, with three-course repasts costing from $4 (for omelets) to $7 to $8 (for beef Stroganoff or a shrimp-filled salad). Dinner menus follow the classic tradition, but with fascinating digressions and additions: frog legs in garlic have a splash of Pernod added in the cooking ($14.50), and duck cooked in a wine sauce comes accompanied by sliced pears ($10.50). Figure to spend $5 to $15 at lunch (wine included), $15 to $25 at dinner, also with wine.

MODERATELY PRICED RESTAURANTS: No one can afford to dine in Montréal's top restaurants all the time, and in fact you'd be missing a great deal if you did, for this city's moderately priced restaurants and bistros offer excellent food, congenial and informal surroundings, and French-style service all at value-for-money prices.

Crescent St. is lined with expensive restaurants, trendy restaurants, places where the food is only an excuse to see and be seen (and is therefore pretty awful), and places serving almost no food at all. In the midst of this maelstrom is a cheerful and attractive place without pretensions but with a friendly and down-to-earth ambience. **La Marguerite** (tel. 284-0307), 1472 Crescent St., corner of Maisonneuve, features an interesting menu moderately priced. You can order lapin aux pruneaux (rabbit with prunes, $8), rognons de veau Dijonaise (veal kidneys, $6.75), saumon marine aux herbes (salmon flavored with herbs, $4.75), or any of half a dozen other unusual dishes. If you just want a light lunch or supper, salads are priced at $2.50 to $4.25, and a cheese or pâté portion is $2.50. But the specialty of the house is Breton-style crêpes, made before your eyes on a hearth in the inner dining room. About as large as a family-style pizza, and filled with asparagus, ham, cheese, mushrooms, fruit, preserves, or even a combination of the above, a crêpe can make a good light meal or a fantastically tempting dessert. Prices range from $1.50 for a plain one to $6 for one stuffed with seafood; the most elaborate dessert crêpe comes filled with ice cream and flamed in liqueur for $6. Wine, beer, and cocktails are served, and it's open from noon to midnight daily. Menu in French only.

Passing the corner of Crescent and Maisonneuve, you'll notice that the glass facade of **Casa Pedro** shields two levels of tiny cafe tables, and that most of these tables are full most of the time. It's not just the view of the sidewalk action that draws the crowd to 1471 Crescent St., it's the paella ($5.50) and the daily special meals for about $3.50. This low price includes soup, a main course such as roast beef au jus, and a dessert, perhaps crème caramel (or flan). But Pedro's is no fast-food place. The dinner menu lists a host of good things, most of them Spanish, with main courses priced from $5 to $13, most costing about $7 to $9. If you want to join the young and sophisticated crowd at Pedro's and you're not sure of finding a table, you can call for reservations: 288-1314.

On the relatively quiet upper reaches of Mountain St. north of Maisonneuve you'll find the **Coffee Mill** (tel. 288-3546), 2049 Mountain, where coffee and light meals are reminiscent of Vienna and Budapest. Tables are scattered through an enclosed room overlooking the street, a small open-air terrace several steps below street level, and various spaces behind these two. Drop in for coffee (40¢ for American, to $1.20 for Viennese mit schlag) and pastry: the specialty is an immensely fattening and sybaritically delicious chocolate cake with cherries and jam call Ludlub ($1.30), but dobosch torte and other Central European regulars are always on hand, too. For something more filling, try a brace of Debreceni sausages with horseradish or mustard and bread and butter for $2.75, or the daily special plate for about $3. You can spend up to $10 per person here if you have a full-course dinner with dessert, coffee, and wine or beer, but there's no need to spend that much. The Coffee Mill is open from 8 a.m. to 1 a.m. daily, closed Sunday.

Just about every first-time visitor to Montréal treats himself to lunch or dinner in the manner of Old Montréal at **Les Filles du Roy** (tel. 849-3535), 415 rue St-Paul Est at rue Bonsecours, next to Calvet House. Housed in a restored stone building decorated with antiques and period pieces, the restaurant gets you in the mood for exploring the city's historical treasures by serving some of the best traditional Québecois cuisine. If you're not hungry enough to charge into a grand portion of petit cochon de lait farci (stuffed suckling pig, $10.50), or a ham steak braised in maple syrup ($7.50), by all means try the assiette canadienne (Canadian assortment plate) with samples of pigs' feet stew, meatballs, and the game-and-fowl pie called tourtière, for $6.75. Gaspé salmon, grilled or poached, costs just a bit more. All main courses come with vegetable and potato, and constitute one of the best high-quality lunch or dinnertime bargains in Old Montréal.

For drinks, you might want to experiment with a maple sugar cocktail ($2.25); as for Caribou, the native rocket-fuel made from red wine and whiskey (or plain grain neutral spirits!), you can get a portion for $2.75, but you'd better do it at dinner only.

The restaurant takes its name from the shiploads of single girls and women who were given dowries by the king of France and who braved the wild Atlantic to provide the men of New France with companionship and families. Waiters and waitresses wear period costumes, and will bring you a drink in the delightful little glass-covered court if you must wait for a table. A better idea is to reserve in advance. Touristy? Yes, because the food is good, prices are very reasonable, and the atmosphere is just right.

When it comes to seafood, **Chez Delmo** (tel. 849-4061) is a Montréal institution. Although the restaurant's location at 211 rue Notre-Dame Ouest, near the corner of St. Francis Xavier, would make it a good place to draw in the heavy tourist crowds, Delmo's still dedicates itself to the task of serving the local business clientele. This means it is closed Saturday noon, all day Sunday, and Monday evenings when business people are not around, but it also means food quality will be maintained because the clientele is local. Old-fashioned, serviceable but not elegant surroundings are the setting for lunches (Monday through Friday, 11 a.m. to 3 p.m.) and dinners (Tuesday through Saturday, 6 to 11 p.m.) of delectable lobster bisque ($5.75 for two), Canada's famous filet de doré amandine ($6.75), or trout meunière, in season, for a bit less. Fried oysters are delicious and different ($7.75). Salads, cheeses, and desserts—fresh fruit au Kirsch is especially tasty—are yours for about $2 the portion. Be sure to consider the daily specials, which always provide the freshest and tastiest seafood for the most reasonable price. At lunchtime Delmo's is usually pretty crowded, and a reservation is a good thing to have. Alternatively, come early.

Among Montréal's many excellent delicatessens, one stands out as any deli-fresser's idea of heaven. The pearly gates, in this instance, are lined with dozens of huge pickle bottles, pendulous würsts, bagels, and rye breads. In fact, the sidewalk display window at **Dunn's** (tel. 866-4377), 892 rue Ste-Catherine Ouest, always draws admiring stares from the curious and the hungry. Inside, booths and a long lunch counter are always occupied by Dunn's fanatically loyal clientele who know that whatever their insatiable craving, Dunn's can satisfy. Where else could you find a sandwich made of chopped liver, chicken fat, Spanish onion, corned beef, and smoked tongue, served with cole slaw for $4? Or Polynesian steak, chicken in the basket, knockwurst, sauerkraut and baked beans, shish kebab, and of course such deli standards as pastrami, latkes, and knishes? Many filling plates are priced around $4; others such as salmon steak and shish kebab hover around $9 to $10. Beer, wine, and cocktails are served. For dessert, there are lots of things offered, but only one to have: strawberry cheesecake, each piece piled high with whole berries. Dunn's is good for a snack, a lunch, or a hearty evening tuck-in. Dunn's *never* closes. Years ago when Mr. Dunn bought the place, he threw away the key.

The **Restaurant Au Quinquet** (tel. 272-4211) is off the beaten track at 354 Blvd. St-Joseph Ouest, corner of Ave. du Parc; it's a favorite with native Montrealers who call well in advance to reserve one of the few small tables in the several equally small dining rooms. A pristine, homey, and unpretentious but very attractive decor sets the mood for traditional Québec dishes such as cretons de campagne, a hearty rough pâté of pork and spices ($2.75), jambon fumé à l'érable (ham smoked with maple wood, $2.75), or a delicious soup. As a main course, try the tourtière de lièvre, a meat pie made with hare in season, with rabbit at other times, for $5.25. The Québecois cipaille, an elaborate pot pie of vegetables and several kinds of meat and fowl, is a special treat at $16 for two persons. Wine comes by the carafe or bottle, with a quarter liter about $2.75; a liter, about $7.25.

If you come in advance of your reservations, stop for a drink in the Quinquet's cozy bar next door to the restaurant. Au Quinquet is not difficult to get to; catch a bus (no. 128, 129, or 80) from the Place des Arts Métro station going north on Jeanne Mance St. If you go to Place des Arts by Métro, remember to grab a transfer from the machine *before* boarding the train, and the bus trip will be yours free. Au Quinquet is open for lunch and dinner on weekdays, for dinner on weekends.

Outdoor Cafes on Place Jacques-Cartier

When the warm weather returns after Montréal's long and chilly winter, the cafe tables are rolled out and set up on narrow terraces all around Place Jacques-Cartier. By the time waiters lug the chairs up from storage, professional and semiprofessional cafe sitters are already lining up and waiting to indulge in their favorite occupation: dawdling over a coffee or a beer, consuming ever so slowly a bowl of onion soup, or a ham-and-cheese sandwich, or perhaps a plate of deep-fried clams or squid. Gazing at the buskers, layabouts, sun worshippers, flower sellers, itinerant artists, and strolling tourists who move through the square can occupy one for hours, and so it's a tough task to find table space at any cafe on any nice day. If you can spot a couple just as they signal the waiter for the bill, and then hover over them to grab their table when they leave, you can have a decent lunch in a delightful setting for $5 to $8, or a beer and a sandwich for a bit less. All cafe prices are in a similar range, and are a bit high—except when you consider location.

Le Tastevin and **Le Nautique** seem to have the highest prices, although they're not extraordinarily high when you consider that food tends to be better, and that Le Nautique specializes in seafood. The **Restaurant des Gouverneurs,** near the northwest corner of the square, usually has the lowest prices as it is located a few steps from (but still in view of) the center of the square's bustling activity. But note this: virtually every cafe has *two* menus, a menu de terrasse with slightly higher prices and less varied offerings, and a menu de restaurant, packed with heartier dishes at lower prices for those content to dine at the indoor tables behind the terrace. Be sure to check out both lists.

Want to escape the exuberance of the square and take it easy in a hidden garden, quiet, amiable, with a choice of shady or sunny tables? Near the southeast corner of Place Jacques-Cartier is a sign on the sidewalk pointing down a short alley to the peaceful courtyard occupied by **Le Navigateur,** a crêperie perfect for a light lunch and a cool refresher. Generous-sized crêpes stuffed with meat, vegetables, seafood, or eggs make good main courses at $4 to $5; dessert crêpes made with jams and fruits are about half as expensive. Beer is $1.25 the mug; wine, $2 the quarter liter (slightly over a pint). Le Navigateur is only for sunny days in summer, of course.

INEXPENSIVE EATERIES (Meals for $1 to $5): Despite Montréal's reputation for Gallic haute cuisine, it's not like Paris where even a hamburger seems to cost an arm and a leg. Mixed with the finesse of French cooking is a very New World hankering for good grub at low prices, and for many of your meals you'll want to spend only a dollar or two for a sandwich, or about $3.50 for a luncheon special plate. It's easy: inexpensive eateries are all over town.

Montréal's Brasseries

Not exactly breweries as the name implies, Montréal's brasseries are in fact the Gallic version of English pubs. Beer is the mainstay, whether by the mug or by the pitcher, but sparkling cider, tart and refreshing, with about the same alcoholic content as beer, is served in bottles at most brasseries. Food is usually simple but tasty and filling, and very reasonable priced.

The **Brasserie Le Tramway** (tel. 875-6300), 1122 rue Ste-Catherine Ouest, between Peel and Stanley, recalls the days when street railways laced Canada's cities and buses or Métros were unknown. Tramcar doors and decorations, lamps, fire buckets, and similar memorabilia surround the tables, booths, and bar, and the menu cover is a blown-up reproduction of an oldtime tram ticket. Mugs of beer appear almost immediately after you sit down, lugged over by a cheerful and comely barmaid. You pay when it arrives, as in all brasseries (85¢ a mug, but add 15¢ as tip for the waitress). Piped-in music and a TV set provide entertainment, and short-order cooks can dish up anything from fish 'n' chips ($2.95) through hamburgers with french fries and pickles ($3.25) to a small filet mignon ($7.50). You get a small salad with each main dish. Cheerful atmosphere, youngish and easy-going crowd, friendly and efficient service.

You can find the outdoor cafe atmosphere of Place Jacques-Cartier at a lower price, and still not wander far from the square by seeking out the **Brasserie Lambert Closse** (tel. 866-0537), down an alley off rue St-Vincent at no. 435B. From Place Jacques-Cartier, just walk one block west to St-Vincent —the brasserie is more or less right behind the Hotel Iroquois. A modern building with two floors of tables overlooking the courtyard through plate-glass windows is open all winter. But in summer the court's wooden deck is filled with white umbrella-topped cafe tables and a solidly local clientele (overwhelmingly French-speaking) who come for luncheon specials priced at $3.75 to $5, main course, vegetables, dessert, and coffee included. Mugs of beer are 90¢, but it's customary to give the waiter a dollar, with 10¢ as tip. After 3 p.m., the luncheon specials give way to a supper menu until closing at 7 p.m. Plates of sausages and beans ($3.50), beef liver, seafood, and salads fill the list. Sandwiches are simple as tomato ($1) or complex as club ($5). Try out your French if you come here: menus and waiters are all francophone.

Although at first its presence seems an alien element in Gallic Montréal, **Old Munich** (tel. 288-8011), 1170 rue St-Denis at the corner of Dorchester, soon becomes a welcome old-world addition to the city's restaurant lineup. It's delightfully authentic: a simply cavernous beer hall of dark wood is spruced up with Bavarian blue and white, and a raised bandstand at the center is surmounted by a gigantic replica of the crown of the Holy Roman Empire. Dirndl-clad waitresses carry fistfuls of beer mugs to thirsty singers as the bandleader coaxes newcomers and regulars alike into a song (songsheets provided). The miles of long wood tables are rarely all filled, except perhaps during Oktoberfest time, and the food is hearty, simple, and inexpensive. A plate of sausages and sauerkraut costs $4.50, one of pig's knuckles, mashed potatoes and sauerkraut just a bit more, and the special Bavarian buffet of various meats, sausages, potatoes, and kraut is served to four people or more at $5 per person. For dessert, apfelstrudel ($1.25) is a natural. It's all great fun, an inexpensive place for dinner and a show, and *you* end up being the show. Old Munich oompahs its way through every evening of the week, opening at 4 p.m. and going strong till midnight or after.

Crêpes

Crêpes, those marvelously thin and delicate French pancakes, are a veritable art form in Brittany, and Bretons who have emigrated to Montréal have brought the art with them. You can sample their artistry in any branch of the restaurants named **À La Crêpe Bretonne** which are scattered throughout Montréal. No fast-food chain, the restaurants are all different, although operated by the same people. There's one in the shopping complex called Les Terrasses, another at 1440 Peel St., right across the street from the main entrance to the Sheraton Mount Royal Hotel. But the original restaurant is the nicest. It's at 2080 Mountain St., north of Maisonneuve (tel. 842-3481).

Now, about Breton crêpes: they're made with either froment (wheat) or sarrazin (buckwheat), and they come stuffed with tomatoes and sausage, shrimp, bacon, cheese, liverwurst, cottage cheese, strawberries, apples, ice cream—over 100 varieties in all, priced from $2 to $5. The restaurant's heavy wooden door, rough-plastered walls and coarse wood accents, and waitresses in traditional Breton costumes complete with starched lace headdresses, make it all delightfully adventurous. After your crêpes you can move to the little "Bistro" a few steps below sidewalk level, with a view of the street, for salads, cakes, and coffee. À La Crêpe Bretonne is open from 11 a.m. until past mid-night every day of the week. Other locations include 360 St. Francis Xavier St., corner of St. Paul, in Old Montréal, and 808 rue Ste-Catherine Est.

Delis

The cavernous interior of **Ben's Delicatessen and Restaurant,** at the inter-section of Metcalfe and Maisonneuve, may or may not be where Montréal's famous smoked-meat (pastrami) sandwich originated, but it is certainly where hundreds of inexpensive and tasty breakfasts, lunches, and suppers originate daily. After beginning with the inevitable smoked-meat sandwich ($1.85) and giant smoked-meat sandwich plate with cole slaw and pickles ($4), Ben's menu rambles on in a fit of multiethnic culinary madness: smoked-meat egg rolls for instance (two for $1.60), or smoked-meat fried rice ($3.60); then spaghetti, then latkes, then chicken pot pie and Virginia ham, all at bargain prices. The atmosphere at the tiny Formica tables or the long lunch counter is that of dining in a railroad station without the tracks, but you'll love it. Ben's is right next to the Sheraton Mount Royal Hotel (which is right above the Peel Métro station). The deli-restaurant is open every day, and hours are so long that it's easier to tell you when it's *closed:* from 4 a.m. to 7 a.m. Sunday through Thursday, from 5 a.m. to 7 a.m. on Friday and Saturday.

The throbbing heart of busy St. Lawrence Blvd. has got to be **Schwartz's Montréal Hebrew Delicatessen,** at no. 3895. Behind an unimposing facade lies a long, narrow, bare room with a lunch counter and a collection of beat-up tables and chairs, all usually jammed with fanatically loyal fans. They come for the smoked meat, served in a huge sandwich ($1.80), a small plate ($3.20), or a large plate ($4.20). Other meats are offered, from a jumbo frank (70¢) to the top-priced rib steak and trimmings ($7.20), but smoked meat is the real treat here. Order a small plate—I don't know who could ever finish a large one—and it comes heaped with the succulent stuff, accompanied by a tall stack of dark bread. A side order of french fries and one of pickles (two mammoth garlicky specimens), plus a soft drink, will bring the bill for this gargantuan repast to $6, tip included. Schwartz's is open every day; it has no liquor license. If the place is simply too jam-full to get in, a very suitable substitute is the **Main Deli,** two doors down at no. 3887. Greater selection of dishes, comparable prices.

Cafes

In Montréal's Latin Quarter, rue St-Denis between Maisonneuve and Ontario is packed with little restaurants, cafes, and eateries in all price ranges. In summer every single one has sidewalk tables, and at lunchtime on sunny days every table is sure to be filled. If you come here for lunch, try to arrive before 11:45 or after 2 to avoid the crowds.

A young and happy crowd gathers at **Le Faubourg St-Denis,** at the corner of rues St-Denis and Emery. One of the largest and airiest sidewalk cafes in this student area, Le Faubourg provides lots of outdoor tables as well as two levels of seating in its cavernous interior. Rock music, held to a decent volume, twangs from speakers here and there, and waiters circulate with cold bottles of beer and carafes of wine. The blackboard menu features sandwiches (cheese, pâté, sausage, etc.) for about $3, apple pies (tarte aux pommes) for $1. But besides being a cafe, Le Faubourg is also a moderately priced French restau-rant. An interior dining room several steps up from street level serves full lunches and dinners for about $10 to $14 per person.

International Fare

Montréal's Chinatown, centered on rue Lagauchetière Ouest between rues St-Urbain and Clark, harbors dozens of tiny Chinese restaurants featuring fast service, tasty food, and incredibly low prices. Perhaps because Chinese cuisine —one of the world's great cuisines—is not based on the individual portion (as in countries that favor steaks and chops) bulk preparation allows prices to remain low while quality remains high. Whatever the reason, the proof is in the eating, and Montrealers flock to Chinatown for delicious food at very low prices.

To confirm this one has only to drop into the **Jasmine Cafe** (tel. 861-4501), 62 Lagauchetière, an unpretentious place with the predictable red booths and Chinese knickknacks. Waiters clad in black trousers and white shirts circulate swiftly with pots of tea, trays of egg rolls, and plates of piping hot chow mein, spare ribs, and rice. You can have a voluminous six-course meal, beginning with soup, proceeding through all the good things just mentioned, and ending with an almond cookie, for $3.25 (with tea, tax, and tip, the total is $4.50). If you have a party of four the savings are even greater, for the Jasmine's menu lists no fewer than six various full-course dinners costing from $10.40 to $30—that's the complete cost *for four people,* plus tax and tip. À la carte items cost more, relatively speaking, than the complete dinners. The Jasmine Cafe is open every day of the week for lunch and dinner, and is especially crowded on Sunday afternoons, when whole families pack in for the feast. No liquor is served here.

If the Jasmine's too crowded, try the upstairs dining room at **Tai-Sun,** right next door at 70 Lagauchetière, where a full-course set meal for two is priced at $7.50, and $3 for each extra person. There's a complete à la carte menu as well.

Weekend visitors to Place Jacques-Cartier flock to the **Old Spaghetti Warehouse,** 2½ blocks west of Place Jacques-Cartier on St. Paul St. They fill the many rooms of what in fact looks to be an old warehouse dressed up modishly with stained glass, hanging plants, well-worn tables, and barrel-back chairs. They come for mountainous plates of steaming spaghetti, almost a dozen varieties in all, priced from $3.25 to $4.25, with lasagne, veal parmigiana, and a few other Italian favorites priced somewhat higher. It's a convivial if down-to-earth place with quick service, low prices, and filling meals, and it's open for lunch and dinner every day of the week.

For a romantic late-night supper or after-the-show snack, try **Le Bistro** and **La Mansarde,** two establishments under the same glass roof at the corner of St. Catherine and McGill College Sts., one flight up. Something light, like a cheese fondue, is $2.90; more substantial plates of spaghetti ($3.90) and "butcher's steak" ($3) are served until 6 a.m. Fourteen different salads are priced from $1.75 to $4.50. Service goes on 24 hours a day in the plant-filled greenhouse-like restaurants, with the crowd slowly changing from daytime shoppers to show-goers to late-nighters to early birds. The entrance is right next to Dunn's, another 24-hour eatery.

Casse-Croûte

Although it is not unusual these days in French-speaking countries to grab a bite at *le snack-bar,* the traditional French quick lunch is called **casse-croûte** ("break a crust"). Gnawing a dry crust of bread has nothing to do with it, however, as Montréal's casse-croûte establishments are actually short-order lunch counters on the American model, complete with lunch counter and rows of chrome-plated stools. Hot-dogs steamés (also called chiens chauds) are a staple here, as are plates of fèves au lard (pork and beans), and frites (french fries, served with cider vinegar—tasty!—or American-style ketchup). Prices in a casse-croûte are low and service is quick. There's a casse-croûte on Place Jacques-Cartier, for instance, and a hot dog, with a plate of beans and a soft drink, will cost only about $2.25.

3. The Sights of Montréal

Montréal has sights and attractions to fill up all the days you spend here. You can get a taste of the city in a short weekend stay, but to appreciate fully all the things Montréal has to offer, you'd better plan at least five days or more. Summer is undoubtedly the best time to see Montréal in its glory, with autumn a close second. But even if you come in winter or spring, there will always be plenty to see and do.

The first place visitors make for when they come to Montréal is the oldest part of town, called **Vieux Montréal** (Old Montréal), dating from the 1700s. Then, for contrast, it's nice to stroll through the downtown sections of the modern city, perhaps with an eye to shopping. **Mount Royal Park,** just a few blocks from downtown, is the place to get away from the city's bustle if you have a mind to. On rainy or very hot days, descent to the climate-controlled world of Montreal's **Underground City,** a labyrinth of passages, subway tunnels, and building complexes where you can amuse yourself for days without ever stepping out into muggy humidity or chilly slush. For a lark, take off to **Man and His World** (that's what Montréal's world-famous Expo became after 1967), a permanent display of natural and man-made wonders and amusements. **La Ronde,** Montréal's fabulous amusement park, is right next door. The center for spectator sports is obviously the incredibly ambitious **Olympic Complex,** the most architecturally daring assemblage of its kind in the world. Nearby, the **Botanical Gardens** provide the perfect haven for an hour's peaceful meditation. To get into the Montréal of the Montrealers, you'll have to take a stroll along **St. Lawrence Blvd.** the axis of the city's ethnic neighborhoods, then through **Place St.-Louis** to the "Latin Quarter," center of French-speaking student activity. Finally, a visit to **St. Joseph's Oratory** will give you a glimpse of Montrealers' religious life at one of the city's most noteworthy shrines.

Here, then, are details on all these exciting places. But before you plunge into the marvels of Montréal, perhaps you'd like to take an introductory tour to get your bearings. For complete information, check back to the section on "Guided Tours" near the beginning of this chapter.

OLD MONTRÉAL (VIEUX MONTRÉAL):
Picture, if you will, Jacques Cartier and his little band sailing up the broad St. Lawrence River in 1535, approaching a large island bearing a small Indian settlement. Cartier, not much interested in large islands or Indian settlements, pushes onward in his search for the sea route to China, but gets hung up at the rapids just west of the island. In a fit of mingled optimism and frustration, the great explorer bestows the encouraging name of La Chine (China) on the rapids—assuming that China was just the other side of them—and then decides to check out the large island after all.

He landed at a spot in Old Montréal, paid his respects to the local dignitaries, and mounted the hill to plant a cross and claim the place for the French king. He named it Mont Royal (Royal Mountain).

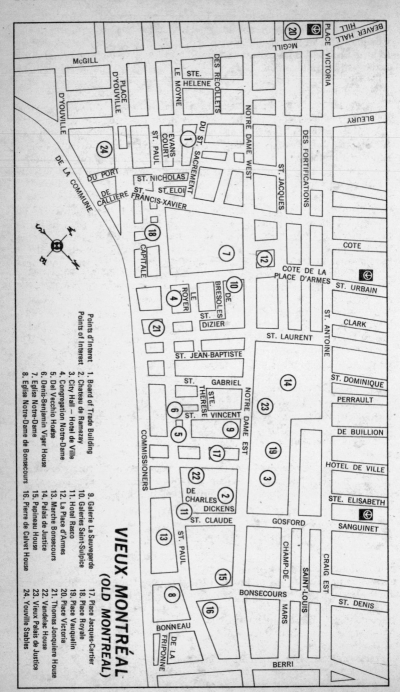

Points d'intérêt
Points of Interest

1. Board of Trade Building
2. Chateau de Ramezay
3. City Hall — Hotel de Ville
4. Congregation Notre-Dame
5. Del Vecchio House
6. Denis-Benjamin Viger House
7. Eglise Notre-Dame
8. Eglise Notre-Dame de Bonsecours
9. Galerie La Sauvegarde
10. Galeries Saint-Sulpice
11. Hotel Rasco
12. La Place d'Armes
13. Marche Bonsecours
14. Palais de Justice
15. Papineau House
16. Pierre de Calvet House
17. Place Jacques-Cartier
18. Place Royale
19. Place Vauquelin
20. Place Victoria
21. Thomas Jonquiere House
22. Vandelac House
23. Vieux Palais de Justice
24. Youville Stables

VIEUX MONTRÉAL
(OLD MONTREAL)

So ended Cartier's contribution to the city. Over 100 years later Paul de Chomeday, Sieur de Maisonneuve, arrived (1642) to establish a colony. All Chinese fantasies having been laid to rest, Maisonneuve knew he was coming to live in a land uncharted by Europeans and inhabited by local peoples both fierce and friendly. He and his band of settlers came ashore and founded Ville-Marie, dedicated to the Virgin Mary, at the spot now marked by the Place Royale. They built a fort, a chapel, stores, houses; and the energetic Jeanne Mance made her mark forever by founding the hospital named Hôtel-Dieu-de-Montréal, which still exists today.

Life was not easy. Unlike the friendly Algonquins who lived in nearby regions, the Iroquois in Montréal were not about to live in peace with the new settlers. Maisonneuve had said he would settle at Montréal "even if the very trees of the island turn to Iroquois," and it's a good thing he was thus prepared, for it must have seemed to the handful of inhabitants of Ville-Marie that the trees had done just that. Fierce battles raged for years, and it's a good thing for the settlers that their numbers included such undauntable souls as the Cavelier de la Salle, du Luth, la Mothe-Cadillac, and the brothers Lemoyne, all of whom later left their marks, and their names, on territories in the Great Lakes and Mississippi. In the **Place d'Armes** you'll see a statue of Maisonneuve, marking the spot where the settlers defeated the Iroquois fighters in bloody hand-to-hand fighting, with Maisonneuve himself locked in mortal combat with the Iroquois chief. Maisonneuve won.

From that time the settlement prospered, but until the 1800s the city was still all within what is today called Old Montréal. Over half of Montréal's long and colorful history is preserved in the old city's ancient walls and streets, and in its picturesque churches and houses.

A Walking Tour

Start your visit by taking the Métro to the Champ-de-Mars station. Follow the signs pointing to Vieux Montréal, and mount the hill to the old **City Hall** building. It's a modern building by Old Montréal standards, having been finished in 1877, although its Renaissance French design makes it look as though Maisonneuve brought it with him, stone by stone. By the way, the Champ-de-Mars of the subway station name refers to the City Hall parking lot, which at one time was a parade ground for the local men at arms.

Just over the hill from City Hall is the focus of summer activity in Old Montréal—**Place Jacques-Cartier.** Without doubt the most enchanting of the old city's squares, its cobbled streets and ancient buildings instantly transport you back to the 1700s, while its outdoor cafes, street musicians, flower sellers, and horse-drawn carriages tug you forward at least to the Montréal of a century ago. Young, old, hang-loose, and upwardly mobile Montrealers all mingle with the crowds of tourists on nice days, each enjoying the circus of activity in the square in his own way.

But once you've taken in the square's carnival atmosphere, take a closer look at the ancient buildings which surround it.

Just across rue Notre-Dame from City Hall is the **Château de Ramezay,** 290 rue Notre-Dame Est. Built by Gov. Claude de Ramezay in 1705, it was the home of the city's royal French governors for four decades, before being taken over and used for the same purpose by the British conquerors. In 1775 an army of American "rebels" invaded and held Montréal, using the château as their headquarters. Benjamin Franklin, sent to persuade Montrealers to rise with the Americans against British rule, stayed in the château and no doubt enjoyed his stay even though he failed to persuade city people to join his cause.

After the short American interlude, the house was used as a courthouse, government office building, teachers' college, and even as a headquarters for Laval University before being converted into a museum in 1895. It's still a museum, and you can visit both the house and its exhibits Tuesday through Saturday from 10 a.m. to 5 p.m., on Sunday from 1 to 5 p.m. Old coins, furnishings, tools, and other memorabilia from early Québec fill the main floor, and in the cellar are the original vaults dating from the house's contruction in 1705.

Walk from the Château de Ramezay along rue Notre-Dame, across the north side of Place Jacques-Cartier. On your right, between City Hall and the imposing domed Old Court House (1800), which houses a tourist information bureau, is the **Place Vauquelin,** complete with a pretty fountain. On your left, across Notre-Dame at the top of the sloping Place Jacques-Cartier, look for the monument to Lord Horatio Nelson (1809), hero of Trafalgar. Past his lordship, turn left to descent into the Place Jacques-Cartier.

Just as you turn, on your right, once stood the famed Silver Dollar Saloon, long since torn down. The drinking place got its name—and its renown—from the 350 silver dollars embedded in the floor, an early publicity stunt that piad off handsomely during the life of the saloon and even afterward: every guide-book to the city mentions the long-lost tavern, although no one seems to know what ever became of the silver loot in the floorboards.

Plaques in French and English will tell you all about the **Vandelac House** (no. 433 on the square), the **del Vecchio House** (no. 404-410), and the **Cartier House** (no. 407). One glimpse shows that these early houses were well suited to the rigors of life in early Montréal: steep roofs shed the heavy winter snows rather than break under the burden, and small windows with double casements let in light without letting in too many wintry breezes or Indian arrows; when shuttered, the windows were almost as effective as the heavy stone walls in fending off hostile attacks or the antics of devil-may-care trappers fresh from an evening's liquid refreshment in nearby taverns. Some of the old buildings in and around Place Jacques-Cartier harbor fine restaurants and cafes (see the restaurant section, above, for full details).

At the bottom of the square, past the artists' booths, guitarists with open cases to welcome a rain of quarters, and old men sitting in the sun, is St. Paul St., oldest thoroughfare in Montréal. You can hire a calèche here for a horse-drawn guided tour of Old Montréal. Rates vary with current business and your bargaining ability, but should be something like $15 to $20 for an hour's ride.

Turn left onto St. Paul St., and at no. 281 was the Hotel Rasco which, like the Silver Dollar Saloon, lives on in story if not in fact: the Rasco was the Ritz of its day in Montréal, hosting the great and famous including Charles Dickens and his wife.

The **Marché Bonsecours** is the imposing building with a colonnaded facade and a handsome dome. Built in the mid-1800s, it was first used as the City Hall, then as the central market (market-day activity centered in Place Jacques-Cartier, but the Bonsecours was for other days), and finally as the home of the municipality's housing and planning offices.

Just past Marché Bonsecours is the little **Church of Notre-Dame-de-Bonsecours** (1771), called the Sailors' Church because of the wooden ship models hanging inside, given as votive offerings by sailors. The first church building, the project of an energetic teacher named Marguerite Bourgeois, burned down but was replaced with the present one. Marguerite did a lot to educate the children of rough-and-ready Montréal in the latter half of the 17th century. She and several sister teachers founded the Congregation of Notre-Dame (a nuns' order). The church has a small museum dedicated to her life and work, and here you'll learn that this pioneer of education was recognized as a saint in 1953. Don't miss the view of the harbor and the town from the church's tower, called **le Monument.**

Right across St. Paul St. from the church is one of Old Montréal's most fascinating places to visit as it offers a detailed look at what life was like in the Montréal of about 1725. **Calvet House** was built in that year, although the centuries took their toll before being restored recently as a museum. It's now furnished with authentic antique pieces made or used in Québec out of the collection of the Montréal Museum of Fine Arts. Beautiful, quaint, homey, rustic, elegant—all these words apply to life at that time, but remember that such a house would have been inhabited by some fairly well-to-do people. One of the most surprising items on display is a copy of the local newspaper from Thursday, February 9, 1786, with bulletins from Constantinople, Berlin, and The Hague, and printed in both French and English. Calvet House, at 401 rue Bonsecours, is open from 10 a.m. to 4:45 p.m. daily, from 12 noon to 4:45 p.m. on Sunday, closed Monday. Admission is free.

Now, walk north on Bonsecours to rue Notre-Dame, turn left, and go six blocks to get to the **Place d'Armes,** centerpiece of which is the Monument to Maisonneuve mentioned earlier. But the real attraction here is the magnificent **Notre-Dame Church** (1829), big enough to hold 5000 worshippers, and breathtaking in the richness of its interior furnishings. It was designed by an American architect named James O'Donnell who, the story goes, was so inspired by his work that he converted to Roman Catholicism after it was done. The main altar and pulpit were the work of Victor Bourgeau; the church's monster bell, named Le Gros Bourdon, weighs over 12 tons—its ring is a deep, low vibration which seems to shake your soul. The splendor of Notre-Dame's main altar will dazzle you; for a more restful but still impressively lofty sight, go around behind the main altar to the Chapel of the Sacred Heart, and the small museum dealing with the history of the church and of Roman Catholicism in Québec. Take a close look at the near-surrealist paintings of Father Guindon (1864–1923). You'll have to pay a small fee (50¢) to see the exhibits in the museum.

Montréal's oldest **stone walls** (1658), enclosing the Seminary of Saint-Sulpice, are right next to Notre-Dame Church. The clock on the facade, by the way, had a movement made almost entirely of wood.

You might want to have a glance in the grand old **Bank of Montréal** building, facing the Place d'Armes. It's Montreal's oldest bank building, and besides being solid and impressive to look at (inside and out), it has a small banking museum to show what its early operations were like.

Walk by the Seminary of Saint-Sulpice, heading west on rue Notre-Dame, and turn left onto rue St-François-Xavier. Three blocks down, turn left again onto St. Paul St. and walk the short distance to the ancient **Place Royale,** site of the early settlement of Ville-Marie. An obelisk commemorates the founding of the great city in 1642.

South of the obelisk, the conjunction of streets makes a sort of open square which extends almost three blocks to the west and which is used these days as—what else?—a parking lot. Wander westward through the cars and soon on your left you'll see the bull's-eye windows high in the old stone walls of the **Youville Stables,** which have stood in this spot for almost two centuries. Actually, the rooms within the iron-gated building compound were offices, storerooms, and workplaces; the actual stables, next door, were made of wood and disappeared long ago. Like much of the waterfront area, Youville "Stables" was rundown and disregarded before a group of businessmen decided to buy and renovate the property. Today the compound is an elegant office and shopping area, complete with its own well-known steakhouse. Feel free to look around inside the gates whenever they're open, which is most of the time.

That's the heart of Old Montréal. To look at the heart of the new, 20th-century city, take the Métro from either the Place d'Armes station or the Champ-de-Mars station, and go to the Bonaventure stop. From there it's only a block and a half to the center of the downtown shopping and business district, Dominion Square.

MODERN MONTRÉAL: The modern city's recent history is almost as fascinating as its colorful early days, for Montréal was a "wet" town when the United States was "dry" due to Prohibition. Bootleggers, hard drinkers, prostitutes, and the rest all flocked to this large city so well-situated close to the American border, and mixed with the rowdy elements from the port, much to the distress of Montréal's mainly clean and decent folk. For half a century the city's image was off-color, but in the 1950s the cleanup began, and along with it the ambitious building and expansion which has made Montréal the great city it is today. In 1967, Montrealers were ready to welcome the world to Expo, and in 1976 to host the prestigious Olympic Games. The great gleaming skyscrapers and towering hotels date mostly from the last 30 years.

Downtown (West) Montréal

But **Dominion Square** is surrounded by elegant reminders of the Victorian era, such as the Windsor Hotel and the row of patiently waiting calèches. If you'd rather ride in a carriage than walk, bargain with one of the drivers: as at Place Jacques-Cartier, you should pay $15 to $20 for each hour of riding, a bit less per hour if you take the long ride to the top of Mount Royal. In winter, the calèche drivers replace their carriages with horse-drawn sleighs, and charge about the same rates for the ride to the top of the mountain.

Start your walk by going east along Dorchester Blvd., the city's broadest downtown thoroughfare, and the one with the fastest traffic. On the right is a faithful copy of Saint Peter's Basilica in Rome, built (1870) on a smaller scale and named **Marie-Reine-du-Monde** (the Cathedral of Mary, Queen of the World), headquarters for Montréal's Roman Catholic bishop. The **Queen Elizabeth Hotel,** just past the church, stands right above Central Station. Actually, the hotel is a sort of central transportation point for tourists, for you can get the bus to Dorval Airport from here, or catch the sightseeing tour bus, or take a train, or (on the street behind the hotel) get the bus to distant Mirabel Airport.

Across Dorchester Blvd. from the Queen Elizabeth in **Place Ville-Marie,** keystone of the early urban redevelopment efforts. The cross-shaped skyscraper (designed by I. M. Pei) and the square's name recall Cartier's cross, planted to claim the island for France, and Maisonneuve's first little settlement. The complex is sleek and streamlined, but somewhat cold and forbidding except for the pleasant cafe situated below ground level but open to the sky (open in summer only). By the way, it's in a building at the eastern end of the complex that you'll find the **Tourist Information Office.** Place Ville-Marie, to Montrealers, is simply "PVM"—be advised.

Turn left onto University St. and walk the two blocks to rue Ste-Catherine for a look at **Christ Church Cathedral,** a fine Gothic building only about 100 years old, seat of the Anglican bishop of Montréal.

A left on Ste-Catherine will head you northwest, through the center of Montréal's shopping and entertainment district. The giant department stores are here, including "La Baie" (short for Hudson's Bay Company, successor to the ancient and famous fur-trapping firm), Eaton's, Simpson's, and Ogilvy's. Movie houses, restaurants, shops, pinball arcades, and even grocery stores line Ste-Catherine all the way to the chic district centered on Crescent and Bishop Sts. The best dressed men and women, the most expensive or flashy cars, the priciest boutiques, and some of the city's excellent restaurants are jammed into the appealing gabled facades of old row houses. Believe it or not, this center of gilded youth and glamor was once a rundown slum area slated for demolition. Luckily, individual buyers with a good aesthetic sense saw the possibilities of the delightful old houses, and brought them back to life through renovation.

Near the corner of Crescent and Sherbrooke Sts. is the **Musée des Beaux-Arts** (Museum of Fine Arts), Montréal's finest and most extensive collection of artworks. Old Masters, pre-Columbian statuary, eskimo soapstone carving, Islamic artwork, and African masks all find places in the museum's fascinating and ever-growing collection. Special shows add to the attraction. Drop in at the museum any time from 11 a.m. to 5 p.m. Tuesday through Sunday, or call 285-1600 for the latest information on special exhibits.

While you're on Sherbrooke St., perhaps you'd like to do some shopping (or window shopping) in the elegant antique shops clustered near the museum and dotted along the street. If you walk east on Sherbrooke, you'll soon come to the campus of **McGill University,** one of Canada's most prestigious institutions of higher learning. Feel free to wander around the beautiful campus with its green lawns mounting the slopes of Mount Royal. The **Redpath Museum** on campus houses McGill's natural history displays: examples of animal and birds (stuffed) from around the world, geological samples and archeological findings—including skeletons of prehistoric animals. But to learn about things Canadian, seek out the **McCord Museum** at 690 Sherbrooke St. West. Through collected objects, displays, and early photographs, the folk history of Canada unfolds, with special emphasis on the lives of pre-European inhabitants. The McCord is open Wednesday through Sunday from 11 a.m. to 5 p.m.

East Montréal

In earlier days, Montréal was split ethnically between those who spoke English, living in the city's western regions, and those who spoke French, concentrated to the east. For many years now there's been no such line of demarcation in fact or in theory, although the vestiges of this linguistic split still seem to make themselves felt. For some reason you do get the feeling things get more French as you walk east: street names and Métro station names are not Peel or Atwater but instead St-Laurent or Beaudry. While the east-west dividing line for the city's street numbering system is St. Lawrence Blvd. (Blvd. St-Laurent), the "spiritual split" seems to come at Ave. de Bleury / Ave. du Parc.

Place des Arts and Complexe Desjardins

In planning for the "new" Montréal which grew after World War II, the city fathers left nothing out. Cultural centerpiece of the plans was a complex of handsome buildings for opera, concerts, and ballet, to be called **Place des Arts.** In 1963 the designers' plans came to fruition with the Salle Wilfrid-Pelletier, the main concert hall; other halls and galleries were finished in the following years, and today Place des Arts is a fabulous boon to the arts lover. Schedules of current offerings (in French) are issued monthly and distributed in hotels and tourist offices. You can take a tour of the Place des Arts on any

Tuesday or Thursday, at 1, 2, 3, or 4 p.m. The tour takes about 45 minutes. Exactly what you'll see depends on rehearsal schedules, as tours don't go to anyplace where rehearsals are in progress.

Across rue Ste-Catherine from Place des Arts is Montréal's breathtaking **Complexe Desjardins,** the most strikingly beautiful and harmonious of all the city's ultramodern building complexes. Designed by a local firm and built with the aid of the Québec government, the complex was finished in 1977 at a cost of $100 million.

As you enter the lofty glass doors from rue Ste-Catherine, the Complexe absorbs you into its unique world: "street level" turns out to be higher than the level of the complex's central terrace. Waterfalls and fountains, trees and hanging vines, even birds, fill the vast interior world of the central court, sealed off from rain and snow. Music and the sound of falling water fill the air. Lanes of shops go off in every direction and small knots of people wait at elevator doors, soon to whisk up one of the four tall office towers which are part of the complex. Beneath are several levels of parking garage. The Hôtel Méridien is an integral part of Complexe Desjardins, and from its Vieux Marché coffeeshop you can view all the activity in the court while munching toast and coffee or having a cool drink. You'll notice that a crystal shape is the theme for the design of the complex—it turns up everywhere. The crystal-shaped sunken area on the terrace is often used as a studio for live television shows, and you may catch a rehearsal or even the show itself; or the terrace will be filled with a garden show, science fair, or auto exhibition. There's always something going on in Complexe Desjardins, and always people around (it's open 24 hours a day).

Place des Arts and Complexe Desjardins are connected by an underground passage to one another and to the Place des Arts Métro station, all part of Montréal's incredible Underground City. But for now, let's stay above ground for a walk in the Latin Quarter (Quartier Latin), focus of French-language student life. You can shorten your walk, however, by taking the Métro from Place des Arts to the Berri-de-Montigny station and emerging on the rue de Berri.

The Latin Quarter and Place St-Louis

Montréal has several large and renowned universities, and thus an immense student population. Rue St-Denis, axis of the French-language university district, is to Montréal what the Blvd. St-Germain is to Paris. The major difference is that in Paris these days the sidewalk cafes are all glassed in and tend to be expensive, whereas along St-Denis the cafes are still open air, and prices here are moderate to cheap—it's still a student area.

As you emerge from the Berri-de-Montigny Métro station, you'll be near the **Centrale d'Artisanat du Québec** (Québec Handicrafts Center), at the corner of St-Denis and Maisonneuve. Here you'll find the very best selection of Québec handicrafts gathered from throughout the province and sold at moderate, fixed prices.

Walking north along St-Denis will take you through the heart of the sidewalk cafe district, described in detail in the restaurant section, above. If you push on up the hill, soon you'll come to **Place St-Louis,** a delightful park surrounded by Victorian town houses in suitably ornate style. (A Métro shortcut to St-Louis exists: take the Métro to the Sherbrooke station, only a few steps from the square.)

Walk through Place St-Louis. At its eastern end, Prince Arthur St. will take you into one of the city's most colorful and ethnically diverse neighborhoods.

The "Little U.N." of St. Lawrence Blvd.

Prince Arthur St. leads to St. Lawrence Blvd., one of Montréal's foremost north-south thoroughfares and a fascinating potpourri of peoples and cultures. Polish, Greek, German, Jewish, and Italian restaurants serve hungry shoppers, and as many different kinds of groceries provide the ingredients for those who want to cook their knishes, golombkis, raviolis, or souvlakia at home. Most people over the age of 50 here speak at least three languages: Montréal's two tongues, French and English, and also the native tongue of whatever country they've come from. There's nothing fancy about St. Lawrence Blvd., for it's a living part of the city, not an exhibition area or quaintly restored historical district. You'll come away from here with the feeling you've just seen a show that could only be called the "Real-Life Circus."

Chinatown

Chinese immigrants to Montréal tended to congregate along the southern reaches of St. Lawrence Blvd., near the intersection with rue Lagauchetière. Lagauchetière is now Chinatown's main street, lined with Chinese restaurants, groceries, import shops, businesses, and even the stereotypical hand laundry or two. Knots of old men stand on street corners discussing the day's events—all in Chinese, of course. For the benefit of "outsiders," most (but not all) notices are in French or English as well as Chinese. Community spirit is strong, as it's had to be to resist the bulldozers and builders of urban redevelopment. Hedged in by the expressway to the south and the mammoth new building projects to the north, Chinatown's inhabitants are in an island of ancient traditions threatened by a tidal wave of modernism.

You should plan to dine in one of the restaurants, large or small, plain or fancy, but if your stroll through Chinatown is not at lunch or dinnertime, at least do some browsing in one of the Chinese grocery stores. A smiling grocer will do his best (in French or English) to explain about all the exotic and unfamiliar herbs, spices, teas, vegetables, and products packed on his shelves.

Mount Royal Park

The famous American landscape architect Frederick Law Olmsted left his verdant artistic mark on many North American cities—New York's Central Park and similar stretches of greenery in Philadelphia, Hartford, and Boston testify to his skill—but somehow Mount Royal Park is his special triumph. Not many cities can boast of having a mountain right in the center of town. Montréal has the mountain, and it's all one huge and delightful park.

If you don't take a calèche or sleigh from Dominion Square (described above), you can drive your car around the western edge of the park and spiral up the hill to a parking lot on the north side. But the most enjoyable way to get into Mount Royal Park is simply to walk. Go north on Peel, Drummond, or Museum (Musée) Sts. and you'll find stairways and a switchback bridle path leading to the top. Your goal is the **Chalet Lookout,** with its snackbar and, in winter, ski warming room. The terrace in front of the Chalet has a fantastic panoramic view.

If you don't want to scale the steep slope directly to Chalet Lookout, take the road leading left (northwest) shortly after you enter the park from Peel or

Drummond Sts. You can walk at your own speed while slowly gaining altitude, and this route has the advantage of taking you past the pretty **Lac des Castors** (Beaver Lake). Surrounded by sunbathers and picnickers in summer, Beaver Lake is an ice skater's paradise in the cold winter months before the snow sets in. Once the pond is covered with snow, the small ski tow starts operation, tugging novice skiers up the gentle slope for another practice run down and across the pond's face.

Past Beaver Lake is the **Mount Royal Art Centre,** a small building housing art shows both summer and winter. A sculpture park surrounds the centre, and you can wander through it, getting the best angles for viewing the modern pieces.

Soon the Chalet Lookout will come into view. Continue past it for a walk to the eastern edge of the mountain where, tradition has it, Maisonneuve erected his wooden cross over 300 years ago. Today the spot bears a steel structure rigged for illumination at night—it's visible from all over the city.

Joggers, cyclists, Frisbee players, lovers, and everyone in search of a little peace and quiet head for the park in good summer weather. In wintertime, cross-country skiers follow the miles of paths—all within the park—and snowshoers tramp and crunch along other trails laid out especially for them.

The Underground City

Montréal's "Underground City" is world-famous. Most people who have heard of it tend to picture some wildly futuristic maze of tunnels and subterranean buildings. Well, that's exactly what the Underground City is, and the surprising thing is that no one ever thought to do it before.

But Montréal's city planners first conceived the plan several decades ago when designs for the Métro and for the Place Ville-Marie complex were being considered. The Métro promised to alleviate greatly the congestion on Montréal's sidewalks and in its streets, so why not decongest it further by adding a few underground walkways between major downtown buildings? To pay for the upkeep of the walkways, why not set up a few shops in them? The beauties and advantages of the plan soon became clear: no crowded streetcorners, fewer pedestrian-auto accidents, no need to get one's feet wet in winter slush or summer rain. The downtown business and shopping area could be expanded while actually *reducing* congestion!

Although the Underground City is still growing, today you can arrive in Montréal by train or airport bus or car, get out at an underground station or parking garage, take an elevator or underground walkway, find a hotel or restaurant, do business, see a movie, attend a concert, go shopping or swimming —all without every setting foot outdoors. Here's how it works: major building complexes such as Place Ville-Marie, Complexe Desjardins, and Place des Arts have several underground levels, and are connected to one another or to the Métro; you ride the long distances by subway and walk the shorter distances, such as from one to three blocks.

Actually, "Underground City" is not a completely accurate name for this exciting place because some complexes—Place Bonaventure or Complexe Desjardins, for example—define their own spatial levels, which may have nothing to do at all with "ground level." Elevators in these complexes routinely refer to *names* of levels rather than floor numbers: promenade level, mezzanine level, hotel reception level, parking "A" level, and so on. In fact, in Place Bonaventure you may leave the Métro and then wander around on the same level only to find yourself, at one point, staring out a window several floors above the street. (In the 30- and 40-story office towers, normal numbered floors are the rule, though.) While it can be confusing and bewildering at first, there are direction signs everywhere; but you must remember that the Underground City is a vast area, almost a city in itself and without the convenience of a logical street grid. But, to be truthful, getting lost is half the fun.

Place Bonaventure

It doesn't really matter where you "go underground" to begin your explorations of Montreal's amazing labyrinth, but eventually you should make your way to Place Bonaventure (Métro: Bonaventure), the first big complex in which the Underground City concept reached full development. Place Bonaventure holds the huge Hôtel Bonaventure, which is often filled with convention groups. You should seek out its swimming pool, on a little terrace well above street level, open to the sky. Trees and bushes surround it, with deck chairs in summer and graceful snow-drifted "sculptures" in winter. The water is heated in the cold months and, far from having to brave the chill of wintry air, swimmers can enter the pool through a water tunnel from the changing rooms! Other fascinating parts of the Place Bonaventure complex include Montréal's largest exhibition hall, and an international shopping area called **Le Viaduc.** Movies, restaurants, cafes, and nightclubs can keep you busy in Place Bonaventure for hours, if you have the time.

Follow signs to **Windsor Station** (1886) through the underground maze if you'd like a look at the work of Bruce Price, who is most famous for his Château Frontenac in Québec City. **Central Station** also reachable from Place Bonaventure by underground passage, is hardly as romantic, although it is attractively modern and functional. Take an elevator up to the **Queen Elizabeth Hotel,** or continue your underground stroll to Place Ville-Marie's underground shopping arcades.

Other complexes you can walk to from Place Bonaventure are the **Place du Canada,** with the cheese-grater-like Château Champlain Hotel, and **Place Victoria,** on the western edge of Old Montréal.

For explorations farther afield, all still underground, take the Métro to Berri-de-Montigny station, the very heart of the Métro system. The station is where three lines meet, and is full of activity through the day and most of the night. Change trains and head down to Place des Arts and Complexe Desjardins, all accessible underground. Then, near the McGill Métro station, is the multilevel shopping complex called **Les Terrasses,** noted for its elegant shops. Eaton's and the Bay are also accessible from McGill station. If you travel on to Peel station, you'll be directly under the Sheraton Mount Royal Hotel.

Eventually the southern portion of the Underground City at Place Bonaventure and Place Ville-Marie will be linked directly with the northern portion between Peel and McGill stations—you won't even have to board the Métro to get from north to south.

The Olympic Sports Complex

Montréal hosted the Olympic Games in 1976, and Montrealers basked in the warm glow of the world's admiration. More visitors than ever flocked to the "new" Montréal and to its magnificent Olympic Stadium, surrounded by other sports buildings including a Velodrome (for bicycle racing) and a swimming complex with no less than six different pools. The complex was bold, brash, and outspoken in design, a marvel which inspired architectural debate and public admiration. The games were a thrill for participants, visitors, and Montrealers alike.

Then came the morning after. Bills for the construction and design of the sports complex kept rolling in until they topped the billion-dollar mark, and still they grew. Receipts from the gate would never pay off such an amount. Reports of audits and inquiries filled the newspapers and television news shows for several years afterward, and it turned out that the world-renowned Parisian architectural firm, headed by Roger Taillibert, which designed the complex had been told that "expense was no object." The matter is still not settled, and even now some of the bills remain to be paid. The question, as always, is one of who should pay them.

As a visitor, these monumental worries are ones you can blissfully ignore as you take a guided tour of the complex. To get to the Olympic Complex, take the Métro to either the Pié-IX or Viau stations—to the Viau station particularly if you're headed for the guided tour.

The **Swimming Complex,** in the northeast corner of the great Olympic Stadium, has six pools. The competition Olympic pool has an adjustable bottom; then there's a training pool, a warm-up pool, a children's wading pool, a diving pool, and an amazing 50-foot-deep Scuba diving pool. Want to swim where the stars do? Public swim periods are scheduled at various times, with low admission rates: $1 for adults, 50¢ for kids.

Whatever else its critics may call the gigantic **Olympic Stadium,** they've got to admit it's grand, breathtaking, and monumental. Depending on the game or program being staged, the place can seat an astounding 60,000 to 80,000 spectators. Judging from the stadium's amazing flexibility, it must have taken at least that many architects and designers to think out its masterplan. For instance, with Astroturf covering the field and a quickly moved portable pitchers's mound, it's a baseball stadium; move these out and put up the retaining walls and you have a bull ring; flood the floor (as is done every winter) to produce a mammoth skating rink, or put down boards (in summer) for a roller rink. Take up the Astrotruf from the outer ring of the playing surface and you have an Olympic competition track for footraces. Rock concerts, motorcycle shows, football games—you name it, it's held here. Be sure to take a close look at the east-side scoreboard; in fact, it's impossible *not* to take a close look as the thing is as large as a hockey rink! And beneath the stadium are vast exhibition rooms for special shows, not to mention gyms, locker rooms, and the mountains of mechanical and electronic gear needed to operate such a modern marvel.

Actually, the Olympic Stadium is not finished. Money problems may prevent it being finished for some time, and it may suffer the fate of some European cathedrals: to be abuilding for a century and then go steeple-less for another 100 years while more money is raised. The "steeple" in this case is the futuristic tower meant to rise on the northeast edge of the stadium and to hold the removeable roof stretched on cables above the playing area.

Near the Viau Métro station entrance is the **Velodrome,** another outspokenly bold structure in the shape of a gargantuan shell, its transparent roof supported, apparently, by nothing. Inside, a track of Cameroon redwood is canted at a steep 48 degrees to counteract the centrifugal force of a speeding bicycle racer. Besides bike races, the Velodrome is used for ice skating in winter, roller skating in summer, and for exhibitions and shows. The capacity of the place, counting standees, is about 7500 people.

The Olympic Complex, at the time of the XXI Olympiad, also included the nearby pyramid-shaped apartment blocks, called the **Olympic Village.** A thousand apartments and chambers here catered to the rest and comfort of athletes, trainers, and staff.

When you're ready to leave the Olympic Complex, prepare yourself for an adventure of a completely different nature. Leave behind the mountains of concrete and the thrust of architectural inspiration for the quiet, simple pleasures of flowers and plants. Montréal's delightful Botanical Gardens (Jardin Botanique) is accessible right from the Olympic Complex by means of an underground passageway.

The Botanical Gardens (Jardin Botanique)

Right next to the Olympic Sports Complex are Montréal's lovely Botanical Gardens, spread through 200 acres in Parc Maisonneuve. Take the Métro to the Pié-IX station and walk up the hill to the gardens. They were begun in 1931, and have since grown to include an astounding 20,000 different types of plants, each grown in the environment which best suits it. Of course the gardens are at their most eye-catching in spring, summer, and autumn, but even in winter the gardens are well worth a visit. Huge conservatory greenhouses shelter the tropical and desert plants from the cold weather, and a stroll among the cacti and palms does a lot to dispel the gloom of a dark winter day. Make your visit any day of the year from 9 a.m. to 6 p.m. Admission is free.

Man and His World

Expo '67 was the crowning achievement of a decade's redevelopment for Montréal, and in the short seven-month lifetime of this world's fair (April to October 1967) 50 million people explored its shows and exhibits. It was a tremendous success.

But the story of how Expo came to be is almost more fascinating than the exhibits, for St. Helen's Island (Île Ste-Hélène) in the St. Lawrence River changed completely as it became Man and His World. In the four years before Expo opened, construction crews literally reshaped St. Helen's, adding again as much surface area, and then went on to create a brand-new island right next to it, called Île Notre-Dame. Much of the needed earth was dredged up from the bed of the St. Lawrence, and the rest was brought in by truck—some 15 million tons in all!

After the islands had been made, bridges were built and 83 national and theme pavilions were constructed to house exhibits. When Expo closed in the autumn of 1967, the city government decided to preserve the fair as a permanent exhibition ground. Parts of Îles Ste-Hélènes and Notre-Dame were later used for Olympic Games events in 1976.

To appreciate the gargantuan labors that went into making Expo such a success, take the Métro to the Île Ste-Hélène station for a walk around. A number of the pavilions from 1967 have disappeared, and the exhibits in those that remain are changed from time to time. You can stroll around the grounds for free, but if you want to go into the various pavilions you'll need a "visa," $4 for adults, $2 for kids 8 to 18; children 8 and under accompanied by an adult get in free. The visa gets you into La Ronde, the amusement park, too.

Among the outstanding attractions in Man and His World are the marine delights of the **Aquarium.** In the Alcan Pavilion you'll see over a hundred species of marine life, and in the Alcan Marine Circus, trained dolphins perform their antics every day in May through September from 10 a.m. to 10 p.m.; Tuesday through Sunday in winter from 10 a.m. to 5 p.m.

La Ronde

Without even leaving St. Helen's Island, prolong the day's enjoyment by a visit to Montréal's delightful La Ronde amusement park. Rides, sights, places to eat and drink (including a good beer garden) fill the northern reaches of the island, and stay open from noon until past midnight; the park grounds close at 2:30 a.m. La Ronde is open on weekends in May, and every day beginning early in June and continuing until early September.

The St. Lawrence Seaway

Ever since Cartier sailed up the St. Lawrence looking for China, the river has been of prime importance for Canada's economic life. Early trappers ferried their furs out along the same river, and immigrants from Europe and the rest of the world followed Cartier's course upriver to populate the rich interior of the country.

But just as Cartier had his troubles with the rapids at Lachine, later voyagers found parts of the river difficult to navigate. For over 100 years—since the time when immigration increased from a trickle to a flood in the mid-1800s—Canadians had been debating ways to increase the river's usefulness as an inland highway. Finally in 1959 the century of planning and years of construction reached fruition as Queen Elizabeth II and President Eisenhower inaugurated the St. Lawrence Seaway. With the momentous opening of the new system of locks and canals, ocean-going vessels could sail right into the heartland of North America, 2000 miles from the Atlantic.

To see the Seaway in operation, drive or take a taxi across Victoria Bridge to the observation deck overlooking **St. Lambert Lock.** Displays explain the operation of the mammoth lock, 860 feet long by 80 feet wide. Tremendous ships are raised about 50 feet while in the lock, and then the upriver gates are opened for them to continue the journey via the Great Lakes to the center of the continent.

From April through December, you can visit the observation deck for free between 9 a.m. and 9:30 p.m. In January, February, and March, ice on the river prevents ships from sailing, and they sit out the cold weather, waiting for the spring thaw.

St. Joseph's Oratory

You don't have to be a pilgrim to appreciate the impressive shrine built by Montréal's Catholics to the honor of St. Joseph, patron of healers, and to the memory of the city's beloved Brother André. Take the Métro to the Guy station, and don't forget to grab a transfer from the machine before you board the train at your station of entry. Then, hand the transfer to the driver of the no. 65 bus you'll catch outside Guy station; it will take you right to the Oratory at 3800 Queen Mary St.

The story of St. Joseph's Oratory begins when Brother André, a monk of the Order of the Holy Cross, discovered he had the miraculous power to cure illness. The fame of his powers spread and attracted suppliants from all around, and Brother André performed his benevolent work faithfully until his death in 1904. Even after his death, the sick traveled to the site of his tomb hoping for the blessing of healing and few, it seems, went away disappointed. Brother André had dreamed of building a magnificent shrine to his patron St. Joseph, but the dream became a reality only after his death. By 1916 a church had been built above his tomb, and in 1960 a magnificent modern-style basilica was finished, incorporating the earlier "crypt church" as its lower level.

You may have noticed the great dome of the Oratory towering above the northwest side of Westmount. No matter when you go, you'll see pilgrims, especially the ill, coming to seek intercession from the saint and his follower. Besides the crypt church and the lofty basilica, tour the small museum dedicated to Brother André's life and work, and take in the 15-minute film. Services in the churches are usually held in French.

The Oratory is open daily from 8 a.m. to 10 p.m.; the museum has shorter hours, from 10 to 5. If you come on Sunday at 3:30, you get the special treat of a free organ concert.

Wax Museum

Almost across the street from St. Joseph's Oratory is Montréal's best wax museum, a private concern called somewhat misleadingly the Canadian Historical Museum, or, more correctly, the Wax Museum of Montréal. It's at 3715 Queen Mary St. (Chemin de la Reine Marie), and is open from 9 a.m. to 5 p.m. every day of the week; admission cost is $3.50 for adults, $1.50 for children. Far from being merely Canadian in theme, the museum's dioramas peopled by wax figures portray scenes from Roman catacombs in early Christian times through the founding of Montréal by Maisonneuve to the inevitable modern replicas of John F. Kennedy and Charles de Gaulle. Actually, it's not so much the wax figures as it is their costumes one comes to see. If you like wax museums, you'll like this one.

4. Montréal Shopping

No need to journey to London, Paris, or New York when you're in the market for high fashion, solid quality, or a large assortment to choose from. Montréal has all the stores you'd ever want to browse, from the chic to the discount, plus unexpected bonuses such as crafts shops selling Inuit (Eskimo) art and traditional Québec handiwork.

In fact, Montréal has so many shops and stores on its downtown streets, in its building complexes, and along its underground passageways that, shop for shop, there may be more here than in the Champs-Élysées, Regent St., and Fifth Ave. combined.

U.S. readers of this book have the distinct advantage of substantial markdown on all prices encountered in Montréal shops due to the difference in exchange rates between the Canadian and U.S. dollars. If you're traveling on U.S. dollars, be sure to take the trouble to go to a bank to exchange your U.S. cash for Canadian. Banks will give you the very best rate, and the transaction takes only a few minutes. If you spend dollars or U.S. travelers checks in the stores, you'll almost certainly get between 4% and 7% *less* for your money than if you had exchanged it in a bank. Note that if you're buying with a credit card, the charges will automatically be converted at the favorable bank rate before appearing on your monthly credit-card statement. VISA seems to be the most popular bank card in this part of Canada, although MasterCharge and American Express are almost as widely used.

DEPARTMENT STORES: Most of Montréal's big department stores were founded when Scottish, Irish, and English families dominated the city's commerce, and so their names remain Anglophone even though their merchandise and appeal is strictly bilingual.

Simpson's on rue Ste-Catherine between Mansfield and Metcalf, is a huge department store on the traditional model, selling just about everything of a personal nature: clothing, accessories, jewelry, cosmetics, and such luxuries as Cuban cigars. The **Dunhill Humidor,** a small tobacco shop operated by the prestigious London tobacco firm, is on the ground floor near the Metcalf St. entrance. The precious Cuban, Jamaican, and Brazilian products are kept in closely monitored conditions of temperature and humidity. Exotic cigarettes and pipe tobaccos are sold as well. Americans must remember that as of this writing it's still forbidden to bring Cuban products into the United States.

Ogilvy's, at 1307 rue Ste-Catherine Ouest, puts its emphasis on things Scottish, whether produced in Scotland or in New Scotland (Nova Scotia, that is). Here's the place to go for tweeds and tartans, or teas with shortbread and oatcakes in the Tartan Room. Come early, as the store opens, or stay until closing time and you'll hear the skirl of a be-kilted piper ringing through the store.

Eaton's at 677 rue Ste-Catherine Ouest, is much like the large Simpson's in what it offers to shoppers—a good range of goods at good prices—but it also has the distinction of being Montréal's largest store.

No Canadian commercial concern has a name older or more illustrious than that of the **Hudson's Bay Company,** called simply "The Bay" (or "La Baie") by Montrealers. In one form or another Hudson's Bay Company has been doing business in Canada for the better part of 400 years! Although its main store on rue Ste-Catherine Ouest at Phillips Square (near Aylmer) is a full-selection department store in every sense, the emphasis—for historical and sentimental reasons—is on furs and warm wool products for the chilly Québec winters. If you've come with a few thousand dollars to spend on a well-made, good-looking fur wrap or coat, start your search at the Bay. Incidentally, fur coats are not really just a luxury item here in Montréal, something that rich ladies take along to show off on trips to Florida. The coats last and last, and can be retailored at a nominal cost to keep up with current fashions, and (if need be) sold or traded in at a good price much as a good, solid car can be. They even become heirlooms, keeping successive generations of Montrealers warm and toasty during whatever winter may bring. After your browse in the Bay, if you're captivated by the coats but you can't afford a brand-new one, check the classified advertisements in the daily newspapers for offers to sell used coats. Add a sum to the asking price for tailor's fees, and you may find yourself dressed in fur next winter.

Now for the top of the line. What Selfridge's is to London or Saks is to New York, **Holt Renfrew** is to Montréal. The very best men's and women's clothing and furnishings (including original French designers' works), plus a food section stocking delicacies of the caviar-and-truffles kind, fill up this palace of the posh at 1300 Sherbrooke St. West, corner of Mountain St. Anyone with good taste will want at least to take a turn through the store, but the way to buy at Holt's is to find something you think you simply can't live without, and *then* look at the price. To help cure the sinking feeling that may follow, Holt's will accept your credit card as well as their own (some of the big stores accept only their own cards).

All of the stores mentioned above have branches throughout the city, and you may well come upon one during your rambles underground as well as while strolling in the downtown business district.

ART OBJECTS AND HANDICRAFTS: It's hard to tell where the crafts end and the art objects begin when one considers the careful workmanship and inspiration that goes into making Inuit (Eskimo) drawings and carvings, or quaint Québec wood-carved figures and patchwork quilts. Prices are about the best index, the beauty of the piece usually matched by a suitably lofty price. The largest collection of Québec crafts in the city is at the **Centre d'Artisanat de Québec** (Quebec Handicrafts Center), above the Berri-de-Montigny Métro station at the corner of rues St-Denis and Maisonneuve (the traditional gray stone building has a small door to the right on its facade, and that's the entrance to the center). Moccasins and mukluks (fur-and-sealskin boots), snowshoes and baskets, quilts and hand-carved figures and figurines are all nicely displayed in a range of sizes and prices. Rag rugs and other cottage-craft textile items are particularly nice here, and there's a decent selection of Eskimo soapstone (steatite) carvings. The center is the first place to visit if you're in the market for any of these items. It's in a corner of the Institute of Applied Arts (Institut des Arts Appliqués), and is open every day but Sunday.

The **Canadian Guild of Crafts,** 2025 Peel St., has a smaller but choicer collection of craft items than the aforementioned center, and is particularly good in traditional or avant-garde jewelry and soapstone figures. If you just want a small souvenir of your visit to Montréal, you should be able to pick up a little carving for $10 to $20, but if it's a true work of art you're after, a large figure of sensuous curves in the smooth, soft dark stone may cost five to ten times that price.

BOUTIQUES: It's difficult to pin down a single area for fancy boutiques, for in fact they flourish throughout the city from Old Montréal's narrow St. Paul St. to the pretty and pricey reaches of Crescent, Mountain, and Bishop Sts., spilling over onto Sherbrooke at these streets' northern ends. Best thing to do is to keep a sharp eye out for things that interest or intrigue you as you see the sights of the city.

5. Montréal's Nightlife

Montréal's nightlife has got to be the most ebullient, varied, and exciting in all North America. From the chic rendezvous of Crescent St. to the cheap Bingo parlors and girlie flicks of rue Ste-Catherine Est, from posh supper clubs and cloud-level discos to bare but mellow Québecois boîtes-à-chansons (French folk-music clubs), every and any taste can be satisfied. This city is on the concert circuit that includes Chicago, Boston, and New York, and top-name rock singers, orchestra conductors and virtuosos, ballet companies, and entertainers pass through regularly. The hottest songs, the most talked-about films, and the biggest name performers are yours virtually every night of the week.

For details of current performances and events, pick up a free copy of **Montréal Scop,** a weekly ads-and-events booklet, at any large hotel reception desk. Place des Arts puts out a monthly **Calendrier des spectacles** describing concerts and performances to be held in the various halls of the great arts complex; you can pick one up in most large hotels, or near the box offices in Place des Arts. Montréal's newspapers, both English and French, carry full listings of films, clubs, and performances in their Friday and Saturday editions.

Start your explorations of Montréal's glittering after-dark delights with a stroll on Crescent and Mountain Sts. north of Ste-Catherine. The mere act of walking along these streets presents a kaleidoscope of entertainments and all sorts of possibilities for bumping into new acquaintances.

BARS: Of Crescent St.'s myriad bars, restaurants, and cafes, one of the most long-lived and successful is the **Sir Winston Churchill Pub** (tel. 288-0616), 1455 Crescent St. One of the reasons for its longevity is its narrow glassed-in row of streetside tables, and another is its authentic English-pub decor down-stairs. But foremost is its policy of admitting only a well-dressed, well-heeled and adventurous crowd of young professionals out to see and be seen, meet and be met. Thursday through Sunday evenings a very large man with an intimidat-ing scowl stands guard over the Sir Winston's downstairs entrance, and you must show him a reservation, courtesy card (issued to regular patrons), or a generous palm-greaser (a $5 bill will do nicely, thank you) to get in. Also, under no circumstances must you be wearing denim. Once in, order any of the very reasonably priced plates such as asparagus salad ($4, in season), a hamburger (2.50), or maybe barbecued spare ribs ($4), plus a beer, wine, or cocktail, and then try to look like you've been there forever. Food and drink are good, but not important here. Music and meeting members of the opposite sex are impor-tant.

Perhaps the prime watering place of Montréal's young upwardly mobile professional set is **Thursday's** (tel. 849-5634), 1449 Crescent St., a pub connect-ed with the restaurant known as **Les Beaux Jeudis,** in the same building. A sign hung prominently near the front entrance invokes the "No Denim" rule, and indeed most of Thursday's good-looking clients are dressed to kill in the latest "casual" high fashion. Drinks cost $1.75 to $3.50, which is little enough to pay for the priceless opportunities to meet the right person. In the restaurant, the daily luncheon special may cost only about $5, but prices go up—and go à la carte—at night. Thursday's may well take its name from the not-so-ancient Montréal custom of prowling the nightspots on Thursday evening in search of the perfect date for Friday night and perhaps the whole weekend. Thursday's and Les Beaux Jeudis open at noon and stay crowded until about 3 a.m.

You can get into the act at **Stitches** (tel. 842-3713), 1470 Crescent St. beneath a Chinese restaurant. Here, the emcee most likely will extract from the audience the latent comic talent it never knew it had. Not exactly an amateur hour, not really a professional show, the entertainment at Stitches falls some-where in between as a sort of light-hearted and enjoyable auditions session. Food and drink are served, and the place takes its name from what the enter-tainment is meant to keep you in.

FOLK MUSIC: In this sea of ethnic diversity an Irish bar fragrant with the auld sod simply had to exist, and it does: the **Hunter's Horn** (tel. 861-8022), 1214 Peel St., is a combination bar, restaurant, nightclub with live entertain-ment, and dance hall open Monday through Saturday from 11:30 a.m., Sunday from 6 p.m., until the wee hours. There's a hearty daily lunch special such as corned beef hash with an egg (Mondays, $4), or Irish lamb stew ($4.25), but sandwiches ($3 to $4) are served all the time. The folksy atmosphere of rough wood walls, small tables, shirtsleeves, and smoke is perfect for a few pints. The live Irish-style music begins at 8 p.m. nightly. The pub is down a few steps from street level; upstairs in "The Parlour" is room for dancing and a pianist to provide the music from 8 p.m. onward.

For bluegrass, blues, and other styles of North American folk music, try the **Yellow Door,** 3625 Aylmer St. north of Prince Arthur St., near McGill University. The door (and it is, indeed, yellow) opens at 8:30 nightly to let in a mostly college-age crowd come to hear up-and-coming performers who ap-pear for one- or two-night stands. Sunday is hootenanny night. No cover, low prices, good music, good vibes, coffee only (no booze). If you're in the area at lunchtime, the Yellow Door is unlocked from 10 a.m. to 4 p.m. on weekdays, noon to 2 p.m. on Saturdays, serving inexpensive, delicious, and nutritionally balanced lunches. The bulletin board and message board will fill you in on Montréal's college scene.

Québec-style folk music, jolly or soulful songs sung in the local dialect of French ("joual"), sound forth each evening in the city's boîtes-à-chansons (song clubs, literally "song boxes"). Most of these are in Old Montréal, a number being on St. Paul St. Perhaps the best known is **Aux Deux Pierrots**, at 110 St. Paul St. West, where beer is sold by the mug ($1.25) or the pitcher, wine by the carafe, and the music comes by the hour after hour. You may have a good deal of difficulty catching the words to the songs even if your French is good, but during the break a good way to meet people is to ask for a translation. In summer the Pierrots' terrace area, named Terrasse Les Pierrots II, next door, is open when it's not raining. Music fans sit at small cafe tables, and the songsters often inspire a sing-along.

The best German oompah band blasts its way to bliss in **Old Munich** (described above in the restaurant section; 1170 rue St-Denis, tel. 288-8011), and patrons, beer steins in hand, are heartily encouraged to sing along from the songsheets which are delivered with the beer. The echoes in this tremendous beerhall mercifully soften the overall effect of everyone singing, each in his own key. Jollity depends a great deal on the size of the crowd, so Old Munich is best on weekends and during holiday periods, particularly Oktoberfest time.

ROCK MUSIC: Big-name stars and groups are booked into Montréal's **Forum** (tel. 932-6131), 2313 rue Ste-Catherine Ouest between Closse and Atwater Sts. (Métro: Atwater). Call or check the current listings in the newspapers for the latest schedules. If a big name is in town, flyers, radio and TV ads, and general informational osmosis will let you know.

Otherwise, **L'Imprévu** (tel. 878-9397), in the ground floor of the Hotel Iroquois in Place Jacques-Cartier, has local groups noted for their high decibel levels which threaten the integrity of the Tiffany-style lamps hung to dispel—slightly—the cozy darkness. Shows are at 10 p.m. and midnight, and drinks cost around $2.50. The club called **L'Évêché**, in the Hotel Nelson across the square, is open Thursday through Sunday evenings as well.

DISCOS: Fickleness rules when it comes to disco popularity, and no single place seems to hold top spot for long. Crescent St. harbors **La Bicyclette** (tel. 288-2512), 1465 Crescent; **Le Rally Club** (tel. 844-4003), 1423 Crescent; and **Stitches** (tel. 842-3241), 1470 Crescent, which has comic entertainment (see above) Monday through Thursday when the dance crowds aren't packing in. Other discos are scattered throughout the downtown area, some specializing in men-only and women-only clienteles, others going the gamut from teens (no alcohol served) almost to the geriatric set (most hotel discos). **The Rendezvous** (tel. 861-6224), 1112 rue Ste-Catherine Ouest, is hot at this writing, but please understand if the crowd has passed on by the time you arrive there. For a sure thing, go to Place Ville-Marie, enter the skyscraping Royal Bank Building by its eastern door, and take the elevator to the 44th floor where you'll find the **Altithèque 727** (tel. 861-3511). Designed and decorated to look like the interior of a jumbo jet, the disco's location 727 feet above street level provides its own between-dance entertainment. You relax in aircraft-type seats and look through plane-size windows at the fabulous nighttime cityscape. Drinks are $2.25 (beer) to $3.75 (cocktails), and hours are 9 p.m. to 3 a.m. The crowd is college students and young professionals, the mood relaxed and good-natured.

THE GREAT MONTRÉAL TIME MACHINE: At least once in a lifetime, everyone should chuck inhibitions and dive into the sort of antiquarian folly offered up at **Le Festin du Gouverneur** (tel. 514/879-1141), in an old fortress on the Île Ste-Hélène in the St. Lawrence River. In a stone-lined chamber deep within the old fort, servants in period costumes serve dishes, grog, and revelry such as one could have enjoyed here in the year 1691. Whole roast chickens, slabs of tourtière (traditional meat-and-fowl pie), aged cheeses, and similar hearty fare are consumed Tom Jones–fashion, with a bare minimum of eating utensils and according to the hearty rough-and-ready table manners of frontier Québec. Jesters and musicians entertain, the wine flows as freely as the merriment and revelry, and new friends are made all along the great expanse of rough-hewn banquet table.

It's as much a show as it is a meal, and in fact you must buy tickets in advance and get there at the appointed time. The whole evening costs under $20 per person. Buy tickets at any "TRS" (electronic ticket service) booth in Canada, Ticketron outlet in the U.S., or at the Festin's convenient ticket booth in Dominion Square at no. 1025 (Montréal, PQ H3B 2T9). The "Governor's Feast" is held nightly during the summer from May through October, Thursday through Sunday in winter. Take the Métro to the Ste-Hélène station, then follow Path No. 1 through the park to Le Vieux Fort (The Old Fort).

BARS WITH A VIEW: Actually, you can go to a skytop lounge for a drink, a dinner, or a dance, depending on your inclination. The **Château Champlain's** rooftop bar is one of the best, with a breathtaking view. Drinks cost about $2.25 for beer, $3 to $4 for liquor and cocktails. In **Place Ville-Marie,** you can drink and/or dine beneath the revolving beacon with the city at your feet. The dinner is buffet style, so you'd better go hungry when you come. The price is $18.75 plus tax and tip, it's on from 6 to 9 each evening, and it's good to have reservations: phone 861-3511.

SUPPER CLUBS: Because of the number of luxury hotels to be found in Montréal, the number of supper clubs is also large as these two go together. Usually the evening includes a table d'hôte dinner (or you can choose from the more expensive à la carte menu) and one or two performances of the show. At the **Salle Bonaventure** (tel. 861-3511) in the Queen Elizabeth Hotel, an elegant table d'hôte meal costs $20.75 plus tax and tip, and is offered every evening except Sunday. Just for the show, you pay $6.50 cover charge. The show goes on at 9:30 and 11:30 p.m. on weekdays, 9:30 and midnight on Saturdays. For current notices of who's performing, see the local listings, or call the Salle Bonaventure.

In the Château Champlain's **Caf' Conc'** supper club (tel. 878-1688) the table d'hôte costs $19.50 plus tax and tip, but for this you may get snails, lobster, steak, and fresh fruit salad au Kirsch—no inexpensive fare. If you choose to go just for the show, a drink at the bar will run about $3.50, and you'll have to pay the $7 cover charge. The Caf' Conc' is a nice little mockup of a Gay '90s theater, with shows to match.

BALLET, SYMPHONY, OPERA, CHAMBER MUSIC: High season for high culture is during the winter months, of course, but Montréal's good-music fans don't go away in summer—and neither does their music. For the best performances with top-name performers, check at the **Place des Arts** box office (tel. 842-2112). If you don't find what you crave, don't despair. Even during the summer you may find concert activity at McGill University's **Pollock Hall** (tel. 392-8224), 555 Sherbrooke St. West, or at other even smaller halls throughout the city. The best place to look for current information is in the Saturday editions of the Montréal *Star* or the *Gazette.* Tickets, by the way, may cost anywhere from $3 to $10. By the way, if the listings note that a concert or recital is taking place in the Théâtre Maisonneuve, Théâtre Port-Royal, or Salle Wilfrid-Pelletier, you should know that these three halls are all part of the Place des Arts complex.

THEATER: Pick your language before you set out for a night of theater in Montréal, as both English-and French-language performances are given regularly. Although the city has a long history of thriving dramatics in both languages, recent legislation passed by the Québec National Assembly has made it increasingly difficult for English-language companies to garner the subsidies needed to guarantee a successful season. Even so, if you'd like an evening at the theater, you won't be disappointed.

The best place to look for current productions is in the Saturday newspaper listings. The **Centaur Theatre** in Old Montréal at 453 rue St-François-Xavier (tel. 288-1229) has an outstanding English-language company, and productions at **La Poudrière** (tel. 526-0821), in the powder-magazine of the Old Fort on St. Helen's Island, are usually given in both French and English (on different nights, of course). For children's theater, contact the **Children's Theatre** at Victoria Hall, 4626 Sherbrooke St. West (tel. 484-6620).

It's difficult to imagine that one would get tired of Montréal, but an occasional escape from the city is a tonic to Montrealers and visitors alike—especially when the getaway spot is in the delightful villages scattered among the Laurentian Mountains, north of Montréal.

THE LAURENTIANS

ANY GEOLOGIST will tell you that the mountains making up the Laurentian Shield are among the oldest in the world. Over the eons which mark geological time, while titanic earth upheavals were forming jagged mountain ranges in other parts of the world, the Laurentians were being worn down by wind, water, fire, and ice.

No one will say (out loud, at least) that all this geologic sculpting was being done just so Montréal would have a suitable forest playground next door, but the way Montrealers love their Laurentian Mountain hideaways one might come to just such a conclusion.

Actually, the lake-sprinkled hills and valleys between Montréal and Mont Tremblant, the Laurentians' highest peak, were first settled more than a century ago by farmers, foresters, and would-be miners in search of instant, or at least quick, wealth from the depths of the unexplored ground. The mineral boom soon became a bust, the farming proved difficult, and lumbering suffered from intense competition by neighboring regions. The Laurentian villages soon feel into a depression both economic and spiritual all their own.

Then came skiing. The city grew and grew, and Montrealers needed some healthful outdoor exercise in winter. A half century ago the first ski schools, rope tows, and trails were established, and the boom which started then has never let up. Today the posh Laurentian resorts and modest lodges and inns are packed each winter with skiers from not only the nearby metropolis, but indeed from all over the continent and throughout the world.

But skiing is only half the Laurentians' story. As transportation improved, people saw the alluring opportunities for water sports, golf, tennis, hiking, and every other kind of summer sport. Resort hotels sprang up on vast wooded estates—even today, these places sit on thousands of acres—and bus and train-loads of Canadians and Americans filled all the rooms, staying all summer. Before long the region gained a far-flung reputation for good dining, refined service, and genteel atmosphere which survives to this day. At the top resorts, jacket-and-tie formality still reigns at dinnertime, and in the words of one sports director, tennis attire other than the standard whites "will not be tolerated."

PLANNING YOUR VISIT: Winter or summer, a visit to any of the little villages and luxurious resorts in the Laurentians is sure to yield unforgettable memories. Just so they'll be good memories, here are some important things to keep in mind:

Many Laurentian hostelries are sybaritic bits of paradise with every conceivable service, sport, game, attraction, and diversion. Others are plainer but more personal. Whichever you choose, you'll find that the busiest times are in July and August, during the Christmas–New Year's holiday period, and in February and March. Outside these times, reservations are easier to get, prices of virtually everything are lower, and crowds less dense. Many of the larger resorts and some of the smaller inns and lodges close down after the Easter weekend until late May, and again after Canadian Thanksgiving through November or even until early December.

As for prices, they are sometimes incredibly difficult to pin down: the large resorts have so many various types of rooms, cottages, meal plans, discounts, and packages that you may need a travel agent (who will be glad to help you at no charge) to work your way through the thicket. But knowing about all the details is important if you are out to have the most fun for the least money.

When you call for reservations, for a room, a dinner, a seat on the train or bus, remember that Montrealers crowd the highways north on weekends, particularly during the good skiing months of February and March: plan accordingly, plan ahead.

A final note: Pet lovers, despair! Few Laurentian resorts will accept your dog or cat on the premises.

GETTING THERE: Some people hitchhike, others fly in by private plane, but however you travel, the Laurentians are easy of access. Skiers especially have lots of options open to them.

By Bus

Voyageur buses depart Montreal's **Terminus Voyageur** (tel. 514/842-2281) almost hourly between 8 a.m. and 10:45 p.m. for the trip along the Laurentian Autoroute and Hwy. 117 to Ste-Adèle, Val Morin, Val David, and Ste-Agathe. Others start out on the 93-mile (146-km) run to the base of Mont Tremblant about nine times a day, although not all the buses make all the stops. A local bus, making all the stops (32 of them!) will take almost three hours for the trip, but an express bus can shave almost an hour off this time. From Montréal to Ste-Adèle takes about an hour and a half, 15 minutes more to Val Morin and Val David.

On Friday, Saturday, and Sunday during the busy months of ski season, **Autobus Le Promeneur, Inc.** (tel. 819/425-3096), based in St-Jovite, operates buses between Montréal's Dorval Airport and the various resorts at Ste-Adèle, Val David, and St-Jovite / Mont Tremblant. Rates are slightly higher than the train or Voyageur bus, but still very reasonable. Round-trip tickets save you several dollars over two one-way fares.

If you go all the way to St-Jovite and Mont Tremblant, you should know that six Voyageur buses a day operate in each direction on the road from St-Jovite past Gray Rocks, Villa Bellevue, Lac Mercier, Lac Tremblant, and Mont Tremblant, touching at most of the Mont Tremblant area resorts and lodges. From St-Jovite to Mont Tremblant Lodge (and its ski slopes), the trip takes 25 minutes.

By Train

Ski trains are a thing of the past in most of North America, but as of this writing Montréal and the Laurentians are still served by this eminently sensible and enjoyable means of conveyance. **Le P'tit Train du Nord** ("The Li'l Northern Train") chugs out of Montréal's Windsor Station on winter weekends from early December through mid-March, leaving each Friday evening. Another train leaves Saturday morning, and yet another Sunday morning; return trips run Saturday and Sunday evenings, allowing skiers to spend one or two nights in the mountains, or if they prefer, just all day Saturday or Sunday.

Fares are low and competitive with the bus, and special excursion rates make the price even lower. From Windsor Station to Piedmont takes 1¼ hours, to Ste-Marguerite / Ste-Adèle 1¾ hours, to Val Morin and Val David just a few minutes more; after two hours the train pulls into Ste-Agathe, and before three hours have passed you're in St-Jovite or Mont Tremblant. For full information on Le P'tit Train du Nord, contact VIA Rail Canada at Windsor Station (tel. 514/395-5151). By the way, Le P'tit Train usually hauls its own dining car, with bar attached.

By Limousine

Taxis and limousines await your arrival at both Dorval and Mirabel Airports in Montréal, and will gladly whisk you off to any Laurentian hideaway —for a price. Coming with a group, the taxi trip is not outrageously priced as four or five people sharing the cost brings the price down considerably. But to pay $50 to $70 alone. . . . You might want to ask the standard fare to the inn or lodge you'll be staying at; do it when you call the inn for reservations. In most cases, the inn will take the responsibility for seeing that a taxi or limo is indeed waiting for you, and they may even help you find other guests arriving at the same time to share the cost.

If you find yourself at the airport caught without a ride, talk to the person at the **Murray Hill airport bus** counter. The Murray Hill company often runs limousines to the Laurentians, and may be able to arrange transport for you.

By Car

Nothing could be simpler: the fast and scenic **Autoroute des Laurentides** (Laurentian Autoroute). Hwy. 15, goes straight from Montréal to Ste-Agathe-des-Monts. Running parallel to it nearby is the older Hwy. 117, along which are the motels and towns of the region. North of Ste-Agathe, 117 becomes the major artery for the region, passing through St-Jovite and continuing deep into Québec's north country, ending finally at the Ontario border hundreds of miles from Montréal.

The Laurentian Autoroute is a toll road, with four toll booths along its 90-km (58-mile) length.

Canada's major car-rental firm, **Tilden Car Rentals,** has service desks at both Montréal airports, and in the city. You can reserve a Tilden car ahead of time through any Tilden office in Canada, or through any National Car Rental office in the U.S., or call the reservation office in Montréal (tel. 514/842-9445). At Dorval, the number is 514/636-9030; at Mirabel, 514/476-3460; the rental office in Montréal is at 514/878-2771.

Once out of the thicket of expressways surrounding Montréal, the countryside grows greener as you head north, and before long the first foothills of the Laurentian range come into view. The Laurentian Autoroute gives one a sweeping, panoramic introduction to the mountainous vastness, but on Hwy. 117 you get to know the villages.

Summer weekend day trippers course up and down 117 past innumerable Go-Kart tracks and flea markets ("marché aux puces"), stopping frequently at small roadside stands. "Patates Frites" ("french fries") is emblazoned on almost every little shack, and while no one lives by fried potatoes alone, tasting the ones from various stands along this road certainly tempts one to try such a one-item diet. Have them with ketchup, American style, or with tart white cider vinegar as the Québecois do.

As you approach each town along the road north, signs will direct you to the local tourism information office, good for tips on hotels, restaurants, and things to do. The first settlement which is truly "in the mountains" is aptly named: Piedmont.

1. Piedmont–Mont Gabriel

As the highways north enter the foothills of the Laurentian range you'll come upon two eminently recommendable places to stay, one right by the roadside and the other perched atop a nearby mountain.

The **Hôtel-Motel Le Totem** (tel. 514/227-2618; in Montréal, call 514/866-4249) is easily identifiable by its namesake, a very convincing and colorful totem pole perched out front. Despite its antique symbol, the Totem's rooms are all bright and modern, even stylish, and the buildings are positioned perpendicularly to the roadway in order to reduce the traffic noise level. An outdoor patio where drinks are served and two swimming pools (one is for children) are at the center of attraction in summer, although most guests move inside in the evening for dinner and live entertainment in the dining room named Les Palissades. Specials served every day make Les Palissades a favorite: on weekdays, a full-course dinner with a one-pound rib steak as main course costs just $10; on Saturdays it's prime rib of beef for $12.50 the complete dinner, and on Sunday roast beef—all you can eat—for a mere $6.50. Later in the evening, the hotel's L'Imprévu piano bar is the scene of dancing from traditional to disco.

All 50 of the Totem's rooms have private baths, color TVs, and AM-FM radios, plus the very unmotel-like luxury of room service from the bar and restaurant. Two people pay $32 for all this on any night in the busy summer or winter seasons except Saturday, when the price rises to $35 double. If you come in summer, bring your tennis outfit to use on the three new courts; if they're occupied, pass the time playing the other outdoor games such as Ping-Pong, shuffleboard, or volleyball. In winter, cross-country ski trails start right on the motel grounds, and downhill slopes are only a few minutes' drive away. When you call for reservations, ask about the special ski packages if you intend to stay more than a night or two. The Hôtel-Motel Le Totem is right on Hwy. 117 at Piedmont, on the right-hand side as you travel north.

Perched atop Mont Gabriel, commanding the highways and the valley occupied by Le Totem, is the **Auberge Mont-Gabriel** (Mount Gabriel Lodge, tel. 514/229-3547; in Montréal, call 514/861-2852). Coming north on the Laurentian Autoroute, take the Mont Gabriel exit, no. 64, about 40 miles north of Montréal. Set on a 1200-acre forest estate, the auberge is a full-fledged resort complex featuring golf-tennis week programs in summer, ski packages in winter, and motel-style resort accommodations and fun year round. The swimming pool (summer only) is heated, and for summer ski-like thrills Mont-Gabriel has

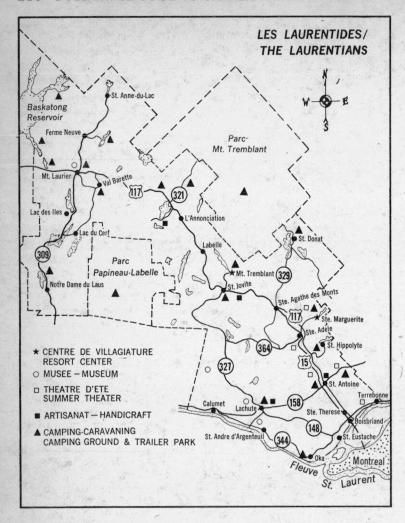

**LES LAURENTIDES/
THE LAURENTIANS**

Baskatong
Reservoir

St. Anne-du-Lac

Ferme Neuve

Mt. Laurier

Val Barette

117

Parc-
Mt. Tremblant

321

L'Annonciation

Lac des Iles

Lac du Cerf

309

Parc
Papineau-Labelle

Labelle

St. Donat

Mt. Tremblant **329**

St. Jovite

Notre Dame du Laus

Ste. Agathe des Monts

117

Ste. Marguerite

Ste. Adele

364

St. Hippolyte

15

327

St. Antoine

Terrebonne

Calumet

Lachute

158

Ste. Therese

Boisbriand

148

St. Andre d'Argenteuil

344

St. Eustache

Oka

Montreal

Fleuve St. Laurent

★ CENTRE DE VILLAGIATURE
  RESORT CENTER
○ MUSEE — MUSEUM
□ THEATRE D'ETE
  SUMMER THEATER
■ ARTISANAT — HANDICRAFT
▲ CAMPING-CARAVANING
  CAMPING GROUND & TRAILER PARK

Map Courtesy of The Association Touristique des Laurentides

its own "Superglissoire" (Super Slide), a half-mile-long trough-like track down the mountainside which you descend on a little one-person "sled," shooting down the straightaways and leaning into the corners as fast or as slowly as you wish. In the evenings, there's dancing in the main lodge.

Accommodations are arranged in four price classes, and prices include breakfast and dinner each day. Cabins with private bath and TV cost $73 double per day; standard-grade motel rooms with similar facilities are $83 for two per day; with the addition of a fireplace and/or a color TV the price rises to $93 double; and for the newest, largest, and most luxurious rooms two people pay $101 per day. You can save about 20% by signing up for a week-long stay, whether or not you're a golf or tennis addict.

Although it's a popular resort destination and convention spot in summer, Mont-Gabriel comes into its own each winter when guests schuss down its 18 trails and slopes and then slide back up again on the nine T-bar lifts, the double-chair or the triple-chair lift. Snowmaking equipment keeps the slopes slippery, and six of them are lit for nighttime skiing. Cross-country trails girdle the mountain and range through the surrounding countryside. When you tire of Mont-Gabriel's own trails, you can take a short drive to reach any of several other mountains in the region.

2. Ste-Adèle

Although quaint Laurentian villages line the upper reaches of Hwy. 117, Ste-Adèle is almost a metropolis compared to these smaller settlements. What makes it "big" is not so much its population as its services: police, doctors, ambulances, shopping center, art galleries, and a largish collection of places to stay and to dine.

Forty-five miles (70 km) from Montréal, Hwy. 117 goes directly into Ste-Adèle to become its main street, the Blvd. Ste-Adèle. As the road mounts the hill to Lac Rond, Ste-Adèle's resort lake, you'll see why the town is divided into a lower part ("en bas") and an upper part ("en haut"). But once you arrive at the shores of the lake and gaze across its placid surface, you'll understand what makes Ste-Adèle such a popular summer resort. Canoes, sailboats and "pédalos" (pedal powered watercraft) glide here and there, and swimmers splash and play near shoreside beaches. In winter the surrounding green hills are swathed in white, and the ski trails come right down to the frozen lake.

WHERE TO STAY: Ste-Adèle's most sumptuous place to stay, summer or winter, is the famous resort named **Le Chantecler** (tel. 514/229-3555; in Montréal, call 514/866-6661). It's a fabulous domain set on a 700-acre estate and centered in the stone-turretted hotel at lakeside. You can swim in the lake or in the indoor pool—in winter, you can swim inside and gaze at the snow-covered lawns and lake through huge poolside windows. Extensive lawns and gardens, hiking and ski trails, and summer sports including golf, tennis, and horseback riding are all on tap for guests. Outdoor dining terraces and indoor elegant dining rooms share the same breathtaking view of the lake and the forest, and the Cocorico club will entertain you when you want a touch of city-style showtime or a band to dance to.

Le Chantecler is a complete and self-contained summer or winter resort, and comes at a complete price, with two meals per day included. Besides the castle-like hotel, Le Chantecler guests can choose to stay in a less imposing clubhouse, or a four-room cottage, or a two-room apartment. Daily rates in the hotel are $39 to $44 single, $68 to $78 double, depending on whether you prefer a lakeside view (the more expensive rooms) or a forest view. Suites cost $5 more per person; an additional person in a room, with the two meals included, is $27. If you pay by the week, you'll have almost 20% on these rates. Clubhouse rooms are about $2 cheaper per person than hotel rooms, although all rooms at Le Chantecler come with private bath, radio, and color TV. Four-room cottages are priced at $156 a day, $888 a week. The two-room apartments, which like the cottages have fireplaces, cost $88 per day, $504 per week, for two people. For children 10 and under Le Chantecler has special rates if the kids share a room with their folks: $19 per day, or $102 per week. By the way, a fully supervised children's program and day-care center will provide the kids with amusements and supervision while you're out sampling the pleasures of this fabulous resort. Important note: The resort will add a 15% service charge to your final bill, and while this saves you the bother of tipping, it also raises the price of a room in the hotel from $68 to $78 double to $78.20 to $89.70.

These summer rates will give you an exact idea of accommodations and basic costs at Le Chantecler, but you can do even better if you sign up for a special package deal such as a ski week in winter, a golf week in summer, or the honeymoon specials which are offered during all but the busiest times. On the honeymoon specials, for instance, you and your spouse (recently married or not!) can pay only $420 for six nights' lodging, three meals a day—including breakfast in bed, if you wish—and all the resort's activities, and to usher you into the vacation, a chilled bottle of champagne will be waiting in your room when you arrive. A similar but shorter three-night plan costs $210 per romantic couple. Add the inevitable 15% service, and these rates come to $483 and $241.50, respectively. When you call about winter ski-week packages, be sure to ask whether the rates quoted include this substantial service charge.

Is all this completely out of your range? Are you rocketing through Ste-Adèle on your way to Mont Tremblant? You can just stop for a table d'hôte dinner in Le Chantecler's sumptuous dining room and pay $15.53, service (but not tax) included. The table d'hôte meal is what all the guests will be having, and you can order à la carte if you wish, but your final bill will be about twice the table d'hôte price as main courses here range from $11 to $16.

The resort called **Sun Valley** (tel. 514/229-3511; in Montréal, call 514/861-4801), is five miles (7 km) north of Ste-Adèle. If you're driving, you'd leave the Laurentian Autoroute at Exit 67 and go north on Hwy. 117 until you see the Sun Valley sign directing you to a side road on the left. Back from the highway, secluded in its own mountain dale, is Sun Valley's Hostellerie Suisse (Swiss Inn), a complex of alpine-style buildings with rustic trimmings but all the modern conveniences, not to mention the resort activities on which the place thrives: three tennis courts (bring your whites), horseback riding, badminton, volleyball, shuffleboard, and—nearby—two 18-hole golf courses. A large heated swimming pool is yours in summer, and when the snow falls the resort's chair lift, two T-bars, and Poma lift cart skiers to the top of Sun Valley's own trails and slopes. In the evening, visitors tend to wander to the hotel bar, cozy in a very alpine way, or to the disco which is open every night. Summer visitors get the bonus of being right next door—literally—to the Théâtre Sun Valley, a French-language summer stock theater which stages light-hearted comedies from mid-June onward.

Staying at Sun Valley gives you the choice of modern accommodations in one of three buildings: the Swiss chalet-style hotel has smaller rooms with private bath and balcony; in "The Chamois" motel-style units are Swiss-inspired as well, but include a small refrigerator and two double beds in each room besides the bath and balcony; and in the "William Tell" building, latest built of the resort's hostelries, there's a private bath, one double bed and one hide-a-bed, and a fireplace in each room. All rooms are equipped with radios, phones, and color TV sets. Rates are based on the building you stay in and the number of people sharing a room as well as on length of stay, making for complex calculations worthy of a computer specialist. In short, however, two people coming for a weekend in summer will pay $144 to $160, plus 15% service, as the total amount for two nights in a room plus two meals (breakfast and dinner) each day. Weekly stays for two cost $340 to $410, plus 15%, for five nights and two meals a day. You can have lunch each day for an additional $6 per person per day; children under 12 sharing their parents' room pay half price. Tennis and horseback riding cost extra: $5 per hour per court for the tennis, $7 per hour for a mount. You should also know that rooms at Sun

Valley are capable of housing two, three, or four people, and a party of four can profit by sharing one room: each *couple* would pay not $144 but rather $132 in such a double-up situation for a summer weekend. Prices, then, work out to be very close to those at the aforementioned Le Chantecler, and while Sun Valley doesn't have the grand scale of its imposing neighbor, it has an equally charming coziness, alpine seclusion, and informality which make it just as appealing, in a different way. As at most resorts, honeymoon, tennis, and ski packages offer reductions on these basic rates. Sun Valley is Ste-Adèle's best and most charming place to get away from it all.

Considerable savings can be worked into your holiday budget if you choose a place offering accommodations alone, without the extras such as sports possibilities and meals. Ste-Adèle's **Auberge Champêtre** (tel. 514/229-3533), at 1435 Blvd. Ste.-Adèle (that's Hwy. 117), is somewhere between a resort motel and a condominium block, boasting three different kinds of modern, rustic-decor accommodations. The least expensive for two people are the "President" rooms equipped with a double bed or two twin beds, a Franklin fireplace, color cable TV, and AM-FM radio for $35 per night. "Family" rooms have all these plus a small sitting area and kitchenette, as well as beds for up to four people. These deluxe rooms cost $44 for two, $51 for three, or $58 for four people. Finally, the "Chalet" rooms have a living room with all the comforts on the ground floor, and a sleeping loft above capable of putting up four people. The Chalets are extra-commodious and thus cost the most: $50 for two, $58 for three, $66 for four. Besides the Franklin fireplace (with firewood) in each room, the auberge has its own little pool surrounded by a terrace and bar. In spring and fall special off-season rates can save you money, as can an extended stay of a week or more. Better than a motel, cheaper than a resort, the Auberge Champêtre is just the sort of place to base yourself while you explore the Laurentians.

Should you just be passing through, Ste-Adèle can accommodate you in any of several motels for a night or two. The **Motel Altitude** (tel. 514/229-2919) is a new, modern, fully equipped hostelry perched up a slope above Hwy. 117 about a mile north of Ste-Adèle. Rooms are a bit darkish but attractively furnished and spotlessly clean, and all share the luxuries of color TV, modern bathrooms, and a little heated swimming pool surrounded by lounge chairs (open in summer only). A standard room costs $25 per night; one with a fireplace and kitchenette is $10 more per night. Although you're not right in the town of Ste-Adèle, the amusements of the Seraphin Village (see below) are only a five-minute stroll up the road next to the motel. Coming directly from Montréal, take Exit 72 from the Autoroute to get to the Motel Altitude.

Staying right in town means you can walk to most of Ste-Adèle's attractions, and if this is what you have in mind, look for the **Hôtel/Motel Châtel Boisé** (tel. 514/229-2953) at 1997 Blvd. Ste-Adèle, just beside the turnoff for the Mont Alouette ski area. Take Exit 69 from the Autoroute. The Châtel Boisé is a modern two-story frame motel building with attractive touches of stonework attached to an older hotel unit with a quaint dining room and a big lounge and bar. Rooms are of the standard motel type, with private bath, radio, and color TV, and prices ranging from $25 to $33 per couple per day. During summer days guests can enjoy the motel's private swimming pool, and in the evening all year round a disco provides lively diversions. As for meals, the Châtel Boisé's dining room features Québec specialties at very reasonable prices, plus frequent daily specials. A full roast beef dinner can cost as little as $8, a lobster feed (in season) as little as $13.

WHERE TO EAT: Among Ste-Adèle's dining spots, **Le St-Trop** (tel. 229-3298), right on the lakeshore at 251 rue Morin, is a perennial favorite. Keeping to its country setting, Le St-Trop is rustic in inspiration but plush in its furnishings, with a half-timbered facade hiding a deep-carpeted interior wealthy in plants, and with an exceptionally fine view of the lake. The cuisine, as the restaurant's name implies, is French with the occasional North American concession; dinner, beginning at 6 p.m., is the only meal served. The menu changes frequently, but recently it offered starters such as shrimp cocktail or cream of mushroom soup, followed by dorade aux herbes de Provence (dorado flavored with Provence spices: rosemary, thyme, and sage), or perhaps a daube provençale (a knuckle of meat in a rich dark wine sauce). To finish up there was lemon pie. With coffee, but without wine, the bill came to $16.50 per person. With tax, tip, and wine, the tab for two might be $40 to $45, but careful choosing could bring the price as low as $35. Le St-Trop is an easy walk from town, only a fifth of a mile past the Chantecler driveway.

All-around favorite dining place in Ste-Adèle is **TJ's** (tel. 229-4417), 179 rue Morin at the intersection with the Chantecler road. You'll spot the outdoor roadside patio bar as you approach, and if the weather's not good enough to have your breakfast or lunch outside, there's plenty of room in the L-shaped dining room. Marvelously ingenious macramé plant hangers serve as lamps also and provide something beautiful to look at, as the dining room has no view. TJ's chef is Greek, explaining the menu listings of moussaka ($5) and shish kebab ($9), or souvlaki sandwiches ($1.75). But spaghetti and hamburger plates are offered as well, providing less expensive alternatives. The daily special plates, which are liable to follow any cuisine, be it Greek, Italian, Canadian, or Québecois, allow you to have a full three-course meal for about $10, wine not included. TJ's is nice without being formal, so you needn't worry about dress requirements, and kids are always welcome.

The cheapest Ste-Adèle lunch of all is the one you carry away from **Mike's Sub Shop** (tel. 229-2838), 1791 Blvd. Ste-Adèle. Local representative of an ever-growing chain, the "sous-marins" (subs) come hot or cold, in lengths from 7 to 14 inches, priced at $1.50 to $3.50. Stuffings can include steak, cheese, pepperoni, mushrooms, salami, ham, fried onions, lettuce, tomatoes, etc.—a dozen different combinations in all. Pizza, in four sizes priced from $2.50 to $11, is another Mike specialty. Sharing a large 16-inch pizza, four people could have a light lunch for as little as $1.50 per person.

WHAT TO DO: The lake is the center of activities during a Ste-Adèle summer. Besides the numerous water sports offered by Le Chantecler, "pédalo" pedal-powered watercraft may be rented at several lakefront docks.

For an excursion into the Laurentian past, go a mile north of Ste-Adèle on Hwy. 117 to **Seraphin Village** (tel. 514/229-4777), a recreation of the sort of village found throughout the Laurentians almost 100 years ago. Rude log cabins and slightly more refined public buildings set within the forest on crude dirt streets allow you to imagine what life was like during the period of large-scale settlement in the region. The amusement park takes its name from a novel by Claude Henri Grignon entitled *Un homme et son péché,* ("A Man and His Sins"), which depicts the demanding life of the Laurentian frontier and how one man—Seraphin Poudrier—failed to meet its challenge, responding to its demands with greed rather than generosity. Children will love the park's oldtime atmosphere, and for a thrill they can have a ride on "Le Petit Train du Nord," a miniature train which chugs under a covered bridge and sets out for a 20-minute run through the village and the forest. Plan your visit anytime from May 15 through October 15 from 10 a.m. to 5 p.m., but note that from mid-May through mid-June and from mid-September through mid-October the park is closed on Fridays. You'll pay $1 to park your car, and then $2 for every person over 12, $1 for every person from 5 to 12. By the way, Seraphin Village has a bakery which turns out fresh bread (for sale), a restaurant serving Québecois dishes, and a bar where you can taste Québec oldtime favorites like "caribou" and cider.

STE-ADÈLE SKIING: Le Chantecler resort has its own ski trails, 13 of them in all, served by two double-chair lifts and five T-bars. You can rent equipment and sign up for lessons right at the resort. Some of the well-groomed trails end right by the main hotel.

On the other side of Hwy. 117 and a bit farther north is **Mont Alouette** (tel. 514/229-2717; in Montréal, call 514/861-6572), with ten trails, three T-bars, and a Teleski lift. Rental skis are available, as are lessons.

At **Sun Valley** resort, described above, you can profit from ten downhill trails served by one double-chair lift and four T-bars, plus snowmaking machinery, a rental shop, and a ski school. At the town's more modest **Centre Municipal** (tel. 514/229-2757) the trails are good for beginners: three T-bar lifts will slide you up the slopes for the run down three different trails.

3. Ste-Marguerite

In the center of Ste-Adèle you may notice a street going northeast named the Chemin Ste-Marguerite. After crossing the Laurentian Autoroute at Exit 69, this little road bridges the Rivière du Nord and leads into a beautiful lake-sprinkled resort area dotted with imposing luxury holiday estates.

Just by the river stands the outspokenly Swiss-style **Alpine Inn** (tel. 514/229-3516; in Montréal, 514/861-3258), a resort complex which is actually located in the town named Ste-Marguerite-Station. Peeled and varnished tree trunks serve as posts, rafters, and beams throughout the inn's baronial reception hall, and hand-painted folk motifs dance along railings and borders and cover the cathedral ceiling.

But for all its aggressive rusticity, the Alpine Inn is a very luxurious place to spend your vacation. The least expensive rooms are in the main lodge, and two persons in a room sharing a bath with another room will pay $60, breakfast and dinner included. Private shower or bath can bring the price up to $62 to $76 for two. In the Alpinette chalet, two persons pay $68 for a room with television, bath, and air conditioning. The inn's deluxe cottages come with bedroom and living room, fireplace, TV, and bath for $94 double, $114 triple, or $132 for four; one super-deluxe cottage rents for a few dollars more in each case. Remember that these rates include two meals a day, and as is the custom in Laurentian resorts, that a 15% service charge will be added to your bill, raising the final figure substantially. An extra person in any room or cottage pays $18 daily; children 12 and under pay half price if they stay in their parents' room.

Once you're bedded down in the Alpine Inn's ever-so-rustic charm, the fun begins. Both the indoor and outdoor swimming pools are heated; a private golf course and tennis court are yours in summer; the inn's own four-sheet curling rink is close by, and in winter the cross-country trails are marked according to difficulty. Trail fees are only a few dollars a day, and you can rent your skis and take lessons right on the spot. Speaking of golf and skiing, the Alpine Inn offers special rates for devotees of these sports who stay at least two days (but not on Saturday): $32 to $33 per person per day, with two meals, taxes, and service all included. Feel free to sign up for these special rates even if you aren't a skier or golfer—here, one could spend days just wandering through the green valley sniffing the air and admiring the views.

At the nearby **Auberge Yvan Coutu** (tel. 514/228-2511; in Montréal, 514/861-5212), the pleasures are many and the prices eminently reasonable. Smaller than many other Laurentian resorts, it still has its own 365 acres of forest and ski slope, with a 72-room main lodge plus seven small cabins. For a double room, breakfast and dinner included, you can expect to pay $55 to $60. Sports at the lodge and on nearby lakes and mountains range from down-hill and cross-country skiing through golf, archery, canoeing, tennis, and swimming.

Empress of Ste-Marguerite resorts is the one past Ste-Marguerite-Station, and past Ste-Marguerite, in the town of Esterel. Almost a town in itself, **L'Esterel** (tel. 514/228-2571; in Montréal, 514/866-8224 to 866-3594) is a fabulous year-round holiday hideaway capable of accommodating 300 guests on an immense 5000-acre estate offering almost unlimited activities. Perched dramatically right on the lake shore, L'Esterel's modern hotel rooms all have private baths, color TV, and air conditioning, and are rented at three basic rates: rooms with a view of the lake cost most, of course, going for $108 double, two meals included. If you're willing to take a room on the other side of the hotel with a forest view, you pay $94 for two; and a block of "economy" rooms goes for $78 double. At any time other than mid-July to mid-August, room rates are about $8 lower per day. Weekly (five-day) rates save you about 9% over daily rates. Add 15% for service (no tax).

But about those activities: the list includes downhill and cross-country skiing, golf, tennis, nature trails, sailing, "pédalo" peddling on the lake, bad-minton, volleyball—and on and on. Exceptions such as L'Esterel's health club, winter sleigh rides, and snowmobile rentals are just the icing on the cake, but even the most used-to-luxury visitor will be surprised to learn that he can trundle out to L'Esterel's own sugar bush in early spring, tap the trees, and make his own maple syrup in the resort's private sugar house! Some of these activities—pédalos, sailboats, ski equipment, electric golf carts, and the like—are subject to rental charges, and golf and tennis cost extra if you stay less than a five-day "week," or if you just come up to sample L'Esterel's pleasures for a day. By the way, Voyageur buses from Montréal go right to L'Esterel's remote doorstep, 50 miles from the metropolis.

4. Val Morin and Val David

VAL MORIN: This Laurentian hideaway is truly that: a hideaway almost three miles beyond the village, nestled among the hills. The **Far Hills Inn** (tel. 819/322-2014; in Montréal, 514/866-2219) soon becomes your very own posh estate as your imagination accepts the dignified old New England–style stone-and-frame mansion as "home." All of the resort activities are here, including lots of skiing in winter, and summertime fun like indoor and outdoor swimming pools, sauna, tennis and squash courts, hiking and mountain climbing, and canoeing and sailing on the inn's motor-free lake. But the inn's particular sort of getaway spirit is best expressed in things like its outdoor barbecues in good weather, indoor nature talks, recorded classical music "concerts," and library for rainy days. A piano bar and disco bring a note of social excitement to this otherwise completely laid-back atmosphere.

Rates for the 75 comfortable, modern rooms are simple: $49 to $59 single, $78 to $98 double, $25 for each child under 12 sharing its parents' room; $78 per night double for a two-day "Laurentian Weekend," or $318 to $478 double for a Sunday-to-Friday five-day vacation "week." The customary 15% service is added to room and board charges, and all of these rates include breakfast and dinner daily. If you drive to Far Hills Inn, leave the Autoroute at Exit 76, go through Val Morin, and follow the signs up into the hills to reach the inn.

VAL DAVID: Montrealers, who know the Laurentians well, think of several lovely things at the mention of Val David's name. Summer hideaway chalets; winter ski cabins; neighbors who paint, or carve, or write for a living; and elegant dinners at the renowned luxury resort of La Sapinière—all have a part in the mystique of this village, even though the sheer beauty of abruptly rising hills, scatterings of ponds, creeks, and lakes, and a fragrant forest lushness are attractions enough.

Driving north on 117 from Montréal, make your first contact with Val David by stopping for a meal at the roadside restaurant named **Au Petit Poucet** (tel. 819/322-2246), on the right-hand side just a short distance before the Val David turnoff. A country-ish place with minimal formality, Au Petit Poucet still manages to be charming, particularly because of the large windows which expose a simply marvelous view of the Val David region. Red-and-white checked table cloths, natural wood, and other homey touches set the scene for the house specialty: maple-smoked ham. Six set-price meals are priced from $5 to $11, although you can dine here for even less if you order, say, barbecued chicken with french fries ($3.30). Tourtière and other Québec delicacies share the menu with North American and continental dishes both familiar and exotic. Au Petit Poucet is open from 8 a.m. to 11 p.m. daily; on Fridays and Saturdays it stays open until 1 a.m.

Turn right off the highway to reach the center of the village, and the street you follow will soon be named the rue de l'Église (it runs right by the little church). As you pass through the center of town, note the location of **Le Bistrot des Campagnards** on the left at the corner of rue de l'Académie. It's Val David's favorite "local" eatery, serving everything from breakfast eggs to late-night (1 a.m. on weekends) snacks and suppers. The breaded veal cutlet will run about $6.25, but a ham steak with pineapple, or fish and chips, or spaghetti, or any of several sandwiches cost only $2 to $3.50. The Bistrot is licensed, so you can have wine, beer, or a cocktail with your supper.

For fancier cuisine, and also to rent a room for the night, follow the signs through the town to the **Auberge du Vieux Foyer** (tel. 819/322-2686), a pristine Swiss-style inn which makes you happy even when you just look at it. In the tidy living room, comfortable armchairs are drawn up to the little fireplace, and in the nearby dining room the predominance of honey-colored natural wood is strangely soothing. A small bar provides a focus for après-ski conviviality, and a billiard and Ping-Pong room is available for rainy days. The guest rooms are smallish and plain, without private bath, but with fine views of the surrounding forested hills. The price is no drawback: one person pays $34 per day, or $37 for a room with a little private balcony; two pay $48, or $54 with balcony; and of course breakfast and dinner are included in the price. Weekly rates are $214 to $233 single, $302 to $340 double, and except for the high summer season there's a special five-day Sunday-to-Friday price of $210 for two people. Add 15% for service. The auberge is located on its own private little pond, good to swim in or sun by, and equipment for outdoor games is always yours for the asking.

If you're so unlucky as to be speeding through Val David, you can still sample the auberge's tranquility by dropping in for a supper of Swiss-style fondue, served between 6 and 8 p.m. each evening, and priced about $12 to $18 for two people. By the way, Val David is so beautiful, and the Auberge du Vieux Foyer is so popular (although so small), that advance reservations are an absolute necessity at most times of the year—in winter, claim your room at least two months in advance if you can. The several ski slopes of Mont Plante are only a short stroll away.

Val David is mostly the domain of the vacation homeowner, but you can join this privileged group for a week or a season by renting a cabin in **Le Village Suisse** (tel. 819/322-2205; in Montréal, 514/527-1293), a small cluster of alpine cabins right at the beginning of the lane which leads to the prestigious Hôtel La Sapinière. The fully equipped cabins rent by the week, the month, or the season, and cost $255 per week, a bit less when rented for the longer term. In high summer and winter seasons all the cabins are usually rented well in advance, while off-season you may be able to find one vacant the day you call.

As one of the most delightfully beautiful villages in the Laurentians, Val David deserves—and has—a top-notch, world-class luxury resort hotel famed throughout Canada for the finesse of its cuisine and the graciousness of its service and accommodations. The **Hôtel La Sapinière** (tel. 819/322-2020; in Montréal, 514/866-8262) is a dignified dark-wood forest lodge set in emerald lawns right at the shore of a little lake. Even the Québec government attests to the excellence of the hotel's hospitality, granting it five fleurs-de-lis (out of a possible six) for the comfort of its rooms, and four forks (out of four) for its dining room. Private swimming pool, boating and canoeing, tennis, sunbathing, or winter skiing at nearby Mont Plante are the activities, but the feeling one gets here is much more of a refined mountain rest spa than of an activity-filled resort.

And then there's the dining: classic French with Canadian accents, it concentrates on the best there is to offer: recently the table d'hôte listed marinated New Brunswick herring or smoked salmon as an appetizer, gazpacho or vichyssoise for the (summer) soup course, and lobster or stuffed rack of lamb as the pièce de résistance, accompanied by assorted vegetables and concluded with rhum baba and coffee. Guests find such a dinner included in the daily room rates; others can reserve for dinner and have such a meal for $24, tax and tip (but not wine) included. As for the wine, the list runs to 200 choice items priced from $15 per bottle and up (mostly up). For two, then, the bill for dinner with wine would certainly be above $60, with wine, tax, and tip; choosing from the menu rather than from the table d'hôte offering increases the final tab substantially. But what a meal!

La Sapinière can offer you rooms in the main lodge, in motel-style buildings, or in four- or five-person cottages, and contrary to the practice in most Laurentian resorts, prices here include not two, but rather *all three meals* each day. All accommodations have private baths, color TV sets, and air conditioners, and are priced at $62 to $70 single, $94 to $110 double, $52 to $55 per person in the cottages, plus the customary 15% for tips. Note that La Sapinière is basically an adult resort, and so reductions for children staying in their parents' room are offered only for children under 7 years old. Also, for dinner men will be expected to come in jacket-and-tie formality, women in similarly suitable attire, although casual vacation wear or sports clothes are acceptable for breakfast and lunch. It is probably safe to say that no pair of denim jeans has ever polished a chair seat in the dining room of La Sapinière. For sheer beauty and gentility, there may be no better place to visit in all the Laurentians than La Sapinière.

5. Ste-Agathe-des-Monts

With a population of something like 6000, Ste-Agathe-des-Monts is the largest town in the Laurentians. Early settlers and vacationers must have flocked here in search of precious lakefront footage on the beautiful Lac des Sables, and local business and industry followed the crowds. Ste-Agathe's main street, the rue Principale, is the closest you'll come to citification in these timeless mountains, but don't be concerned by this touch of urbanity. If you follow the rue Principale from the highway through town, you'll end up back in vacationland, at the town dock on the Lac des Sables.

The dock and surrounding waterfront park make Ste-Agathe a fine place to stop for the day, and the summer waterskiing activities and lake cruises may lure you into a stay of a week or more. For a night or two, the motels near town on Hwy. 117 provide comfort and convenience, but for longer stays you may want to consider putting up at a lakeside lodge.

WHERE TO STAY AND EAT: The deluxe **Motel Ste-Agathe** (tel. 819/326-2622) is a modern 40-room motel right on Hwy. 117 with a heated swimming pool out front and private baths, television sets, and radios in all the rooms. You'll pay $28 to $33 for a room here, and the town is only a short drive away.

Just to the northeast of the town dock, at no. 83 on the road called Tour du Lac ("Around the Lake"), is the charming old **Auberge Colonial Inn** (tel. 819/326-4791). The stone entryway superimposed on the frame building catches your eye as you drive or walk from town, and through that stone portal lies an establishment with an ambience hovering between the gracious and the cozy. Popular with retired vacationers because of its cool, quiet, pine-shaded location just across the road from the lakeshore, the Colonial is a quaint reminder of the gentility which once prevailed earlier in this century. The basic charge for two people in a room without private bath is only $20, rising to $60 for two if all three meals are taken in the inn's tall-windowed dining room.

For some of the best dining to be had in Ste-Agathe, go to the town dock and scan the end of the rue Principale for the **Salle à Manger Girard,** open for lunch and dinner daily except Mondays (on Sundays, it's brunch from 11 a.m. on). The Girard is a Ste-Agathe classic, a humble eatery with blue-ribbon cooking located in a small Québec-style house. In good weather diners can sip a pre- or postprandial drink on the small patio on the lake side of the house; a glass of kir (crème de cassis and white wine), for example, costs $2. On the less than frantically busy days of Tuesday through Friday, the Girard offers set-price meals which go for $2.75, $3.50, or $5, but if you're willing to spend $8, it will buy you something like this: fresh cantaloupe for a start, then cream of broccoli soup followed by sirloin en brochette (on skewers, with a wine sauce), vegetable and potato, a coffee mousse for dessert, and coffee or tea. The Salle à Manger (that's "dining room") Girard is quaint, but the food is fancy.

WHAT TO DO: Get your bearings by taking a cruise on the **Alouette boats** (tel. 819/326-3656) which depart the dock at the foot of the rue Principale seven times daily from mid-May to mid-October. After the 50-minute, 12-mile voyage on a boat equipped with a bar and running commentary of the sights, you'll know, among other things, that Ste-Agathe and the Lac des Sables are famous for waterski competitions and "hydravion" (seaplane) flights. In fact, the lake is a virtual "airport" for these trusty little craft which buzz here and there in the lake-filled and often roadless reaches of northern Québec. Cost for the Alouette cruise is $3 per adult, $1 per child 10 years of age or younger.

Want to take a buzz in one of those amphibious planes? **Air Ste-Agathe** (tel. 819/326-1365) will be glad to oblige, taking you aloft for a turn around the lake for a mere $5. Longer trips of 20 minutes ($10 per person) and an hour ($20 per person) are yours for the asking. Actually, while these airborne tours of the Lac des Sables are a thrilling way for tourists to get their bearings, Air Ste-Agathe really specializes in flying hunters and fishermen to destinations in the backwoods where the streams are choked with fish and the moose seem to be behind every hill and tree.

6. St-Jovite–Mont Tremblant

Without doubt the most famous and popular of all Laurentian locales is the one surrounding Mont Tremblant, highest peak in the Laurentians (3150 feet, or 960 meters). Mont Tremblant's fame and popularity are not new, however, as the provincial government set aside almost 1000 square miles of wilderness in 1894 to be Mont Tremblant Park, and the foresight of this early conservation effort has yielded unlimited outdoor enjoyment to vacationers past, present, and future.

The mountain's curious name reportedly comes from an Indian legend: a hunting party ended a successful day's efforts by feasting on the catch, after which they all fell asleep. Streams tumbling down the mountainside made such a thunderous booming that the whole mountain seemed to be in motion, thus giving rise to the Indian name which translated into French as *la montagne tremblante* ("trembling mountain"). Well, this isn't the first time that the stuff of legends has proved to be exceptionally flimsy!

St-Jovite (pop. 4000) is the commercial center for the area, providing all the modern services. The village of Mont Tremblant, several miles nearer the large resorts and the mountain itself, has only the most basic services. Highway 117 passes straight through St. Jovite to continue northeast; Mont Tremblant lies in the northern loop of Rte. 327. The town of St-Jovite harbors a few interesting restaurants and a motel or two, but most vacationers make their base at one or another of the resorts or lodges scattered along 327.

Water sports in summer are as popular as the ski slopes and trails in winter, because the base of Mont Tremblant is surrounded by no fewer than ten lakes: Lac Tremblant, a gorgeous glacial stretch of water ten miles long; and also Lac Ouimet, Lac Mercier, Lac Gelinas, Lac Desmarais, and five more, smaller bodies of water, not to mention rivers and streams.

THE RESORTS: Mont Tremblant's dowager, famous as the mountain itself, is **Gray Rocks** (tel. 819/425-2771; in Montréal, 514/861-0187) on Lac Ouimet. Pages and pages could be devoted to a detailed account of what there is to see and do at Gray Rocks in summer and winter, but perhaps a brief mention of several exceptional features will say it all. For instance, Gray Rocks not only has its own airport for guests who fly in by wheeled aircraft, but in addition it has its own seaplane base on Lac Ouimet. Of course Gray Rocks has tennis courts, but would you have guessed it has *16* of them? And you'd expect some amusements for children, but would you be surprised to find a complete playground, with attendants to care for the children while you have fun elsewhere, and even a program of free swimming lessons for the kids? Horseback riding, sailboat rentals, golf, shuffleboard, croquet—not to mention Gray Rocks' own ski slopes, lifts, and cross-country trails right at your door, make this the most "compleat" vacation community in the Laurentians.

Prices for a stay at Gray Rocks are almost as bewildering as the list of things to see and do. Here are the basics: accommodations are in the huge old rambling main lodge or in the cozier, more modern lodge called Le Château, or in one of the resort's four-person cottages. Rates per day include three meals and the relevant taxes, but a service charge of 12½% will be added to the basic daily room-and-board charge to cover tips to dining room personnel and chambermaids. Single guests, then, pay $35.50 to $52.50; couples pay $56 to $97; parties of four pay between $164 and $210. Stays of six nights are cheaper than six times the normal day rate, and a single guest would pay $185.50 to $200 at the least, $274 to $296 at the most for six nights, with the higher figures applying during the busiest vacation periods. For couples, six-night prices are between $371 to $506 off-season, and $400 to $547 in high season. At the lowest of these rates, your room would share a bathroom with at least one other room. Children 12 and under sharing their folks' room pay half rate, but during off-season each couple can have one child 6 years old or less sharing their room for free—meaning the little one dines courtesy of Gray Rocks. Golfers and tennis players can pay one flat rate for a week's use of the facilities, and perhaps even some lessons; skiers get a similar deal. But bonafide honeymooners get the best deal of all: a free bottle of champagne, a bouquet of fresh flowers, and free use of golf, tennis, rowboat, and canoe facilities (off-season only) during a six-night stay.

All this is bewildering, perhaps, but once through it you can take in the entire Gray Rocks scene by hiring the resort's own seaplane pilot to take you aloft for a scenic flight above Lac Ouimet, Mont Tremblant, and the entire Laurentian region. Four people can go up at once, and the total cost for the 20-minute flight is $24 per planeload.

Last stop on the Voyageur bus run from Montréal is right at the base of Mont Tremblant. Here, the bus pulls right up to the front door of the **Mont Tremblant Lodge** (tel. 819/425-2711; in Montréal, 514/861-6165), a sprawling holiday village which rests not just on the mountain's skirts, but on the shores of Lac Tremblant as well. Mont Tremblant Lodge seems to attract the most diversified and fascinating clientele from all parts of Canada and abroad, especially during the winter ski season. When the snow is deep (as it usually is), skiers here like to follow the sun around the mountain, making the run down slopes with an eastern exposure in the morning and the western-facing ones in the afternoon. The lodge boasts 20 trails in all, served by three double-chair lifts and two T-bars. In summer, guests have the choice of pool or lake swimming, and ten-mile-long Lac Tremblant is perfect for waterskiing (at a small extra fee). The chair lifts up the Laurentians' highest mountain operate in summer as well (for a few dollars per trip), just so vacationers can enjoy the panoramic view. Six tennis courts and a nine-hole golf course are on the lodge's estate, along with a dozen other indoor and outdoor amusements.

Mont Tremblant Lodge lists its maximum high-season rates in its public notices, and then with a bit of accountant's legerdemain the off-season rates are quoted as rebates or discounts (of 10% or 20%) on the top rates. As with other great Laurentian resorts, you can choose from a variety of accommodations. The inn—Mont Tremblant's main building—has twin-bedded rooms with washbasins and shared bathrooms; the adjacent building, named Les Cèdres, has single rooms with or without private shower, and also double-bedded rooms with private bath. Most expensive of all are the twin-bedded rooms in the lodge proper, all of which have private baths, some of which are corner rooms with the most light and the best views. Then there are the cottages, a half-dozen styles in all, including tiny ones for a single couple, more capacious ones with living room as well as bedroom and bath, others with several bedrooms, perhaps with a living room equipped with color TV. The largest and finest have several bedrooms, a living room with a fireplace, color TV, and bath, and can accommodate from six to nine people. In summer, guests can choose to have either two or all three meals per day, the difference between the two- and three-meal prices being a mere $3 per person. In winter, the ski-week packages include all three meals, daily lessons, and unlimited use of the lifts. In summer, then, a couple can expect to pay $58 for a room without private bath, three meals included, or up to $82 for the most luxurious room with private bath (the one-bedroom Honeymoon Cottage costs $10 more). Single guests pay $32 to $35 per day for room and all three meals. For seven-day stays, prices are $202 to $220 single, $358 to $516 double, plus the customary 15% service, but no tax. Winter ski-week prices are higher: single rooms cost $283 to $322, doubles are $289 to $389, and dormitory bunks sell by the week (meals and lifts included) for $238 per person. On New Year's weekend these rates rise somewhat, but in mid-December and through January to early February they're actually 10% to 20% lower. But don't let all these details daunt you. Once you arrive at Mont Tremblant Lodge for a week of skiing (on water or snow), the sheer breathtaking beauty of the place will make it all worthwhile.

Actually, you don't have to stay right at Mont Tremblant Lodge in order to schuss down its slopes, for the ski school, ski shop, and lifts are open to visitors staying at other Laurentian hostelries, and to those just up for the day from Montréal. There's a charge, of course, and it's a daily one with no ski-week discounts. For use of all the lifts all day, you pay $8 on weekdays, $12 on Saturday, Sunday, and through the Christmas–New Year's busy period.

Other resorts near Mont Tremblant are smaller than these two giant places, but in exchange for the lack of a few exotic activities you gain a coziness and small-group conviviality which only a smaller establishment can give. The resorts below still offer a long list of things to do in summer and winter, although you may have to drive to Gray Rocks or Mont Tremblant Lodge for a golf game, seaplane ride, or ski lift.

The **Villa Bellevue** (tel. 819/425-2734; toll free in Québec, 800/567-6744) is designed more like a motel than a huge, rambling old mountain inn, but don't let the word "motel" conjure up some garish highway hostelry hung with neon signs. Rather, Villa Bellevue is the one-story housing plan adapted to the shores of Lac Ouimet, and guests profit from the efficiently designed, cheerfully decorated modern rooms, all of which have large, sunny windows. There is an older lodge, however, where rooms have washbasins but share adjoining baths, and although these rooms are not as modern and spacious as the "motel" rooms, they constitute a real bargain for resort-goers on a tight budget. Such a hotel room can cost as little as $25 for two persons per night, breakfast included, or $131 for two for a six-night week. With breakfast and dinner, the weekly (six-night) rate for two is $240. For larger rooms in the hotel or for the modern motel rooms, all with private bath, two pay $36 to $47 daily, $202 to $258 for six nights, breakfast included; add about $9 per person per day if you'd like dinner as well. The breakfast-and-dinner plan at the Bellevue doesn't tie you to just this resort's dining room, however. Four hotels in the area (of which the Bellevue is one) have agreed to let guests from any one hotel dine at any of the others without payment of any extra fee. Package plans for weekends and ski weeks are always offered, and the Villa Bellevue seems especially to like kids: children 14 and under can share their folks' room for free, and a children's menu in the dining room keeps the cost of meals reasonable. A few rooms have one double and one single bed and a kitchenette, making it even easier to bring a child. In summer, hotel staff will watch the kids during the afternoon and evening while you go sailing or do your yoga. By the way, the same 15% service charge is added to room and board prices here as at other resorts.

Le Manoir Pinoteau (tel. 819/425-2795) has a marvelous location, perched on a hillside above the road and overlooking Lac Tremblant. A diving school occupies the lakeshore at the foot of the Pinoteau's hill, and guests divide their time between water sports down below and tennis, archery, badminton, volleyball, and other games atop the short slope. The quaint half-timbered lodges of the Pinoteau fit right into the Laurentian landscape. In the dining room, tremendous wood beams, the stone fireplace, and large murals depicting wine cellar scenes inspire frequent fits of romantic fancy. Should these flights of fancy become too frequent, you can move on to the Villa Bellevue, the Mont Tremblant Lodge, or Cuttle's Tremblant Club for your evening meal, as the Pinoteau is one of the four "Variety Dining" hotels in the Tremblant area.

Least expensive units are the motel-style rooms, all with private bath, for $35 double with breakfast, $56 double with breakfast and dinner. By the week (six nights), these prices are $185 and $296, respectively. Small cabins and slightly more deluxe rooms cost about $7 more per night, and prices rise even more for the Pinoteau's luxurious multibedroom cabins with living room and fireplace which take a minimum of four persons. A penthouse, one of the relatively small number of rooms to enjoy a sweeping view of the lake, has its own bedrooms, living room, and private bath, and costs a somewhat daunting $58 daily for two with breakfast, $92 for breakfast and dinner. Add 15% for service. Le Manoir Pinoteau lists special Friday-and-Saturday weekend rates, five-night "week" stays, honeymoon weeks, and ski-week packages, too. Off-season reductions can save you 10%. Children, by the way, are granted a discount of 25% if they're between 7 and 12 years old if they share their parents' room; younger tots can stay for free.

LODGES AND INNS: The Laurentians, and Mont Tremblant in particular, are justly famous for their luxurious resorts. Less renowned but equally delightful are the much smaller lodges and inns which, like their New England counterparts, provide a very different sort of ambience. In a smaller hostelry you're virtually forced to meet your fellow guests, and friendships tend to grow quickly at close quarters. Everyone else in an inn or lodge has chosen to stay there for reasons similar to your own, and you shouldn't be surprised to find yourself having dinner, exchanging tennis partners, or sharing a ride to the slopes with interests much like yours.

Prettiest of Mont Tremblant's inns is the **Château Beauvallon** (tel. 819/425-7275), a white gambrel-roofed and gabled structure set in a swath of emerald lawn and bordered by a log fence. The château's own lake beach is a short stroll away on Lac Beauvallon, and the château's boats are moored nearby. Built in 1942 as part of the Mont Tremblant Lodge resort, the handsome château was later sold—perhaps because it is some distance from the rest of the resort. Today this seclusion is a major attraction, and hardly anything happens to disturb the tranquility of life at Château Beauvallon.

In summer, the rustic but comfortable Québec country-style rooms are rented on a daily basis with breakfast and dinner included: doubles are $40. In winter, ski-week packages are the most popular plan. Children 12 and under pay $10 a day when sharing their parents' room. The cozy dining room seats only 30 guests, and the tiny bar vies with the pine-paneled lounge (with fireplace) in attracting before- and after-dinner conversation groups.

Smallest and coziest of Mont Tremblant's inns is the **Auberge Sauvignon** (tel. 819/425-2658), next to the Chalet des Chutes (same bus stop), and only a short stroll from Lac Tremblant's shore. The eight guest rooms at the auberge are all different: one has a private bath and a king-size bed, and costs $40 for two in summer, $60 in winter, the difference in price being in the meal plan. In summer, auberge rooms come with a full Canadian breakfast; in winter, with breakfast and dinner. Other, simpler rooms, which share showers, are less expensive at $30 double in summer, $52 in winter.

Owners of the Auberge Sauvignon, Grant and Katie Moffat, are also chefs de cuisine, with Grant doing the main courses and Katie seeing to the desserts in the snug 36-seat dining room. Guests at the auberge are served the table d'hôte meal of the day, which in the past has meant such delights as fondue on Tuesdays, a barbecue on Wednesdays, leading up to a sumptuous Sunday-night repast of roast prime rib of beef with Yorkshire pudding. The dining room is open to the public, by the way, and while an à la carte listing is offered all the time, the daily table d'hôte dinners are bargains not to be missed: the prime rib dinner from soup to coffee, for example, is only about $15.

The **Chalet des Chutes** (tel. 819/425-2738) is a 27-room hotel and motel with the feeling of a mountain inn and the services—including a private swimming pool (summer only)—of a modern roadside hostelry. Over the years the chalet's owners have built a reputation for good food, conviviality, and friendliness which brings guests back every year, winter and summer. The piano bar called L'Ambiance, with its massive stone fireplace and spirited nightly crowd, is a major attraction. The 15 modern motel-style rooms are rented at a basic two-person rate of $27 to $29 per day; the older but very comfy rooms in the Swiss-inspired hotel come without private bath for $20 to $22 per day for two. These basic rates include no meals, although you can avail yourself of meal-inclusive rates and ski-week plans if you wish. Water sports on Lac Tremblant, and the ski lifts and slopes of Mont Tremblant, are only a few minutes' drive away. Some guests even walk.

MOTELS: Although hardly replete with mountain charm, the several motels near Mont Tremblant and St-Jovite offer the undeniable advantages of modernity, predictable comfort, and very reasonable prices. Bonuses can include kitchenettes—great money savers for groups of skiers who are willing to cook and eat in common—and private swimming pools open in the summer months. And if the motels don't have the spacious grounds, comfy lounges, or long lists of activities of other Laurentian hostelries, all these things are easily available nearby. Often, motel ski-week rates provide you with access to slopes and après-ski soirées for no additional charge.

Closest motel to everything is the **Mont Tremblant Motel** (tel. 819/425-3505), in the village of Mont Tremblant right across the road from the Hôtel de Ville (City Hall). Here, you'll go to sleep after enjoying an hour with the color cable TV, and will wake to a panoramic view of the lake through your room's picture window, or from your own little private balcony. For breakfast, just wander down to the motel's own little dining room, and later in the day relax in the built-in cocktail lounge. Basic daily rates are $16 single, $19 to $21 double; or with breakfast and dinner, $28 single, $34 to $40 double. By the week these rates are even cheaper, and one of a variety of weekend or ski-week packages with lift tickets included should fit itself exactly to your needs.

Just over a mile from the center of St-Jovite stands the **Mountain View Motel** (tel. 819/425-3429), on Rte. 327 as you travel toward Mont Tremblant. The 20-unit motel is set perpendicular to the highway, minimizing the noise problem; half of the rooms have kitchenettes, and all share use of a nice little heated pool (in summer only). All have modern private baths and color TV sets.

As the Mountain View is open all year, rates vary from period to period depending on demand (as at virtually all vacation hostelries), but in general a double room with kitchenette is priced at $40 per day. Rooms without kitchenette are $2 per person per day cheaper. Ski and family groups take note: the Mountain View's rooms can sleep up to four people, and so for a $60 room with cooking facilities, a family or group of four would be paying a mere $15 per person. In the slack off-season period and when most other Laurentian lodging places are closed, the motel lowers its rates substantially, by 20% to 40%, depending on the dates and the number of people sharing the room.

RESTAURANTS: Although most Laurentian lodging places have their own dining facilities, and—at least in wintertime—require that you use them, anyone exploring the surroundings of Mont Tremblant should know of a few good independent dining places for the odd night out, lunchtime snack, or stop en route. Here are some local favorites:

Before visiting the modest little building containing **La Table Enchantée**, call 425-7113 and see about reservations. This tiny restaurant doesn't look like much from the outside, and those who know no better might think they were in for fish and chips. Not so. The small tables neatly set support some of the most carefully prepared and tasty dishes in the region, served each evening from Tuesday through Sunday in the busy summer season; on Friday, Saturday, and Sunday off-season. The owners, Ghislaine and Leopold Handfield, stick to traditional and authentic Québec cuisine with the occasional excursion into the realms of the French (cuisses de grenouilles, frogs' legs) or the Anglo-Saxons (steak), for instance. But a full traditional dinner would start with fresh bigorneaux (periwinkles or whelks) in season, or crème de palourdes (clam chowder). Then comes the Québec pâté called creton, followed by authentic cipaille, a many-layered pot pie made with pheasant, guinea hen, rabbit, veal, and pork—but too often these days consisting (in other restaurants) of chicken, beef, and pork. The fèves au lard à l'érable (maple-sugar-cured pork and beans) is a cheaper alternative to the cipaille. Dessert might be fresh apple pie or grand-pères au sirop d'érable (dumplings in maple syrup). The price? For soup, pâté, main course, dessert, coffee, wine, tax, and tip, about $22 per person (much less if you have only three courses and are content to drink beer). This may be the most memorable single meal you'll have during your stay at Tremblant. But don't forget to make those reservations. La Table Enchantée is near the settlement of Lac Duhamel, exactly 1 4/5 miles northwest past the steel river bridge in St-Jovite, on Hwy. 117.

Less expensive and elaborate fare is the specialty of **Petite Europe** (tel. 425-5557), right downtown in St-Jovite at 804 Ouimet, the main street. In French it's what's termed a charcuterie, which is classically a pork butcher's shop, but today signifies a delicatessen. Besides selling uncounted delicacies—five dozen sorts of cold meat, three dozen cheeses, two entire cold cases full of various pastries, cakes, and tarts, racks of jams and jellies, coffee beans, alcohol-free beer, even clam juice—Petite Europe has a few small booths and tables where you can have sandwiches ($1.50) made from any of these good things, or assorted cold-meat-and-cheese plates ($3) or desserts (75¢), not to mention fresh coffee. Although there's no liquor license, you may develop a taste for that thirst-quenching if spirit-less beer. Petite Europe is open, much to hungry travelers' delight, from 9 a.m. to 5 p.m. and from 6 p.m. to 9 p.m. every day but Sunday.

SKIING MONT TREMBLANT: It's Mont Tremblant that draws the biggest downhill ski crowds in the Laurentians, and **Mont Tremblant Lodge** has the slopes: 20 downhill runs and trails in all, plus a ski school, ski shop, and snack cafeteria; three double-chair lifts and two T-bars ferry skiers up the mountainside for $8 per weekday, $12 on Saturday or Sunday, with reductions, as is customary, for children or half-day skiers.

But Tremblant is not the only place in the area to ski. **Gray Rocks** has slopes overlooking Lac Ouimet and ending in the inn's backyard, at rates comparable to Mont Tremblant's. And besides these heavily patronized downhill trails, there is plenty of cross-country action. Organized by **Le Club de Ski de Fond Mont Tremblant St-Jovite, Inc.** (tel. 819/425-3300), the area has 100 km (60 miles) of trails cleared and maintained through cooperation of the ski club, various lodging places, and civic organizations. The Villa Bellevue, for instance, has its own "Centre de Ski de Randonné" (Cross-country Ski Center) affiliated with the ski club, as does Gray Rocks. Fees for the trails are only a few dollars a day, and rental equipment is readily available at the two inns mentioned, and at sports shops in St-Jovite.

7. The Eastern Townships and Sherbrooke

Southeast of Montréal lies Québec's breadbasket, a flat and fertile region broken by rolling hills and by the 2600-foot (792-meter) peak of Mont Orford, centerpiece of an enchantingly beautiful provincial park and ski area. Only a short distance from Mont Orford stands Sherbrooke, industrial and commercial capital of the Eastern Townships (Cantons de l'Est), and throughout the Mont Orford–Sherbrooke area are serene glacial lakes which attract summer fishermen, sailors, and swimmers from all around. Touristically, the Eastern Townships are Québec's best kept secret, so it's mostly Montrealers and Québecois who come here to rent summer cabins or to launch their boats or to ski.

Unlike the Laurentians, which virtually close down in "mud time" when spring warmth thaws the ground, the Eastern Townships fairly bustle with activity as crews penetrate every "sugar bush" (stand of sugar maples) to tap the sap and "sugar off." Autumn, likewise, has its special attraction here, for in addition to the glorious autumn colors, the Eastern Townships brim to overflowing with apples of every variety, and the cider mills hum day and night to produce the "wine" of Québec. It's not unusual for visitors to help with the autumn apple harvest, paying a low price for the basketful they collect themselves. And the cider mills throw open their doors for tours and tastings. As for maple sugar time, local towns and villages often have maple sugar festivals, and numerous farms host "sugaring parties" at which guests partake of a gargantuan country repast, and claim their dessert out by the sugar house: boiling maple sugar is poured on the fast-melting winter snow and cooled instantly to produce a unique maple sugar candy. Montréal newspapers and local tourist offices and chambers of commerce keep current lists of what's happening where and when.

GETTING THERE: Leave the island of Montréal by the Champlain Bridge, which leads to Autoroute 10, heading for Sherbrooke. Don't fret if you're carless, just call the **Terminus Voyageur** (tel. 514/842-2281) in Montréal and ask for the departure time of the next bus on bus route no. 47, from Montréal to Granby, Magog, Sherbrooke and St-Georges. Those in a breathless rush can remain on Autoroute 10—and plenty of express buses do this too—but to get to know the countryside, turn off the Autoroute at Exit 37 and go north the short distance to join Hwy. 112. Local buses leave Montréal to follow Hwy. 112 about ten times a day, arriving in Sherbrooke, 100 miles (160 km) away, 3¼ hours later.

VIA Rail Canada operates rail service daily from Central Station in Montréal along a track which is more northerly than the highways mentioned. Diesel railcars make a trip a day in each direction, taking about 2¼ hours to reach Sherbrooke. But for a fascinating rail adventure, take the *Atlantic,* which chugs out of Montréal's Windsor Station each evening just after the close of the business day on its way to Saint John, New Brunswick. The *Atlantic*'s route is along and slightly to the south of the Autoroute. It drops you in Sherbrooke two hours and 40 minutes after departure from Montréal, and then heads out on an international route which cuts across the forests of Maine to reenter Canada at McAdam, New Brunswick. The *Atlantic* hauls sleeping cars (which, presumably, you won't need if you're just going to Sherbrooke), a restaurant car, and a lounge car with snack and beverage service.

ON THE ROAD: Although town names such as Granby, Waterloo, and Sherbrooke are obviously of English origin, the Eastern Townships today are overwhelmingly French-speaking. Tidy little towns along the road through apple country are filled with houses kept neat as a pin, and surrounded by carefully tended orchards and farmland.

Rougemont, 22 kilometers from Autoroute Exit 37 along Hwy. 112, is a major apple orchard and cider-mill town, and at all times of the year the main street is dotted with little stands selling various sorts of apples, apple products, other vegetables, and homemade bread. At St-Césaire, a few kilometers farther along, the little stands and shops specialize in handicraft items made locally. The next town is Saint-Paul-d'Abbotsford, founded in the late 1700s by Scottish settlers. Abbotsford became the name of the town in 1829, the Saint Paul being added later by the French inhabitants. To apple growers of the Eastern Townships, Saint-Paul-d'Abbotsford is something of a mecca, for it was here in 1896 that the Société de Pomologie du Québec was founded—the local apple-growers cooperative.

Granby (pop. 35,000) is an industrial town with a surprising attraction—surprising to find in this agricultural region, at least. The **Granby Zoo** (tel. 514/372-9113), at rues Bourget and Pare, is a sprawling wooded park harboring beavers, zebras, mountain goats, gorillas, giraffes—even a yak or two. Local and visiting children come not just to look at the animals, but also for the games in the amusement-park section, and for the pony rides. Open from mid-April through October, the zoo charges $3 admission for adults, $2 for seniors, $1.50 for students 14 to 18, $1 for kids 6 to 13.

For an overnight stay, the **Motel Le Granbyen** (tel. 514/378-8406), a few blocks west of the center of town at 700 rue Principale, is modern and fully equipped, but moderately priced at $30 per night for two. The town's **tourist information office** is just on the other side of the traffic lights from the Granbyen at 650 rue Principale (tel. 514/372-7273). Nearby are representatives of just about every fast-food chain on the continent.

MONT ORFORD: While the park is a small one compared to the vast protected areas in northern Québec, **Mont Orford Provincial Park** is among Québec's loveliest and most popular for camping and hiking. In high summer season, campsites fill up quickly, especially on weekends. Winter visitors come for the more than 20 miles of ski trails and slopes, with a vertical drop of 1500 feet, or for the extensive network of cross-country ski and snowshoe trails.

Orford has its own special claim to fame in the **Centre d'Arts d'Orford** (tel. 819/843-3981), set on a 222-acre estate within the park and providing musical and dramatic classes for young people throughout the year. Québec's answer to Vermont's Marlboro Festival, the **Jeunesses Musicales du Canada** has a formal arts festival each summer, drawing talented performers and teachers from throughout Canada and the world.

Skiing Mont Orford

The ski area is superbly organized, and will do all the work for you in setting up accommodations and transportation from almost anywhere. A call to **Mont Orford Reservations**, P.O. Box 248, Magog, P.Q. (tel. 819/843-4200), allows you to select and reserve a room, chalet, or efficiency apartment at one of the many motels, hotels, or vacation villages nearby. You pick a category of accommodation—deluxe, standard, second, or third, priced from $115 to $190 per week for two people—and the bureau finds the room and mails you all the particulars.

Want to do it yourself! Try the **Auberge Cheribourg Inn** (tel. 819/843-3308), which is actually a collection of up-to-date mountain chalets very near the Orford Arts Center and the road to the Lac Stukely Campground. Single rooms are for rent by the day at $36 to $46 double, up to $58 for up to five people; or hire one of the boldly designed and brightly colored chalets by the week ($150 to $235 off-season, $225 to $370 in-season) or by the month, or by the season. Except for the smallest one-room studio ("garçonnière") chalets, all the others can sleep up to six people in varying degrees of luxury, and all are equipped with a fireplace, kitchenette, linens and utensils. The Cheribourg is open year round, and in the slow periods lots of special money-saving package deals are up for grabs. To get to the Cheribourg, take Exit 118 from Autoroute 10.

When it comes to paying lift rates, you're in for a pleasant surprise, as Mont Orford has joined with three other nearby ski centers to form **Ski East** (Mont Orford, Mont Sutton, Bromont, and Owl's Head). Instead of the $10 to $12 daily lift rates you might pay at any one center, you can purchase an all-inclusive five-day ticket for $38 good anywhere, anytime. Similarly cheap lesson plans are yours for the asking.

MAGOG AND LAKE MEPHREMAGOG: Orford is where the people go, but Magog is where the people live. How did a nice little Eastern Townships town at the northern tip of a beautiful lake get such a name? Certainly this isn't the place inhabited by the nations of Gog and Magog who, according to the Book of Revelations in the New Testament, will follow Satan into battle against the Kingdom of God in the Last Days. As with 1000 other incredible Canadian and American place names, Magog came by its handle through corruption of a much more romantic Indian name. In this case the Abenaki name Memrobagak ("Great Expanse of Water") was corrupted to Mephremagog, from which was extracted Magog.

In fact, Magog and the lake are noted for their sanctity: the **Benedictine Abbey of Saint-Benoit-du-Lac,** about halfway down the western shore of the lake from Magog to the Canada–U.S. frontier, is a spellbinding spot where the ancient art of Gregorian chant is kept alive by the monks in their daily services: Mass at 11 a.m., Vespers at 5 p.m. (at 1:30 p.m. on Thursdays in winter; 1:30

p.m. on Tuesdays and Thursdays in summer), and Compline at 7:45 p.m. Visitors will want to be decently dressed to attend services, of course. A hostel for men and a separate one for women provide lodging for visitors. The Canadian blue cheese known as L'Ermite, among Québec's most famous, is produced at the monastery, and is for sale in a little shop.

Although Saint-Benoit-du-Lac dates only from 1912, the serenity of its monks and of their way of life is timeless—and inspiring.

SHERBROOKE: Seat of an archbishopric, university town, and home of about 150 different manufacturing firms, Sherbrooke is the "metropolis" of Québec's Eastern Townships. It's a hilly city, built where the Magog and Saint-François Rivers meet. Just before the Magog River flows into the Saint-François, it widens to form the Lac des Nations—a lake right in the center of town.

Every year at the end of May and beginning of June, Sherbrooke hosts the **Festival des Cantons,** an explosion of dancing, music, drama, oldtime games and fun, pony and hay rides, banquets, and contests of all conceivable sorts—perhaps the closest thing Québec has to a state fair.

It's easily possible to use this city of 100,000 as the base for your explorations of the "Cantons de l'Est," and if you come by train, bus, or air, you may have to do just that.

Yes, Sherbrooke has air service: **Air Bar Harbor** (alias Bar Harbor Airlines), of Ellsworth, Maine, operates flights between Boston, Hartford/Springfield, New York (La Guardia), points in Maine, and Sherbrooke and Québec City. Note that although you can fly to Québec City or Sherbrooke from the U.S., you cannot fly *between* Sherbrooke and Québec City—unless it's just to set down in Sherbrooke on a flight to Québec City, of course. For information, fares, and schedules, call Zenith 62930; or 819/566-4545 in Sherbrooke, 418/872-4344 in Québec City, or 800/341-1504 in Boston.

Where to Stay and Eat

Most of Sherbrooke's accommodations are aimed at the business traveler, and so you'll find a grand and luxurious **Holiday Inn** (tel. 819/563-2941), at 3535 King St. West, which is actually the continuation of Hwy. 112 in the city. Rooms—all 125, the standard modern best—go for $35 to $39 double, and there's no extra charge for use of the beautiful indoor swimming pool, or the sauna. When the business crowd is not filling the inn, try suggesting a slight reduction in rates.

The Holiday Inn's main competition comes from the brand-new **Auberge des Gouverneurs** (tel. 819/565-0464), a similarly impressive roadside hostelry at 3131 King St. West, one of a chain of Québec hotels and motels of the highest quality. Prices are similar to those at its rival: single rooms, $32.50; double rooms, $38.50 to $40.50, depending on whether you desire one bed or two; each extra person pays $8 in the same room. Come for a two-day weekend and you need pay only $30 for two the first night, $25 the next.

The budget-minded travelers, the older but serviceable **King George Hotel** (tel. 819/569-2581), 380 King St. West, is at the top of the hill on King St., very near the center of town. Although the hotel's facade is anything but impressive, the rooms are clean and simple, and cost only $16.50 for two, or $17.50 with a color TV set—all have private baths. The hotel's dining room retains a tradition of good food born of another age, and you may want to drop in some evening for, say, their filet de turbot aux câpres (turbot filet with a caper sauce, $6.75), or tournedos Rossini ($11.50). A metered municipal parking lot is right across King St. from the hotel.

A favorite Sherbrooke dining place is the **Restaurant Le Provençal** (tel. 819/864-9124), a quaint mansard-roofed stone building at 5156 Blvd. Bourque (Hwy. 112, west of the city, in disguise), corner of rue Kennedy. For all its Québecois decor, the menu is more hearty Canadian, featuring things like grilled trout with garden salad ($7.75), tenderloin tips for about the same price, a surprising number of calves brain and sweetbread dishes, and a half-dozen sorts of filet mignon priced about $11.

Attracted to the **Restaurant Yildiz**, in the King Shopping Center ("Centre d'Achat") on King St. West, by dreams of delicious and exotic Turkish dishes, I found that the name (Turkish for "star") survives from earlier owners, and that now the cuisine is international. The prices are very reasonable, especially at lunchtime. For $7.75 at lunchtime, tax (10%) and tip included, I had one of two proffered soups of the day, a brace of grilled pork chops served with potato and vegetables, apple pudding for dessert, a bottle of beer, and a cup of coffee. Items on the à la carte menu are slightly more expensive, but still quite reasonable.

From Sherbrooke, roads lead to the capital of Québec, which many people (the present writer among them) consider to be the most enchanting city in all North America.

QUÉBEC CITY AND THE GASPÉ PENINSULA

THE SOUL OF FRENCH CANADA is in Québec City, as it has been for almost 400 years. The first settlement to be founded by the claimants of New France, it has always been the center of French national feeling. Montréal was the inland port, nearer to the riches of the trappers and the timbermen, and it became the brains and muscle of Québec. But the soul of Québec was always here.

This is not to say that Québec City is entirely an antique town, filled with sentimental old people and a pension economy. It is, after all, the first large port up the St. Lawrence, as well as a manufacturing town, and, foremost, the center of government for this huge and increasingly independent province. The modern section of Québec City sits cheek-by-jowl with city walls of a medieval cast, but in the large sister cities of Ste-Foy to the southwest and Levis on the opposite bank of the St. Lawrence, modernism reigns supreme.

Québec is almost solidly French in feeling, in spirit, and in language, although many of its citizens speak English as well. And even if they don't, you can put aside at once any fear of being looked on as an outsider. In Paris the people may be sticky about using the language, but not in Québec. Every attempt on your part to speak French, or on a Québecois's part to wrap his tongue around the unfamiliar sounds in English, always ends in mutual smiles and more often than not in mutual understanding.

But so much for Greater Québec. The part of town most people envision when the city's name is mentioned is the jumble of ancient, picturesque houses clustered around a castle out of Hans Christian Andersen. The old city, with its marvelous Château Frontenac, is every bit as romantic as you could ever imagine. Perched atop the steep cliffs of Cape Diamond, its present-day tranquility hides a turbulent past.

When Jacques Cartier sailed up the St. Lawrence in 1535, he recognized at once the tremendous strategic potential of Cape Diamond, "the Gibraltar of the North," especially as it commanded a *kebec,* the Indian word for "narrowing of the waters." But he was exploring, not empire building, and after setting foot here he reembarked for the trip upriver.

Samuel de Champlain arrived 73 years later, determined to settle at Québec. His first settlement, or "Habitation," was down near the riverbank beneath the cliffs of Cape Diamond. It grew to become Québec's Lower Town. But almost from the beginning there were rivals: first the Iroquois, then the English, and much later the Americans. The Québecois constructed a fortress atop the cape, and gradually the center of urban life moved to the easily defensible top of the cliffs.

In the 1750s, the struggle for control of the rich North American lands raged between Britain and France, with strategic Québec as a prize of the highest value. The French sent Louis Joseph, Marquis de Montcalm, to command their forces here. The British sent an expedition in a fleet under the command of a hot-headed, 32-year-old brigadier general named James Wolfe. The battle for Québec, fought on the Plains of Abraham southwest of the city on September 13, 1759, is one of the most famous in North American history. As every Canadian schoolchild knows, both valiant generals perished in the fighting, but the British under Wolfe were victorious, and the fate of Québec was sealed for the next two centuries.

In this chapter you'll find tips on where to stay and where to dine, what to do and what to see in the city itself. After Québec, you might want to consider a day-trip to the Laurentian Mountains very close by, to the garden-like Île d'Orléans, or to the popular shrine of Ste-Anne-de-Beaupré, with the nearby provincial park of Mont Ste-Anne. For skiers, Mont Ste-Anne is a must. Those readers lucky enough to be off on a tour along the southern bank of the St. Lawrence will find complete descriptions of where to stop and what to do all the way around the Gaspé Peninsula, a breathtaking land of incredible unspoiled beauties.

GETTING TO QUÉBEC CITY: Direct bus and air routes serve Québec City from Montréal, New England, New York, and the Atlantic provinces; if you come by rail from the west or south of the city, or by jet from overseas, you'll probably have to pass through Montréal.

By Car

Montréal and Québec City are linked by Autoroute 20, a fast, four-lane highway which can speed you along the 166-mile distance between the cities in three hours or so. From the Atlantic provinces, the fastest route is up the Saint John River Valley in New Brunswick to Rivière-du-Loup, Québec, from which Autoroute 20 brings you to Québec City.

From the south, Québec City is a lot more accessible than it looks from a brief glance at the map. It's only slightly over 500 miles from New York, and less than 400 miles from Boston. New Yorkers (and others from farther south along the coast) will want to pick up Interstate 91 at New Haven, and follow it right up to the Canadian frontier; from Boston, take I-93 right out of the city and link up with I-91 at St. Johnsbury, Vt. After crossing the border, you'll be on Québec Autoroute 55 almost to Sherbrooke. From Sherbrooke you have a choice: if speed is your object, take Rte. 143 to Autoroute 20, and whiz right along. But Rte. 116, which leaves 143 north of Sherbrooke, is more scenic if a bit slower, passing through small and neat French Canadian towns along the way. As you approach the city, follow signs for Pont (Bridge) Pierre-Laporte.

After you've crossed the bridge, turn right onto Blvd. Wilfrid-Laurier (Rte. 175), which later changes names and becomes the Grande-Allée; after it penetrates the old city walls it's named the rue St-Louis, and it goes straight to the Château Frontenac.

By Bus

Québec's capital city is served by **Voyageur Lines** operating out of the Gare Centrale d'Autobus, 225 East Charest Blvd. (tel. 524-4692). Voyageur has daily buses to Rivière-du-Loup and Edmundston, N.B.; at Edmundston, Atlantic province travelers connect with SMT lines.

The bus traffic between Québec's Gare Centrale and Montréal's Terminus Voyageur is intense, with a bus almost every hour. You can call for times, or just drop down to the station when you're ready to go; chances are you won't wait more than a half hour.

In summertime, **Autobus Fortin Poulin** and **Greyhound Lines** team up to provide Boston to Portland to Québec City service along I-95, U.S. 201, and Québec Rte. 173. Coming from Boston, you change buses at Old Orchard Beach, Me. If you're enroute from New York, the best thing to do is to change at Boston for the Old Orchard Beach bus, then again at Old Orchard Beach. The trip between Boston and Québec City is a full-day trip taking about 11 hours.

By Rail

It used to be that one chose his route between Montréal and Québec City by the railroad he selected: Canadian National went the southern route via Drummondville, and Canadian Pacific went the northern route via Trois-Rivières. Now that Canada's passenger rail services are unified under the VIA logo, you have to choose your route by train rather than by company. The trip takes anywhere from slightly under three hours to almost four hours, depending on the train you choose. Fastest are the Rapidos on the southern (Drummondville) line; slowest are the named trains on the same line.

The southern line serves Montréal's Central Station and Québec's Ste-Foy Station. Morning and evening Rapido trains connect with buses at Ste-Foy to take you to the Château Frontenac. You'll find a club car and snack and beverage service on these commuter trains. On the *Scotian* and the *Ocean* you can sit down to a meal, or buy a snack, or rent a reclining seat, or get a berth in the sleeping car. From Montréal, only the *Scotian* is of interest, as the *Ocean* gets in after 2 a.m. If you're coming to Québec City from the opposite direction —from the east or north—the *Scotian* and *Ocean* serve (with connections) Halifax, Sydney, Charlottetown, Saint John, and Gaspé, plus points along the way. For Québec City information: call 418/653-6422.

On the northern route, via Trois-Rivières, diesel railcars leave Montréal's Windsor Station three times daily on the three-hour-plus trip, stopping on signal at intervening stations. The Québec City terminus for these trains is at 200 St-Sacrément, northeast of the center of town. Taxis wait to whisk you downtown. For information, call 418/687-4729 in Québec City.

By Air

Although Québec City is served by a number of major airlines, most air traffic comes by way of Montréal. Of special interest (and not widely advertised) are the several regional and commuter lines which serve the city, outlined below.

Québecair (tel. 418/692-1031 in Québec City) has flights between Québec City and Boston, Chicago, Miami, Montréal (Dorval), New York (JFK and LaGuardia), Ottawa, Paris, Toronto, and most major cities within the province; the long-distance flights are carried out in conjunction with major carriers such as Eastern, Delta, Air Canada, and CP Air.

Bar Harbor Airlines (tel. Zenith 62930; airport, 418/872-4344) has flights to Québec City from New York (LaGuardia), Boston, Hartford/Springfield, and Portland, as well as several points in Maine, but note that you'll be in for at least one stopover, maybe two, and perhaps even a change of planes on these flights. From New York the flight takes about three hours, from Boston between two and three hours depending on which flight you pick.

Should you be coming to Québec City from the North Pole—the town of Resolute—you'll be flying on **Nordair** (tel. 418/694-0281 in Québec City), but you may also choose this carrier if you're coming from Pittsburgh, Windsor, Hamilton, Ottawa, Winnipeg, Dryden, Thunder Bay, Sault Ste-Marie, or Toronto. Nordair also operates most of the routes to remote points in northern Québec—like Resolute, near the North Pole.

There's an airport bus ($3) to bring you from Québec City's airport northwest of the city right into the center of town.

ORIENTATION: Believe it or not, you could spend almost all your visit to Québec in the old city, as most tourist hotels and tourist homes, restaurants, and tourist-oriented services are based here. The **Upper Town,** at the tip of lofty Cape Diamond, is enclosed by the old city's fortification walls. The **Lower Town,** at the foot of Cape Diamond, is similarly colonial in large part. Several ramp-like streets and an elevator ("funiculaire") join the two parts of the colonial town.

For a panoramic look at the city, seek out the Québec government's office building called Edifice "G" at 675 St-Cyrille Est (tel. 643-6017). On the 31st floor is an observatory open from 9 a.m. to 4 p.m. on workdays March through October. Other good places for an overall view are the top floor of the Hilton International Québec (site of the Eden disco), and the revolving restaurant atop Loew's Le Concorde Hotel. Nothing ties it all together like being able to take in the entire city at once.

Tourist Information

The city operates a well-staffed tourism information service at **60 rue d'Auteuil** (tel. 692-2471), just inside the city walls near the Porte St-Louis. Another center is run by the provincial Ministry of Tourism near the **Place d'Armes** (which is right beside the Château Frontenac) at 12 rue Ste-Anne (tel. 643-2280). If you're in the Lower Town, drop in at **Picard House** in the Place Royale (tel. 643-6631).

GETTING AROUND IN QUEBEC CITY: It's simple: walk. Once you've reached the center of town, virtually no place of interest and no tourist-oriented hotel is out of walking distance. If it's raining hard or if you've got a game leg you may be obliged to take the occasional taxi, but in general shoeleather is the way to go.

Although you can walk between the Château Frontenac (top of the cliff) and Place Royale (bottom of the cliff), you can also allow yourself the luxury of a ride on the **funicular** (tel. 692-1132) which operates up the cliff face between those two points along a 210-foot track. The cost for the short trip is

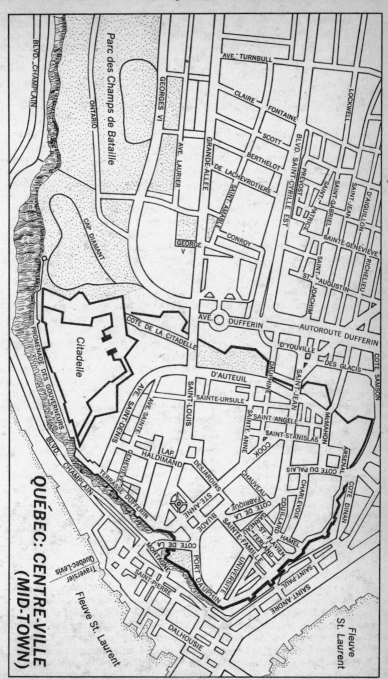

QUÉBEC: CENTRE-VILLE (MID-TOWN)

50¢, and the car operates daily until 11:30 p.m. Note that the upper station is just off Dufferin Terrace near the front of the Château Frontenac and the Place d'Armes; the lower station is in Maison (House of) Louis-Jolliet on rue Petit-Champlain, a block or two from the Place Royale.

Parking

It's a problem in Old Québec, where almost every available space seems to be marked with the ominous words "Terrain Privé—Remorquage à vos Frais" ("Private Property—Cars Towed at Owner's Expense"). Some smaller hotels have their own lots, for which the charge is usually about $2.50 per day. Otherwise, large underground public lots exist behind City Hall: two lots are entered from Ave. Chauveau, and prices are 40¢ to 50¢ per hour up to a maximum daily charge of $4. The **Garage Haldimand,** on the one-block-long street called Haldimand between St-Louis and Mont-Carmel, charges $1 for the first hour, 50¢ for each additional hour up to a daily maximum of $4. Right around the corner on the Jardin des Gouverneurs, the parking lot of the **Château Frontenac** is the old city's most expensive at $1.25 for the first hour, $4.75 for up to seven hours. Right outside the St. Jean Gate at **Carré d'Youville** is another large public lot priced like those at City Hall.

Bicycle Rentals

I'll stick to my earlier statement that the best way to see Québec City is on foot, but if you must have wheels, two will do very nicely. Bike rentals cost about $1.75 per hour, cheaper (per hour) if you rent for a half day or a day or even longer. Actually, some agencies rent adult tricycles and quadricycles as well as bicycles, and thus even the unsteady can join in the fun. Couples can save 25¢ per hour by renting a tandem bike at $3 per hour. Here are some rental agencies: **Agence Cyclotour,** rue Tache and Grande-Allée, next to Loew's Le Concorde Hotel and Plains of Abraham (tel. 529-1493); **Velocation,** 1169 rue St-Jean in the old city (no phone); **Location de Bicyclettes,** 641 Grande-Allée Est, between the Citadelle and Loew's Hotel on that street (tel. 522-2040).

Calèches

These horse-drawn carriages congregate in the **Place d'Armes** by the Château Frontenac and in the parking lot next to the **Municipal Tourism Information Office** by the city walls. Your driver acts as your tour guide if you like, and charges $20 for a city tour taking between 45 and 60 minutes. In rainy weather, the top and perhaps a plastic sheet draped over the front will protect you; the driver gets to sit in the rain.

1. Québec's Hotels

By far the nicest—and the most economical—place to stay in Québec City is in one of the small hotels or guest houses within the old city walls. In many of these establishments every room is unique, and the standards of comfort, amenities, and prices vary so much from one small hotel to another that it is truly difficult to imagine one couldn't find just what is wanted here. From rooms with private bath and color TV down to plain but surprisingly inexpensive rooms, the old city has everything. There's even a modern motor inn.

But if grand-hotel luxury is your wish, you may have to search in the new city on the other side of the ancient walls. The Château Frontenac offers big-time luxury at comparable prices, but for the glitter and sheen of a Hilton or a Loew's, go to the new city. However, even these luxury hostelries are still easily within walking distance of the old city gates. In fact, the only places to stay which are not within walking distance are the chain motels which line the Blvd. Wilfrid-Laurier between the Pont Pierre-Laporte and the Cité Universitaire.

In the sections which follow, hotels are arranged according to price category, and then within each category by general suitability: the most highly recommendable places are listed first, followed by other suitable—if not quite unique or exceptional—places to stay.

BIG AND FANCY (Doubles for $56 and up): Although Québec City has many fewer luxury palaces than Montréal, there are still enough of them to provide handsomely for the crowds of businessmen and well-heeled tourists who flock to the city both winter and summer. In line with policies at luxury hotels throughout the world, the top hotels in Québec City have rate structures which only a computer can understand: peak-period high rates, slump-period discounts, special arrangements for weekend stays, for honeymooners (whether newlywed or not!), for ski weeks (the slopes of Mont Ste-Anne are not far away). In fact, while calling to confirm these prices before press time, I was quoted several different "basic" rates for the same hotel. All this is just to convince you that luxury hotels will demand what the traffic will bear, and if you're not coming on Christmas or New Year's or during Winter Carnival, and if you know to ask for specifics on weekend stays, honeymoon specials, or discounts for extended stays, you can bring the price of luxury down to very moderate levels. Remember also that for families, luxury hotels can prove to be surprisingly moderate because most rooms have two double beds, and if your children use one bed and you use the other, there should be no extra charge above the normal price for a double room with two double beds.

Québec's magnificent **Château Frontenac** (tel. 418/692-3861; toll-free reservations through CP Hotels or LRI Reservations) is usually the very first place visitors consider when looking for a place to stay. The opportunity is difficult to pass up, for few people have more than one chance to stay in a 500-room baronial castle perched atop a cliff towering over one of the world's great rivers. Queen Elizabeth and Prince Philip, a half dozen other British and foreign monarchs, even Madame Chiang Kai-shek—all have put up at the Château Frontenac. During World War II, Churchill and Roosevelt had a conference here, and because of wartime security measures they had the entire 500 rooms to themselves.

As for services, the Frontenac is virtually a city in itself, consisting of the main tall-towered building and a semicircle of lower buildings around it. The location is without doubt the best in town, right next to Dufferin Terrace, the Place d'Armes, the Jardin des Gouverneurs, and the funicular to the Lower Town. In winter, the Dufferin Terrace toboggan and skating rink are just out the Frontenac's door. Of the hotel's half dozen restaurants, the most famous is Le Champlain, certainly one of the city's finest places to dine (see the restaurant section further along). The public rooms reflect their elegant turn-of-the-century heritage.

As for the guest rooms, periodic renovations over the years have kept them up to snuff so that they're fully as comfortable and attractive as any in town, although they cannot be called brand new as can those at the Hilton, Loew's, or the Auberge des Gouverneurs. Prices depend on size and location of the room, with the best views costing more (natch!). Single rooms with bath at the Frontenac cost $46 to $49, double rooms are $56 to $59, and an extra person pays $9 in a double room. The greatest disadvantage of staying at the Frontenac is that you can't gaze at the beautiful place when you're inside it.

Québec's own chain of luxury hotels and motels is named the **Auberge des Gouverneurs,** and in Québec City the auberge (tel. 418/647-1717) is a towering luxury palace of breathtaking modern design reminiscent of Montréal's multilevel building complexes. And indeed the auberge is part of Québec City's first such complex, called the Place du Québec, and is also connected to the city's Convention Center. The location is good, not far from the Québec National Assembly, at 690 Blvd. St-Cyrille Est, and only a block or so from the old city walls and Porte (Gate) Kent. While the decor of the auberge is outspoken and ultramodern, it is perhaps the most successful and tasteful of Québec City's large new hotels. The 400 rooms and suites have color TV, of course, plus individual climate controls and shower-tub bathrooms—as you'd expect. The bonus here is an outdoor swimming pool, heated and open right through the year, including during Québec City's ebullient Winter Carnival. The sauna stays open year round, too. For a single here, expect to pay $50 to $56; for a double, $60 to $66; $10 for an extra person in the room.

The **Hilton International Québec** (tel. 418/647-2411; toll-free reservations through Hilton International) has almost 600 modern rooms in its towering building, and the ones on the upper floors have marvelous views of the old city. But if you can't get into one of these rooms, never mind, for the rooftop disco-bar is the perfect vantage point for taking in the panorama, and is one of the city's most popular nightspots as well (see my nightlife recommendations). At the Hilton you get the high standards of comfort and service which have made the chain of hotels famous throughout the world. The location is excellent, considering that the Hilton is outside the city walls. Near the Québec National Assembly and connected to the Place du Québec complex, you're only a few minutes' walk from the city walls, about ten minutes or so from the heart of the old city.

Room rates, basically, are $46 to $58 single, $56 to $68 double, and $10 for an extra person, but these rates are subject to so many changes and special deals that you'll have to check on them when you reserve. For instance, availability of rooms can change the price, and if there's hot demand for rooms the price will be toward the upper part of the figures quoted. But Hilton also offers several very attractive special-price arrangements for weekends and slow-demand periods, and utilizing one of these can bring the weekend price for a double room down to as low as $45. Be sure to ask about these specials when you reserve. If you plan to visit in winter, ask also about ski-week and ski-weekend deals. With these, up to four friends can share a Hilton room and end up paying as little as $20 per person per night, lift tickets included! Families traveling together will also want to note that Hilton in Québec does not charge for children—of any age—traveling with their parents and staying in the same room with them. Thus, on a special weekend deal, a family of four might stay for as little as $12 per person.

Certainly Québec City's most prominent new hotel is **Loew's Le Concorde** (tel. 418/647-2222; toll-free reservations through LRI), 1225 Place Montcalm off the Grande-Allée next to the Plains of Abraham. The reason for its prominence is its great bulk towering above the battlefields where Wolfe and Montcalm fought it out; atop its daring asymmetrical structure is a wheel-shaped revolving restaurant justly noted for the magnificence of its views. Boldness is the thing in both its design and decor and—if it doesn't overwhelm you—you'll find yourself noticing new elements of this boldness throughout your entire stay. As for luxuries, Le Concorde has them: sauna and heated outdoor, year-round pool, disco, bars, and restaurants—including the revolving rooftop aerie.

Rooms cost between $45 and $59 single, $55 and $70 double; an extra person (not a child) pays $10. As in other luxury hotels, these rates are subject to special highs (during peak and holiday periods) and lows (during off periods, on weekends and ski weeks). Although you're still walking distance from the old city here, it's something like a ten-minute walk to the walls and then another five or ten minutes to the center of the old city as this is the farthest out of the hotels mentioned in this book.

MODERATE HOTELS (Doubles for $20 to $40): Québec City is unique in North America for having such a large number and wide range of small, cozy hotels each with its own special character and charm, and to know the city well you should try to stay in one of these. The range of prices can vary even from room to room in each establishment, and so our guidelines of "moderate" and "budget" are only approximate: you may find a $40 room and a $15 room right next to one another, although this is the exception. Almost all of the hotels recommended below are in the Upper Town of the old city; the few that are outside the city walls are within a five-minute walk of the walls. As with the luxury hotels, prices can vary greatly with the season, and if things look to be slow, a polite suggestion for a special deal often produces a welcome discount. If you're shown a room for $28, just the mention that "we were only going to budget $25" might get you your price.

Start your search for a moderately priced room right in the shadow of the Château Frontenac's towers, on the Jardin des Gouverneurs. If you draw a blank, try right on the other side of the Frontenac at the Place d'Armes.

On the Jardin des Gouverneurs

The facade of the **Manoir Ste-Geneviève** (tel. 418/694-1666) tells you all you need to know about this charming place: a tasteful light-gray color, it's broken by flower boxes in the windows (in summer) and the name of the hotel done in cursive wrought-iron lettering. It's completely charming and exceptionally well kept, and with its location at 13 Ave. Ste-Geneviève, corner of Laporte, Québec, PQ G1R 4A7, it faces the Jardin des Gouverneurs and the Château Frontenac. All the rooms are done in a comfortable, homey style (no. 6 has a bay window with a fantastic view of the park and Château Frontenac). Some rooms have air conditioning and all have TVs, many in color. Prices depend on season and the press of trade, but in general a double with bath is $28 to $34, and well worth it. A few rooms have kitchenettes.

Don't let the antique facade of the **Château Bellevue** (tel. 418/692-3092) fool you, for behind the graceful old stone are 40 ultramodern guest rooms. The interior of the buildings at 16-18 rue Laporte, Québec, PQ G1R 4M9, overlooking the Jardin des Gouverneurs, has been completely transformed into a modern mini-hotel with central air conditioning, wall-to-wall carpets, and a decor of bright basic colors. All rooms have brand-new bathrooms and television sets, and the hotel's bellboy will park your car in the private lot behind the hotel ($2.50 per day) after he's unloaded your luggage out front. Room prices are $25 to $30 single, $30 to $36 double, with the higher prices charged for rooms with views of the Jardin and the Château Frontenac. The Bellevue is easily the most modern hotel on the Jardin, and perhaps even in all downtown Old Québec.

The quaint antique exterior of the **Hôtel Jardin du Gouverneur** (tel. 418/692-1704), painted white with blue trim, catches every visitor's eye at the corner of Mont-Carmel and rues Laporte/Haldimand on the Jardin des Gouverneurs. Although the hotel is closed at the "slow" times of year, in the busy seasons it offers 16 rooms with private bath or shower, some with air conditioning and/or TVs, for $16 to $20 single, $22 to $30 double. The address is 16 rue Mont-Carmel, Québec, PQ G1R 4A3, right next door to the Château Frontenac's parking garage and indeed the Château Frontenac itself.

Of the town houses converted to lodging houses which surround the Jardin des Gouverneurs, only one has the advantages of the grand Château Frontenac without the grand prices. It's the **Château de la Terrasse** (tel. 418/694-9472), and its special advantages come from its location around the corner from the Jardin, overlooking Dufferin Terrace, at 6 Place Terrasse Dufferin, Québec, PQ G1R 4N5. If you can pay $28 to $32 for a double room, you can have the breathtaking view of the St. Lawrence River and the city of Levis on the opposite bank; if you're content with a room at the back of the hotel, you'll save money as double rooms with bath there cost $20 to $22. Some rooms have kitchenettes, and the hotel has several parking places reserved for clients.

At the **Château View** (tel. 418/692-2692), 8 rue Laporte, Québec, PQ G1R 4M9, most of the 17 rooms have small, neat showers, although a few rooms have bathtubs. Fresh wallpaper and paint keep the rooms tidy, and the simple furnishings provide adequate comfort. Prices vary with the room, the season, and the number of people occupying a room together, but generally two people pay $30 to $32 for a room with shower. Two rooms without private shower are a good deal cheaper at $18 to $22 double, $26 triple. Château View has its own limited parking facilities, and others are handy less than a block away. Here you're right on the Jardin des Gouverneurs.

Near the Jardin on Ave. Ste-Geneviève

There are three establishments in Old Québec which have "fleur-de-lis" in their names, but only the **Château Fleur de Lys** (tel. 418/694-1884) is just off the Jardin des Gouverneurs, at 15 Ave. Ste-Geneviève, Québec, PQ G1R 4A8, right at the corner of rue Laporte. The 15 rooms are tidily furnished with pieces one might also find in a small motel, but a motel could never have such a variety of accommodations. From the two small double-bedded rooms with washbasin ($24) through the larger rooms with private bath or shower ($30 to $34), to the very large rooms capable of sleeping four or five people ($38 to $42) complete with kitchen and bath, whatever you need you'll find it here. All rooms have air conditioners and TVs, many in color. Note that continental breakfast is included in the prices quoted above.

Immaculate, graceful rooms decorated with classic Gallic taste are the forte of **Le Château de Pierre** (tel. 418/694-0429), at 17 Ave. Ste-Geneviève, just off the Jardin des Gouverneurs. Marble fireplaces, sconces with crystal prisms, and other elegant touches highlight the very fine decor, but the modern conveniences aren't forgotten. In larger rooms, for instance, you may have two washbasins in the large bathroom (much appreciated if a family or group of four are in the same room). All rooms have air conditioners and TVs, most of which are color sets. Rooms are priced at $30 double for a smaller room with a double bed, $38 for two in a larger room with two double beds, $42 for four in a large room with two double beds. Parking is available, but costs extra.

Just a short walk of one block from the Jardin des Gouverneurs brings you to the **Maison du Fort** (tel. 418/647-9357), 21 Ave. Ste-Geneviève, at the corner of rue des Grisons. The 11 rooms have tile showers or baths, TV sets, and unexpected treats like big old fireplaces (not working, alas) or pretty wood floors. Smaller rooms cost $20 for one or two persons; larger ones are $25 with either double bed or twin beds. The street is a fairly quiet one.

Besides being a charming and comfy place to stay, the **Cap Diamant Maison de Touristes** (tel. 418/694-0313) is almost a bona-fide "museum of domestic decoration." The rooms are all different, and hold an astounding assortment of furniture: brass beds, Victoriana, things from grandma's attic, pieces from the '30s, and all as neat and clean as can be. All rooms have televisions; one has a small refrigerator. The baths and showers are not part of the "museum," however, as all are very modern. Prices are $20 single, $25 double, with some larger rooms going for $30. The big front room can sleep up to six people. The Cap Diamant is at 39 Ave. Ste-Geneviève, only 2½ blocks from the Jardin des Gouverneurs. Free Parking. The grassy lawns of the Plains of Abraham are right behind the house.

Near the Place d'Armes

The **Gîte de la Place d'Armes** (tel. 418/694-9485 or 647-9304) couldn't have a more prestigious location: at 24 rue Ste-Anne, Québec, PQ G1R 3X3, it's virtually a dozen footsteps from the curb of the square, right next door to the Wax Museum, and facing the Anglican cathedral. Rue Ste-Anne is closed to car traffic in this block, an added bonus. The rooms are not fancy, but quite modern and conscientiously maintained. They tend to be small but comfy, some with TVs and air conditioners. Those without private bath rent for $15 to $18 single, $20 to $25 double; with bath (and that means a tub), the price rises to $30 double. No parking, but the inexpensive City Hall lot is just a block and a half away.

The **Hôtel Clarendon** (tel. 418/692-2480) must have been Québec's second-best place to stay (first was the Château Frontenac, of course) several decades ago, and although its boxy brick facade and art deco lobby accents can't compete with the modern gigantism of a Hilton or Concorde, its prices and location can't be beat. Right beside City Hall at 57 rue Ste-Anne (corner of Desjardins), Québec, PQ G1R 3X4, it's at the geographical center of Old Québec. The rooms are all renovated and quite modern, and moderately priced at $28 to $34 single, $36 to $42 double, $40 to $46 twin. All 104 rooms have television sets, some in color, and many have city views that are quite nice. You can park across the street in the City Hall underground lot. A good, centrally located choice.

A Modern Motor Inn

In the midst of Québec City's quaint antiquity, the **Auberge Fleur-de-Lys Motor Inn** (tel. 418/694-0106) is an oasis of bold modernity. Although its exterior doesn't clash unduly with its old-fashioned neighbors, the interior is one of unabashed up-to-date decor. Bright solid colors and decorator touches are in every room; all are air-conditioned; and continental breakfast comes with the price of the room, which is $32.50 double. Free parking, of course, in the inn's street-level lot. You'll find the inn at 115 rue Ste-Anne, Québec, PQ G1R 3X6, not far from the corner of rue Ste-Ursule.

On rue d'Auteuil by the City Walls

The rue d'Auteuil borders the southwestern walls of Old Québec, and while it's a five- or six-minute walk from the Place d'Armes and Jardin des Gouverneurs, it's right next to the Parc de l'Esplanade, Cité Parlementaire, and Place du Carnaval (where the snow sculptures stand in winter).

The **Hôtel Manoir d'Auteuil** (tel. 418/694-1173 or 692-0730), 49 rue d'Auteuil, Québec, PQ G1R 4C2, has the character of a small and efficiently run hotel rather than of a family pension. Decorations and furnishings tend to be straightforward, comfortable, and commodious, although each room has its own special character. Depending on the room you choose, you can have a simple double room with washbasin for $25, or one with bath and color TV for $30, or a larger one similarly furnished for $35 to $40, the higher priced one being for a family of three or four. The Municipal Tourist Bureau is right across the street in the park, and a large parking garage is just on the other side of the sturdy city walls, through the Porte St-Jean.

The **Auberge de la Chouette** (tel. 418/694-0232), 71 rue d'Auteuil, combines a French-Canadian restaurant, a coffeehouse-theater, and a lodging house all in one. The six rooms share three baths; all are air-conditioned, and cost $30 single or double. Combining forces with the seafood restaurant below, called Renoir, the auberge offers meal plans guaranteed to please, at $38 single, $50 double, for breakfast and either lunch or dinner; or $45 single, $60 double, for room and all three meals. This may be the only place in Old Québec to have such a cozy, oldtime inn ambience.

The place called **Au Petit Hôtel** (tel. 418/694-0965) is not all that "petit," encompassing three buildings for a total of 26 rooms. But it preserves the atmosphere of a small family-run pension, and prices to match. Two of the three buildings are on the peaceful dead-end street named rue des Ursulines, the other is on the larger rue Ste-Ursule. Most rooms have private bath, color TV, and telephone, and cost $25 to $35 double, about $5 less single in summer, with cut rates during the winter season. The official address is 3 rue des Ursulines, Québec, PQ G1R 3Y6. Rue Ste-Ursule is parallel to rue d'Auteuil, but one block closer to the center of the old city.

Just a few blocks outside the Porte St-Louis is the **Hôtel Château Laurier**, 695 Grand-Allée Est, Québec, PQ G1R 2K4 (tel. 418/522-8108). A sturdy old stone structure well kept up, the Laurier's 52 rooms are all in good condition and have recently been equipped with color TVs. Some rooms have air conditioning. Single rooms cost $18 to $32, depending on size, accoutrements, and view (it could be of the Assemblé Nationale, the Plains of Abraham, or the old city walls); doubles are $27 to $35 in a double bed, $32 to $35 in twin beds. An extra person in a room pays $4. An elevator serves the several floors, a well-regarded restaurant occupies the basement, and parking is free to hotel customers. The location is excellent for Winter Carnival, and not bad at all for summer visitors as the Château Frontenac is only a 15-minute walk away.

In the Latin Quarter

The **Hôtel Louis-Jolliet** (tel. 418/692-2056) is at the edge of Old Québec's Latin Quarter, at 3½ rue des Remparts, overlooking the battery of cannons, the port, and the towering grain elevators. A medium-sized, older hotel, the Louis-Jolliet's rooms are kept in good shape with new wallpaper, drapes, and bedspreads, and the furniture is still very serviceable. Expansion into the house next door at 3¼ rue des Remparts will give the hotel even more than its present 50 rooms, and will add a good number of rooms with a view. Prices are very reasonable: $20 single, $25 to $30 double for a room with bath and TV. The hotel has its own bar and dining room on the ground floor.

BUDGET ROOMS (Doubles for $15 to $20): The lowest priced rooms in the city are in establishments very similar to those mentioned in the preceding section on moderate hotels, the difference being that budget places have not spent as much in renovation or modernization or creature comforts as the moderately priced places. In budget-priced hostelries, it's a good idea to inspect the room before you register because often the owner will consent to show you several rooms, in which case you'll be sure to get the best value for your money. The people who come in after you and who don't ask to see a room or two will be lodged in the room you rejected. Although you probably won't have a television set in a budget hotel, you should still get the friendly, personal warmth a small hotel can offer, whatever the price.

On the Jardin des Gouverneurs

Of the hostelries overlooking the Jardin des Gouverneurs, none has lower prices than the **Manoir Sur-le-Cap** (tel. 418/694-1987), 9 Ave. Ste-Geneviève. Like most of the guest houses in Old Québec, the Manoir Sur-le-Cap has guest rooms made by partitioning the large and lofty rooms of an elegant town house, and so you may well have a run of ornate frieze or a marble mantlepiece in your room. Because of this gerrymandering, all rooms are different shapes and sizes, and different prices as well: singles start at a very reasonable $10, doubles at $15, and increase in price as size gets greater and extras multiply. Even so, for $20 double you can have a room with a view of the park, and for $24 double you'll get a full bathroom. You can't go wrong here.

Each hostelry on the Jardin des Gouverneurs has its own special character, and at the **Hôtel Château Normandie** (tel. 418/692-2676) it's hominess. Each of the nine rooms looks as though mother has cared for it—mother, in this case, being the proprietress Mme. Gauthier, a genial lady who will see to your comfort and happiness. Rooms are thoughtfully fitted out with TVs, private bath or shower, and in summer with electric fans, and cost a very reasonable $16 to $18 single, $20 to $22 double, certainly among the best prices to be found on the Jardin des Gouverneurs, considering the comfort and cleanliness of the facilities. Château Normandie is at 10 rue Laporte. Parking is available.

Two houses facing the Jardin des Gouverneurs offer an assortment of 17 accommodations at very moderate prices. **Le Manoir de la Terrasse** (tel. 694-1592) and **Beau Site** (same phone) are under the same management. Le Manoir, at 4 rue Laporte, specializes in clean if plain rooms without private bath for $15 single, $18 to $20 double; Beau Site, next door at 6 rue Laporte, has more rooms with private bath or shower, priced a bit higher at $22 to $24 double.

The rooms at the **Manoir Dufferin** (tel. 418/694-0025) have seen better days, but it must be admitted they have their advantages. The building is at 3 Ave. Ste-Geneviève, Québec, PQ G1R 4A7, right next door to the American consulate on the Jardin des Gouverneurs, facing the Château Frontenac. Front rooms, carved up from immense, lofty chambers of a bygone era, have French windows opening onto a balcony overlooking the park and château. All rooms have either shower or bath-shower, and the facilities determine the price: with shower, a double room is $22 to $24; with bath-shower, $24 to $25.

On rue Ste-Anne

Maison Doyon (tel. 418/647-9335), at 109 rue Ste-Anne, Québec, PQ G1R 3X6, is an informal guest house, spare though quite clean and presentable, where frills and extras do not drive up prices. Singles can cost as little as $12 ($15 with bath), and doubles are about $15 with just a washbasin, $18 with a shower; weekly rates bring down these low prices even further. While the location on rue Ste-Anne offers no doorstep attractions or panoramic views, it is only a five-minute walk from anything in Old Québec, and the prices are virtually unbeatable.

On rue St-Louis

Rue St-Louis is one of the old city's busiest—and therefore noisiest—streets. The small hotels and guest houses along the street have refrained from costly renovations, choosing instead to add yet another coat of paint to the woodwork to keep things presentable. These two facts, the busy street and the lack of renovations, combine to make the accommodations on rue St-Louis among the best lodging bargains in Québec, because for all their coats of paint and unrenovated longevity the rooms are quite presentable; and as for noise, only the few front-facing rooms have that problem, and even then only during the daytime.

La Maison du Général (tel. 418/694-1905), at 72 rue St-Louis, Québec, PQ G1R 3Z3, has rooms priced at $13 to $14 single, $14 to $16 double. None of the rooms has private bath or shower, but all have washbasins, some have TV sets, and a few even have small refrigerators. The trick here is to try to get a room on the same floor as the showers, but not in the front of the building (if you're a light sleeper).

The **Manoir Fleur-de-Lys** (tel. 418/694-0066), 43 rue St-Louis, is just one block off the Place Royale, and although the rooms here have seen a lot of use over the years, they come at good prices in a good location. The 25 rooms are of all sorts, from tiny singles at $12 without private bath, to roomy suites complete with private bath and kitchenette for $28 double. Don't expect anything fancy or ultramodern, but the lack of investment in modern fanciness keeps the prices low. The hotel doesn't have its own parking, but there are lots within a block. You can speak English, French, Spanish, German, Russian, or Ukrainian here and the friendly staff will understand you.

2. Dining in Québec

Québec City is unquestionably the capital of haute cuisine in North America. Were it not for this city's myriad other delights, chances are that the hotels would be filled with people coming here just to sample its culinary pleasures.

Why is the dining so good here? First and foremost, the people involved in running a restaurant, large or small, modest or elegant, look upon it as their métier—their profession—and not merely as a job. Then, the Québec countryside, its rivers, woods, and streams, produce such bountiful and high-quality edibles that they seem to inspire good chefs. Finally, the French tradition of haute cuisine, of food prepared with exceptional care, of service as a serious business, is the legacy of both restaurateurs and diners. Very rarely will you come upon a chef or maître d' or waiter who doesn't put *your* enjoyment uppermost. If you find someone who seems condescending or inattentive, he's probably from out of town.

The respect is a two-way thing, however, and a pleasant dinner can depend on following a few traditional rules. Make reservations for busy periods (weekends and holidays especially), and either keep them or cancel them promptly. Dress well—informally, if you wish, but presentably. And note the restaurant's hours of operation: snack shops and cafes may stay open throughout the day, but in general Québec's restaurants like to stick to regular mealtimes. Generally, this means 11:30 a.m. to 2:30 p.m. for lunch, 6:30 to 10:30 p.m. for dinner. Then, relax and enjoy some of the best dining ever. The waiter will be a happy person if he (or she) has been able to please you, and the chef will peek out the kitchen door at least once in an evening to see if everything's going right. In fact, it's not unusual for the chef to send an assistant—or even to come himself—to ask if you've found a particular specialty to your liking. It's a rare thing in most cities these days, but it makes for unforgettable dining.

In general, this love of good food pervades all Québec eating places, even the inexpensive ones, and you may be surprised to see the care taken with a simple sandwich. But stay away from anyplace emblazoned with huge posters advertising "Hamburgers, Hot Dogs, Cheap!" That's not Québec. And speaking of price, you may find the cost of a meal here to be higher than at home, although Québec's prices are certainly in line with those of Montréal. But while the price may be a bit higher, remember that the quality more than makes up the difference. In terms of value for money, Québec is still a very good place to dine. The one item which will hike up the price of a meal more than any other is the cost of wine; in many cases this can't be helped as wine prices even in liquor stores here are a good deal higher than in other provinces or in the United States.

The restaurants recommended below are arranged according to price category. Is your budget tight? You can still enjoy the upper-bracket establishments by going to them for lunch, which is always a bargain. Choose the daily special, which is often a full three-course meal at one low, fixed price. The ingredients will be fresh, the recipe will be one of the chef's specialties, and the bargain will be unbeatable.

When estimating costs, add in the 10% provincial meals tax and 10% to 15% tip.

THE TOP RESTAURANTS (Complete Dinners for $25 and up):

Here are the city's most famous restaurants, where menus boast the most delicate and exotic treats, waiters show the most personal concern, and dinners are most sumptuous. Jacket-and-tie or cocktail-dress formality is the custom, although no strict "dress regulations" apply. Go here for a special occasion, but don't be afraid to return for lunch, which will be surprisingly reasonable in price.

While hotel restaurants are often good enough, rarely do they surpass the majority of independent local restaurants. The exception to this rule in Québec City is the Château Frontenac's dining room, **Le Champlain** (tel. 692-3861). The decor is inspired by Canada's early history, although it is doubtful Samuel de Champlain ever dined with the benefit of the tremendous chandeliers, painted ceilings, high-backed chairs, and grand windows overlooking the St. Lawrence which grace the dining room today. You can sample the cuisine at Sunday brunch (noon to 2:30 p.m.) for only $7.50 per person, plus tax and tip. But to truly savor the chef's accomplishments you must call and get reservations for one of the dinner seatings at either 6 to 6:30 or 9 p.m. Then you get to order, as an opener, the fantastic casserolette d'escargot solognote (snails in a sauce of mushrooms and sliced almonds, $5), then go on to lobster soufflé, Arctic char, steak tartare, or quails, although the salmon steak ($10.40) will never let you down. For dessert, a smooth crème renversée au caramel (caramel custard, $2.10) will do very nicely. The Champlain's wine list is impressive, perhaps even daunting, as are the prices per bottle—but you may not find some of these bottles anywhere else. If you can afford a splurge, dine at Le Champlain once before you leave the city.

Usually the restaurants right in prime tourist areas such as the Lower Town's Place Royale leave something to be desired, but not **La Traite du Roy** (tel. 692-0793), 25¼ rue Notre-Dame, right on the Place Royale. Under the tiny yellow awning and down the dark corridor is a charming throwback to rustic Old Québec, and were it not for the elegant table settings you'd think you were in some modest 17th-century Québecois inn. A glass caseful of *Holiday* magazine dining awards bears witness to the finesse of the cuisine here. The dinner menu includes all the classic French dishes: onion soup gratinée ($2) and escargots au Pernod (snails flavored with anise liqueur, $3.50) for appetizers, escalope de veau ($10.50) and cuisses de grenouille (frog legs, $11.50) as well as beef, fish, lobster, and fowl dishes. If you're going all out, you've got to finish up with flaming crêpes Suzette ($6.50 for two people); if not, the pêche Melba is more modestly priced at $1.75. If nothing on the menu catches your fancy (a near impossibility), the chef will be glad to prepare the dishes of your choice, to your order, if you give him 24-hour notice. With wine, a dinner for two at La Traite du Roy could easily cost upward of $75 if you include tax and tip. If you'd rather not go that high, come at lunchtime when you can have soup, such things as asparagus omelet or beef brochette, dessert, and coffee for $6 or less per person, tax and tip included. By the way, La Traite du Roy has its own bar with dancing in the stone-arched cellar, which bears the somewhat inappropriate name Le Cloître des Nonnes ("The Nuns' Cloister"), and which may have been crowded with *tuns* (barrels of wine) but never, I suspect, with nuns.

The perfect place for a cozy, romantic dinner of the finest French food is in Québec's Latin Quarter, at **L'Ancêtre** (tel. 692-2137), 17½ rue Couillard at the corner of rue St-Flavien. Small rooms filled with high-backed wooden chairs, tables with brown-and-white checked cloths, and gold napkins set the scene for a true culinary experience. It all begins when you begin your study of the intriguing but equally bewildering menu, which lists such delicacies as rabbit, oysters, lobsters, and the like in the loftiest of High Gallic culinary language. Don't feel bad if your high school French is not up to the task: even local native speakers are often mystified by the delicious-sounding names. A waiter is always ready to explain. As for price, you can limit yourself to one of the daily table d'hôte menus at $15 (five courses), $18.50 (six courses), or $28.50 (ten courses—a minimum of two persons must order it; the price is *per person,* however). Or you can choose to order à la carte. Either way, you won't forget your evening here. Be sure to have reservations.

THE MIDDLE RANGE (Complete Dinners $15 to $25): Many of Québec's medium-priced restaurants serve dinners fully as memorable as in more expensive places. If you choose carefully, and if you share the bottle, you should be able to dine within the quoted range and still have wine with dinner. Remember: the price range reflects evening-meal costs, not those of the much less expensive lunches.

Le Marie Clarisse (tel. 692-0857) opened in 1979 to rave reviews from Québec's most demanding culinary critics, and has already established a reputation as the city's prime seafood restaurant. It's located at 12 Petit Champlain, next to the lower station of the funicular, in the Lower Town, and like other establishments in and around Québec's historic Place Royale it has rough stone walls and ancient wood ceiling beams. But the "olde tyme" atmosphere is not overdone, and paintings or plants brighten up the stone here and there. Recorded classical music provides background sound.

Luncheon prices are low: a cold-meat plate ($3.25) or lapin à l'estragon (rabbit cooked with tarragon, $4.50), with soup, dessert, and coffee included. But the dinner seafood menu reveals the true Marie Clarisse. I recommend starting with the feuilleté de fruits de mer (a light, flaky pastry filled with scallops, shrimp, and lobster in a cream sauce, $2.75), or the equally delicious coquilles St-Jacques ($2.50). As a main course, the filet de doré amandine is delicious: two filets of Canada's renowned walleyed pike cooked in butter and covered with shaved almonds ($7.25). The quenelles de brochet, light and airy "dumplings" of fish with a hint of cheese ($8.50), are sheer ambrosia. For dessert there's always fresh fruit and whipped cream, or fruit tarts, or perhaps soufflé glacé aux framboises, a chilled soufflé of raspberries ($2). Portions are not huge, but rather just the right size because of the richness of the food. The wine list is short, well chosen, and moderately priced ($7.50 to $15 per bottle), indicating that the management serves wine to enhance the cuisine, not to make a killing. In every way, Le Marie Clarisse deserves the highest praise, although I expect prices will rise somewhat in the future. Be sure to have reservations for Friday or Saturday evenings—and they're not a bad idea on other nights, either.

Few visitors to Québec depart without having had at least one meal at the cafe-restaurant called **Au Chalet Suisse** (tel. 694-1320), 26 rue St-Anne just off the Place d'Armes and rue du Trésor. Outside, umbrella-shaded cafe tables provide the perfect vantage point for people-watching on the pedestrian street, St-Anne. Inside, a warren of tiny, low-ceilinged rooms is painted with murals of Swiss country scenes or wine cellars, or paneled in knotty pine. An espresso machine steams and hisses in a passageway, and hard-working waitresses scurry to provide for the numbers of local and foreign visitors. The menu is bewildering to say the least, with over 200 drink selections (apéritifs, wines and beers, cocktails, digestifs) alone, and a similarly daunting array of dinner choices: lobster, bratwursts, Caesar salads, raclette, and fried chicken all share the same page. Last time I was there the brochette sauce bordelaise (shish kebab with a rich gravy sauce, $7.25) was particularly good; it comes with french fries, salad, rolls, and butter. But fondues are the house specialty: Swiss (cheese, $6.60), bourguignonne (beef, $8.40), or Chinese (thin slices of meat dipped in a simmering fondue pot of broth and then flavored with various sauces, $8.75). The Chalet Suisse is open every day. Note that the sidewalk cafe, or "mezzanine," has its own separate, limited, light-lunch menu.

Le Vendôme (tel. 692-0557) has been at the same location, 36 Coté de la Montagne, for over 30 years, serving the flood of tourists and Québecois hiking up and down the hill between Québec's upper and lower towns. The decor consists of ancient movie and theater posters and murals of Paris street scenes, and looks as though it hasn't been touched since it was devised in the early '50s. The food is dependably good, the service quite friendly and attentive, and the prices reasonable, even in this prime touristic location; and these three characteristics keep Le Vendôme busy most of every day. At dinner, expect to find classic French dishes: hors d'oeuvres ($2.50 to $3.75), soups ($1, up to lobster bisque at $2.75), and such main courses as canard à l'orange (duck in orange sauce, $11.50), steak au poivre for the same price, a seafood brochette for $8.75, and carré d'agneau (rack of lamb, $21 for two people). Some North American favorites such as filet of sole and lamb chops with mint sauce slip into the menu at lower prices ($6 to $7). Cocktails and wines are good if a bit expensive: wine prices start at $7 a bottle. Luncheon prices are well below dinner prices, of course. Le Vendôme is open seven days a week from 11 a.m. to 12 midnight.

You can go to the **Café d'Europe** (tel. 692-3835), 27 Ste-Angele just off St-Jean, for pizza or pasta, even though the menu lists more expensive items like filet mignon. The pizzas are fresh and delicious, priced at $4 to $5.25, pasta dishes run the gamut of spaghettis ($6) up to canellonni ($7), and for just a bit more you can treat yourself to authentic veal scaloppine alla Marsala ($9). The Cafe is neither a cafe nor a pizza-parlor, but a moderately priced restaurant with somber lighting, padded booths, and rows of paintings decorating the walls reminiscent of the better class of trattorias. Wine and beer are served, and the restaurant is open every day but Monday; on Sundays, opening is at 5 p.m.

Along rue St-Louis

Although all Québec restaurants look to tourism for at least part of their business, the ones along rue St-Louis seem particularly tourist oriented. But before you flip the page to look for "nontouristy" places, you should note that several restaurants on St-Louis draw tremendous crowds because they offer just what visitors want: good food, or low prices, or entertainment, or atmosphere, or a combination of all these. While clip joints do exist, you can avoid them by following the recommendations below, and by observing the cardinal rule of good dining: never sit down in a restaurant that is virtually empty at prime mealtime hours.

The Jacquet House (1675) at the corner of St-Louis and des Jardins was once the home of Québec author Philippe-Aubert de Gaspé, who wrote *Anciens Canadiens*. A restaurant now occupies the rough old stone house, but de Gaspé would no doubt still feel right at home, because **Aux Anciens Canadiens** (tel. 692-1627), 34 rue St-Louis, is an extremely warm and welcoming place. Low ceilings, antique sideboards, Québec carved-wood bas reliefs, and antique glass collections decorate the two dining rooms, striking a balance between rusticity and elegance. The waitresses in traditional dress couldn't be friendlier. As for food and prices, Aux Anciens Canadiens has hit on a formula guaranteed to please. Between 11 a.m. and 4 p.m. every day a set-price three-course "brunch" is served for $5 (plus tax and tip), starting with juice, grapefruit, or soupe d'ivrogne ("hangover soup" of onions and garlic!), progressing to a large plate of assorted meats, pâté, and meat pie, or buckwheat crêpes with maple syrup, or pork and beans with sausages and potatoes, or any of several other choices. Dessert is fruit, yogurt, or cake. Coffee, tea, or milk is included (refills free), and drinks are available at an extra charge. At dinnertime (5 to 11 p.m.) the plan is similar, with a delicious four-course table d'hôte meal priced at $13.50 per person, plus tax and service. I can't recommend the restaurant highly enough—you're sure to love it.

Breton-style crêpes, those pizza-size pancakes spread with any of various fillings and folded into a square, are the specialty at **Les Crêpes des Vieux Murs** (tel. 692-3847), 49½ rue St-Louis. They cost between $1.50 (plain) and $5 (shrimp, eggs, and béchamel sauce all in one), with 20 different varieties of main-course crêpes, and almost a dozen types of dessert crêpes: flaming crêpes Suzette, or apple crêpes flamed in Calvados, the French apple brandy ($4.25 to $5.50). Salads, sandwiches, breakfast plates, and the like provide for other appetites. Open all day, every day.

Despite its Italian-sounding name, the **Restaurant au Parmesan** (tel. 692-0341), 38 rue St-Louis near Haldimand, serves an international selection of dishes, although the service takes place in the midst of more wine bottles of more shapes and sizes than you've ever seen in one place before. In the sidewalk windows, in wine racks, on shelves along the walls, on the tables as wax-bedripped candle holders, the bottles are everywhere throughout the two long, narrow dining rooms and small bar. As for the food, Genoa salami ($3) or a fondue parmesan ($2.50) provides the proper Italian start, but then for a main course lots of guests here have the surf and turf (steak and lobster tail, $13.50) or the saumon grillé (grilled salmon, $9.25) rather than the veal parmigiana. Dessert can turn another international corner, ending up at Black Forest cake ($2.50). All main courses (and you must order at least the main course) come garnished, large portions are the rule, and wine, beer, and cocktails are served.

THE ECONOMY RANGE (Meals for $2 to $10): No one dines in fancy restaurants all the time. For those times when a quick sandwich and salad or a light meal is just right, here are Québec City's inexpensive eateries. They offer the advantages of informality, fast service, low prices, and (usually) continuous hours of operation so you needn't wait for specific lunch or dinner sittings.

Hidden on the relatively little-traveled rue Ste-Ursule is an excellent new restaurant as yet undiscovered by anyone other than les Québecois. It's named **Le Saint-Amour** (tel. 694-0667), 48a rue Ste-Ursule, and it is simply delightful. The restaurant opens at noon every day, and serves the same very reasonably priced dishes until after midnight. As you enter, you'll pass a small and very woody cafe-bar on the right. Then you proceed to a small, sunny dining room, or a larger one with a vaulted wooden ceiling, whitewashed walls, and Renoir reproductions, or out into the high-walled terrace at the back, shaded by four enormous trees. Classical music fills the air, and delectable dishes fill you: on my last visit I had the soup of the day, lapin à la moutarde (rabbit in a light but slightly peppery mustard sauce), an unusually delicious chocolate pudding with whipped cream, a beer, and coffee, and the bill (tax and tip included) was $9. All the dishes served here are accompanied by soup and dessert, and so if you order quiche au jambon (ham quiche, $3.50), or coquille de fruits de mer (a shell filled with seafood, with cheese on top, $6.25), you're actually getting a three-course meal. Soups, seafood cocktails, salads, cheese plates, and pastries are always offered; wine and beer are very reasonably priced. Highly recommended.

For moderate prices, good food, simple and attractive surroundings, and friendly service, high marks go to **Chez Faniole** (tel. 694-0425), 73 rue St-Louis at the corner of rue Ste-Ursule. Come early to get one of the little window-side tables, and then order from the short but varied menu which includes honey fried chicken ($4), filet de sole ($4.25), or two grilled pork chops with apple sauce and fried potatoes ($3.50). Salads and sandwiches are even lower in price. Combine a main dish with the soup of the day (75¢) and a piece of tarte au sucre et aux pommes (maple sugar and apple pie, 85¢) for a hearty, three-course meal costing around $6. You can dine here any day of the week between 11 a.m. and midnight.

Starting at the fringe of Québec's Latin (student) Quarter and extending all the way to the walls at Porte St-Jean, the broad thoroughfare of rue St-Jean is the city's culinary fairground. Doughnut shops, pastry shops, restaurants serving hamburgers, spaghetti, soups, and salads at student prices line both sides of the street, crowding the few more expensive places. The cheapest thing to have is a sandwich, and the cheapest place to get it is at the **Fromagerie-Patisserie Pierre & Denis**, 1023 rue St-Jean. An egg sandwich costs a mere 80¢, a nearly foot-long sub only $1.50. The prices are low because the store has no sit-down facilities. Paradoxically, the fromagerie-patisserie name ("Cheese and Pastry Shop") is misleading, as Pierre and Denis's place stocks not only a vast assortment of delectable French pastries and imported cheeses, but also cold cuts, jams and croissants, french bread, condiments, even apples and oranges—everything you need for a first-class, high-quality picnic.

Rue St-Jean's most versatile eatery has got to be **Le Figaro**, 1011 rue St-Jean right near the Porte St-Jean. A lunch-and-supper restaurant, nightclub, and café-terrasse are all rolled into one, and the menu, although short, covers all bases: cheeseburgers ($2.15) take their place next to spaghetti ($2.85), sandwiches, stews, and salads, while on Wednesdays you can have couscous ($4.35) and on Fridays roast beef ($4.60). But lots of people come just to have a beer ($1) or to share a bottle of the house wine ($5.50). The cafe's outdoor tables are on rue d'Auteuil, by the way, not on St-Jean.

Au Petit Coin Breton, 1029 rue St-Jean, is another restaurant specializing in the Breton crêpes which make a perfect breakfast, light lunch, snack, or dessert. Stone, brick, and wood in the decor set the mood, and when the waitress approaches your table dressed in her traditional costume of lace cap, long dress, and apron, you really begin to think in Breton terms. Don't be surprised at the "menu"—it's shaped like the huge crêpes it advertises. You get to choose any one (or several) of the 87 varieties of crêpes offered. One with ham, for instance, costs $1.60; with mushrooms and béchamel sauce, $3; with apricots and ice cream, $2.30. Drinks are served here, and run about $1.75 for an apéritif; same price for imported beers. Wine is $7 the bottle and up. If the place looks crowded, note that there are two levels, and thus there may be tables free. Au Petit Coin Breton opens at 10 a.m., early enough for a late breakfast, and stays open until 2 a.m. in summer, which is late enough for an early breakfast.

The **Café de la Cour,** 1117½ rue St-Jean, will do nicely for a pick-me-up during a hectic or tiring day's sightseeing. An outdoor terrace and some indoor booths provide a choice of surroundings, and the menu provides sandwiches for $2.25 to $3, or espresso and croissants ($1.75), or a late-afternoon or evening drink ($2 to $3). It's open from noon to 3 a.m., and draws an interesting crowd almost all the time. Come especially to meet other travelers or locals while you rest your weary feet.

Stop dreaming of a submarine sandwich (hoagie, hero, grinder, etc.) and go to the corner of rue Ste-Angèle and St-Jean, where you can buy the sandwich of your dreams. Look for the sign that says **Sous-Marin** (submarine, of course), and then prepare yourself for some novelties: besides the regulation roast beef sub ($2.80), you can have one stuffed with shrimp ($3.25) or other good things, depending on the season. A side order of potato salad (45¢) and a dish of ice cream (50¢) make a filling and delicious meal for a mere $3.75 or so. The place has a half dozen outdoor tables, and stays open from 10 a.m. to 11 p.m.

Québec's gilded student set hangs out at **Croque-Mitaine,** 33 rue d'Auteuil very near the Porte Kent (gate) in the city walls. In good weather the outdoor terrace filled with tiny tables is well attended as the young and good-looking come to see and be seen, to read newspapers, and to pass an hour in conversation and wine or beer sipping. The short, sweet menu lists various cold-meat plates for $2.25 and luncheon salads for $3.25 to $3.75, but the best bargain is the daily lunch special of, say, onion soup, truite meunière (trout sauteed in butter), and fresh strawberries and cream, all for something like $3.25. But the special is served only between 11:30 a.m. and 2:30 p.m., so get there on time. You get no choice of dishes if you order the special lunch, but with such food at such a price, who needs it?

Easily accessible for a quick, inexpensive meal any time of day is the **Brasserie Le Gaulois** (tel. 694-1582), at the corner of Buade and des Jardins, almost facing City Hall. Heavy wood-and-leather chairs and wagonwheel chandeliers give Le Gaulois a rather Wild West flavor, although the clients sitting at small tables by the windows sipping beer look more like students than cowpersons. Café au lait and a filling omelette nature (plain omelet) will cost about $3, a chef's salad is $1.50, and the massive club sandwich is $3.25. The glasses of draft beer in evidence, so crucial to the well-being of a brasserie, cost 80¢ apiece. If the downstairs room is too crowded, head upstairs. In any case, come back in the evening for the live entertainment offered at no extra charge almost every night.

For Petit Déjeuner

A real French cafe, with wood floor, rough wood beams, checkered table-cloths, and walls plastered in posters both political and artistic, inhabited by bearded and bespectacled early-morning newspaper readers and students in earnest conversation—it must exist in Québec, and it does, at the **Café Chez Temporel**, 25 rue Couillard, a half block off rue St-Jean / Coté de la Fabrique in the city's Latin Quarter. To relive fond moments spent in Paris, or to have the quintessential French breakfast of croissants (75¢ for one, $1.25 for two), jam, butter, and strong French coffee (80¢) or café au lait, no place is better than Chez Temporel. You can drop by later for a sandwich or salad, but breakfast is best just because it's so typically French.

3. What to See in Québec

This city is its own greatest tourist attraction, and simply strolling through the winding, picturesque streets could delight one for days. Unlike Montréal, a huge city in which it pays to have specific sightseeing goals such as Notre-Dame Church or Place des Arts, in Québec a list of things to see is merely the excuse for a stroll. If you have only a single day here (perish the thought!), don't feel guilty about setting out without a plan. Go and experience Québec.

For the fortunate visitor with several days or even a week to spend, the itineraries below will fill in the background of this fascinating, historical place. Seeing Québec on foot, the impressions you gain are much more vivid than in a car, and so the following guide to the sights is set up as a walking tour. Distances are not great, and the old city is so compact that you can break off your walk at any time and return to your hotel in just a few minutes' time.

Should rain, fallen arches, or general disinclination keep you from exploring Québec on foot, don't despair. Good guided tours make a suitable substitute.

GUIDED TOURS: If you don't take a tour by calèche (described above in the beginning of this chapter), the thing to do is contact **Maple Leaf Sightseeing Tours,** 16 rue Laporte (tel. 418/692-3654; for reservations, call 653-4460). They'll pick you up at your hotel in a mini-bus—large buses can't squeeze through the narrow streets—and take you on a comprehensive tour of Québec, old and new, Upper and Lower Towns, for $10 per adult, $5 per child. Other tours trundle out of town to the surrounding districts of Île d'Orléans, Ste-Anne-de-Beaupré, and the Laurentians north of the city. You can even sign up for an evening tour to Montmorency Falls, a restaurant, and a nightclub, all for one price.

In the Lower Town, the **tourist information center** in Picard House, right in the Place Royale, offers free tours in English and French. They're given by enthusiastic student guides from 9 a.m. to noon and 1 to 4 p.m. daily in summer. The only catch is that each of the half-dozen volunteer guides on hand can handle only about two dozen tourist at once, and in peak season demand may exceed supply. You can reserve in advance, though, by calling 643-6631.

Self-Guided Tours

You can rent a tape cassette machine, plug your ears in, and walk at your leisure through the city while the machine tells you all about what you're seeing. The cost is $8, and the place to rent your machine is at **Le Kiosque** (tel. 694-0665), next to the Place d'Armes and the Château Frontenac. They also have a tape on the sights of Ste-Anne-de-Beaupré and the Île d'Orléans for the same price; or, you can rent both tapes at one time for $14. Ask for the Sonore Tour.

River Cruises

Nothing will bring back the wilderness days when Cartier sailed up the St. Lawrence and stood on the deck gazing in wonder at the "Gibraltar of the New World." In Cartier's day the pristine ruggedness of Cape Diamond was marked only by the small Indian settlement of Stadacona. But you should be able to visualize what the city looked like when General Wolfe and his army approached by water in June of 1759. All you need is a boat. The M/V *Louis Jolliet,* 900 tons, will take you on a motor-cruise up the St. Lawrence past Ste-Foy, or down the St. Lawrence around the tip of the Île d'Orléans. The latter of these two cruises is called "Les Découvreurs," ("The Discoverers"), and lasts for 2½ hours in the afternoon: $5 per adult, $2.50 per child under 12. The former cruise, "Les Trains de Bois" (Timber Rafts), is a three-hour evening trip up the river past the Citadelle, the Plains of Abraham, and as far as Cap Rouge which used to be a marshalling point for the rafts of logs floated downriver—sometimes from hundreds of miles away. Dancing spices up the evening. Cost: $6 per adult, $3 per child under 12.

Cruising season is from mid-May to mid-September, with extra cruises laid on before and after that time depending on demand. For information and tickets, call 418/692-1159, or drop in at **Le Kiosque** next to the Place d'Armes and Château Frontenac. Then, board the boat at Quai Chouinard, 10 Dalhousie St., near Place Royale in the Lower Town.

QUÉBEC'S FABULOUS WINTER CARNIVAL: In the grim depths of winter when Florida, California, and various Caribbean islands are on the minds of most Canadians, Québecois are madly planning to stay put. The reason? The marvelous cold-weather blowout known as Winter Carnival (Carnaval d'Hiver), when the entire city blazes with lights, shines with snow, and glitters with icicles. Lasting two weekends and the intervening week, usually near the end of February, the revelry is centered on fabulous ice and snow sculptures carved in the Place du Carnaval (otherwise the Parc de l'Esplanade). Concerts, dances, parades, and general brouhaha carry right through the week, leaving good memories and uncountable hangovers throughout the region for several hundred miles around. Shops sell plastic trumpets and canes filled with a spirit of questionable palatability but proven warmup properties: it's called "Cariboo," and although the formula varies, the principal ingredients are cheap whiskey and sweet red wine—hence, those hangovers.

Québec is courtly, dignified, and serene through most of the year, but all that is cast aside when the statue of the snowman with the red *tuque* (cap) and multicolored sash is erected. This genial fellow, named Bonhomme Carnaval, presides over the revelry. Have reservations for transportation and accommodation well in advance of Carnival time or you'll never find a place—the city is always packed full up.

STROLLING THROUGH OLD QUÉBEC: The colonial city was first built right down by the St. Lawrence, for it was here that merchants, traders, and boatmen earned their livelihoods. But in the 1700s, enemy cannonades leveled the town so many times that the inhabitants grew tired of rebuilding, and so this Lower Town became merely a wharf and warehouse area as residents moved to safer houses atop Cape Diamond. The Upper Town, Québecois later discovered, was not immune from cannonade either, as General Wolfe was to prove. Nevertheless, the division into Upper and Lower Towns persisted for obvious topographical reasons.

The place to start your walk is the **Jardin des Gouverneurs** (Governors' Garden) right next to the Château Frontenac. The park takes its name from the site of the mansion built to house the French governors of Québec. Nothing remains of the mansion, and whatever ruins there may have been were buried under the great bulk of the Château Frontenac. The obelisk monument at the center of the park is dedicated to *both* generals in the momentous battle of September 13, 1759, when Wolfe (British) and Montcalm (French) fought it out for what would be the ultimate destiny of Québec. The British were victorious. Wolfe, wounded in the fighting, lived only long enough to hear of his victory. Montcalm died after Wolfe, knowing the city was lost. In summer, the Jardin des Gouverneurs is the scene of various shows and musical programs sponsored by the municipal government just for fun. By the way, the handsome building near the southeast corner of the Jardin is the American consulate.

It's impossible to resist the urge to run down and have a look at the river. **Dufferin Terrace,** the boardwalk-lookout, leads to the **Promenade des Gouverneurs** (down to your right as you face the river). Sometime during your visit, follow the promenade which skirts the sheer cliff wall and takes you all the way past Québec's Citadelle, a ten-minute walk away.

Walk up **rue Mont-Carmel,** which runs between the Jardin des Gouverneurs and the Château Frontenac, and turn right onto Haldimand. At the next corner, with rue St-Louis, is the blue-and-white mansion called **Kent House** (1648), one of the oldest buildings in Québec. Although it is most famous for being the place in which France signed the capitulation to the British forces, its name comes from the Duke of Kent. The duke, Queen Victoria's father, lived here for a few years at the end of the 18th century. A few doors down from Kent House, at 17 rue St-Louis, is the **Maillou** (or Mailloux) **House,** the foundations of which date from 1736. The house was much improved and enlarged in 1799, and later restored in 1959. Now it houses the Québec Board of Trade and Industry.

Head northwest down rue St-Louis and a few steps will bring you to the **Place d'Armes,** once the military parade ground right outside the governors' mansion. By this time you've seen almost every angle of the bewitching Château Frontenac, which was built as a hotel in 1892–93 by the Canadian Pacific Railway Company—they still own it today. The architect, Bruce Price of New York, raised his creation on the site of the governors' mansion and named it after Louis de Buade, Comte de Frontenac. Monsieur le Comte was the one who, in 1690, was faced with the threat of an English fleet under Sir William Phipps. Phipps sent a messenger to demand Frontenac's surrender, but Frontenac replied, "Tell your lord that I will reply with the mouths of my cannons." Which he did. Phipps sailed away.

While you're here next to the château, take a glance along Dufferin Terrace at the monument to Champlain, who founded Québec City in 1608, and another glance at the Monument to the Faith in Place d'Armes. The latter recalls the arrival of Recollets monks from France in 1615. The Recollets claimed a large plot of land hereabouts for their church and monastery; today the land is occupied by the Courthouse and the Anglican **Cathedral of the Holy Trinity.** You can visit the church, which dates from 1804, any day between noon and 5 p.m. Enter on the rue des Jardins. The cathedral's interior is simple but spacious and handsome, with pews of solid English oak and a latticed ceiling in white with a gilded chain motif. You may get to enjoy an organ recital, or at least the rehearsals for one, when you visit the church.

Facing the Place d'Armes you'll notice the **Musée du Fort,** where a sound-and-light diorama outlines the six sieges of Québec ($1.50 for adults, 75¢ for kids); and the **Musée Historique,** which is actually a wax museum in which the subjects of displays range far beyond Québec. Not far from a scene wherein Columbus discovers America you'll find Iroquois torturing Jesuits, and then Paderewski meeting Toscanini. Entry fees are $1.50 for adults, $1 for children and over-65s, 75¢ for students. By the way, the wax museum building is actually the old Vallee House, built in 1692.

When a Quebecois speaks of **rue du Trésor,** he's referring to the narrow street between Ste-Anne and Buade where artists good and bad hang up their paintings beautiful and not-so-beautiful. Rue du Trésor is always lively with buyers and sellers, and prices are kept within the means of the average visitor. So are the works of art: you won't find any masterpieces here, and in fact the artists who sell here are probably saving up the money so they can have time to work on avant-garde projects which might not appeal to the public taste. Several artists here do paintings sure to appeal—portraits or caricatures. They can chalk you onto a large piece of paper in no time at all.

At the northern (downhill) end of rue du Trésor is rue Buade. Turn left and you'll see the Renaissance-Victorian turrets of Québec's **City Hall** looming not far away. City Hall was built in 1883. In the small park next to it is a statue to the idealistic Parisian druggist Louis Hébert, who became Québec's first farmer. He's shown offering his first harvested sheaf of wheat to God in thanksgiving, but even in his boldest dreams he must never have imagined that one day Canada would export in a single year more wheat than Old Europe could grow in a decade. **City Hall Park** was designed for easy conversion into an outdoor show area, and in summer—especially during the Festival d'Été (Summer Festival)—concerts, dance shows, and other programs are staged here.

Go south on rue des Jardins to reach an entrance to the **Ursulines Convent,** built originally in 1639 as a girls' school. Look for the small metal door bearing the notice "Entrée Libre"—it's just beyond the large sign which tells you the museum is closed indefinitely for restoration. Through the door is the seven-acre Ursuline estate. On the right as you enter is one of the oldest buildings in the complex, which served as the home of the illustrious Monseignor Laval from 1659 to 1661. What you see of the convent today is actually a succession of different buildings added and repaired at various times (fires were frequent) up to 1836. To visit the **Ursuline Chapel,** you'll have to use the entrance at 12 rue Donnacona. The chapel, which shelters the remains of Montcalm, has been restored to its Louis XIV brilliance.

At the corner of des Jardins and St-Louis is the **Jacquet House,** dating from 1675, a charming traditional old Québec dwelling which now houses the restaurant Aux Anciens Canadiens (described in the restaurant section, above).

THE LATIN QUARTER: In 1663, the powerful Msgr. François-Xavier de Laval-Montmorency saw to the founding of a seminary in Québec. Laval, a major force in the building of early Québec, was to be remembered when the seminary he founded grew to become a full university. It was named for him, and for many years Laval University (1852) occupied the much-expanded seminary campus. By the middle of our century, however, Laval University had outgrown its 17th-century campus, and a new, modern university city was constructed west of the city in Ste-Foy. In 1972 the administrative and faculty offices and most other functions were moved to the new campus, although a few classes are still held in the ancient seminary buildings. And even though the main campus is now miles away, many students and artists cling tenaciously to their tiny houses and apartments in the streets near the seminary. The entire area is still known as the Latin Quarter.

Start your tour on artist-jammed **rue du Trésor.** At its northern end is the **Basilica of Notre-Dame** (1647), which has seen a tumultuous history of bombardment, reconstruction, and restoration. Its interior is ornate, the air rich with the scent of burning candles. Many valuable old paintings and ecclesiastical treasures still remain from the time of the French regime. The basilica is actually connected to the complex of old buildings which makes up Québec Seminary. To enter the complex, though, you must go to 7 University St.

The inner quadrangle of **Quebec Seminary** is fantastically impressive: a quiet, grassy place surrounded by beautifully cared-for stone and wood buildings. If you get the chance, peek into some of the buildings to see the lavish use of stone, tile, brass, and great gilt-framed oil paintings, all symbols of the church's power and influence at that time. A delightful and completely unexpected surprise in this awesome setting is a **Museum of Playthings of Yesteryear,** housing a collection of dolls and other toys made between 1840 and 1940. The little museum is open daily from noon to 5 p.m., on Sunday from noon to 9 p.m.; adults $1.50, children (under 10) free.

Off to the right of the main quadrangle, up a small driveway, is another quadrangle with a different grace, this one surrounded by stark white buildings on three sides. A sundial on one of the buildings dates back to 1773. It came in handy for the American officers who, having failed in their attempt to capture Québec in 1775–76, were held prisoner in the seminary here. Near the heavy doors between the street and this quadrangle is an entrance to the chapel dedicated to Monseignor Laval. It's small but quite lovely, and the tomb of the highly respected churchman is off to the left. Finished in 1948, the tomb displays the height of Québec craftsmanship: cut stone, yellow marble, gilt mosaic ceiling, and bronze croziers surround the recumbent marble sculpture of Laval.

You may want to take a glance in the old **University Museum,** at 6 University St. (open 10 a.m. to 5 p.m. weekdays, 50¢ entry), simply because its collection is so eclectic. Made up when university scholars needed a place to store curiosities of whatever nature from near and far, today it houses old coins, paintings, religious relics and articles, and—of all things—an authentic Egyptian mummy.

Stroll through the student quarter, bounded by rues Couillard, Garneau, and Ste-Famille, and you could swear you were in Paris. To bring your thoughts back to Québec, head for the Lower Town by way of the **rue des Remparts.** Not only the ramparts, but the tremendous guns which defended them are still mostly in place. At Port Dauphin and and Côte de la Montagne is **Montmorency Park,** a welcome patch of green. Although it's a park today, in past centuries it was the property of the early French intendant (governor) Jean Talon, later built on by Quebec's second bishop (after Laval), Monseignor de Saint-Vallier; Québec's first legislature met in a building on this site, and then Canada's Fathers of Confederation held talks here. No sign of any of these structures remains.

Before you trundle down the steep slopes of Côte de la Montagne, take a few minutes to enjoy the view. The mammoth grain elevators—those rows of upright cylinders down in the harbor—have a capacity of eight million bushels. Beyond the harbor and the river, the Laurentian Mountains rise in the distance.

LOWER TOWN: After battles had destroyed or heavily damaged the Lower Town several times, the governors and important folk moved to the top of **Cape Diamond** and fortified it well. Thus began the Lower Town's decline, for it soon became a rough waterfront district peopled by sailors and merchants. The 19th- and 20th-century commercial boom had no time for preservation of crumbling colonial buildings, and new structures often were built on ancient ruins.

Recently the Lower Town has seen a renaissance of rebuilding and refurnishing, and dozens of old houses, taverns, and places of business dating from colonial times have been beautifully restored. You'll notice it right away, whether you descend by means of the **funicular** or walk down the **Côte de la Montagne** and turn right onto **Breakneck Stairs.** Both methods of descent take you to the same place: **Louis Jolliet House** (1683). The lower funicular terminus is actually inside the house of the great Québecois-French explorer who, with Father Jacques Marquette, was the first man of European parentage to explore the upper reaches of the Mississippi.

Jolliet House is at the junction of rue Petit-Champlain and rue Sou-le-Fort, a place busy with restaurant-goers, cafe sitters, strolling couples, and groups of children out to learn their Québec history firsthand. It's reminiscent of New York's SoHo: a once-rundown district where the young, energetic, and artistically minded have moved in to fix up, live, and enjoy. Wander down Petit-Champlain, but then return to go down Sous-le-Fort. Turn left onto Notre-Dame.

Just half a block up the grade is the heart of the Lower Town, the **Place Royale.** In the early days, Place Royale was alive with activity all day and much of the night, because this was the town marketplace, not to mention the center of business and industry. The superb restoration work has returned it to very near its oldtime appearance. Folk dances and impromptu concerts are often held near the bust of Louis XIV (he's the "Roy"—king—in Place Royale). As restoration work is still going on, you'll be able to see and appreciate the amount of work, time, and money involved. For a more detailed look, though, head for 27 rue St-Pierre, the **Fornel House.** An information and interpretation center has been set up here, with before-and-after photographs and display cases filled with artifacts recovered during the rebuilding work. You won't believe the photos of **Picard** and **Dumont Houses,** which stand in the Place, and you may find yourself carrying a visual image back to the square—and finding that several entire levels had to be removed from the two houses to restore them to 17th-century appearance.

The **Church of Notre-Dame-des-Victoires** is the oldest stone church in Québec, built in 1688 on the site of Champlain's original stockade, the "Habitation." The wonderful paintings, the castle-like altar, and the large model boat suspended from the ceiling were votive offerings brought by early settlers to ensure a safe voyage. The little church faces directly on the square, and is open during daylight hours for your inspection.

The interiors of restored houses near the Place are as revealing as the exteriors. Search out **Amiot House,** on the Marché Champlain, open free and currently sheltering shows by local artists in a gallery called **L'Anse aux Barques** (hours: 9 a.m. to 5 p.m. daily, until 11 p.m. Wednesdays). At the corner of Marché Champlain and rue Notre-Dame is the striking **Hôtel Chevalier,** originally built as three houses in 1699, and later joined into one huge house by Jean Baptiste Chevalier (1752). Now it's the **Musée de l'Habitation.** Inside, among the wood beams, wide board floors, and stone fireplaces are 17th- and 18th-century furnishings: on a handcrafted wooden table, an eight-place setting in pewter. Don't miss the bedroom set with four-poster and a delightful "double chair" for ma and pa. In another room, displays show what was necessary to turn flax into cloth: cleaning, carding, spinning, and weaving.

At the river end of rue Sous-le-Fort is the **Royal Battery,** from which a dozen mighty cannons once defended the Lower Town. The battery was put up in 1691, and the cannons moved in during the year 1712. They got the chance to speak their minds in 1759, but the English victory silenced them, and the general move to the Upper Town left the cannons to rust. Sunken foundations were all that remained of the Royal Battery by the turn of the century, and when restoration work began the Royal Corps of Engineers of New France was called upon to rebuild the battery from the bottom up. Next to the battery, that largish parking lot used to be the Finlay Marketplace, site of hectic buying and selling on colonial market-day.

The Ferry to Levis

At the Royal Battery, you're only a few steps from the car and passenger ferry across the St. Lawrence to Levis. Boats leave every half hour between 6 a.m. and midnight on the 15-minute voyage, and the cost is only 75¢ per adult, $1.50 per car one way. Children under 12 sail for free.

The Antique-Shop District

Along with the general rejuvenation of the Lower Town came a very appropriate development. Dealers in antiques began to move into the shops on St. Paul St. (follow rue St-Pierre from the Place Royale, then go west on St. Paul). Today there are close to a dozen shops, chock full of old brass beds, colonial furnishings and knickknacks, Québec furniture, candlesticks, old clocks, even Victoriana and art deco kitsch. Besides antique objects, this area is filled with the troubled ghosts of gallant but defeated soldiers, for it was along here that Benedict Arnold and his misguided band of American troops marched to their defeat at the hands of Québec's defenders. Arnold—who is not exactly remembered with kindness by Americans anyway—met defeat behind a barricade at the corner of rues St-Pierre and St-Jacques. Earlier he had received a wound nearby.

You can return to the Upper Town by finding the street called **Côte de la Canoterie,** parallel to St. Paul but right against the cliff. It climbs the slope to join the rue des Remparts near Québec Seminary.

The Citadelle

Going toward the modern city on rue St-Louis, turn left just after you cross the rue d'Auteuil and before you come to the Porte St-Louis. This somewhat forbidding road leads to an even more forbidding place, the Citadelle. It stands 360 feet above the banks of the St. Lawrence on a grassy, spacious plateau with the regulation commanding position. The great star-shaped fortress was the equivalent of an atomic missile in its day: expensive to build, and built more as a deterrent than in preparation for any expected war. Bastions had been built here by the French as part of Québec's defenses, but it was the British who gave the huge fortress its present shape, beginning in 1820. Construction went on for 30 years. But just over 30 years after its completion the Citadelle was obsolete. The British garrison marched out in 1871, and Canadian units took their place.

Since 1920, its been the impressive home base of the Royal 22nd Regiment, a battle-tested unit that fought in both World Wars and the Korean War. You can visit the regimental museum, and watch the Changing of the Guard or the ceremony called Beating the Retreat for free. The guard changes daily at 10 a.m. in the summer months; Retreat is at 5 p.m. on Tuesday, Thursday, Saturday, and Sunday in the months of July and August. Guided tours of the Citadelle (for a fee) are given daily except in November when tours leave on weekdays only, and in December through March, when there are no tours. Exception: During Winter Carnival the tours are resumed.

OUTSIDE THE WALLS: Rue St-Louis leaves the old walled city by the Porte St-Louis (built in 1873 on the site of a gate dating from 1692, Frontenac's time), and broadens to become the Grande-Allée. On the right is the **Parc de l'Esplanade,** site of Québec's famous Winter Carnival, held right under the somber gaze of the Québec National Assembly.

Québec's provincial legislature, named **L'Assemblée Nationale du Québec** since 1968, occupies the imposing neo-Renaissance castle which is the center of the Cité Parlementaire—Québec's government complex. The Assembly building was constructed in 1886. Along the facade are 22 bronze statues of the most illustrious figures in Québec's colorful—not to mention tumultuous— history; the fountain in front of the door is the work of Philippe Hébert (1890), and was dedicated to Québec's original Indian inhabitants.

You can tour the gilded and sumptuous rooms of the Assembly building with a guide for no charge. Times change depending on the availability of guides, but in general the tours run in English on the hour, in French on the half hour, from 9 a.m. to 9 p.m. on weekdays, 9 to 5 on weekends and holidays. Highlights are the magnificent Blue Room, where the Assembly sits, and the Red Room, once the seat of the now-disbanded upper house called the Legislative Council. Throughout the building, symbols of the fleur-de-lis, the initials "VR" (for Victoria Regina), and the maple leaf remind visitors of Québec's trinational heritage.

BATTLEFIELD PARK (PARC DES CHAMPS DE BATAILLE) AND QUÉBEC MUSEUM: Covering 235 acres of grassy knolls, sunken gardens, monuments, fountains, and trees, Québec's Battlefield Park is a fantastic swath of green almost at the heart of the city. It stretches over the Plains of Abraham, where Wolfe and Montcalm fought to the death, and is a favorite place for joggers, strollers, kids, and picnickers. Take in the view from the top of the escarpment overlooking the St. Lawrence, and don't miss the fine gardens and statue of Jeanne d'Arc (Joan of Arc) just off Ave. Laurier between Loew's Le Concorde Hotel and the Ministry of Justice.

The **Québec Museum** is in the southern reaches of the park at the intersection of George VI and Wolfe Sts.—you'll see the monument to Wolfe there. On the first floor, visiting exhibits on various subjects fill the rooms, while the second floor holds the museum's own collection of Québec memorabilia, paintings, and sculpture. The museum is free, and is open from 9 a.m. to 5 p.m. daily; Thursday evening, it stays open until 11 p.m.

THE GRAND THÉÂTRE: Have your wits about you when you pay a visit to Quebec's Grand Théâtre, bounded by the streets named St-Cyrille, Turnbull, St-Amable, and Claire-Fontaine. It's not merely a theater, but a bold, massive, tumultuous creation by the Polish-born, English-trained architect Victor Prus. An immense three-part mural in concrete by Spaniard Jordi Bonet (who now lives in Québec) dominates the three foyers of the theater. Bonet's aggressive work won't please everyone, and as Guy Robets has described it, the mural is "a colossal work which involves an exhausting game of hide-and-seek, and its analysis . . . can only exacerbate the frenzy of the whole." It won't even cost you the price of a theater ticket to wrestle with the creations of Prus and Bonet, because free tours are given daily except Monday at 2:30 in English, 10:30 a.m. and 4 p.m. in French. Watch it, though: once you begin, you'll have to deal with *Death, Space,* and *Liberty*—the three parts of the tremendous mural—for a full hour.

4. Québec City's Nightlife

For all its sedate colonial charm, Québec can get very lively at night—if you know where to look. For general sitting and gazing, **Dufferin Terrace** is the place to go. To stroll, see, and be seen, **rue St-Jean** is the best place. In summer, the upper portion of the street near **Porte St-Jean** is closed to cars and made into a pedestrian promenade. Dancing and cruising at the same time is a distinct possibility for those who join the M/V *Louis Jolliet* on its evening cruise (see above under "River Cruises"). But if you're content to stay a confirmed landlubber, here are some specific recommendations.

First, drop in at the tourism information offices in Place d'Armes or on rue d'Auteuil for a list of special summertime or wintertime events. Early in July, Québec City holds its annual **Festival d'Été** (Summer Festival). Free concerts and shows are staged all over town in the evenings, and you should be up on what's happening each night. If neither the Summer or Winter Carnivals is on while you here, check out these places:

SIDEWALK CAFES AND BARS: On rue Ste-Anne near the Place d'Armes are two very congenial sidewalk cafes where it's easy to meet new people or just to relax with a coffee or a drink. **Au Chalet Suisse** is a restaurant as well as a cafe, while its neighbor on rue Ste-Anne, named **Mokador,** has some edibles but specializes in things to drink.

Prices are on the high side on rue Ste-Anne, but a lot lower if you just want to sit and sip something at **Le Zeppelin** on rue St-Jean, corner of Côte du Palais. Your neighbors at the next table here will doubtless be young, free, and French-speaking. But if it's raining Le Zeppelin's no good so go to the **Café de la Cour** at 1117½ rue St-Jean, where you can sit inside with a similar, convivial group of people. The upwardly mobile and artistically inclined young professional set will be gathered around the corner and up the hill at **Croque-Mitaine,** 33 rue d'Auteuil, and if you can break through the considerable thickness of ice and in-group cohesiveness, you'll meet some fascinating people. Croque-Mitaine has outdoor tables for good weather, but plenty of indoor space as well.

WITH MUSIC: At **Le Figaro,** near the corner of rue St-Jean and rue d'Auteuil (at 1011 St-Jean), eating, drinking, and listening to music both live and recorded are the evening passers. Different nights bring different delights, such as Wednesday's couscous ($4.35), or Friday's roast beef special ($4.60), but cheeseburgers ($2.15) and spaghetti ($2.85) are always offered. Beer costs $1 a glass, the house wine is $5.50 per bottle, and the music is free. If Le Figaro is absolutely packed, try **Le Gaulois** at the corner of Buade and Desjardins—but chances are this place will be just as full. Prices and entertainment are similar in both establishments.

A much different set congregates at **L'Ostradamus,** 29 rue Couillard (not far from the corner of Côte de la Fabrique) in the Latin Quarter. Although breakfast, light lunches, and snacks (sandwiches, salads, and so on) are served, the mostly intellectual, mostly university crowd comes for the Québecois musicians. Beer, wine, and drinks are sold, and posters put up throughout town advertise the act currently appearing.

DISCOS: The young and dance-crazy all head for **Le Bistro,** where it's impossible to count all the light bulbs even if you spend a week in the city. Beer is the most popular beverage ($1.25 a bottle), the people are wall-to-wall and top-to-bottom (there's a mezzanine floor), and mirrors everywhere make the place seem five times as big and ten times as crowded. The dance floor, topped by whirling spotlights and flashing neon tubes, is the most active in town, and I guarantee that standing in front of the gigantic speaker cabinets will cause you to forget completely who you are in 15 minutes or less. Le Bistro is easily the most popular disco in town.

More sedate and a lot more pricey is **Eden,** atop the Québec Hilton. They'll check your outfit, and if it's not some sort of dress or jacket and tie they may let you in only if things aren't busy. The music is good and expensive sounding, the treestump tables are eye catching and expensive looking, the drinks are good and expensive, but the view of Québec at night is priceless. Beer, brought by a young lady to whom you will want to give a large tip, is $2; a gin and tonic, $2.75; cognac, $3.50 to $4—but there is no cover and no minimum. The light system looks like something out of Skylab, but is not nearly so frenetic as it could be.

Most sedate "disco" of all is in the basement of **La Traite du Roy,** on Place Royale in the Lower Town. Priced something like the Hilton's Eden, the subterranean cavern called **Le Cloître des Nonnes** (The Nuns' Cloister) is hardly ecclesiastical. No mind-boggling lights here, just a cozy bar, a small dance floor, and an atmosphere which is so relaxed one wonders how the tag "disco" ever got tied to this place.

A REVOLVING RESTAURANT: There is only one in town, and it's at **Loew's Le Concorde.** Although revolving restaurants rarely get on any gourmet's short list of favorite places, that's to be expected as the big attraction is the chance to dine while gazing at an ever-changing and incredibly romantic panorama. At Loew's, the bonus is that the evening meal is either à la carte or buffet. Choose the buffet and take what you like, all for $13.75 plus tax (10%) and tip.

5. One-Day Trips from Québec City

LAC BEAUPORT: Just as Montréal has its Laurentian Mountains resorts at Val David and Mont Tremblant, Québec City has its Laurentian hideaways. But there are differences: the Laurentians sweep down very close to the St. Lawrence, and so Québecois need drive only 30 minutes or less to be in the woods. And as Québec City is much smaller than its metropolitan sister city, the Québec resorts are more modest in size and fewer in number, although their charm is equal to anywhere else in the Laurentian range.

Should you want to rent a car to explore the countryside around Québec City, contact **Tilden Car Rentals** (tel. 418/687-3322), 1303 Maguire Ave., in the suburb of Sillery, Québec. The office has extra-long hours, and someone's there between 8 a.m. and 10 p.m. on weekdays.

In summer, it's less than a half-hour drive to Lac Beauport, the most accessible of the several resort lakes. In winter, the city "Skibus" brings skiers from city hotels to the modest slopes. The lake is small, but exceptionally pretty. The best way to enjoy it is to stay right on its shores.

Where to Stay

Lac Beauport's prime hostelry is the **Manoir St. Castin** (tel. 418/849-4461), a modest castle of a place right on the lakeshore. With its own tennis, rowing, canoeing, putting, and swimming facilities (and golf course and indoor tennis courts nearby), the manoir is the lake's most complete, and expensive, resort. In winter, the manoir's ski lifts (right across the street) take skiers to the top of ever-snowy slopes; cross-country trails begin right off the grounds. Besides all this, the dining room rates four forks (the highest rating) from the Québec government for its elegant, although expensive, haute cuisine. The price you pay depends on when you stay, on which view (mountain or lake) you choose, and on whether or not you have breakfast and dinner here. Spring and fall, rates are $25 to $35 single, $35 to $52 double, without meals; add $16 per person for breakfast and dinner. In high season (late June to Labour Day), prices are $35 to $45 single, $46 to $64 double, with the same markup for the two meals. In winter, special ski-package or ski-week rates apply. In the restaurant, the renowned cuisine is unabashedly expensive, and a number of the choicer items offered at lunch and dinner carry a supplemental price tag for those who've bought meals with their room. Main courses hover around $10 to $12, with a full dinner at least twice that figure.

More economical, if not so elaborate, is the **Auberge Normande** (tel. 418/849-4486), just slightly farther around the lakeshore than the Manoir St. Castin. Although it takes its name from Normandy, the auberge has borrowed its architecture from the Swiss Alps, and added such new-world conveniences as an indoor heated swimming pool, saunas, and modern guest rooms boasting wall-to-wall carpeting, private baths, television sets, and, in some, even fireplaces or kitchenettes. In high season (July through mid-September), two people pay $32 for a standard room, $38 for one with fireplace or kitchenette; add $15 per person if you want breakfast and dinner. The auberge has several 2½-room apartments with kitchenette, and in one or two a fireplace, for $250 to $280 for six nights. Up to four persons can share the apartment. Off-season, rates go down by $3 to $4 per room. The auberge has its own lawns on the lakeshore, terrace, bar, and dining room. Winter rates are on the ski-package plan.

STE-ANNE-DE-BEAUPRÉ:
Legend has it that French mariners were sailing up the St. Lawrence River in the 1650s when they ran into a terrifying storm. Up against the Ultimate Cruise, they prayed for their patroness, Ste. Anne, to intercede for their deliverance. Surviving the storm, they dedicated a wooden votive chapel to Ste. Anne near the sight of their perils, on the north shore of the St. Lawrence 22 miles northeast of Québec City. Not long afterward, a pilgrim to the spot was cured of an affliction while praying there, and since that time pilgrims have come to pay their respects to Ste. Anne, the mother of the Virgin Mary.

Ste-Anne-de-Beaupré is an easy day's outing from Québec City, and you can combine a visit to the church with a look at Montmorency Falls, higher than Niagara, and a pleasant drive on beautifully pastoral Île d'Orléans. Guided tour companies (see above) offer day trips on this route, a good bet if you're in the city without a car.

Get on Autoroute 40, north of the city, going east. At the end of the Autoroute, where it intersects with Hwy. 360, is **Montmorency Falls.** The waterfall is surrounded by a provincial park where you can stop for the view and a picnic. You'll hear the proud boast that the falls, named by Samuel de Champlain for Charles de Montmorency, governor of New France, are well over the height of Niagara. The falls are an impressive sight in summer, but even more so in wintertime, when the freezing spray sent up by the plunging torrent builds a huge mountain of white ice at the base.

Opposite the falls is the bridge to the Île d'Orléans, described below.

From Montmorency Falls, it's a 20-minute drive along Hwy. 360 east to the small town of Ste-Anne-de-Beaupré—you can't miss it as the highway goes right past the magnificent **basilica** which is the most recent building raised in Ste. Anne's honor. After the sailors' first modest wooden chapel was swept away by the flooded St. Lawrence in the 1600s, another chapel was built in a safer place. Floods, fires, and the ravages of time dealt with later buildings, until a tremendous and impressive structure was put up in 1887. In 1926 it too lay in ruins, gutted by fire. The present basilica was begun shortly after that disastrous fire—of stone this time, and in a streamlined and altogether beautiful variation of the traditional Romanesque design. It combines modern art and traditional grandeur, using the best of materials: marble, granite, cut stone, mosaic, stained glass, and hand-carved wood. No sterile monument, the basilica exhibits the craftsmanship of Québec's master artisans. The pews, for instance, are of wood with hand-carved medallions at the ends, each portraying a different animal in God's creation; the realism is surprising, and goes so far as to portray the monkey hanging upside-down—his natural pose.

Behind the main altar are eight side chapels and altars, each different, each excellent in its artistic harmony. Be sure not to miss the very fine ceiling mosaics in the nave, surely an outstanding achievement of 20th-century art. Whether you come to pay your respects to Ste. Anne or just out of curiosity, the magnificent artistry of the basilica will make your visit worthwhile.

Note that the church, and in fact the whole town of Ste-Anne-de-Beaupré, is particularly busy on days of significance to the saint: first Sunday in May, mid- to late-July, fourth Sunday in August, and early in September.

Besides the basilica, **Fountain of Saint Anne, Scala Santa Chapel,** and **Old Chapel,** other attractions in town include the **Historical,** a wax museum, and the **Cyclorama,** a 360-degree painting of Jerusalem—but these you must pay to see.

Parc du Mont Ste-Anne

Past Ste-Anne-de-Beaupré along Hwy. 360 is the large Parc du Mont Ste-Anne, surrounding a 2625-foot-high peak which has become Québec City's best skiing area. In summer, there's camping, and the gondola to the top of the mountain operates any day (between June 24 and September 8) when it's not too windy. Tickets cost $1.50 for adults, $1 for children, and the view is worth many times the price.

In winter, a dozen lifts (gondola included) take downhill skiers to the starting points of two dozen trails and slopes. Lift tickets cost from $36 to $45 for a ski week, depending on the month you ski, or $9 to $10 per day (a dollar more on weekends and holidays; reduction for children and for adults over 65 years of age). Miles of cross-country trails lace the park, dotted with heated rest huts, all yours for free. If you rent your equipment, it'll cost you only about $6 a day, $30 a week.

The **Québec City Skibus** network serves the slopes at Mont Ste-Anne, so you can stay downtown and ski at the mountain with no trouble.

Île d'Orléans

The 21-mile long island just downstream from Québec City in the St. Lawrence was spotted by the intrepid Jacques Cartier in his early navigations up the river, but over a century was to pass between his first stop here and settlement by Frenchmen. Many of the half-dozen villages on the island have already celebrated their tricentennial anniversaries of foundation.

Less than 50 years ago, the only way to the island was by boat in summer, by boat or by tromping over the ice in winter. The present highway bridge has allowed the fertile fields of Île d'Orléans to become Québec City's market garden district, the fruits and vegetables being picked fresh on the farms and trucked into the city daily. If you take a drive out here in mid-July, you'll notice lots of crude, hand-painted signs with the cryptic but telling phrase "Fraises: cueillir vous-même" ("Strawberries: pick 'em yourself"). Don't pass the invitation up. Spot a good field, wander to the farmhouse nearby, and the farmer will hand you a basket and quote a figure, usually about $2, which you'll pay when the basket's full. You'll need a bag or box to empty your hoard into, then some heavy cream (crème à fuetter, whipping cream).

If you'd rather have someone reap and prepare the bucolic wealth of Île d'Orléans for you, head for the restaurant called **L'Âtre** (tel. 829-2474), in the village of St-Pierre, 12 miles from the bridge on the northern shore of the island. Park in the lot marked by a sign, then wait for the horse-drawn carriage to come from the restaurant across the road and down the slope. The short carriage ride is free, although you may want to tip the driver. L'Âtre is open from noon to 10 p.m., and you may want to have reservations (especially in the evening, and even more especially on weekends) rather than chance being turned away. When you arrive, you'll find a charming old Québecois house with rough board floors, rustic decorations, and a marvelous view of the river and the northern shore, with the Laurentians in the distance.

The menu is the same all day, and is short but to the point: you start with soupe aux legumes et fines herbes (vegetable soup flavored with herbs, $2.15), or perhaps creton (Québec pork pâté) or pâté de foie gras (goose liver pate) at $3.50. Boeuf en cocotte (beef stewed in red wine) or tourtière (Québec meat-and-game pie) provide the main course, at $8.75. For dessert you can have maple sugar pie, but in summer you'd be well advised to opt for fresh fruit—remember those strawberries! All in all, a meal at L'Âtre could cost $20 to $25 per person with wine or beer—not cheap, but certainly a unique experience. By the way, the restaurant demands you spend at least $7 from noon to 5 p.m., and from $10 between 5 and 10 p.m. It's no hard task, as you should really come here for a culinary treat, not for a snack or light lunch.

THE SOUTHERN BANK: Several towns on the southern bank of the St. Lawrence are within easy range of a day's excursion, and in good weather the beautiful views of the river and its islands are by themselves worth the drive. Head for the artisans' village of St-Jean-Port-Joli, about 60 miles from Québec City. You can take Autoroute 20, but then you miss seeing all the villages along the way. A much better plan is to follow Hwy. 132 on your way out, and then return by the faster Autoroute. Both roads are fairly close to the riverbank.

The long Île d'Orléans lies just off the southern bank for the first 25 miles of the drive, a fertile garden in midstream with the Laurentian Mountains on the north bank as a backdrop. The first big town you come to is **Montmagny,** a farming and industrial center. Offshore from Montmagny are the **South Shore Islands,** known best as a wildfowl hunter's paradise. There are six islands in all, the largest being two islands joined by an isthmus: Île aux Grues (Cranes' Island) and Île aux Oies (Geese Island). A ferry goes out to the Île aux Grues from Montmagny.

About 14 miles past Montmagny is the fishing town of **L'Îslet-sur-Mer.** The pretty church in the center of town, **Notre-Dame-de-Bonsecours,** was built in 1768, and beautifully restored in the 1940s. The pristine white interior gleams with gold-leaf trim. Pews and floor are of naturally finished wood, and the Stations of the Cross are bas-relief woodcarvings done by Médard Bourgault (see below). You can visit the church from 9 a.m. to 6 p.m. any day, free of charge (donations accepted).

Also in L'Îslet-sur-Mer, half a block from the church, is the **Musée Maritime de la Côte Sud** (South Shore Maritime Museum), featuring memorabilia of the town's most famous favorite son, the Arctic explorer Captain Bernier, and other nautical artifacts from the town's seagoing past. The museum, housed in a former 19th-century convent, is open in the summer months from 9 a.m. to 5 p.m.

From L'Îslet-sur-Mer it's only eight miles to **St-Jean-Port-Joli,** famous throughout Québec for the quality of woodcarving done here. It all started in the early days when much of the decoration for local churches was done in carved wood. But in the 1930s, three brothers in St-Jean-Port-Joli began carving other things as well: bas reliefs, statues, figurines, even portraits. The fame of the brothers—Médard, André, and Jean-Julien Bourgault—spread and attracted dozens of students. A wood-sculpture school was established, and the town became the heart of Québec's woodcarving artistry (Jean-Julien is the only surviving brother). Today the town is filled with artisans' shops and galleries, and pottery and textiles are produced as well as carved wood. First thing to do is to stop at the **Musée des Anciens Canadiens** (Old French-Canadian Museum), on the left side of Hwy. 132 in the village, open from 9 a.m. to 9 p.m. daily (75¢ admission). Works of the Bourgault brothers and of other artisans are displayed with explanatory pictures and capsule histories. The woodcarving is just incredible. Once you've marvelled at these masterpieces, wander into any of the woodcarving shops in town for a look at what's on sale. Pieces by the famous Bourgaults and their descendants will carry slightly higher prices than those by fledgling craftsmen, of course, but a bas relief of one or two square feet in size should be priced around $40 to $60.

Other artisans in the town include Mme. Edmond Chamard and her school of weavers. Madame sells examples of the best weaving in the region, and other crafts, at her shop on the way out of town to the east.

Another place to admire the artistry of the town's citizens is in the church, built in 1779 and decorated by early woodcarvers. The Bourgaults did the pulpit in 1937. The much-mentioned author of *Anciens Canadiens,* Philippe-Aubert de Gaspé, was the last in a line of seigneurs ("lords of the manor") who owned and governed St-Jean since 1633. He's buried in the church under the seigniorial pew; nearby is a plaque with a list of all the town's seigneurs, back to the time when the original land grant was made by the king of France.

Where to Stay and Eat

St-Jean-Port-Joli's foremost hostelry is the **Auberge du Faubourg** (tel. 418/598-6455), just west of the town proper. The 140 modern, wood-paneled motel rooms all have private baths or showers, and a swimming pool and golf course take your mind off woodcarvings a while. The motel's restaurant is a good bet for any meal, or you can try the French-Canadian fare at **La Boustifaille,** in the complex called **La Roche à Veillon.** The building contains a summer theater, and a boîte à chanson (Québec folk-music club) as well as the restaurant. But personally, my favorite for a light lunch or coffee and pastries is the **Café La Coureuse des Grèves,** 300 Rte. de l'Église (which is Hwy. 204), a block along 204 from the junction with 132. The cafe's strange name comes from a legend, which tells of a beautiful maiden who would run ("la coureuse") along the river's shores ("des grèves"), tempting fishermen and mariners. She might be caught in a net, but no man could hold onto her for more than a single evening. The cafe is a gathering place for local artists and crafts workers, and so the décor of carved-wood tables and stained-glass lamps is appropriate. Films and exhibitions of works are held from time to time, but the nourishment is available daily: coffees ranging from the plain, hearty café du maison (75¢) to the espresso with whipped cream Vienna ($1). Croissants are 75¢ apiece, pastries are similarly priced, and the luncheon special costs about $3.75. On the last visit, it consisted of cream of pear soup, ham cured in maple syrup, apple pastry, and coffee.

If you've still got some time after your lunch in St-Jean-Port-Joli, head up the coast along Hwy. 132 a bit farther, to the picture-postcard village of **Kamouraska.** One of the southern shore's oldest settlements, it has few "attractions," but lots of charming old houses, riverbank panoramas, and photographic angles to discover.

The next big town along the highway is Rivière-du-Loup, gateway to the Gaspé Peninsula. From here ferries cross the St. Lawrence to St. Simeon on the North Shore.

FARM VACATIONS: The Québec Ministry of Agriculture and the Agricotour Federation sponsor a farm vacation program with marvelous possibilities: spring maple sugaring parties; summers filled with country sights, scents, and sounds; an autumn week when the foliage is ablaze; or a winter getaway to a cozy, snowbound farmhouse. About 150 farms and farmers participate in the program, offering accommodations either in their own farmhouses or in cottages nearby. A week in a farmhouse, all country-style meals included, may cost only $150 per adult, $75 per child, or about $20 per adult, $15 per child, for just an overnight stay, with meals. If you don't have that much time, for a few dollars you can camp on the farm's grounds or take a day tour to the barns and fields. For full information and reservations, contact the **Fédération des agricotours du Québec,** 515 Ave. Viger (2e étage), Montréal, PQ H2L 2P2 (tel. 288-8090 in Montréal, 800/361-6196 in other parts of Québec).

6. To the Gaspé

The southern bank of the St. Lawrence sweeps north and then eastward toward the Atlantic. At the river's mouth the tongue of land called the Gaspé Peninsula juts into the Gulf of St. Lawrence. Gaspé is a region of rugged hills, forests blanketing hundreds of square miles, and a dramatic rocky coastline. It's pointless to compare the Gaspé to the Maine coast or Big Sur, for nowhere

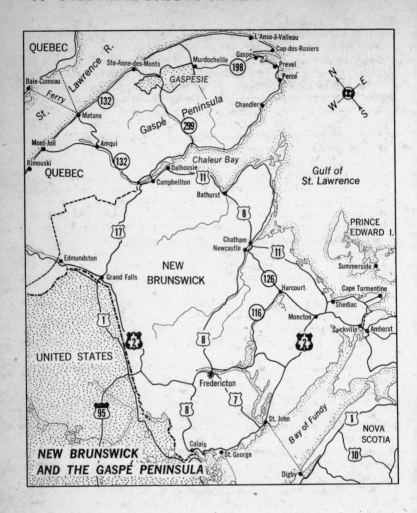

else will you find the same tidy fishing villages nestled in coves cut from the rocky coast, or lumber towns at the mouths of rivers brimming with salmon. It's a land for hikers, hunters, fishers, bicyclists, campers, and anyone who loves the outdoor life. You don't need much equipment to enjoy the Gaspé, however, as almost every little town has a modest but clean and comfortable motel and a restaurant to match. As for things to do, the breathtaking scenery will absorb your interest every minute of the way, and the picturesque villages, each with its church spire towering over a cluster of simple houses, provide interesting variations to the scene.

Coming from Québec City, you can plunge right into the outdoor life by taking a short detour from Hwy. 132 on Hwy. 289 to the **Open-Air Center at Pohenegamook,** on the beautiful lake of the same name. It's about a 30-mile detour, one way. On Hwy. 289 you'll pass through the **Parke Game Reserve** (camping and picnicking) and then the town of St-Eleuthère. In Estcourt, at the end of the lake, turn left and follow the road which starts beside the church to get to the center. Children's camps, nature walks, sailing, canoeing, and fishing are on the program here, and you can enjoy them even if you have no camping equipment. There are family chalets for rent, and even full camping outfits, by the piece. Rental tents cost $5 to $6, sleeping bags $2.50, pots and pans about 50¢ each, and two people should be able to set up camp in style for about $20, total. To reserve a chalet or to get more information, phone 418/859-2405, or write to: Base de Plein-Air Pohenegamook, Estcourt, Ville Pohenegamook, Cté. Kamouraska, PQ G0L 1J0.

RIVIÈRE-DU-LOUP: Unless you're planning to take the ferry across the St. Lawrence to St. Simeon, there's little to hold you in Rivière-du-Loup. Schools and businesses, courts and governmental offices provide for the surrounding region, but with the beauties of the Gaspé waiting, you'll want to press on.

Should you need a picnic break, the best place is in the **Parc de l'Ancrage**, on the river near the ferry dock: follow Hwy. 132 through town until you see signs for the ferry operated by Clark Transport Canada. But instead of following the ferry road, take the road down the hill just to the right of it. This'll take you to the park, and if you keep on going, to the ferry as well.

If you must stay overnight here, the **Motel Loupi** (tel. 418/862-6898), just off the inland (as opposed to the waterfront) road to the ferry dock, is clean and cheerful, with many rooms having a fine view of an inlet from the river and the city beyond. A swimming pool is just the thing in which to cool off, and a modest restaurant can provide breakfast, lunch, or dinner. All 27 rooms have TVs, mostly in color, and private baths. Prices are from $27 to $32, mostly depending on view. Note that the Loupi is open only in the warm months.

Ferry to St. Simeon

The car ferry across the St. Lawrence operates between mid-April and early January, weather permitting, with seven sailings a day in each direction during the busy summer period from late June to early September; in April, May, early June, and mid-September through November there are three crossings each way; in December, two. Fares are $4.25 for adults, $2.25 for children (6 to 11), $9.50 for a car, one way. The boat takes 100 cars and 500 passengers on the 1¼-hour voyage. For the latest information, call 418/862-5094 or 862-9545 in Rivière-du-Loup, or 418/638-2856 in St. Simeon, on the northern shore. (Note: If you're staying the night in Rivière-du-Loup and you just want a chug on the river, take the "sunset cruise," across and back for only the one-way fare, offered on a sailing late in the day when business is slack.)

ON THE ROAD: Past Rivière-du-Loup along Hwy. 132, the country slowly grows more typically Gaspésian. Peat bogs on the river side of the road yield bales and bales of famous Canadian peat moss, shipped to gardeners throughout the continent. At **Trois-Pistoles** (the name allegedly comes from a French coin, the pistole, and not from firearms) there is another **ferryboat** across the river, to Escoumins on the northern shore. Boats operate from the beginning of April through November two or three times a day in each direction, more times if the traffic demands. Times and fares: 1¼ hours one way, $4.25 per person, $9.50 per car. Call in Trois-Pistoles 418/851-3099, or in Escoumins 418/233-2512, for information on exact times.

Past Trois-Pistoles are miles of lush wood-post-fenced fields and low rolling hills. Along the roadside, hand-painted signs advertise pain de ménage (homemade bread) and other baked goods for sale (about $1 to $1.25 per loaf). If you're lucky, you can pick up some homemade cretons, Québec country pork pâté, at the same time to go with the fresh bread.

Approaching **Bic,** prepare for a sight. As you come over the hill to the town the view of the settlement, bay, and islands is a bewitching sight.

Rimouski (pop. 30,000) is the largest city in the region, boasting regional business and governmental headquarters. One gets the feeling of a boom town, with lots of new buildings going up. The highway skirts the center of town along the riverbank. Hunters and campers pass through Rimouski on their way to the 300-square-mile Rimouski Reserve, filled with moose, deer, fish, and small game. It's about 30 miles southeast along Hwy. 232.

Past Rimouski, the Gaspé begins in earnest. Some say the highway between Matapedia and Mont-Joli actually marks the boundary of the peninsula proper. The highway's number is 132—the tail end of the road which loops all the way around the peninsula to join itself again at Mont-Joli. Thus the confusing signs: 132 *est* (east) and 132 *sud* (south). If you choose 132 sud, go to the end of this section and read backward. Otherwise, on 132 est, read on:

MÉTIS PARK: Near Grand Métis is the former Reford estate, last owned by a lady with such a passion for gardening that even in the relatively severe climate of Gaspé she was able to cultivate a fabulous botanical wonderland: 100,000 plants of 2500 varieties. It all started in 1886 when the first president of Canadian Pacific bought the land and built the mansion so he could angle for salmon in the Métis River nearby. His niece, Mrs. Reford, got it as a gift in 1910. By 1929 her army of gardeners had produced, under her guidance, a garden fine enough to get her admitted to the Royal Horticultural Society in London. The provincial government took over in 1962, and you can visit the park from mid-June through September from 8:30 a.m. to 8 p.m. Visit the mansion while you're here—you can even stay for supper: meals are served during park opening hours.

As you approach Matane, the foothills off to the right of the highway get larger and larger, and roadside communities are farther apart. When you reach Matane, you know you're well into the Gaspé.

MATANE: At first Matane can fool you: the highway enters town and passes spic-and-span gas stations and a brand-new shopping center reminiscent of the bustle in Rimouski. But turn right and head up Ave. St-Jérôme along the Matane River, and this small city on a salmon river reveals itself. Before you get that far, however, you may want to stop at the phare (lighthouse) a short distance before the aforementioned shopping center. The town maintains an **information bureau** here, open daily from 9 a.m. to 8 p.m. The bilingual person at the desk will give you a map of the town, answer your questions, and tell you about the small museum in the next room.

Before getting into what makes Matane so delightful—in a word, salmon —here are some hints on where to stay and where to dine.

Where to Stay and Eat

Matane has several motels in the higher price range, the most delightful of which is the **Motel & Hôtel Belle Plage** (tel. 418/562-2323), on the road called Matane-sur-Mer not far from the car-ferry dock. The 50 rooms cost $36 double with private bath and color TV. The combination hotel-motel is on a quiet road; vines cover the porch and climb the walls. Across the street are several small smokehouses for salmon, the products of which are served in the dining room. The menu is table d'hôte, including soup and coffee with whatever main course you select: the salmon, if available, is right up there with boiled live lobster at $17; grilled or poached scallops are less expensive at $11. The dining room has walls of glass overlooking the river, and at first glance you'll think you're actually floating just above the water. After lunch or dinner, wander into the lounge to a seat near the crackling wood fire, lit on any day when there's the slightest suggestion of a chilly breeze. The Belle Plage is not immediately noticeable as there's no sign right on the building (as of this writing), but look for the two red spinning wheels at the entrance and you won't miss it.

The **Motel Vigie** (tel. 418/562-3664), on Hwy. 132 before town, is right next to the left turnoff for the car-ferry dock. Most of the 30 rooms are perpendicular to the highway and therefore very quiet; a few face the highway. Rooms have color TVs, and cost $32.50 in the back, a dollar less facing the highway (take a room in back). The motel's restaurant-bar is usually busy with local people who come for good food and good company.

Downtown on Ave. St-Jérôme, the **Hôtel Bernier** (tel. 418/562-0236) is a well-maintained small hotel built in the 1930s but renovated and spruced up several times since then. Rooms are not fancy, but clean and adequate, all with TVs and baths. Prices are very reasonable: $15 single, $18 double. The address is 335 Ave. St-Jérôme, but in a town this small there's no chance you'll miss it. The Bernier's rooms are good, but the hotel's real reputation comes from its restaurant, called **La Terrasse.** Some of the best food in town issues from its kitchens, and the prices are good: fresh salmon steak cooked in butter, with soup, dessert, and coffee, goes for only $8.65, plus tax and tip. The salmon come right out of the river only a block away. Shrimp, cod, and halibut, also on the menu at equally affordable prices, are locally caught.

Although the decor is surprisingly up-to-date, there's a backwoods feeling about the **Brasserie au 21 du Vieux Port,** in the modern shopping center at the mouth of the Matane River. Fishermen gather to discuss the day's possibilities or disappointments over a pitcher of beer and Canadian-style food (served from 11 a.m. to 11:30 p.m.). The fisherman's platter (assiette de pêcheur) assembles all of Matane's marine wealth in one place for $4.75; fish and chips is only $3.15; the three-course daily special (menu du jour) usually costs around $3.25.

Matane even has an artists' cafe where you can have morning coffee and croissants (two) with butter and jam for $1.60. It's **Le Café d'à Côté,** at about 150 (no number marked, really) on the Ave. d'Amours which runs along the eastern riverbank. A dozen or so tables and a stack of newspapers fill the interior, and in good weather several tables are brought outside, with a view of the river. Come for sandwiches or perhaps a shrimp-and-rice salad ($4.25) later in the day. The cafe is in the same building as the APGA Photo Studio—enter around the left side.

What to Do

Matane is a fishing and logging town. If you're here in mid-June you may get to participate in the **Shrimp Festival:** shrimp of excellent quality are caught out in the St. Lawrence. (If you miss the festival, no matter.) Wander up Ave. St-Jérôme to the bridge across the Matane River. The modern architecture of the **Hôtel de Ville** (City Hall) is an unmissable landmark. Behind it, on an island in the river, is a beautiful **municipal park** with an open-air theater for summertime evening entertainments, as well as a playground and picnic grove. There's a footbridge to the island near the City Hall. But even before the island park, right next to City Hall and the river dam, is a fascinating, very Gaspésian sight you won't want to miss. Starting in June and continuing through September, **Atlantic salmon** swim up the Matane River to get to their spawning grounds. The dam, built in the early 1970s, would have blocked their passage were it not for the ingenious construction of a "migratory passage," a sort of backdoor through which the salmon could swim. The passage, right beside the dam, simulates the rushing channels a salmon might have to battle when swimming upstream between huge boulders—only here the rushing waters swirl among wood-and-concrete stalls. In the little building at the top of the passage, a plate-glass window in one stall lets you watch the salmon—sometimes up to three feet long and weighing 25 pounds—shoot themselves up the rapids with a single powerful push from the tail. Push the button marked "Anglais" (English) for a short explanation of the whole marvelous phenomenon.

The salmon's life cycle is nothing short of amazing. Hatched during the winter months in small hollows of chilly rivers like the Matane, the small fish spend three or four years maturing in the shallow river before heading downstream and out into the Atlantic, sometimes traveling as far as Greenland. After several years at sea, both male and female salmon get the urge to return to their freshwater breeding grounds, so they swim back across the ocean, and *leap*, rapid by rapid, rock by rock, up the river during the summer months. In October the female digs a hole in a shallow riverbed, lays her eggs (which will be fertilized by the male), and then sometimes dies of exhaustion from the trip upriver—all the eggs make her up to 35% heavier than normal. If she survives, she heads downstream again for another Atlantic vacation.

The authorities in Matane monitor the number of salmon that pass through the migratory passage. Their number can vary from 334 to 2881 in any given year. Some are caught and banded so their movements can be traced. You can fish for salmon below the dam, but you need a license ($15 a day), available in the fisheries bureau across the street from the dam. Otherwise, the fish-packing plant on St-Pierre, at the intersection with Ave. Fraser, will sell you some fresh-caught salmon if there's any available the day you're in town. Even if there's no salmon, there will be delicious cod filets (morue) and smoked cod (morue fumé), halibut (flétan), and shrimp (crevettes). For a picnic, take your fixings down to the mouth of the river, on the eastern bank, where there's a nice picnic area right on the St. Lawrence shore.

Car Ferry

Here's your last chance to ferry across the St. Lawrence to the northern shore. After Matane, the river widens to become virtually a sea. The trip over to Baie-Comeau or Godbout takes just under 2½ hours, and costs $5 per adult, $2.50 per child (5 to 12), $5 for a motorcycle, and $1.25 to $2 per linear foot for a car (longer cars pay the top price; trailers pay $1.25 per foot). You can go across and back the same day for only $6. People over 65 years old are charged half price on passenger fares—have identification ready. From the beginning of May through October there are five daily sailings in each direction, two to four at other times of the year (no boats in November or December). For reservations, call: in Matane 418/562-2500; in Baie-Comeau, 418/296-2593; in Godbout, 418/568-7575.

STE-ANNE-DES-MONTS: Ste-Anne, like Matane, is a fishing town, and if you missed buying fresh salmon there, you might be able to get it here. Try the **Poissonnerie Ste-Anne,** opposite the church and right next to the fishing-boat docks in the center of town. Smoked salmon, if they have it, will cost around $10 a pound (it's worth twice the price, if you ask me).

For an overnight break, the town's most recommendable hostelry is the **Motel Manoir-sur-Mer** (tel. 418/763-2201), on the waterfront street. Coming from Matane, follow the sign that points to "Ste-Anne-des-Monts" as you enter town, turning left to go along the water. The motel is on this street before you come to the church and the center of town. The Manoir-sur-Mer is not exactly a manor house, but it is certainly on the water: all rooms have a fantastic river view, and cost $26 to $30 for two, depending on whether you want one bed or two. In the restaurant, sandwiches are around $3, but main courses such as salmon ($6.75) and halibut ($5) give you more for your money.

In Ste-Anne, you'll find a local **tourism information** booth just past the church, and also stores, garages, gas stations, and the other necessary services.

PARC DE LA GASPÉSIE: The enormous parks of Matane and Gaspésie, Cap-Chat and Chic-Chocs, cover much of the mountainous land south of Hwy. 132 from Matane to Anse-Pleureuse, 60 miles up the road. You can spend a day picnicking, hiking, or camping in the Parc de la Gaspésie by turning onto Hwy. 299 in Ste-Anne-des-Monts and heading for the Gîte du Mont-Albert, 25 miles inland.

The road climbs into the steep mountains called the **Chic-Chocs** (that's "sheek-shocks"), some of which are naked rock at the summits. Back in the mountains, the rivers brim with baby salmon and speckled trout, and the forest hold large herds of moose, caribou, and deer. The **Gîte du Mont-Albert** has a hotel, cottages, restaurant, and nature center as well as camping and picnicking areas. Trails start from here. Get maps and regulations from the information office on the road before coming to the Gîte.

Should you want to stay overnight or even to have a meal, reservations are almost essential as the Gîte du Mont-Albert has acquired an excellent reputation both for the quality of its cuisine and the tranquility of its accommodations. The large main lodge, white with a black roof, is right in the valley up against the mountains. Rooms for two persons cost $16 in the lodge, $31 in the small cabins ("chalets") next to the lodge. In a chalet, each extra person above two pays $6. Telephone 418/763-2288 or 763-2289 to hold your room.

The restaurant here is surprisingly elegant for being deep in the forest, and it has cuisine to match this elegance. Breakfast is served between 7:30 and 9 a.m.; late toast and coffee from 9 to 9:30. Lunch, from 12 noon to 2:30 p.m., is table d'hôte. For about $4.75 you can have, say, the soup of the day, ham smoked in the chef's own smokehouse, vegetables, dessert, and coffee. At dinner the table d'hôte still reigns, although your choice of entree determines the price: everyone starts with lobster bisque (who wouldn't?), and ends with peach shortcake and coffee. As a main course you can choose among poached cod filet ($7.25), coq au vin ($8), or crab salad or cold lobster with mayonnaise ($11). For reservations, call the same number for rooms, above.

BACK ON HWY. 132: From Ste-Anne, the highway becomes a narrow band of asphalt at the base of a sheer rock wall. Offshore, sea birds perch on rocks, pecking at tidbits in the water. Each Gaspésian village resembles the last: a pretty church with a graceful spire, white houses with black roofs which catch the heat of the sun. The setting of each village is unique, though, and gives each a special charm. It's all reminiscent of other northerly areas: Iceland, Norway, British Columbia, or even Alaska.

Mont-St-Pierre

Around a rocky point and down a slope, Mont-St-Pierre is much like other Gaspesian villages except for the eye-catching striations in the rock of the mountain east of town.

As you look at the elliptical patterns in the rock, you may notice a strange flying object soaring in the currents which sweep in from the river and up the mountainside. It's a man with wings: believe it or not, the tiny village is one of the most popular hang-glider spots on the continent because of the perfect updrafts. Each year at the end of June the town holds its annual two-week **Fête du Vol-Libre** (Hang-Gliding Festival), when the sky is filled with birdmen (and birdwomen) who take their ungainly nylon-and-aluminum contraptions up the steep road just east of town to the cross at the top of the mountain. A few minutes of assembly, a harness hookup, the right moment, and they're in flight hundreds of feet above the town, looping and curving as they like for as long as they like, then finally coming down to a belly-landing in the sports grounds behind city hall. A bat-like metal sculpture near the mouth of the small Pierre River commemorates the town's popularity with winged men.

If you'd like to stay, the **Motel-Restaurant Au Délice** (tel. 418/797-2850) will provide for your needs, renting its 17 rooms with bath and TV for $27 double (during the warm months only—closed otherwise).

To Forillon National Park

At Gros Morne the colored banding in the rocks is spectacular. Soon the road winds into the mountains, up to a rise, down into the valley, and again up to the next. Settlements get smaller, but still there are roadside stands advertising fresh-baked homemade bread and fresh fish. At Petite-Rivière-au-Renard, Hwy. 197 heads southwest toward the town of Gaspé while Hwy. 132 continues eastward to the tip of the peninsula. Motels, restaurants, and services line the roadside in Rivière-au-Renard, Anse-au-Griffon, Jersey Cove, and Cap-des-Rosiers before the highway enters Forillon National Park.

Chosen because of its representative terrain, the park's 100 square miles capture a surprising number of the features characteristic of eastern Canada. A rugged coastline, dense forests, and rich flora and fauna attract hikers and campers from all North America. On the northern shore are sheer rock cliffs carved by the sea from the mountains. On the south, the Bay of Gaspé has warmer waters than you'd normally find at this latitude because of warm ocean currents. The park has a full program of nature walks, trails for hiking, cross-country skiing and snowshoeing, beaches, picnic spots, and campgrounds. You must pay a fee of $1 (for one day) or $2 (for four days) to bring your car into the park. After that, all is free except camping ($3 per night). As you enter the park, the bilingual ranger will give you maps and information, including a topographic map of the park's trails.

Of the park's two camping grounds, the one at **Petite-Gaspé** is the more popular; the one at **Le Havre** is subject to a gentle but persistent breeze from the sea. For swimming, the beach at **Penouille** is best because of the warm waters in the Bay of Gaspé.

With the approval of the park officials, a few private boats operate deep-sea fishing trips and **boat cruises** from Cap-des-Rosiers seven days a week in the warm months. Twice a week, a park naturalist comes aboard to describe the flora and fauna observed on the cruise. A cruise costs $5 per person, a fishing trip (tackle included) $9 per adult, $5 per child. It's a good idea to reserve your place in advance, especially for the popular cruises with the park naturalist. Drop down at the dock (*le havre*) not far from the campground at Cap-des-Rosiers.

Town of Gaspé

The little town of Gaspé has a momentous place in Canadian history, for it was here that Jacques Cartier stepped ashore in 1534 to claim the land for the king of France. He erected a wooden cross to mark the spot, but it disappeared long ago. Today a granite cross commemorates Cartier's landing, and the **Historical Society Museum** just north of town on Hwy. 132 tells the whole story.

You'll also want to take a look at Gaspé's modernistic wood cathedral, built in 1969. Other than being Cartier's first foothold, and the seat of a bishopric, Gaspé today is important because of the three salmon rivers whose mouths are here, for the government fish hatchery, for its deep-water port, and its railhead. It's an important but unprepossessing town with altogether too many gas stations. Unless you have business here, you'll want to head south to the resort town of Percé.

PERCÉ: As you wind through the hills and along the water toward Percé, you'll be greeted by the dramatic view of the **Pic de l'Aurore** (Peak of the Dawn) which dominates the northern reaches of the town. Over the hill from the Pic, famous **Percé Rock** and the bird sanctuary of **Île Bonaventure** come into view. The rock is Percé's most famous landmark and most dramatic accent, and it's especially beautiful when the golden sunlight of late afternoon warms up all its colors.

The town of Percé is not large, and except for a few quiet, well-groomed inland residential streets, it's confined to the highway which winds along the shore. Little private museums, cafes, snackbars, gift shops, restaurants, and motels line both sides of the highway, and young people in bathing suits or shorts and T-shirts give it all a beach-party ambience.

Where to Stay and Eat

Percé's most elegant place to stay is the **Hôtel-Motel La Normandie** (tel. 418/782-2112), right in the middle of town on the water. The building is brand new, of tasteful weathered wood in a simple attractive traditional design. The rooms are all very new and modern, with generous use of light natural wood. All rooms have bath-shower combinations, color TVs, and little sitting areas. Rooms on the water side have decks for sitting and taking in the view, and cost $45 double; on the land side the price is $40 double. The Normandie's dining room is well respected both for its food and its tasteful decor. Bentwood wicker chairs and black circular tables keep to the mood of simplicity. The menu is "table d'hôte," that is, you order your main course and you get soup, dessert, and coffee included in the price. The seafood au gratin, a favorite in these nautical parts, costs $13.50; the salmon, fresh from nearby Gaspé rivers, is $15.50. The dining room is open to the public, of course, for breakfast, lunch, and dinner. The view of the water and Percé Rock is very fine.

The **Hôtel-Motel Bleu-Blanc-Rouge** (tel. 418/782-2142), downtown but to the north a bit, is another place noted for its comfortable rooms and fine food. The motel units, in two buildings set perpendicularly between the highway and the water's edge, hold well-kept if older rooms with TVs, and in some cases kitchenettes. The office and restaurant are across the highway in a predominantly blue and white (*bleu, blanc*) house with red (*rouge*) accents. Mme. J. E. Boulanger keeps a close eye on it all, especially the renowned kitchen. Although the menu lists meat and poultry items as well, seafood is the main fare: a cod filet is as cheap as $8.50; lobster is most expensive at $15. The price of the main course includes appetizer or soup, dessert, and coffee (some of the more elegant appetizers, soups, and desserts are subject to a surcharge—lobster bisque, for example). The dining room is cheerful and cozy, with crocheted covers on the backs of all the chairs. It might be good to call for reservations during the busy season. The Blue-Blanc-Rouge is open all year.

The **Maison Avenue House** (tel. 418/782-2954), on Church Ave. (rue de l'Église) only a few steps from the church itself, has five fine rooms all done in narrow strips of wood—floor, walls, ceiling—back when pretty wood and honey-colored lacquer could be had at a better price. All are very clean, and equipped with washbasins. Bathrooms are in the hall. One person pays $7 to $9; two pay $8 to $12. It's quiet back by the church as all the traffic is on the main highway.

Want to stay a while? Of the many establishments in town renting cabins on a daily or weekly basis, those belonging to the hotel named **Au Pic de l'Aurore** (tel. 418/782-2050) certainly have the most commanding views of the town and Percé Rock. Just north of town on Hwy. 132, the hotel is built into a ledge up against the Pic de l'Aurore, and the larger cabins with fireplace, living room (with couch-beds), and bedroom have a simply fantastic view. They can sleep up to four people, and cost $50 double ($60 in early August), plus $5 for each additional person. Smaller cabins without the same view are $10 less.

If you want to take a drive out of town for a splendid dinner of what may be Percé's best cuisine, call for reservations at **L'Auberge de Gargantua** (tel. 418/782-2852), famous for its French cuisine with Gaspésian ingredients and its extensive collection of wines. Take money: a dinner for two could easily cost $60, and no credit cards are accepted.

Besides the aforementioned dining places, Percé holds many which offer good food at lower prices. **Au Pigalle,** for instance, is on Hwy. 132 in the center of town. The restaurant has two dining areas, upstairs and down, with booths as well as white-clothed tables. Red drapes, waitresses in costume, and soft music set the mood for lunch or dinner. You can have an hors d'oeuvre of shrimp sauteed in garlic butter for $3, followed by lobster reasonably priced at $7.50. They serve breakfast here as well, and a full morning meal need cost only between $1.50 and $3.

You can't beat the breakfast prices at **Biard's,** on the highway slightly north of the center of town. For $1.75 you can get two eggs, ham, and coffee. Later in the day, sandwiches are only $1.25 to $1.75, and more substantial fare such as roast pork chops ($6.50) and liver and bacon ($5.50) are on the menu. Biard's is unpretentious: standard offerings on the menu, pine walls, plastic-covered booths, but the food and service are fine, and prices are right.

Similar in tone and price is **Flynn's Restaurant,** in the center of Percé. The whole place is done in brilliant-colored knotty pine, and the booths are more like picnic tables and benches—although the benches manage to be less comfortable than a picnic table's. A large club sandwich with a heap of french fries costs $3.25, and a crab crêpe absolutely packed with crabmeat is a bargain at $3. A quarter roast chicken costs $3.25, an omelet only slightly more, and both come with vegetables. Flynn's is open for breakfast, lunch, and dinner every day.

Being a resort town, Percé has got to have its places for seeing and being seen, hanging out, and meeting members of the opposite sex. The prime one here is the complex north of the center of town which comprises a **Terrasse** (patio) with umbrella-shaded cafe tables, a bistro and a nightspot. Come here for light meals (hamburgers, $1.10; hot dogs, 75¢) or just for a glass of beer ($1.10) or a drink ($2).

What to Do

Enjoy the scenery, first thing. Take a picnic up to the roadside rest just north of the **Pic de l'Aurore** for that view, then take in different views of **Percé Rock.** At low tide you can walk out to the fossil-filled rock without getting your feet wet by going along a sand bar.

Île Bonaventure, the low, green island beyond Percé Rock, is a provincial park and bird sanctuary. The Canadian Wildlife Service sponsors **walking tours** of the shore and the island, led by a naturalist, and they also operate the **Percé Wildlife Interpretation Center** (tel. 418/782-2240). The center is south of town off of the highway, on the Rte. d'Irlande road; open 10 a.m. to 5:30 p.m. in late June, July, and August.

There's a provincial park camping facility and swimming pool (separate locations) in town.

HEADING EAST AND SOUTH: After Percé, Hwy. 132 heads southeast. The southern shore of the Gaspé, on the Baie des Chaleurs, is very different from the north, with much more farming and industrial activity, and none of the picturesque rock formations or fishing villages. The air is warmer and more humid. After passing through New Richmond, Hwy. 299 heads north into **Gaspésie Provincial Park** to the Gîte du Mont-Albert (see above), and then to Ste-Anne-des-Monts on the St. Lawrence shore. Highway 132, though, continues southeastward as far as Matapedia, where it turns northeastward to take you back to the St. Lawrence at Mont-Joli. Long before Matapedia, but after passing through New Richmond, you'll come to **Carleton,** a pretty port and resort town. A few miles later at **Nouvelle** you'll see signs for the Miguasha-Dalhousie (New Brunswick) car ferry, which cuts 67 kilometers (40 miles) from the drive around the eastern reaches of the Baie des Chaleurs. If you're heading south to New Brunswick and Canada's Atlantic provinces, this is a good shortcut. It runs from Miguasha (Québec) every hour on the hour between 7:30 a.m. to 7:30 p.m. The ferry ride costs $5 for car and passengers, and takes 15 minutes. The boat can take about 12 to 14 cars—if you're 16th in line, you'll almost certainly end up waiting for the following voyage.

Part Two

CENTRAL CANADA

by Marilyn Wood

To my Mother and Father

Chapter X

OTTAWA

1. Orientation
2. Hotels of Ottawa
3. Restaurants
4. The Sights
5. Culture and Nightlife
6. Side Trips from the Capital

IT WOULD BE SILLY to compare Ottawa (pop. 669,000) with such lively and cosmopolitan capitals as London and Paris, but this city certainly possesses a unique and strangely alluring beauty of its own.

First, it has been blessed with a striking natural physical beauty, set high on a bluff above the confluence of the Ottawa, Gatineau, and Rideau Rivers, with the gently rolling contours of the Gatineau Hills as a northern backdrop.

On top of such natural assets, the Gothic Parliament Buildings brood romantically above the city, reminiscent of a Turner painting; the Rideau Canal cuts a vibrant swathe through the city, worthy of any Dutch palette in summer or winter; while Wordsworth would surely have sung of the daffodils in Rockcliffe Park had he seen them.

In short, Ottawa has not yet really been visited by choked downtown streets and that imprisoned feeling so often the hallmarks of experience in most modern North American cities. You can still see the hills and the rivers from downtown.

And for the tourist coming to Ottawa, where else in North America can you see soldiers in scarlet and bearskin changing the guard just as they do at Buckingham Palace; skate and boat on a canal reminiscent of Amsterdam, and wonder at the three million tulips that blaze and sway throughout the city in early May; ski, fish, and hike through wilderness only 12 minutes away from downtown; watch the dramatic debates and pomp of parliamentary proceedings; and then visit a rustic French inn across the river in Québec? Well, you can do all these things and more in Ottawa.

SOME HISTORY: Ever since European explorer Samuel de Champlain discovered the Ottawa River in the 17th century the waterway was used by the French and their allies for transporting furs from Michigan to Montréal. The first European settlement was not established until 1800, however, by one Philemon Wright who had come from Massachusetts, built a settlement, and pioneered the log route to Québec City in the early 1800s when the timber supplies for the British navy, normally gotten from Scandinavia, had been cut off by Napoleon's blockade in the Baltic Sea.

The Ottawa side of the river didn't really develop until 1826 when it was chosen as the site for the development of a canal to safeguard the transport of troops and communications between Kingston and Montréal as an alternative route to the St. Lawrence Seaway, then so vulnerable to American attack. When Colonel By came to construct the canal, the town took the name Bytown, and during and after the construction grew into a reckless backwoods lumber town where many a raucous brawl broke out among the lumberjack and navvy population, especially between the French and the Irish.

In the mid-19th century the two Canadian provinces of Upper Canada (Ontario) and Lower Canada (Québec) were fused into the United Provinces of Canada, but the fierceness of their rivalry continued to such an extent that the legislature had to meet alternately in Toronto and Montréal. Casting around for an acceptable site for the new capital, in 1855, Queen Victoria selected the brawling village as the new capital, probably with the implicit wish that, located smack on the Ontario-Québec border, it would resolve francophone and anglophone differences.

Her choice was not exactly praised: essayist Goldwin Smith commented tersely, "A sub-Arctic lumber village, converted by royal mandate into a political cockpit," while the American press merely remarked that it was an excellent choice because any soldiers who tried to capture it would get lost in the woods trying to find it.

Certainly, for nearly a century the city languished in provincialism as dull as its gray-flanneled denizens and developed a reputation for sobriety and propriety. Nightlife, then, was something you indulged in across the river in Hull, and even today Ottawa is no nightlife capital of the world. Still, during even that period it managed to throw up some colorful characters, not the least of whom was Mackenzie King (who conducted World War II with the help of his dog, his deceased mother, and frequent spiritual consultations with former prime minister Sir Wilfrid Laurier), and later Charlotte Whitton, Ottawa's mayor in the '50s and early '60s, about whom I have this favorite tale. When she met the Lord Mayor of London, both formally decked out in their chains of office, he bent down and asked permission to smell the rose pinned to her shoulder, saying, "If I smell your rose, will you blush?" To which she replied: "If I pull your chain, will you flush?"

Anyway, in the 1960s perhaps because of Canada's newly expressed nationalism and independence of spirit or perhaps because the government wished to create a real capital, Ottawa changed. The National Arts Centre was built (Hull also underwent a massive transformation), ethnic restaurants popped up, the Byward Market area and other old buildings were renovated, and public parks and recreation areas were created. And still the process continues. . . .

1. Orientation

Ottawa is located on the south side of the Ottawa River, which arcs around the city. The downtown area is divided into an eastern and a western section by the **Rideau Canal,** which comes up from Kingston and sweeps past the National Arts Centre and eventually out into the Ottawa River.

In the western section you'll find Parliament Hill, the Supreme Court, the National Gallery, and the National Museum of Man. In the eastern section are located Ottawa University, the Byward Market, a vital center for restaurants and nightlife, and just north of there, along Sussex Dr. (which follows the

Points of Interest
1) Parliament Building
2) National War Memorial
3) National Arts Centre
4) Visitors Information Bureau
5) National Gallery
6) Bytown Museum
7) Byward Market
8) Canadian Ski Museum
9) Nepean Point
10) Canadian War Museum
11) Royal Canadian Mint
12) Ottawa City Hall
13) Rideau Falls
14) Rideau Hall
15) Laurier House
16) University of Ottawa
17) Supreme Court of Canada
18) National Library and Public Archives
19) Garden of the Provinces
20) National Museum of Man
    National Museum of Natural Sciences
21) Chaudiere Falls
22) Majors' Hill Park
23) Lester B. Pearson Building
24) Sparks Street Mall

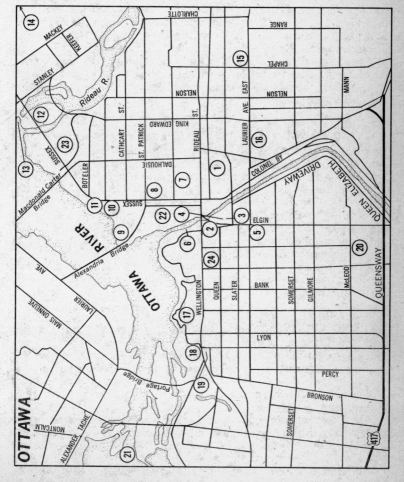

Map Courtesy of Ottawa Visitors and Convention Bureau

Ottawa River's course), the Canadian War Museum, the Royal Canadian Mint, the prime minister's residence, and finally Rockcliffe Park and diplomats' row. The area south of downtown is referred to as the **Glebe** and is currently sprouting some interesting restaurants and clubs.

North across the river in Québec lies **Hull,** reached by the MacDonald-Cartier and Alexandra Bridges from the east end of town, and the Portage and Chaudière Bridges from the west end. Here you will find some of the best French restaurants and also a vibrant nightlife (thanks to the more relaxed liquor laws enabling places to stay open seven nights a week until 3 a.m.). North of Hull stretch the Gatineau Hills and glorious ski country.

Getting around can be a mystifying experience for the visitor. Streets have a habit of disappearing and reappearing a few blocks farther on, while some streets change their names several times. For example, the main street starts in the west as Scott St., changes to Wellington St. as it passes through downtown west in front of the Parliament Buildings, changes again to Rideau St. in downtown east, and finally to Montréal Rd. on the eastern fringes of town. Such phenomena make it advisable not to leave your hotel room without a map, unless you know Ottawa or find getting lost an adventure.

Just a few pointers: The main east-west streets going south from the river are Wellington, Laurier, and Somerset; the Rideau Canal demarcates the east from the west; the main north-south streets starting in the west are Bronson, Bank, and Elgin.

GETTING TO AND FROM OTTAWA: Located about 20 minutes south of the city, the **airport** is surprisingly and pleasantly small and compact: a single terminal with two gates and the usual conveniences. Airport bus service to and from various downtown hotels is operated by **Blue Line** (tel. 746-8741). Fare: $2.75. Air Canada (tel. 237-5000), CP Air (tel. 237-1380), and Eastern (tel. 613/733-5430) are the main airlines serving Ottawa.

The old downtown Union Station has been converted into a conference center so that **VIA trains** now come in at the station on St. Laurent Blvd. in the southeastern area of the city. From here buses connect to downtown. For VIA Rail information, call 613/236-7581.

Buses come into the **Central Bus Station** at 265 Catherine St., between Kent and Lyon. **Voyageur Colonial** (tel. 613/238-5900) provides service to other Canadian cities and the U.S.

GETTING AROUND: The city has a complex network of **bus** routes operated by the **Ottawa-Carleton Regional Transit** Commission (OC Transpo). Pick up a map (50¢) at their downtown office at 294 Albert St. between 8:30 a.m. and 5 p.m. weekdays. For daily information about schedules, where to buy tickets, etc., call 741-4390 from 7 a.m. to 11 p.m. Tickets can be bought at certain outlets (tobacco stores, etc.); otherwise you need the exact fare, which is 60¢.

Bus stops are color coded to indicate the type of route: black for regular routes, red for limited stops, green for express routes; Sunday service is indicated by orange. Routes start closing down at midnight and there's no service after 1:30 a.m.

In **Hull,** buses are operated by **Outaouais Transit** (tel. 819/770-7900). Transfers between the two systems are obtainable when you pay your fare on the bus.

Car-rental prices vary so much that it's impossible to keep track, but just to give you some idea, here are **Tilden**'s rates for a compact: $21 daily, $128.65 weekly, including 200 free kilometers per day (10¢ per kilometer thereafter). Their offices are at 199 Slater St. (tel. 232-3536), the airport (tel. 521-3367), and 1599 Carling Ave. (tel. 729-2068).

Thrifty Rent-a-Car, 328 Kent St. at Somerset (tel. 238-8000) has compacts for $17.95 a day, $118.50 per week, with 250 kilometers per day free and 10¢ per kilometer thereafter.

When driving, remember that Ontario has a compulsory seatbelt requirement. Be warned also that you can spend 20 or more minutes trying to extricate yourself from the maze of one-way streets, which can make arriving on time at a destination difficult. Parking is also a problem, and the best deals (50¢ per hour) are available at city parking lots at: Gloucester and Nepean, west of Bank; Somerset, east of Elgin; between Second and Third Aves. in the Glebe; at 222 Queen St., 70 Clarence St., and Nicholas and Besserer Sts. The National Arts Centre also has underground parking—65¢ per hour; $3 maximum from 6 a.m. to 7:30 p.m.; $2 from 5 p.m. to 2 a.m.; $1 from 11 p.m. to 8 a.m.

Taxis as usual are expensive, $1.05 when you step in and 85¢ per mile thereafter—call **Blue Line** at 238-1111 or **Diamond Taxi** at 235-1821.

USEFUL INFORMATION: For **police,** call 230-6211 in Ottawa, 777-1661 in Hull. . . . For a **medical emergency,** call 236-2545. . . . For an **ambulance,** call 237-4545 in Ontario, 771-7343 in Québec. . . . For **late-night snacking,** Fullers Restaurants at 809 Richmond St. (tel. 722-2336) and 1515 Bank St. (tel. 731-0034) are open 24 hours. . . . The **U.S. Embassy** number is 238-5335. . . . The most conveniently located **post office** is at 59 Sparks St. at Confederation Square (tel. 992-4779), open Monday to Friday from 8 a.m. to 6 p.m., and Saturday from 9 a.m. to 1 p.m. . . . The most conveniently located **liquor stores** are at: 140 George St., 181 Bank St., 105 O'Connor St., 22 Isabella St., and 640 Bank St. Hours: from 10 a.m. to 6 p.m. Monday to Wednesday and Saturday, until 9 p.m. on Thursday and Friday. . . . Most convenient **beer outlets** are at: 157 Dalhousie St., 400 Rideau St., 564 Bronson Ave., 515 Somerset St. West, 20 Isabella St., and 900 Bank St. Hours: noon till 8 p.m. Monday to Saturday (until 9 p.m. Friday). . . . The **telephone area code** of places in Hull is 819, and is needed to call from Ottawa (the area code in Ottawa is 613).

TOURIST INFORMATION: The friendly personnel at the **Tourist Information Centre** in the National Arts Centre will answer all your queries from 9 a.m. to 5 p.m. daily, until 7 p.m. from mid-May to Labour Day (tel. 237-5158 or 237-5159). The **National Capital Commission's Information Centre** at 10 Metcalfe St. is also an excellent source of information for Ottawa and the surrounding area. Open in winter from 9 a.m. to 5 p.m. Monday to Saturday; from 8:30 a.m. to 6:30 p.m. daily during the summer.

The **Visitors and Conventions Bureau,** 222 Queen St., can also be of help (tel. 237-5150).

2. Hotels of Ottawa

Ottawa accommodations do not come cheap. It's far and away Canada's highest priced city for places to stay—and I wouldn't like to speculate why. Luxury and expensive hotels there are aplenty; downtown there are several moderately priced establishments and apartment hotels where you can get a double for $35, but there's really only one downtown budget hotel. Otherwise, you can check in at the university, the YMCA, or the youth hostel.

On the outskirts some full-facility hotels still manage to charge over $50 for a double, and quite frankly many of the motels are no longer cheap—$45 double for a basic motel room during the summer?

In the section that follows I have picked out as many moderately priced establishments as possible. If it's nightlife and gourmet dining you're after, stay over in Hull.

LUXURY HOTELS: If you're going to splurge in Ottawa, then I suggest you hop over the river to the opulent **Auberge de la Chaudière,** 2 rue Montcalm, in Hull (tel. 819/778-3880), a small personal hotel in the grand European manner, but with ultramodern conveniences. Built by Monsieur Campeau (who also built Toronto's Harbour Castle Hilton), it has all the elements of a dream hotel. The lobby sets the tone with a three-story-high ceiling of oak, a rich Oriental carpet, and a waterfall cascading over solid blocks of marble, surrounded by greenery.

Just off the lobby you'll find the premier restaurant, Le Châteauneuf, extravagantly but exquisitely furnished with red oak paneling, walnut-framed velvet Queen Anne chairs, and tables appointed with the finest linen, crystal, silver, and china. Luxury is maintained by a 15th-century Gobelins tapestry, and a working marble fireplace whose mantel supports two Ming vases—a decor certainly suited to the romance and soothing strains of a strolling harpist. To capture the ambience fully, dine after 8 p.m. Dinner might begin with one ounce of Beluga caviar ($20), or more modestly with the escargots Châteauneuf, cooked in white wine, peppercorns, garlic, parsley, tarragon, truffles, and finished with fresh cream and a touch of Pernod ($4.75). For main course, there's a select choice of fish—sole, salmon, lobster, and frog legs—grills, and game, plus such dashing dishes as entrecôte muscovite ($15.25), a prime sirloin scented with crushed peppercorn, a touch of cognac, red wine, essence of juniper berries, and sultana, and served with a sprinkle of pine kernels. Desserts are classically extravagant. Before dinner you can relax over an apéritif and listen to the soft strains of the piano in the adjacent intimate Bar Avignon.

Across the other side of the lobby you'll find Le Jardinière, one of the most opulent coffeeshops ever. It's a beautiful spot for breakfast, lunch, or dinner with its cushioned wicker banquettes and bamboo chairs set against bright greens, including a tasteful number of plants. In summer you can even sit outside and have your morning coffee.

One floor up, La Boîte has nightly entertainment amid a sea of red decor and copper tables. Outside La Boîte between 3 and 5 p.m., take afternoon tea on the balcony area around the fountain and garden. The hotel also has outdoor areas for dining and drinking—including a terrace on the 11th floor with glorious views over the Gatineau.

And finally, the 240 rooms. All have been gorgeously decorated, and not only feature all the modern conveniences—color TV, bedside AM-FM radio, individually controlled air conditioning and heating—but also those little extras, such as a second telephone in the bathroom, an additional vanity, and an extra door that secures the sleeping and sitting areas from the entrance to ensure extra quiet and privacy.

The hotel also should have a glass-enclosed pool for your recreation by the time you arrive.

Rates: $55 to $60 single, $65 to $70 double. Children under 18 stay in their parents' room free. Weekend packages are available at $40 per night. For toll-free reservations, call 800/223-6800; in New York State, call 212/838-3110 collect; in Canada, 800/567-1991.

Don't worry about getting into Ottawa—there's a regular courtesy shuttle service back and forth.

A fairytale castle—that's the **Château Laurier,** Confederation Square (tel. 613/232-6411), one of those gloriously old character hotels, which has attracted kings, queens, potentates, and such celebrities as Marlene Dietrich, Duke Ellington, and Nana Mouskouri. This granite and sandstone replica of a French château, opened in 1912, with its copper roof and cylindrical turrets, is magnificently situated at the bottom of Parliament Hill, with many rooms offering glorious views over the Ottawa River to the Gatineaus.

Here, you may very likely rub shoulders with the mandarins, most likely in the renowned beamed and elegant Canadian Grill, where you can have a deluxe prix-fixe dinner for only $15 that might feature as a main course Brome Lake duckling with prunes. Otherwise, choose from the extensive continental fare on the à la carte menu. Moxie Whitney and the Château Laurier Orchestra provide music for dancing Tuesday through Saturday (cover charge $2 on weekdays, $4 on Saturday). At lunchtime prix-fixe meals begin at $5.50. The Cock and Lion, a pubby-type place, is a popular lunch spot for business people on the run and at night becomes an equally popular dance spot featuring live popular/rock music. To complete the dining scene, there's the rustic-style coffeeshop L'Auberge, and a charming summer sidewalk cafe overlooking the canal, plus the Cross Keys Lounge, one of the most authentic-looking pubs I have ever seen, with its wheel-back Windsors. Then, for recreation, there's a large indoor swimming pool, sauna, steam room, massage salon, and exercise room.

The 460 rooms have all recently been renovated and are furnished very elegantly with antique reproductions and tones of gold and pink. The rooms are large, high ceilinged, have enormous bathrooms equipped with phones, plus that old-fashioned luxury—solid mahogany doors. In addition, all have the usual modern appurtenances. The turret rooms are oddly charming in shape, consisting of a rather long corridor and a small space filled with bed and TV in the turret window.

Rates: $40 to $55 single, $50 to $65 double. Weekend packages for two nights are $28 per night, single or double.

Entertainers (most recently André Gagnon and Buddy Rich) and other notables seem to enjoy the **Four Seasons Hotel,** 150 Albert St., at O'Connor (tel. 613/238-1500), a lavishly appointed accommodation that emphasizes personal service. Inside, the lobby with its comfortable leather chairs for lounging, wood slatted walls and ceiling, earth-tone tapestries, and fluid spiral staircase, provides a dramatic yet gracious welcome.

The Carleton Room is exquisitely elegant with its embroidered wallpaper, Eskimo wall hangings, Chippendale chairs, and plum-colored banquettes, and offers fine continental cuisine ranging from veal medallions in a light cream sauce with mushrooms ($12.50) or grilled lamb chops, to quails in port wine sauce with raisins ($17).

Sascha's is probably the most fashionable disco on this side of the river, with its gleaming brass railings, raised dance floor, pulsating music and light show, and soft comfortable armchairs on the balcony overlooking the dance floor. It is unique also in having a skylit area decorated with hanging plants. At lunchtime there's a good salad bar ($3.75) and also one or two other snacks.

The 236 rooms spread over 17 floors are beautifully furnished with marble-top desks, color-coordinated brown and pink decor, and color TV, AM-FM clock radio, bedside control panel, telephone, and individual climate control. There's a refrigerator in the bathroom, and 24-hour room service.

An indoor heated swimming pool with saunas and exercise room completes the facilities.

Rates: $70 single, $80 double; an extra person is $10. A weekend package is available at $38 per night, single or double. For toll-free reservations, call 800/828-1188 in the U.S.; in New York State, 800/462-1150; in Canada, 800/261-6282.

DOWNTOWN FIRST-CLASS HOTELS: There are two things that you will notice immediately at the **Inn of the Provinces,** 360 Sparks St. (tel. 613/238-6000): first, the skylit lobby filled with trees, flowers, and street-lamp-style lighting, which has obviously been carefully designed to blend with the Sparks St. Mall outside; and second, the friendliness that pervades the atmosphere.

Similar signs of care are found in L'Artisan, an understated but nevertheless rich dining room with blue velour chairs and, Royal Doulton or Royal Worcester art sculptures framed in octagonal mirrored cases placed around the room. The chandeliers and such additional touches as personalized matches on your table (if you reserve ahead) complete the effect of a gracious room dedicated to fine dining. Your meal might begin with stuffed crab creole or salmon rosemary (smoked salmon, topped with cream and Swiss cheese, wrapped in thin crêpes), both $4.75. Main courses include a selection of classic seafood, meat, game, and flambé dishes, all under $15 (most around $12), and the desserts are simply scrumptious.

Adjacent, for that relaxed cocktail, stop in at the piano bar L'Allegro, or if you prefer more frantically paced surroundings, Le Quadrille, a dance spot that features live bands ($1 cover on weekends). At lunchtime, the Quadrille also features an excellent buffet lunch, usually with a large hip of beef ($3.45). For light dining the Kitchen Garden offers bright parklike surroundings, even to the point of having live trees.

Two squash courts add cachet to the usual recreational facilities of indoor swimming pool, saunas, and exercise room.

All 188 rooms are spacious and contain balconies and kitchenettes, with dining area. The decor is primarily earth tones, and all are appointed with color TV and individual climate control.

Rates: $50 to $60 single; $55 to $70 double (the higher prices are for a one-bedroom suite). Weekend packages run $45 per night, single or double.

Just down the street, the **Holiday Inn (Center),** 100 Kent St., at Queen and Kent (tel. 613/238-1122), has Ottawa's only revolving rooftop restaurant, La Ronde, on the 29th floor, which offers superb and romantic views over the Gatineau Hills and the city. Along with those views come some fine dining and dancing nightly except Sunday, with such dishes as rack of lamb ($26 for two) and veal kidney dijonnaise ($10.25) offered at dinner, and omelets and lighter fare at lunchtime, plus a very popular buffet-style brunch on Sundays from 11 a.m. to 3 p.m. Downstairs on ground level there's the International Room, which offers a seafood buffet every night for $11.50 and a $5.50 luncheon buffet in decidedly purple surroundings. At the Blind Pig, which has a pubby air, there's dancing to live music nightly, except Sundays.

All of the 504 rooms have the usual appurtenances associated with the chain, plus vanity sinks and mirrors. The decor is color coordinated in blue/beige or brown. There's also an indoor pool, and a cabana-style bar outside, plus a game room for family entertainment.

Rates: $49 to $53 single, $52 to $58 double. An extra person in a room is $4.

Across town, located near the Byward Market, there's another older smaller **Holiday Inn (Downtown)**, at 350 Dalhousie St. (tel. 613/236-0202), with 170 pleasant rooms set around a courtyard with an outdoor heated swimming pool, plus lounge, dining room, and coffeeshop. Rates are lower: $38 to $42 single, $41.50 to $47.50 double. An extra person is $4.

The **Skyline**, 101 Lyon St. (tel. 613/237-3600) is currently undergoing extensive updating and redecorating. So far the lobby has been redone with rock pools, red and mauve wall tapestries, and some interesting chandeliers that look rather akin to sea urchins.

Off the lobby you'll find two very different dining rooms: Alfredo's, where you can enjoy some good Italian cuisine in elegant surroundings, and Henry VIII, where colorfully costumed servers will load your table with steak and lobster amid a Tudor-style decor. Downstairs there's the large Trellis Room, a light and airy coffeeshop-cum-restaurant that serves moderately priced meals all day, plus a Sunday brunch from 11 a.m. to 2:30 p.m. for $5.95. At the English Pub, which may well be a wild disco by the time of your visit, you can currently get good, thick, and well-filled sandwiches at lunchtime and listen to the nightly entertainment.

The 420 rooms have yet to be upgraded and could do with some brightening, but they have all the facilities expected of a large hotel—color TV, radio, telephone, and modern furnishings. For recreation there's an indoor swimming pool.

Rates: $51 to $53 single, $59 to $61 double; an extra person is $6. Weekend packages are $30 a night, double occupancy; other packages are available. For toll-free reservations, call 800/268-1332 in Canada.

Although the **Park Lane**, 111 Cooper St., east of Elgin (tel. 613/238-1331) is only six years old, it has a certain old-world air. The small lobby has a thick red carpet, soft couches, and warm modern wall tapestries.

The 235 rooms are all very beautifully decorated, in brilliant reds with matching geometric design curtains and spreads. All have color TV, phone, individual climate control, and a touch of luxury in the bathroom—heated floors for those cold winter mornings. The executive rooms with a kitchenette and small sitting area, and the small one-bedroom suites with full kitchen, are only a little more than standard rooms. Executives even contain pant pressers!

Off the lobby there's a small cozy lounge, and a stylishly modern dining room that serves a seafood buffet in the evening Thursday to Saturday for $12.95, and a roast beef buffet from Sunday to Wednesday.

Rates: $37.50 to $51 single, $49.50 to $62 double (the higher prices are for *large* one-bedroom suites. An extra person in a room is $10; cots or cribs are $2.

DOWNTOWN MODERATELY PRICED HOTELS: Only three blocks from Parliament Hill, next door to the National Gallery and right across from the National Arts Centre, the **Lord Elgin**, 100 Elgin St. (tel. 613/235-3333), offers one of the city's top values—not surprising, given its sturdy Scottish flavor and demeanor. This dignified stone edifice with its green copper roof was built in 1940 and named after the eighth Earl of Elgin who was governor general of Canada. The lobby has a quiet, respectful air about it, which is perhaps encouraged by the busts of Lord and Lady Elgin and one or two showcased family mementos, including the coat, hat, and snowshoes worn by the governor general and the silver presentation spade given to Lady Elgin in

1851 when she opened the Simcoe-Huron railroad. The place attracts men of substance—Sir Michael Redgrave and Sir John Mills, for example.

The whole hotel has recently been renovated, and the 355 rooms are all tastefully decorated and have red and green tartan bedspreads, the family tartan woven in Scotland under the supervision of His Lordship. The rooms tend to be a little small, with gray-red decor and modern furniture, appointed with color TV and phone. Most of the bathrooms have a shower only; some have tub only.

Off the lobby you'll find a comfortable library-style cocktail bar called the Uskey Houff, which naturally has a very wide selection of rare and single-malt whiskeys, and some very inviting wingbacks to sink into. Also on the ground floor, Paxton's, an atrium-style dining room complete with butcher-block tables, cane bentwood chairs, and greenery, offers elegant dining—breakfast, lunch, dinner, and after-theater supper. You might find many of the theater people working across the road staying and dining here. Downstairs there are two very plain tavern-style rooms.

Rates: $30 to $32 single, $34 to $36 double; children under 18 stay free in their parents' room. For toll-free reservations, call 800/323-1776 in the U.S. 800/267-4298 in Canada.

The **Embassy Apartment Hotel,** 25 Cartier St. (tel. 613/237-2111), has 147 sizable and really very lovely rooms with large double closets, and balconies, decorated in color-coordinated earth tones, and equipped with color TV and phone. Bachelor rooms have separate fully equipped kitchens and a bed-sitting area. For the price, these accommodations are excellent. On the premises you'll find a study-lounge and a dining room.

Rates: $30.50 single, $35.50 double, for a bachelor; $36.50 single, $41.50 double, for one-bedroom apartment; $58.50 for a two-bedroom apartment. An extra person is $4. Weekly and monthly rates are available.

For a different kind of bargain—a home away from home—head straight to the **Aristocrat Apartment Hotel,** 131 Cooper St. (tel. 613/232-9471), which has 106 one- and two-bedroom suites with fully equipped kitchens. All the rooms are beautifully decorated in shades of brown and orange, and have plenty of closet space and all the conveniences: air conditioning, color TV, and telephone. There's a laundromat in the basement and a party room with Ping-Pong. But there's no maid service on weekends.

Rates: $32 single, $38 double, for a one-bedroom suite; $49, single or double, for a two-bedroom suite; an extra person is $5. Weekly and monthly rates are available.

The same management runs the **Westbury,** just down the street at 141 Cooper St. (tel. 613/236-7500), which has similar facilities except that all the rooms have balconies and there are some bachelor studios available.

Rates: $27 single, $33 double, for a bachelor studio; $36 single, $40 double, for one-bedroom suites; an extra person is $5.

Similar accommodations, but not furnished or kept up quite so nicely, are to be found at the **Algonquin Apartment Hotel,** 225 Lisgar (tel. 613/238-1616). Suites have modern basic furniture, sizable living rooms, small bedrooms, and fully equipped kitchens. Facilities include color TV, telephone, and air conditioning.

Rates: $28 single, $34 double.

In the southern part of the city, located behind the National Museum of Man and near Dows Lake, you'll find the **Sheraton El Mirador,** 480 Metcalfe St. (tel. 613/237-5500), which has, as its name suggests, a somewhat Spanish flavor with its white arches and wrought-iron staircase leading off the stone-floored lobby.

The 158 rooms are large and pleasantly decorated in burnt-orange tones, with matching curtains and spreads, often with a sitting area. They have all the modern conveniences of color TV, phone, and individual climate control. For fun, there's an outdoor enclosed heated pool, coffeeshop/dining room, and lounge.

Rates: $36 single, $42 double; an extra person is $6; children under 17 stay free in their parents' room. For toll-free reservations, call 800/325-3535 in the U.S., 800/261-9393 in eastern Canada, 800/261-9330 in western Canada.

DOWNTOWN BUDGET ACCOMMODATIONS: For truly budget accommodations, seek out the **Bytown Hotel,** 127 Metcalfe St. (tel. 613/237-5171) at Laurier St. West. Originally the Ottawa Y, it has just been renovated and rooms have been pleasantly decorated in earth tones with floral-print bedspreads and matching curtains. Some of the rooms are a little small (try to avoid the back rooms which are rather dark, having only one small window). There's a laundromat and coffeeshop on the premises, and the management intends to install a lounge bar.

Rates: $20 single, $23.50 double. Weekly and monthly rates are available.

In southern Ottawa at the corner of Argyle and O'Connor there rises a five-star luxury 15-story **YM-YWCA,** at 180 Argyle St. (tel. 613/237-1320), with 300 air-conditioned rooms. Most rooms are single, some have a TV and bath; a few doubles are available. All rooms have telephone and free local calls. There's a TV lounge and laundromat, plus the added attractions of an indoor pool, gym, exercise rooms, handball and squash courts, a small but well-stocked library, cafeteria, and even resident counselors available 24 hours a day.

And, of course, the price is right: $18 single with private bath, $14 with shared bath, and $10 per person in a double room with shared bath. Three in a double room pay $7 per person. Children under 12 stay free when accompanied by an adult.

If you like, while you're in the city you can stay in jail at the **Youth Hostel,** 75 Nicholas St. (tel. 613/235-2595). The gray stone building was opened in 1862, gradually became outmoded as a prison facility, and was taken over and renovated by the hostel. The old chapel is now used as a dining room, and the bunk beds in the dorms are located along the corridors of the old cell blocks. A limited number of rooms for couples or families are offered, but only to members. Checkers, chess sets, and cards are readily available. Rates are $3.50 per night for members; $4.50 for nonmembers. From May to September you'd do best to reserve.

During the summer **Ottawa University Residences** (tel. 613/231-7055) offers accommodations. The reception area is at 100 Hastey Ave., just off Laurier St. East. Rates are $18 for a double room; $13 to students. For information write: 648 King Edward Ave., Ottawa, Ontario. Besides the room, you can also get a cheap meal at the cafeteria or restaurant.

Right downtown, the **Beacon Arms Hotel,** 88 Albert St. (tel. 613/235-1413), is a family-run place that offers 158 basically furnished but clean large rooms with kitchenettes, good closet space, and black-and-white TV, plus free local phone calls. Many of the casts performing at the National Arts Centre stay here. There's a dining room, coffeeshop, and several bars, all of which feature $2 lunch specials, including the friendly library-style La Bibliothèque that usually has a singer of some sort in the evening. In the main lounge, rock bands perform and people dance from 9 p.m., on, Tuesday through Saturday nights.

Rates: $26 single, $31 double; children under 14 can stay free in their parents' room.

OTTAWA WEST: For a dash of Oriental style, the grounds at the **Talisman Motor Inn,** 1376 Carling Ave. at the Queensway (tel. 613/722-7601), have been landscaped as a Japanese garden built around a large ornamental pond with stepping stones and a picturesque waterfall. The two outdoor swimming pools are also built into the design.

Inside the peak-roofed wooden buildings you'll find an entertainment complex. The Village Dining Room overlooks the rock garden and falls, and you can sit out on the balcony to dine. Decorated with Oriental art and high-backed banquettes, the room offers lunch and dinner buffets ($6.95 and $11.95) and entertainment Friday and Saturday nights. The atrium-topped Greenery, with its cascading philodendrons and other plants blending with the bamboo furniture, makes a refreshing place to have breakfast, lunch, or dinner, while the Beachcomber makes a great Tahitian-style disco with live entertainment.

All 292 rooms have balconies; ground-floor rooms, opening on the gardens and pool, are very desirable. They are all pleasantly decorated with Oriental-style furnishings and color schemes of blue or melon, plus color TV, high-fidelity music, air conditioning and telephones.

Rates: $45.75 single, $52.75 double; an extra person is $6; children under 12 stay free with their parents. Weekend package: $29.95, single or double, per night.

The other good and more moderately priced establishment in the west end is **Webbs Motel,** 1705 Carling Ave. just west of the Queensway (tel. 613/728-1881), easily identified by its white walls and gray mansard-style roof. It's a friendly place, where the rooms are sparkling clean, tastefully decorated in reds and oranges, furnished in Danish modern or colonial style, and fully equipped with color TV, air conditioning, and telephone. Several efficiencies are available with dining and living areas. There's a licensed dining room on the premises.

Rates: $26 single, $29 to $31 double; an extra person is $3; an efficiency goes for $37, single or double.

The **Embassy West Motor Hotel,** 1400 Carling Ave. at the Queensway (tel. 613/729-4331), is a friendly, modern place. The lobby with its burnt-orange carpet, natural stone walls, and check-in counter lit by a row of vanity lights, has a bright feel, and the 121 rooms are as pleasant with their gold-and-brown spreads and matching curtains. The ground-floor rooms facing the front have motel-style entrances as well as an inside entrance. All are equipped with color TV, radio, air conditioning, and phone (local calls are free).

For entertainment and dining there's a dining room-cum-coffeeshop, a lounge bar, and Disco Reflections, which has a good light show and live entertainment (cover charge $3 on weekends; free to hotel guests). The kidney-shaped outdoor pool is surrounded by gardens that create some privacy.

Rates: $31.50 single, $37.50 double; an extra person is $5; children under 12 stay free with their parents. Weekend package: $26, single or double, per night.

Macies Ottawan, 1274 Carling Ave. at Merivale Rd. (tel. 613/728-1951) has been built in two stages. At the back of the site stands a modern four-story block which houses large rooms with sitting areas, nicely decorated in orange tones and fully equipped with air conditioning, color TV, alarm clock, massage unit, and phone (local calls free). Opposite stands an older unit, where the rooms are decorated in shades of green and have that basic motel-style appearance. There's a pleasantly secluded outdoor pool.

Rates: $27 single, $29.50 double; an extra person is $3.

OTTAWA EAST: About two miles from downtown, the **Concorde,** 333 Montreal Rd. (tel. 613/745-2112) has just been completely remodeled and the new rooms are so color coordinated that even the armchairs are upholstered in the same fabric as the drapes. Furniture is modern; the rooms are equipped with color TV and telephone; and all rooms face the swimming pool and have motel-style entrances.

Just off the main building lobby, there are two cozy lounge-piano bars, one with a raised fireplace with a copper chimney, the other with a small fountain and relaxing music from 8 p.m. to 1 a.m. Tuesday to Saturday. Downstairs you'll find Stage East, a country-and-western music club.

Rates: one bed, $27 to $33; two beds for two people, $35 to $38; an extra person is $3 or $5 (the higher rates refer to the summer only).

A little closer to town, you'll find the **Butler Motor Hotel,** 112 Montreal Rd. (tel. 613/746-4641), a large modern place probably most famous for Bogey's, where the over-30s swing to good country and rock bands amid a few Bogart blow-ups.

The hotel has 99 rooms, some with balconies and all with color TV, telephone, and air conditioning. Furnishings are Danish modern, with color-coordinated carpets, shades, and spreads. The outdoor pool area with patio and barbecue facilities is shaded by beautiful silver-birch trees and fenced off for privacy. There are also a dining room and lounge bar.

Rates: $25 to $30 single, $30 to $36 double; an extra person is $3; children under 14 stay free in their parents' room. To get there, take the Alta Vista exit north off the Queensway and turn right on Montreal Rd.

Carleton University, four miles southwest of the city, has summertime double accommodations that rent for $11.50 per person, including breakfast. A snackbar and some sports facilities are available. For information, write: Carleton University, Conference Centre, 1233 Colonel By Dr., Ottawa, ON K1S 5B7 (tel. 613/231-5510).

HULL: Five minutes across the river just off the Alexandra Bridge, the **Sheraton Le Marquis,** 131 rue Laurier (tel. 819/770-8550), provides 131 moderately priced accommodations, many with a glorious view of Parliament Hill. The rooms are large with modern furniture, and are tastefully decorated in shades of burnt orange and brown. All have color TV, telephone, and air conditioning. There's a pleasant dining room and an entertaining piano bar that is open *seven* days a week (remember, we're over the border here), until *3 a.m.*

Rates: $33 to $40 single, $37 to $42 double; an extra person is $4. Weekend package: $22, single or double, per night.

3. Restaurants

Not so long ago it was difficult to find a good meal in Ottawa. Most people dined at home and hence there were few, if any, exciting restaurants—and they were over the river in Hull. It's still true that the best French restaurants are in Hull, but downtown Ottawa has been sprouting many ethnic restaurants—Chinese, Malaysian, Italian, Greek, Turkish—of her own, so that now you can find whatever your palate desires.

In the section that follows I have categorized about 70 of my favorites by location, price, and type of food.

HULL: Because the top French restaurants are clustered over in Hull I am kicking off the section with the following expensive dining rooms.

French

When people need a reliable spot offering classically good cuisine, they often head for **Le Pied de Cochon,** 248 Montcalm St. (tel. 819/777-5808). It's a small, unpretentious place. There's no awning outside, and if you didn't know about it you'd probably walk on by. Inside, there are two rooms, both very simply furnished in a rustic style. Part of the second room has a cozy lounge area for apéritifs before dinner.

Here you will dine on simple, exquisitely prepared, and finely served cuisine, starting perhaps with an aspic de foie gras en gelée ($3) or coeur d'artichaut ravigote ($1.75), followed by côte de veau à l'Armagnac or cailles aux pruneaux, both $8.75. For dessert, try the calorie-laden Vacherin glacé au kirsch ($1.75). Or you can opt for the special, which will include appetizer, salad, and dessert for the grand sum of $11.50.

At lunchtime the place is so popular that people even dine at the long bar on omelets, steak, and fish, priced between $4 and $6 and including soup, dessert, and coffee.

Open noon to 2 p.m. Tuesday to Friday; 6 to 10 p.m. Tuesday to Friday and Sunday; until 11 p.m. Saturday.

"Let's go to Burger's" used to be a byword in Ottawa in the early '20s when Henri Burger, chef at the Château Laurier founded his restaurant, **Cafe Henri Burger,** 69 rue Laurier (tel. 819/777-5646). Although he died in 1936 the name still attracts people to this landmark brick building with its Italianate windows, side porch, and finialed entrance overlooking the river. Inside, there are five small dining areas—three downstairs—each woodpaneled and simply decorated, often with engravings of, for instance, Les Cinq Sens.

Gracious service and a convivial atmosphere top off the superb cuisine. The menu changes daily, and at dinner, besides a small à la carte selection of such delicacies as sweetbreads with mushrooms and olives in Madeira sauce ($10) and chateaubriand ($30 for two), there are variously priced table d'hôte dinners to choose from. For example, you might have avocado vinaigrette and vichyssoise followed by coq au vin de Bourgogne and coupe aux fraises sorbet for $11. Similar style luncheons from $4.50 make this an excellent lunch stop.

Open Monday to Saturday from noon to 2:30 p.m. and 6 to 10 p.m.

The son of a baker, André Dupuis always had a weakness for food and his weekend hobby was cooking, so it seemed natural that he should open his own **Café Restaurant Kian,** 651 Blvd. St-Joseph (tel. 819/770-3880) and cook, which he did for the first six years.

Here you can dine in any one of the four stuccoed small rooms, simply decorated with one or two farm implements like pitchforks, and feast on such tasty dishes as lapin chasseur ($8.95) or mignonettes de boeuf bordelaise ($10.95), plus the calorific pastries or crêpes Suzette.

At lunchtime you can have a complete meal (soup, dessert, and beverage) with a main course of pork filet provençale for only $3.95. The little front room serves as a cafe where you can get good sandwiches, but best of all, simply scrumptious french toast for breakfast, or if you prefer, two eggs with bacon plus good thick toast, fried potatoes, and coffee for $2.20. This section only is open from 6 a.m. to 3 a.m. Tuesday to Saturday, from 8 a.m. on Sunday.

Regular restaurant hours are from 11:30 a.m. to 2:30 p.m. Tuesday to Saturday, 6 to 11 p.m. Tuesday to Friday, 6 p.m. to midnight Saturday, and 6 to 10 p.m. Sunday.

Set in a Victorian house at 138 rue Wellington **Oncle Tom** (tel. 819/771-1689) is the place to go for that intimate dinner. Inside, candy-stripe wallpaper provides the backdrop for heavy drapes, stained glass, one or two gilt-framed pieces of art, and French provincial chests in the downstairs dining areas. Upstairs, you can settle into a cozy little alcove amid a warm rose and burnt-orange decor.

The cooking is as classic as the decor: frog legs provençale ($9.50), entrecôte au poivre ($12.50); for starters, the terrine du chef and the escargots au parfum d'ail ($3.60) are both excellent choices. Save room for the enticing French pastries or the mousse au Tia Maria, both around $2.

Open noon to 2:30 p.m. and 6 to 10:30 p.m. Monday to Friday, 6 to 10:30 p.m. on Saturday.

Greek

Knossos, 509 Blvd. St-Joseph (tel. 819/771-4669), can sometimes be filled in the wee hours with a whirling, singing crowd of Greek revelers, dancing to the sounds of the guitar and balalaika amid brilliant red tables set against white stucco walls.

Such excitement may well follow a meal that might begin with stuffed vine leaves ($1.50), or more exotically with octopus in vinegar ($2.75), and continue with delicious moussaka, lamb shish kebab, or souzoukakia (from $4.50 to $6). Greek coffee and some galaktoboureko, both 80¢, will round out such a meal, and a little ouzo will set your feet tripping onto and over the small dance floor.

Open Tuesday to Sunday from 5 p.m. to 3 a.m.

Italian

For first-rate Italian food, people hurry to **Da Parisi,** 24 rue Eddy (tel. 819/776-5531). Here, in a large, comfortable stuccoed room decorated with brilliant pictures of Italy, you'll find an extensive array of Italian fare. There are seven soups alone to choose from, and an impressive list of appetizers—the antipasto makes an excellent choice. Various spaghetti and fettucine dishes plus cannelloni and lasagne are all from $4 to $5, while the specialties—scaloppine francesca, marsala, Siciliana, and so on, are only $2 more. Desserts include the usual spumoni plus a delicious cassata au rhum and tarte à l'orange ($1.50).

The lilting refrains of Neapolitan and Latin American songs will entertain you through the evening, thanks to the strolling guitarist. At lunchtime you can get a complete meal of roast beef soup or salad, dessert, and beverage for only $4.25.

TWO SPECIAL QUÉBEC CHOICES: L'Echelle de Jacob, 27 Blvd. Lucerne, Aylmer, Québec (tel. 819/684-1040), is currently the talk of the town and one of the most popular Ottawa area restaurants. And it's not surprising, for it is truly a delightful spot. Ex-teachers Peter Brice and Daniel Lepage, who journeyed to Paris to learn the art of cooking, have created an authentic French inn filled with antiques which they brought back from France.

The small (only 16 tables) dining room, set not surprisingly upstairs, has a warm rustic air created by beamed ceiling, natural stone walls, and candlelight burnishing the oak chairs and china-filled breakfronts. Simplicity is the keynote here, where even the menu is handwritten. It might contain such enticing appetizers as marinated shrimp and a short selection of entrees such as chicken stuffed with ham and cheese, steak au poivre, or roulade of sole stuffed with crab and mushroom sauce, ranging from $7 to $10. A succulent roast suckling pig is available on Saturdays only. For dessert you might try such treats as green figs in their own syrup, parfaits, and a variety of seasonal fruit dishes.

If you have one chance to splurge, do try and visit. It's a little difficult to find, but worth it. From Ottawa, drive over the Champlain Bridge and make a sharp left immediately off the bridge. Drive about 2½ miles to the first cluster of buildings and pull into the parking lot on the left. The restaurant (there's a tiny inn sign hanging) is in the old stone building farthest from the road. From Hull, take Blvd. Tache and turn left on Vanier Rd. (just past the ChâteauGay Motel) and follow the previous instructions.

Open Tuesday to Saturday from 6:30 to 10 p.m. Reservations are essential, and should be made well in advance.

Unless you knew about the **Auberge Le Mileu de Monde,** rue Principale, Limbour (tel. 819/827-2112), you'd drive right past this unpretentious suburban-looking low white house set a little way back off the road. Inside are several warm wood-paneled dining areas and simple brown-checked tablecloths on sturdy tables. The food is exquisite. You can either order à la carte or else take advantage of the table d'hôte dinner that might offer a choice of celery or cauliflower soup, followed by an entrecôte béarnaise, fruit salad au kirsch, and tea or coffee, for $14.50 ($2 less if you choose duck à l'orange).

Probably, the best time to sample some of the cuisine without busting your budget is to enjoy the lunchtime fare, from $4.75 to $5.50, for a whole meal that might include such main dishes as perch provençale or lapin à la moutarde.

Open 11:30 a.m. to 2:30 p.m. and 6 to 10:30 p.m. Tuesday to Friday, 6 to 10 p.m. on Saturday, and 6 to 9 p.m. on Sunday.

To get there, take Hwy. 5 out of Hull. Exit at the Pont Alonzo-Wright and follow the signs for the bridge. Once over the bridge, turn left and it's a mile up the road on the left-hand side.

Now let's look at the restaurant offerings of Ottawa itself.

DOWNTOWN WEST—MODERATELY PRICED: First, let's discover a few Canadian and steakhouse places.

Many is the Ottawan who swears by **Al's Steakhouse,** 327 Elgin St. (tel. 233-7111), especially for its prime rib. It's a warm, inviting place where the low lighting flatters the cedar ceiling, the velour banquettes, the cane-seated armchairs, and the waterfall and tiny fish pond. The delicious charcoal-broiled steaks are brought sizzling and juicy to your table—from $6.25 for a rib to $13.95 for a 22-ounce T-bone. Shish kebab and pepper steak round out the menu, along with an eclectic collection of hors d'oeuvres (from chopped chicken liver and pickled herring to snails) and fresh pies and gâteaux for dessert.

From noon to 3 p.m. you can benefit from Al's lunch special—a small filet mignon served with mushroom caps, accompanied by a tossed green salad, french fries or a baked potato, and beverage.

Open noon to 1 a.m. Monday to Saturday, to 10 p.m. on Sunday.

At the **Tiffany,** 64 Queen St., only 250 paces from the arts center (tel. 235-0426), a plush atmosphere prevails created by (you guessed) 33 original Tiffany lamps, heavily carved antique furniture, and two huge stained-glass window murals.

The food consists primarily of steaks and seafood including such complex dishes as prawns Marseillaise—jumbo shrimps sauteed with chives and tomato, flamed with Pernod and white wine sauce, and served on rice—plus the usual offerings from the broiler priced from $6.75 to $13.95. Lunchtime entrees fall into the $4 to $6 range.

Open noon to midnight Monday to Saturday, 5 to 10 p.m. on Sunday.

The **Old Vic Steakhouse and Tavern,** 39 Queen St. (tel. 232-1119) puts on a very good show—moderately priced meals in a pleasantly upbeat setting of bentwood cane chairs, butcher-block tables, and black-and-white photographs of Shakespearean scenes.

The menu-playbill presents the fare in acts. Act I might consist of onion soup or New England clam chowder; Act II would follow with either Hamlet, a $7.95 sirloin, or a thicker Falstaffian portion for $10.95. All the steaks are served with a potato and salad. From 4 to 7 p.m. there's a special Cassius cut ($5.95)—a top sirloin served with potato salad. Lunchtime features a $4.25 special and a selection of entrees all under $6.50.

Open 11 a.m. to 1 a.m. Monday to Friday, noon to 1 a.m. on Saturday, noon to 10 p.m. on Sunday.

You won't miss **Friday's Roast Beef House,** 150 Elgin St. (tel. 237-5353), a dramatic black and white Victorian house with dormer roof which was built in 1875 by Dr. (later Sir) James Alexander Grant, physician to the governors-general of Canada. The downstairs rooms are spacious, and the fine marble fireplaces, heavy Victorian newel post, and the thick rounded door and window trim attest to the status of its original owner. The dining rooms blend with the dignified atmosphere of the house—military pictures are on the walls, and table mats depicting hunting themes grace the tables. Upstairs there are two lounges decorated with heavy Victorian drapes, old London engravings, wing-back chairs, and tufted couches; in one lounge you can relax to the tinkling of piano music.

Steaks and prime rib (from $9.75 to $13.75) dominate the menu, which also lists a complete dinner of soup or juice, salad, prime rib with vegetables, Yorkshire pudding, Victorian chocolate cake, and coffee for only $11.75. Luncheon and late-night snacks are also available at reasonable prices.

Open from noon to midnight Monday to Friday, from 5 p.m. on Saturday.

The Mill, 555 Ottawa River Parkway (tel. 237-1311), on the Ottawa River, offers a delightful setting for a selection of beef cuts and one or two seafood dishes. Erected in the 1840s when Ottawa was a lusty, hell-raising lumber town, it now provides an outdoor dining terrace, an atrium dining room, and several other dining areas upstairs and down with a magnificent view over the river.

The fare is definitely traditional—prime rib plus Dublin Bay scampi, king crab, or filet of sole amandine, all from $7.50 to $12.95. All entrees include a large salad, an individual hot loaf, kosher-style pickles, potatoes, and Yorkshire pudding. At lunchtime, small portions of the same are available for half the prices. *Note:* This is a popular spot—even lunchtime reservations are required.

To get there, either take the no. 62 bus from the Public Archives Building to the Place de Portage, or else, more pleasant, walk through the gardens. Open noon to 2:30 p.m. and 5 to 11 p.m. Monday to Friday, 5 to 11:30 p.m. on Saturday, and noon to 10:30 p.m. on Sunday.

The National Arts Centre's **Le Restaurant** makes an excellent and relaxing spot for either a drink or dinner, and certainly for lunch where there's an excellent buffet offering a whole range of salads, plus one or two hot dishes and some superbly irresistible desserts, all for $5.95 from noon to 2:30 p.m. Monday to Friday. At dinner the fare ranges from $5.50 for an asparagus omelet to $13.95 for pepper steak Madagascar.

Open noon to 2:30 p.m. Monday to Friday, and 6 p.m. to 1 a.m. Monday to Saturday.

French

A plush antique decor set in a historic town house makes **Café de la Bonne Fourchette,** 442 Gilmour St. (tel. 233-3661), the only downtown spot for elegant French dining. Madame, who has been here for 12 years, brought from Belgium the stunning silver and china collection which is now housed in elegant breakfronts. Tables are intimately lit by candelabra and gilt-framed oils grace the walls. Such is the appropriate setting for a table d'hôte dinner that might have as its main course rabbit Flemish style with prunes, veal marengo, veal brains with butter and capers (all around $13.75), including soup, vegetable, and dessert. Or you can order à la carte—lobster newburg ($13.25) or tournedos aux champignons ($11.25). At lunchtime there's a full menu with entrees in the $6 to $10 range.

Open 11:30 a.m. to 2 p.m. and 6 to 10 p.m. Monday to Thursday, 5:30 to 10 p.m. on Friday and Saturday.

A far cry from the traditional decor associated with French cuisine—that's **Willy's,** 356 McClaren St. (tel. 233-7777), which consists of a downstairs wine bar and an upstairs restaurant, located in a red brick house with a neon sign in the window.

It's a uniquely personal restaurant, run by one of Ottawa's most colorful characters—Willy herself—who would have no trouble getting into Studio 54 in New York. She is quite likely to greet you decked out imaginatively in a wonderful blue-purple-orange combination. The decor exhibits the same flair with stuffed satin lips of all hues, from lurid pink to blue, stuck around the walls, paisley couches and rich blue-puce chairs in the downstairs wine bar, which offers the finest selection of wines in the city. Upstairs the mood continues with brown lips and upturned parasols, oak furniture, and several separate dining areas. The atmosphere is distinctly casual, even to the point of having handwritten on the wall "Welcome to Willys. Come on in. Bar downstairs. Restaurant upstairs."

The food is good and has the same unique quality, the menu listing such appetizers as green eggs (hard-boiled eggs stuffed with capers and anchovies and served with sauce, $1) and Nell Gwynne (tomato and Stilton tart, $2). Main courses offer you a choice of Anita's Folly (filet marinated in orange juice, coriander, and garlic $11) and "Mary had a little sautee of lamb with mushrooms, onions, garlic, wine, etc., with tomato ($7.50"). When you reach the final admonition "coffee, tea, etc., as always, sometimes available for a price!" you know this is a very personalized place. As with all such places, strong personalities can cause strong reactions!

Open noon to 1 a.m. Monday to Saturday, until 10 p.m. Sunday.

Classical red, white, and blue decor establishes the mood at **La Parisienne,** 196 Laurier Ave. West (tel. 238-7759). Red and white leather chairs, and modern French posters complete the setting for some reasonably priced French cuisine. There's an $8.50 table d'hôte which includes soup, plat du jour, dessert, and coffee, or else you can choose from the à la carte menu which features such dishes as boeuf bourguignon ($9.50) or coquilles St-Jacques. For a real dessert treat there are strawberry crêpes ($8 for two) or less expensive, the crème caramel ($1.50).

Open noon to midnight Monday to Saturday.

Hungarian

There's no doubting you're in a **Little Hungarian Village,** 164 Laurier Ave. West (tel. 238-2827), when you see the gaily dirndled waitresses, hear the stirring gypsy music, and look around at the cuckoo clocks and brightly painted wood and ceramics in this cozy cheerful spot.

Here you can start with a cold cherry, cabbage, or goulash soup ($2.25) or any of the appetizers such as Russian egg à la casino, pickled herring, cabbage roll, smoked sausage—all around $3. Entrees are all priced at $7.25—goulash, Stroganoff, pot roast, cabbage rolls—except for the true delicacy of suckling pig served with red cabbage ($13.75). Save some room for those delicious apple, cherry, or cheese strudels ($1.75), or else the palacinta ($3.25). And on the way out, add your name and comments to those that already cover the entryway walls.

Open 11:30 a.m. to midnight Monday to Friday, 4:30 p.m. to midnight on Saturday, 4 to 10 p.m. on Sunday.

Italian

As far as Italian restaurants go, **La Roma,** 673 Somerset St. West at Bronson Ave. (tel. 234-8244), is one of my favorites primarily because of the reasonably priced first-class fare. It's not especially decorous—heavy red velour drapes, simple wooden chairs, and green tablecloths, a mural of the Spanish Steps and another of the Castel St. Angelo, and the usual Italian musical background, but it's convivial—the kind of place you might fall into warm conversation with someone at the next table.

There's plenty to choose from: seven hors d'oeuvres including green asparagus with pimento, hard-boiled egg and tomato ($2.95), and sweetbreads with wine, prosciutto, and mushrooms ($4.75); six soups; and a marvelous array of delicious spaghettis—with tomato sauce, chicken livers, green peppers, and mushrooms, or with tomato, anchovies, olives, and hot chilies—all between $5 and $6. Then there are the seafood and meat specialties: ossobuco milanese, veal piccata (both $6.50), and a host of others, most under $8.

This is a popular place, so you might have to wait on line. Reservations accepted only for six or more. Open 11:30 a.m. to 2:30 p.m. and 4:30 p.m. to midnight Monday to Saturday; 4:30 to 10 p.m. on Sunday.

Light and airy **Alfredo's Terrace,** Sparks St. Mall (tel. 233-1183), has in addition to its plants a full complement of grape and chianti bottles. Stucco walls and green placemats with orange-seated chairs provide a strangely pleasant setting for an assortment of Italian fare which includes the regular appetizers, soups, and pastas (in the $3.75 to $5 range), plus such specialties as saltimboca alla romana ($6.75), chicken cacciatore, and stuffed trout (both $5.75).

Open 11 a.m. to 11 p.m. Monday to Friday, from 5 to 11:30 p.m. on Saturday. It's especially nice in summer when the restaurant overflows into a sidewalk cafe where you can sit and sip a Campari and soda while the crowds drift by.

You almost need shoulder pads to get into **Mamma Teresa's,** 281 Kent St. (tel. 263-3023), and it's no wonder when you look at the menu and see that for $7.95 you can get a full dinner that includes hors d'oeuvres, minestrone soup, chicken parmigiana with spaghetti, spumoni, and coffee or tea. There are several such, plus a whole host of antipasti, pastas, and main dishes to tempt the palate as well as the wallet. It doesn't really matter much about the neighborhood Italian decor, with red and white or black checked tablecloths and wine-bottle candelabras, because you can hardly see it for the people.

The veal dishes—with ham and cheese, vermouth sauce and olives, parmigiana, marsala, pizzaiola—are all under $7, most under $6. Most of the pastas are under $4, while there are some more expensive items, such as the sirloin steak pizzaiola at $9.25. For dessert take the smooth zabaglione ($3) or the delicious cheesecake ($1.50). You should by this time be eminently satisfied.

Open 11 a.m. to 11 p.m. Monday to Friday, 5 p.m. to midnight on Saturday, and 4 to 10 p.m. on Sunday.

Japanese

Visitors approach the downstairs dining room over stepping stones to find a delightful series of anterooms with sliding partitions (shoji) at **Suisha Gardens,** 208 Slater St. (tel. 236-9002). It's a very pretty place to enjoy traditional Japanese fare. Outside, a waterwheel turns to the strains of Oriental music, while inside the rooms are decorated tastefully with authentic Japanese artifacts—fans, stone lanterns, a samurai sword, a parasol used for the tea ceremony, and even a fearsome lion mask used to welcome the New Year.

Sashimi, sunomono, shrimp tempura, and yakitori make up the appetizers (from $2.95 to $4.25) which you can then follow with a choice of various tempura or teriyaki dishes (from $7 to $9), as well as sukiyaki ($11.75) and shabu-shabu ($12.75). Or if you prefer, there are several combination dinners such as the Royal, consisting of soup, salad, tempura appetizer, and suisha-yaki, plus dessert and tea ($11.95). At lunchtime all the dishes are under $5.

Open 11:30 a.m. to 2:30 p.m. and 4:30 to 11 p.m. Monday to Friday, 4:30 to 11 p.m. on Saturday, and 4:30 to 10 p.m. on Sunday.

At **Japanese Village,** 170 Laurier Ave. West (tel. 236-9519), you can watch the chefs dramatically cook your meal at one of the 11 teppan tables. The decor is restrained—a showcase of samurai swords over the bar, and some fans, ceremonial dolls, lanterns, and ceramics.

Here, everything is served as a dinner. You start with some really delicately seasoned shabu-shabu soup and yaki-yaki shrimp. Then you can choose from eight entrees ranging from $8.95 for chicken teriyaki to $15.95 for lobster teppan style. It's a sizzling experience that you can top off with a refreshing sherbet or ice cream and some Japanese tea. At lunchtime most of the dishes are under $5.

Open noon to 2 p.m. and 5 to 10:30 p.m. Monday to Friday, 5 to 10:30 p.m. on Saturday, and 5 to 10 p.m. on Sunday.

Seafood

Appropriately enough the **Three Caravels,** 340 Elgin St. (tel. 233-1244), serves some really tasty seafood in some very Spanish-flavored surroundings. Downstairs on the ground floor you'll find three stuccoed rooms, one with a lovely high cathedral-style ceiling, and each separated by Spanish-style arches and wrought-iron work. Cane armchairs and bright red or white tablecloths complete the decor.

From the appetizers you might select a fresh oyster stew ($4.50) or a Spanish fish soup ($3.25), or more modestly the mussels vinaigrette ($2.50).

Although there are a few meat dishes, you'd do better to stick with such specialties as the zarzuella catalana (whole live lobster, filet of sole, filet of perch, mussels, clams, and king crab, marinated in mushrooms, wine sauce au gratin, and béchamel sauce, and served with rice at $26 for two) or any of the more modest fishes—trout, perch, salmon steak, or halibut (all under $9). At lunchtime you can enjoy a shrimp Louisiana with soup and dessert for only $4.75.

Upstairs, there's a very tastefully furnished lounge-disco with art deco design fabric couches, mirrored walls, and a good sound system. A comfortable spot for meeting friends. Open noon to midnight daily.

DOWNTOWN WEST—BUDGET DINING: First, one or two Chinese eateries.

Chinese

Local aficionados of Peking- and Shanghai-style cuisine are well acquainted with **Pine Tree Village,** 354 Elgin St. (tel. 232-6126), a small and basically decorated restaurant. The only real bow to decor is a carpet. But the food is good, and cheap. There are six soups to choose from, the most interesting being Chinese radish and pork ($2.50) enough for two or three, piping hot-and-sour soup, and fishballs and vermicelli.

Some of the other specialties include shrimps with sizzling rice (shrimps with green peppers, mushrooms, and bamboo shoots, with tomato and sweet red sauce) and imperial shrimps, cooked with a hot-and-spicy sauce and stir-fried with small green onions and diced ginger root (both $4.35). The standard chop suey, chow mein, and sweet-and-sour dishes are also available, along with a dinner for two for as little as $7.95.

Open noon to 2:30 p.m. and 4:30 p.m. to 1 a.m. Monday to Saturday, and noon to midnight on Sunday.

Shanghai, 651 Somerset St. West (tel. 233-4001), offers a little more comfort and decor—Chinese wall paneling, lanterns, red tablecloths, and stucco walls—plus some very good Chinese cuisine, which may be why it's popular with some prominent government figures.

Soups include Chinese melon ($1.25) and Chinese greens (95¢), which you might follow with one of the more dashing specialties such as gee bow guy (breast of chicken rolled around sweet ham, green onions, and almonds, covered with rice paper, and deep-fried in peanut oil, $5.75, steamed pickerel served with green onions and their own sauce, or beef or barbecued pork with bean curd and oyster sauce (both under $4.75). Some Canadian dishes and regular dishes like beef with broccoli (all between $3.50 and $5) flesh out the menu.

Open 11 a.m. to 12:45 a.m. Monday to Thursday, 11 a.m. to 2:45 a.m. on Friday and Saturday; and 11 a.m. to 11 p.m. on Sunday.

At the **Lantern House,** 175 Lisgar St. at Elgin (tel. 238-4618), Szechuan and Cantonese specialties share the limelight. Try the fried beef with ginger in hot pot, the pa jin bean curd in hot pot, or the fried beef with oyster sauce (all around $6). The sesame shrimps are an extravagance at $7.25, but worth it. Special dinners for two ($8.50) are also available, along with the usual expected Chinese fare in a modestly decorated room with brown tablecloths and Chinese lanterns.

Open 11 a.m. to 10 p.m. Sunday to Tuesday, to 11 p.m. on Wednesday and Thursday, to 1 a.m. on Friday and Saturday.

Italian

Tell me, seriously, where can you get a smooth, tasty cappucino for the honest sum of 60¢? At **Ciccio's,** 330 Preston St. (tel. 232-1675), a tiny down-home neighborhood place with red tablecloths where Italian men gather in the afternoons to sip a glass of wine and exchange their vibrant opinions.

Leone Eramo, the owner, is a passionate sports fan, which accounts for the team photos of Milan's soccer team and other baseball and hockey stars, relieved only by a map of Italy. In the back there's a small room with wine-bottle candles on the tables. One young man left his wedding reception and brought his still-dressed-in-white bride here to dine—such loyalties and sentiment does this warm, friendly place conjure.

The prices help—specials change daily but will read something like chicken cacciatore served with bread and butter and a glass of wine for $4.50—and the same goes for gnocchi, ossobuco, stuffed peppers, or Italian sausages. Most of the pastas are under $4, and there's a selection of sandwiches.

Open 11 a.m. to 11 p.m. Monday to Saturday.

Similarly friendly family-style dining takes place over at **Sorentos,** 326 Elgin St. (tel. 234-7896). There are two rooms, each festooned with grapes (they're even painted on the walls), chianti bottles, and murals of Sorrento and southern Italy.

Owner Mike Chi had a nightclub in Argentina for years before coming here to offer good honest limited fare—veal parmigiana, canneloni, chicken cacciatore, lasagne, and so on, all under $6. For that family calorific feast you can enjoy any one of the several pizzas—from $6 to $8.25 for large ones.

Open 10 a.m. to 1 p.m. Monday to Saturday, 10 p.m. on Sunday.

Turkish

Don't be put off by the unprepossessing exterior, set off by a large Coca-Cola sign, of **Topkapi,** 209 Kent St. at Gloucester (tel. 232-5992), a family-run place, whose 12 tables are sure to be packed, often with civil servant moguls. Inside there's a small homey room full of tables with red checked tablecloths, plain chairs, a few Turkish artifacts, and a rather touristy-looking tapestry.

The owners will welcome you and immediately make you feel at home while offering you an array of Turkish specialties—homemade soup with a base of lemon and mint (60¢), cucumber and yogurt salad, doner kebab ($3.25), pilic sis (chicken grilled on a skewer with onions, tomatoes, green pepper, and mushrooms), and other dishes, all $5. At these prices you can afford to have a bottle of Turkish wine and top off with baklava (60¢) and Turkish coffee.

Open 11:30 a.m. to 2 p.m. Monday to Friday, and 5 to 10 p.m. Monday to Saturday.

Soups, Salads, Etc.

A stock market ticker-tape-style electronic advert flashes in the window of the **Brokerage,** 320 Queen St. (tel. 238-5213), a light and airy and very popular lunch spot located in the ground floor of a high-rise office building. Butcher-block tables and greenery abound, and even the menu is a delicate shade of green, a fetching background for the salads, sandwiches, and desserts displayed at this healthy, happy place.

A vast bowl of crunchy romaine lettuce, green pepper, spinach, celery, red onion, string beans, broccoli, cauliflower, cucumbers, and a sprinkle of sesame seeds is just one of the huge imaginative salads available for $3.35 (large). Or you can opt for a hot dog on a whole-wheat bun with diced tomato, diced onion, and strips of swiss cheese; another exciting sandwich and homemade soup; plus some dangerously tempting desserts—pies, cakes, ice creams, and a delicious frozen strawberry yogurt sundae—all under $3.

Open noon to 7:30 p.m. Monday to Thursday, to 9 p.m. on Friday, to 5 p.m. Saturday.

For soups, sandwiches, quiches, and delicious pies and pastries (linzer torte, for instance) to take into the park or out on a boat in the canal, stop in at **Les Gourmets,** a takeout place just north of Laurier St. West on O'Connor. Open Monday to Friday from 7 a.m. to 4 p.m.

Just two doors away at 113 O'Connor is **Kars,** your basic coffeeshop, where you can get two eggs, toast, ham or bacon, and coffee for only $1.15.

DOWNTOWN EAST—MODERATELY PRICED: They've all been here, or so the photographs show—Ted Heath, Luciano Pavarotti, John Diefenbaker, Tom Jones, Engelbert Humperdinck, and Liberace—to this warm log-cabin-style spot called **The Place Next Door,** 320 Rideau St. (tel. 232-1741). What's it next door to? Nates, a famous Ottawa deli institution. Here, though, you'll find hearty, filling char-broiled treats—rib, New York, filet mignon, from $6.95 to $21.95 for a chateaubriand bouquetière for two. Seafood choices are also available, and you can kick off with anything from pickled herring and chopped liver to artichoke hearts, all around $2.75. There are also plenty of bargains around at lunchtime.

Open noon to 1 a.m. Monday to Saturday, to 10 p.m. on Sunday.

Although the **Hayloft,** 200 Rideau St. at Waller St. (tel. 232-7161), specializes in large parties, you can still get a very good, reasonably priced steak or seafood dinner here in a warm convivial atmosphere enhanced by the strawboatered friendly waiters.

The several rooms are all large and have squared beams, barnboard floors, and a combination of candlelight and imitation gaslight falling onto the Pennsylvania Dutch hex signs scattered around. Salad bar and coffee are included with all entrees which run from $6.95 for a grilled boneless chicken breast to $11.45 for an 18-ounce New York sirloin.

Open Monday to Saturday from noon to 2:30 p.m., Monday to Thursday from 5 to 11 p.m., Friday and Saturday from 5 p.m. to midnight, and from 5 to 10 p.m. on Sunday.

You don't exactly go to the **Marble Works,** 14 Waller St. just off Rideau (tel. 235-6764), for the gourmet cuisine but rather for a hearty evening's entertainment that may even burst into communal singing of the good old songs. Located in an old stone building originally built in 1866 that has served variously as a stable, marble workshop, and furniture warehouse, the place is now decorated with Victorian oak chairs, plants in the windows, and etchings of old Ottawa. It's famous for its Canadian feast.

Tie on your bib and dip your fingers into a pile of chicken, steak on a skewer, pork ribs, lamb chops, corn on the cob, breaded mushrooms, onion rings, potatoes, grapes, and nuts, plus soup and a loaf of bread—all served on a wooden platter for $7.95. Other entrees range from liver for $4.75 to prime ribs for $9.50. Whatever you choose, a wandering minstrel will stir your spirit —and the kids will just love to get in there and eat with their fingers.

Open 11:30 a.m. to 2:30 p.m. Monday to Friday, 5 to 10 p.m. Sunday to Thursday, to 11:30 p.m. on Friday and Saturday.

Japanese

For truly authentic Japanese cuisine, served in the proper manner with a koto musical background, there's only one place to go and that's **Yakītori House,** 544 Rideau St. (tel. 233-1850). Two Western-style tables are the only sign of compromise.

All dinners run from appetizer, soup, and rice, to tea. Appetizers include the usual sashimi and sunomono, plus takosu (sliced octopus with special sauce) and kanisu (snow crabmeat cocktail). Try the soybean paste soup. Then you can choose from various dinners. The Zen dinner is an especially exciting conglomeration of shrimp and vegetable tempura, deep-fried salmon, scallops, and ocean perch, all served on a Japanese tray for $13. The sukiyaki and various teriyaki dinners are between $8 and $10. For dessert, try a carrot sherbet ($1).

Open 5 to 10:30 p.m. Monday to Thursday, to 11 p.m. on Friday and Saturday, to 10 p.m. on Sunday.

DOWNTOWN EAST—BUDGET DINING: Most budget sections begin with a Chinese restaurant or two, and this one is no exception.

Chinese

The **Golden Dragon,** 176 Rideau St. (tel. 237-2333), has been in business 19 years, serving Ottawa some of the best and most various Chinese food ever. It's a large place, divided up into areas by partitions and decorated in the usual basic Chinese style, but somehow with more warmth and comfort—perhaps it's the red walls, Chinese panels, and the red tablecloths.

There are two menus here. Make sure to ask for the Chinese menu—a red one—not the black one, which lists only chow mein, chop suey, and other more Westernized dishes. Then you can go wild and choose from 18 soups (ever had bean cake and preserved turnip soup, or mustard green and salt egg with sliced pork soup?—both $3.75). Other exciting flavors follow—fried beef with ginger and green onions, diced chicken with kung bo and chili, Szechuan style (both $5.25). Real specialties like steamed doré fish are priced according to size. At lunchtime you can order a special combination plate of basic dishes for as little as $2.95.

On weekends make reservations. Open Monday to Saturday from 11 a.m. to midnight, until 10 p.m. on Sunday. And don't miss the Sunday dim sum from 11 a.m. to 3 p.m.

Farther along Rideau you'll find the **New Star,** 496 Rideau St. (tel. 236-1669), where arborite tables, turquoise plastic chairs matched with red flocked wallpaper and crystal lamps still do not alter the family atmosphere—the children might even be sitting and doing their homework while father watches the TV.

The food is good and plentiful, from the bowls of hot-and-sour soup ($3) to the steamed chicken with Chinese winter mushrooms ($4.95), or the fried chicken balls with black bean sauce ($3.85). Everything on the menu, in fact is under $5. This place has been around for 20 years, which says something about the quality and the price ratio.

Open noon to 2:30 a.m. and noon to 1:30 a.m. on Sunday. Good dim sum here also on Sundays.

Across the street, **Emerald Gardens** (tel. 234-3322) has a little better decor than most of Ottawa's other Chinese restaurants, and some very good food. Most of the meat dishes are all under $4—fried chicken with black mushrooms in oyster sauce, diced pork with cashew nuts, for example. More exciting fare includes tom so fish (fresh boneless codfish with papaya, pineapple, and ginger, $5.50) and hoho scallops (fresh scallops with snow peas, water chestnuts, and seasonal greens, $5.25).

Open noon to 1 a.m. Monday to Friday, 11 a.m. to 1 a.m. on Saturday and Sunday. Dim sum are especially good on weekends.

The **Chinese Village,** 415 Rideau St. (tel. 233-6947), is perhaps the only such Ottawa establishment that has shown a real concern for its decor—a ceremonial Chinese robe, showcased Chinese artifacts including ivory figures, a laughing Buddha sculpture by the bar, Chinese paintings, and elegant brown tablecloths.

Emphasis is on Mandarin cuisine, with such dishes as pork in Shanghai sauce ($4.25) and woa mein (Chinese stew filled with fish balls, barbecued pork, chicken, and shrimps, $3.95). For dessert you can try what is called toffee apple or toffee banana—wedges of apple or banana coated with sesame seeds and candied in a sweet sauce, then hardened in ice water before serving.

Open noon to 1 a.m. Monday to Thursday, to 3 a.m. on Friday and Saturday, until midnight on Sunday.

Crêpes

Choose from over 40, sweet or savory, at **La Crêpe de France,** 263 Rideau St. (tel. 235-2858), a cute little place with two small rooms each with checkered tables. Crêpes range from $2 to $3.75 (for one with tomatoes, sausages, and onions). The raspberry, cherry, or peach crêpes make a super nightcap after a visit to the Little Theatre, right around the corner.

This one's unlicensed. Open 11 a.m. to midnight Monday to Thursday, to 1 a.m. on Friday and Saturday, and from 10 a.m. to 11 p.m. on Sunday.

Deli

An Ottawa institution—that's **Nates,** 316 Rideau St. (tel. 236-9696), where you can get what has to be the cheapest breakfast in town—95¢ for eggs and sausage. Then there are the really good things: cheese blintzes, cheese bagels, potato latkes, meat kreplach, boiled potato varenikes with stuffed kishke (all under $3.50), plus a whole host of sandwiches under $2 (pastrami included, of course) and a bagel and nova with cream cheese ($3.95).

Just as the sign says, "You don't have to be Jewish to enjoy Nates." And you don't have to have low lights and tablecloths to fress well. Open 7:30 a.m. to 2 a.m. Monday to Friday, 8 a.m. to 3 a.m. on Saturday, and 8 a.m. to 2 a.m. on Sunday.

Indian

In the foyer of **Le Pousse-Pousse,** 408 Rideau St. (tel. 238-1204), you'll find a magnificent red Indian garden umbrella with tassles and some Indian art, and probably a crowd of people being greeted at the door. Inside, the low-lit dining area is warm, comfortable—modern pine upholstered furniture, orange-brown lampshades over the tables—and has a certain elegance. Upstairs, there's a lounge bar with a wood-burning fireplace blazing in winter and soft couches to relax on either pre- or postdinner.

Dal soup, samosa, or shrimp pakoras are some of the dishes you could tease your appetite with, before moving onto the tandoori specialties and curries—the murgh shahnaz (chicken marinated in yogurt, pounded ginger, and garlic, and roasted, $5.50) or lamb, beef, chicken, or vegetable curry from $3.75 to $4.75.

Open 11 a.m. to 3 p.m. and 5:30 to 11 p.m. Tuesday to Sunday. No reservations accepted.

The decor is less plush at **Shahzan,** 111 Mann Ave. (tel. 235-7759)—one or two Indian-style arches, some brass plates on the walls—but the Pakistani food is really good and cheap. The menu offers an interesting selection of curries, biryanis, pullaoos, and tandoori dishes. The murgh kharamasala (chicken pieces cooked with onion, garlic, and whole Oriental spices, $3.25) is delicious, and so too is the specialty murgh korma shahi (chicken seasoned with yogurt, onion, garlic, and Oriental mild spices, $3.25). For a change, why not spice up the rice with a pullaoo mutton dehlvi (rice cooked in a special stock of lamb and Oriental spices, $3)? And don't forget those fantastic Indian bread accompaniments.

For dessert there's an exotic shahi tukra—a slice of bread fried until golden brown and garnished with almond powder, milk, and silver leaf, served chilled or warm ($1.50).

Open 11 a.m. to 11 p.m. Tuesday to Sunday.

Malaysian

People in the know go to the **Tropical Dining Lounge,** 599 Sussex Dr. (tel. 233-9388), not for the aesthetics—plywood paneling, arborite tables, and plain kitchen chairs—but for the food, the prices, and the rijsttafel, served every Friday and Saturday. For $9.45 per person, it includes 14 courses of such dishes as satay, curry beef, sambal shrimp, chicken lemak, and fried banana.

On the à la carte menu, most dishes are under $5: satay ($3.95), mee goreng and nasi goreng, Malaysian sweet-and-sour tomato shrimp or fish. Desserts include a banana donut, and you can experience drinking sugarcane juice.

Open noon to 2 p.m. and 5 to 10 p.m. Monday to Friday, and 5 to 10 p.m. on Saturday and Sunday.

Middle Eastern

Cedars of Lebanon murals and bright banners create some atmosphere at **Lebanese Village,** 538 Rideau St. (tel. 238-1108), a welcome haven for the lover of hummus, falafel, and other Middle Eastern goodies, most around $3.

The kibbi bi sanieh (baked lamb, onion, and pignola nuts between layers of raw kibbi and salad) is delicious, and so are the stuffed grape leaves (both $5.95). Don't forget that thick, smooth coffee, and honey-sweet baklava to finish. Lunch specials come as cheap as $3.50 for chicken and lamb dishes.

Open 11 a.m. to 1 a.m. Monday to Saturday, to 10 p.m. on Sunday.

Oriental

At **Asia House,** 460 Rideau St. at Chapel (tel. 234-8398), the welcome signs are everywhere: outside in the window and inside on the placemats, and certainly in the warm smiles of owner Keng Chiam, who came from Singapore to study at Ottawa University, but decided to open her own restaurant instead, serving delicacies from China, Vietnam, Singapore, and Malaysia. The look is simple but warm, with plain red plastic chairs and red tablecloths, fringed lampshades, and a small bar at the back of the room.

You can start your meal with a 1000-year-old egg ($1.95) or one of the soups, and follow with one of the various curries, or some satay, or more unusual fried scallop, quail eggs, and carrot (all around $5). Full-course dinners that include appetizer, soup, dessert, and beverage start at $8.45 for a curry main course. Even more exciting, you can have the steamboat, a typical Singapore dish which includes shrimp, squid, beef, fish balls, and vegetables, all cooked ceremoniously at your table ($10.95).

Certainly, this is one of Ottawa's more unusual restaurants. Open noon to 11 p.m. Monday to Thursday, until midnight on Friday and Saturday.

BYWARD MARKET—MODERATELY PRICED: Going to the guillotine in Ottawa is not half as bad as it was in Paris at the turn of the 19th century, for at **La Guillotine,** 531 Sussex Dr. (tel. 236-8183), you can dine on good French cuisine without even having the prospect of an inflated bill hanging over your head. The atmosphere is very Parisian cafe: red banquettes, white bentwood chairs, and blue tablecloths, with one or two brightly be-postered Parisian kiosks. Just to complete the scene, Napoleon sits on one side of the room and Dr. Guillotine on the other.

At dinner, daily specials, such as beef bourguignon, veal marengo, coq au vin, and even couscous, are all under $10, and come with soup, salad, and beverage. Of the desserts I'd opt for the crème caramel or the vacherin, both around $1.50. Or else you can order à la carte from such dishes as rabbit in red wine sauce, quails à la Régence ($9.95), or ($1 more) tournedos béarnaise. Various crêpes, omelets, salads, and fish dishes complete the menu, plus, of course, the appetizers which include an assiette de charcuterie ($3.95).

The best choice at lunch is the daily special for $4.95—chicken or beef in white wine sauce, for example, plus soup or juice, salad, and beverage.

The popular French music adds greatly to the Parisian gaiety of this spot frequented by many an M.P., diplomat, and newsman, each probably wishing he was back under the bridges.

Open 11:30 a.m. to 10 p.m. Monday to Thursdays, to 10:30 p.m. on Friday, 5 to 10:30 p.m. on Saturday.

The atmosphere is a little more formal at **Le Jardin,** 127 York St. (tel. 238-1828), as befits its setting in a beautiful old Victorian gingerbread house. In summer you'll find a small terrace in front with tables topped by bright umbrellas; inside you'll find two small tastefully decorated rooms, with chintz fabric-covered walls (one with a fireplace), highlighted by antiques, greenery and fresh flowers, and among other things, a magnificent Gaspé quilt.

Owner Roy Bullock takes great care to select the freshest ingredients for his small menu which changes daily. At dinner you might choose from three or so hors d'oeuvres (perhaps avocado and shrimp or fowl liver pâté, $3.10) before selecting one of probably three main courses, including a meat, a fish, and fowl dish—filet of pork tenderloin with a peppercorn sauce ($11.50) or salmon with white wine and caper sauce ($12.50) served with the freshest of vegetables. Besides a crème caramel, desserts are sure to include some fresh fruit concoctions.

At lunchtime there's a small selection of quiches and crêpes (all under $4), and on Sundays, brunch (served between 11 a.m. and 3 p.m.) features kippered herring and oeufs Madelaine with smoked salmon, fresh-poached salmon, and white wine sauce, over an English muffin (both under $5).

Open noon to 3 p.m. and 6 to 10 p.m. Tuesday to Friday, 11 a.m. to 3 p.m. and 6 to 10 p.m. on Saturday and Sunday.

BYWARD MARKET—BUDGET DINING: **Daphne and Victor's,** 47 William St. (tel. 235-3881), is the kind of place that's always crowded with young and not-so-young people devouring really good burgers, salads, and other wholesome fare in two small but light and airy rooms with the current plants-and-brick look.

Daily specials, all under $5, are chalked on a blackboard while the regular fare consists of a selection of esoteric burgers (from $2.50) including a teriyaki specimen and a pecan burger made with a rich filling of pecans, almonds, and vegetables, topped with mornay sauce. Salads are a little less unusual—broccoli, or watercress and mushroom (under $2). For dessert there's good old-fashioned hot apple crumble and a super soft frozen-yogurt sundae with seasonal fresh fruits. On Sundays, stop in for the brunch—eggs Benedict with juice and coffee or tea ($3.75).

By the way, you can also dine upstairs in the William St. bars (more about them in the nightlife section).

Open 11:30 a.m. to 2 a.m. Monday to Friday, 10 a.m. to 2 a.m. on Saturday, to midnight on Sunday.

The **Old Fish Market,** 54 York St. (tel. 563-4954), seems to have found the magic formula for serving fresh fish in a simple way to the delight of the crowds who pack this place daily. The original Old Fish Market is in Toronto; Ottawa's is smaller but along the same lines, with a shellfish bar upstairs where you can sit and watch the chefs cleave oysters, clams, and mussels.

Downstairs, the two rooms bedecked with rope decoration, lobster pots, and other nautical regalia, feature fresh fish—haddock, black sea bass, snapper, porgies, rainbow trout—all under $7, plus a bouillabaise for $6.99 and a selection of chowders and seafood appetizers. Cheesecake and ice cream choices complete the dessert menu.

Open 11:45 a.m. to 2:30 p.m. Monday to Friday, 5:30 to 11 p.m. Monday to Thursday, until midnight on Friday and Saturday, and from 4 to 10 p.m. on Sunday. On Saturdays there's a special market-day breakfast served from 8:30 to 11 a.m., and on Sunday you can enjoy some finnan haddie, kippers, and omelets stuffed with crab for around $4 between 11 a.m. and 3 p.m.

Various other chains have clustered around the market—among them the **Old Spaghetti Factory,** 126 York St. (tel. 238-6441), specializing in spaghetti with different sauces, veal parmigiana, and a chicken dish (all under $6), and served among a vast assembly of Canadiana. Lunchtime brings forth burgers and subs under $3.

Open 11:30 a.m. to 2:30 p.m. Monday to Friday, 4 to 10 p.m. Monday to Thursday, 4 to midnight on Friday, noon to midnight on Saturday, and noon to 10 p.m. on Sunday.

Mother Tucker's, 61 York St. (tel. 238-6525), employs a slightly different formula in a warren of low-lit rooms hung with various wooden kitchen and farm implements. A dinner of chicken ($7.95) or deep-fried shrimp ($8.95) will include several treks to the salad bar (gloriously arrayed on a haywagon replica), fresh-baked bread, and dessert.

Open from 5 to 11 p.m. on weekdays, until midnight on Friday and Saturday, and from 4:30 to 11 p.m. on Sunday. No reservations are accepted.

THE GLEBE: The Glebe refers to the southern part of Ottawa, an area stretching from just north of the Queensway to the Rideau Canal and from Bronson Ave. to Bank St.

Chinese

Regarded by many as one of the best Chinese restaurants in Ottawa is **Wan Wah,** 1098 Bank St. (tel. 235-0670), a small and very simple place with arborite tables, plain furniture, and flocked wallpaper, but turning out some really excellent cuisine and a vast selection of it.

Choose from 12 soups and as many fried noodle dishes before moving into the sliced beef with oyster sauce or with ginger and green onion, the pork spare ribs with plum sauce, the fried duck webs with Chinese mushrooms, the bean curd dishes, and various congee dishes (all under $5). On Sundays dim sum are served from 11 a.m. to 3 p.m. This one is unlicensed.

Open 11 a.m. to 1 a.m. Monday to Thursday, until 2 a.m. Friday to Sunday.

Canadian

As the guy who runs the place puts it, "everyone from politicians to jailbirds" crams into **Patty's Place Pub,** 1070 Bank St. (tel. 235-1020), to raise a jug or two, tuck into some real fish and chips or Irish stew (both under $4), and listen to the stirring Irish ballads from long ago as rendered by a folksinger (resident Thursday to Saturday). Small, it's the kind of place where you're tossed into the fray and wind up having a good old time playing darts, rapping, singing, and wassailing. Real atmosphere requires little decor.

Open 11:30 a.m. to 1 a.m. Monday to Saturday, to 10 p.m. on Sunday.

Peppers, 360 Elgin, just north of Frank St. (tel. 236-5915), is the kind of small, two-room place where students like to hang out and read while they sip a coffee or a beer—it's that casual. One of the reasons why, of course, is the cheap food. Daily specials, including potatoes, vegetables, soup or juice, and bread and butter, are all under $4, while regular entrees are a little higher—$6.95 for pepper steak for example. Burgers and sandwiches served in pita bread make up the rest of the menu.

It's not fancy by any means, functioning as a 1960s-flavor coffeehouse cum entertainment center. The acrylic art on the walls is for sale; one wall is covered with apéritif labels; there are plants in the window but no carpet; the tables are arborite and the chairs plain. Rock or popular music provides the background sound for the young bohemian crowd.

There are usually some popular singers on Thursday, Friday, and Saturday nights. It's also quite famous for its weekend brunches, where all items are under $3.

Open 8 a.m. to 11 p.m. daily.

Greek

Many Greeks gather at the **Parthenon,** 589 Bank St. (tel. 232-3912), where they know they can get good honest Greek food and convivial Greek dancing. It's owned by two families, the Mandrapiliases and the Mimikopouloses, who will make you feel at home and take you on a tour of the kitchen, where with the chef's help you can select your dish. Stuffed zucchini, roast lamb with potatoes, moussaka, meatballs with egg and lemon, or lamb fricassee might be some of the dishes available. Such a dinner, including coffee, will cost $6.95. During and afterward you can capture the spirit of Greece in the music and dancing (from Tuesday to Saturday).

Open 11:30 a.m. to 1 a.m. Monday to Thursday, to 2 a.m. on Friday and Saturday, to 10 p.m. on Sunday.

Mexican

Despite the name **Mexicali Rosa's,** 895 Bank St., at Fifth Ave. (tel. 236-9499), the Southern Californian owners of this friendly place have taken pains to show that the food is derived more from the great southwest than south of the border. Walls are hung with old photographs of border country scenes, various artifacts, and wooden implements, cooking pots, and cornhusks suggesting pioneer days; and the music is more likely to be country and western than anything else.

The food still retains that Mexican flavor, however, with a selection of tacos, enchiladas, tostadas, burritos, and various combinations thereof (between $4.25 and $6.25), served with rice and beans.

Open 11:30 a.m. to 11 p.m. Monday to Saturday, to 9 p.m. on Sunday.

Middle Eastern

Bright-orange curtains and plants in the window draw passersby to **Kamals**, 845 Bank St. (tel. 234-5223), a friendly hangout where young student types and families both repair for good Middle Eastern fare, mixed with some American favorites—an eight-ounce hamburger with onion and vegetable ($3.50), for instance.

More interesting are the Lebanese-style sandwiches—shaivarma (lamb marinated in wine mixed with tomato, onion, and tahini sauce, $2.75) or the falafel—plus the entrees which include the usual shish kebab and something called shishtaouk (consisting of chicken cubes marinated in garlic and wine sauce, and served on rice).

Open 11 a.m. to 1 a.m. Monday to Saturday, to 10 p.m. on Sunday.

Across the street, pity the dromedary at **Camel Humps**, 840 Bank St. (tel. 232-7769), which specializes in Egyptian food. Photographs of ancient Egypt grace the walls. There's only one puzzling note in the decor—the chianti bottles around the small split-log bar (Africa begins at Rome?).

Lahm mashwie (roast beef served on Oriental rice and Egyptian salad combined with seasoning, $5.95) and kowffta tarbb (ground lamb, korendall, parsley, eggs, and spices, charcoaled and served with rice and salad, $8.50) are just two of the specialties, besides the usual falafel, etc. American-style sandwiches and steaks are also available.

This is also a good place to indulge in some exotic coffee like the délice du café—espresso, coffee ice cream topped with whipped cream, and a drop of cocoa ($1.50).

Open noon to midnight Monday to Saturday, until 10 p.m. on Sunday.

OTTAWA WEST—MODERATELY PRICED: The Green Valley, 1107 Prince of Wales Dr. (tel. 225-8770), is the kind of place that families repair to for nostalgic family affairs and for afternoon tea with scrumptious hot tea biscuits and toasted cinnamon buns. Its three conservatively attractive dining rooms, the tables finely appointed with linen, pretty china, and fresh flowers, overlook the experimental farm.

Here you can enjoy a complete dinner of vegetable soup, chicken Kiev with sherry wine sauce, pepper, squash, and potatoes, plus butterscotch cream pie and coffee, for $8.95, or else branch out into the more continental menu (frog legs, scaloppine marsala, around $10). Desserts include various liqueur parfaits, and peach Melba. Tea is served daily except Sunday from 2:30 to 4:30 p.m.

Open noon to 10 p.m. Monday to Saturday, until 9 p.m. on Sunday.

OTTAWA WEST—BUDGET DINING: Mostly international fare here.

Austrian

Tyrolean murals of the mountains form a natural backdrop for the waitresses in their pretty dirndls at the **Austrian Inn,** 278 Richmond Rd., near Churchill (tel. 722-1048), as they carry hearty Austrian fare to the green checkered tables. Owner Fred Eder dreamed of one day serving his country's authentic cuisine, and that is certainly what you find.

You can start your meal with some head cheese with onions, oil, and vinegar ($1.25), or any of the soups—leber knodl, potato, or goulash (each around $1.50). To follow, there are various schnitzels (priced from $5.95 to $7.95), Viennese and Hungarian goulash (both $4.95), several other specialties, and some seafood dishes. At lunchtime there are daily specials that might be a small schnitzel, cabbage rolls, or stuffed pepper (usually $3.25); there's also a short-order and sandwich menu. On Friday and Saturday evening jolly accordion music will help you on your way.

Open from 11 a.m. to midnight Monday to Saturday.

Canadian

Easy listening and easy singing is as much a part of **TJ's Speakeasy,** 91 Holland Ave., between Wellington and Scott Sts. (tel. 729-4765), as easy eating and easy paying. Owners John Stott and Tony Gilchrist are both young musicians and so there's folk music on Tuesday to Saturday nights from 9 p.m. If you've toted your guitar, Monday night is talent night. In summer the music is piped out to the patio.

Floral tablecloths, fringed lampshades, and walls bespattered with such homilies as "Good Humor Makes All Things Tolerable" set the casual scene in the small room for light, low-priced fare—hamburgers and sandwiches all under $3.

Open 11 a.m. to 1:30 a.m. Monday to Saturday, until 10 p.m. on Sunday.

Continental

Simply but tastefully decorated, the **Bistro,** 1268 Wellington St. (tel. 723-3111), reflects owner Les Lucas's theatrical interest with National Arts Center posters and costume renderings on the stucco walls. Tables are covered with blue striped tablecloths appointed with blue napkins and fresh flowers, and set under a blue-painted ceiling (the glitter upon it was inherited from the former denizens, who offered Mexican fare).

Here you can get some good continental fare at low prices—for instance, a tasty chicken cacciatore with braised celery and boiled potatoes for $4.

Open 6 a.m. to 10 p.m. Monday to Wednesday, to 1 a.m. Thursday to Saturday.

German

The **Cafe Black Forest,** 1323 Wellington St. (tel. 722-0659), is just what the name implies—an authentic Black Forest inn. The exterior looks like one, and inside the painted wood bar, the simple woody decor with beamed ceiling continues the theme. Upstairs are three dining rooms, each with red tablecloths on the tables and cane-backed chairs for seating. The menu comes encased in a beautiful hand-carved leather binding.

Dinner might begin with an egg salad with tomato ($1.95) or marinated herring ($2.10), and follow with a choice from several schnitzels ($5 to $7), Bavarian sausage with sauerkraut and potatoes ($3.65), or beef rouladen served with red cabbage and potatoes ($5.65).

The place started out as a pastry shop, and the rich and tempting pastries are still all made here—Black Forest cake, chocolate cake, strawberry torte—all 95¢. In summer you can sit out under an umbrellaed table.

Open noon to 2:30 p.m. and 5 to 10 p.m. daily.

Mexican

There's no doubting the origin of the food at **Pancho's,** 311 Richmond St. (tel. 722-8325). Owner Fanny Peschard used to run a restaurant in Mexico City before being lured to Ottawa by her family, where she continues to serve the cuisine of that sun-seared country even in the subzero temperatures of Ontario.

Here, among the stucco arches, on straw-seated chairs facing a bar with a terracotta tile roof, you can select from the sombrero-shaped menu a cool gazpacho to start, and follow with the camarones al ajillo (shrimps sauteed with garlic, chili, and olive oil), the real treat, mole poblano (both $5.75), or the more common combination plate containing an enchilada, taco, burrito, or tostada ($5.25).

For dessert try the ice cream cake with liqueur and cherries. On Saturday and Sunday, mariachis entertain.

Open 11:30 a.m. to 10 p.m. daily.

OTTAWA EAST—MODERATELY PRICED: There's not too much to signal that **Maxi Plate,** 320 McArthur Ave. (tel. 745-3995), is Czechoslovakian except for a couple of photographs and two costumed dolls on the bar. Then there's the homey, rustic decor and the menu: goulash with dumplings, sauerbraten, or pork chops à la Robert, prepared in a sauce with a subtle hint of anchovies, capers, and French mustard (all under $6.50); even more characteristic are the Czech country birds—lean pork chunks seasoned and roasted with onions in a nest of wine, sauerkraut with potato dumplings ($5.95), or the Prague meatloaf served with potato dumplings ($3).

At lunchtime, specials hover around $3.50 for chicken paprikash, liver, etc. On weekends a Czechoslovakian guitarist entertains.

Open noon to 11 p.m. Monday to Saturday.

La Rose des Sables, 439 MacArthur Rd. near St. Laurent Blvd. (tel. 741-4987), is named after the rose-like rock sculptures created by the wind in the Sahara Desert. Set in a suburban-looking house, the restaurant consists of three intimate rooms separated by an arcade, and decorated simply with large, beautiful photographs of the Algerian landscape.

Mrs. Bemmiloud is from Algeria, and takes much delight in serving the specialties of her native land. The couscous are really highly recommended—they're only $8 on Sundays ($13 otherwise). Then there are such specialties as brik Tunisien (crêpes stuffed with meat and fried); dolma (stewed lamb with zucchini, stuffed with meat and rice, $9) or chicken pastilla (chicken pie stuffed with almond, raisin, sugar, egg, and onion, and flavored with ginger and cinnamon, $10.50). On Thursdays and Fridays there's an extra-special treat: mechoui—a whole lamb broiled on a spit ($12.50).

Desserts include baklava and such classic affairs as soufflé Grand Marnier ($6 for two).

Open Tuesday to Saturday from 6 p.m. to midnight, on Sunday from noon to 10 p.m.

4. The Sights

Ottawa has plenty of interesting sights which have the added attraction of being free. But the city also provides a great mecca for the outdoors person: skiers, tobogganers, and skaters in the winter; cyclists, walkers, and boaters in the summer. First, the historic sights.

PARLIAMENT HILL: Standing on a bluff jutting into the Ottawa River, the Parliament Buildings with their high, pitched copper roofs are truly spectacular. As you enter the grounds by the central gate, you will pass by the **Centennial Flame,** lit on New Year's Eve of 1967 by Lester Pearson, encircled by the shields of the ten provinces and two territories.

In front of you rises the pride of the capital: the **Parliament Building** (commonly referred to as the Centre Block) and the Peace Tower, with the East Block on the right and the West Block on the left, which contain offices for Members of Parliament and their staffs.

The 291-foot **Peace Tower** forms part of the main entrance to the Parliament Buildings and is dedicated to the 66,650 Canadians who sacrificed their lives in World War I. The Memorial Chamber not only contains the Book of Remembrance, but lodged in the walls and the floors are stones from the very battlefields. The tower also contains a 53-bell carillon, with bells ranging from 10 to 22,400 pounds, and a four-face clock 16 feet in diameter. Atop the tower rises a bronze mast, 35 feet high, crowned by a cluster of lamps which are lit when Parliament is in session.

Here, in the Centre Block, the Commons and the Senate sit. The original building was constructed 1859–66, but was destroyed by fire in 1916. Only the **Library** at the rear was saved. This is a glorious 16-sided dome supported outside by huge flying buttresses and beautifully paneled inside with Canadian white pine. Note the magnificent carvings around the room—gorgons, crests, masks, and hundreds of rosettes. The original floor was an intricate pattern of oak, cherry, walnut, and ash.

You may sit in the Visitor's Gallery in the **House of Commons,** where you can tune in on translations of debates in both English and French. Parliament does not usually sit during July, August, and September, or during the Christmas and Easter holidays. Otherwise, sessions are held on Monday, Tuesday, and Thursday from 2 to 6 p.m. and 8 to 10 p.m., Wednesdays from 2 to 6 p.m., and Friday from 11 a.m. to 1 p.m. and 2 to 5 p.m. The liveliest part of the session is usually the question period, which follows soon after the Speaker's parade through the Hall of Honor to the Commons Chamber, which opens the proceedings.

You may also attend **Senate** sessions, which usually take place on Tuesday at 8 p.m. and Wednesday and Thursday at 2 p.m. Call ahead to make sure that there will be a session: 593-4328 or 992-2049.

If you are Canadian, you can find out who your M.P. is (if you don't know) by calling the main entrance at 992-4793, and then reach him/her by calling the number for all government offices, 232-8211. Your M.P. may arrange for you to sit in the Members' Gallery—don't be surprised if he comes to greet you.

You can also take a tour of the Centre Block which includes the Memorial Chamber, the Library, and the Peace Tower lookout. These tours leave daily from 9 a.m. to 9 p.m. Monday to Saturday, and 9 a.m. to 6 p.m. on Sunday during the summer (July 1 to Labour Day); 9 a.m. to 4:30 p.m. daily during winter.

The East Block is open to the public on Sunday only from 10 a.m. to 4 p.m. For information, call 992-3594.

After you have taken these tours, you can stroll the terrace with its splendid views over the river and wander around the grounds, keeping an eye out for the many statues—William Lyon Mackenzie King, Sir Wilfrid Laurier, Sir John A. MacDonald, and George Étienne Cartier among them.

Changing the Guard

During the summer, witness the pageantry of an ancient military ceremony performed by Her Majesty's Canadian Guards on the lawns of Parliament Hill daily at 10 a.m. from June 24 to Labour Day. The ceremony includes inspection of dress and weapons, parading of the Colour, and the exchange of compliments. If you can understand what some of those sergeant majors yell, you're a natural-born soldier. It's a very colorful spectacle to watch the 125 soldiers in busbies and scarlet jackets.

THE SUPREME COURT: Created in 1875, and until 1949 only the penultimate stepping stone on the route of appeals to the Judicial Committee of the Privy Council in England, the Supreme Court today is Canada's ultimate court of appeal.

The exterior of the Supreme Court building, with its steep copper roofs, blends with the rest of Parliament Hill. Two magnificent bronze doors lead into the impressive entrance hall which gives access to the main courtroom on the first floor, where you can see the Court sitting. Three sessions are held during the year: the first session begins on the fourth Tuesday in January and ends just before Easter, the second begins on the fourth Tuesday in April and continues to the end of June, and the third begins on the first Tuesday in October and ends just before Christmas. The Court does not normally sit during July, August, and September. While in session, the Court usually hears appeals on Mondays, Tuesdays, Wednesdays, and Thursdays from 10:30 a.m. to 1 p.m. and from 2:30 to 4 p.m. The first and third Mondays in each month are usually reserved for the hearing of motions for leave to appeal.

NATIONAL GALLERY OF CANADA: Located in the Lorne Building on Elgin St., between Albert and Slater Sts. (tel. 992-4636), the National contains six floors of galleries devoted to contemporary European and Canadian art, prints, drawings, and photographs, and various changing exhibitions, such as the recent tribute to Paul Klee. Among the paintings in the European collection are works by Rembrandt, Chardin, El Greco, Cézanne, Van Gogh, Monet, and Picasso. The Massey Collection provides a survey of English painting from about 1900 to 1950.

The gallery also runs a full program of lectures and films. There is a pleasant cafeteria on the eighth floor and a bookstore on the ground floor.

Open 10 a.m. to 6 p.m. weekdays (to 10 p.m. on Thursday), and 2 to 6 p.m. on Sundays and holidays. Closed Mondays from September 1 to May 1. Admission is free.

THE RIDEAU CANAL: Built to avoid using the St. Lawrence River, so vulnerable to American attack, for transporting troops and supplies to the interior of Canada should another war like that of 1812 break out between the United States and Britain, the canal is one of Ottawa's greatest assets. In summer you can either walk or cycle along the canal paths, or else canoe or boat your way along before stopping in at the canalside beer garden at the

National Arts Centre. In winter it's turned into a glorious skating rink worthy of any Dutch artist's palette as people come and go to work, skating with their briefcases, and families take to the ice with children perched atop their backs or drawn upon sleighs. For daily information on the state of the ice, call 992-1234.

The construction of the canal began under the direction of Lieutenant Colonel By of the Royal Engineers in 1826. The 123-mile engineering feat was completed in 1832. For many years Parliament Hill served as the barracks site for the regimental soldiers involved.

Starting in Ottawa, the canal follows the course of the Rideau River to its summit on Upper Rideau Lake, which is connected to Newboro Lake where the canal descends the Cataraqui River (through a series of lakes controlled by dams) to Kingston. In Ottawa there's a flight of eight locks that carry boats the 79-foot difference between the man-made portion of the canal and the Ottawa River—a sight not to be missed, and almost adjacent to the Château Laurier Hotel.

NATIONAL MUSEUM OF NATURAL SCIENCES and THE MUSEUM OF MAN: Both of these museums are in the old Victoria Memorial Building at Metcalfe and McLeod Sts., which has a rather beautiful facade encrusted with stone carvings around the porticos and a series of stained-glass windows above. You'd do best to tour each half separately.

The **Natural Sciences** half of the building features exhibits about geology and the evolution of life, including the dinosaur court that houses several impressive specimens mounted in realistic poses amid the subtropical vegetation typical of western Canada 75 million years ago. Other exhibits depict mammals and birds in Canada, and the evolutionary development of the animal kingdom. This last is demonstrated by a huge tree of life, which you can operate yourself to trace the evolutionary threads from more than 500 million years ago.

The **Museum of Man** emphasizes the history of man in Canada. Here you can see the artifacts and lifestyles of the Iroquois Indians, the Central Plains Indians, and the exceptional art of the Northwest Coast Indians—the Haida, Tlingit, Tsimshian, Bella Coola, Kwakiutl, Nootka, and Sliash. Eskimo traditions and culture are also explored—you may see a film of an Eskimo caribou or seal hunt. One exhibit outlines the history of Canada from the early voyages of discovery and the fur and timber trade days through the Depression to modern times, while another gallery examines the various folk traditions that play a role in every individual's journey from birth to death.

Open 10 a.m. to 6 p.m. Tuesday through Sunday, except Christmas Day. Admission is free. For information about the Natural Sciences Museum, call 996-3102; the National Museum of Man's number is 992-3497.

CENTRAL EXPERIMENTAL FARM: There are numerous parks in the city, but the biggest and possibly the most attractive isn't a park at all—it's the Central Canada Experimental Farm, 1200 acres of green open space, now completely surrounded by Ottawa suburbia.

Located at the Driveway and Carling Ave. (tel. 995-5222), its greenhouses are famous and every November a spectacular chrysanthemum show is held. The farm itself has tree-shaded roads, barns, and fields with lots of farm animals which the kids' will love to see. There's also a flower garden, ornamental garden, and the arboretum with clusters of trees and shrubs from all over the world. During the summer, from May to Thanksgiving, you can take rides in wagons drawn by Clydesdales, weather permitting, at 10 a.m. and 2 p.m. Monday to Friday. Guided tours are given from 8:30 a.m. to 3:30 p.m. weekdays. This is a lovely place to sit down and have a picnic.

BYTOWN MUSEUM: Housed in a small gray stone building—the oldest in Ottawa, in fact, and originally erected to serve as a storage place for food and equipment for the men who came to construct the canal—located near the entrance to the Rideau Canal, it is now appropriately filled with artifacts—furniture, clothes, guns, tools, old toys—used during the early days of Ottawa. It also contains some possessions of Colonel By, the man who supervised the building of the canal.

Open mid-May to mid-October from 11 a.m. to 5 p.m. Monday to Saturday (closed Sundays, holidays, and from October to early May), it is located on the Driveway near the junction of the Rideau Canal locks and the Ottawa River (tel. 234-4570).

CANADIAN WAR MUSEUM: Kids love to clamber over the tanks that are stationed outside the War Museum, 330 Sussex Dr. (tel. 992-2774), and they seem to love almost as much imagining themselves in the life-size replica of a World War I trench.

The collection, which traces Canadian military history, contains airplanes, cars (the command car of Field Marshal Goering, for example), guns, torpedoes, mines, uniforms (including that of Canadian air ace Billy Bishop), and tools, plus several large displays complete with sound effects showing famous battles such as the American invasion of Québec in 1775 and the Normandy D-Day landings.

Open 10 a.m. to 6 p.m. daily from early May to Labour Day, to 5 p.m. Tuesday to Saturday, and noon to 5 p.m. on Sunday during the winter. Admission is free.

ROYAL CANADIAN MINT: You must have an appointment to visit the mint at 320 Sussex Dr. (tel. 992-2348 or 236-3132). Tours are given every half hour between 9 and 11:30 a.m. and 1 and 3 p.m. weekdays. Along the way, you'll see machines stamping blanks out of long sheets of metal and being processed into coinage, which you can watch flow into cloth money bags.

LAURIER HOUSE: Outside the house at 335 Laurier Ave. East there's a stone by the curb which was used as an aid for getting in and out of carriages. From 1897 to 1919 this mansion was the home of Canada's seventh prime minister (and first French-Canadian P.M.), Sir Wilfrid Laurier. From 1923 to 1950 it was Mackenzie King's home, and the house is crammed with mementos of them both. In the library where King held séances you can see the crystal ball that King supposedly had seen and coveted in London but said he couldn't afford and which an American bought for him when he overheard. You can also see the portrait of his mother by whom he used to place a red rose daily, and also the program Abraham Lincoln held the night of his assassination, plus copies of the death mask and hands of the president. Lester B. Pearson's library has also been recreated, where you can see the Nobel Peace Prize medal he won for his role in the 1956 Arab-Israeli dispute.

Open 10 a.m. to 5 p.m. Tuesday to Saturday, and 2 to 5 p.m. on Sunday. Admission is free.

NATIONAL AERONAUTICAL COLLECTION:

At Rockcliffe Airport (tel. 998-4566) you can walk through three hangars filled with more than 50 real aircraft including the Lancaster bomber, the Supermarine Spitfire (which helped win the Second World War), the Vickers Viscount (the first turbine-powered plane to be used for passenger service), and the Star Fighter, with its rapier-like nose. The ones with the pans underneath collecting oil are still being flown.

You can also see a replica of the *Silver Dart,* which rose from the ice of Baddeck Bay, Nova Scotia, in February 1908 performing the first powered flight in Canada. It flew for nine minutes—not bad considering it looks as though it was built out of bicycle parts and kites.

Open 9 a.m. to 9 p.m. Tuesday to Sunday in winter, daily during the summer. Admission is free. To get there, take the Queensway East. Exit at St. Laurent Blvd. and drive north (past Montréal Rd.) to the collection, which will be on your right.

NATIONAL MUSEUM OF SCIENCE AND TECHNOLOGY:

This museum, at 1867 St. Laurent Blvd. at Russell Rd. (tel. 998-4566), offers fun and learning through involvement. You can pull levers to demonstrate physical principles such as viscosity, climb aboard a steam locomotive, look at the heavens through Canada's largest refracting telescope, watch people coming and going in the adjacent parking lot through a couple of periscopes, see chicks hatching, and try to walk through the Crazy Kitchen, where everything looks normal but the floor is tilted at a sharp angle.

The museum also houses a collection of antique trains, streetcars, fire engines, and autos, including the Bricklin, the safest car on the road which was produced in Canada in 1974 to 1975.

Open 10 a.m. to 9 p.m. Tuesday and Wednesday, to 6 p.m. Thursday to Sunday; closed Monday (during the winter it is also closed on Tuesday). Admission to the museum is free. For reservations for evening programs at the Observatory, call 998-9520. Closed Monday.

NATIONAL POSTAL MUSEUM:

If you're a stamp lover, then this museum's for you. Inside, you'll find the weathered boards, beamed ceiling, and hanging lamps of a reconstructed 19th-century general store and post office where you can buy the latest mint stamps, first day covers, and drop a letter or souvenir postcard into the cast-iron Victorian mailbox. In the west wing, floor cases and wall cabinets display ornate brass letter balances, old mailbags, hand-canceling hammers, plus a detailed model of the sail and paddle-wheel steam packet *Brittania,* built for the North Atlantic mail service in 1840. The east wing houses one of the world's finest collections of Canadian and British North American stamps, plus documents and memorabilia relating to Canadian mail history.

Open 9 a.m. to 5 p.m. Tuesday to Saturday, and noon to 5 p.m. on Sunday. Closed Christmas Day. Admission is free. To get there, take Bronson Ave. south to Heron and turn right. The museum is in the Sir Alexander Campbell Bldg., Confederation Heights (tel. 998-8451) at Heron Rd. and Riverside Dr.

ALONG THE PARKWAY AND SUSSEX DRIVE: This makes for a very picturesque and interesting drive. The **Ottawa River Parkway** starts in the west end at Carling Ave. and runs along the river into Wellington St., all the way offering glorious views over the islands in the river.

From Confederation Square, proceed along Sussex Dr. to St. Patrick St., where you can turn left into **Nepean Point Park.** Here, you and the statue of Samuel de Champlain can share a beautiful view over the river, and in summer you can attend concerts and drama at the 700-seat **Astrolabe amphitheater** (check the newspapers for programs).

Across the road is **Major's Hill Park,** where the noonday gun is fired (10 a.m. on Sundays to avoid disturbing church services). You can, if you wish, watch the lighting of the cannon.

Just beyond the MacDonald Cartier Bridge stands **Earnscliffe,** originally the home of Sir John A. MacDonald and now the impressive residence of the British high commissioner.

Farther along Sussex Dr. you cross the Rideau River, whence you can look down upon the modern Ottawa City Hall pat in the middle of Green Island, before proceeding past the prime minister's house, well sheltered by trees at 24 Sussex Dr., and on to **Government House,** still often referred to as Rideau Hall, the residence of the governor general. You cannot go inside the residence, but you can enjoy the 88-acre grounds when His Excellency isn't there, where you'll find a red oak tree planted by the late President Kennedy and also a sapling planted by President Nixon (which local wags note has grown rather crooked).

The Drive then becomes the National Capital Commission Driveway, a beautiful route along the Ottawa River and through **Rockcliffe Park.** Where the road forks in the park, follow the right fork to Acacia Ave. to reach the **Rockeries,** where carpets of daffodils and narcissus herald the spring in April.

GATINEAU PARK: Only two miles, about a 20-minute drive, from the Houses of Parliament, lie 88,000 acres of woodland and lakes named after notary-turned-explorer Nicolas Gatineau of Trois-Rivières. The park began in 1934 when the federal government purchased some land in the Gatineau Hills to stop destruction of the forests brought on by the demand for cheap firewood during the Depression. Now there are white-tailed deer, beaver, and more than 100 species of birds in the park. The black bear, timber wolf, otter, marten, and raccoon are regular residents. If you're lucky you might spy a moose, lynx, or wolverine.

Facilities in the park include 90 miles of **hiking trails,** supervised **swimming beaches** at Meach Lake, Lac Philippe, and Lac Lapêche and a tough seven-mile bikeway up to Pink Lake. Boats can be rented at Lac Philippe and Lac Lapêche. Motorboats are not permitted on park lakes except on Lac Lapêche, where motors up to 10 h.p. may be used for **fishing.** Most lakes can be fished (if it's not allowed, it's posted). A Québec license is required and can be obtained in Hull at the Québec Department of Tourism, Fish and Game, 653 Blvd. St-Joseph (tel. 819/711-7768).

Camping facilities are at or near Lac Philippe accessible by Hwys. 5, 105, and 366, and the Masham road. Sites are filled on a first-come, first-served basis. For information, call the park headquarters at Old Chelsea (tel. 819/827-2711) or the park entrance (tel. 819/456-2259).

In winter the hiking trails become cross-country ski trails, marked by numbers on blue plaques with châlets along the way. Winter camping is available at Lac Philippe.

While you're in the park, visit the country estate of Mackenzie King at **Kingsmere.** You can have tea in a summer cottage there and inspect the architectural fragments he dragged here from the parliamentary building after the 1916 fire and from London's House of Commons after the 1941 Blitz. The tearoom is open only in summer from noon to 6:30 p.m.

To get to the park you can take several routes: cross over to Hull and take the Blvd. Tache (Rte. 148) to the Gatineau Parkway which will lead you to Kingsmere, Camp Fortune (a ski resort), and eventually to Meach Lake. To reach Lac Philippe you should take Hwy. 105 north out of Hull up to Wakefield. Beyond Wakefield, take Rte. 366 west. Just before you reach Ste-Cécile-de-Masham you can turn off to Lac Philippe; to reach Lac Lapêche, keep going along the Masham road to St-Louis-de-Masham and enter the park just beyond.

OTHER THINGS TO DO: In addition to the museums and historic sights, Ottawa is very much an activity-oriented city.

Cycling

In all, there are over 60 miles of bike paths along the Ottawa and Rideau Rivers, the Rideau Canal, and in Gatineau Park, and more miles are being added. All bikeways are marked with a blue, black, and white cyclist logo. For information, write to: Information Services, National Capital Commission (NCC), 48 Rideau St., Ottawa, ON K1N 8K5.

You can rent cycles from **Rent a Bike** in the parking lot behind the Château Laurier Hotel (tel. 233-0268) at $10 per day for a five- or ten-speed bike, or $7 for a three-speed machine; at **Bike Rental,** Fifth Ave. at the Driveway by the canal (tel. 232-2023); and at Dows Lake. Single bikes are $1.75 an hour and tandems are $3 an hour.

Boating/Cruising

You can rent boats on the Rideau Canal at the following locations: **Hog's Back Marina,** on Hog's Back Rd. between Riverside Dr. and Hwy. 16 (tel. 733-5065), rents canoes and rowboats for $35 per week, $20 for a two-day weekend $25 (three-day) or $2.50 per hour.

The NCC at **Dows Lake boathouse** (tel. 232-2023), at the Driveway and Preston Ave., also rents canoes, paddleboats, and rowboats for $4 per hour. Paddleboats are available at the National Arts Centre, and at Fifth Ave. on the Rideau Canal in the Glebe.

Paul's Boat Lines Ltd., 3244 Riverside Dr. (tel. 733-5186), operates two cruises: the Ottawa River cruise, which takes you along Embassy Row to Rockcliffe Park, departing from the dock opposite the Château Laurier, and the Rideau Canal cruise, which leaves from the docks opposite the Arts Centre and goes down the canal to the Experimental Farm and Carleton University.

River cruises leave at 11 a.m., and 2, 4, and 7:30 p.m. Adults pay $4.50; children, $2.25. The trip lasts 1½ hours. The canal trip leaves at 11:30 a.m., and 1:30, 3, 4:30, 7, and 8:30 p.m., and takes 1¼ hours. Adults are charged $4; children, $2.

Skating

During the winter the **Rideau Canal** is flooded to a depth of three feet, becoming the longest and most romantic skating rink in the world—it stretches five miles from the National Arts Centre to Dow's Lake and Carleton University. (Every morning the state of the ice is reported on the radio news.) Along the way there are changing rooms and a canteen to warm up in. Skates can be rented at the **Park Lane Hotel,** 111 Cooper St. (tel. 238-1331), near the canal, for $4. Call ahead to make sure they have them, for supplies are limited. For daily ice condition reports, call 232-1234.

Downhill and Cross-Country Skiing

Both are only minutes' commuting distance away from this capital city. Closest spot is **Camp Fortune** (tel. 819/827-1717) only 12 miles from the city up the Gatineau Parkway. The resort has 16 slopes—five beginner, four intermediate, and seven expert—which are reached by eight lifts including a triple chair, double-chair, poma, four T-Bars, and rope tow. The longest run is 4000 feet. There are five day lodges, one with a scenic bar overlooking the slalom hill, night skiing from Monday to Saturday, and a ski school and ski shop. Daily passes on weekdays are $7.50 for adults, $11 on weekends, with long-term packages available.

Camp Fortune also has good access to the cross-country trails in the Gatineau Park and maintains a cross-country skiing lodge with full facilities. White fees are $2 per weekday, $4 per weekend day, $6 per weekend.

Mont Cascades, just across the Gatineau River outside of Cantley (tel. 819/827-0136) has eight trails, one triple- and one double-chair lift, two T-Bars, and one poma. The longest run is 3000 feet. There are two day lodges with cafeteria, restaurant-bar, and disco at the hill. During the summer you can enjoy the thrill of coming down the superslide, careening around corners in real bobsled style at your own pace. Night skiing is available. Lift rates: $7 for adults on weekdays, $10 on weekends.

Eighteen miles from the city, **Edelweiss Valley,** Rte. 366, Wakefield (tel. 819/827-0552 or 819/459-3052), has 15 slopes, seven lifts (including a double chair and two pomas), and a warm cozy lodge, plus overnight accommodations. You can also ice skate here and take sleigh rides through the snow. Lift rates: adults pay $6 on weekdays, $9 on weekends.

Mont Ste-Marie, 55 miles from Ottawa at Lac Ste-Marie (tel. 819/467-2812), is the fullest facility resort in this area. Winter activities include twin peaks, 1250-foot vertical skiing with the longest run at two miles. There are three double-chairlifts and one poma. Other facilities include cross-country skiing, skating, and tobogganing, plus an overnight lodge, L'Auberge L'Abri (tel. 819/467-5200). Lift rates: adults pay $7 on weekdays, $11 on weekends.

Summer facilities include four tennis courts, a nine-hole golf course, three private lakes where you can swim, and canoe, a volleyball court, stocked trout lakes, and, of course, miles of hiking trails through the mountains.

A five-day ski package at the auberge usually averages a little over $235 in winter, including accommodations, breakfasts and dinners, lift fees, and ten hours of ski instruction. Two-day weekend packages are about $100. In summer, a five-day stay might run $170 per person; a two-day weekend, about $70.

SPECIAL EVENTS: Ottawa's biggest event is, of course, the **Festival of Spring** in May when the city is ablaze with 200 varieties of tulips stretching along the driveways, around public buildings, monuments, embassies, and private homes. (Probably the best viewing is to be had at Dows Lake). The festival began in 1945 when the people of the Netherlands sent 100,000 tulip bulbs to Canada in appreciation of the role Canadian troops played in liberating

Holland. Queen Juliana of the Netherlands, who had spent the war years in Canada during Holland's occupation, arranged thereafter for a personal annual presentation of bulbs to celebrate the birth of her daughter, Princess Margriet, in Ottawa in 1943 (to ensure that the princess was born a citizen of the Netherlands, the Canadian government proclaimed her room in the Ottawa Civic Hospital to be part of Holland).

Over the years the festival has grown, and each year a flurry of spectacular events follows the opening ball and the crowning of the Tulip Queen: fireworks displays, parades, regattas, car rallies, special productions at the National Arts Centre, craft shows, and so on.

Throughout July, **Festival Canada** celebrates the nation's birthday with a host of summer events: canoe and sailing regattas, concerts, theatrical productions, music and dance, and art and craft demonstrations. For information, write: Box Office, National Arts Centre, P.O. Box 1534, Station B, Ottawa ON K1P 5W1 (tel. 613/237-4400).

5. Culture and Nightlife

Ottawa's culture and nightlife pickings are somewhat meager, really only extending to the National Arts Centre, several bars, and one or two discos, the raciest of which are concentrated in Hull.

NATIONAL ARTS CENTRE: Ever since the Centre opened in 1969 it has acted as a catalyst on the Ottawa, and indeed the Canadian, cultural scene. Situated in the center of Ottawa on a triangular site bounded by Confederation Park, Confederation Square, and the Rideau Canal, the building itself is interesting. It is not an intimidating palace to culture. Rather, architect Fred Lebensold created three interlocking hexagons which have been placed to form a series of attractively landscaped pedestrian terraces which take advantage of the sloping terrain, offering a spectacular panorama of Ottawa. A cafe below lobby level which faces the canal opens onto a covered terrace in summer.

Inside there are three auditoriums. In the **Opera House,** seating 2300, the eye is immediately drawn to Micheline Beauchemin's curtain that flames and glitters across the great expanse of the proscenium. The 800-seat **Theatre** has an apron stage that thrusts 23 feet into the auditorium, while the smaller **Studio** provides great flexibility for experimental works. The theater is hexagonally shaped and the stage can be raised above the floor, set level, or sunk into the floor. A cafe and restaurant complete the public facilities.

A tremendous variety of programs are produced here. The Centre acts as an impresario in dance and variety shows, hosting such visiting companies as the National Ballet of Canada, the Royal Winnipeg Ballet, and the Grands Ballets Canadiens, and such variety artists as Nana Mouskouri, Tom Jones, B. B. King, Gilbert Becaud, Andy Williams, Jose Feliciano, and so on.

But in music the Centre has its own **National Arts Center Orchestra,** directed by Mario Bernardi, which in ten short years has, as the *New York Times* noted, been "brought to front-rank standing." Two main series of 12 concerts each are presented. In the past such guest artists as Isaac Stern, James Galway, Philippe Entremont, and Barry Tuckwell have performed. The musical season culminates in the Festival Canada, which usually features opera and chamber concerts. Within these festivals, NAC credits have included such productions as the Josef Svoboda–designed *Queen of Spades* with Jon Vickers and Maureen Forrester, and Britten's *A Midsummer Night's Dream* staged by

Covent Garden's John Copley. And you'll be pleased to note that the top price for an opera ticket is $17.50.

The Centre also has a theatrical ensemble working in two languages. In the past the English series has ranged from such classics as *Hamlet* through contemporary English contributions such as *Travesties* by Tom Stoppard and *Equus* by Peter Shaffer, to modern Canadian plays. The French ensemble has produced everything from Feydeau farces through classics like Corneille's *Le Cid* to modern offerings by Arnold Wesker.

Tickets at the Centre range in price from $3.50 to $17.50 depending on the presentation. For information, call 237-4400.

THEATER: Besides the ensemble at the National Arts Centre, **Ottawa Little Theatre**, 400 King Edward Ave. (tel. 233-8948), offers some good productions of such popular shows as Neil Simon's *Come Blow Your Horn*, Emlyn Williams's *Night Must Fall*, and Agatha Christie's *The Unexpected Guest*. The company started in 1916 in an old church which burned down in 1970, but it now has a fully equipped, modern theater. Tickets are $3.50 or $4.

FOLK, ROCK, AND JAZZ: At **TJ's Speakeasy** (see my restaurant recommendation), a small homey spot, you can catch some soft country folk sounds. For a more rollicking Irish mood, there are two cavernous pubs where the bands belt out Irish ballads and the crowds kick up their heels among the trappings of the green: **Molly McGuire's**, 257 Rideau St. (tel. 235-1972), where a pint of beer runs $1.35; and **Elaine's Pub**, 1075 Bank St. (tel. 238-2780), where beer is $1.10 a bottle. Just across the street, **Patty's Place Pub,** a much smaller spot with dartboard and mirrors etched with advertising, gathers a friendly crowd on Thursday, Friday, and Saturday nights for folk entertainment of the Irish persuasion.

The Imperial Theatre (1914) now houses Ottawa's most startling rock emporium—**Barrymore's**, 323 Bank St. (tel. 238-5691). The place has been renovated so that there are five levels from which to view loud, driving punk and progressive rock bands, two standup bars, and a capacity of over 300. On weekends there's a $2.50 cover and drinks average $2.25; snacks, such as hamburgers, are available. During the week, the cover is $1 (except for Monday when there's none). The **Black Swan**, 275 Rideau at King Edward (tel. 235-3407), features such progressive rock groups as Lighthouse from Toronto, Wayne Cochran and the CC Riders, and the Dutch Mason Blues Band, in a large, carpeted room with one or two Tiffany lamps. A draft beer will cost about $1; there's also a $2 cover.

Jazz is a somewhat elusive entity in Ottawa. In summer the cafe terrace at the NAC features a swinging Dixieland-style band, but there are none of those smoke-filled stomping jazz joints. **La Parisienne**, 196 Laurier Ave. West (tel. 238-7759), features jazz of one sort or another on Tuesdays from 9 p.m. on; while **Chez Lucien**, 59 Clarence St. (tel. 233-9356), offers the Capital City Jazz Band riproaring its way back to Basin St. every Friday night from 8 p.m. Cover is $2.

Saucy Noodle, 409 Somerset St. West (tel. 234-4332), offers an eclectic mix of all three, plus an occasional comedian or magician. The place is upstairs and presents a rustic shingled atmosphere complete with dartboard. Entertainment begins at 7 p.m. nightly. From Wednesday to Sunday there's a cover charge which varies with the performer.

DINING AND DANCING: For classic dancing, Moxie Whitney's Orchestra has been providing the sounds at the **Canadian Grill** for good old-fashioned cheek-to-cheek dancing. Cover charge is $4 on Saturday, $2 otherwise.

Le Restaurant at the NAC provides a more up-to-date sound and surroundings for similar-style dancing, only the music is provided by a jazz trio.

La Ronde, atop the Holiday Inn, also offers the same.

DANCING TO LIVE MUSIC: Most of the middle-of-the-road rock groups perform in hotel and motel rooms around the city, providing a kind of live disco atmosphere. The most crowded are currently **Le Quadrille,** a large singles dating scene, at the Inn of the Provinces; the pubby **Cock and Lion** at the Château Laurier; and the more intimate **La Boîte** at the Auberge de la Chaudière in Hull. **Bogey's,** in the basement of the Butler Hotel, 112 Montréal Rd. (tel. 746-4641), draws a 30-ish crowd to dance to country-rock bands amid a few blowups of Mr. Cool himself.

DISCOS: The hippest discos are to be found across the river in Hull, where nightlife swings till 3 a.m. Certainly, **Viva,** 259 Blvd. St-Joseph (tel. 819/770-2216), is Ottawa's closest answer to Studio 54, a glitter palace housed in a converted church basement where avant-garde costumes are de rigueur. The bar stretches practically around the full length and breadth of the mirrored room with its velvet banquettes. Drinks average $2.25; cocktails, $3.50. Cover charge runs from $1 on Sunday to $2.50 Saturday.

On the opposite side of the street is **Le Globe,** 194B Blvd. St-Joseph (tel. 819/771-5050). Although it's jam-packed, it has a much less frantic aura than most, and practically a rustic feel with hanging baskets of dried flowers, candles on the tables, and a small but nevertheless spectacularly lit dance floor. The crowd here seems as much into talking and relaxing as into showing off. Drinks average $2.25. No jeans allowed Thursday to Sunday. No cover.

Le Club, 77 rue Wellington (tel. 819/771-9813), doubles as a lunch spot and nighttime disco. The atmosphere is plush: high velvet banquettes, two marble bars accented with polished brass, and a small, well-lit dance floor. Drinks average $2.50.

In Ottawa proper, the most sophisticated disco thrives at the Four Seasons hotel—**Sascha's,** where amid the gleaming brass you can watch the dancers from a plush couch or chair placed on the balcony around the room.

Studley's, 1820 Carling Ave. (tel. 725-3066), doubles, would you believe, as a deli-disco. During the day you can get a smoked-meat sandwich, chicken pot pie, and so on, all under $5. Stained-glass lamps, a few hanging plants, high tables, and bentwood chairs set the scene for dancing on the brass-railed dance floor under the high chalet-style ceiling. Cover charge Thursday to Saturday is $2. Drinks average $2.25.

Brandy's, 126 York St. (tel. 232-2621), packs in the flesh with its Tiffany lamps, "exposed brick, and hanging plants" magic formula, plus the latest music and a small dance floor. A young singles crowd stands around and talks. Cover charge is $2; a pint of beer costs $1.20; hot and cold snacks under $4 are on hand. No jeans allowed.

Plants also hang everywhere in the beamed room at **Stoney Mondays,** 62 York St. (tel. 236-5548). There's a tiny dance floor in the back, plenty of comfortable couches scattered around, and a central bar. Drinks average $2.75.

BARS: The latest addition to the nightlife scene are the wine bars. Ottawa has three of them at the moment. **Willy's** (356 McClaren St.) has already been discussed in the restaurant section. At the **William Street Bars,** 49 William St. (tel. 235-3881), people, wine, and conversation are the important ingredients. Downstairs, there's a bar that has been imported from Ruthvin, Wales, plus one or two chairs—the idea being that people should circulate. Upstairs, the decor is more sophisticated—almost art deco, with mirrored walls, gleaming black bars, and chrome accents. Rare wines mingle with vins ordinaires, and you can savor your wine with a rabbit or provincial pâté or any of several quiches. Certainly this is one of the city's most interesting spots to imbibe.

Also in the Byward Market area, **Vines,** 54 York St., affects a cellar-like atmosphere with its downstairs setting, stone floors, and red checked tablecloths. Five different house wines are featured (from $1.35 a glass) plus over 100 different varieties. Snacks are available too.

For quiet drinking with a piano background, **Friday's Victorian Music Parlour,** 150 Elgin St. (tel. 237-5353), with its clubby atmosphere, old London engravings, and comfortable wingbacks, plus an inviting fire in winter, is a good choice, especially for single women who just want to have a quiet dignified drink.

In the Beacon Arms Hotel, 88 Albert St., **La Bibliothèque** provides one of the warmer, friendlier atmospheres in town; the Inn of the Provinces, 360 Sparks St. has the chic **L'Allegro** piano bar. For drinking sans music, the Château Laurier's **Cross Keys Lounge** is the closest thing to an English pub I know, while **Alfie's Pub,** downstairs at the Marble Works, 14 Waller St. (tel. 235-6764) affects a gay '90s air for convivial elbow exercising.

6. Side Trips from the Capital

KINGSTON: This handsome town, 103 miles south of Ottawa, retains much of its 19th-century charm in the form of its many well-preserved stone houses and old defense constructions, such as the Martello Towers on the waterfront.

The town is rich in history. Looking like an active fortress, **Old Fort Henry** dominates the town from its high promontory. Here, all summer long the Guards, complete with their goat mascot named David, perform 19th-century drills, including the spectacular Ceremonial Retreat every Wednesday and Saturday at 7:30 p.m., when both infantry and artillery perform detailed maneuvers creating a cacophony of rifle and cannon fire. Admission is $2.25 for adults; 75¢ for children 6 to 16. Open mid-May to October 15 from 9:30 a.m. to 5 p.m.

The **Royal Military College,** Canada's West Point, is also located here not far from the fort. Although you can tour the grounds, the only building open to the public is the **Fort Frederick Museum,** located in a large Martello Tower which houses displays pertaining to the college's history and Kingston's Royal Dockyard, plus the Douglas collection of small arms and weapons. Admission: $1 for adults, 50¢ for seniors, 25¢ for children 8 to 16. Open June through Labour Day from 9 a.m. to 9 p.m.

On July 1, 1867, the Canadian Confederation was proclaimed in the Market Square and the chief architect, Sir John A. MacDonald, who became Canada's first prime minister, lived here at **Bellevue House,** 35 Centre St. This Tuscan-style house, jokingly called "Pekoe Pagoda" or "Tea Caddy Castle" by the local citizenry, has been restored to the style of the mid-1800s, containing displays highlighting the career and life of Sir John. Open June 1 to Labour Day, 9 a.m. to 6 p.m.

Kingston is very much a waterfront defense town. Along the waterfront, **Confederation Park** stretches from the front of the old 19th-century city hall down to the magnificent yacht basin (worth looking at). Rising on the waterfront is one of the finest Martello Towers, built during the Oregon Crisis of 1846 to withstand the severest of naval bombardments. The **Murney Tower** is now a museum where you can see the basement storage rooms, the barrack room, and the gun platform. Admission is 50¢. Farther west along the waterfront you'll find **Portsmouth Harbor,** site of the 1976 Olympic sailing events.

Then, of course, the famous **1000 Islands** holiday area is right on the town's doorstep. Known to the Indians as Manitonna (Garden of the Great Spirit), it is alive with cruise boats in summer which meander through the over 1800 islands past such extraordinary sights as **Boldt's Castle,** built by millionaire George Boldt at the turn of the century as a gift for his wife. (When she died suddenly, the work was abandoned, and so it stands a relic to lost love.) The **cruise boats** leave from various points along the St. Lawrence. From Kingston Harbour at City Hall, you can take a 3½-hour cruise on either the *Island Queen* or the *Island Princess* during the day, or a special Starlite cruise at night. The cost for adults is $6; for children 6 to 12, $3.50.

Staying Over

Two chains have commandeered the spectacular position overlooking the harbor—the Holiday Inn and the Howard Johnson's **Confederation Place Hotel,** 237 Ontario St. (tel. 613/549-6300), whose ultramodern pine lobby is a decorous masterpiece. There are 88 rooms on six floors, all very tastefully decorated and fully appointed. Whiskers is a popular disco lounge where the bar is supported by mock silver-birch trunks! Rates: $36 single, $44 double, in summer; $34 single, $42 double, in winter. An extra person is $5. The **Holiday Inn,** 1 Princess St. (tel. 613/542-7311), has all the facilities expected of the chain, including a heated swimming pool, lounge, and rooftop restaurant. Rates: $36.50 to $40 single, $46.50 to $50 double. An extra person is $4.

La Salle Hotel, 2360 Princess St. (tel. 613/546-4233), has 35 exquisitely decorated, brand-new units accented with cedar wall strips and decorated in brown and beige, fully appointed with a remote control switch for the color TV, a double vanity with theatrical-style lighting, a massager, and sliding glass doors. The rest of the 75 units consist of pleasantly decorated motel-style rooms. There's a dining room on the premises, and an outdoor pool, and the management is currently putting in a cocktail lounge with a mirrored cedar bar, comfortable couches, and working fireplace. Rates: $35 single, $39 double, in the new units; $28 and $35, respectively, in the motel section.

Catercorner from the La Salle, sheltered behind a stand of walnut trees, lies the **Walnut Grove Motel,** 2327 Princess St. (tel. 546-2691). The ten units are beautifully set around a grove with picnic tables. Rooms are bright and pretty with plywood paneling. There's an outdoor heated pool which is fenced off and sheltered from the roadside. Rates: $24 single, $27 to $31 double, off-season; $26 single, $30 to $33 double, in July, August and September. There are also eight efficiencies available for a $3 extra charge. Cots are $4.

The latest addition to Kingston's hotel scene, and the cheapest choice, lies at **Journey's End,** 1454 Princess St. (tel. 549-5550), in a two-story motel-style building. There are 58 units. Downstairs rooms have sliding glass doors, and all the rooms have up-to-the-minute decor, queen-size beds, loveseats, and large writing tables. Added attraction: local phone calls are free. Rates: $17.88 upstairs, $19.88 downstairs.

Where to Eat

True to its name, the **Firehall**, 251 Ontario St. (tel. 549-5167), is located in a firehouse. It consists of three very different rooms. Downstairs, the first room contains a magnificent collection of old toys—from rocking horses and dolls to smaller wooden toys—matched with bentwood chairs, magnolia tablecloths, and brown napkins, each table appointed with fresh flowers. Beyond this room lies the Greenhouse, with its bamboo furniture, tile floor, plenty of plants, and botanical prints on the walls. It overlooks the lake and the ferry dock. The original metal red staircase leads up to Pumpers, where the hoses still hang in a comfortable, chic lounge-pub where you can catch a pub lunch of shepherd's pie or soup and sandwich and at night be entertained by folk singers. The menu in the main restaurants stresses continental fare. Try the medallions of pork tenderloin with onions, red wine, and a touch of garlic ($7.50), or the roast duckling with sage and onion dressing served with apple sauce ($10.50).

Open noon to 2:30 and 5:30 to 10 p.m. Monday to Saturday, and 11:30 a.m. to 2:30 p.m. for Sunday brunch.

Just off Princess St., along a narrow passageway in what is known as the Old Stones, a complex of old buildings that have been renovated and now house interesting stores and boutiques, you'll find **Chez Piggy**, 68 Princess St. (tel. 549-7673), occupying an early 1900s building that probably served as a stable. In front there's a crazy paved courtyard where you can sit outdoors. Inside, on the ground floor there's a long bar with brown high directors chairs, while in the loft, white Italian metal furniture provides a classical setting where the only real decor consists of two glorious Tunisian rugs. The menu is small and might feature five or so entrees at dinner. Try the baked ham with fruit sauce ($6) after you've sampled either the hummus ($2) or the Stilton pâté ($2.50). Salads, omelets, and sandwiches are offered at lunch, all under $4.

Open 11 a.m. to midnight Tuesday to Saturday, with lunch served until 2 p.m. and dinner from 6 to 9:30 p.m. Sunday brunch from 11:30 a.m. to 2:30 p.m.

Kingston has its own wine bar—**The Vaults,** 21 Queen St. (tel. 546-2414), run by two young owners. The main dining room has an eclectic assortment of Victorian oak furniture, while upstairs there are three rooms with polished wood floors adorned with throw rugs. In one area wicker furniture and placemats set the tone, while the other room (at the back) is the wine bar with an assortment of Regency-style tables and a Pennsylvania Dutch clock chiming over all. There's folk, jazz, or piano music in the wine bar from Thursday to Saturday, while on Fridays a lutist accompanies diners in the main dining room. Open 11:30 a.m. to 10 p.m. Monday to Saturday (wine bar until 1 a.m.).

The dinner menu offers a $7.75 special with pâté, salad, entree, and tea or coffee. Or else you can choose from such dishes as chicken marengo, cod au gratin, prime rib with Yorkshire pudding (ranging from $4 to $8.50). Desserts are all homemade. Such snacks as ploughmans' lunch, even bagel and lox, are available at the noon hour, and you can always stop by for morning coffee or afternoon tea.

Gencarelli, 629 Princess St. (tel. 542-7976), is the family name synonymous with really good Italian food, and also real Italian style. Upstairs there's a rooftop patio, complete with a bright orange and white striped awning, a flaming show of geraniums in window boxes, and white wrought-iron furniture with yellow seats. The inside is less flamboyant—a series of rooms with stucco walls and arches, a handful of Italian posters, and one or two chianti bottles draped around the bar.

Start with a plateful of antipasto ($2.25) and follow with the smoothest of smooth scallopine alla marsala or any of the other classics: veal cacciatore, Cordon Bleu, or milanese (all $8.95). Steaks and seafood are available for the nonbelievers. At lunchtime, pastas, soups, and sandwiches are all under $4.

Open 11 a.m. to 11 p.m. daily, until 10 p.m. on Sunday.

The **Hungry Lion,** 303 Bagot, La Salle Mews (tel. 542-5466), is a combination dining room-lounge-disco. In the dining area you can select your own private alcove in a garden-like setting with wicker chairs and upturned parasols hanging above the black-topped tables. Over near the dance floor, with its Rousseau-esque lion and lily stained-glass floor motif, the tone is set by plush banquettes, gleaming brass, two or three stained-glass lamps, and exposed brick walls. Food consists of steak and seafood, from $6.95 for fried scallops to $12.95 for pepper steak.

Open 11:30 a.m. to 1 a.m. Monday to Thursday, until 3 a.m. Friday and Saturday (no liquor from 1 a.m.). Closed Sunday.

UPPER CANADA VILLAGE: Located 60 miles southeast of Ottawa, just east of Morrisburg, Upper Canada Village is Ontario's Williamsburg, illustrating pioneer history. All of the 35 structures and their contents have been restored with painstaking accuracy and devoted attention to detail—hand-forged nails and wooden dowel pegs, for instance, hold them together. All of the authentic buildings were scattered through eight village sites that bordered the St. Lawrence River; when the river's course was changed, they were all assembled here.

Even the personalities seem to inhabit them. In the schoolmaster's house, slate and sponge await the unwilling attention of a young boarder, while the doctor's lap robe hangs by the door. In the woollen mill the waterwheel spins, the old machinery turns, and the wool is woven into soft blankets; the clang of hammer on anvil rings out from the blacksmith's shop, while a heady smell of fresh bread wafts from the bake shop near Willard's Hotel. Stop at the hotel for lunch or dinner. The village craftsmen, dressed in period costume, who operate the 19th-century machinery will explain any questions you may have. Meanwhile, you can experience what it was like to ride a stagecoach or watch the horse ply the tow path dragging a barge behind it on the canal.

Open May 15 to October 15: 9:30 a.m. to 5 p.m. until June 15 and from Labour Day to October 15; to 6:30 p.m. June 15 through Labour Day.

Admission is $3 for adults, $1 for children 6 to 15; the family rate is $8.

Chapter XI

TORONTO

1. Orientation
2. Toronto's Hotels
3. The Restaurants of Toronto
4. The Sights
5. Culture and Nightlife
6. North from Toronto

ONCE LAMPOONED as dull and ugly, a city whose inhabitants fled to Buffalo for a good time and where the blinds were drawn on Sundays at the main department store (Eaton's) to stop anyone from sinfully windowshopping, Toronto has burst forth from its stodgy past and grabbed attention as one of the most exciting cities on the North American continent. Already the subject of rave reviews by the media and visiting foreign experts, I can only add this whole enthusiastic chapter.

How did it happen? Unlike most cities, Toronto got a second chance to change her image with a substantial blood transfusion from other cultures. Once a quiet, conservative community dominated by sedate Anglo-Saxons, who either entertained at home or in their clubs, Toronto was given a huge infusion of new energy by the post-World War II influx of 400,000 Italians, 80,000 Chinese, 65,000 Portuguese, plus Germans, Jews, Hungarians, Greeks, Indians, West Indians, and French Canadians, so that now the place is vibrating with street cafes, restaurants, cabarets, boutiques, theater, music, and life—ad infinitum.

And somehow, perhaps because of its past, it has become a model city where conservative traditions have tempered the often runaway impulse to destroy in order to create anew. When you see the old church and one of the oldest houses in the city standing proudly against the futuristic Eaton Centre, retained because the people wished it so, you know that certain values, qualities, and a great deal of thoughtful debate have gone into the making of this city.

As I said, it has become a model city. Indeed, Jane Jacobs, the urban planner, historian, and sociologist, chooses to live here to watch her theories actually working on the downtown streets—where people walk to work from their restored Victorian town houses, where no developer can erect downtown commercial space without including living space, where the subway gleams and the streets are safe, where old buildings are saved and converted to other uses, where the architects design around the contours of nature instead of just bulldozing the trees, where 200 parks invite you to "Please Walk on the Grass," and where close to three million people live graciously in harmony, surrounded by a city created with flair and imagination but also a sense of traditional values.

A HISTORICAL NOTE: In 1615 French explorer Étienne Brûle was the first European to visit the site of Toronto, then referred to by the Indians very simply as "a meeting place." Friction between the Indians and the eastern colonists delayed the establishment of a settlement until 1749, when Fort Rouillé was erected. The tiny fort became a scene of contention between the French and the English in the mid-1700s, and eventually became known as Fort York in 1793, and the capital of Upper Canada in 1797.

During the War of 1812, Fort York was occupied and set afire by American troops, in retaliation for which some Canadians went down and torched the American president's residence. With the cessation of war in 1814 the town really began to grow. Yonge St. was opened as a public thoroughfare and military road, the Bank of Upper Canada was founded, and in 1834, with a population of 9000, the city was incorporated and renamed Toronto.

Thereafter industrialization continued apace and Toronto boomed as lake travel increased and the railroads arrived. Between 1834 and 1884 the foundations of an industrial city were laid: water works, gas, and later electrical lighting were installed, public transportation organized, and the first telephone exchange established.

By World War II, because of its prime location on Lake Ontario and its nearness to raw materials, power, and fuel, Toronto had become a prosperous city. After the war the tremendous European influx turned it into the exciting cosmopolitan city it is today.

1. Orientation

Toronto is laid out in a grid system. **Yonge St.** (pronounced Young) is the main south-north street, stretching from Lake Ontario in the south to Hwy. 401 in the north; the main east-west artery is **Bloor,** which cuts right through the heart of downtown. Yonge St. divides western cross streets from eastern cross streets.

Downtown usually refers to the area stretching south from a few blocks north of Bloor to the lake between Spadina Ave. in the west and Jarvis St. in the east. Because this is such a large area, for the purposes of this book I have divided it into downtown (from the lake to College/Carlton Sts.) and **midtown** (College/Carlton Sts. to Davenport Rd.). In the first you will find all the lakeshore attractions—the Harborfront, Ontario Place, Fort York, Exhibition Place, the Toronto Islands—plus the CN Tower, City Hall, Chinatown, the Art Gallery, and Eaton Centre. Midtown includes the Royal Ontario Museum, the University of Toronto, Markham Village, and ultrachic Yorkville, a prime area for browsing and dining al fresco.

Because metropolitan Toronto is spread over 634 square kilometers and includes the suburban boroughs of (from west to east) Etobicoke, York, North York, East York, and Scarborough, some of her primary attractions exist outside the core, such as the Ontario Science Centre, and the Metropolitan Zoo—so be prepared to journey somewhat.

It is not enough to know the streets of Toronto; you also need to know the warren of subterranean walkways that enable you to go from Union Station in the south to City Hall without going outside—at least that's what is planned. Currently, you can walk from Yonge and Queen St. Station west to the Sheraton Centre, then south through the Richmond-Adelaide Centre, where you

SHEPPARD AVE. W.

SHEPPARD AVE. E.

Downsview Airport

Earl Bales Pk.

MACDONALD-CARTIER FREEWAY

WILSON

YORK MILLS RD.

LESLIE ST.

DON MILLS RD.

LAWRENCE AVE.

ST.

AVENUE RD.

BATHURST

DUFFERIN ST.

ALLEN EXPY.

DON VALLEY PKY.

Sunnybrook Pk.

EGLINTON

AVE.

BAYVIEW AVE.

LAIRD DR.

YORK

VAUGHAN RD.

SPADINA AVE.

ORIOLE PKY.

HIGHWAY 11

MOORE

OVERIEA BLVD.

EAST YORK

ST. CLAIR AVE. W.

MOUNT PLEASANT RD.

DAVENPORT RD.

DUPONT ST.

OSSINGTON AVE.

ST.

BLOOR ST.

DONLANDS

GREENWOOD

WOODBINE

DANFORTH AVE.

YONGE ST.

COLLEGE

CARLTON

PAPE

COXWELL

UNIVERSITY

JARVIS

PARLIAMENT ST.

GERRARD ST. E.

QUEEN

ST.

W.

DUNDAS ST.

QUEEN ST. E.

KING ST. W.

FRONT ST.

GARDINER EXPRESSWAY

LAKE SHORE BLVD.

Toronto Is. Airport

Woodbine Beach Pk.

Toronto Islands

N
W   E
S

Aquatic Park

LAKE ONTARIO

METROPOLITAN TORONTO

emerge briefly on Adelaide St., take a few steps east, and dive down into First Canadian Place whence you can walk all the way (through the dramatic Royal Bank Plaza) to Union Station. En route, branches lead off into the Toronto Dominion Centre and Stock Exchange. So if the weather's bad, you can eat, sleep, dance, and go to the theater without even donning a raincoat.

GETTING TO AND FROM TORONTO: Metropolitan Toronto, like any other major city, is easily accessible.

By Air

Over a dozen airlines serve Toronto with regularly scheduled flights departing and arriving at the International Airport, located in the northwest corner of Metro Toronto about 30 minutes (17 miles) from downtown. Two terminals serve the traveler and offer the full services expected at international airports: Terminal 2 for Air Canada, Air France, SwissAir, Air Jamaica, and Air Mexico, and Terminal 1 for other airlines.

Facilities at the airport include the exceptionally useful **Transport Canada Information Centres** in both terminals, where a staff fluent in 12 languages will answer queries about the airport, airline information, transportation services, and tourist attractions (tel. 416/676-3506).

Here are a few useful airline addresses: **Air Canada,** 130 Bloor St. West (tel. 969-5330); **US Air,** 100 Front St. West (tel. 364-6471); **American Airlines,** 40 St. Clair Ave. West (tel. 961-9291); **CP Air,** 69 Yonge St., 6th floor, (tel. 869-6714); **Eastern Airlines,** 2200 Yonge St., Suite 1703 (tel. 487-5477).

Getting to and from the Airport: The most convenient way of course is to order your own **limousine,** which will cost you about $15 to downtown—call 249-3368.

Otherwise, you can use the **Airport Bus Service,** which leaves from the Royal York and Sheraton Centre Hotels every 20 minutes from 5:40 a.m. to midnight. Fare is $3.75 for adults, $2 for children under 12. For more information, contact Charterways Transportation (tel. 416/677-3840).

The cheapest way to go, however, is by **subway and bus,** which will probably take about 50 minutes from downtown. You can either take the Bloor subway west to Islington and board a Gray Coach which leaves every 30 minutes from 6:30 a.m. to midnight—fare: $1.50. The bus leaves the airport every 30 minutes from 7 a.m. to 12:30 a.m. A bus also leaves from Yorkdale Station on Spadina extension line every 30 minutes from 6:20 a.m. to 11:50 p.m.; it runs from the airport between 6:45 a.m. and 12:15 a.m. Or else you can take the Yonge St. subway north to York Mills, whence the buses run every 30 minutes from 6:15 a.m. to 11:45 p.m.; they run from the airport every 30 minutes from 6:45 a.m. to 12:15 a.m. Fare: $2 one way. For information call 979-3511.

In addition, most first-class hotels inside and outside the downtown area run their own **hotel limousine services,** so check when you make your reservation.

If you're driving to the airport, take the Gardiner Expressway and Queen Elizabeth Way to Hwy. 427 north; then follow the airport expressway signs.

By Rail

Both Canadian Pacific and Canadian National (VIA) trains pull into the massive classically proportioned **Union Station** on Front St. (near the lake), one block west of Yonge. The station, of course, has direct access to the subway so that you can easily reach any Toronto destination from here (for **VIA Rail** information, call 416/367-4300). By the way, a one-way economy ticket from Montréal will cost you only $24, and the journey will take only a little under five hours—which is faster than driving.

By Bus

Out-of-town buses arrive and depart from the **Bus Terminal,** 610 Bay St. at Dundas St., and provide fast, cheap, and efficient service to Canadian and American destinations. **Gray Coach Lines,** 700 Bay St. (tel. 979-3511), **Greyhound, Travelways,** and **Voyageur Colonial** operate from here. For information and schedules, call 487-5111.

By Car

From the U.S. you are most likely to enter Toronto from the west via either Hwy. 401, or Hwy. 2 and the Queen Elizabeth Way. If you come via Montréal from the east, you'll use also Hwys. 401 and 2. Here are a few approximate road miles to Toronto: from Atlanta, 977 miles; from Boston, 566; from Buffalo, 96; from Chicago, 534; from Cincinnati, 501; from Dallas, 1452; from Detroit, 236; from Minneapolis, 972; and from New York, 563.

GETTING AROUND: Public transit is operated by the Toronto Transit Commission (tel. 484-4544, 7 a.m. to 11:30 p.m.), which provides an overall interconnecting subway, bus, and streetcar system.

Fares (including transfers to buses' or streetcars) for adults are 60¢ (or six tickets for $3), for children under 12, 20¢ (or six tickets for $1). You can purchase from any subway collector a special $1.50 Sunday or holiday (except Labour Day) pass good for unlimited travel, which may be used by one person or up to a family of five (maximum of two adults). On surface transportation you must either have the exact fare or a ticket. Tickets may be obtained at subway entrances or authorized stores that display the sign "TTC Tickets May be Purchased Here."

The Subway

It's a joy to ride—fast, quiet, and sparkling clean. The floors glisten in stations; you have to look for litter. It's a very simple system to use, designed basically in the form of a cross: the **Bloor St. east-west line** runs from Islington Ave. in the west to Warden Ave. in the east. The **Yonge St. north-south line** runs from Finch Ave. in the north to Union Station (Front St.) in the south. From here, it loops north along University Ave. and connects with the Bloor line at the St. George Station. A new **Spadina extension** runs north from St. George to Wilson.

Note: The subway operates from 6 a.m. to 2 a.m. Monday through Saturday, and on Sundays from 9 a.m. to 2 a.m.

Buses and Streetcars

Where the subway leaves off, buses and streetcars take over to carry you east-west or north-south along the city's arteries. When you buy your subway tickets, always pick up a transfer as well, so that if you want to board a streetcar or bus at the end of your subway ride you won't have to pay another fare (ditto when boarding the bus). For complete TTC information, call 484-4544.

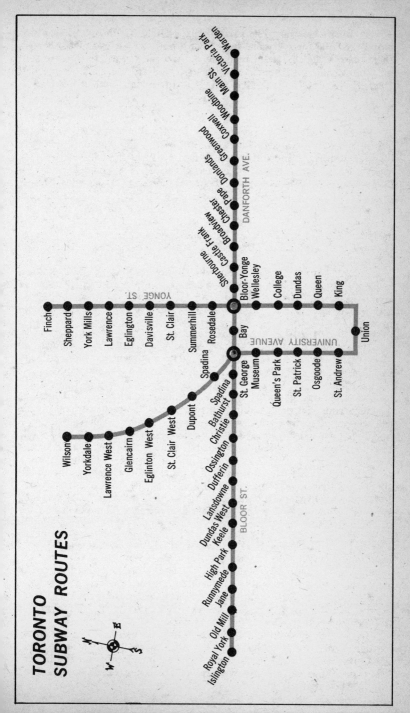

TORONTO
SUBWAY ROUTES

Taxicabs

As usual, an expensive mode of transportation: 70¢ the minute you step in and then 10¢ for every one-seventh of a mile (or 10¢ every 50 seconds). There's also a 10¢ charge for each bag. As you can see, cab fares can mount up, especially in rush hours. Nevertheless, here are the major companies: **Diamond** (tel. 366-6868), **Yellow** (tel. 363-4141), **Metro** (tel. 363-5611).

Car Rentals

Prices change so frequently and vary so widely that probably your best bet is to shop around via the *Yellow Pages*. Still, just to give you some idea, here are a few companies and their rates: **Budget** (161 Bay St., tel. 364-7104; 627 Bay St., tel. 597-0181; 1269 Bay St., tel. 964-6383; 1128 Yonge St., tel. 964-7202) charges $20.95 (including 200 free kilometers) per day plus 10¢ per kilometer, or $130 per week, for a subcompact. **Hertz** (123 Dundas St. East, tel. 245-2211) charges $22.95 (including 100 free kms) plus 16¢ a km per day for a compact. **Avis** (80 Bloor St. East, tel. 964-2051) charges $17.95 per day (including 200 free kms) plus 10¢ per km, $107.70 per week (unlimited kms). **Tilden,** (920 Yonge St., tel. 922-2600), charges $16.95 per day (including 200 free kms) plus 10¢ per km.

Note: If you're under 25, check with the company—many will rent on a cash-only basis, some only if you have a credit card, and others will not rent to you at all.

Driving in Toronto

It can be very frustrating because the traffic moves slowly downtown and parking costs are extremely high. Generally, the city-owned lots, marked with a big green P, are slightly cheaper. Still, if you can't do without your car, note the following:

You can turn right on a red light after coming to a full stop and checking the intersection, but watch out for those signs forbidding such turns at specific intersections. The driver and front-seat passenger must wear seatbelts or, if caught, pay a fine that starts at $28. The speed limit within the city is 30 m.p.h. You must stop at pedestrian crosswalks. If you are following a streetcar and it stops, you must stop well back from the rear doors so that passengers can get off easily and safely. (Where there are concrete safety islands in the middle of the street for streetcar stops, this rule does not apply, but still exercise care.)

The **Ontario Motor League,** 2 Carlton St. (tel. 964-3111), provides reciprocal aid to any driver who is a member of a recognized auto club.

TOURIST INFORMATION: A trip or note to the **Convention and Tourist Bureau,** Toronto Eaton Centre, Suite 110, P.O. Box 510, 220 Yonge St., Toronto, ON M5B 2H1 (tel. 416/979-3143), will elicit top-notch friendly guidance and a wealth of printed matter, including a good map of the city. Open 9 a.m. to 5 p.m. Monday to Friday. You'll find the bureau in Suite 110 of the Galleria at the Eaton Centre (take the escalator to the second floor and then the glass-enclosed elevator to the first stop).

During the summer, look for the bureau's information booths at various locations, including **City Hall,** outside the **Eaton Centre** at Dundas, and in **The Colonnade** at 131 Bloor St. West. For quick information, use the **Infoline** (tel. 979-3143) Monday to Friday from 9 a.m. to 5 p.m. (until 7 p.m. in June, July, and August).

The **Ontario Ministry of Industry and Tourism,** 900 Bay St. at Wellesley, open from 9 a.m. to 5 p.m. Monday to Friday (tel. 965-4008), has all the information you need on Ontario destinations.

Sport Ontario (tel. 964-8655) provides basic information on sports.

The **Community Information Centre,** 110 Adelaide St. East (tel. 863-0505), specializes in social and health service info, but will try to answer any question, and if they can't, will direct you to someone who can.

USEFUL INFORMATION: The Ontario sales tax is 7%. . . . **Banks** are open generally from 10 a.m. to 3 p.m. from Monday to Thursday, and on Friday to 6 p.m. To get the most advantageous rate of exchange, go to a bank. . . . The main **post office** is at Bay and Front Sts. For a full list of postal stations, look in the white pages under "Government of Canada" or call 369-3164 to find out which is closest to you. Hours are from 8 a.m. to 5:45 p.m. Monday to Friday. Only the main office is open on Saturday, from 10 a.m. until 2 p.m. Some post offices are open Thursday until 8 p.m. and closed Saturday. . . . Dial 361-1111 for **ambulance, fire, police,** or Harbor Police Services. . . . For **medical and dental emergency,** the Toronto General Hospital provides 24-hour emergency service (tel. 595-3946). Entrance is at 150 Gerrard St. West. . . . For **one-hour dry cleaning,** try Best Serve–One Hour Cleaners, 531 Yonge St. at Wellesley (tel. 921-9016), which gives one-hour dry cleaning service until 1 p.m. Open 7 a.m. to 7 p.m. weekdays, to 6 p.m. on Saturday. . . . **Lost and Found Office** is at the Bay St. subway station (tel. 924-2136), open 8 a.m. to 5:30 p.m. weekdays.

A NOTE ON LIQUOR: Toronto still maintains a somewhat conservative approach to the marketing of alcoholic beverages. Beer is sold in **Brewer's Retail Stores,** most of which are open 10 a.m. to 10 p.m. weekdays, to 8 p.m. on Saturdays. Check the *Yellow Pages* under "Beer and Ale" for locations. Liquor and wine can be purchased at the **Liquor Control Board of Ontario** outlets. Most are open 10 a.m. to 6 p.m. Monday to Saturday. Handy downtown locations: Toronto Eaton Centre, Union Station, Mann Life Centre, 55 Bloor St. East. The following are open 10 a.m. to 10 p.m. Monday to Friday and to 6 p.m. on Saturday: York Centre at 145 King St. West (tel. 363-0489); 101 Richmond St. West (tel. 364-6500); 1121 Yonge, (tel. 922-0403).

Some quiddities of the local law: Drinking hours are from noon until 1 a.m. Monday to Saturday, until 10:30 p.m. on Sunday. Liquor-only establishments are usually closed Sundays. It is illegal to transport an open case of beer or an opened bottle of liquor. Furthermore, you are not allowed to carry an unopened bottle of liquor to a friend's place as a gift, but he or she can collect it from your residence. That's a little difficult to enforce I imagine, but take note all ye drinkers who enter metropolitan Toronto. Oh, yes—the minimum drinking age is 19.

2. Toronto's Hotels

Toronto abounds in hotels. You can choose from the $400-a-day International Suite at the Hotel Toronto (with a grand piano, billiard table, and wood-burning fireplace) to more modest accommodations in downtown hotels, motels, and hostels.

You're wise to reserve ahead. The **Hotel Association of Metropolitan Toronto** runs a free seasonal reservation service providing information on rates,

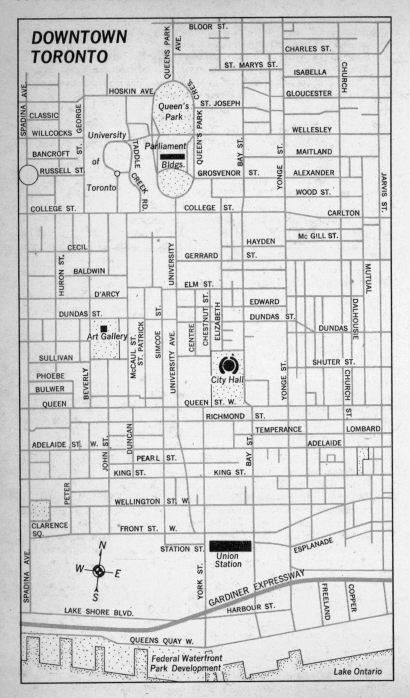

DOWNTOWN TORONTO

type of accommodation, and vacancies. Call 961-2544 from 1 p.m. to 8 p.m. Monday to Friday from mid-May to November.

In the pages that follow I have categorized my favorites according to price and location. Downtown runs from the lake shore to College/Carlton Sts. between Spadina and Jarvis; midtown refers to the area north of College/ Carlton Sts. to where Dupont crosses Yonge, also between Spadina and Jarvis; North, west, and east simply designate areas outside the city core; I have included a substantial selection of airport hotels because the "Strip," as it's called, has nine major hotels and functions as a large entertainment center, not only for visitors but also for natives who think nothing of popping out there to a disco or dining spot.

Note: There used to be a hotel and accommodations tax. Thank goodness it has been removed, but already there is much speculation that it may return in 1980.

The financial categories for a double room are roughly as follows: luxury, $60 and up per day; first class, from $50 to $60; moderate, from $30 to $50; budget, under $30. I emphasize that these are only very rough categories, and subtle distinctions of taste, clientele, and reputation must also be taken into account.

DOWNTOWN HOTELS: The downtown area runs from the lakefront to College/Carlton Sts. between Spadina and Jarvis.

The Luxury Leaders

No expense has been spared at the $45-million **Harbour Castle Hilton,** One Harbour Square (tel. 416/869-1600), to provide the ultimate in glamor and luxury. From the minute you enter the spacious richly furnished lobby with its marble floors, English oak paneling, sparkling fountains, and glittering crystal chandeliers facing a glorious view of Toronto harbor, you know. Unique in design, two 35-story towers rise from a five-story podium which houses the main public areas, and somehow the overall effect reminds me of London's Tower Bridge enlarged and turned into a magnificent hotel.

Just off the lobby in the Quayside Lounge you can enjoy that civilizing meal, afternoon tea; while in the definitely masculine atmosphere of the library-style Chartroom bar you can relax over cocktails and catch the soft piano entertainment.

The premier dining room is the Châteauneuf, modeled after a salon in a French château. Coromandel screens, rare pickled elmwood paneling, a mirrored panel ceiling, English and French original oils and watercolors enhancing the walls, and soft candlelight flickering off silver, Rosenthal crystal, and Royal Doulton: this is the mood of the richly romantic Châteauneuf, where no woman leaves without carrying a rose, a special gift from the maître d'. French and European dishes of game, meat, poultry, and fish are prepared and served with finesse. The wine cellar is extensive and contains some rare vintages, with prices peaking at $250 a bottle. Dining here will likely cost $80 and up, so save it for that strictly special occasion.

Two gilded dolphins set the theme for the Poseidon, with its tasteful nautical decor—ship chandler's ropes, lobster traps, whaling lamps—that provides the background for fish and seafood dining. An average dinner for two (with wine) will run $50 to $60. Reached by glass-walled elevator, to the top of the south tower, the Lighthouse is a revolving restaurant which turns completely every hour to provide a breathtaking panorama of 1970s fairytale

Toronto. Even the coffeeshop, the Peppermill, with its earth-tone weavings from Lisbon provides a delightful setting for cheerful nourishing fare. Downstairs, Jacqui's disco is perhaps the most innovative in the city, able to provide a dazzling display of lighting effects—from fog, light sculptures, neon lightning flashes, high-intensity light curtains, etc.—and pulsating light rhythms for the young, sophisticated crowd that gathers here. The sensational light and sound show, coordinated and designed by a British D.J. who delivers a unique patter, is coupled with quiet, softly lit seating areas. Drinks average $3 for cocktails, $1.82 for domestic beer; there's a $3 cover charge on Thursday, Friday, and Saturday. No blue jeans.

If you prefer to indulge in real exercise rather than disco dancing, Monsieur Campeau, architect-builder has provided a complex with an indoor pool, Jacuzzi whirlpool, steam and sauna baths, squash courts, exercise room, and even an outdoor heated running track.

Finally, we come to the rooms. Each of the 983 rooms overlooks the Toronto Bay and islands—a design feat in itself. Every room has individually controlled air conditioning and heating units, direct-dial telephone (including a bathroom extension), a bedside console for controlling the radio and TV (housed in a gracious wooden cabinet), and in-room movies. The furnishings are plush with heavy floor-to-ceiling drapes, marble-top furniture, and cut velvet spreads—all, of course, color coordinated. Oversize mirrored closets and large-size beds add to your comfort. Some rooms are specifically designed for the handicapped, and there is even a nonsmoking floor. Works of art—oils, watercolors, mixed media—give that added touch of luxury. And of course there's 24-hour room service.

To bask in such luxury, rates are: $53 to $73 single, $75 to $95 double, depending on the height location of the room. An extra person is $13; two children stay free in their parents' room. Weekend packages are $55 per person (double occupancy) for two nights. Additionally, there are 191 suites, including the Royal Suite (which, besides other opulent decor, contains a huge black marble mirrored bath with gilt faucet, which apparently caused visitor Prince Andrew some good-humored consternation).

The hotel operates a complimentary shuttle-bus service every 15 minutes around downtown shopping and sightseeing areas. Parking is $5, however.

A city in and of itself, that's the **Sheraton Centre,** 123 Queen St. West (tel. 416/361-1000), whose 43 stories with 1466 rooms stand super-conveniently across from City Hall at the center of a network of subterranean shopping malls. It contains one of the largest in-hotel shopping villages: 40 boutiques and restaurants on three levels, plus two movie theaters. At the back of the bustling lobby are landscaped gardens, the domain of two ornamental pheasants who evidently enjoy the waterfalls cascading to a wishing well, silver birches, and shrubs.

The hotel has six restaurants and lounges, plus a super-efficient meal species known as the "Flying Breakfast," served from a kitchen-equipped elevator that flies back and forth between floors, delivering phoned-in breakfast orders to your room in minutes.

In the shopping concourse you'll find a very authentic-looking English pub (it was shipped from England in sections), Good Queen Bess, complete with toby jugs and cozy fireplaces, one of the few places you can enjoy a mug of Newcastle brown. Off the lobby, Traders Lounge offers the chance to check the Toronto and New York stock quotations for the day on an electronic display panel, as you sip a cocktail at the oblong bar amid an imperial atmosphere of bamboo chairs, polo sticks, and clipper-ship models. On the mezzanine level, at the Long Bar (70 feet, in fact) you can watch the sun set over City Hall.

On the mezzanine, Le Pavillon coffeeshop, brightly decorated in apple green and white, serves an excellent breakfast buffet from 7 a.m., while the two premier restaurants—Pinnacle, atop the tower offering spectacular views, especially of the CN tower, and the Cafe of the Redwoods—offer both dining and entertainment. The cafe has a resident dance band, while the Pinnacle lounge adjacent to the restaurant offers two floor shows a night with disco dancing in between. Diners enjoy complimentary entry; otherwise the cover is $3 on weekdays, $5 on weekends.

An indoor/outdoor pool (20 feet inside, 60 feet outside), replete with $20,000 worth of tropical plant atmosphere, sauna, a game room, and health clinic complete the facilities.

Last but not least are those 1466 spacious rooms with all the modern accoutrements, plus in-house movies. If you're looking for a full-facility hotel super-conveniently located where you can function come rain or shine, then this is the place for you. For toll-free reservations, call 800/325-3535 in the U.S., 800/261-9330 in western Canada, 800/261-9393 in eastern Canada.

Rates: $47 to $60 single, $58 to $70 double; an extra person is $5; a roll-away bed is $10; two children under 17 stay free in their parents' room. Various packages are also available including a weekend break for $76.50 per couple for two nights. Parking is easily accessible in the underground City Hall parkade which connects to the hotel, but it will cost you $4.75 a day—more if you choose valet parking.

If you approach the **Hotel Toronto,** 145 Richmond St. West (tel. 416/869-3456), from the rear you'll see the steam rising from this plush hotel's show pool, just one of the luxury facilities available at this stylish, personalized, 600-room, 32-story, $40-million establishment, which is part of the Western International chain. Inside the comfortable lobby, 20-foot-tall trees separate it from the Terrace Grill, a super-grand coffeeshop, or rather, an open garden, landscaped dining room, created by an atrium which allows daylight to filter down from louvered windows two levels above. To complete the light atmosphere, a fountain plays, green filaments drift down from the plants placed around the balcony above, and a filigree light curtain consisting of seven panels, each with 2200 lights, sparkles overall. A 60-foot collage mural picks up the outdoor theme in a combination of hemp, cork, brass, and tiles, while the walls at the back are made of swirling rope art—quite mesmerizing somehow. Here you can enjoy breakfast, lunch, afternoon tea, and dinner seated on high-backed or low-backed rattan chairs with soft cushions.

If you wish, you can take the glass-enclosed elevators to your room, which will be large and impeccably decorated with all the expected conveniences—Touch-Tone phone, color TV, AM-FM radio, individual temperature control—plus unusual touches such as scales and alarm clocks. Rooms are currently furnished in white French provincial or dark wood contemporary with blue-green or melon and gold color schemes. In the '80s the management is redecorating in bright patterns, tending to Chinese-style bedspreads and so on.

Besides the Terrace Grill, the hotel houses the renowned Trader Vic's, with Polynesian fare and decor; the adjacent lounge offers over 90 potent exotic drinks such as the Scorpion (with a fresh gardenia floating in the glass). Stop in for complimentary tidbits Monday to Saturday from 5 to 7 p.m. The Barrister's Bar is, as might be expected, clubby and masculine, with wonderful leather armchairs and couches to sink into, and even comfy armchairs at the bar itself, which is sunken to accommodate such self-indulgent tipplers. Leather-bound legal volumes abound. Here, if you order the Barrister's Cocktail (vodka and light rum with a blend of lemon and pineapple), you can keep the fun swizzle stick with the porcelain head of a bewigged barrister. Barristers also has jazz concerts on Saturday afternoons from 1 to 4 p.m., and a Sunday sports spectacular when you can watch your favorite sport on a seven-foot TV screen. And the hotel has 24-hour room service, practically Western International's trademark.

Rates: $54 to $63 single, $64 to $74 double, $10 for each additional person. One child under 18 may stay free in the parents' room. On a weekend package you can stay for $49 per night, single or double. Overnight parking costs $4. For toll-free reservations, call 800/228-3000 in the U.S., 800/268-8383 in Canada.

Moderately Priced Hotels

Undoubtedly Toronto's best buy is Delta's **Chelsea Inn,** 33 Gerrard St. West between Yonge and Bay Sts. (tel. 416/595-1975), offering all the facilities of a luxury hotel at modest prices. A zesty doorman in blue and yellow tricorn and red uniform will usher you into what will surely be a crowded lobby, where if you peer round the bodies you'll make out a grandfather clock and one or two antique pieces. Off the lobby there's a small conservatory with a fountain surrounded by ferns, cacti, ivy, and ficus, through which you'll reach two of the hotel's four restaurants, Wittles and the Kitchen Garden. The first, seating only 42, offers French service and intimate dining in a room furnished with wingback dining chairs and a fireplace graced with pheasants and pepper mills. Classic grills, roasts, and seafood dishes are served and a dinner for two averages $50 with wine. Throughout the hotel, telltale signs reveal the overwhelming welcome given to children and you'll find one such sign in the light and airy, shrub-filled Kitchen Garden restaurant where there's a special children's menu with a hunting picture that the kids can take home and color.

There's nightly entertainment in the Chelsea Bun, stuffed with Victoriana and a lot of headgear, including bearskin helmets which you might find useful on the crowded dance floor (or on Saturday or Sunday when the place fills for a Dixieland session between 3 and 6 p.m.). Hors d'oeuvres (three for $1) are available from 4 to 7 p.m. Entertainment runs from 9 p.m. to 1 a.m., with a piano bar from 6 to 8 p.m. Then there's the Spotted Cow, a self-service fast-food eatery where you can get a soup and sandwich for $2.95 plus other familiar fare.

Hotel facilities include a swimming pool, whirlpool, sauna, exercise room, lounge, and game room (with three pool tables), and—a blessing for parents—a children's creative center where 3- to 8-year-olds can play under close and expert supervision. There's a nominal charge for this service. Babysitting service costs $2.50 per hour.

Rooms vary in size and facilities, perhaps because the building used to be an apartment house. Some rooms have fully equipped kitchens and rent for as little as $47 double. All of the 995 rooms have queen- or twin-size beds, color TV, direct-dial phones, wall-to-wall carpeting, and bright, modern decor and furnishings in shades of beige, brown, and orange. Half the rooms have balconies.

Rates: $34 to $38 single, $42 to $46 double; one-bedroom suites start at $55 single, $62 double. An extra person is $7; children under 18 can share their parents' room free. A weekend package costs $72 for two nights, single or double, in a deluxe room. Indoor parking costs $3 a day.

The **Holiday Inn Downtown,** 89 Chestnut St. (tel. 416/367-0707), right behind City Hall, has all the earmarks of the chain, plus a little extra. Not usually touted for food accomplishment, the inn has six restaurant-lounges, and certainly the buffet spread for $5.95 at Uncle's is a masterpiece, featuring cold cuts, two hot dishes, salads galore, homemade bread, fruits and cheeses, and fantastic desserts. At night the spot turns into a steakhouse with its checked carpeting, brass railings around curtained booths, and photographs of turn-of-the-century Toronto.

La Ronde started the revolving restaurant syndrome in the city and offers sophisticated cuisine while you watch the city sparkle and enjoy the nightly entertainment and dancing. Up above, on the 28th floor awaits the Top of the Inn, where popular rock, disco, and jazz music groups entertain from 9 p.m. amid stainless-steel tables that glisten in the low-lit room. Meanwhile, for real kaleidoscopic disco-style entertainment where you can literally watch the walls float by, stop downstairs to the very popular Floating World Disco. You don't even have to have a few here before you think you're flying as the clouds drift by. Cover charge on Friday and Saturday nights is $2.50.

All 715 rooms have tiny triangular balconies for that breather when you need it, and most have startling views of the CN Tower. They are large and well furnished, and have a console control panel by the bed for the color TV and radio, vanity mirrors or sinks outside the bathroom, and individual climate control. An added bonus: local phone calls are free. Parking is also included in the room price. Recreational facilities include indoor and outdoor swimming pools, sauna, exercise room, games area, and sun terrace.

Rates: $43.50 to $49.50 single, $49.50 to $59 double, depending on the number of beds and height location. An extra person is $4. Children under 12 and teens stay free with their parents.

There are five other Holiday Inns in the Toronto area: rates and facilities are pretty much the same at the inns at the **Airport,** 970 Dixon Rd. (tel. 416/675-7611), **Yorkdale,** 3450 Dufferin St. (tel. 416/789-5161), just off Hwy. 401 en route to the airport, and **Don Valley,** 1250 Eglinton Ave. East (tel. 416/449-4111 at the Don Valley Parkway. At the inns designated "West" (on Hwy. 427, en route to the airport, 2 Holiday Inn Dr.; tel. 416/621-2121) and "East" (on Hwy. 401 at Warden Ave., out in **Scarborough;** tel. 416/293-8171), rates are lower: $35.50 to $39.50 single, $39.50 to $45.50 double.

Note: The Airport branch is famous for its nightly buffet.

That other well-known chain is also well represented in Toronto and environs—the **Ramada Inn Downtown,** 111 Carlton St., near Jarvis (tel. 416/869-0099), also has partners at the airport and Don Valley. At the downtown location, opened in 1977 and just minutes from Maple Leaf Gardens, there are 350 spacious rooms, all with wall-to-wall carpeting and chic color-coordinated furnishings, color TV, and individual climate control. All the singles contain sofas for that comfortable at-home look.

For a magnificent view north over the city, whisk yourself up to Fiddler on the Roof Dining Room, which lays on superb lunchtime buffets and intimate (primarily steak and seafood) dining at night, plus an adjacent disco. The downstairs coffeeshop charmingly evokes the atmosphere of a Viennese cafe with its painted Austrian wood decor and dirndl-clad waitresses. For recreation, there's an outdoor heated pool and saunas.

Rates: $39 to $41 single, $43 to $47 double; an additional person is $6. Weekend packages are $30, single or double, per night. Parking costs $3.50 overnight.

The brand-new inn at 5444 Dixie Rd. (tel. 416/624-1144), on a six-acre woodland site ten minutes from the airport, exhibits all the current chic design modes—natural oak walls or trim in the lobby, coffeeshop, and Forest dining room, plenty of plants scattered throughout, warm earth tones and modern pine furniture in the 140 rooms, and gleaming brass and kinetic light shows in Big Daddy's disco. It has even kept abreast of sports fads, providing an indoor/outdoor pool, squash courts, and the usual saunas, exercise room, and billiard room.

Rates: $38 to $41 single, $45 to $48 double; an extra person is $7. Free parking.

The **Ramada Inn–Don Valley,** at 185 Yorkland (tel. 416/493-9000), has 286 rooms and a range of facilities including dining room, coffeeshop, live entertainment disco, and an indoor-outdoor pool. Rates: $39.50 to $41 single, $44.50 to $46 double; an extra person is $6.

Budget Hotels

Ideally located just a few blocks from Yonge St. and Eaton Centre, **Bond Place Hotel,** 65 Dundas St. East (tel. 416/362-6061), is an independently owned, medium-size modern place offering all the appurtenances of a first-class hotel at ridiculously low prices. The small triangular lobby is welcoming with its natural oak reception desk. The 281 rooms, all pleasantly decorated with bright orange-yellow floral bedspreads and curtains, caned headboards, Scandinavian-modern furniture, and wall-to-wall carpeting, contain color TV with in-house movies available, individual climate control, and direct-dial phone— and local calls are free.

Off the lobby, the Garden Cafe, always ablaze with flowers, has a bright orange-brown-yellow decor and Roman blinds, and serves from 7 a.m. to 1 a.m. daily. Downstairs, Freddy's serves a $3.50 buffet lunch, then turns into a piano bar at night (where you can enjoy complimentary hors d'oeuvres from 5:30 to 6:30 p.m. and later dance on the small dance floor).

Rates: $27 to $28 single, $31 to $32 double; suites are $45 to $50; $4 for an extra person. Weekend packages are offered, and parking is available nearby at $3.50.

As Toronto has thrived, the city center has been expanding into and reclaiming old rundown neighborhoods. This is beginning to happen on Jarvis St., until recently a skid-row neighborhood. Certainly, there still are a number of fleabag hotels either still operating or else boarded up, but one or two are being given a new lease on life, such as the **Essex Park Hotel,** 306 Jarvis St. just south of Carlton St. (tel. 416/368-4823), facing the glorious Allan Gardens.

Still under renovation when I visited, the hotel will have 110 rooms on ten stories, all decorated in the latest California "natural oak and earth tones" look with corduroy armchairs, and appointed with color TV, phone (local calls free), and individual climate control. Besides the standard rooms, some bachelorettes and one- or two-bedroom suites with full kitchen and dining area, living room, and bedroom, will be available for monthly rental. There will also be a small English-pub-style bar and a coffeeshop.

Rates: $25 to $27.50 single, $27.50 to $33 double, $55 for a one-bedroom suite, $60 to $80 for a two-bedroom suite. Children under 18 sharing parents' room stay free; an extra person is $4. Weekly and monthly rates available.

Basically furnished rooms with modern conveniences at rock-bottom prices are the hallmark of the **Carlton Inn,** 30 Carlton St. (tel. 416/363-6961), a modern, centrally air-conditioned high-rise where all 500 rooms contain studio couches (instead of beds), arborite furniture, color TV and in-house movies, phone, and a small bar with refrigerator.

Besides the economic accommodations, the inn is well located, only a few steps from Yonge St., right next door to Maple Leaf Gardens, which explains why the couches in the bar-disco are designed to resemble hockey goals and the decor consists of ice hockey gear, memorabilia, and photographs. The forefront of the bar-disco functions as a self-service coffeeshop. And the inn has an indoor pool and sauna.

Because of its location and rates, the Carlton does a flourishing transient trade. Rates: $23.95 single, $28.95 double; an extra person is $4. Children under 12 stay free in their parents' room. Parking is available for $3 at an independent garage on Wood St.

For truly economical (if somewhat musty) accommodations where the front-desk clerk will pop out to operate the elevator that takes you to your room, there's the **Victoria Hotel,** 56 Yonge St., just north of Wellington (tel. 416/363-0501), still retaining some of the charm of the Edwardian era in which it was built. The small lobby has high marble walls and polished brass railings, and a grandfather's clock stands by the old oak fireplace. Just off the lobby there's the Old Vic Restaurant and Lounge, serving lunch and dinner during the week only.

Room sizes vary and so do facilities. Some rooms have washbasin only and a shower-bathroom down the corridor; others have private bathrooms, and still others are very large, have a view of the city, and contain color TV and AM-FM radio. All are modestly furnished.

Rates: room without bath, $15 single, $20 double; room with bathroom, $20 single, $27.50 double; a large front room (with a city view), $27.50 single, $33 double.

From mid-May to September the **Neil Wycik College Hotel,** 96 Gerrard St. East between Church and Jarvis (tel. 416/367-0320), has basic accommodations available to tourists and families at extremely reasonable rates. Since these are primarily student accommodations, rooms have no air conditioning and no TV, and contain only the most essential furniture—bed, chair, and desk. Family rooms have three single beds and room for a cot. Bathrooms and kitchen facilities are down the corridor. If you want to cook, you have to furnish your own utensils.

Other facilities in the building include a TV lounge, rooftop sundeck, sauna, a game room with Ping-Pong and pool tables, a laundry room on the 22nd floor, and a cafeteria.

Rates: $13.75 to $14.75 single, $20 to $21 double, $20 to $28 for a family room (depending on the number of adults). Parking is $2.25.

The rather grim-looking **YMCA,** 40 College St. (tel. 416/921-5171), offers cheap overnight basic accommodations to both men and women. Rates: $12 to $14 single, $18 double; weekly and monthly rates available. Staying here entitles you to use the swimming pool, gymnasium, exercise rooms, and sauna. A cafeteria providing cheap but decent meals is open from 8 a.m. to 6 p.m., and there's a TV lounge on the main floor.

MIDTOWN HOTELS: The midtown area runs north from College/Carlton Sts. between Spadina and Jarvis, to where Dupont crosses Yonge.

The Luxury Leaders

Celebrities like George Peppard and Donald Sutherland stay at the **Four Seasons Hotel,** 21 Avenue Rd. (tel. 416/964-0411), whose 32 stories tower over the heart of the Bloor-Yorkville area. Having developed a reputation for the fine art of attention to detail, it is a highly personalized, 500-room hotel exmphasizing excellence of service, quiet but unimpeachable style, and total comfort.

Large accommodations are furnished with king-size beds and elegant furniture, even down to the brown-beige and velvet-trimmed lampshades. Conveniences include color TV and phone, plus such niceties as a clock radio, fine-grade linens and towels, a Persian rug wall decoration, louvered closets, a retractable clothesline, complimentary shoeshine, and 24-hour room service. Large bay windows in every room provide panoramic views of the city.

Truffles is one of the premier restaurants of the city. The handsome menu graced with a reproduction of a 17th-century Flemish painter's rendering of the Four Seasons lists such gourmet dishes as foie gras de Strasbourg truffle en terrine ($15 for two), Gordon's gin tomato soup ($6.50 for two), and pheasant perigourdine ($30 for two), as well as nouvelle cuisine specialties like salmon served with a light sorrel sauce ($11.50) and filet of beef with prunes ($15). The decor is worthy of such luxurious fare: antique chests and tables greet diners before they enter an atmosphere created by a huge French antique tapestry, gilt-framed oils, high-backed Chippendale chairs, and curvilinear French-style banquettes, whose tables are separated by wooden partitions to provide privacy.

There's also an elegant wood-paneled piano lounge with leather couches and wingback and gilt-framed portraits of Wellington and other haughty-looking generals, known as the SRO (Standing Room Only), and the Odyssey (on the 32nd floor) for dancing and nightly entertainment. The Cafe Coco serves as a brass-chandeliered coffeeshop.

The management is currently revamping and lightening the decor throughout so that by the time you arrive you'll probably find less masculine decor in all the public areas. Other facilities include an outdoor heated swimming pool with a large sundeck, and an adjacent garden with a delightful Renaissance maze.

Rates: $60 single, $80 double, suites from $128. Weekend packages are available. Parking costs $4.50 a day.

The **Sutton Place,** 955 Bay St. at Wellesley (tel. 416/924-9221), has 12 years of experience in providing gracious and personal service to its guests. The 319 rooms here are exceptionally large, and tastefully furnished in mono-chromatic tones with velour bedspreads, wingback chairs, and contemporary furniture. Amenities include bathroom telephone extensions, a bedside remote control panel for the color TV, in-house movies, and individual climate control. Half of the rooms (which are spread over 17 floors) have wet bars and refrigera-tors. The management is currently renovating and refurbishing, so don't be surprised if certain aspects have changed.

The renowned Tony Roldan is currently executive chef, and every Tues-day evening you can savor a special gourmet dinner featuring the nouvelle cuisine for $21.50 per person that might include a vegetable pâté with clamato sauce, frog legs simmered in white wine and sour cream sauce, grape sherbet, noisette of lamb with kiwis and macadamia nuts, turnips with watercress sauce, Belgian endive with mint sauce, and assorted fresh fruit with raspberry sauce. Such a gustatory treat will be served in the Royal Hunt room, which should be refurbished by the time of your visit, but will still retain the fine crystal and china and magnificent displays of fresh fruits, cheeses, breads, and other fresh ingredients.

Other entertainment and dining facilities include the English-style pub, the Bull and Bear (free snacks at cocktail time), a coffeeshop with an outside cafe, and on the 33rd floor, Stop 33, where the management is spending three-quarters of a million dollars to install a splendiforous dining/entertainment area with fountains, waterfall, hanging fireplace, raised dance floor, leather car seats, and a futuristic sound system. The magnificent view from up there requires no additional investment. Indoor pool, health club, and sauna are also available.

Rates: $50 to $60 single, $62 to $74 double; suites from $105. No charge for children under 12 sharing their parents' room; an extra adult is $10.

Weekend packages that include free overnight parking cost $46 per couple per night. Parking normally costs $4 per day.

The **Park Plaza,** 4 Avenue Rd. at Bloor (tel. 416/924-5471), retains much old-fashioned elegance, starting with the gracious forecourt which is often crammed with Rollses and Mercedeses depositing guests, through to the nightly turn-down service. Past denizens, by the way, have included Charlton Heston, Prince Philip, and Jerry Lewis.

The hotel consists of two wings. The original south wing was built in 1937, while the north wing was added in the 1950s. In the newer wing, spacious rooms, each with a little entrance corridor, have king-size beds, marble-top dressers, three closets, and handsome color-coordinated fabrics, plus all the expected accoutrements of any luxury accommodation. South wing rooms are a little smaller but still furnished with simple elegance.

The Prince Arthur Dining Room offers chic dining in an 18th-century French-style room with chandeliers. Such dishes as roasted partridge with glazed onions, mushrooms, and bacon served with red wine sauce and wild rice, are among the many specialties found here. The lounge features the large, whimsical contraptions of *Punch* cartoonist Rowland Emmett. They're wonderful, but they might have disappeared by the time you visit, should the hotel alter the decor (as is presently planned). The KCR disco (King Cole Room), Birdy's Pub, and a rooftop lounge and outside terrace complete the relaxing and entertainment picture.

Rates: $42 to $50 single, $52 to $60 double, suites from $65. An additional person is $8; children under 14 stay free in their parents' room. Parking will cost $4 a day. For toll-free reservations, call 800/323-7500 in the U.S., 800/261-6353 in Canada.

Her sister along the street has all the modern chic that such a three-year-old should have. **Hotel Plaza II,** 90 Bloor St. East (tel. 416/961-8000) has 256 rooms on six floors only—the rest of the red brick tower in which it's housed is devoted to apartments.

The hotel is designed around an inner cobblestone courtyard with flowers, shrubbery, and trees. The Greenery Dining Room picks up the theme, adorning itself with $20,000 worth of exotic plants that receive light through a vast solar-panel-style atrium. A harpist provides soft musical background for some fine expensive hotel dining featuring such specialties as steak Diane, or quails wrapped in bacon and served with Curaçao and raisin sauce ($15.25). The adjacent Greenery Lounge provides a sophisticated piano bar atmosphere where you can enjoy oyster and shrimp nibbles between 5 and 7 p.m., while the ground-floor lounge (just off the lobby) features nightly entertainment in a purple on red and natural oak setting highlighted with modern lithographs. Nibblers Coffeeshop has no windows but makes up for it with attractive spotlights and again a purple on red decor, compounded by colorful original lithographs. On the concourse level, Mingles disco is one of the most crowded spots in town, featuring a supersonic light show.

All the rooms have double beds and are decorated in burnt orange and yellow or brown and yellow, highlighted with modern original lithographs. Appointments include color TV, Touch-Tone phone, in-house movies, individual climate control, a retractable clothesline, and pushbutton bedside controls for TV and lights. For $300 you can rent an exquisite duplex suite that will have a bathroom with a marble-encased tub and cushioned marble banquettes—and a skylight over the bed—among other wonderful touches. All guests are entitled to use the pool, sauna, and health club facilities of the Bloor Park Club in the building.

Rates: $44 to $62 single, $55 to $73 double, suites from $95. Weekend packages are available. Children under 14 stay free in their parents' room; an extra adult is charged $8. Parking costs $4.50 a day. For toll-free reservations, call 800/323-7500 in the U.S. (except Illinois, 800/942-7400) or 800/661-1262 in Canada.

First-Class Hotels

In this category are two of my favorite Toronto hotels. The **Windsor Arms,** 22 St. Thomas St., one block west of Bay just off Bloor (tel. 416/979-2341), is a unique 82-room hostelry opened in 1928 and brimming with character, from its ivy-encrusted Gothic exterior and creaking oak-paneled Tudoresque elevator to the gleaming brass knobs and number plaques on the oak-paneled doors.

Many famous people have been won over by its charms and have returned time and time again (sorry, but I vowed not to reveal their names lest I spoil the hotel's reputation for discretion and old-fashioned good taste).

Authenticity is the hallmark throughout. Every room is different, although each contains predominantly Canadian antique pieces—pine cabinets, brass beds, a Victorian wicker drink trolley, a chess table—supplemented by European antiques, and even a collection of African spoons. The front-desk staff have fun assigning rooms to a particular personality and many patrons do indeed have their own specific favorite. The bathrooms, by the way, are equally unique, usually exorbitantly large, and have tub or shower or both. All rooms have air conditioning and color TV.

Besides the accommodations, the hotel has achieved a supreme dining reputation with its four restaurants. The Courtyard Cafe, opened in 1974, is *the* place to see and be seen. Stars and celebrities tumble in here to sit under a huge glass roof open to the sky among lots of greenery and sigh over the outstanding pastries and terrines (not to mention the ices, made from pure fruit, which are truly a sensual experience).

The other three restaurants are collectively known as the Three Small Rooms, and have long been held the top Toronto dining spots. Despite much stiff competition, the Restaurant is still regarded as a superb 50-seat low-lit dining room featuring haute cuisine, excellent service, and a wine cellar that offers 135 different varieties at prices ranging from approximately $10 to $275 for an Imperial, with better than 40% of them privately imported. Dinner for two here will run $65 and up. The least of the three, the Wine Cellar, set down a flight of stairs, offers a limited menu that is written daily on a blackboard. Dinner for two will run $25 to $40. The Grill completes the collection, an open room with another chalkboard menu and an on-the-spot chef for grilled items. Dinner here will run $25 to $40 for two. The hotel also has a very popular piano bar called the "22."

Rates: $36 to $56 single, $44 to $66 double, suites from $60 to $120. An extra guest is $8. Free indoor overnight parking.

In 1978 Loew's $5½-million rejuvenation program converted the 22-year-old **Westbury Hotel,** 475 Yonge St. (tel. 416/924-0611), into a modern luxury establishment that emphasizes gracious personal service. And that is the key-note from the minute you enter the lobby with its 40-foot stained-oak reception desk trimmed with brass and marble that acts as a backdrop for the huge brilliant glass chandelier. Nutmeg suede wallpaper, mirrored walls, and green planters add the finishing touches. Throughout the hotel, dark oak, brass railings and moldings, geometric carpet patterns, and wall suedes impart a luxurious feel.

The 550 rooms are wonderfully large and have little entrance halls which make them seem more like home. All except corner rooms have balconies, and all have the usual accoutrements—color TV, in-house movies, air conditioning, Touch-Tone phone. They also contain oversize beds, wall-to-wall carpeting with a border, and contemporary furnishings with a burled wood effect. The bed-sitting rooms are especially handsome, and convenient if you require more than a bedroom. Excess closet space has been converted into large vanity counters with mirrors and lights.

The contemporary coffeeshop is a joy for breakfast or lunch, with its upholstered booths surrounded by diagonal oak paneling, mirrors, and green hanging planter boxes. And Beaton's quickly became a sophisticated nightspot where people gather around the mahogany and brass standup bar or sink into the velvet banquettes and pub chairs scattered around this primarily rust and green, multilevel room.

But the pièce de résistance of the new Westbury remains the renowned restaurant Creighton's, which has nurtured so many of Toronto's now top chefs, including Tony Roldan. At the center of this elegant room hangs the shimmering gold and crystal chandelier imported from the Palais d'Orsay Hôtel in Paris. Clear mirror columns and beams with solid mahogany edges and a mirrored ceiling create drama in the room, while the velvet high-backed banquettes and chairs provide relaxing comfort for dining off Rosenthal china and Zwiesel crystal. Such a setting of course brings forth haute cuisine dishes such as suprème de volaille flambé Jeanne d'Arc (breast of chicken stuffed with oysters sauteed in Canadian whiskey and cream, topped with king crabmeat and mushrooms, and flambed with cognac at your table, $12) or the scampis amoureux retained by popular demand from the former Westbury menu (these are shrimps, mushroom, and spices flambeed with Pernod and cognac, finished with fresh cream and hollandaise sauce, and prepared at your table, $13.50). A separate dessert menu lists some extra-special desserts including three soufflés: Grand Marnier, chocolat, and Rothschild ($3). Fine wines complement the excellent cuisine.

Guests have access to an indoor swimming pool, sauna, and health club in an adjacent apartment complex for $3.

Rates: $38 to $48 single, $46 to $56 double, $52 single and $60 double for a bed-sitting room, from $90 for suites. Children under 14 stay free in their parents' room; an extra adult is $8. Weekend packages are available. Overnight parking is $3.75.

Moderately Priced Hotels

Billed as an oasis in the heart of downtown Toronto, the **Hampton Court Hotel**, 415 Jarvis St., just north of Carlton St. (tel. 416/924-6631), certainly has that air: the four-story blocks are built around a courtyard containing a swimming pool and dotted with rose bushes, shrubs, and pines. The summer patio cafe by the pool provides a stunning setting for relaxing. Ideally located right downtown, the Hampton Court offers the rare boon of free parking.

This 163-room establishment was originally a Four Seasons hotel, and it still retains a certain class. All the rooms are attractively furnished with modern furniture, floral drapes, and modern poster art, in color-coordinated tones. Some 50 rooms have a sauna/steam gadget in the bathroom, while all rooms have individual climate control, color TV (with a remote control panel), and phone. There's a small dining room which looks out over the courtyard, and a piano bar.

Rates: Singles from $33, doubles from $39; an extra person is $6; no charge for children under 14 occupying a room with their parents. A weekend package is available at $69 for two nights, double accommodation, with a continental breakfast. For toll-free reservations, call 800/828-1188 in the U.S. (except in New York, 800/462-1150), or 800/261-6282 in Canada.

Because the **Town Inn,** 620 Church St. (tel. 416/964-3311), was originally built as an apartment house, all the rooms are suites and have bedroom, living room, dining area, kitchenette, and balcony. They also feature color TV, in-house movies, and individual climate control. Unfortunately, as is so often the case, such accommodations get a lot of wear and tear, and some of the furniture and appointments could do with a little neatening up. Still, the prices are reasonable enough so that it's still an excellent bet, especially for families.

The Inn has a fine indoor swimming pool with solarium roof, saunas, and an outdoor tennis court. Downstairs, there's an attractive piano bar, standing bar, and lounge, each with patterned broadloom, bookcase, and comfy armchairs, and highlighted by a working fireplace, hunting trophies, and pewter mugs. A dining room and disco complete the picture.

Rates: $35 to $42 single, $42 to $52 double, $80 for a two-bedroom suite accommodating up to four persons. An additional person is $8; children under 14 stay free in their parents' room.

Across town, the **Village Inn,** 89 Avenue Rd. (tel. 416/923-1116) in the heart of Yorkville, offers 63 rooms at more than fair prices. Although the rooms are not fancy, they are all newly redecorated in earth tones, and have all the usual appointments, including color TV, air conditioning, and phone. Renovations, still under way at the time of writing, include a bar, restaurant, and disco under construction.

Rates: $26 single, $30 to $34 double, from $40 for a suite. An extra person is $4; children 14 and under stay free in their parents' room.

NORTH CENTRAL (MODERATELY PRICED) HOTELS:

The six-year-old **Roehampton Place Hotel,** 808 Mount Pleasant Rd. (tel. 416/487-5101) at Eglinton Ave. East, is a comparatively small (112 rooms), friendly place. A ten-story tower shaped flatiron fashion rises atop the podium base. This makes the corner rooms especially large and attractive. All rooms have pleasant modern decor and furnishings, color TV and remote control console, in-house movies, and individual climate control; some come with their own bars and refrigerators, others are equipped with saunas in the bathroom, and a few have waterbeds.

Facilities include a coffeeshop/dining room and the Koutoubia Disco, where live groups entertain ($2 cover charge weekends after 9 p.m.) while the young crowds fill the two dance floors.

Rates: $36 to $44 single, $42 to $50 double (the higher prices are for corner suites and waterbeds). No charge for children regardless of age occupying the same room as their parents. An extra adult is $6. Free parking. A weekend package of $59.95, based on double occupancy, includes two nights' accommodation, breakfast, and free admission to the Koutoubia Disco.

The **Muir Park Hotel,** 2900 Yonge St. just south of Lawrence Ave. (tel. 416/488-1193), stands opposite the park named after Alexander Muir who wrote the anthem "O Canada." An older, yellow brick hotel, it offers 122 rooms which are modestly furnished with modern pieces, all with color TV, phone, and air conditioning. Some of the studios with kitchenettes and the suites are good value, despite such signs of age as chipped paint (especially on door frames). The hotel also has an indoor unsupervised swimming pool and hot tub, and a lounge and dining room.

Rates: $27 to $37 single, $33 to $43 double (the higher prices are for studio apartments). One-bedroom suites start at $55, two-bedroom suites at $70. An extra person in a room is $5; children under 12 stay free in their parents' room. Weekly and monthly rates are available. Free parking.

AT THE AIRPORT: Airport hostelries range from luxury to budget.

The Luxury Hotels

For really personal service—the kind that caters to the idiosyncrasies of each guest—and beautiful ultrachic surroundings, the spot out here is the **Bristol Place,** 950 Dixon Rd. (tel. 416/675-9444), a select 285-room hotel where contemporary architecture and facilities blend with old-fashioned attention to detail and service. Outside, the red brick building is striking enough, looking like a concertina from a distance, but step into the lobby and it's stunning. It soars three stories to a skylit ceiling through which the sun dances on the trees, sculptures, mosaics, and contemporary wall hangings. The sound of the waterfall alone makes me want to stay.

Le Cafe, raised slightly to overlook the lobby is a coffeeshop with comfortable banquettes and handmade ceramic tiles, while in the Perroquet Pub, a barrel-vaulted room decorated with Victorian posters, you can tuck into a very English shepherd's pie. Also overlooking the lobby, the quiet lounge just happens to have a coromandel screen by which you can relax on really comfy chairs.

Zachary's dining room is delightfully contemporary and graced with a kaleidoscopic tapestry hung over white tile. Here executive chef Tony Roldan specializes in the nouvelle cuisine, and every Friday creates a $17 gourmet dinner, which in the past has featured such exciting dishes as a mussel soup with saffron, julienne of leeks and truffles, thin slices of salmon sauteed in butter with sorrel sauce, and a pineapple and mango soufflé. The hot and cold Sunday buffet brunch is also known for its distinguished sweets table and the chance to savor, (among other things), a salmon and caviar omelet.

At night, head for Dr. Livingstone's, where you can plow through the jungle of sophisticated bodies in search of whomever, surrounded by African decor and chrome—chrome bar, chrome balustrades, chrome lightbulbs—and dance the night away. The indoor/outdoor pool is crowned by a skylight dome and is complete with sundeck, flower gardens, reflecting pools, and a children's play area. The health club has an exercise room, sun room, and sauna.

And now the rooms. If you can't afford to stay in the Prime Minister's Suite, usually reserved only for the Aga Khan and Duke of Kent, a $600-a-day triplex furnished with a baby grand, antiques (many of them Chinese), a skylit bathroom with Jacuzzi whirlpool, and a private sundeck, don't despair. For the regular rooms are beautifully designed, decorated, and appointed. Each room has custom-made contemporary furniture, twin, double, or king-size beds, geometric design throws, two telephones, color TV, bedside console, alarm clock, individual climate control, and large parlor lights in the bathroom. Twenty-four hour room service? Of course.

Rates: $54 to $58 single, $60 to $66 double, suites from $100. Children under 12 stay free with their parents; an extra person is $10. Many special packages are available, including a weekender priced at $35 per night, single or double. Free parking. For toll-free reservations, call 800/828-7491 in the U.S., 800/462-7330 or 800/261-7100 in Canada.

First-Class Hotels

Looking like a huge white cliff, the **Constellation Hotel,** 900 Dixon Rd. (tel. 416/677-1500), although built 16 years ago, has been added to so often that it offers a myriad of different styles in its rooms. Providing top-notch facilities and personal service, it has a certain traditional elegance (real copper and leather throughout, for instance)—Lester Pearson liked to stay here when he came to Toronto.

The hotel is a veritable entertainment complex. The Woodbine Inn with its jockey regalia and racetrack decor has long been known for its Las Vegas–style floor shows and dancing to a big-band-style orchestra. And note—there's no cover charge. The Burgundy Room is a popular local dining spot that offers classic grills and seafood in an elegant French provincial setting. It has an especially fine selection of wines.

The hotel has an indoor/outdoor pool, shaped like a river around a Tropical Island reached by small wooden footbridges. You can sit under the spreading banyan tree overlooking this tropical garden and enjoy a cocktail or dance in the Banyan Terrace bar. During the summer, the poolside cafe and trilevel garden patio burst into life to the pulsating rhythms of a West Indian steel band while bikini-clad waitresses bop back and forth transporting exotic coolers. Weekend barbecues also add to the fun.

Or else you can waft up to the Magic Carpet lounge with its *Scheherazade* theme, overlooking the airport, and watch the planes take off—you might even catch a stewardess waving to a pilot in the cockpit. Before you reach for your earplugs, note that the room is soundproofed—and very effectively too.

The rooms are in various styles, and to add to the confusion the management is about to renovate those in the original tower. Color schemes run from beige-brown to brilliant red-mauve or green, but all have queen-size beds, color TV with in-house movies, air conditioning, and phone, and most have a sitting area for added comfort.

Besides the pool there's a full recreation complex: indoor tennis, exercise room, game room, table tennis, and saunas. A convenient touch: there's 24-hour room service, and the coffeeshop is open around the clock.

Rates: $37 to $47 single, $42 to $55 double. An extra adult is $6, and children under 16 stay free in their parents' room. Weekend and honeymoon packages are available. Free parking.

The **Airport Hilton,** 5875 Airport Rd. (tel. 416/677-9900), has all the comfort and conveniences associated with the name. Currently, perhaps the most talked-about part of the establishment is Misty's, a disco that on weekends draws capacity crowds of people whose average age hovers around 30 and who come to drift in and out of the magical illusions created by the art of projection coupled with supersonic lighting effects. On Wednesday and Thursday the cover charge is $2; on weekends, $3.

Above, in the 11-story tower, the 263 rooms have all the expected appurtenances: queen-size beds, crushed-velvet geometric design bedspreads and curtains (all color coordinated), bedside remote control console, color TV and in-house movies, louvered closets, bathroom with bidet and telephone, and a European-style minibar so that you have your drinks right there. There are a number of $85-a-day theme suites with mirrored ceilings over the beds and bathtubs for two.

Other facilities include an outdoor heated pool with poolside deck, the Coffee Pot for moderately priced meals, the Candlelight Dining room for romantic intimate dining, and the Bachelor's Lounge.

Rates: singles from $48, doubles from $58; an extra adult is $10, and children stay free with their parents. Weekend and honeymoon packages are available for as little as $35 per person, double, for two nights' accommodation. Free parking.

Moderately Priced Hotels

The **Cara Inn**, 6257 Airport Rd. (tel. 416/678-1400), offers facilities similar to other larger hotels on the airport strip, but at lower prices. It's a small, friendly place with 210 rooms, set in a streamlined seven-story block. The lobby has a comfy air with its natural-stone fireplace.

The rooms are bright and airy, and feature natural-pine furniture and headboard, burnt orange, brown, and yellow color schemes, color TV, phone, individual climate control, and a vanity outside the bathroom.

A heated pool is the focal point of an outdoor patio and garden area sheltered by pines. In the Greenhouse Restaurant, carefully tended plants and flowers are set in an actual greenhouse wall, and are complemented by exposed brick and a host of Canadian artifacts—a steeple clock, Staffordshire figures, and other ceramics. A pianist entertains from 5:30 to 9 p.m., and the fare is exceptionally reasonably priced. The Bishop's Landing, an intimate piano bar and dance spot, always crowded at the cocktail hour, is appropriately enough decorated with international flying memorabilia and named after World War I flying ace Billy Bishop, whose son and grandson sometimes still pop in.

For more formal dining, a mirrored ceiling and very private booths provide the background at La Résidence for such dishes as suprème de faisan Rob Roy ($14.25) and some excellent seafood.

Rates: $33 to $38 single, $40 to $46 double, suites from $60. An additional adult is $5, and children under 12 stay free in their parents' room. Weekend packages are $50.60 per couple for two nights. Free parking.

Howard Johnson's Airport Hotel, 801 Dixon Rd. (tel. 416/675-6100), is a pretty place. The foyer looks out over a pebbled rock garden with waterfalls and silver birches, and down to the solarium dome of the pool.

A chic wicker and chrome atmosphere prevails at Faces International Club, a swinging place for sipping and dancing. The average price of a drink is $2.25. The TallyHo dining room lays on a soup, sandwich, and salad bar lunch, and nightly entertainment, usually a folk singer.

The 250 rooms have every modern convenience—color TV, bedside panel, individual climate controls, even vibrators—and are pleasantly decorated in shades of blue.

Rates: $38 to $42 single, $44 to $48 double. Children under 18 stay free in their parents' room; an extra adult is $7. Weekend packages are available. Free parking.

At the city end of the airport strip, the **Cambridge Hotel,** 600 Dixon Rd. (tel. 416/249-7671), has 200 spacious guest rooms and more than adequate facilities—but low rates! All the rooms have color TV, bedside control panel, individual climate control, modern furnishings that might include a comfy leatherette recliner, and bright decor—brown and gold or red and mauve. Some of the rooms overlook the courtyard with an outside heated pool.

Rounding out the facilities are a lounge, dining room, coffeeshop, and Sadie's disco, which alternates live and recorded entertainment.

Rates: $26 to $30 single, $32 to $36 double; children under 12 stay free in their parents' room; an extra adult is $5. Weekend packages are available. Free parking.

The drive to reach the **Ascot Inn,** 534 Rexdale Blvd. at Hwy. 27 (tel. 416/677-3101), will bring you from runways and highways to ravines and fields where horses graze peacefully—until you decide to ride them, that is. Here, set in sprawling grounds that encompass golfing and riding facilities stands a chalet-style inn built in 1955 by two Swiss brothers, where the light streams into the lobby through a glazed multicolored glass front.

Besides the resort-style facilities the inn has a renowned dining room, Once upon a Porch, where you can enjoy steak and seafood in a distinctly Victorian atmosphere of oak furniture, brass table lamps, Staffordshire figures, and even an old carriage dangling from the ceiling. Downstairs there are two lounges—one with pine and cane-seated stools, pool table, pinball, and backgammon; and the other called Spats, which has three stained-glass-mirrored standup bars and nightly rock entertainment for dancing.

The 88 rooms are set well away from the entertainment areas and all have balconies or patios and views over the surrounding parkland. They are attractively decorated with wall-to-wall carpeting and floor-to-ceiling drapes, and have large closets, air conditioning, and color TV. For $80 double you can rent a duplex suite, beautifully furnished and appointed with cedar ceilings, a double Jacuzzi bath and mirrored surround, bar, and refrigerator.

The Health Club has a beauty salon, exercise room, massage salon, sauna, sun room, and Ping-Pong table, while outside there's a swimming pool and two tennis courts. Golf and horseback riding are nearby. The management is planning to put in a jogging track and also a children's play area. No doubt, the Ascot Inn makes a super country-city stopover vacation spot.

Rates: $30 single, $38 double. An extra person is $5, but children under 18 can stay free in their parents' room. Weekend and other packages are available for as little as $58 per couple for two nights, plus little extras. Free parking.

An Airport Budget Hotel

Also off the airport strip, but close enough to be convenient, **La Plaza Hotel,** 240 Belfield Rd. at Hwy. 27 (tel. 416/241-8513), has 70 modern rooms with up-to-date, color-coordinated decor and pine furnishings, plus individual climate control, color TV, and direct-dial phone. The hotel also has some motel units which rent for $2 less. There's a dining room which serves honest fare, a coffeeshop, and a downstairs entertainment lounge.

Rates: $24 single, $28 double, $3 for an extra person.

TORONTO WEST: Accommodations listed here are either along Hwy. 427, the route to the airport, or along Lakeshore Blvd., once a prime motel row before new motorways lured away the business.

Moderately Priced Hotels

If you want to experience a real smorgasbord along with many in-the-know Torontonians, go to the **Valhalla Inn,** 1 Valhalla Inn Rd., Hwy 427 (exit at Burnhamthorpe Rd.; tel. 416/239-2391). Without being obvious, the inn does have Scandinavian touches—a cedar-roofed lobby, a large dragonhead rising from the lounge bar, and of course those Scandinavian specialties in the Nordic dining room.

The lower rooms open out to a landscaped courtyard of trees, bushes, flowers, and fountain, while the upper ones have balconies overlooking the scene. All 160 rooms are tastefully covered with grass-cloth wallpaper that sustains the woody effect, and are decorated in burnt-orange/brown and blue combinations. Phones, radio, color TV, and individual climate control complete the room features.

There are three dining areas: the Terrace Cafe, overlooking the garden courtyard; the Mermaid, which features steak and lobster; and the Nordic, where the Sunday smorgasbord (between 5 and 9 p.m., $12.50) produces a sumptuous array of Swedish marinated salmon, roast chicken or beef, Scandinavian-style sausages, and masses of Scandinavian salads—shrimp, lobster, cauliflower, herring and onion, cucumber, bean, and pickled apples, plus breads, cheeses, and scrumptious desserts. For entertainment you can dine, drink, and dance in the Mermaid lounge. Recreation facilities include an indoor pool and sauna.

Rates: $38 single, $42 double, $6 for an extra person. No charge for children under 12 occupying their parents' room. Weekend packages are available. Free parking.

Overlooking the sweep of Lake Ontario stand two closely associated hotels, the **Seaway Towers,** 2000 Lakeshore Blvd. West (tel. 416/763-4521) and the **Seaway Hotel,** 1926 Lakeshore Blvd. West (tel. 416/766-4392).

The younger of the two, the Towers (built in 1963) has a fraction more style than its neighbor, especially reflected in the carpeted comfort of its lobby. Here, all 145 rooms face the lake and have balconies. They are furnished in Scandinavian modern and are fully appointed with color TV, phone, and individually controlled air conditioning. For relaxation there's an attractive outside pool, a dining room with nightly (except Monday) piano entertainment, and a lounge. The coffeeshop is open from 7 a.m. to noon only.

Rates are a reasonable $35 single, $41 double, in summer, dropping to $27 and $33, respectively, in winter.

The 26-year-old, four-story Seaway has very pleasant front rooms furnished with burled-wood-style furniture and a red and ochre decor, and fully appointed with color TV, phone, and air conditioning. Although the back rooms are cheaper, they are rather small, dark (having just one high small window), and practically abut the highway, so I'd stick to the front.

In the Marine Room dining room there's an excellent Ukrainian singer who entertains from 9 p.m., while the Backstage functions as a 400-capacity rock dungeon with a no-frills decor.

Rates: $35 single, $40 double; an extra person is $6. The back rooms are $29 single, $35 double. Free parking at both hotels.

Budget Hotels

Just off the Queen Elizabeth Way, at the junction of Browns Line and Hwy. 427, stands the small stuccoed and shingle-roofed, independently owned **Motel 27,** 650 Evans Ave. (tel. 416/255-3481).

All 44 units have just been completely redecorated with brown wall-to-wall carpeting and special carpet on the walls, light-brown spreads, and brown and orange patterned drapes. They all have individual climate control, color TV, and air conditioning. The motel also has what it calls its "special" room, containing a circular bed with bronzed mirror walls and ceiling, and a bathroom with a Jacuzzi whirlpool, bathtub, and a real sauna—yours for only $49.95 double. Some rooms also have waterbeds.

Rates: $19.95 to $23.95 single, $22.95 to $30.95 double; and an extra person is $3. Children under 12 are half price. Free parking.

Along Lakeshore Blvd. stretches a whole motel row's worth of accommodations which saw their heyday when Hwy. 2 was the main route into the city. Today only a few of these motels deserve a mention, and these primarily for a clean but basic accommodation. The **Silver Moon,** 2157 Lakeshore Blvd. West (tel. 416/251-4801) for instance, has rooms with black-and-white TV, no room phone, and only a shower, for $17 single, $21 double, in winter; and $26 single, $30 double, in summer.

Or there's the **Hillcrest Motel,** 2143 Lakeshore Blvd. West (tel. 255-7711), which offers clean and neat utilitarian accommodations with color TV and air conditioning. Its rates are $20 and $24 (for one and two double beds, respectively) in winter; in summer, these prices go up to $24 and $28.

Perhaps the best of the bunch are the Beach Motel and the West Point Motor Inn. At the **Beach Motel,** 2183 Lakeshore Blvd. (tel. 416/251-5591), all rooms face the lake; they are air-conditioned and have black-and-white TVs, but no telephones. Furnishings are adequate but pleasant. Rates in winter run from $22 to $26, but can rise to $40 in summer for a room with two double beds.

The **West Point Motor Inn** 2285 Lakeshore Blvd. West. (tel. 416/259-1138), is larger and is set L-shaped around a courtyard-parking area that has an outdoor swimming pool. There's a coffeeshop and dining room with nightly entertainment. The rooms are quite pleasant and some of them face the lake. Rates run from $26 single, $32 double ($3 for an extra person), in winter, to $32 and $40, respectively, in summer.

Perhaps there are travelers who prefer motel-style accommodations if they're just passing through town. But otherwise, for real value, I'd say settle for reasonably priced downtown hotels like the Chelsea Inn or Bond Place.

TORONTO EAST: This area, to the east of the city's core, offers several hotels in the luxury and moderately priced brackets.

The Luxury Hotels

Its name simply describes the setting of the **Inn on the Park,** 1100 Eglinton Ave. (tel. 416/444-2561), without conveying its charm, luxury, and resort atmosphere. This is a very lively and beautiful establishment only 15 minutes from downtown, just a quick run up the Don Valley Parkway, and conveniently located for the Ontario Science Centre (not something to be sneered at since to enjoy this sight fully you have to get there at opening time and beat the crowds).

Set at the top of a ravine overlooking the city and surrounded by parkland, the inn takes advantage of its natural setting—for example, the comfortable Copper Lounge piano bar faces west to capture the magnificent sunsets. And when you enter the lobby, ahead lies a landscaped courtyard with Douglas firs, silver birches, pruned trees, a rock garden and duck pond, all criss-crossed by walkways and dotted with benches. Beautiful in summer, the courtyard walkways are flooded in winter for ice skating.

The facilities here seem endless. Eight dining and entertainment rooms include the Café de l'Auberge, famous for elegant French cuisine and dinner dancing in a wood-paneled, candlelit ambience, one of the top restaurants in Toronto. The Vintage Room and Harvest Room take care of casual dining. In the Copper Lounge, a truly comfy spot, Indian-style hors d'oeuvres (like pappadums, and breaded shrimp with hot sauce) are served from 5 to 7 p.m. to the strains of soft piano music. Jazz takes over on Saturdays from 2 to 5 p.m. Potted palms and bamboo set a regal atmosphere in the Terrace Lounge, another piano bar, while Le Club presents an equally lavish spread of couches with wine and emerald pillows, an almost decadent setting for disco and supper dining. The cover is $5 and there's a sophisticated professional crowd.

Facilities include an indoor pool decorated with Rousseau-like murals, an outdoor pool and diving pool, a game room with Ping-Pong and pinball, badminton, shuffleboard, indoor tennis, a children's play area, and a health club with saunas and gym. A racquet club with squash and racquetball courts, running track, lounge, and gym is under construction. Meanwhile, with 600 acres of park across the road, in the summer bicycles are available, and in winter you can cross-country ski and toboggan. And if you want to get your nose (or anything else) fixed there's even a plastic and cosmetic surgeon on the premises!

Finally there are the 550 rooms, located in a 12-story low-rise and a 23-story tower, all of which have beautiful views (those facing west have balconies). All are superbly decorated with contemporary pieces and have those extra little features like alarm clocks, a retractable clothesline, and 24-hour room service, as well as the usual color TV, in-house movies, phone, and individual climate control.

Rates: $46 to $54 single, $60 to $80 double; an extra adult is $12; two children under 18 can stay free in their parents' room. Weekend packages are also available. There's free parking for 1000 cars, and even an on-the-spot gas station. For toll-free reservations, call 800/828-1188 in the U.S. (800/462-1150 in New York State), or 800/268-6282 in Canada.

The other luxury resort hotel in this area is much quieter, having an almost ethereal serenity, which may derive from its Japanese connections. The **Prince Hotel,** 900 York Mills Rd. (tel. 416/444-2511), is located 20 minutes from downtown and set in 15 acres of private parkland where you can wander nature trails and catch sight of rabbits, squirrels, ground hogs, and muskrats.

A warm and soft decor will greet you in your room, which may have a beautiful bay window or balcony with soft velvet window seat in salmon pink. Each oversize room has a marble bathroom, color TV, in-house movies, individual climate control, and 24-hour room service.

Velvet-covered booths and copper-colored walls create a certain "je ne sais quoi" ambience in Le Continental, a restaurant for haute cuisine and dancing, but really unique dining awaits you in Katsura, which houses four separate dining experiences: a tempura counter and sushi bar, tatami-style dining, a teppanyaki-style cuisine, and a garden room adjacent to the crystalline pool complete with stepping stones and waterwheel. A beautiful atmosphere prevails. Every Sunday and Monday, family hour specials are available between 6 and 7 p.m. when, for instance, a teppanyaki special consisting of salad, a combination of sirloin, chicken, and scallops, prepared with beansprouts, onions, zucchini, and mushrooms, served with rice, and tea and ice cream, will cost $7.50.

The blending of indoors and outdoors is well accomplished in the Coffee Garden by an earth-tone color scheme and magnificent textural wall tapestries. The restaurant overlooks a grove of 30-foot-tall trees, as does the Brandy Tree, a sophisticated piano bar, restfully decorated in gray and plum, which, in summer, overflows onto an outside patio where you can sip under blue parasols while seated on wide garden furniture.

Summertime is glorious here, and every year the hotel holds a theme festival outside, usually for three to five weeks around July. Previous years have produced Japanese, Philippine, and Hawaiian festivals, with lunchtime performances in the hibachi garden.

Mature over-30s male and female executive types gather at night in Raffles disco, where 12 projectors and a complex lighting system produce pyrotechnics in which to shine. Drinks average $2. Recreational facilities include an indoor-outdoor pool, sauna, and outdoor floodlit tennis court, putting green, and nature trails. Bicycles are available to explore the surroundings.

Rates: $46 to $52 single, $57 to $63 double, suites from $90. An extra person is $6; no charge for children under 14 occupying their parents' room. Weekend packages are available. Free outdoor parking. For toll-free reservations, call 800/323-7500 in the U.S. (in Illinois, 800/942-7400), or 800/661-1262 in Canada.

Moderately Priced Hotels

If you want to stay only ten miles outside the city in a unique and beautiful 50-acre setting, then try the **Guild Inn**, 201 Guildwood Parkway, Scarborough (tel. 416/261-3331). You'll enter through broad iron gates, forged in England in 1839, which served as the entrance to Toronto's main military fortification, the Stanley barracks, until they were brought to rest here. Follow the circular drive shaded by trees and bordered with flowers, and walk into the original entrance hall, which retains the character of an English manor with its broad staircase, oak beams, wrought-iron chandeliers, and oil paintings.

As you may have guessed, besides serving as an inn, the place has become a repository for art and architecture, so that the grounds are dotted with historic architectural fragments—limestone Ionic columns rescued from Toronto's Bankers Bond building, torn down to make way for the futuristic Canadian Place, for instance—as well as sculpture, fountains, and even a wishing well. Inside you'll also find wonderful collections of Liverpool jugs, Staffordshire, Meissen, carved oak sideboards and Tudor blanket chests, and pieces of sculpture and art. I can't begin to list the treasures within and without. Suffice it to say that anyone with artistic and aesthetic sensibilities and an eye for antiques would love to stay here.

Part of the reason for this plethora of art lies in the fact that the property was occupied from 1932 by the Guild of All Arts, which established art and craft workshops here. So many visitors were attracted that dining facilities were added and guest rooms soon followed, until the Guild became a flourishing country inn. During these halcyon years many notables visited, including Queen Juliana, Dorothy and Lillian Gish, Moira Shearer, Rex Harrison, Sir John Gielgud, and Lilli Palmer, to name just a few. The dining room is still a popular gathering place for Sunday brunch, and serves primarily grills, roasts, and seafood in pleasant surroundings.

The original central portion of the inn was built in 1914 and the rooms here are less modern, (without air conditioning, with black-and-white TV) and have simple functional furnishings. The new wing, however, has all the modern conveniences you expect, plus sunlamps in the bathrooms, picture windows, and private balconies. The gardens at the rear sweep down to the Scarborough Bluffs rising 200 feet above Lake Ontario, and for a room with this view you'll pay a little extra. For recreation there's an outdoor swimming pool. Otherwise the grounds and art are pleasure enough.

Rates in the main inn: $23 single, $28 double, $4 for an extra person; in the new wing: $34 single, $40 double, $5 for an extra person. Weekend packages at $59.50 per couple for two nights are available, as is free parking.

3. The Restaurants of Toronto

Food prices are high and dining in Toronto can be rather expensive. First, there's a 10% provincial sales tax on tabs over $6.

Then, if you enjoy wine with your meal, the cost will increase dramatically: the government places a *100+%* tax on all imported wines, primarily to protect and promote the Canadian wine industry in British Columbia and Ontario. Thus you may pay as much as $2.50 for a glass of house wine in the better restaurants, and $10 or more for a one-liter carafe. And doubtless the way the government continually seems to be upping the prices arbitrarily, you can expect the cost of wine to be even higher by the time of your arrival. Suffice it to say that any wine list rapidly becomes obsolete.

And as if that weren't bad enough, there's also a 10% tax on all alcohol— and the prices quoted often do not reflect that tax. Just be aware—these are the facts!

Furthermore, rather old-fashioned attitudes control the purveyance of alcohol. The law states that food has to be available in order to qualify for a liquor license, and on Sundays liquor cannot be served after 10 p.m. even in a first-class restaurant, so that midway through your meal the waiter may approach and ask for your last order. Better think about it, because you won't get another chance for a drink until Monday morning.

Ever since Toronto became *the* growth city of the North American continent, restaurants have been springing up like the proverbial weed—look around and signs saying "Opening soon!—French and Italian cuisine" stare back at you from every nook and cranny.

In the section that follows I have selected over 100 of my favorites and categorized them according to location, price, and type of cuisine. Locations are as follows: downtown refers roughly to streets from the waterfront to and including College/Carlton Sts. between Spadina Ave. and Jarvis St.; midtown refers to the area north of College/Carlton Sts. to Davenport and Yonge Sts., also between Spadina and Jarvis; Toronto North covers Yonge-Davenport and north.

Prices are rather broad categories: at luxury establishments expect to pay $60 and up for dinner for two; upper bracket, $40 to $60; moderate, $20 to $40; and budget, under $20. These, I stress, are only rough guidelines, and at many of the moderately priced and budget-priced establishments you can pay much less by choosing carefully.

HOTEL DINING: Currently considered the top haute-cuisine rooms are: **Café de L'Auberge** at the Inn on the Park, **Creighton's** at the Westbury, **Châteauneuf** at the Harbour Castle, and the **Three Small Rooms** at the Windsor Arms.

Other top-notch dining spots include the Park Plaza's **Prince Arthur Room**, Bristol Place's **Zachary's**, and Sutton Place's **Royal Hunt Room** (the latter two presided over by Tony Roldan—although the way chefs move around that might not be true by the time of your visit), the Four Seasons' **Truffles**, and Plaza II's **Greenery.** Out at the airport, the **Burgundy Room** at the Constellation and **La Résidence** at the Cara Inn offer less grand but excellent cuisine.

And then there are those two special spots—the Windsor Arms' **Courtyard Cafe** for gourmets and gossips, and the very British-Canadian **Guild Inn.**

A DOWNTOWN LUXURY RESTAURANT: Winston's, 104 Adelaide St. (tel. 363-1627), is one of the last bastions of grande cuisine in Toronto. Two small brown awnings mark the entrance to what could be an over-$100 dining experience where the burgundy decor is opulently heavy—mirrored ceilings, oak paneling, art nouveau and Tiffany lamps in excess—and food to match.

To start your dinner you might choose the quenelles of pheasant foie gras with truffle sauce ($6) if you're in a moderate mood, or really indulge with some caviar ($22). Even richer dishes might follow: escalopes de veau Winston (veal cutlets in a white wine and Cointreau sauce served with glazed banana and grapes, $13.75), or a soufflé de sole Gretna ($11.50). Top off with a Grand Marnier soufflé ($12) and don't forget to doff your hat to Winnie (who, remember, was rumored to suffer from gout) on the way out.

Lunchtime offers a chance to sample the atmosphere and cuisine at lower prices—for instance you could have a paillard of veal with mushrooms ($6.50) and Winston's terrine ($2), and still escape solvent.

Open noon to 2:30 p.m. Monday to Friday, and 6 p.m. to 1 a.m. Monday to Saturday.

DOWNTOWN UPPER BRACKET RESTAURANTS: Steakhouses, as far as I'm concerned, are usually rather dull establishments, but **Barberian's,** 7 Elm St. (tel. 597-0225 or 597-0335), if the crowds are anything to go by, is perhaps the best and brightest in town. The front half of the restaurant, both inside and out, remains essentially as built in 1860, and the three cozy interconnected rooms with candy-striped wallpaper house a superb and authentic collection of Canadiana that includes several originals by the Group of Seven, a bust of Canada's first prime minister, Sir John A. Macdonald, one of the original grandfather clocks made in Canada, along with pre-Confederation money, coal-oil lamps, and firearms.

Despite the traditional air, the friendliness and lightness of touch are reflected in the irreverent attitude expressed toward the dreaded dress code (one of Toronto's stodgier aspects). A note reads: "In the beginning, the Lord created Light, Heaven, Earth and, among other things, the Fig Leaf. He never created the Jacket. The Tie. Or the rest of that ridiculous array of formal and semi-formal attire present-day restaurateurs demand their hungry clientele wear. Not being one to mess with Divine Wisdom, Barberian's wishes to announce the following dress restriction—you must wear something."

This nonchalance does not extend to the food, however, which revolves around ten or so steak and seafood dishes, from $9.25 for a brochette of beef wrapped in bacon to $15.50 for a thick and juicy New York sirloin. After 10 p.m. a fondue and dessert menu awaits the after-theater or late diner.

The place is so popular that reservations are imperative. Open Monday to Saturday from 5 p.m. to 1 a.m., on Sunday to midnight; and Monday to Friday for luncheon from noon to 2:30 p.m.

If you'd like to dine aboard ship without shelling out for a cruise, then head down to the harborfront to **Captain John's,** 1 Queen's Quay West (tel. 363-6062 or 366-6713) at the foot of Yonge St., and hoist yourself up the gangplank and into any one of three deck restaurants, aboard the *Normac,* formerly a fireboat in Detroit.

Start your evening with a cocktail in the Cargo Hold and follow with a candlelit dinner of gourmet seafood: bluepoint oysters ($4.25), lobster marinated in cream and Pernod with mushrooms and clams ($15.95), or baked Spanish mackerel marinated in white wine, sauteed in garlic butter, and served with a baked potato ($5.95). A parfait of your choice or some cherry cheesecake might complete your meal.

From the Passenger Deck and the outside Top Deck (open for lunch only) you can gaze out over the harbor and skyline.

Open Monday to Thursday from noon to 2:30 p.m. and 5:30 to 10:30 p.m.; Friday and Saturday from noon to 1 a.m., to 10 p.m. on Sunday.

DOWNTOWN MODERATELY PRICED RESTAURANTS: There's a whole host of such species, arranged here according to the type of cuisine.

Balkan

One of my personal favorites, the **Balkan,** 12 Elm St. (tel. 597-0424), has been on the Toronto dining scene for 25 years, ever since it was opened by Joseph Sutulovie and his wife Magda, whom you can see cooking behind the counter at the back of the restaurant. As you open the door, a bell rings announcing your entrance into a small intimate dining room with a wonderful gypsy-style tented ceiling and decorated with Balkan artifacts. The menu, shaped like a fez, lists a mixture of Turkish, Yugoslav, Roumanian, Bulgarian, Greek, and Middle Eastern specialties. It also features a $19.90 dinner for two consisting of Serbian bean and smoked-meat soup, Serbian chef's salad or pecena paprika (broiled sweet pepper in spice), cabbage rolls or stuffed green peppers, rasnici kebab of veal, baklava, and Turkish coffee. The wine list features a wide selection of Balkan vintages—retsina included ($6.95).

Open for dinner only, Monday through Saturday from 5 p.m. to 1 a.m.

Basque

Another of my favorites for gracious dining in a very romantic atmosphere (created by flattering pink lights), the **Maison Basque,** 15 Temperance St. (tel. 368-6146), is just that. Step up the stone stairs past the area festooned with hanging cauldrons, pots, and ladles, into a long, narrow beamed room where the banquettes are plush and soft, the tables are appointed with Basque-style tablecloths and napkins, and the walls are festooned with pictures of costumed Basque workers in the mountain pastures, china, pottery, plates—even the basket glove of the national sport, jai alai. The waiters complete the scene with their Basque costumes and dashing sashes.

Here you'll find one of the best buys in Toronto—a delicious fixed-price $9.95 dinner that will include an appetizer, such as asparagus vinaigrette, salad with a tart vinaigrette dressing, a main course (perhaps chicken Basque style cooked with tomatoes and pimientos, and served with two fresh vegetables and potatoes, or coquille de fruits de mer), plus dessert—my choice was a succulent slice of gâteau Basque, a cake with fresh fruit and Pernod. Finish with espresso or cappucino, and complement with a glass of the excellent house wine or a selection from the good wine list.

Open noon to 2:30 p.m. Monday to Friday, 6 to 10 p.m. Monday and Tuesday, until 11 p.m. Wednesday to Saturday.

Canadian

That very English sleuth appears on the menu at **Sherlock's,** 12 Sheppard St. (tel. 366-8661), a very popular luncheon spot where you can get a full roast beef lunch downstairs in the Chelsea Room (named after the owner's dog) for only $6.95. Here, you can enjoy "gewgaws and scrimshanks" that range at lunchtime from beef hash, fish 'n' chips, and chicken pot pie (all around $5), to lamb chops, veal parisienne, and barbecued spare ribs (all $10.95) at dinner, in a very Holmesian atmosphere created by English china and prints, old copper and kitchen utensils, and a carved fireplace in front of which you can relax on comfy lounge chairs.

Reservations are a must, especially at lunchtime. Open noon to 2:30 p.m. Monday to Friday, and 5:30 to 10:30 p.m. Monday to Saturday. Closed Sundays and holidays.

Toronto has always been known as the capital of English Canada and while much about it has changed, it's not surprising that **Simpson's-in-the-Strand** decided to clone itself in the basement of First Canadian Place (tel. 368-2761). An oak staircase flanked by leather wingbacks leads down to the vast very proper, dignified replica of this august English institution founded by John Simpson (1801–1862).

The restaurant specializes in sirloins of beef and saddles of mutton and other joints which will be wheeled to your table on a silver dinner wagon. You might start your dinner with smoked filet of eels ($4.50) or potted shrimps ($3.50), and if you avoid the joints, sample the delectable steak, kidney, and oyster pudding ($9.25) or a delicacy, stewed tripe and onions ($7.50). At luncheon such English favorites as Lancashire hot pot, shepherd's pie, and bangers and mash (here referred to as grilled pork sausages) are available. Sweets include such delights known and cherished by the English as treacle roll, bread-and-butter pudding, and sherry trifle (all $1.75), which I'm told are largely an acquired taste, but one that can be heartily satisfying.

On the back of the menu you'll find an amusing cartoon depicting a fierce-looking chef responding to the query as to whether the meat is English or Foreign.

Open noon to 2:30 p.m. Monday to Friday, and 6 p.m. to 10 p.m. Monday to Saturday.

A listing of Canadian restaurants would not be complete without one or two representatives from Honest Ed Mirvish's clan. I'll tell you more about Toronto's famous Ed Mirvish later; meanwhile, hop down the stairs past the walls plastered with signed photographs of such celebrities as Liberace, Lorne Greene, Jane Asher, and Anne Murray, into **Ed's Warehouse**, 270 King St. West (tel. 366-6676) where enormous fringed Tiffany lamps, stained-glass panels, old amusement arcade slot machines, and huge (larger than you or me) porcelain vases join together in a glorious array of Victorian kitsch.

Start with Ed's barley vegetable soup and follow with any one of several cuts of prime rib ranging from $5.95 to $8.95, each served with rolls and butter, kosher dills, mashed potatoes, Yorkshire pudding, and green peas. Apple pie and ice cream for dessert.

Note that as at all of Ed's establishments (Ed's Lobster, Old Ed's) men are required to wear jacket and tie—if you don't, they'll pin a bowtie on you. Open Monday to Friday from noon to 2 p.m., from 5 p.m. daily for dinner.

After dinner you can stop in at Ed's Folly, seat yourself in a private courting parlor, and only emerge to dance if you want to. No cover.

Hordes of meat lovers flock to the **Market Grill,** 15 Market St. (tel. 366-7743), for reasonably priced grills, roasts, and poultry. The actual cuts greet you at the door, laid out for your edification, before you proceed either for a cocktail at the sunken bar or else into the large dining room with its teak salad bar, behind which are shelves of storage jars filled with pickles of all kinds.

Soups and salads precede the grills and roasts, which are priced from $3.95 for chopped steak to $7.45 for roast duck with apple sauce. I can also recommend the mixed grill, an array of sirloin steak, lamb chop, pork filet, sausage, kidney, bacon, tomato, mushroom, and french fries, all for $7.55. Luncheon specials are all under $4; brunch is served from 11:30 a.m. to 3 p.m. for $5.95.

Open daily, noon to midnight.

Chinese

The downtown area includes Chinatown, which stretches all along Dundas from Bay St. to Spadina Ave., and is spreading north and south on Spadina. Most of these Chinese eateries classify as budget establishments.

The decor is nothing special at **Young Luk Gardens,** 416 Spadina Ave. (tel. 861-1869), but it's still one of Toronto's most highly rated and popular restaurants, serving superb Mandarin cuisine. Kick off with hot-and-sour soup, and follow with a simply delicious beef in oyster sauce or palace shrimp (under $6), spiced to perfection. Open from 11 a.m. to 11 p.m. Wednesday to Monday.

Especially recommended by a Chinese friend of mine, **Jade Court,** 419 Dundas St. West (tel. 861-1634), specializes in Hakka-style cooking—a southern province in Canton. You come here for the chicken baked in spiced salt ($9 for a whole chicken), the fried chicken in paper wrapper ($10 or $5), or the bird's nest with chicken puree (from $5.50).

Most of the other dishes are around $4; there are 14 soups to choose from and 16 rice dishes. The dining room upstairs has solar-type windows, making it light and airy, and it's decorated in simple style. Open daily from 4 p.m. to midnight.

The **Pink Pearl,** 142 Dundas St. West (tel. 363-9339), is an example of the new plush Chinese restaurants—thick carpeting, exquisite table linen and napkins, and such little details as bronze chopstick holders and separate dishes for sauces. The cuisine is also rather interesting, including such appetizers as crispy fried fresh milk ($1.70), stuffed crab claws ($1.75 each), and chili and vinegar soup ($1.50), just one of ten soups. Specialties include something called "rainbow chopped in crystal fold," which is in fact a delicious blending of pork tenderloin with five vegetables sauteed with crispy noodles and wrapped in lettuce ($5.75), and a sizzling and very tasty beef tenderloin with oyster sauce served in a hot iron plate ($5.95).

Reservations recommended. Open 10 a.m. to 11 p.m. daily.

Continental

Another one of my favorites, **Crispin's,** 64 Gerrard St. East (tel. 366-4136), is one of those rare finds—a place that offers a supremely tasteful atmosphere, excellent cuisine, and a moderate tab. At dinner a harpist, classical guitarist, or some other similar gracious entertainment will provide the background—along with a setting of exposed brick and mirror (highlighted by modern graphics), marble-top tables with placemats, and cane chairs—for such creative dishes as rabbit morsels marinated in port, red wine, bay leaves, and juniper berries with prunes ($7), or Cornish hen crapaudine in sauce diable, which is as delicious to eat as it is humorous to look at ($8.25). Some really tasty appetizers are available, and you must save room for the bittersweet chocolate mousse topped with crème de cacao and almonds, or the watermelon bombe, a combination of lime sherbet, vanilla ice cream, and raspberry yogurt, both $2. By the way, don't ignore the salads. At lunchtime you'll find salmon and sole pie, ratatouille, fettucine Alfredo, beef bourguignon, salads, and soups, all under $4.

Open noon to 2:30 p.m. Monday to Friday, and 6 to 10:30 p.m. Monday to Sunday; Sunday brunch is from noon to 3 p.m.

French

Les Copains, 48 Wellington St. East (tel. 869-0898), is a handsome spot for lunch, dinner, or after-theater dining. It consists of a downstairs luncheon cafe and cabaret-style nightspot, and an elegant upstairs restaurant. Pink tablecloths, cane chairs, exposed brick, French posters, much greenery, and a centerpiece of fresh flowers—glorious red roses when I visited—provide the upstairs ambience.

Here you can order à la carte such hors d'oeuvres as fish soup Breton style served with gruyère, croutons, and rouille ($3.95), and follow with filet of white snapper cooked in seaweed ($10.75), or roast quail or sweetbreads with crayfish ($12.95). Or you can take advantage of a fixed-price dinner. The menu changes daily and you may choose from three main courses—the prices ranging from $10.95 for a brochette of scallops, onions, and mushrooms in lemon-and-butter sauce, to $14.50 for an entrecôte bordelaise. This price will include the soup of the day, the hors d'oeuvre of the day, the house salad, and a choice of dessert, a splendidly tempting array—crème caramel, chocolate mousse, and apple tart. A similar fixed-price menu is offered at lunchtime for $6.95.

At lunchtime French popular music and at night a chanteuse or similar entertainer provides the mood downstairs, along with marble-top tables, cushioned cane chairs, and a long natural-oak bar for light fare. This spot is especially popular with the publishing crowd.

The restaurant is open noon to 2:30 Monday to Friday and 5:30 to 10:30 p.m. Monday to Saturday. The cafe is open from noon to 1 a.m. Monday to Friday and 5:30 p.m. to 1 a.m. on Saturday, with entertainment from 9:30 p.m.

French restaurants which serve an excellent, reasonably priced cuisine are hard to find, but one such is the Château D'Orsi, 712 Bay St. (tel. 595-1785), where your table will be yours all night. You can relax in the lounge downstairs in front of the brick fireplace before climbing the walnut staircase with its large newel post to the elegantly but not pretentiously French provincial dining room. Here the tables are beautifully set and the room finished with chintz wallpaper, carved wooden mirrors, framed tapestries, some Napoleonic guns, armor, and dueling swords, and a stained-glass panel executed by Mrs. Orsi (who is an art teacher).

Robert Orsi, a Parisian, and Judi Fraser oversee the kitchen which produces classic hors d'oeuvres—escargots bourguignons, crevettes sauté a l'ail, pâté de foie maison—main courses such as civet de lapin ($9), faisan en Salmis 1855 ($12.50), cuisses de grenouille Provençale ($9.50), and petit filet mignon Bordelaise ($6.50). For dessert there's a scrumptious gâteau, baba chaud au rhum, and other delights ($1.50). There's also a table d'hôte dinner that includes soup, salad, a main dish (which might be duckling with black currant sauce, veal, or steak with anchovy dressing), dessert, and coffee or tea, all for $9.25. Daily luncheon specials run from $3.95 and always include a meat and fish dish, soup or juice, and vegetables and potato.

Open noon to 2:30 p.m. Tuesday to Friday, 5:30 to 10 p.m. Tuesday to Thursday, until 11 p.m. on Friday and Saturday, and from 4 to 10 p.m. on Sunday.

German

At Zum Gasthof, 403 Roncesvalles, you'll find a very German guest house atmosphere where the wine is served in broad-stemmed glasses and a cuckoo clock occasionally chants. Beamed ceiling, green gingham tablecloths, and stucco walls lined with wooden crests from the Rhineland and elsewhere in Germany complete the very homey decor.

The fare runs to various schnitzels, including a tasty Tiroler with tomatoes and bacon, all around $6, and accompanied by salad and fried potatoes. Other dishes—steak tartare, sausage plate, goulash, a Bauern omelet range from $4.50, and all make excellent meals washed down with a glass of good German beer ($2).

Open noon to 11 p.m. Monday to Thursday, to midnight on Friday and Saturday, to 10 p.m. on Sunday.

Hungarian

For years people have been flocking to **Csarda,** 720 Bay St. (tel. 597-0801), for a hearty meal made festive by stirring gypsy music and costumed waitresses. In the four small areas, wrought-iron lamps cast a warm glow over the peach table settings and room appointed with costumed dolls, painted wood artifacts, and handsome colorful plates. In winter, the blazing fire in the stone fireplace makes it even cozier.

Here, you can experiment with such delicacies as rantott borjulab (muscle of calf's foot, cooked three hours, breaded, and served with tartar sauce, $6). The goulash will come in a wrought-iron cauldron served over a flame, but the best introduction is the Transylvanian wooden platter, which includes filet mignon, veal and pork, sausages, bacon, and cabbage rolls, with vegetables, braised potatoes, and various salads—all for only $8.75. For dessert, palacsinta is a must.

Open noon to 2:30 p.m. Monday to Friday, 5 to midnight Monday to Saturday, and 4:30 to 10 p.m. on Sunday.

Indian

Serenity, a charming hostess, and some excellent Indian cuisine can be found at small and intimate **Samina's Tiffin Room,** 326 Dundas St. West (tel. 362-0350). The simple tasteful elements of the decor reflect the three components of Indian culture: the rugs that grace the wall are Muslim from Pakistan, the wood sculptures are Hindu, and the prints are taken from a book that was sent to the Queen by the British general who crushed the 1857 uprising, showing how he did so.

Crystal candle holders, brown tablecloths, cane chairs, and classical background music (most likely Bach), complete the peaceful dining atmosphere created by Samina herself, who started the restaurant four years ago after she gave up her chartered accountant career to spend more time with her children. It's the kind of personal place where the liquor is served from a small cabinet and the hostess will stock particular favorites for her customers.

You can start your dinner with samosas (85¢) or harira, a cold yogurt soup with walnuts, raisins, and cucumber ($1.55). Besides the curries (which range from $2.25 for curried lentils to $5.75) there are such interesting seafood dishes as fish moli, which is grouper poached in coconut milk with tomatoes and lime ($4.95), various charcoal barbecues, plus the very special karhai gosht, veal cooked in karhai with hot peppers, fresh tomatoes, and green coriander ($5.95). You'll need several napkins and tissues for this one. Mango ice cream and Indian sherbet (iced milk with almonds and pistachios) are among the desserts that range from $1.35, and you can finish with any one of a full range of exotic teas.

By the way, Tiffin is a coinage that was used in the Raj during the '20s and '30s to mean lunch, so it's a little surprising that Samina's is open for dinner only—from 5 to 11 p.m. Monday to Saturday. During the summer you can dine outside in a garden setting.

Indonesian

You won't find a better place for an introduction to the exciting flavors of Indonesian cuisine—or crafts, for that matter—than **Java,** 14 Richmond St. East (tel. 364-7666). Showcased puppets from West Java and Balinese masks and headresses dominate the main dining area, supplemented by buffalo-hide fans and Indonesian dolls.

Here, seated on rattan chairs, you can sample the magnificent range of two rice tables—one with 15 ingredients for $8.75 per person, and the other with 24 ingredients for $12.75 per person. To name only a few: pork sate, spiced egg in Bali sauce, vegetables cooked in coconut sauce, shrimp crackers, Indonesian beef curry, deep-fried fish with sweet-and-sour sauce, fried banana. Or else you can choose the à la carte specialties—various sates ($3.50), nasi and bami dishes (from $4.25 to $6.25), and meat, poultry, and seafood dishes. Finish with a special fruit dessert of mixed tropical fruit with shaved ice and a special sauce ($2.75).

This is also an excellent spot for lunch, when you can experiment with Indonesian specialties priced as low as $2.50. Open 11:30 a.m. to 11 p.m. Monday to Friday, 5 p.m. to midnight on Saturday, and 5 to 10 p.m. on Sunday.

Italian

A restrained and elegant modern decor differentiates **La Cantinetta,** 322 King St. West (tel. 869-1040) from the usual Italian restaurant, festooned with chianti bottles, plastic grapes and unholy images of the Bay of Naples. Here, a festive air is created by large blue and yellow banners waving from the crossbeams of this cavernous converted warehouse now tastefully decorated with plenty of plants, exposed brick, bentwood cane chairs, and large globe-style lights. A strolling trio rendering Neapolitan songs and operatic arias adds to the lively atmosphere, where tuxedoed waiters scurry back and forth carrying mounds of pasta and other Italian specialties.

What's going to make *you* festive, though, are the prices. For only $8.95 you can have a full dinner beginning with a generous antipasto, followed by either lasagne verde or soup, then vitello Vesuviana, veal with eggplant, ham and cheese sauteed in a red wine sauce, and finally homemade Italian ice cream and coffee. The pasta, by the way, is made fresh daily and you can watch the process right there in the dining room. If you prefer, you can order à la carte: pastas range from $4.50 to $6.50, and meat dishes from $5.95 to $13.95 (for pepper steak).

Most lunchtime entrees are under $5; and you can sample them in the Wine Garden, with its hanging plants and wrought-iron tables and chairs. There's a very fairly priced (for Canada) wine list.

Open noon to 2:30 p.m. and 5 p.m. to midnight Monday to Friday, 5 p.m. to midnight on Saturday, and 5 to 10 p.m. on Sunday. La Cantinetta is conveniently located two blocks north of the CN Tower.

Japanese

At **Masa,** 195 Richmond St. (tel. 863-9519), you can choose either to seat yourself at the sushi bar (and choose from a whole assortment at 80¢ to $1 apiece), or dine Western style or tatami style. Sake containers, Japanese prints, fans, and screens are scattered around the large room, which has a rock garden and pool stocked with goldfish at the entrance.

There's a full range of appetizers—sliced fishcake, oysters in rice vinegar, seaweed pasted crab leg, to name only a few—that range from 80¢ to $3.50. Or you can preface your dinner with one of the many fascinating soups—seaweed "kobu" tea for instance. The best deal, though, is to opt for the prix-fixe dinner, which for $6 or $7 will include clear soup, a small appetizer, rice, and such main courses as salmon teriyaki, raw tuna sashimi, or garlic beef yakiniku. More elaborate dinners are available for around $10. Don't miss the mitsu mame dessert—jelly made from seaweed with black peas.

Masa is well-known to Toronto aficionados of Japanese cuisine. Open noon to 2:30 p.m. Tuesday to Friday, and 5 to 10 p.m. Tuesday to Sunday.

Mongolian

The latest unique dining experience to hit Toronto comes from Mongolia via Taiwan, thanks to Y. C. Yen, owner of **Genghis Khan,** 346 Spadina Ave., between Dundas and College (tel. 363-0000), where you can taste the barbecue created by that famous conqueror whose empire once extended from the Pacific to the northern shores of the Black Sea. Here's how—after some soup, and rather interesting garnishes of pickled vegetable, garlic peanuts, and northern Chinese-style sesame bread, step up to the table display of beef, lamb, pork, chicken, and an assortment of eight seasonal vegetables. Assemble your own selection, and then blend your own sauce from among 12 condiments. Take your bowl to the chef who in a few dramatic sweeps will cook it atop huge pine-wood-stoked stoves that are heated to a blistering 600° temperature before flipping it into your bowl and returning it safely to you. It's quite an adventure—one that adults and children both enjoy. You can repeat the process as many times as you like. Follow with dessert and coffee, and for this superb and fun feast you'll pay $12.75 per person ($6 for children under 9 and nothing for children under 5). There's also a similar shish kebab complete dinner for $9.75.

The massive high-ceilinged room with a dramatic bronze frieze of galloping horses, hung with Chinese lanterns and furnished with cushioned bamboo swivel chairs, provides the appropriate background. So, too, do the hostess and waitresses clad as ladies in waiting in brilliant red and gold shimmering costumes. Open 6 to 11 p.m. Tuesday to Sunday.

Portuguese

Any Portuguese worth his (or her) salt will tell you to seek out the rather out-of-the-way **Vasco da Gama,** 892 College St. (tel. 535-1555), for really authentic Portuguese cuisine—which means primarily seafood. Cream of lobster soup or jumbo shrimps with a marvelous garlic flavor make excellent previews for such dishes (ranging from $6 to $13), as calamaries maître d'hôtel or seafood and fish in cream sauce. And where else can you get a char-broiled lobster for only $13? For the nonbelievers, there's a selection of Portuguese-style meat dishes.

Open noon to 3 p.m. and 5:30 to 10:30 p.m. daily.

At **Imperio,** 349 College St. (tel. 922-0954 or 922-1145), you'll find in front a lunch counter usually crowded with Portuguese, and in back a restaurant decorated with Portuguese pottery and plates, and a tiled mural of Portuguese fishing boats, where the tables are appointed with orange tablecloths and a single flower with fern.

This is the place to come for really tasty seafood—sole à la Costa Rica ($9.75) served with clams, shrimps, and a special sauce, and garnished with spinach-washed potatoes, or the "Discover Portugal" plate ($9.75), which combines lobster tails, clams, shrimp, and baby squid with potato, onions, and eggs. If you like squid, then the squid à la Sevillana are ($6.75) especially good, and the carne de porco a Alentejana (marinated pork and clams with a special sauce, $8.50) is very tasty.

Finish your meal with crêpes Suzette ($8 for two), or more modestly with a pastry ($1), and top it off with a Portuguese coffee, a delicious blend of cognac, Tia Maria, Grand Marnier, and Cointreau with coffee and cream ($4.50).

At lunchtime there's a substantial selection of meat and seafood entrees, all around $5. Tuesday to Saturday from 7:30 p.m. a flamenco guitarist entertains. Open noon to 3 p.m. and 6 to 11 p.m. Monday to Saturday, and from noon to 10 p.m. on Sunday.

Seafood

Although the city has several seafood establishments, most of them are super expensive, so local seafood lovers repair to the **Mermaid,** 724 Bay St., just south of Hayter St. (tel. 597-0077), where they can still dine on fish without losing their shirts. Furthermore, it's regarded as the best seafood going, much of it cooked Danish style.

Start with any one of the oyster appetizers, the excellent smoked eel, the thick clam or fish chowder, or the lobster bisque with cognac ($4.25). Follow with either shellfish—curried lobster Waikiki (curry with pineapple, coconut, and mango chutney, $11.50), stuffed shrimps with crabmeat ($8.75), or fish, which includes the unusual poached cod with a mustard sauce ($8.75) as well as turbot, char, salmon, sole, trout, and whitefish. All dinners include a tossed salad.

The place is always busy. The decor is eclectic—a statue of Copenhagen's Mermaid, a model of the *Blue Nose,* an Indian bark canoe almost abutting the beamed ceiling, plus two Royal Copenhagen porcelain sculptures. There's a little back room if you want some intimacy.

At lunchtime there's a selection of dishes (most under $7) served with fish chowder, dessert or cheese, and coffee. Most famous is the Tivoli platter, consisting of Copenhagen fish chowder, herring, sole filet with tartar, smoked salmon, small shrimp, queen crab, and smoked eel, plus dessert and coffee for only $6.95.

Open noon to 2:30 p.m. Monday to Friday, 5:30 to 10 p.m. Monday to Thursday, and 5:30 p.m. to midnight on Friday and Saturday.

The other seafood place that packs them in lies across town by the St. Lawrence Market, and is the original in a chain of similarly named establishments that are popping up throughout eastern Canada. The **Old Fish Market,** 12 Market St. (tel. 363-0334), set in a converted warehouse now topped by a boat with a red and white funnel, is a cavernous place. Downstairs on the ground floor there's a small oyster bar and a large restaurant with comfortable booths and wooden tables, and decorated with numerous photographs of old salts and fishing scenes, plus nautical regalia such as lobster traps and foghorns. Upstairs you'll find Coasters, a black arborite shellfish bar where you can relax and eat while seated on low sofas if you prefer that to a table. Here the decor consists of exposed brick and painted plumbing warmed by a huge fire blazing in the back during the winter.

Coasters offers oysters baked on the half shell or in a stew (priced daily), plus a selection of mussels, smoked whitefish, marinated herring with sour cream, shrimp, langustine, and escargots (all under $3). Wash down your choice with a carafe of the white wine ($3 to $10).

Downstairs you'll get a selection of the freshest fish, usually pan-fried or broiled. Start with one of the chowders, and then choose from the night's fresh fish offerings: rainbow trout, snapper, halibut filet, pacific shark, or tile fish, for example (from $5 to $7), all served with sourdough roll and butter, mackerel pâté, house salad, and boiled or french-fried potatoes.

Open daily noon to midnight Monday to Thursday, to 12:30 a.m. on Friday and Saturday, to 9 p.m. on Sunday.

Soul Food

How many of the following do you know: Benjamin Banneker, Henry Highland Garnet, Sojourner Truth, Richard Allen, Harriet Tubman, and Frederick Douglass? If you don't know them, then you really should; and if you do, then you'll probably want to head for the **Underground Railroad,** 225 King St. East (tel. 869-1400).

Ten years ago, this was very much an underground restaurant, known only to a few who enjoyed large portions of succulent ribs and so on at ridiculously low prices. Now it has celebrated its tenth anniversary and expanded, but people still flock here for a really tangy southern fried chicken, or ribs, baked ham and hamhocks, and more. To accompany these southern dishes (ranging from $6.25 to $9.50), you can choose two vegetables, from collard greens, casper squash, blackeyed peas, yams, okra, and snap beans. Start with an order of some chitlins, seasoned pig tails, codfish cakes, hush puppies (crunchy corn-meal fritters with a dash of onion), or corn bread. For a soul dessert, try sweet potato pie.

Such cuisine, in slavery days, ingeniously created from the master's left-overs and any foodstuffs found growing wild in the fields, deserves a simple farm flavor background, which is what you'll find here—horse collars, farm implements, hanging lanterns, old oil lamps, gourds, and portraits of some of those figures mentioned above. At lunchtime, there's a selection of omelets, sandwiches, and special entrees (all under $6); on Sundays from 10 a.m. to 2:30 p.m., enjoy a southern-style brunch menu from $3.25. Open 11:30 a.m. to 1 a.m. Monday to Friday, 10 a.m. to 1 a.m. on Saturday, and 10 a.m. to 10 p.m. on Sunday.

Spanish

Right in the heart of the Kensington Market stands **Casa Baldo,** 15 St. Andrews, just off Spadina Ave. near Dundas (tel. 362-7535), a red and green Victorian-turreted town house wherein owner Baldo Salmoral presides over a simple dining room. Baldo has been in the restaurant business since he worked for his uncle in Cordoba when he was 11 years old. Now, after years in Argentina and Canada working in top French restaurants, he is able to produce what is closest to his heart: spectacular Portuguese/Spanish seafood, plus several continental dishes.

The paella valenciana is stuffed with poultry, meats, seafood, and vegetables, and flavored with saffron ($12.50), the paella marinera similarly so with seafood ($18), while more modest dishes include a tasty casserole of red snapper, shrimps, asparagus, hard-boiled eggs, clams, and red pepper in a brandy sauce ($5.20), or a roasted Cornish game hen with eggplant, green peppers, onions, and tomatoes, sauteed in butter, brandy, and herbs ($6.75).

At lunchtime there's a wide selection of entrees (all under $4), and this is the time to enjoy the gazpacho ($1). Open noon to 2:30 p.m. Tuesday to Saturday, and 5:30 to 10:30 p.m. Tuesday to Sunday.

At **Don Quijote,** 300 College St. (tel. 920-2523), a statue of this famous character stands quietly presiding over a long, narrow, beamed and stucco-walled room hung with brilliant tapestries and paintings of windmills.

There's a good selection of appetizers, primarily seafood (around $3), which you can follow with one of the specialties: seafood casserole, leg of lamb segoviana, or frog legs cordobesa (all around $8.50); or paella valenciana ($15) or paella marinera ($20), both for two. Lunchtime dishes are all around or under $5.

Upstairs there's a tavern that features flamenco-style entertainment and dancing at 9:30 and 11:30 p.m. ($2.50 cover charge on weekends). Open Monday to Friday for lunch from noon to 3 p.m. and on Saturday from 1 to 3 p.m.; for dinner, 5:30 to 11:30 p.m. Monday to Saturday.

DOWNTOWN BUDGET RESTAURANTS: First, the Canadian species:

Canadian

You may not agree with Thomas Fuller's dictum "Of soup and love the first is best—love has its charms, but soup nourishes the young, stokes the fires of manhood, and comforts the old," but you'll surely relish the really steaming hot bowls of it at the **Great Canadian Soup Company,** 149 Yonge St. (tel. 362-0020), at Richmond St.

The French-Canadian pea soup is always available plus two others that change daily—a total of 19 soups (average price, 95¢). Sandwiches are also on hand at this self-service establishment that is decked out with butcher-block tables, bentwood chairs, and Canadiana. The morning muffins are extra-special too. There are other branches at: First Canadian Place (tel. 362-4641), 8 Dundas St. East (tel. 368-6302), and 13 Bloor St. West.

Open 7:30 a.m. to 7:30 p.m. (until 8:30 p.m. on Wednesday, Thursday, and Friday). Closed Sunday.

At the **Great Canadian Beef Company,** 145 Mutual St. (tel. 368-2877), you can get a full dinner with soup, salad bar, sourdough bread and butter, baked potato or fries, and peppermint ice cream for as little as $5.95. Barbecued chicken, ribs, breaded shrimp, and fried scallops are just a few of the dishes you can sample amid a Canadiana complex where old-fashioned bathtubs serve as salad bars. Stop in also at the company store for old-fashioned candies, home-made peanut butter, etc., and into the lounge for a drink. Try the barber's chairs for size. Open 11:30 a.m. to 3 p.m. Monday to Friday, 4 to 10 p.m. Monday to Thursday, 4 to 11 p.m. on Friday and Saturday, and 11 a.m. to 3 p.m. and 4 to 10 p.m. on Sunday.

In the adjacent **Town and Country,** part of the same organization, you can have an all-you-can-eat smorgasbord for $7.95—an endless spread of shrimp and cold cuts, hot dishes, and desserts. Booths, Tiffany lamps, and vinyl table-cloths provide the no-frills decor. The buffet is served from 4:30 to 9:30 p.m. Monday to Thursday, until 11 p.m. on Friday and Saturday, and until 10 p.m. on Sunday. There's also a Sunday brunch, from 11 a.m. to 3 p.m.

Crêpes

There'll probably be a line of eager young folks outside **Le Papillon,** 61 Jarvis St., just north of King (tel. 363-0838), a pretty place to repair for a candlelit dinner and crêpes of all kinds. Exposed brick, mirrors, some greenery, bentwood chairs, gingham tablecloths, and modern lithographs set the tone. Ever since Sandra Kane started this place four years ago it has been a roaring success, so she's expanding elsewhere in Ontario.

Before you taste the imaginative crêpes, you can start with a vegetable cocktail or a bowl of vichyssoise ($1.20) and a salad. There are 12 savory crêpes ranging from crêpe Marie Claude (with sausages, apples, and cheddar cheese, $3.70) to crêpe continental (chicken, mushrooms, and peppers in béchamel, $4.90), which comes with a small green salad. Then there are those luscious dessert crêpes with apricots, or banana and hazelnuts with ice cream and chocolate rum sauce (both $2.20), and fruit crêpes for around $3.20.

Open noon to midnight Tuesday to Friday, to 1 a.m. on Saturday, to 11 p.m. on Sunday. Licensed for beer and wine only.

Chinese

You can't leave Toronto without a visit to **Sai Woo,** 124 Dundas St. West (tel. 856-9594), a noisy, cavernous, easy-going place where you hang your coat on a wire hanger and sit down at a Formica-top table to some of the best and cheapest Cantonese food in the city. If you like, you can request a tablecloth and it will be gracefully given.

The menu runs to five pages, plus there are daily specials that run from $3.50 to $7.75 (for baked Vancouver crab with fresh ginger, green onion, and garlic flavor). Other dishes run from $3.75 for loon fong wing (chicken wings wrapped in bacon) to $17.50 for Peking barbecued duck, the skin, meat, and bone served separately with hoi sin sauce and ginger (enough for four). You can order a dinner for one for a mere $2.75, which will include consommé, egg roll, chicken chop suey, sweet-and-sour ribs, rice, and Chinese pastries. Weekday lunchtime means dim sum—a choice of 20 priced at 95¢, served from 11:30 a.m. to 3 p.m.

If you're lucky, you can write ahead and put yourself on the mailing list for the now-famous biannual banquets given at Sai Woo. Owner Bill Wen, undoubtedly one of Toronto's most genuinely gracious hosts, began these in 1972 when he duplicated the banquet served to Prime Minister Trudeau by Chou En-lai. Often running to 22 courses, it takes three months to plan, five days to prepare, and five hours to eat, and features such rare delicacies as swallows' nest, snow fungi (dug out of the ocean), and 1000-year-old egg spiced with ginger. Such a feast will cost $17.50 per person.

Open 11 a.m. to 3 a.m. daily, until 2 a.m. on Sunday.

Much smaller and less well known is **Manwall,** 404 College St. (tel. 967-0635), which offers the best tasting Chinese food I've ever had. It's likely to be crowded with Chinese families dining on deep-fried garoupa with tomato sauce ($4.50), diced chicken with walnuts, spare ribs Cantonese style, or any of the other specialties between $3 and $4. There are 21 soups to choose from, 17 rice dishes, and the menu stretches for seven pages. Dim sum are also available from noon to 4 p.m. The decor is practically nil except for two copper characters on one wall.

The owner, now 81 years old, ran a restaurant in Hong Kong for 50 years, speaks no English, but will give you gracious salutations, as will his daughter Alice, who will most likely be running the cash register. Open 11 a.m. to 10 p.m. weekdays, until 10:30 p.m. weekends. Closed Monday.

Chungking, 428-430 Spadina Ave. (tel. 367-1101), has become the spot to go to for Szechuan-style food, where you can get tasty tangy broccoli with garlic sauce, shrimp, orange chicken, or beef in unpretentious surroundings. Most dishes are between $4 and $5.

Open noon to 10 p.m. Monday, Tuesday, and Thursday, to 11 p.m. on Friday, 1 to 11 p.m. on Saturday, and 1 to 10 p.m. on Sunday. Closed Wednesday.

Stop any Chinese on the street to ask for a real Chinese restaurant and more than likely you'll be told to go to **Ho Yuen,** 135 Dundas St. West (tel. 366-4577). Down a flight of stairs you'll find a tiny place with only six Formica-top tables and a blackboard full of Chinese characters. If there's one or two of you, join someone at one of the tables, ask for the English menu, and then write your choices down on the little pad provided. The Chinese come here primarily for the seafood—where else can you get a Chinese-style lobster for $11.50, crab or squid with Chinese mushrooms for $3.25, or a whole steamed fish for $5? Moreover, you might meet some new friends—I did.

Open 4 p.m. to 12:30 a.m. Monday to Thursday, to 1:30 a.m. on Friday and Saturday, to 12:30 a.m. on Sunday. Unlicensed.

Continental

Currently ensconced in two rooms of a town house with a warm red decor, gingham tablecloths, and candles in wine bottles, **Bodega** will have moved to its new location at 30 Baldwin St. (tel. 977-1287), two blocks south of College and two west of University Ave., by the time you read this. But it will still be serving French food at rock-bottom prices. Entrees range from $5.95 to $7.95, including vegetables; daily specials chalked on a blackboard when I was there listed calf liver provençale, lapin au vin blanc, côte de veau normande, and even carré d'agneau aux herbes for only $14 (for two). Desserts are homemade and include the fascinating La Réligieuse—an eclair with chestnut puree—and a delicious apple tart with Calvados.

At lunchtime, when it's especially popular, there's lighter fare with such things as coq au vin or beef tongue for $4.25, including soup or salad.

Open noon to 2:30 p.m. Monday to Friday, and 5 to 11 p.m. Monday to Saturday.

Chic simple surroundings in a Victorian town house, well-chosen cuisine and wine, and attention to detail are the key to the success of **Parkes,** 226 Carlton St. (tel. 925-8907), one of the first restaurants to offer fairly priced continental cuisine. Young owner David Rowlands not only changes the menu frequently, but also rotates the modern graphics and art on the walls (these are for sale). The pine furniture, floral cushions, brown linen, and "Fat Albert" lighting, are not for sale.

The menu is definitely select and will usually contain two soups, five or so appetizers (a terrine and a pâté among them), and some eight or so main courses offering a full range of tastes and flavors from curried shrimps, through rabbit in red wine sauce, to poached salmon, sauce hollandaise. And where else can you find a roast rack of lamb for $6.95? Similar miracles are performed at lunchtime.

Open noon to 2:30 p.m. Monday to Friday, and 6 to 10:30 p.m. Monday to Saturday.

Surrounded by car washes and other less salubrious industrial outlets, **Le Pigalle,** 315 King St. West (tel. 367-0698), conveniently located for the CN Tower and Royal Alexandra Theatre, blots them out and lets in dreams of Paris, and that tucked-away bistro. Not that the decor—lace curtains in the window and bentwood chairs—contributes much. Rather it's the menu which lets you follow a fish soup ($2.95) or a terrine des chefs ($1.95) with chicken flambé with Calvados and apples ($4.95) and the aptly named dessert "Tentation" (apple cake with rum and almonds, $1.50). The prices, too, lead you to dream of your lost bohemian youth on the boulevards.

Open noon to 2:30 p.m. Monday to Friday, and 6 p.m. to 11 p.m. Monday to Saturday. No reservations. Be prepared for a lineup—as with all good things, people catch on fast.

Along Queen Street: This is another one of the city's up and coming neighborhoods where several moderately priced bistros are clustered around quaint junk-turned-antique stores.

Past the unprepossessing exterior of **Le Select,** 328 Queen St. West (tel. 869-3405), and the people thronging the entrance waiting for a table, you'll find a real French bistro decorated in French-provincial style with breakfronts, fringed fabric lampshades over the tables, tollware, French posters, and a jazz musical background.

What draws the young artistic crowd here is the chance to dine on cheap but good French food—rôti de porc à la crème et aux champignons ($4.75), rognons de porc, sauce moutarde ($5.30), and pavé de boeuf au poivre vert flambé au cognac ($9.80). There's always a dish of the day and a full fixed-price $7.50 dinner which includes soup or salad, choice of main course, dessert, coffee or tea, and rolls and butter. At lunchtime the menu extends to include a selection of quiches and omelets (all under $4).

No reservations are accepted. Open Monday to Saturday from noon to 2 a.m. Licensed for beer and wine only.

A glorious art deco interior and the witty lyrics of Cole Porter and George and Ira Gershwin set the mood for dining at the **Blue Angel,** 269 Queen St. West (tel. 593-1521). Breuer cane chairs, shiny black tabletops, Erte posters, tulip-shaped standing lamps, and of course mirrors, create a very effective decor. The food is just as imaginative, with such salads as Cleopatra (consisting of romaine, tomatoes, mushrooms, sprouts, anchovies, and cheese, with croutons or guacomole borracho) or avocado with bacon, pimiento, chilis, and tequila. Choose from a selection of entrees such as puffed shrimp ($5.95), carpaccio ($4.25), or the fish, pasta, or meat dish of the day. Luscious desserts like torte sorrano—an almond with chocolate truffle filling—should be experienced.

Open noon to 1 a.m. Monday to Thursday, to 3 a.m. on Friday and Saturday. Remember, though, that it's not licensed between the hours of 1 and 3 a.m.

A very friendly atmosphere prevails at **Chives,** 339 Queen St. West (tel. 368-0227), which certainly derives from its young owners, Tim Peel and Sophie. The decor also has a very personal flavor—truly phenomenal color photographs of mushrooms and other works of art (which are for sale), plus dolls, weavings, art on silk, jute carpet on the lower portion of the walls, and an eclectic collection of Victorian oak tables and chairs.

Ditto for the food, which is prepared by Tim. Dinner entrees might feature rouladen (top round steak, pounded thin with chopped onions, mustard, dill pickle, and bacon, then rolled, braised, and served with red cabbage and potatoes, $6.75), veal sweetbreads in a cream sauce, or duck with plums and brandy (both around $8). There's always a daily special that includes soup or salad and coffee or tea for around $4.50 at lunchtime, along with a selection of light entrees from $3.25. Salads include wonderful eight-ingredient blendings of endive, escarole, fennel, dandelion, and red and green peppers (from $1.25 to $3), while the desserts and fresh fruit tortes are all homemade and delicious.

Open from noon to midnight Monday to Saturday.

A neon sign marks the **Parrot,** 325 Queen St. West (tel. 366-4147), and the waiters all wear black aprons graced with the same parrot emblem. Here, the menu changes weekly, although the sandwich specialties remain a constant—combinations of all different kinds of cheeses and salads (for $1.25 to $2). In the past this spot has been known as a vegetarian restaurant and the dinner menu still reflects that approach to food, with such dishes as mushrooms stuffed and baked with black olives, capers, cream, fresh herbs, and romano cheese; polenta pasticciata; or fettucine con Parma e funghi (all around $2 to $5). But the management intends to serve more Mediterranean dishes and fish. All kinds of teas are available. Black plastic tablecloths, exposed brick, modern graphics, and red, yellow, and black chairs create an oddly satisfying, almost punky decor.

Open Tuesday to Saturday from noon to 2:30 p.m. and 6 to 9:30 p.m. Sunday brunch is served from noon to 4 p.m., when nine different omelets are available with salad for $3.95.

Peter Pan, 373 Queen St. West (tel. 364-3669), still remains the favorite of many who know this budget gourmet row intimately. A bare-bones '30s look of sheet-metal ceilings, high booths, and a spider plant here and there provides the background for truly juicy, tender burgers, crisp salads (broccoli, bacon, and mushroom), and a cheesecake smoother than the patter that passes any politician's lips. Open noon to midnight Monday to Wednesday, until 1 a.m. Thursday to Saturday.

Czechoslovakian

A bright atmosphere obtains at the **Mountain Hut,** 67 Hayter St. (tel. 597-0600), where traditional red tablecloths, matching curtains, colored-glass ball lamps, and pictures of Old Prague set the scene for some hearty dining. Start with tripe soup or the borsc (both 70¢), and follow with such specialties as veal brains with eggs, potatoes, and mixed salad; stewed beef with cream sauce, dumplings, and cranberries; or grilled cauliflower with eggs, fried potatoes, and salad (all under $5).

Apple strudel and palacinka are just two of the traditional desserts at $1. Take the opportunity, while you're here, to toss off a burning slivovica. Open noon to 11 p.m. Tuesday to Saturday, and 6 to 10 p.m. on Sunday. Closed Monday.

Deli

Aficionados favor either **Shopsy's,** 295 Spadina Ave. (tel. 366-5401), or **Switzers,** across the street at 322 Spadina Ave. (tel. 364-2309), and fierce rivalries exist between patrons of one or the other. Both are vibrant places which serve really thick corned beef and pastrami sandwiches, plus soups, knishes, gefilte fish, and so on. Switzers is open from 8 a.m. to midnight daily; Shopsy's from 10 a.m. to 8 p.m. Monday to Thursday, 10:30 a.m. to 3 p.m. on Friday, and 10:30 a.m. to 8:30 p.m. on Sunday.

You have to be a member of the "clean plate club" if you want to eat at the **Bagel,** 285 College St. (tel. 923-0171); otherwise the waitresses will get after you with "C'mon, eat already." Blintzes, bagels, lox, and cream cheese are the tops at this really characterful spot. Open 7 a.m. to 10 p.m. daily.

Just around the corner at 289 College St., just west of Spadina Ave., there's the less authentic but nonetheless dirt-cheap **Mothers Sandwich Shop** (tel. 925-4579 or 925-4570), a college hangout where you can gorge yourself on a corned beef, pastrami, or roast beef on rye for $1.85 in pleasant surroundings of Victorian photographs and pinewood booths lit by fabric-fringed lamp-shades. You can also get Italian sandwiches and really good subs for $1.75 up. On Tuesdays, free soup or fries are provided with your order (good to know). Open Monday to Saturday from 11 a.m. to 1 a.m.

In the heart of downtown, **Smokey's Restaurant,** 27 Carlton St. (tel. 363-6813), provides a full range of deli sandwiches on rye from $1.65, plus potato latkes, cheese blintzes, knishes, hamburgers, and full meals that start at $3.25 for baby beef liver served with bacon, french fries, and cole slaw. It's large, bright-red on orange, and furnished with pine. Open 8 a.m. to midnight Monday to Saturday, to 10 p.m. on Sunday.

Greek

At the **Acropole,** 50 Edward St. (tel. 598-4542), the menu changes from day to day. In fact there is no menu, for you choose your food from the daily specials on the steam table (all $4.75), which might be marinated octopus, taramosalata, saganaki appetizers, moussaka, dolmades, stewed lamb, and sweetbreads for main dishes.

Greek music, gingham tablecloths, Venus de Milo, and pictures of the Acropolis provide the atmosphere. Instead of the usual baklava, why not try the revani (walnut cake) or the special custard (galatobouriko)?

Open 11 a.m. to 11 p.m. daily, until 10 p.m. on Sunday.

Italian

The **Old Spaghetti Factory,** 54 The Esplanade (tel. 864-9761), turns out spaghetti—$2.95 with tomato sauce to $4.65 with meatballs—supplemented with veal parmigiana, chicken cacciatore, and lasagne. It's a huge space, divided into separate areas, all of which are cluttered with Canadiana—a good place to go with the kids.

Even better, next door at 54 The Esplanade is the **Organ Grinder,** (tel. 364-6517) a vast musical pizza parlor where David Lobban and Don Thompson bash out popular tunes on the theater pipe organ that has a fascinating array of gadgets—submarine sirens, sleighbells, bird whistles, horse hooves, all kinds of drums, chimes, cymbals, and a glockenspiel—and over 1000 pipes made of wood, zinc, lead, and tin.

To the tunes of this rare monstrosity you and the kids can chew any one of nine pizzas (from $2.75 to $4.25). Burgers, sandwiches, and other specials are available.

You should also look out for **Frank Vetere's Pizzerias** (there's one at Carlton just east of Yonge), where you can get a small pizza for $2.85 and up, pasta from $2.50, and special bargains such as the half-price dinner of spaghetti with meat sauce plus all the salad you can eat for only $1.87 every Wednesday from 4 p.m. to closing. Open 11:30 a.m. to midnight; to 1 a.m. Friday and Saturday; to 10 p.m. Sunday.

Salads and Sandwiches Plus

Crowded with shoppers, business people, and others attracted at lunch-time by a superb buffet, **Cornucopia,** 101 Richmond St. (tel. 360-1954), in the lanes of the Richmond-Adelaide Centre, offers an atrium-capped dining room festooned with greenery. Besides the buffet that features salads and hot dishes ($4.50), there's a selection of salads and light entrees at lunchtime (all under $4). Dinner brings more or less the same menu except that sandwiches with potato salad and cole slaw ($3.25) replace the buffet, and you can have such entrees as coq au vin, beef bourguignon, shish kebab, or prime ribs (all under $8). Open Monday to Saturday from 8 a.m. to midnight.

There's a larger branch at 277 Victoria St. (tel. 862-7617) serving the same food at the same prices in a little plusher surroundings—mirrored pillars, crystal chandeliers, statues standing on marble bases supporting plants, and white wrought-iron chairs give you some idea. Open noon to 5 p.m. Monday to Friday, and 6 p.m. to midnight Monday to Saturday.

On weekends you might have to wait two hours to get into **Mr. Green Jeans Emporium and Restaurant,** 120 Adelaide St. (tel. 363-3809), so your best bet is to call ahead and get put on the waiting list. Once inside, you'll be surrounded by open-style stores selling soap, candles, glass, novelties, stuffed animals, cards, and plants, all under one roof. The restaurant itself is bulging with plants, upturned parasols, and green-painted plumbing, and is appointed with bentwood cane chairs and green drop lamps over each butcher-block table.

The menu is massive and features monstrously large sandwiches (tuna, club, dagwood, reuben—all $3.95), omelets from $2.65, hamburgers with chips and cole slaw from $3.25, and a variety of salads from $2.95 for a "whole earth" featuring spinach, sprouts, mushrooms, walnuts, apples, raisins, etc. Finish with a swish sundae.

Open 11:30 a.m. to 1 a.m. Monday to Saturday, and 10:30 a.m. to 10 p.m. on Sunday.

Ukrainian

Any New Yorker knows that one of the best places in that city to get gargantuan portions in a warm and bustling atmosphere is to head down to the Lower East Side's Ukrainian neighborhood for a healthy diet of dumplings, borscht, etc. A Torontonian will make a beeline for **Yevshan Zillia** (tel. 366-2350), where $8.95 will buy a full dinner that includes an appetizer plate called zakusky—beets in cream and horseradish sauce, sausage, pickled mushrooms, sauerkraut salad, and a piece of fish in a piquant sauce. There's a full range of veryanke ($2.25) and salads. Main choices run to pechena kachka (duckling roasted in wine with apricots), poladvycza (pork filet with braised vegetables), and others, which you can accompany with either boiled potatoes, cabbage rolls stuffed with rice, kasha (baked buckwheat groats), or nachynka, a corn-meal soufflé. The house dessert consists of a sweet bread served with fruit and a yevshan (a herb) and brandy sauce.

Open 11:30 a.m. to 11 p.m. Tuesday to Thursday, until 1 a.m. on Friday and Saturday, and until 3:30 p.m. on Sunday and Monday.

MIDTOWN LUXURY RESTAURANTS: Napoleon, 79 Grenville St. (tel. 929-5938), has become so much *the* French restaurant at which to dine that you're lucky if you can get a table even by booking a week or more in advance. Two Egyptian sphinxes guard the entrance to the town house wherein you will find several rooms, all extremely elegant in the French manner, lit by crystal chandeliers, with luscious drapes and Empire-style furniture and Napoleon in one form or another everywhere: equestrian statues on the mantel, gilded portraits on most walls, and a statue at the top of the staircase.

Despite the opulent surroundings, the food is—surprisingly—not outrageously priced. The classic hors d'oeuvres include a pâté aux trois gibiers ($4.95), a terrine de ris de veau aux noisettes ($5.25), and a soup de poisson marseillaise ($3.50). Entrees cluster in the $12 to $15 range for tournedos

Napoleon, faisan aux marrons, a rather intriguing poulet au vinaigre de framboise.

Open 5:30 to 11:30 p.m. Monday to Saturday.

For many locals and out-of-towners, **Auberge Gavroche,** 90 Avenue Rd., is still their dearest dining spot, although prices are very high. Set in a town house, the auberge has a simple and tastefully decorated room downstairs with blue floral patterned upholstered chairs, lace curtains in the bay window, and a scattering of plates on the walls. Fresh flowers add a special touch to the tables. Here you might start your dinner with one of the classic terrines ($3 to $5.25), before selecting from the 13 fish and meat entrees that range from $13.50 for canard à l'orange to $18 for navarin de homard "Bocuse." There's a choice selection of desserts that runs to the extravagant chef's hot soufflé which will cost $10.50 and take 30 minutes. At lunchtime you can sample plat du jour with salad and coffee ($5.50) or any one of the entrees (which range from $6 to $9).

Upstairs, there's the more modest L'Entrecôte Bistro where a charming rustic atmosphere prevails: stuccoed walls, a pitchfork or two, wicker baskets hanging from the crossbeams, Victorian treadle tables with marble tops, and Windsor-style chairs, plus a small cozy bar area with comfortable banquettes. The same menu is offered every night, that is, either steak or salmon (which might be an entrecôte grilled with sauce de chef or a poached salmon with mussel sauce). Fruit and coffee will complete your meal for around $6.

Open 5 p.m. to midnight Monday to Saturday.

You'll need a wad of banknotes to entertain at the city's plushest Italian extravaganza, **La Scala,** 1121 Bay St. (tel. 925-1216), set in a matte black and white gabled town house with glorious Italianate windows. Everything about the decor is opulent: the marble entrance, the chandeliers, the red velvet chairs, the candlelit alcoves, the wood paneling, the antiqued mirrors, the Italianate statues, the gold menu with an embossed imprint of the name.

The cuisine features Italian dishes such as veal piccata ($12.95) plus steak and fish dishes (from $13.95). During the week there's a flambé specialty—steak Diane au sherry ($17.95), for example. Lunchtime prices dip substantially.

Behind the restaurant there's an equally opulent cocktail lounge complete with comfy couches, Regency-style chairs, damask drapes, gilt-framed portraits, and a marble-tiled bar.

Open noon to 2:30 p.m. Tuesday to Friday and from 5 p.m. Tuesday to Saturday for dinner.

MIDTOWN UPPER BRACKET RESTAURANTS: Most of the restaurants I've put in this category serve continental fare, so let's begin with them.

Continental

If I had one choice for dinner I'd probably, as do many others, head for **Fenton's,** 12 Gloucester St. (tel. 961-8485), the creation of two very talented and artistic men, David Barrett and Nicholas Pearce. There are in fact two dining rooms here: the first, small and intimate, and known as the Restaurant, which is downstairs; and Fenton's Garden, which has to be the most delectable place to dine in Toronto.

In both, freshness is the hallmark, from the flowers that radiate everywhere—huge arrangements of white hyacinths, tulips, daffodils, stocks, lilies anemones—to the magnificent spreads of bread, exotic cheeses, shining strawberries, nuts, peppers, celery, etc., that greet you at the entrances. With so much color provided by the flowers and ingredients, the rest of the downstairs decor is blissfully understated: exposed brick, mirrored walls, brown tablecloths, white wooden chairs, and banquettes with armrests.

The same creative energy is brought to the food, whether it's such hors d'oeuvres as rillettes of rabbit served with gherkins and pickled onions, a simple salad of lettuce, scallion, and tomato with a walnut dressing, mussel salad with saffron and hearts of lettuce, or camembert fritters with fresh tomato sauce and fried parsley (all under $3). For soup connoisseurs, the cream of leek with Stilton is heavenly ($1.75). An equally imaginative selection of meat and fish dishes follow. Just one selection should give you an idea: breast of chicken filet with veal, nuts, and ginger, blazed in Curaçao and sauteed with oranges, grapes, and raisins ($8.25).

In the garden large Ficus trees strung with tiny white lights, a balcony draped with shrubs, and an atrium arching over the tiled floor creates a fairytale setting in the grand manner of the European cafe. The same flair found downstairs inspires the cuisine, and some of the dishes are in fact the same. Desserts are justly proclaimed—syllabub, lemon cheesecake with fresh berries, or chestnut ice cream with hot chocolate sauce ($1.75 to $2).

Don't miss Fenton's—but do reserve so you won't be disappointed.

Brunch at the **Hazelton Cafe,** in Hazelton Lanes (tel. 923-6944), simply should not be missed by anyone visiting Toronto looking for a memorable dining experience. Also the domain of the aforementioned Barrett and Pearce, it shares the same distinguishing characteristics as Fenton's: glorious fresh-flower arrangements and food displays, and exquisitely understated decor—one Persian chest, one Venetian mirror, Philippine fans lit from behind, and Bauhaus design chairs of French velvet.

Every morsel of the $9.25 brunch is worth it. Although it changes from week to week, you might start with a terrine or prosciutto with fresh fruit (not just melon). Then you can choose from quenelles, omelets, roulades, and even a veal curry that is quite exquisitely served with coconut and an array of condiments, including kumquats. The desserts can only be adequately described in erotic terms, but if the blanc et noir—a combination of chocolate mousse with meringue such that you will never taste the likes again—is on the menu, have it. And the whipped cream is whipped just to that point. . . .

To complete the experience, you can gaze onto (or sit in) a courtyard miraculously transformed in summer into a medieval scene, with brilliant blue and yellow jousting tents. Similar wonderful experiences can be had at lunch or dinner.

Open from noon to 4 p.m. for lunch, from 6 to 10 p.m. for dinner. Sunday brunch is served from noon to 2:30 p.m. Closed Sunday evening. Reservations are vital at all times.

At **L'Hardy's,** another town house restaurant at 634 Church St. just north of Charles St. (tel. 967-1818), an ornate French-style decor of chintz wallpaper, Louis XV chairs, and gilt mirrors provides the background for expensive but excellent (the menu is limited to ensure it) dining. A prix-fixe dinner runs from $17 to $21.95 depending on your choice of entree, which might be rabbit in red wine sauce, or veal baked in cream and Madeira sauce. You can choose from three soups—my favorite, a cucumber and watercress vichysoisse—and several appetizers including a quiche of crabmeat Florentine.

Again, reservations are absolutely vital. Open 6 to 9:30 p.m. Monday to Saturday.

Across the town, **Glossops,** 39 Prince Arthur Ave. (tel. 964-2440), provides a similar $18.75 five-course prix-fixe dinner, but in rather different surroundings. Set in a beautiful red brick town house, the series of dining rooms is splendidly light and airy, appointed simply with leather banquettes, brown tablecloths, silver candelabras, fresh-flower arrangements, and a soft classical music background.

Dinner might start with broiled oysters (with bacon, finely chopped red and green peppers, onion, breadcrumbs, and garlic, with a dash of Tabasco) and continue later with either sole with butter, sprigs of fresh herbs, and lemon, or fresh baby pheasant cooked in vine leaves with grapes and then poached in French sauternes and cream. At lunchtime, the entrees range from $3.55 for an omelette chasseur to $7.50 for filet steak with sauce béarnaise.

Open noon to 2:30 p.m. Monday to Friday, and 6 to 10 p.m. Monday to Saturday.

In the heart of Yorkville, **L'Aiglon,** 121 Yorkville Ave. (tel. 925-8612), has been serving continental cuisine for 20 years. Elegantly decorated with shield-back chairs, gracious table settings, and chintz wallpaper which matches the menu cover, L'Aiglon is noted for such rich specialties as coeur de filet de boeuf sauté ambassade ($11.75), a filet mignon stuffed with fresh oysters sauteed with vermouth and Calvados cream sauce and garnished with baby shrimp, as well as the classic entrecôte bordelaise ($12.50), or the frog legs sauteed with garlic and tomato ($10.50). Dessert specialties include, of course, crêpes Suzette au Grand Marnier ($5.75 for two).

Given its style and the standard of its cuisine, L'Aiglon is one of the more reasonably priced continental restaurants. Lunchtime is ideal for sampling veau normande or oysters Florentine, both around $5. Open noon to 3 p.m. and 5 p.m. to 1 a.m. Monday to Saturday.

The **Corner House,** 501 Davenport Rd. (tel. 923-2604), is interesting not only for its excellent cuisine, but also for its location. Set at the foot of a hill only minutes from Casa Loma, it looks like any other suburban single-family house, except for the discreet sign outside on the lawn. Inside, there are four rooms for dining: two small ones downstairs, and two upstairs (one with only four tables), each decorated very simply with oil paintings and some china plates.

Chef Peter Colberg spent 11 years at that bastion of grande cuisine, Winston's, and continues to turn out an excitingly rich array of dishes: veal Oscar that consists of two medallions of veal, one topped with white asparagus bathed in a white wine, cream, and mushroom sauce, and the other topped with Alaska king crab and a generous dollop of sauce béarnaise ($14.95); a breast of chicken sauteed and simmered in a sauce with bananas, pineapple chunks, and Mandarine, a Belgian liqueur ($12.25). The price includes an appetizer, salad, dessert, and coffee or tea. At lunchtime there's a daily $5.50 special which includes soup and dessert.

Open noon to 2:30 p.m. Tuesday to Friday, and 6 to 11 p.m. Tuesday to Saturday.

French

One of the older Toronto French restaurants, **Le Provençal,** 23 St. Thomas St. (tel. 924-3721), offers not only a charming, unpretentious French-provincial setting complete with its large fireplace and beamed ceiling hung with brass skillets and pots, plus warm golden table settings appointed with fresh flowers, but also an excellent table d'hôte dinner for $14.50. This includes soup or appetizer, a choice from such main courses as an entrecôte grilled with herb butter or veal escalopes with white asparagus tips and cream sauce, a dessert which you can choose from a tempting array, and coffee or tea. You can also order à la carte, where entrees range from $9.50 to $16 for the lobster specialties.

Lunch, very conveniently served from 11:45 a.m. to 4:30 p.m., is a good time to stop in for a variety of entrees (from $4 to $8) or the daily special, which might be pork loin roast with vegetables, soup, and coffee or tea included for only $5.

Open noon to midnight Monday to Saturday.

Italian

Another truly unique dining place that should not be missed, **Noodles,** 60 Bloor St. West (tel. 921-3171), has an ingenious decor, and although I have classified it as Italian, it actually specializes in . . . ?

Somehow or other the designer managed to take the high-ceilinged mirrored room with a gallery, tile it with glowing burnt-orange Italian tile, and fill it with elongated appointments all reminiscent of noodles—from the tubular chrome chairs with tubular upholstery to the very long, dangling lights and the heavier rounded stainless-steel columns and exhaust ducts. It's one of the most glorious, truly inspired decors around. And the food matches it. The dishes are original, superbly prepared and served. At dinner you might start with the carpaccio (marinated veal, lemon, ground pepper, and fresh herbs) or the snails in mushroom caps (both around $4), before moving on to the veal scaloppine with chanterelles and green fettucine ($8.75) or the tutto mare—scallops, shrimps, and clams in a white wine and cream sauce—served with green fettucine ($7.50).

At lunchtime I can highly recommend the fettucine with a brochette of shrimps, scallops, and scampi with pesto butter ($6.90), although you will just as surely enjoy the fettucine with pesto ($2), a meal in itself. Do save room for the zabaglione with marsala or the deep-fried ice cream flamed with rum at $2.85 (I warned you everything about the place was original).

Open noon to 2:30 p.m. and 6 to midnight Monday to Saturday, and 5 to 10 p.m. on Sunday. Reservations recommended, especially at lunchtime.

Seafood

Simple cozy surroundings (but note the art deco lamp in one corner) of brown checked tablecloths, assorted chairs, and sandblasted brick walls covered with copper molds and other cooking paraphernalia set the background for some luxurious seafood at **Quenelles,** 636 Church St. (tel. 967-6131).

Appetizers include the usual moules marinières, shrimps in garlic and lemon butter, plus a really superb seafood pâté of scallops, sole, shrimps, molded with sherry and herbs. If you prefer soup, try the fascinating crabmeat and saffron ($3). Entrees cluster in the $8 to $11 range with such treats as bass amandine, grouper à la Basque, coquille of scallops with mustard sauce, quenelles of snapper, pickerel, and sea bass served with cream of lobster sauce, and a truly thick bouillabaisse loaded with crab, lobster, mussels, snapper, sea bass, shrimps, and clams, and served in an elegant china tureen.

Since Quenelles is regarded as the city's top seafood restaurant, reservations are vital. Open 6 to 10 p.m. Monday to Saturday.

MIDTOWN MODERATELY PRICED RESTAURANTS: Much international fare here. Let's start with—

Danish

The **Copenhagen Room,** 101 Bloor St. West (tel. 920-3287), is the only place in Toronto where at lunchtime you can get authentic Danish open-face sandwiches—53 varieties and combination plates in fact, all priced between $2 and $4 (more for the combination plates). At night the wood-paneled room, with its hanging brass planters and little Danish flags on the tables, is transformed into a warm candlelit dining room serving Danish gourmet cuisine.

Start with Danish bleu cheese soup or a consommé with meatballs, dumplings, and vegetables (both $1.50), or gravlaks, the specialty of the house (cured salmon with dill and mustard sauce, $4.10). Tempting main courses include a filet of plaice served with shrimps, diced tomatoes, mushrooms, green peppers, and cubed potatoes ($8.50), the classic chicken samsø covered in cream sauce with ham, pimiento, and parsley, and grilled with samsø cheese ($7.50), or the Danish meatballs served with red cabbage and boiled potatoes ($6).

Every second Tuesday of the month the Copenhagen holds a deluxe five-meter Danish buffet with musical entertainment for the fair price of $12. You must reserve early, because these affairs are very popular. Oh, and don't forget to quaff down a Tuborg or a Carlsberg—just the right accompaniment for the food.

Open 11:30 a.m. to 2:30 p.m. and 5:30 to 11:30 p.m. Monday to Saturday.

French

The owner-chef of **Le Trou Normand,** 90 Yorkville Ave. (tel. 967-5956), Mr. Herget, has been variously pastry cook to the French president, cook for the Kennedy's aboard their private yacht, and chef at the Ritz Carlton in Montréal before he created his present post. Here his dishes are served in three very simple rooms decorated with Italian floor tiles, Windsor chairs, and breakfronts housing china plates.

You may choose from a dozen or so appetizers, most between $2 and $3—beef tongue served with vinaigrette, and chopped onions and celeriac in a mustard mayonnaise are two of the more unusual. Entrees are similarly fairly priced and very tasty—I can recommend the beef bourguignon Escoffier style ($7.45), or the similarly priced marinated rabbit served in a sauce with gooseberry jelly and prunes. Desserts are all under $2.

Luncheon fare changes daily, but ranges from $2.65 to $4.50. Open noon to 5 p.m. Tuesday to Saturday, and 5:30 to 10 p.m. Tuesday to Sunday.

La Chaumière, 77 Charles St. East, at the corner of Church St. (tel. 922-0500), must be one of the original homey French bistros that opened in Toronto. It's been going for 43 years and some of its customers have been coming for 25. The reason? Because you can get a meal for under $10, which I defy you to finish, so generous are the portions.

First, you can select any number of hors d'oeuvres from the trolley—sardines, tomatoes and anchovies, herring, cucumber, beets, and numerous other salads, plus a pâté served with hot bread. Soup will follow, and then a main course that might be veal or chicken chasseur, sweetbreads, plus dessert and coffee all for $9.75. Price is determined by the choice of your entree, but there are at least six selections under $10.

And all this will be brought to you in warm, wood-paneled surroundings, amid French scenes and posters, at your red gingham-topped table by a friendly waitress. Open 5:30 to 10:30 p.m. Monday to Saturday.

Indian

The name **Le Tandur,** 151 Avenue Rd. (tel. 928-0422), refers to the tandoori oven that takes up a glass-encased corner of this rather elegant Indian restaurant where you can watch the chefs hook out the breads from the side of the oven. Sitar music sets the mood for the various lamb, chicken, and beef specialties cooked in the specially imported clay oven—for instance, tandoori chicken ($10.95 full, $6.50 half) and boti kebab ($6.75), the Indian equivalent of shish kebab. The menu is rounded out with various other specialties—rogan josh, lamb vindaloo, chicken do piaz, mughlai biryani—plus some vegetarian delights like aloo gobhi masala (cauliflower and potatoes cooked with spices), one of my favorites.

The management has spared no expense on the decor, chic with its bentwood chairs, broadloom, and simply exquisite rosewood Indian sculptures. Upstairs there's a very comfortable lounge with comfy couches, a tented ceiling, and a cozy fireplace.

Open 11 a.m. to 3 p.m. Monday to Friday, and 5 to 11 p.m. Monday to Sunday.

Italian

Mister Tony's, 100 Cumberland St. (tel. 964-2222), has more of a continental or French air with its French-style chairs, gilt-framed pictures and mirrors, and chintz wallpaper—and in fact the primarily Italian menu is peppered with intruders. Still, the prime attractions are the reasonably priced Italian veal dishes—piccata, parmigiana, milanese, Cordon Bleu—from $6 to $8, and the various pastas at $2.50 that may precede them. You can also get a good beef Wellington, duck à l'orange, and scampi alla marinara for $9. The desserts include the Italian Sicilian cheesecake, zuppa inglese, and zabaglione, all under $2.50.

At lunchtime there's a daily special that includes soup for $4.95 and a long list of appetizers, soups, egg dishes, pasta, salads, and light fish and meat entrees, most under $6.

Open noon to 2:30 p.m., and 6 to 11 p.m. Monday to Saturday.

No such compromise is made at **Luigi's Trattoria,** 819A Yonge St. (tel. 966-5321). Strictly Italian fare holds forth in this room with its red checked tablecloths and murals depicting old Rome and the Trevi fountain. Mandolin and accordion will accompany your dinner nightly from 7 p.m. to midnight. Here, the special of the day might consist of a filet of sole capriccio, plus minestrone or lasagne bolognese, for $9.95. A complete veal parmigiana dinner will cost $11.50. Appetizers, soups, and pastas complete the à la carte menu. The lunchtime special at $4.25 includes soup or salad and coffee or tea; there are other entrees from $3.95 to $6.95 (for a beef paillard served with spinach).

A small patio out front provides summer al fresco dining. Open Tuesday to Friday from noon to 3 p.m., and 5 to 11 p.m. Tuesday to Saturday. Reservations are recommended, unless you want to wait an hour in the cocktail lounge, especially on weekends.

At **Mario's Hideaway,** 137 Avenue Rd. (tel. 929-3341), the usual plethora of chianti bottles, Neapolitan murals, and red checked tablecloths provides the background for a full selection of pasta dishes from $4.25 to $6, and more substantial meat dishes that hover around $8. Some of the fancy drinks are worth a try—the Godfather, made with scotch and amaretto ($2.50), or Virgio's White Lie, a combination of amaretto, crème de cacao, and cream. Daily lunch specials present a bargain at $2.50 to $3.50. Open noon to 2 p.m. Monday to Friday, 5 to 11 p.m. Monday to Thursday, until midnight on Friday and Saturday.

Japanese

Simple Japanese decor, including some straw-matted (tatami-style) booths, along with popular Japanese music provide the atmosphere at **Michi,** 459 Church St. (tel. 924-1303 or 924-7501), between Carlton and Wellesley.

If you opt for the $8 sukiyaki dinner, kimono-clad waitresses will bring you an iron pan and burner and Michi's special sukiyaki sauce in which *you* cook: bamboo shoots, Chinese cabbage, mushrooms, bean sprouts, onion, spinach, yam noodles, bean curd, and paper-thin slices of beef sirloin. A raw egg will be served on the side into which you dip the hot beef before eating. Seafood dinners like ushio nabe, houroku yaki, and a kind of Japanese meat fondue (shabu-shabu), plus various complete tempura and teriyaki dinners are served for around $9. Accompany each with a small carafe of sake ($1.90).

At lunchtime, several tempura, sukiyaki, and teriyaki dishes are served (from $2.50 to $4.60), including a clear soup, rice-vinegared small salad, and rice. Open noon to 2 p.m. Monday to Friday, and 5 to 11 p.m. Monday to Saturday.

Middle Eastern

Climb the stairs at 1280 Bay St. and you'll find yourself in **Mamounia,** or the Sultan's Tent (tel. 961-1601), amid opulent and exotic surroundings—a tented ceiling, sensually cushioned banquettes, leather hassocks, Oriental rugs from the Atlas Mountains and Marrakesh, and brass and copper artifacts, bought by the kilo in Fez. (Mamounia is in fact the name of a hotel in Marrakesh where Winston Churchill stayed, according to owners Mustapha and Hafid Zniber.)

Weave your own fantasies while waitresses in kaftans bring huge bowls of couscous with either lamb or chicken and vegetables, and a dancer moves to the sounds of the kanoon and oud. For $11.75 you can select a soup, appetizer, salad, entree (including such delights as lamb with prunes and almonds, or rabbit with honey and tomatoes), dessert, and mint tea or Moroccan coffee. If you order 24 hours ahead they'll prepare a whole leg of lamb for a minimum of four persons at $7.95 per person. At lunchtime entrees run from $2.95 to $4.95.

Open noon to 2:30 p.m. Monday to Friday, 5:30 to 10:30 p.m. Monday to Thursday, and 5:30 to midnight on Friday and Saturday.

Seafood

Yugoslav Joseph Spralja of Malka and Joso has appeared on the "Johnny Carson Show" and performed at Carnegie Hall, but since he gave up folk singing and playing the guitar because of an ulcer he has taken to combing the fishmarkets for his restaurant **Joso's,** 202 Davenport, just east of Avenue Rd. (tel. 925-1903). Besides having a fascinating owner, this place has some interesting seafood and also a rather idiosyncratic decor (which might offend some, so I have to mention the erotic ceramic sculptures of golf-ball-bosomed females).

If you don't care a fig about such indelicate matters, but you do care about fresh seafood prepared to retain its flavor, then stop by Joso's. At dinner a selection of fresh fish will be presented to you, from which you can choose the specimen that appeals to you. It will then be grilled and served with a salad (such dishes are priced by the pound). Or else you can have octopus steamed in garlic and parsley sauce, deep-fried squid with salad (both $6.50), or spaghetti with an octopus, clam, and squid tomato sauce for $5. A selection of exotic coffees is available, as are French pastries for dessert.

Bentwood cane chairs and pale-lemon tablecloths complete the decor of the tiny downstairs room. A larger room upstairs is similarly appointed. Remember, this cosmopolitan bistro makes a very personal statement: you can either take it or leave it, but you should know about it.

Open 11:30 a.m. to 3 p.m. Monday to Friday, 5:30 to midnight Monday to Thursday, and 5:30 to 1 a.m. on Friday and Saturday.

Swiss

Husband and wife Kurt and Charlotte Leumann run the charmingly rustic **Auberge Montreux,** 1315 Bay St. at Scollard (tel. 923-1005), specializing in their native Swiss cuisine. A small and cozy stucco room with wood trim provides an Alpine feel for such dishes as escalope de veau zingara (with julienne of ham, mushrooms, pickles, pimientoes, laced with Madeira and cream), rabbit marinated in white wine, simmered with diced vegetables, pearl onions, and croutons, or breast of chicken St. Raphael, stuffed with mushrooms, dipped in egg, and served with browned butter (all between $6 and $7). To start, try the Swiss air-dried thinly sliced cured beef, pickles, and cocktail onions, and finish with a Swiss torte.

Open noon to 10 p.m. Monday to Thursday, until 11 p.m. on Friday, and from 5 to 11 p.m. on Saturday.

Vietnamese

Salmon-pink tablecloths and a simple decor with a bamboo-style bar topped by a cabana welcomes you to the **Saigon Village,** 4 Collier St. (tel. 922-5840). Start with one of the appetizers that range from $1.50 for spring roll to $4 for the crab claws wrapped with shrimp, or else try the truly tasty crab and asparagus soup. Follow with chicken and rice in a clay pot, or beef allspice (both around $6), or a Vietnamese fondue for two ($15). Do save room for that beignet of bananas flambed in Grand Marnier.

Open 5:30 to 10:30 p.m. weekdays, until 11:30 p.m. weekends. Closed Sunday.

MIDTOWN BUDGET RESTAURANTS: Here we have several establishments offering continental fare, two with health/vegetarian offerings, and one serving Hungarian specialties.

Continental

As the name suggests, **Jacques' Omelettes,** 126A Cumberland St. (tel. 961-1893), specializes in omelets, plus one or two dishes such as escalope de veau normande ($6.50).

Upstairs above a boutique in the heart of Yorkville, everything about the small room is tasteful—the fresh-flower arrangement gracing the bar, the warm carpet, the French prints and pictures of Paris. But the prime attractions for the crowds are the omelets—15 selections (all between $3 and $4), including a three-ingredient bacon, mushroom, and onion, and a shrimp with garlic variety. Salads, cheeses, and soups and a small selection of hors d'oeuvres, plus some dinner entrees make this an ideal and charming dining spot for lunch or dinner.

You don't have to pay through the nose for taste and well-prepared food, not even in Yorkville. Open noon to 3 p.m. and 5 to 10 p.m. from Monday to Saturday.

At **Tramps,** 649 Yonge St., just south of Charles St. (tel. 961-8078), you can get a beef brochette, plus soup or salad and tea or coffee for a mere $4.25, and take in all the blow-ups of tramps pasted along the walls of this narrow room—from Charlie Chaplin (the original) through Fred Astaire and Ginger Rogers to Marilyn Monroe.

Besides the special mentioned above, the menu lists three or four appetizers and seven or eight entrees, including mussels cooked in white wine, onions, thyme, and parsley, and oxtails braised in a red wine sauce (both $3.75).

Not exactly Maxim's, but it's very hard to beat. Open 11 a.m. to 11 p.m. Monday to Saturday.

A similar approach is taken by Michael Rowlands at **Barrows,** 640 Church St. (tel. 923-7032), but in a more elegant sandblasted town house setting. If you can't afford to dine at L'Hardy's or Quenelles, then Barrows (next door) will provide some good continental fare—sole Véronique, veal à la Parisienne—priced from $5 to $7.50. A small selection of appetizers, salads, and soups completes the menu.

The place is delightfully light and airy; a philodendron climbs over the marble mantel; and the swivel-back (yes, back) pine chairs are super-comfortable because you can adjust them to fit your particular torso. Reproductions of Brueghels, Picassos, and others make a welcome change.

At lunchtime, entrees run from $3.50 to $5.50; a special including soup or salad and coffee is $3.95. Open noon to 2:30 p.m. Monday to Friday, and 6 to 10:30 p.m. Monday to Saturday.

Health and Vegetarian

Four years ago at the request of his spiritual leader Sri Chinmoy, Shivaram Trichur opened the **Annapurna Restaurant,** 138 Pears Ave., behind the Avenue Place Hotel and downstairs (keep looking—it's there). A bell announces your arrival. Beyond the counter where you can purchase various goodies including a loaf of banana bread, along with books on yoga and copies of *Inner Life,* you'll find a room with no particular decor to speak of but some superb low-priced food.

For instance, when I was there the dinner of the day was $2.50 and consisted of cream of spinach soup, cannelloni, and steamed broccoli. There's always a soup and several salads such as mixed bean with tamari, or raita (cucumbers and tomatoes covered in yogurt). Various breads accompany the South Indian food—masala dosai (a crêpe made from rice and urad lentil flours, filled with a spicy mix of potatoes and onions, and served with coconut and chutney, $1.75) or sambar (mixed vegetables and toor dahl in spicy sauce, $1). Various herbal teas and desserts like carob balls with dates, raisins, and cashews complete the menu.

A young and rather intellectual, interesting crowd gathers here. Open from noon to 9 p.m. Monday to Saturday.

The **Bay Streetcar** is far from being attached to any spiritual movement. Set in the lower level of Cumberland Terrace on Bloor St., it serves fresh and healthful food in a setting designed to resemble its name.

At the self-service counter there's a plentiful supply of salads—julienne of pepper and onions (75¢), for example—open sandwiches, including a rather creative peanut butter, bananas, and strawberry jelly (95¢), plus various herbal infusions and shakes (such as hazelnut with milk, and honey juice with zest of lemon, $1.25). All the breads, cakes, and cookies are homemade.

Open 8 a.m. to 6 p.m. Monday to Wednesday, until 7 p.m. on Thursday and Friday, and from 10 a.m. to 6 p.m. on Saturday.

Hungarian

Tarogato, 553 Bloor St. West, at Bathurst (tel. 536-7566), named after an ancient double-reed wind instrument, is the place to hie if you're a strudel fancier. At the front counter five types are available—apple, cheese, cherry, poppyseed, and walnut.

In the back there's a warm and traditional Hungarian dining room where the colorful costumed waitresses heft large plates of cabbage rolls, paprika chicken with dumplings, and more (between $3 and $5).

Budget aficionados know this place and so also do Latin Americans—note the South American newspapers in the window. (Explanation? The owner spent much of his life in Argentina.)

Open noon to midnight Monday to Thursday, until 1 a.m. on Friday and Saturday, to 10 p.m. on Sunday.

TORONTO NORTH—MODERATELY PRICED DINING: Let's begin our dining adventure in the northern section of Toronto with French cuisine.

French

Step beyond the lush drapes into **Antoines,** 553 Eglinton Ave. West (tel. 483-8161), an intimate dining room handsomely decorated with gilt pictures and mirrors, gingerbread clocks, chandeliers and chintz wallpaper, and rich blue needlepointed chairs. The low lighting provides a romantic setting for such dishes as sweetbreads with apples and Calvados or canard rouennaise (duck served in a black cherry Madeira sauce), both $8.95. Any entree will come with pâté maison and green salad. Although the desserts change daily, you can reckon on the best of whatever is in season—fresh strawberries, for example, plus a smooth crème caramel or chocolate mousse. An extensive and fairly priced wine list is available.

Open 5:30 to 10 p.m. Monday to Saturday.

Italian

Outside of Noodles and the high-priced La Scala, the next two listings offer the best opportunity for moderately priced Italian food.

At **San Marco,** St. Clair Ave. West (tel. 654-8482), there's always a daily dinner special for around $10 that includes an antipasto choice, perhaps veal marsala and vegetable as a main course, tartufo, and coffee. You dine on wrought-iron chairs, in a stuccoed room with a chianti-festooned bar at the back. The waiters are impeccably charming and attentive, and the food well prepared.

Besides the special, you can order à la carte with familiar dishes priced from $6 to $7; seafood specialties run from $9.50.

A singer adds to the warm Mediterranean atmosphere. Open Monday to Saturday noon to 1 a.m., Sunday 4 to 9:30 p.m.

More pricey but worth it, **Sabatinos,** 1144 Eglinton Ave. West, between Dufferin and Bathurst (tel. 783-5829), is crowded with Italian food fanciers who can dine in a low-lit romantic atmosphere where Tiffany lamps hang over the tables and paintings grace the walls. For a special treat, ask for the table in the alcove.

The cannelloni florentina, stuffed with spinach-flecked ricotta cheese and topped with nutmeg, makes a highly recommended pasta intro or main course ($2.50). Entrees range from $7.50 to $11.75 (for steak pizzaiola), and most of the veal dishes will be served with fried green and red peppers and cubed potatoes sprinkled with rosemary.

For dessert, the profiteroles al cioccolato ($2) are especially delicious. Open from 5 to 11 p.m. Tuesday to Sunday.

Russian

Mother Russia steals the scene at **Barmalay,** 994 St. Claire St. West (tel. 651-5415), one of my favorite ethnic restaurants, where Paris emigré Sergei Boldireff charges the atmosphere and stirs the blood with his singing, and ex-actor/owner Gregory Bruskin adds some tambourine excitement. Here, an open grill sizzles with Caucasian shashlik, Moscow basturma (tenderloin of beef) served with garnish and delicious potatoes roasted on the grill for around $8.

Downstairs warm red tablecloths, yellow lanterns, and a room decorated with painted wood artifacts and murals of matrioschka dolls, plus balalaika music, set a jovial atmosphere for a feast of satsivi (cold pieces of chicken in a thick nut and garlic sauce, $3.95) or borscht ($1.50), followed by such main courses as really tasty cabbage rolls with mashed potato and sour cream ($4.25), or Jarkoia stew served with kasha ($5.35). For dessert you can take your chances on a Russian potato, which will turn out to be made of chocolate with prunes and walnuts inside.

A samovar graces each table. The tea is brewed in a china pot atop the samovar. Pour a small amount of tea into a glass cup (put a spoon in to keep it from cracking), and dilute from the samovar. Russians usually add strawberry jelly, but here you'll find sugar.

Truly, this is a lively and inexplicably touching spot to spend an evening. Open daily from noon to 2 p.m. and 6 to 10:30 p.m., until midnight on Friday and Saturday.

Seafood

People wend their way north to the **Lobster Trap,** 1962 Avenue Rd. just north of Lawrence (tel. 787-3211), for *one* reason only—and that really should be stressed—because it's the only place in the city where you can still pick out a live lobster for an honest and fair price. Look around, you may even be sitting next to a celebrity of some sort in this room where the tables have green gingham tablecloths, and most are sheltered under a shingled construction to evoke that maritime province atmosphere.

For a dinner that includes clam chowder or lobster bisque, salad, rolls and butter, french fries or rice, and beverage, and a one-pound lobster, steamed or broiled and served with drawn butter, you will pay $13.50. Prices rise gradually to $23.95 for a 2¼-pound crustacean. Other fish dinners are available, but I'd stick to the lobster if I were you.

Open 4 to 10:30 p.m. daily.

Soups, Salads, Sandwiches Plus

Capture those childhood dreams of milkshakes, Coke floats, and a good burger forever, along with the rest of the crowd at '50s-flavor hamburger joint **Toby's Goodeats,** 91 Bloor St. (tel. 925-2171). The decor suits: a schizophrenic combination of arborite tables, cookie jars, and funky posters, and the voguish sandblasted brick-and-plant look. It's very crowded at lunchtime.

Open 7:30 a.m. to 3 a.m. Monday to Saturday, and 11 a.m. to 1 a.m. on Sunday.

Diet books, the Scarsdale diet, and Overeaters Anonymous may be ubiquitous but, bold enough to buck the trend, **Just Desserts,** 306 Davenport Rd. (tel. 922-6824), is open round the clock on weekends for those in need of that sugar fix.

Around 40 desserts are available—as many as nine different cheesecakes, six or so assorted pies, plus a whole array of gâteaux, tortes, meringues, etc. I don't need to describe them—just go, order with a cappucino or coffee, savor every bite, and feel bad afterward.

Open 24 hours on weekends, until 3 a.m. on weekdays.

A really good downtown spot to repair to at lunchtime as many shoppers, business people, and others do is the **Fare Exchange,** 4 Irwin Ave. (tel. 923-5924), between Wellesley and Charles St.

Complete the saying and you won't be disappointed. The bric-a-brac—Victorian chests, old clocks, telephones, and painted signs—go well with the prices: quiche Lorraine, lasagne, and bratwurst with potato salad, all under $2.25 at lunch. Dinner prices soar to $3.50 for baby beef liver with wine sauce, and $5.25 for barbecued spare ribs, both served with potatoes and fresh vegetables.

Open 11:30 a.m. to midnight Monday to Saturday, and 4:30 p.m. to midnight on Sunday.

Pine, plants, cane chairs, butcher-block tables, and rotating modern graphics are the now-familiar surroundings at **Pears,** 138 Pears Ave. (tel. 961-5272), one block north of Davenport just west of Avenue Rd. The food is similarly light and also reasonable. Soups, salads, omelets, and a whole range of hamburgers at lunchtime are supplemented by such dishes as pepper steak, wienerschnitzel, and cheese and vegetable pie from $3.50 to $7 at night. All the desserts are homemade (you might enjoy the Mennonite cheese pie, $1.75).

One other aspect distinguishes Pears from its many brothers and sisters—it shows free first-run films on Sundays and Mondays. Open noon to 2 p.m. Monday to Friday, and 6 to 10 p.m. Monday to Sunday.

TORONTO NORTH—BUDGET DINING: First a Chinese selection:

Chinese

Whether you fancy Cantonese, Mandarin, or Szechuan cuisine, you'll find it all at **China House,** 925 Eglinton Ave. West (tel. 781-9122), a more-than-usually decorous spot. Enter on a dainty footbridge over a pool with water lilies, into a room at the center of which stands a glorious pine tree hung with Chinese lanterns. Chairs are Chippendale shape and the table appointments attractive.

Start with hot-and-sour soup ($2.95) or sizzling rice ($4.30). The king shrimp in ginger sauce and the chicken with cashews in hot sauce (both around $6) are highly recommendable. At lunchtime, various combination platters are offered, all in the $2 to $4 range.

Open noon to midnight Monday to Thursday, until 1 a.m. on Friday and Saturday, and until 11 p.m. on Sunday.

Continental

In a plain but stylish decor of exposed brick, painted wooden chairs, and wine-colored tablecloths, highlighted by some modern graphics and historical Toronto prints, at **Mount Pleasant Lunch,** 604 Mount Pleasant Rd. (tel. 481-9331), for the princely sum of $4.75 you can have veal Cordon Bleu plus soup, salad, potatoes and vegetables, hot garlic bread, dessert, and beverage. At lunchtime, daily specials like veal pizzaiola, chicken cutlet, and wiener-schnitzel are under $2.50, and include soup, bread and butter, and beverage. No wonder you practically have to fight your way in.

Open 11:30 a.m. to 2:30 p.m. Monday to Friday, 5 to 10 p.m. Monday to Thursday, to 11 p.m. on Friday and Saturday.

Palestinian

At **Jerusalem,** 955 Eglinton Ave. West, just west of Bathurst (tel. 783-6494), it's the food and prices that count. All the appetizers are $1.25—falafel, kubbeh (a cracked-wheat roll stuffed with ground meat, onions, and pine nut), various styles of hummus, taheena, tabbouleh (a delicious blend of cracked wheat with chopped tomatoes, onions, parsley, mint, lemon and olive oil).

You can follow them with liver fried in garlic and hot pepper sauce ($4.50) and siniyeh (mixed ground lamb and beef with onions, parsley, and pine nuts, and oven baked with taheena sauce).

The decor is simple—just some brass tabletops on the walls—but the atmosphere is extremely warm, the service friendly and unhurried.

Open noon to midnight daily; until 10 p.m. on Sunday. No reservations.

4. The Sights

ONTARIO PLACE: When this 96-acre recreation complex at 955 Lakeshore Blvd. (tel. 965-7164), on the shores of Lake Ontario, opened in 1971 it seemed futuristic, and eight years later it still does.

From a distance you'll see five steel-and-glass pavilions, suspended 105 feet on columns above the lake, straddling three man-made islands and alongside a huge geodesic dome that looks like a golf ball magnified several thousand times. The five pavilions contain three multimedia theaters and other displays that tell the story of Ontario in vivid kaleidoscopic detail. The dome houses a **cinesphere** where a 60- by 80-foot screen shows specially made movies—for example, a thrilling minute-by-minute depiction of the last massive Icelandic volcanic eruption entitled *Volcano.*

Located under an enormous orange canopy, the **Children's Village** provides a well-supervised area where children aged 4 to 14 can scramble over rope bridges, bounce on an enormous trampoline, and slide down a twisting chute, or most popular of all, squirt water pistols, garden hoses, swim, and generally drench one another in a water-play section. Afterward, parents can just pop them in the conveniently available dryers before moving on.

A stroll around the complex will unearth a marina full of yachts and other craft, the HMCS *Haida,* a World War II and Korean War destroyer which can be toured, a miniature 18-hole golf course, plenty of grassland for picnicking and general cavorting, and a whole array of restaurants and snackbars serving everything from Chinese, Italian, German, and Canadian food to hot dogs and hamburgers. And don't miss the wildest ride in town—the Water Slide.

At night the **Forum,** an outdoor theater which accommodates 8000, either inside under the translucent vinyl canopy or outside on the grassy slopes, comes alive. During the summer a whole myriad of entertainments are held here, everything from the Hamilton Philharmonic or the 48th Highlanders Pipes and Drums Band to Melba Moore and Blood, Sweat, and Tears. For information, call 965-7711.

The park is open from mid-May to early October from 10 a.m. to 1 a.m. Monday to Saturday, until 10 p.m. on Sunday. Admission: $2.50 for adults ($1 after 9 p.m.), $1.50 for under 18s (50¢ if accompanied by an adult), seniors free. Located on the shores of Lake Ontario west of downtown, Ontario Place can be reached by taking the subway to either Bathurst or Dufferin, and the buses south from there to Exhibition. Or call TTC Information (tel. 484-4544) for special bus service details.

EXHIBITION PLACE: Cross the bridge over Lakeshore Blvd. from Ontario Place and you're in Exhibition Park, 350 acres of grounds, and home of the **Canadian National Exhibition,** which began as an agricultural fair in 1878. It still retains both a Victorian flavor—the exhibition halls are superb examples of Victorian excess—and an agricultural flavor, with livestock and poultry shows, horse events, and magnificent food halls. Other attractions include the aerobatics of the Canadian International Air Show, the aquatic highjinks of Aquarama, the fearsome whines of pipes at the Scottish World Festival Tattoo, and the fun of a midway and star-spangled grandstand show. All this takes place during three weeks ending on Labour Day. For more information, write: Canadian National Exhibition, Exhibition Place, Toronto, ON M6K 3C3.

Also on the grounds of Exhibition Place stands the **Marine Museum** (tel. 595-1567), which describes the history of the Great Lakes and St. Lawrence waterways, and offers the chance to clamber over the fully restored *Ned Hanlon,* the last steam tug to sail on the Great Lakes.

Open daily Monday to Saturday from 9:30 a.m. to 5 p.m., on Sunday from noon to 5 p.m. Admission: adults, 75¢; children and seniors, 50¢.

At the **Hockey Hall of Fame,** Exhibition Place (tel. 595-1345), genuine ice hockey nuts can see the original Stanley Cup, donated in 1893 by Lord Stanley of Preston, Terry Sawchuck's goalie gear, Newsy Lalonde's skates, the stick that Max Bentley used, along with photographs of the personalities and great moments in ice hockey history.

Open every day except Christmas, New Year's, and the day before the annual Exhibition, from 10:30 a.m. to 4:30 p.m.; until 8:30 p.m. from May 24 through Labour Day, Tuesday through Sunday. Admission free.

FORT YORK: Established by Lieutenant Governor Simcoe in 1793 to defend "little muddy York," as Toronto was then known, Fort York (Fleet St. between Bathurst and Strachan Ave.; tel. 595-1567) was sacked by Americans in 1813. In retaliation some Canadians went down and torched the president's house. To hide the burn marks, the Americans painted the house white, which explains that edifice's color and name in Washington. At the fort you can see the soldiers' and officers' quarters, clamber over the ramparts, and watch the men drilling in full-color early 19th-century uniform.

Open all year from 9:30 a.m. to 5 p.m. Monday to Saturday, and noon to 5 p.m. on Sunday. Admission: adults, $1.50; children and seniors, 50¢. To get there, take the Bathurst streetcar south to the gate.

HARBOURFRONT: Since the federal government took over a 96-acre narrow strip of prime waterfront land in 1972 to prevent developers from obliterating the waterfront vista, Torontonians have been rediscovering their lakeshore. The abandoned warehouses, shabby depots, and crumbling factories have been refurbished and an urban park created on and around the old piers.

The focal point of Harbourfront activities is **York Pier,** at 235 Queen's Quay West (tel. 364-5665), where you'll find the main information office, a gallery of contemporary Canadian art, various arts and crafts workshops, theater and cafe, and a host of happenings that include: Tuesday night poetry and novel readings, Wednesday evening films, a Thursday night open sing-in of folk and blues, Friday night square dances, Saturday matinee movies, and good old-fashioned ballroom dancing on Sunday, plus jazz and an antiques market, and all kinds of family programs and expositions. To find out what's happening at the Harbour, either pick up a copy of *Harbourfront Happenings,* published every two weeks, at the main office at York Pier, or look for it in the Saturday *Globe and Mail.* Most of the activities are free; admission to the area is also free.

Farther west, reached by a footbridge, lies **Quay 4,** which offers a complex of marine outfitters and other related businesses, plus the **Storehouse Restaurant** (tel. 863-1440), where you can sit out on the deck and dine at waterside on seafood and steaks, or else enjoy a drink in the upstairs lounge. Open noon to 11 p.m. Monday to Friday, and 5 to midnight on Saturday.

At the **Pier 4 Sailing School,** 245 Queen's Quay West (tel. 366-0390) you can take a week-long adult beginner sailing course which includes 15 hours instruction for $50. The **Harbourside Sailing School** (tel. 368-4000), also on the pier, runs intensive 25-hour weekend, weeknight, or week-long courses for $190.

At the next pier, Spadina, you'll find the **Canadian Railway Museum** (tel. 297-1464), which consists of several locomotives retired from the railroads which you can tour (open from June to October) and also the **Centre Francophone,** 435 Queen's Quay West (tel. 367-1950) at the bottom of Spadina, a good place to stop and have some delicious crêpes, salad, or soup in a very French atmosphere. The Centre also hosts French cultural affairs. On the pier you can also watch experts restoring old ships or else set up your own barbecue in the pits provided.

At the west end of the park stands **Bathurst Pier,** which most resembles a park. Here you'll find a large sports field for romping around, plus two adventure playgrounds, one for older kids and the other (supervised) for 3- to 7-year-olds.

To get to Harbourfront, take the 77B bus from Union Station or Spadina subway station. Or the 6 or 6A bus to the foot of Bay St. and walk west.

THE TORONTO ISLANDS: A stolid little ferry will take you across to 612 acres of island park criss-crossed by shady paths and quiet waterways—a glorious spot to walk, play tennis, cycle, feed the ducks, mess about in boats, picnic, or just sit.

Children will find **Centreville,** a 19-acre oldtime amusement park, built and designed especially for them. But you won't find the usual neon signs, shrill hawkers, and the aroma of greasy hot-dog stands. Instead you'll find a turn-of-the-century village complete with Main St., tiny shops, firehouse, and even a small working farm where the kids can fondle lambs and chicks, and enjoy pony rides. They'll also love trying out the miniature antique cars, fire engines, old-fashioned train, the authentic 1890s carousel, the flume ride, and the aerial cars. Admission is free, but there is a charge for the rides. Open from May 18 to Labour Day, 10 a.m. to sunset.

Ferries leave from the docks at the bottom of Bay St. To get there, take a subway to Union Station and the Bay St. bus south. Fare: adults, $1; children 14 and under, 25¢; seniors, 50¢. For ferry schedules, call 367-8193.

Cruising the Islands

Boat Tours International, 5 Queen's Quay West (tel. 364-2412) offers cruises of the harbor and islands in glass-covered boats modeled after Amsterdam's canal cruisers. Tours leave from either the foot of Yonge St. and Queen's Quay right beside the Harbor Castle Hilton, or from the marina at Ontario Place; and you can cruise in and out of the lagoons spying Canadian geese and other wild fowl during the day, or else at night when the star-spangled skyline unfurls before you. Adults pay $3.50; children under 12, $1.75.

ROYAL BANK PLAZA: Shimmering in the sun on the corner of Front and Bay Sts., it looks like a pillar of gold—and in a way it is. More important, it is a masterpiece of design and architectural drama. Two triangular towers of bronze mirror glass flank a 130-foot-high glass-walled banking hall. The external walls of the towers are built in a serrated configuration so that they reflect a phenomenal mosaic of color from the skies and surrounding buildings.

In the banking hall, hundreds of aluminum cylinders hang from the ceiling —the work of Venezuelan sculptor Jesús Raphael Soto, while two levels below there's a waterfall and pine tree setting naturally illuminated from the hall above.

If you want to see modern architecture at its most imaginative, then don't miss Royal Bank Plaza. It's a free visual inspiration.

CN TOWER: As you approach the city, the first thing you will note is this slender needle-like structure and the tiny colored elevators that look like jumping beans gliding to the top of this 1815-foot-high tower—the tallest free-standing building in the world.

As you enter the base of the tower at 301 Front St. West (tel. 360-8500), just look up through the atrium to the top . . . yes, that's where you're going. Glass-walled elevators on the outside walls of the tower whisk you to the 1200-foot-high seven-level sky pod in just over one minute. From here, on a clear day you can't quite see forever but you can see, I'm told, all the way to Niagara Falls, even Buffalo, if you wish. One of the two observation levels is partially open to allow you to experience that dizzying sensation of height (vertigo sufferers beware).

The pod also contains broadcasting facilities and a revolving restaurant. Atop the tower sits a 335-foot antenna mast which took 3½ weeks to erect with the aid of a giant Sikorsky helicopter. It took 55 lifts to complete the operation.

While you're up there, don't worry about the elements sweeping it into the lake: it's built of contoured reinforced concrete covered with thick glass-reinforced plastic, and designed to keep ice accumulation to a minimum. The structure can withstand the highest winds, and the effects of snow, ice, lightning, and earth tremors, which is more than you can probably say about your own house.

Back down at the base of the tower you'll find a futuristic fun center furnished with a host of slot machines, fairground games, and "the world's tallest free-standing clown," plus snackbars, ice-cream parlors, and a taffy-producing store.

Open daily from 9 a.m. to midnight. Admission: adults, $3; children 13 to 17, $2.25; seniors, $1.50; children, $1.50. To get there, take the subway to Union Station and walk west along Front St.

CITY HALL: Another architectural spectacle houses the Mayor's Office and the city's administrative offices. Daringly designed by Finnish architect Viljo Revell, it consists of a low podium topped by the flying-saucer-shaped Council Chamber enfolded between two curved towers. In front stretches Nathan Phillips Square (named after the mayor who initiated the project), where in summer you can sit and contemplate the flower gardens, listen to concerts, and consider the fountains and reflecting pool (which doubles as a skating rink in winter). Here also stands Henry Moore's *Three-Way Piece No. 2,* locally referred to as *The Archer,* purchased through a public subscription fund.

The interior is as dramatic as the exterior, and tours are conducted daily, 10:15 a.m. to 5:15 p.m. For information, call 367-7999. A cafeteria and dining room are located in the basement; the 27th-floor observation deck on the East Tower provides a good view of the city. In contrast, to the east stands the Old City Hall, a green-roofed Renaissance-style building.

To reach City Hall, take the subway to Queen St. and either take the Queen streetcar west or else walk.

OSGOODE HALL AND CAMPBELL HOUSE: To the west of City Hall extends an impressive, elegant wrought-iron fence in front of an equally gracious mansion, Osgoode Hall, 130 Queen St. West (tel. 362-5811), currently the home of the Law Society of Upper Canada. The fence was originally built to prevent the cows from getting in and trampling the flower beds. On a conducted tour you can see the splendor of the grand staircase, the rotunda, and the Great Library. Building began in 1829 on this structure, which now houses legal offices, government offices, and occasionally serves as a courthouse (appeals to the Supreme Court of Ontario are heard here).

Just across the street, on the opposite corner of University and Queen, sits Sir William Campbell's mansion, 160 Queen St. West (tel. 597-0277), built in 1822 by this Loyalist and subsequent chief justice of Upper Canada. He retired to his mansion in 1829 where he resided (happily, it seems) with his pet alligator until he died in 1834 despite a diet of snipe prescribed by his physician. Today you can still see the little wooden snipe cages in the house's kitchen.

For a tour of Osgoode Hall, call Mr. Campion at 363-4101. Campbell House is open from 9:30 a.m. to noon and 2:30 to 5 p.m. on weekdays; from May 19 to Labour Day noon to 5 p.m. on weekends. Admission: adults, 75¢; seniors and students, 50¢; children, 25¢.

EATON CENTRE: Buttressed at both ends by 30+-story skyscrapers, this hi-tech center, which cost over $250 million, stretches from Dundas and Yonge Sts. south to Queen St., and encompasses six million square feet. Eaton's

Department Store takes up one million square feet, and the rest is filled with 150 stores, restaurants, etc., and two garages.

Inside, the structure opens into the marvelous **Galleria,** a long glass-domed arcade with marble floors dotted with benches, orchids, palm trees, and fountains where life flows in colorful waves. Three tiers rise above, reached by escalator and glass elevators, giving glorious views over this Crystal Palace / Milan-modern-flavored masterpiece designed by Eb Zeidler (who also designed Ontario Place). Here, no matter what the weather does you can enjoy the sights, sounds, and aromas in comfort—and don't be surprised by the twittering of the sparrows, some of whom have decided that this new facility is as pleasant as the outdoors.

One more amazing fact stands out about this new construction: it was built around two of Toronto's oldest landmarks—Trinity Church (1847) and the Scadding House (home of the rector, Dr. Scadding)—because the public demanded that the developers allow the sun to continue to shine on the church's twin towers. It does.

ART GALLERY: The low massive pile at 317 Dundas St. West between McCaul and Beverley Sts. (tel. 361-0414) gives no hint of the light and openness inside this beautifully designed gallery.

The highlight of the place has to be the **Henry Moore Sculpture Centre,** which numbers more than 300 pieces—original plasters, bronzes, maquettes, woodcuts, lithographs, etchings, and drawings—given to Toronto by the artist, supposedly because he was so moved by the citizens' enthusiasm for his work (remember, public donations bought the sculpture that decorates City Hall square). In one room, under a glass ceiling, 20 or so of his large works stand like silent prehistoric rock formations. Along the walls flanking a ramp are color photographs showing Moore's major sculptures in their natural locations, which really reveal their magnificent dimensions.

Next, the gallery has an excellent and comprehensive collection of Canadian paintings by Cornelius Krieghoff, Paul Peel, Tom Thomson, David Milne, F. H. Varley, and Emily Carr, as well as such moderns as Harold Town, Kenneth Lochhead, John Chambers, and William Kurelek.

The collection of Old Masters ranges from the 14th century through such works as Tintoretto's *Christ Washing His Disciples' Feet,* 17th-century Dutch painters, 18th-century Italian works, to the French impressionists.

In the gardens stands the **Grange** (tel. 361-0414), an elegant Georgian home built in 1818 by D'Arcy Boulton, which you may saunter through to glimpse the lifestyle of the 19th century's beautiful people. Open 11 a.m. to 5:30 p.m. Tuesday, Friday, Saturday, and Sunday; 11 a.m. to 9 p.m. on Wednesday and Thursday. Admission: $1 for adults; students, 50¢; children, free.

The gallery has a comfortable restaurant, cafeteria, a gallery shop, plus a full program of films, concerts, and lectures. It is open 11 a.m. to 5:30 p.m. on Tuesday, to 9 p.m. on Wednesday and Thursday, to 5:30 p.m. on Friday, Saturday, and Sunday. Closed on Christmas and New Year's Days. Admission: adults, $1; students and seniors, 50¢; children under 12, free.

The nearest subway stop is at St. Patrick on the University line. Or else you can take the subway to Dundas and the streetcar west.

CHINATOWN: Stretching along Dundas St. from Bay St. to Spadina Ave., and north and south along Spadina, Chinatown is a wonderful place to spend time browsing in the fascinating shops and eating at the restaurants. Even the street signs are in Chinese here. While you're in Chinatown, try to visit **China Court** at 210 Spadina Ave., a traditionally designed Chinese shopping center, whose exterior looks like a pagoda.

MARKETS: Toronto has a colorful and lively tapestry that should not be missed—the **Kensington Market** (between Spadina Ave. and Bathurst St. just south of College St.). If you can struggle out of bed to get there around 5 a.m., you'll see the squawking chickens being carried from their trucks to the stalls. Here, in what used to be primarily a Jewish market in the heart of the then garment center, you'll find the accents of Portuguese, Italians, and others, stallowners who spread their wares before them—squid and crabs in pails, chickens, pigeons, bread, cheese, apples, pears, peppers, ginger and mangoes from the West Indies, salted fish from Portuguese dories, lace, fabrics, and other colorful remnants. The place seethes with crowds on its narrow streets, a cacophony of bargaining and shrieking—a veritable bazaar.

As I said, if you want to capture the essence of the market then go in the early morning; if you're a bargain seeker, go later in the day when the vendors are anxious to be rid of their wares (I know—I once lived that way, carping and bargaining with these merchants, buying shiny smelts and other wonders for half the price).

The other market has a far more staid atmosphere. The accents are clearly English at the **St. Lawrence Market,** held every Saturday from 7 a.m. to 5 p.m. Ontario farmers gather here to offer meat and produce for sale, and you can capture the aroma of cheese, meat, and fish mingled with the scent of flowers and freshly made candies and pastries. It's a good place to pick up your picnic fare for a day at the Islands.

While you're here, seek out the restored St. Lawrence Hall. In the 19th century it used to be the focal point for Toronto's social life—everything from Jenny Lind performances to temperance and antislavery meetings—a glorious building designed in the Renaissance style.

ROYAL ONTARIO MUSEUM: The galleries at the **ROM** (Avenue Rd. at Bloor; tel. 978-3690), as it's affectionately called, cover three acres. As you probably suffer from museum fatigue at the end of a maximum of two hours, let me suggest a few highlights.

The objects displayed on the third floor make up the most outstanding collection, Chinese art—bronze vessels, carved jades, red and black lacquer, pottery, textiles, rare porcelains, and hundreds of burial figures lined up in cases like warriors in battle formation. Also on the third floor you'll find Shinto and Buddhist sculpture, tea ceremony wares, decorated screens, and other representative pieces of Japanese arts and crafts, as well as artifacts displaying the Islamic period of Egypt, Syria, Mesopotamia, Turkey, and Iran, and a whole Indian collection. Tucked in there also are mounted specimens of Canada's mammals, birds, and fishes.

Egyptian mummies, a remarkable lion from the throne room of Nebuchadnezzar, and state dresses of the British queen are just a few of the exciting objects found on the second floor in the Greek, Roman, Etruscan, Coptic, Syro-Palestine, and textile and costume galleries. The kids will love the dinosaur gallery.

On the first floor there's a potpourri that ranges from Chinese wall paintings and medieval silver, to antique musical instruments, weapons and armor, and geology and rock displays.

Dive down to the lower floor and you'll unearth North American Indian totem poles and Eskimo and other Canadian native art, along with the Discovery Room where kids can shake hands with a skeleton, try on a gladiators' helmet, or pick up the world's largest cell (an ostrich egg, for your and my information).

To glimpse the history of Ontario, don't miss the ROM's Canadiana collection, housed at 14 Queen's Park Crescent, quite a way south, exhibiting furnishings and materials from the 16th to 19th centuries and an impressive collection of Canadian paintings, watercolors, and drawings. Open Monday to Saturday from 10 a.m. to 5 p.m.; Sunday from 1 to 5 p.m. Admission is free.

The main museum is open daily, except Christmas and New Year's, from 10 a.m. to 6 p.m. Monday, Wednesday, and Saturday, to 9 p.m. on Tuesday, and 1 to 9 p.m. on Sunday from September through June; during July and August, from 10 a.m. to 9 p.m. Monday to Saturday, and 1 to 9 p.m. on Sunday.

Admission: adults, $1.50; students and children, 75¢; family rate, $3 (maximum); seniors, 50¢.

Adjacent to the museum stands the **McLaughlin Planetarium,** where you can see a regular show that focuses on diverse aspects of the universe presented daily except Monday (cost: $1.75 for adults, $1 for seniors, students, and children), or a special show such as the latest "Heavy Water Light Show," which required the viewer to wear heavy water goggles to achieve a 3-D effect and the sensation of flying through space. For this the admission is $3.25, and show times are 8:30 p.m. Thursday through Sunday, with extra shows on Friday and Saturday at 9:45 p.m. For more detailed information, call 978-8550. Children under 6 are not admitted.

To get there, either take the Yonge-University line subway to Museum or the Bloor-Danforth line to St. George; if you are going directly to the Canadiana Building, get off at Queen's Park.

UNIVERSITY OF TORONTO: Just south of the Royal Ontario Museum sprawls the main campus of the University of Toronto, with its quiet wooded walkway, ivy-covered buildings, and spreading lawns populated by 55,000 students and staff. Insulin was discovered here, the first heart pacemaker was built here, and even baby's pablum was developed here.

Wander through and note the architecturally interesting buildings, such as the Gothic-inspired Hart House.

ONTARIO LEGISLATURE: East of the university, at the top of University Ave., lies Queen's Park surrounding the rose-tinted sandstone and granite Ontario Parliament Buildings (tel. 965-4028), profusely carved, with stately domes, arches, and porte cochères. Drop in between 2 and 3 p.m. when the legislature is in session (March to June) for some pithy comments during the Question Period. Tours are also conducted from 9 a.m. to 12:30 p.m. every half hour on Monday, Tuesday and Thursday; from 9 a.m. to 3:30 p.m. on Wednesday; and from 1 to 3:30 p.m. every Friday (when the legislature is in session). From May 19 to Labour Day, tours are given Saturday, Sunday, and holidays on the hour from 9 a.m. to 4 p.m. Free.

THE GREAT TORONTO ADVENTURE: One way to get a handle on Toronto's history in an easily digestible form is to pay a visit to the Great Toronto Adventure, a multimedia show that uses 40 separate slide and motion-picture projectors showing 3200 transparencies and thousands of feet of film in a kaleidoscopic portrait of the city's history, attractions, and people. At this show you'll even feel the wind as it blasts off the lake on a cold winter's morning.

Shows are presented in the theater in the Colonnades Shopping Centre on Bloor St. between Bay and University (tel. 922-1212). Admission: adults, $3; children, $1.50. Shows run daily from 10 a.m. to 10 p.m., every hour on the hour.

YORKVILLE: In 1853 Yorkville became a village, then surrounded by trees and meadows; in the 1960s it became Toronto's Haight Ashbury, the mecca for young suburban runaways; in the 1970s it has become the focus of the chic. Hermès, Courrèges, Fabiani, Cartier, names with more than simply cachet, inhabit the restored town house boutiques which draw the well-heeled crowds into the area, now filled with art galleries, cafes, and restaurants.

Stroll around and browse; sit out and have an iced coffee in the sun at one of the cafes on Yorkville Ave. and watch the parade go by. Make sure you wander through the labyrinths of Hazelton Lanes between Avenue Rd. and Hazelton Ave. where you'll find a maze of shops and offices clustered around an outdoor court in the center of a building which is topped with apartments—the most sought after in the city. In the summer, the court becomes excitingly alive when the Hazelton Cafe erects colorful medieval-style jousting tents for one and all to relax under.

And while you're in the neighborhood (especially if you're an architecture buff), take a look at the red brick building on Bloor at the end of Yorkville Ave. If more libraries had been built like this one in the past, then perhaps study and learning would have come out of the dim and fusty closets and into the world where they belong. Step inside—a pool and a waterfall gently screen out the street noise and pine fence-like partitions undulate through the area like those you find along the sand dunes. Step further inside and the space opens dramatically to the sky. Every corner is flooded with light and air. I envy the citizens of Toronto their designer-architect Raymond Moriyama.

MARKHAM VILLAGE: One of Toronto's more famous characters is **Honest Ed Mirvish,** who originally started his career in the '50s with his no-frills shopping at the store at the corner of Markham St. (one block west of Bathurst) and Bloor, where the signs screaming bargains leap at you from everywhere. Among other things, Ed Mirvish rose to save the Royal Alexandra Theatre from demolition, established a whole row of adjacent restaurants for theater patrons, and finally created this block-long complex with numerous art galleries and restaurants. Stop by and browse, and don't forget to step into Honest Ed's on the corner.

CASA LOMA: Every city has its folly (some have several, while some . . .) and Toronto has a charming one, complete with Elizabethan-style chimneys, Rhineland turrets, secret panels, underground passageways, and a mellifluous-sounding name: Casa Loma, 1 Austin Terrace (tel. 923-1171).

Sir Henry Pellatt, who built it between 1911 and 1914 at a cost of $3 million, had a lifelong and incurably romantic fascination with medieval castles, and so he decided to build his own. He studied European medieval castles, gathered materials and furnishings, bringing marble, glass, and paneling from Europe, teak from Asia, oak and walnut from prime areas of North America;

and he imported Scottish stonemasons to build the massive walls that surround the six-acre site.

It's a fascinating place to explore: the majestic Great Hall with its 60-foot ceiling; the Oak Room, where three artisans worked for three years to fashion the paneling; the Conservatory with its elegant bronze doors and stained-glass dome; the battlements and Tower; Sir Henry's suite, containing a shower with an 18-inch diameter shower head; the 1700-bottle wine cellar; the 800-foot tunnel to the stables, where horses were quartered amid the luxury of Spanish tile and mahogany. As you go through the house, a tape recording in each room explains what you are seeing.

Open 10 a.m. to 4 p.m. daily. Admission: $2 for adults, 50¢ for seniors and children 12 and under, $1 for students 13 to 18.

ONTARIO SCIENCE CENTRE: Variously described as everything from the world's most technical fun fair to a museum of the 21st century, the Science Centre, at 770 Don Mills Rd. (tel. 429-4100), really does hold a series of wonders for adult and child.

First, the building itself is another one of architect Raymond Moriyama's miracles. Instead of flattening the ravine and bulldozing the trees on the site, Moriyama designed to the contours of the ravine so that a series of glass-enclosed escalators providing views of the natural surroundings take you down the escarpment to the main exhibition halls. Supposedly Moriyama built penalty clauses into the subcontractors' contracts for each and every tree destroyed!

Then the fun begins. Wherever you look there are things to do: test your reflexes, balance, heart rate, grip strength; play with computers and binary system games and puzzles; shunt slides of the tadpole, butterfly wings, and fired and unfired bullets under the microscope; try to prove wrong those optical illusions (you can't, but we all try); learn from the simple demonstrations which show that the shortest distance between two points is not necessarily the fastest (thanks to the inverted cycloid) and other graphically clear demonstrations of the rules of physics and mathematics; watch the bees work for a change; try to lift sponge building blocks with a mechanical grip; see how many lights you can light or how high you can force a balloon with your own pedal power—and on and on, through more than 450 participational exhibits. It's a wonder I ever made it home.

Throughout, there are tiny theaters showing film and slide shows on various topics, while at regular times demonstrators present 20-minute expositions on such subjects as lasers, elementary chemistry, and high-voltage electricity (watch your friend's hair stand on end). Facilities include a licensed restaurant and lounge, cafeteria, and bookstore.

Open daily from 10 a.m. to 6 p.m. Summer hours are extended (call 429-4423). When 1,600,000 people visited last year, you know that the best time to get to the museum is promptly at 10 a.m.—that way you'll be able to play without too much interference and negotiation.

Admission: adults, $2; students, $1; children 12 and under, 50¢; family rate, $4. Parking costs $1.

To get there, take the Yonge St. subway to Eglinton and then the Eglinton bus going east. Get off at Don Mills Rd. If you're driving from downtown, take the Don Valley Parkway and follow the signs from Don Mills Rd. north.

THE METROPOLITAN ZOO: In winter you can give the animals a show by skiing past the dozens of hardy types—lions, elephants, caribou—which stay outside during the winter.

How so? Because the zoo covers 700 acres of parkland around which many of the animals—tigers, polar bears, camels, and others—roam in their close-to-natural habitats, and across which beginners and intermediate cross-country ski trails run.

Then there are many indoor exhibits, marvelously housed in glass-roofed pavilions brimming with lush vegetation (all identified), free-flying birds, and exotic mammals, fishes, and reptiles. Follow the pine walkway from one pavilion to the next amid beautiful natural surroundings. Giant footprints lead the way. Ride the train down into the Rouge River Valley to see the Canadian animals; take a picnic and enjoy; drop into the pet park. You can spend the whole day, or if you have limited time, keep to the walkways that lead to the African Pavilion and Indo-Malayan pavilions.

Ample parking is available. There are restaurants and snackbars including a MacDonald's that has outdoor picnic tables. Strollers are available for $1. In winter, skis can be rented.

Open daily, in winter except Christmas Eve and Day from 10 a.m. to 4:30 p.m.; in summer, from 9:30 a.m. until dusk. Admission: adults, $3; seniors and youths, $1.50; children under 12, 50¢; under-5s, free.

For ski information, call 284-9781. For zoo info, write Metro Toronto Zoo, P.O. Box 280, West Hill, ON M1E 4R5 (tel. 284-8181).

The zoo is located at Meadowvale Rd. north of Hwy. 401 in Scarborough (tel. 284-0123). To get there, take the subway all the way to Warden on the Bloor-Danforth line. Then take the bus from there north. Check with the TTC for schedules (tel. 484-4544). By car from downtown, take the Don Valley Parkway to Hwy. 401 and exit on Meadowvale Rd.

BLACK CREEK PIONEER VILLAGE: Life here moves at the gentle pace of rural Ontario as it was 100 years ago. You can watch the authentically garbed villagers as they go about their chores—harrowing, seeding, rail splitting, sheep shearing, threshing. Enjoy the fruits of their cooking, wander through the cozily furnished homesteads, visit the working mill, shop at the general store, and rumble past the farm animals in a horse-drawn wagon. There are over 30 restored buildings to explore in a beautifully landscaped village.

Open in summer Monday to Thursday from 10 a.m. to 10 p.m.; Friday from 9:30 a.m. to 5 p.m. weekends from 10 a.m. to 6 p.m. Admission: adults, $3; seniors, $1.50; students, 75¢; family rate (maximum), $6. In winter it's open weekends only—for outdoor fun in the snow.

The village is located at Steeles Ave. and Jane St. (tel. 661-6600) northwest of the city. To get there, take the Yonge St. subway north to Finch and transfer to the no. 60 bus that runs along Steeles Ave. West to Jane St.

THE McMICHAEL COLLECTION: Located at Kleinburg, 25 miles north of the city (tel. 893-1121), this collection of Canadian, Inuit, and Indian art is worth a visit for the setting alone.

You'll approach the two-level gallery through quiet stands of pine trees to a log-and-stone building specially designed to house the Canadian landscapes within. The lobby itself is a work of art: a pitched roof soars to a height of 27 feet on massive rafters of Douglas fir. In the center stands a huge clefted granite column down which water pours to a reflecting pool at the base. At the west end towers a magnificent Bella Coola long house entrance post, dating from about 1875, while panoramic windows look south over white pine, cedar, ash, and birch.

In the 30 galleries that follow, the vividly and often thickly coated whirling color landscapes of the Canadian Group of Seven and their contemporaries glow against warm pine in room after room of smooth oak floors, rough hewn stone, and floor-to-ceiling windows that look out over the woods—you may even be distracted by a thrush looking for a worm.

The gallery contains only Canadian art, much of it by the Group of Seven—Franklin Carmichael, Lawren Harris, A. Y. Jackson, Frank Johnston, Arthur Lismer, J. E. H. MacDonald, and Frederick Varley—plus works by Tom Thomson, David Milne, Clarence Gagnon, and J. W. Morrice. Most, if not all, of these were inspired and moved to paint the landscapes of northern Canada, especially northern Ontario as they found it in Georgian Bay and Algonquin Park.

Collected in the Gallery of the West Coast Indian are totem poles, vividly carved and painted masks, pottery, and the paintings of Emily Carr. A gallery devoted to the Woodland Indian features their traditional silver, carving, beading, and quill work, plus their brilliant art depicting scenes from Indian legends. Until about 20 years ago painting among the Woodland Indians was taboo; so what you are given the opportunity to look at here is quite a phenomenon.

Downstairs in the first gallery, solid dramatic Eskimo sculptures carved from gloriously veined green or black soapstone polished to a brilliant sheen demand attention, while the often wry (to the non-Eskimo) visions of their art adorns the walls. To explain that last parenthesis, let me just say that the Eskimo is fully aware of his mammalian nature and circumstances.

Started as a personal collection by the McMichaelses in 1954, the museum retains their personal stamp. Throughout are reminders that this unique gallery began its life as a loved and loving home—polished floors, hooked rugs, earthenware pots laden with flowers and leaves, a cauldron over the fire, and by the stone fireplace a wooden rocking chair. Take your coat off and stay a while.

Open noon to 5:30 p.m. Tuesday to Sunday. Admission is free.

Note: After your visit, do try and have lunch or dinner at the nearby **Doctor's House & Livery** (tel. 893-1615) a delightfully rustic and atmospheric spot.

SPECIAL EVENTS: The prime events and dates to remember when planning a visit to Toronto are:

The **Mariposa Folk Festival,** staged on the Toronto Islands in mid-June, attracts performers and artisans from all over the world.

In the last week of June, the city is swept into an ethnic celebration lasting nine days entitled **Metro International Caravan.** It includes about 60 "international cities"—from Amsterdam to Zagreb. Reasonably priced "passports" ($6) enable holders to visit an English pub, Paris cafe, or German beer hall set up in community halls, churches, and clubs. The food, drink, and dance are as diverse as the cities themselves—Budapest, Kiev, and Amsterdam.

On the last Saturday in June, the **Queen's Plate** is run at Woodbine Racetrack. Dating back to 1859, it is the oldest stakes race in North America.

At the end of July to the beginning of August, Toronto's Caribbean community celebrates with **Caribana**—which features moonlight cruises, carnival balls, and on the Islands, music, dancing, picnics, and tropical fun. High point of the celebrations is the Saturday's grand parade when the city throbs to the beat of steel drums, as the colorful befeathered and sequinned retinue snakes its way downtown, singing and dancing in best Mardi Gras fashion.

And finally, taking the population up to Labour Day, there's the **Canadian National Exhibition,** described earlier under Exhibition Place.

SPORTS: Some wag once said that there's only one really religious place in Toronto and that's **Maple Leaf Gardens,** where the city's ice hockey team wield their sticks to the delight and screaming enthusiasm of fans. Tickets are nigh impossible to attain because they are sold by subscription. Your only hope is to find a scalper.

Exhibition Stadium in the Canadian National Exhibition grounds is the home of the Blue Jays baseball team. Admission prices run from $2 to $7. For information, write Toronto Blue Jays Baseball Club, P.O. Box 7777, Adelaide St. P.O., Toronto, ON M5C 2K7 (tel. 595-0077).

Racing takes place at **Woodbine Race track** (Rexdale Blvd. and Hwy. 427; tel. 675-6110), famous for the Queen's Plate (contested in June) and the Canadian International Championship, a world classic grass race, contested in October. Admission: $2 for the grandstand, $4 for the clubhouse. For further information, call 675-6110.

For information on golf courses, tennis, swimming pools, beaches, and picnic areas, call: City Parks (tel. 367-7251) and Metro Parks (tel. 367-8186).

5. Culture and Nightlife

Toronto has the National Ballet of Canada, the Canadian Opera Company, and the Toronto Symphony, two large arts centers, a concert hall, theaters galore (with a second-to-Broadway reputation), plus enough bars—plush, pub, wine, jazz, casual, and otherwise—discos, cabarets, and other entertainments to keep anyone spinning. For local happenings, check *Key to Toronto, Toronto Life,* and *Toronto Calendar* magazines, as well as the *Globe and Mail,* the *Toronto Star,* and the *Toronto Sun.*

OPERA, BALLET, AND SYMPHONY: The **O'Keefe Centre,** 1 Front St. East (tel. 363-6633), with its 60- by 130-foot stage and 3155-seat theater, provides the home for the Canadian Opera Company and the National Ballet of Canada.

The **Canadian Opera Company** began its life in 1950 with ten performances of three operas. It now stages six different operas spread over two seasons from September to December and April to May. Ticket prices range from $7 to $25. For tickets, call 923-3080.

Most famous of all Toronto's culture contributions is perhaps the **National Ballet of Canada.** It was launched at the Eaton Auditorium in Toronto on November 12, 1951, by English ballerina Celia Franca, who served initially as director, dancer, choreographer, and teacher. Over the years the company has achieved great renown, and among the highlights of its history have been the invitation to perform at Expo '70 in Osaka, Japan, its 1973 New York debut (which featured Nureyev's full-length *Sleeping Beauty*), and Baryshnikov's appearance with the company soon after his defection in 1974.

Besides its tours of Canada and its annual summer season at the Metropolitan Opera House in New York, the company performs its regular seasons in Toronto at the O'Keefe Centre in the fall, at Christmas, and in the spring, as well as summer appearances before enormous crowds at the open-air theater at Ontario Place. The repertoire includes both the classics and many modern works, among them Jerome Robbins's *Afternoon of a Faun,* Sir Frederick Ashton's *The Dream, The Two Pigeons,* and *Les Patineurs,* and Kenneth MacMillan's *Elite Syncopations.* Plans for 1979–1980 include a season at the Royal Opera House, Convent Garden, which marks the first occasion on which a Canadian ballet company has been invited to appear in that famous theater.

The senior modern dance company, **Toronto Dance Theatre** performs at the St. Lawrence Centre, where tickets are usually from $5 to $8.50 (tel. 967-1365).

The **Toronto Symphony** (tel. 363-7301), with Andrew Davis as music director, usually performs at Massey Hall, 178 Victoria St. (tel. 363-0374), a large piece of Victoriana (a new hall, scheduled to open in 1981, is currently being constructed on the west side near the Royal Alexandra Theatre). Tickets range from $5 to $13.50 depending on the featured international guest artists. The symphony also supports a Youth Orchestra, whose concert tickets sell for between $3 and $6.

Other classical music concerts, recitals, and chamber music featuring internationally famous artists are given at the **St. Lawrence Centre,** 27 Front St. East (tel. 366-7723), most often in the Town Hall, where tickets run from $5 to $9.50.

THEATER: The city's biggies include the O'Keefe Centre, the St. Lawrence Centre for the Arts, and the Royal Alexandra Theatre, fondly referred to as the Royal Alex. Then there are a number of small theater groups producing exciting offbeat drama—a slowly burgeoning Toronto equivalent to Off-Broadway. As there are a great number of these smaller companies, I have picked out only the few whose reputations have been established. If you'd like to do some talent scouting of your own, pick up the local newspaper or a local magazine, scan the myriad of productions and find the next Sir Laurence Olivier.

Shows from Broadway migrate to the **Royal Alexandra Theatre,** 260 King St. West (tel. 593-4211). For the 1979–1980 season, *Ain't Misbehavin',* *Deathtrap,* and *Dancin',* plus four more will be offered. Tickets, which range from $6 to $15, are often snapped up by subscription buyers, so your best bet is to write ahead to the theater at the above address (Toronto, ON M5V 1H9).

The theater itself is quite a spectacle. Constructed in 1907, it owes its current lease on life to owner Ed Mirvish, who refurbished it in the 1960s (as well as the surrounding area). Inside it's a riot of plush reds, gold brocade, and baroque ornamentation, with a seating capacity of 1493. Apparently, you're wise to avoid the second balcony and also sitting under the circle.

Prime tenant at the **St. Lawrence Centre for the Arts,** 27 Front St. East (tel. 366-7723), is **Toronto Arts Productions,** which presents a season of drama, including both classics and Canadian plays, and also a series of recitals and chamber music concerts in the smaller Town Hall auditorium. Tickets usually range from $5 to $9.50. For most shows, remaining seats are sold to seniors and students 30 minutes before curtain time for $4.

The **O'Keefe Centre** also presents such musicals as *Man of La Mancha* and *Anne of Green Gables,* plus diverse artists such as Joan Armatrading and Phoebe Snow. Ticket prices range from $5 to $25 depending on the star or the show.

Three theater groups—Open Circle, New Theatre, and Le Théâtre du P'tit Bonheur—use the **Adelaide Court,** 57 Adelaide St. East (tel. 363-6401). The two theaters (one upstairs and one downstairs) are located in the old York County Court House, built in 1852. Many of the original door and ceiling trims and moldings as well as the judge's bench, the graceful spiral staircase, and even the basement jail cells, were restored and made an integral part of the theater. Besides the two theater auditoriums, the building houses a restaurant, lounge, and summer cafe. The Open Circle, founded in 1972, provides entertainment with a strong social consciousness; Le Théâtre du P'tit Bonheur performs French-language plays; and New Theatre presents plays new to Canada. Telephone for tickets (usually $5 and $7), but there are no reserved seats.

Toronto Workshop Productions, 12 Alexander St. (tel. 925-8640), is housed in another completely redecorated warehouse, and is the city's oldest indigenous theater. It gained its reputation with the North American premier of *Chicago '70* and *Che Guevara,* and its resident company currently offers a season of original Canadian plays between October and May. Tickets are $6 Monday through Thursday and $8 on Friday and Saturday. Telephone for tickets; there are no reserved seats.

Théâtre Passe Muraille, 16 Ryerson Ave. (tel. 363-8988), started in the late '60s when a pool of actors began experimenting and improvising original Canadian material. Set in another warehouse, there's an upstairs and a downstairs theater each seating 300 and a back space for 100. Again, no reserved seats. Take the Queen streetcar from Bathurst.

The **Tarragon Theatre,** at 30 Bridgeman Ave. (tel. 531-1827), near Bloor and Bathurst, opened in the early '70s and continues to produce original works by Canadian playwrights—Michel Tremblay, David French, James Reaney, Roland LePage, Rick Salutin, and Steve Petch, for example—and an occasional classic like their recent productions of Racine's *Bajazet* and Lillian Hellman's *Toys in the Attic.* One of their most notable successes was David Freeman's *Battering Ram.* It's a small intimate theater where you can get coffee and apple juice in the foyer. Tickets are $5 to $6.50, and again there are no reserved seats. On Sunday you pay what you can afford.

At 24 Berkeley St., in a century-old building that was once part of Toronto's gas works, is the **Toronto Free Theatre** (tel. 368-2856), which was started in 1972 and presents original Canadian works as well as such plays as Sam Shepard's *Angel City* and the occasional classic. This highly experimental group also puts on poetry readings, and playwriting and directing workshops. Tickets are usually $4.50 and $6.50; on Sunday there's a pay-what-you-can matinee.

The **Bayview Playhouse,** 1605 Bayview Ave. (tel. 481-6191), has a 500-seat theater and delivers light modern musicals—one of its most successful productions was *Godspell*—as well as such modern serious plays as David Mamet's *Life in the Theater.* Tickets range from $7 to $9; seats can be reserved. Again, there's a pay-as-you-can matinee on Sunday.

Started in 1970, the experimental **Factory Theatre Lab,** 207 Adelaide St. East (tel. 864-9971), is the home of Canadian playwriting, where promising new authors get the chance to develop and showcase their works. In the past it has presented festivals of Canadian plays in London, and premiered David Freeman's *Creeps,* which ran Off-Broadway.

Toronto Truck Theatre, 94 Belmont St. (tel. 922-0084), is currently enjoying a long run—22 months of the *Mousetrap* in a renovated church. Tickets are $6 and $8. Previous seasons have included such hilarious productions as *Private Lives, The Owl and the Pussycat, Barefoot in the Park,* and even *The Imaginary Invalid.*

Children's Theater

In Toronto there's no problem about kids' entertainment, for the city has taken its children's theater very seriously by opening a **Young People's Theatre Centre** on Front St. East (tel. 864-9732), which includes a main theater accommodating up to 330, the studio theater on the third floor holding 100, a lobby for art shows and mini-performances, and a restaurant. Here, they put on such harum-scarum nail-biting visions as *Curse of the Werewolf* or enchanting musicals about Hans Christian Andersen. There might be one problem: kids have been known to weep when the show ends.

FILM: Generally in any city, it's easy enough to find a movie theater either from the *Yellow Pages* or the local daily newspapers, but Toronto has such an exciting futuristic film buffs' heaven that I simply have to tell you about it. It's called **Cineplex.** Always chary of describing any animal, vegetable, or mineral as the biggest, let me just say that the film complex houses 18 theaters with seating capacities ranging from 57 to 137.

Located in Eaton Centre, exterior screens over the Cineplex entrance display on-going slide presentations and an annunciator board in the lobby lists all movies and starting times. By staggering the starting times and selling tickets in advance, this celluloid wonderland avoids the modern film-goers bugaboo of standing on line. Furthermore, the complex can respond to lulls and swells in the crowd flow because it has the ability to show the same movie in anywhere from one to ten screening rooms, depending on demand.

Revivals, theme series, foreign films, and second runs of big hits are the staples; tickets are $3.50.

The **Ontario Film Institute** at the Ontario Science Centre, 770 Don Mills Rd., is the place to go for golden oldies of the film industry—William Powell and Carole Lombard comedies, Max Ophul's *Letter from an Unknown Woman,* or W. C. Fields and Mae West in *My Little Chickadee.* For film times, call 429-0454; for information, call 429-4100. Admission: adults, $2; students, $1; children, 50¢; seniors, free.

SUPPER CLUBS: Perhaps the most famous and glamorous of these is the **Imperial Room** at the Royal York Hotel, where you can still catch such stars as Tony Bennett, Pearl Bailey, Rita Moreno, Lorna Luft, Des O'Connor, and the Lettermen performing on stage under the exotic Sultan's tent in true Las Vegas style. The decor leans to heavy draperies, classical columns, plenty of gilt, and pumpkin velvet. Complete dinner and show prices vary depending on the artist. Recently for Pearl Bailey's appearance it was $32.50 plus tax ($18 to attend the show only). In the past the room has been closed during the summer, but in the future the management intends to bring in revues.

The other Las Vegas–style entertainment can be found at the Constellation's **Woodbine Inn,** where singers, dancers, magicians, and big bands entertain amid the racetrack and jockey regalia. Here, you can dine and dance, and there's no cover charge.

The **Café de L'Auberge** at the Inn on the Park also has a resident orchestra for dancing while you dine.

CABARETS: **Second City,** one of Toronto's zaniest theater groups, which specializes in improvisational comedy, works in the **Old Firehall,** an impressive building at 110 Lombard St. (tel. 363-1674) dating back to 1867. The skits are always funny and topical. Originally a fire station, the building now houses a theater seating 200 and a restaurant, and the shiny gold firepole remains. Second City has had a marked impact on Canadian entertainment with its various workshops, touring company, seasoned resident company, and internationally syndicated TV series. It offers reasonably priced dinner-theater packages: $14.48 Monday to Thursday, and $15.48 on Friday and Saturday. Shows-only prices are $6 and $7, respectively.

Toronto's oldest and most successful cabaret-style theater has been **Theatre-in-the-Dell,** over the Dell Restaurant at 300 Simcoe St. (tel. 598-4802), which features musical revues. Its reputation was established by the Noel Coward revue which ran for 18 months. Tickets are $6 on weekdays and $8 on weekends.

Recently it has been joined by others. **Basin Street Cabaret,** 180 Queen St. West (tel. 598-3013), kicked off in October 1978 with a resounding success entitled *Indigo,* a gutsy revue of the history of black music that had audiences clapping and roaring for more. Combination dinner-show tickets were $12.95 to $14.45; show only, $6 to $7.50.

The other major club is **Yuk-Yuk's Komedy Kabaret,** 1280 Bay St. (tel. 967-6425), situated in the heart of Yorkville, an ideal location for amateur and professional standup comics to puncture a few contemporary social pretensions in a stream of totally unpredictable monologue. Comic Mark Breslin founded the place following the trend of New York's Catch a Rising Star and Los Angeles's The Comedy Store. Besides the comics, other bizarre and hilariously grotesque troupes find their way to this spotlight. Tickets are usually $3 to $4.50.

Razor-edged lyrics and biting satirical monologues are also the fare offered at **Pears Cabaret,** 138 Pears Ave. (tel. 961-4698). Tickets are $4.50 Tuesday to Thursday, $5.50 on Friday and Saturday. Often breathlessly paced and cleverly written satirical revues also occur at **Teller's Cage** (tel. 862-1434), Commerce Court South (at King and Bay), where a recent show entitled *Tonight at 8:30 . . . 9:30 in Newfoundland* featured a male and female smiling their way through the most gruesome dissection of the nation's inferiority complex. Dinner-show tickets are $13.95 on weekdays, $14.95 on weekends; show only, $6 and $7, respectively.

Often a visit to any one of these tart revues is as good a crash course as any in Canadian history, politics, and society.

More quietly, you can float on a wave of Broadway melodies and patter at the **Captain's Quarters Lounge,** aboard Captain John's Flagship, 1 Queen's Quay West at the foot of Yonge St. (tel. 363-6065). Scheduled usually from 9 p.m., there is a $3 cover.

At the **Café des Copains,** 48 Wellington St. East (tel. 869-0898), you're also likely to catch more musical acts—duos singing haunting songs of love, loss, madness, and melancholy in almost Brechtian spirit. There are usually three shows an evening Monday to Saturday for which there's a $2 cover charge.

JAZZ: The city is really big on jazz—especially on Saturday afternoons when many a hotel lounge or restaurant lays on an afternoon of rip-roaring rhythm. Here are just a few of the top jazz spots in the city.

Bourbon St., 180 Queen St. (tel. 598-3020), is probably the most famous jazz joint around, owned by Doug Cole, former New York Rangers hockey player and a jazz nut. There's jazz every night, except Monday, from 9 p.m. to 1:30 a.m. (Sunday from 6 to 10 p.m.). There's no cover charge except for the Saturday matinee from 3 to 5 p.m. when it's $2. There is, however, a $3 minimum that can either be quaffed in the bar (on the side, away from the artists), or in the restaurant where you can get a veal parmigiana with salad and beverage for around $5. Remember that in this low-lit spot with a jazz-band silhouette on the wall, it's the sound that matters, and if past stars are anything to go by—violinist Joe Venuti, tenor saxophonist Buddy Tate, trombonist Al Grey, saxophonist Zoot Sims, and more recently, Gerry Niewood (who was for a long time with the Chuck Mangione Quartet)—then you'll be catching some hot sounds.

George's Spaghetti House at Dundas and Sherborne features local jazz groups, including Moe Koffman and his quintet.

In a rather unlikely setting of white and green walls, lattice work, and wrought-iron chairs, famous jazz pianist Joel Shulman entertains at the **Garden Party,** 82 Avenue Rd. (tel. 961-1114), which is his and his wife's domain. You can catch Joe and a good light lunch or dinner—poached salmon, rock Cornish hen à l'orange (both $6), from noon to 2:30 p.m. and from 6:30 on. But the excitement is really generated every second Sunday when there's a featured guest artist and the place takes on the aura of a genuine jam session. Joel played for years at New York's Village Gate opposite the Bill Evans trio, and in the past his jam partners have included Hagood Hardy, Don Thompson on bass and vibes, guitarist Ed Bickert, and Guido Basso on trumpet and flugelhorn. The whole evening will be very informal, about $4 per person, and desserts only are usually available. As the place only seats about 36 people you must reserve. But certainly this is one place to learn about the Toronto jazz scene and talk to the people in the know.

Saturday afternoon hops at **Malloney's,** 85 Grenville St. West (tel. 922-4106), one of the best known singles bars, between 3:30 and 6:15 p.m. where a swing-along older crowd fills the two bars for a traditional and Dixieland session. From 8:30 p.m. to 12:30 a.m. there's disco dancing on Thursday, Friday, and Saturday.

Other Saturday afternoon jazz spots include: **Barrister's,** at the Hotel Toronto; the **Chelsea Bun,** at the Chelsea Inn; and the **Northgate,** at the Ports. Upstairs at the **Brunswick House,** 481 Bloor St. West (tel. 924-3884), there's always a good smorgasbord of '30s, '40s, Chicago- and New Orleans–style jazz, nightly from 9 p.m.

ROCK, FOLK, AND POP: El Mocambo, 464 Spadina Ave. (tel. 961-2558), is *the* rock/blues emporium. Behind the somewhat tacky exterior there's a long bar, a young beer-quaffing and noisy crowd, but who cares when this is the place the Rolling Stones chose to make an impromptu appearance in 1978, and Long John Baldry, John McLaughlin, Sonny Terry and Brownie McGhee, Lou Reed, and others rip it up here. Cover varies depending on the guest.

Across town, the **Edge,** 70 Gerrard St. East (tel. 366-9401), long a student hangout, is shaping up as the punk and New Wave rock palace in a similarly rather scruffy ambience. Again, the cover varies.

For live rock and roll in a cavernous room, try the **Gasworks,** 585 Yonge St. (tel. 922-9367) Monday to Saturday.

For less harsh and driven sounds, try the **Stable,** 5 St. Nicholas St. (tel. 923-5854), where in a Danish-style bierstube decked out in a horse motif—prints, brasses, collars—a resident guitarist sings country and folk from 9 p.m. to 1 a.m.

Scoops, 136 Yorkville Ave. (tel. 923-9820), offers a potpourri of visiting popular-folk-country entertainers Tuesday to Saturday from 8:30 p.m. There's no cover. Monday is "sing for your supper" night, so if you have your guitar along, why not give it a try? Eccentric musicians also often seem to flourish at the **Groaning Board,** 1057 Bay St. (tel. 922-9876), from Thursday to Saturday.

DISCOS: As you know, discos come and go—the hottest spot can turn into the coldest potato almost overnight, so bear with me if some of those listed below have disappeared or changed. Meanwhile, here are some of the currently crowded spots on the Toronto scene.

First, let me just remind you of those hotel discos already mentioned: **Misty's,** at the Airport Hilton; **Jacquis,** at the Harbour Castle; **Raffles,** at the Prince; and the **Floating World,** at the Holiday Inn Downtown. For live-music discos, there's **Dr. Livingstone's,** at the Bristol Place; **Beaton's,** at the Westbury; and the awaited transformation of the old **Stop 33** on top of the Sutton Place Hotel.

On weekends you'll have to line up to get into the **Ports,** 1145 Yonge St. (tel. 961-7678), wherein you'll find the one disco Studio 54's Disco Sally recently chose to grace with her presence. Here a D.J. sits in a resurrected elevator and spins the most up-to-the-minute music to a capacity crowd. In between boogying you can relax on the red velvet banquettes and watch the scene and the flashing lights either on the ground level or from the balcony above. The average price of a mixed drink is $2.50. Under the same roof there's a series of restaurants, each with a different theme from western saloon to San Francisco fresh, which you may or may not wish to patronize, plus a number of singles bars. Open Monday to Saturday from 5 p.m. to 1 a.m., with a cover Thursday to Saturday.

At **Arviv,** 15 Bloor St. West (tel. 964-0242), you'll find tasteful creamy walls with wood trim, big mirrors everywhere, and plenty of brass railings. You can either dine upstairs or simply head downstairs to the small dance floor. There's a sophisticated flair at this place and the crowd reflects it—along with the light and sound system. Average price of a drink is $3.

Similar happenings occur (but on one level only) at **Christopher's,** 1240 Bay St. (tel. 961-4422), corner of Cumberland and Bellair in Yorkville, where you can dine in high-backed booths and other cozy nooks away from the deafening sounds of the dance floor. There's also a separate room for dining. Tiffany lamps, plants, and lush surroundings at this disco diner, where your classic French/continental meal could cost you $35 to $40 for two (entrees begin at $9.75 for royal squab marinated in wine with aromatic herbs).

At **Katrinas,** 5 St. Joseph St. (tel. 922-4188), a straight-gay crowd mingles on the dance floor in a melee of excitement, luminous projections, kaleidoscopic lighting effects, and a light organ that hangs over the dance floor. Dancing goes on until 1 a.m. Monday to Thursday, and until 4 a.m. Friday and Saturday. During the day Katrinas serves a very good buffet lunch for $3.50—a spread of marinated artichokes, Chinese baby corn, herring salad, roast beef, cabbage rolls and soup, and dessert. There's also a similar $6.50 dinner buffet served from 6 to 10 p.m. on Sundays only, and a brunch buffet on Sunday from noon to 4 p.m. for $3.50. Outside buffet hours, there's a $2 cover.

Brandy's, 58 The Esplanade (tel. 366-0780), is a singles spot that packs them in in droves. Somehow the management seems to have found a successful formula for capturing the younger crowd in an ambience created by exposed brick, masses of plants, and as many Tiffany-style lamps, occasional chaise lounges, and wingback chairs. During the early hours the place serves light fare such as quiches and salads, but from 9 p.m. to 1 a.m. the lines are champing at the doors to dance up a storm on the small dance floor. Drinks are fairly expensive: cocktails, $2.50; special cocktails, $3.25; a bar shot, $1.85; and domestic beer, $1.14—all plus 10% tax.

Thank Goodness It's Friday, 204 Eglinton Ave. East (tel. 485-1222), offers a very large disco restaurant crammed with the younger crowd.

PUBS AND BARS: First, let me repeat some of my favorite hotel bars. The fairly formal **Chartroom** at the Harbour Castle Hilton has a good view of the lake and the islands ferry; publishers, artists, and other professionals gather at the comfortable **Club 22,** the extremely conducive-to-conversation bar at the Windsor Arms; **Barristers** offers a clubby atmosphere, an oyster bar from 5 to 7 p.m. along with a pianist, and jazz on Saturday afternoons; the **Chelsea Bun** at the Chelsea Inn has a fine selection of single malt whiskeys and good musical entertainment. If you prefer a pubby atmosphere then there's **Dick Turpin's** at the Royal York, or the **Good Queen Bess** in the Sheraton. White-collar singles seem to collect at the **SRO** at the Four Seasons. The **Roland Emmett lounge** has a unique atmosphere at the Park Plaza Hotel, while there's dancing to a trio at the **Copper Lounge** at Inn on the Park. At the airport, check out the **Banyan Terrace** and the **Magic Carpet,** both at the Constellation, and the **Bishop's Landing** at the Cara Inn, all comfortable piano bars.

And now for the independents:

Bemelman's, 83 Bloor St. West (tel. 960-0306), with its mirrors, marble, gleaming brass rails, and plants, has a certain slice-of-Manhattan air about it, and the characters that inhabit it are dramatic and definitely trendy too. A long standup marble-top bar is where the action focuses; in the back you can get a decent meal—egg dishes, salads, spare ribs, which can add up to $10 or $20 for two. This is also a popular place for brunch from 11 a.m. to 3 p.m. Sunday. Open noon to 3 a.m. Monday to Friday, 11 a.m. to 3 a.m. on Saturday, and 11 a.m. to midnight on Sunday.

Another rather voguish watering spot cum French bistro is **Jingles,** 467 Church St. (tel. 964-7722), where you can perch at the semicircular teak bar along with the rest of the young attractive professional but arty types. On the other side of the bar you can have a fairly priced meal (dinner entrees $5 to $9) and in summer dine al fresco on the patio out back.

Then there are a whole series of veddy British-type pubs, designed in England and shipped and assembled here, where you can get as many as 28 beers and ales on tap (usually about $1.25 a half pint, $2.50 a pint, for imported brands; around $2 for bottled imports). In First Canadian Place, appropriately enough next door to the Simpsons-in-the Strand entrance, the **Duke of Westminster** offers a very classy English atmosphere which seems to attract those very English types for a good frothy English pint. The **Duke of York,** downstairs at 39 Prince Arthur Ave. (tel. 964-2441), offers similar plush surroundings and snacks such as steak-and-kidney pie, and Melton Mowbray from $2.50 to $3.50. Both offer the secluded, select air of a good English country pub/lounge bar. The **Duke of Richmond,** 220 Yonge St. (tel. 598-4454), in Eaton Centre's Galleria on the ground floor, has a more citified air with its Victorian etched-glass windows and models of the Royal Scot and various other railway memorabilia. (Similar ales and snacks available as at the Duke of York.) So also, does the **Duke of Gloucester,** upstairs at 649 Yonge St. (tel. 961-9704), which is crowded and noisy most of the time. Only someone who responds to the subtle nuances of locality and class can quite explain the differences.

Scotland Yard, 58 The Esplanade, (tel. 363-2301), with its Victorian bric-a-brac and heavy bar with phony beer pumps, has very much the flavor of a casual English local where you go to stand around the bar and josh or play a game of darts in between pints. The young crowd that gathers here take their game very seriously and some even bring their own set of arrows. Good mixed crowd. At nights there's a small dance floor that resounds to the good old tunes—like Elvis and the Beatles? Domestic beer is $1; cocktails average $2.60. Open daily noon to 1 a.m., Sundays until 10 p.m.

For some really good raucous Irish entertainment and joviality, stop in at **Dooley's**, 23 Bloor St. East (tel. 922-2626), which also has a proper down-to-earth pub area. Plenty of Harp lager and Guinness to imbibe here, and some hearty fare too, if you wish—good Irish stew, for instance. Live entertainment from 9 p.m. to 1 a.m. Monday to Saturday.

For a truly unique experience, step into the **Brunswick House**, 481 Bloor St. West (tel. 924-3884), a cross between a German beer hall and an English north country working men's club. Waitresses move through the arborite tables in this cavernous room carrying high trays of frothy suds to people of all sizes, shapes, ages, and lifestyles. And while everyone's quaffing or playing bar shuffleboard, they're entertained by anyone who wants to hop up onto the stage and live the fantasy of being Edith Piaf, Sophie Tucker, Gracie Fields, or Harry Lauder. You'll be treated to some semirecognizable renditions of "You Made Me Love You," "Buttons and Bows," and other staples of the music hall genre. An inexpensive place to down some beer. Upstairs, there's a good jazz spot.

Finally, there are the latest sophisticates on the watering hole scene: the wine bars. **Vines**, down the stairs at 38 Wellington St. East (tel. 869-0744), provides a pleasant atmosphere to sample a glass of champagne for $3.50. There's a list of 54 wines priced between $1.60 and $4 for a small four-ounce glass. Salads, cheeses, and snacks, served with fresh french sticks (from $2.50 to $5) are available.

The **Vineyard Bistro**, 5 Hayden St. (tel. 960-3053), lets you imagine you're sitting in a candlelit cellar surrounded by barrels and wine racks filled with bottles of wine. Perhaps more than a wine bar—there's an oyster bar plus a full lunch and dinner menu (five-course continental dinner for $9.75)—it nevertheless has the earmarks of the vintage—a wine of the week, which when I was there was a 1970 Rubesco Riserva at $16 a bottle, and also a vin du jour, both red and white that might range from $1.40 for four ounces to $2.80 for eight ounces (that's a healthy wine-globe full).

The **Hop and Grape**, 14 College St. (tel. 923-2715), provides, not surprisingly, beer on one level and wine on another, and is one of the most popular wine bars in the city. On the ground floor the pub offers 35 types of beer with four varieties on draft (imported beers $1.80 and up). Upstairs, the wine bar offers a selection of 100 wines, some by the glass and some by the bottle. Closed Sunday.

Upstairs at the **Hind Quarter**, 23 St. Thomas St. (tel. 924-3163), amid rustic decor retained from its days as a French-style restaurant, you can sample some 40 wines by the glass, unaccompanied or else heightened by light shellfish and seafood snacks such as snow crab claws with artichoke and tartar sauce (from $3), various pies, and light entrees like salmon with sorrel à la Troisgros (with herbs, shallots, fish fumet, and white wine, cream, and sorrel sauce, around $8). In the afternoon you can meet a friend and converse over a fine vintage port sherry, or Madeira, accompanied by light pastries. Closed Sunday.

COCKTAILS IN THE SKY: For obvious reasons the **CN Tower Lounge**, 301 Front St. West (tel. 360-8500), can be difficult to get into because of the crowds. But it's worth the wait to sip that drink and gaze at the panoply of Toronto's lights. Open noon to 1 a.m. Monday to Saturday, to 10 p.m. on Sunday. No jeans allowed. Sure to be another crowd pleaser is the disco atop the tower, which opened as this book went to press.

Or you can glide up to the **Lighthouse lounge** atop the Harbor Castle and listen to the vocalist from 7:30 p.m. to 12:30 a.m. daily, except Sunday. The bar itself is open Sunday until 10 p.m., and daily from noon to 1 a.m.

6. North from Toronto

And where do Torontonians go when they want to flee their high-rises or downtown dynamic energy-packed streets? Primarily, they head north—toward Georgian Bay, the wilderness of Algonquin Provincial Park, or the cottage and resort country of Huronia and the Muskokas, about 130 miles north of the city, where they can ride, hike, play golf, boat, fish, go antiquing, and swim in summer, and ski, snowmobile, and ice fish in winter.

Of course, from Toronto any visitor can also explore the cities and towns that ring the southwestern shores of Lake Ontario from Kitchener–Waterloo to Niagara Falls, which I'll do in the next chapter. But first, find Hwy. 401 and turn north on Rte. 400 to Barrie.

BARRIE: This is the gateway to the north and primarily a convenient overnight stopping place 66 miles north of Toronto. If you do stop in Barrie, go into the **Simcoe County Museum and Archives,** R.R. 2 Minesing (tel. 705/728-3721), about five miles north of Barrie on Hwy. 26, which traces the history of the area—Indian, pioneer, and Victorian—in displays and reconstructions. Open daily 9 a.m. to 5 p.m. Admission: $1.25 for adults, 50¢ for children.

Staying Over

Natural stone and chalet styling make the **Brookdale Park Inn,** 150 Dunlop St. West (tel. 705/728-1312), the most inviting place to stay. Chalets are arranged around a tree-shaded court at the back of which is a secluded pool area sheltered by lilac and shrubbery. There's also a tennis court and barbecue equipment by the pool.

Several different types of accommodation include regular singles and doubles, efficiencies, full kitchenettes, and double doubles with small refrigerator and bar. Rooms are all pleasantly furnished with Scandinavian-modern furniture and fully appointed with color TV and phone.

There's a dining room and tavern on the premises, where, among other things, you can get a good breakfast for $1.50.

Rates: $21 to $27.50 single, $25 to $32 double (the higher rates for the double doubles with refrigerator).

For budget accommodations, try the **Lake Simcoe Hotel,** 114 Blake St. (tel. 705/728-3704), where Orville and Elsie Evans maintain 20 nicely kept units set well back from the road overlooking Lake Simcoe. Some of the units have shower only, and there are some double units with common bath ideal for families. Rooms are decorated in golds and browns, and have TVs (some color), and phone.

Rates: $19 single, $21 double.

Where to Eat

There are two first-class restaurants in the town where you can dine in style.

Maude Koury's Steak House, 126 Collier St. (tel. 705/726-6030), will even send a chauffeured limousine for free to pick you up and take you home. You will be deposited in front of a white stucco Victorian house with black shutters and a Doric-columned portico. Just off the front entrance there's a lounge area where you can relax in front of the fireplace over an apéritif. Downstairs, the dining room is rustic in style with heavy beamed ceiling, knotty-pine paneling, and simple ladderback chairs. Upstairs, the rooms have plush Louis XV–style blue armchairs, and crystal chandeliers gilding the gilt-framed portraits on the walls.

The only odd thing about the menu is that it is prefaced with 15 soups—everything from French-Canadian pea to goulash and cream of celery. Otherwise, specialties are steaks (from $5.95 to $14.95 for an 18-ounce New York cut) and seafood (ranging from $7.95 for deep-fried shrimp to $16.95 for lobster tails).

Open noon to midnight Monday to Saturday, and 4:30 to 9:30 p.m. on Sunday.

Shannons, 149 Bayfield St. (tel. 705/737-3492), is located in a very large gray brick Victorian house, also with Doric-pillared portico. The entrance is magnificently oak paneled, even the ceiling, and a gracious staircase sweeps off it.

Inside there are three beautifully appointed rooms, each with fireplace—one especially ornate with Ionic pilasters at each end. Chintz wallpaper, heavy brown drapes at the Italianate windows, drawings and prints by local artists, and handmade furniture compliment the vintage surroundings. Oak tables are graciously appointed with Staffordshire china, crocheted placemats, and brown napkins.

Food runs to steaks and seafood. Try the breaded Digby scallops or the honey-basted ham steak (both $6.95). All dishes are served with kosher dills, french loaf, pickled beets, and baked, french-fried, or Suzette-style potatoes.

For budget dining you won't find better than the **Schnitzel Haus,** 29 Dunlop St. (tel. 705/726-3831), where a warm, woody atmosphere provides the background for such appetizers as rolled pickled herring ($1.25), which you can follow with Bavarian fried sausages with sauerkraut and pan-fried potatoes ($3.75), or any of several schnitzels (from $4.75). Try the strudel for dessert ($1).

Open 11:30 a.m. to 10 p.m. Monday to Saturday, and 4 to 10 p.m. on Sunday.

COLLINGWOOD (AND BLUE MOUNTAIN): Named after Admiral Collingwood, Nelson's second in command at Trafalgar, Collingwood first achieved prosperity as a Great Lakes port and shipbuilding town which turned out large lake carriers, and the many mansions and the Victorian main street are reminders of those days. Nestled at the base of Blue Mountain, today Collingwood is the center of Ontario's largest skiing area.

Blue Mountain

At the ski resort there are 27 trails and 18 tows, including eight chair lifts, one T-bar, six pomas, and three rope tows. At the base of the mountain there's the 20-room **Blue Mountain Inn,** plus a host of entertainment facilities including a licensed cafeteria, dining room, the Inn Place for dancing and entertainment, and a disco. In addition, there is a restaurant atop the mountain and three more base lodges. Five-day ski packages are available for as little as $139.50, including five nights' accommodation, breakfasts and dinners, lift tickets, 12 hours of ski lessons, plus a free nursery. Lift rates are $12 on weekends, $9 on weekdays. For more information, call 705/445-0231, or write Blue Mountain Resort.

Ever since the **Great Slide Ride** was installed in 1977 the resort has become a summer center. Now anyone from 6 to 76 can zoom down 3000 feet of asbestos-cement track aboard a molded fiberglass sled, weaving in and out of trees, and careening around high-banked hairpin curves. Naturally, you don't *have* to go at breakneck speed.

Riders ascend the slope in a leisurely ten-minute ride aboard the triple-chair lift, which treats you to a glorious panoramic view over Georgian Bay. The slide is open 9 a.m. to dusk (adults pay $3; children, $1.50).

During the summer, the resort also hosts poetry weekends and other cultural activities, and features musical concerts in the outdoor bandshell. For schedules, call 705/445-0231.

Besides skiing, Blue Mountain is also famous for its **pottery,** and you can take a tour and watch it being made and perhaps buy a few seconds. Many of the creations have been inspired by the natural life of the area—the wing of a bird, the graceful neck of the heron, the silver-scaled fish of the rivers and lakes. A small group of artists began in 1949 using the native red clay dug along creek beds on the mountain. The pottery outlet is located at Hwy. 26 in Collingwood (tel. 705/445-3000).

Three miles east of Collingwood on Hwy. 26 at Theatre Rd., the kids can enjoy testing their mettle and skills at **Blue Mountain Go-Karts.** For the really small fry there are mini-karts plus a mini-golf, a small touch-and-pet animal park, and a games arcade.

And just east of Blue Mountain sweeps nine miles of golden sands at **Wasaga Beach.**

Staying Over

The **Heidelberg Inn,** 461 Hume St. (tel. 705/445-4280), specializes in family accommodations. The 32 rooms are all furnished in modern style, appointed with TV, radio, and phone, and facing out on a grass courtyard where there's an outside pool. The dining room offers an excellent buffet lunch and some interesting German specialties, as well as steaks and seafood.

Rates: $35 per room for families in summer and winter; $22 per room from March to July and September to December.

The **Mariner Motel,** 305 Hume St. (tel. 705/445-3330), has 22 pleasantly decorated rooms arranged in an "L" shape overlooking grass, trees, and (in season) lilacs. The rooms have the latest grass wallpaper, double beds with cane headboards, color TV, direct-dial phone, air conditioning, and radio. The Mariner also has the added touch of a coffee room where you can have coffee or tea free, plus a breakfast room which is as spic and span as any you'd ever wish to see.

Rates: $24 double, $26 twin; an extra person is $5. During May and June, rates are $2 less.

The **Highwayman Inn** stands at the corner of First and High Sts. (tel. 705/445-6630), only minutes from the mountain. Built in a mock Tudor style with lattice windows, in winter a fire blazes in the lobby's brick fireplace studded with horse brasses, collars, and bridles, providing a warm welcome to chilled skiers coming off the mountain. The Flaming Hearth Restaurant offers the same glow. Rooms are ultramodern, fully appointed, and local telephone calls are free. For entertainment there's an outdoor pool, a sauna, and also a floodlit tennis court.

Rates: $25 single, $30 double, on weekdays; $29 single, $37 double, on weekends. An extra person is $5. Children under 18 stay free in their parents' room.

Of course, you can stay right at **Blue Mountain Inn,** R.R. 3 (tel. 705/445-0231), which has 20 rooms, enabling you to beat the lift lines in winter. Rooms are simply furnished, and have white cinder-block walls, color TV, and telephone. All have little balconies facing the mountain and overlooking the tennis courts.

Rates: $22 to $26 single, $26 to $30 double.

There's a warm welcome for you at the **Alpine Motel,** R.R. 3 (tel. 705/445-0988), which Austrians Joe and Anne Kablinger built themselves, five miles west of Collingwood on Hwy. 26. The 20 units are all beautifully maintained, are decorated in earth tones, and have color TV and inside and outside access.

Anne produces one or two of her native specialties in the warm barnboard dining room (for guests only) where a bright fire blazes in winter. And for summer play there's an outdoor pool and tennis court; in winter you can splash around in the indoor pool, hot tub, and sauna.

Rates: $20 single, $27.50 double, on weeknights; $24 single, $30.50 double, on weekends. Three-night weekend and weekly packages are available.

You'll find a home away from home at **BeaconGlow Motel,** R.R. 3 (tel. 705/445-1674), which has nine nicely furnished efficiency units that range in size from a compact two-bedroom with kitchenette to a spacious housekeeping unit that sleeps six and rents for $66 to six adults. There are also nine rooms in the guest lodge which rent for $28 to $36 double.

It's a warm, casual, and friendly place. For fun there's an outside pool, plus whirlpool and sauna, shuffleboard, horseshoe pitch, and a game room with a pool table, as well as a TV room where people gather for a cozy chat. Special weekly rates are available.

Note: In booking any of the accommodations above for weekends or holidays, you should reserve at least three months ahead.

Staying in Wasaga Beach: If you've ever been to the Black Forest, you won't miss the **Hotel Waldhorn,** Mosley St. at 32nd St. (tel. 705/429-4111), a delightful chalet-style inn with a roof garden where you can sit out and dine or snack at umbrella topped tables.

There are only 15 rooms, but they are large and modern, complete with color TV, phone, and air conditioning. The dining room is decorated with hunting and fishing trophies and a cuckoo clock or two, and waitresses in colorful dirndls serve the German specialties.

Rates: $23 single, $27.50 double; an extra person is $4.

Where to Eat

Sweep up the gravel drive past the well-manicured lawn and herbaceous borders to the **Spike and Spoon,** 637 Hurontario St. (tel. 705/445-2048), set in an elegant 120-year-old red brick house with peaked roof and dormer windows. The house used to belong to a Chicago millionaire named Hodgson who owned, among other things, a circus in Mexico. The wife of one of the Hodgsons was a music publisher in New York, which accounts for the music covers around the walls bearing such titles as "Loves and Frollics."

The three dining rooms are each different and feature an eclectic assortment of chairs including Windsors. One room has a fireplace with a stained-glass window above it where you'd expect to find the flue.

The food is not quite so eclectic, but does offer some unusual touches—home-baked bread, for example, a hors d'oeuvres table, and three fresh vegetables accompanying each main course. One or two specialties are featured each night (for example, fresh trout from the aqua farm, a rack of lamb, or tournedos en croûte topped with sauce chasseur and mushrooms), and served as part of a five-course fixed-price dinner for $14.50.

Open Tuesday to Sunday from 5:30 to 9 p.m. Closed in April and November. To get there, you'll probably enter Collingwood on Rte. 26; follow the signs to the business section past the Heidelberg Inn and Mariner Hotel to Hurontario St., where you turn left. The Spike and Spoon is on the left.

Red-haired and mustachioed Ray Sheffer returned from Barbados, where he had several restaurants, to open one in his hometown—the **Governor's Table**, 143 Pine St. (tel. 705/445-7771). Set in a red brick bungalow with bay windows, the Table offers several rooms each tastefully decorated with a few old artifacts like stone water bottles and Staffordshire ware, and a bar-bistro area furnished with rattan furniture and comfy loveseats. Here, after a classic appetizer of oysters Rockefeller ($4.95) or an oxtail soup ($2.25), try the rainbow trout in lemon butter ($6.75) or the rack of lamb ($8.95).

Open noon to 2:30 p.m. Monday to Friday, and 6 to 9 p.m. Monday to Saturday.

Practically next door, in a warehouse redevelopment, **Christopher's**, Schoolhouse Lane (tel. 705/445-7117), specializes in crêpes (all under $4), plus a soup and salad bar. The bar area, with its pine trimmings and bentwood cane chairs, serves cheese and crackers—and backgammon—as well as potables. In the cafe, rose banquettes and gray walls complemented by gray print tablecloths and art deco prints set an elegant tone. In summer, there's an outdoor patio for that European-style staring.

The really unique eatery in Collingwood is the **Depot** at Craigleith, six miles northwest of Collingwood on Hwy. 26 (tel. 705/445-4829): first, because it's located in an 1879 burgundy-colored clapboard station with Rhineland-style turrets; second, because it's surrounded by a huge patch of wild lilacs; third, because it offers reading material from the 1800s in the form of a superb collection of U.S., Canadian, and British newspapers. I think you get the picture.

Don't go there just to eat—take a look at the books on local and railway history that are there for you to peruse, and talk to owner Ken Knapman about the area. Every antique piece gathered here has a story: the Tiffany lamps and oak chests, the memorabilia of Sir Sanford Fleming (who designed the first Canadian postage stamp), even the carved mantel (which came out of a castle Sir William Osler built for his wife who died).

The food consists of juicy steaks—a New York or rib eye for $8.95—which you can follow with one of the delicious pastries. The restaurant is not licensed, and no reservations are taken.

Open noon to 2:30 Monday to Friday, and 6 to 9 p.m. Monday to Saturday.

For budget dining, go to **Peppis Upper Crust**, 390 First St. (tel. 705/445-0541), on Hwy. 26 in downtown Collingwood, for a pizza feast. Fifteen-inch pizzas range from $4.55 to $8.35, while various pastas (all under $4), and a range of steaks (under $10) are also available. Booths, stained-glass lamps, and a pine interior create a comfortable atmosphere. Open daily from 11:30 a.m. to 10 p.m., until 11 p.m. on Friday and Saturday.

Barnboard siding, a wagonwheel chandelier, and swinging saloon-style doors are just part of the western flavor inculcated at the **Gateway Tavern and Restaurant** (tel. 705/445-6262), opposite Blue Mountain Pottery showroom at Hwy. 26 and Blue Mountain Rd. It's a good place to stop for some barbecued chicken, steak, and seafood at reasonable prices.

On Hwy. 26 before you reach Collingwood (just west of Wasaga Beach Rd.), stop in at the **Pioneer Restaurant** with its log-cabin-style walls and heavy knotty-pine furniture, for some real home-style cooking at pioneer prices—a burger with bacon and cheese for $1.35, sandwiches from 80¢ to $2.85, plus half a barbecued chicken for $3.85. While you tuck in, the walls will keep you entertained too—for they're covered with such aphorisms as "Love Your Enemies—It Drives Them Nuts," and even more apropos, "How to have a successful vacation—take along less clothes and more money." Don't omit the homemade butter tarts (25¢).

MIDLAND: Some 33 miles east of Barrie and 90 miles north of Toronto, this city's history goes back to 1639 when the Jesuits established a fortified mission to bring the Word of God to the Huron Indians. The mission retreat of Sainte Marie among the Hurons flourished for one decade only, for the Iroquois, jealous of the Huron-French trading relationship, increased their attacks at the end of the 1640s. In 1648, 2000 Hurons and Father Daniel were killed, and in March of 1649 two villages were destroyed within six miles of Sainte Marie, and Father Brebeuf and Father Lalemant were tortured to death along with hundreds of Hurons. Eventually, the Jesuits burned their own mission and fled with the Hurons to Christian Island, about 20 miles away. But the winter of 1649 was harsh: thousands of Hurons died, leaving only a few Jesuits and 300 Hurons to straggle back to Québec whence they had come. Their mission had ended in tragedy and martyrdom. Had it been otherwise, the course of history might have changed, for it was 100 years before the Indians saw whites again, and then they spoke a different language.

This history is captured at **Sainte Marie Among the Hurons**, P.O. Box 160 (tel. 705/526-7838), where 22 structures have been built using 17th-century French skills. The blacksmith stokes his forge, the carpenter squares a beam with a broadaxe, the ringing church bell calls the missionaries to prayer, while a canoe enters the fortified water gate. A film also explains the life of the missionaries.

To get there, take Hwy. 12 to three miles east of Midland and follow the Wye Heritage signs. Open 10 a.m. to 6 p.m. daily from mid-May to Labour Day, until 5 p.m. from Labour Day through October 9. Admission: $1.75 for adults, 75¢ for students, 25¢ for children.

Just east of Midland on Hwy. 21 rise the twin spires of the **Martyr's Shrine,** a memorial to the eight North American martyr saints. As six of these were missionaries at Sainte Marie, this imposing church was built on the hill overlooking the mission, and thousands make a pilgrimage here each year. The bronzed outdoor Stations of the Cross were imported from France. Admission: $1 per car. Open mid-May to mid-October from 8 a.m. to 9 p.m.

Across from the Martyr's Shrine, the **Wye Marsh Wildlife Center** offers viewers the chance to explore the marshland along special trails guided by naturalists.

Midland is also the center for cruising through the beautiful scenic thousands of Georgian Islands. **30,000 Island Cruises,** P.O. Box 546 (tel. 705/526-6783), offers three-hour cruises which follow the route of Brûlé, Champlain, and La Salle up through the inside passage to Georgian Bay. During July to Labour Day, boats leave the town dock.

Where to Eat

Just past the Martyr's Shrine, set atop a hill commanding a wonderful view east over the lakes, stands **Bavarian House** (tel. 705/534-3202). Bavarian music, a mural of mad King Ludwig's fairytale castle, pine chairs, and wood paneling highlighted by gold tablecloths and red napkins, create the cozy atmosphere of a country inn which serves some really good sauerbraten, numerous schnitzels, and cabbage rolls (all under $7). Try the apple strudel for dessert. Lunch consists of fewer German specialties (all under $4), served from noon to 5 p.m.

Open noon to 10 p.m. daily. Closed in January and February.

Freda runs **Freda's**, 325 King St. (tel. 705/526-4857), almost as a hobby, but I don't mean that to detract from the quality of the food. It simply means that the restaurant is on the ground floor of her residence and that you must make reservations for dinner, when you can choose from a list of surf-and-turf and fowl dishes which include Stroganoff ($6.50), Cornish hen, and coquilles St-Jacques (both $7.50).

Lunchtime offers a vast array of sandwiches (most under $2), and snacks like shepherd's pie and chili ($2.80).

THE MUSKOKAS: En route to this beautiful lakeland region, whether or not you come from Midland you will probably pass through **Orillia,** where you can visit **Stephen Leacock's house,** a green and white mansard-roofed and turreted house with a central balcony overlooking the beautiful garden that sweeps down to the lake. The interior is stuffed with heavy Victorian furniture and seems to evince no particular sense of humor.

From Orillia, head north on Hwy. 11, keeping a lookout for **Paul Weber's** hamburger place at the side of the road. Here, you can get a real burger with real french fries, not the frozen variety, for $1.10 and 60¢, respectively. I heartily recommend it. Take a breather and sit out under the trees at the picnic tables provided.

Keep following Hwy. 11 north to **Gravenhurst,** a Victorian gateway to the Muskoka Lakes, where you can visit the house of **Dr. Norman Bethune,** 235 John St., who died tending the sick in China during the Chinese Revolution.

The Muskoka Lakes were for many years havens of the rich. Back in the balmy days before World War I, wealthy families built summer palaces on Lakes Muskoka, Rosseau, and Joseph. The way in was by steam train and steamboat, and even if you didn't have your own mansion you could vacation in one. An eccentric New Yorker had the wild idea that the rich could be enticed into the Canadian bush for a vacation, and he built a mansion on Lake Rosseau in 1870 and dared to charge visitors $5 a day (sound familiar?). It was a huge success and Muskoka never looked back. By 1903 there were eight big lake steamers, countless steam launches, and supply boats (floating grocery stores) serving a flourishing resort area. And it continues today. The rich are still here but so are the many families in their summer cottages and the sophisticated young professionals from Toronto who also flock to the larger resorts. You'll note that many of the resorts don't look so impressive from the road—but just take a look at the other side and remember that they were built for steamship approach. The corridors are often still very wide because, of course, they were originally built to accommodate huge steamer trunks.

Gravenhurst is the gateway town, while **Bracebridge** and **Huntsville** are the two main centers, around which cluster many of the resorts.

At Bracebridge one stop you should make is at **Santa's Village,** P.O. Box 398 (tel. 705/645-2512), a must for kids from 7 to 70. It's an imaginatively designed fantasyland full of delights, not the least of which are the frog litter bins that advertise "I love waste" and the Lost Adults Depot. You can wander through stands of pine trees to Elve's Island, a unique children's play area where the kids can crawl on a suspended net and over or through various modules—Punch Bag Forest, Cave Crawl, and Snake Tube Crawl for instance. Stop in to see the Gingerbread Lady, or Old MacDonald's Touch and Pet Animal Farm, or board either the Candy Cane Express or Paddlewheel boat up and down the river, or any one of many rides and attractions.

Rides are purchased with tickets which cost 40¢ each (or 20 for $6). And of course don't forget to visit Santa's House and his dog Sno Bo.

Open weekends only from May 19 to June 16 and from September 8 to October 7; from June 16 to September 2 open daily from 10 a.m. to 6 p.m. Admission: adults, $2, children under 17, $1.

Huntsville is the center for cruising the Fairy and Peninsula Lakes. **Muskoka Boat Tours,** R.R. 2 (tel. 705/635-2443), offers three-hour cruises aboard 40-foot *Miss White Pines,* past the palatial summer homes and in and out of the islands. You can really see the area as it was intended, when the steamers used to ply back and forth (adults pay $6; children up to 12, $3).

In the fall Muskoka has such dazzling scenery that Walt Disney had aerials made of the region for the filming of his *Littlest Hobo,* story of a vagabond cat. To celebrate its autumn beauty Muskoka stages a **Cavalcade of Color** that runs from the last two weeks of September to the Canadian Thanksgiving on October 10. Nearly all of Muskoka's prime centers put on something during the cavalcade—fall fairs and carnivals, invitational golf tourneys, concerts, and dancing. This is an especially good time to drive the Algonquin Route, that section of Hwy. 60 from the west gate to the east gate of Algonquin Park, known as the Frank MacDougall Parkway.

Bracebridge Accommodations

For a secluded, not overdeveloped casual lodge, ideal for families, **Paterson Kaye Lodge** (tel. 705/645-4262) fits the bill. Located on Lake Muskoka, the main lodge has a variety of rooms while cottages of various sizes accommodating a total of 100 people are scattered around the property.

Free waterskiing with instruction is run from the dock; there are two tennis courts, and a number of activities are arranged which you may participate in. Of course, there's plenty of fishing, golf, and riding nearby, and boats and bicycles are available.

Rates are quite moderate, in peak season running from $125 to $145 per person per week, including breakfast and dinner daily, depending on the type of accommodation. Special weekend packages are available, and also special reductions at certain weeks.

Tamwood Lodge, R.R. 1 (tel. 705/645-5172), is also fairly small and a real log lodge, where all the interiors are furnished with heavy knotty-pine furniture, often arranged around a granite fireplace. The main lodge has 40 units, all simply but nicely decorated; there are a few cottages, and then there are four deluxe loft accommodations stunningly appointed with pine interior, two bedrooms with a skylight, plus a loft area, an upstairs and downstairs bathroom, and a living room with Franklin stove leading out onto a balcony from which you can dive into Lake Muskoka.

There are facilities for swimming (both indoors and outdoors), fishing, tennis, volleyball, badminton, and shuffleboard, plus boat and canoe rentals, and all the winter sports imaginable.

Rates: These range from $33 to $37 daily (from $174 to $222 per week), depending on type of accommodation. Special discount weeks and weekend packages are available.

The very name **Clevelands House,** Minett near Port Carling (tel. 705/765-3171), has a gracious ring to it, and indeed this resort has been providing the ultimate in luxury since 1869. It is much larger than the two above (it can accommodate 360) and is very much a full-facility resort—17 tennis, four shuffleboard, and three badminton courts, a nine-hole golf course, a lovely dance floor set out on the dock with a sundeck on top, a children's playground and other activities, a heated outdoor swimming pool, and good fishing, swimming, boating, and waterskiing on Lake Rosseau. The lodge itself is a truly magnificent brick and clapboard structure with a veranda that runs around the lakeside giving views over the well-kept flower gardens. Accommodations vary in size and location and have solid old-fashioned furniture.

Rates: regular accommodations in various lodges run from $174 to $366 per person per week with three meals daily, depending on the number of people in the room and whether bathrooms are shared. Bungalow and cottage accommodations run from $192 to $294 per person per week. Special discount family weeks are available.

On Lake Joseph, **Elgin House,** Port Carling (tel. 705/765-3101), is equally majestic although built a little later (in the early 1900s). There are four lodges, the main building, plus cottage accommodations, all pleasantly furnished with solid pine furnishings.

This is a full-facility resort, with six tennis courts, a nine-hole golf course, waterskiing, boating, and canoeing, an outdoor heated pool, and the Deck, right down by the lakeside for dancing and cocktails. Children are well looked after, and there's even a nondenominational chapel on the grounds.

Rates (including breakfast and dinner) range from $195 to $295 per person per week, the higher price for a 700-square-foot lakeside suite with fireplace. Special weekend rates are available.

Huntsville Accommodations

The prime luxurious resort is undoubtedly **Deerhurst Inn and Country Club,** P.O. Box 1950 (tel. 705/789-5543), which caters less to families and more to swish and chic Torontonians.

The lodge itself has maintained a tradition of gracious hospitality and impeccable service since its opening in 1896. Modern comfort and style are the hallmarks throughout. Accommodations consist of 17 cottages from bed-sitting to five-bedroom, the main lodge, and a number of ultramodern luxurious motel-style units. Most of the cottages have stone wood-burning fireplaces and balconies, and are super stylishly decorated (as are the public areas in the main lodge). The lounge has a massive stone fireplace stretching the length of one wall, and comfy velvet and leather chairs. The adjacent bilevel dining room offers romantic dining overlooking the lake, while the piano bar creates a chicly modern rattan environment.

Facilities include a disco (which is also used for performances by Second City, the theater group), a billiard room, four tennis courts, outdoor and indoor heated swimming pools with whirlpool, sauna, plus the usual swimming, sailing, boating, waterskiing, and fishing opportunities, and a full winter program including skiing at nearby Hidden Valley.

Rates: In the summer and winter seasons, rates run $61.50 per person per day for a package that includes accommodation and two meals per day plus free use of all facilities; modified American plan is $54; European plan, $34.50. In spring and fall, rates are $43, $40, and $23, respectively. A fireplace is $3.50 extra.

Fine old trees and rolling fields flank the approach to **Grand View Farm,** P.O. Box 1089 (tel. 705/789-7462), which offers a totally different experience. You won't find racy discos or facilities to fill every minute of the day, but rather tranquility and some of the most exquisitely furnished, decorated, and maintained accommodations I've ever seen. Many of the cottage accommodations have antique brass beds and antique reproduction furnishings. In the main lodge the rooms are all bright and different, although many have louvered closets and iron bedsteads. One delightful room has a four-poster and a balcony, while kids love the oddly shaped attic room which contains three beds that pull out of drawers.

The Farm (the stables are still there, albeit empty) has been a resort since 1909, but the Craiks, who run it now, took over in 1970 with their six children.

Facilities do include two tennis courts, dock, sailboats for rent, canoes for free, and waterskiing. Certainly, this is a glorious place to be far from the madding crowd. Open May 24 to a week after Canadian Thanksgiving in October, and then from December 27 to March 31.

Rates: from $35 to $45 per person in the cottages; from $35 to $46.25 per person double in the inn; from $92.50 to $98.50 per couple for certain luxurious rooms (with fireplaces, refrigerators, and sliding glass doors leading to a balcony overlooking Fairy Lake). All rates include three meals a day.

The **Holiday Inn** at Hidden Valley (tel. 705/789-2301) is unlike any other member of that chain. Located on a sheltered bay on Peninsula Lake, the chalet-style rooms offer glorious views over the lakes to crimson hills in fall.

It's located right at the base of the mountain which offers two chair lifts, a T-bar and rope tow, and ten slopes. Snowmobiling and cross-country skiing are also available. Facilities include an indoor and outdoor pool, sauna, dock, waterskiing and sailing instruction, boat rentals, lounges, and dining room.

Rates: $34.50 to $36.50 single; $49 to $51 double, from December 18 to April 15; $27 to $29 single; $30 to $36 double, from April 16 to June 12 and October 9 to December 16; $36 to $38 single, $42.50 to $52 double, June 13 to October 8.

Pow-Wow Point, P.O. Box 387, R.R. 4 (tel. 705/789-4951), is a small family resort with regular rooms and several simple cozy cottage accommodations, none of which has TV or phone, plus a rustic lodge with pine interior, a deck overlooking the lake, and a recreation room and snackbar. Facilities include one tennis court, an inside pool with whirlpool, and free waterskiing during July and August. Boat rentals and other sports are available nearby.

Rates (including three meals) range from $32 to $34 per person, double, in summer; $30 to $32 per person otherwise. In the cottages (depending on the size), each of the first two adults pays from $38 to $44 in summer, from $36 to $39 otherwise. Weekly rates are available. An additional adult sharing a room or cottage is $24.

Where to Eat

Overlooking the hills and lakes of Hidden Valley, **A Touch of Dutch,** Muskoka Road 23, Huntsville (tel. 705/789-7886), offers precisely that. In an atmosphere created by locally made pine furniture and a knotty-pine interior and rafters, the blue and white lampshades and the Dutch tiles around the salad bar add just that hint of flavor. The cuisine consists of steak and seafood with several Dutch specialties, including the pork rolladen in a mushroom cream sauce with a touch of sour cream and mustard ($8). For dessert, try the strawberries Romanoff ($2.50). At lunchtime there are omelets, sandwiches, and light entrees (all under $4).

In winter it's especially inviting to sit around the large open fireplace and look out over the pastoral scene outside under a soft coat of snow. Open noon to 2:30 p.m. and from 5 p.m. During the summer there are sittings at 6 p.m. and 8 p.m. The place is closed in November and April. Hours are sometimes erratic—you must make a reservation.

You might not expect to find a classic top-notch restaurant up in the hills, but indeed there is one—**Ascona Place,** on Bethune Drive in Gravenhurst (tel. 705/687-5906), named after a small picturesque village in southern Switzerland. The menu features appropriately classic cuisine plus one or two Swiss specialties, such as an émincé of veal Swiss style in white wine and cream sauce ($9.25). Entrees range from $7.75 for wienerschnitzel to $12.25 for Dover sole bonne femme. You may either dine in the wine cellar, a cozy nook hung with wine bottles, or else in the larger Ascona Room, hung with Swiss banners, wicker lampshades, and a set of Swiss cow bells. Gateback chairs with blue seats and gold tablecloths complete the scene.

Owner Ernest Zingg is a wine connoisseur and the wine list is very extensive, offering over 300 choices, some going back to 1911. Desserts are truly exquisite—puree of chestnuts with whipped cream, homemade meringues, or an iced soufflé with French Marc de Bourgogne (all around $2.25). Lunchtime is a good time to try the cuisine, when most entrees are under $5.

Open noon to 1 a.m. daily.

Cottage Accommodations

Cedar Rail Resort, Woodington Rd., R.R. 2, Port Carling (tel. 705/765-5789), on Lake Rosseau, has pine log chalets all facing the water, and all fully equipped for housekeeping. For extra comfort each has a fireplace and electric heating. Open from mid-April to mid-October. Rates: Three-bedroom chalets sleeping six are $310 weekly; two-bedrooms sleeping four are $280; in July and August, $235 and $210, respectively.

Farther north and on the fringes of Algonquin Provincial Park, **Blue Spruce Inn,** R.R. 1, Dwight, ON P0A 1H0 (20 miles northeast of Huntsville; tel. 705/635-2330), has nicely kept motel efficiencies and cottages. The lodge has a cozy lounge, and there's a beach, boating, sundeck at the lake, two tennis courts, game room, and snowmobiling for recreation. Rates: One-bedroom cottages and the efficiencies are $30 per night, $162 per week; two-bedroom cottages are $42 and $220, respectively; three-bedroom cottages are $64 and $310.

Pine Dale Efficiency Motel has bright, spacious bed-sitting rooms and cottages, both equipped for light housekeeping, with balconies and picture windows overlooking Gull Lake. Family units are also available, and there are tennis, table tennis, shuffleboard, boating, and waterskiing facilities. Write P.O. Box 760, Gravenhurst (tel. 705/687-2822).

Rates in season are from $27.50 to $28 double per night; a family room sleeping four costs $36 per night; suites sleeping six are $42 per night. Weekly rates are available.

Camping

Gravenhurst Reay Park and Koa Campground, R.R. 3 (tel. 705/687-2333), has 200 acres of pine trees and meadows, plus a trout pond, swimming pool, store, heated washrooms, hot showers, and laundromat. The 135 sites are $5.50 for two persons, plus $1 for electricity and water service. For recreation there's a nine-hole golf course, hiking trails, and boats for rent. Sites have fireplaces, firewood, electricity, and convenient water taps. The campground is located between Gravenhurst and Bracebridge on Hwy. 11.

Sports

The Muskoka District and Algonquin Provincial Park boast more than a thousand beautiful lakes, many of them with miles of connecting systems of waterways ideal for canoeing. For **canoe route information** in the park, write: Superintendent, Algonquin Provincial Park, Ministry of Natural Resources, Whitney, ON K0J 2M0. For information in the Muskoka Lakes, write: Ministry of Natural Resources, P.O. Box 1138, Bracebridge, ON P0B 1C0.

Hiking trails abound in Arrowhead Provincial Park at Huntsville and the Resource Management Park on Hwy 11, north of Bracebridge, and of course, in Algonquin Park.

More and more **snowmobiling** trails are being opened through wilderness country. For information, write: MTA, P.O. Box 58, Gravenhurst, ON; or Muskoka Winter Association, P.O. Box 1239, Huntsville, ON.

ALGONQUIN PARK: Immediately east of Muskoka lie Algonquin Park's 3000 square miles of wilderness—a haven for the naturalist, camper, fisherman, and sports enthusiast, whether canoer or cross-country skier. The park is a game sanctuary and moose, beaver, bear, and deer roam freely, but there is plenty of fishing for speckled, rainbow, and lake trout, and small-mouth black bass.

There are several lodges in the park, the most beautiful and rustic being **Arewhon Pines,** very popular with young people. Also recommended is **Killarney Lodge,** (tel. 705/633-5551), which has 28 modern cottages and excellent recreation facilities for swimming, canoeing, and fishing. Open May to October.

Enter the park on Hwy. 60 from either Dwight or Whitney.

Chapter XII

AROUND LAKE ONTARIO

1. Kitchener–Waterloo
2. Elmira, Elora, and Fergus
3. Stratford
4. Hamilton
5. Niagara-on-the-Lake
6. Niagara Falls

WITH TORONTO AS your base, you can explore nearby Ontario attractions that range from the Mennonite farming communities of Elmira, Elora, and Kitchener–Waterloo, and the fruit-growing and wine-producing areas around Niagara-on-the Lake to the steel town of Hamilton and the honeymoon capital of the world—Niagara Falls.

All these destinations are within easy driving distance of Toronto and can be enjoyed individually as day trips or, better yet, covered in a counterclockwise tour from Toronto.

1. Kitchener–Waterloo

The twin cities of Kitchener (pop. 135,000) and Waterloo (pop. 50,000) lie 69 miles or about an hour's drive from Toronto along Hwy. 401 west, in the heartland of rural Ontario. Travel a few miles out of town and you can see fields being plowed by four-horse teams and families traveling to market by horse and buggy—the people of the Twin Cities are never far from their Mennonite heritage.

About 60% of the population is of German origin. The first German settlers were Pennsylvania Mennonites who came in Conestoga wagons around 1800. Abraham Erb, founder of Waterloo, left Pennsylvania with his family and possessions in 1806, while Benjamin Eby purchased the land on which Kitchener stands in 1807. Descendants of the Mennonites are still living and farming the area. Some still adhere to the old values—they do not drive cars, drink alcohol, vote, hold public office, serve in the armed forces, or use the courts to enforce personal rights. Listen for the gentle clip-clop of hooves upon the highway; look up and you will probably see an Amish couple, he in black suit and hat and she in bonnet and ankle-length skirt, riding proudly in an open buggie (with an umbrella if it's raining).

German immigration continued throughout the 19th and 20th centuries, and still Kitchener–Waterloo's two drawing cards, the Farmer's Market and the Oktoberfest, reflect the cities' ethnic heritage.

WHAT TO SEE: As you come into town along King St. (Hwy. 8) past the colorful Rockway Gardens with their rockeries, flower beds, and illuminated fountains, you'll find the **Farmers Market** located on the right at the junction of King and Frederick Sts. in the ultramodern Market Square Complex which also houses 36 stores, among them, Eaton's department store. The market started on May 25, 1839, and has been going strong ever since. The best way to see the market is to get up early on a Saturday morning, because by 8 a.m. the 200 stalls are booming with business and some of the best deals have already been made. Savor the sights, sounds and scents. Sample some shoofly pie, apple butter, kochcase (a cooked cheese ordered with or without caraway seeds), Baden limburger, Wellesley cheddar, blueberry fritters, and in a class by itself, the region's sauerkraut. No cellophane packages here. Purchase homemade rugs, quilts, woodcarvings, paintings, custom-made knives, hand-carved toys, slippers, vests, mitts—the handsome creations of the local folk. Open Saturdays all year from 5 a.m. to 2 p.m., with a smaller market on Wednesdays during May to December, 6 a.m. to 2 p.m. Admission is free.

While you're visiting the market, you might pop over and see Canada's first **glockenspiel,** which is located at King and Benton Sts. right across from the Valhalla Inn lobby entrance. It depicts the fairy tale of Snow White and the Seven Dwarfs, and the 23 bells that form the carillon play a song each day at noon and 5 p.m.

Drive down King St., turn into Wellington St., and continue until you come to **Woodside National Historic Park,** 528 Wellington St. North (tel. 519/742-5273), the teenage home of William Lyon Mackenzie King, prime minister of Canada from 1921 to 1930 and 1935 to 1948. The Victorian home with its 11½ acres of grounds has been restored to represent the interior and atmosphere of an uppper-middle-class home in Ontario in the early 1890s. Large subtropical potted plants compete for space and attention with plaster busts, wax flowers, beadwork, hanging plates, gilt-framed pictures suspended from picture rails, and other bric-a-brac. One can imagine the King family gathered around the piano in the parlor singing hymns and popular airs or playing cricket or croquet on the front lawn. The house is open Monday to Sunday from 9 a.m. to 6 p.m. from June 1 through Labour Day; Monday to Sunday from 10 a.m. to 5 p.m. from September through May 31. Closed winter public holidays. Admission free.

Many of the relics of the pioneer past are preserved in **Doon Pioneer Village,** R.R. 2, Kitchener, ON N2G 3W5 (tel. 519/893-4020), just south of Kitchener, where you can see 23 buildings including a blacksmith, cooper, and butcher shop, a general store, a sawmill, a model of an original Mennonite village in Russia, and a saddlery. Plus you can ride on the Mini Steam train, an exact replica of the Grand Trunk engine and track operating in 1856 from Guelph to Kitchener. To get there from downtown Kitchener, drive south on King St. (as if you're going back to Hwy. 401), turn right on Fairway, proceed to Manitou Dr. and turn left, and then turn left again onto Homer Watson Blvd. until you see Doon Pioneer Village. Open May 1 to October 31 daily from 10 a.m. to 5 p.m. Admission: $2 for adults, $1 for senior citizens and students, 50¢ for children under 12.

In Waterloo you might like to stop in at the **Farmers Market** held one mile north of Waterloo (just off Hwy. 85) on Weber St. every Saturday from 6 a.m. to 1 p.m. and on Wednesdays from June through October 5 from 3 to 9 p.m. The kids might also enjoy **Waterloo Park** with its small animal menagerie of bears, deer, foxes, hawks, owls, peacocks, and wolves. Located off Albert St., it's open all year and free, and the whole family can enjoy a picnic and a swim (in summer only). The **University of Waterloo,** Ontario's third-largest university, with 22,000 students, has much to offer the casual visitor—an art gallery, a biology–earth sciences museum, an optometry museum (both open weekdays from 9 a.m. to 4 p.m.), and professional and amateur theater. Stop in at the information kiosk at the campus entrance on University Ave. south of Albert St. and ask for a campus map, a walking-tour guide, and parking information.

For maps and more detailed information on the area's attractions, stop in at the **Kitchener Chamber of Commerce,** 67 King St. East (on the second floor of the Canada Permanent Trust Building) between 9 a.m. and 5 p.m. on weekdays only (tel. 576-5000), or the **Waterloo Chamber of Commerce** at King and Bridgeport Sts., Waterloo (tel. 886-2440).

THE OKTOBERFEST: Where you find Germans, there you find beer. From small beginnings in 1969, this festival now attracts over 350,000 people annually. There are over 30 festival halls and tents serving frothy steins of beer, thick juicy sausages, sauerkraut, and oompah music in the best Bavarian tradition, as well as special entertainments—plays, satirical revues, art shows, concerts, folk-dance displays, and sports—all culminating in a three-mile Oktoberfest parade. Admission to the festival halls is $3.

As the festival is so popular, rooms have to be reserved *at least* six months in advance and even then you may not be able to find accommodations in Kitchener–Waterloo itself but may have to stay in Stratford, Guelph, Cambridge, or Hamilton and drive in.

For information and reservations, call or write K-W Oktoberfest Inc., P.O. Box 1053, Kitchener, ON N2G 4G1 (tel. 519/576-0571).

WHERE TO STAY: First, a couple of downtown possibilities.

Downtown

The **Valhalla Inn** at King and Benton Sts. (tel. 519/744-4141), whose entrance lies across from the glockenspiel, offers 130 modern rooms with balconies equipped with dark colonial-style furniture, burnt-orange wall-to-wall carpeting, pretty print spreads and curtains, and the usual amenities—direct-dial telephone, color TV, individually controlled air conditioning and heating, and a full bathroom. The hotel also has an indoor pool surrounded by Astroturf and covered with a solarium dome (open from 10 a.m. to 10 p.m.), a sauna, a coffeeshop (open 7 a.m. to midnight Monday to Saturday, and 8 a.m. to 11 p.m. on Sunday), a cocktail lounge that has entertainment from 9 p.m. to 1 a.m. daily, except Sunday, and the Black Walnut Dining Room, so called because of the heavy walnut pillars that support the ceiling, where you can enjoy a buffet-style lunch for $3.95 on weekdays.

Rates: $29.50 single, $33.50 double. An extra person in a room costs $4. Weekend packages for two nights go for $52, single or double (note that they are *not* available during July and August or the week of Oktoberfest). Free parking is available.

The other hotel worth looking at downtown is the old **Hotel Walper,** 1 King St. West (tel. 519/742-3531), which was built in 1886 and has retained the marks of that era—a gracious crystal chandelier-lit lobby with carved Charles II–style chairs and a brass-railed marble staircase that leads to the 97 high-ceilinged rooms (currently being renovated) furnished with elegant floor-to-ceiling drapes, matching spreads and wallpaper, comfy velour sitting chairs, and modern darkly finished furniture.

Rates: $26 single, $30 double (these are expected to rise after the renovation has been completed).

The hotel's Baroque Room has long been a local dining landmark with its eight crystal chandeliers, ornate French-style gilt mirrors, Corinthian columns, and baroquely carved chair backs. The extensive menu includes fish, fowl, pork, and beef dishes, and features several German specialties. Prices start at $7.50 for kasseler rippenspeer (smoked pork served with sauerkraut) and run through to roast goose stuffed with chestnuts and apples and served with red cabbage and potato dumpling. Desserts are notoriously good and fattening.

Along King St. (Hwy. 8)

As you come along Hwy. 8 from Toronto into Kitchener–Waterloo, there are many motels and accommodations along each side of the road. There's the good old standby, the **Holiday Inn,** 30 Fairway Rd. South (tel. 519/893-1211), which has 117 large standard rooms decorated in modern style in hues of either blue, gold, or red, and all the modern conveniences. This particular inn has a very pleasant outside pool, a slide and play area with climbing bars for the kids, and even barbecue facilities. It also has an outdoor cafe (serving subs and burgers from $2 to $3.50) where you can sip a drink and enjoy the scent of the lilacs, a dining room, coffeeshop, and lounge.

Rates: $35 to $41 single; $40 to $46 double.

If you're looking for a more distinctly local flavor, then pop into the **Conestoga Inn,** named after the finely crafted wagon introduced into the area by the Pennsylvania Dutch in the 1800s and located at 2668 King St. East (tel. 519/743-4171). It offers 54 motel-style units with outside/inside access, furnished colonial style and decorated in shades of aqua/purple with matching curtains and bedspreads. A few smaller rooms are finished in super-fashionable earth tones. Fourteen rooms have balconies and six have direct access to the outdoor pool. All rooms are fully air-conditioned, and have color TV and direct-dial phones.

Rates vary according to how many beds are used. For one double bed: $23 single, $26 double; one double and sofa bed: $27 single, $30 double; two double beds: $27 single, $32 double; suites: $30 single, $35 double. An additional person is $3 extra; a crib, $2. No charge for children under 16 in the same room as their parents. Free parking and an extra bonus: no charge for local telephone calls.

The Rib room with its cathedral-style cedar ceiling and large fireplace serves an excellent buffet lunch for $3.75 (cold meats, salads, and breads, with a different hot meat daily), from 11:30 a.m. to 2 p.m., a dinner buffet from 5 to 8 p.m. for $8.50, and a Sunday breakfast buffet served from 9:30 a.m. to 1:30 p.m. at $4 for adults, $2 for children. Otherwise, try the house specialties— steak-and-kidney pie and seafood Newburg.

A small but warm pine-paneled lobby greets you at the **Old Dutch Inn,** 4278 King St. East (tel. 519/653-3269), where you'll find 40 motel-style units with off-white wallboard paneling and walls that are semicarpeted with blue shag. All rooms have switchboard phones, color TV, and full baths. Rates: $22.95 single, $25.95 double; an extra person is $4.

The rustic-style pine dining room has a conical fireplace at its center and serves an array of sandwiches (from $1.65 to $3.95) for lunch, and burgers, pork chops, fried chicken, and steaks (ranging from $3.95 to $6.75) for dinner. Open from 7 a.m. to 10 p.m. daily. There's also a downstairs lounge where a variety of entertainment (usually piano) is offered.

For a really nicely kept motel along this route, try the **Riviera Motel,** 2808 King St. East (tel. 519/893-6641), with its 45 chalet-style units, each sporting a brightly painted orange door, and all set around an outdoor pool with its own small garden area. The rooms are very tastefully decorated in green and gold, with one wall papered in a green/gold/orange stripe, and contain modern furnishings, color TV, air conditioning, and switchboard phones (26 of the 45 units have refrigerators).

Rates: $22 single, $26 to $28 double. An extra person is $3. There's a coffeeshop open from 7 a.m. to 10:30 p.m. on weekdays, from 8 a.m. to 11 p.m. on weekends.

WHERE TO EAT: Most of our dining choices are in the Kitchener part of the Twin Cities, so we'll begin there.

Dining in Kitchener

In downtown Kitchener you'll find two most interesting restaurants, both of recent vintage. At 24 Eby St. North, just off King St., the **Brittany** (tel. 745-7001) was opened two years ago by owner-chef Jean-Pierre Guillet, who hails from Brittany. Located in a lovely old two-story white brick town house with rust-colored trim, the downstairs and upstairs dining areas are divided into three separate sections by the natural contours of the house. Brown tablecloths are exquisitely set and accented by flowers on every table, while the stucco walls show the Peter Snyder watercolors to advantage. It's simple, the essence of good taste, and an excellent setting for the superb food.

For dinner you might start with a cold salmon marinade (raw salmon marinated in brandy and dill, served with mustard dressing) or champignons à la Grecque (cooked mushrooms marinated in white wine with onions and coriander), or perhaps a mussel soup with leeks seasoned with saffron and served with garlic croutons. Then you might progress to civet de lapin (rabbit stewed with spices and simmered in red wine sauce with bacon, mushrooms, and pearl onions, $8.50) or the medaillons de veau chatelaine (veal slices sauteed with shallots and diced artichoke bottoms, and finished with cream, $9) or any of the other imaginative dishes. Finish off with an excellent crème caramel, cheesecake, or whatever Jean-Pierre is offering the day you visit.

To partake of this delicate fare without paying too highly, come for lunch when you'll find a selection of crêpes for $2.95 and one or two more unusual dishes, like lamb printanière (braised cubes of lamb simmered in a red wine sauce with mushrooms, onions, and carrots, $3.95). The Brittany is open Tuesday to Saturday from noon to 2 p.m. and 5:30 to 10 p.m. Reservations recommended.

While you're in Kitchener–Waterloo you shouldn't miss a visit to **Market Village,** where a number of old town houses have been restored and now contain boutique and specialty shops or restaurants like **Bottles,** 1 Market Village (tel. 744-3041), where hanging plants and vines, stucco walls, butcherblock tables with bentwood chairs, and blue placemats create a light and airy setting for the light and moderately priced fare. Upstairs the same decor prevails, plus woven wall hangings, a conical fireplace, an old Victorian oak sideboard, and some uncommonly good modern graphics. At night the track lighting is dimmed to create an intimate atmosphere.

At dinner you might try one of the cold dishes, like salmon aspic with lemon and green peppercorns ($3.50), served with bread and whipped butter, or an entree like suprême of chicken, poached in light tomato sauce, flavored with white wine and Pernod ($5.65). For dessert try Bottles's almond cake ($1.25) or sabayon ($1.50). At lunchtime the same cold dishes are offered at the same prices, but the entrees consist of lighter dishes, such as ratatouille with cheese ($2.95) or mushroom caps stuffed with spinach and cheese and served with tomato sauce ($4.95). And don't forget to order a bottle of wine, which may be pulled from the clay drainage-pipe wine rack that takes up one wall downstairs. Open 11:30 a.m. to 2:30 p.m. Tuesday to Friday, 5 to 10 p.m. Tuesday to Thursday, until midnight on Friday and Saturday.

Another convenient downtown eating spot, located in the same complex as the Farmers Market, is **Sir John's,** 160 King St. East (tel. 744-8311), named after Sir John Eaton, philanthropist, sportsman, and second son of the founder of Eaton's department store. The decor is appropriately rich and attractive. Half the dinner menu concentrates on beef: two sizes of prime rib served with Yorkshire pudding ($7.95 and $10.95) and shish kebab ($5.95), while the other half offers chicken pie, half a chicken teriyaki, and seafood (from $3.95 to $7.35 for a seafood combo of jumbo fantail shrimp and deep-fried scallops). Main courses include tossed salad, roll and butter, and choice of potato. This is also a good place for lunch, when soup and a sandwich or a burger will satisfy the craving for food. As for the desserts, try the scrumptious cheesecake with strawberries ($1.35) or a parfait crème de menthe ($1.95). Open Monday to Friday from 11 a.m. to 9 p.m., and Saturday until 5:30 p.m. Closed Sunday.

A little way out along King St. toward Hwy. 8 you'll find another really excellent dining choice. Don't be put off by its rather unprepossessing exterior, for the **Café Royale,** 729 King St. East (tel. 579-5510), has been providing excellent continental—French, German, and Canadian—cuisine for many years at very reasonable prices in unostentatious surroundings. Here, a couple of large wooden spoons and a cuckoo clock are pretty much the only complement to the captain's chairs, gold tablecloths, and brown napkins.

Choose one of the more traditional dishes like coq au vin or sauerbraten (both $5.95), or experiment with the carbonade petite filet (medallions of beef sauteed with onions demarara, dark beer, and fines herbs, $8). All entrees include a choice of potato. Appetizers and soups offer comprehensive choices including a turtle soup for $1.65. Various fish dishes round out the menu. As for dessert, it's hard to get past the glass case displaying Black Forest, mocha, or chocolate layer cakes, and apple and praline tortes (which are all made here), without ordering immediately. One slice will cost you $1. Luncheon fare consists of omelets (from $2.50 to $2.95), various sandwiches, a fish dish (for example, trout in garlic butter at $4.95), plus a crêpe dish. Menus change weekly.

Open Tuesday to Friday from noon to 2 p.m., Saturday from 4 p.m. to midnight, and Sunday from 4 to 9 p.m. Closed Monday. Always crowded, so reservations are essential.

Farther out on King St., the **Swiss Castle Inn,** 1508 King St. East (tel. 744-2391), takes you to a Swiss Alpine chalet whose main dining room is dominated by an octagonal open hearth and the colors red and white—red tablecloths and white napkins, red and white striped curtains over lattice windows—and cow bells. In this cozy atmosphere you can sample Swiss specialties, including bundnerfleisch appetizer (thin slices of beef air cured, $3.50), Berner platte (one smoked pork chop, one white sausage, and one piece of bacon served on a bed of sauerkraut, $6.95), and various fondues—beef bourguignonne ($9.95), seafood ($11.95), and cheese ($7.95). The super-special raclette (cheese, which you grill yourself in a special table oven, served with boiled potatoes, pickles, and onions) is available only if ordered in advance. Fish and steak dishes are also on the menu. For a perfect finale, try the Swiss chocolate cherry cake ($1.50). At lunchtime, try the daily special which usually goes for $3.60 or so, the wienerschnitzel, or a William Tell sandwich (corned beef, cheese, and sauerkraut, $3.45). Open Monday to Friday from noon to 11 p.m., Saturday from 4 to 11 p.m., and Sunday from 4 to 9 p.m.

Still farther out along King St., opposite the Holiday Inn in fact, stands the **Charcoal Steak House,** 2980 King St. East (tel. 893-6570), a large complex of six rooms each decorated in a different style—the wine cellar with barrels set in brick vaults, the hunt room with a stone fireplace and a mural depicting mallards and geese in flight, the hearth room with a French tapestry on one wall, and a room with a definite English flavor with its Windsor-style chairs with needlepointed backs and antique china everywhere. Each one provides a warm, attractive ambience for some really good steaks that range from $5.50 for a chopped sirloin to $12.95 for a 12-ounce New York sirloin. If you're feeling adventurous, try a local delicacy—roasted pig tails (roasted in fruit juices, spices, and browned over charcoal, and basted with barbecue sauce). For dessert, try the nesselrode pie, a light fluffy rum- and fruit-flavored dessert. All dinners include tossed salad, potato, and rolls. On Sundays there's an excellent-value family buffet for $8.50. At lunchtime there's a similar but shortened menu, offering burgers, small steaks, barbecued ribs, and chicken from $3.95 to $6.95; those prices include appetizer, potato, and coffee.

The dining areas are open from 11:30 a.m. to 11 p.m. Monday through Thursday, to midnight on Friday, from 4 p.m. to midnight on Saturday, and from noon to 9 p.m. on Sunday.

If you have to wait for a table or you just want a snack like a burger or a sub for under $3, then you'll be ushered into the **Library Lounge,** which also doubles as a piano bar where you can sit in a rust-colored wingback or sink into a comfy low armchair, watch the gas lamps shed a glow on the wood paneling and bookcases, and listen to the dulcet airs of a few decades ago. The lounge is open from 8 p.m. from Tuesday to Thursday, until 1 a.m. on Friday and Saturday.

Where to Eat in Waterloo

As you drive west along King St., you probably won't even notice that you've crossed a boundary into Waterloo. One of the first budget eateries you'll come to is **Marbles,** 8 William St. (tel. 519/885-4390), just catercorner across from the Labatts brewery. Everything is a variation on a marble theme—there are brilliant colored marbles under glass at the serving counter, a marble clock with marble digits, and photographs everywhere of kids playing marbles.

The kids will enjoy the decor *and* the food—a foot-long hot dog smothered with fresh tomatoes and bacon slices ($1.90), a basic burger with tomato, onion, and pickle slices ($2.45), or the savoryburger, topped with tangy tomato barbecue sauce ($2.45), both burgers served with french fries. There's a wide variety of salads also available, from spinach with bacon, mushrooms, bean sprouts, and cheddar cheese ($2.35) and a meal in itself, to whole pear with shrimp ($3.90). It's hardly elegant with stark-white walls, Formica tables, and exposed pipes supporting hanging plants, but it's cheap and cheerful, and the food is really fresh and imaginative. You don't have to join the assembly line for budget fare. Open Monday to Wednesday from 11:30 a.m. to 11 p.m., Thursday to Saturday until midnight, and Sunday from 5 to 10 p.m.

For another affordable dining experience just a little farther west on King St., penetrate the plain exterior of **Willies Too,** 64 King St. South (tel. 886-4160), and sample some of young Bill Weirmier's hospitality and Italian cuisine at hard-to-believe low prices. Pizzas, submarines (from $1.65), and a number of spaghetti dinners (from $2.75) are available, but the taste treats come with the pasta dinners that begin at $3.90. They all include soup or a trip to the salad bar, and you might choose rigatoni, ravioli, or lasagne ($4.75), veal parmigiana ($5.25), or chicken cacciatore ($5.50). Dinners for two that include antipasto, soup, main course, rolls and butter, dessert, and beverage start at $14.55. Such prices can only add to the already warm atmosphere of the two rooms with the captain's chairs and golden tablecloths.

Open Monday to Thursday from 11 a.m. to 1 a.m., on Friday and Saturday until 2 a.m., Sundays from September to June, noon to midnight (July and August, from 4 p.m. to midnight).

Pierre's Steak House, 32 King St. North (tel. 519/886-5770), is named after the owner, who has been in the restaurant business for 28 years, and decorated to his fastidious taste with plush red velvet highbacked semicircular nightclub-style banquettes that ensure privacy, and a series of mirrored domes cut into the ceiling, each sheltering a crystal chandelier. The menu features an array of steaks and seafood—12- to 14-ounce prime ribs ($9.95), 8-ounce ground sirloin with mushroom sauce ($4.95), and deep-fried shrimp with cocktail sauce ($7.25). It also includes some showy dishes like steak Diane ($11.95), prepared at your table, and chateaubriand bouquetière for two ($23.95). All dinners include relish tray, roll and butter, and choice of potato. If you still have room for dessert, then choose a French pastry from the wagon ($1.50) or splurge and have the waiter make you cherries jubilee ($5.25) or crêpes Suzette ($5.75), both for two. A short menu features sandwiches, omelets, butterfly shrimp, deep-sea scallops, and small steaks, at lunchtime, with most dishes under $5. Downstairs, Pierre is planning an intimate piano bar, so look in—it should be open by the time you visit. Open Monday to Thursday from noon to midnight, Friday from noon to 1 a.m., Saturday from 4:30 p.m. to 1 a.m., and Sundays and holidays from 4:30 to 9:30 p.m.

2. Elmira, Elora, and Fergus

These three small towns in the heart of the Mennonite farmlands can be visited from Kitchener–Waterloo or from Toronto (many Torontonians, in fact, come out for some fine country dining which I'll detail ahead).

ELMIRA: A charming town, Elmira (pop. 6800) was one of the earliest settlements of Upper Canada. Set amid the rich farmlands of the Grand and Conestoga River Valleys, it is a focal point for Mennonite farmers and craftsmen and home of a famous spring maple syrup festival, held the first Saturday in April, when the population swells to 40,000 and black-bonnetted Mennonite women serve up flapjacks with syrup and offer hand-crafted goods to all and sundry, while horse-drawn wagons take visitors off to the maple bush to see the sugaring off, from the tapping of the trees to the boiling of the syrup. Festivities usually start around 7 a.m.

In the town itself, **Brox's Olde Town Village,** 10 Church St. West (tel. 519/669-5121), is a new shopping complex housing oldtime stores: Brubachers, an authentic example of a 19th-century general store; Ye Olde Ice Cream Parlor, where you can have super-special sundaes and local fare; the Village Loft, a clothes store; Krafts by Us; the Fudge Machine; Die Quilt Frau, with one of the largest selection of quilts in the area; the Festive Touch, for flowers and plants; the Country Cheese Haus; and the Larder Box. In the basement, the **Elmira market** is held every Saturday from 7 a.m. to 1 p.m. offering such Mennonite specialties as cooked cheese, homemade butter, bread, and pastries, and excellent handicrafts. Open Monday to Wednesday from 9 a.m. to 6 p.m., Thursday and Friday until 9 p.m., and Saturday from 8 a.m. to 6 p.m.

From June to August, Monday through Friday, harness racing is held at the Elmira Raceway in the Elmira fairgrounds.

For further information on the area, contact the **Elmira–Woolwich Chamber of Commerce**, 5 First St. East, Elmira, ON N3B 2E3 (tel. 519/669-2605).

To reach Elmira, which is 14 miles north of Kitchener–Waterloo, take Rte. 85 north until it meets Rte. 86.

A Mennonite Restaurant and Gift Shop

Be sure to stop in at the **Stone Crock**, 59 Church St. West (tel. 519/669-1521), for a savory taste of the past. The cold buffet consists of a delightful selection of Waterloo County salads, cold cuts, cheeses, and fresh homemade bread. The hot buffet includes the above plus two or three hot savory meats, potato, and vegetable. In an early Canadian atmosphere created by pine furniture and some artifacts like butter churns and stone crocks, you can enjoy the noon cold buffet with dessert and beverage for $4.65 or the noon hot buffet with dessert and beverage for $5.75. There are usually luncheon specials also, for example, liver and onions when I last visited ($2.95), or you can have soup and a sandwich or salad. The evening buffet runs $6.40 including beverage, $7.35 for buffet, dessert, and beverage. The evening buffet is served from 3:30 to 8:30 p.m. on Saturdays, Sundays, and holidays, from 4:30 to 8:30 p.m. Monday to Friday.

There's another Stone Crock restaurant and gift shop at 41 King St., in the small village of St. Jacob's (about seven miles south of Elmira on Rte. 85), where the traditional family-style dinner is served with a variety of salads and homemade bread with apple butter. Steaming platters of meats, potatoes, and succulent vegetables are passed around the table, and the waitresses are happy to refill them. Choose two of the following meats per group: roast beef, barbecued spare ribs, farmer's sausage (made on the premises), roast turkey, and fried chicken with dressing. Price is around $8.

And don't forget to check out the gift shops at both establishments for a fantastic array of super-fine crafts and hand-woven quilts.

ELORA: This picturesque village (pop. 2589), located at the falls of the Grand River, was founded in 1832 by a retired British soldier who named it after a ship that belonged to his brother, a tea trader who must have been familiar with the Elora caves in India. Various mills, breweries, and furniture manufacturers lured by the water power are gone, but today many of the old 19th-century buildings have been restored and now house many quaint shops and restaurants.

Besides picturesque **Mill St.,** where you can browse and chat in peace with only the sound of the river rushing by, Elora has the **Elora Gorge,** a 300-acre park on both sides of the 70-foot limestone gorge. Overhanging rock ledges, small caves, a waterfall, and the evergreen forest on its rim are just some of the scenic delights of the gorge. The park has facilities for **camping** and swimming, as well as nature trails, picnic areas, and playing fields. Located just west of Elora at the junction of the Grand and Irvine Rivers, it is open from May 1 to October 15. Admission is $2 per car. To camp, for both tents and trailers, it's $2 per unit per day, plus the admission fee.

Staying and Dining in Elora

Torontonians make the 72-mile journey just to eat at the **Elora Mill Inn,** 77 Mill St. West (tel. 519/846-5356), a former five-story grist mill built in 1859 overlooking the beautiful Elora Gorge. Downstairs is a lounge overlooking the falls with the original exposed beams, a huge stone fireplace where a warm fire burns in winter, and pine Windsor-style chairs that go with the raw stone walls of the interior. Similar furniture and rusticity are retained in the upstairs dining areas.

Dinner might start with mushrooms Metcalfe (broiled mushrooms with a tantalizing mixture of smoked ham and onions topped with hollandaise sauce au gratin, $2.75) or the gazpacho or vichyssoise ($1.50). Specialties include veal scaloppine marsala or veal italiano (with smoked ham and tomatoes smothered with emmenthaler cheese; both $9.50), roast duck Grand Marnier ($12.95), and roast rack of lamb ($11.50). Seafood dishes (ranging from $8.95 to $15.50) and steak dishes (from $8.95 to $25.95) round out the menu. All dinners include vegetables, potatoes, and rolls. Chocolate mousse ($1.50) or a liqueur parfait ($2.25) with a luxurious Spanish coffee ($3.50) make delightful desserts.

Lunchtime offers some interesting country dishes (all under $4), like ham-and-leek pie, Wellington County beef stew, pioneer chicken in a crock, or a farmer's omelet.

Open for lunch Monday to Friday from noon to 2 p.m. and from 6 to 9 p.m., on Saturday from noon to 3 p.m. and 6 to 10 p.m., and on Sunday from noon to 3 p.m. and 5:30 to 8:30 p.m.

If you're not rushing anywhere, you can stay in one of the 16 rooms, each one furnished and shaped differently, some with brass bedsteads, others with canonball pine beds, most containing a quilt, wingback chair, and a mixture of antiques and reproductions. None of the rooms has a TV, so you can really enjoy the rural retreat. Singles range from $38 to $56, doubles from $42 to $60. The more expensive rooms overlook the gorge. An additional person in a room is $5.

Many in-the-know people go to the Mill to dine, but just as many take a quick walk along the street to the **Cafe Flore,** 26 Mill St. (tel. 519/846-5631), to sample the tempting, moderately priced delights: strawberry tarts and pastries (75¢), cheese croissants (40¢), and gâteau Basque—all baked daily right here on the premises. The menu is chalked on a board, the dishes displayed and you pick from possibly quiche Lorraine, ratatouille, boeuf bourguignon, Cornish hen, various salads, or macaroni and cheese (ranging from $1.95 to $6.50). Dine on the sturdy pine tables and chairs looking at the photographs and weavings on the walls, or if the weather's clement, sit on the terrace overlooking the river. In the evening the fare remains the same, but if you make a reservation you can choose from beef Wellington, rack of lamb, and canard à l'orange, and the soup, salad, dessert, and cappucino will be included in the $15.50 price tag. Licensed for beer and wine only. Open from 9 a.m. to 9 p.m. daily.

FERGUS: A pleasant little town on the Grand River, Fergus (pop. 6001) was originally known as Little Falls, but its name was changed for its Scottish immigrant founder Adam Ferguson. There's not a lot to see, but it happens to contain a favorite accommodation and dining establishment that appeals to those who are familiar with the warmth, style, and fare of English bed-and-breakfast inns. The other noteworthy Fergus event is the **Fergus Highland Games,** featuring pipe band competitions, caber tossing, tug-of-war contests, and Highland dancing, held usually on the second Saturday in August. For more information on the games, write to: Fergus Highland Games Association, P.O. Box 3, Fergus, ON N1M 2W7 (tel. 519/846-9254).

Superb Dining in Fergus

You can't miss the **Breadalbane Inn,** 686 St. Andrew St. West (tel. 519/843-4770), because it's such a delightful gray stone structure with ornate grill-work around the front porch, a bay window jutting into the street, and a gleaming door knocker. Built by the Honorable Admiral Ferguson in 1860, it had variously served as a residence, nursing home, and rooming house for derelicts when Philip Cardinal, a mechanical engineer, and his wife Jean, a home economics graduate, took it over three years ago. Inside you'll find two dining areas with French doors leading into the garden which, if you're lucky, will be full of roses. Here you can dine on darkly polished tables off cork placemats depicting hunting scenes or birds, to the strains of a Mozart or Mendelssohn violin concerto, and sip your coffee afterward from Royal Doulton china.

Philip and Jean quite obviously love what they are doing: they bake their own bread and take pains with everything. I can fiercely recommend the steak-and-kidney pie—it's one of the best I've ever had outside of England. At lunchtime Philip also turns out really exquisite omelets which are very popular and are served with relishes, baked potato Cardinal or french fries, and a loaf of home-baked bread ($3.50). Super-large sandwiches are also available, like the open-face hot corned beef topped with melted cheese on rye bread with dill pickle ($2.95) or the "Breadalbane Sooper Dooper Sandwich," with generous slices of country smoked ham, Muenster cheese, fresh tomatoes, and lettuce in a loaf of home-baked bread with special dressing ($2.95). For dessert, leave room for those homemade butter tarts. At dinner, try the French onion soup ($1.75), and follow it with a fine-quality steak (from $8.50 to $12.95), or the char-broiled back ribs with honey maple sauce ($8.95). All entrees include relishes, home-baked bread, and baked potato Cardinal or french fries. Open Tuesday to Friday from noon to 2 p.m., and from 5:30 to 9:30 p.m. Tuesday to Sunday.

You can also enjoy an informal stay with Philip and Jean in one of their six rooms, each extremely comfortable and elegantly furnished with early Canadian-style furniture. There are four bathrooms available, each luxuriously appointed. For a large double with continental breakfast, expect to pay the grand sum of $28 double; for a smaller room, $22 double. If you enjoy this English bed-and-breakfast style of accommodation and a role as a responsible house guest, then this is the place for you.

3. Stratford

Home of the world-famous Stratford Festival, this small town manages to capture the prime elements of the Bard's birthplace, from the Avon River and the swans to the green lawns that sweep down to the river where you can picnic under a weeping willow before attending a Shakespearean play.

THE STRATFORD FESTIVAL: Since its modest beginnings on July 13, 1953, when *Richard III,* starring Sir Alec Guinness, was staged in a huge tent, artistic directors Michael Langham, Jean Gascon, and Robin Phillips have all built on the radical but faithfully classic base originally provided by Tyrone Guthrie to create a repertory theater that ranges from classic Elizabethan productions to contemporary and experimental performances.

Stratford has three theaters: the **Festival Theatre,** 55 Queen St. in Queen's Park, with evening performances on its dynamic thrust stage from the first week in June to the second week in October, Tuesday through Sunday, and matinees Wednesday and Saturday; the **Avon Theatre,** 99 Downie St., with evening performances on its proscenium stage from early June to the second week in October, with evening performances Tuesday through Saturday and matinees on Wednesday, Saturday, and Sunday; and **Third Stage,** Lakeside Dr., with evening and matinee performances throughout the season. Festival Theatre prices run from $3.50 to $14.50; Avon, from $3.50 to $12.50; Third Stage admission is $5. In each theater, if you book a preview the seats sell at a 20% discount. Tickets usually go on sale the first week of March, and you can order them by writing to: Festival Theatre Box Office, P.O. Box 520, Stratford, ON N5A 6V2. Allow at least four weeks for processing. Telephone bookings are accepted after April 30 at 519/273-1600.

The 1980 season will include Shakespeare's *Coriolanus, Twelfth Night, Henry V,* and *Henry VI,* John Vanbrugh's *The Relapse,* Chekhov's *The Seagull,* Carlo Goldoni's *The Servant of Two Masters,* O'Neill's *Long Day's Journey into Night,* Sheridan's *The Rivals,* John Gay's *The Beggar's Opera,* and three premieres: John Murrell's *Parma,* Sheldon Rosen's *Choices,* and Susan Cooper and Hume Cronyn's *Foxfire.* And if 1980 is anything like 1979 when Dizzy Gillespie, Sarah Vaughan, and the Preservation Hall Jazz Band performed, then there should be some exciting jazz on hand, too.

WHAT TO DO: Summer pleasures in Stratford beside theater? Walking through the park, of course, paddling a boat or canoe from the boathouse at the Orr Dam, or browsing around the downtown shops. Within sight of the Festival Theatre, **Queen's Park** has picnic spots beneath tall shade trees or down by the water's edge where the swans and ducks will gather too. To the east and west of the theater, footpaths follow both shores of the Avon River and Lake Victoria. Past the Orr Dam and the 90-year-old stone bridge, through a rustic gate once straw-thatched but now (for want of a thatcher) cedar shingled, lies a very special park, the **Shakespearean Garden.**

Here in this formal English garden, where a sundial presented by the former mayor of England's Stratford-on-Avon measures out the hours, you can relax and contemplate the herb and flower beds and the tranquil river lagoon, and muse upon Shakespeare's bust by Toronto sculptor Cleeve Horn.

If you turn right onto Romeo St. North from Hwys. 7 and 8, as you come into Stratford, you'll find the **Gallery/Stratford,** 54 Romeo St. (tel. 519/271-5271), located in a beautiful old building on the fringes of Confederation Park. Since it opened in 1967 it has naturally adopted a Canadian focus, mounting such shows as *Coasts: The Sea and Canadian Art,* which featured, among others, the works of Emily Carr, Benjamin Leeson, F. H. Varley, and Jack Shadbolt; *Twentieth-Century Canadian Drawing,* and shows of individual artists like Tony Urquhart or Norval Morriseau, the Ojibway nation artist from Lake Nipigon and Thunder Bay in northern Ontario. The gallery has also created some very exciting exhibitions like *Fantastic Shakespeare,* which revealed interpretations of Shakespearean themes from Dali and Ben Shahn to Delacroix and Benjamin West, and the delightful *History of Children's Book Illustration 1750–1940,* which showed Arthur Rackham, Edward Cruickshank, Kate Greenaway, Beatrix Potter, William Blake, and others at their whimsical best. If you're an art lover, do stop in, for you're sure to find an unusual, personally satisfying show in one of the three galleries. Open Sunday and Tuesday to Friday from 1 to 5 p.m., on Saturday from 10 a.m. to 5 p.m.

from September through May; June through August, open Monday through Saturday from 10 a.m. to 8 p.m., and Sunday noon to 5 p.m. Admission: adults, $1.

Just along Romeo St. at no. 339 lies another attraction, **Shakespeareland** (tel. 519/273-2000), a one-tenth scale reproduction of the town of Stratford-on-Avon, which includes among the 60 replicas Anne Hathaway's Cottage and the Garrick Inn, as well as free boating and fishing, a contact zoo, and a ducking stool, stock, and pillory for wrongdoers of either sex. Open daily, May 15 to September 30 from 9 a.m. to 7 p.m. Admission: adults, $2.75; students and senior citizens, $2; children, $1.

WHERE TO STAY: As with any festival town, accommodations are at a premium and the prices and, sad to say, standards reflect the situation. Still, if you have to stay in Stratford here's a selection:

No doubt the nicest place to stay is the **Festival Motor Inn,** 1144 Ontario St. (tel. 519/273-1150), with its 102 black and white motel-style units set back off Hwys. 7 and 8 in ten acres of landscaped grounds around an outdoor pool with adjacent patio. The place has an old English air with its stucco walls, mock Tudor beams, and high-back red settles in the lobby. The Tudor style is maintained throughout the large modern rooms, all with wall-to-wall red carpeting, matching bedspreads and floor-to-ceiling drapes, reproductions of Old Masters on the walls, direct-dial telephones, color TV, and full bathroom. Some of the bedrooms have charming bay windows with sheer curtains, and all rooms in the main building have refrigerators. Other facilities include two tennis courts, shuffleboard, dining room, and coffeeshop.

Rates: In the main building, single or double $46, $49 twin double; outside units (with no inside access and no refrigerator), $36 single, $41 double, $45 twin double. For an extra person you'll pay $3; cots are $4. During the winter rates drop by about 40%.

The **Victorian Inn,** 10 Romeo St. (tel. 271-4650), the largest hotel in town with 115 rooms, is ideally situated only ten minutes' walk from the Festival Theatre. In fact, some of the back rooms overlook the Festival. Rooms are spacious and comfortable, decorated in greens and golds, and have all the modern features: color TV, direct-dial phone, air conditioning, full bathroom. Most have balconies. The place practically doubles as an entertainment complex—there's the Library Lounge overlooking the indoor pool for relaxed drinking, the Rosewood Lounge offering nightly entertainment and dancing from jazz to rock, the Honky Tonk Room in the basement for sing-along fun Tuesday to Saturday from 9 p.m. to 1 a.m., and the dining room overlooking the river, which also has a dance floor.

Rates: $38 single, $42 double. A twin double occupied by one person is $42; by two persons, $50; by three, $54, by four, $56. Suites are $70 and up. From October 16 to May 13 rates are slashed by as much as 35%.

For a moderate-priced accommodation, you won't find a cleaner, friendlier place than **Majer's Motel,** 858 Ontario St. East (tel. 519/271-2010), just ten minutes out of Stratford, right next door to the Festival Inn. Run by the Memmel family, the rooms are pleasantly appointed with clock radio, color TV, phone, color-coordinated spreads, carpet, and drapes, and even carpeted bathrooms. There are 31 motel-style units set around an outdoor swimming pool and lawn area dotted with shrubs. There is an older and a newer section, but very little difference in the rooms except fractionally in size.

Rates: $26 to $32 single, $28 to $33 double, $36 to $41 twin double, $39 to $44 triple, and $43 to $46 quad.

WHERE TO EAT: Stratford's restaurants are certainly more exciting and top drawer than its accommodations, but before describing my favorites, there are two outstanding dining places that you might stop at en route to Stratford.

In New Hamburg

Only 11 miles east on Hwy. 8 in the tiny village of New Hamburg, at 17 Huron St., stands **Waterlot,** a fascinating, oddly shaped cream-painted brick building with an ornate turret atop, surrounded by gardens and weeping willows that sweep down into the river. Inside, you'll find four dining rooms, all with fireplaces and bay windows, and one looking out to the river. Each of the wood-paneled rooms contains cane bentwood chairs, brown tablecloths, and art (for sale) on the walls. Built around 1846 by a Scottish immigrant and entrepreneur (who left New Hamburg in 1862 and moved his family to New Zealand to break up a romance between his daughter and an unsuitable suitor), the house had various owners, each playing an important role in the history and development of the area until Gordon Elkeer who served 22 years as a secretservice Royal Canadian Mounted Policeman, took it over and made it his dream restaurant, qualifying for a liquor license only after he had held a local plebiscite (the area was dry). It was worth it.

The menu is especially innovative in the choice of soups and appetizers, which include pain de poissons (a light and savory blend of fresh and smoked fish), beignets d'huîtres (oysters poached in white wine, battered, deep-fried, and served with cocktail sauce, $4.25), or velouté de pommes (a blend of apple, onion, and curry in a cream and chicken broth, garnished with nuts, $1.95). Entrees are few but impressive, ranging from caneton aux prunes (duckling glazed with plum juice and brandy, served with a Madeira sauce and plums sprinkled with toasted almonds), to a brochette of pork with apple sauce (both $9.75). Or you can have the $13.95 prix-fixe which includes a vegetable crêpe, house salad, main course (perhaps Cornish game hen), dessert, and beverage.

Sunday is family day, when brunch is served at two sittings—11:30 a.m. and 1:30 p.m. For $7.25 you'll receive the usual brunch items plus pâtés, smoked fish, crêpes, chicken livers, and other unusual brunch delicacies. Sunday evenings there's always prime rib and two hot specials for $9.95. Children 12 and under eat for half price. Luncheon items start at $2.95 for whole-wheat crêpes filled with fresh vegetable.

Open Tuesday to Saturday from noon to 2 p.m. and 5 to 10 p.m. Sunday brunch is served at 11:30 a.m. and 1:30 p.m., and dinner from 5 p.m. Reservations are absolutely necessary for lunch, dinner, or brunch. Call 519/662-2020.

Cambridge's French Country Inn

The **Bouquet Garni,** 285 Fountain St. (tel. 519/653-1108), will tempt the most fastidious gourmet. There are numerous interesting fish dishes including a bouillabaisse ($11), delicious entrees like pork tenderloin simmered in apple brandy with cream, diced apples, and chives ($5.95), and super-specialties like the entrecôte de boeuf double moscovite (double slice of New York sirloin roasted and garnished with marinated sultanas, raisins, and almonds in red wine sauce, scented with juniper berries, and served with a slice of egg and caviar, $20.75 for two). Desserts are equally enticing, especially the chocolate mousse. An excellent and extensive wine list includes a 30-year-old Madeira.

Not only is the food wonderful but the setting is also exquisite, for you'll dine upstairs in a lovely 160-year-old creeper-encrusted house that has served as a button factory and apartment house, seated on light pine Windsor-style

chairs, and surrounded by exposed brick walls, plants, and watercolor landscapes. If you have to wait for your table, you can enjoy a quiet apéritif in the
downstairs lounge with its imitation burled wood tables and comfy sofas.
Luncheon gives you the chance to sample poached eggs Florentine or crêpes
à la reine (stuffed with chicken and mushrooms and topped with sauce suprême) for $3.25.

Open noon to 2 p.m. Monday to Friday, and 5 to 10 p.m. Monday to
Sunday. Reservations necessary. Take Hwy. 8 south off Hwy. 401 for 800 feet.

Stratford Dining

The Church, corner of Brunswick and Waterloo Sts. (tel. 519/273-3424),
must be the only restaurant in Canada where you have to reserve six months
in advance—and pay a deposit. Still, it's a unique privilege because the food
is so good and the decor is, well, awesome. The organ pipes and the altar are
still intact, along with the vaulted roof, carved woodwork, and stained-glass
windows, and you can sit in the nave or the side aisles and dine to the appropriate sounds of, usually, Bach. Fresh flowers, elegant table settings, and a huge
table in the center graced with two silver samovars further enhance the experience.

The menu changes summer and winter, weekdays and weekends, but there
is always a prix-fixe $19.50 dinner. Otherwise, you can order à la carte and
perhaps start with potted rabbit with cognac and apricots ($3.45) or fresh hot
asparagus with a mousseline sauce ($4.55), continue with chicken drumsticks
dijonaises ($10.95) or fresh lobster Newburg ($14.75—flown in from Nova
Scotia), and finish with any one of a dozen superb desserts—mille feuilles
marquise (thousand-leaves cake filled with chocolate mousse and served with
a coffee cream sauce), sherry trifle, oranges in brandy (all under $4). As a final
treat, taste the Mandarin coffee, a Church specialty of hot coffee with Mandarin
liqueur and Triple Sec, topped with heavy cream. Now say a prayer. Weekend
menus are equally stimulating and the $9.50 luncheon buffet well worth the tab.
There's also a shorter after-theater buffet worth considering if you prefer to stay
awake during the play.

The Church is open Tuesday to Saturday from noon to 2 p.m. and 4:30
p.m. to 1 a.m. It is closed Monday unless there is a musical performance or
some other special event at the theaters. Make your reservations in March or
April when you buy your tickets, otherwise you'll be disappointed.

The other first-class dining establishment in Stratford is far from awesome
and its large windows take advantage of its beautiful setting overlooking Lake
Victoria. You'll know **Rundles,** 9 Cobourg St. (tel. 519/271-6442), by the lilac
umbrellas outside. A very creative Britisher, Jim Morris, runs this place. His
father insisted that he learn something useful before he would pay for Jim's
drama school education, so Jim went to a hotel management school before
coming to Canada in 1970 where he worked for Toronto's top restaurant,
Winston's.

Now he serves a $16.50 prix-fixe dinner at two sittings, 5:30 and 8:30 p.m.
The menu changes daily but Jim has a great penchant for game, so you might
be treated to roast stuffed pheasant served with a delicate vegetable garnish, or
else a leg of lamb stuffed with ham and anchovies and braised, or else duck with
black currants. When you dine here, you are greeted at the gate and given a
complimentary glass of sherry on the terrace before moving into the simple
graceful dining area with its gray tables, salmon-pink striped napkins, good
cutlery and crystal, contemporary art (including some oddball sculptures by

Victor Tinkl), and an operatic singer at the piano rendering a few Italian or French songs.

There's also a supper menu that might offer a cold salmon plate or a game pie (priced from $6.50 to $14). At lunch, egg and fish dishes predominate. Perhaps Jim's most dashing contribution to culinary art is the gourmet picnic which for dinner might include cold pheasant, or salmon with watercress mousseline sauce, pâté, fruit and cheese, and wine, of course. Delectable. And only $4.50 to $10, depending on the ingredients.

Rundles follows the theater schedule exactly, opening from noon to 2 p.m. and 5:30 p.m. to 1 a.m. Tuesday to Saturday, and 5:30 to 10 p.m. on Sunday. Closed Monday unless there's a performance. During the winter the restaurant closes and functions as a cooking school until theater season comes again. Reservations, of course.

For more moderately priced dining, search out the **Terrace,** 10 Downie St. (tel. 519/271-7114), located on the second floor of what is known as Festival Square, an old historic building in the center of Stratford that used to hold offices and medical and dental surgeries before it became a store emporium. The lounge, with its fan chairs and wicker tables, sets the tone for the three large dining rooms that follow, with their exposed brick walls and plumbing, plants, contemporary art and wall weavings, modern light-wood chairs, beige table tops, and green napkins.

The place offers a plethora of menus and activities: the Attitude Adjustment Hours from 4 to 6 p.m., when crocks of pâté, fresh shrimp, and cheese accompany sippables served from the knotty pine bar; the Terrace Ensemble, which interprets baroque music, jazz, popular tunes et al.; the Sunday night Stratford Roast from 5 to 8 p.m., with either prime rib ($10.95) or a fish or white meat dish ($8.95) with buffet and dessert; Sunday brunch from 11:30 a.m. to 2:30 p.m., which includes appetizer and dessert buffet and a choice of egg dishes like poached eggs Passmore (arranged on artichoke bottoms on toast, and topped with mozzarella cheese and glazed); an after-theater supper menu that might include soups, salads, appetizers (like escargots, fantail shrimp, or crêpes), and desserts.

Then there's the regular menu, with unusual soups like Danish port and blue cheese ($1.25), curried mussels in a crust (as an appetizer, $2.75), and some interesting, very reasonable main dishes: casserole of rabbit in cream and mustard ($7.95), or half a rack of lamb dijonnaise (deviled with mustard, rosemary, and basil, $6.75). Top that off with a lemon syllabub and a pot of good coffee or Orange Pekoe tea and. . . . At lunchtime the menu offers a selection of salads, soups, crêpes, omelets, and a daily special (all under $5).

This casual but stylish place is open Monday to Friday from 11:30 to 2 p.m., for Saturday brunch from 10 a.m. to 2 p.m., for tea Monday to Saturday from 2 to 4 p.m., for dinner Monday to Saturday from 5 p.m. on, for Sunday brunch from 11:30 a.m. to 2 p.m., and for the Stratford Roast from 5 to 8 p.m.

Almost as broad a repertoire holds a little way down the street at the **James Inn,** 108 Downie St. (tel. 519/271-8181), where you'll find three different rooms for dining. The Carvery, which is reminiscent of an 18th-century colonial chophouse with a stuffed pheasant soaring above the brick fireplace and Windsor-style chairs, is open for lunch from noon to 2 p.m. and from 5 p.m. for dinner, and offers a champagne supper after 9 p.m. Lunch includes light dishes like shrimp remoulade served in a fresh avocado with hot crusty rolls ($5.95), oysters, salads, bagels and lox, corned beef on rye ($2.99), gazpacho, or colonial bean-and-bacon soup (both $1.95). Dinner offers specialties such as squab chicken gourmet ($8.95), pheasant ananas ($12.95), veal, fish, and lamb dishes, and a selection of steaks (from $11.95). All meals include rolls and butter, vegetables, and potato. The champagne supper ($16) includes roll and butter, salad bar, choice of potato and vegetable, dessert, coffee, and the choice of pheasant, beef tenderloin and green peppers, or fresh salmon filet.

Upstairs, in the Carvery Room with its oak chairs and gold tablecloths, you can feast at a dinner buffet ($14) that includes an unhealthy amount of salads, roasts, seafood, cheese, and desserts, or you can indulge in the equally decadent Sunday champagne brunch buffet from noon to 2 p.m. with an exorbitant amount of relishes, seafood, hash browns, bacon, chicken, eggs, pineapple fritters, and pastries ($8.75).

Finally, downstairs you'll find Stratford's first wine bar, offering good wines and food, in a cellar-like setting, concentrating on cheeses, quiches, and oysters.

The main dining rooms are open strictly according to theater schedule, from noon to 2 p.m. and from 5 p.m. to midnight (the wine cellar stays open till 1 a.m.).

4. Hamilton

Situated on a landlocked harbor spanned at its entrance by the dramatic sweep of the Burlington Skyway, Hamilton (pop. 312,000) or "Steeltown" as it has long been known, is only 42 miles southwest of Toronto on the Queen Elizabeth Way.

Although it certainly has steel mills and smoke-belching chimneys, it has recently received an extensive facelift, the most remarkable results being Hamilton Place, a huge cultural center, Lloyd D. Jackson Square, a new City Hall with splashing fountains afront, and many an urban-renewal project, the most notable being Hess Village. Such a renaissance has also spawned restaurants and other facilities that a cultured city naturally possesses.

WHERE TO STAY: There are really only two hotels in Hamilton: one is the Holiday Inn, and the other, more interesting because it's not a Holiday Inn, is the **Royal Connaught,** 112 King St. East (tel. 416/527-5071), a grand old hotel with classical details. The lobby is a panorama of glass, marble, and hand-rubbed wood dramatically set off by huge crystal chandeliers, Corinthian columns, and a flying staircase. Note the gleaming old-style brass royal mailbox. Built in 1904, the hotel has undergone a series of renovations, the most recent in 1973, and the 222 spacious rooms currently feature modern brown decor, dark-toned furniture, color TV, and direct-dial phone. The bathrooms are exceptionally large.

The hotel has a number of entertainment and dining spots. O'Sullivan's, its entryway studded with photographs of the celebrities who have dined here—Pierre Trudeau, George Hamilton, Liberace—offers a super-elegant atmosphere, for lunch or dinner, with its brown Louis XV–style chairs and Tiffany-style lamps (the specialty is prime rib). A pianist entertains at night. In the Duke's lounge there's live entertainment, usually a middle-of-the-road group, occasionally some jazz, six days a week from 9 p.m.

Rates (depending on the number of beds in your room) are: $41 to $45 single, $47 to $52 double. Suites start at $95. For an extra person in the room you'll pay $8 (no charge for children under 14). Free parking available—an asset in downtown Hamilton.

The **Holiday Inn,** 150 King St. East (tel. 416/528-3451), has 230 comfortable guest rooms each equipped with every modern facility. For afternoon relaxation and evening entertainment there's the Wunderbar lounge, the El

Toro dining room, and the Dutch coffeeshop for sustenance, plus an outdoor heated swimming pool for recreation.

Rates: $38 to $42 single, $43 to $49 double.

If you can't get in at either of the above hostelries, then drive out east along Main St. about five miles to the **City Motor Hotel,** 1620 Main St. East (tel. 416/549-1371), which has 98 motel units set around a tarmac courtyard with an outdoor heated pool in the center. Rooms are clean, air-conditioned, and fully equipped with TV, telephone, wall-to-wall carpeting, and private bathroom. There's a coffeeshop and dining room on the premises.

Rates: $24 to $28 single, $26 to $30 double.

WHERE TO EAT: A little short on hotels, Hamilton has some excellent dining spots, and one place to explore immediately is Hess Village, which is Hamilton's, rather nicer and less chichi in a way, answer to Toronto's Yorkville.

Hess Village

Here among the boutiques you'll find two moderately priced restaurants and one deluxe dining experience—**Tiffany's,** 115-117 George St. at the corner of Queen (tel. 416/528-6781), housed in two 19th-century white brick gabled semidetached fused into one, and flanked by two courtyards where you can dine or drink under umbrellaed tables. You'll enter from a large porch supported by Corinthian columns to find a series of brown-on-white rooms with fireplaces, where old engravings and prints, immaculate linen, and cut flowers complement the continental menu.

Specialties include tournedos done in several ways (for $12), for example, Strasbourg (stuffed with goose liver and served with wine sauce) or Henri IV (garnished with heart of artichoke and served with demiglace and Madeira wine), plus veal, poultry, lamb, steaks, and fish dishes ranging from $9.50 to $15.95 for surf and turf. At lunchtime you can enjoy coquilles St-Jacques ($3.75) or any number of omelets and crêpes, with one or two entrees such as chicken livers sauteed in red wine sauce with mushroom and rice ($4.75). At the outdoor patio café, tasty burgers, barbecued ribs, and open-face sandwiches are available.

Situated right around the corner from Hamilton Place, many a celebrity stops in for dinner so don't be surprised if that's Liberace with his mother at the next table. They all come here. Open Monday to Saturday from noon to 1 a.m. and Sunday from 4 to 10 p.m.

Hesse House, 24 Hess St. South (tel. 416/527-5164), a red brick structure with a front porch and upstairs balcony, was the pioneer project of the Village. Downstairs or on the outside patio you can partake of salads (from $3.50 to $6), chicken, shrimp, or scallops in a basket (from $3.50 to $4.50), and snacks like a ploughman's lunch of cheese, roll, and butter, pickles and greens, and a mug of beer or wine ($3.25).

Up the walnut staircase with its fanciful newel post you'll find more leisurely dining in lavishly decorated rooms with velvet drapes, chintz wallpaper, and Louis XV chairs in shades of soft blue. For that truly intimate dinner there's a bay window cum balcony with two or three tables. You might begin with a pâté maison or vichyssoise ($1.75), and follow with beef bourguinonne ($6.95) or coq au vin ($7.50). Assorted pastries, peach Melba, and pear Belle Hélène are just some of the delicious desserts (from $1.25 to $2.25). At lunchtime there's a "daily inspiration" for $4.50, and a selection of soups, salads, sandwiches, and light entrees (all under $5). Open 11 a.m. to midnight Monday to Saturday, and 4 to 10 p.m. on Sunday. Reservations for upstairs only.

Right around the corner at 100 George St., **Le Papillon** (tel. 529-6590), in yet another sandblasted town house decorated with great flair (cedar paneling, track lighting, exposed brick walls, yellow check overlays on white tablecloths, cane-seated chrome chairs, and interesting graphics for sale), specializes in crêpes. Choose from 25 fillings—for example, asparagus and cheddar cheese; bacon, cheddar cheese, and tomato; sausages, apples, and cheddar cheese; beef, mushrooms, and onions in red wine; bananas, hazelnuts, and ice cream with chocolate rum sauce and whipped cream; or mandarins or apricots. Savory crêpes run from $3.25 to $4.50; fruit crêpes, from $1.95 to $2.90. Soups, imaginative salads, and quiches are also mainstays. Reservations are accepted *only* Tuesday to Thursday evening and all day Sunday. Open Tuesday to Thursday from noon to midnight, Friday and Saturday from noon to 1 a.m., and Sunday from 10 a.m. to 10 p.m.

Downtown Dining

Currently the most talked about Hamilton restaurant, **Flavours,** at 16 Jarvis St. (tel. 527-5050), consists of an upstairs art nouveau–style dining room, a top-floor dinner theater with a Venetian feel provided by mirrors and billowing gray/pink drapes, and a downstairs lounge with comfy sofas and armchairs and a small dance floor. The kitchen prepares superb French cuisine, and the waiters, in their long brown aprons blending with the brown tablecloths, carpet, and rather unique dried fern and flower arrangements, serve it with impeccable style. Appetizers include hearts of palm remoulade ($2.75) and escargots Pernod or chablis ($3.25). Steak and seafood dishes compete with escalopes de veau à la King Oscar (sauteed in butter and white wine, served with Alaska king crab, white asparagus, and béarnaise sauce, $11.50) or coq au vin ($8). For a final flourish have the cherries jubilee or crêpes Suzette for two ($4.50), and an extra-special coffee like rustic almond (brandy, amaretto, Tia Maria, and whipped cream topped with brown sugar and cinnamon, $3.50).

Open Monday to Saturday from noon to 1 a.m., and Sunday from noon to 10:30 p.m. The lounge sometimes has entertainment, usually on weekends, and the dinner theater is most often open Thursday, Friday, and Saturday, but as the schedule is erratic, check before you go.

Shakespeare's Steak House and Tavern, 181 Main St. East (tel. 416/528-0689), is a Hamilton dining institution, serving good beef and seafood. Not surprisingly, the decor is very English, with dark wooden beams, horse brasses, a gilded portrait of Shakespeare over the fireplace, and Shakespearean characters from Bottom to Falstaff around the walls. The menu continues the theme with a full reprint of the poem "The Passionate Pilgrim" that ends with the familiar and much used (and misquoted) "Live with me and be my love." From it you may select marinated Bismark herring to start ($1.95) or consommé au sherry ($1.50), and graduate to a Salisbury steak with bordelaise ($6.95) or a 16-ounce New York sirloin ($14.95), both of which will be served with garlic bread, kosher dills, and french fries or a baked potato. For dessert the apple beignets ($1.75) are irresistible. At the end of your meal you will be presented with a huge goblet of candies to rummage through—it even contains Liquorice. Allsorts—Bassett's, of course, for all you Anglophiles. For lunch you'll find various sandwiches served with potatoes and pickles for under $5.

Open Monday to Thursday from noon to 2:30 p.m. and 5 to 11:30 p.m., Friday from noon to 2:30 p.m. and 5 p.m. to 1 a.m., and Saturday from 5 p.m. to 1 a.m. Closed Sunday.

The blue and white sign outside **Pappa's Dining,** 309 Main St. East (tel. 525-2455), hints at the Greek delicacies to be found within among the Corinthian columns, the blue wall friezes, and classical statues in the wall alcoves. Waitresses in white Grecian robes will serve you fried feta cheese ($3.25) or avgolemeno soup ($1.25) to start, followed by souvlaki or kokinisto (tenderloin with peppers, onions, and rice, sauteed over a low flame with light Greek wine), both $7.50. Steaks and seafood are also available, and Greek feasts for two which include soup, salad, chicken riginato, spare ribs kokinisto, fresh fruit bowl, and coffee for two ($22). Lunchtime finds a selection of omelets and sandwiches from $1.50 to $3.85, and entrees for around $6. Open Monday to Thursday from 11 a.m. to 11 p.m., Friday from 11 a.m. to midnight, and Saturday from noon to midnight. Closed Sunday.

At the **London Fishery and Oyster House,** 157 Main St. East (tel. 528-1433), nauticalia fills every nook and cranny in this cavernous place where an old Newfoundland dory functions as a soup and oyster server, and ships horns, lobster pots, lanterns, and old pumps help create the ambience for those dining in the cafe-curtained booths. The menu sticks mostly to fish, with a couple of items listed for the nonbeliever. At lunchtime there's a daily special which the day I visited was a seafood casserole for only $1.99. The balance of the lunchtime menu is under $5, like the broiled filet of ocean perch, fish and chips, a whole mess of smelts, etc.

At night there are usually three specials, for example, broiled filet of Boston bluefish with creole sauce ($3.49), plus favorites like the fishery grill (fresh fish, smoked fish, snow crab, stuffed shrimp, oysters Rockefeller, and scallops, broiled and presented on a platter with onion rings, smelts, half a tomato, and french fries $6.99). Chowders, escargots, pecan pie, and ice cream complete the picture. The bar offers oysters on the shell or prepared Rockefeller and casino styles, as well as clams, shrimp, and escargots. Live music adds a seaworthy touch. Open Monday to Saturday from 11:45 a.m. to 1 a.m., and Sunday from 4:30 to 10 p.m.

The **Black Forest Inn,** 255 King St. East (tel. 416/528-3538), provides an eminently festive background for good budget dining. Here among the warm wood paneling and the painted wood furniture of southern Germany, served by waitresses in colorful dirndls, you can sample all manner of schnitzels (from $3.50 to $5.70)—paprika, jaeger, wiener, à la Holstein—and various sausages including Bock, Bavarian white, Hungarian country, Thueringer, and farm sausage, all served with home fries and sauerkraut ($1.50 to $1.80). Naturally, for dessert have Black Forest cake or Dobash torte (70¢).

This place is so crowded that you'll probably have to wait on line no matter what time you arrive on whatever day of the week. No reservations. Open Tuesday to Saturday from noon to 1 a.m., Sunday to 10 p.m. Closed Monday.

Hamilton's Italian Palace

For a large slice of La Dolce Vita, head for **Caesar's,** 30 King St. East (tel. 416/526-1060), a Roman entertainment complex that houses **Big Julie's Disco** (open 7 p.m. to 1 a.m.; closed Sundays; no cover; average price of drink, $2), Paesano's Italian Deli, a penthouse dinner theater, and fine continental dining in a very Roman atmosphere created by solid brick walls, Roman arches and pillars, classical oil paintings, terracotta pots, male and female statuary, red velvet chairs, and white tablecloths.

The menu is extensive and highly imaginative. Why not try the smoked sturgeon Bostonaise ($3.25) or the rillette of partridge with pickled onions ($2.25)? It's very hard to choose an entree for they're all outstanding, and range in price from $7.50 to $14.50. Breast of chicken Curaçao (chicken breast filled with veal, nuts, and ginger, blazed in Curaçao and sauteed with oranges, grapes, and raisins), or tournedos Marquis de Sade (filet marinated in sherry and wine, filled with crabmeat, and served with a wine sauce) are just two examples from the 15 or so entrees.

At lunchtime there's a selection of appetizers, soups, egg, crêpe, meat and fish dishes, and salads (most under $5). In **Paesano's Italian Deli,** on the ground floor amid the red, white, and green lamps, Italian staples like pasta and salami sandwiches are served.

The **Penthouse Dinner Theatre** presents comedies, dramas, and musicals (when I was there, Neil Simon's *The Star Spangled Girl* was playing) from Tuesday to Saturday. A five-course dinner (soup, salad, choice of three main courses, dessert, and coffee) plus the show will cost you $15.95 on Tuesday through Thursday, $17.95 on Friday and Saturday. You can see the show only from Tuesday to Thursday for $6.75.

Open noon to 2:30 p.m. Monday to Friday, and 5 to midnight Monday to Saturday. Reservations recommended.

A Unique Polish Table

Four and a half years ago you would have found Stefan and Bernice Lazowski running a coffeeshop. Then they felt that Hamilton was ready for a real Polish restaurant, so **Sir Stefan's,** 436 Aberdeen Ave. at Dundurn St. (tel. 416/528-0878), was born. Here you'll find lashings of hearty fare: bigos mys-lywski (hunter's stew) golobki (cabbage rolls; both $4.95), pierogis, which come boiled or fried (cheese and potato, cabbage, cottage cheese, meat and mushrooms; all about $4.75), brace of roast quails stuffed with seasoned rice and mushrooms, baked in white wine sauce, and served with potatoes or homemade egg noodles and fruit relish ($8.95), or Stefan's special plate introducing kielbasa, cabbage rolls, pierogi, with fried onions and sour cream ($7.50). Start with borscht, cabbage soup, or marinated herring with sour cream ($1.35), and end with a plum pieroszki, poppy-seed strudel, or crêpes with peaches, cherries, or raspberries. Burgers are also available, and there are eight or so different vodkas to try, ranging from aromatic herb to the natural potato-based variety.

And while you're enjoying these eastern European delights you can contemplate pictures of costumed Polish dancers holding their zapigi in the mountains, and watch the waitresses moving around in their brilliant costumes. So popular has the place become that unless you have a reservation, especially on weekends, you will have to wait.

Open Tuesday to Thursday from 11 a.m. to 9 p.m., on Friday and Saturday, to midnight. Closed Sunday and Monday.

The Most Elegant Pub Imaginable

A pub in an old bank building? Why not? But a pub with an ornate stone staircase with bronze figurines and chandeliers . . . ? That's the **Duke of Hamilton,** 54 King St. East (tel. 416/527-7777), where you can toss back many a tankard of imported beer—Bass, Beamish, XXX Stout, Worthington E, Tennent's lager—for $1.60 apiece, $2.40 for a pint. There are also 37 varieties of bottled beers alone. Then, of course, there's the pub grub to go with the ale—a ploughman's, veal, ham, and egg pie, scotch egg and salad, Melton Mowbray or shepherd's pie, or bangers and mash (all under $4). In the upstairs dining room a buffet is served from noon to 2:30 p.m. and from 5:30 to 9 p.m.

Open Monday to Saturday from noon to 1:30 a.m.

WHAT TO DO AND SEE: Hamilton offers a wide range of sights and attractions, from the most obvious industrial tours to an unlikely bucolic retreat. For information, stop in at the **Hamilton and District Visitor's and Convention Bureau,** 58 Jackson St. West (tel. 416/525-7011).

The Royal Botanical Gardens

These gardens (P.O. Box 399, Hamilton; tel. 416/527-1158) on the northern approaches to the city provide almost 2000 acres of stunning horticultural exhibits: the rock garden features spring bulbs in May, a fantastic display of summer flowers from June to September, and chrysanthemums in October; the Spring Garden blazes during June and July with iris, peonies and lilies; the arboretum fills with the heady scent of lilac from the end of May to early June, and the exquisite color bursts of rhododendrons and azaleas thereafter; the Centennial rose garden is at its best from late June to mid-September.

Some 25 miles of nature trails crisscross the area inviting exploration, while nearby, and still part of the gardens, is **Cootes Paradise,** a natural wildlife sanctuary with trails leading through some 12,000 acres of water, marsh, and wooded ravines. For a trail-guide map, stop in at either the Nature Centre (open 10 a.m. to 4 p.m.) or at headquarters at 680 Plains Rd. West (Hwy. 2), Burlington.

Refreshments can be had at the Tea House overlooking the Rock Garden.

Open all year from dawn to dusk. Admission free. To get there from Hamilton, take Main St. West to Hwy. 403, and then Hwy. 403 north. Exit at Hwy. 6 and follow the signs.

Downtown

Aside from steel, Hamilton is probably best known for its professional football team, the Hamilton Tiger Cats. It is not surprising, therefore, to find the **Canadian Football Hall of Fame** located in City Hall Plaza, 58 Jackson St. West. Opened in 1972, this national shrine to Canadian professional football traces the last 100 years of football history; Labatt's Theater offers regular showings of an ever-changing selection of football films and documentaries, while one room has push-button CFL statistics available.

The **art gallery,** 123 King St. West (tel. 627-6610), has an excellent collection of Canadian, American, British, and European paintings, graphics, and sculpture, and offers several special exhibitions that change monthly. Open Tuesday to Saturday from 10 a.m. to 5 p.m., on Thursday from 7 to 9 p.m., and on Sunday from 1 to 5 p.m. Admission is free.

Don't forget to explore **Hess Village,** a four-block area of restored clapboard houses now containing boutiques, galleries, and restaurants.

Dundurn Castle

For a glimpse of the opulent life as it was lived in this part of southern Ontario in the mid-19th century, visit Dundurn Castle, Dundurn Park, York Blvd. (tel. 416/522-5313). Built between 1832 and 1835 by Sir Alan Napier MacNab, prime minister of the United Provinces of Canada in the mid-1850s, a founder of the Great Western Railway, and knighted by Queen Victoria for the part he played in the Rebellion of 1837, the 36-room mansion has been restored and furnished in the style of 1855. The cream exterior with its classical Greek portico is impressive enough, but inside from the grand and formal dining rooms to Lady McNab's boudoir the furnishings are equally rich. The museum contains a fascinating collection of memorabilia. During the summer months special children's entertainment is provided in the **Cockpit Theatre,** and in the Castle Courtyard concerts are held every Wednesday evening in July and August at 8 p.m. You may dine before the concert in the **McNab Arms** restaurant (tel. 416/527-3303), which is also open during regular castle hours.

Open 10 a.m. to 5 p.m. daily from mid-June to Labour Day, and 1 to 4 p.m. from Labour Day to mid-June. Closed Christmas and New Year's Day. Admission: adults, $2.25; students, $1; children under 12, 50¢.

To get there from downtown Hamilton, take King St. West to Dundurn St., turn right, and Dundurn will run into York Blvd.

Steel Tours

While you're here you really ought to take a tour of a steel plant. You can do so Monday to Friday from 8:30 a.m. to 5 p.m. at **Dominion Foundries and Steel Co. of Canada,** where you will see the dock area with the huge equipment used for unloading boats, blast-furnace operations, the oxygen steel-making process, followed by hot rolling, cold rolling, and finishing. A similar 2½-hour tour is available at **Steel Co. of Canada,** Tuesday to Friday from 9:30 a.m. to 1:30 p.m. At both places visitors must be over 16, and you must make an appointment ahead of time. Admission is free.

For appointments, write: Manager, Guest Relations, DOFASCO, Box 460, Hamilton, ON L8N 3J5 (tel. 416/544-3761); or Chief Guide, Public Relations, Steel Co. of Canada, Ltd., Hamilton, ON L8N 3T1 (tel. 416/528-2511).

Nearby Attractions

Just a half-hour drive northwest of Hamilton off Hwy. 8, you can drive through the **African Lion Safari** (tel. 519/623-2620), at Rockton, keeping an eye out for rhinos, cheetahs, tigers, elephants, giraffes, zebras, and many, many more. Inside the park there's a cafeteria, snackbar, souvenir shop, picnic areas, playground, and pets' corner. Open July and August from 10 a.m. to 5:30 p.m.; otherwise from noon to 4:30 p.m. on weekdays, from 10 a.m. to 4:30 p.m. on weekends. Closed Christmas Day. Admission: adults, $3; children 3 to 17, $1.50. To get there, take Hwy. 8 from the west end of Hamilton.

A little farther west along Hwy. 8 you can visit the **Wentworth Pioneer Village** (tel. 416/526-4154), where you'll find 27 buildings dating from 1814, including a log church, railway station, drugstore, and general store. Enjoy the picnic areas and adjoining nature trails. Open from the second Sunday in May to September 30. Hours: weekdays in July and August and weekends and holidays year round from 11 a.m. to 6 p.m.; weekdays in May, June, and September from 10 a.m. to 5 p.m. Admission: adults, $1.50; students, 75¢; children, 50¢; preschool children free. Take Hwy. 52 off Hwy. 8.

Nightlife

For symphony concerts, top-class entertainers, theater, and dance, go to **Hamilton Place,** a super-modern $11-million arts complex housing two theaters: the Great Hall, holding over 2000, and the smaller, more intimate Studio seating 400. The **Hamilton Philharmonic Orchestra** and **Theatre Aquarius** are the prime tenants, plus a whole cavalcade of visiting entertainers who have included Nana Mouskouri, Kenneth McKellar, Joan Armatrading, and the Shevchenko Dance Company. Ticket prices range from $2 to $13, depending on the show. Hamilton Place is at Main and James Sts. (tel. 416/525-3100; box office: 416/525-7710).

For jazz, try the downstairs lounge of **Flavours** on weekends (tel. 416/527-5050) and Wednesday to Saturday, the **Duke of Hamilton.** For pop and middle-of-the-road music, drop in at the Royal Connaught's **The Duke's Lounge** (tel. 527-5071).

For discoing there's Caesar's **Big Julie's,** and across the street, **Bannister's,** 95 King St. East (tel. 545-4318), an art deco experience where a massive stained-glass lampshade hangs over the main bar, brass railings surround the raised dance floor, and a gallery provides a bird's-eye view of the action pyrotechnics. No cover charge. Cocktails average $2.50. Check out the computer bar. Downstairs for your dining pleasure when you tire is **Tudor House** (tel. 527-1230), offering steak and seafood dishes (from $8.75) served in a red-carpeted beamed, mock-Tudor atmosphere, complete with decorative warming pans and brass. Open daily from noon, Sunday from 5 p.m.

The loveseats and greenery at **Feathers,** 10 Young St. (tel. 416/528-7511), provide a posh background for disco dining. Entrees concentrate on steaks, seafood, and chicken (from $4.75 to $12), and include garlic bread, baked or french-fried potatoes, vegetable, and salad bar. Open Monday to Friday from noon to 1 a.m., on Saturday 6 p.m. to 1 a.m.

My favorite watering hole is that strangely cross-bred English-French pub, the **Duke of Hamilton,** 54 King St. East.

And don't forget the dinner theaters at **Caesar's,** 30 King St. East, and at **Flavours,** 16 Jarvis St.

5. Niagara-on-the-Lake

Niagara-on-the-Lake has a lot of firsts: first capital of Upper Canada, first grist mill (1782), first census taken (1792), first newspaper (1792), and now certainly first in line for being the best preserved and prettiest 19th-century village in North America, with its lakeside location and tree-lined streets bordered by gracious clapboard and brick period houses. Such is the setting (only 80 miles from Toronto, 35 miles from Buffalo) for one of Canada's most famous festivals:

THE SHAW FESTIVAL: Brian Doherty, a local lawyer, conceived of the Shaw Festival, which saw its first performance of *Don Juan in Hell* in the summer of 1961. The theater company that occupies the Shaw Festival Theatre and the beautiful old creeper-encrusted Courthouse theater is the only one in the world devoted to presenting the plays of Bernard Shaw and his contemporaries. An evening spent at the red brick **Festival Theatre** dramatically designed by Ron Thom will provide excellent dramatic entertainment and elegant intermissions spent looking out over or experiencing the courtyard with its reflecting pools, shade trees, and tubs of flowers.

The Festival Theatre opens in the second or third week of May and runs through the first week of October with evening performances Tuesday through Saturday at 8:30 p.m., and matinees on Wednesday and Sunday at 5 p.m. and Saturday at 2 p.m. The **Courthouse** is open from the third week of June to the second week of September presenting usually the plays of Shaw's contemporaries. Performances are at 8:30 p.m. Tuesday through Saturday, with matinees on Saturday at 2 p.m. and Sunday at 5 p.m. There are also lunchtime performances and Sunday afternoon concerts during the summer, as well as winter programs from October to April. Ticket prices run from $8 to $12.50 at the Festival, $6 to $8 at the Courthouse; for previews, there's a $2 discount.

For more information, write: Shaw Festival, P.O. Box 774, Niagara-on-the-Lake, ON L0S 1J0 (tel. 416/468-3201).

WHERE TO STAY: As one might expect, Niagara-on-the-Lake has several exquisite old inns to choose from. First, probably *the* place to stay, with a prime location overlooking the lake, is the **Oban Inn**, 160 Front St. at Gate St. (tel. 416/468-2165), located in a charming white Victorian house with a black dormer-style roof and windows, and a veranda that extends around the side and front of the house—quite adequate for the old lake captain for whom it was built in 1824. The gardens are a joy to behold and a source of the bouquets on each table in the dining room.

Each of the 20 rooms is different. Some have the old pine floors exposed, others have more of a chintz flavor, but all have antique chests and early Canadian-style headboards. None has TV or telephone, but all are air-conditioned. Downstairs in the pubby piano bar, with its leather-seated Windsor-style chairs and hunting prints over the blazing fireplace, hangs an oil portrait of Shaw and photographs of the inn's best loved and many guests—the stars of the Festival stage. The dining room has three different areas—one with carved-back chairs and needlepointed seats, another with royal-blue walls and white ruffled curtains, chandeliers, and a gilded portrait of Queen Elizabeth II, and the third, which is in fact the glass-fronted veranda furnished with white-painted chairs, hanging plants, and lace placemats. In any one of these rooms you may taste the $9.50 prix-fixe dinner starting with homemade soup or tomato, and followed by a choice of fish or meat main course. A similar luncheon is available for $4.25. Meals are served only in sittings.

Rates: $27.50 single, $36 double, and $40 for a room overlooking the lake. Weekend packages and midweek packages are available during the winter from November 1 to April 1. The $76 per person weekend package includes all meals from Friday dinner to Sunday lunch, the room (double occupancy), and a bottle of Bright's champagne. Ditto for the midweek package at $66 per person.

For a more lively atmosphere that still retains the elegance and charm of a Victorian inn, the **Prince of Wales Hotel**, 6 Picton St. (tel. 416/468-3246), has it all: full recreational facilities including an indoor pool, sauna, whirlpool, sun and exercise room, and platform tennis court, Vikki's disco, lounges, bars and restaurants, and 58 rooms, some with colonial-style furniture, others with brass bedsteads, and all beautifully decorated with antiques or reproductions and color-coordinated carpeting, drapes, and spreads. The large bathrooms are equipped with bidets.

The original section of the hotel was built in 1867 and contains the room where the Prince of Wales supposedly slept (hence the Prince of Wales feathers carved on the headboard), complemented by Louis XV–style chairs and a marble-top chest. In the newer south wing, huge wardrobes house the TVs and botanical prints on the walls set the tone. The newer wing has been extremely well designed to match as closely as possible the original red brick and cream exterior with its slate dormer roof.

An impressive old oak bar that came from Pennsylvania dominates the quiet bar off the lobby, where a businessmen's lunch is served for $3. The main dining room exudes elegance with its mirrored walls and French Empire aquamarine chairs contrasting with the airiness of the greenhouse patio overlooking Simcoe Park. Dinner might begin with pâté served with Cumberland sauce ($2.75), followed by a ratatouille of seafood—crabmeat, scallops, and shrimp in a Mornay sauce ($9.75)—or roast rack of lamb with diable or mint sauce ($13.25), and finish with one of many cakes, pastries, and ice creams.

Lunch offers lighter fare: tomato, herb, and bacon quiche with salad ($3.75), sandwiches, and dishes like medallions of pork with seasonal vegetables and potatoes ($5.25).

The coffeeshop must be the only such named establishment with wingback chairs and couches, tiled floors, oak paneling, and bamboo-style chairs where you can enjoy soups, salads, and pastries. Vikki's Disco offers sophisticated disco dancing in a chic atmosphere created by bentwood cane chairs, beige velvet banquettes around the walls, some wicker furniture in one corner, and a minimum of stained glass and hanging plants, mirrors, art deco prints. The speakers are trained directly onto the dance floor so that one can talk easily off the floor. Open 8 p.m. to 1 a.m. Proper dress required.

Rates are seasonal: May 15 to October 15, singles are $43; doubles, $49; at other times, $37 single, $43 double. An additional person is $8. Suites in season start at $70, off-season at $60.

Rustic to every last inch of barn board, the **Pillar & Post Inn,** 48 John St. at King St. (tel. 416/468-2123), has 60 lovely rooms, 19 of them with wood-burning fireplaces. Although each room is decorated slightly differently, any room will certainly contain early Canadian-style furniture, Windsor-style chairs, and a color TV tucked into a pine cabinet, historic engravings, plus the usual modern conveniences. One of the suites (with cathedral ceilings, red brick wood-burning fireplace, pine settle with cushions, and other pine furniture) goes for only $72.

The lobby sets the tone for the place with its brick floor and pine reception desk, opening onto a tiny courtyard with tubs of flowers, an old pump, and wooden rakes and hay forks on the walls. In the back there's a secluded grass-surrounded pool—some rooms facing the pool on the ground level have bay windows and window boxes—a sauna and whirlpool. The Pillar lounge is a pleasant place to relax on a plush red couch or a high-backed settle under an old beamed ceiling, lit by soft lamps in old-style candle holders. Bask for a while in the firelight emanating from the huge inglenook fireplace. There's nightly entertainment, usually gentle folk, and a small dance area if the spirit moves you.

The dining room has the pine flooring of the original building, which in the 1890s was known as Factory No. 13, a canning factory that turned out peaches and tomatoes carted in by nearby farmers. The last can came down the line in 1957, and baskets were then manufactured and stored here until 1970, when the building was converted to a restaurant and craft center. The rooms were added in 1972. If you sit in the dining area off to the right of the entrance you can look down and see one of the craftsmen at work over a metal sculpture in a studio, and after your meal (which might have been roast chicken at $7.95 or shrimp creole at $10.50), wander through into the craft shop full of stunning quilts, kitchenware, pine furniture, toys, dolls, etc.

Rates: $43 single, $47 double; fireplace rooms $5 extra. Winter weekend packages including two nights' accommodation, two breakfasts, and champagne, are $87.50 per person, double occupancy.

WHERE TO EAT: The Buttery, 19 Queen St. (tel. 416/468-2564), of course, either on the terrace reddened by hanging geraniums or inside the beamed dining room off copper-topped tables with medieval knights careening around the wallpaper. Besides the regular menu, you may already have guessed that a Henry VIII–style feast is taken upstairs at the Buttery on weekends at 9 p.m., when serving wenches will "cosset" you with food and wine, "and being most amiable call your attention to the jongleurs, musickers and those who have been summoned expressly for your entertainment." There you will in fact receive four removes—broth, chicken, roast lamb, roast pig, sherry trifle, syllabub, and cheese, washed down with a goodly amount of wine, ale, and mead. This will cost you $18.50, including tax and gratuity for Henry VIII.

The Tavern Menu, offered from noon to 5 p.m. and 9 p.m. to midnight, has a tempting array of snacks like Welsh rarebit, mushroom quiche, and a real Cornish pasty, worthy of the name, stuffed with meat, onion, and potato (ranging from $2.50 to $3.95), as well as heartier fare like steak, kidney, and mushroom pie and Williamsburg spare ribs for $4 to $4.50. Afternoon tea is served from 3 to 5 p.m., and dinner from 6 p.m., when you can enjoy entrees (from $7.75 to $12) that include chicken breast in champagne sauce, duckling Montmorency, entrecôte bordelaise. The price will include soup and salad, and you can finish with warm apple dumplings or chocolate cream roll ($1.25). And if you're wise, you'll take home some of the fresh baked goods available—pies, strudels, dumplings, cream puffs, scones, etc. Reservations only for the medieval feast. Open daily noon to midnight.

In a colonial village one takes tea, and you can do that (or lunch) at **McCrae Hall Tea Room,** 65 Queen St. (tel. 416/468-7187), off glass tables either in the garden under the trees or inside seated on wrought-iron, black-and-white striped furniture, enjoying scones with preserves (95¢), buttered fruit bread, various sandwiches, peach shortcake ($1.65), and a variety of teas and coffees. The front is a gift shop crammed with Royal Doulton, Royal Worcester, and other china artifacts. Open 10 a.m. to 6 p.m. daily.

WHAT TO DO AND SEE: First, a stroll along Queen St. will reveal the Niagara Apothecary Shop, a restored 1866 shop; McClelland's Store, which has operated since 1835; the Fudge Shop, where they make fudge on a marble slab while you watch; Greaves Jam, fourth generation jam makers; and period houses, many dating back to the 1820s and 1830s.

The **Niagara Fire Museum** on King St. has a collection of fire equipment that dates from 1816 to 1926. Open daily except Monday from July to Labour Day. The **Niagara Historical Museum,** 43 Castlereagh St. (tel. 416/468-3912), fronted by a white picket fence, is one of the oldest and largest of its kind in Canada, having about 19,000 artifacts pertaining to local history—possessions of United Empire Loyalists who first settled the area at the end of the American Revolution, mementoes of John Graves Simcoe (Upper Canada's first lieutenant governor), Laura Secord, and many other exciting exhibits. Open May 15 to October 15 from 10 a.m. to 6 p.m. daily; the rest of the year, open Wednesday, Saturday, and Sunday only, from 1 to 5 p.m. Admission: adults, $1; children under 14, 50¢.

See the fort that played such a stormy role in the War of 1812. **Fort George** (tel. 416/468-2741), which had been built in the 1790s to replace Fort Niagara as British headquarters, was destroyed by American artillery in 1813, rebuilt by 1815, abandoned in the 1820s, and only restored in the 1930s. Step inside and imagine yourself part of the daily life of a British military post manning the sentry posts and bastions, sleeping on the hard shelf beds in the guard room, attending a civilian dinner in the officers' quarters, and relying on the carpenter and the blacksmith. Note the powder magazine where several hundred barrels of gunpowder were stored. To avoid the possibility that a stray spark might ignite the powder, there are no metal fitments here—even the floorboards are secured with wooden pegs instead of iron nails, and soldiers working in the magazine wore special smocks and wooden clogs.

Open mid-May to Labour Day from 9 a.m. to 6 p.m.; from Labour Day to October 31, open daily from 10 a.m. to 5 p.m.; from November 1 to mid-May, open weekdays by appointment only. Admission: adults, $1.50; children, 75¢; children under 5 and senior citizens, free; family rate, $4. Located on the Niagara Parkway not far from Niagara-on-the-Lake.

One of the best ways to experience the river and its frontier history is to take a **Lower Niagara Cruise** that sails from the Ricardo St. dock in Niagara-on-the-Lake. The two hour cruises that leave daily at 1:30 and 4 p.m. (check when you get there) will take you past Fort Niagara, Youngstown, N.Y., Lewiston, N.Y., Queenston Heights, and Fort George. Or you can watch the ship cut gracefully through the night and dance to the sunset every Saturday night. Daytime cruises cost $6 for adults, $3 for children; moonlight cruises cost $8. For reservations, call 416/468-3253, or write Lower Niagara River Cruises, P.O. Box 13330, Niagara-on-the-Lake, ON L0S 1J0.

6. Niagara Falls

Just a 20-minute drive down the Niagara Parkway from this 19th-century tranquility lies a tourist nugget—Niagara Falls, with its gimmicks, amusement parks, wax museums, daredevil feats, and a million motels, each with a honeymoon suite somewhere, somehow. . . .

To some, Niagara Falls may seem rather ticky-tacky and certainly over commercialized, but somehow there are still the falls and the parks and the gardens—nature manages to survive with grace.

WHERE TO STAY: Every other sign in Niagara Falls advertises a motel, so what follows is a very small selection of favorites:

First-Class Establishments

It could almost fit into Niagara-on-the-Lake and it's the only really old-world accommodation of character at the falls—the **Old Stone Inn,** 5425 Robinson St. (tel. 416/357-1234), right across from the Skylon Tower and Pyramid Place. Built only two years ago, it was designed to create the atmosphere of a country inn by using natural rough-hewn stone, heavy crossbeam supports, and barn-style paneling. The 114 rooms set in a three-story L-shaped configuration are spacious, furnished in shades of burnt orange with modern white furniture and yellow chairs, and contain the usual conveniences. Three rooms have fireplaces and double sunken showers; 36 ground-floor rooms face the outdoor heated pool. The lounge with its burnt-orange wingbacks and loveseats, tile floor, stone walls, and rustic paneling leads right out to the pool while the dining room with its huge working fireplace, brass chandelier, bookcases, and high cathedral-style ceiling provides a super-cozy atmosphere for such specialties as maison kebab, tournedos Rossini, escargots bourguignonnes. The rustic coffeeshop with tile floor and early Canadian artifacts like a milk churn, butter churn, and coffee grinder, makes a pleasant change from the usual.

Rates are seasonal: May 15 to September 15: singles, $42 to $65; doubles, $48 to $70; an extra person is $4; September 16 to May 14: singles, $25 to $35; doubles, $28 to $38; an extra person is $3. Children under 14 free. Prices depend on whether it's a room with twin doubles, king-size, or queen-size bed. Some rooms have special facilities for the handicapped.

For an unblemished view of the falls, you have a choice of either the Sheraton Brock or the **Sheraton Foxhead,** 5875 Falls Ave. (tel. 416/354-7441).

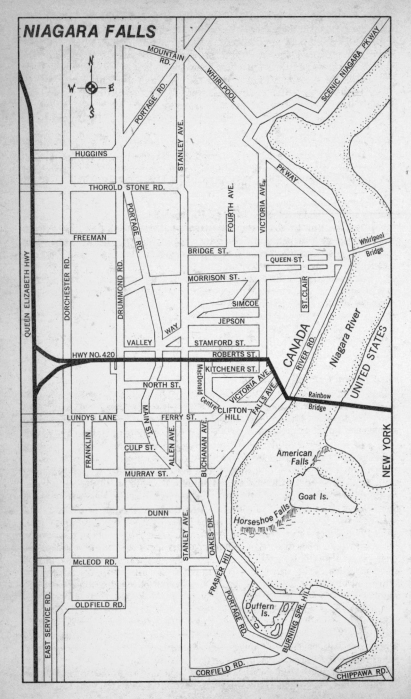

The Foxhead, built ten years ago, has 406 rooms spread over 12 floors. Floors 9 through 12 have just been renovated and sport the currently fashionable earth tones; elsewhere the rooms might have aquamarine with floral drapes, or gold or red combinations. By the time you visit the whole place should be done in browns and beiges. (Honeymoon suites have black leather waterbeds and white fur spreads). The 14th-floor penthouse Dining Room takes fair advantage of the view with its large glass windows, and serves a daily hot buffet from 5 to 10 p.m. for $9.95. For entertainment, step into the Pickwick Lounge on the ground floor; for recreation try the outdoor rooftop swimming pool.

Rates are seasonal: May 25 to October 7, $54.50 to $79.50, single or double; October 8 to May 24, $34.50 to $52.50, single or double. Prices depend on whether it's a room with a view of the falls, gardens, village, or city. An extra person is $5. No charge for children under 18 sharing a room with their parents.

Right next door, with only Maple Leaf Village separating it from the Foxhead, stands the **Sheraton Brock**, 5685 Falls Ave. (tel. 416/354-7441), that has been hosting honeymooners and falls visitors since 1928. It still has a certain air of faded splendor—a huge chandelier and marble floors in the lobby—but with an emphasis somehow on the faded. Rooms are decorated with burnt-amber wall carpet, and orange-brown and yellow spreads and curtains, and colonial-style pieces. Some 100 of the 258 rooms overlook the falls. City-view rooms, which are smaller, are also cheaper.

For dining there's the Rainbow Room on the tenth floor with a lovely view over the falls, serving a continental menu of such entrees as filet of sole amandine ($8.50) or center-cut double lamb chops ($9). An unusual dessert of deep-fried ice cream (tortoni with candied fruits dipped in batter and deep-fried, then topped with rum-flavored sauce) is worth trying. The coffeeshop is light and airy with green carpeting and hi-tech-style furniture and pine partitions, and for that quiet drink there's the Golliwog Lounge.

Rates are seasonal: $43.50 to $64, single or double, May 25 to October 7; at other times, $26.50 to $45.50. Prices depend on the room's view. An additional person is $5, and children under 18 stay free in their parents' room.

The other Sheraton property, the **Sheraton Motor Inn**, 5685 Falls Ave. (tel. 416/354-7441), is behind the other two and ideal for families—all 208 rooms are large. Some family suites have 700 square feet that includes a bedroom with double double beds and living room for only $39.50. There's an outdoor heated swimming pool and an eating facility.

Rates: $32.50 to $54.50, single or double, depending on room type.

For reservations at any of these Sheraton accommodations, call toll free in the continental U.S., 800/325-3535 (in Missouri only, 800/392-3500); in eastern Canada, 800/261-9393; in western Canada, 800/268-9330. Honeymoon packages and special winter packages at really low rates are available at both the Brock and the Foxhead.

Just up Clifton Hill around the corner from the Foxhead, window boxes with geraniums attract the eye to the **Honeymoon City Motel**, 4943 Clifton Hill (tel. 416/354-2613). The 77 units on two floors are set around a courtyard with an outdoor heated pool (22 of the rooms are honeymoon suites with canopied beds and extra-plush decor). The other rooms have colonial-style furniture and pink walls, clock radios, full bathrooms, and color TVs (none has a telephone). Rooms 54 through 58 have a direct view of the falls; 12 rooms have private balconies. Convenient facilities include a washer-dryer, gift shop, and the Jolly Brewer Lounge and Restaurant that features an outdoor patio and nightly entertainment.

Rates are seasonal: in season, $40 to $50, single or double; off-season, $30 to $35, single or double. Honeymoon suites are the most expensive.

Across the street the **Fallsway Motor Hotel,** 4946 Clifton Hill (tel. 416/358-3601), is a veritable entertainment complex, with an indoor and outdoor swimming pool, the Thunderbird lounge for dancing and live entertainment, a dining room and coffeeshop, and 172 attractive rooms with white cinderblock walls, modern aluminum furniture, and orange and yellow color schemes. There are 12 poolside rooms.

Rates are seasonal: from June 16 to September 15: $44.50 to $50.50 single or double, $64.50 for a bridal suite, $60.50 to $72.50 for a family suite (three beds); from March 16 to June 15 and September 16 to November 14: $32.50 to $42.50 single or double, $54.50 for a bridal suite, $48.50 to $58.50 for a family suite; November 15 to March 15: $30.50 to $36.50 single or double, $44.50 for a bridal suite, $44.50 to $48.50 for a family suite. A roll-away bed is $5, cribs are free, an additional person is $4, and children under 14 stay free.

The mock-Tudor style of the **Inn of the Falls,** 5525 Victoria Ave. (tel. 416/357-2011), differentiates it from the rest of the motels on motel row. The four older units are not particularly special, but the 36 new units arranged on three floors around a kidney-shaped outdoor pool are extremely stylish—with beige wall-to-wall carpeting, beige striped wallpaper on one wall, matching blue/beige curtains and spreads, and dark-toned wood furniture to complement the Tudor trim. Honeymoon suites have circular beds (some with brass bedsteads) and white bamboo-style furniture. All rooms have color TV, air conditioning, and full bathrooms (there are no telephones, although the owner is planning to install them).

Rates are seasonal: April 1 to April 27, $24.50 to $28.50, single or double; April 28 to June 15, $28.50 to $32.50; June 15 to September 17, $40.50 to $44.50. An additional person is $4. Off-season rates drop as low as $25 across the board. Within walking distance of the falls (turn right at the top of Clifton Hill along Victoria Ave.).

Holiday Inn by the Falls, 5339 Murray St. (tel. 416/356-1333), has a prime location right behind the Skylon Tower, only minutes from the falls. Note that although it sports the familiar green-and-yellow Holiday Inn sign, it is *not* a Holiday Inn (the owner had the name first and still refuses to sell it to that chain). Externally this is a good-looking place and the rooms live up to expectations, for they are large, have good closet space, coin-operated massagers, an additional vanity sink, color-coordinated modern furnishings, telephone, and color TV. Most of the 77 rooms on six floors have balconies. Dining facilities and an outdoor heated pool and patio are available.

Rates are seasonal: from June 8 to September 23: $52 to $56 single or double, $76 for family suites (three beds); March 12 to June 7 and September 24 to October 27: $45 to $46 single or double, $55 for the family units; October 28 to March 11: $38 single or double; $46 for a family unit. Roll-away beds are $4; cribs, $3. An extra person is $4. Honeymoon packages are available.

Budget Accommodations

For budget accommodations—correction, accommodations period—you can't beat the home-away-from-home feel of the **Nelson Motel,** 10655 Niagara River Parkway (tel. 416/295-4754), run by Paul and Betty Solose who live in the large house adjacent to the motel units. Betty keeps those 25 units as spic and span as her own place, and the outdoor pool even sparkles. The units have character, especially the family units with a double bedroom adjoined by a twin-bedded room for the kids. These two-room units go for $40 and $50. Regular units have modern furniture with black-and-white TV. Singles have showers only, and all units face the neatly trimmed lawn with umbrellaed tables and shrubs (none has a telephone). Open April 1 to October 31.

Rates: April 15 to May 15, $16 to $22 single or double, $20 to $24 triple, $22 to $26 quad; May 16 to September 15, $22 to $28 single or double, $26 to $30 triple, $28 to $32 quad. Roll-aways and cribs are extra, and the above rates do not apply on U.S. or Canadian public holidays. It's located a short drive from the falls overlooking the Niagara River, away from the hustle and bustle of Niagara itself.

The farther away from the falls you go, the more likely you will encounter good accommodations for reasonable rates—as at the **Detroit Motor Inn,** 13030 Lundy's Lane West (tel. 416/227-2567), five miles west of the falls at the city limits. The inn has 37 modern air-conditioned units with black-and-white TV, wall-to-wall carpeting, and full bath. There's an outdoor heated pool, miniature golf, barbecue facilities, and a licensed dining room and cocktail lounge.

Rates are seasonal: June 15 to September 7, $25 to $29, single, double, triple, or quad; otherwise, $18 to $22. To get there, drive out Lundy's Lane past the Beechwood Golf Course and open fields, and you'll see it on the right.

Also on Lundy's Lane in the heart of the motel strip stands the pleasant-looking white brick two-story units of the **Arkona Motel,** 8450 Lundy's Lane (tel. 416/356-8450), arranged around a courtyard with a pool and play area in the center. Rooms have wall-to-wall carpeting, color-coordinated drapes and spreads, white brick walls and plywood paneling, color TV (some have black and white), and air conditioning. None has a telephone.

Rates are seasonal, with rooms going for $22 single, $26 double, $32 for a family during July and August; $18 to $22 double in winter.

Another super-budget place is the **Surfside Inn,** 3665 Macklem St. (tel. 416/295-4354), where the 32 units have sliding glass doors, colonial-style furniture, and either royal-blue, powder-blue, or gold decor, telephones, and full bathrooms. Sixteen of the units have black-and-white TV.

Rates during the summer are: $29.50 single, $32.50 double, $6 for an extra person; in winter, $2 or $3 less. There's a public beach across the street in Kings Bridge Park. To get there, follow the Niagara Parkway south.

The **Americana,** 8444 Lundy's Lane (tel. 416/356-8444), is one of the nicer moderately priced motels on this motel strip, set in 25 acres of grounds with a pleasant tree-shaded area for picnicking right across from the office, and two tennis courts and an outdoor swimming pool to use. The 180 very large rooms are fully equipped with telephone, color TV, vanity sink, and full bathroom, and are decorated in aquamarine-plum or rust and gold combinations. A dining room, lounge, and coffeeshop are on the premises.

Rates are seasonal: June 28 to September 4: $34 single or double; two-room family suite, $70; suites from $38.50; September 5 to June 27: $26 to $28, single or double; a two-room family suite, $60; suites from $28.50. An additional person is $3.

Long and fine traditions of hospitality stretch back for **Michael's Inn,** 5599 River Rd. (tel. 416/354-2727), a four-story white building overlooking the Niagara River gorge. The 130 rooms are large, have all the modern conveniences, and are decorated in aquamarine/blue or gold/orange combinations. There's a solarium pool out back. The Open Hearth Dining Room is just that—the charcoal pit is enclosed behind glass so you can see all the cooking action.

Rates are seasonal: June 16 to September 15: one double bed, $43 to $55; two double beds, $43 to $58; three double beds, $60 to $70; bridal suite, $60; March 16 to June 15 and September 16 to October 31: one or two double beds,

$27 to $45; three double beds, $33 to $65; bridal suite, $56; November 1 to March 15: one or two double beds, $25 to $37; three double beds, $28 to $45; bridal suite, $38 to $48. A roll-away bed is $5; a crib, $3.

WHERE TO EAT: The Niagara Parkway Commission has commandeered the most spectacular scenic spots and there operate some reasonably priced dining outlets. **Table Rock Restaurant** (tel. 416/354-3631), only a few yards from the Canadian Horseshoe Falls, offers entrees from $2.85 to $6.25, all served with vegetable of the day and french fries. There's also the special feature: soup or juice, salad, roast beef and Yorkshire pudding, with vegetable and baked potato, for only $6.95. Breakfast is also a good bet here.

 Victoria Park Restaurant (tel. 416/356-2217), also within spitting distance of both the Canadian and American falls, offers not only a terrace with a green awning where you can sit and dine, but an inside dining room warmed by its burnt-orange tablecloths and globe lights, a downstairs cafeteria, plus a fast-food outlet pushing hot dogs and ice cream. Here, at least in the dining room and terrace, you'll find quite an elaborate menu with a whole range of appetizers (escargots bourguignonnes, smoked salmon, white asparagus tips vinaigrette) from $1 to $3.75, entrees that include steaks, deep-fried Canadian lake perch ($7.50), beef Stroganoff served with rice ($7.75), and the house specialty, rock Cornish game hen marinated in white wine and served with wild rice stuffing and Niagara sherry sauce ($9.25). The entree prices include choice of soup or juice, salad, fresh-baked rolls, and tea, coffee, or milk. Half-price portions are available for children. Open May 12 to June 22 and September 4 to October 8 from noon to 2:45 p.m. and 5:30 to 9:30 p.m.; June 23 to September 3 from noon to 10:30 p.m.

 Along the parkway toward Queenston lies the rather delightful **Whirlpool Golf Club Dining Room** (tel. 416/356-1159), at the commission's 18-hole golf course. It has a fine view of the first tee, the 18th green, and the 6945-yard championship course, and serves a hearty breakfast and eminently reasonable lunch as well as dinner. Open all year.

 The last star of the commission's eateries stands dramatically atop **Queenston Heights** (tel. 416/262-4266), and that's its name. Set in the park among fir, cypress, silver birch, and maple, the open-air balcony affords a magnificent view of the lower Niagara River and the rich fruitland through which it flows. Or you can sit inside under the cathedral ceiling with its heavy crossbeams where the flue of the stone fireplace reaches to the roof. At lunchtime, light entrees like steak-and-kidney pie, quiche Lorraine, and open-face roast beef sandwich (from $3.95 to $6.75) are offered. At dinner, specials include filet of Arctic char, roast quail with wild rice stuffing, sauteed rabbit (all $9.75), plus a selection of fish and seafood, roasts, and broiled and grilled dishes. Open noon to 2:30 p.m. and 5 to 9 p.m. Monday to Friday, noon to 10 p.m. on Saturday, and noon to 9 p.m. on Sunday from May 14 to September 23.

Dining with a View

 Besides the view from atop the 520-foot tower, the **Skylon Tower Restaurant** (tel. 356-2651, ext. 271) specializes in continental cuisine: chicken Cordon Bleu or Arctic char Grenobloise (both $9.25), for example, plus various steak dishes. At night, if you go at 5:30 p.m. you can dine for a minimum of $6 instead of the regular minimum of $9.15 that applies later. Similar fare is offered at lunchtime for around $5. In addition to your food bill, you will have to pay an entrance fee at the base of the tower of $2 for adults, $1 for children and seniors. Open daily for lunch from 11:30 a.m. to 2:30 p.m. and from 5 to 8:30 p.m. for dinner.

International Fare

If any of you have been to Britain and tasted *real* fish and chips, then head for a local favorite, **Betty's Restaurant & Tavern,** 8911 Sodom Rd. (tel. 416/295-4436), for here you'll find fish and chips ($3) such that I haven't tasted since I left merrie old England. It's a plain and simple family dining room with arborite dining tables with souvenir paper placemats. The art and generosity surface in the food—massive platters of scallops and chips, breaded pork chops, fried chicken (from $3.75 to $4.50), all including soup or juice, vegetable, and potato. If you can, save room for dessert for the pies are home-baked and the portions are enormous. Certainly it's a marvel that Arthur Treacher survives.

Open 7 a.m. to 10 p.m. Monday to Saturday, and 9 a.m. to 10 p.m. on Sunday. Breakfast and lunch also offer superb low, low-budget eating.

Restaurateur Frank Kovalec, who comes from Budapest, has gone to great lengths to create a really authentic Hungarian atmosphere at his **Hungarian Tavern and Restaurant,** 5329 Ferry St. (tel. 416/356-2429), even to the extent of importing a gypsy musical trio from Budapest who play violin, double bass, and cimbalom. The front is designed to resemble a village inn with an outside courtyard garden with pleasant grape arbors and intimate nooks, while off to the left there's a room that resembles a roadside inn with hand-woven placemats and tokaj (rustic paintings on canvas, all with a wine and grape theme). At the back awaits the more formal Franz Liszt Room, studded with a few prime Hungarian tapestries and a cimbalom in the center. Here, to the stirring sounds of gypsy music or Liszt melodies, you can sample Hungarian specialties ranging from $6.25 to $8: chicken paprikas, veal goulash, cabbage rolls "Kolozavar style" (served with pork chop and potatoes), gypsy steak, or the Transylvanian wooden platter (beef tenderloin, pork chop, veal cutlet, cabbage roll, and sausage, piled high on a bed of rice and served with french fries and sweet-and-sour cabbage, $18 for two). For dessert, palacsinta ($2) or Viennese pastries, of course. Continental dishes are also available.

Open Tuesday to Friday from 4 p.m. to 1 a.m., Saturday from noon to 1 a.m., and Sunday from noon to midnight. Closed Monday. Super-popular, so reservations are a must on weekends.

Real gemütlichkeit greets you at the chalet-style restaurant the **Happy Wanderer,** 6405 Stanley Ave. (tel. 416/354-9825), where you can lay your knapsack down and tuck into a host of schnitzels, wursts, and other German specialties. Transport yourself back to the Black Forest among the beer steins and the pheasant, duck, and other game trophies on the walls in one of several rooms, including the Black Forest Room, with a huge, intricately carved sideboard and cuckoo clock, and the Jage Stube, with solid wood benches and woven tablecloths. At lunch there are omelets from $3.65 and cold platters, and sandwiches from $1.65 for a hamburger to $4 for a deluxe Schwarzwaldschinken sandwich. Dinner might start with goulash soup ($1.75), proceed with bratwurst, knackwurst, or rauchwurst (all $5.95), served with sauerkraut and potato salad, or a schnitzel—wiener, Holstein, jaeger ($8.95 to $9.75). All entrees include potatoes, salad, and rye bread. Desserts include, naturally, Black Forest cake and apple strudel (under $2).

Open 8 a.m. to 11 p.m. daily. No reservations.

For truly fine dining amid opulent surroundings one goes to **Casa d'Oro,** 5875 Victoria Ave. (tel. 416/356-5646), to savor Italian delights amid an overwhelming array of gilt busts of Caesar, Venetian-style lamps, statues of Roman gladiators, Roman columns, and murals of Roman and Venetian scenes. Taste the splendors of clams casino ($4.75 for six) or the brodetto Antonio (a giant crouton topped with poached eggs and floated on savory broth garnished with parsley and accompanied by grated cheese). Follow with specialties like saltimboca alla Romana ($9.95), pollo cacciatore ($7.95), or sole basilica (flavored with lime juice, paprika, and basil, $10.25). Then, if you can bear it, choose from the dessert wagon or really spoil yourself with cherries jubilee or bananas flambé ($5.95) and an espresso (75¢). At lunchtime there's a shorter menu offering Canadian and Italian dishes under $5.

Open Monday to Saturday from noon to 1 a.m., Sunday to 10 p.m.

At the back of the Casa d'Oro, stroll over the bridge of sighs and onto the disco floor of the **Rialto Room,** where you can dance from 9 p.m. to the wee hours. Drinks average $2.50.

TOURIST INFORMATION: Visit or write the **Niagara Resort and Tourist Association,** 5433 Victoria Ave., Niagara Falls, ON L2G 3L1 (tel. 416/356-6061); the **Regional Niagara Tourist Council,** 227 Church St., St. Catharines, ON L2R 3E8 (tel. 416/685-1571); or the **Niagara Parks Commission,** Queen Victoria Park, P.O. Box 150, Niagara Falls, ON L2E 6T2 (tel. 416/356-2241).

Summer information centers are open at Table Rock House, Victoria Park Restaurant, the School of Horticulture, and the Princess Elizabeth Building.

WHAT TO SEE AND DO: Ever since the falls were first seen by Fr. Louis Hennepin, a Jesuit priest, in December 1678, people have come to see the seventh natural wonder of the world. More than 12 million visit annually. Many are honeymooners, although how the trend got started no one quite knows—legend has it that Napoleon's brother started it when he came on his honeymoon, having traveled all the way from New Orleans by stagecoach.

Viewing the Falls

Still, whoever started it all, people do come to see the falls and that can be done from many vantage points above, below, and in the middle when you take a trip on the **Maid of the Mist** 5920 River Rd. (tel. 416/358-5781), which takes you practically into the maelstrom through the turbulent waters around the American Falls, past the Rock of Ages, to the foot of the Horseshoe Falls where the 34.5 million imperial gallons fall per minute over the 176-foot-high cataract. Your nose will probably drip, your sunglasses mist, but that will not detract from the thrill of the experience.

Boats leave from the dock on the Parkway just down from the Rainbow Bridge.

Trips begin in mid-May and operate as follows: mid-May to June, 10 a.m. to 5 p.m. on weekdays, 10 a.m. to 6 p.m. on weekends; July to Labour Day, 9:15 a.m. to 8 p.m. daily; Labour Day through mid-October, 10 a.m. to 5 p.m. on weekdays, 10 a.m. to 6 p.m. on weekends.

Rates: adults, $3.75; children 6 to 12, $2.25; children 5 and under, free.

Take yourself down under the falls by going into the elevator at Table Rock House which drops you 150 feet down through solid rock to the **Table Rock Scenic Tunnels** and viewing portals. Do put on the black oilskin mackintosh. Open all year. Admission: adults, $2.25; children 6 to 12, 75¢; children under 6, 25¢.

To view the falls from above most spectacularly, take a 12-minute or half-hour spin in a chopper over the whole Niagara area. Helicopters leave from the **Whirl-a-Port,** adjacent to the Whirlpool at the junction of Victoria Ave. and Niagara Parkway, from 8 a.m. to dusk during summer and from 9 a.m. to 5 p.m. (weather permitting) during winter. Admission: 12-minute trip, $17.50 per person, $22.50 for two; 30-minute trip, $45 for two. Contact Niagara Helicopters, Ltd., 3731 Victoria Ave. (tel. 416/354-2751).

Or else you can ride up in the external glass-fronted elevators 520 feet to the top of the Skylon Tower observation deck at 5200 Robinson St. (tel. 416/356-2651). At the base of the tower there are 30 boutiques and stores to browse in, and an indoor amusement park with a ferris wheel, several carousels, and appropriate vending outlets. The Observation Deck is open from 9 a.m. to midnight daily; 8:30 a.m. to 1 a.m. June through Labour Day. The basement amusement park is open daily from noon to 6 p.m. July through Labour Day; weekends only at other times.

Admission: adults, $2.75; seniors and children under 18, $1.25; children under 5, free. A special family entertainment plan for $8.95 buys up to five tickets to Skylon, four tickets to the amusement park, and discounts in the shops.

A similar perspective can be gained from the top of the 325-foot **Panasonic Centre and Marine Aquarium,** 6732 Oakes Dr. (tel. 416/356-1501). On-site attractions include the Burning Springs Wax Museum and the Waltzing Waters. Open May through September, daily from 9 a.m. to midnight; October through April, daily from 10 a.m. to 6 p.m. Closed Christmas Day and New Year's Day. Admission: adults, $3; students, $2.

The Falls by Night

Jean Francois Gravelet (or Blondin, as he was known), the famed tight-rope walker, is believed to have inspired the first effort to light the falls in 1859 when he walked across the river on his rope at night, setting off fireworks that illuminated the gorge. Various installations have been run since then.

Today, don't miss the stunning vision of the falls lit by 22 Xenon gas spotlights (each producing 250 million candlepower of light), in shades of rose pink, red magenta, amber, blue, and green. You can see it any night of the year as follows: November to February, 7 to 9:30 p.m.; in March, 7 to 10 p.m.; in April, 7:30 to 10:30 p.m., in May, 9 p.m. to midnight; in June, 9:15 p.m. to midnight; in July, 9:15 p.m. to 12:30 a.m.; in August, 9 p.m. to 12:30 a.m.; September 1 to Labour Day, 8 p.m. to 12:30 a.m.; in September and October, 8 to 11 p.m.

Attractions Along the Niagara Parkway

The Niagara Parkway—conceived in 1867 by a group of Americans which included Frederick Law Olmsted, designer of New York City's Central Park, who had become outraged at the peddlers, hawkers, and barkers of freak sideshows that inhabited and preyed upon Niagara's tourists—provides a 35-mile stretch of parkland and gardens that are exquisitely kept and a delectable sight.

You can drive all the way to Niagara-on-the-Lake taking in the attractions en route. The first attraction you'll come to is the **Great Gorge Trip and Daredevil Exhibit,** 4330 River Rd. (tel. 356-0904), where you can learn about Niagara's daredevil history, who died and who survived, and examine several of the actual barrels used to ride over the falls. Then you can stroll along the scenic boardwalk beside the raging white waters of the Great Gorge Rapids and wonder how it must have felt to challenge this mighty torrent, where the river rushes through the narrow channel at an average speed of 30 m.p.h.

Half a mile farther north and you'll arrive at the **Spanish Aero Car,** a red-and-yellow cablecar contraption which will whisk you on a 3600-foot jaunt between two points in Canada, high above the whirlpool, providing excellent views of the surrounding landscape. Open from May 1 to the third Sunday in October: from 9 a.m. to 6 p.m. in May; until 8 p.m. in June; until 9 p.m. in July and August; from 10 a.m. to 7:30 p.m. in September; and 9 a.m. to 5 p.m. in October. Admission: adults, $2; children 6 to 12, 75¢; children under 6, 25¢.

From here you'll pass the **Whirlpool Golf Club,** an outstanding public course: greens fees: 18 holes for $9 (after 4 p.m., $7); 9 holes for $6; from October 1 to the second Sunday in November, $6 for 9 or 18 holes.

Next stop is the **School of Horticulture,** and a free view of the vast gardens there before going onto look at the Floral Clock, containing 25,000 plants in its 40-feet-in-diameter face.

From here you can drive to **Queenston Heights Park,** site of the battle of that name during the War of 1812 and of the 210-foot-high monument to General Isaac Brock who was killed in the battle. Picnic or play tennis ($3 an hour) in this shaded arbor before moving finally to the Georgian-style **McFarland House,** built in 1800 and home to John McFarland, "His Majesty's [George III] Boat Builder" (which ends our trip north along the parkway unless you want to continue to Niagara-on-the-Lake). Open 11 a.m. to 6 p.m. Saturday through Wednesday from June 30 to September 3; weekends only from September 4 through 29 and May 19 to June 29.

A trip south along the parkway will take you by the Table Rock complex to a stop at the **Park Greenhouse,** which is a year-round free attraction (open daily 9:30 a.m. to 4:30 p.m.).

Farther along, visit **Dufferin Islands,** where the children can swim, rent a paddleboat ($2.50 per half hour), and explore the surrounding woodland areas while adults visit mining magnate Sir Harry Oakes's **Oak Hall Mansion,** which he built in 1928 with 38 rooms, 17 bathrooms, and its own private swimming pool and billiard room. It holds an interesting collection of early Niagara paintings and prints. Open noon to 5 p.m. daily from June 30 to September 3, weekends only from September 4 to 29 and May 19 to June 29. Admission: adults, 75¢; children 12 and under, free. Or else you can play a round of golf on the illuminated nine-hole par-three course (adults: 18 holes, $3; 9 holes, $2.50; children: $2.50 and $2, respectively). Open the second Sunday in April to the last Sunday in October.

A little farther on you can stop for a picnic in **King's Bridge Park** and mess around on the beaches before driving on to **Fort Erie,** a reconstruction of the fort that was seized by the Americans in July 1814, besieged later by the British, and finally blown up as the Americans retreated across the river to Buffalo. You will be conducted through the museum and display rooms by guards in 1812–1814 period uniforms of the British Eighth Regiment. These guards also stand sentry duty, fire the cannons, and demonstrate drill and musket practice. Open the second Saturday in May to the second Monday in October from 9:30 a.m. to 6 p.m. daily. Admission: adults, $1.25; children 12 and under, 50¢.

Then if you feel like it, you can continue to one of Canada's largest amusement parks—**Crystal Beach,** Erie Rd., where you can lose your stomach on the roller coaster and your dignity on the Crown Mountain water slide. Open from the last Tuesday in June through Labour Day from 12:30 to 11 p.m. Tuesday to Saturday, on Sunday from 1:30 to 11 p.m.; during June, on Thursday from 11 a.m. to 6 p.m., on Friday to 11 p.m., and on Saturday from 12:30 to 11 p.m. Closed Mondays, Tuesdays, and Wednesdays in May and June. Closed Monday throughout the season.

Two Top Attractions

Maple Leaf Village, (tel. 416/357-3090), which opened in 1979, is a large, $18-million shopping, dining, entertainment complex modeled after San Francisco's Ghirardelli Square. Three floors of restaurants and unique old-world boutiques offering everything from British woolens to fine china and exotic furs are topped by the 350-foot Maple Leaf Tower, which offers a breathtaking view from its observation deck.

In the back of this complex is the prime attraction, a 1920s theme amusement park complete with English bobbies, Scott Joplin music, costumed sweepers, operators, and fare takers and featuring the largest ferris wheel in the world outside of Vienna (175 feet high), bumper cars, and 11 other exciting rides. A dramatic laser light show, two multimedia theaters (the Hollywood Experience and the Niagara Experience), and a puppet theater are just some of the additional entertainment found here. Admission to the village is free. Already a calendar of special events has been drawn up that includes fashion shows, winter festivals, and dazzling feats like Henri Rechatin walking from the Maple Leaf Village Tower to the top of the Maple Leaf Village Giant Wheel. Drop in and see what's happening on your visit. Ride coupons cost 30¢ each, and discount books at $5 and $10 are available.

As the village is an integral part of the Sheraton complex that includes the two Sheratons and the Sheraton Motor Inn, it stands between the Foxhead and the Brock on Falls Ave. In the future it will be physically linked to both.

Just across from the base of the Skylon Tower rises a pyramid-shaped building and beside it a totally renovated factory complex which are together known as **Pyramid Place** (tel. 416/357-4442). The pyramid houses the IMAX theater with its vast six-story-high screen that currently features the movie *To Fly,* a spectacular experience of the skies. Showtimes start at 12:30 p.m. and every 45 minutes thereafter until 8 p.m. Admission: adults, $2.50; children 12 to 18, $1.50; children under 12 and senior citizens, $1; under 6, free.

When you've seen the wonders of the big screen, hop into the factory complex to restaurants that run from the **Old Fish Market** and **Coasters Shellfish Bar** to a **Wine Garden** and the **Oasis,** a fast-food eating spot that has separate counters offering Chinese-food, submarines and Italian snacks, pizza, fish and chicken, and hamburgers—all at very reasonable prices in bright and imaginative surroundings. The complex also contains a multimedia presentation **Legend Niagara,** a **Good Times Room** with pinball machines and electronic games, and **Good Times Jamboree,** an animated musical show, plus many boutiques and gift shops.

Marineland and Game Farm

This is not to be missed on your trip to the falls. At the aquarium, enjoy dolphin aquabatics and a competition between four-ton male Kandu and three-ton female Ms. Nootka in their Annie Oakley–style killer whale contest, or tap along with a musical combo of madcap sea lions. During the summer these aquatic stars are joined on the Aqua Theatre Stage by tigers jumping through flaming hoops, bears on uni- or motorcycles, and dancing elephants.

In contrast, at the game farm you'll see wildlife living and roaming freely —lions, bears, Canadian elk, timber wolves, buffalo. There are four restaurants available or you can spread your picnic lunch on one of the many tables provided.

Open from June 15 to Labour Day from 9 a.m. to one hour before sunset; at other times, from 10 a.m. to one hour before sunset. Admission: October 15 to March 31: adults, $4.25; children under 12, $2. April 1 to June 16: adults, $4.75; children, $2.25. June 17 to September 10: adults, $6.25; children, $3.25. September 11 to October 15: adults, $5; children, $2.50. To get there, drive south on Stanley St. and follow the signs.

Other Attractions

Niagara Falls Museum, 1651 River Rd. (tel. 416/356-2151), has an interesting collection that includes the Daredevil Hall of Fame and houses exhibits ranging from Eskimo and Indian life to animal, bird, reptile, and mineralogical exhibits, as well as Egyptian mummies and Oriental curios. Open all year (except Christmas Day): May 20 through October 9 from 9 a.m. to midnight; the rest of the year, from 9 a.m. to 6 p.m. Admission: adults, $3; students 12 to 18, $2; children under 12, 75¢; under 6, free.

There's a whole slew of sideshows on Clifton Hill ranging from **Ripley's Believe it or Not, Castle Dracula, Houdini Museum, Movieland Wax Museum, Louis Tussaud's Wax Museum**—all of them charging about $3 for adults, $1.50 for children. On the whole block perhaps the most entertaining for children might be **Circus World,** 4848 Clifton Hill (tel. 416/356-5588), where you can be your own ringmaster. You can walk a tightrope, have your picture taken on a tiger or with your head in the mouth of a lion, test your strength, and find your way out of a mirror maze. The highlight for children, however, is being shot out of the Whizzo Cannon (which is really a slide plus sound and light effects). Open from 9 a.m. to 1 a.m. Admission: adults, $3; students, $1.25; children under 12, $1.25; under 5, free.

Camping

The Niagara Parks Commission operates a superb campsite at **Miller's Creek Park,** P.O. Box 150, Niagara Falls (tel. 416/871-6557 June to Labour Day, and 416/356-2241 off-season), that provides 54 sites, each with 2500 square feet of privacy and a fireplace. The park has running water, showers, a laundry, a trading post, ice, a playground, and a marina and launching ramp across the road. Electricity is available. Open weekends only from 1 p.m. Friday to noon Monday, May 18 to June 15; daily from June 16 to Labour Day. Fee: $5.50 per day; electricity, $1.50 per day. There are no water hookups.

There's also a **Niagara Falls KOA** at 8625 Lundy's Lane (tel. 416/354-6472), which has 300 sites (240 electric, 238 water, 58 sewage) plus a dumping station. Facilities include water, flush toilets, showers, fireplaces, store, ice, pool, sauna, and game room. Fees: $6 minimum for two; each additional person, 75¢. Open May 1 to November 1.

Cross-Country Skiing

Niagara Falls is a four-season resort with most of the attractions open all year. The falls ice formations and the ice bridge formed in winter is quite remarkable (you'll know how remarkable if you've ever seen a building in winter after the firemen have put out the fire). At the **Whirlpool Golf Course** you can ski cross country on the three trails: one for beginners, one for intermediates, and a five-miler for advanced skiers. Use of the ski trails is free, and you can rent equipment at $6 a day for adults, $4 a day for children 14 and under (after 1 p.m. the price goes down to $4 and $2, respectively). Five-day rental packages are available at $25 for adults, $15 for children. The clubhouse is open from 8 a.m. to 5 p.m. daily for food, shelter, and a welcome fire. Tobogganning also.

TOURS: One of the best ways to see the sights of Niagara is on an organized tour—either the Queen Victoria **Viewmobiles** or the **Niagara River Sightseeing Package Tour.** The Viewmobiles will take you around all the sights within Victoria Park, while the package tour includes all the sights described above from the Canadian Horseshoe Falls north to Queenston Heights. Viewmobiles charge $2 for adults, 75¢ for children under 12. The Package tour is available to individuals and families only on weekends from May 24 to the last Friday in June, and daily from the last Saturday in June to Labour Day (adults, $20; children 6 to 12, $11). The price includes admission to *Maid of the Mist* boat tour, Table Rock Scenic Tunnels, the Great Gorge Trip and the Daredevil Gallery, the Spanish Aero Car, and a meal at either the Whirlpool Golf Clubhouse or Queenston Heights Restaurant. It will take approximately six hours, the first half in a Viewmobile and the second half by double-decker bus. Either one of these tours can be purchased at Table Rock House, Victoria Park Restaurant, Princess Elizabeth Building at the foot of Clifton Hill, or at the Whirlpool Spanish Aero Car.

Winery Tours

Niagara is set in the fruit- and wine-producing area of the Niagara escarpment. The Niagara peninsula has over 25,000 acres of select vineyards cultivating some 45 varieties of wine grapes. There are six wineries in the region: Barnes, Château Gai, Inniskillin House, Andres, Brights, and Jordan. At **Brights,** the oldest winery in Canada, you can see champagne processed in the European method by fermenting the wine in the bottle, and at any of the wineries you can view the winemaking process from the moment the grapes enter the crush house to the fermentation, bottling, and packaging stages. And then comes the fun part—the wine tasting.

Probably the best time to visit is during vendange or harvest season, from the first week in September to the end of October. At Brights, free tours are offered Monday through Friday at scheduled times between 9:30 a.m. and 3:30 p.m. Call 416/357-2400, or write: Brights Wines, 4887 Dorchester Rd., Niagara Falls. For other winery tours, write to: Andres Wines, Kelson Rd., Winona, Grimsby (tel. 416/643-1203); or Jordan Wines, 120 Ridley St., St. Catharines (tel. 416/688-2140).

WINNIPEG, MANITOBA

TOUGH, STURDY, MUSCULAR—midwestern Canada's Chicago—that's Winnipeg, capital of Manitoba, with its solid cast-iron warehouses, stockyards, railroad depots, and grain elevators, symbols of its role as a distribution and supply center, first for furs and then for agricultural products. It's a toiling city where 650,000 inhabitants sizzle in summer and shovel in winter.

That's one side. The other is a city and populace that have produced a symphony orchestra which triumphed in New York, the first "Royal" ballet company in the British Commonwealth, and a theater and arts complex worthy of any national capital.

Many Winnipeggers have left their city, fanning east or west in search of fame—Marshall McLuhan, Margaret Laurence, Len Cariou, Neil Young, John Hirsch, and Monty Hall—but they still talk about going back to Portage and Main, the windiest corner on the North American continent, to the city that nurtured them. There's something about Winnipeg that inspires gut loyalty and pride. Perhaps it has something to do with size, the human scale and communal spirit, or to quote stage director John Hirsch: "You can still be a mensch in Winnipeg—it's very difficult to be a mensch in a lot of places in the world today." And, you know, he's right.

SOME HISTORY: Indians, herds of buffalo, a few trading posts and forts were all that Lord Selkirk's first group of 70 colonists found in 1812 when they arrived on the banks of the Red River. The going was tough, and even after the first formal government of the Red River Settlement, centered on Fort Garry, was formed in 1835, it was another 24 years before the first steamboat navigated the upper Red River and reached the inhabitants.

During these early years it was the 1869 Métis rebellion led by Louis Riel against the eastern government that threw the colony into prominence and brought the Redcoats under Lord Garnet Wolseley to the region.

By 1873 the population had grown to 1869 and Winnipeg was incorporated as a city. With the coming of the Canadian Pacific Railway in 1886, Winnipeg became the gateway to the west and the destination for a tide of European immigrants from the Ukraine, Iceland, Germany, Poland, and Eastern Europe. The rush for land was on and the city boomed. Speculation drove the cost of land to fantastic figures, and from 1904 to 1914 the population tripled, from 67,000 to 203,000. Those were colorful days when the streets thronged with farmers, prospectors, trappers, speculators, promoters, immigrants, and the like.

Of these halcyon years and those that followed in the 1920s oldtime residents recall the shunting CPR steam engines heard day and night, and cattle being driven through the streets on the way to the stockyards. Although the city has yielded its position as the world's most important grain center to Chicago, you can still see the Exchange and the stockyards that laid the foundations for the thriving industrial city that Winnipeg is today.

1. Orientation

A native Winnipegger who had come east once said to me, "I still can't get used to the confined and narrow streets in the east." When you see Portage and Main, each 132 feet wide, and the eerie flatness that means no matter where you go you can see where you're going, then you'll understand why.

Portage and Main is the focal point of the city, which is situated at the junction of the Red and Assiniboine Rivers. The Red River runs north-south, as does Main St.; the Assiniboine and Portage Ave. run east-west. Going north on Main from the Portage-Main junction will bring you to the City Hall, Warehouse Restoration Area, the Centennial Arts Centre (including the Manitoba Theatre Centre), the Museum of Man and Nature, the Ukrainian Museum, and on into the North End, once a mosaic of cultures, and still dotted with bulbous church domes and authentic delis visited by lost souls from Edmonton and west. (*Warning:* At night you are advised to stay away from Main St. north beyond the Arts Centre, unless you enjoy fleabag hotels and skid row.)

From Portage and Main, if you go six blocks west along Portage, the main shopping drag, and two blocks south, you'll hit the brand-new Convention Centre. From here, one block south and two blocks west brings you to the Legislative Building, the Art Gallery, and south, just across the river, Osborne Village.

GETTING IN AND OUT OF WINNIPEG: Winnipeg International Airport is only about 20 minutes west-northwest from the city center. If there are three or more of you and you take a **taxi** downtown, you'll pay the same $2.50 per person that you would if you took the **airport limousine** that runs from 9:15 a.m. to 12:55 a.m. Cheapest of all is the city bus (40¢), which runs approximately every 15 minutes during the day, every 22 minutes in the evenings to Portage and Garry.

The following **airlines** have regular flights to and from Winnipeg: Air Canada, Lombard Pl. (tel. 943-9361); CP Air, 1610 Portage Ave. (tel. 957-1060); Northwest Airlines, 419 Portage Ave. (tel. 475-2730); Pacific Western, at the airport (tel. 632-1250); and Nordair, also at the airport (tel. 632-6625).

VIA Rail Canada's depot is at Main St. and Broadway. For information on CN train arrivals and departures, call 944-8785; for CP info, call 944-8780.

Greyhound Bus Lines and the bus depot are at 487 Portage Ave. (tel. 775-8301).

If you're **driving**, just to give you some idea of distance it's 432 miles from Minneapolis, 146 miles from Grand Forks, N.D.

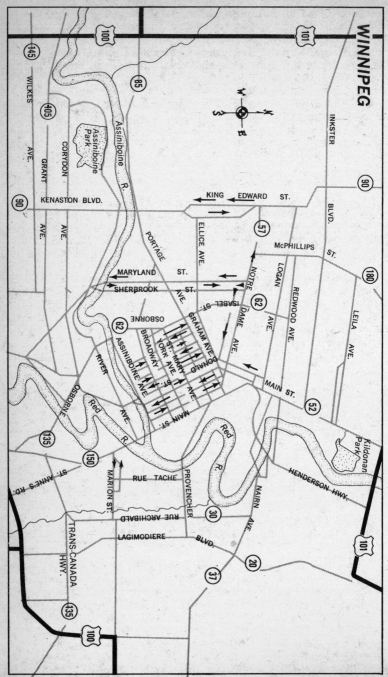

GETTING AROUND: The extensive Winnipeg Transit system makes it easy and cheap. Monday to Friday from 9 a.m. to 4 p.m. a 10¢ **DASH shuttle** operates, each bus traveling a continuous route enabling you to stop and visit all the attractions. For a DASH route pamphlet, call **City of Winnipeg Transit,** 421 Osborne St. (tel. 284-7190), or else look for the DASH bus stop signs.

For regular buses, you need 40¢ in exact change (15¢ for children, 10¢ for seniors) to board. Call the above number for route and schedule information.

Racetrack service out to Assiniboine Downs costs $1 each way, and runs from City Hall, stopping at express stops only out to Polo Park Shopping Mall.

Taxis can most easily be found at the downtown hotels. As usual, they're an expensive form of transportation: $1.25 when the meter drops and 10¢ every one-seventh mile thereafter. Herewith a few sample numbers: **Duffy's Taxi,** 772-2451 or 775-0101, **Moore's Unicity Taxi,** 947-6611 or 942-3366; **Yellow Cab,** 947-6611 or 942-7555.

Driving is no problem in Winnipeg, but do watch out for the pedestrian walks marked with an X, and note that Manitoba has a stringent drunken driving law. A blood-alcohol level of 0.08 or higher means a conviction—don't take chances.

For car rentals, **Tilden** is located downtown at 283 Ellice at Smith St. (tel. 942-3525) and also has an office at the airport (tel. 772-2854). **Budget** has three offices: downtown at the corner of Ellice and Edmonton (tel. 947-1551), at the airport (tel. 772-9109), and at Polo Park (tel. 772-0475). **Avis** has offices at the airport and at 350 St. Mary's Ave. in the Holiday Inn (tel. 775-8911).

TOURIST INFORMATION: The following will load you down with information: the **Legislative Building Tourist Reception Center** (tel. 946-7131), open 8:30 a.m. to 4 p.m. Monday to Friday in winter, to 9 p.m. daily from the third Monday in May to Labour Day; the **Convention and Visitors Bureau** on the second floor of the Convention Centre (tel. 943-1970), and the **Mayor's Office,** City Hall (tel. 946-0196), both open from 9 a.m. to 5 p.m. weekdays; the **Department of Tourism,** 304-200 Vaughan St. (tel. 944-3777), open 8:30 a.m. to 4:30 p.m. Monday to Friday.

For **parks information,** call 885-1500; and for taped instant tourist info, call 942-2535.

USEFUL INFORMATION: For a city its size, Winnipeg is lucky to have two **newspapers,** the Winnipeg *Tribune* and the Winnipeg *Free Press,* 14 foreign-language weeklies, plus eight community newspapers. Get the idea that Winnipeggers enjoy politics? . . . **Liquor** can only be bought from the Manitoba Liquor Control Commission stores. Main downtown locations are: 325 Ellice Ave., 755 Portage Ave., 471 River at Osborne, 1020 Main St., The Bay, and 515 Main St. On Sundays drinks may only be served with food, and the tab for drinks must not exceed the tab for food—otherwise forget it. . . . For **medical assistance,** dial 911 or call Winnipeg General Hospital (tel. 774-6511). . . . The main **post office** is at 266 Graham Ave. and is open from 7 a.m. to 6 p.m. Monday to Friday. The general delivery window is open 8 a.m. to noon on Saturday (tel. 985-5481). . . . Winnipeg is on **Central Standard Time** except from April 26 to October 30 when the city is on daylight saving. . . . **For weather information,** dial 786-4125.

2. Winnipeg's Hotels

As has been pointed out, many hotels have been established in the past primarily to serve liquor, not to provide hospitality. As far as possible I have avoided such places, but it's still true that every hotel, first class or no, will have a large beverage room attached, which will be purely functional, somewhat loud, and often too boisterous for the average traveler.

Note: To all the rates that follow, add the 5% hotel tax.

FIRST CLASS CHOICES: When Delta remodeled the **Marlborough Inn,** 331 Smith St. (tel. 204/942-6411), originally built in 1914, they retained the vaulted ceilings, beams, stained-glass windows, and Victorian Gothic exterior of that elegant era and simply added modern amenities. In the 144 air-conditioned rooms you'll find campaign-style furniture, plush chocolate-brown or beige carpeting, Touch-Tone phones, color TV, and huge closets.

Off the gracious lobby with its antique wall clock and antique sideboards you'll find the most beautiful dining room in the city, Churchill's, a two-story-high room with Gothic arches, stained-glass windows, oak paneling, brass chandeliers, wingback chairs, and loveseats for gracious and romantic dining (a classical guitarist plays nightly on the balcony). Here, you might begin your meal with prawns Armagnac ($4.75) or bouillabaisse ($3.25), and follow with steak Diane ($13.20) or else enjoy the four-course table d'hôte selections like chicken breast Wilhelm (stuffed with a blend of apples, almonds, fine herbs, and spices, $9). What was originally the bar has been turned into Flanders Cafe, a coffeeshop which consequently features a solid oak hammerbeam ceiling, a row of iron lamps, and a distinctive clock. Down the marble stairway lies Colonel Webb's lounge where you can sink into a sofa, listen to the piano, and enjoy some free hors d'oeuvres in an atmosphere created by exposed brick walls, oak fireplace, and heavy beamed ceiling. And finally, for boogying, there's the Iron Duke cabaret which features live entertainment Monday to Saturday from 8 p.m. to 1:30 a.m.

Rates: $33 to $39 single, $39 to $46 double; suites from $85. An extra person is $5; children under 18 in their parents' room stay for free. A weekend package is $30 double, per night.

Right at the corner of Portage and Main rises the 21-story white concrete **Winnipeg Inn,** at 2 Lombard Place (tel. 204/957-1350), a few minutes' walk from the Centennial Arts Centre. It's a modern Western International hotel which was built in 1970, offering 350 rooms furnished with white colonial-style pieces and the usual modern appointments. The Velvet Glove dining room is one of the top restaurants in the city and offers truly luxurious dining in a plush atmosphere of gilt-framed portraits, wood paneling, brass torchères, semicircular booths, and the soothing sounds of a harpist. Start your dinner extravagantly with caviar Beluga Molossol ($15) or less extravagantly with the pâté maison ($3.25), and continue with the Manitoba delicacy, Winnipeg goldeye ($8.95), breast of pheasant stuffed with lobster and served with a champagne sauce, or any of the other gourmet dishes. Chocolate cherries, served with your coffee, are just part of the impeccable service, and if you desire that over–$100 bottle of wine, it's available. Table d'hôte dinners start at $9.95.

For postdinner dancing, stop in at the Stage Door, with live entertainment from 5 to 10:30 p.m. and disco from 10:30 p.m. to 1 a.m. among wall-to-wall black-and-white caricatures of Marilyn Monroe, W. C. Fields, Gloria Swanson et al. There's a one-drink minimum and you can dine if you like. Drinks are half price from 5 to 8 p.m. For a top-notch nighttime view of Winnipeg, have a drink at the Top of the Inn piano bar. There's an indoor pool on the 21st floor, and a sauna too. Downstairs in the shopping concourse you'll find the Cafe Lombard coffeeshop open from 6:30 to 10 p.m. daily, where you can get a good buffet dinner ($12.95 for two).

Rates: $51 to $57 single, $62 to $68 double; suites from $115. An extra person is $10. A weekend package is available at $35 per night, single or double. For reservations, call toll free 800/268-8383 in Canada, 800/228-3000 in the U.S.

Two blocks west along Portage stands the rather severe-looking gray concrete **North Star Inn,** Portage Ave. at Smith St. (tel. 204/956-0410). Somewhat unusually designed, the first nine floors provide parking so that when you enter the street-level lobby you take an elevator to the 12th floor reception area. On floors 15 through 29 you'll find 272 rooms, all brightly decorated in browns and orange, with color TV, air conditioning, telephone, and pine furniture.

All the dining outlets have good views over the city. These include the candlelit, oak-paneled Selkirk Room, for dining and dancing from 6 p.m. to 1 a.m.; the sunny Garden Cafe, with its wicker chairs and planters; and the Step 33 lounge that offers piano entertainment from Monday to Saturday from 5 to 7 p.m. and 9 p.m. to 1 a.m. There's a lovely indoor pool area on the 13th floor.

Rates: $42 to $46 single, $54 to $58 double. The weekend package ($29.50 per night, double occupancy) includes $1 off on tickets to the adjacent movie theater. For reservations, call toll free 800/323-8811 in the U.S. (in Illinois, 800/942-8880).

Right downtown and connected by skywalk to the Convention Centre, you'll find the **Holiday Inn,** 350 St. Mary's Ave. (tel. 204/942-0551), with 410 rooms spread over 17 floors. The rooms are decorated in warm red or burnt orange, and besides the usual accoutrements offer remote control for the TV. There's a skylit indoor as well as an outdoor pool, and both have been super-attractively designed with potted plants, terraces, even a little putting area. There are 26 smashingly located poolside rooms that are a couple of dollars more than standard rooms.

Dining facilities include the Oriental-style Tea House coffeeshop, open 7 a.m. to 11 p.m. daily, the Park Lane Dining Room, serving a $3.95 lunch buffet, the Park Lane lounge, and Uncle's, one of the more popular nightlife spots in town (drinks average $2.30) which may have gone disco by the time you arrive ($1.50 cover charge on Friday and Saturday).

Rates: $46 to $48 single, $51 to $57 double. Weekend packages offer a 25% discount. This is the only hotel in the city that offers a hostess desk where you can pick up all kinds of useful information and have your special needs catered to.

One can imagine the people streaming from the nearby railroad station—men in their wing collar suits and women in ankle-length dresses—to the **Hotel Fort Garry,** 222 Broadway (tel. 204/942-8251), now a landmark from another era. Built between 1911 and 1913 and named after one of the first Hudson's Bay posts, it is a strikingly handsome French-château-style building with bay windows and a copper-covered peaked roof. Inside, the magnificent chandeliered lobby has a wide marble staircase with gleaming brass railing and cast-iron work leading to a gold-ceilinged mezzanine dotted with rich red couches. Not quite as central as it might be (it's six blocks from the Convention Centre), it offers 265 very large air-conditioned rooms that have old-fashioned heavy oak doors with moldings opening onto elegantly furnished rooms with green pile carpets, floor-to-ceiling heavy green drapes, either red or mauve bedspreads, a comfortable couch and armchairs, extra-large bathroom, and the usual color TV and phone.

Its public areas include a super-elegant circular lounge bar with a billowing tent canopy, the Country Kettle (open from 7 a.m. to 8:30 p.m.) coffeeshop that uses attractive willow-pattern china, and the Left Bank, that sports an octagonal dance floor and live entertainment (drinks average $2.25). The Factors Table restaurant is legendary not only for its food and rustic atmosphere of stone and beams with a moose keeping an eye on everything, but also for its maître d', who is very quick on the draw with his cigarette lighter (and once mistakenly lit a bread stick). Your meal might begin with curried snails Madras ($3.95) followed by the specialty of the house, a baked darne of salmon coulibiac (baked in a puff pastry with wild rice, fresh mushrooms, green onions, egg, and a lemon-butter sauce). For dessert don't miss the crêpes Suzette ($6.50).

Rates: $35 to $45 single, $44 to $54 double. A weekend package is offered at $28 per night, single or double. For reservations, call toll free 800/327-3384 in the U.S., 800/268-8136 in Canada.

A New Hotel near the Racetrack

Five minutes from the Assiniboia Downs Racetrack, and a 15-minute drive from the airport, the spanking new **Wandlyn Birchwood Inn**, 2520 Portage Ave. (tel. 204/885-4478), offers 160 superb double-double rooms plus 37 large suites, all with air conditioning, color TV, clock radio, vanity mirror, and pamper panel, and furnished in Danish-modern style. Each has a rather lovely nature mural. The deluxe one-bedroom suites have a fully equipped kitchen and rent for only $65.

Facilities include the brass-railed SOS, a piano bar where you can relax on comfy sofas and be entertained, the Château dining room, and the Orangerie coffeeshop. The stunning tropical atrium contains an indoor pool, sauna, exercise room, shuffleboard area, and deck for that poolside drink. Note the tropical fish that add a dash of color to the elevators.

Rates: $40 to $43 single, $46 to $50 double. Children under 18 stay in their parents' room free. The weekend package is $30 a night, double occupancy. A racing package that includes admission to the track is also available for $36. The higher rates are for eighth-floor rooms that are beautifully decorated in pale blue with Delft lamps and have the added convenience of a refrigerator. The suites start at $80. For reservations, call toll free 800/561-0000.

Winnipeg's Best Value

Right in the heart of downtown Winnipeg there's a bargain that shouldn't be passed up. At the **Place Louis Riel Apartment Hotel**, 190 Smith St. at St. Mary (tel. 204/947-6961), you can stay in a studio or a one- or two-bedroom beautifully furnished suite with fully equipped kitchen and dining area, color TV, phone, air conditioning, security intercom, and weekly maid service (daily maid service available for $3.50 a day). The doors are brightly painted in swathes of orange, beige, and gray, and the interiors are all exquisitely furnished in earth tones and pine furniture in the bedroom, and stylish couches and armchairs in the living room. For convenience there's a laundromat, grocery store, beauty salon, coffeeshop, swimming pool, and sauna located on the ground floor of the 18-floor building.

Rates: bachelor suites (with a sleeping/living area partitioned from the kitchen), $27.50 single, $33 double; one-bedroom suite, $33 single, $38.50 double; two-bedroom suite, $45 double. Each additional person is $5. No charge for children under 16 sharing with parents. Monthly rates are available, and a weekend package is offered at $21 per night, single or double.

MODERATELY PRICED ACCOMMODATIONS: Right downtown, the **Charterhouse,** at York and Hargrave Sts. (tel. 204/942-0101), opened its doors in 1962 but has since been extensively remodeled and now offers 90 rooms spread over four floors. Standard rooms come with all the modern accoutrements and may well be furnished in brilliant-red carpet and drapes, psychedelic bedspread, and red floral wallpaper in the bathroom. Some 45 of the rooms have balconies.

The Rib Room is well known locally for really good steaks, roasts, and live lobster. Dinner might begin with snails flavored with Pernod ($3.75) and continue with rack of lamb ($12) or duckling Robert ($10.50) served in a copper dish with vegetables. Reasonable table d'hôte meals are also available in this warm, wood-paneled room with its large copper-flued fireplace and otherwise simple table settings. The coffeeshop is open from 7 a.m. to midnight.

Rates: $33 single, $40 double; an extra person is $4. A family rate is offered at $27, with children under 16 free in their parents' room. For cooling off there's an outdoor swimming pool with water chute, and a deck/patio for relaxing.

In the lobby of the **St. Regis,** 285 Smith St. (tel. 204/942-0171), you'll find a rack holding a large selection of local Manitoba papers and you'll probably find a few farmers and local businessmen from Winnipeg's surrounding area chatting and reading. It's a simple, friendly family place with 107 rooms on three floors. Rooms are neatly furnished with red carpets and curtains, stick-style furniture, and contain air conditioning, phone, and color TV. The Front Page, as the name suggests, offers not only good honest food but some of the best reading in town—a collection of daily and weekly newspapers from Canada, the U.S., and Europe. Front-page reports of major disasters seem to rate high as attractions—the Halifax explosions, the Winnipeg flood, the sinking of the *Titanic,* the assassination of President Lincoln.

On the menu, look for the specials: coq au vin ($6.95), barbecued ribs ($7.25), or the Winnipeg goldeye ($6.75)—and note the salad bar. There's also a good selection of reasonably priced lunch dishes. For a country and western flavor there's the Outside Inn pub; other facilities include a coffeeshop.

Rates: $27 to $29 single, $32 to $34 double. An extra adult is $4, and children under 18 are free when sharing their parents' room. The St. Regis is a Flag Inn and so you can call toll free for reservations: 800/426-7774 in the U.S., 800/663-9191 in Canada. Weekend discount, 20%; senior citizens discount, 10%.

The **Sheraton Carlton,** 220 Carlton St. (tel. 204/942-0881), has an excellent location, right across from the Convention Centre, but lacks the elegance one usually expects at Sheraton. Opened in 1961, it has 107 rooms each brightly decorated with chrome furniture, Formica-top tables, and the usual phone, color TV, and air conditioning. It does have an interesting restaurant, however, the Beachcomber, for dining under the Polynesian stars sheltered by palm trees while seated on fan-style chairs; taste the succulent treats that come out of the steak pit: steaks from $6.95, or else Polynesian specialties such as drums of heaven (chicken dipped in batter, fried golden brown, and served with sesame seeds and sweet-and-sour sauce, $4.50) or Hawaiian barbecued baby rib ($7.75). Complete dinners that include appetizers, and entrees start at $5.95 per person. Why not try the seaweed soup? At lunchtime, similar Polynesian dishes are all under $3.50.

Rates: $30 single, $35 to $45 double. The weekend package is $25 per night, single or double.

Away from the Center

The **Viscount Gort,** 1670 Portage Ave. (tel. 204/775-0451), offers 85 very nice rooms on six floors. Rooms on floors two through four have balconies; the top-floor rooms do not, and so they are a little larger. The top two floors have a burnt-orange/brown decor with modern pine furniture, while the other rooms are decked out in dark colonial-style furniture, and some have full-length mirrors on stands—an unusual touch. There's a sauna on the fourth floor. Westside rooms overlook the highway, so try to get a quieter eastside room. Situated off the tile-floored lobby with its little fountain awaits the lounge, It's a Gas, where comedian Pat Riordan entertains, along with Laurel and Hardy in black-and-white blow-ups. At Teddy's dining room you can sample a smorgasbord Sunday dinner from 5 to 8 p.m. for $4.95, but you'll have to make a reservation because it's always jam-packed. At other times there are good sandwiches and burgers (all under $5).

Rates: $28 single, $32 double. An extra person is $2; cots, $3. Children under 18 stay free in their parents' room. The Viscount is out on Portage near the airport, the Polo Park Shopping Centre, and the racetrack.

The **Ramada Inn,** 1824 Pembina Hwy. (tel. 204/269-7700), occupies a U-shaped complex and offers a variety of rooms—huge double doubles that can accommodate eight, poolside rooms that overlook the extremely well-appointed Reef Room with its palm trees and wrought-iron furniture, and a cabana bar, whirlpool, sauna, and sunlamps. All of the rooms are decorated in orange shades and contain color TV, phone, and air conditioning. Facilities include a coffeeshop (open from 7:30 a.m. to 11:30 p.m.), lounge with dancing and nightly live entertainment, and dining room that serves a 16-salad (plus three hot dishes) smorgasbord at lunch for only $4.45 and becomes a cozy dining room at night with a solo guitarist on Thursday through Saturday.

Rates: $34 to $38 single, $38 to $42 double. An extra person or a cot is $6. The weekend package, available only from January 1 to May 15 and September 22 to December 30, is $25 per night, single or double.

TraveLodge Niakwa is located off on its own St. Anne's Rd. at Hwy. 1 East (tel. 204/253-1301) near the new Canada Mint. Set well back from the highway, the large rooms have all the expected conveniences and are pleasantly decorated in browns and earth tones with good modern furniture. There's a very nice solarium pool area that has a spiral staircase leading to poolside rooms, sauna, and exercise room. Off the small, cozy lobby with its leatherette couches there's a cocktail lounge and dining room (for steaks, veal, and chicken from $6.75), as well as a large German-style beverage room where a Bavarian band plays oompah music six nights a week. Shots are $1.25.

Rates: $29 to $33 single, $35 to $40 double; an extra person is $4. Weekend packages are $58 for two nights, double occupancy. Oh yes, and you can swing your arm at the automatic 12-lane bowling alley.

BUDGET HOTELS: Probably the best budget downtown hotel is the **Gordon Downtowner,** 330 Kennedy St. (tel. 204/943-5581). Don't be put off by the somewhat faded neighborhood and the very plain exterior. Inside there are 40 rooms where the wall fabric on one wall matches the curtains, and dark Spanish-style furniture combines with louvered closets and a couch. Added touches in the bathroom include a phone, clothesline, and sliding panels on the shower-bath. Amenities include the comfortable coffeeshop-dining room (open from 7 a.m. to 9 p.m.) where you can get bacon, eggs, toast, and coffee for $1.29.

For such accommodations rates are incredibly low: $24 to $26 single, $28 to $30 for bed-sitting double; for a two-room suite, $28 single, $32 double. An extra person is $3.

Just around the corner stands the **City Centre Hotel,** Carlton at Ellice (tel. 204/956-0100), a seven-floor squarish white building with black trim. Each of the rooms has good modern furniture, color-coordinated carpets, spreads, and curtains (usually red), and extra-large bathrooms and louvered closets. Some of the rooms have a couch that opens into a bed. For dining and entertainment there's a lounge (with piano entertainment from 5 to 7 p.m. and 9 p.m. to 1 a.m.), a dining room that serves steak, seafood, and chicken dishes, and a $3.95 buffet lunch, and a down-home disco and coffeeshop.

Rates: $31 single, $36 studio single, $36 double, $44 studio double. The weekend package at $59.95 per person, double occupancy, is for two nights. No charge for children under 12 occupying the same room as their parents.

Along Pembina Hwy.

Along the Pembina Hwy. there's a wealth of motels, many of them offering budget accommodations. The **Montcalm Gordon Motor Hotel,** 2280 Pembina Hwy. (tel. 204/269-1406), built 17 years ago, was recently renovated and has 21 very nice rooms with modern conveniences (color TV, phone, air conditioning), colonial-style furniture, and color-coordinated decor. There's a lounge, coffeeshop, and beverage room with down-home dancing and entertainment nightly. Rates: $22 single, $28 double; an extra person is $4.

The **Townhouse,** 1844 Pembina Hwy. (tel. 204/269-6230), has 30 standard motel rooms, with colonial-style decor, phone, color TV, and air conditioning. Four of the units have shower only. In the new wing the rooms are exceedingly nicely decorated with brown crushed-velvet spreads and color-coordinated carpet and curtains. These rooms rent for $24 single, $27 double ($27 and $30 in summer). Rates for standard units: $20 single, $23 double ($22 and $25 during the summer). An extra person is $3. Kitchenettes are available for $3 extra.

On Portage Ave., for a basic, clean motel accommodation with color TV, air conditioning, and phone (somewhat ancient in style), stop at the **Boulevard Motel,** 3120 Portage Ave. (tel. 204/837-5891). Rates: $20 single, $22 double.

Near the Airport

The **Airport Motor Hotel,** Ellice Ave. and Berry St. (tel. 204/783-7035), less than five minutes from the airport, has 55 large modern color-coordinated rooms with the usual conveniences. It also has a coffeeshop, lounge, and the inevitable beverage room, both with live entertainment, plus an indoor pool. Rates: $25 single, $30 double, $40 to $45 for a suite.

The **Canadiana,** 1400 Notre Dame Ave. (tel. 204/786-3471), is a larger, two-floor establishment that has been operating for seven years providing 75 large rooms, most of them decorated in oranges and golds set off by dark furniture. The usual features are available. Facilities include a sauna, coffeeshop (open from 7 a.m. to midnight), cocktail lounge with a small dance floor (and entertainment six nights a week), and a beverage room. Rates: $24 single, $27 double; an extra person is $3.

STAYING ON A FARM: To really get the feel of the prairies there's no better way than to stay for a while on a farm. The **Manitoba Farm Vacations Association,** 437 Assiniboine Ave., Winnipeg, MB R3C 0Y5 (tel. 204/943-8361), is the organization to contact for detailed information about farm accommodations. Rates average $20 a day for adults, $10 for children—a very reasonable price for such an exciting experience.

3. The Restaurants of Winnipeg

Not so long ago guidebooks would counsel that if you wanted to eat anything besides steak and potatoes you'd be out of luck in Winnipeg. Now, and I suspect for quite some time, you can eat very well and adventurously in Winnipeg.

Note: There's a 5% sales tax on any food bill above $2.99.

THE TOP RESTAURANTS: **Victor's,** 454 River St. at Osborne (tel. 284-2339), is the kind of place to take an out-of-towner who thinks there are no imaginative restaurants, either decor-wise or food-wise, in Winnipeg. For owners Victor and Margaret Gouriluk and Heinz and Johanna Kattenfeld have set about providing both in the ground floor of a restored apartment building in Osborne Village that now also houses unique shops and some offices.

The entrance to the restaurant is off a central, sun-roofed courtyard leading into three intimate stucco-walled rooms, each with a sophisticated, understated atmosphere achieved by bentwood cane chairs, oak tables, natural brick and wood, and stained-glass panels. Dinner might start with escargots with champignons or crêpes St-Jacques, stuffed with scallops, shrimp, and tomatoes. Do have the watercress and mushroom salad, dressed in a tasty light curry dressing. Entrees are likely to include at least two schnitzels, and more unusual, a nasi goreng or bouillabaisse (both $11). Save room for some lemon crème crêpes or my favorite, the peppermint chiffon, with an Oreo cookies base, crème de menthe, whipped cream, and marshmallows (both around $2). Prices include soup and salad (three bean, creamy coleslaw, or tossed). At lunchtime such interesting dishes as Maharani toast—an omelet topped with curried shrimps, fried bananas, and pineapple ($4.25)—stand alongside salads and sandwiches.

In 2½ years the restaurant has achieved such popularity that you'll have to reserve for lunch or dinner. Such success has led to the planned opening of another place on Portage Ave. Check it out. Open for lunch Monday to Friday from 11:30 a.m. to 2:30 p.m. and for dinner Monday to Saturday from 5:30 to midnight.

For some really fine-quality French cooking, seek out **Chez André,** 426 Main St. (tel. 957-1629). Ignore the plain street entrance and Chinese restaurant downstairs and take the elevator up to the low-lit dining room above, decorated in rich royal blue (down to the napkins) and hung with carved gilt-framed pictures. Start your meal with a classic coquilles St-Jacques ($4.25) or an equally classic consommé double au sherry ($1.40). Sample entrees include frog legs provençale ($9.75), veal tongue in tomato and caper sauce ($8.25), or civet of rabbit ($11.25). For the less adventurous there are steaks, chicken Kiev, roast duckling, etc. All entrees include soup, salad, vegetable, and beverage. Try one of the assorted pastries ($1.25) or the fresh strawberry Romanoff, if it's available. At lunchtime the menu ranges from omelets and sandwiches to such specialties as shrimp Parisienne (shrimp and mushrooms caressed with sherry, finished with cream, and served over a pastry shell) and beef burgundy, all under $5.

Open Monday to Friday from 11:30 a.m. to 2:30 p.m.; Monday to Thursday from 5 to 10 p.m., on Friday and Saturday to 11 p.m. Closed Sundays. Reservations are recommended, especially on weekends.

There are two dining spots over the river in St-Boniface (Winnipeg's twin French city) that both offer something unusual—one an unusual decor, the other an amusing specialty.

La Vieille Gare, 630 Des Meurons at Blvd. Provencher (tel. 247-7072), is just that—a restaurant set in a 1914 railway station, and alongside is a 1912 dining car retaining its original fittings and glorious walnut interior, which serves as a cocktail lounge at night and a lunch spot during the day. I can heartily recommend the lunch specials, such as chicken à la king (plus soup) for $3.95, and I defy you to finish, so generous are the servings. In the main gold-on-brown dining room with its Louis XV chairs and a large central fireplace, you can enjoy the finer touches of fresh flowers on your table as well as beginning your meal with a terrine of duckling ($2.25) or pâté de foie gras truffé ($4.50). Other larger tasty morsels will follow: coq au chambertin ($8.95), filet mignon béarnaise ($10.75), and naturally crêpes Suzette ($5.50 for two).

Open Monday to Friday from noon to 2:30 p.m. and 5 to 11 p.m., and Saturday from 5 p.m. to midnight. Closed Sunday.

A frog with a bib wielding knife and fork sets the tone for **La Grenouillère,** 150 Blvd. Provencher (tel. 233-0422), and that frog has been attracting customers for 26 years. So what do you expect? Among the specialties of course are frog legs—provençale ($9.95) or Grenobloise, ($10.50). And around the circular stuccoed walls there are frog cartoons—the King and Queen of Frogs, frogs in ice hockey outfits, and a special Golden Boy frog. However, if you're not partial to frogs and prefer to leave them burrowing in the mud, you can choose from French and Canadian entrees that range from $6.95 for pork charcutière or ham and maple syrup to $12.95 for beef tenderloin with shrimp, lobster, and a béarnaise sauce. Main courses include soup and salad. For dessert, stick to French pastries ($1.25) or a parfait of your choice ($2.50).

Open Monday to Friday for lunch from 11:30 a.m. to 2:30 p.m., and for dinner Monday to Thursday from 5 to 10 p.m., to midnight Friday and Saturday. Closed Sunday. To get there, find Portage and Main, go south on Main and turn off onto Hwy. 57, which will take you over the Red River and onto Blvd. Provencher.

Now for one of my favorite Winnipeg restaurants—**Restaurant Dubrovnik,** 390 Assiniboine (tel. 944-0594), where owner Milan Bodiroga has gone to great lengths to create a romantic setting for fine Balkan cuisine. Having chosen a beautiful Victorian brick town house with working fireplaces and leaded glass windows, he has enclosed the veranda to create a two-level dining area, set tables in what used to be the living room, dining room, and center hall, and decorated them all tastefully with a few plants and colorful Yugoslav weavings, dolls, and gusle (ancient beautifully carved musical instruments, often inlaid with mother-of-pearl).

Instead of opting for one of the schnitzels or steaks (from $11.50), experiment with the exciting eggs ruski (Russian salad, eggs, smoked salmon, and caviar, $3.95) and follow with Russian shashlik ($10), or the huge chef's special of veal or pork scallops filled with kajmak cheese, breaded, baked, and coated with tartar sauce ($11.75). For dessert there are the usual super-sweet delicacies —palacinke ($2.50) and baklava ($1.25). Finish with a coffee Dubrovnik (sljivovica, kruskovac bitters, with coffee, whipped cream, and chopped walnuts) and you'll feel as though you've just returned from a vacation on the Dalmatian Riviera. Lunchtime offers Russian borscht and pirojak (meat-filled pastries, $3.50) along with omelets, sandwiches, and some more substantial dishes (all under $5).

Open Monday to Friday from 11:30 a.m. to 2:30 p.m. and 5 p.m. to midnight, Saturday from 5 p.m. to 1 a.m. Make reservations.

For really top-flight hotel dining, visit the **Velvet Glove** at the Winnipeg Inn. **Churchill's** at the Marlborough or the **Factor's Table** at the Fort Garry also have very attractive dining rooms. (See the hotel section.)

DOWNTOWN DINING: First, the moderately priced selections:

Moderately Priced Restaurants

Expectations should match experience at the **Old Swiss Inn,** 207 Edmonton St. (tel. 942-7725), if a Swiss inn signifies unpretentious Alpine warmth, wood paneling, pictures of mountain scenery, and Swiss specialties, for this is precisely what you'll find. You might start with Swiss onion soup or cheese fondue ($4.40), and follow with pollo in Pardella alla Ticinese (pan-fried chicken breast topped with Mediterranean-style tomato sauce, $9.75), sole pizzaiola ($8.45), or any of the other tempting beef and seafood dishes. At lunchtime you can have a familiar corned beef on rye ($3.30) or bratwurst mit rosti ($3.95).

Open Monday to Friday from 11 a.m. to midnight, Saturday from 5 p.m. to midnight. Closed Sunday.

A clubby atmosphere prevails at **Hy's Steak Loft,** 216 Kennedy St. (tel. 942-1000), probably Winnipeg's most popular steakhouse. It has been here 21 years. Dining here can be extremely intimate, for the semicircular booths can be curtained off by heavy velour drapes, leaving you and whoever pleasantly ensconced in a candlelit alcove full of books. Hy's menu plays variations on a theme of steak—pepper steak ($10.75), steak teriyaki ($14), steak Diane ($15), filet of beef Wellington ($15), plus your basic cuts and some seafood dishes (from $11). At lunchtime, old favorites include the calorie counter—a hamburger served with cottage cheese, hard-boiled egg, and tomato slices ($4.35), grilled crab 'n' cheese ($5.35), and other small steaks and salads. For a quick nightcap after dinner or apéritifs there's a lounge downstairs where you can relax on one of the many leather couches.

Open Monday to Friday from 11:30 a.m. to midnight, Saturday from 5 p.m. to midnight, and Sunday from 5 to 9:30 p.m. Reserve.

Just down the street you can go into **Café de Paris,** 236 Edmonton St. (tel. 943-7438), and find some interesting French cuisine. The front part of this place has a coffeeshop flavor to it, while the back dining room has few distinguishing marks, except for the food. You might begin dinner with a salad russe with lobster and shrimp medallions ($3.95) or tassette Lady Nelson (slightly curried turtle soup), and continue with lapin in wine sauce ($8.25) or game hen masked with mustard and honey ($8.25), or you can choose a rainbow trout from the tank—all of which will include soup of the day, salad, and vegetables and potatoes. Finish with a coupe Romanoff ($2.25) or one of the tempting Swiss pastries ($1.15). At lunchtime the menu features veal, seafood, chicken, and beef dishes, as well as soups, salads, omelets, and sandwiches, with most dishes under $5.

Open Monday to Friday from 11:30 a.m. to 2:30 p.m., Monday to Thursday from 5 to 11 p.m., and Friday and Saturday from 5 p.m. to midnight. Closed Sunday. Reserve.

Ichi-ban, 189 Carlton St. (tel. 942-7493), delights the eye as well as the taste buds with its garden atmosphere, the sounds of Japanese music, water splashing over a waterwheel, and bird song among the almond blossom. You'll also love it if you're gregarious and have to share a teppan table where you watch the chef prepare your meal, producing steak Ichi-ban ($11.50), ebi shrimp (prepared in butter, soya, lemon, and sake, $9.50), chicken sesame ($8.50), or the imperial dinner, which consists of gyunku (prime tenderloin), ise ebi (baby lobster), and niwatori (chicken), for $13.50. These dishes will also include an appetizer, soup, and sunomono (a salad of marinated cucumbers with shredded crabmeat).

Open Monday to Saturday from 4:30 to 11:30 p.m., Sunday to 10 p.m. Reserve.

Nazare, 423 Portage Ave. (tel. 957-1576), takes its name seriously, and by lighting tries to create the effect of sitting inside a ship and looking out its windows. It's a simple large room with red chairs and white tablecloths, and some really good authentic Portuguese cuisine. Such appetizers as camarao a Nazare (shrimp sauteed in butter and spices, simmered in seafood sauce, $3.50) set the whole tone for a menu that specializes in treasures of the sea: bacalhav a Braz (dry cod mixed with potatoes, egg, onions, and parsley, $8.95), stuffed squid ($9.95), and trout, salmon, and sea bream when they're available. For the carnivores there are some lamb, chicken, and veal dishes that include borrego grelhado (broiled lamb steak marinated in white wine, $9.75). All these dinners are served with soup, salad, vegetable, and coffee or tea.

Open Monday to Friday from 11:30 a.m. to 11:30 p.m., on Saturday from 5 to 11:30 p.m. Closed Sunday. Reservations recommended.

On October 9, 1877, a 32-ton steam engine, the *Countess of Dufferin,* barged into Winnipeg practically declaring it the gateway to the west. Its memory survives at the **Countess of Dufferin,** 375 York (tel. 956-1139), in the Convention Centre on the second floor, where an authentic replica stands, and behind it several trucks filled to the brim with salads. The restaurant is divided into three coach sections with railway-style banquettes and curtains on the simulated windows. Every 20 minutes or so you'll hear the sound of a train swooping by. The prices even capture the steam era—$7.95 for a selection of prime rib, baked Virginia ham, roast turkey, all with potatoes and vegetables, and as many servings of salad as you like, plus bread. At lunchtime you'll find a variety of sandwiches from $2.95 to $5.45.

The restaurant provides free indoor parking in the parkade for a maximum of two hours. Get the waitress to validate your parking ticket. Open 11:30 a.m. to 2:30 p.m. Monday to Friday and 5 to 10 p.m. Monday to Saturday.

A racing tout in a trilby with a large moustache and bushy brows grins from the menu at **G. Willaker's,** 175 Carlton St. (tel. 944-8297). To enter you have to go down a flight of stairs above which hangs a wicker basket carriage presaging the mass of Canadiana and the old advertising prints below. The place specializes in seafood and steaks at honest prices: a whole lobster at $11.25, deep-fried shrimp at $8.95, baked breast of chicken at $6.95, a ten-ounce steak for $8.95. There's also a variety of sandwiches from $3.45.

Open 11:30 a.m. to 2 a.m. daily.

Not so dissimilar is **Mother Tucker's,** 335 Donald St. (tel. 943-5539), another fictional character who specializes in giving the customer plenty of good plain food. She has taken over an 1895 temple to do it, and installed log-cabin decor, an old-fashioned general store that serves as a lounge, and a bake shop and salad bar placed on a wooden cart inside a log cabin structure. The menu is short and features country-baked half chicken ($7.45), broiled New York strip steak ($9.95), and deep-fried shrimp or roast prime ribs (both $8.95). All dinners include freshly baked bread, any number of trips to the salad bar (which is a truly magnificent spread of colorful salads, vegetables, fruits, and cheeses), and choice of potatoes, vegetables, and homemade dessert.

Open Monday to Thursday from 5 to 11 p.m., Friday and Saturday from 4:30 p.m. to midnight, and Sunday from 4 to 9 p.m. No reservations accepted.

Budget Dining

The **Garden Crêperie,** 349 York (tel. 957-0221), makes an ideal lunch spot. It's situated in the Convention Centre complex and offers an endless variety of savory and dessert crêpes, plus soups and salads. Savory crêpes (ham palacsintas and asparagus soufflé, chicken suprême, ratatouille) range from $3.45 to $4.25, and dessert crêpes (apple crêpe Calvados, or vanilla ice cream wrapped in a crêpe, smothered in hot caramel sauce, and topped with chopped roasted pecans, for example) run from $2.15 to $2.95. At night dessert crêpe prices remain the same but the dinner menu has more substantial dishes, like tenderloin of beef brochette served with a mushroom crêpe and mixed green salad ($6.95).

Open 11 a.m. to 3 p.m. Monday to Friday, 5 to 11 p.m. Monday to Thursday, Friday and Saturday to 1 a.m., and Sunday from 5 to 9 p.m.

Also in the Convention Centre, on the second floor, **Shangri-la** (tel. 942-2281) offers elegant Anglo-Cantonese dining. Having started his first restaurant in 1972, Park Lee, who once worked as a bellhop at the Winnipeg Inn, has moved rapidly for this is his second of five restaurants (one of which is in St. Cloud, Minnesota). The menu is extensive with some of the more unusual dishes like pork spare ribs in black bean and garlic sauce ($4.90) or bean cake and barbecued pork ($4.80), along with chop suey, chow mein, and egg foo yung dishes.

Popular as it is, make reservations, especially on weekends. Open 11:30 a.m. to midnight Monday to Thursday, to 1 a.m. on Friday and Saturday, until 10 p.m. on Sunday.

You'll find many Chinese at **Kum Koon Garden,** 426 Main St. (tel. 943-4655), a large room divided in half by an open slatted-wood partition where the tables sport red tablecloths. The menu is long and varied, offering eight soups including egg drop with mushrooms ($2.50) and special bean curd in a bowl ($4.50). For main dishes there's a yummy shrimp with black bean and garlic sauce ($5.50), chicken in lemon sauce ($5.75), beef with broccoli ($4.75), and a most unusual fish lips with vegetable and assorted meat ($5.75). At lunchtime, the self-service cafeteria goes into action where you can find daily specials and dim sum—sweet lotus bun, chicken in a bun (two for $1.60), and so on.

Open 11 a.m. to 3 p.m. Monday to Friday, 5 p.m. to midnight Monday through Thursday, Friday and Saturday until 1 a.m., and Sunday till 10 p.m.

Austrian yodeling and light music provide the background for sipping coffee and tasting the scrumptious tortes that line the showcase at the **Café Mozart,** 221 Garry St. (tel. 942-3825)—Black Forest cake, mocca torte, Vienna marble cake, all around $1.30. At lunch there are sandwiches such as roast beef, club, reuben, and toast Mozart (topped with mushrooms, ham, and Swiss cheese, and melted in the oven). The real delights, however, are the pastries and the Swiss cheese fondue ($10.75) or the chocolate fondue ($4.25). This makes a fine after-theater spot.

Open from 9 a.m. to 12:30 a.m. Monday to Saturday. Wine only served.

Moskovitz and Moskovitz, 101 Mayfair at Main St. (tel. 474-2410), serves anyone who's yearning for nosherai—bagel and cream cheese, chopped liver on rye, pastrami on rye (ranging from $1.80 to $4), all served with potato salad or steak fries and coleslaw or pickle. It's cafeteria-style self-service, where you take your victuals back to pine tables which stand under burlap lampshades amid many hanging plants. Besides the nosherai there's a selection of beef (eight-ounce steaks, $5.90 to $7.05), egg dishes (from $2 to $3), and blintzes and pancakes, including potato latkes with sour cream ($2.50). Mahlzeit.

Open Monday to Saturday from 11 a.m. to 5 a.m., Sunday to 1 a.m.—a good place to know about when there aren't too many eating establishments in Winnipeg that stay open these hours.

OSBORNE VILLAGE: This area is just behind the Legislative Building across the Assiniboine River, where old buildings have been renovated and now house some unique shopping (the Elegant John, for example), and some of the prettiest and most reasonable restaurants in Winnipeg.

Moderately Priced Dining

Swallows (tel. 452-6654) is one of them. Creative owner Lynne Buchanan returned from several years spent learning weaving in Bergen and London, found a building that appealed to her, and installed a very attractive, light, and airy restaurant that is set on the top floor of 100 Osborne St. (the same building that Victor's occupies). The hardwood floor, butcher-block tables, bamboo blinds, sandblasted white brick walls, pot lights, and a smattering of plants seem to go with the food, which consists of quiches (like crabmeat, parsley, and chives, $4.50 to $5), and Scandinavian sandwiches (such as Norwegian jarlsberg with green pepper, $2.15 to $3). At night the menu is expanded. Daily specials are chalked on a blackboard and might include rabbit in mustard sauce ($7.95) or curried shrimp ($6.95). All the main dishes come with fresh salad, brown bread, and a crock of herb butter. Save room for the pumpkin pecan pie, or cheesecake with pineapple or apricot topping ($1.75). Across the hall Lynne has opened a quiche bar that offers various sandwiches and smoked meats and a fine continental breakfast. Licensed for wine only, Swallows has some excellent inexpensive wines available.

Open Monday to Thursday from 11:30 a.m. to 11:30 p.m., Friday and Saturday to 1 a.m. The quiche bar is open 9:30 a.m. to 11:30 p.m.

Two Budget Cafes

The boast on the menu "We do the unusual right" is very apropos of **Basil's,** 117 Osborne St. (tel. 453-8440), and refers equally well to the food and the decor. As soon as you walk in you're faced with a cabinet full of delicious bakery items—eclairs, almond croissants, apple strudel, and various cakes such as obst torte, almond chocolate, or Swiss zuger kirsch (85¢ to $1.65). Beyond the dessert showcase there are three sitting areas, each with wonderfully textured wall hangings, macramé lampshades, and a lowered cedar ceiling. The food focuses on super-fresh salads (from $2.85 to $3.50) and some imaginative open-face sandwiches that use the prime ingredients of various national cuisines —for example, the Gordon (Spain), which combines tuna with lemon on rye with onion slices and capers, or the French treat, which is camembert with lettuce and chopped onions, and oil and vinegar dressing with rye bread ($3.45). Hot dishes and platters, such as an enormous platter of imported cheeses with a basket of breads, fresh vegetables, and olives ($4.85), are also available. Savory and dessert crêpes go well with any of the 12 different coffees (85¢ to $1.35).

Open Monday to Saturday from 10:30 a.m. to 11:30 p.m., Friday and Saturday to 12:30 a.m., and Sunday from 2 to 9:15 p.m. Wine only.

Roggis, 129 Osborne Lane (tel. 452-4571), offers a warm village-type coffeehouse atmosphere but the flavors here are Middle Eastern: falafel ($1.95), tahina, hummus, kufta, or couscous (all around $3). Quiches, sandwiches, and pita plates (beef or vegetable curry or chili on pita) are also available. A good place to hang out behind the bamboo blinds, basking in the red glow of the lamps and talking with the jukebox turned down low.

Open Monday to Thursday from noon to midnight, Friday and Saturday to 2 a.m. Wine only.

An Expensive Austrian Chalet

Painted wooden slats separate the upper and lower dining areas of **Engl's,** 159 Osborne St. (tel. 453-5670), where not only all the decor (cow bells, photographs of Austrian folk, carved roots) is authentic, but so also is chef-owner Heinz Engls' food, even to the extent that all the entrees are served with a mixed salad of red cabbage, lettuce, carrots, tomatoes, and potato salad. Besides the expected schnitzels ($8.50), Heinz offers bauernschmaus (smoked pork rib knackwurst served on a bed of sauerkraut and Tyrolean roast potatoes) and chicken dolomiten (chicken breast covered in almonds, flamed in brandy, and served with a mango cream sauce and Viennese rice, $9.50). For an appetizer, try the filled eggs that contain pureed ham, butter, and egg yolk filling, and are served with rolls of ham and olives ($2.15), and for dessert there's always Viennese pastries. At lunchtime, dishes are usually under $4, with a daily soup and open-face sandwich special going for $2.75. Open for dinner only.

THE WAREHOUSE DISTRICT: This area stretches north from Portage and Main to City Hall and the Centennial Arts Centre, and is filled with old cast-iron buildings that are being restored and developed into shopping complexes, restaurants, discos, and so on.

Upper Bracket Dining

Jose Lavilla of Barcelona used to have restaurants in Sitges and his home city before he came to Winnipeg to convert an old warehouse into a Spanish enclave with its toreador posters, red tablecloths, and flamenco guitarist entertaining on Thursday to Saturday nights. At **Los Españoles,** 167 Bannatyne St. (tel. 943-5171), dinner might begin with mushrooms or prawns ajillo, mussels or clams marinera, or any of the other appetizers from $2.25 to $3.95. To follow that there's of course paella ($10.50) or bouillabaisse Catalana ($13.95), or any one of various lamb, veal, and beef dishes in the $8.75 to $10.75 range. Entrees include soup and salad. For dessert, do try the brazo de Gitano, a special Spanish cake, or the flan al rum (caramel custard with a touch of rum). Lunch offers a mixed bag of Canadian and Spanish specialties, all under $4.

Open Monday to Friday from 11:30 a.m. to 2:30 p.m., and Monday to Saturday from 5 to 11 p.m. Closed Sunday.

It seems fitting that **Oliver's,** 185 Lombard (tel. 943-4448), should now inhabit what was once the offices of Great West Life Insurance because its decor is certainly rich, somber, and masculine enough. In the downstairs lobby there's a glass case containing Blackstone's *Commentaries,* and arrayed behind the coat-check desk are leather-bound English statutes taken supposedly from the Old Bailey, while upstairs in the three dining rooms stand 300-year-old hand-carved sideboards among wooden Corinthian columns, gilded portraits, and red velvet chairs. The food also reflects the same taste: you might start your dinner with a pâté maison ($2.50) or turtle soup Madeira ($3), and continue with Winnipeg goldeye ($8.50) or any one of several steaks (from $10.95 to $15.50). Cheesecake or casata Napolitane would make a good dessert. At lunchtime you'd find corned beef on rye ($2.85) and several other Canadian sandwiches. Downstairs there's an elegant lounge-piano bar where even the bar stools are upholstered. An after-theater menu is available here until 1 a.m.

Open for lunch Monday to Friday from noon to 2:30 p.m., for dinner Monday to Saturday from 5 to midnight. Closed Sunday.

Moderately Priced Dining

Ever wanted to sit in a bath in public? If you have, then **Lock Stock and Barrel,** 171 McDermot St. (tel. 943-5411), is the place to do it, either in the basement lounge or upstairs in the dining area, where one or two old baths have been converted into loveseats. The place is chock-full of Canadiana—old photographs, horse collars, and farm implements, and the vast area has been divided, by stained-glass partitions, into more intimate areas. Here you can feast on either a $7.95 dinner that will include stuffed baked potato, bread, salad, and tea or coffee, as well as a choice of prime rib, barbecued ribs, veal parmesan, or steak and shrimp; or a $9.95 dinner that will offer a choice of king crab legs, New York sirloin, or a 12-ounce prime rib as the main course. Sandwiches and burgers dominate the lunch menu ($1.95 to $3.85), which will include soup and either cottage cheese, tomato, french fries, or baked potato.

Open Monday to Friday from 11:30 a.m. to 1 a.m., on Saturday from 4:45 p.m. to 1 a.m., and on Sunday from 4:30 to 9 p.m.

At the **Old Spaghetti Factory,** 291 Bannatyne Ave. (tel. 943-2433), the usual plethora of Canadian effects overcomes you—stained glass, old carriages, brass instruments, a dining area that is in fact designed as a tram car's interior —and the usual array of inexpensive food is available—spaghetti with various sauces (from $2.95 to $4.25), veal cutlet parmigiana ($5.65), and New York steak ($7.95). All dinners include salad, sourdough bread, coffee or tea, and spumoni ice cream. All the luncheon sandwiches and burgers are under $3.50.

Open Monday to Friday from 11:30 a.m. to 2 p.m. and 5 to 10 p.m., till 12:30 a.m. on Friday and Saturday, and Sunday from 3 to 9 p.m.

CHINATOWN: There is no real Chinatown in Winnipeg, although Winnipeg-

gers refer to one—an area where several Chinese restaurants are concentrated along King St. between Bannatyne and McDermot Aves. Here you will find some of the finest Cantonese food at the **King's Palace,** 260 King St. (tel. 943-1077), a small place that seats only 36 and will most likely be full of Chinese families. The menu is written in Chinese on a blackboard; you may select from an English menu. There's really no decor to speak of, just red vinyl chairs. The menu, however, is extensive, and you can sample barbecued duck with plum sauce, deep-fried chicken with green onions and ginger, dried spare ribs with spiced salt, steamed minced pork with salted duck egg, or scallops and snow peas. Each dish will cost between $3.50 and $4.50 (except for the fried crab with garlic and black bean sauce, $7).

Open from 4 p.m. to 2 a.m. Monday to Thursday, until 3 a.m. on Friday and Saturday.

At the **Unicorn,** 224 King St. (tel. 943-3933), dim sum (about 40 of them) are the lunchtime specialty on Saturday and Sunday when you can sample such delicacies as stuffed sweet rice wrapped with lotus leaf (90¢ each). As for the regular menu, Alan and Ann Wong are trying to woo people away from the old chop suey tastes by providing more diverse Chinese cuisine—Unicorn honey garlic ribs ($4.25), bean cake with vegetable ($4.75), diced chicken with walnut ($3.45)—in a pleasant atmosphere created by Chinese prints on bamboo around the walls and Chinese guitar (peipa) music in the background. Remember, the Unicorn is a lucky symbol.

Open 11 a.m. to 4 p.m., daily.

For Chinese food in elegant surroundings, go to **Imperial Gardens,** 245 King St. (tel. 944-9400), in Chinatown Plaza, and sit yourself down in a modern brown upholstered chair that goes with the orange tablecloth and broadloom and there sample some of the dim sum ($1.25) from the trolley at lunchtime or else choose from the extensive regular menu. There are ten soups to choose from—hot and sour ($6.50), beancake with pork ($4.50), or if you're really extravagant, bird's nest or shark's fin (from $17.95). Otherwise there's beef with chili and black bean sauce ($6.25), steamed garlic spare ribs ($6.95), or diced shrimp with cashew nuts ($7.25), just to give you some idea of the possibilities.

Open 11 a.m. to 1 a.m. daily.

BROADWAY AND SHERBROOK ST. AREA: A little off center west, beyond the Legislative Building, Sherbrook St. offers some good moderate-priced dining.

Moderately Priced Choices

Norman Gladstone, a Manitoban, was a brewmaster who went to visit Denmark for obvious reasons. While there he met and married Birgit Westergaard, who in turn persuaded her sister and husband Mogens Kristiansen to come to Winnipeg. The result is the **Bistro Dansk,** 63 Sherbrook St. (tel. 775-5662), a lovely, warm chalet-style bistro with bright-red gate-back chairs with red checked upholstery that go with the wooden tables and raffia placemats. The classical background music complements the unusually friendly and serene atmosphere. And so do the food and the prices. Main courses include seven superlative Danish specialties, such as frikadeller (Danish meat patties, made from ground veal and pork, served with red cabbage and potato salad, $5.75) or aeggekage (a Danish omelet with bacon, garnished with tomato and green onions, and served with home-baked Danish bread, $4.75). There are also daily specials chalked up on a blackboard (when I was there, such exciting fare as turkey breast filled with apples and onions, served with sweet potato, hazelnuts, and fruit salad, at $7.50). Dessert specials included hazelnut pie tart and puff pastry with whipped cream and chocolate ($1.50). At lunchtime, besides salads and an omelet or two, there are eight or so open-face sandwiches available, served on homemade rye or white bread, most priced at $2.25.

Open Tuesday to Saturday from 11:30 a.m. to 2:30 p.m. for lunch, from 2:30 to 5 p.m. for tea, and 5:30 to 9:30 p.m. for dinner. Closed Sunday and Monday. Wine only.

Not far around the corner on Broadway you'll find some excellent Indian cuisine at the **India Curry House,** 595 Broadway (tel. 786-2728). Behind the unprepossessing exterior you'll find a large, very low-lit room separated down the middle by a curtain of beads. The walls are decorated with batik pictures depicting mythology (lit creatively from behind), and a small display of sitars, brass statuettes, and Indian dolls. You can't beat the lunchtime buffet that always offers two curries for only $3.50. In the evening, start your meal with samosa or bhujia (spiced vegetable fritters, 50¢), and proceed with one of the curries, from $3.50 to $4.60 for a beef vindaloo which will take your breath away and leave you awash in sweat, with the tears running down your face. Or else you can sample a biryani or the house specialty of tandoori chicken ($9.50). All dinners include rice, onion, salad, and papadum. This place is very popular and reservations are especially necessary on weekends.

Open Monday to Friday from 11:30 a.m. to 2 p.m., Sunday to Thursday from 5 to 11 p.m., Friday and Saturday to midnight. Closed Tuesday.

Zorbas, 228 Maryland St. (tel. 775-5807), comes close to being an authentic Greek taverna with its stucco walls, red checked tablecloths, and arcades—and certainly Katerina and Michael Tsalatsidis help to make it even more so. Katerina loves to cook the dishes of her native land, and you can sample her keftedes, moussaka, yemesta (tomatoes stuffed with rice, minced beef, onions, parsley, and oregano, and served with Greek-style potatoes), souvlaki, or kreas (braised meats in tomato sauce, onions, and spices), all ranging from $5.75 to $7.50 for a combination plate. The homemade baklava is out of this world ($1). All you need now is to find a Zorba to brighten up your life. At lunch the Greek dishes take a back seat to hamburgers and sandwiches (all under $3).

Open 11:30 a.m. to 1:30 a.m. Monday to Saturday, and Sunday from 4 to 9 p.m. No reservations taken.

The name gives it away; the statues, fountains, and arcades merely confirm that **Acropolis,** 172 Sherbrook St. (tel. 775-8927), serves Greek-style food. Here, you can watch a whole lamb turn on the spit and the gyro slowly spinning, while you begin your meal with avgolemono soup ($1.25), or more adventurously with octopus ($2.50). Choose your main course from such specialties as arni souvlas (barbecued lamb, $9.25), moussaka, souvlaki, and grape leaves (all around $8). For those who don't enjoy Greek food there are also steaks and seafood (from $7.50). If you've tasted baklava, try kataifi (shredded wheat stuffed with walnuts and covered with honey sauce, $1) just for a change. At lunchtime all the entrees are under $4, and you can enjoy such things as a mini souvlaki in a pita, or a Ulysses boat (gyro in a pita, $2.75), as well as sandwiches, salads, and omelets.

Open Monday to Thursday from 11:30 a.m. to 11 p.m.; until 1 a.m. on Friday and Saturday, and from 4 to 10 p.m. on Sunday. Reservations recommended on weekends.

Budget Eating

For Shanghai and Szechuan specialties, there's no better place to go than **Fortuna Gardens,** 253 Sherbrook St. (tel. 772-1786), to gorge yourself on fried shredded beef or pork with hot garlic sauce ($4), bean curd with hot sauce ma poo ($3.75), or the more exotic sea cucumber with mixed meats ($5). Try also the tangy pork and Szechuan cabbage soup or one of the cold appetizers like pong-pong. If you long for something sweet after Chinese food, have the pineapple or banana fritters ($1.80). As usual it's the food that attracts—the arborite tables, aluminum and vinyl chairs, and paper placemats are far from alluring.

Open Sunday through Tuesday and Thursday from 5 to 10 p.m., until 11 p.m. on Friday and Saturday. Closed Wednesday.

The Good Old Days, 143 Sherbrook St. (tel. 774-4255), brings them back in tea-room style. Situated in a town house, part of which is turned into a boutique stuffed with home craft items (shawls, knitting, quilts, woodwork), the tea room is decorated with pale blue painted wood chairs and lace curtains, and serves light fare such as homemade soup and salad with brown bread (75¢), beef or pork pie with coleslaw; quiche ($1.75) and such teatime treats as Welsh teacakes, bran muffins, and scones with strawberry jam, all homemade and only 40¢ each.

Open Monday to Saturday from 10 a.m. to 5 p.m., until 9 p.m. on Friday.

THE NORTH END—A BUDGET HAVEN: One place the locals will tell you about is **Betsy's Place**, 1134 Main St. (tel. 582-7685), a two-room restaurant which is the expression of Betsy de Boer's phenomenal determination and vitality. She started it eight years ago when, her children having grown up, she felt somewhat empty, and against many odds went ahead and bought a grubby lunch counter. The first room still looks rather like a lunch counter with its Formica tables, plastic tablecloths, and aluminum vinyl chairs. The second room has only a little more decor—oleander in the windows, red walls, tablecloths, a couple of New Guinea hunting spears, Indonesian wall posters . . . but it's the cheap and delicious Indonesian food (and Betsy's bubbling personality) that brings in the crowds—the pork and chicken sate ($4), oedang goreng (fried shrimp with sauce and salad, $4.50), tahoe goreng (fried beancake garnished with beansprouts, celery, and sauce, $2.70), and the pièce de résistance, the eight-dish rijsttafel ($6), which you have to order in advance. All dishes include rice. For dessert there are apple or banana fritters that just melt in your mouth (80¢). Make sure you say hello to Betsy—you'll love her.

Open 11 a.m. to 10 p.m. Monday to Wednesday and Friday, to 8 p.m. on Thursday, and Saturday from 4 to 10 p.m. Closed Sunday. Wine only.

As I mentioned before, the North End was once a thriving mosaic of cultures and the evidence remains today in the delis that stretch along Main St. to which ex-Winnipeggers who have gone to Montréal, Chicago, or Vancouver still return because there's not a corned beef sandwich as good or as thick as those at **Oscar's**, 1304 Main St. (tel. 582-7128), anywhere else on the North American continent. Get your own Coke or 7-Up out of the machine and sit down at your Formica-top table with its aquamarine vinyl and aluminum chairs, and wait for your doorstep-thick slices of rye stuffed with either corned beef, pastrami, or salami—and then thank God you're only paying $1.25 for the treat.

Open 9:30 a.m. to 5:30 p.m.

Simon's, 1322 Main St. (tel. 589-8269), has greater variety. Besides the sandwiches you can order cheese blintzes, cheese kreplach, potato veranekes (all for $3), or a large bowl of borscht in a lunch-counter-plus-tables ambience.

Open 6 a.m. to 6 p.m. Monday to Saturday.

Kelekis, 1100 Main St. (tel. 582-1786), is also famous and always crowded, but not for deli fare. Hamburgers and hot dogs (ranging from $1 to $2) are the attraction. More substantial dishes are available, for example two grilled pork chops ($4), deep-fried jumbo shrimps ($3.75), or grilled ham steak ($3.75), all served with coleslaw and either french fries or mashed potatoes.

ALONG PORTAGE AVE.: For Italian food people swear by the **Paradise Restaurant**, 789 Portage Ave. (tel. 772-2539), where you can either order a pizza (from $4.90 to $7 for a 15-incher) or dine by candlelight in a warm room split down the middle by exposed brick walls with wrought-iron gates. The usual selection of pastas—cannelloni ($4.25), spaghetti alla Napoletana ($3)—plus such specialties as veal scallopine alla marsala ($9), chicken cacciatore ($6.50), or veal chops pizzaiola ($9.75) are available, along with special Paradise dishes such as melenzane plene (eggplant with meat filling, $4), cavatelli with homemade sausage and tomato sauce ($5), and coniglio (rabbit) alla cacciatora ($9.50). For dessert there's always spumoni.

Open Monday to Thursday from 11 a.m. to 1 a.m., Friday and Saturday to 2 a.m., Sundays and holidays from 4 p.m. to midnight.

Rae and Jerry's Steakhouse has been and remains a veritable Winnipeg institution—even the entertainers Harry and Leon, a pianist-singer and saxophonist-trumpeter have been entertaining here for 20 years. Set in a large low-lit room with slatted wood walls and simple furniture, the restaurant serves complete dinners that include soup or juice, salad, potato, and choice of sundae. Main dishes run from $8.95 for grilled Manitoba goldeye to $16.75 for broiled lobster tail, with a lot of steaks, chicken, and fish in between. There's also a selection of sandwiches, hamburgers, and omelets (all under $5), and a fairly reasonable lunchtime menu featuring more of the same.

Open 11:30 a.m. to midnight Monday to Saturday, to 8:30 p.m. Sundays and holidays. Reservations suggested.

Another venerable institution that really marks the spot where the race-track used to be in the good old days is the **Paddock,** 1540 Portage Ave. (tel. 772-0727). The mural in the circular coffeeshop actually depicts the vista that existed from 1925 to 1956 when the stands at the old Polo Park racetrack used to rise across the road before Polo Park Shopping Mall rose in its stead. The restaurant is also historically significant because it was the first cocktail lounge to open in 1957—before that no liquor could be served by the glass and the only bars were men-only beer parlors. The place has been in the Orestes family for years and the family still owns five racehorses—two of their old favorites have their portraits on the walls, Eternal K and Kenny K. In the three dining rooms there's plenty of horse memorabilia and some good steaks to go with it. The restaurant roasts its own turkeys, naturally ages its steaks, and home-bakes its pies and desserts, which are superb. Try the strawberry shortcake ($1.50). At dinner you might begin with herring cutlets in sour cream or shrimp cocktail ($3.25), and then sample one of the steaks ($7.95 to $10.95) or beef liver and onions ($5.25), all served with salad, bread and butter, and beverage. From 6:30 to 7:30 and then from 9 p.m. to 1 a.m. there's piano entertainment in both the lounge and the dining room with its red tablecloths and black wood chairs. It gets very crowded on weekends, so you'll need a reservation.

Open 11:30 a.m. to 1 a.m. Monday to Saturday. Closed Sundays and holidays.

AROUND TOWN: The restaurants that follow fit into no particular area but are well-known local eateries.

A Renowned Chicken Shack

It's a small white house in the middle of a residential area somewhere between downtown and the airport called **Haynes Chicken Shack,** 257 Lulu St. (tel. 774-2764), and it's really worth seeking out for some good home-style cooking and a family welcome. Percy Haynes grew up in this house, and he and his wife have been running their family-style restaurant with its neat white tablecloths since 1952. A lowboy piano stands in the corner and Percy will play on and off through the evening—ballads or blues or soft dinner music, recalling the days when he was a jazz musician working the U.S. and Canada. The really tasty home-style cooking includes southern fried chicken ($6), barbecued spare ribs ($5.95), shrimp creole or breaded shrimp ($5.95), and T-bone steak ($7.10).

All these dishes come with french fries, potato salad, or rice. For dessert there's ice cream.

Open Monday to Saturday from 5 p.m. to 1 a.m.

Gemütlichkeit on Ellice

The owners of the **Happy Vineyard,** 719 Ellice Ave. at Toronto St. (tel. 783-6837), have gone to great lengths to recreate a German stube and village atmosphere. A replica of a wine press greets you at the door, and there are several wood carvings of figures who have made great contributions to the cultivation and production of wine—Charlemagne, Bernard of Clairvaux, Dom Perignon. The large area has been divided up into several small rooms, each with red checked tablecloths. An accordionist entertains. German specialties naturally prevail: sauerbraten with dumplings, rinds rouladen (thin slices of beef rolled with bacon, pickles, onion, and mustard, and served with dumplings or potatoes), smoked pork hock with sauerkraut, or wienerschnitzel (from $8.25 to $10.25). All dinners are served with beet borscht, German-style pea soup, salad, and coffee. At lunchtime there's a German-style buffet with cold cuts, salads, potato pancakes, perogi, and sauerbraten (it varies) for only $5.50.

Open 11:30 a.m. to 1 a.m. Monday to Friday and 5 to 1 a.m. on Saturday. Closed Sunday.

Continental Cuisine in St. Boniface

Over in St. Boniface there's a delightful little house called the **Red Lantern,** 302 Hamel Ave., (tel. 233-4841), that does indeed sport a red lantern without, and a long, narrow two-tier dining room within that is cozy with its red tablecloths. The food is excellent and very reasonable, with coq au vin going for $6, veal Cordon Bleu at $5.75, and barbecued steak for $7.75—and these prices include salad, potato or rice, fresh vegetable, and bread. For dessert you can choose any kind of sundae. You might start with onion or fish soup ($1.25), or frog legs ($3.25). At lunchtime light snacks like hamburgers ($1.75) or salmon salad on french bread ($2.50) are available. Wine and beer only.

Open daily, except Monday, from 11 a.m. to 2 p.m. and 5 to 10 p.m.

On the Pembina Hwy.

From the Tudoresque surroundings—stucco walls, heavy beams, stained glass, and fireplaces in each of the five dining rooms, and a lounge festooned with heraldic banners—you might expect it to be called the Round Table, but in fact it's the **Round Window,** 800 Pembina Hwy. (tel. 453-3631). Nevertheless, the restaurant seems to have a certain fascination for history as the menu opens with a quote from Lord Byron—"All human history attests that happiness for man—the hungry sinner—since Eve ate Apple much depends on dinner"—and is placed between an 1842 edition of the *Illustrated London News.* Your dinner will depend very largely on the price and quality of beef, for this is essentially a steakhouse: New York sirloin ($12.65), filet mignon ($12.95 to $14.95), prime rib ($8.25 to $10.55). Other specialties include lamb chops ($9.35), chicken Kiev ($8.55), and Winnipeg goldeye ($8.25). All dinners come with soup, salad, bread and butter, and baked potato or french fries. For dessert, try Eddas brown cake ($1.85), a spicy layer cake with cream frosting filling topped with cream, or a chantilly banana crêpe ($2.25). At lunchtime you can resort to the soup and salad bar ($2.85), a sandwich, or any one of several crêpes, all under $5.

Open Monday to Friday from 11:30 a.m. to 2:30 p.m., and Monday to Thursday from 5 to 10 p.m., Friday and Saturday to 11 p.m., on Sunday from 5 to 9 p.m.

Szechuan-Style Dining

Owner Hu Wang hails from northern China and so **Mandarin,** 613 Sargent Ave. (tel. 775-7819), specializes in Szechuan-style cuisine—bean curd and green pepper with black bean sauce ($3.75), shredded beef with Mandarin hot sauce ($4.50), fish with sweet-and-sour sauce ($4.50). Try one of the unusual soups such as sliced fish with fresh tomato soup ($3.25), or shredded meat and hot pickle soup ($3.25). The two most famous dishes here, however, require one day's notice—the sizzling rice shrimp ($18 for two) or Harvest in Snow, which can only be described as golden puffs of chicken and pork with other ingredients on a bed of angel-hair vermicelli, and served with salad and eight pancakes. The room is fairly small and basically decorated with golden tablecloths, vinyl and aluminum chairs, and plyboard wall paneling.

Open Tuesday to Sunday from 4 p.m. to midnight.

4. The Sights

THE GOLDEN BOY AND THE LEGISLATIVE BUILDING: Author Jack Ludwig probably has captured the meaning of the Golden Boy to Winnipeggers when he said: "I was thinking about it as something corny and silly that has always been corny and silly. Yet, at the same time, it's spatially fixed. People change, people come, people go, people die. But the Golden Boy is like Keats' nightingale. Something so fixed it seems eternal, almost immortal. Golden Boy becomes as mythically important as a Keats nightingale or a Hopkins windhover."

There he stands, 240 feet above ground atop the Legislative Building's dome, clutching a sheaf of wheat under his left arm and holding aloft in his right an eternally lit torch symbolizing the spirit of progress (remember, he was sculpted in 1914 or thereabouts, before progress became a dirty word). French sculptor Charles Gardet created this five-ton, 13½-foot bronze statue during World War I, which caused it a somewhat rough passage getting to Winnipeg. First the foundry was bombed, but the statue survived. Then the ship bound for New York was commandeered as a troop ship and the Golden Boy rolled around in the hold for two years, until he was safely delivered after the war to his current perch.

The building below is a magnificent classical Greek structure designed by British architect Frank Worthington Simon, who also designed the Liverpool Cotton Exchange, Liverpool University, and the buildings of the Edinburgh International Exhibition. Construction was completed in 1919. Enter the main lobby and you will be confronted by a grand marble staircase flanked by two enormous bronze buffalos, also the work of Gardet. Climb to the top of the staircase and look down from the legislative antehall into the Pool of the Black Star on the floor below. This chamber, with three steps leading down into it, is a perfect circle surrounded by 16 pillars, and is just one of many examples of the Egyptian influence evident in the building. Note also at the back of the antehall the Frank Brangwyn mural commemorating the First World War. The focal point of the whole building is, of course, the Legislative Chamber, where the 57 members of Manitoba's legislative assembly meet.

Before leaving the area, wander through the 31-acre grounds full of many species of trees, geraniums, and petunias, and note the statues that pay respect to Manitoba's many ethnic groups—Scotland's Robert Burns, French-Canadian Georges-Étienne Cartier, Iceland's Jon Sigurdson, and Ukrainian poet Taras Shevchenko. The building is open from 10 a.m. to 4 p.m. Monday to Friday.

MACDONALD HOUSE (DALNAVERT): Just behind the Legislative Building at 61 Carlton St., between Broadway and Assiniboine, stands one of the few surviving gracious Victorian homes that used to dominate the Winnipeg streetscape. The house has been restored to 1895 when it was built by Hugh John MacDonald, the only son of Canada's first prime minister. It's a fine example of a late Victorian gingerbread house with wraparound veranda. At the time of construction the latest innovations—electric lighting, indoor plumbing, central steam heating, and walk-in closets—were included. Throughout the house are beautiful stained-glass panels (whose softness of color cannot be duplicated today), elaborate wood paneling, ceilings, wainscoting, and staircases, and masses of overstuffed furniture and ornate drapes. As you go through the house you'll probably wonder at the extraordinary amount of muscle power needed for housework in those days to operate such gadgets as the Dowswell washer, and how even functional appliances were things of beauty—note the waffle iron with its diamonds, hearts, clubs, and spades design. You can play a guessing game of "What Is It?" as you go around.

Open 10 a.m. to 6 p.m. during summer, noon to 5 p.m. during winter. Closed Mondays and Fridays. Admission: $1 for adults, 75¢ for students 13 to 17, 25¢ for children under 13.

WINNIPEG ART GALLERY: Easily identifiable because of its triangular site and its bold prismatic mass (it looks like an iceberg or some other ocean-going object afloat on Memorial Blvd.), the gallery, opened in 1971, is most famous for its excellent collection of Eskimo art and sculpture handsomely arranged on the mezzanine. Note the wry vision of an artist such as Leah Qumaluk Povungnituk as contained in a stonecut of *Birds Stealing Kayak from Man.*

The main thrust of the remaining collections are Canadiana—important recent shows have included *Frontiers of Our Dreams: Quebec Painting in the 1940s and 1950s* and *Eskimo Narrative.* Two galleries are devoted to prints and photography, and the contemporary gallery will probably have some very interesting sculpture—perhaps even video sculpture.

Besides permanent and changing exhibits, the museum also organizes many artistic and cultural events: lectures, concerts (from folk to chamber and contemporary music), dance performances, films, and children's theater. For information, call 786-6641.

Open Tuesday through Saturday from 11 a.m. to 5 p.m., and Sunday from noon to 5 p.m. Closed Monday. Admission is free.

MUSEUM OF MAN AND NATURE, AND THE PLANETARIUM: Part of the Centennial Arts Centre on Main St., the museum galleries depict aspects of local history, culture, and geology. The Earth History Gallery portrays the creation of the universe, the prehistoric era, Ice Age, and geologic formation of Manitoba, while the Grasslands Gallery traces the history of the prairies from the days when Indian tribes hunted the buffalo, through the fur-trading era, to the early settlement and the immigrant boom of the late 1800s. In the Urban Gallery you can walk down a 1920s Winnipeg street past typical homes and businesses of the era and climb aboard the *Nonsuch,* a full-size replica of the 17th-century ketch that returned to England in 1669 with the first cargo of furs out of Hudson Bay. In each of these areas you'll find lifesize exhibits of the buffalo hunt, prehistoric creatures, pioneer life, pronghorn antelope, tepees, sod huts, log cabins—a fascinating place to perform acts of imagination.

Open mid-May to mid-September, Monday to Saturday and holidays from 10 a.m. to 9 p.m., and Sunday from noon to 9 p.m.; mid-September to mid-May, open Monday to Friday from 10 a.m. to 5 p.m., Saturday to 9 p.m., and Sundays and holidays from noon to 6 p.m. Admission: 75¢ for adults; senior citizens and children under 6, free; family, $3 maximum. For information, call 943-3139 or 947-5601.

The **planetarium,** whose entrance is downstairs from the museum, unlocks the mysteries of the universe in an exciting series of (usually) six different shows a year. One of the best places to see the last total solar eclipse of the century on February 26, 1979, was in Manitoba. Hence the show *Eclipses: When Worlds Align,* which prepared the audience for this dramatic event demonstrating how to observe the eclipse safely, and recreated eclipses as seen from Jupiter by the Apollo astronauts. The two current shows when I visited were *Cosmic Evolution,* which investigated theories about the evolution of galaxies and stars, and looked at such mysteries as black holes, quasars, and pulsars, and *Laserock,* a gyrating blaze of color choreographed against a blanket of stars to such artists as Fleetwood Mac, Yes, and Earth, Wind and Fire.

Admission to Laserock is $3.25. Admission to the planetarium is $2 for adults, $1.50 for students, $1 for children 6 to 12 and senior citizens. For information and show times, call 943-3142. Show times are: July and August: Saturday, Sunday, and holidays, 1, 2:30, 4, 7:30, and 9 p.m.; Tuesday to Friday, 11:30 a.m., and 3:30, 7:30, and 9 p.m. September through June: Sunday, 1, 2:30, and 4 p.m.; Tuesday to Friday, 3:15 and 8 p.m.; Saturday and holidays, 1, 2:30, 4, 7:30, and 9 p.m. Closed Mondays (except holidays).

THE UKRAINIAN CENTRE: Just up the street from the Museum of Man and Nature, the Ukrainian Centre, 184 Alexander Ave. (tel. 943-3045), devotes itself to conserving the artifacts and heritage of the Ukrainian people. Now housed in a restored old cast-iron building, on the ground floor, you'll find a boutique and small exhibition area featuring fine art paintings and musical instruments like the cymbaly, the multistringed bandura, the lyre-like kobza. On the second floor is an art gallery containing M. Muchin's wax sculpture of *Prince Ihor,* A. Pavlos's bronze *Prince Roman of Halych,* and Jacque Hnizdowsky's woodcuts entitled *Field and Cabbage,* just part of a collection that ranges from an anonymous 18th-century icon to contemporary graphics. In the fifth-floor museum, besides the folk art collection (embroidery, weaving, Easter eggs, woodcarving, ceramics, and native costumes), you can see a reproduction of the interior of a peasant hut with its decorative ceramic stove, icons, and hand-carved woodwork, as well as a collection of coins and stamps issued by the Ukrainian National Republic in 1918. The center also offers lectures and film programs.

Open weekdays from 9 a.m. to 5 p.m., Saturday and Sunday from 2 to 5 p.m. Admission is free.

ROYAL CANADIAN MINT: The drive to the mint, which lies south of Winnipeg, will sketch and capture the feeling of the west—as you pass the Union stockyards, grain elevators, and boxcars etched against the horizon. At the end of your trip the mint rises as a gleaming glass pyramid, glistening in the sun or purple on a dull day. Inside the foyer, light falls dramatically on the plants, rock garden, and paths leading between the fountains.

At the mint you will be taken on a truly mind-boggling tour of the engineering processes required to make money—the 14 stages involved in producing one die, a roof crane lifting 4000-pound strips of bronze and nickel, three 150-ton presses stamping out up to 8800 coin blanks per minute, and the coining presses turning out up to 18,000 coins per hour to the telling machines which count the number for bagging. A bag of 10,000 dimes, by the way, weighs 46.487 pounds. The whole process from start to finish represents an extraordinary engineering feat, from the overhead cranes to the conveyor belt that carries the blanks up and down into the furnaces, dropping under the floors to deliver the metals from one room to the next, to the overhead monorail that delivers those same blanks to the coining presses. You will also see a film on the history of coin making.

Open 9 a.m. to 3 p.m. weekdays only. Admission free. To get there, take Main St. south over the Assiniboine/Red Rivers, turn left onto Marion St., and then right onto Lagimodière. You'll see the mint rise up just beyond the Trans Canada Hwy. (Rte. 135).

ASSINIBOINE PARK AND ZOO: Comprising 362 acres for playing, picnicking, or bicycling, the park also contains a miniature railway, a duck pond, and English garden (which opens in June), a conservatory, and a small 100-acre zoo where the animals—bears, tigers, zebras, flamingos, buffalos, elk, moose—are kept in as natural an environment as possible. The children will enjoy Aunt Sally's Farm and the young animals there during the summer.

The zoo is open every day from 10 a.m. to dusk. Admission is free. The park is open from 8 a.m. to 10 p.m. During the winter you can enjoy skating on the pond, tobogganing, and sleigh rides.

To get there, take Portage Ave. west, turn left onto Kenaston Blvd. (Rte. 90) south, and then turn right onto Corydon.

THE COMMODITY EXCHANGE: Organized in 1887 originally as a grain exchange, it changed its name in 1972 to reflect its expansion into oilseeds, rapeseed, flaxseed, and gold. The very crux of Winnipeg was right here: the world's premier grain market.

Come early, around 9:30 a.m., or late, at 1:15 p.m. when you're more likely to see some feverish action on the floor. You don't have to view the proceedings through glass but can actually get down on the floor, almost into the pit where buyers and sellers are jostling, yelling out figures, and gesticulating in apparent confusion, while above markers race up and down chalking up the current Winnipeg and Chicago prices on blackboards. The pits themselves are raised octagonal platforms, with descending steps on the inside—a shape that permits all buyers and sellers to see each other.

If you go before October 1980 you'll be seeing such action closeup for the last time, since the exchange is moving into brand-new quarters with a fully electronic system, and any visitor will probably be back behind those familiar distancing glass panels. Today the commodities traded include feed wheat, oats, barley, rye, rapeseed, flaxseed, corn, and gold. There are 340 members and 110 companies are registered for trading privileges. The Commodity Exchange is at Lombard Ave. right next door to the Winnipeg Inn. Go to Room 608 and someone will take you around and explain everything that is happening. Open from 9:30 a.m. to 1:15 p.m. Admission is free.

ST-BONIFACE CATHEDRAL AND MUSEUM: Across the Red River in St-Boniface, one of the oldest French-Canadian communities in Canada, stands the Cathédrale de St-Boniface originally built in 1818. Fire destroyed the interior in 1968 so that only the exterior facade remains. The interior has been rebuilt as a modern chapel. The body of Louis Riel, leader of the Métis and president of the provincial government formed in 1869 to 1870 to prevent the transfer of the Red River settlement to Canada, lies in the cathedral close.

Next door is the St-Boniface museum, 494 rue Tâche, located in a white oak-log structure with green shutters, an early example of Red River frame construction, which was originally built for the Grey Nuns between 1845 and 1851. It houses a very large collection of French and Métis artifacts, including the blue and green tuque Riel wore the day he was hanged in Regina. Open from late May to Labour Day, Monday to Friday from 10 a.m. to 5 p.m., on Sunday from 1 to 5 p.m. Otherwise, Sunday to Friday from 1 to 5 p.m. Admission: Free will offerings.

GRANT'S OLD MILL: At the corner of Portage Ave. and Booth Dr. stands the reconstruction of the original watermill built on Sturgeon Creek in 1829, which is believed to be the first watermill west of the Great Lakes and the first instance of the use of hydropower in Manitoba. Grist is ground daily during the summer and you can buy some in a souvenir bag if you like. Open daily from July 1 to September 1, 10 a.m. to 8 p.m., Sunday from 2 to 8 p.m., and weekends during May, September, and October by appointment only. Admission: adults, 50¢; children, 25¢.

RIVERBOAT TOURS: The cruise ships M.S. *River Rouge* and M.S. *Lady Winnipeg* depart daily from Dock 312, Nairn Ave. at the Louise Bridge (tel. 669-2824). The M.S. *Lady Winnipeg* cruises to Lower Fort Garry Wednesday through Sunday, departing at 10 a.m. and returning at 4:30 p.m. (adults pay $6.75; children 11 and under, $3.75; children under 2, free). The M.S. *River Rouge* cruises the Red and Assiniboine Rivers offering a spectacular view of Winnipeg. Daytime cruises leave Monday through Saturday at 2 p.m. and Sunday at 1, 3, and 5 p.m. (adults pay $3.50; children 11 and under $1.75). Nighttime cruises that include dancing to a live band depart Monday through Saturday at 7 and 10 p.m., and Sunday at 7:30 p.m. (adults are $4.50; children 11 and under, $1.75).

Or you can cruise on M.S. *Paddlewheel Queen* or *Paddlewheel Princess,* two replicas of the sternwheelers that helped to open the west. An afternoon sightseeing cruise departs at 2 p.m. daily, May through October (adults, $3.75). A sunset dinner-dance cruise departs at 7 p.m. daily, May through October (adults, $4.75). The moonlight dance cruise leaves at 10 p.m. (adults, $4.75). Both boats depart from the Redwood Bridge. To get there, drive north on Main St. to Redwood Ave. and turn right. Operated by Gray Line, 285 Enniskillen Ave.; call 589-4318 for more information.

A STEAM TRAIN RIDE: A 1900 steam-era train, the Prairie Dog Central, will take you on a two-hour, 36-mile round trip to Grosse Isle, Manitoba. En route you really get a feel for the prairie and what it must have been like for late 19th-century immigrants to travel to and through the west. The train leaves on Sunday at 11:30 a.m. and 3 p.m. June through September (adults, $5; senior citizens, $4; children 3 to 11, $2.50; children under 3, free).

To reach the station, drive west on Portage Ave. to just beyond St. James St. For more information, write P.O. Box 1182, Winnipeg, MB R3C 2Y4 (tel. 204/284-2690).

THE RACETRACK: Assiniboia Downs, 3975 Portage Ave. (tel. 885-3330), is open from the end of April to the end of October, and offers thrilling evening entertainment, where besides the racing you can either dine in the Futurity Room or drink in one of the four lounges. Post times are Monday, Wednesday, Friday, and Saturday at 7 p.m.; Sundays and holidays at 2 p.m. Admission: adults, $2; children 5 to 15 and seniors, $1; under 5, free. Clubhouse admission is $4.

The track is located nine miles west of the city at the junction of Hwy. 1 West (Portage Ave.) and Hwy. 100 (Perimeter Hwy.). For transit information, call 885-3330.

5. Culture and Nightlife

CENTENNIAL ARTS CENTRE: The shining star on Winnipeg's cultural scene is the $7½-million Centennial Arts Centre, a little way north of Portage on Main St. The huge complex includes the Centennial Concert Hall, Manitoba Theatre Centre, the Museum of Man and Nature and the Planetarium, the Warehouse Theatre, and the Playhouse Theatre. There is also a skating rink/playground and a serene outdoor courtyard with fountains, the scene of an annual free summer festival. In the concert hall itself, works of art are highlighted. In the lobby Greta Dale's vast tile mural brilliantly represents the three major performing arts—dance, music, and drama—while the orchestra-level foyers are enhanced by the murals of Tony Tascona representing the mathematical precision of music. Three magnificent chandeliers made of Norwegian crystal flood all the lobbies with light—a breathtaking sight from without. Each weighs 7600 pounds and contains 600 pieces of crystal and 140 lightbulbs. The 2263-seat auditorium is in the continental style with no center aisle, and has fully retractable seats. It is known for its acoustical excellence. Behind the gold mesh of the ceiling and walls there are 28 sets of acoustical curtains which are fully extended or retracted for electronic amplification or nonamplification events.

OPERA, SYMPHONY, AND BALLET: Of the three arts, the longest established has of course been the world-renowned **Royal Winnipeg Ballet,** which was founded in 1939 by two British immigrant ballet teachers. By 1949 it was a professional troupe, and in 1953 was granted a royal charter. Today the company's repertoire contains both contemporary and classical works. One of the most exciting recent choreographies was the world premiere of Salvatore Aiello's *Journey;* performed to a concerto for organ and orchestra by Malcolm Arnold, it was the first major Canadian work for an all-male cast. Otherwise, the repertoire includes such works as *Don Quixote,* Balanchine's *Glinka Pas de Trois,* and Paddy Stone's joyous *The Hands.* The company performs at the Centennial Concert Hall, usually for four days only in October, November, December, March, and May. Tickets range from $3.50 to $9. There are usually discounts for students and senior citizens on Wednesdays, Thursdays, and Sundays.

The **Winnipeg Symphony Orchestra,** 117-555 Main St. (tel. 942-6954), established 1947, had its greatest triumph perhaps only last year when it made its debut at Carnegie Hall in New York City. The prestige of the orchestra and the genuinely superb acoustics of the Centennial Concert Hall (555 Main St.; tel. 947-5611) have enabled the orchestra to attract such guest artists as Philippe Entremont, Maureen Forrester, Van Cliburn, Yehudi Menuhin, and Ruggiero Ricci. For information, call 942-4576. Tickets range from $5.75 to $9.50, and the season usually runs from early November to early May.

The **Manitoba Opera Company** (tel. 942-4567) gave its first performance in 1970 and has now settled down to a season of three operas at the Centennial Arts Centre—for 1979–1980, *La Traviata, The Merry Widow,* and *Turandot;* for 1980–1981, *Tosca, The Barber of Seville,* and *Nabucco.* Tickets range from $6 to $21.

THEATER: Acclaimed as the best regional theater in Canada, the **Manitoba Theatre Centre** began in 1958, operating in the rickety but spirited atmosphere of the old Dominion Theatre on Portage and Main. Today, it has an ultramodern theater seating 785 people on Market Ave., adjacent to the Centennial Arts Centre. Ever since Tom Hendry and John Hirsch founded the group it has been dedicated to producing good serious theater, and over the years has performed all kinds of works: *Juno and the Paycock, A Midsummer Night's Dream, Who's Afraid of Virginia Woolf?, Heartbreak House, Galileo* (with Paxton Whitehead), *The Three Sisters, Dance of Death,* and more recently, *Sleuth, The Dybbuk, Equus, Private Lives,* and *Cyrano de Bergerac.* Probably the most famous actor to have emerged from Winnipeg onto the Broadway stage and film is of course Len Cariou. The season usually contains seven productions and runs from mid-October to mid-May.

A second stage called the **MTC Warehouse** performs the more experimental works in an intimate, 220-seat setting. It offers a four-play season from mid-October to mid-May. Such productions have included *Endgame, Berlin to Broadway with Kurt Weill, Waiting for Godot, Ashes,* and in 1979, *Sizwe Bansi Is Dead.*

Tickets range from $3.50 to $8.50 on weeknights, $6.50 to $9.25 on weekends, $3 to $8.50 for matinees. For information, call the box office at 942-6537.

At the Warehouse, tickets are usually $4.50 for adults, $3 for students and senior citizens.

CONCERT POTPOURRI: Other places where you might find concerts being performed include: **Centennial Concert Hall,** 555 Main St., which also features such artists and rock groups as Kenneth McKellar, Ivan Rebroff, Joan Armatrading, and Oscar Peterson; the **Winnipeg Art Gallery,** which often features blues/country singers, chamber music, and contemporary music groups, where tickets are usually only $2.50 to $5; the **Playhouse Theatre,** 180 Market Ave. (tel. 942-4037), which has recently hosted such jazz greats as Roy Eldridge and Budd Johnson, and foreign folk-music groups; the **Convention Centre,** 375 York Ave. (tel. 956-1720), for popular and folk artists, and light orchestral musical concerts.

DANCING TO LIVE MUSIC: Most of the nightlife action takes place at the main downtown hotels: for dancing to live music, **Stage Door** at the Winnipeg

Inn, the **Iron Duke** at the Marlborough Inn, the **Left Bank** at the Hotel Fort Garry, and **Uncles** at the Holiday Inn are the most popular spots.

Otherwise, the **King's Plate,** 2727 Portage (tel. 832-4996), is a cavernous place that seats close to 200 and offers dining and dancing on a larger than usual dance floor. Your dinner might begin with a shrimp cocktail ($3.75) and continue with smoked Winnipeg goldeye ($8.50) or a king-size New York steak ($10.95). Soup, salad, potato, and beverage are included in the price. The live entertainment, usually a local or out-of-town rock group, begins at 9:15 p.m. If you just want to sit in the lounge and use the dance floor, you can—drinks average $2 for a gin and tonic, $1.55 for beer, and $2.50 to $3.50 for cocktails.

DISCO DANCING: The hottest disco is undoubtedly **Bogart's,** 159 Albert St. (tel. 942-1143), which is always jam-packed with a sophisticated 30-ish crowd. On the ground floor, next to the raised dance floor with its fantastic light show, there's elegant dining with bentwood cane chairs and exquisite table settings. Upstairs there's a cocktail lounge. The average price of a drink is $3. To enjoy the disco legally you have to eat, and so here's a brief rundown on the menu: appetizers include escargots, shrimp cocktail, pâté, or coquilles St-Jacques (from $2.75 to $3.50); steaks from $8.50, veal with Madeira sauce ($8.25), and barbecued ribs ($7.75) are featured main dishes. You select your pastry from the cart or have the crème caramel or ice cream. Open from 6 p.m. to 1 a.m. daily, except Sunday.

Ever danced at a disco without a liquor license? Well, you can do that at **Disco Inferno,** 293 Nairn (tel. 668-6688), where you'll find a young but pleasant enough crowd. The floor has a sophisticated pyrotechnics show operated by an English disc jockey. The tables nearest the dance floor are mirrored. Open from 8 p.m. to 2 a.m. Wednesday through Sunday. There's a cover charge of $4 Wednesday through Saturday (except Thursday, when women can get in free). No liquor is served. Nonalcoholic beer and wine are available ($1.10), or else soft drinks (75¢).

The most popular cabaret spot, the **Town and Country Cabaret,** 317 Kennedy St., has been closed while the management converts it into an ultra-flashy disco. Check it out and let me know.

PIANO BARS: Again, most of the piano bars are found at the hotels—the **Drummer Boy** at the Hotel Fort Garry, the **S.O.S.** at the Wandlyn Birchwood Inn, **Step 33** at the Northstar Inn, **Top of the Inn** at the Winnipeg Inn. For a very English atmosphere, drop in at the **Old Bailey,** downstairs at Olivers. The **Paddock** also has a middle-of-the-road pianist in the lounge and dining room. (For additional details, see the descriptions in the restaurant section.)

DINING ON THE RIVER: Sit back with shipboard friends and watch the city drift by as you glide along the Red and Assiniboine Rivers on the M.S. *River Rouge* and dance to a live band. Dinners are available from $5.75. For more information, call 669-2824.

OUTDOOR THEATER: Canada's largest and oldest continuously operating outdoor theater, **Rainbow Stage,** marked its 25th anniversary in 1979. During July and August the stage presents two musical classics running about three weeks each. Some typical productions have been *Fiddler on the Roof, Oklahoma!, My Fair Lady,* and *Hello Dolly.*

Located in Kildonan Park on the banks of the Red River, Rainbow is easily accessible by bus or car north on Main St. The park itself is quite delightful and contains landscaped gardens, picnic spots, cycling paths, outdoor swimming and wading pools, as well as a restaurant and dining room, overlooking a small artificial lake. Also in the park, look for the Witch's House from *Hansel and Gretel*.

For information about shows and ticket prices, call 942-2421 or 942-2091; or write: Rainbow Stage, 500-352 Donald St., Winnipeg, MB R3B 2H8.

6. Around Winnipeg

LOWER FORT GARRY: Only 20 miles northeast of Winnipeg on Hwy. 9, at this stone fort you'll find costumed personnel reenacting life as it was back in the days of the fur trade. The fort was constructed in the 1830s as a Hudson's Bay Company supply center. You can see the big house—the first building completed on the fort site in 1832—home of the company's governor, the retail store, the fur loft and sale shop building (that once served some 1800 customers from the area), the unique York boats that were used to navigate inland waters and carry furs and trade goods.

Open daily from mid-May to mid-October from 9:30 a.m. to 6 p.m. Admission: adults, $1.25; children 16 and under, 50¢.

AROUND LAKE WINNIPEG: This 264-mile-long lake is the continent's seventh largest, and its shores harbor some interesting spots to visit: **Gimli,** 60 miles north of Winnipeg, a farming and fishing community and the hub of Icelandic culture in Manitoba, which was established a century ago as the capital of New Iceland and for many years had its own government, school, and newspapers, and still celebrates an Icelandic festival on the first long weekend in August; **Gull Harbour** (130 miles northeast of Winnipeg) on Hecla Island, once a part of New Iceland and until recently home for a small community of Icelandic-Canadian farmers and fishermen, but now the site of Manitoba's newest provincial park, providing natural wilderness and excellent sporting opportunities—hiking, golf, fishing, camping, bird watching, canoeing, swimming, hunting, cross-country skiing, snowshoeing, snowmobiling, tobogganing, and curling—as well as first-class resort facilities at Gull Harbour Resort Hotel (for more information on the resort, write to: Gull Harbour Resort Hotel, General Delivery, Riverton, MB R0C 2R0); **Grand Rapids,** 266 miles north of Winnipeg, the home of a fish hatchery, major electric power-generating station, and a thriving Indian community; and **Berens River,** on the eastern shore of the lake, a remote (no all-weather roads connect it to the rest of Manitoba) community where one of Manitoba's largest and best known Indian reservations is located.

Cruising the Lake

One of the best ways to see the places mentioned above is to take a cruise out of Selkirk, only 22 miles northeast of Winnipeg. The M.S. *Lord Selkirk II* visits all these ports of call and has two-, and three-, and four-, and five-day cruises from June to September. Two-night cruises start at $139 economy to $259 luxury, while five-night cruises run from $359 to $579, respectively. For more information, write to: Sub-Arctic Expeditions Inc., 1065 Ellice Ave., Winnipeg, MB R3G 0E1 (tel. 204/786-6588).

WHITESHELL PROVINCIAL PARK: Less than two hours' drive from Winnipeg (90 miles east) lies a network of a dozen rivers and over 200 lakes in a 1000-square-mile park. Whiteshell offers unlimited opportunity for outdoor activity—swimming, scuba diving, sailing, waterskiing, fishing, hiking, golfing, riding, tennis, and bird-watching, as well as winter sports. Within the park lies one of Canada's most modern recreational townsite developments, **Falcon Lake,** where tennis courts, an 18-hole golf course, and a ski resort are just some of the facilities. Most of the resorts and lodges in the park charge anywhere from $20 to $50 double ($100 to $200 per week) for a cabin. Camping facilities abound. For more information, write to: Department of Tourism, Recreation and Cultural Affairs, Legislative Building, Winnipeg, MB R3C 0P8.

RIDING MOUNTAIN NATIONAL PARK: About 175 miles northwest of the city you can indulge in the same outdoor activities plus downhill skiing at Mt. Agassiz on the east side of the park, but in dramatically different surroundings. Riding Mountain is set in the highlands, atop a giant wooded escarpment. Accommodations and facilities are centered in Wasagaming; there is only one year-round lodge, **Elk Horn Ranch** (P.O. Box 40, Wasagaming, MB R0J 2H0; tel. 204/848-2802). You'll find tennis courts, lawn bowling greens, a children's playground, and a log-cabin movie theater in the Wasagaming Visitor Centre beside Clear Lake. At the lake itself you can rent a boat, canoe, or paddleboat, and swim at the main beach.

For campers, the Wasagaming campground has electricity and three-way hookups, toilet buildings with showers, kitchen shelters, and a sewage disposal station nearby. Other campgrounds are at Lake Katherine, Moon Lake, and Lake Audy.

The park information bureau is open daily from mid-May to mid-September, and on weekends during the ski season. For information, call or write: Superintendent, Riding Mountain National Park, Wasagaming, MB R0J 2H0 (tel. 204/848-2811). Camping rates are $3 unserviced, $5 with electricity, and $6 with electricity, sewer, and water. Entry to the park is $1 daily, $2 for a four-day permit.

THE FAR NORTH: The best way to explore the north is by rail on one of VIA's tours taking the *Hudson Bay Explorer* from Winnipeg, through the Pas, a fisherman's mecca, and the mining communities of FlinFlon and Thompson to **Churchill** on Hudson Bay. No other land route has yet penetrated this remote region covered with lakes, forests, and frozen tundra.

One of the largest grain-exporting terminals in the world, grain elevators dominate the Churchill skyline and you can watch the grain being unloaded from boxcars onto ships—perhaps 25 million bushels of wheat and barley clear the port in only 12 to 14 weeks of frantic nonstop operation. Other attractions in Churchill include the chance to see Beluga whales cavorting inshore, an excellent Eskimo museum, and the 18th-century Fort Prince of Wales, accessible via boat during the summer and by dog team during the winter.

The trip takes six days and six nights and costs $495 from Winnipeg (including accommodations, sightseeing, and specified meals). So popular has this trip become that you will have to make reservations a year in advance. For more information, contact your travel agent or a local VIA office.

Chapter XIV

THE TWIN CITIES OF SASKATCHEWAN

1. Regina
2. Saskatoon
3. Special Saskatchewan Events and Activities

FIVE TIMES THE SIZE of New York State, with a population of under one million, Saskatchewan is the center of Canada's prairie provinces and produces 60% of Canada's wheat.

For the tourist it provides a hunting and fishing paradise in the northern lakes and forests, several summer playgrounds, including Prince Albert National Park and 17 provincial parks, and the cities of Regina and Saskatoon.

SOME PROVINCIAL HISTORY: The first settlers of the province were hunting and gathering Indian tribes—Chipewyans, Blackfoot, and Cree. At the end of the 17th century, Henry Kelsey entered the prairies and Saskatchewan—the first white man ever to do so. Soon others followed in search of furs, and among the first to settle were the Métis, of mixed European and Indian blood. In 1872 the Canadian government offered free land to anyone who would settle what was then known as the Northwest Territories, but it was not until the arrival of the Central Pacific Railway in 1882 that the floodgates of immigration were opened and the British, Germans, Ukrainians, Scandinavians, French, and other Europeans poured in. Regina was established as the seat of the territorial government and headquarters of the Northwest Mounted Police. The Métis did not accept the takeover of the area by the eastern government, and in 1885 Louis Riel led them in a rebellion in northern Saskatchewan, which was suppressed by Major-General Middleton at the Battle of Batoche (later, Riel was executed in Regina). Immigration continued apace, wheat production soared, and in 1905 Saskatchewan was created with its capital at Regina.

Her steady growth was interrupted by the Depression, when Saskatchewan was even more badly hit than other provinces because of nine years of drought and crop failure. After driving through southern Saskatchewan in the summer of 1934, a Regina newspaper reporter wrote: "for miles there was scarcely a thing growing to be seen. . . . Gaunt cattle and horses with little save their skins to cover their bones stalked about the denuded acres, weakly seeking to crop the malign Frenchweed which seemed to be maintaining some sickly growth. When the miserable animals moved it seemed as if their frames rattled. The few people in evidence in the little towns appeared haggard and hopeless."

The worst year of all was 1937, when the temperature reached 114°. In Regina, according to Edward McCourt's book *Saskatchewan,* bathers in Wascana Creek could not get from the water to the bathhouses without being coated with dust, and legend has it that a baseball player set off from the batting square and wound up three miles out on the prairies.

Such hardship breeds a stoical pride, independence, and pessimism, which may account for both the suspicion of government and the willingness to indulge in political and social experiments that has characterized the province's recent history. Saskatchewan, for example, elected the first socialist government in Canada—in 1944.

A NOTE ON CLIMATE: Summers can be simply magnificent, with warm sunny days and cool refreshing evenings and nights. The climate is dry with only 30 to 40 centimeters of rain per year. Summer temperatures average 24° to 27°C. Average winter temperatures are −18° to −23°C with about 100 to 125 centimeters of snowfall each year—I think you can guess the best time to go.

A NOTE ON SASKATCHEWAN LIQUOR LAWS: Saskatchewan seems to have cast (and still does) a jaded eye on "devil drink" as the current laws indicate. No standup bars are allowed—you cannot stand up and walk around with a glass of liquor; beverage rooms have to be connected to hotels; no liquor can be served anywhere unless food is available. Until July 1, 1979, dancing to recorded music was forbidden if liquor was available on the premises (which explains the province's lack of discos). Not until 1961 were women allowed in beverage rooms. And, of course, all lounges and beverage rooms are closed on Sunday. You may, however, drink on Sundays provided you are in a restaurant and your liquor bill does not exceed your food bill. This can take a bit of getting used to—so better you should know now.

1. Regina

Originally named Pile O'Bones after the heap of buffalo skeletons the first settlers found (the Indians had amassed the bones in the belief that they would lure the vanished buffalo back again), the city has to thank Princess Louise, daughter of Queen Victoria, for its more regal name. She named it in her mother's honor in 1882 when it became the capital of the Northwest Territories.

The original town site was not widely acclaimed. It was severely criticized by the Canadian press: "There is no water in the creek, a series of shallow stagnant pools . . . of a dark brown, brackish appearance," reported the Toronto *Globe,* while an exasperated editor of *Forest and Stream* wrote, "I have never in all my travels seen so wretched a site for a town."

Despite the questionable water supply, the barren prairie landscape, and the infamous Regina mud, the town grew. It only really hit the national headlines three times: first, when Louis Riel was hanged in November 1885; second, in June 1912 when a cyclone tore through the city killing 28 and injuring 200, and third, when the Royal Canadian Mounted Police (RCMP) clashed with strikers from the labor camps of British Columbia who were en route to Ottawa. Hundreds were injured when stones, bricks, and clubs were met with gunfire and tear gas.

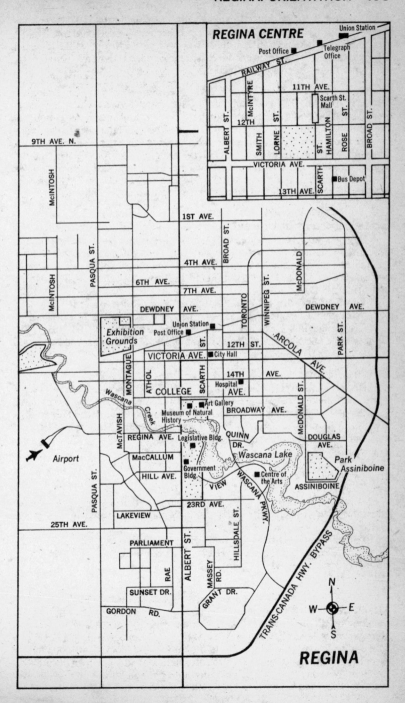

REGINA CENTRE

Union Station

Post Office ■

Telegraph Office

RAILWAY ST.

11TH AVE.

McINTYRE

Scarth St. Mall

12TH

ALBERT ST.

SMITH

LORNE ST.

ST. HAMILTON

ROSE ST.

BROAD ST.

VICTORIA AVE.

SCARTH

■ Bus Depot

13TH AVE.

9TH AVE. N.

McINTOSH

McINTOSH

PASQUA ST.

1ST AVE.

4TH AVE.

BROAD ST.

6TH AVE.

7TH AVE.

McDONALD

DEWDNEY AVE.

Exhibition Grounds

Union Station

Post Office ■

TORONTO

WINNIPEG ST.

DEWDNEY AVE.

PARK ST.

12TH ST.

ARCOLA

MONTAGUE

ST.

VICTORIA AVE. ■ City Hall

AVE.

ATHOL

SCARTH

14TH

Hospital

AVE.

McDONALD ST.

COLLEGE

AVE.

McTAVISH

■ Art Gallery

BROADWAY AVE.

Museum of Natural History

DOUGLAS AVE.

REGINA AVE.

Legislative Bldg.

QUINN DR.

Park Assiniboine

MacCALLUM

Wascana Lake

■ Centre of the Arts

ASSINIBOINE

Airport

HILL AVE.

Government Bldg.

VIEW

WASCANA PKWY.

PASQUA ST.

23RD AVE.

HILLSDALE ST.

25TH AVE.

LAKEVIEW

ALBERT ST.

PARLIAMENT

MASSEY RD.

RAE

TRANS-CANADA HWY. BYPASS

SUNSET DR.

GRANT DR.

N

GORDON RD.

W — E

S

REGINA

Wascana

Creek

Today it is the provincial capital with a population of 160,000, and although it still has a certain prairie feel, it is becoming a rather zippy, sophisticated city. So take no notice of those who whisper of Regina as the last stop on any itinerary. It has some good hotels, a burgeoning selection of restaurants, and some rather interesting attractions.

ORIENTATION: The two main streets are Victoria Ave., which runs east-west, and Albert St., which runs north-south. South of their intersection lies the Wascana Centre, a 2500-acre park that also contains the Legislative Building, the University of Regina, the Diefenbaker Homestead, the Natural History Museum, Norman Mackenzie Art Gallery, Saskatchewan Arts Centre, and the waterfowl park. Most of the downtown hotels stretch along Victoria Ave. between Albert St. on the west and Broad St. on the east. The RCMP barracks are located to the north and west of the downtown area.

Getting in and out of Regina

Regina's **airport** is located only 15 minutes from downtown west of the city. For a limousine to the major downtown hotels you'll pay $2. **Air Canada** has offices at 2015 12th Ave. (tel. 525-4711) and has flights going east-west. **Norcanair** (tel. 525-8711) offers flights to and from Saskatoon, Prince Albert, and Minot, N.D.

VIA Rail operates out of the station at South Railway and Rose St. (tel. 522-2626). Some sample fares: $13 one way to Saskatoon, $27 to Winnipeg.

Greyhound Bus Lines are located at 2041 Hamilton St. (tel. 565-3340). Some sample one-way ticket prices: to Winnipeg, $20.40; to Saskatoon, $9.45.

Getting Around

Regina Transit, 1157 Albert St. (tel. 569-7777), operates eight or so bus routes that make it easy to get around. For schedules and maps, either go to the address above or else to the transit information booth at Broad St. and 11th Ave., open Monday to Saturday from 9 a.m. to 11 p.m. Fares are: adults, 45¢; children up to elementary school age, 25¢; students, 20¢. You must have the exact fare.

Taxis can most easily be found at downtown hotels. They are of course expensive—$1.20 when you get in and 80¢ per mile thereafter. **United** (tel. 543-3333) is the most used.

Driving is no problem in Regina, but do note that the province requires all motorists to wear seatbelts. Otherwise, you may be fined anywhere from $20 and up.

For **car rentals,** here are a few addresses: **Budget Rent-a-Car** is in the Regina Inn Mall (tel. 527-5623); **Hertz,** 3405 South Railway (tel. 525-3377); **Tilden,** Victoria Ave. at Hamilton (tel. 527-4696); **Avis,** 2010 Victoria Ave. (tel. 527-1653).

Tourist Information

For on-the-spot information, go to the **Regina Tourist and Convention Bureau,** 2145 Albert St., Regina, SK S4P 2V1 (tel. 527-6631), which is open Monday to Friday from 8:45 a.m. to 5 p.m. It's 1½ blocks south of Victoria Ave. From June 1 to August 31, two **information booths** are open from 8 a.m. to 8 p.m. Monday to Saturday and noon to 8 p.m. on Sunday at Gordon Rd. and Albert St. on the southern approach to the city, and at 101 Victoria Ave.

Or else go to the **Department of Tourism and Renewable Resources,** 1825 Lorne St., Regina SK S4P 3V7. This department (known as Sask Travel) offers an in-province toll-free travel counseling service during the summer, usually from the first week of June to Labour day. Call 565-2300 if you're in Regina; 800/667-3674 if you're elsewhere in the province.

Useful Information

Regina's **daily paper** is the *Leader Post*. . . . There are six **liquor stores** in the city—the most convenient downtown location at 416 Albert St. North, which is open from 11 a.m. to 10 p.m. weekdays, to 6 p.m. on Saturday (closed on Sunday, of course). . . . Regular **store hours** are from 9 a.m. to 6 p.m. Tuesday through Saturday and Thursday evening until 9:30 p.m. . . . **Banking** hours are Monday through Thursday from 10 a.m. to 3 p.m., and to 6 p.m. on Friday. . . . The main **post office** is at 220 South Railway at Cornwall St., and is open Monday through Friday from 8 a.m. to 5:45 p.m., on Saturday from 8 a.m. to noon (tel. 569-5640). . . . For **telephone information,** dial 113. . . . Saskatchewan **climate** can vary from 100°F in summer to −50°F in winter, with an average of 50 inches of snow per year.

REGINA ACCOMMODATIONS:

REGINA ACCOMMODATIONS: The **Regina Inn,** at Victoria Ave. and Broad St. (tel. 306/525-6767), stretches almost one full block—a whole entertainment complex complete with dinner theater, Tikis piano bar/disco, and a pub-style lounge, the Old Posthouse, with its authentic Liverpool jugs, wood paneling, and bookcases. Built in 1967, the inn's 240 rooms on 14 floors were completely renovated last year and decorated in color coordinations of brown and rust. The rooms are large, have louvered closets, clock radio, and some have a bar while others have a vanity area. Only 20 do not have balconies. The pool area has a solarium dome, an outside sundeck, and white garden furniture for relaxing over that postswim cocktail, plus two saunas and a small exercise room.

The Inn Steakhouse, where you can watch your steaks sizzling in the steak pit in a setting of warm wood paneling, gilt-framed portraits, leather chairs, and gas-style table lamps, has an excellent dining reputation. A sample dinner might start with escargots piperade (snails prepared with fresh tomatoes, mushrooms, peppers, and a hint of garlic, $4.95) or Lady Curzon soup (half turtle, half puree of peas, mildly spiced with curry and topped with cream, $4.25), and follow with duckling bigarrade ($9.95), steak Diane ($14.95), or a charcoal-broiled steak (from $10.50 to $12.95). Top off the meal with the house specialty—bananas cooked in foil with apricot puree and vanilla ($3.25), and a special coffee to go with it. At Tikis, the Polynesian-style lounge/dance spot, I can heartily recommend the Tiki special—a combination plate of steak, ribs, and shrimp served with feta cheese—delicious. On Friday and Saturday there's a $2 cover charge; drinks average $2.50.

Rates: $39 to $43 single, $45 to $50 double. An extra person is $5, and children under 18 stay free with their parents. A weekend package is available. Free indoor parking.

Only two years old, the **Sheraton Centre,** 1818 Victoria Ave. (tel. 306/ 569-1666), has a natural and graceful air which you'll notice the minute you walk into the lobby with its earth-color wall hangings, natural wood walls, small waterfall, and open-area coffee plaza with plants scattered around. Off this lobby lies the Cellar, where you can dine seated inside a vat under lamps created from wine casks—you even have your personal lighting control. In the fireside lounge you can sit around an open firepit on soft velour banquettes before dropping into the French Quarter, one of the city's most popular nightspots, with live entertainment, stainless-steel dance floor, and terraced seating. To complete the picture there's a really luxurious Oasis on the second floor housing saunas, sunlamps, whirlpool, miniature golf, and indoor pool under a solarium dome. Rooms are attractively decorated in the current fashionable browns and oranges with modern furnishings and all the usual facilities, including Touch-Tone phones.

Rates: $36 to $44 single, $42 to $60 double (the $60 double price is for a petite suite which has a partition between the bed and the living area). Children under 12 stay free in their parents' room. An extra adult is $5. Free indoor parking.

The creeper-encrusted limestone exterior of the **Hotel Saskatchewan,** Victoria Ave. at Scarth (tel. 306/522-7691), has a rather solid old-world air about it that provides a satisfying prelude to the modern comfort within. The large, almost heart-shaped clock that hangs in the lobby is original to the 1927 Georgian-style building. The long narrow lobby leads to the L-shaped Ranch Room, with terraced seating highlighted by brick archways, wooden pillars, stately windows, and a coffered oak ceiling with brass chandeliers. The menu specializes in grills, seafood, veal, and chicken dishes (from $7 to $11) at dinner and a lighter selection at lunchtime. In the Spanish lounge, period furniture (sofas, tables with carved pedestal bases) creates a tasteful and restful setting for a quiet drink.

The 252 rooms have all been recently renovated, furnished with contemporary pieces, and decorated in gold, green, and beige combinations, but still retaining the graceful high ceilings, wall moldings, and large bathrooms. Corner rooms have been turned into especially comfortable bed-sitting rooms with a pull-out couch.

Rates: $34 to $42 single, $41 to $50 double. No charge for children under 14 occupying their parents' room. Free parking.

A Moderate Downtown Choice

Standing across from the Regina Inn is the seven-story-high **Westward Inn,** 1717 Victoria Ave. (tel. 306/527-0663), part of the Best Western chain. All 126 rooms were renovated 1½ years ago and feature contemporary furniture, orange, yellow, and green spreads with matching curtains, and the usual accoutrements—direct-dial phone, color TV, and radio. Rooms at the back of the hotel are quieter and might be preferred. There's a dining room/coffeeshop and lounge/bar on the premises.

Rates: $27 to $32.50 single, $33.50 to $37.50 double. Children 12 years and under free; an extra adult is $5. Free parking.

Along Albert St. South

If you are coming from the U.S. border you will probably come into Regina along Albert St. South, which presents several accommodations choices.

First class: The most luxurious accommodation on the strip is the brand-new **Landmark Inn,** 4150 Albert St. (tel. 306/586-5363). From the road it looks long, low, and sleekly modern, and the interior consolidates that impression. It offers a selection of dining and entertaining establishments from the Blade and Barrel, where red fringed lampshades and butcher-block tables set the scene for steak and lobster, to the authentic English pub, Checkers, with its horse brasses, hunting prints, and banquettes, plus a very English dartboard in the corner. There's a beer garden also. Beer is $1.05, cocktails about $1.75, and pub fare runs from $2.25 to $3.95. A super-sophisticated atmosphere prevails at Bogart's, achieved by extensive use of natural pine, plants, wicker and fan chairs, and a touch of wrought iron. Here you can dine and dance in the style of Humphrey himself (surrounded by his scenes and his portraits). Start with shrimp provençale ($3.45) or a seafood bisque ($2.25), and follow with veal Oscar ($9.75) or rack of lamb, or any of the fish dishes. Save room for a hot chocolate crêpe à la mode ($1.95). On Thursday, Friday, and Saturday there's a $2 cover charge if you come in just to dance—it's waived if you dine. Mixed drinks average $2.50. Open 6 p.m. to 1 a.m. Monday to Saturday and also for Sunday brunch, served from 11 a.m. to 2:30 p.m. There's also a coffeeshop.

The 186 rooms are pleasantly decorated with floral spreads and curtains, modern furniture, and Touch-Tone phones, clock radio, and color TV. An indoor pool, whirlpool, and saunas are available.

Rates: $31 to $33 single, $37 to $39 double.

Moderately Priced: A Spanish-American flavor prevails at the **Vagabond Motor Inn,** 4177 Albert St. (tel. 306/586-3443), from the brick arcaded lobby with a wrought-iron balustered staircase to the Casa Terrace dining room, which offers entertainment (occasionally revues) as well as a selection of seafood, steak, and chicken, with daily complete dinners for as little as $7.95. Rooms are furnished in dark wood colonial style, often with burnt-orange carpet, floral curtains, and green and yellow spreads. Each has direct-dial phone and color TV.

Rates: $27.50 single, $31 double, $33 triple, $35 quad. Children under 18 stay free in their parents' room.

When you enter the **Bell City Inn,** 4025 Albert St. (tel. 306/586-2663), you're quite likely to see people splashing around in the tropical indoor pool, visible off the lobby. The area is tropically landscaped with Polynesian masks on the walls and poolside dining and dancing at the Blue Lagoon, where you can also sip one of the very special drinks, like Chichi (vodka, coconut syrup, and pineapple juice) or a mai tai (both $3.20). Beyond the pool area you'll find the Black Angus dining room, where vat-shaped booths and lighting from wine casks provide the setting for good steak and seafood dining with entrees ranging from $8 to $12.50. There's also a coffeeshop, open from 7 a.m. to 8 p.m.

Red tartan carpeted corridors lead to the 210 rooms, which are decorated colonial style in shades of aqua and purple. All have direct-dial phones and color TVs. Rates: $30 single, $33 double (for two beds: $34 double, $36 triple, $38 quad).

Pine shingle seems to be the identifying mark for the **Imperial 400 Motel,** 4255 Albert St. (tel. 306/584-8800), which offers 204 ultramodern rooms with orange/brown striped headboards, matching spreads and curtains, a vanity outside the bathroom, and the usual trimmings of Touch-Tone phone, clock radio, and color TV. Rooms are located either in the main building with an inside hallway or else in motel-style units. There's a coffeeshop/dining room on the premises, and also an indoor pool, whirlpool, and sauna.

Rates: $28 single, $33 double. An extra person is $2, a cot is $3, and children under 16 stay free in their parents' room.

Budget: For budget accommodations the **Sherwood Motel** offers 62 rooms set around a courtyard, all with direct-dial phones, color TVs, basic modern furniture, wallboard paneling, and color coordinated wall-to-wall carpeting, spreads, and curtains. Rates are $22 single, $26 double (one bed), $30 double (two beds). Rooms with kitchenettes are available at $32 (one bed), $38 (two beds). Cots are $4. There's a fenced-in outdoor pool on the frontage near the highway.

Along Albert St. North

Guest rooms at the **Holiday Inn** 777 Albert St. (tel. 306/527-0121), are located in separate wings enclosing an outdoor swimming pool. Currently being renovated on my visit, the rooms are being decorated with burnt-orange shag and orange curtains and spreads. All 105 rooms have direct-dial phone and color TV. The management is planning to construct a bilevel restaurant called the Saskatchewan Wheat and Beverage Company, with a pioneer-style decor of shingles, and chuck-wagon salad bar.

Rates: $32 single, $33 to $38 double; an extra person is $4.

Budget: The management of the **Intowner Motor Hotel,** at Albert St. and Fourth Ave. (tel. 306/525-3737), have started remodeling their 42 rooms with earth-tone drapes, spreads, carpeting, and new wallpaper. All rooms have direct-dial phone, color TV, clock radio, and an added touch—a phone in the bathroom. A licensed dining room is on the premises. The setting is not particularly picturesque, although you may appreciate being right next door to the gas station.

Rates: $20 to $24 single, $22 to $26 double. The cheaper rates apply on weekends.

Along Victoria Ave. East

The **Relax Inn,** 1110 East Victoria Ave. (tel. 306/565-0455), had just opened its doors when I visited to display 190 rooms spread over three floors, all with color TV, direct-dial phone, stucco walls, ultramodern furniture, and aqua-and-brown or burnt-orange and brown decor. Bathrooms have colorful patterned floor tiles. Off the lobby is an indoor swimming pool and whirlpool.

Rates: $19 single, $20 double ($21 double with two beds), $23 triple.

REGINA RESTAURANTS: Not so long ago travelers in Regina had to content themselves with steak and Chinese food or else go hungry. Not quite so any more, although it's still predominantly meat-and-potatoes and chop suey country.

Moderately Priced Downtown Dining

The most interesting restaurant to appear on the Regina scene is located in a delightful town house. Since it opened a few months ago, **Upstairs Downstairs,** 2305 Smith St. (tel. 525-1496), has become so successful that it's nigh impossible to get a reservation. Taste and elegance are the hallmark of this establishment, right from the gracious awning and exterior of this detached Victorian house to the maroon burled-leather menu holder and the original lithographs that are scattered throughout. Downstairs there's a lounge area with fireplace, bookcases, marble-top tables, lit by a small Steuben chandelier and torchères over the fireplace. Up the oak staircase are three refined dining areas, one with a white ceramic-tile fireplace and all with Louis XV–style chairs covered with Sanderson chintz and long drapes to match. The menu is limited. Among the more unusual hors d'oeuvres are beef scallion rolls ($2.75), scampi sharif ($3.50), and tomato and anchovies vinaigrette ($2.25). For a main course you can choose from several meat and poultry dishes like breast of chicken in champagne ($8.75) and steak marchand de vin ($13), to seafood specialties such as lobster Pernod ($14.50). The desserts are all homemade—the strudel is especially good ($1.75). There's also a reasonably priced selection of fine wines.

Open Tuesday to Saturday from 5:30 to 10:30 p.m.

For really fine French cuisine, find **Le Parisien,** 1770 Québec St. (tel. 569-2743), where Swiss owner-chef Monsieur Boehm creates a number of dishes with great flair and serves them in a downstairs stucco-walled room dotted with French posters and Parisian scenes. The red tablecloths and fresh flowers on every table are highlighted by candlelight at night. To start, there's a selection of hors d'oeuvres (from $2) or you can splurge on grenouilles à la provençal ($4.50) or the 12 escargots bourguignonne ($7.80). If you like bouillabaisse, don't pass it up ($7.50). For a main course try the entrecôte Parisien with a Dijon mustard sauce ($9.50) or the tournedos maître d'hôtel. All dishes include salad, vegetables, and potatoes. For dessert there are those tempting crêpes Suzettes ($5.50) or sabayon ($2). At lunchtime you can have an omelet with salad (from $4 to $5).

Open noon to 2 p.m. Tuesday through Friday, from 5 p.m. to midnight Tuesday through Saturday, to 11 p.m. on Sunday.

Golf's Steak House, at Victoria and Hamilton (tel. 525-5808), is one of those venerable Regina institutions. The atmosphere is decidedly plush (note the grandfather clock as you enter, the large fireplace, the piano and antique organ, and the heavy gilt-framed pictures and high-backed carved-oak Charles II–style chairs). The menu offers traditional steakhouse fare. Start with smoked salmon ($3.75) or shrimp cocktail ($3.95), before moving on to stuffed trout ($6.75), baby back ribs ($7.50), or any number of steaks (from $7.50 to $11 for an 18-ounce T-bone). All dishes are served with salad, hot garlic bread, and baked potato with sour cream, chives, and crisp Canadian bacon. For dessert there's crème caramel ($1.50) or a special treat, baked Alaska ($4.75).

Open 4:30 p.m. to midnight daily (Sundays and holidays to 9 p.m.).

Another venerable institution that has moved into more modern surroundings is **L'Habitant,** 1711 Victoria Ave. (tel. 525-1551), where similar fare is offered in a rather different atmosphere (remember, L'Habitant is Québecois for "the woodsman"). At the center of the room are several totally private ashwood booths with butcher-block tables and brass lanterns, surrounded by four small intimate areas—one of them the original restaurant room, with ox-yoke light fixtures. The front of the restaurant provides a display area for a thick profusion of plants and shrubs.

For dinner, start with shrimp cocktail ($3.95) or smoked oysters ($2.50), and proceed with perhaps trout meunière ($8.50) or ham steak ($7). If you choose the table d'hôte, you can select various steaks (from $10.75 to $16.50 for steak and lobster), and the price will include an appetizer, salad, garlic bread, and coffee. Chocolate mousse ($1.50) and fresh apple pie await the diner with a sweet tooth. At lunchtime there's an extensive selection of sandwiches, salads, and light entrees (most under $5).

Open 11:30 a.m. to 2:30 p.m. and 5 to 11 p.m. Monday to Friday, from 5 to 11 p.m. on Saturday and Sunday.

Barry Armstrong and his partners have amassed a wealth of Victoriana and assembled it at **Bartleby's,** 1920 Broad St. (tel. 565-0040), to create an interesting, lively eating spot. Old fairground games, such as "Test Your Love," a videoscope, etc. are in the lobby, to the left of which is a long oak bar, rescued from Montana, studded above with stained-glass lamps and furnished with oak furniture and hanging plants (note the tin ceiling, which came from an old Montana bank). In the vast restaurant itself there's a whole warren of nooks and crannies, each with a different look—country store or Victoria room with fireplace, etc.—and each festooned with Canadiana that ranges from stained-glass panels, treddle tables, and old advertisements to bicycles hanging from the ceiling.

At dinner you can have scrivener prime rib ($7.95), roast chicken ($7.50), lasagne ($6.75), and one or two other dishes, all served with soup or salad bar and fresh bread. Try the mud pie for dessert (a base of crushed chocolate cookies, coffee ice cream with fudge topping, whipped cream and chocolate, and shaved almond). At lunchtime there's a selection of sandwiches for $2.95, plus soups and burgers. The brunch on Sunday (from 10 a.m. to 2 p.m.) for $4.95 features such old-fashioned prairie breakfast items as porridge, eggs, and sausage. The "Good Time Hour" (from 5 to 6 p.m. weekdays and 2 to 6 p.m. on Saturday) features smoothies of amaretto and Swiss chocolate for 99¢, highballs for $1, and a half liter of caesar for $4.50.

Open 10 a.m. to 11 p.m. Monday to Saturday; 10 a.m. to 2 p.m. and 4:30 to 9:30 p.m. Sunday. No reservations.

Right in the heart of downtown, opposite Victoria Park, is the family-style **Copper Kettle,** 1953 Scarth (tel. 525-3545). The front part serves as a comfortable carpeted coffeeshop with red Formica tables. The back has been turned into a steak room with copper artifacts—ladles, torchères, jugs, pitchers—with Hogarth prints on the stucco walls and tables with golden tablecloths. The menu ranges from $7.25 for an eight-ounce New York steak to $16.85 for steak and lobster tail, with many chicken and beef dishes in between, all served with salad, garlic bread, and stuffed baked potato. Saturday night is Greek night, when owner Robert Gardikiotis serves a full meal of avgolemono soup, Greek salad, taramosalata, main course, and baklava, for $7.50. At lunchtime you can select any number of sandwiches (all under $4) and a full range of pizzas (going from $8.70 for a large 13-inch pie with backbacon to $11, fully dressed).

Open Monday to Saturday from 7 a.m. to 1 a.m., Sunday from 9 a.m. to midnight.

Downtown Budget Dining

As I mentioned before, Regina has recently become a much more exciting spot to dine in, and certainly the first two restaurants that follow justify such a statement.

Mieka's Kitchen, 1810 Smith St. (tel. 522-6700), belongs to 22-year-old Mieka Wiems Bertoia who, upon her return from studying at the London Cordon Bleu cookery school, decided to open a rather different and experimental restaurant. The decor, created by her architect father to her specifications, is light and airy, somewhat stark, but rather effective because it distracts neither from the food nor from the lithographs and tasteful contemporary art on the white walls. The ceiling has been dropped and the place is lit at night by fluorescent and spot lamps. Fig trees and geraniums in the window add splashes of color to the evenness of tone provided by the white arborite tables and Eames chairs.

But it is the food that is really exciting—light and fresh, seasonal, and homemade. For instance, in August or September you're likely to find pumpkin soup featured on the blackboard menu. Otherwise, there's a selection of imaginative sandwiches—savory beef (brisket cooked in spices and vegetables, and served with potato salad, $3.50) or a Dagwood, with herb-and-spice creamy pâté, cucumbers and tomatoes, alfalfa sprouts garnished with green pepper rings ($3). Then there's usually a crêpe of some sort on the menu, served with soup, salad, and a thick slice of home-baked bread for around $5. Also featured are various salads—carrots, raisins, and cashews, for example—and an array of interesting teas like wild strawberry or brambleberry (50¢). Desserts are simply yummy—chocolate or coffee cake, fresh fruit delight ($2), and do try a smoothie (a blend of fruit, yogurt, milk and egg, and cinnamon, $1.50). Don't miss this place while you're in Regina.

Open 8 a.m. to 8:30 p.m. Monday to Saturday. Closed Sunday.

A friend of mine told me not to miss Sunday Brunch at **Gretta's,** 1427 11th Ave. (tel. 569-3177), and so I'm passing it along to you because you really shouldn't either. You'll be treated to eggs Pacific, a very rich concoction of shrimp, asparagus, poached eggs, and hollandaise served on a toasted English muffin, or eggs Benedict and such desserts as hot banana rum crêpes (all between $4.50 and $5.50). Gretta is another young contributor to the Regina restaurant scene who returned home after a stint on the West Coast where, among other things, she ran a food coop in Vancouver. The restaurant's look is very much a cooperative effort—Gretta and friends put up the cedar paneling and bar, someone else made the red-and-white gingham curtains and table-cloths, another friend contributed the stained-glass lamps; the art and photographs on the wall are from artist friends and are all for sale.

If you can't make brunch, try lunch or dinner. The menu changes daily but there are some constants you can reckon on: crêpes, chicken, baked meat, and vegetarian dishes, for example, ham and cheese crêpe ($4.50), apricot, or tangerine, or lemon honey crêpes ($1.95), shish kebab ($7.95), or quiche Lorraine ($4.25). On weekdays at luncheon you'll find various sandwiches, all under $3.

Open 11 a.m. to 2 a.m. daily.

Wah-Kua, 1717 Tenth Ave. (tel. 352-0367), must be pleasing somebody because it's been serving Chinese food for 30 years (the name in fact means "people from overseas"). Little stone pagodas mark the entrance which leads, past a case containing a magnificent Chinese lantern and figurine, into a low-lit, low-ceilinged room with red tablecloths, red napkins, and a few Chinese prints. When you come here, do have the wonton soup because it's one of the few places that still makes it own wontons. The Cantonese specialties include almond chicken ($4.75), lichee chicken ($5.25), subgum fried wonton ($6.25), and a whole range of other special dishes and family dinners.

Open from 5 p.m. to 2:30 a.m. weekdays, to 4 a.m. on Friday and Saturday, and from 4 to 8:30 p.m. on Sunday.

Less decorous but nevertheless an excellent place for Chinese food is **Pagoda Garden,** 1745 Broad St. (tel. 352-1110). Strictly a no-frills decor obtains—linoleum flooring, Formica tables, aluminum-vinyl chairs, and red checked plastic tablecloths. The Cantonese dishes include wonton soup ($1.30) and winter melon soup ($3.95), plus a selection of chop suey and chow mein dishes (under $4). More interesting are the beef with oyster sauce ($5.25), beef with snow pea pods ($4.95), and the specialty, tai dop voy (diced chicken, shrimp, meat, barbecued pork, and mushrooms, sauteed with Chinese vegetables, bamboo shoots, and water chestnuts, $5.75). Combination dinners from $3.95. Unlicensed.

Open from 4:30 p.m. to 2 a.m. Monday, Tuesday, and Thursday, to 3 a.m. on Friday and Saturday, to midnight on Sunday. Closed Wednesday.

Along Albert St. South

Natural elements—pine siding, macramé wall hangings, plants, butcher-block tables—hold key positions at **Waldos,** 3970 Albert St. at Parliament Ave. (tel. 584-9119). You can sit on the cut velveteen banquettes or the eclectic collection of oak furniture gleaned from attics, farmhouses, and antique stores. Dinner might start with the soup and salad bar, and continue with perhaps rainbow trout ($7.25) served on rice with tartar sauce, chicken Kiev, or veal Cordon Bleu (both $8.25). All dinners are served with a mini-cob of corn, vegetable, and baked potato. For lunch there's light fare such as soup and salad ($3.95) or quiche Lorraine ($4.75). On Sundays a $5.95 brunch of soup and salad bar plus omelets, crêpes, and quiches is served from 11 a.m. to 3 p.m.

Open Monday to Saturday from 11 a.m. to midnight, and on Sunday from 11 a.m. to 3 p.m. and 5 to 10 p.m.

There's no mistaking where you're supposed to be when you enter the **Mediterranean Restaurant**, 3926 Gordon Rd. in the Albert Park Plaza (tel. 585-1177), as you're confronted with Doric columns, a fountain, statue of Aphrodite, and a spread of grapes and wine. You can either dine in the semicircular booths or in the center of the room on red leatherette chairs off white tablecloths. The menu offers mostly steaks, including steak Diana ($15), seafood such as salmon steak ($7.50), and chicken Cordon Bleu ($7.50), among other dishes. Only the appetizers reflect a touch of Greek inspiration—saganaki ($2.95), squid marinated in red wine ($2.45), and stuffed grape leaves ($2.25).

Open Monday to Saturday from 4 p.m. to 12:30 a.m., Sundays and holidays from 4 to 9 p.m.

The **Chimney**, 2710 Montague (tel. 584-7777), is definitely one of Regina's more interestingly decorated steakhouses. The room focuses on a huge conical fireplace, around which you can sit and dine (unless you prefer to sit in the warm brown tartan booths set against the log-cabin-like walls) under an A-frame ceiling with heavy crossbeams. Oil lamps flicker over the booths, and pistols are the only decoration on the walls. Dinner might start with shrimp cocktail ($4.50) or asparagus tips with hollandaise ($3), and proceed to steaks (from $9.95 for a 12-ounce dinner steak) or lobster tails ($17.50). All dinners include onion soup or salad, garlic toast, and baked potato. For dessert, try the smooth cheesecake ($1.25). Pizzas are also available, along with various pasta dishes (from $4.50). Lunchtime provides a concentrated choice of sandwiches and snacks (all under $4).

Open 11 a.m. to 1 a.m. Monday to Saturday, and 4 p.m. to midnight on Sundays and holidays.

Despite its name so often associated with wild debauchery, **Dionysus**, 2727 Parliament Ave. (tel. 584-2551), is quite elegant and sophisticated. The tone is set at the entrance where, if you have to wait, you may sit either on one of the brown velvet wingbacks or a low comfy couch before going to your candlelit table. Still, the food is most definitely Greek. Start your meal with garithes Uvetsi (whole prawns baked with fresh tomatoes and cheese in a light wine sauce, $3.75), taramosalata ($2), or the spinach or cheese pie ($1.50). You can watch the spit turning and the chef preparing such dishes as sarmathakia (grape leaves stuffed and topped with sauce made from eggs, oil, and lemon, $6.25) and gouvetzaki (filet mignon pieces with special noodles and fresh sliced tomatoes, baked in the oven, $7.25), as well as more familiar steaks and bar-becued chicken ($6.50). Finish with a baklava or rizogalo rice pudding with cinnamon (both $1).

Open Monday to Saturday from 11 a.m. to 12:30 a.m., Sunday from 4 to 10 p.m.

Along Albert St. North

Locals rave about the lasagne served at **Geno's**, 1515 Albert St. (tel. 352-3655), and they've been doing so for ten years. Far from being an Italian-flavor place, it's stuffed with Canadian artifacts—old photographs, advertise-ments, clocks, telephones, washboards, and so on—hung on the walls behind the upper level oak booths, each lit by drop lamps with fringed shades. On the lower level, captain's chairs and tables are arranged around a fireplace. Besides the lasagne ($5.25), you can order spaghetti and meatballs ($4.50), fettucine ($4.95), or a 12-ounce T-bone steak ($8.95). Pizzas are also available, both with the regular thin crust as well as the Chicago-style deep-dish pie with an extra-thick crust. A 12-inch pie runs from $4.70 to $8.10 (with six toppings). At lunchtime, spaghetti ($3.50), small pizzas, and sandwiches are the primary fare.

Open Monday to Thursday from 11 a.m. to midnight, Friday and Saturday to 12:30 a.m., and Sunday from 4 p.m. to midnight.

At the pub next door, **The Last Spike,** you can build your own burger at the bar. The appearance relates to the railway era and the role it played in opening the west. The serving area is set up as if it were a railroad station, Pullman booths provide seating, and two murals by local artist Frances Pedley depict working on a railroad and a locomotive hurtling down the tracks toward the viewer. This is a pleasant spot for a drink—beer is 90¢ and bar drinks $1.20. Burgers, sandwiches, fish and chips, shrimp dinners, and pizzas are available (all under $5) and served from 11 a.m. to 7 p.m. daily.

Another oldtime Regina favorite has been serving a smorgasbord for 17 years—**Viking Smorgasbord,** 1032 Albert St. (tel. 522-8368). There's nothing distinctive about the decor except for the wooden cutout of a Viking ship on one wall—it's the buffet and the people that create the atmosphere. At noon the spread of cold cuts and salads, plus three hot dishes (usually fish, barbecued ribs, and chicken), costs $4.50 ($5.50 in the evenings). There's also a regular breakfast menu where you can order Canadian bacon, ham, or sausage, egg, and hash browns for $2.85. Sandwiches (around $1.60) and other short orders are available, ranging from $2.75 for fried chicken with french fries or a hot turkey or beef sandwich, to $6.75 for a 12-ounce T-bone.

The smorgasbord is served from 11:30 a.m. to 1:30 p.m. and 5 to 8 p.m. Monday to Saturday. The other menu is offered from 7:30 to 9 p.m. Monday to Saturday.

On the Northern Fringes

The **Dragon Palace,** 101 Hodsman North (tel. 545-6616), is the first Regina restaurant to branch out into more interesting northern Chinese cuisine. Pass the downstairs coffeeshop and go up to the large dining room, which although carpeted has a minimum of decor—red tablecloths and napkins, red kitchen-style chairs, and two pictographs which mean "double happiness." Here you can sample hot-and-sour soup ($3.75), barbecued duck in mustard green soup ($4.50), dung kong–style bean cake hot pot ($5.50), sliced whelk with celery ($6.25), and minced pork with Chinese sausages ($4.95). You can even have a jellyfish cold plate, and if you order in advance, a special baked chicken with salt ($14.50). There's a Canadian menu available, and the usual chow mein, egg foo yong, and lo mein dishes and combination dinners. Open daily from 6 a.m. to 1 a.m. (Sundays until 11 p.m.).

The **China Doll,** in the Northgate Shopping Center (tel. 545-1221), sticks to the more familiar food but has branched out when it comes to decor. Fetching bamboo fans shield the wall lamps; Chinese dolls in showcases add interest; and cane-backed chairs with cushions and elegant table settings complete the scene. The menu includes many familiar dishes—crushed almond sou gai ($6.45), tai dop voy ($6.95), spare ribs with garlic sauce ($5.50), and the usual chop suey, chow mein, and egg foo yong (from $4 to $6). Luncheon special combinations are available for under $5.

Open from 11:30 a.m. to 2 p.m. and 5 p.m. to midnight Tuesday to Saturday, and from 4:30 to 8:30 p.m. on Sunday.

THE SIGHTS: The best place to begin your sightseeing is at:

Wascana Centre

Certainly Regina did not start out with a bounty of natural assets, which is what makes Wascana Creek, a 2500-acre park right in the middle of the city, practically a testament to the indomitable will of the human spirit. The muddy little creek has been turned into a glorious parkland, where every tree that grows was physically planted by man.

Within the centre lies a **waterfowl park** frequented by 60 or more species of marsh and water birds. A really interesting project was begun here in 1953 with the introduction of a pair of geese. Now there are more than 150 breeding pairs, some of which remain during the winter, while others pop off as far afield as New Mexico. An elevated boardwalk leads out over the marsh and there's a naturalist on duty from 9 a.m. to 5 p.m. weekdays; call 522-5535 for information.

Another delightful spot is **Willow Island,** a picnic island reached by a small ferry from the overlook west of Broad St. on Wascana Dr.

Forty-five minute tours of the center in a British double-decker leave from the northern front of the legislative center every hour from noon to 7 p.m. daily, except Tuesday and Wednesday. Call 523-6131. No stops are made along the way though. Adults, 50¢; children, 25¢.

For information on Wascana Centre itself, call 532-6131 (summer only), or stop in at the **information guide office** at Lecture Hall, west of Broad St. on Lakeshore Dr. Open daily 9 a.m. to 8 p.m.

Besides the natural features mentioned above, the center also contains the bulk of the city's attractions:

Start at the **Legislative Building** (tel. 565-5357), a stately building that was built in 1909 for only $3 million in an English Renaissance and Louis XVI style (parts of the building also strongly remind one of the Palace of Versailles). Designed in the shape of a cross, the building is crowned by a 226-foot-high dome. Once inside, note that on the main floor and main rotunda 34 kinds of marble were used—white veined from Québec for the staircase, Italian on the walls, Vermont on the floor and baseboards, and Connemara for the pillar bases. The pillars were obtained from Cyprus, and were cut and shaped in Québec.

The mural above the rotunda, entitled *Before the White Man Came,* depicts the Qu'Appelle Valley where Indians are preparing to attack a herd of buffalo on the opposite shore. Rooms of interest include the Legislative Assembly Chamber, the 90,000-volume library, and the Executive Council Chamber and galleries on the first and second floors, which show rotating exhibitions.

The building is open from 9 a.m. to 9 p.m. during the summer and from 9 a.m. to 6 p.m. in the winter. Tours leave on the hour from 9 to 11 a.m. and every 30 minutes from 1 to 4 p.m. and 6 to 8 p.m.

The **Museum of Natural History's** (tel. 565-2815) exterior is faced entirely with blue Tyndall stone from Manitoba, and along the top of the two-winged building runs a 457-foot frieze displaying more than 300 figures of mammals, birds, and fish, most of which are native to Saskatchewan. There are 24 large diorama showcases in the upper gallery displaying true-to-life exhibits—bugling elk on the Saskatchewan River, woodland caribou in a La Ronge setting.

The lower gallery has over 100 showcases featuring exhibits on geology, paleontology, archeology, and human history. (An amusing aside: Of this area that contains some of the world's best agricultural land, Captain John Palliser reported in 1857–1858 that soil, rainfall, and other conditions made the area unsuitable for successful farming!) The Zoology Hall contains hundreds of specimens of mammals, birds, fish, reptiles, amphibians, and insects, and explicatory exhibits on flight, camouflage, and so on. Open 9 a.m. to 9 p.m. daily during the summer; from 9 a.m. to 5 p.m. Monday to Friday, and from 10 a.m. to 6 p.m. on Saturday and Sunday during the winter. Admission is free.

Norman Mackenzie Art Gallery (tel. 523-5801), just a short walk north of the Museum of Natural History, is in fact part of the University of Regina which takes up a 300-acre site in the park. The collection has been built upon the legacy of Norman Mackenzie, a Regina lawyer who began collecting works of art about 1900, but it was not until 1953 that the gallery was built. The approximately 600 works concentrate on Canadian artists, especially such Saskatchewan painters as James Henderson and Inglis Sheldon-Williams, contemporary American art, and 15th- to 19th-century European paintings, drawings, and prints. The gallery also offers a round of cultural events—films, music, dance, lectures. Open Monday to Friday from noon to 5 p.m., Saturday and Sunday from 1 to 5 p.m., and Wednesday and Thursday from 7 to 10 p.m. Admission is free.

Also in the park stands the **Diefenbaker Homestead House** (tel. 584-8660), the original home of Prime Minister Diefenbaker, which has been moved from Borden, Saskatchewan. It is furnished in pioneer style and contains some original family articles. Open daily 10 a.m. to 8 p.m.

RCMP Barracks and Museum

Located out on Dewdney Ave., this fascinating museum traces the history of the Mounties from 1874 when they began the Great March West to stop the liquor traffic and enforce the law in the western territories. They did so at a time when organized law enforcement anywhere in the world was less than 50 years old. The museum uses replicas, newspaper articles, uniforms, and mementoes to display the lives of the early Mounties and the pioneers, and goes on to trace their role in the 1885 Riel Rebellion, the Klondike Gold rush (when the simple requirements laid down by the North West Mounted Police probably saved the lives of many foolhardy golddiggers who came pitifully ill-equipped), the Prohibition era (when they sought out stills), the First and Second World Wars, the 1935 Regina strike (when they faced weapons made out of solid-steel pipe and the like), and in the capture of the mad trapper (who was chased in Arctic temperatures for 54 days in 1937) right up to the last dog patrol in 1969, the entry of women into the force in May 1974, and the use of the snowmobile.

Kids and adults too will probably love to role-play in the cockpit of the de Havilland, one of the originals from the founding of the Air Division in 1937. Open 8 a.m. to 8:45 p.m. June 1 to September 15, 8 a.m. to 4:45 p.m. otherwise.

Besides the museum there is a tour which takes in the chapel and the drill, where you can see and hear the trainees getting hell for doing what's wrong while practicing the mounted cavalry drill. The schedule is highly tentative, so check before you go by calling 569-5838 or 569-5777.

The Trial of Louis Riel

Louis Riel was tried and hung in Regina in 1885. Bitter arguments have been fought between those who regard Riel as a patriot and martyr and those who regard him as a rebel. Whatever the opinion, Riel certainly raises some extremely deep and discomforting questions. As G. F. Stanley, professor of history at the Royal Military College, Kingston, has written, "The mere mention of his name bares those latent religious and racial animosities which seem to lie so close to the surface of Canadian politics."

Even though he took up the cause of the mixed-blood population of the west, French-speaking Canadians often regarded him as a martyr and English-speaking Canadians damned him as a rebel. Written by John Coulter, *The Trial of Louis Riel* is a play based on the actual court records of the historical trial. It is presented in the ballroom of **Saskatchewan House,** the former residence of Saskatchewan lieutenant governors, which is transformed into a courtroom where the audience become real spectators to the trial. Certainly thought-provoking, it raises such issues as language rights, prejudice, and justice.

The *Trial* is presented on Tuesday, Wednesday, and Friday at 8:15 p.m. from late June to late August. Tickets are $4, and you can pick them up at the Chamber of Commerce at 2145 Albert St., preferably in advance, although some tickets are available at the door. To get to Saskatchewan House, go north on Albert St. to Dewdney Ave. Turn left, keep going west, and you'll find the house just past Pasqua St.

Saskatchewan Conservation House

As we enter an era of shortages, some of the more serious-minded might find a visit to this house particularly rewarding. Built by the government of Saskatchewan as a prototype, it has an experimental solar-heating system, special energy-recycling systems, super-insulation, enclosed porches, energy-efficient appliances, shuttered windows, and many other features that can be applied to homes today. In this house the usual rate of heat loss—and therefore energy consumption—has been reduced by 85%.

Open daily from 1 to 5 p.m., except holidays, and from 7 to 9 p.m. during June, July, and August. For information, call 565-3031; or write: Office of Energy Conservation, 1914 Hamilton St., Regina, SK S4P 4V4. The house is located at 211 Rink Ave. in northwest Regina. To get there, take Albert St. north to the Ring Rd. or Ninth Ave. North. Turn left and go west to McIntosh St. Turn right onto McIntosh and then left at Rink Ave.

REGINA NIGHTLIFE: Hardly Canada's nightlife capital, the city does have one or two spots for dancing, most often located in the hotels, plus a marvelous cultural center in the middle of Wascana Park.

Saskatchewan Centre of The Arts

On the southern shore of Wascana Lake stands the ultramodern Saskatchewan Centre of the Arts, which was opened in 1970 and contains two theaters and a large hall: the 2029-seat Centennial Theatre; the smaller Jubilee Theatre, used for theater in the round, proscenium performances, and recitals; and Hanbridge Hall, 12,200 square feet of convention and banquet space. Offerings at the center are varied—from Ivan Rebroff to Dr. Hook, to dance performances and the Regina Symphony Orchestra. Tickets vary in price depending on the show, and can be as low as $4 for local dance and theater companies or from $9.50 to $12.50 for the Regina Symphony. The center box office at 200 Lakeshore Dr. is open from 11:30 a.m. to 6 p.m. Monday to Saturday (tel. 584-5555).

Theater

The **Globe Theatre,** founded in 1966, is housed in the Merchants Bank Building on 11th Ave. between Scarth and Cornwall Sts., and presents serious drama as well as works of local playwrights. For tickets, call 525-9533.

Dinner Theater

One of the truly successful cultural spots belongs to the Regina Inn where **Stage West** has been packing the audiences in for over a year to see such stars as Gail Gordon, Nancy Culp, Jane Kean, Lloyd Bochner, Henry Jones, and Sid Caesar. When I was visiting, Dana Andrews and Mary Todd were performing in *Marriage-Go-Round,* a wry commentary on the contemporary war between the sexes. A superb buffet is served between 6 and 8 p.m., and the show starts at 8:30 p.m. Tickets are $14.95 from Monday to Thursday, and $16.95 on Friday and Saturday. For information, call 565-0611.

Disco Dancing

The hottest disco in town is part of **Waldo's** restaurant at 3970 Albert St. South. At night there's a fairly glitzy light show on and around the large dance floor which is set among trees draped with macramé and a ceiling that is also hung with the same. Bar drinks are $2; mixed drinks, $2.50; and beer, $1.50. There's a cover charge on Thursday, Friday, and Saturday of $2, but it's waived for women. Open from 8 p.m. to 1:30 a.m.

2. Saskatoon

As you come in from the airport, the focus of Saskatoon (pop. 145,000) becomes quite apparent: massive pieces of farm machinery stand silently, row upon row, and once in town you'll find saddlers and trappers and hunters supplies stores exhibiting metal objects in the window that look like instruments of torture, plus pelts, and charts showing all the conceivable varieties of Winchester bullets. Farming and hunting—that's Saskatoon's background. More recently, manufacturing has increased and the uranium and potash boom is right around the corner.

Meanwhile, there's a distinctly western air to the town. Downtown streets are broad and dusty, and dotted in summer with many a pickup truck. Those same downtown streets just seem to disappear on the edge of town into the prairie, where grain elevators and telegraph poles become the only reference points and the sky your only company.

Small, western, but also a very pretty city, Saskatoon takes advantage of the natural sweep of the Saskatchewan River and the many bridges that span it create a dramatic backdrop for those only-in-the-west sunsets.

SOME HISTORY: Saskatoon was originally founded in 1882 as a teetotaler's haven by Ontario Methodists, who were granted 200,000 acres on and about the present site of the city. Since the grant stipulated that odd-numbered sections of the land had to be reserved for free homesteads, the colony did not remain teetotaler for long, although traces of its sober antecedents are quite clearly visible today.

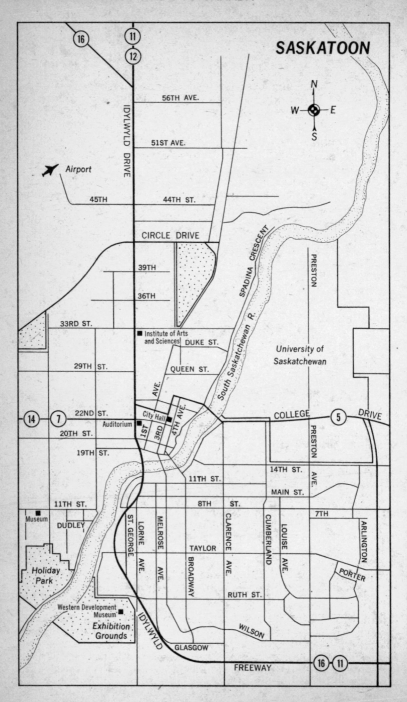

In its early days the settlement lost out in the struggle for the railroad, which passed 150 miles south, thereby leaving Saskatoon in the backwaters until 1890 when the railroad finally penetrated from Moose Jaw. Even then it was not until the 1900s when the agricultural potential of the surrounding area was realized that the city was incorporated (1906) experiencing a boom that brought forth, among other things, the University of Saskatchewan in 1907.

Today, it stands poised in anticipation of a great potash boom.

ORIENTATION: The main thing to remember when moving around town is that 22nd St. divides the city into northern and southern sections, and Idylwyld Dr. divides east from west.

The South Saskatchewan River cuts a diagonal north-south swathe through the city. The main downtown area lies on the west bank, the University of Saskatchewan and the long neon-sign-crazed 8th St. dominates the east bank.

Streets are laid out in a numbered grid system—22nd St. divides north and south designated streets; Idylwyld Dr. divides, in a similar fashion, east from west. First St. through 18th St. lie on the east side of the river, 19th St. and up on the west bank in the downtown area. Spadina Crescent runs along the west bank of the river, where you'll find such landmarks as the Bessborough Hotel, the Ukrainian Museum, and the Art Gallery.

Getting In and Out of Saskatoon

Air Canada (tel. 652-4181) and **Norcanair** (tel. 652-7741) fly in and out of the one-terminal airport. **VIA rail** (tel. 382-0211) trains leave from and arrive at the station in the west end of the city on Chapel Drive. **Greyhound Bus** services can be reached at 565-3340. Buses depart and arrive at the terminal at 50 23rd St. East.

Getting Around

You probably won't need to use transportation too often except to visit the University of Saskatchewan and the Western Development Museum, but there's a perfectly adequate system of **buses** operated by the Saskatoon Transit System (tel. 664-3133) which require 30¢ exact change. For a bus map, go to City Hall at 23rd Street and Third Ave. It will cost you 50¢.

Taxis are, as usual, expensive—$1.10 when you step inside and 80¢ a mile thereafter—but here are the names of two companies: **Saskatoon Radio Cab** (tel. 242-1221), and **United Cabs** (tel. 652-2222), which also operates the limousine to the airport.

Car rental companies: **Holiday Rent-a-Car**, 350 Third Ave. North (tel. 244-5548); **Avis**, 610 Spadina Crescent (tel. 652-3434); **Budget**, 2215 Ave. C North (tel. 244-7925); **Hertz**, 2323 8th St. East (tel. 373-1161); and **Tilden**, 321 21st St. East (tel. 652-3355).

Tourist Information

For an answer to all your travel problems, drop into the **Tourist and Convention Bureau** on the mezzanine at the Bessborough Hotel, open from 8:30 a.m. to 4:30 p.m. Monday to Friday (tel. 306/242-1206). The **Department of Tourism** for the province is at 122 Third Ave. North, on the tenth floor (tel. 664-6240). During the summer (from around May 18 to the end of August), **tourist booths** are open at 25th St. and Kinsmen Park, 8th St. and Circle Dr., and Idylwyld Dr. and 51st St.

Useful Information

Banking hours are Monday to Thursday from 10 a.m. to 5 p.m., Friday to 6 p.m. . . . The **post office** is located at 202 Fourth Ave. North, and is open Monday through Friday from 8 a.m. to 5:45 p.m. (tel. 652-9080). . . . **Stores** are open Monday through Saturday from 9 a.m. to 6 p.m., Thursday until 9 p.m. (closed Wednesday afternoons). . . . **Hospitals** include St. Paul's, 1702 20th St. West (tel. 382-3220); Saskatoon City Hospital, Queen St. (tel. 242-6681); and University Hospital, University Grounds (tel. 343-2112). . . . The daily **newspaper,** the *Star-Phoenix,* has a circulation of 55,000; there are two weekly newspapers, the *Western Producer* and the *Commentator.* . . . **Liquor stores** are located at 401 20th St. West (open 11 a.m. to 6 p.m. daily except Wednesdays and Sundays), 1701 Idylwyld Dr. North (open 11 a.m. to 6 p.m. daily except Mondays and Sundays, to 9 p.m. Thursdays), and in the Westgate Shopping Centre (open 11 a.m. to 10 p.m. Monday to Friday, to 6 p.m. on Saturday).

SASKATOON HOTELS: The city has a surprising range of accommodations from which to choose.

The Top Choices

Even the name the **Bessborough Hotel,** 601 Spadina Crescent (tel. 306/244-5521), has an elegant and gracious ring to it, which suits this old hotel built in 1930 and opened in 1935. It was dashingly constructed to look like a French château, with copper roof and turrets. Inside, each of the 225 rooms is different, although all have beautiful oak entrance doors and traditional furniture. Front rooms are large and most have bay windows that house a sofa (the whole bay can be closed off by floor-to-ceiling drapes), antique furnishings (often wingbacks), and the usual accoutrements, such as telephone and color TV. Riverside rooms are smaller but the views across the Saskatchewan River are simply magnificent, and so romantic! Other facilities include an outdoor swimming pool set in beautiful grounds that sweep down to the river. In the future, the hotel plans to construct an indoor pool with whirlpool and sauna, tennis courts, a Japanese steakhouse in the basement, and a brand-new coffeeshop. Some of these facilities should be open by 1980.

The hotel also houses the best seafood restaurant in the city—Aerial's Cove, named after fisherman Aerial Gray from Halifax, who provided the nets and lobster traps that complement the warm red tablecloths and ladderback chairs where 45 people can be seated. If you really want to splurge, start with the caviar ($19.50), or less extravagantly with "angels on horseback" (oysters wrapped in bacon and broiled, $4.50). Then you can choose a lobster from the tank or else enjoy such delights as scallops mornay ($10.50), curried shrimp ($12), or the rack of lamb (marinated in wine and garlic and served with mint sauce, $13.50). Save some room for the cheesecake served with brandied pineapple sauce ($2.75), or the fresh pineapple with kirsch ($2.50). At lunchtime, sample various sandwiches and seafood specialties (from $4.95 to $6.95). Trudi's Coffeeshop is open daily; there's a comfortable pubby lounge, and a beverage room. Free indoor parking is available.

Rates: $30 to $40 single, $36 to $46 double. The weekend package is $29, single or double, per night. There is no charge for children staying in the same room as their parents. Free local phone calls.

The stiffest competition to the Bessborough stands across the street, the **Sheraton Cavalier,** 612 Spadina Crescent (tel. 306/652-6770), a white eight-story structure that contains 250 rooms, all decorated in super-modern style in shades of burnt orange and brown, with louvered closets, radio, TV, and pushbutton phone. The hotel also has a top range of facilities, including a complete resort complex with adult and kiddy swimming pools, saunas, whirlpool, exercise room, sundeck and sunlamps, game room, and a small Astroturf putting area.

On the ground floor, just off the lobby, dine at the Cellar, where you can sit in barrel-shaped booths, each with its own individually controlled light dimmer, and enjoy various steak and seafood dishes as well as specialties like the cellardwellar—a six-ounce bacon-wrapped filet, topped with asparagus tips, hollandaise, and melted cheese ($9.95).

At the Top of the Inn, which takes advantage of a glorious view over the Saskatchewan River, live entertainment runs from 9 p.m. to 1:30 a.m. nightly except Sunday. The purple and red decor coupled with copper-top tables and Las Vegas–style booths make for a showy nighttime atmosphere. On Fridays and Saturdays there's a cover charge of $2. Drinks average $2; beer, $1.75. And for that end-of-the-day cocktail there's the Tent 'n' Tavern lounge, where you can relax on a low-slung sofa; the coffeeshop is light and airy and overlooks the park sweeping down to the river.

Rates: $30 to $44 single, $36 to $50 double, depending on the view. Bed-sitting rooms are $45 single, $50 double. A weekend package is $30, single or double, per night. Free indoor parking is available.

Downtown Hotels

Moderately Priced Accommodations: Really conveniently located, the **Holiday Inn,** 90 22nd St. East (tel. 306/244-2311), stands opposite the new Eaton's complex and Centennial Auditorium. The 200 rooms feature the usual Holiday Inn appurtenances: large double or queen-size beds, radio console and alarm clock, cane headboards, a clothesline in the bathroom, Scandinavian-modern furniture, and color-coordinated fabrics.

In the blue Tamarack dining room with its Windsor-style chairs you can sample a super luncheon buffet for only $3.95 or else dinner fare that concentrates on steak and seafood (from $7 to $12.50). At night, go downstairs to Flanagan's where you might find rock, disco, or jazz music being played from 9 p.m. on, daily except Sunday. Captain's chairs and hunting prints set the unpretentious, mildly Irish tone of the place. There's a cover charge ($2) on Thursday, Friday, and Saturday. Drinks average $2; beer is $1.75. The coffeeshop completes the dining facilities. And there's an indoor pool and sauna available, and a game room and amusement arcade to pacify the kids.

Rates: single $35.50 (one bed), $38.50 (two beds); double $40 (one bed), $45 (two beds); an extra person is $4; children under 19 stay free in their parents' room. The weekend package is $28, single or double, per night.

The **King George Hotel,** 157 Second Ave. North (tel. 306/244-6133), is an outstanding example of an old downtown hotel that has survived the vicissitudes of time and changing economies and continues to provide traditional hospitality. Don't be put off by the somewhat austere exterior, erected in 1905. The whole place was totally renovated in 1961 and the rooms are continuously upgraded. Each of the 104 air-conditioned rooms has color-coordinated fabrics and decor, often in burnt-orange and brown combinations, as well as all the modern conveniences—pushbutton phone, color TV, radio, large closets, and a shuttered shower instead of the usual curtains.

A great deal of imagination has gone into the dining complex in the basement of the hotel—a whole area that represents a medieval castle-fortress.

Enter through the portcullis to the Great Hall, a comfortable spot for breakfast, lunch, dinner, or a quick coffee; in the Jousting Lounge you can relax with friends amid booths enclosed by striped jousting tents and a bar that has a stained-glass panel above depicting a jousting tournament, before going into Hanover's, the dining room that resembles a castle. The tables are set in stone alcoves, each with its own individually controlled light dimmer, and the room is divided into various sections. The Abbey for example, has a mirrored ceiling, while the Tower table is indeed set in a turret with slit windows that overlook the center of the room. All in all, this is a fun place to sample an assortment of steak, chicken, or seafood dishes that range from $7.50 for chicken Cordon Bleu to $13.95 for lobster tail with beef kebab—prices including potato, garlic toast, and tea or coffee.

Rates: $26 to $30 single, $33 to $39 double; an extra person is $4. Weekend packages are $23, single or double, per night. Free indoor parking is available.

Another moderately priced accommodation, not quite so central to downtown but still conveniently located, is the **Park Town Hotel,** 924 Spadina Crescent East (tel. 306/244-5564), a modern establishment, part of which was built in 1955, the rest in 1977. It stands just by the bridge over the river to the university, and offers 70 ultramodern rooms with dark Spanish oak-finish furniture, matching orange bedspreads and curtains, color TV, Touch-Tone phone, and a tub in the bathroom. The 40 older rooms are being remodeled and should be color coordinated and shipshape by the time of your visit.

Facilities include an attractive pool area with a kidney-shaped pool, surrounded by carpeting dotted with garden furniture, various shrubs, and potted plants; colorful banners hang from the ceiling girders. There's also a pleasant dining room where you can enjoy a good lunchtime buffet (for $4.50) or a steak, seafood, or poultry dinner (from $8.75), a lounge, and a coffeeshop.

Rates: $27 to $35 single, $31 to $40 double, depending on which section you're in; an extra person is $4. There's a weekend package of $27, single or double, per night.

The hotel also has the zippiest entertainment spot in town on the premises. **Fast Freddies** (tel. 665-7500) provides a sophisticated setting for dancing and dining complete with flashy light show. Everywhere you look in this multilevel room good taste predominates—clear-cedar ceiling and bar, bamboo-style chairs, bar stools with cushions, good-looking tiles on the bar, comfortable couches on the raised terrace area, stained glass in the ceiling, and healthy plants. Currently the entertainment consists of live groups, but by the time you visit it should have gone disco. At night cocktails average $2.25 to $2.75; beer is $1.75. During Happy Hour (from 2 to 7 p.m.) highballs are $1; beer, 75¢.

Freddie's also functions as a creative sandwich bar where you can choose a variety of fillings—cucumber, crab, avocado, salami, pastrami, etc.—and accompaniments such as tomatoes, onions, lettuce, and alfalfa sprouts, served on either four-grain, sprouted-wheat, or sourdough rye. Prices run from $2.25 to $2.75. Other snacks are also available, among them chicken liver plate ($2.95), savory shrimp, and finger ribs (both $3.95).

Open daily from 11:30 a.m. to 2 a.m. Closed Sunday.

Budget Selections: The **Senator** is another oldtimer that has withstood the test of time and continues to cater to a primarily local family trade. Built in 1908 at the corner of 21st St. East and Third Ave. South, you'll recognize it by its tiled exterior and portico with Corinthian columns. In the old red carpeted lobby there's a wonderful marble newel post at the bottom of the mirrored staircase that leads to the 45 rooms on the two floors above. Only eight or so of these have showers—the rest have good honest tubs. The rooms are furnished with Scandinavian-modern furniture, color TV and radio, and switchboard phone, but each one is different in size and style. A mammoth double with sitting room goes for as little as $24.50.

The unlicensed dining room with its large chandelier, gilt-framed pictures, wood paneling, and gold-leaf ceiling is one of the best spots to enjoy a hearty breakfast or dinner. Remember, the hotel caters to local farm families who demand good, wholesome, large meals at honest prices, and the menu reflects the customers' needs—bacon, and ham, or sausage, two eggs, toast, coffee, and jam for $3.25 at breakfast; or breaded veal cutlets or pork chops with apple sauce, each served with tomato juice or soup of the day, roll, and coffee, for $4.95 at dinner. There's also a wide selection of hot sandwiches (from $1.45) and salads (around $4). *Note:* The dining room is only open from 7 a.m. to 7 p.m.

Rates: $20 to $21 single, $23 to $25 double. Family rate available. Free parking.

Hotels Around Town

Moderately Priced Choices: The **Imperial 400,** 610 Idylwyld Dr. North (tel. 306/244-2901) is easily identified by its red brick, shingle-roofed, two-floor, motel-style units, each of which contains modern furniture, color-coordinated curtains and spreads, and the usual color TV, clock radio, and phone. These rent for reasonable prices, and there are even a few suites with fully equipped kitchen and a double double-bedded room for only $44. A two-bedroom suite goes for $50 double. Other facilities include an indoor swimming pool surrounded by Astroturf, a restaurant/coffeeshop, and a lounge overlooking the pool.

Rates: $29 single, $33 double; an extra person is $4. Children under 12 stay free in their parents' room. There's a weekend special for only $24 per night, single or double.

Farther north, at 806 Idylwyld Dr., stands the **Sands Motor Hotel** (tel. 306/665-6500), which opened its 183 rooms on six floors in August of 1978. All are immaculately furnished in modern style, with brown wall-to-wall carpeting and patchwork-style bedspreads and matching curtains. Color TV and Touch-Tone phone are in each room.

Just off the contemporary lobby there's a Spanish-style stucco-walled coffeeshop highlighted with Mexican pottery, weavings, and posters. In the dining room, a smorgasbord is the only meal served, from 5 to 11 p.m. on weekdays and from 5 to 9 p.m. on Sunday. A cocktail lounge and beverage room are available as well. There's a decorous pool area that adopts a nautical theme expressed via ropes, sunken timber posts, and murals of fishing boat and harbor. The area also contains a whirlpool and sauna.

Rates: $29 single, $33 double, suites from $44. An extra person is $4, and children under 16 stay free in their parents' room.

Still farther north on Idylwyld Dr., at the junction with Circle Dr., you'll find the rounded white stucco building of Saskatoon's **Travelodge,** 106 Circle Dr. (tel. 306/242-8881), offering 130 extra-large rooms, each with either a vanity or a small bar area. The rooms are decorated in earth tones, with modern furnishings, color TV, and Touch-Tone phone.

The hotel has an especially attractive pool area with skylit ceiling, tropical gardens, whirlpool, sauna, and poolside rooms with balconies. Dining facilities include a coffeeshop with pleasant poolside terrace, a cedar-walled dining room that offers a $3.95 lunch smorgasbord, a lounge, and beverage room.

Rates: $28 single, $33 double, $36 poolside. A weekend special is available at $25 per night, single or double. Children under 12 sharing their parents' room stay free. Cribs are free; roll-away beds are $4 extra.

In the southern part of town across the Saskatchewan River, you'll find **Holiday House Motor Hotel,** 2901 8th St. East (tel. 306/374-9111), which has an older and a newer section. The 32 rooms in the new section are quite exquisitely furnished with cane headboards, matching brown/orange curtains and spreads, modern furniture, color TV, and direct-dial telephone. In the older motel section, standard basic accommodations rent for $20 single, $22 double.

The hotel houses one of Saskatoon's most relaxing drinking and dancing spots, Foxy's, which features cabaret-style entertainment from 9 to 1:30 a.m., usually consisting of eminently listenable folk-type music, occasionally jazz or bluegrass. Owner Bill Lowe has quite a reputation as a hunter and his trophies decorate the walls—black bear, silver fox, red fox skins, and elk heads and pronghorn deer antlers. There's no cover and drinks average $2. Happy Hour runs from 11 a.m. to 8 p.m., when beer is 90¢; shots, $1.10; and doubles, $2. Also on the premises are a coffeeshop and restaurant. For relaxation there's an outdoor pool, exercise room, and sauna.

Rates: $24 single, $30 to $32 double.

Budget Accommodations: Certainly, the best buy in Saskatoon has to be found at the **Confederation Inn,** 3330 Fairlight Dr. (tel. 306/384-2882), which opened in August 1978. Standing well back from the road, the inn has 40 rooms, all decorated in red with Spanish-style modern furniture, Touch-Tone phones, and color TV. The restaurant on the premises is open from 7 a.m. to 9:30 p.m. daily, while the beverage room offers a noon buffet for $2.75.

Rates: $24, single or double; an extra person is $3. Children under 12 stay free in their parents' room.

Other strictly no-frills standard, clean motel accommodations are offered at several places. The **Westgate Inn Motel,** at 22nd St. and Ave. Y (tel. 306/382-3722), has 42 pleasantly furnished and decorated units in red or blue shades, each with color TV and switchboard phone. Rates: $20 single, $26 to $28 double, depending on the number of beds in the room. An extra person is $2. A nice touch here is the courtesy coffee.

The **Skybird Motel,** 16 33rd St. East at Idylwyld Dr. (tel. 306/242-4234), offers similar basic motel accommodations. Most of the units have color TV, but a few have black and white; some have shower only, but all have switchboard phone. Rates: $20 single, $23 double, $25 triple.

At the **Greystone Motor Hotel and Motel,** 2921 8th St. East (tel. 306/374-6222), you'll find color-coordinated drapes and bedspreads in the rooms, with modern furnishings, switchboard phone, and color TV. Rates are $22 single, $24 double; an additional person is $2. The motel units, which are similarly equipped, rent for $20 single, $22 double. There's a restaurant serving Chinese-American food on the premises (open from 7 a.m. to 11 p.m. daily).

SASKATOON DINING: Saskatoon is primarily steakhouse country. If you don't like steak and seafood, you won't relish Saskatoon's restaurant scene, for that's all you're going to find (except for one or two unlikely choices which I'll describe first).

Ethnic Choices

Sami Ullah did not expect to preside over his **Shaheen,** 135 20th St. West (tel. 244-8807), but despite his graduate degree in animal physiology somehow or other he became a restaurateur and not a veterinarian. Because he is a native of Lahore, Pakistan, his restaurant specializes in North Indian dishes, offering 11 curries (from $4.25 to $7.50), all served with rice and a yogurt salad. Delicious Indian breads—chappaty, stuffed paratha, poppadum—are available, plus other side dishes like samosa (65¢) and pea pulao ($1.65). For the uninitiated, the menu lists a variety of hot and cold sandwiches, burgers, and salads, from 85¢ to $4.75 for a meal of pork chops. The decor is strictly no frills, with chrome-vinyl chairs and red tablecloths on the tables.

Open Monday to Saturday from 11 a.m. to 10 p.m. Closed Sunday.

Spartako, 225 Third Ave. North (tel. 665-1767), is the latest attempt to diversify Saskatoon's cuisine. A large airy restaurant arranged in three tiers, where the stucco walls support Greek rugs, aprons, and other bright tapestries, it has the air of a Greek bistro with red checked tablecloths and Greek music in the background. Besides the predictable souvlaki ($6.95) and moussaka ($5.95), the menu also offers such exciting seafood dishes as kalamaria tiganita (pan-fried baby squid, $6.25) or kovouri (crab legs broiled in lemon sauce, $11.50). To start, you might try the taramosalata, a tangy mullet fish roe dip blended with lemon juice and olive oil, and garnished with black olives ($1.75). At lunchtime there are daily specials, for example, pita stuffed with baby shrimp salad, and various Greek dishes that range from $2.95 for char-broiled ground beef (wrapped in pita, garnished with tomatoes, onions, and parsley, and served with potatoes) to $4.25 for stuffed grape leaves. Finish with a baklava ($1.25) and some really thick Greek coffee (75¢).

Open 11 a.m. to 11:45 p.m. daily, on Sunday from 5 to 10:30 p.m.

Saskatoon has a fairly large Ukrainian population yet **Karpatia,** 343 20th St. West at the corner of Ave. D South (tel. 652-2191), seems to be the only spot serving such fare as cabbage rolls and perogies. Named after the Carpathian Mountains that run through the Ukraine, the restaurant has two murals of that mountains area, which are the only attempt at decor. Otherwise, it's strictly functional with brown tablecloths and vinyl-aluminum chairs. You can have your perogies with sauerkraut, deep-fried, or with sausage ($3.75). Cabbage rolls are $3.50. Because of the clientele the menu also lists breakfast items, sandwiches, and Canadian fare, such as barbecued spare ribs or fish and chips ($2.25).

Open from 9 a.m. to 9 p.m. Monday to Saturday. Closed Sunday.

Several Chinese restaurants cluster around Ave. C South, including **Wah Qua,** 402 Ave. C South at 19th St. West (tel. 244-2939). Specialties include beef fried with green onion ($8.50), cashew chicken ($7.50), and sliced fish with wine sauce, which must be ordered in advance ($14.50). The rest of the menu consists of various chow mein, chop suey, and egg foo yong dishes (from $3.25 to $4.75) plus various dinner combinations. A complete dinner for one of chicken chow mein, sweet-and-sour ribs, egg rolls, and rice can be had for the low price of $3.95. There's nothing especially outstanding about the decor— white tablecloths cover the tables and the ubiquitous vinyl-aluminum chairs complete the picture.

Open Monday to Thursday from 4 p.m. to 1:30 a.m., Friday and Saturday to 3 a.m., and Sunday to 10 p.m.

Bamboo Gardens, 263 Second Ave. South (tel. 652-7788), offers perhaps more interesting Chinese dishes. Again the decor is nothing to go into raptures about, but the food is excellent. Here you can have hot-and-sour soup ($2.95)— a meal in itself—or equally interesting, winter melon and pork soup, which you can follow with spare ribs with black bean sauce ($4.95), beef in Peking sauce ($4.50), or paper-wrapped beef ($5.25). Seafood lovers will probably be tempted by cuttlefish in chili sauce ($4.95) or the whole fresh steamed pickerel ($8.25). The full complement of more familiar Chinese dishes is also available.

Open 11 a.m. to 2 a.m. Monday to Saturday, and 4 p.m. to midnight on Sunday.

For light fare, stop in at the ultramodern self-service-style **Sandwich Works,** 303 22nd St. East (tel. 652-7330), that has the latest bricks, macramé planters, and Breuer cane chair look. Interesting sandwiches are, unsurprisingly enough, available for from $1.65 for lettuce and tomato to $2.95 for smoked turkey, cucumber, lettuce, tomato, and mayo, or shrimp, avocado sprouts, and mayo. Fresh garden salad ($1.25) and fresh fruit salad are really super, as is the homemade cheesecake ($1.50), the honey bran muffins (50¢), and carrot cake (65¢). As for me, I'll take the ice cream and hot raspberries ($1.50).

Open Monday to Friday from 9 a.m. to 7 p.m., and Saturday until 5 p.m.

When Mr. Gibson (an ex-Canadian Royal Air Force chap) retired from the service, he came back from England with a secret recipe for fish and chips and established a very authentic **fish and chips** outlet in Cumberland Shopping Square on 8th St. Here you can either sit down at Formica tables on bentwood chairs or else take out good helpings of fish and chips ($2.30), haddock and chips ($3.20), or scallops and chips ($3.20), which will be placed in a box and wrapped in real newspaper as well as doused in real malt vinegar. Certainly worth stopping by if you appreciate real fish and chips.

Open Monday to Saturday from 9 a.m. to 8 p.m.

Steakhouses

When I was in Saskatoon, locals swore up and down by **John's Prime Rib,** 401 21st St. East (tel. 244-6384), and certainly the house does serve the best the Canadian prairies can offer. The room has been partitioned to provide intimate dining, and the pleasant surroundings are enhanced by a breakfront with china, rural prints, and even some weathervanes—a cow and a horse—on the walls. Do have the prime ribs ($9), unless you really prefer a seafood dish which might be filet of sole ($6.95) or broiled lobster tail ($15.95). Appetizers run from $1.50 for onion soup to $4.50 for a jumbo shrimp cocktail. Desserts include an intriguing congo pie, a rich combination of chocolate cake with custard filling and chocolate icing, topped with whipped cream and chocolate sauce ($1.50). At lunchtime there are special luncheon dinners (under $6), all served with soup, rolls and butter, and potatoes, and also a selection of sandwiches (most under $4). No reservations are taken at lunch, but they are recommended for dinner.

Open Monday to Friday from 11 a.m. to 2:30 p.m. and 5 to 10:30 p.m., and Saturday from 4:30 to 11 p.m. Closed Sunday.

The other favorite steakhouse is **Hy's,** Midtown Plaza (tel. 653-3322), which never fails to deliver succulent steaks in a plush atmosphere of wood paneling and elegant table settings somberly lit by brass chandeliers. Steaks run from $12.50 for a 12-ounce New York cut to $16.50 for a 16-ounce sizzler. If you're not a beef fancier, then try the rack of lamb ($12.50) or the chicken Cordon Bleu ($9.75). At lunchtime a delicious grilled crab 'n' cheese sandwich will cost you $5.25, while most other sandwiches are under $4. There's a pleasant cocktail lounge for relaxing, where between 4:30 and 6:30 p.m. beer is only $1.05 and shots are $1.25.

Open Monday to Saturday from 11:30 a.m. to 2:30 p.m. and 5 to 11:30 p.m. Closed Sunday.

A warm ranch-style candlelit atmosphere prevails at **Mr. Steer's,** 145 Third Ave. North (tel. 653-5550), created by the barnboard-siding walls, horse brasses and collars, and an area signposted as the livery stables. Sink into one of the comfortable couches in the cocktail lounge before partaking of such dishes as ham steak with pineapple ($7.50), barbecued ribs ($8.25), or any of various steaks (from $8.95). Fish and chips ($3.95) and pizzas are also available (from $7.95 to $10.55 for a large pie). Luncheon fare is under $4 and includes such plates as barbecued beef on a toasted french loaf with Spanish onions, coleslaw, dill pickle, french fries, and a special dip.

Open Monday to Saturday from 11:30 a.m. to 1 a.m., on Sunday from 4 p.m. to midnight.

Beer barrels, ships' lanterns, and mooring posts mark the entrance to **Smugglers,** 416 21st St. East (tel. 652-0074). Inside, the theme is continued throughout several rooms. In the lounge bar with its low couches and cozy nooks, a ship's bell stands on the bar and models of ships are dotted about. Elsewhere, blocks, sailing sheets, compass, and so on are just a few of the embellishments, while upstairs the main dining room focuses on a mast with thick ropes and blocks streaming down from the top. The tables are really solid and the fare is similarly so—a 13-ounce cut of prime rib, which includes salad bar and bread and butter ($9.50), steak teriyaki ($7.45), or kebab ($6.60). At lunchtime you can have a barrel of bones, which is in fact baked prime rib bones with barbecue sauce and salad bar ($2.95) or various sandwiches and daily specials (all under $4). Because of the quality, size, and price of the meals here, this is an extremely crowded place and you may find yourself waiting as long as 1½ hours on weekends. Unfortunately, you can't jump the queue by making a reservation—they don't take them.

Open Monday to Thursday from 11 a.m. to midnight, Friday to 12:30 a.m., Saturday from 5 to 12:30 a.m., and Sunday from 4:30 to 9:30 p.m.

If you can't get in, then you can always go across the street to **Golf's Steak House,** 317 21st St. East (tel. 652-7733), where you might be served by a waitress in tuxedo in a plush atmosphere created by gilded picture frames, crushed-velvet chairs with heavily carved backs, and a beamed ceiling. Start your dinner with chicken livers ($3.25), heart of artichokes, or broccoli topped with lemon butter ($3), before moving on to the real reason for dining here—the steaks (from $9.95). Top off your meal with a parfait of your choice ($3.95) or a smooth crème caramel ($1.95).

Open from 4:30 p.m. to midnight Monday to Saturday, and from 5 to 10 p.m. on Sunday.

At **Copperfields,** 121 Second Ave. North (tel. 244-7677), ranch-style decor is crossed with views of Dickensian London to provide a western-style chophouse. The tables are separated by pine slats so that dining is intimate. Probably the best buy here is the hearty buffet, brimming with cottage cheese, macaroni salad, rice, potato salad, tossed salad, bean salad, onion and cucumber salad, cauliflower salad, fruit salad, cheese and mushroom salad, and seafood salads, plus two hot dishes, oven-roasted potatoes, and either hot apple pie or peach Melba—all for $6 (half price for children under 12). To partake of this feast you have to come between 5 and 8 p.m.

At other times you might start your meal with beef barley broth ($1) or escargots bourguignonnes ($4.50), and follow with perhaps the house specialty of baked Cornish game hen stuffed with rice and mushrooms, served with a demi-glacé sauce ($8.75).

Open Monday to Saturday from 8 a.m. to 11:30 p.m.

A Steakhouse with a Difference

Perhaps the most originally designed Saskatoon restaurant is **The Cave,** 2720 8th St. East (tel. 374-5090), for speluncular dining among stalagmites and stalactites. The restaurant has three dining areas, each with intimate semicircular booths and each part of a labyrinthine design. At the very back of the restaurant is an area filled with plants, where water spills down over the rocks and light comes in from above via tiny potholes. The kids will adore it and the food as well, for they can gorge themselves on 10- or 14-inch pizzas (ranging from $5.50 to $7.95), or spaghetti with clam, tomato, mushroom, or meatball sauce (all under $5), while the older folks can savor the charcoal-broiled steaks (from $7.95), or the liver and onions ($5.25).

Open Monday to Saturday from 5 p.m. to 1 a.m., and Sunday from 4 p.m. to midnight.

SASKATOON SIGHTS: The **Mendel Art Gallery,** 950 Spadina Crescent East (tel. 652-8355), housed in a visually striking modern building overlooking the South Saskatchewan River, a short walk from downtown, has a good permanent collection of Canadian paintings, sculptures, watercolors, and graphics, including works by Emily Carr, David Milne, and Lawren S. Harris, as well as more recent figures like David Craven, Greg Curnoe, Toni Onley, and Dorothy Knowles.

The gallery also arranges special shows such as the recent *Images of the Prairie, Eskimo Prints and Sculpture,* and the works of British artist Richard Smith, plus lecture, recital, and film programs. It also houses a very refreshing conservatory with fountain cooly playing amid a variety of exotic plants and tropical trees.

Open from 10 a.m. to 10 p.m. daily. Admission is free.

The **Ukrainian Museum of Canada** is housed in a brand-new building at 910 Spadina Crescent East (tel. 242-0429), which is reminiscent of a Ukrainian home in western Canada at the turn of the century. The museum preserves the Ukrainian heritage as expressed and contained in such irreplaceable items as clothing, linens, tools, books, photographs, documents, wooden folk art, ceramics, pysanky (Easter eggs), and other treasures and art forms brought from the "old homeland" by Ukrainian immigrants to Canada. The museum is open Tuesday to Sunday from 1 to 5 p.m. Admission free.

The **Western Development Museum,** 2610 Lorne Ave. (tel. 652-8900), presents early Saskatchewan history in an imaginative recreation of a western Canadian town. The street is lined with 19th-century businesses: a saddler, carpentry shop, blacksmith, barbershop, Chinese laundry, law office, dry goods store, drugstore, church, and so on. Besides the town model/replica, the museum also houses a collection of vintage cars, from the 1905 Cadillac Touring Car to the Edsel, the Fairlane, and an electrically powered car. While you're here, contemplate the old farm machinery and imagine the huge steam tractors slowly chugging across the horizon, their whistles tooting and funnels pumping steam.

To get to the museum, take Idylwyld Dr. south to the Lorne Ave. exit and follow Lorne Ave. south until you see the museum on the right. Or take bus no. 1 from Second Ave. and 19th St. Open 9 a.m. to 9 p.m. Monday to Saturday, and Sunday from 10 a.m. during the summer from Victoria Day to Labour Day; 9 a.m. to 5 p.m. on weekdays and noon to 5 p.m. on weekends during the winter. Admission: adults, $1.50; children under 16, 50¢; families, $4.

The **University of Saskatchewan** occupies a dramatic 2550-acre site overlooking the South Saskatchewan River and educates some 12,000 students. The actual campus buildings are set on 435 acres while the rest of the area is given over (naturally enough) to the University Farm and experimental plots. Tours of the university campus can be taken. Some of the more interesting highlights include: the biology museum (open weekdays from 8:30 a.m. to 5 p.m., Saturday from 8:30 a.m. to 12:30 p.m.), which the kids will really appreciate for they can view close up bush babies, ferrets, rattlesnakes, crocodiles, various fish and bird species, and beautiful sea anemones and sponges; the Observatory (open to the public every Wednesday evening from 8 to 11 p.m., and Sunday from 2 to 5 p.m. and 8:30 to 11:30 p.m.) housing the Duncan telescope; the Little Stone House, which was built in 1887 and served as the city's first school and community center (open May 22 to June 7 from 1 to 6 p.m. daily; June 8 to August 31, Tuesday to Saturday from 1 to 5 p.m., and Sunday from 2 to 5 p.m.). To arrange a guided tour of the university campus, contact Ruth Dunford, University Secretary's Office, University of Saskatchewan, Saskatoon, SK S7N 0W0 (tel. 343-5175).

To get there, take bus no. 7 from downtown at 23rd St. and Second Ave. or (summers only) bus no. 2 from 19th St. and Second Ave.

While you're in Saskatchewan, you really should take the time to visit a **potash mine.** Don a hard hat, get into the "cage," and travel 3250 feet below ground and then another eight kilometers through subterranean tunnels to the mine face, where you can watch machines mining up to 11 tons of potash per minute. Then you can explore the underground warehouses and maintenance shops before returning to the surface to see the raw potash refined and loaded for shipment to North American and offshore markets. For a tour, write: Tours, Public Affairs Department, Potash Corporation of Saskatchewan, 728 Spadina Crescent East, Saskatoon, SK S7K 4H7 (tel. 306/664-5543). Arrangements have to be made four to six weeks ahead.

For a change of pace, head for the bandstand south of the Bessborough Hotel and hop aboard the 28-foot luxurious pontoon riverboat the *Little Northcote* and **cruise** for an hour along the South Saskatchewan River. Cruises begin every hour on the hour from noon to 8 p.m. during June and July, from noon to 7 p.m. from August to September 15.

Forestry Farm Park, Forest Dr. (tel. 373-0494), is an excellent destination to head for for a barbecue while you wander around and view the 300 or so species of Canadian and Saskatchewan wildlife gathered here. Wolf, lynx, coyote, fox, bear, racoon, eagle, owl, and hawk, different kinds of deer, caribou, elk, and bison have their home here.

During the winter you can cross-country ski the 2½-mile trail. During the summer there's a large sports field to practice throwing a ball or Frisbee around. And if you don't feel like picnicking, there's a food concession in the park.

To get there, cross the University Bridge and head along College Dr. to Central Ave., where you turn left. At 115th St., turn right and drive until you come to Forest Dr., which will lead you into the park.

CULTURE AND NIGHTLIFE: There's not an awful lot of nightlife activity in Saskatoon but the **Centennial Center,** Auditorium Ave. and 22nd St. (tel. 653-3722), provides a superb 2003-seat theater where the **Saskatoon Symphony** performs. Tickets are available from the Saskatoon Symphony box office (tel. 665-6414).

The two professional theater companies are the **Persephone Theatre** (tel. 343-7141), which works from its own theater at Ave. H and 20th St. West, offering five shows a season (from October 20 to March 31); and **Twenty Fifth Street Playhouse** (tel. 343-9966), which stages its productions at various locations so that you'd best check in the local newspaper for details.

For dining and dancing there are one or two clubs. Probably the spiffiest is **Fast Freddie's** in the Park Town Hotel (tel. 244-5564), 924 Spadina Crescent East (see my hotel description). Otherwise, you might try **Dominic's,** 710 Idylwyld Dr. North (tel. 665-6644), a large two-tier room with a sizable dance floor furnished with Breuer-style chairs. Large portraits of artists like Ray Charles and Liza Minelli stare down from the walls and prompt you into action. Here, groups provide top-40 disco sounds from 9 p.m. on. The cover, only charged on Thursday, Friday, and Saturday, varies with the group from $1.50 to $3. Cocktails average $2.25; beer costs $1.65. If you like, you can enjoy a good dinner here at reasonable prices—a ten-ounce top sirloin for $8.95, veal cutlets at $6.95, deep-fried shrimp for $8.25. Open Monday to Saturday from 5 p.m. to 2 a.m.

The **A-Four Club** (tel. 242-4225) is another cavernous spot providing dancing to live entertainment. Drinks average $2.25; beer, $1.50. Weekdays from 11 a.m. to 8 p.m. and Saturday from 5:30 to 8 p.m. is Happy Hour, when beer is $1, ditto wine, and a Harvey Wallbanger is $1.70. Dinner entrees begin at $4.25 for ground beef steak, to $5.45 for boneless ham steak and $7.95 for spare ribs Greek style. There may or may not be a cover charge depending on the group's fame. Primarily rock and roll groups appear here—Charity Brown, for instance.

AROUND SASKATOON: Saskatoon is a jumping-off point for two interesting trips.

Fort Battleford National Historic Park

This lies about 86 miles (a 1½-hour drive) northwest of the city on Hwy. 5. In 1876 when the district headquarters of the North West Mounted Police was established here, the area was still the exclusive domain of Indians, buffalo, and a handful of white traders. The government, which had received the North West Territories from the Hudson's Bay Company in 1870, wanted to settle the land with farmers, thereby opening the west. Policing the area was necessary and so the fort that you see today was built in 1876 and remained in use until 1924.

Inside the palisade you'll find five buildings that can be visited, but first stop in at the interpretative gallery where you can walk through a display that relates the role of the Mounted Police in the history of the area from the fur-trading era through early settlement and treaty negotiations with the Indians to the panorama of events that led to the North West Rebellion of 1885. You'll see a Red River cart, the type that was used to transport police supplies into the west, excerpts from the local Saskatchewan *Herald,* a typical log cabin settler's home which is amazingly tiny, articles of the fur trade, and an 1876 Gatling gun.

Besides the guard house (1887) containing a cell block and the sick horse stable (1898), visit the Officers' Quarters (1886), which now contains a music display of vintage instruments, Mounted Police uniforms, and various artifacts of Indian culture, European trade goods, a Cree Bible, and articles of dress. Perhaps the most interesting house is the Commanding Officer's residence

(1877), which even though it looks terribly comfortable today was certainly not so in the 1880s, as Superintendent Walker lamented in 1879: "this morning with the thermometer 37 degrees below, water was frozen on top of the stove in my bedroom, notwithstanding there was sufficient fire in the stove to start the morning fire." Stuffed with Victoriana, the house shows some interesting items—like the early steam irons and irons into which you put coals before using them.

Open 9 a.m. to 5 p.m. Monday to Saturday, and 10 a.m. to 6 p.m. on Sundays and holidays.

Prince Albert National Park

This is a stunningly beautiful wilderness area in which to get away from it all only 103 miles north of Saskatoon, 15 miles north of Prince Albert, the gateway to Saskatchewan's north. The park's headquarters is at **Waskesiu,** where lodges, hotels, motels, and cabins are located. Most of the cabins and lodges are old, quaint, and rustic in style—often containing stone fireplaces. Rates start at $12 single, $20 double, for accommodation with bathroom down the hall; rising to $30 for accommodation with kitchenette, sitting room, and two bedrooms, including all cooking utensils (no maid service). Within the park there's an 18-hole golf course, paddlewheelers on the lake, camping for 500, horseriding, bowling greens, and tennis courts. Don't be surprised if the elk just casually wander through your backyard. Vehicle entry to the park costs $10 for an annual permit, $2 for a four-day permit, $1 for a daily permit. Unserviced campsites cost $3 (with electricity, $5; with electricity, sewer, and water, $6).

For more information, write: Prince Albert National Park, Waskesiu Lake, P.O. Box 100, SK S0J 270 (tel. 306/663-3511).

3. Special Saskatchewan Events and Activities

SPECIAL EVENTS: Saskatoon's **Pioneer Days,** usually held the second week of July, provides some grand agricultural spectacles, such as the threshing competition in which steam power is pitted against gas, sometimes with unexpected results, and the tractor-pulling competition, when standard farm tractors are used to pull a steel sled weighted down with a water tank. The fair also includes a grandstand show, various displays and animal judging, and thoroughbred horse racing.

Regina's **Buffalo Days,** usually held the first week of August, recalls the time when this noble beast roamed the west. Events include livestock judging, the heavy horse show, various demonstrations, a beard-growing contest, and a grandstand show.

STAYING ON A FARM: Obviously one of the best ways to see, understand, and enjoy the prairies is to visit one of Saskatchewan's farms. Here, you're certain to find really warm hospitality, fresh home-grown, home-cooked food, and a chance to pitch in and help with the chores, ride horses, or watch a prairie sunset emblazon and fade from the sky. For example, at Marie Moldenhauer's farm in Allan, about an hour outside Saskatoon, you'll find 1280 acres run by her young son, where you'll become part of the family and stay in rooms in the farmhouse. **Saskatchewan Farm Vacations Association** publishes a list of farms offering accommodations. Write to: Mrs. Irene Lightbody, Secretary, Saskatchewan Farm Vacations Association, P.O. Box 24, Bateman, SK S0H

OE0 (tel. 306/648-3530). Rates are set as follows (although they may vary depending on the facilities available): room plus three meals and horseback riding, $16 a day for adults, $12 for children under 12. Campers with electricity are charged $5 a day, $3 without. Bed-and-breakfast rates can often be negotiated.

CANOEING: To some it comes as a surprise that Saskatchewan has 31,000 square miles of water. Her northern water routes offer a challenge to both novice and expert. So, 55 canoe routes have been mapped which will take you through terrain that has not changed since the era of explorers and fur traders. You can get to all but three of the routes by road. Various outfitters will supply tent, camping equipment, and canoe, look after your car, and transport you to the starting point for your canoe trip. Most of them are located in either Flin Flon or Lac La Ronge, 250 miles north of Saskatoon.

Churchill River Canoe Outfitters P.O. Box 26, La Ronge SK (after May 15) and 913 10th St. East, Saskatoon, SK S7J 0H6 (tel. 306/664-3400) offers also a selection of canoe camping tours. Four-day packages that include lodge accommodations and equipment (no meals) start at $90 per person for adults, $60 for children 12 to 16 with parent, $45 for children under 12 with parent. For seven-day packages, the prices are $150, $100, and $75, respectively.

For more general information about canoeing vacations and lists of canoe outfitters, write to the **Department of Tourism and Renewable Resources,** 1825 Lorne St., Regina, SK S4P 3N1 (tel. 306/565-2300).

FISHING: For the fisherman the same clear cold northern lakes hold out the chance of catching walleye, northern pike, four species of trout, and Arctic grayling. There are over 200 northern outfitters—both fly-in and drive-in camps—offering equipment, accommodation, and experienced guides to take you to the best fishing spots. And while you're in the north you might catch the spectacular aurora borealis.

Rates for accommodation vary, but you can reckon it will cost between $15 and $30 a day per person. Boat and motor will cost about $35 a day, and guide services run about $25 to $35 a day. For more information, write to the Department of Tourism and Renewable Resources (see above).

Adults 16 and over must obtain a fishing licence: $10 for nonresidents, $3 for Canadians. These can be purchased at special vendors, including most stores selling fishing equipment, and from the Department of Tourism and Renewable Resources.

THE PROVINCIAL PARKS: Saskatchewan has 17 such parks where you can camp for $3 unelectrified, $5 electrified.

Duck Mountain, Cypress Hills, Greenwater Lake, and Moose Mountain offer cabin accommodation: rates are usually $24 to $26 for a one-bedroom cabin, $28 to $30 for a two-bedroom, with some nonmoderns (that is, with an outdoor toilet) renting for $16 double, $10 single.

For information, write to the park superintendent at each: **Cypress Hills Provincial Park,** P.O. Box 850, Maple Creek, SK (tel. 306/667-2981); **Duck Mountain Provincial Park,** Kamsack, SK (tel. 306/542-3482); **Greenwater Lake Provincial Park,** Porcupine Plain, SK (tel. 306/278-2972); **Moose Mountain Provincial Park,** P.O. Box 100, Carlyle, SK (tel. 306/577-2131).

I recommend you call ahead to **SaskTravel** at 306/565-2300 (toll free within Saskatchewan at 800/667-3674) to rate your chances of getting a campsite.

Part Three

WESTERN CANADA

by John Godwin

Chapter XV

ALBERTA

1. **Calgary**
2. **Banff and Jasper National Parks**
3. **Edmonton**
4. **Elsewhere in Alberta**

STRETCHING FROM the Northwest Territories to the U.S. border of Montana in the south, flanked by the Rocky Mountains in the west and Saskatchewan province in the east, Alberta is a very young, very big, very beautiful chunk of North America. Also a very empty one. Measuring 255,285 square miles, the province is almost as large as Texas, but with under two million inhabitants it has fewer people than Philadelphia.

More than half the population lives in Edmonton and Calgary, leaving the rest of the province a tremendous amount of elbow room, breathing space, and unspoiled scenery.

The country was originally called Rupert's Land, a fur franchise of the Hudson's Bay Company first explored by a white scout named Anthony Henday, who penetrated far enough to see "shining Mountains" in the distance—the first glimpse of the Canadian Rockies. Although fur traders and trappers formed the vanguard of white penetration, it was missionaries like Fr. Albert Lacombe who opened the country to settlement.

They did it by making friends with the Indians, particularly the powerful Blackfoot Nation, a union of warrior tribes as formidable as the Sioux. Rupert's Land only became part of Canada in 1869, when the Hudson's Bay Company sold out to the government. Law and order, in shape of the North West Mounted Police, didn't arrive until five years later. Meanwhile Alberta went through its wildest and bloodiest period, with fur and whiskey traders moving up from Montana Territory and establishing aptly named outposts like Fort Whoop-Up.

While the Mounties threw out the whiskey peddlers, Father Lacombe established schools, churches, and good relations with the Blackfeet. So good, in fact, that an agreement with the tribes in 1880 made it possible to build the transcontinental railroad without firing a shot.

There isn't much left of earlier sources of Alberta's wealth, furs and gold. But the later ones are in evidence wherever you go: cattle, wheat, and oil. To which, in fairness, we must add tourism.

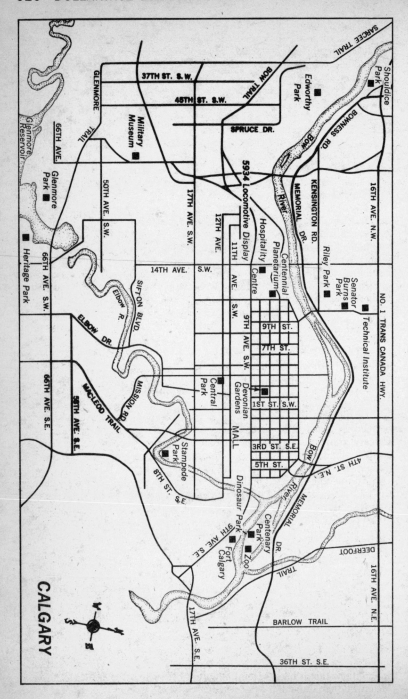

1. Calgary

Calgary is a phenomenon—the only metropolis in the world founded by a police force, and surely the only city of half a million people anywhere whose inhabitants refer to her affectionately as a "cowtown."

It takes a little while before you catch on to what they mean by that. At first glance this young urban giant, flexing steel and concrete muscles, seems as far removed from anything pastoral as Los Angeles is from the angels. What the locals are saying is that the *spirit*—the heart and soul—of their town has remained rural—wealth, high-rises, and traffic jams notwithstanding.

And in that they are right. Calgary is the friendliest place on the map, a city whose population consists of welcoming committees, where motorists smile after getting their fenders dented, where everybody seems to be competing for a National Niceness Award, and bus drivers tell you to "have a happy day" as if they cared.

It's a city that lives largely on oil but lives *for* that huge annual razzle-dazzle celebrated as the **Calgary Stampede.** A place where high-powered business executives who have never ridden a horse wear cowboy boots and invite you home for dinner after bumping into you at a street corner. Where a cop, seeing you lost, will walk you all the way to wherever you want to go and give a running commentary on the sights en route. Where a waitress may show you photos of her kids between courses and a total stranger may offer to share his umbrella to save you a drenching.

Niceness, however, doth not a city make. One famous Canadian author described Calgary as "looking like it was uncrated only an hour before you got there." And he isn't altogether wrong.

Historically Calgary dates back just over a century. It was born in the summer of 1875, when a detachment of the North West Mounted Police, advancing westward, reached the confluence of the Bow and Elbow Rivers. They built a solid log fort there, and by the end of the year the fortified spot had attracted 600 settlers.

Gradually the lush prairie lands around the settlement drew tremendous beef herds, many of them from the overgrazed U.S. ranches in the south. Calgary grew into a cattle metropolis, a big meat-packing center, large by cowboy standards—but not by any other. When World War II closed, it numbered barely 100,000 souls and life was placid.

The oil boom erupted in the late 1960s, and in one decade utterly changed the pace and complexion of the city. Alberta produces nearly all the oil in Canada, earning provincials the nickname of "blue-eyed Arabs." And about 80% of the country's oil and subsidiary companies have their headquarters in Calgary—or are trying to get them there. Modern Calgary is thus a little over ten years old, the diaper stage of urban development.

The population shot up to 506,000 and is growing at a pace that makes statisticians dizzy. In 1978 alone, $1 billion worth of construction was added to the skyline, creating office high-rises, hotel blocks, walkways, and shopping centers so fast even locals aren't sure what's around the next corner.

In another decade downtown Calgary may be a motorist's Nirvana but currently it's a madhouse. Half the area is under construction, half the streets have detours, a good proportion lead nowhere. Traffic lights run riot, like tropical fungi, blossoming in clusters of six or more at intersections. Some road junctions are festooned with so many signs, arrows, instructions, warnings, and admonitions that it takes several minutes of reading before you dare proceed. Meanwhile the traffic has piled up for two blocks behind you. In every other city your fellow drivers would have lynched you by osmosis. Here they smile. By conditioned reflex.

ORIENTATION: Central Calgary lies between the **Bow River** in the north and the **Elbow River** in the south. The two rivers meet at the eastern end of the city, forming **St. Georges Island,** which houses a park and the zoo. South of the island stands **Fort Calgary,** birthplace of the city. The Bow River makes a bend north of downtown, and in this bend nestles **Prince's Island** with another park. Between Ninth and Tenth Aves. run the Canadian Pacific Railway tracks, and south of the tracks stretch **Central Park** and **Stampede Park,** scene of Calgary's greatest annual festival.

For sheer muddle, central Calgary's street-numbering system is matched only by central London—which has the excuse of being some 900 years older. The city is divided into four segments: Northeast (NE), southeast (SE), northwest (NW), and southwest (SW), with avenues running east-west and streets north-south. The north and south numbers begin at **Centre Ave.,** the east and west numbers at **Centre St.**—a recipe for confusion if ever there was one.

Even if you faithfully remember that downtown Calgary consists of one-way streets and make sure of driving the right way, you're in for a hair-raising shock. For Seventh Ave., which goes west-east, has *one* lane on which buses and taxis hurtle toward you east to west! That's their privilege. So pull over, try to control your shaking hands, and *smile.*

Beyond the downtown area the going gets easier. In fact, beautiful. Calgary nudges the foothills between the Rocky Mountains to the west and the endless prairies to the east. A short drive northeast lie the **Drumheller Badlands,** an awesome configuration that yield the dinosaur skeletons you'll see in the city museums. This is also the direction of the **International Airport.** Northwest, just across the Bow River, spreads the lovely campus of the **University of Calgary.** Southwest runs a vast pattern of parks, golf courses, and nature trails surrounding the sparkling **Glenmore Reservoir.** And farther south begins the rich rural landscape of farming communities and baronial cattle ranches.

Because of her high altitude the city is dry and very sunny as well as windy, and even in the heat of summer it tends to be cold in the shade. Summer "heat" is a relative matter here. July and August, the warmest months, rarely climb above 75°F. or so.

Your best orientation point is the cloud-pushing **Calgary Tower,** at Ninth Ave. and Centre St. Looking across the avenue you're facing due north. You have the post office on your left, the Convention Centre opposite, and City Hall two blocks up on the right.

Inside the Tower you'll find **Hospitality House,** which provides you with cheerful and gratis literature, maps and information about the city. This is run by the Calgary Tourist & Convention Association, also in charge of **Hospitality Centre,** 1300 Sixth Ave. SW. The centre operates an extremely useful, no-charge **Accommodation Bureau** (tel. 403/263-8518), something of a rarity in Canada. For information about the province in general, you have one of the finest, most amiable of government services in **Travel Alberta,** Alberta Hotel Bldg., 808 First St. SW. (tel. 403/261-6574), an outfit that represents the quintessence of Calgary's welcome mat.

Transportation

Calgary, as befits an oil metropolis, has excellent connections with the outside world. **Pacific Western** (tel. 265-6540) maintains the unsurpassed

Airbus service to Edmonton: planes leaving on the half hour mornings, and every hour the rest of the day for the 36-minute hop (costing $33). **CP Air** (tel. 269-8257) links major Canadian cities, the U.S., Europe, and the Orient. From the airport a limousine bus gets you downtown for $2.50. By taxi the trip costs around $9.40.

The **C.P. Rail Depot** is at Palliser Square, behind the Calgary Tower (tel. 266-9541), and the **Greyhound Bus** depot is at 222 First Ave. SW (tel. 265-9111). Within the city, bus transportation is provided by the **Calgary Transit System** (tel. 276-7801) with the smilingest drivers extant. The standard fare is 45¢ for adults, 30¢ for children.

Calgary taxis charge $1.10 at flagfall, then 10¢ per mile. The largest cab fleet in town is **Yellow Cab** (tel. 276-8311).

Car-rental firms include: **Tilden,** 520 Centre St. South (tel. 263-6386); **Budget,** 407 Centre St. South (tel 263-0505); and **Hertz,** 113 Seventh Ave. SE (tel. 263-8400).

THE CALGARY STAMPEDE: This is a special event of such magnitude that it rates a section to itself. Every year, July 6–15, Calgary puts on the biggest, wildest, woolliest western fling on earth. To call the Stampede a show would be a misnomer. The whole town, plus several more towns of visitors, participate by going mildly crazy for the occasion, donning western gear, whooping, hollering, dancing, and generally behaving uproariously.

The organized events spill over into the streets, but most of them take place in **Stampede Park,** a show, sports, and exhibition ground built for just that purpose. Portions of the park become amusement areas, whirling, spinning, and rotating with the latest rides. Others are set aside especially for kids, who romp through Little Britches Land and the Petting Zoo. Still other areas have concerts, livestock shows, food and handicraft exhibitions, free lectures, and dance performances.

The top attractions, though, are the Stampede regulars, drawing immense and fanatically enthusiastic audiences, some held in daytime, some in the evenings. The world-famous **Chuckwagon Race** has oldtime cowboy cook wagons thundering round the track in a fury of dust and pounding hooves, competing for the $125,000-plus in prize money.

The **rodeo** events are the biggest and roughest of their kind in North America. Cowboys from all over the continent ride bucking broncos and bulls, rope calves, and brand steers for prize money totaling more than $150,000. At night the arena becomes a blaze of lights when the **Stampede Stage Show**—the largest outdoor extravaganza in the world—takes over with precision kicking dancing girls, clowns, bands, and glamor spectacles.

On top of that, the Stampede offers a food fair, an art show, dancing exhibitions, an International Bazaar, a gambling casino, car contests, and the chance of winning the Stampede Dream Home.

Let me tell you right now that Calgary is *packed* for the occasion, not just to the rafters but way out into the surrounding countryside. Booking ahead for accommodation is essential—as many months ahead as you can possible foresee your arrival.

The same applies to reserving tickets for the park events. They cost from $4 to $19.50, depending on the event and the seats, afternoons or evenings. Tickets can be booked for any number of particular events or in one block covering all of them. For mail-order bookings, write to the **Calgary Exhibition & Stampede,** P.O. Box 2890, Calgary, AB T2P 2M7.

ACCOMMODATIONS: Alberta, you'll be glad to hear, has no sales tax. You won't have to add any percentage onto either hotel or restaurant bills, which brings even deluxe establishments down to fairly reasonable levels. Calgary is mushrooming with new and very swank hotels, but unfortunately many of the older budget hostelries are marked for demolition. So if you find a high-rise palace where I described a modest three-floorer, don't blame me—blame the oil boom.

Luxury

The **International,** 220 Fourth Ave. SW (tel. 403/265-9600), is a soaring white tower with a breathtaking view from the upper balconies: 35 stories of sheer spendor mellowed by good taste. The hotel has no rooms—only 254 suites of various sizes, all with separate bed and living rooms, private balconies, and superb bathrooms; most with dinettes and refrigerators as well. The decor is in carefully matched colors, the modernistic prints on the walls chosen with an expert eye, plus the accoutrements—caressing carpeting, wide and wonderful beds, huge-walk-in closets, plus electric blankets and lighting arrangements that can be concentrated or diffused at will.

The International features a most intriguing three-level piano bar that blends with the hotel, a grill decorated in the richest 1930s style, indoor pool and saunas, and an all-pervasive aura of low-key luxury.

Singles cost $44; doubles, $54; two-bedroom suites, $66; and penthouse suites, $110.

The **Four Seasons,** Ninth Ave. at Centre St. (tel. 403/266-7331). Like all Canadian hotels in that chain, this is a haven of discreet gorgeousness with the accent on personalized service (like 24-hour room service that *really* functions around the clock). It has a tropical garden terrace and an indoor pool with greenery that makes it resemble a jungle setting; two dining rooms with distinct personalities: one a family-style buffet, the other a temple for gourmets (and priced accordingly); a fireside cocktail bar, the Traders Lounge, for cocktails and conversation; and the ultra-plush Scotch Room, with show bar entertainment and one of the best jazz combos in town.

The 400 bedrooms and suites come in restful greens and browns with in-room movies as well as color TV. Each has enough space for a theatrical wardrobe, lighting fixtures to suit your moods, bathrooms equipped for starlets. And the hotel connects with the promenade boutiques, stores, and theaters of Palliser Square, in case you want to go shopping without facing the weather. Telephones here are Touch-Tone; clock radios and electric blankets are taken for granted.

Singles range from $48 to $56; doubles, from $60 to $68; suites start at $120.

The **Calgary Inn,** 320 Fourth Ave. SW (tel. 403/266-1611) is a massively modern luxury block in the heart of the financial district. You could hold a diplomatic reception in the huge scarlet and gold lobby connected with an indoor shopping concourse. There's a fabulous panoramic swimming pool with saunas and whirlpool at the rooftop. And a very "in" nightspot called Marco's, featuring big-name entertainers and—which is rare—acoustics that live up to their talents, as well as a very plush and expense-accountish restaurant and a pleasantly simple terrace grill with wooden chairs and checked tablecloths.

The 550 bedrooms and suites are completely air-conditioned and decorated in light and delicate pastel hues. They have oversize beds, equally roomy closets, unusually comfortable armchairs, and Touch-Tone telephones. The suites incorporate just enough slightly old-fashioned ornaments to make them homey.

Singles go from $46 to $49; doubles, from $56 to $63; while suites start at $105 and climb all the way to $210 for three-bedroom units.

Moderately Priced Hotels

The **Palliser,** Ninth Ave. and 1st. St. West (tel. 403/266-8621). A squat and squarish building that forms the core of Palliser Square, next to the Calgary Tower, this hotel gives a great feeling of spaciouness so often lacking in the newer structures. Not quite old enough to play the "grande dame" role, the Palliser has enough rich marble and cherished wood to pass for the part. The dining room boasts a magnificent fireplace and impressive wall murals, and the cocktail lounge gets international vocalists singly or in groups. Additionally, the management accepts pets and arranges for babysitters.

The 330 bedrooms have all been refurbished, which luckily has not lessened their family-size dimensions. Each is handsomely furnished with period touches, vast beds and convertible couches, attractive writing desks and beautiful shaded lamps, all featuring radio and color TV.

Singles range from $33 to $37; doubles from $42 to $46; suites from $65 to $85.

The **Sheraton Calgary,** 202 Fourth Ave. SW (tel. 403/262-7091). An unusual building—a tower rising from a ground-level platform—the Sheraton is a hostelry as well as Calgary's major entertainment center, a family hotel and a convention, seminar, and exhibition complex. It houses a cabaret, a disco, the unique Library Lounge cocktail bar, and the city's sole legal gambling casino (see the nightlife section). It offers a heated outdoor pool with large sunbathing patio, a stylish restaurant, and a very fast-service coffeehouse.

The bedrooms are fully air-conditioned, each and every one with a view. They are not large but very modern, with writing desks, excellent mirrors, color TV, comfortable armchairs, and waterbeds on request (reserve ahead, they're extremely popular).

Singles cost from $38 to $49; doubles, from $42 to $55. No charge for children under 18 staying in their parents' room.

The **Empress,** 219 Sixth Ave. SW (tel. 403/262-1141), is a small gem of a hotel, Calgary's earliest downtown hostelry but newly renovated in a way that left its charm intact. An old-world front with Parisian awnings leads into a contrasting modern lobby, paneled in Scandinavian light-wood patterns which you'll find reflected in the bedrooms. The tavern is stylishly western, the garden dining lounge fringed with romantic greenery, the paneled Rectory Lounge a quiet retreat with Chesterfield nooks.

Only 60 bedrooms are offered, all delightful in light wood and pastel tones, air-conditioned, with springy beds, armchairs beside low tables, artistic drapes, and rich carpeting, plus cable TV and dial telephones.

Singles cost $25; doubles, $30 to $32; children under 12 stay free with their parents.

Macleod Trail: Once this was a cattle track but now it's a roaring expressway that runs from downtown Calgary south through wide-open suburbia until it becomes the highway leading to the U.S. border. The northern portions of this endless, pulsating roadway are lined with inns and motels—from upper middle range to economy. I'll give a few samples from each bracket (all of them have fast and frequent bus connections to downtown).

Stampeder Inn, 3828 Macleod Trail (tel. 403/243-5531), underwent extensive rebuilding in 1979 and is now a mirror image of modern Calgary. From a modest little establishment it expanded into a vast, highly contemporary assemblage of restaurants, bars, hair salon, retail stores, dry-cleaning shop, convention facilities, and two wings of guest rooms. The dining room serves a buffet dinner that rates separate mention in the culinary bracket—it's famous.

The 150 bedrooms are separated into the simpler old wing and the deluxe new wing, and priced accordingly. The 100 new rooms combine spaciousness with conveniences like automatic wake-up service, air conditioning, Touch-Tone telephones, extra-long beds, color TV, clock radios, and "bedssage" (an intriguing vibration device that hums you gently to sleep). Furnishings are elegant, bathrooms have automatically timed ventilators, and the management supplies thoughtful trifles like miniature sewing kits and complimentary shampoo.

New rooms cost $29 single, $36 double; old rooms, $20 single, $25 double. No extra charge for children to 16.

Holiday Inn, 4206 Macleod Trail (tel. 403/287-2700). An excellently designed link in the famous chain and built in a contemporary western style that sits nicely with the environment, it has lawns with deckchairs and sunshades on the outside, a cozy lobby in rust colors with inviting circular settees and Muzak in the air, and an outstanding steak restaurant on the premises, plus a bar unfortunately named Fort Whoop-Up Lounge (actually it's a pleasantly restful spot, minus military trappings). Indoor swimming pool, one-day valet service, and temperature control throughout help keep the inn's seven conference rooms thronged with business conventions.

The guest rooms are cheerfully furnished in superior motel taste, which includes ample wardrobe space, good carpeting and lighting, dial telephones, and color TV.

Singles cost $32.50 to $33.50; doubles, $37.50 to $38.50. There are also special weekend rates of $29.50 per single.

Continental Motel, 4637 Macleod Trail (tel. 403/243-7791). Set well back from the roaring Trail, this smallish motel stands on rather bare grounds but offers very good facilities at even better rates. The brown and orange structures enclose an indoor pool and 37 units, 12 with their own kitchens, plus a coffeeshop. All come with bathrooms, color TV, and dial telephones; water beds are available. The units aren't large, but are nicely furnished, paneled in wood and equipped with writing desks. The rear portion of the grounds, where most units are located, is higher than the front part and doesn't get much traffic noise.

Singles cost $21; doubles, $23; triples, $28; and self-contained family units, $40.

The **Atlanta Motel,** 3620 Macleod Trail (tel. 403/243-4651), is a two-story pastel-colored place, as attractive inside as out. A large swimming pool is set amid green lawns sprinkled with bushes, tables, and sunshades. The 43 units (six with kitchenettes) are air-conditioned with individual temperature controls, and fitted with decorative orange carpets in pleasing contrast to the white plaster walls. Each sports prints on the walls, a small writing desk with lamp, open hanging spaces, intimate bedside lamps, and compact bathrooms. Razor plugs are outside the bathroom, but within cord range of the mirror. Color TV and dial telephones (no charge for local calls) are included. The management here is unusually attentive, even by Calgary standards of niceness.

There's only one rate—$24, single or double.

Back in the heart of downtown, the **York Hotel,** 636 Centre St. South (tel. 403/262-5581), is a red brick corner building of older vintage, but recently renovated and excellently maintained. In a rather drab part of Centre St., the York sets exceptional standards. The lobby is spacious, well carpeted, lit by many-armed chandeliers and decorated with illuminated wall murals. There's a pleasant lounge and a fast-service grill restaurant open seven days a week.

The newly refurbished bedrooms are cheerful and nicely fitted with neat corner dressing tables and mirrors, wide beds, twin bedside lamps, and walk-in closets. Several of the rooms have discreetly disguised Murphy Beds. The bathrooms are small, with showers only, but every room has color cable TV.

Singles run from $23 to $25; doubles, $27 to $30. Children under 14 stay free with their parents.

The **Motel Village,** northwest of downtown, is a triangle of 14 motels, plus restaurants, stores, and gas stations, forming a self-contained hamlet near the University of Calgary. Enclosed by Crowchild Trail, the Trans Canada Hwy. and Hwy. 1A, the Village is arranged so that most of the costlier establishments flank the highway, the more economical lie off Crowchild Trail. Plenty of accommodation choice in a small area with good public transport connections. A few samplers:

Mt. Eisenhower Motel, 2227 Banff Trail (tel. 403/289-6626), is an open rectangle of pretty white-and-green units, with patches of lawn and scrubs, sprinkled with garden furniture in the center. The 44 units come with bath or shower, color TV, and telephones. The motel has a heated pool, accepts pets, and serves complimentary coffee to guests. The rooms are covered with fluffy green carpets, bathrooms are red tiled and quite spacious, and furnishings and lighting facilities are ample. There are large walk-in closets and electric coffee pots in the units. Some also have kitchenettes.

Singles range from $22 to $24; doubles, $24 to $30. Children stay free in their parents' room.

The **Anchor Motel,** 1816 Crowchild Trail (tel. 403/289-6606), has 39 units, 8 with kitchenettes. Behind a simple layout of pink-toned structures there are very pleasant living quarters: walls paneled in dark woods, deep-brown carpeting, beds flanked by nighttables and reading lamps. The rooms however, are fairly small, and the bathrooms are rather old-fashioned and equipped with tubs only. All units have color TV and switchboard telephones.

Singles cost $20; doubles, $24 to $30; additional occupants pay $5.

The **Sunset Motel,** 2112 Crowchild Trail NW (tel. 403/289-4401), has an open layout with a small patch of lawn and one tree in the center. The white and yellow structures house 40 units, 10 of them with kitchenettes. All have bath or shower, color TV, and switchboard telephones. Accommodations here are compact, nicely furnished and decorated: wood-paneled walls, green carpets, a little makeup niche with mirror, a couch but no chairs, a large closet with folding doors. An ice machine and soft drink and cigarette dispensers are on the premises. The management accepts pets.

Singles cost from $20 to $22; doubles, $24; additional occupants, $2.

Budget

Fairly slim pickings in this category, since many of the older buildings which usually supply economy lodgings are in the process of being torn down. That's the reverse side of the coin in any boom. On the other hand, there's no tax on hotel bills, so some of the lower-medium-priced establishments actually fall into the budget category.

The **Success Hotel,** 318 Fourth Ave. SE (tel. 403/266-8893), has a cozy green cottage front flanked by trees, and a small lobby with leather chairs, potted plants, and vending machines. All of the 59 rooms are air-conditioned and 17 are kitchen units, but none has a private bath (shared bathrooms are in the halls). The corridors are neatly kept and the bedrooms, though smallish, are quite trim. There are good red carpeting, good beds, TV sets, and telephones in all rooms, but no sinks, and only ceiling lights.

Singles cost $11; doubles, $14; kitchen units (on a weekly basis) $60 to $85.

The **St. Louis Hotel,** 430 Eighth Ave. SE (tel. 403/262-6341). The lobby, adjoining the downstairs tavern, is somewhat bare and is decorated mainly with vending machines. The 51 rooms, however, come compact and cozy, equipped with wall-to-wall carpeting, TV, and writing desks, and 15 of them have little bathrooms with showers only. There are bedside lamps but no ceiling lights, no room telephones. There's a restaurant on the premises and a food bar in the tavern.

Singles run $8.50 to $12; doubles, $10 to $15.

The **Chinook Motel,** 6106 Macleod Trail (tel. 403/255-8211), has 15 units, all with kitchenettes and showers. A supermarket across the road keeps your refrigerator filled (the management supplies the essential kitchen gear). The kitchens have gas stoves and the units come with separate little bedrooms and TV. Furniture is rather basic. No room telephone, and no shaver plug in the bathroom.

Singles cost $16; doubles, $18; additional occupants pay $2 each.

The **Bluebird Motel,** 3912 Macleod Trail (tel. 403/243-0393), consists of scattered blue-and-white shingle-roofed buildings around an open yard. The setup is spacious if fairly bare, and you can park your car right outside your unit. The 17 units have showers, and 11 also have kitchenettes. All come with TV, but minus telephones. Furniture includes all the essentials, good hanging space, but no extra frills.

Singles cost $18; doubles, 20; weekly rentals, $95.

The Ys

Calgary's YM and YW stick to their titles inasmuch as neither takes residents of the opposite sex. Both are in central downtown locations.

The **YMCA,** 332 Sixth Ave. SW (tel. 403/268-6701), has a handsome brick and marble front, but a very plain and small lobby decorated chiefly with athletic plaques. The cafeteria keeps rather restricted hours and closes on Sunday. The 67 bedrooms are spotless and rather spartan: linoleum on the floors, narrow beds, bedside and table lights, and a chest of drawers, plus a good-sized closet. The building has no private baths, but washrooms with showers are on each floor. No curfew hours for residents.

Singles pay $9; doubles, $8.50 per person.

The **YWCA,** 320 Fifth Ave. SE (tel. 403/263-1550), is a much frillier affair. There's a visitors' lounge with tables, magazines, and TV, and a charming lobby with gleaming tile floors, leather settees, and globular chandeliers. The cafeteria, though, closes at 5:30 on weekdays and stays closed weekends, presumably on the assumption that ladies fast Saturdays and Sundays. The bedrooms are nicely carpeted and equipped with dressing tables, wardrobes, and bedside lights, all in cheerful color patterns. Accommodation ranges from rooms with private baths to four-bunk rooms and simple sleeping-bag space, giving a wide choice of rates.

Singles from $14 to $16; doubles, $10 to $12 per person. Bunk rooms run from $5.50 to $9 per person.

College Accommodations

The **University of Calgary,** 2920 24th Ave. NW (tel. 403/284-5110), lies in a California-style campus setting of 314 acres. The grounds are park-like and offer a vast variety of sports and cultural attractions. Visitors are accommodated during term holidays, and facilities are excellent. All rates include breakfast. Singles pay $16.85; doubles, $11.85 per person.

Campgrounds and Trailer Parks

Bow Bend Trailer Park, 5227 13th Ave. NW (tel. 403/288-2161). Located beside Shouldice Park and the Bow River, it has washrooms, showers, and laundry. Rates per site are $7 to $8 for two persons.

Max Bell Park, 2425 Memorial Dr. NE (tel. 403/248-4868), is in the triangle between Deerfoot and Narlow Trail, 1½ miles east of the zoo. Facilities include hot showers, toilets, and grocery stores. A bus stop is close by. Sites with electricity hookups cost $6.50

Sunalta Trailer Park, P.O. Box 6531, Stn. D. (located two miles west of the city limits at Happy Valley turnoff on Hwy. 1; tel. 403/288-7911), the Sunalta has a laundromat, store, toilets, and playground as well as hot showers. Full hookups cost $8; power and water, $1; tenting, $6.

MEALS: The only thing "cowtown"-like about Calgary's culinary scene is the profusion of steakhouses serving the superlative Alberta beef. This is certainly a red-meat metropolis, not a very happy hunting ground for vegetarians. But one of the brighter side effects of the oil boom has been the restaurant boom that accompanied it. In the course of five or six years Calgary changed from a determinedly parochial eating spot to an astonishingly cosmopolitan one, catering to the taste buds of the United Nations.

Most of the international establishments are very new, very plush, and rather expensive, tailored for an executive clientele. In the cheaper brackets the fare gets more conservative, and in the cheapest it's the old hamburger–hot dog routine, but with the redeeming feature that the quality of the meat, even there, is unusually high.

The Top Choices

The Three Greenhorns, 4th St. and Fourth Ave. SW (tel. 264-6903). A velvety combination of pioneer Canadiana, nautical decor, gourmet cuisine, and smooth service has made this establishment one of the preserves of Calgary's smart set. It looks in parts like an enlarged ship's cabin with curved rafters overhead and coils of rope along the walls, illuminated by boat lanterns that give just the right atmospheric glow. But the seating facilities are definitely not quarterdeck—no sailing skipper ever sat so comfortably. Do take time to admire the marine prints, antique maps, nautical instruments, and superb ship models. The dining area is adjoined by a very chic cocktail lounge for pre- or postdinner refreshments. The menu is a fine balance between meat and seafood, both of top quality. Soup comes as part of your meal, as do the best and crispest rolls in town. Try the pâté of the house, the outstanding cucumber salad. Then perhaps the "baked salmon Jim"—a secret recipe. Your meal would come to around $15, not including liquids, of course. Open till 11:30 p.m. Closed Sunday.

Panorama Room, Calgary Tower (tel. 266-7171). A vast revolving restaurant seating 200 diners, this place offers a different vista with each course as the view from the tower top slowly changes from city to prairies to mountains and back again. The romantic impact is strengthened by subdued lighting effects and sentimental background music. The decor here is highly contemporary, but the scene from the curved picture windows is the main decoration, not to be surpassed by any interior designer's efforts. The clam chowder makes an ideal starter, then a small salad, climaxed perhaps by coquilles St-Jacques, with maple leaf pie (magnificent) as the fitting finale. You'll pay about $14 for a memorable meal. Open six nights a week till midnight, Sundays till 11 p.m.

Oliver's, 609 Seventh Ave. SW (tel. 264-1000), named after the little waif who wanted "some more," is part of a carousel complex that also includes a posh pub called **Old Bailey** and a diabolical disco named **Lucifer's.** Oliver's, to be sure, bears no resemblance whatever to a Dickensian workhouse. In fact it's among the silkiest dineries in town, a haven of soundless carpets, shining table linen, leather settees, and the most flattering lights in the province. Its extremely cosmopolitan menu is heavy on lobster, chateaubriand, and other goodies young Master Twist never heard of. I'd suggest you commence with the delicate filet of herring for $2.75, and proceed to the filet mignon for $10.50. Open till 11 p.m. six days a week. Closed Sunday.

Maxim's, 7105 Macleod Trail (tel. 255-1155). You don't expect a dinery named after one of the world's most illustrious hostelries along an erstwhile cattle trail—but this is Calgary and there it is! And the designers didn't go overboard with phony Parisian knickknackery. Instead they created a beautifully subdued restaurant whose elegance doesn't jump at you, but enfolds you slowly in a velvet embrace—literally, because the upholstery *is* velvet. And the wall paneling is pecan wood, and the cutlery silver. The *Mona Lisa* painting, however, was not hijacked from the Louvre, at least so the management says. You can't do better than to start with the lobster bisque, with a tingling touch of champagne. Followed by either lapin chasseur (rabbit in cream and wine sauce) or tournedos Henry IV (beef stuffed with goose liver pâté). With various suitable trimmings, your meal should hover at around $17. Closed Sundays.

The Eye-Opener, corner of Third Ave. and 2nd St. SW (tel. 264-2000). The original *Eye-Opener* was one of the most unorthodox periodicals ever published anywhere. It came out "semi-occasionally" and had a staff of one—Editor-Everything Bob Edwards—who, when his paper failed to appear, blithely informed his readers in the next edition that he'd been too drunk to produce the missing number. They loved it, and when the news sheet did get out, enjoyed the largest circulation in Alberta. The restaurant by that name is considerably more reliable, but likewise places a strong accent on liquid inspiration. Calgary cuts of steak (all fat meticulously trimmed off) cost $8.95, the same as the Cornish hen stuffed with wild rice and served in brandy sauce. Soup, salad, and sourdough bread come with the meal, but you pay extra for vegetables. There's an enormous list of potables, from Bob's Special cocktail (with a scotch base, $4) to imported Médoc (at $10.95 a bottle). At the back of the newsprint menu there's a sample page from the *Eye-Opener,* vintage 1912.

The Rimrock Room, Palliser Hotel, Ninth Ave and 1st St. SW (tel. 266-8621). The decor here is "cattle baron western," the menu international, but weighted in favor of some of the finest Alberta beef served in the province. The wall murals, depicting the Old West, provide a panorama of their own. There's a small dance floor beneath shimmering chandeliers for use between courses or afterward. Table linen glows scarlet to match the upholstery. The French onion soup is outstanding and comes with your dinner. But the pièce de résistance here is the roast prime rib, a pink and rare masterpiece for $13.50. Open seven days a week till 10:30 p.m.

I would have to stretch this bracket over twice its length to include all of Calgary's culinary top rankers. There's the **Inn on Lake Bonavista** (tel. 271-6711), with superlative views to accompany the food; the **Balalaika,** 5809 Macleod Trail (tel. 253-9260), with gypsy violins to add atmosphere to the shashlik; the **Iron Gate,** at the downtown Holiday Inn; **Gatsby's,** the International Inn's Roaring '20s dinery; the **Omar Khayyam,** 301 16th Ave. NW (tel. 277-2110), for some of the finest East Indian fare served in Canada; **Caesar's,** 512 Fourth Ave. SW (tel. 264-1222), a sumptuous steakery with a Roman motif; etc., and so forth.

Moderately Priced Restaurants

The **Long Bar,** Eighth Ave. and 1st St. West (tel. 232-1799). Located downstairs in a pedestrian mall, this plush little dinery becomes a plush little disco later at night, boasting Calgary's first computerized dance floor. It has a distinct European flavor, both in the decor and the menu. From Monday to Friday it serves a wildly popular businessmens' buffet lunch for $4. At night the fare gets costlier. The trout with salmon mousse runs $8.75, which should be followed by the Black Forest cherry cake, $1.10. Open till 3 a.m. Thursday through Saturday for dancing.

Monty's, 606 1st St. SW (tel. 265-8008). This is the wealthier offshoot of a little deli that outgrew its premises. Come and taste, and you'll see why. The new Monty's (after owner Jim Monument) has Czech white oak furniture, draped street windows, romantic lighting, and hanging greenery, enclosed by cozy paneling. The barbecued spare ribs melt in your mouth for $5.75. And don't miss the 85¢ blueberry pie. Open till midnight weekdays, till 6 p.m. on Sundays.

Gasthaus, 2417 4th St. SW (tel. 266-6288). As German as its shingle, this is a vast and immensely elaborate "wursthaus" with one of the biggest bars this side of Bavaria. Waitresses wear dirndl costumes, garlanded pillars support the low ceiling, and one wall is entirely covered with highly colored Bavarian town and country scenes. A three-piece lederhosen band blows, beats, and squeezes Teutonic airs interspersed with tangos. The dance floor is always in use and the atmosphere is as gemütlich as huge helpings of beer can make it. The food is not only excellent but authentic. You get the rarely encountered—and quite delicious—Pilsner beer soup for $1.50. A wonderful steak tartare is $8.25. If that's too raw for your palate, pick the rindsrouladen (stuffed beef slices) for $8.80. The Gasthaus offers an encyclopedic list of German beers and wines, including the celebrated "boot of beer," a glass boot that holds six ordinary bottles. Open till 1 a.m. six days a week. Closed Sunday.

The **Alberta Meat & Beverage Company,** Holiday Inn, 4206 Macleod Trail (tel. 287-2700), is a lunch-dinner-breakfast operation with a rustic pioneer air. The entrance is guarded by barrels and the wood-paneled walls are hung with intriguing old photographs of rural Alberta in the bygones. There are deep leather seats, intimately orange lighting, and an informative menu showing the corss section of a cow (it explains where the various cuts of meat come from, in case you want to know). The top sirloin steak sandwich comes in at $6.50, and a mighty steerburger with sauteed mushrooms, for $5.25. Rich and creamy pie à la mode costs $1. Open daily from 7 a.m. till midnight.

Calgary's **Chinatown** occupies a little over two blocks at the south end of the Centre St. Bridge. Although small, it is packed with stores and restaurants and—like everything in this town—is busily transforming itself. The eateries are of very good quality, but unfortunately don't put their menus in the window (a serious omission when it comes to catching tourist trade). Another thing: I couldn't see anybody except the Chinese patrons and yours truly eating with chopsticks. Perhaps the waiters should give some impromptu lessons to their Occidental clientele.

The **Mandarin Village,** at Centre St. and Third Ave. (tel. 264-1642), is easily recognizable by its pagoda roof. Supremely comfortable and air-conditioned, the place has a stylish (not garish) Oriental decor. Mellow lights, shielded candles on the tables, red carpeting blending with the red drapes, murals resembling Chinese silkscreens along the walls—the restaurant exudes an air of quietly contemplative table pleasure. The pace is leisurely and the dishes take time, as good food will. And they're worth a wait. A fine mustard-green soup with pork is served for $4, tasty shrimps in sesame seeds for the same price. You could follow this up with either the duckling with green onions for $5.25 or the green beef and beans for $4.25. As you'll note, this isn't the standard sweet-and-sour pork fare, although you can get that as well. Open till midnight seven days a week.

The **Jade Garden,** 130 Third Ave. (tel. 261-0000), has a definite touch of Shangri-la. Vast and elaborate, with scarlet lanterns, scarlet chairs, and pillars wreathed in gilded dragons, the Garden offers a huge and elegant waiting room equipped with upholstered chairs and a fascinating display case of Chinese delicacies, such as a golden bowl filled with shark fins. The place is famous for its remarkable businessman's lunch buffet, served weekdays from 11:30 p.m. to 2 p.m. Six courses, including tea or coffee, cost only $4.95. Hard to beat at that price and quality.

The **Chinatown Inn,** 207 Centre St. South (tel. 269-7783), is the latest arrival on the scene at the moment (although I'm sure it won't be by the time you read this). The feature here is a nine-course Chinese smorgasbord served Tuesday till Sunday until 10 p.m. for $4.95. But the unique attraction is the midnight smorgasbord, available Fridays and Saturdays from 11 p.m. to 1:30 a.m.—six courses for $3.95. The fare is rather westernized, quantities unlimited, and the premises air-conditioned.

Only a part of Calgary's Chinese establishments are situated in Chinatown, which is way too small to house them all. The **Lin Yen Garden,** 5802 Macleod Trail (tel. 253-2721), hides behind plum-colored drapes and has a split personality. Oriental touches are supplied by bamboo partitions and Chinese prints on the walls. Western influences come in the form of taped pop music, metal chairs, and table mats showing (of all things) an illustrated "Century of Fire-fighting." The Garden serves chop suey, chow mein, and other standards, but also a variety of connoisseur pleasers. Try the diced chicken livers and kidneys with walnuts for $4.95. Or the steamed pork spare ribs in sweet plum sauce at $4.50. Or the chow steak kue, steak fried in oyster sauce with Chinese greens, for $8.95. Open six days a week till 1 a.m., Sundays till 9 p.m.

My Marvin's, 2208 4th St. (tel. 266-4679), is a delightfully relaxed and permanently thronged deli restaurant dedicated to overeating in maximum comfort. The kind of place where the staff gives you learned tips on what to order and where the clients all seem to know each other—or *get* to know each other. A striped awning welcomes you, the shaded orange lights flatter you, the service pampers you, and the fare makes you grow up big and strong. So what more do you want? There's a fresh-daily soup pot at $1.50 per dip. Lox and cream cheese omelets cost $4.75; deluxe bagels with corned beef, pastrami, and salami are the same. There are rows of appetizers including gefilte fish, potato latkes, and chopped liver; and vast plates of apple, blueberry, or cheese blintzes served with sour cream and cinnamon for $3.50. And a fairly unique drink called a sunburst—champagne and orange juice—costing $1.95. And the menu tells you to "Have a nice day!!!" with triple exclamation marks.

The **Old Spaghetti Factory,** 628 Ninth Ave. SW (tel. 264-7614). Another link in the chain of zany eateries that encircles Canada, this one is crammed with genuinely beautiful wrought iron, stained glass, and wood pillars acquired from stately homes and old churches around Calgary. The dining car that forms the centerpiece is an accurate reproduction, lifesize, of a 1910 vintage streetcar that rumbled the gaslit avenues before the first high-rise. All dinners include green salad, sourdough bread, garlic butter, coffee, and spumoni ice cream. The eight breeds of spaghetti run from $2.95 (with tomato sauce) to $4.65 (with meatballs). But you also get a lovely chicken cacciatore (with spaghetti) and veal cutlets (with spaghetti) for $5.45.

Stampeder Inn Buffet, 3828 Macleod Trail (tel. 243-5531). This famous spread is laid on seven days a week till 9 p.m. The Stampeder's new dining room is partitioned into small sections to create intimacy, and paneled in light woods, scattered with greenery, the tables lit by glass-shielded candles, with an organist to provide lilting background music. The buffet is one of the best arranged I've seen: an impressive choice of salads flanked by cold cuts of ham, beef, pork, and salami. Then the hot portions: piles of roast beef, fried chicken, fried fish, breaded veal, and roast pork accompanied by mashed potatoes and four kinds of vegetables. Finally there are the fruit tarts, French pastry, and cheeses. The entire feast goes for $9.25, with children paying half.

Budget Meals

The **Tower Inn,** Calgary Tower (tel. 266-7171), is one of the smaller and considerably cheaper breathren of the revolving dining lounge on top. You get succulent Tower burgers for $3.25, or roast beef sandwiches for $2.55. An innovative touch here is the **Tower Breakfast Club:** you join by paying $4.40 for a ticket, which entitles you to a free elevator ride plus breakfast at 626 feet above ground level.

Moshe's Delicatessen, 522 Eighth Ave. SW (tel. 265-7736), is a large, bare, and businesslike eatery with metal chairs and plastic tabletops; the walls are hung with current movie posters. The character of the place is in the menu: chicken soup for $1, a "Montreal hot smoked meat sandwich" for $4 (well, not quite Montréal but pretty good); also a very tasty apple strudel for $1.25. Open till midnight six days a week. Closed Sunday.

Altaco, 4th St. at 19th Ave. SW (tel. 266-4759), reads the huge sign with a small vaguely Mexican-style building behind it. The dining room is equipped with exceptionally comfortable wooden armchairs, lit by ornate wrought-iron lamps, but otherwise strictly streamlined and undemonstrative. The Mexican pepperiness has been suitable toned down for Anglo palates, but the fare is tasty and the helpings generous. Taco burgers cost $1.70; enchiladas, $1.50. Or you can order a combination dinner featuring the house specialties for $3.90. Open seven days a week till 11 p.m.

Finally, here are two places on Eighth Avenue SE, chosen for contrast, economy, quality, and in order to disprove the notion that Calgary lacks interesting eateries in the budget bracket:

The **Whitworth Inn,** 323 Eighth Ave. SE (tel. 261-5646), has a country-cottage exterior and looks equally rustic inside, with a low-beamed ceiling above highly polished wooden tables and brown carpeting, white plaster walls shining in the light of roof lanterns and hung with color photos of street scenes, and very comfortably unholstered chairs. And the management informs you that the house specialty, Hog & Donkey, is made from a recipe "stolen from the Hog & Donkey Pub." It's pork chops with tomatoes, onions, green peppers, and roast potatoes—and tastes delicious ($4.25). They also serve very good, very English shepherd's pie for $2.25. The hours are a wee bit complicated: open from midnight till 4 a.m. Wednesday to Saturday, for lunch only on Monday, and closed on Sunday.

The **Tokay,** 331 Eighth Ave. SE (tel. 262-4992), is small, plain, and spotless, heavily patronized by local Magyars, which speaks for the authenticity of the menu. You enter the small counter section, which adjoins the actual dining room, with its whitewashed walls bearing Hungarian peasant jugs, painted plates, and gleaming copperware. The menu is written in Hungarian, but thoughtfully with English translations. Most of the dishes cost a standard $4.35, which includes a cup of the wonderfully thick barley soup. Choose between cabbage rolls, sweetly spiced paprika chicken, and pork goulash—all excellent and ample. Open six days a week till 8 p.m. Closed Sundays.

DAYTIME ACTIVITIES: **Glenbow Centre,** Ninth Ave. and 1st St. SE, is a most impressive complex created in order to exhibit, under one roof, the art and history of man. Beautifully displayed and spread over four floors, this ambitious museum devotes one floor to art, one to the history of western Canada, another to military equipment. You can spend days in there, constantly finding fascinating items you'd overlooked before: exotic carvings and ceramics from every part of the globe; hundreds of Indian and Eskimo artifacts; paintings and statuary by famous artists, both local and on tour; a stunning array of medieval armor, including mounted knights looking like apparitions from *Star Wars;* one of the largest gun collections in existence; trophies and weapons from two World Wars; historic Canadian prints, letters, and documents, and so on. Open from 11 a.m. to 9 p.m. daily. Admission: $1 for adults, 50¢ for children.

Fort Calgary, 750 Ninth Ave. SE. On the occasion of the city's centennial in 1975, Fort Calgary became a public park of 40 acres, spread around the ruins of the original Mounted Police stronghold. The focal point is the **Interpretive Centre,** a fantastic lifesize kaleidoscope that produces visual, audio, and sensory experiences, taking you back from modern Calgary to the sights, sounds, and—you'd swear—smells of the prariries. The auditorium features multi-screen presentations of the life, adventures, and hardships of the Mounties a century ago—the rigors of their westward march and the almost unbelievable isolation and loneliness these pioneer troopers endured. The park is open all week, and admission is free.

Just across a bridge from Fort Calgary Park, on St. George's Island, lies the **Zoo,** the largest and by far the finest in Canada. The enclosures, housing 400 species of animals, reptiles, and birds, are scenic gems, each simulating the creatures' natural environments. You can watch polar bears, otters, beavers, and penguins cavorting above and under water through safety-glass windows. There are rare snow leopards from the Himalayas, crocodiles, snakes, and gila monsters, 19-foot giraffes and minuscule anoles. There's a jungle-like tropical aviary awhirr with birds like flying jewelry, plus a children's zoo where kids can pet and cuddle baby goats, donkeys, racoons, and bear cubs.

The **Prehistoric World** is a patch of parkland populated by 46 dinosaurs that peer over the hedges and graze among the foliage. So lifelike they scare you, these full-size reproductions from the dawn of time blend amazingly with their surroundings. Open every day. Admission is $1 for adults, 25¢ for children.

Heritage Park, west of 14th St. and Heritage Dr. SW. On a peninsula jutting into Glenmore Reservoir some 60 acres have been turned back in time. It's a Canadian pioneer township of the early 1900s, painstakingly recreated down to the almost-forgotten but then-popular sarsaparilla served over the counters. Walk down the main street and admire the "latest" fashions, drop in at the authentically curlicued soda fountain, stop at the elaborate hotel, watch the blacksmith at work, or sit on the cracker barrel of the general store. The layout includes a Hudson's Bay Company fort, an Indian village, mining camp, oldtime ranch, steam trains, streetcars, a horse-drawn bus, and a paddle-wheeler that chugs you around Glenmore Reservoir. The town is not just for looking—you can join in. Open daily till 6 p.m. Admission is $1.50 for adults, half price for children.

Calgary Tower, Ninth Ave and Centre St. South. Reaching 626 feet into the sky, this Calgary landmark is topped by an observation terrace offering unparalleled views of the city and the mountains and prairies beyond. A stairway from the terrace leads to the cocktail lounge for panoramic liquors. Photography from up there is fantastic—on a clear day you can snap tomorrow. The high-speed elevator whisks you to the top in just 63 seconds. The tower is open daily till midnight. The elevator ride costs $1.50 for adults, half price for children.

Planetarium, 11th St. at Seventh Ave. SW. A veritable chamber of marvels housing the **Aero-Space Museum,** a live theater, an observatory, and the **Star Chamber,** offering a remarkable melange of historical flying machines, films, concerts, and variety performances. The main attractions are the educational "star shows" put on by means of a wondrous Zeiss projector and 100 special-effects projectors plus a hemispheric sound system. These shows explore the mysteries of the universe in dramatic and immensely impressive one-hour segments that hold audiences of all age groups spellbound. Permanent special-effects exhibits include a close-up of the "solar furnace" of the sun, the "galaxy wall" that takes you some three million light years into space, and a circular display that gives an overall view of the incredible vastness of the known universe with its billions of galaxies. This is one of the most modern and lavishly equipped planetariums in North America, and certainly the most versatile. Open six days a week. Closed Tuesday. Admission is $1.65 for adults, 85¢ for children.

Stampede Park, 17th Ave. and 2nd St. SE. This is the center of action for the annual Calgary Stampede, held every July. But it also has a vast variety of events throughout the rest of the year. These include ice shows, circuses, rock concerts, dog, horse, and livestock shows, antique sales, ice hockey matches, wrestling, boxing, gymnastics, harness racing, and the famous Rodeo College where professional cowboys teach youngsters the ins and outs of rodeo riding. For information on what's going on currently, consult the newspapers or call 261-0101.

The **Military Museums,** situated on the Canadian Forces base on Crowchild Trail between 33rd and 50th Aves. and open to the public, are dedicated to the history of the two Calgary home regiments: Lord Strathcona's Horse and Princess Patricia's Light Infantry. They show collections of military gadgetry from this century and the last, trophies and souvenirs brought back by soldiers from every corner of the world, plus the uniforms worn, the weapons used, and the flags flown by the two regiments through the years. Fascinating for military buffs, both museums are open on weekdays only, the Lord Strathcona till 3 p.m., the Princess Patricia till 4:30 p.m. Since this is a military security area, you may be asked to produce some personal identification.

Lunchbox Theatre, Bow Valley Square, at the corner of Sixth Ave. and 1st St. SW. An absolutely delightful Calgary feature which other cities, not known as "cowtowns," should copy, the Lunchbox is a regular second-floor theater, with live professional performers and remarkable repertoire, catering to downtown shoppers, workers on their lunch breaks, and sundry tourists. Shows change irregularly, depending on public interest, and range from straight drama and comedy to musicals and specialty turns, such as the tribute to the immortal Paris sparrow in *Edith Piaf—Her Songs, Her Loves*. The shows are shrewdly timed: 12:10 p.m. Monday to Friday, with a shopper's special every Thursday at 1:30 Admission is $2. Check newspapers for programs or call 265-1894.

Devonian Gardens, Eight Ave. Mall between 2nd and 3rd Sts. SW. Another almost-unique attraction in downtown Calgary, the Gardens are a patch of paradise, an enclosed 2½-acre park, like a gigantic glass house, 46 feet above street level. Laid out in natural contours with a mile of pathways and a central stage for musical performances, the gardens contain 20,000 plants (mostly imported from Florida), a reflecting pool (that becomes a skating rink in winter), a sun garden, childrens' playground, sculpture court, and water garden. In this lushly green retreat Calgary has found the perfect antidote to the din and dust of its building boom. And to make matters perfect, it's *free*. Open every day from 9 a.m. to 9 p.m.

The **Fish Hatchery,** 1440 17A St. SE., was designed to provide 8.6 million fish per year to stock Alberta's lakes and streams. It's the focal point of the province's expanding sport fishing industry and calculated to satisfy fishing requirements for the next decade—hopefully.

The **Hospitality Centre,** Ninth Ave. and 14th St., SW, is built like a miniature railroad station and crammed with everything you want to know about Calgary (and aren't afraid to ask). Beside the "station" stands the biggest steam locomotive in the British Commonwealth. Officially known as the *5934,* this steel mammoth was built in prediesel days to haul trains over Canada's huge mountain ranges. They don't make 'em this big any more. Bring your camera—she poses free of charge.

The last two attractions are on the outskirts of town, but easily accessible:

Fish Creek Park, Canyon Meadows Dr. and Macleod Trail SE, is one of the largest urban parks in the world (actually, a kind of metropolitan wildlife reserve). Spreading over 1800 acres (and due to expand another 1000 acres) it provides a sheltered habitat for a vast variety of animals and birds. You can learn about them by joining in the walks and slide presentations given by park interpreters. For information on their schedules and planned activities, visit the Administration Office or call 278-0111.

The **Alpine Slide,** Trans Canada Hwy. West at Bowfort Rd., is located in the Paskapoo ski area, but works without snow. You go up by scenic chair lift and come down in a kind of miniature dry-land bobsled, getting all the thrills and none of the risks entailed in that sport. The little sleds are completely spillproof and controllable; you can start, stop, accelerate, or slow down at will as you go around the hairpin turns, dips, and straight-aways. Children can ride these sleds on their own. Open daily from June through August, weekends in September and October. Adults pay $2.50; children, $1.50; and there are concession tickets for multiple rides.

CALGARY AFTER DARK: If there is any characteristic that will effectively demolish Calgary's "cowtown" image, it's the performing arts scene. Calgary offers far more in the music and live stage line than most U.S. cities her size or bigger. The trouble is that these low-key pleasures tend to be overshadowed by the more garish aspects of nightlife—meaning that they only get a fraction of the publicity and none of the neons. The listing below will give you an idea of the selection available. For current programs, check the newspapers or the little weekly *Action,* a publication devoted to the city's leisure and available in hotel lobbies.

The Performing Arts

The **Jubilee Auditorium,** 14th Ave. and 14 St. NW., is a magnificent performance hall seating 2760 people. An acoustic marvel, the auditorium is located high on a hill with a panoramic view no other institution of its kind in the world enjoys. Open for visitors daily (no charge), the auditorium is also the home of the **Calgary Philharmonic,** which presents music series ranging from the classics to pop. The **Southern Alberta Opera Association** performs three operas each year at the auditorium. Periodic productions by the young **Alberta Ballet Company** are also part of the auditorium's varied programs.

Alberta Theatre Projects puts on five plays a year at the Canmore Opera House in Heritage Park.

The **Pumphouse Theatre,** 2140 Ninth Ave. SW., is the showcase for a variety of play styles, such as the innovative and experimental **Loose Moose Theatre,** which performs regularly, and the weekend matinees of the **Story Book Theatre.**

Theatre Calgary, QR Centre, 830 Ninth Ave. SW., offers two types of fully professional plays: standard theatrical productions in a main-stage series and avant-garde performances on the second stage.

The **University of Calgary Theatre,** U. of C. Campus, has a remarkable variety of presentations, ranging from solo guitar concerts to chamber music, unusual groups like the Renaissance Singers, and traditional stage plays.

Discos, Bars, Lounges

Calgary's nightlife, like that of every other Canadian city, is awash with disco. Here, however, disco fever is a brand-new phenomenon and the various D.J.s set their own styles in a more determined fashion than elsewhere. They even talk of "educating" their clientele to this or that musical concept. Most of them eventually realize the futility of such ambitious endeavors and get back to just spinning the platters, minus philosophy. But while their high hopes last they're amusing to watch. And they have succeeded in giving some discos a definite character, although the majority is the standard melange of rock/pop that represents the customary fare of discoland the world over.

The bulk of Calgary's after-dark action takes place in the larger hotels. Many of them have developed entertainment complexes that cater to a variety of tastes under one roof, like nightlife supermarkets.

The most versatile is the Sheraton, 202 Fourth Ave. SW. There you'll find the **Daddy's Money** disco (tel. 262-7901), where the cover charge is $1.50, the music progressive, and the action goes from 4 p.m. till 12:30 a.m. On the same premises, but strictly separated, is the **Casino,** Calgary's one and only legal gambling spot (it's legal because it's run for the benefit of charities). A very jolly and friendly no-frills operation, minus any Las Vegas touches, the Casino offers roulette and blackjack only, for stakes ranging from $1 to $25. Open six days a week from 12 noon to midnight. Closed Sunday.

The **Airliner Inn,** 4804 4th St. NE (tel. 276-3391), has no less than four entertainment rooms: the Tavern, featuring live talent, the Telstar Lounge, with performers Monday through Saturday, the Cabaret, which swings Thursday through Saturday, and the Prop Room, a quiet retreat with quiet music.

The **Highlander,** 16th Ave. and 17th St. NW (tel. 289-1961), features one of Calgary's top D.J.s, Rodd Wayne, who spins platters and patter in the Fling Tavern. Changing bands and vocalists perform in the hostelry's Black Bull Tavern; there's a Thursday through Saturday cabaret and, for good measure, an excellent organist named Bruce Bristowe in the Black Angus dining room.

Lucifer's, 609 Seventh Ave. SW (tel. 265-9000), is a nightclub-disco, and among Calgary's best in both departments. Big and plush, this nitery has relays of name bands, a neat dance floor, and excellent buffet service. It's in action nightly till 2 a.m., with Tuesdays designated as Ladies Night.

New York–New York, 131 Ninth Ave. SW (tel. 265-1234), a combination disco and lounge, has some New Yorkerish sophistication but none of the uptightness. Beautiful light plays and sound effects and lavish aquariums swarming with tropical fish that seem to dance in rhythm with the rock. Plus comfortable settees to rest your dance-weary bones. No admission charge and the music is on Monday through Saturday from 7 p.m. till midnight.

The **Tiki-Tiki,** 718 Eighth Ave. SW (tel. 265-2214), presents lavish Polynesian floor shows along with South Pacific food. Loaded with Hawaiian decor and blessed with romantic atmosphere, the Tiki gets hula and steel guitar groups direct from the Islands. I watched more couples holding hands there than anywhere else in Alberta. There's a dance floor for use between shows. No cover charge. The action starts at 8:30 p.m., and goes on till 2 a.m. Open seven days a week.

Lonnie's, 306 Fourth Ave. SW (tel. 262-5554), is both a seafood restaurant and singles-type lounge—the first of its stripe to open in Calgary. Delightfully atmospheric, the place features highly polished pianists-vocalists (usually male) with extensive repertoires and remarkable knacks for improvising request numbers. A big fireplace helps the ambience.

Ba-Ba's Saloon, Hotel Regis, 127 Seventh Ave. SE (tel. 262-4641), has a unique trio that plays its way from Beatles classics to 1950s nostalgia, country music, and back again. Good to dance to. The music goes Monday through Saturday, 8 p.m. till midnight.

The Refinery, 1117 1st St. SW (tel. 265-3673), gets top-name performers like Fats Domino, Ricky Nelson, and the CC Riders. A disco nitery with a very elegant lounge attached, the spacious premises reverberate with rock and soul, a-flickering with light plays and pulsating with youngish humanity. It goes till 2 a.m. six nights a week.

The above represent only a thin slice of Calgary's nightlife, top-heavy with discos as it is. There are dozens more, including a special one for teenagers (**Bianca's,** on the lower floor of the York Hotel, Seventh Ave. and Centre St. tel. 262-1032, serves soft drinks only and stops jumping at midnight).

Most of the larger hotels have entertainment in their dining rooms or lounges, or nightclubs on the premises. The **Scotch Room** of the Four Seasons features Las Vegas–style acts till 2 a.m. The **Trade Winds,** Macleod Trail and Glenmore Trail, operates the Red Slipper Cabaret. The Calgary Inn has **Marco's,** with top-ranking decor and entertainers. And the **Tower Inn,** at the Calgary Tower, provides nightly performers in an English-pub atmosphere.

There's a very basic minimum of nudity connected with Calgary's bright lights. Strip clubs somehow never made it big in this town. I found only two in action. The **Pink Panther,** 725 Eighth Ave. SW (tel. 261-6028), operates Monday through Saturday and starts its shows at 9:30 p.m. The **Blue Mouse,** 705 1st St. SE (tel. 262-6772), is an all-nighter where you can dine and dance from 10 p.m., waiting for the undraped ladies who make their appearance about two in the morning.

SHOPPING: Calgary's retail scene is, like everything else, in a surge of expansion and flux. As more and more small stores give way to high-rises, retailing is becoming concentrated in huge shopping centers and arcades. One fine feature of this growth explosion is the "Plus-15" system, a series of enclosed walkways 15 feet above street level connecting buildings, which enables you to conduct a shopping expedition in living-room comfort, regardless of weather conditions.

A major portion of Eighth Ave. has been turned into a pedestrian mall, closed to most vehicles. While not terribly chic or impressive as yet (Canadians lack the Dutch or German touch in mall design), it's a very comfortable stretch for shopping.

The city is not too well endowed with boutiques and specialty stores, although there are a number of interesting ones. And because of the absence of a sales tax, your money goes further here.

The **Calgary Cabin,** 264 Palliser Square East, is run by a nonprofit society and offers a great range of crafts articles made by local artisans. Materials range from leather and silver to dinosaur bone.

The **Wolf Den,** 114A Eighth Ave. SE, looks like the trophy room of a sumptuous hunting lodge. Realistically stuffed wolves, cougars, lynxes, porcupines, pelts and skins, mounted game birds and Indian artifacts make for a fascinating display.

The **African Art Centre,** 17th Ave. and 5th St. SW, provides a novel highlight in this prairie city. It could pass as a museum. It's filled with masks, drums, sculptures, handmade pieces of furniture, tribal ornaments and batiks, rugs, elephant-hide wallets and shoes from many parts of Africa, beautifully displayed and chosen by experts. Equally intriguing for exotica hunters and just-browsers.

Western Outfitters, 128 Eighth Ave. SE, could be called Calgary's cowboy headquarters since it stocks everything that a cowpoke (working or dude) might need, with the exception of cows. Apart from the more glamorous western duds, it also offers a big range of blue jeans, which most cowhands wear anyway these days.

Cottage Craft Gifts, 6503 Elbow Dr. SW, has one of Canada's largest selections of Eskimo sculptures, carvings, and prints, and Indian artifacts—all absolutely authentic and marked with official labels to prove it. It also runs a picture-framing service for your treasured prints and prize travel photos. Closed Mondays, open Fridays till 9 p.m.

ATTRACTIONS OUT OF TOWN: There are several sightseeing attractions outside Calgary worth the trip.

Drumheller and the Badlands

Drumheller lies 88 miles northeast of Calgary amid a landscape that resembles a canvas by Salvador Dali. The so-called Badlands is a patch of semiarid desert sprinkled with cacti and weird pillars called hoodoos that give you the impression of walking on the surface of the moon. Adjoining this eroded scenery, however, are lush prairie farmlands with sparkling waters and roadside campgrounds. In a single day you can tour two entirely different worlds.

The Drumheller Valley was a tropical marshland some 150 million years ago, a stomping ground for the colossal reptiles scientists have been digging for out there at an amazing rate. The town prides itself on the prevalence of these long-dead lizards, and you meet them all over the place. At the bridge crossing the Red Deer River on Hwy. 9 stands a lifesize replica of the fearsome *Tyrannosaurus rex*—great to be photographed with.

The **Dinosaur Museum** houses prehistoric fossils and the only mounted dinosaur specimen in Canada—the *Edmontosaurus*—over 30 feet long. The **Dinosaur Trail** is a scenic loop leading past most of Drumheller's attractions. These include the **Homestead Antique Museum,** where hundreds of items from the everyday life of Old West pioneers are displayed.

Further along stands the "Largest Little Church in the World," a famous edifice that seats 10,000 people—but only six at a time. The **Prehistoric Park** has exhibits of lifelike dinosaurs set among the hills that their ancient counterparts actually roamed.

Fort Macleod

South of Calgary, a little over two hours by Greyhound, stands what was the western terminal of the North West Mounted Police in 1884. Named after Colonel Macleod, the redcoat commander who brought peace to Canada's west, the fort is still patrolled by Mounties in their traditional uniforms, one of the few places in Canada to see them. The fort is filled with fascinating material on the frontier period. Among its treasured documents is the rule sheet of the old Macleod Hotel, written in 1882: "All guests are requested to rise at 6 a.m. This is imperative as the sheets are needed for tablecloths. Assaults on the cook are prohibited. Boarders who get killed will not be allowed to remain in the house."

Lethbridge

East of Fort Macleod lies Lethbridge, a delightful garden city and popular convention site (it gets more annual hours of sunshine than most places in Canada). The pride of Lethbridge is the **Nikka Yuko Japanese Garden.** Its pavilion and dainty bell tower were constructed by Japanese craftsmen without nails or bolts. One of the largest Japanese gardens in America, the place has Japanese hostesses in kimonos who pose for photos by the beautifully carved bridge.

The Leighton Foundation

This combination art gallery and crafts center is located 15 miles southwest of Calgary. Based in a charming family home, the center displays an outstanding collection of paintings, sculpture, graphics, and ceramics by Alberta artists. Part museum and part workshop, the center has students of all age groups taking courses in a large variety of art forms including weaving, batik, jewelry, and metalwork (run by a nonprofit organization). For information, call 931-3633.

Organized Tours

Grayline 'of Calgary, International Airport (tel. 276-0766), offers city sightseeing tours as well as 7- to 12-hour excursions to the Canadian Rockies.

Tour C1 takes in the city sights, covering 30 miles in 4½ hours; a running commentary provides the historical background. You start at the Calgary Inn at 9 a.m. or the Greyhound Depot at 9:30 a.m., and go to Fort Calgary, Heritage Park, Scotsman's Hill, which overlooks Stampede Park and the core of downtown. Fares include admission prices: adults are $6; children, half price.

There are three tours to the Rockies, Calgary's western neighbors, all of them touching Banff. Tour C3 is the longest, covering 400 miles in 12 hours and visiting the famous Columbia Icefield (optional snocoach ride on the glacier). The tour starts at the Greyhound Depot at 7 a.m. Adults pay $29.75; children, $15.

Ski Spirit is a highly individualized little outfit, fun by two very enterprising, very attractive young ladies. Originally intended to organize ski tours only, it has since expanded to arranging river-rafting and trail-riding excursions as well, taking groups of up to 30 people. For details, call Lois Hager or Marla Hedman at 246-9836.

2. Banff and Jasper National Parks

Straddling the border between British Columbia and Alberta are two of the greatest nature reserves on the face of the globe. I say two because these wonderlands were founded at different times and have separate administrations. But for all practical purposes they are one very big unit and should be regarded as such.

The Banff and Jasper National Parks comprise 6764 square miles carved out of the Canadian Rockies and boast a resident population of around 8000. Their annual tourist flow, however, tops two million. The Rocky Mountains spill over into British Columbia to the west and the adjoining **Willmore Wilderness Park** to the north. But geographically both parks lie within Alberta, a province that has set aside 4% of its entire surface for national parkland.

Describing these parks is one of the most frustrating tasks that can face a writer. It's like trying to picture a tropical sunset on a black-and-white photograph or conveying the soul-stirring grandeur of a Beethoven symphony on typewriter keys. The feeble best I can say is that you will take those impressions of white peaks towering over green forests, of river torrents and silent blue lakes, of leaping mountain sheep and waddling bear cubs home with you to warm your heart on the gray and dismal city days that are sure to follow.

ORIENTATION: Banff is the senior of the two parks, founded as a modest ten-square-mile reserve by Canada's first prime minister, Sir John Macdonald, in 1885. Jasper, now Canada's biggest mountain park, was established in 1907, although it already boasted a "guest house" of sorts in the 1840s. A visiting painter described it as "composed of two rooms of about fourteen and fifteen feet square. One of them is used by all comers and goers, Indians, voyageurs and traders, men, women and children being huddled together indiscriminately, the other room being devoted to the exclusive occupation of Colin Fraser (postmaster) and his family, consisting of a Cree squaw and nine interesting half-breed children."

The parks form an irregular ribbon running from **Mt. Sir Douglas** in the south to **Resthaven Mountains** in the extreme north. They are traversed by one of the finest highway systems in Canada, plus innumerable nature trails leading to the more remote valleys and peaks. The two "capitals," Banff and Jasper, lie 178 miles apart, connected by Hwy. 93, one of the most scenic routes you'll ever roll on. **Banff** lies a mere 81 miles from Calgary via Hwy. 1A, **Jasper** 225 miles from Edmonton on Rte. 16, the famous Yellowhead Hwy.

Air Canada and **CP Air** fly regular services to the parks. Alternatively, you can come by **VIA Rail** or **Greyhound Bus** from Calgary or Edmonton or from Vancouver and Prince Rupert in British Columbia. **Rental cars** are obtainable from **Tilden** (corner Cariboo and Lynx Sts., Banff; tel. 762-2688) or **Budget** (corner Wolf and Bear Sts., Banff; tel. 762-3345).

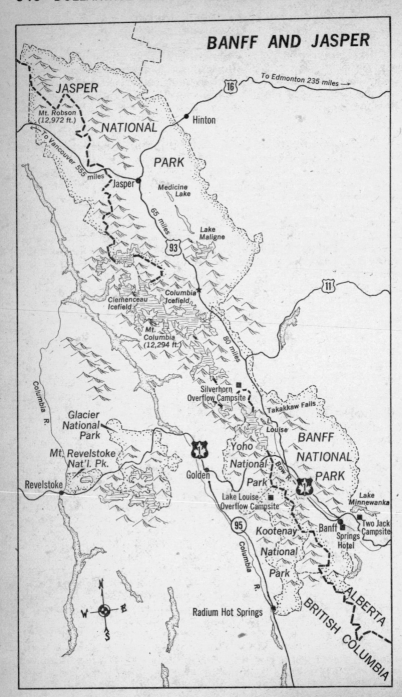

BANFF AND JASPER

JASPER

To Edmonton 235 miles →

16

Mt. Robson
(12,972 ft.)

NATIONAL

Hinton

To Vancouver 555 miles

PARK

Jasper

Medicine
Lake

65 miles

Lake
Maligne

93

11

Clemenceau
Icefield

Columbia
Icefield

Mt.
Columbia
(12,294 ft.)

80 miles

Columbia R.

Silverhorn
Overflow Campsite

Takakkaw Falls

Glacier
National
Park

Louise

BANFF

Mt. Revelstoke
Nat'l. Pk.

1

Yoho

National

Bow R.

NATIONAL

Revelstoke

Golden

Park

1

PARK

Lake
Minnewanka

Lake Louise
Overflow Campsite

Two Jack
Campsite

95

Kootenay

Banff

Columbia R.

National

Springs
Hotel

Park

ALBERTA

Radium Hot Springs

BRITISH COLUMBIA

Admission to both parks costs $2 per vehicle and is good for four days.

LOOKING AT ANIMALS—AND VICE VERSA:

The parklands are swarming with wildlife, some of it meandering along and across highways and hiking trails, within easy camera and often patting range. Here I would like to pass on the fervent plea uttered all summer long by the game wardens: **Don't feed the animals, and don't touch them!** There is, for a start, a fine of up to $500 for feeding *any* wildlife. There is also a distinct possibility that you may end up paying more than cash for disregarding this warning.

It isn't easy to resist the blissfully unafraid bighorn sheep, mountain goats, soft-eyed deer, and lumbering moose you meet. (Very little chance of meeting the coyotes, lynx, and occasional wolves, since they give humans a wide berth.) But the stuff you feed them may kill them, if only indirectly. Bighorns get accustomed to summer handouts of bread, candy, potato chips, and marshmallows, when they should be grazing on the high-protein vegetation that will help them survive through the winter. As a result, scores of sheep and goats, weakened by improper nutrition, lie dying in the Rocky Mountain snows.

Moose entail additional risks. They have been known to take over entire picnics after being given an initial snack, chase off the picnickers, and eat up everything in sight—including cutlery, dishes, and tablecloth.

But it is the bears that pose the worst problems. The parks contain two breeds: the big grizzly, standing up to seven feet on its hind legs, and the smaller black bear, about five feet long. The little one, strangely enough, causes most of the trouble—or rather, human behavior toward it does.

The grizzly spends most of summer in high alpine ranges, well away from tourist haunts. As one of North America's largest carnivores, its appearance and reputation are awesome enough to make visitors beat a retreat on sight. But the less formidable black bear is a born clown with tremendous audience appeal, and takes to human company like a squirrel.

At the Jasper Lodge golf course, a bear mother taught her cubs how to turn on water sprinklers so they could enjoy cooling showers. The cubs liked it so much that eventually the management had to hire a boy to follow behind the bear family—at a safe distance—and shut off the sprinklers.

The black's cuddly looks and circus antics, plus his knack for begging and rummaging around garbage cans, tend to obscure the fact that these are *wild* animals: powerful, faster than a horse, and completely unpredictable. They are omniverous, meaning that they can eat anything—including *you*.

Hiking in bear country (and virtually all parkland is bear country) entails certain precautions which you can only ignore at your peril. Never hike alone, and never take a dog along. Dogs often yap at bears, then when the animal charges, run toward their masters for protection, bringing the pursuer with them. Use a telephoto lens when taking pictures. Bears in the wild have a set tolerance range which, when encroached upon, may bring on an attack. Above all, *never* go near a cub. The mother is usually close by, and a female defending her young (she doesn't know you mean no harm) is the most ferocious creature you'll ever face—and quite probably your last.

BANFF:

The town lies 4538 feet above sea level at the foot of **Cascade Mountain,** which looms so close that it seems to be peering into your bedroom window. Actually there are mountains all around, but the others aren't nearly as intrusive.

Getting your bearings is easy. *The* main street—**Banff Ave.**—starts at the southern end of town at the **Bow River** and runs north for the entire length until it is swallowed by the Trans Canada Hwy. Just beyond the river stands the **Administration Building** and about halfway up the avenue is the **Park Information Centre.** Along that broad, bright, and bustling thoroughfare, which looks like an alpine village street without potholes, you'll find most of the hotels, restaurants, stores, office buildings, and nightspots the town possesses. At the northwestern edge of town is the **Railroad Station,** and a little farther northwest the road branches off to **Lake Louise** and Jasper. In the opposite direction, northeast, lies the **Airstrip** and past it the highway going to Calgary.

The **Greyhound Bus Depot** is at the corner of Banff Ave. and Cariboo St. (tel. 762-2241). **Banff Taxi & Tours** is in the Sundance Mall, Banff Ave. (tel. 762-4444). For **VIA Rail** information, phone 762-3255.

In passing, let me introduce you to **Rocky M. Ram,** Banff's town symbol and official greeter. Rocky is an enormous bighorn sheep, wearing hiking shorts, horns, and an expression of permanent incredulity. He's hard to get away from.

Accommodations

Let's start with some good news: Alberta has no sales tax, which means that you don't have to add 5% to your hotel bill as in most other provinces.

The **Banff Springs Hotel** (tel. 403/762-2211) stands south of the Bow River where it joins the Spray River, and could pass as a suburb under one roof. Resembling a cross between Camelot and a Scottish laird's stronghold, the place even has a mysterious "sealed room" somewhere on the premises (during rebuilding in 1928 the workmen neglected to put in the required door and later forgot the location of the chamber!).

Set in a fabulous landscape of twin rivers ringed by mountain ranges, the Springs greets you with a reception hall of such baronial splendor that you're not in the least surprised to learn that it maintains a staff of 700 and holds medieval banquets weekly ($14 per feaster, including wine). It houses four dining rooms, one more palatial than the other, an espresso bar, three cocktail lounges, post office, beauty salon, barbershop, 22 stores and boutiques, an Olympic-size indoor pool and a panoramic one outside. The golf course is considered one of the most scenic in the world and has an added attraction in the shape of a lady bear named Victoria, who visits it regularly, accompanied by her latest crop of cubs.

The 600 guest rooms are decorated in matching orange, white, and red, some with canopy beds and lanterns on the walls, all of them charming.

Singles cost from $51 to $65; doubles, from $61 to $75; and suites (regal is the word for them), from $85 to $250.

The **Mount Royal** (tel. 403/762-3331) occupies the central corner of Banff Ave. and constitutes the hub of downtown. The hotel is much larger than its 84 guest rooms indicate because everything in it is generously proportioned. A hive of holiday activity, the Royal has an appropriately alpine cocktail lounge, smartly modern lobby, deluxe-rustic dining room that stars country-rock-folk entertainers nightly, and a bus terminal at the rear. Bedrooms are spacious and excellently furnished with clusters of overhead lights, writing desks, large walk-in closets, lots of bed pillows, night desks with lamp and telephone, and color TV. Beautiful scenic prints form the wall decorations, and the bathtubs come with handy hand showers.

Singles and doubles are a standard $38, triples go for $43, and children under 8 stay free with their parents.

Rundle Manor, Martin and Moose Sts. (tel. 403/762-2707), is a handsome hewn-stone structure with Swiss-style wooden balconies that houses 23 self-contained units. All of them are large (capable of accommodating six to eight persons), grandly carpeted, and exceptionally well equipped for vacation living. There are plenty of roomy walk-in closets with folding doors, streamlined bathrooms, all-electric kitchens with utensils and dinettes, balconies with views, color TV, writing desks, good lighting arrangements, and a general feeling of being able to swing a dozen or so cats in your living quarters. No restaurant or room telephones.

Units cost from $40 to $75, depending on size—regardless of the number of occupants.

The **Homestead Inn,** Lynx and Wolf Sts. (tel. 403/762-4471), looks and feels like an alpine chalet but actually stands two blocks from the center of town, with **Melissa's Missteak,** one of Banff's oldest and best restaurants, right next door. You have a choice between two styles of rooms at the same price, differing in decor and sleeping facilities but each tastefully furnished and equipped with couches, armchairs, telephone, color TV, and stylish bathrooms.

Rates here change no less than six times yearly, according to season, subseason and mini-subseason. Peak summer prices are $42 per room, single or double, with each additional person paying $5 extra.

The **Driftwood Motor Inn,** 340 Marten St. (tel. 403/762-3727), is a downtown hostelry in a quiet block, offering 24 guest rooms and 8 kitchen units. The rooms are very pleasant, small and compact, with red plush carpets, elegant black sinks, bath and shower, writing desks, and color TV. There are no room telephones and no restaurant on the premises, but any number of eateries in the vicinity. You get queen-size beds and individual heat control, as well as a soothingly tranquil atmosphere that goes with the scenery.

Prices run $30 to $36 for bedrooms and $40 for two separate bedrooms and kitchenette.

The **Cascade Inn,** 124 Banff Ave. (tel. 403/762-3311), has a rather plain frontage, attractive interiors, a largely young clientele, and the lion's share of Banff's social action. There's a Japanese restaurant that serves Western breakfasts, one of the biggest taverns in the Rockies, and a jumping disco that draws the eligibles in town. Of the 60 guest rooms, half have private baths (no showers) and all have TV. Scarlet bedspreads and carpets, and black-and-red drapes make for a pleasant decor—but why the Spanish bullfight and flamenco scenes on the walls? There's ample hanging space and a desk mirror with individual light.

The rate structure is of typical resort complexity, varying with the seasons and according to whether the room has a bath, half bath, or merely a sink. Prices range from $15 to $39.

The **Stafford Motel,** 229 Beaver St. (tel. 403/762-2492), is a small and simple cluster of blue-and-white cabins fringed by strips of lawn. The cabins are self-contained, furnished modestly but sufficiently. Kitchens come with gas stoves, refrigerators, and all utensils, and most of the units have their own showers, although two merely have hot- and cold-water sinks. There's a TV in all rooms, but no telephones. Double occupancy costs $20; four people pay $30.

Magee's Cabins, 426 Banff Ave. (tel. 403/762-2892), another budget hostelry, offers two simple cabin suites, complete with kitchens, linoleum flooring with rugs, a small open hanging space, small bathroom with shower and sink, plus a gas stove, refrigerator, and kitchen utensils. The cabins are basic but self-contained, and a real money saver—$20 per double occupancy. No TV in the rooms and no pay phone on the premises.

Out of Town: The **Château Lake Louise** (tel. 403/522-3511) lies 35 miles west of Banff in a setting that can only be described as magical. It's a storybook castle perched a mile high in the Rockies, surrounded by forest-clad snow-capped peaks, mirrored in a lake green as an emerald—a lake undisturbed by the screech of outboard motors, shimmering like a gem amid the towering mountains.

The Château is a massively graceful structure, blue roofed and furnished with Edwardian sumptuousness. The two restaurants have enormous stone fireplaces as well as a spectacular view of Victoria Glacier. The lake-size outdoor swimming pool is sheltered by glass walls and heated. The lake is too chilly for swimming but ideal for canoes (rentable at $4 an hour). Château guests get tea dancing in the afternoon, cabaret entertainment at night, memorable cuisine, and facilities like a post office, bank, cafeteria, beauty salon, barbershop, boutiques, and outstanding room service.

The 374 bedrooms are kept in modern pastel hues, superbly carpeted, temperature controlled, and furnished with discreet elegance. The mountain view from the windows should rank as part of the decor—perhaps the best part. All have dial telephones, but none contains either TV or radio—that's Château policy (there's a plush TV lounge downstairs for addicts, as a kind of compromise). But the round of outdoor action and social events keeps most of the patrons too busy for much viewing.

Singles range from $51 to $65; doubles, from $61 to $75; suites, from $175 to $250.

Meals

For a place its size, Banff is remarkably well supplied with dineries in all price brackets, and the culinary standard is well above the usual tourist-resort level. As in most resorts, however, prices tend to be slightly higher than their urban equivalents. You pay for the mountain air that gives you an appetite.

The **Ticino,** 205 Wolf St. (tel. 762-5848), features a dual menu, Swiss-Italian, with roughly equal selections for both. Elegantly paneled in dark woods, it has impeccable Swiss service, an impressive list of imported wines, and some of the best laid tables in the Rockies. The fare, understandably, concentrates on veal dishes, fondues, and steaks. The veal cutlet Cordon Bleu is $9.75, and you get a wonderfully aromatic cheese fondue for two persons for $15. Do leave room for the zabaglione dessert—light, frothy, and irresistible. Open from 5 p.m. to 11 p.m.

The **Paris Restaurant,** 114 Banff Ave. (tel. 762-3554), is a large alpine eatery with lights hanging from raw wooden beams, upholstered peasant chairs, and intimate dining niches. At the entrance there's a big tank with live lobsters —you know you're getting them fresh. You can also watch your steaks being cooked on an open grill behind the counter. All entries come with help-yourself soup and half a dozen breeds of salad from two salad bars. Your meal price, therefore, is the price of your main dish. Every night here is lobster night. You get a whole one—broiled or thermidor—plus baked potato, coupé Paris, and coffee for $14.75. For those not lobsterish inclined there's English mixed grill (very English), and German bratwurst (not very German). Open seven days a week till 10 p.m.

The **Drifter's Inn,** Sundance Mall, Banff Ave. (tel. 762-4524), is a deluxe log cabin, sort of, serving food that no log cabin dweller ever got. You're surrounded by natural wood, which blends appetizingly with the sizzling steak aroma. The cuisine is divided between beef and seafood, capped by a terrific dessert list. The self-service salad bar is one of the best in town. The thick and hearty beef barley soup hits the right spot in a mountain climate. Followed, perhaps, by the even heartier prime rib of beef ($7.95) or the mahi mahi rainbow trout ($7.50). In conclusion, I'd recommend either the maple walnut sundae or the pecan pie—both gorgeous, loaded with calories, and $1.50. The mountain view is on the house. Open daily.

Guido's Spaghetti Factory, Banff Ave. (tel. 762-4002), serves a lot of things beside pasta. Every meal is accompanied by a wooden platter with crusty Italian bread, butter, and cheese, as well as salad. The dining room is one floor up, so you get a lively view of *the* street below as you dine. It's a large, handsome place with a low wood ceiling, leather upholstered chairs and eating booths, and lights disguised as gas lanterns. A well-stocked bar in the background and a very Italian rear wall festooned with copperware gleaming in the "candle" light add to the mood. A glass of the goodly house wine is a must at $1.50. Spaghetti with mushroom sauce is not only outstanding but arrives in enormous heaps ($5.50). If you're not in the mood, try the veal parmigiana ($8.95). Open daily

The **Banff Café,** Banff Ave. (tel. 762-2553), is a cafe only insofar as it serves exceptionally fine coffee at 40¢ a cup. Actually it's a big plastic restaurant of no particular character, with orange walls, framed landscapes, and two carved bighorns guarding the entrance—very popular, bright and lively. The food is as hearty as the service is fast. You get a char-broiled sirloin steak, soup de jour, garlic toast, baked potato, and coffee for $5.50. Or pan-fried rainbow trout amandine for $6.25. Do fit in the homemade cheesecake with cherry topping as a finale. Open seven days a week till 11 p.m.

Grizzly House, 207 Banff Ave. (tel. 762-4055), looks like a mountain log cabin inside and out, lit by lanterns and filled with a very relaxed crowd. At night silent movies of the Dick Turpin–Charlie Chaplin genre are projected on the wall in such a well-chosen position that you can watch them or ignore them as it pleases you. Not that the food needs distraction—it's first rate (the packed cabin will attest to that): classic French onion soup ($1.75), and prime tenderloin beef in "cub," "momma bear," and "boar" portions ($5.65 to $15.95), plus lobster platters, fondues, or steak sandwiches. Baked potatoes and vegetables come extra here. Don't miss the special dessert, apricots confit à l'Armagnac (marinated in French brandy) for $1.50, and memorable. Open seven days a week.

The **Banff Buffeteria,** 219 Banff Ave. (tel. 762-3214), operates as a cafeteria till 4 p.m., and with table service from then till midnight. An unpretentious and very friendly eatery with lightning service, it provides Western breakfasts and an even split between Chinese and American lunch and dinner selections. On one side there's sweet-and-sour pork or house special chow mein for $5.50, and on the other, roast turkey ($3.95) or corned beef and cabbage ($3.50). Even the tea is split between standard and jasmine (both 35¢). Open daily.

While I'm talking about Oriental fare. . . . Every Friday and Saturday from 6 to 9 p.m. the dining room of the **Mount Royal Hotel** puts on an extensive Chinese smorgasbord—all you can put away for $5.95.

Daytime Attractions

Apart from helicopter excursions (which can be bumpy and are always expensive), the only way to get an overall view of a mountain landscape is by cable car. Banff Park is well provided with them, ranging from open chair lifts to glass-enclosed gondolas. The **Sulphur Mountain Gondola Lift** has its lower terminal two miles southeast of Banff on Mountain Ave., by car, cab, or Grayline bus. The gondolas are roomy, safe, and fully enclosed; the panorama is stunning. At the upper terminal there's the famous **Tea House in the Clouds** for refreshments, hiking trails along the mountain ridges, and picnic grounds. Rides cost $3 for adults, $1.75 for children (those under 5 ride free).

Banff Cable Cars float up to **Mt. Norquay,** ten driving minutes north of town, along Norquay Rd. You start at a mile-high cafeteria, choose an enclosed gondola or open chair, and get hoisted to the 7000-foot level in about seven minutes. A restaurant awaits you or you can bring your own lunch and eat it at one of the equally panoramic picnic tables. Adults pay $2.50; children, half price; those under 5, free.

The **Whitehorn Gondola** offers the longest skyride in Canada—over two miles in 20 minutes. This ride is located at **Lake Louise,** just off the Trans Canada Hwy., 35 miles west of Banff. From the Château the route is marked in red. The cars here are Swiss gondolas, probably the most comfortable anywhere. You arrive at the **Whitehorn Lodge,** 1700 feet above the valley floor. The round trip costs $3 for adults, half that for children, but there's a $2 "hiker's special" for one-way riders.

The **Buffalo Paddocks** are located just outside Banff across the Trans Canada Hwy., a large enclosure housing a small herd of the big shaggies that once ruled America's prairies in countless millions. (Strictly speaking, though, there never were any buffalo on this continent. True buffalo are indigenous only to Africa and Asia—the American version were bison.) Now, they're nearly all gone except for the scattered groups in nature parks. The best time to visit them is early evening, since the bison stay hidden among the trees during the heat of the day.

The **Natural History Museum,** Clock Tower Village, Banff Ave., has interesting displays of early forms of life on earth, dating back to the Canadian dinosaurs of 350 million years ago, plus the "authentic" model of a Sasquatch, local version of the Abominable Snowman. The museum makes regular film and slide presentations on the origins of the earth—the birth of our planet. Open daily till 10 p.m., admission is $1 for adults, half price for children.

The **Luxton Museum** is housed in a log fort south of the Bow River, just across the bridge. Devoted to Canada's Indians, it shows realistic dioramas, a sun dance exhibit, Indian artifacts, weaponry, and ornaments. Adults pay $1; children, half price. The museum is closed Mondays, other days open till 5 p.m.

The **Peter Whyte Foundation,** Lynx St., stands as a memorial to the pioneers of the Canadian Rockies. It houses the historical archives, the Banff library, and an art gallery with changing exhibits—prints, paintings, and statuary pertaining to the mountains of western Canada. Afternoon tea is served in front of a fireplace and every Friday there are nature films and lectures in the gallery.

The **Upper Hot Springs Pool,** top of Mountain Ave. south of Banff at Sulphur Mountain is a beautiful big modern pool fed by natural hot-water springs, highly sulfurous and marvelously relaxing. Opinion is divided on whether it's meant for swimming or just soaking. In any case there's a lifeguard on duty, with heated change and shower rooms.

Auto Tape Tour, Rundle Photographic, Banff Ave. This is a rental tape plus player that gives you a running commentary to accompany several scenic routes while you're driving over them, and offers an enormous amount of incidental information: Indian and animal facts and legends, what and why are glaciers, the various life zones of the parks, about mountains, trees, and plants you see. The driver sets the pace, so you start and stop as you wish. It costs $6.95 for either Banff or Jasper, $10.95 for both.

The most popular daytime activities in **the parks** are hiking, fishing, boating, horseback and bicycle riding, although not necessarily in that order. All of them are lavishly catered for. Most of the lakes and streams in the parks are open to fishing (a license costs $4 and can be bought at all information centers and park warden offices).

Hiking trails abound, 18 easy ones in the vicinity of Banff alone, all taking less than half a day to complete. My favorite one is the **Golf Course Loop,** five miles round trip to the Spray Bridge, because at dawn and dusk you often see coyote, elk, and deer in the area. **Rental bikes** are available at 229 Wolf St. for $1.25 an hour for ordinary models, $1.75 for five- or ten-speed jobs. Horses for trail riding by the hour, half day, or full day, at the **Stables** across from Banff Recreation Grounds.

After Dark

The **Banff Centre of Fine Arts,** St. Julien Rd. and Tunner Mountain Dr., is a remarkable institution for a small park resort. Founded in 1933 as a theater school, it grew, prospered, and developed into a performing arts complex. Now consisting of two modern theaters—one large, the other intimate—the center attracts well-known artists, apart from its function as a showcase for students and faculty members. The repertoire is wide and varied—dramas, comedies, concerts, films, ballets, all get their turn. There's a summer festival held in August that includes opera, chamber music, jazz, musicals, and straight plays, performed on a highly professional level. Tickets run from $5 to $7; children are half price. Look up the current programs in the periodical *Banff,* available at hotels and restaurants.

Banff also has considerable action in the dance and live-entertainment line, most of it on the premises of the larger hotels.

The **Cascade Inn,** 124 Banff Ave. (tel. 762-3311), has a live band Monday to Wednesday and becomes a disco (with D.J.) Thursday to Saturday. **Grizzly House,** 207 Banff Ave. (tel. 762-4055), features slow and easy dinner dancing till 2 a.m. every night except Sunday. There's more dinner dancing at the **Banff Park Lodge,** Lynx St. (tel. 762-4433), while the **Banff Springs Hotel** offers a so-called dinner disco that goes from 6 p.m. to midnight.

You get live performers, solo or in groups, in a dozen places. The Saloon of the **Silver City** (tel. 762-3337), has a singing trio nightly from 9 p.m. (you'll find it in the Clock Tower Village Mall on Banff Ave.). The **Voyager Inn,** 555 Banff Ave. (tel. 762-3301), presents a frequently changing lineup of talent Monday through Saturday till midnight. The **Rimrock Inn,** 340 Marten St. (tel. 762-3356), has a piano bar with a panoramic view, while **Melissa's Missteak,** 217 Lynx St. (tel. 762-5511), serves singers and instrumentalists, together with great Alberta steaks, every Friday and Saturday till 2 a.m.

JASPER: It's not really fair to say that the best thing about Jasper is the trip from Banff, except that the journey between the two park "capitals" is so grandiose that nothing—or very little—can match it as an experience.

Despite the excellent grading of the highway, it's a slow road—because you can't help stopping every few minutes to gaze at what surrounds it—animals: ambling bighorn sheep, mountain goats fighting head-banging duels, elks with huge shovel antlers, momma bears with cubs . . . all guaranteed to halt traffic and set cameras clicking.

From Lake Louise on, you travel the **Columbia Icefields Parkway,** which commands the most majestic scenery in the Rockies. The highway snakes through deep valleys between mountain ranges, skirted by the glaciers spawned by the icefield. You pass within a mile of the **Athabasca Glacier,** a white tongue of the Columbia Icefield that once covered most of Canada. It began retreating about 10,000 years ago but still forms the largest accumulation of ice in the Rocky Mountains. All around, the jagged rocks rise upward, striped with gushing waterfalls, dotted at intervals by calm green lakes. Occasionally you can watch the mountain goats picking their way with their delicate little hoofs over seemingly vertical stone walls as if they were treading level ground.

Jasper Townsite is smaller and cozier than Banff. The main street, **Connaught Dr.,** runs alongside the Canadian National Railway tracks. There's a tiny trim railroad station, looking as if designed for electric toy trains, where Jasper the Bear, symbol and mascot of the town, waves you a welcome.

The tracks run due north before they start the long easterly sweep that leads to Edmonton. Jasper, in fact, is the hub of the **Yellowhead Highway System** that links it with Vancouver, Prince George, and Edmonton, and is therefore an important communication point. Luckily you don't notice much of that—the little town has retained all the tranquility you'd expect from an alpine resort. Right in the center, surrounded by delightful shady gardens, are the **Parks Information Offices.** East of town flows the **Athabasca River,** and beyond it lies **Lac Beauvert** with Jasper Park Lodge, adjoining one of the world's finest golf courses. That's the scene of the annual Totem Pole Golf Tournament in which the most celebrated competitor was Bing Crosby. The totem pole in question, named after Queen Charlotte, stands at the railroad station and is reputedly the largest in existence today.

The post office is at the corner of Patricia and Elm Sts., **Avis Rental Cars** on Connaught Dr. at Pacific (tel. 852-3970). Taxis and buses can be caught at **Brewster Transport** on Connaught Dr. (tel. 852-3146). Rental bicycles, canoes, fishing supplies, and licenses can be found at **Sandy's,** Jasper Park Lodge.

Accommodations

The **Lobstick Lodge,** Geikie and Juniper Sts. (tel. 403/852-4431), has the mountain-chalet look that blends beautifully with the peaks framing it like a picture postcard. Big and modern, with swimming pool, whirlpool, patio, guest laundry (but no room service), the Lobstick is an ideal family hostelry featuring babysitting arrangements among its other attractions. There's a game room to keep youngsters occupied on rainy days, plus a splendidly designed lounge with fireplace for adult relaxation. Of the 137 guest rooms, 30 have all-electric kitchenettes, and all have color TV and dial phones. The rooms are generously proportioned, decorated in pleasing oranges and browns, equipped with day couches and such thoughtful extra touches as a special reading corner with a three-way hanging lamp (a hotel rarity). The bathrooms have virtually splash-proof folding shower screens.

Singles cost $34; doubles, $38 ($4 more with kitchenette); while children under 12 stay free in their parents' room.

The **Tonquin Motor Inn** (tel. 403/852-4987) stands at the eastern end of Connaught Dr., well away from any "midtown" bustle. Built in deluxe log-cabin style, surrounded by shady trees, the place also houses the plush **Prime Rib Village** restaurant. Sundecks and lawns for sprawling, a pool and sauna, a coin laundry and a gift shop, combined with room service and babysitting arrangements, as well as several executive suites, make this a pretty velvety holiday spot. Of the 72 units 22 have their own kitchens. All feature individual thermostats, color TV, and telephones. The bedrooms are on the small side, tastefully furnished and delightfully quiet.

No single rates here; doubles run from $40 to $48; with kitchens, $50.

The **Andrew Motor Lodge,** Connaught Dr. (tel. 403/852-3394) in the central block of Jasper, is a white, bright new establishment with little balconies and glassed-in stairways. All rooms are centrally air conditioned and elevators service the three floors. There's nothing alpine about the pastel-colored dining room or ultramodern cocktail lounge with body-hugging swivel chairs and large leather settees. The 99 guest rooms are quite spacious, excellently carpeted and equipped with huge sliding-door closets, color TV, and telephones. The streamlined bathrooms have heat lamps; the bedrooms come with armchairs, writing desks, and unusually good bedside lighting fixtures. No room service.

Singles pay from $36 to $38; doubles, from $40 to $42; and several units can house up to four people and cost $50.

Whistlers, Connaught Dr. (tel. 403/852-3361), occupies the central corner of town and is correspondingly busy. With a pavilion-shaped drugstore in front and a restaurant, lounge, coffeeshop, and pancake house on the premises, Whistlers is probably the most walked-through patch in the Rockies. The lobby has comfortable armchairs and is an ideal situation for a rendezvous. The same building also houses the **Wildlife Museum.** The 41 bedrooms are nice and airy, hung with landscapes and equipped with color TV, radio, telephone, and very good bathrooms. The open hanging space is large, and the hotel does provide room service.

Singles or doubles cost $37, with additional persons paying $5.

The **Athabasca,** Patricia and Miette Sts. (tel. 403/852-3386), has a lobby like a hunting lodge, with a stone fireplace, rows of trophy heads of deer, elk, and bighorn, and a tavern alongside that converts into a disco at night. A gray stone corner building with a homey oldtimer's air, the hotel has a large beautiful dining room, a small and trim coffeeshop, and a handsomely decorated lounge with nightly entertainment. Each of the 60 bedrooms has a mountain view, although only half have private baths. The rooms are fair sized, furnishings ample but not luxurious—armchairs, writing table, and walk-in closet, plus TV, radio, and telephone.

The tariff rate ranges from economy to "superior." Singles cost from $20 to $30; doubles, from $24 to $34; triples, $38.

Out of Town: The **Black Cat Guest Ranch,** P.O. Box 542, Hinton (tel. 403/866-2107), is a wilderness retreat 35 miles northeast of Jasper. Set in superb mountain scenery, this rustic relaxer offers 16 guest units, each with private bath, huge windows, and an unspoiled view of the Rocky ranges. There's a big central living room grouped around a large fireplace, and a separate dining room where the fare is family-style home-cooking, the portions measured for fresh-air appetites. Activities include hikes, horseback riding, canoe trips, and fishing. Part of the ranch is devoted to a young people's riding camp, where 9- to 18-year-olds get separate facilities. Ranch staff will meet your train or bus at Hinton, or your plane at the Jasper airport.

Rates include three hearty meals a day, based on double occupancy: $30 per person.

Meals

The **Villa Karouzo's** (tel. 852-3920), is a very handsome Italian hostelry overlooking Connaught Dr. and the mountains beyond. Dark-wood ceilings and light-wood walls and pillars combine stylishness with an air of leisurely dignity accented by gleaming white table linen, upholstered armchairs, and mellow candle flames. An elegant little bar in the corner and appropriate Italian background music add to the flavor. The cuisine is—not surprisingly—outstanding. Your order comes accompanied by onion soup or salad, memorable garlic toast, and coffee. The specialty is spare ribs served on a wood platter with baked potato for $9.95. Alternatively, try the veal scallopine for $6.90. Half a bottle of a fitting chianti costs $4.85. Open every night till 11:30 p.m.

Also facing Connaught Dr., the **Iron Horse** is a brightly wood-paneled dinery, decorated with genuine old "Wanted" posters ("Dead or Alive") and pictures of historical locomotives. It offers a special lunch buffet seven days a week: for $5.25 you can gorge on hot perch, beef, half a dozen cold cuts, and salads. The dinner menu at night has excellent veal Zurichoise (with mushrooms in white wine cream sauce) for $8.75, or trout la mer for $6.75. Helpings from the salad bar are included.

Still on Connaught Dr., the **Holiday Restaurant** (tel. 852-4378), radiates good cheer, reinforced by service both fast and amiable—a rare combination. The windows view street and mountain ranges, but unfortunately there are few window tables. The wine list is extensive and you sit very comfortably in white chairs with green leather upholstery. Main dishes are accompanied by either soup or tomato juice, green salad, and baked potato. A charcoal-broiled steak sandwich on garlic bread costs $7.50; the T-bone steak with mushrooms, $10.75. Open seven days a week till 11 p.m.

For budget eating, there's the **A & W,** Connaught Dr. (tel. 852-4930), which doesn't look the part at all. Brand new and wood paneled, with fringed lights above the tables and an inner ring of upholstered wooden seats grouped around a coal fire, the place is both cozy and comfortable, and invites lingering. The fare includes "Grandpa" and "Mama" burgers ($2.30 and $1.05), fish and chips ($2.85), and tacos (85¢). Open seven days a week, weeknights till 10 p.m., Sundays till 8 p.m.

Daytime Activities

One of Jasper's delightful sidelights are the framed descriptions of local attractions from the laborious but highly evocative pens of Grade 4 elementary school students, tacked up all over the place. Read and chuckle.

The **Sky Tram** starts at the foot of **Whistler's Mountain,** four miles south of Jasper off Hwy. 93. The large red cars, each carrying a conductor in attendance, are the only reversible type found in the national parks. Each takes 30 passengers and hoists them 1¼ miles up to the summit in a breathtaking sky ride. The size of the cars permits them to take on baby carriages, wheelchairs, or the family dog. The unfolding panorama is grandiose. At the upper terminal you step out into alpine tundra, the region above the tree line where some flowers take 25 years to blossom, a wonderful picnic area carpeted with mountain grass and alive with squirrels. But *please* don't pick the flowers. The ride costs adults $4.25; children, $1.75.

At the Sky Tram's upper terminal you can encounter the beasties Whistler's Mountain is named for. The **"whistlers"** (actually hoary marmots) are furry little critters that grow up to two feet long. They live in rockpiles near the terminal and warn each other with sharp whistles when you approach their domain (hence their name). Whistlers are gentle and cuddlesome, but very shy. The terminal is one of the few places where they'll let you get within camera range before diving into their burrows. In winter the marmots hibernate en masse, sealing the entrance of their home, clustering into tightly packed clumps and snoozing until spring.

Maligne Lake is an incredibly blue mountain lake 45 minutes east of Jasper. The Maligne Narrows are one of the most photographed beauty spots in the world. The Indians, who called it Chaba Imne, had a superstitious awe of the region. The white man (in this case a white woman, Mary Schaffer) did not discover Maligne until 1908. Today regular buses go to the "hidden lake," and a summer lodge at the shore provides edibles, potables, and fishing equipment. Boat cruises—in either glass-enclosed or open craft—show you the entire lake area. Tickets cost $9 for adults, half price for children.

A phenomenal body of water is **Medicine Lake,** northwest of Maligne, which exists only in summer! The lake appears regularly every spring, grows five miles long and 60 feet deep, then vanishes in the fall, leaving only a dry gravel bed through the winter. The reason for this annual wonder is the drainage from the Maligne system, which remains constant during warmer weather but is reduced to a trickle when cold stops the melting process of the snowfields.

The **Columbia Icefield** sprawls over an area of 130 square miles and in places reaches depths of 2000 to 3000 feet! It thrusts out slowly moving rivers of ice into the valleys below—the glaciers, which rank among the most awe-inspiring spectacles nature provides. One of them, the enormous **Athabasca Glacier,** is six miles long and about 1100 feet deep near the center. The **Columbia Icefield Chalet** stands adjacent to this mass on the Icefield Parkway, 63 miles south of Jasper. The chalet is the base for a fleet of peculiar vehicles specially designed to crawl around glaciers. They come in two sizes: big sno-coaches, looking like tour buses mounted on sets of caterpillar tracks, and the small snowmobiles, which resemble enclosed army half-tracks with round bull's-eye windows. Operated by expert drivers familiar with the crevasses, moraines, and moulins of the terraine, they give you a 45-minute tour of Athabasca with a fascinating commentary on its characteristics. At the turnaround point you get a chance to stomp around on the ice, toss a few snowballs (in midsummer) and take half a million pictures. Adults pay $5.50; children $2.50.

The **Miette Hot Springs** lie 36 miles northeast of Jasper by one of the best animal-spotting routes in the park. Watch for elk, deer, coyotes, and moose en route. The hot mineral springs can be enjoyed in a beautiful swimming pool, surrounded by forest and a grandiose mountain backdrop. They are adjoined by campgrounds and an attractive lodge for refreshments. During summer the pool remains open from 8:30 a.m. to 11 p.m.

Jasper After Dark

Most of Jasper's nightlife consists of the conviviality engendered by local bars, since most tourists get too much outdoor action during the day to keep late hours. What entertainment there is takes place in lounges attached to hotels or motels.

The **Trophy Room** of the Athabasca Hotel becomes a disco nightly, and gets packed with a young crowd that has sufficient energy to dance till around midnight. Drinks at bar prices.

The **Marmot Motor Lodge** (tel. 852-4471), a svelte and charming wood structure at the far end of Connaught Dr., puts on a nightly "cabaret," and has a dance floor. "Cabaret" here is the usual Canadian misnomer for various name bands giving guest performances (one at a time) until 1 a.m. Admission is $1.50.

The **Crater Theater,** across the Miette River, south of town, is an outdoor stage performing **The Jasper Story** nightly during the last week of July and the first week of August, highly enjoyable musical "historama" makes the valley's past come alive with dramatic effects.

PARK CAMPGROUNDS: There are over 20 campgrounds in the region of Banff and Jasper National Parks, providing a total of some 5000 campsites. You need a special permit to camp anywhere in the parks outside the regular campgrounds—a regulation necessary because of fire hazards. The campgrounds range from completely unserviced sites to those providing water, power, and sewer connections, laundry facilities, gas, and groceries. The usual fees are $3 per night at unserviced sites and $6 for full-service hookups.

TOURS AND EXCURSIONS: The **Brewster Transport Co.** operates tours from Banff (tel. 762-2286) and Jasper (tel. 852-3332), covering most of the outstanding beauty spots in both parks. A few sample packages:

Banff to Jasper (or vice versa): Eight hours through unmatched scenery, the trip takes in Lake Louise and a view of the icefield along the parkway. Box lunches are required on this journey. One-way fare is $25; round trip, $37.

Columbia Icefield: A six-hour tour from Jasper. You stop at the Icefield Chalet and get time off for lunch and a snocoach ride up the glacier (not included in the tour price). Adults pay $13; children, half price.

Mount Norquay Cablelift: The trip from Banff takes two hours and the fare includes a lift ride, providing superlative views of Banff townsite, Bow Valley, and the Vermilion Lake. Tickets are $6 for adults, half price for children.

Whistler's Mountain Tramway: A two-hour jaunt from Jasper with a ride on the aerial tram included in the fare. You can get off at the top, take a stroll along the alpine trails, and return on a later bus. The fare is $7.50 for adults, $3.75 for children.

Athabasca River Raft Tour: Starts from Jasper and takes three hours. You shoot the rapids—in complete safety but with a lot of thrills—on big, sturdy rafts steered by professional rivermen. The raft ride is included in the fare. Rates are $15 for adults, $7.75 for children.

On Horseback

One of the most exhilarating experiences the parks can offer is trail riding. It has the added advantage of being available to the tenderest of tenderfeet—those who have never sat on a horse before. The guides take your riding prowess (or lack of same) into account and select foothill trails slow enough to keep you mounted. And the special mountain trail horses used are steady, reliable animals not given to sudden antics.

One of the largest riding outfits in Alberta is **Warner & McKenzie**, Trail Rider Store, Banff Ave. (tel. 762-4551). They offer local rides by the hour and half-day and six-day pack trips that include with the seasons, as do the rates. From May through June it's $275 per rider; July to August, $330; and September, $295—for six days, including guides, horses, tents, meals, etc. You supply your own sleeping bag and personal articles.

3. Edmonton

A standing joke in Alberta has it that *no* rivalry exists between the province's two major cities, Edmonton and Calgary. Because both towns are utterly devoted to the cult of "niceness," they can't possibly admit to anything as abrasive as competitiveness. In point of fact, however, they're at it hammer and tongs, each scoring off the other at every given opportunity, running a neck-and-neck race for supremacy.

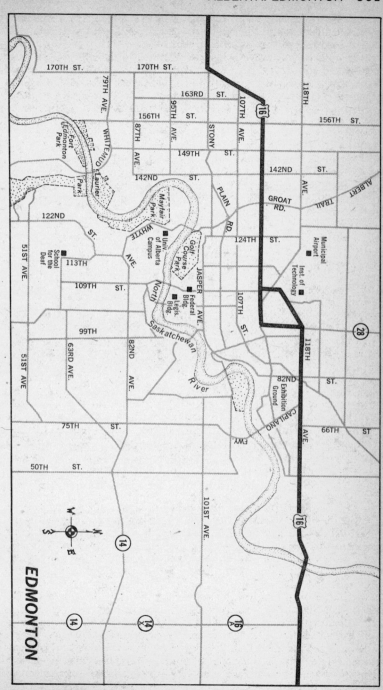

This works out splendidly for visitors, since the two places are constantly trying to outdo each other in hospitality. But it makes it hard—nay, impossible —to assess which of them is actually ahead.

Edmonton is the provincial capital and has a slight edge in population, currently around 515,000. But Calgary is growing faster and may take the lead any moment. Edmonton has slightly more political clout, but Calgary slightly more money. Calgary offers the world-famous annual Stampede, Edmonton is coming up fast with its yearly **Klondike Days** shindig. Edmonton is the technological and scientific center of the oil industry, Calgary the business and administrative one. Calgary smiles at you more, Edmonton feeds you better. . . .

In one respect Edmonton has gained a very visible advantage. She began rebuilding her downtown area a decade sooner. Which means that her core is now comfortably streamlined, whereas Calgary's is chaotic. But in a few years Calgary will have completed reconstruction and may emerge even more impressive from the cement dust.

Edmonton was founded as an armed and pallisaded trading post of the Hudson's Bay Company in 1795. Her customers were the formidable warriors of the Blackfoot tribal confederacy, and trading could be a somewhat nervous enterprise. When 2000 mounted and feathered braves appeared on the skyline you never knew for certain whether they came to trade or to storm the stockade. So you primed the cannon and brought out the merchandise simultaneously—just in case.

Actually Edmonton House, as the post was called, had less trouble with its clients than with the supply line. Every scrap the outpost used had to come by freight canoe over 2000 tortuous miles, and nothing got through in winter. From season to season the existence of the 165 men, women, and children in the "house" depended on whether they'd laid in enough supplies to last the winter months. Potatoes and vegetables were luxuries. The staple diet was buffalo meat—5 pounds a day for men, 2½ pounds for women, 1¼ pounds per child. The beef-eating habit has stayed with Edmontonians ever since.

Until 1870 Edmonton remained the most lucrative fur-trading post in the Hudson's Bay empire. Then the company sold the land to the Canadian government and the area was opened to pioneer settlement. The "house" expanded into a township, joined the outside world by means of telegraph wire, founded a newspaper, and got the law in the shape of the scarlet-coated North West Mounted Police, who put an end to the habit of settling disputed land claims by "Winchester arbitration."

In 1891 electricity and the railroad arrived from Calgary and utterly changed the little settlement. Floods of newcomers poured in, some to stay, others to populate the rich land all around. The Klondike Gold Rush made Edmonton the major supply center for goldseekers on the perilous Klondike Trail routes overland to Dawson City in the Yukon.

By 1905 when the Province of Alberta was created, Edmonton had around 8000 souls and was one year old as a city. She got the nomination as capital of the new province largely because of her geographically central position. The older, bigger, and more southerly Calgary never quite got over the shock.

Edmonton grew in spurts, following a boom-and-bust pattern as exciting as it was unreliable. One moment people were lining up to buy blocks of land in the city and the next moment they were lining up outside soup kitchens. During World War II the boom came in the form of the Alaska Hwy., with Edmonton as material base and temporary home of 50,000 American troops and construction workers.

The ultimate boom, however, gushed from the ground on a freezing afternoon in February 1947. That was when a drill at Leduc, 25 miles southwest of the city, sent a fountain of dirty-black crude oil soaring skyward. Some 10,000 other wells followed, all within a 100-mile radius of the city. In their wake came the petrochemical industry and the major refining and supply conglomerates. In two decades the population of the city quadrupled, her skyline mushroomed with glass-and-concrete office towers, a rapid-transit system was created, and a $150-million Civic Centre arose. Edmonton had become what she is today—the Oil Capital of Canada.

ORIENTATION: Edmonton is located almost exactly in the center of Alberta, some 350 miles north of the U.S. border. The Rocky Mountains stretch 200 miles to the west, to the south lie the foothills prairie, to the north the beautiful lake country and the Alaska Hwy. The city tends to be sunny, windy, and cool. Midsummer temperatures average between 70° and 80° Fahrenheit, and at an altitude of 2182 feet, even summer nights can be nippy.

The winding **North Saskatchewan River** flows right through the heart of the city, dividing it into roughly equal portions. One of the young capital's greatest achievements is the way in which this river valley has been kept out of the grasp of commercial developers. Almost the entire valley has been turned into public parklands, forming 17 miles of greenery, sports, picnic, and recreation grounds within earshot of the busiest thoroughfares. You never lose sight of one or another of these multiple oases for office workers. Future generations will bless those powers that be for stubbornly hanging onto scenery that could so easily have withered into parking lots and factory sites. The river valley is ingeniously interwoven with a network of freeways connecting the two city portions, but so cleverly that the roadways above don't affect the green serenity of the parks below.

Edmonton's main street is the wide and seemingly endless **Jasper Ave.** (actually 101st Ave.), running north of the river. For some mysterious reason the high-numbered streets and avenues are the central ones while the low-numbered thoroughfares lie way out in the suburbs.

At 100th St., one block north of Jasper Ave., rises the superb **Civic Centre,** the only completely planned complex of its kind in Canada. At the northern approach to the **High Level Bridge,** surrounded by parkland, stand the buildings of the **Alberta Legislature,** seat of the provincial government. Across the bridge, to the west, stretches the vast campus of the **University of Alberta.** Running south in a straight line from **Queen Elizabeth Park** on the riverside is 104th St., which becomes **Calgary Trail** and leads to the International Airport.

Jumping back to the north shore of the river, you'll find the **Visitor Information Bureau** at 10145 100th St. Three blocks to the west, at 102nd St. and 102nd Sve., is the **Greyhound Bus Depot.** Farther north, but amazingly close to downtown, lies the **Municipal Airport.** The main post office is located at 103A Ave. & 99th St. (These "A" designations for certain streets and avenues are a nuisance for anyone trying to get his bearings, since they interfere with block counts. But otherwise the layout of downtown Edmonton is a model of clarity.)

Beneath the downtown core stretches a network of pedestrian walkways—called pedways—connecting hotels, restaurants, and shopping malls with the library, City Hall, and the **Canadian National Railways Station.** These pedways not only avoid the surface traffic, they're also climate controlled.

Getting Around

Edmonton sits astride the **Yellowhead,** Western Canada's great new inter-provincial highway. This is an east-west route with excellent access from every compass point to other Canadian highways and U.S. interstate highways. The Yellowhead route is also followed by the Canadian National Railway's trans-continental line through most of western Canada, using the famous domed lookout cars. Just west of Edmonton the Yellowhead is linked to the Alaska Hwy. VIA Rail goes from the CNR Station, 104th Ave. and 100th St. (tel. 429-5431).

Edmonton is served by six major airlines, including **CP Air** and **Pacific Western.** The latter operates the outstanding **AirBus** shuttle to Calgary, a no-reservation service of 13 flights a day, making the hop in 36 minutes. The **International Airport** lies ten miles south of the city on Hwy. 2., about 45 driving minutes away. The trip, by cab, costs $16 to $20; by Yellow Coach, $3.50.

Edmonton's public transport is handled by **Edmonton Transit** (tel. 432-1234 for information), one of the finest outfits of its kind not only in Canada but on the American continent. Transit operates the city buses as well as the brand-new, silent, streamlined, and supremely comfortable **LRT** (Light Transit Line). This partly underground partly aboveground electric rail service connects downtown Edmonton with northeastern Belvedere and has (as yet) only five stations. The downtown terminal, **Central Station,** lies underground at Jasper Ave. and 101st St. It's spacious, spotless, handsomely decorated, and right in the heart of the busiest commercial section. The other end of the 4½-mile line is at 129th Ave. and Fort Rd.

The LRT and the Transit buses have the same fares, 50¢ for adults, half price for children. You can transfer from one to the other from any given station on the same ticket.

Taxis: Edmonton cabs charge $1.20 at flagfall, then 80¢ a mile.

Car Rentals: Budget, 10018 103rd St. (tel. 428-6155); **Hertz,** 10815 Jasper Ave. (tel. 424-6408); **Airways,** 10140 109th St. (tel. 423-5281).

Cycling: With the possible exception of Amsterdam, no city in the world takes such tender care of her pedal pushers as Edmonton. The entire metropolitan area is sprinkled with cycling routes specially designed for clear visibility and for access to recreational facilities, schools, parks, commercial centers, and places of employment. They come in three clearly marked types: (1) bike paths, reserved exclusively for cyclists; (2) bike lanes, delineated portions of roadways meant for cyclists; and (3) bike routes, where cyclists have to share the roadways with other types of traffic. The **Capital Recreation Park,** the long ribbon of parks enfolding the North Saskatchewan River Valley, is a biker's paradise and the most ideal cycling area in Canada. The city has published a special Bikeways Map, showing cycling facilities, which you can get at the Visitor Information Bureau.

You can rent your pedal steeds at **George's Cycles,** 9350 118th Ave. (tel. 474-2421).

ACCOMMODATIONS: Having started her downtown facelift ten years before her rival, Edmonton is that much better off than Calgary when it comes to providing tourist beds. This doesn't mean that the capital boasts many more hostelries. It does mean that her accommodations are better balanced at the lower-medium and budget end of the scale. Here even the older buildings now enjoy a measure of permanence and aren't threatened with bulldozing at any moment. So you're fairly safe in assuming that a hotel mentioned below will still be standing by the time you get there. As already stated, Alberta has no sales tax, which means no sneaky additions to either your hotel or restaurant bills.

Luxury

Hotel Macdonald, Jasper Ave. and 100th St. (tel. 403/424-5181). Just forget about "golden arches." This establishment was named after Sir John Macdonald, Canada's first prime minister, and is the oldest, most distinguished luxury hotel in town. A blue-roofed Victorian charmer, the Macdonald reserves all its sumptuousness for the interior, combining 19th-century chic with Nuclear Age comfort.

The lobby is a haven in deep reds and browns, where you sink into leather settees and contemplate a visit to the special "Quiet Bar," which looks like an Edwardian drawing room. The Inglenook, the main dining room, is subtly gorgeous yet intimate. The fast-service snackery and open-air Terrace are quite informal, and the glass-walled swimming pool and sun patio overlook the river valley below. The 450 guest rooms, furnished with tasteful timelessness, have closets large enough to sleep in, bathrooms big enough to dance in, combination TV and radio, and individually controlled air conditioning.

Singles cost $41 to $55; doubles, $49 to $63; and suites, $53 to $60.

Four Seasons, 10235 101st St. (tel. 403/428-7111). This, by contrast, is the latest arrival on the deluxe scene, and opened its portals in June 1978. It has the unique feature of having one entire floor—the 14th—reserved for nonsmokers. The Four Seasons is connected via overhead walkway with the Edmonton Centre shopping complex, so you can reach the stores without stepping outside. The showpiece here is the superlative Garden Lounge in the center of the lobby, lit by a skylight and set amid palms, ferns, and flower beds. An indoor pool with with whirlpool and sauna, two celebrated restaurants, plus a disco complete the hotel facilities, plus the 24-hour room service.

The 314 guest rooms breathe discreet elegance. The decor is light gray and powder blue, and writing desks and bathroom sinks are topped with genuine marble. Despite the air conditioning, one window opens, a blessing for oxygen addicts like myself. You get direct-dial Touch-Tone telephones, bedside controls for TV and radio, extra-large towels, and thoughtful touches like hideaway clotheslines, extra plugs for hair dryers, complimentary shower caps and shampoos.

Singles cost from $49 to $59; doubles, $61 to $71; but there's also a Weekend Special at $35 *per room* (single or double).

The **Edmonton Plaza,** 10135 100th St. (tel. 403/426-3636), is an immense brown block of titanic beauty that manages to appear both huge and graceful. The softly lit lobby has picture windows overlooking Churchill Square outside, and a delightful cocktail bar in the center that's at least half garden, illuminated by star showers encased in waving nets. Impressive! The staff of this streamlined palace commands 29 languages. An underground shopping complex bustles, unheard, beneath your feet. The Carvery is the intimately stylish main restaurant, but there's also the less formal Terrace Grill and the *very* informal Stage Door, rocking with, well, rock. And, of course, a luxurious swimming pool.

The 350 rooms and suites are large, air-conditioned, and decorated with some of the finest prints found on hotel walls, and contain burnt-orange carpeting, immense beds, Touch-Tone telephones, alarm clocks, color TV, and a lot of other pampering gadgets. The bathrooms follow the pattern, with hideaway clotheslines, shower caps, and free shampoos, plus heating lamps with attached timers (you can set them for just as long as it takes you to shower and dry yourself).

Singles cost from $51 to $57; doubles, $63 to $70. The Weekend Special here costs $32 per room per night, single or double occupancy, but does not operate June through August.

Château Lacombe, 101st St. at Bellamy Hill (tel. 403/428-6611), is a round ivory-colored tower soaring up 24 stories from the surrounding greenery, its dancing lights reflecting in the river below. One of the most beautiful modern hotels in Canada, the Lacombe blends perfectly with the city's dramatic skyline as well as her green river belt. The huge lobby is a soothing and strangely serene study in beige, brown, and amber suffused with the soft glow of mighty chandeliers. The adjoining Garrison Lounge has an interesting military air, decorated with oldtime Mounted Police equipment and guarded by a genuine brass Maxim machine gun, vintage 1895.

There are a boutique and a barbershop on the premises, plus a revolving restaurant, appropriately named La Ronde, at the top of the tower. The 330 bedrooms and suites come in delicate pastel tints and with excellent black-and-white pencil sketches on the walls. The tiled bathrooms come with shower caps, shampoos, and detergents—a nice little extra. Color TV, radio, full air conditioning, and telephone might be taken for granted, but the lighting fixtures that can be arranged from concentrated bright to subdued intimate are a tomorrow touch.

Singles range from $43 to $45; doubles, from $53 to $55.

Moderately Priced Hotels

The **Sheraton-Caravan,** 100th Ave. and 104th St. (tel. 403/424-0011), is a sparkling white structure resting on blue pillars, and a frontage dominated by little balconies give the local Sheraton a distinctly Mediterranean flavor. The lobby is busy and undistinguished, but the guest rooms are charming and the hotel a hive of action: a fast and economical restaurant for busy travelers, a plush piano bar for leisurely relaxers, and a jumping dance spot called, strangely enough, Yesterdays, for the young in leg.

The 141 guest rooms are spacious, each with private balcony, TV, radio, and individually controlled air conditioning. Both elevator and room service function fast and smoothly. The beds convert into daytime couches, there's ample storage space in eight drawers and a walk-in closet, and the rooms are colorfully decorated, softly carpeted, and supremely comfortable. Bathrooms are fluorescently lit, while ceiling and bedside lamps are suitably soft.

Standard rates—all year—are singles from $34 to $38; doubles, from $36 to $40. No extra for children.

Midtowner Motor Inn, 105th St. and 100th Ave. (tel. 403/429-5111). Smallish, smart, and streamlined, this central hostelry offers remarkable facilities at surprisingly humble rates. A low white stone structure with flaring torches as shingles, the Midtowner welcomes you with a neat little lobby, tavern adjoining. The hotel's Cave Lounge features a volcanic rock wall with a waterfall tumbling down: a unique touch. There's a small pool alongside a tree-studded sun patio and a very pretty dining lounge with candlelight atmosphere.

The 60 guest rooms look chic in russet and brown tones. They have beds and couches, low tables and armchairs, springy carpeting and one wall handsomely paneled in brown wood. Plus hanging space behind a sliding curtain, beds with free Magic Finger vibrators, air conditioning and bedside controls for lights, TV, and radio. The bathrooms are green tiled and come fluorescently lit and with electric ventilators.

Singles cost a standard $26; doubles, $31; but at the special weekend rates you pay $24 for either.

Convention Inn West, 16625 Stony Plain Rd. (tel. 403/484-7751), is located about ten minutes from downtown on the Yellowhead route to Jasper Park. A huge, massively modern accommodation and entertainment complex, the inn contains a bar, restaurant, coffeeshop, cocktail lounge, tavern, cabaret, a truly grand ballroom, and every conceivable convention facility, including an excellently laid out lobby that combines vastness with comfort.

The inn has only 60 guest rooms, few for its size, but these are large and nicely furnished. Big front windows give maximum daylight, the decor is a pleasant brown and orange, hanging space is ample, and room service is excellent. The decorations are somewhat puzzling: framed stanzas from the *Rubaiyyat* of Omar Khayyam—in 12 languages and six different scripts yet! Nothing Persian about the bathrooms, however. They're big and modern, with complimentary shower caps and boxes of tissues. (In Canada it's Scotties instead of Kleenex.)

Single rooms cost $25; doubles, $27.

The **Saxony Motor Inn,** 156th St. and Stony Plain Rd. (tel. 403/484-3331). Also about ten minutes from downtown, this dazzling white-and-blue structure with a display of international flags offers outstanding value. With sumptuous Spanish decor throughout, as well as air conditioning, the Saxony houses a first-rate restaurant, smart coffeeshop, cozy tavern, and the El Gato lounge for nightly entertainment, as well as a heated rooftop swimming pool and sun terrace, and extensive convention and banquet facilities. A rare touch is the complimentary breakfast for guests, served from 7 to 9 a.m. in the dining lounge: juice, eggs, bacon, hash browns, coffee or tea—all on the management.

The 59 rooms are large, with tiny balconies, all air-conditioned and very well appointed. You get king-size beds, leather armchairs, macramé on the walls. Indian prints, plus cable TV, radio, writing desk with dial telephone, and an open hanging niche. Bathrooms are compact and streamlined.

Singles cost $25; doubles, $28.

Travelodge, 9650 102nd Ave. (tel. 403/424-0961). We're back in the heart of downtown with this cubistic white motel, part of the chain that stretches across America. The exterior is utilitarian with no extra frills, but the 67 guest rooms are pleasantly spacious, individually heated, and air-conditioned. The deep green or red carpeting matches nicely with the paneled wood along the wall. Furnishings are good motel standard, with armchairs, writing desk, and open hanging space. There are ample bedside and table lights, but no overhead illumination. The bathrooms have electric ventilators and fluorescent lights, but most come with showers only. Color TV and dial phones are in all rooms, and there's a coffeeshop on the premises.

Singles cost $27; doubles, $31.

The **Greenbriar,** 10209 100th Ave. (tel. 403/428-6442), is a motor hotel with an unassuming front and surprisingly smart interior. The lounge is very attractively decorated with outstanding sports photographs, the armchairs and settees lit by Tiffany lamps. The 73 guest rooms, all with bath and shower, have black couches as well as beds, and are completely air-conditioned. The furniture is highly contemporary, with intriguing little desks, standard lamps, and brand-new carpeting. Additionally you'll find a big open hanging space, color TV, and dial telephone. Bathrooms have fluorescent lighting and excellent fixtures.

Singles come at a standard $26; doubles, $30. Children under 13 stay free in their parents' room.

Hotel Vega, 10815 Jasper Ave. (tel. 403/424-7265). Sitting on Edmonton's main street, the Vega is a square beige corner building offering a lot of facilities. The Grieg dining room has splendid Scandinavian decor and gourmet fare. The Café Camille puts on an extensive daily buffet—all you can eat for $4.30. The Terracotta is a garden lounge with an oasis atmosphere, ideal for a quiet drink or three. The adjoining Norseman Tavern and Longboat pub provide somewhat noisier conviviality, helped at night by assorted male vocalists and items like genuine Swedish "Bolle Suppe."

The 150 guest rooms are not large, but bright and cheerful in green and beige, with light-wood furniture and French Utrillo prints on the walls, and bedside TV selection, desk, small table, armchairs, and standard lamp in one corner. Bathrooms are small and have either bath or shower. The entire hotel is air-conditioned.

Singles go from $26 to $30; doubles, from $30 to $34; and the special bridal suites, from $35 to $50. Children under 12 stay free with their parents.

Ambassador, 10041 106th St. (tel. 403/429-4881), is a very attractive small motor inn with tavern attached (the tavern portion is kept completely separate from the hotel so none of the bar hurly-burly penetrates the living quarters). The smartly red-carpeted lobby has black leather armchairs and white cube tables, and an adjoining coffee shop doubles as a restaurant. The elevators are speedy and the 76 guest rooms are models of contemporary comfort, all air-conditioned with individual controls, wall-to-wall carpets, and writing desks with lamp and mirror. The bathrooms, with tubs and showers, have separate rooms for the sink and open hanging space. Color TV and dial telephones throughout.

You pay from $27 to $29 for singles, $30 to $32 for doubles, $4 for each additional person.

Budget Hotels

The **Corona,** 10625 Jasper Ave. (tel. 403/422-7106). A brownstone building in the busiest part of downtown, the Corona has a large, somewhat bare, half-carpeted lobby, but nicely appointed rooms. There's a good restaurant on the premises (serving a smorgasbord), a fast-service coffeeshop, plus a fairly sumptuous lounge, dishing out cocktail-hour hors d'oeuvres and nightly band entertainment (dancing till 1 a.m.) A bank and barbershop are in the baths or showers. All come equipped with color TV and telephones. Furnishings include wall-to-wall carpets, big and comfortable beds, large closets, good lighting, and writing desks. Bathrooms are rather old-fashioned but well maintained.

Singles run from $18 to $27; doubles, $23 to $32. Additional occupants pay $5 each.

Stones Motel, 16220 Stony Plain Rd. (tel. 403/489-7731), a short distance from downtown, is an open rectangle of red-roofed, white units, most with kitchen facilities. (There's a shopping center a few blocks away, but no restaurant on the premises.) All units have baths or showers, color TV, and telephones. The rooms are adequately furnished, although by no means glamorous: big beds, writing desks, ample closets, bedside and desk lamps. The kitchenettes have gas stoves and refrigerators. Bathrooms are fairly simple and come minus razor plugs.

Singles cost $20; doubles, $22; and $2 for each additional person.

Klondiker Hotel, 153rd St. and Stony Plain Rd. (tel. 403/489-1906), has a distinct gold rush flavor. The lobby resembles a log cabin, wood paneled and illuminated by lovely antique lanterns. A huge mural and bronze statue symbolize the Klondike epoch. Appropriately, there are three taverns in the building, providing liquid refreshments, conviviality, and nightly entertainment. Most of the 37 guest rooms come with baths or showers and TV sets, and all have telephones. The whole building is spaciously designed, the room decor quite attractive. You get a smallish wardrobe, good carpeting, armchair, bedside and desk lamp, but no razor plug.

Singles range from $14 to $16; doubles, from $17 to $19. Small children stay free in their parents' room.

Hotel Cecil, 10406 Jasper Ave. (tel. 403/428-7001). Back to midtown for this small corner building with hewn stone front and a tavern on the premises. The lobby is a rather spartan affair, but the 59 bedrooms are furnished nicely enough. Twenty of them have private baths or showers, the others hot- and cold-water sinks. Carpeting is wall to wall, and there's fair hanging space in either closets or open arrangements, a small work desk, bedside lamps, room telephones, and color TV. A coffeeshop is in the building.

Singles go from $12 to $15.50; doubles, $15.50 to $19.50, with additional persons paying $3 to $4.

Gateway Hotel, 10038 106th St. (tel. 403/424-8055), is a small brick building with an attractive lobby-lounge, fitted with ornamental fireplace and TV set, leather chairs, and cigarette and soft-drink machines. No elevator here, and the stairs are rather steep, but *up* isn't very far. Of the 43 rooms half have baths or showers. The rooms are smallish, adequately and plainly furnished: wall-to-wall carpets, dresser with mirror, wall telephone, bedside table with lamp, armchair, and a good-sized closet. No TV, and no razor plugs in the bathroom.

Singles pay from $10 to $12.50; doubles, $12.50 to $14.50; additional persons, $2.50.

The Ys

Both of Edmonton's Ys are housed in modern, pleasant buildings without any hint of the barracks flavor that permeates some of their fellows elsewhere. Neither of them accommodates residents of the opposite sex, which avoids a lot of confusion.

The **YMCA,** 10030 102A Ave. (tel. 403/424-8047), has a cafeteria, pool, gymnasium, and racquetball court, plus a spacious lobby with good seating facilities. Of the 134 rooms a minority have private baths (tubs only). The rooms are small and trim, nicely carpeted, and cheerfully furnished with a small writing desk, a bedside table with lamp, and friendly curtains. Telephones are in the lobby only. Singles run from $9.50 to $13.50; doubles, $11.50 to $13.50.

The **YWCA,** 10305 100th Ave. (tel. 403/422-3451), has a cafeteria that sells good breakfasts seven days a week for $2, as well as a pool and a fine range of sports facilities. Five floors of accommodations range from a ten-bed dormitory to singles with bath. Laundry facilities and TV lounge are available in the house. The public bathrooms are sparkling and the staff is exceptionally friendly. Private rooms range from $13 to $16, dormitory bunks cost $5, and sleeping bags are $3.

MEALS: Edmonton, as I said before, is very much a beef town, with a restaurant scene basking in the aroma of sizzling steaks. But over the past decade other, more cosmopolitan styles of cuisine have gained popularity, although not to the point of dominance. The city today has achieved a fine balance between the native American palate and its international alternatives—meaning you can get both in every price bracket.

The following selections come from such a lengthy list of choices that they can only serve as samples. A handful among them are unique, one-of-a-kind establishments. The majority merely indicate a certain culinary genre which has a dozen or two other representatives, which I had to omit for purely space reasons.

The Top Choices

Oliver's, 117th St. at Jasper Ave. (tel. 482-4888). Ironically named after the little workhouse waif with the growling stomach, this quite gorgeous dinery caters to diametrically opposite types. Just to remind patrons of the restaurant's namesake there's a glass case displaying an ancient copy of the Dickens classic, with the inimitable Cruikshank illustrations. This touch is indicative of the style of the place: only top quality will do. The carpets caress you, the seating upholstery feels sensual, the table linen is dazzling, the wall decorations exquisite. It's divided into the dining room on one side, bar lounge on the other, with superb service in both portions. And it's hard to decide which is finer here: the beef tournedos at $12.95 or the delicately grilled Dover sole for $11.25. Open for lunch and dinner.

Yeoman Steak House, 10030 107th St. (tel. 423-1511), is an unusually handsome establishment consisting of four dining rooms, each furnished in a subtly different style, all blending into a harmonious whole. You don't realize the size of the place—the glass partitions allow diners to see each other yet provide an air of intimacy for each section. The walls are hung with beautifully framed oils and prints, individually illuminated. The lower room has an open grill arranged rather like an altar to the gods of gastronomy. The Service is silently attentive—and leisurely. Every entree comes with onion soup, garlic toast, and salad (excellent Bismarck herring for appetizers). Then, perhaps, the sweetbreads gourmet ($9.45) or the charcoal-broiled New York steak ($11.95). Finally—a must—the hot apple pie with rum sauce, which will give you an idea just how delicious dessert can be. Open seven days a week till midnight.

1001 Nights, 103rd Ave. and 104th St. Mid-Eastern cuisine of the highest order, an impressive wine list, and one belly dancer combine to make this establishment a must among those Edmontonians ready to forego their steaks for an evening. The decor is both smart and delicate: light-wood chairs and shutters, chestnut-hued table linen, and what amounts to an indoor garden of plants and ferns—all understated and intimately elegant. The fare is *maza,* which doesn't imply a dish but dozens of them, a kind of Levantine smorgasbord. But the way they are served is delightfully original: you get sample plates loaded with feta cheese cubes, chicken hearts, kebab, vine leaf rolls, calf liver slices, ground beef cakes, mashed eggplant, stuffed peppers, etc. You can either order full servings of whichever tidbits you fancy ($5 to $10) or get the entire range ($24.95 for two very hungry people).

Fujiyama, 121st St. and Jasper Ave. (tel. 482-5494), is a classical Japanese beef-chicken-seafood house run by an immensely popular and concerned restaurateur named Sam Walsh. Part of his popularity is undoubtedly due to his habit of announcing the scores of major sporting events over the intercom. Very large tables (with ample room for long legs underneath) center around a sizzling grill. The food is prepared at your table by a chef, triple-trained as cook, juggler, and comedian. You see the creation of your entire meal, accompanied by astonishing feats of knife play and wrist-flicking saucer magic. The cocktail lounge serves all western libations plus the restaurant's own concoctions, as pretty as they are potent. Price? Teppan shrimp and hibachi steak for (respectively) $10.25 and $10.75, hokusai-combi for $10.95. The sunimono salad here is outstanding. Do leave room for the pineapple yama, a tropical dessert of memorable quality.

The **Steak Loft**, 9974 Jasper Ave. (tel. 426-6226). One of the handsomest steakeries in Canada and definitely a stronghold of the executive echelons, the Steak Loft is subtly lit, so that the table linen gleams as brightly as the lamps. Permeated with the aroma of vintage wines, Paris perfumes, and charcoal-broiled beef, decorated with oil portraits in heavy gold frames, served by silently gliding waiters, and patronized by some of the best dressed, best heeled folks in town, it's famous for expense-account lunches and equivalent dinners. Both the pepper steak and the filet mignon are outstanding, even in this beef metropolis. The former costs $10.95; the latter, $12.50.

Moderately Priced Restaurants

Hungarian Village, 10110 107th St. There's nothing in the least rustic about this svelte temple of Magyar gourmetry, a singular misnomer. The red brick walls form an intriguing contrast to the dark-brown table linen, the candles glowing in scarlet glass covers, and the deep green upholstery of the chairs. A big, beautiful dining room, graceful with vaulting arches, is divided into intimate portions by carved wooden railings. The air is unobtrusively filled with Hungarian folk strains and the menu features a brief essay on the art of Hungarian cooking—enough to make you give up counting calories for the occasion. Both food and service are of the essence. The cucumber salad, sprinkled with paprika, is positively poetic. If you're alone, try the superb stuffed pork for $8.55. If you're accompanied, it's the heaped wooden Transylvanian platter: a minor mountain of smoked, roasted, and boiled meats, prepared only for two and costing $12 per person. Open till 11 p.m. six nights a week. Closed Sunday.

The **Crêperie**, 10220 103rd St. (tel. 420-6656). Located in the Boardwalk Building downtown, this dinery has a large comfortable waiting room, and needs it—the curse of popularity. A charming, softly lit dining room wafting with delicious aromas is undoubtedly the magnet that keeps people rooted in those leather waiting chairs. All crêpe dinners include either onion soup (not to be missed) or salad, and range from $7.50 to $9.75. A vast selection of crêpes, including beef and chicken bourgignonne or ham Cordon Bleu. If you can manage dessert, there's a memorable Swiss chocolate fondue at $2.50. Open weekdays till 11:30 p.m., Sundays till 9 p.m.

In the same Boardwalk Building, which is a complex of shops, offices, and eateries, you'll find the **Steakboard** (tel. 429-0886). Divided into a large lounge and small dining room, both beautiful, it has a low black ceiling and brick walls decorated with movie-quality photos of Canadian scenes from the 1920s. An extensive salad bar occupies a central position, and glass-shielded candles glimmer on the tables. The svelte and cozy lounge features entertainers six nights a week. The dining room features food: escargots champignon at $3.25 per half dozen, filet mignon for $11.50, medallions of veal for $10.50. Also, a package-dinner deal—a complete meal, including coffee and dessert—is offered for $8.50. Open six days a week till midnight, Sunday till 9 p.m.

Mother Tucker's Food Experience, 10184 104th St. (tel. 424-0351), is a weird and wonderful place, not so much frequented as besieged by the local populace. Dedicated to home-style cooking, homemade bread, and country atmosphere (the staff are known as the "Tucker kin"), this establishment almost makes you believe that there really is a "Mom" somewhere in the background, whippin' up them vittles. Even the liquor lounge comes in character disguise as "Tucker's general store." Nothing to disguise about the cuisine, though; it's homey, hearty, tasty, and awesomely abundant. Dinners include straight-from-the-oven bread, a vast salad bar selection (they encourage you to eat, eat), and homemade dessert. The prime ribs of beef buffet costs $8.95. The country-baked half chicken comes for $7.45, scintillatingly seasoned rainbow trout for $8.45. No reservations accepted here. Open seven days a week.

Bistro Praha, 10164 100A St. (tel. 424-1046), is unique in Edmonton—a European-style cafe-restaurant so relaxed, charming, and convenient that you can't help thinking how much the texture of life would be improved if the town had half a dozen more of the same. Spacious and quite simple, the Praha has one wall covered by a landscape mural, some small framed pictures of Prague, and the kind of tables and chairs you'd find in a private home. The background music is Bach and Beethoven, the clientele cosmopolitan, appreciative, mainly young and mostly attractive. The cuisine is dreamy and the portions are colossal (the wienerschnitzel covers the entire plate—in two layers!). The Praha serves the finest tomato and onion salad in the west, and it comes as part of your meal. Choices include a rich cabbage soup for $2, steak tartare for $11, and a superb natur schnitzel (meaning minus crumb crust) for $9.50. You get to choose among 12 brands of tea, and the Sacher torte is the way they dished it up in Old Vienna. Drop in for a meal or just a cuppa. The hours are ideal for either: 11 a.m. to 2 a.m. seven days a week.

Also on 100A St. is **The Granary** (tel. 424-4795). A vaguely rustic establishment that looks vegetarian but isn't, the Granary has wooden shutters (but no windows), vaulted arches, whitewashed walls, classical guitar music, rural prints as wall decorations, and a very friendly staff. While as yet it's unlicensed, the management hopes to rectify that. It serves a meal combination of soup, salad, and whole-wheat roll for $2.50 (14 varieties of soup), a fine quiche Lorraine for $3.75, chicken and mushrooms fricassee in pita bread for $3.25, and sandwiches ranging from shrimp and avocado to Bavarian meatloaf. Open from 11 a.m. to 8 p.m., but will keep later hours when licensed.

Blue Willow, 10041 Jasper Ave. (tel. 426-1410), is an unusually beautiful Chinese restaurant that looks like a Chinese tea house with Western trimmings (such as a bar). You enter over a little bridge spanning a wishing well. The dining room lights filter through bamboo screens on the ceiling. You get a love story on your paper serviette and a hot, moist towel to refresh you after the meal. The menu includes some rare items such as the savory bacon rolls (chicken liver and water chestnuts wrapped in crisp bacon) for $2.50. Both the almond chicken ($6.75) and the pea pods and beef ($6.25) are excellent. Unfortunately they charge you 35¢ for two fortune cookies. Open seven days a week.

The **Pepper Mill,** 15912 Stony Plain Rd. (tel. 484-1812). Tucked away inside the Jasper Pl. shopping center, this family-style steakhouse offers an excellent bargain in the shape of a $7.95 steak dinner special. It comes on a wooden platter, accompanied by salad, toast, and baked potato. The restaurant is large yet cozy, with tables and eating booths of natural wood and *very* dim lighting (so dim, in fact, that I had trouble making out the furnishings). Prime rib goes for the same price as the special, along with salad, potato, and a soft bun. The best items on the dessert list are the banana and chocolate cream pies.

Edmonton has two eateries claiming to be a "San Francisco experience," which they are, give or take a few touches. The **Grinder,** 10957 124th St. (tel. 453-1709) and 110th Ave., has some of the correct trimmings: Tiffany lamps, belle époque posters, Casablanca-style ceiling fans, a genuine Wurlitzer jukebox, enormous wooden pepper grinders on the tables (very S.F.), etc., plus a pleasant laid-back atmosphere. The effect is somewhat weakened by red-and-blue beer ads and the absence of crispy sourdough bread. Still, the food is home-cooked and the clientele predominantly young and attractive. All entrees are served with salad or soup, vegetable, and potato or rice. The house special is barbecued ribs with a deliciously tangy sauce for $5.95. Escargots, served with mushrooms in herb sauce, come at $3.95. And the grinderburger is guaranteed the biggest of its breed in town. Open till 11 p.m. six nights a week. Closed Sunday—a decidedly un-San Francisco deviation.

The **Gas Pump,** 11402 Jasper Ave. (tel. 488-4841), features menus in the shape of a gas pump, perhaps a subtle dig at what's currently short in San Francisco. The place is delightfully decorated: the windows are half-curtained from the street, the space above your head filled with Tiffany lamps and hanging ferns. Elaborate pub mirrors proclaim 19th-century Coca-Cola slogans. Deep red carpets flow beneath wooden pillars. On the walls is an array of pictures ranging from delicate miniatures to an almost lifesize photo of W. C. Fields dangling a baby he is obviously about to parboil. Try the spare ribs ($7.35; this is one of the few places to serve them with corn fritters and a fingerbowl). Soup comes from the Sausalito Soup Kettle, and the Fisherman's Wharf salmon steak is excellent, served with crab snacks for $6.75. And pay attention to the appetizer tray, loaded with enough savory munchies for two.

The **Black Bull,** 102nd St. off Jasper Ave. (tel. 426-5456). Although mainly devoted to pizza, this is quite a step or two above the usual pizza parlor. In fact, it's a long narrow dining room, smartly decorated with oak beams and ferns, leather upholstery on the chairs, bullfight oil paintings on the walls, and soft Latin music in the background. The pizzas come in 20 varieties: from ham with tomatoes ($4.80) to an architectural feat of bacon, mushrooms, pepperoni, olives, peppers, and shrimp ($7.40). While pizza forms the backbone of the menu, it also extends to shish kebab, steaks, and barbecued chicken. The Bull keeps great hours for hungry tourists: open till 2:30 a.m. every morning.

Finally in this bracket we have a theater restaurant that puts on one of the best and most economical lunch spreads in town. The **Intermission,** 9828 101A Ave. (tel. 424-6627), is part of the huge glass lobby of the Citadel Theatre. Ideal for precurtain dinners and after-play snacks, the Intermission gets a business lunch clientele quite different from its evening customers. Quite simple but very comfortable, busy but relaxed, it caters to company executives, secretaries, rehearsing actors, and visitors. The big draw here is the $4.25 buffet, an impressive presentation of mushroom soup, roast beef, chicken wings, beef stew, parsley potatoes, salads, cheeses, and fruit. Aside from the buffet, it also has a variety of luncheon crêpes and the justly famous Citadel jumbo: a four-ounce beef sandwich on country rye bread for $3.95.

Budget Meals

Deli's Restaurant, 10124 Jasper Ave., is a rather smart delicatessen, long and narrow, with a single line of tables in front and a small restaurant area in the back. The front portion is very brightly lit, the rear wrapped in discreet semidarkness, and the Deli serves traditional lox and cream cheese bagels for $3.75, quiche Lorraine and hot potato salad for $3.95. The cheese blintzes are exceptionally rich, even for veteran deli diners like yours truly. Open Monday to Thursday till 9 p.m., weekends till midnight. Closed Sunday.

Tivoli Gardens, at 10432 Jasper Ave. (tel. 429-0867), overlooks one of downtown's mini-parks, and some of the plants seem to have crept inside to decorate the walls. The Danish touches can be found in the food and the array of beautiful posters of Copenhagen's Tivoli. A long and narrow cafeteria occupies the front, tables and chairs the rear section. White walls and fluorescent lighting make the Tivoli a bit overbright, which is further accentuated by the bare and sparkling floor. But the atmosphere is Copenhagen convivial, the food good and cheap, the coffee outstanding. The roast beef sandwiches, lean and tangy as they should be, cost $2.30. There's also a large vegetarian spread, including alfalfa sprouts, avocado, asparagus, and cucumber, that tastes garden fresh. The apple pie is Danish to the core, easily the finest of its species in town, and costs $1.50. The Tivoli starts serving breakfast at 6:30 a.m. and stays open till 6:30 p.m. Closed Sunday.

Ponderosa Steak House, Stony Plain Rd. at 160th St. (tel. 489-5609). You don't get too many steakeries in the budget bracket since the price of beef decided to emulate oil (or vice versa)—but this one qualifies. Under the slogan "Steak at Family Prices," it offers T-bone dinners at $4.39. For weekday lunch you can get a strip loin steak plus generous helpings from the salad bar for $2.59. The place that seems to be fighting a lone battle against inflation has a small patch of arranged "desert" out in front, decorated with carts and wagon wheels. Inside, it resembles a very attractive bunkhouse: wood paneled and hung with western gadgetry—but air-conditioned. Open four nights a week till 9 p.m., Fridays and Saturdays till 10 p.m.

Fuller's, Jasper Ave. at 122nd St. (tel. 482-3211). Under a vivid red roof that serves as a landmark, this large and plastic eatery serves simple food at very handy hours. Huge picture windows survey the street, and you get a choice between eating at the counter or in dining niches. The roast half chicken comes with all the trimmings for $5.45—enough for two people. Five species of burgers range from $2.75 to $3.85. The service is fast and the turnover rapid. Open all week: Sunday through Thursday till 1 a.m., Friday and Saturday till 2 a.m.

Finally, we have a couple of fast-service family eateries keeping the kind of hours and charging the kind of prices roaming tourist groups are always asking other roaming tourists about (a case of the halt seeking guidance from the blind). **Smitty's,** 109th St. and Kingsway Ave. (tel. 479-1313), is a big, bright, and air-conditioned pancake house–restaurant, with lots of seating space, indestructible tabletops, and a menu that extends from breakfast to dinner. It offers 16 kinds of pancakes, ranging from $1.80 to $4, plus egg dishes, steak sandwiches, burgers and bacon. Smitty's opens every day at 7 a.m.

Rafina, 10346 107th St. (tel. 425-9373), calls itself a pizza and spaghetti house, but offers a range of other dishes as well, and gives special rates on large delivery orders. It makes pizza in 10-inch and 13½-inch sizes and 23 varieties (from $3.50 to $7.90), plus baked lasagne, barbecued spare ribs, and pasta with or without meatballs. Open daily from 11 a.m. to 2 a.m.

Sunday and Other Specials

The Sunday brunch habit has spread across Canada like a benevolent epidemic. By and large this is because families are abandoning the traditional Sunday roast at home, along with the big leisurely breakfast, and combining both meals in one restaurant outing. As more hostelries opened up for Sundays and reaped full houses, the idea of such specials extended to later hours and slid into the afternoon and evening. Today these Sunday treats reach well into the dinner hour. The great advantage for the eating public is the fact that they're invariably cheaper, giving even the moderately heeled a chance to taste some grandiose cuisine in places they wouldn't ordinarily frequent. Some of the top-bracket hotels and dineries make it a point of honor (and propaganda) to lay on superlative spreads for the Sabbath feast at very moderate tabs. Word, as they say, gets around.

The specials listed here merely give an idea of what's available. The Saturday newspapers carry entire pages of other similarly priced ones:

The **Capilano Motor Inn,** 9125 50th St. (tel. 465-0765), has Sunday family smorgasbords—five hot dishes, six cold collations, plus salads—at $6.50 per adult, $3.75 per child. Tables spread from 12:30 to 7 p.m.

The **Corkscrew,** 10210 142nd St. (tel. 452-0160), features a buffet brunch from 10:30 a.m. to 2 p.m. Adults eat for $4.95, children for $3.50.

Deluxe brunch at the **Executive House,** 10155 105th St. (tel. 423-4811), runs from 9 a.m. to 1 p.m. costing adults $4.95; children, $3.50.

At the **Rex Motor Inn,** 6107 101st Ave. (tel. 466-2155), the family buffet goes from 4:30 to 8:30 p.m., offering a carved hip of beef, cabbage rolls, roast turkey, and pepper steak, all at $5.75 per adult, $3 per child.

The **Highway Inn,** 4520 76th Ave. (tel. 469-2351), has a family smorgasbord from 4 p.m. to 8 p.m. at $5.25 for adults, $2.95 for children.

Our last special is unconnected with Sunday. This is "New York Nite" at the **Saxony Motor Inn,** 156th St. and Stony Plain Rd. (tel. 484-3331). The night is every Tuesday and the scene the sumptuous Matador dining lounge of the inn. You get a ten-ounce New York steak, tossed salad, baked potato, vegetables, and garlic toast for $7.50 (also, top-rated entertainment by singers and bands, local and imported, as part of the menu).

DAYTIME ACTIVITIES: Edmonton's daylight action centers around that marvelous undulating ribbon of parkland that is the North Saskatchewan River Valley. The valley runs through the heart of the city, twisting, bending, and lush, providing totally unexpected vistas at every curve. The entire green belt on both sides of the river is a series of parks, sports grounds, recreation areas, and showplaces, and is in the process of developing more. By the time you get there, you may find a batch of new attractions which didn't exist when I researched this book.

Parks and Attractions in the River "Green Belt"

It's impossible to lump the area into one segment. You have to take it piece by piece, park by park. The point to remember is that they all form one continuous strip along the river, connected by roads, bridges, bike paths, hiking trails, and for boating folks, by the river itself. Dividing the actual parks from the other attractions, we have:

Borden Park: swimming and wading pools, baseball diamond, fully equipped playground.

Victoria Park: 18-hole golf course, horseshoe pitch, picnic facilities, free outdoor skating in winter.

William Hawrelak Park: a unique childrens' fishing lake, stocked with rainbow trout. Only kids—or adults accompanied by such—can fish there. In winter the lake becomes a skating rink. The park also has paddleboats, an "Adventure" playground, picnic and barbecue areas.

Emily Murphy Park: on the south bank of the river, with picnic facilities and two toboggan runs in winter.

Whitemud Park: on the south bank, with natural picnic areas around the creek, a riding academy with horses for trail rides, also a hang-gliding area— one of the biggest attractions for spectators and participants alike.

Kinsmen Park: the main feature here—the "Fitness Trail" for jogging, with interim exercise spots (less energetic folks can picnic).

Rundle Park: a new development at the eastern edge of the city, still in the process of completion, with a vast family recreation center, eight tennis courts, 18-hole golf course; also paddleboats, canoeing, fishing.

The above are by no means all the parks or all the facilities they offer. But they'll give you an idea of how wonderfully Edmontonians are utilizing the natural green belt they have so carefully preserved from becoming another strip of cement. Some of the attractions located within these park areas are:

Fort Edmonton, south bank over Quesnell Bridge, is a beautifully detailed reconstruction of the old Mounted Police stronghold and surrounding township, circa 1885. Inside the fort are the men's quarters, horse yard, and Indian trading store. Step outside and you're in a frontier town—homes, farmstead, stores, including McDougall's General, where you can buy some real old-fashioned stick candy (although not at 1885 prices). An oldtime steamboat lies moored to the riverbank, a trolley clanks through the street, and on the south side there's a small Indian encampment. Open till 6 p.m. daily. Admission is $2 for adults, 75¢ for children.

Valley Zoo, in Laurier Park, at the south end of Buena Vista Rd., is a charming combination of reality and fantasy, mingling real-live beasties with fairytale creations. Over 500 animals and birds are neighbors to the Three Little Pigs, Humpty Dumpty, and the inhabitants of Noah's Ark. Open till 6 p.m. daily. Admission is $1.50 for adults, 50¢ for children.

Nature Centre, adjoining Fort Edmonton, offers lectures and lessons on anything dealing with the great outdoors through programs run by qualified naturalists. You can learn to canoe on the river, go bird watching with a professional, learn about the causes and effects of the weather, get a crash course in astronomy, and so forth. Open till 4 p.m. weekdays, till 5 p.m. weekends. Admission free.

Queen Elizabeth Planetarium, Coronation Park, 135th St. and 112th Ave., uses a fascinating "Star Projector" with 32 optical systems as well as slide, movie, and special-effects projectors. With their aid you get closeups of some 2800 stars, the sun, moon, and planets of our solar system. In essence this is a multimedia theater putting on polished and immensely entertaining productions that blend astronomy with drama and superb artistry. Phone 455-0119 for show times (this is important, since late-comers are not admitted). Admission is $2 for adults, 75¢ for children.

Muttart Conservatory, off James MacDonald Bridge at 98th Ave. and 96A St., is housed in a group of four pyramidical pavilions that look like science-fiction structures. Actually they house one of the finest floral displays in America, but in a style quite different from other conservatories. Each pyramid contains a different climatic zone—the tropical one has an 18-foot waterfall as well. The Arid Pavilion has desert air and shows flowering cacti and their relatives. The temperate zone includes a cross section of native Canadian plants. The fourth pyramid features changing ornamental displays of plants and blossoms. Open till 9 p.m. Admission is $1 for adults, 25¢ for children.

John Walter Museum, south of the 105th St. Bridge at 10627 93rd Ave., is the site of the first home on the south side of the river, built in 1874. It gives a glimpse of early Edmonton as well as knowledge of one of its first settlers. It is also the site of the town's first telegraph station. Admission free.

The **Alberta Legislative Building,** 109th St. and 97th Ave., rises on the site of the early trading post from which the city grew. Surrounded by lovingly manicured lawns, formal gardens, and greenhouses, it overlooks the river valley. The seat of Alberta's government was completed in 1912, a stately Edwardian structure open to the public throughout the year. Conducted tours tell you about the functions of provincial lawmaking; who does what and where and for how long.

Elsewhere in the City

Now we step outside the park belt for daytime action throughout the city. This being Edmonton, several of these attractions are also located in parkland, separate from the river valley.

The **Provincial Museum,** 12845 102nd Ave. Modern and expertly laid out, this museum displays Alberta's natural and human history in four permanent galleries. The Habitat Group shows wildlife in natural settings, Indians and Fur Trade offers a glimpse of the region's original inhabitants, Natural History has fossils and dinosaurs, and History tells the pioneer story. The museum also puts on live artists and craftsmen and free film showings. Open till 9 p.m. Admission free.

Vista 33, 10020 100th St. Actually the head office of Alberta Government Telephones, this soaring square tower rises to 441 feet and has a helicopter landing pad on the roof. Vista 33, on the 33rd floor, commands an unsurpassed view: on clear days you can overlook some 2500 square miles. Within this radius lives nearly a third of the population of Alberta! Part of Vista is the **Man and Telecommunication Museum.** An intriguing mini-museum, this displays telephonic instruments, starting with a tiny manual switchboard from 1906 to the fully automated marvels used today. You have to pay 50¢ for the elevator ride up (half price for children). Vista stays open till 10 p.m. every night, when the lights of the city create a spectacular sight.

The pride of Edmonton, a $150-million hub of municipal government, industry, and art, the **Civic Centre** occupies the rectangle between Jasper and 103A Ave. at 100th St. This is the only formally planned civic center in Canada and includes:

City Hall (open Monday to Friday till 4 p.m.); the **Aviation Hall of Fame,** temporarily housed in the Law Courts Building, and a monument to the achievements of Canada's flying pioneers, inventors, and explorers (open Monday to Friday till 4 p.m., admission free); the **Edmonton Art Gallery,** which has a permanent art exhibition plus changing programs of lunchtime theater, film screenings, and concerts (open seven days a week till 5 or 10 p.m., admission free); and the **Public Library,** which apart from the customary books, offers live animals in the Children's Art Department, concerts, puppet shows, film screenings, and theater programs, and admission to all functions is free. (For the magnificent theater block called **Citadel,** see the "After Dark" section.)

The **Antique Motorcycle Museum,** 12510 82nd St., is an unusual showcase for classical two-wheelers and a magnet for every motoring buff. It contains 35 restored bikes dating back to the spidery, spluttering contraptions of 1901. Open Monday to Saturday till 6 p.m. Admission for adults is $1.50; children, free.

Dolls in Costume, 10462 82nd Ave., is a wonderful display of 3000 dolls wearing historic, ethnic, fairytale, and fantasy costumes, some of them superb. Open seven days a week till 5:30 p.m. Admission for adults is $1.75; for children, 75¢.

Northlands, 118th Ave. and 74th St., is a complex of parks, arenas, and buildings housing the Coliseum, Sportex, and Northland Parks racetrack, hosting a vast variety of sports events and other shows. The racetrack is the scene of the annual Canadian Derby as well as thoroughbred and harness racing. In May there is the annual Horse Show, followed nightly by a musical ride of the Royal Canadian Mounted Police—a superb equestrian spectacle. Tickets are $4.

EDMONTON AFTER DARK: The **Citadel Theatre,** 9828 101A Ave. A masterpiece of theatrical architecture, this is not a playhouse in the conventional sense but a community project encompassing virtually every form of stage-craft. The building looks like a gigantic greenhouse—more than half is glass walled; even the awnings are glass. The two-floor foyers, stage, restaurant, and seating facilities are ideal, the acoustics outstanding. But the best feature of the complex is that it houses several entirely different theaters and that it isn't confined to its premises but reaches out into the community.

The building has three auditoriums, workshops, and classrooms. It forms the home of the **Citadel Theatre Company,** which puts on performances ranging from Shakespeare to contemporary Canadian playwrights. The **Rice Theatre** uses a more adventurous style with emphasis on action and imagination. The **Shoctor Theatre** spans the stage gamut from classical Molière to musicals like *Hey Marilyn,* based on the career of La Monroe. The **Citadel-on-Wheels** is a mobile unit that takes plays—especially children's plays—to communities in Alberta, the Yukon, and Northwest Territories that have no resident live theater. Tickets range from $7 to $16. Watch for news of the programs in the newspapers and make a point of seeing at least one.

For good measure, the Citadel also contains the Alberta branch of the **National Film Theatre,** the exhibiting arm of the superlative Canadian Film Institute, by far the best of its kind on the American continent. Apart from commercial products, the institute also screens obscure film gems that hardly ever reach the ordinary box office outlets. Tickets cost from $2.75 to $3.50 for adults, $1 to $2 for children.

Edmonton also has formidable live theater action outside the Citadel. The **Northern Light Theatre,** 10189 99th St., is a new and very enterprising group of professionals using different stages for their productions. Their 1979 season, for instance, included *Piaf,* performed at the Art Gallery Theatre, and the jazz age *Eight to the Bar,* a musical put on at the Studio Theatre, University of Alberta campus. Tickets cost from $6 to $7.

Stage West, Mayfield Inn, 10910 Mayfield Rd., is a charming theater restaurant that combines excellent food with light-hearted, often sumptuously equipped, stage productions. Shows go on at 6 p.m. nightly, but there's also a highly unusual Sunday brunch show, starting at 11 a.m. Tickets (including meals) cost $16.50 at night, $11.95 for brunch.

Theatre 3, 10426 95th St., puts on contemporary plays like *P.S. Your Cat is Dead.* **Théâtre Français,** 8406 91st St., specializes in French plays from both sides of the Atlantic.

The **Jubilee Auditorium,** 87th Ave. and 115th St., is the setting for a great variety of concert and ballet performances. They range from the **Edmonton Symphony Orchestra** to the **Conservatoire de Ballet** and jazz specialties like *A Nite in New Orleans.*

Discos, Bars, Cabarets

Edmonton isn't quite as overrun with discos as other Canadian cities, although they're multiplying rapidly. At the moment they are more or less balanced out by "cabarets," which in Canada is strictly a licensing term.

Occasionally it may indicate a melange of different acts, but usually it means one live performer or band appearing the entire evening.

At the **Kingsway Inn,** 10812 Kingsway Ave. (tel. 479-4266), you get a taste of both styles. This entertainment center gives you a choice between hearing top Canadian and U.S. bands in their dining room, cabaret dancing in the Sumplacelse Cabaret, or romantic vocalists in the Tavern. Shows six nights a week.

The **Palms Cafe,** 10010 102nd St. (tel. 422-8205), is the home of the Edmonton Jazz Society, an outstanding group that plays till 1 a.m., although not regularly. Admission is $3 to $6 depending on the combo performing that night.

The **Tiki-Tiki,** 11723 Jasper Ave. (tel. 482-5478), serves up Islands cuisine together with Hawaiian and other Polynesian spectaculars. The Bora-Bora duck is outstanding here at $8.25. So was the big, drum-throbbing, grass skirt–swirling *Oto Ataonga Review* I saw there in a very romantic bamboo and lantern setting. Shows are seven nights a week.

The **Chevalier Grill** at the luxurious Château Lacombe (see hotel section) has an unusually versatile group called Etcetera: two ladies and two men singing and strumming through oldtime favorites, current pops, and occasional bouts of country music, a melange that manages to please nearly everybody some of the time. No cover charge on weeknights; Friday and Saturday, $1.50.

The **Discovery,** 9929 108th St. (tel. 929-6294), is an all-rounder, serving businessmen's lunches, stylish dinners, and late-night entertainment. The piano bar has an atmospheric keyboard artist in the person of Scott Alexander. The lounge features various performers, sometimes solo, sometimes in groups.

The **El Gato and Matador Lounges** at the Saxony Motor Inn (see hotel section) get some of the best variety acts in town, using both local and imported talent. Typical of their lineup for a given month was Armagh, one of Ireland's top bands, an Edmonton combo called Red Wyng, and a young Texas guitar and harmonica artist named Buddy Knox with his band.

Lucifer's, 9974 Jasper Ave. (tel. 425-0303), is a faintly devilish disco with the slogan "Just for the hell of it." It gets a youngish and well-dressed clientele and top show bands (which change every week). Dancing goes till 2 a.m. Monday to Saturday. Thursday is "Ladies Night" with no cover charge. Otherwise it's $3.

Edmonton has a trio of striptease places going by the label of burlesque, which is not strictly accurate. They feature nude dance acts—topless and bottomless—but hardly any of the variety and comedy routines that make a real burlesque show. In fact, few of the dancers even inject the "tease" part. They'll do one dance fully dressed, disrobe down to the last postage stamp, and dance another routine naked. The music is rock or disco, the dancing can be pretty good—bordering on a kind of erotic interpretive ballet—but of genuine striptease there mostly isn't a trace. Stripping while dancing is a highly specialized art, perhaps an almost lost one (like wheelwrighting or roof thatching).

Tracy Starr's, 10307 82nd Ave. (tel. 439-0883), features mini-Las Vegas–style shows from midday to 2:30 a.m. over steak and seafood dinners. No admission charge till 6 p.m., then $5.

Embers, 10052 106th St. (tel. 422-0609), has continuous shows and dining from 6:30 p.m. to 3 a.m. Cover charge is $5.

Chez Pierre's, 10615 Jasper Ave. (tel. 423-2707), calls itself "King of Striptease" and comes closest to the real thing, with shows from 9:30 p.m. to 2 a.m. The place is unlicensed, but your $5 admission pays for the entire evening and you can slip out, have a drink somewhere else, and get back in for the next number.

The above survey barely skims the surface of Edmonton's nightlife. For a more extensive coverage of the dining-dancing-entertainment scene, look for *Billy's Guide,* one of the slickest publications of its kind in the country. It comes out twice each month, and is available—gratis—in most hotels.

ATTRACTIONS OUT OF TOWN: Elk Island National Park, located on the Yellowhead Hwy. 20 miles east of Edmonton, is one of the most compact and prettiest of the national parks system. It is the home and roaming ground to North America's largest and smallest mammals: the wood buffalo and the pygmy shrew (a tiny creature half the size of a mouse, but with the disposition of a tiger). The park has hiking trails, campgrounds, golf courses, a lake, and sandy beach.

Alberta Game Farm, nine miles southeast of Edmonton on Hwy. 14, contains a collection of wildlife from every part of the world. Founded by Dr. Al Oeming, this reserve served as a remarkable study of how large animals—even from tropical climes—can adapt to the changing seasons of temperate Canada. Most of them grew winter furs although their original habitats had no winters. The farm is open till dark, and admission is $3 for adults, $2 for youths, free for children under 7.

Ukrainian Cultural Heritage Village, 30 miles east of Edmonton on Yellowhead Hwy. 16, is one of several exhibitions highlighting the great contribution made by immigrant Ukrainians to the art and cultural pattern of Alberta. Within Edmonton you'll find two more: The **Ukrainian Canadian Museum,** 9543 110th Ave., containing an array of ethnic artifacts and is open Saturday and Sunday only, and the **Ukrainian Museum,** 10611 110th Ave., open on Sundays and showing colorful peasant costumes, artistically painted Easter eggs, dolls, and hand-woven tapestries. Admission to all three sites is free.

Father Lacombe Museum, at St. Albert, 12 miles north of Edmonton on Hwy. 2, is housed in the original log chapel built by Father Lacombe in 1861 in what was then a howling wilderness. One of the earliest pioneer structures in the province, it's open daily till 9 p.m., admission free.

Klondike Days

The gold rush that sent an army of prospectors heading for the Yukon in 1898 put Edmonton "on the map," as they say. Although the actual gold fields lay 1500 miles to the north, the little settlement became a giant supply store, resting place, and "recreation" ground for thousands of men stopping there en route before tackling the hazards of the Klondike Trail that led overland to Dawson City in the Yukon. Edmonton's population doubled in size, and her merchants, saloon keepers, and ladies of easy virtue waxed rich in the process. Very few prospectors made their fortunes in the gold rush, but those who supplied them with equipment, food, liquor, and sex made theirs.

Since 1962 Edmonton has been celebrating the event with one of the greatest and most colorful extravaganzas staged in Canada. The Klondike Days are held annually in late July. Street festivities last five days, and the great Northlands Klondike Exposition goes on for another five.

Locals and visitors dress up in period costumes, street corners blossom with impromptu stages featuring anything from country bands to cancan girls, stage coaches rattle through the streets, parades and floats wind from block to block. Buildings all over town disappear behind false storefronts displaying merchandise from yesteryear. Clerks and bank managers work disguised as camp gamblers, waitresses become red-gartered saloon cuties. "Klondike Dollars" are the accepted coin of the realm for the duration (you can take those not spent home as souvenirs).

The new 16,000-seat **Coliseum** holds nightly spectaculars of rock, pop, or western entertainment, using imported top stage stars and superstars. Northlands Park turns into **Klondike Village,** complete with oldtime general store, barbershop, post office, and gambling saloon—iegal for this occasion only. The Citadel Theatre drops serious stage endeavors for a moment and puts on hilarious melodramas with mustachioed villains to hiss and dashing heros to cheer.

City Hall serves up immense "miners breakfasts" in the open air, massed marching bands compete in the streets, and down the North Saskatchewan River float more than 100 of the weirdest looking home-built rafts ever seen, racing for the "World Championship of Sourdough River Rafting." Presiding over all the action is "Klondike Kate," chosen from all of America's nightclub talent for cyclonic energy, a leather larynx, Junoesque figure, and a wide repertoire of Klondike-style songs and dancer.

Tourist Information

For any emergency calling for police, doctor, ambulance, fire brigade, or poison control, dial 911.

For information regarding Alberta Province, contact **Travel Alberta,** Capital Square, 10065 Jasper Ave. (tel. 427-4321)

For information concerning Edmonton, contact the **City Visitors Bureaus:** downtown at 10145 100th St. (open Monday through Friday till 4:30 p.m.; tel. 422-5505); or southside at 5068 103rd St. (open seven days a week till 4:30 p.m.; tel. 434-5322).

Tours and Excursions

The simplest and cheapest of all sightseeing tours in town is operated by **Edmonton Transit,** the city bus service. This is **Route 123,** the Discovery Ring. Run on Sundays and holidays only (afternoons), and only in one direction, Route 123 buses (clearly marked) take in a circular tour you can board at any of the stopping points, which include the city's main attractions: Government Centre, Provincial Museum, Valley Zoo, Fort Edmonton, Nature Centre, and University of Alberta. Tickets cost the normal bus fare of 50¢ for adults, 25¢ for children. For further information about this tour, call 432-1234.

Multipak Excursions, 15041 85th Ave. (tel. 483-0949), offers five different jaunts, including a rather unusual one. The **Edmonton Overview** covers most of the inner city sights and includes a drive through the river valley to the University of Alberta campus and a tour of the Provincial Museum. Tours depart daily in summer from three major hotels and take three hours. Tickets are $6.50 for adults, $3 for children.

Edmonton as It Was puts the accent on historical sites such as Fort Edmonton, 1885 St., and the John Walter Site (the original residence of one of the first families to settle in Edmonton and containing all the period furniture, the artwork, and much of the hardware then in use). Tours operate daily and take three hours. Adults are charged $7.50; children, $3.50.

A quite unique excursion for travelers with pampered palates and a leaning for luxury, **Epicurean's Delight** gives you Edmonton in a velvet package by twilight and includes cocktails, hors d'oeuvres and a gourmet dinner as well as the sights. The trip starts each evening appropriately at the Château Lacombe Hotel and has a cocktail intermission at the Edmonton Country Club.

The finale is a glorious repast at La Ronde, the largest revolving restaurant in Canada. It costs $30 per person, and reservations are required 72 hours in advance.

The **Grayline,** 102022 102nd St. (tel. 423-2765), offers a choice of three main tours, all running daily during the summer months. The **Parkland Drive** covers 30 miles in 2½ hours, visits Muttart Conservatory and Botanical Gardens, and goes through the river valley as well as taking in city sights. Admission prices are included in the ticket costs: adults pay $6.50; children, half price.

The **Deluxe City Tour** visits the Civic Centre, the Legislative Buildings, University of Alberta, and Jubilee Auditorium. You get a stop at Fort Edmonton and the view from Vista 33 in the Telephones Tower. The tour takes 3½ hours, and admission prices are included in the cost. Tickets for adults are $8.50; children, half price.

The **Alberta Game Farm** tour takes you over the 1600-acre habitat of big game animals and exotic birds from other parts of the world. It involves considerable walking, so wear comfortable shoes. The trip lasts 3½ hours and covers 45 miles. Admission prices are included. Adults pay $8.75; children, $4.50.

4. Elsewhere in Alberta

The main magnets for visitors to Alberta (apart from the Calgary Stampede and Edmonton's Klondike Days) are the 53 provincial and 5 national parks. We have already dealt with Banff and Jasper, and mentioned Elk Island.

Wood Buffalo National Park is the world's largest, measuring 17,300 square miles—bigger than Switzerland. Two-thirds lie inside Alberta, one-third in the Northwest Territories. The park was created for the specific purpose of preserving the last remaining herd of wood bison on earth. At the turn of the century these animals were near extinction. Today some 8000 of the big shaggies roam their habitat, where you can see and snap them in droves.

The park is also the only known breeding ground for the majestic whooping crane. Some 50 of these birds live there from April until October before migrating to their winter range along the Gulf of Mexico.

Waterton Lakes National Park, in the southwestern corner of the province, is linked with Glacier National Park in neighboring Montana. Once the hunting ground of the Blackfoot Indians, this 203-square mile sanctuary has Upper Waterton Lake straddling the U.S. border. A lake steamer links the Montana with the Alberta shore. The park nestles against the eastern slopes of the Rockies and its animal life includes cougars, coyotes, big horn sheep, and white-tailed deer.

Alberta has the greatest variety of geographical features among Canada's provinces: soaring mountain ranges, table-flat prairies, huge lakes, dense forests, and even a patch of subtropical oasis called **Cypress Hills.**

You can divide the province into four distinct areas, each with its special scenic attractions: first, the Canadian Rockies, in the west; then the land of rolling prairies and rich agriculture that starts at the U.S. border and reaches some 300 miles north; next the so-called parkland, with broad valleys, high ridges, lakes, streams, and small stands of timber; finally, the region comprising the whole northern half of the province—huge lakes and forests broken by tracts of open prairie and the sweeping terraces of the **Peace River Valley.**

Across the exact center of the province, east to west, runs the **Yellowhead Hwy.,** from Saskatchewan to British Columbia. This scenic route is named after an Iroquois trapper and scout with a trace of white blood that gave a blonde tinge to his hair. His real name was Pierre Hatsinaton, but the French voyageurs called him Tête Jaune—yellow head. Tête Jaune worked as a guide for the Hudson's Bay Company and explored much of the route now followed by the highway that bears his name. Guiding ranked among the highest of high-risk occupations. In 1827, on the British Columbia side of the mountains, a swarm of Beaver Indians fell upon Tête Jaune, his brother, their wives, and their children, and killed them all.

Rocky Mountain House, halfway between Edmonton and Calgary, is actually a town. Established in 1799 as a fort of the North West Company, the place exported great bales of otter, sable, fox, and other furs annually. Today this is one of the fastest growing towns in the province, but has taken great care to preserve the landmarks of its colorful history.

At **Innisfail,** to the southeast, the Royal Canadian Mounted Police has its dog training center. Unfortunately the kennels are open to the public only on Sundays between 2 and 3:30 p.m. But if you can manage to be in the area then, don't miss seeing the magnificent police shepherds go through their paces.

Land of the Mighty Peace is the name given to the region around the confluence of the Peace and Smoky Rivers. This is a land of gold-rush trails and explorers' passages, where summer twilight lingers till midnight and monuments to early explorers dot the landscape. The center of the region is the **Peace River,** some 300 miles northwest of Edmonton. A landmark of the town is the statue and grave marker of "Twelve-Foot Davis," on the river's east bank (Davis was a prospector who staked out a 12-foot claim between much larger ones during the Cariboo gold rush and dug out a bonanza). The **Peace River Museum** contains, among other memorabilia, a riverboat which used to ply the stream between Fort St. John and Vermillion.

Each July the annual jet boat river races are run from Grande Cache to Peace River, with contestants coming from as far as Mexico and Australia. You can ride a jet boat yourself by going on the **Tar Island River Cruise** which runs from the town to Tar Island, about 40 miles downstream, and stops there overnight.

Alberta's lake country stretches from St. Paul, about 130 miles northeast of Edmonton, to the border of the Northwest Territories. Vast and beautiful, it gets emptier the farther north you go, and includes the Wood Buffalo National Park. This is *big* country in every sense of the word—the lakes are big, the fish are big, and the largest oil deposits in Canada are located here. There's wonderful lake and river fishing for trout, pike, perch, goldeye, and walleye.

The trading center of the area is **St. Paul,** which has constructed a world-famous centennial project—a "Flying Saucer Landing Pad," ready to receive whatever creatures may materialize from a *Close Encounter of the Third Kind.*

At **Vegreville** stands the world's largest Ukrainian Easter egg, gaily painted and towering over 30 feet tall in Elk Park. This "pysanka" was constructed in 1974 to commemorate the 100th anniversary of the arrival of the Royal Canadian Mounted Police in Alberta. You can camp all around the egg and, if you get there early in July, watch the annual Ukrainian Festival with singing, music, and leg-throwing folk dances.

Lac La Biche is the communal heart of one of the greatest fishing areas in Canada. There are 50 shimmering lakes around the town, teeming with game. In July and early August the Blue Feathers Fish Derby is held here, the biggest such event in the province.

If you want to get the feel of oil sand—more treasured than gold these days—go to **Fort McMurray.** The home of the Athabasca tar sands, the stuff is so rich in "black gold" that you can pick up a handful of sand and squeeze out oil. It's also a large and thriving community with motor hotels and golf courses.

RANCH AND FARM VACATIONS: Alberta offers a variety of ranch and farm vacations, divided into guest ranches, working ranches, working farms, and hobby farms. Typical of the guest ranches is **Rafter Six,** about 50 miles west of Calgary. There is a log chalet, stables, swimming pool, and barbecue facilities, with accommodations for 60 people in the lodge and individual cabins. The rooms cost $26 for singles, $30 for doubles. Contact Rafter Six Guest Ranch, Seebe, AB T0L 1X0 (tel. 403/673-3622).

For a working farm, there's **Broadview,** which has accommodations in the farm home as well as tent and trailer camping. Apart from farm activities, you can swim, boat, and golf nearby. Rates for room and board are $15 a day (children up to 6, half price). Contact R. Young, R.R. 2, Milet, AB T0C 1Z0 (tel. 403/387-4963).

A hobby farm is a somewhat different proposition, more like a country retreat. While most hobby farms have horses and some raise cattle and feed, their main source of income doesn't stem from farming. **Tanglefoot Lake Farm** has a lodge and a small cabin for its guests, with outdoor toilets, and bathroom facilities in the farmhouse. There's boating, swimming, lawn games, and hiking. The lodge and cabin have their own cooking facilities, and rates range from $15 to $25 a day. Contact K. Keates, P.O. Box 407, Alix, AB T0C 0B0 (tel. 403/747-2247).

Chapter XVI

BRITISH COLUMBIA

1. Vancouver
2. Victoria and Vancouver Island
3. Elsewhere in British Columbia

CANADA'S MOST WESTERLY PROVINCE can be all things to all men—or pretty nearly so. Its outstanding characteristic is variety; scenically, climatically, and socially.

In the southwest, near the Washington State border, the country is densely populated, with large sophisticated cities, a sunny coastline dotted with resorts and belts of rich farmlands raising dairy cattle on lush pastures. But in the north, where the province borders on Alaska and the Yukon, the settlements are tiny, and most of the land is a starkly beautiful wilderness ruled by bush pilots and frontiersmen. In between these extremes you get wide-open ranch-lands with cowboys riding herd, ocean fjords as deep and blue as those of Norway, glacier icefields, huge birch and maple forests, thousands of lakes, valleys glowing with ripening fruit, vineyards on the hillsides, and a patch of genuine sand desert—the only one in Canada.

Holding the province together like two immense bolts are the Coast Mountains along the Pacific and the Canadian Rockies straddling the border with Alberta, culminating in their highest peak, Mount Robson.

British Columbia is a huge province of 366,255 square miles, more than twice the size of California—but with a mere 2½ million people, most of them concentrated in the southern portion. This leaves the bulk of the province a thinly settled haven of natural wonders, a place to clear your eyes and lungs of the grit and grime of industralized society and to reattune noise-deafened ears to bird calls, rustling winds, and the burble of mountain streams.

Over a million acres of the province has been set aside in five national parks—four in the mountainous wilds of the east-central region, one on the west coast of Vancouver Island. Add to this the 11 million acres of provincial parks, which range from handkerchief proportions to huge, and you'll get an idea of how the Columbians cherish and preserve their natural heritage.

And their historical as well. Throughout the province you come across so-called petroglyph sites. These are rock drawings made by unknown tribes in the primordial past, now carefully maintained as the earliest indicators of a human presence in the area.

The later explorers, fur traders, and pioneer settlers have their mementos in Fort Langley, a fully restored fur-trading post, in Fort Defiance on Vancouver Island, and in Fort James near Prince George. The Cariboo gold rush of the 1860s is preserved at Barkerville, a township that seems to have stepped out of a photograph of the gold dust boom years. Fort Steele is a living memorial to the North West Mounted Police, the entire fort recreated as a settlement of the 1890s, complete with steam train, general store, smithy, and saloons.

But let's begin in the populous south, with the bustling city of—

1. Vancouver

In the extreme southwestern corner of British Columbia, just 25 miles above the U.S. border, there is a place where mountains and ocean seem to have had a love affair and given birth to a city. The city is Vancouver, and few towns have been quite so wonderfully blessed with their setting as this one. Among the world's great harbor towns only Rio de Janeiro can match her scenic combination of mountain peaks towering over silver-green waters, with the city nestling between.

Vancouver is a metropolis of unforgettable views, vistas of ocean and mountains that spring on you suddenly, when you least expect them. Because her streets are hilly and her harbor splintered into scores of inlets, you can turn a busy downtown corner and find yourself faced with a panorama less fortunate urbanites have to drive for hours to glimpse.

Combine this setting with a relatively balmy climate, one of the world's finest natural deep-sea ports, and a native passion for parks and greenery, and you'll understand why Vancouverites take a positively narcissistic delight in their habitat—an opinion, incidentally, which is continually reinforced by the legions of visitors flocking in summer and winter from every part of the continent.

With around 1.2 million inhabitants Vancouver is—after Montréal and Toronto—the third-largest city in Canada. To complete her delights she has—after Montréal—the best restaurants in the land. On top of that she has a fascinatingly cosmopolitan population: her Chinatown is (after San Francisco's) the biggest in America, and portions of her main drag are so thoroughly Europeanized that it bears the unofficial title of Robsonstrasse.

Vancouverites also possess that reverence for their past without which a city very quickly loses its character and becomes an anonymous assembly kit. Instead of leveling their oldest patch, which had deteriorated into a wino-ridden slum, they lovingly restored its crooked alleys, brushed, painted, and dry-cleaned them, and thus turned Gastown into a major tourist attraction, crammed with boutiques, galleries, and eateries, and boasting the only working steam clock on the continent.

Until about 15 years ago, Vancouver had the reputation of being as dull as she was pretty. But as her downtown area changed from pokey provincial to streamlined splendiferous, the texture of her nightlife kept pace. Nowadays it's not only alive, but kicking up its heels in no uncertain fashion. Vancouverites have learned to eat late, drink late, and play late and hard. And in this they're merely treading in the footsteps of their colonial forebears who were—by all accounts—a rather rambunctious lot.

The city was named after Capt. George Vancouver, who took over the minute settlement of Nootka from the Spaniards in 1790. (Puget Sound, incidentally, got its name from Vancouver's lieutenant, Peter Puget, who helped him explore the area.) However, Vancouver was preceded by the township of New Westminster (today practically a suburb) and didn't come into being until the arrival of a very colorful Yorkshireman named John Deighton.

Mr. Deighton stepped ashore from a canoe, accompanied by his Indian mistress, a dog, and a barrel of whiskey. With the aid of the barrel's contents,

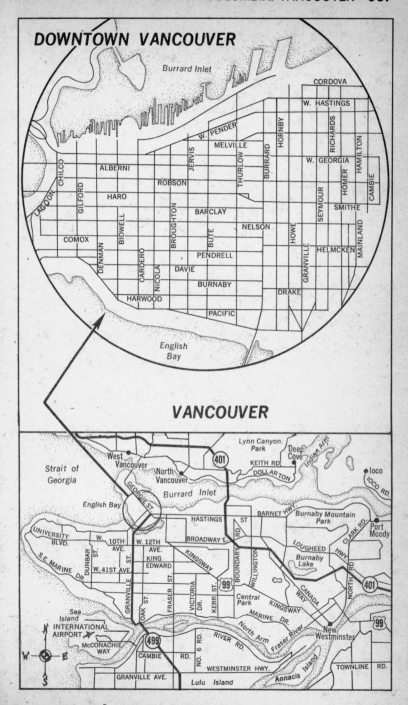

DOWNTOWN VANCOUVER

VANCOUVER

plus a natural gift of gab, he persuaded some local sawmill workers to help him build a saloon—the first structure of future Vancouver! Other saloons, plus stores and a hotel, followed, the development attracted mainly by Deighton's unceasing eloquence, which earned him the nickname of "Gassy Jack."

By 1871 the community known as Gastown, after its honorary mayor, was as notorious for knifings and fistfights as for its indefatigable spokesman. But four years later respectability caught up with it. Gastown was incorporated as the city of Vancouver—counting 2500 souls and a dozen saloons. Over the decades the center shifted south and Gastown became Vancouver's Skid Row, shunned by the saintlier majority, until its recent resurrection.

ORIENTATION: Today's Vancouver, Canada's gateway to the Pacific, is centered on a tongue of land between the Burrard Inlet to the north and the Fraser River to the south, but sprawls out into vast suburbs in both directions. A galaxy of bridges—some magnificent, some mediocre—span the waterways, which cover the entire area like lacework. Overlooking the scene are the peaks of the Coast Mountains, which loom so close that they seem within climbing range from downtown. The nearest, Grouse Mountain, actually lies 20 driving minutes away.

Vancouver has a brand-new (in fact, unfinished) focus and orientation point—**Robson Square.** A three-block complex of terraces, gardens, waterfalls, restaurants, exhibition halls, skating rink, theaters, and government buildings, this is an absolutely ideal spot from which to get your bearings. It's almost the city's dead center and also houses the **Visitors Information Bureau,** where a highly knowledgeable and angelically patient staff will answer any—well, nearly—question you might hurl at them.

Stand on the square's top terrace and look toward the old **Court House,** soon to become an art gallery. You are now facing due west, the direction of the Pacific Ocean and **Stanley Park,** a wonderful green oasis the size of the entire downtown area.

To the north of you lies the **Burrard Inlet,** spanned by the First Narrows and Second Narrows Bridges, which take you to suburban West and North Vancouver and, farther away, to Grouse Mountain. Your southern view is encircled by the crescent shape of **False Creek,** spanned by the Burrard and Granville Bridges. On the far side lies **Vanier Park,** containing the Maritime Museum and the Planetarium. To the west stretches the big and beautiful acreage of the **University of British Columbia.** Southwest, across an arm of the Fraser River and yet another bridge, is **Sea Island,** Richmond, on which the International Airport is located. Due south there's a lot more of residential Vancouver and the road leading to Tsawwassen, departure point of the ferries sailing across the strait to **Vancouver Island,** seat of the provincial capital.

Due east runs the Trans Canada Hwy., traversing the country from coast to coast, leading to the Fraser Valley and other beauty spots.

Downtown

Now back to your immediate surroundings. Running straight west, all the way to Stanley Park, is **Robson St.,** the main eating and shopping strip. Despite its Teutonic nickname, Robson isn't all that German, but Italian, French, Indian, Polish, and half a dozen other ethnic colorations. You can spend days strolling its length and constantly discover new variations.

Running vertically to the east is the **Granville Mall,** a reserve for the infantry carved out of Granville St. As pedestrian malls go, it doesn't work too well: there are too few benches, too little greenery, not enough outdoor cafes (compared to, say, Rotterdam or Cologne), and portions of it have become rather tacky stomping grounds for teenagers, reeking of soggy chips and chicken batter. And although the mall is closed to all but privileged vehicles, there are so many of those—including cabs, squad cars, buses, ambulances, and delivery vans—that you still have to look right and left before crossing over. Creating a real mall means more than just marking a few blocks (Europe and Australia are way ahead of Canada there).

Running west and east of you, through the mall, is **Georgia St.,** which contains the post office as well as some of the city's poshest hotels and stores. Northeast, close to the harborfront, lies **Gastown,** and adjoining it, **Chinatown.** A few blocks to the west of them is the VIA Railway Depot, the terminal for the Seabus, and the superbly designed **Harbour Centre,** which ranks as a major sight.

About half of the downtown streets, incidentally, are one way, and if you're driving you'd better reconcile yourself to never getting from point to point by the shortest route.

Transportation

Vancouver is serviced by **B.C. Hydro,** an excellent if rather expensive system of single-decker buses and trolleys, and by a variety of harbor ferries. These include the famous **Seabus,** a science-fiction apparatus that skims you from the Granville Waterfront Station across the Burrard Inlet to Lonsdale Quay in 12 breathless minutes. It runs every quarter hour during the day and costs 50¢.

The **Downtown Hustler** runs from the airport and costs $3 (the same trip by cab would set you back about $9). Standard **bus** fare is 50¢ for any distance, including transfers—and remember to have the exact change. The Hydro also operates the **Shopper Freebus,** a gratis lift for shoppers that functions at ten-minute intervals, six days a week, between Royal Centre, Harbour Centre, Gastown, Chinatown, and Granville Mall. For further bus information, call 683-2421.

Cabs are plentiful (except when it's raining) and cheap compared to the rates we'll encounter way up north. Flagfall is $1, and each mile after that costs 80¢. Some of the major taxi companies are: **Advance Cabs** (tel. 876-5555), **Diamond Cabs** (tel. 683-2111), and **Yellow Cabs** (tel. 681-3311).

There's also a vast choice of rental-car outfits. But before giving you some sample addresses, a few words on driving in Vancouver. The city has a blitz mechanism for pedestrians—a little walking figure—which appears for about 15 seconds. Given the generally broad streets, not even the nimblest footslogger can scuttle across in the time permitted. So watch out for pedestrians dashing over after you've been given the go sign. Otherwise, traffic is very well regulated and urban speed limits are *enforced.* As in California, you're allowed to turn right against a red light. Motorists, on the whole, are well disciplined and bear no resemblance to the wheeled maniacs you'll meet in Québec. For **rental cars,** try: **Tilden,** 1058 Alberni St. (tel. 685-6111; for out-of-town reservations, tel. 273-7755); **Budget,** 450 W. Georgia St. (tel. 685-0536); **Hertz** (Canamerican), 898 Burrard St. (tel. 688-2411); or **Avis,** 757 Hornby St. (tel. 682-1621).

Vancouver generally, and her vast acreage of parks in particular, is good **cycling** territory. No U.S. city I know of pays as much heed to the needs of the pedal pushers. Every park and a good many ordinary thoroughfares have special bike tracks. Bicycling today is one of the leading Canadian sports, and every second kid seems to be riding one, with more and more adults getting into the saddle as well. This is by far the best way to cover the city's green portions, quite apart from the healthy exercise involved. At 676 Chilco St., opposite the Stanley Park bus loop, you'll find **Bicycle Stanley Park** (tel. 681-5581). They'll rent you a three-speed bike for $1.75 an hour or $7 a day, and a ten-speed for $2.50 an hour, $9 a day. Each rented bike requires a $10 deposit.

ACCOMMODATIONS: Vancouver is a tourist town par excellence, but even so the accommodation scene tends to get pretty tight during peak season, July through the first half of September. The best way of assuring a pillow for the night is to book ahead. Please note that all rates given below are subject to a 5% provincial tax.

Luxury

The **Four Seasons,** 791 W. Georgia St. (tel. 604/689-9333), is a midtown palace so discreetly blended into the Pacific Centre complex that you could walk right past it without noticing. This is no accident—the entire international Four Seasons chain has this aversion to glaring neon signs and a penchant for subtly understated luxury that gives them a special mark of their own, like a tiny artist's signature on a priceless painting.

The same leitmotif permeates their bedrooms. They're unostentatiously beautiful, graceful and sleek in pastel hues, with a lot of little touches that caress you like velvet: thick, fluffy bath towels, sink tops of genuine marble, a clock radio that wakes you with music, bedside TV controls, complimentary shampoos of top quality, 24-hour room service that is really *service.*

Apart from bedrooms you'll never want to leave, the Seasons has a world-class restaurant (see the dining section) and possibly the most gorgeous cocktail bar in all Canada. The Garden Lounge, beneath a huge skylight, is an indoor setting of trees, shrubs, and flowers, with a shimmering fountain at the center and a pianist in the background. The hotel also cleans your shoes overnight, runs its own for-hire limousines, and boasts a service desk that organizes anything—from bridge partners to bodyguards.

Rates run from $46 to $60 for singles, $60 to $74 for doubles, with suites ranging from $140 to $365.

You can't, on the other hand, possibly miss the **Hotel Vancouver,** 900 W. Georgia St. (tel. 604/684-3131). A stately, massive landmark, dominating the skyline against a backdrop of mountains, this is the oldest and most traditional of the city's deluxe hostelries. Designed on a generous scale, the Vancouver has big everything: bedrooms, bathtubs, hallways, elevators—all give you a feeling of wonderful spaciousness. The hotel breathes old-style comforts, starting with the mighty armchairs and svelte showcases in the brown-russet lobby, large enough to swallow up all bustle and retain an oasis-air of contemplative serenity.

The decor of the bedrooms is tastefully subdued—brown tones and light-gray carpets—and the thick, soundproof walls guarantee good slumber. You get magnificent views from the windows, magnifying shaving mirrors in the bathrooms, and impeccable service. Plus, of course, air-conditioning, color TV, and superbly sprung beds. In the same building (which could house an entire village) there are three cocktail lounges, each with a distinctive atmosphere, a couple of gourmet restaurants, and high above you the **Panorama Roof,** one of Vancouver's plushest nightspots.

Rates go from $40 to $60 for singles, $52 to $72 for doubles, with suites running from a mere $70 to $350.

Like all hotels by that name, the **Hyatt Regency,** 655 Burrard St. (tel. 604/687-6543), greets you with a stunning lobby. Vast and gleaming subtly in brown and beige, it sprawls into a sumptuous shopping arcade and features an outstanding hostess service, prepared to answer questions like "Where can I play racquetball?" in about 17 languages, including Czech and Indonesian.

The Hyatt is a gleaming white tower built over a huge shopping mall, which means that you need never stir from shelter. It also houses an ultra-sleek disco, the Truffles Exchange (of which more in the nightlife segment). The 656 rooms, all brightly elegant, come with electric blankets, carpeted bathrooms, digital clock radios, and refrigerators. The color TV sets screen house feature films on request, and the soundproofing is an engineering feat. The hotel also offers two saunas, a deluxe dinery, a charmingly intimate bar, and the Polaris Lounge, which you reach in a glass elevator rising on the outside of the building, and which presents a panoramic view from the 34th floor that almost interferes with your dining, drinking, and dancing activities.

Singles go from $48 to $76; doubles, from $62 to $80; and the suites, from $100 to $400.

The **Bayshore Inn,** 1601 W. Georgia St. (tel. 604/682-3377), rises ivory-white against a resort-like background of ocean and mountains, with Stanley Park as a kind of garden extension. Yet it's almost right downtown, with the main shopping streets a few walking minutes away—a combination of every advantage Vancouver has to offer.

There is a distinct Mediterranean touch about the place, particularly in the scenic Marine Lounge. Somehow the Polynesian trimmings of Trader Vic's blend nicely with the premises. So does the circular outdoor swimming pool, surrounded by a sundeck, lush greenery, and rock gardens. The bedrooms, beautifully light, have individual climate control, electric blankets, alarm clocks, and picture windows covering an entire wall. And the view below shows a dazzling array of luxury yachts bobbing at anchor along the marina.

You pay from $45 to $61 for single rooms, from $57 to $73 for doubles, with suites starting at $95 and climbing to $235.

Moderate

Several of the establishments in this bracket have bottom rates as high as those rated luxury. The reason why they can rank as "moderate" is that they offer suites or apartments for the price of a room in the deluxe category.

This goes for the **Château Granville,** 1100 Granville St. (tel. 604/669-7070), an impressive white structure housing 100 very attractive suites. Each consists of a living room, a bedroom and bathroom, a "wet bar" with sink tucked away behind a screen, and a few extra touches like two telephones, refrigerators, bathrooms with heat lamps, and small balconies.

The hotel opened in 1977 and has all the modern conveniences you'd expect from its youth, including a Xerox machine in the lobby. The lobby is quite small, the hotel very large, with a lot of space devoted to the Coffee Garden, a splendidly traditional dining room (leather settees and ancestral paintings in gold frames), a flag-decked cocktail bar, plus conference and penthouse boardrooms.

The rates, based on floor elevation, run from $45 to $55 for singles, $50 to $60 for doubles, with children under 18 free in their parents' room.

The **Sheraton-Landmark,** 1400 Robson St. (tel. 604/687-0511), prides itself on being Vancouver's tallest hotel—a soaring tower of 42 floors, with a revolving restaurant at the peak (see my dining recommendations). The lobby is fairly small and unimpressive, but the hotel houses 356 rooms, saunas, a tavern-nightclub, cocktail lounge, penthouse suites, and no fewer than 20 meeting rooms, apart from a coffeeshop, underground garage, and a foreign exchange bank. It also has airport limousine service, super-fast elevators, and excellent soundproofing.

The bedrooms are medium sized, air-conditioned, and very well equipped. All have private balconies, cable TV and radio, piped-in music, and walk-in closets. The bathrooms come with heat lamps to give you an after-shower glow, and some boast refrigerators as well.

Rates go from $33 to $43 for singles, $38 to $48 for doubles, while the suites range from $125 to $200.

Directly opposite the Sheraton stands the **Riviera Motor Inn,** 1431 Robson St. (tel. 604/685-1301). An up-to-the-minute former apartment block converted into an apartment hotel, this is an exceptionally good nest for lengthier stays, with its small lobby, impeccably maintained corridors, and a total of 40 units (14 studios and 26 one-bedroom apartments). The units have everything that makes for complete independence: kitchens fully equipped with cooking and eating utensils, all-electric ranges with ovens, dining areas, and refrigerators. The bedrooms are spacious and airy, with little balconies, three hanging closets, wide beds, color TV, dial telephones, and lots of elbow room, all in bright, modern pastel shades. Maid service is included in the rates, and the beautiful views from the upper floors come free.

You pay $30 for singles, $34 for doubles, $3 for each additional person in a unit.

The **Mayfair Hotel,** 845 Hornby St. (tel. 604/687-6751), is another converted apartment building, situated opposite Robson Square. Don't be misled by the no-frills frontage and drab lobby of this establishment—it's among the best accommodation deals in town. Of the 89 rooms, about two-thirds have their own kitchens with every cooking and eating gadget except coffee pots.

The bedrooms are large and homey as well as excellently maintained, lots of lights overhead, at the tables, and bedside, and lots of wardrobe space in the walk-in closets, plus small balconies overlooking the heart of downtown, bathrooms with electric ventilators to get the steam out, a separate eating area, dial phones, wall-to-wall carpeting, and an exceptionally attentive management. The airport bus stops just a block away, and you have a first-rate restaurant on one side and a swinging disco on the other in the same building.

Singles go from $21 to $31; doubles, from $26 to $38; with special weekly rates, from $133 to $245.

The **Hotel Grosvenor,** 840 Howe St. (tel. 604/681-0141), is also a quite unostentatious reddish brick building that hides high-quality comfort behind a plain facade. The manager, Robert Lyon, takes tremendous pride in his hostelry, which shows at every step. Above the spacious, comfortable lobby (with coffeeshop-restaurant) there are 130 rooms in restful brown and orange colors, special fire stairs (rated among the best of their kind in Canada), and ceilings with acoustic tiles designed to muffle noise.

Hallways and corridors are lovingly groomed. The medium-sized bedrooms come with color TV and dial telephones, some with radios as well. And you'll find no wire hangers in the closets—Mr. Lyon insists on wooden ones in his hotel. The bathrooms have heat lamps, big soft towels, and complimentary shower caps.

Rates depend on whether you want extra-long or standard beds, ranging from $24 to $30 for singles, $28 to $30 for doubles (triple bedrooms from $34 to $36).

The medium-sized, medium-priced **Hotel Devonshire,** 849 W. Georgia St. (tel. 604/681-5481), has a pleasant brown lobby, softly lit, plus some of the most popular eateries and drinkeries in Vancouver's downtown area. These include the Dev Seafood House, the gourmet-oriented Carriage Room, a coffee-house overlooking a sparkling fountain, and an entertainment lounge titled El Beau. There are also gift shops, a hairdresser, men's wear stores, a complete convention center, and a panoramic wall map with buttons you can push to light up the major landmarks of the city.

The 145 bedrooms, serviced by speedy elevators, include a proportion with telephones in the bathroom and two double beds pushed together to provide an enormous sleeping space. Otherwise the fittings are good, tasteful standard, with ample wardrobe space, color TV, and better than usual lighting arrangements.

Singles range from $30 to $37; doubles, from $36 to $43.

There's a distinct nautical air about the **Nelson Place Hotel,** 1006 Granville St. (tel. 604/681-6341), which invites you to "lay anchor" there and provides a Quarterdeck Lounge, rope-coiled pillars in the lobby, and a Nelsonian nine-pounder gun covering its pub. It also offers free limousine service from the airport by reimbursing the fare to its guests. The 100 bedrooms are rather narrow and have no ceiling lights, only table and bedside illumination. The bathrooms are spacious, modern, and fluorescently lit, there's lots of hanging space, the decor is a pleasing soft brown, and the walls are hung with intriguingly ancient maps of the globe.

Single rooms go from $20 to $22; doubles, from $22 to $28; and children under 12 stay free when using their parents' room.

The **Centennial Lodge,** 1111 Burnaby St. (tel. 604/684-8763), is a charmer of an apartment hotel, located in a quiet backwater of the busy West End. A tall green modern structure, the lodge offers 50 brand-spanking-new units, either studios or one-bedroom suites. Each apartment is completely self-contained, nicely furnished in striking contemporary color schemes, and has a little balcony, dial phone, color TV, and thermostat heat control.

Kitchens and bathrooms are excellently equipped; all-electric, with every utensil you might need, including toasters, can openers, and knives that actually cut. The living rooms are spacious and designed to catch all the sunshine available. The beds are well sprung, closet space more than ample, the carpeting deep green and wall to wall. There are leather settees and armchairs as well as a dining table, with handy shelves hidden behind folding doors. The entire layout keeps the correct balance between clutter and bareness, and the lighting fixtures could serve as models for those establishments which assume that tourists never do anything but watch television in their abodes.

Studios rent for $24 to $28 per night, $120 to $140 weekly, while the one-bedroom suites cost from $28 to $32 nightly, from $160 to $180 weekly.

Yet another apartment hotel, the **Greenbrier,** 1393 Robson St. (tel. 604/683-4558), features a very indifferent lobby and exterior, but surprisingly good living quarters. A smallish three-story building, the Greenbrier has 31 self-contained units, each with large kitchen, medium-sized sitting room, and small bedroom. The furniture is neither new nor glamorous, but ample. Each unit has one huge walk-in closet plus a little one, bedrooms, with dressing tables and good bedside lights, kitchens with dining tables, electric ranges, and wonderfully spacious refrigerators, and spick-and-span bathrooms with tubs and showers. The units are nicely carpeted and equipped with color TV and dial phones. They'll accommodate up to five persons, although this maximum may be a bit of a crunch.

Singles go for $24, doubles for $28, with each additional person paying $4.

Finally in this bracket we have the **Skyline Airport Hotel,** 3031 No. 3 Rd., Richmond (tel. 604/278-5161). As the name indicates, this is an airport hostelry and maintains a courtesy limousine service to the terminal. About 15 driving minutes from downtown, the Skyline is ideal for overnight stops, featuring an outdoor pool, a large, sumptuous dining room, sauna, and coffeeshop, with well-oiled room service catering to those poor wretches who have to catch early-morning flights.

The 130 bedrooms are remarkably immune to jet screams, furnished in good motel style and equipped with luxuriously spacious beds guaranteed to get the economy-flight cramps out of your knees. They come in singles, doubles, twins, double doubles, family, mini-suites, deluxe executive, etc., and start at $27 for singles, $32 for doubles.

Budget

The **Austin Motor Hotel,** 1221 Granville St. (tel. 604/685-7235), is a very pleasant hostelry in central but rather drab surroundings. The lobby is large, the dining room quite chic (and open every day), the corridors wide, airy, and well kept. Most of the 145 bedrooms have private baths. For those without, there's an excellent bathroom on each floor. The rooms are comfortably furnished, featuring walk-in closets, good overhead and bedside lights, black-and-white TV sets, and telephones. The bathrooms are rather old-fashioned, but have exceptionally large tubs.

Rates depend on whether or not you want a private bath. Thus singles go from $13 to $20; doubles, from $16 to $23.

The **Abby,** 921 W. Pender St. (tel. 604/681-4335), has a fairly stark lobby with linoleum-covered floor and chrome chairs, but 94 attractive bedrooms. This is a good family hotel, protected by an elaborate sprinkler system. The rooms have switchboard phones and color TV, but rather small closets. Those with baths (the majority) are as comfortable as most you'd find in the higher price brackets.

Single rates go from $16 to $19; doubles, from $19 to $22; with children under 10 years free, and $3 extra per cot.

On the same street, at no. 435, stands the **Niagara Hotel** (tel. 604/681-5548). The Niagara has an attractive hewn-stone facade, no restaurant on the premises, but a busy pub that serves cafeteria lunches daily except Sunday. Of the 102 bedrooms, 40 come with private baths. For the others there's a bathroom on each floor. The rooms are small and rather sparsely furnished; all of them, however, have wall-to-wall carpets, bedside lights, dressing tables, and color TV. They have large open closets with ample hanging space, although the rooms themselves are fairly small.

Singles range from $12 to $16; doubles, from $14 to $18; children stay free in their parents' room.

The **Gifford Hotel,** 1348 Robson St. (tel. 604/688-5451), has 61 rooms and 16 apartment suites, the latter completely self-contained. Half of the standard rooms come minus private baths (but with hot- and cold-water sinks). Some of the others only have small shower stalls. The suites consist of bedroom, living room, kitchen, bathroom, all necessary utensils, TV, and telephone, and will house families of up to six people. Furnishings are economy style throughout, with some of the rooms having only luggage racks; others, good-sized closets. The fittings are quite comfortable, there are sufficient lighting fixtures, and the carpeting is wall to wall in the entire hotel. There's a restaurant in the building, plus a number of vending machines.

It has a somewhat complex rate structure: singles are $10 to $16; doubles, $14 to $19; with children living free with their parents. For seven days' residence you get one day gratis. The suites rent only by the week, costing $150 to $175 for that period.

The **Alcazar,** 337 Dunsmuir St. (tel. 604/681-5241), is a solid red brick building with a glaring orange entrance. A vast lobby adjoins the bar, generously equipped with resting facilities. The hotel has a coffeeshop open seven days a week, and 163 rooms, most with private baths. The bedrooms are rather attractive, fitted with excellent carpeting and an abundance of lights. All come with telephones, black-and-white TV, and spacious walk-in closets behind sliding curtains. The bathrooms have electric ventilators and fluorescent lights. The entire place is spacious, impeccably kept, and very busy.

Singles cost from $13 to $17; doubles, $17 to $22. Children stay free with their parents, while cots cost an extra $3.

The most inexpensive establishment in this bracket is the **Hotel Ambassador,** 773 Seymour St. (tel. 604/684-2436). The place has a very plain lobby and somewhat spartan fixtures throughout, but spick-and-span maintenance and 120 cheerful rooms. The bedrooms have telephones, but neither TV nor radios, and none has private bath, although the bathrooms on each floor are models of cleanliness, also quite large. Furniture consists of the essentials, including walk-in closets, bedside lamps, and good chairs. Unfortunately some of the rooms lack plugs for electric razors.

Singles go from $8 to $8.50; doubles, from $10.50 to $11; twins, $13. Children under 12 stay free in their parents' room.

The Ys

For some mysterious reason the Vancouver YMCA takes only male residents, while the YWCA welcomes both sexes. Which means that men get roughly twice as much Y space as women. Both establishments are downtown on Burrard St.

The **YMCA,** 955 Burrard St. (tel. 604/681-0221), has a vast and somewhat bleak guest lounge, with steel furniture, linoleum floors, a showcase full of athletic trophies, half a dozen pay phones, and as many vending machines. There are also a swimming pool, gym, steamroom, racquetball court, etc., plus a coffeeshop that closes at 3:30 p.m. The 100 bedrooms are spotless, bright, and equipped with the basics. No liquor is allowed on the premises, and the rooms rent at $9 a night.

The **YWCA,** 580 Burrard St. (tel. 604/683-2531), is considerably frillier. Housed in a brightly modern residence, 13 stories high, it has a welcoming lobby with comfortable settees, a cozy TV lounge, kitchen facilities, swimming pool, and sauna. The cafeteria is a neon-lit, linoleum-floored affair, but the bedrooms come with potted plants, armchairs, and (most) private baths. Rates depend on whether you want your own bathroom. Singles range from $11 to $17; doubles, from $8 to $11 per person. Dormitory accommodation costs $5 per night. And the cafeteria sells meals like pork chops with fried rice for $1.90 per helping.

College Accommodations

The **University of British Columbia** has a gorgeous near-shore setting overlooking English Bay, about 15 minutes from downtown by the no. 10 bus, which runs to the campus every ten minutes. The layout embraces 100 acres of rose gardens, alpine trails, and wooded paths, the second-largest library in

Canada, a superb Aquatic Centre, the Museum of Anthropology, botanical gardens, jogging tracks, tennis courts, and golf courses. The entire location is a tourist attraction in its own right.

The UBC has 2200 single and double rooms at the **Walter Gage Residence,** 2075 Westbrook Mall (tel. 604/228-5441). Singles run from $12 for rooms to $24 for suites; doubles, from $21 for rooms to $31 for suites. Youths (under 19) pay $8.50 per night. Lodgings are available from May 7 to August 27, and you can get very good and fairly cheap meals on campus.

MEALS: Vancouver boasts such a profuse variety of eateries (over 1500) that it's quite impossible to include more than a fraction of them in the space available. Assume, therefore, that for each establishment listed there are three, four, or a dozen more that had to be omitted. This applies especially to the French and Chinese restaurants, which flourish all over town like delectable fungi.

It was also impossible to find a clear dividing line between dining and entertainment spots, since some of the best eating houses also put on great entertainment at night. Consequently you'll find some of them mentioned here, others in the nightlife pages.

Taken as a whole the culinary standard is excellent, in patches superlative, with a few reservations—bread and coffee, for instance. The bread, except for the brands served in continental restaurants, has the tang and flavor of pure cotton wool; the coffee frequently resembles hot tapwater (occasionally, cold tapwater). You would also do well to forego the so-called pub lunches, made up chiefly of cellophane-wrapped sandwiches and dubious meat-and-dough concoctions. You fare much better buying rolls and fillings at delicatessens, which are numerous and generally a joy.

Above all, you should sample the Sunday brunches, a local institution so highly competitive that it inspires every hostelry to lay on its best. And to end this introduction on a high note: there is no tax on restaurant meals! What you see marked on the menu is all you pay.

The Top Choices

Le Pavillon, in the Four Seasons Hotel (tel. 689-9333), is a spectacularly elegant temple of haute cuisine with an international reputation. The menu changes with the seasons and is completely revamped four times a year. Even the menu cover is a 17th-century Flemish masterpiece. The place wraps you in an aura of seductive luxury: deep scarlet settees, huge wall mirrors, an immense mural depicting wintry splendor, superb prints in gold frames; and the service is silent, smooth, and unobtrusively attentive. Executive chef Michel Clavelin turns his offerings into a kind of culinary symphony, artistically atuned to the last lettuce leaf.

You can start, say, with genuine Russian caviar or truffles soup Élysée, go on to a classic boneless pheasant Souvaroff (stuffed with goose liver), and conclude with a dessert selection from a trolley brimming with glazed fruit, mocca icing, whipped cream, and calories. The whole feast will come to around $33, not including wine, of course. Open six days a week till 11 p.m. Closed Sundays.

Vancouver has the unique distinction of possessing two revolving restaurants offering changing panoramas along with the comestibles. One crowns the top of the Harbour Centre (tel. 669-2220) (see "Daytime Activities"), the other is **Cloud 9,** (tel. 687-0511), 42 stories up in the Sheraton-Landmark Hotel. It's hard to decide here what's more impressive, the fare or the view. The dinery, 564 feet above sea level, takes one hour to complete a turn, weighs 200 tons, and is propelled by two remarkably tiny electric motors.

Between gazing in turn at the city, the bays, and the islands beyond, we imbibed rich green turtle soup with sherry, Alaska king crab with saffron rice, sauté mushrooms, and a scrumptiously cosmopolitan selection of cheeses (six nationalities). Altogether, the cost was only $22 per diner. Cloud 9 is open six days a week till 1 a.m., Sunday till 10 p.m.

There are a couple of top-notch restaurants set in idyllic positions in Stanley Park. One, the **Beach House,** at the Beach Ave. entrance (tel. 681-9951), offers superb crab legs in brandy sauce and filet of sole Russian style, as well as one of the grandest wine selections in the entire city. The other, misnamed **The Teahouse** (which it was once but is no longer), stands at Ferguson Point (tel. 669-3281), and originated as a World War II military installation.

You'll find this hard to believe when you enter the pint-sized white cottage with the beautiful pillared dining room overlooking English Bay. The decor is unostentatiously stylish: a wonderful open fireplace, hanging ferns, subtly flattering mirrors, and a dual view showing the bay full of ships on one side, the park landscape on the other. The clientele is trendy, the atmosphere relaxed, the meals leisurely and quite delicious. I had the escargots in garlic sauce, followed by the unusually succulent rack of lamb, finally the guaranteed best pecan pie I ate in Canada—so rich that your conscience pricks you with every bite and so supreme that you can't stop eating. The meal came to $18. The Teahouse is open seven days a week till 10 p.m.

Le Napoléon, 869 Hamilton St. (tel. 688-7436), has an unusual claim to culinary fame. The owners raise their own game birds and serve them up to their clients, which accounts for both their quality and their freshness. A distinct Bonapartist flavor permeates the entire establishment: the dining room is decorated in imperial scarlet and gold, the enchanting little garden terrace in front is called Désirée (after one of N's tempestuous sisters), and the plush private salon upstairs is the Josephine. The cuisine, however, probably ranks several notches above Napoleon's (who had no palate and ate *anything*). Huîtres Prince Albert (oysters baked with caviar), braised duck with special herbs, and strawberries soaked in champagne as a grand finale—the repast would come to about $26, but *not* if you follow your host to the impressive wine cellar to select your own vintage. Open six days a week till 11 p.m. Closed Sundays.

Don't let the name mislead you into thinking that the **Crêpe Machine,** 1480 W. 11th Ave. (tel. 732-3411), is some sort of snackery. The crêpes here are gourmet nuggets, served with as much savoir-faire as flavor, amid hanging plants and cedar decor. You get oysters Rockefeller crêpes, shrimp and mushroom crêpes, chicken and beef crêpes, and downright wicked cream dessert crêpes, topped with almonds. Your bill would depend on your appetite (most of the crêpes are lightweights), but in the region of $21 to $24. Open till 11 p.m. or midnight six days a week, closed Sunday.

As indicated earlier, the above are merely a smattering of what's being dished out on Vancouver's groaning board. Some others in the same class would be the **Three Greenhorns,** 1030 Denman St. (tel. 688-8655), for seafood; the **Hungry Pilgrim,** 835 Hornby St. (tel. 688-2255), for rustic atmosphere and legendary rack of lamb; the **Fado,** 881 W. Broadway (tel. 874-6531), for Portuguese specialties; **Alfredo's,** 815 Burrard St. (tel. 669-2946), for Italian charm and old-country cuisine; the **Château Madrid,** 1277 Howe St. (tel. 684-8814), for bodega setting and Spanish palate delights; **Hy's Steak House,**

1755 Davie St. (tel. 683-2251), for grandiose beef; the **Park Royal,** 440 Clyde Ave. (tel. 922-2828), for famed tournedos; and so forth.

If you have time for only one buffet dinner, make it to the **Bayshore Inn,** 1601 W. Georgia St. (tel. 682-3377). It's not cheap as buffets go, but amazingly so for what it offers. Staged in a vast dining room, the walls covered with immense blowups of 1930s memorabilia, it features the sort of service usually confined to miniature deluxe nooks. Your used plates vanish as if by magic whenever you leave the table for another gluttonous round. The buffet has umpteen cold cuts, seven kinds of salad, four breeds of cold fish, then hearty beef stew, fried chicken, cold breast of chicken, pâté, *then* huge juicy cuts of roast beef carved before your eyes. And if you're still breathing, the richest, most rum-soaked of French pastry or six varieties of cheese. Sum total bill—$9.75.

Moderately Priced Restaurants

The **Schnitzel House,** 1060 Robson St. (tel. 682-1210), is not solely for breaded veal fans, although the menu centers around eight kinds of schnitzels, from Holstein (with fried egg on top) to pork, all priced between $5.75 and $5.95. But you also get excellent rindsroulade (beef wrapped around chopped meat) with dumplings and red cabbage for $6.70. The entrees include soup of the day, but not the imposing array of imported German, Danish, English, Australian, and Scottish beers. You dine in three rooms, heavily decorated with Austrian and Bavarian pictorials, until 10 p.m. every night.

Robson St. is one of the world's most versatile eating strips, as you'll see by the string of samples below. All of them fall into the middle price range, maintain very good quality, and add up to only a slice of what this thoroughfare has to offer.

The **Pyrogy Inn,** 1536 Robson St. (tel. 684-2816), is a handsome Russian, with thick oak roof beams, gleaming chandeliers, red carpets, and amber wall lanterns illuminating the shining white tablecloths. It specializes in pirogi, the Russian version of ravioli, which come with a variety of tangy interiors—from minced meat and onion-bacon to sweet cheese. An order of a dozen costs $4.95. These should be preceded by borscht or/and a plate of six mildly spiced cabbage rolls for the same price. Open for dinner only, all week till 10 p.m.

The **Tanzanite,** 1674 Robson St. (tel. 681-1612), is a rare hybrid serving "genuine Indian and African cuisine." It's smallish and rather smartly decorated in a neuter fashion that looks neither Indian nor African, except for a few animal skins on the walls. The Indian menu portion features half a dozen curries with all the correct trimmings (all under $5), plus tandoori chicken. The African palate gets mishkaki Tanzanite (beef marinated in yogurt with African spices) and chicken Tika (marinated in bean curds, ginger, and garlic), both $4.50. It also offers Swahili specialties and a range of wonderfully spicy apéritifs.

Similar but different is the **Indian Tea Centre,** 1335 Robson St. (tel. 669-4641), where you get East Indian cuisine prepared in East African style. Tea, in fact, is a sideline here, although it comes in ten varieties. There's a great range of snacks (all $1.50) including somosa (chopped beef and onions wrapped in pastry). Excellent vegetarian curries and thadis, and very spicy fried prawns ($6), are offered, and also an outstanding soup made of chick peas and potatoes. Open seven days a week till 10 or 11 p.m.

The **Prague,** 1429 Robson St. (tel. 688-9044), makes up in the fare what it lacks in atmosphere. A narrow, bare, and plastic dining room, the sole ethnic touches consist of some beautiful prints and photos of Prague city scenes. Even the taped music is strictly elevator stuff. But the solid Czech meals dished out here are unmistakably genuine, the potato salad among the best going. Try the steak in mushroom sauce or the roast duck with potato dumplings. Soup and salad comes with the entrees and the whole meal costs you $6.25. Open six days till 10 p.m. Closed Monday.

Le Cous Cous, 1141 Robson St. (tel. 683-2925), breathes French Morocco, with the accent slightly on the French. The Moorish arches, tiled tables, and aroma are North African, the belle époque posters, farming implements, and wine bottles decidedly French—as is the service. A long narrow room, crammed and cozy, is animated by ceiling fans and the waitresses. Not a good place if you're in a hurry, but ideal if you're hungry. Couscous is steamed semolina flour, served coarse and grainy, and wonderfully tasty when mixed with lamb, chicken, spicy meatballs, prawns, or sausages, any of which you get for $6.50 to $7.50. Also French hors d'oeuvres, steak bordelaise, and a magnificent dish of mussels cooked in their own juice with wine and cream. Open seven days a week till 10 p.m.

You can regard the **Robsonkeller,** 1400 Robson St. (tel. 687-9312), as either a food or a jazz dispensary—it's equally famous for both. It's a vast and rambling beer cellar, with mottos in pure Bavarian along the walls ("There's no beer in Heaven, therefore guzzle down here," etc.), with two dartboards going at all times, games of chess, cribbage, and checkers sporadically. There's also a genuine oldtime popcorn machine on wheels to accompany the jazz. The food is solid stuff: steak-and-onion pie, knackwurst and sauerkraut, weisswurst and red cabbage (from $3.60 to $4.25), with beer, ale, and cider flowing at around $1 a bottle. The bands strike up every Monday and Wednesday night, as solidly enjoyable as the fare. Open till 1 a.m. six days a week. Closed Sunday.

The next batch of eateries are all in **Gastown,** where the numbers and variety are almost as profuse as on Robson St., although considerably more touristy.

Brother Jon's, 1 Water St. (tel. 685-3285), has a delightfully rambunctious monastery setting, with a bunch of rakishly robed "brothers" providing "libations for stomachs and ears alike"—meaning that every evening they break into most un-monkish musical offerings. The place is a feast for the eyes as well, displaying stained glass, painted frescoes, and carefully modeled "medieval" chandeliers. You eat from heavy-hewn wooden tables and benches. The menu is vast, ranging from a canonized cheeseburger called the Archbishop ($4.24) to the Cardinal's Choice—a steak Delmonico described as "a plot to break anyone's vow of frugality" ($7.95), and some of the finest, richest, most lavishly ladled soups in Christendom (at $3.45 per bottomless bowl). Open all week, like most Gastown fixtures.

Leo's, 170 Water St. (tel. 682-1235), is a large seafood establishment divided into oddly scattered dining areas, flanked by aquariums whose tropical inhabitants are *not* on the menu. The bar mirrors are so arranged that you can watch the passing parade outside without twisting your neck. The place is festooned with curious antique furniture and photos, and the only jarring note comes in the form of constant canned pop music. A dinner of oysters marinated in white sauce, followed by pan-fried salmon, costs $12.70.

More seafood, but mixed with piano music, live bands, and occasional cabaret, is offered at the **Town Pump,** 66 Water St. (tel. 683-6695), a rollicking and relaxed pub setting, with complimentary hors d'oeuvres handed out in the piano lounge. The entertainment ups and downs considerably, but the food remains consistently good. Try the thick seafood chowder and the "house special" omelet—the whole treat costing $5.95, although the menu also climbs into more expensive regions.

La Brasserie de l'Horlage, 300 Water St. (tel. 685-4835), ranks among my personal favorites, a faithful reproduction of the real Parisian article, correct to the white muslin curtains, red awnings, and ornate golden wall clock that rarely tells the right time. Tiled floors, brass-topped tables, bistro chairs, and wondrous kitchen aromas combine to give me sharp pangs of nostalgia for the left bank of the Seine. "Nos Spécialités" include oven-baked onion soup, brochette d'agneau (roast lamb on skewers), and fraises au vin rouge (strawberries soaked in red wine)—all memorable and amounting to $7.60. Open till around 1 a.m. six days a week. Closed Sunday.

The **Old Spaghetti Factory,** 53 Water St. (tel. 684-1288), is an eye-shattering melange of antique trappings, gadgets, and contraptions which would take the rest of this chapter to list. The main item is a genuine 1910 streetcar, which once rattled around Vancouver but now serves as a dining car. Do make a point of having your leg pulled by the menu's glowing description of "vintage spaghetti harvests" in southern Italy. And please admire the mustachioed portrait of "Guilelmo Marrconi, Inventor of Wireless Spaghetti." There are nine makes of spaghetti dished out, all of them including salad, sourdough bread, coffee, and ice cream. The top selection is with meatballs for $4.65, plus an allegedly secret-recipe homemade lasagne for $5.25. Open six days a week till 10 p.m., Sundays till 9 p.m.

Climb aboard a genuine railcar for dinner at **Frisby's,** at the foot of Carrall St. (tel. 682-6888), and eat while watching the action at the adjacent Canadian Pacific Railway switching yards. The vehicle is a 12-wheeler built in 1929 for the use of general superintendents, and includes an observation deck, restaurant-bar, and enough iron horse trappings to make a railroad buff's evening. You feast on boxcar steak sandwich ($4.95), engineer's barbecued ribs ($6.95), or executive car chicken ($6.25), and finish off with caboose coffee. Open seven days a week.

It's only a block or so from Gastown to **Chinatown,** which virtually consists of eateries. The cuisine is mostly Cantonese and generally excellent, although you do miss the Mandarin, Hunan, and Mongolian subtleties if you happen to hail from San Francisco. On the other hand, the Vancouver clan has come up with a few innovations of its own—such as Chinese smorgasbord. To pick just a few grapes from this bunch:

The **Yen Lock,** 67 E. Pender St. (tel. 681-3925), is a huge place and so concerned with authenticity that the menu caption "Special of the Day" gives the dish in Chinese characters only! Otherwise there's a minimum of Oriental decor, exceptionally bright lighting, and enough elbow room to stage half a dozen simultaneous banquets. A meal of dry spare ribs, braised chicken wings in oyster sauce, and shrimps in lobster sauce (accompanied by a family-size pot of tea) comes to $12.75. Open till 10 p.m. six days, closed Wednesday.

The **Marco Polo,** at the corner of Pender and Columbia Sts. (tel. 682-2875), is an example of the highly popular Chinese smorgasbord style. An ornately decorated red, black, and gold eating palace, with more curlicues than a rococo bedchamber, it charges a standard $6.25 on weeknights, 50¢ more on weekends, for which fee you can eat yourself into oblivion. The buffet offers unlimited helpings of wonton soup, chow mein, shrimps in cashew nuts, egg rolls, sweet-and-sour pork, chicken chop suey, fried prawns, etc., ending with fruit cocktails. You can also help yourself to such un-Chinese sidelines as potato and macaroni salads. Open every night till 10:30 p.m.

The **Noodle Makers,** 122 Powell St. (tel. 683-9196), could pass for a museum and certainly constitutes a landmark. Run by four noodle-making brothers, the establishment is filled with artifacts used by the early Chinese immigrants in Canada. But the place of honor goes to a beautiful 30-foot fish pond, glittering with expensive goldfish which are trained to feed at the sound of a gong struck at 7:30 and 9:30 nightly. The background sounds are a soothing blend of running water and soft Oriental music. The restaurant has a small select menu of gourmet dishes—lemon chicken and emperor's filet are outstanding—and is open seven nights a week.

Good moderate-priced dining is not restricted just to these areas of the city, but can be found all over, as the following recommendations show:

The **Scanwich**, 551 Howe St. (tel. 687-2415), is actually a Scandinavian food center and incidentally serves far and away the best coffee downtown. Charmingly decorated with hand-picked prints and posters (the table mats are 19th-century works of art), the air filled with the lilt of pure Viennese schmalz, and airmailed copies of Scandinavian dailies on the racks, it provides style and comfort in equal quantities, plus a great steak tartare for $5.50, Norwegian fish balls, and Danish pot Tivoli. The famous "scanwiches" are justly so—shrimps, Danish salami, house pâté, ham and Danish cheese on thinly shaved slices of excellent bread for $3.95. Unfortunately they're so good and so minute that you need about three to pacify a middling appetite. Nordic beers go for $1.90. Open six days till 10 p.m. Closed Sunday.

The **Little Csarda**, 1345 Kingsway (tel. 872-1116), brings a breath of authentic paprika to the scene. The decor is traditional Magyar peasant—wood paneling, wine bottles, scarlet drapes and table linen. The cuisine has the same flavor. The goulash soup is thick and meaty enough to count as a meal. The paprika chicken comes in cream sauce and surrounded by dumplings at $7.50. But if you're a couple, plunge for the flaming wooden platter: a mountain of pork chops, schnitzels, Hungarian sausages, fried potatoes, and salad at $16.95 for two persons. There's throbbing Gypsy music evenings from Thursday to Sunday. Closed Monday.

Gizella's, 775 Burrard St. (tel. 682-4588), has mixed Swiss, German, French, and Anglo fare, lantern-lit tables, old hunting prints on the walls, and a rustic staircase leading to a second dining room above. The food is fine, although far from ethnic anything. Fresh mushrooms à la crème, with asparagus and egg, is $4.45; the Holstein schnitzel, $5.65. Open all week, on Sundays till 6 p.m. only.

There's a touch of Mexico—California style—at the **Topanga**, 2904 W. Fourth Ave. (tel. 733-3713). It looks like a cross between a cafe and a desert adobe hut, and suggests blazing sunshine even when it's freezing. The Topanga serves nearly all the standard favorites and prepares them in an open kitchen area: chili relleno, enchiladas, burritos, tostadas, and tacos, all including refried beans and rice, mostly topped with avocado sauce and sour cream. They're best imbibed in combination plates starting at $3.50, followed by Mexican hot chocolate or hibiscus-cinnamon tea with homemade cake. Open six days a week. Closed Monday.

Describing the **Attic** as a place of "somewhat chaotic elegance" is an understatement. It can't be described—it has to be experienced. Located at 657 Marine Dr. (tel. 922-3224), over the Lions Gate Bridge in West Vancouver, this dinery cum cocktail bar cum entertainment spot cum museum is the brainchild of a fabulously flamboyant showman-restaurateur named Frank Baker. He crammed it with 1200 antiques in an order resembling an abandoned battlefield, hung a huge collection of Tiffany shades from the rafters, and added live jazz, Gay '90s sing-alongs and cabaret turns to his enormous meals. The result is the kind of place that prints a complimentary newspaper—all about itself, including ads for "pneumatic bust forms." Every entree includes heavy helpings from the soup tureen (all house soups come from Grandma Baker's "secret file"), salad, hot corn muffins, and roast potato chunks. Entree choices include baked ham steak ($7.95), sirloin steak, and poached salmon. Open all week.

Venetian cooking is relatively rare among Italian dineries, but at **Il Cappuccino,** 774 Denman St. (tel. 669-0545), you get the real thing. Boss Sandro Romano is the guarantor (as well as the chef). Sandro claims, "In my town the food is so good it makes you want to cry." Well, hardly anyone cries in his small, darkly chic restaurant that serves, among other things, the finest possible cappuccino (at 85¢ per cup). Also prima chicken cacciatore and saltimboca for $7.99, with the menu running full English explanations for every Italian delicacy. Cappucino, incidentally, is said to be a Venetian invention ranking next to the gondola. Open six days a week. Closed Monday.

Le Bistro, 747 Thurlow St. (tel. 681-3818), has scrubbed wooden floors, tiled tables, carved chairs, incongruously cozy fringed lamps, and a profusion of French posters, paintings, graphics, and photographs on the walls. The general impression is that of a village dwelling set up for a very large family dinner. The menu is limited but choice. You'll probably not get better soup anywhere than the rich, thick, and aromatic beef, rice, and vegetable brew that comes with the spécialités. It's hard to choose among them, but given only one selection I'd pick the lapin au vin blanc (rabbit in white wine with mushrooms and bacon) for $4.80. Don't forget to try the pâté maison (homemade, i.e., really maison). The coffee is outstanding as well, for good measure. Open six days a week, closed Sunday.

Budget Meals

The **Food Fair** in the basement of Robson Square puts a cosmopolitan row of economy eateries right at your fingertips, so to speak. They're all self-service, absolutely spotless, very tasty, but unfortunately cease operations at 5 p.m. **Señor McTacos** (tel. 669-2338), dispenses Mexican frito meat and burritos for $1. At **Golly Gee's,** (tel. 688-9018), every Chinese delicacy—from broccoli chicken to egg rolls—costs 95¢. Its Ukrainian neighbor has tangy cabbage rolls for $2.50, while the English fish and chips counter sells—well, fish and chips, gorblimey, for $2.95. On the right flank there's a very appetizing Swedish delicatessen where the roast pork goes for $2.79. How's that for a five-in-one combination?

Isshin, 946 Granville St. (tel. 684-3023), is an attractively simple little Japanese eatery in a dark-brown hue, with lights disguised as round lanterns. There's a lunch counter in front, a small dining room in the rear. The lunchtime specials here go for under $4; the oyako-dan (chopped boneless chicken with onions, eggs, and rice) costs $3.50. Open seven days a week, but weekends for dinner only.

The **Fresgo Inn,** 1126 Davie St. (tel. 689-1332), is a superior breed of cafeteria. Handsomely decorated with ferns and creepers, a stained-glass lighting fixture, and a buffet that resembles a tiled cottage, its only jarring note an uninterrupted stream of canned music, it serves quite excellent chicken pot pie for $2.75 and outstanding stew for 20¢ more, plus enormous breakfasts with all the works. A very bustling place, open six days till 3 a.m., Sunday till midnight.

You'll find a **White Spot** in most of suburban Canada, but this one is right downtown at 1025 Robson St. (tel. 683-5100). It's a large and pleasing coffee-shop-style establishment, soothingly decorated, with soft amber ceiling lights, plus leather settees in the windows facing the street. Service is fast, the food tasty and cheap. Turkey pot pie is $2.75; a glass of tangy B.C. apple cider costs 95¢. Open till midnight.

The **Original Dutch Pannekoek House,** likewise part of a chain, with one of its links at 546 W. Broadway (tel. 876-1913), this was the first of its breed in North America, introducing the Dutch version of the French crêpe, which is vastly more substantial—in fact, a solid meal on its own. The house offers 36 varieties of 'em, from bacon, mushroom, and cheese, to apple, ginger, and strawberry with whipped cream—all of them platter sized. The prices start at $2 and go up to $4.25. Open all week.

On the other hand there's nothing very Dutch about the **Frying Dutchman Hamburger House,** 3451 Cambie St. (tel. 894-3831). It's Anglo-Canadian right to the bun. The burgers are *big*—the "Canadian" consisting of a full half pound of beef, bacon, and cheese, costing $3. Others ("Simple Simon," "Gentle John," "Humble Helen," etc.) have more modest proportions, although still on the hefty side, starting at $1.20. Green salad goes with them.

The **Vegetable Patch,** at the corner of Broadway and Granville St. (tel. 738-5233), isn't all that budgety, but has a grandly economical salad bar that ranks as one of the most popular pieces of grazing land in town. The helpings cost $2.85, give you a choice of 30 toppings, and include cheeses. For another 85¢ you get fresh homemade vegetable soup. For further vegetarian delights there are hot quiches, carrot cakes, frozen yogurt, egg dishes, and banana loafs. No banquet for cannibals, but crisp saladeria served in comfortable surroundings.

DAYTIME ACTIVITIES: Vancouver's landmark, the massively soaring **Harbour Centre,** towers at 555 W. Hastings St., on the waterfront. The glass skylift whisks you 40 floors up to the Observation Deck, the trip costing $1 for adults, 75¢ for children. The view up there is stunning, reinforced by angled observation windows and powerful telescopes. For another $1.50 ($1 for children) you can see a panoramic movie of the city's past and present, thrown on a 37-foot screen by 27 projectors and one computer. The center also contains the **Harbour Mall,** with 50 specialty shops and a variety of eateries serving anything from snacks to gourmet dinners. As impressive after dark as in daylight, it's open all week till 10 p.m.

A few blocks away lies **Gastown** and adjoining Chinatown, both bundles of attractions crammed into what is practically one compact area. Gastown radiates out from its brick-paved hub, **Maple Tree Square,** the spot where Vancouver began. It's a charming, chintzy little tangle of eateries, galleries, and boutiques, clutching you like an amiable octopus, offering visual, edible, and audio treasures and junk in equal quantities. The air is filled with jazz, rock, a dozen ethnic aromas, and the chuffing and hooting from the Canadian Pacific tracks in the background. It's a fun place, with far too few seating facilities for footsore wanderers (a plot, mayhap, to make them pay for a chair somewhere?). The wondrous **Steam Clock,** however, works gratis. Operating on a one-cylinder steam engine, the apparatus plays the Westminster Chimes and blows steam whistles every 15 minutes and, incidentally, also tells the time.

You can cover Gastown and **Chinatown** in one easy walking tour—stopping for appropriate refreshments, of course. The commercial center of Chinatown is a three-block area of W. Pender St., between Carrall and Gore. A kind of Oriental "bazaar" quarter, dedicated to shopping and eating, it remains so completely in character that even the public telephone booths wear pagoda roofs.

The wares for sale include ivory and jade jewelry, gorgeous brocades, and exotic delicacies, cheek by jowl with some of the most fatuous rubbish north of the equator. The balcony style of the older buildings suggests instant Hong

Kong or Singapore. One of them you'll find in Mr. Ripley's *"Believe It or Not"* bible. It's at the corner of Pender and Carrall—five feet ten inches wide, two stories high, and designated as the **World's Thinnest Office Building.** Do you know of a slimmer one?

Stanley Park, rolling over 1000 acres of woodlands, gardens, beaches, picnic sites, and nature trails, starts at the foot of W. Georgia St., and ranks as one of the best designed, best run, most thoroughly enjoyable green havens in the urbanized world. You could spend an entire vacation there. Encircled by a seven-mile seawall ideal for walking jaunts, the park houses tennis courts, miniature golf courses, a giant checkerboard, a midget railroad, lawn bowling greens, cricket pitches, a live theater, restaurants, coffeeshops and snackbars, and the **Brockton Oval** sports arena. Just offshore on a rock perches Vancouver's version of Copenhagen's Little Mermaid—the less celebrated but more stacked *Girl in a Wetsuit.*

The park contains Vancouver's fairly unexciting zoo (free) and the far more spectacular **Aquarium,** largest of its kind in Canada. It shows some 9000 specimens of marine life and has a special pool for Beluga whales—white, playful, and astonishingly noisy. The high spot of the exhibition is the Marine Mammal Complex, which stages regular performances by dolphins that look like animated torpedos and two personality-plus killer whales, Skana and Hyak, who jostle each other for the limelight as much as for the fish. Admission is $3.50 for adults, $1.50 for children.

The **Port of Vancouver,** one of the biggest, busiest harbors on earth, can be seen from various angles and vantage points revealing different aspects. From dry land there's the **Vanterm,** at the foot of Clark Dr., which has a public viewing area that shows the ultramodern container terminal in action. Other vantage points for marine buffs are at **Centennial Pier** and **Granville Square.** For a fast glimpse, take the Seabus from the terminal at the foot of Granville St. For a more leisurely jaunt, **Harbour Ferries Ltd.** operates an old-time stern-wheeler that thumps around the port area in 75-minute tours from the north foot of Denman St.

The **Capilano Suspension Bridge,** North Vancouver at Capilano Rd., offers more thrills than a roller coaster. Hanging 230 feet up in the air, stretching 450 feet across the Capilano Canyon, and spectacularly illuminated at night, this is a dizzyingly wonderful experience and the source of some of the most fantastic photos ever taken. Open until 10:30 p.m. Adults pay $2.50 to cross; children, 75¢.

Grouse Mountain could be called an elevated playground, and the greatest of its toys is what gets you up there. At the end of Capilano Rd., in North Vancouver, lies the base terminal of the **Superskyride.** This is a big, modern, 100-passenger aerial tramway that carries you to the top, with the city spread 1000 feet below you and the hang gliders sailing past. The ride costs adults $4; children, $2. On Sunday you can combine the trip with an excellent brunch at the **Chalet** for a total price of $5.95.

Just off Capilano Rd. is the **Capilano Salmon Hatchery.** This "fish farm," nestling in a forest setting, was designed to replenish the salmon population of the Capilano River. You hear all about the salmon's remarkable life cycle and watch the fish, in various stages of development, swim in glass-fronted tanks, with each phase of the process explained in models, diagrams, and the live water denizens.

Museums, Exhibitions, and Such

The **Museum of Anthropology,** University of British Columbia, a masterpiece of specialized architecture, is a multimedia presentation rather than a standard museum. The exhibits include a famous Northwest Coast Indian collection, an international textile collection, and fascinating material from Asia, Africa, the Pacific, and the Americas. Instead of old-style labels it has a theater gallery in which the displays are explained and enhanced by sight and sound programs. It also contains some of the most impressive totem poles you'll ever see. Admission is $1 for adults, half price for children. Closed Mondays.

The **Centennial Museum** and **Maritime Museum** can be visited on the same ticket costing $1.50 for adults, half price for children. The Centennial, at 1110 Chestnut St., shows the story of Vancouver's past as well as a thorough glimpse at warriors and weaponry from all over the world, plus changing exhibitions such as the *World of Children,* with toys and mementos from around the globe. The Maritime, at 1905 Ogden Ave., offers guided tours of the Arctic patrol vessel *St. Roch,* a nautical ugly duckling of amazing strength. Scores of other naval exhibits include a full-size replica of a ship's bridge, which you can visit. Open daily till 5 p.m.

The **Planetarium,** 1100 Chestnut St., features changing but invariably fascinating shows about man's relationship with and views of the universe. Aided by impressive technological gadgetry, shows like *Space Capsule* bring you up to date with the current state of research in the extraterrestrial sciences. Admission is $1.50 in daytime, $2.50 in the evenings. Closed Monday.

The **Vancouver Art Gallery,** 1145 W. Georgia St., is a rather modest affair, considering the wealth of the city. It has some interesting examples of Canadian paintings and drawings from two centuries, contemporary U.S. prints, and 18th- to 20th-century British paintings, drawings, watercolors, and prints. The lighting is strictly so-so, but admission is free. Closed Monday.

The **B.C. Sports Hall of Fame,** Exhibition Park, Renfrew and Hastings Sts., is a fairly grand tribute to British Columbia's contributions to sports. In 115 showcases covering 68 sports, it traces the history and development of each branch—sometimes by means of soundtracks dramatizing its greatest moments. The hall also boasts one of the greatest collections of trophies and medals assembled anywhere. Donations are accepted. Closed Saturdays.

The **Royal Canadian Wax Museum,** 21 Water St., Gastown, has everything a show of this kind should have: historical personages, Bible scenes, vintage movie stars, pioneer heroes, illustrious villains, and—of course—a Chamber of Horrors, complete with skeletons and a monster. Adults pay $2; children, half price.

The **B.C. Sugar Museum,** at the foot of Rogers St., is a surprisingly interesting display, since the development of sugar refining closely parallels the historical growth of Vancouver. Here you can see old sugar-making equipment dating back to 1715, a plantation locomotive, intriguing ancient photographs, and a 25-minute documentary film. Open Monday to Friday. Admission is free.

AFTER DARK: The performing arts are thriving in Vancouver, although visitors from the U.S. often run into shows that closed on Broadway (or Off-Broadway) a couple of seasons ago. Check the daily papers (when they're not on strike) or the gratis weekly publication *Vancouver Guideline* for what's on where, with whom, and for how long.

The Performing Arts

Focal point of the town's live stage is the **Queen Elizabeth Theatre and Playhouse,** 600 Hamilton St. A large, beautiful, expertly designed stage complex, this building is the home of the opera, the **Playhouse Theatre Company,** plus a changing cavalcade of local and imported musical, dramatic, and dance ensembles. Tickets run from $5 to $15.

The **Orpheum Theatre,** 884 Granville St., lovingly refurbished in its old glory, presents the **Vancouver Symphony Orchestra,** visiting artists, and a permanent Wurlitzer console organ. Tickets range from $5 to $8.50.

The **Robson Square Theatre,** ultramodern and highly versatile, serves as a showcase for a fantastic variety of traditional, pop, and avant-garde stage productions, with tickets in the $3 to $6 range. The **City Stage,** 751 Thurlow St., is an intimate little place that offers lunchtime as well as evening performances, often hilariously satiric and very "in" (meaning hard for outsiders to follow). Tickets are $5 to $6.

The **Arts Club Theatre,** 1181 Seymour St., mixes stage productions with musical offerings. Some of the most interesting plays are those by contemporary Canadian writers and may offend patrons with tender ears and sensibilities. The **Metro Theatre Centre,** 1370 South West Marine Dr., is the home of various amateur companies performing "multicultural" plays—productions in English, French, as well as other languages represented in Canada.

Presentation House/Studio Theatre, 209 W. Fourth Ave., North Vancouver, is a modern show complex including an art gallery, museum, and studio stage, offering professional drama for adults as well as children, also musicals and dance performances. Tickets run $4 to $5. The **Vancouver East Cultural Centre,** 1895 Venables St., a medium-size all-purpose performance space, presents adult and childrens' theater, jazz, classical music, ballet, and films seven days a week. Tickets from $4.

Studio 58, 100 W. 49th St., is the stomping ground of Vancouver Community College's Theatre Arts program. It's comfortable and intimate, presenting a year-round cycle of classics, modern stage hits, and occasional musicals.

Discos Galore

Vancouver's nightlife is awash with discos, some genuine, others merely so-called, insofar as they use live bands as much as platters. This is not the place to quibble over technicalities, so I'll just give you a brief tour of what's spinning in town, regardless of exactitude.

The **Truffles Exchange,** Hyatt Regency Hotel, operates as a restaurant until 11:30 p.m., then gets transformed into a super-smart disco. It looks like two portions of a vast drawing room flanking a dance floor with the inevitable jitter lights. On one side you lounge in deep armchairs, backed by library shelves filled with books you can actually take down and read—if that's your inclination. Disco dance lessons from a championship couple at $5 per.

Annabelle's, Four Seasons Hotel, chic and svelte, insists that gentlemen be attired in jackets and recommends that trousers be worn as well, mingling jazz on Thursdays with disco fare the rest of the week. Over-30s feel at ease here among gorgeous photo blowups on the walls, surrounding a superb sunken dance floor. The finest settees in discoland are enhanced by swarms of pretty cocktail waitresses. Admission is $2 on weeknights, $3 on weekends.

Candy Store, Royal Centre Mall, (tel. 688-6266), likewise enforces a dress code of sorts, and provides a small lounge area slightly protected from the worst decibel din. It has an impressive dance floor made of glass, and porno wallpaper (but *only* in the ladies' washroom).

Pharaoh's, 364 Water St. (tel. 681-0541), Gastown, is Vancouver's oldest disco, still immensely popular. It's given to contests of various kinds, plus changing interiors due to frequent renovations, but invariably comes out comfortable and *lively.*

The following group of discos are all located inside a few short blocks of **Hornby St.,** making it possible to disco-crawl through all of them in one, fairly lengthy, night:

Misty's, 633 Hornby St. (tel. 685-4411), has a deluxe entrance—stairs, railings, and walls thickly upholstered in frosty blue, mirrored by chandeliers and a playing fountain, guarded by a doorman in tuxedo. There's a classy interior and even classier VIP lounge, with couches and conversation, for a $3 cover charge.

The Cave, 626 Hornby St. (tel. 682-3677), offers dual musical entertainment simultaneously. Apart from the flesh-and-blood performers, other bands are projected on a giant television screen, giving you a choice between live shows and shadows.

Pal's, 579 Hornby St. (tel. 669-1930), redolent with brass, illuminated by flickering lights from *below,* has scarlet-cushioned niches and dreamy atmospherics. Although tagged a "New York–style disco," Pal's actually presents a style all its own, refreshingly individualistic.

Sneaky Pete's, 595 Hornby St. (tel. 681-9561), up the elevator on the fifth floor of an office building, this unusually situated disco is well worth the ride and the $3 admission charge. It's divided into two seating areas, one filled with hanging plants and rattan chairs, the other discreetly dark and eminently suitable for romance between dance-floor gymnastics. It serves hors d'oeuvres and glasses of excellent white wine.

Jazz and Folk

You get both of them, plus periodic bouts of country rock, at the **Classical Joint,** 231 Carrall St., Gastown. Strictly a coffeehouse serving no booze, but coffee, cider, tea, etc., it draws a mostly young, entirely dedicated *late* crowd—the music doesn't get under way until 10 p.m. There's an amazing decor: a melange of abstracts and stable utensils on brick cellar walls. The cover charge hovers around $1.75. And there's more jazz at the **Hot Jazz Club,** 36 E. Broadway (tel. 873-4131), which really *is* a club, but one you can join at the door. It presents solid local Dixieland bands (a different one every night), tremendously enthusiastic patrons, and a permanently packed dance floor.

The **Blarney Stone,** 216 Carrall St. (tel. 687-4322), is an Irish pub-like creation transplanted to Gastown. A restaurant cum nightspot, it serves savory Irish lamb stew for $4.80. There's no cover charge for dinners, but others pay $1 to $2.50 for admission, depending on the night. The pub atmosphere is diluted by romantic soft lights, the bands switch between full-throated Irish and somewhat less hearty show ensembles, and the atmosphere stays relaxed and rollicking regardless of who's on.

The other side of the Celtic coin spins at the **George V Lounge,** Hotel Georgia, 801 W. Georgia St. (tel. 682-5566). Robert Stuart and the Publicans, a bearded, kilted young singer plus accompaniment, belts out Scottish airs with tremendous gusto, occasionally sliding into American and English ditties. It's by far the best sing-along entertainment in town, the management kindly providing a brochure with the opening verses of "Loch Lomond," "I Belong to Glasgow," "Alouette," etc., so you won't have to just hum. No admission or cover charge, and a beer costs only $1.50.

The **Fabulous Fifties**, 1040 W. Georgia St. (tel. 685-8311), offers exactly what the name implies: the sights and sounds of the 1950s. Admire the montage of minutiae covering the entrance walls. Listen to the Wurlitzer jukebox pounding out big-band rhythms or hear the live entertainers resurrect Elvis, Bill Haley and the Comets, Crosby, etc. If nostalgia is your bag, this is your pouch. Admission is $1.50.

The **Organ Grinder**, 1260 Hornby St. (tel. 689-1401), doesn't really fit into the nightlife section—it's very much a family spot—but is simply too good to leave out. Imagine a pizzeria built around a musical science-fiction monster disguised as a theater pipe organ, and you'll have a notion of what the place looks like. The "organ" is a kind of Frankenstein creation, assembled from the bodies of 50 little organs, an upright piano, glockenspiel, marimba, xylophone, chrysoglott, cathedral chimes, and heaven knows what else. Activated by organ virtuoso Ron Poll, it produces a computer symphony of sound effects that could pass for the background themes of half a dozen de Mille Technicolor epics. You can listen from 5 p.m. till 11, while munching imaginative pizzas ranging from $2.75 to $4.25, all fresh from the ovens.

The **Mediaeval Inns**, 52 Powell St. (tel. 687-7567), Gastown, are three in number—one on top of the other. The prices are *claimed* to be medieval, and the atmosphere comes close. The frontage is mock Tudor, the interiors full of oak beams and roughly hewn wooden tables, the serving wenches comely, and the lights dim. The medieval feast laid on here lasts three solid hours and includes soup, fish, game hen, roast beef, wine, mead, and cheeses (no titlark pie and roast swan, you'll be glad to hear). The entire meal is eaten with your fingers (forks available on special request only), and is enlivened by sundry minstrels, bawdy monks, and a story-telling manor lord, interspersed with rousing sing-alongs and much hilarity. The total price comes to $15.95 per carousing wayfarer—tip included.

Bare Skin

There isn't much nudity in Vancouver's nightlife, which enhances the role of the **Crazy Horse**, 1024 Davie St. (tel. 687-4919), although it lacks any similarity with the celebrated Paris original. The establishment runs continuous shows from 7 p.m. to 2 a.m., two at a time performed on two levels, so you can walk from one to the other until you decide which deserves your undivided attention. The strips, let me add, are *total:* no nonsense with pasties and G strings. Periodically a very good young magician tries to compete for the audience with the disrobed ladies, but it's doubtful whether Houdini himself could have succeeded in such circumstances. Admission is $3.50; a drink comes to $2.10.

SHOPPING: The most impressive feature of Vancouver's retail trade are the magnificent underground shopping malls. They link vast portions of the downtown area in a network of subterranean stores and boutiques you can browse through on the wettest days without having to unfurl your umbrella.

Biggest of the lot is the **Pacific Centre Mall**, which connects with the two main (aboveground) department stores and the Four Seasons Hotel. It also gives direct access to the **Vancouver Centre Mall**. Both these underground shopping towns lie below **Granville Mall**, where you have the majority of downtown movie houses.

The **Royal Centre Mall**, built under the Hyatt Regency Hotel, has two levels of high-class fashion stores, jewelry and gift shops, gourmet foods and restaurants. The **Harbour Centre Mall** lies beneath the aforementioned tower and another huge department store on the waterfront, and connects with Gastown.

From the city's awesome array of specialty stores, a few samples:

Images, 779 Burrard St., is more an art gallery than a shop. Specializing in Indian and Eskimo handiwork—guaranteed authentic—the tastefully displayed treasures range from a superbly sculpted loon priced at $1450 to tiny jade carvings. You can also buy Northwest Indian dance masks, Eskimo graphics, contemporary pottery, original oil paintings, and masses of ethnic jewelry.

More native arts and crafts are found at **Tempo,** 1107 Robson St. The tone of the place is set by a hand-carved chess set, the most beautiful I've ever seen, costing $1000. The Cowichan sweaters beat anything the Scandinavians produce in terms of winterwear. There's also a splendid selection of fur gloves, moccasins, and toques of Canadian native design.

For Eskimo carvings—tiny white figures catching seals, fighting bears, harnessing sled dogs—local pottery, and art reproductions, try the **Arctic Loon,** 3095 Granville St.

In a town of generally dismal coffee, **Murchie's,** 1008 Robson St., beckons like a lodestar—the aroma alone makes it worth entering. It sells a tremendous variety of coffee blends and tea mixtures in a traditional English setting that makes buying less a commercial and more a social transaction. Another branch, at 560 Gambie St., is a kind of museum of the "cup that cheers but not inebriates."

For an inveterate pipe addict like myself, the **Pipe Dream,** 714 W. Hastings St., was a joyous discovery. It sells custom-blended tobacco (including *my* brand) plus a full range of pipe accessories.

There are about half a dozen retailers who specialize in helping tourists take home some of the famous B.C. salmon—indubitably the world's finest. One of them is **Nikka Traders,** 643 Howe St. They gift-pack the fish for travel—soft and hot smoked, fresh frozen, whole, canned smoke, native-style smoked—and will deliver it either to your hotel or to the airport at no extra charge.

USEFUL INFORMATION: For **police** or **ambulance** emergencies, dial 911. . . . For a **doctor,** call 683-2474; for a **dentist,** call 874-9848. . . . The **Automobile Association** (tel. 732-3911) is at 999 W. Broadway. . . . The main branch of the **post office** is at 349 W. Georgia St. (tel. 666-3531). . . . For bus routes, schedules, and other **transport information,** call 324-3211. . . . The **telegraph office** is at 175 W. Cordova St. (tel. 681-4231). . . . For recorded **weather forecasts,** dial 273-8331. . . . There are two **tourist information centers** on Burrard St.: the Greater Vancouver Convention and Visitors Bureau, 650 Burrard St. (tel. 682-2222), and Tourism British Columbia, 652 Burrard St. (tel. 668-2300). . . . The **Youth Hostel Association** is at 1406 W. Broadway (tel. 738-3128).

ATTRACTIONS OUT OF TOWN: **Fraser Canyon,** one of the natural wonders of the province, lies 2½ driving hours from Vancouver, eastbound on Hwy. 1. This is the site of the **Hell's Gate Airtram,** a ride you won't forget in a hurry. Swiss-built, the fully automated red tramcars descend on cables from highway level to directly above the roaring turbulence of the Fraser River where it leaps and roars through the 110-foot gorge—the spot through which some two million sockeye salmon pass each year on their way to the inland spawning grounds. There are fantastic camera angles from up there, plus a restaurant, gift shop, and observation platform. The ride is $3.50 for adults, $1.75 for children.

The **Heritage Village Museum,** Burnaby, is an enchanting time capsule—an entire little township depicting British Columbia between 1890 and 1925. You can stroll along boardwalks, drop in on your grandparents' schoolhouse, watch an oldtime blacksmith at work, shop in the general store, sniff fresh bread being baked in a log cabin, and generally wallow in nostalgia. And it's only 20 driving minutes from Vancouver. Open daily except Monday. Admission is $1 for adults, half price for children.

Fort Langley National Historic Park, 25 miles east of Vancouver along the Trans Canada Hwy., is the restored site of the trading post of the Hudson's Bay Company (1827–1858), which served simultaneously as a military stronghold. You see the furnishings, utensils, decorations, and log palisades of the place where the Crown Colony of British Columbia was proclaimed in 1858. Open all week.

Also in Fort Langley is the **Farm Machinery Museum,** showing the implements of pioneering life in the colony. From crude plows and wooden kitchen utensils to early (hand-powered) stump pullers, pumping devices, vintage tractors, steam cultivators, and the first aircraft—a Tiger Moth—used in B.C. for crop dusting.

The **Vancouver Game Farm** is actually at Aldergrove, eight miles from Fort Langley, 30 miles from Vancouver. Consisting of 120 acres of lush farmland, the place has 60 species of wild animals roaming in large paddocks or free. They include tigers, jaguars, lions, ostriches, buffalo, hippos, elephants, and camels, and those in "Babyland" are eminently touchable. Open daily till dusk.

The **Canadian Military Engineers Museum** stands on the army base at Chilliwack, some 80 miles east of Vancouver along the Trans Canada Hwy. It houses a fascinating collection of military spectacles and gadgetry, including rows of archaic flintlocks and matchlocks—some of them looking more lethal for the user than for the target. There are weapons dating back to 1610, machine guns and mortars from both World Wars, authentic uniforms and medals, many dating back to the Zulu and Boer Wars, and a unique panoramic reproduction of the Battle of Waterloo, containing more than 1400 hand-painted miniature soldiers. Open to the public Monday to Friday till 4 p.m.

The **Sunshine Coast** starts a few miles west of North Vancouver—a scenic mingling of beaches, mountains, ocean inlets, and fishing harbors, where salmon and oysters are plentiful and the boating is superb. (The best time for oyster picking is spring or fall.) The best way to get to the Sunshine Coast is by ferry (tel. 669-1211 for information). The beautiful white boats of the **B.C. Ferry Corporation** are equipped with picture windows, spacious lounges, promenade decks, and cafeterias. They depart from Horseshoe Bay, West Vancouver, 13 miles from downtown. Fares to Earls Cove / Saltery Bay are $2 for adults, $1 for children. And you may come back with enough trout, salmon, oysters, clams, and prawns to take care of your food bills for the next two days.

The **George C. Reifel Migratory Bird Sanctuary** covers 850 acres on Westham Island, six miles west of Ladner, south of Vancouver. A (rather windy) paradise for bird watchers, the sanctuary has an observation tower and two miles of pathways. Over 230 species pass through here, including great blue herons, trumpeter swans, hawks, eagles, peregrine falcons, owls, and coots. The breeds vary with the season, of course, but you get the greatest variety from September to November. July and August are the quietest months. Open in summer to 6 p.m., in winter to 4:30 p.m.

Tours and Excursions

The **Royal Hudson** is a wonderfully cozy steam train that puffs and whistles from the B.C. Rail Station in North Vancouver to the picturesque logging village of Squamish, leaving at 10 a.m. and returning at 4 p.m. The train is a delight for railroad buffs, pulled by one of the mighty "2860" locomotives that huffed their way across all of Canada in the 1930s. The trip goes through some of the grandest scenery in the province. Round-trip tickets for adults are $6.50; for children, $3.75. For reservations, phone 987-5211.

Sternwheeler Tours of Vancouver's spectacular harbor depart daily at 12:30 or 1 p.m. from the Ferry Terminal at the foot of Denman St. (tel. 687-9558). The boats are genuine old paddle-wheelers with tall black funnels, and the tour circles the entire harbor area, accompanied by a running commentary on what you're seeing. Adults pay $4; children, half price.

S.S. Beaver is an exact replica of the 109-ton wooden paddle-steamer (also equipped as a sailing vessel) that sailed the wild Pacific Coast in the 1840s. Today she undertakes very comfortable cruises around Burrard Inlet and English Bay, fitted with observation decks, barbecue gear, and a dance lounge. The cruises run from June 2 to September 9, and cost $26 for adults, $17 for children. For information, phone 682-7284.

City Tours: A variety of sightseeing jaunts in and around Vancouver are run by **Trailways,** 1650 Granville St. (tel. 669-2431). The Vancouver City Tour takes in Stanley Park, Gastown, Chinatown, English Bay beaches, etc., lasts three hours, and costs $7.50 for adults, $3.75 for children. Another version also includes the Aquarium (with the killer whale show), and costs $10 for adults, $6 for children.

Other excursions show you the University of British Columbia, the city parks, Capilano Canyon, and the salmon hatcheries, costing $8, with children paying half price. All tours depart from the Hotel Vancouver and feature free pickups from other large hotels.

Somewhat more turbulent are the river-raft trips organized by **Whitewater Adventures** (tel. 736-2135). These are one- to five-day expeditions on motor-driven rubber rafts, combining the thrills of whitewater rafting with the pleasures of swimming, hiking, picnicking, and sunbathing. The shortest runs are one-day trips through Hell's Gate or on the Thompson River, costing $49 per person. Both depart from the Vancouver Planetarium at 7 a.m. and return at about 7:30 p.m. Prices include transport from Vancouver, a riverside lunch, and a waterproof camera box. You *will* need a complete set of dry clothing for the return trip.

The **Princess Louisa Fjord Cruise,** 1005 Highland Dr., West Vancouver (tel. 922-0709), is a fly-cruise adventure in a luxuriously appointed motor vessel that takes a maximum of 12 passengers. The tour starts at the Bayshore Inn air dock, where a Beaver aircraft picks you up and whisks you to Egmont. There you board the boat and cruise to Princess Louisa, up a magically blue, deep, and clear fjord, fringed by mountains towering to 8000 feet, with waterfalls rushing down vertical granite walls. The cruise runs three hours each way, and a lot of refreshments plus hefty lunch are included in the price. It departs thrice weekly from May through September.

Tour Guide Services: British Columbia's professional guide services are offered by **Alexior,** 726 Richards St. (tel. 681-9385). The guides are multilingual, highly knowledgeable, and very informative, and can be hired for $12.50 per hour for a minimum of three hours.

Special Events

Folkfest, July 1. British Columbia's biggest multicultural festival. Staged partly in Gastown, partly at the Orpheum Theatre, it's a whirl of native costumes, ethnic foods, dance and choir performances. All events are free, but you have to pay for the cosmopolitan tidbits.

Pacific National Exhibition, late August to Labour Day. A compendium of fun fair, exhibitions, displays, shows, and sports, and kicked off by a two-hour grand parade, it's held at the Exhibition Grounds, with free indoor and outdoor entertainment. Highlights are the loggers' contests, with lumbermen from all over the province competing in pole climbing and log burling.

Oktoberfest, weekends, late September early October. Strictly Teutonic and very lively, with eating, drinking, and entertainment from early evening to 2 a.m. at the Exhibition Grounds, it features local and imported dance groups and oompah bands, genuine Tyrolean village music, and the famous Bavarian "pants-slappers" folk dancers.

2. Victoria and Vancouver Island

When you cross from Vancouver to Victoria you could momentarily believe that you've crossed the Atlantic and stepped ashore at an English seaside town. The capital of British Columbia looks so much like a mirror image of Bournemouth, Brighton, or Torquay that you glance at the flags to reassure yourself you're still in Canada.

Those glaring red double-decker buses, Tudor-style homes, manicured lawns, tea shoppes, pubs, antique stores, and bookshops are so inimitably *British* that it takes a while to sink in that they are, in fact, imitations. The massive gray stone edifice of the Parliament Buildings seem specifically designed to house an *English* assembly. Even the street illuminations have the mellow gaslight sheen of Victorian England. It's hard to imagine that this was once a gold-rush town and fur-trading post with a very far-from-genteel clientele.

But imitation or not, Victoria is a charmer, a not-so-little jewel of a town that somehow manages to retain the atmosphere of a seaside resort while edging close to 200,000 inhabitants. Having the mildest climate and the finest gardens in Canada helps. So do the millions of tourists who swarm in annually to wander beneath the baskets of blossoms that hang from the downtown lamp-posts. So does the picture-postcard panorama that Rudyard Kipling once described as "Brighton Pavillion with the Himalayas for a backdrop."

Victoria was founded in the 1840s as the new western headquarters of the Hudson's Bay Company. It changed from a trading post to a rip-roaring boom town when it became the hub of activity generated by the 1858 gold rush in the Cariboo region of British Columbia. When the Canadian Pacific Railway was being built, British Columbia joined the country as a province (with Victoria as capital) on the promise that the railroad would link its seat of government with the others.

That promise, however, went the way of a great many others. The C.P. tracks terminated at Vancouver, on the mainland, leaving the capital a backwater "deprived" of industrial expansion. Today millions of people thank history for this deprivation. The lack of factory chimneys allowed Victoria to remain a garden spot, free from slums, smog, congestion, pollution, and din, and with a bare minimum of high-rises to ruin its pretty profile. Instead it blossomed into the "bit of the old country" dream of prosperous merchants, farmers, and retired company servants from England and Scotland who fell in love with the scenery and climate.

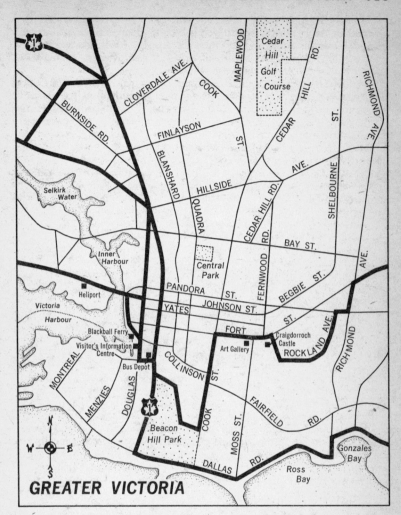

GREATER VICTORIA

And when you see the spotless tiled pavements, green trees, and colored awnings of Government St., the velvet lawns along the oceanfront, the little squares and romantic alleys of Old Town, you'll probably agree that mislaid promises can turn out to be blessings.

ORIENTATION: Victoria sits on the extreme southern tip of Vancouver Island, the largest island on the Pacific coast of North America. Her spectacular doorstep is the Juan de Fuca Strait, a narrow strip of water wedged in between the island and the northern portion of Washington State, dotted with smaller islands and dominated by the snow-capped peaks of the Olympic Mountains. The city actually lies closer to the U.S. than to mainland Canada.

The center and social focal point of the capital is the **Empress Hotel,** a grande dame of such regality that you get the impression the town was built around her as an afterthought. From the portals of this edifice you overlook the **Inner Harbour,** a wonderful bustle of yachts, ferries, fishing boats, launches, and seaplanes. You are now facing due west.

A few steps south rises the green-domed stone majesty of the **Parliament Buildings,** facing an enormous wooden totem pole and housing the legislative apparatus of British Columbia. Cutting through the vast lawns around this building is **Government St.** which, running north, takes you to the post office and the city's main shopping and entertainment area. This is **Old Town** and **downtown,** a tightly entwined duality of arcades, small squares, picturesque alleys, and wide commercial streets.

Farther to the north and east stretches what is known as **Greater Victoria,** more like a patchwork of townships and villages held together by parks and gardens. Northeast lies the University of Victoria, due north the enchanting Butchart Gardens, the airport, and the town of Sidney, and at the very tip of the peninsula **Swartz Bay,** arrival point of the ferry from Vancouver. The ferry from Seattle, for some unknown reason, lands right downtown.

Getting There and Getting Around

Victoria is serviced by three major airlines and several charter outfits, whose buzzing little seaplanes belong to the regular sights of the Inner Harbour. But the most joyous means, from whichever direction you're coming, is by **ferry.** The white, tall-funneled *Princess Marguerite* does the 4¼-hour trip from Seattle daily, the passage costing $13 for adults, $7 for children.

From Vancouver you have a choice of eight daily sailings by **car ferry,** with excellent bus connections between cities and boat terminals. The 100-minute crossing, among little islands and coastal mountain ranges, is one of the nicest ocean jaunts you'll ever make. (Phone 386-3431 for information.) Tickets cost $3 for adults, half price for children, and $9 per vehicle.

The towns of the island are linked by **Pacific Coach Lines,** 710 Douglas St. (tel. 385-4411). There's also the **E & N Railway** that operates daily between Victoria and Courtenay—but never on Sunday (tel. 383-1104). Greater Victoria has the **Vancouver Island Transit** bus service, charging 50¢ per ride (tel. 386-8457). There are also **cab** companies: **Blue Bird** (tel. 382-4235), or **United** (tel. 388-9935). Taxi rides cost $1 at flagfall, then 10¢ every 30 seconds.

Car-rental outfits include: **Tilden,** 767 Douglas St. (tel. 386-1213); and **Budget,** 843 Douglas St. (tel. 388-5525).

ACCOMMODATIONS: Being a resort town has the advantage of a vast selection of hostelries in central locations—mostly along the waterfront. It has the drawback that many of them get packed to the rafters during the peak summer season, July and August. If you intend visiting Victoria in that period, it would be a wise move to book ahead.

Luxury

The **Empress Hotel,** 721 Government St. (tel. 604/384-8111), doesn't need an address. It represents a cornerstone of Victoria, and you can miss it no more than you could accidentally brush past the harbor (although you might, possibly, mistake it for the legislature).

The Empress opened in 1908 and has kept enough period regality to make it an institution as much as a hotel. Tea in the lobby, served at 4 p.m., is an *occasion*—like having a cuppa with a dowager queen: homemade scones and crumpets, Devonshire cream, silver teapots and all, with the chance of a movie star or two hovering in the background. An ivy-ranked gray stone structure, looking like a cross between a château and an art museum, the Empress has a huge lobby that even a couple of simultaneous tour busloads can't clutter completely, plus one of the finest restaurants in town, an informally elegant garden cafe, two bars, and—gracious me!—a disco. The hallways are lofty, the service smooth, with a touch of assured pride. The 416 bedrooms have the stamp of serene and slightly subdued elegance that distinguishes hotels of this class—no screaming murals or canned Mantovani for this lady.

Singles are priced from $42 to $57; doubles, from $51 to $67; and suites, from $65 to $110.

Executive House, 777 Douglas St. (tel. 604/388-5111), is a gleaming glass tower soaring from the downtown area. It features a small, smart lobby and an arcade floor with barbershop and banquet rooms, an English pub-inspired grill, complete with Tiffany lamps and antiques, and an excellent swimming pool, in case you find the ocean too chilly. Mostly ultramodern, but in top taste, the reception area is furnished with black leather settees that not only look good but rank among the most comfortable I've ever relaxed in.

The bedrooms, in matching orange, walnut, and chrome shades, are both elegant and streamlined. The open walk-in closet occupies an entire corner, and the little balconies provide wonderful views. There's a bedside clock radio, caressing carpeting, color TV, and a 19th-story penthouse apartment surrounded by a rooftop garden.

Singles go for $32; doubles, for $38; suites, for $48; and that plush penthouse nest, for $125.

The **Harbour Towers,** 345 Québec St. (tel. 604/385-2405), was designed for views. Every room has one, either across the harbor or the Juan de Fuca Strait, take your pick. Looking like a luxurious apartment block, the Towers' stylish reception lies *off* the lobby of Raven's restaurant in the same building. Also on the premises are a swimming pool, hydrotherapy pool, and sauna.

Victoria's fastest and most silent elevators waft you up to the 100 bedrooms. The decor is orange-russet and beautiful, the English color prints on the walls charming, the compact bathrooms equipped with heat lamps, but the views beat every other type of comfort—they *make* the rooms.

Singles range $30 to $34; doubles, $34 to $46; suites, $40 to $60 (with their own kitchen units for an additional $4).

Moderately Priced Hotels

The **Courtyard Inn,** 850 Blanshard St. (tel. 604/385-6787), has an individualized charm all its own. Small and delightfully intimate, the hotel welcomes you with a lobby that looks like a rustic retreat: light-wood walls, basket chairs, Indian handicraft decorations, and possibly the friendliest staff in town. The rusticality is deceptive, however; at the core it's a pretty plush establishment. The restaurant offers gourmet cuisine, the swimming pool and sauna are luxurious, and the bedrooms come with unique eiderdowns that must be the ultimate in sleeping comfort. Try the Crêperie here for some of the best dessert crêpes on the Pacific Coast.

Singles cost $29; doubles, $34; while children under 12 cost nothing (in their parents' room).

The **Olde England Inn,** 429 Lampson St. (tel. 604/388-4353), lies five minutes by bus from downtown, but seems to have turned back the clock by four centuries. The hotel forms part of an entire Elizabethan village: a thatched, beamed, and shingled replica of Stratford in the rein of Queen Bess. The inn itself is a museum. You enter by a Baronial Hall, replete with suits of armor, ancient weaponry, banners, and a huge copper-canopied fireplace. The 50 bedrooms are all individually furnished; some with exquisite antiques and authentic European canopy beds (used, we are told, by assorted continental monarchs). Standing on a bluff amid five acres of gorgeous grounds, the inn combines Tudor trappings with all-modern bathroom facilities. For good measure, you also get magnificent vistas of sea and mountains.

Rates vary as much as the bedrooms: singles *or* doubles from $20 to $50; the special "Honeymoon Rooms," $35 to $50.

The **Swiftsure Inn,** 427 Belleville St. (tel. 604/386-3451), overlooks the harbor and offers an outdoor terrace cafe from which to watch the marine action with a drink in your hand and a sunshade over your head. A modern, comfortable four-story hostelry, the Swiftsure has a good seafood restaurant, a vaguely nautical cocktail lounge, and 80 bedrooms. The rooms are on the small side, nicely carpeted and comfortable, but not luxurious, with dial telephone, color TV, ornate hanging lamps, and slip-proof bathtubs. While there's only limited hanging space for two people, there are pleasing ocean views and very handy bedside TV switches.

Singles run from $33 to $37; doubles, $37 to $41.

The **Royal Scot,** 425 Québec St. (tel. 604/388-5463), is an attractively contemporary motor hotel with the lobby of a Scottish castle. You are greeted by baronial oak beams, chandeliers disguised as candelabras, royal scarlet carpets and armchairs. The 100 bedrooms, by contrast, are brightly modern, equipped with color cablevision, dial telephones, and excellent bathrooms. There's a large heated indoor pool, Jacuzzi, and sauna. Some of the suites come with full kitchen facilities.

Singles cost $30; doubles, from $34 to $40.

The **Shamrock Motel,** 675 Superior St. (tel. 604/385-8768), is a small corner building facing the vast green expanse of Beacon Hill Park. A large communal balcony runs along the entire front of the structure. Each of the 15 units is self-contained, comprising a big sitting room, bedroom, bathroom, and all-electric kitchen with refrigerator and utensils—a real money saver for two or more people. The furnishings are comfortable if not stylish, with writing desks, sliding-door closets and cupboards, large and springy beds, standing, table, and bedside lamps, and somewhat lurid color prints on the walls.

One or two persons pay $34 to $38 per unit; each additional adult is charged $6.

The **Embassy,** 520 Menzies St. (tel. 604/382-8161), offers bedrooms or self-contained units with full maid service. Guests, however, are asked to wash their own dishes or pay an additional $4 for having the maid do them. An attractive white building with a good-sized pool, the Embassy has a tiny lobby and 36 rooms. Done in bright pastel shades, the airy rooms have big sliding-door closets, ample lighting, TV and telephones, and fine green carpets. Cooking facilities are tucked away in small alcoves.

Singles go for $28; doubles, from $30 to $32; kitchen units cost $4 extra.

Victoria's motel row is **Gorge Rd.,** about a mile north of the city center, with excellent bus connections to downtown. A rather industrialized and not overly handsome thoroughfare, Gorge Rd. is studded with hostelries in the medium and budget price ranges. Some of the selections there belong to the first, others to the second bracket, and you'll find them under the appropriate headings. But they're plenty more along the road:

The **Maple Leaf Inn,** 120 Gorge Rd. (tel. 604/388-9901), resembles a chalet with a swimming pool, sundeck, whirlpool, and sauna. Of the 64 units, about one-third have their own kitchens (costing $4 extra). All come equipped with color TV and dial telephones, queen-size beds or (on request) waterbeds. Very pleasantly furnished, they include bathrooms with heat lamps, large folding-door closets, message service, and complimentary morning coffee (rather rare in Canada).

Singles are $26; doubles, $28; $1 for each additional person.

The **Scotsman Motel**, 490 Gorge Rd. (tel. 604/388-7358), run by an exceptionally hospitable husband-wife team, has a tropical white gleam on the outside and a lobby rather incongruously decorated with hefty Scottish battle axes. Of the 37 units, 20 come with kitchens, all with individual heat control, dial telephones, TV, and heat lamps in the bathrooms. The furniture is ample and new, with carpeting and seating facilities of excellent quality. Waterbeds are available on request. There's a coin laundry for guests, and the kitchens (which cost $4 extra) could serve to illustrate a modern home brochure. Complimentary morning coffee.

Singles pay $24; doubles, $26; and each additional person, $4.

Budget

Still along Gorge Rd. we have the **Chestnut Grove**, 210 Gorge Rd. (tel. 604/385-3488). A small motel with a pretty blue and gray stone frontage, the Chestnut also has a little pool in the rear. The 20 units are modern and neat, 12 of them with private kitchens. You get wall-to-wall red carpets, extra-long beds, walnut-hued writing desks, and bathrooms with fiberglass tubs and heat lamps. Some rooms have an open hanging space instead of a closet, but all have color TV and dial phones.

Singles go for $18 to $22; doubles, $24 to $28.

The **Pacific Isle Motel**, 626 Gorge Rd. (tel. 604/385-3455), looks very simple from the outside but contains 24 good-sized, well-maintained units, and six with kitchens, and all with private bath, new red carpeting, walk-in closets, and color TV, but no room telephones (there's a pay phone in the lobby). The kitchens are quite spacious and there's a little dinette to eat in. The motel has no restaurant, but a 24-hour diner lies just across the road.

Singles cost $16 to $20; doubles, $20 to $26.

Heading back downtown, the **City Centre Motel**, 855 Douglas St. (tel. 604/386-2904), offers 26 self-contained units as well as a restaurant on the premises. A somewhat weathered corner building, the place has a vast dark lobby and spacious but sparsely furnished rooms. The kitchens have electric stoves, refrigerators, and dinettes, while the living rooms have TV, lots of open hanging space, and curious dial telephones on the walls. The decor is green and brown, the carpeting rather worn.

Singles cost $21; doubles, $26.25.

Also on Douglas St., at no. 1001, is the **Sussex** (tel. 604/386-3441). An old-fashioned apartment hotel, the Sussex has several stores, a coffeeshop, and a barbershop on the premises. You have a choice between bedrooms or small apartments with dinettes and kitchenettes, all well maintained, simple, and clean. Some of the apartments come with adjoining bedrooms.

Single rooms run from $17; doubles, from $21. Apartments go for $20 per single, $25 per double occupancy.

At the harborfront, the **Admiral Motel**, 257 Belleville St. (tel. 604/388-6267), is a small, quiet, modern establishment. Some of the 29 units have their own kitchens, and several can house up to seven people. The singles are fairly small, the furnishings basic, lighting arrangements ample. All units have room thermostats, color TV, and dial telephones, as well as bathrooms.

Singles go from $22 to $24; doubles, $26 to $32; with additional persons paying $4 each. Children under 6 stay free with their parents.

The Ys

Victoria's **YM** and **YWCA** are both housed in the same building at 880 Courtney St. (tel. 604/386-7511). Although providing facilities for both sexes, the residence part is for *women only*—primarily single girls from 17 to 22. A massive, modern brown brick building with a brightly spacious lobby and inviting green leather settees, the Y has a cafeteria (closed on Sundays) and a total of 31 beds in single and double rooms. The rooms are bright and quite natty, but have neither private baths nor sinks. There are shared bathrooms on each floor, and the telephone is likewise communal. The management provides lots of towels but no soap—so bring your own, ladies. A cozy TV lounge downstairs and a coed swimming pool on the premises.

Singles rooms cost $9.50; doubles, $14. All rents are payable in advance.

Victoria Trailer Parks and Campgrounds

Oak Park, 616 Goldstream Ave. (tel. 604/478-1823), is a motel-trailer court in 2½ acres of parkland, with swimming and shopping, hot showers, and full hookups. Campsites for two persons cost $4; trailer sites, $5.50.

Inn City Park, 3430 Seymour Ave. (tel. 604/382-4322), has coin-showers, laundromat, sani-station, and full hookups. It's a quiet location near a shopping center. Campsites for two cost $6; trailer sites, $7.

Jackson's Goldstream Estates, 974 Goldstream Ave. (tel. 604/478-5812), has a store adjacent, sani-stations, showers, flush toilets, and a laundromat. Trailer sites cost $5.

MEALS: Victoria has a generally wonderful selection of eateries, ranging from deluxe gourmet chambers to economy quickies. As in most resort towns, the budget meals cost slightly more than the Canadian average, and during the high-pressure summer months they tend to get pretty crowded. There are some—but far too few—outdoor cafes, a deficiency the town shares with every Anglo-Saxon city on the face of the globe.

The Top Choices

Dingle House, 137 Gorge Rd. East (tel. 382-8721), is a jewel of a Victorian mansion, so exquisite that the beauty of the surroundings almost overshadows the excellence of the food. The mansion dates from the 1870s, and has a jovial resident ghost named Charlie and a winsome hostess named Junine Oberg. The dining room, lounge, and stairways are regal affairs, glowing in scarlet and gold, filled with antique furniture and paintings in costly frames. You dine off silver plates and bone china, and the cuisine is on a par with the crockery. Start with the house pâté. Go on to the house specialty, roast prime ribs of beef, and conclude with the house dessert, velvet hammer, an Elysian concoction of ice cream, brandy, and Cointreau, topped with whipped cream. Have your coffee served in the upstairs lounge, sit back, and admire the 14-foot ceilings and stained-glass windows. Your meal will have cost you about $20.

The **Empress Room** (tel. 384-8111), is the palatial dining chamber of the Empress Hotel, where the chandeliers glow amber, the ornately carved wood ceiling might have been transplanted from a royal banquet hall, and George C. Scott could be dining at the next table. A pleasantly subdued four-piece combo plays strict-tempo music, and you can dance off the excess calories between courses. Service is in the grand tradition, and the fare matches the decor: oysters Rockefeller or smoked B.C. salmon for starters; then, say, the veal zingara (fried in butter and served with ham, mushrooms, and truffles); then coffee and Grand Marnier. The meal would come to around $21. Dinner served until 10 p.m.

Still more Victoriana at **Chauney's,** 614 Humboldt St. (tel. 385-4512), although the host and most of the menu are impeccably French. Chauney's foyer is hung with outstanding feasting scenes and uniforms from the Crimean War. The dining room breathes subdued luxury: a combination of swelling settees, soundless carpets, soft lighting, and a general air of total devotion to the pleasures of gastronomy. The menu carefully separates local seafood from the imported delicacies—a practice other establishments should follow. You can start with marinated frog legs and follow up with roast quail. For dessert try possibly the richest and most alcoholic baba au rhum on the island. Total cost—roughly $20. Open for lunch and dinner seven days a week.

The **Captain's Palace,** 309 Belleville St. (tel. 388-9191), has such a nautical trim that it would seem sacreligious to order anything but seafood. The white, pillared, blue-roofed mansion dates from 1897, and you dine in the captain's living room, gazing at the sea through bay windows. The table spreads are works of art, the walls hung with the tall ships bearing the proud names of *Cutty Sark* and *Thermopylae.* The stained glass, frescoes, fireplaces, and built-in buffets evoke the era of the four-masters—at least the plush side of it. The atmosphere is serene and leisurely, and so is the service: plenty of time to admire the superb oak-paneled foyer and vast antique collection of this city landmark. Try the steamed clams—served in their own juice—as gala première, followed by the fresh spring salmon steak poached in a court bouillon. For dessert, the Venetian cream created from creams, brandy, and liqueurs. You'll pay around $19. The Palace, amazingly, is open seven days a week for breakfast, lunch, tea, and dinner.

Moderately Priced Restaurants

The **Rathskeller,** 885 Douglas St. (tel. 386-9348), has the looks of a real "keller" with a low ceiling resting on whitewashed pillars. You sit on wooden peasant chairs, surrounded by candle glow and heraldic emblems, listen to Bavarian brass and zither music, and admire the motto of the establishment: "The boss . . . is the cook!" The fare is authentic German, with a few western dishes for balance: Soup with liver dumplings for $1.50, Kassler rippchen (delicately smoked pork chops) for $7.95, rich cheesecake for $1.45. Instead of the customary beer you might try the delightfully tart B.C. cider. Open all week till 10 p.m.

It's just a few steps to the mellow pub atmosphere of the **Meatmarket,** Nootka Court, Douglas and Humboldt Sts. (tel. 383-4442). The lounge, equipped with deep-cushioned chesterfields, welcomes you with an embrace, fans you with potted plants, and flatters you with the most seductive lighting in Victoria. As the name indicates, this is cannibal heaven, although fitted with an extensive salad bar. Portions range from large to enormous—from the $8.45 Bonanza prime rib to the $10.45 Meatmarket. All entrees are served with potato, *fresh* peas, and crusty sourdough bread. Open seven days a week.

When you see a shining white, red-shingled windmill with turning sails that looks like a direct transplant from Homer's isles, you'll know it's **Millos,** 716 Burdett St. (tel. 382-4422). The interior is a scenario of cool tiles, white walls, and green ferns, waiters in Greek costumes, and an aroma that hones your tastebuds. You can't do better than the egg-and-lemon soup; then either the moussaka ($7.50) or the kota kapama, chicken slowly simmered in tomato sauce with wine. For dessert, try the classic baklava (which is Turkish) and Greek coffee (which is excellent). Open seven days a week.

Chez Pierre, 512 Yates St. (tel. 388-7711), stands in the very heart of Old Town, where it belongs. A small, delightfully authentic French dinery, it's a magnet for those locals who know about Gallic food and the tourists they tell about it. For all its reputation, the Pierre is not expensive—but it's frequently hard to get into. Don't miss the escargots ($3.90); then try to make up your mind between the canard à l'orange (duck in orange sauce) or the lapin casserole (stewed rabbit), both terrific and both $9.75. Open for dinner only. Closed Sunday and Monday.

Pablo's, 225 Québec St. (tel. 388-4255), is housed in a beautifully refurbished old Edwardian home near the Inner Harbour. It's equally famous for its Spanish food and its Spanish coffee, presented with a kind of ritual fire dance by Pablo in person—quite scary if you're unprepared for the spectacle. The lobster here is live, and you can pick out your own feast. If you've had enough of seafood, go for the gazpacho soup, the marinated chicken Tika, and the crème caramel—altogether about $11.50. Open all week till 11 p.m.

Lee's, 1410 Broad St. (tel. 385-6764), offers a Chinese smorgasbord for a sum total of $6.25 per glutton. It's a long, nicely carpeted dining room decorated with hanging plants and Chinese characters, and the Muzak in the background is strictly elevator-neuter, but the buffet choice is good and substantial, although not very authentic: fried rice, fried chicken, fried fish, curry chicken, sweet-and-sour pork, fried rice, mashed potatoes (yes!), lichee nuts, and fortune cookies. But no chopsticks. Open all week till 11 p.m.

The **Mediaeval Inns,** 1005 Broad St. (tel. 386-8317). You get the choice of participating in a medieval feast, complete with minstrels and jesters, or dining to the traditional English, Irish, and Scottish airs delivered by a very talented mandolin-guitar-flute trio called Irish Mist. Both occasions feature pleasing serving wenches in velvet bodices. The fare is varied and excellent, ranging from steak-and-kidney pie ($4.25) to lobster thermidor ($9.95), from French pâté ($2.50) to English trifle ($1.25). There are several dining rooms in assorted sizes and decors, so you can eat in surroundings that fit your mood.

Japanese Village, 734 Broughton St. (tel. 382-5165), features the traditional Teppan tables with the cooking surfaces built into the top. The "tradition," however, is fairly new, since these tables were specifically designed for benighted Occidentals whose legs rebelled against the standard Japanese floor-level facilities. The chefs prepare each meal at the table, combining cooking with juggling skills in a dazzling display of flashing knives and dissected vittles. You get all the famous Teppan delicacies: shrimp, steak teriyaki, scallops, kamaboko, hibachi chicken, etc., fervently hoping that your chef's fingers won't be added to the menu (they haven't lost one yet). Your best bet here is one of the complete dinners—starting at $7.95—that include samplings from most of the items. Open seven nights a week.

Ivanhoe's, 1314 Government St. (tel. 383-0913), shows a knightly frontage to the wayfarers. Inside, crested flags are draped between the oak beams of the ceiling, with shields mounted on the wall above the tables, interspersed with swords and battle axes. Despite all the hardware, the atmosphere is relaxed, the clientele jolly, the service very friendly. Note the artful iron shingle above the doorway. Sir Walter Scott would have approved. The Cornish game hen is mouth-melting and costs $6.45, the rum cream pie exceptional at $1.35.

Budget Eating

Fisgard St. is Victoria's miniature Chinatown: about two blocks long and lined with restaurants. Here you'll find some of the worthiest medium- and budget-bracket dineries in the city. The food, while not very authentic, keeps high standards and the portions are truly generous. Eventually, we hope, Victoria's Chinese gastronomes will learn that they don't have to compromise quite so heartily with Western palates in order to attract the tourists.

The **Golden City,** 546 Fisgard St. (tel. 386-8404), is one of the best finds here. It's vast, modern, and fairly plain, the walls decorated with golden trees, pagodas, and color prints of fat gamboling elf-children riding on goldfish and such-like steeds. The background music is genuinely Chinese and soft enough to leave you undisturbed. The service is fast, the portions huge, and the place very busy. There's a good array of dishes outside the standardized chop suey range: minced pork with salted eggs ($4.50), bean cakes with meat and fish ($4.75), and tangy garlic spare ribs ($5.50). Open every night, but unfortunately only till 8:30 p.m.

The **Nutshell,** 627 Fort St. (tel. 383-6142), a bright, neat all-American establishment which, however, does not serve nuts in any shape or form—except on sundaes. With Dutch doors, a squirrel for a shingle, and rows of red-clothed tables with flowers, the place is as attractive as its heraldic animal. The fare is no-frills Anglo: ham steak with pineapple rings or grilled lamb chops with potatoes and two vegetables ($5.50); nostalgic thick and sweet chocolate sundaes ($1). Open five days a week till 8 p.m. Closed Saturday and Sunday.

The **Old Victoria Fish and Chips,** 1316 Broad St. (tel. 385-5122), is one of several such establishments geared for the Cockney palate, but likewise a wow with U.S. visitors. Housed in a building constructed during the 1890 Klondike gold rush (for which Victoria was the jumping-off point), the place gleams with genuine 19th-century English copperware. The street windows have leaded glass and plants in copper pots, and seating arrangements are a triple row of booths, London style. The helpings of fried fish with the real "giant" English potato chips cost $2.25. You can also get oysters and chips—an unusual combination—and 21 brands of beer, from New Zealand Leopard Lager and Norwegian Frydenlunds to Tsingtao from China. Closes at 7 p.m., worse luck.

On the other hand **Smitty's,** 878 Douglas St. (tel. 383-5612), never closes at all. A big, air-conditioned, and brightly lit pancake house, Smitty's is a family eatery with the accent on the offspring. The place is nicely carpeted, has laminated tables and very fast service, and is generally a godsend for tourist groups. It serves 16 species of pancakes ($1.80 to $3.75) as well as broiled steak sandwiches, fried shrimp, and other such.

DAYTIME ACTIVITIES: Logically and geographically, the best launching pad for sightseeing is the **Visitor Information Centre,** 786 Government St. (tel. 382-2127), right on the waterfront. With a highly knowledgeable staff, unfailing helpfulness, and an immense stock of maps, timetables, brochures, and pamphlets, the centre can save you valuable holiday time and shoe leather, as well as tipping you off to local sights you might have missed otherwise.

Some of the best of these lie on and around Government St., which runs straight through **Old Town.** On the left is **Bastion Square,** once the stomping ground of bearded miners, roistering sailors, and—appropriately—the site of the municipal gallows. Today it's an enchantingly restored pedestrian mall, with the raucousness ironed out and the facelifted old buildings crammed with boutiques and restaurants.

In the 1200 block on Government St., a little byway runs through to Broad St. This is **Trounce Alley,** where those self-same miners and mariners once clustered to spend their gold. A lot of paint, soap, and affection has gone into making this wee thoroughfare a kind of welcome mat. Lit by gas lamps, hung with heraldic crests, ablaze with flower baskets and potted shrubs, Trounce Alley now offers jewelry, fashions, edibles, and greeting cards.

For the city's senior sight, however, you have to backtrack past the Empress Hotel to the **Parliament Buildings.** Opened in 1898, flanked by the awesome wooden totem pole carvings of **Thunderbird Park,** the legislature of British Columbia bears a certain resemblance to the British House of Commons, at least in the ceremonial trappings. The Speaker sits on a kind of canopied throne. He is escorted by a Sergeant-at-Arms, and the symbol of his authority is a golden mace—now purely ornamental, but originally a very handy implement to use on the heads of obstreperous members who disturbed the assembly. Daily guided tours take you through the house, and at night the building is gorgeously illuminated.

Next to Parliament lies **Heritage Court,** a superb combination of concrete buildings and native plant gardens which you enter by stepping over the petrified prints of a dinosaur. The **Netherlands Carillon,** a gift from the Dutch nation, rises like a slender white column 88 feet from the mall floor, carrying bells weighing 10,612 pounds.

One side is occupied by the **Provincial Museum,** the most fascinating of its kind in Canada, perhaps in America. The word "museum" here is a misnomer. It's a magnificently organized, artistically arranged, and magically lit tour of discovery into the past, the very distant past as much as the very recent. You walk among prehistoric Indian groups and extinct animals. See a full-scale, minutely detailed replica of Captain Vancouver's H.M.S. *Discovery.* Peer into the 19th-century "Grand Hotel," with two floors of period rooms containing 5000 artifacts, including the liquor bottles of the time. Gaze at the model "T" Ford in the City Garage of 1913, which looks like a Norman Rockwell cover. Experience the sights and sounds of a steam railway station—I could fill the chapter with this masterpiece of a museum. And it's free!

Behind Thunderbird Park stands **Helmcken House,** the oldest intact dwelling in Victoria. Designed and built by a physician in the 1850s, the place is now a showcase of colonial life in the upper middle strata. It is intriguing to note how much smaller people were only 120 years ago—we bang our heads on their doorways, and all those lovely china doorknobs are slightly below our grasp. Adults pay 25¢; children, 10¢. Closed Monday and Tuesday.

The **Art Gallery,** housed in another Victorian mansion, is located at 1040 Moss St., about a mile east of downtown, and contains an excellent collection of Asian art, some superb Eskimo pieces, Egyptian statuary dating back to the 6th century B.C., and contemporary Canadian works. Admission is 50¢ for adults, half price for children. Open all week.

A mansion of a different ilk is the **Mystery Mansion,** 327 Belleville St., one block west of Parliament. Something decidedly odd in there, my dear Watson. That skeleton in the dungeon—the poor fellow keeps on moving! And that hallway mirror—has the reflection of a young lady hanging herself. Spiders get a bit big, too. Looks like they're feeding on, good gracious, human bones! Did you notice that witch in the courtyard? I think that raven of hers was trying to tell us something. And the owner of the place didn't seem to be, well, quite there. Transparent—that's the word. We'll have to get to the bottom of this sometime, old chap. Meanwhile, kindly pay that character at the cash box $2. And $1 for your young nephew. Fainted, has he? Hm, wonder why?

You walk down a gently sloping stairway to the bottom of the ocean at the **Undersea Gardens,** 440 Belleville St. There, at eye level with the denizens, you see some 5000 marine creatures feeding, playing, hunting, and mating. They include wolf eels, sharks, poisonous stone fish, flower-like sea anemones, and seals. The highlights are the underwater performances of scuba divers, featuring the star of the show: a huge, nightmarish, but remarkably photogenic octopus named Armstrong. Open all week. Admission is $3 for adults, $1 for children.

Directly opposite stands the **Royal London Wax Museum,** with 170 figures from the works of Josephine Tussaud, magnificently gowned, amazingly lifelike, and set in dozens of scenes, including the obligatory Chamber of Horrors and the recent addition of Star Wars. The **Classic Car Museum,** just behind the Empress Hotel, shows 60 years of vintage automobilia. The sheer functional beauty of some of those Rollses, Jaguars, Chryslers, and ancient Auburns makes you itch to get behind their wheels. Also on display are the Crown Jewels of England (in replica, of course). Open all week. Adults pay $2.50; children, $1.

There's a grave risk that you won't be able to get your kids—or yourself— out of the **Miniature World,** 635 Humboldt St. This is not only the most ingenious, but also the most accurate and artistic setup of its kind I've ever gaped at. The layout follows several themes—Fields of Glory, World of Dickens, Fantasyland, Frontierland, etc.—each so overwhelmingly detailed that you can spend hours discovering new minutiae. But the central masterpiece is a 110-foot-long diorama showing the advance of the Canadian Pacific Railway from 1885 to 1915. The steam train chugs across a fantastically realistic landscape, and as it rolls day changes to dusk, then night. Stars appear in the sky and thousands of little lights twinkle in the towns and villages along the track. It's magical—don't miss it. Admission is $3 for adults, $1 for children. Open daily till 10 p.m.

From the Inner Harbour you catch the red double-decker bus going to Oak Bay and Canada's biggest and best oceanarium. This is **Sealand,** 1327 Beach Dr., one of the greatest attractions the island has to offer. Sealand contains razor-toothed eels, aquatic birds, seals, octopi, salmon, and wondrous ocean plants. Above all, though, it has the world's wettest and most appealing killer whale show in a million-gallon pool. The two performers are the giant Haida, who resembles a cavorting submarine, and Miracle, a baby whale who turned to humans to escape from sickness and starvation. Haida is all tail-smacking, leaping horseplay, determined to get spectators as wet as he is. Miracle is gently affectionate, obviously loves everybody, and wants to show it. To watch these two maneuvering for the limelight is something you'll remember. Especially when you get a closeup of those immense armed jaws. It costs $3.50 for adults, $1 for children.

Butchart Gardens, the flowering gem of Vancouver Island, is also a miracle of sorts. An abandoned limestone pit 14 miles north of Victoria has been transformed into a 35-acre Eden of blossoms, flowers, exotic shrubs, lawns, hedges, little bridges, and rare statuary. Actually there are six different gardens, each with an individual character, and each perfection. Illuminations, dancing fountains, and summer-night stage shows make this a spot you simply don't want to leave. At Benvenuto off West Saanich Rd. Open daily.

Ten minutes from Butchart Gardens, on Cordova Bay Rd., is the **Fable Cottage Estate.** An intriguing melange of artistry, craftsmanship, and fantasy, the estate stretches around a fairytale-like home, looking like an illustration from *Alice in Wonderland,* filled with heirlooms and antiques. The surrounding garden is alive with animated dwarfs, quaint floral creations, strange ocean settings, and spectacular blossom arrays. Open daily in summer.

Craigflower Manor, 110 Island Hwy., is a historical site dating back to 1856. The manor was built for a farm bailiff and restored to its original appearance, including the household goods brought over from Scotland by its pioneering occupants. Admission is 25¢ for adults, 10¢ for children. Closed Monday.

The **English Village,** 429 Lampson St., surrounds the Olde England Inn mentioned in the hotel section. It's a row of amazingly accurate Tudor dwelling houses with everything except the 16th-century dirt. The highlights are the painstakingly correct replicas of Shakespeare's birthplace and the equally famous Thatched Cottage of his wife, Anne Hathaway. The whole village was the dream and inspiration of Royal Air Force Squadron Leader Lane and his wife.

Back in Bastion Square in Victoria, the location of the **Maritime Museum** is appropriately marked by a huge anchor. The museum houses a wealth of artifacts and models connected with the province's nautical history, together with old naval uniforms, journals, and photographs—a must for shipping buffs. Open all week till 6 p.m.

The **Tony Burton Sailing Centre,** 1010 Wharf St. (tel. 383-4011), offers more personal maritime action: sailboat rides around the bay as well as instruction courses in coastal sailing. You get two hours on the water for $12.50 per passenger, or three hours at $15 per. Also a great sail-lunch jaunt (food provided) for $16. Children up to 14 come along for half price.

AFTER DARK: Victoria has four live theater auditoriums, my favorite being the **Belfry,** 1291 Gladstone Ave. This is a charming, small and intimate professional playhouse maintaining high standards of acting. Programs span the gamut of serious theater, from Eugene O'Neill and Harold Pinter to Sondheim musicals. Dark on Mondays.

The other houses present considerably more mixed bags—anything from classical ballet to rock concerts, with the quality depending on who's performing what. The **McPherson Playhouse,** 3 Centennial Square, has modern dance groups, musicals, drama festivals, and light opera. The **Memorial Arena,** 1925 Blanchard St., goes for rock concerts, circus performances, and wrestling bouts. The **Royal Theatre,** 805 Broughton St., is mainly devoted to concerts.

You can find the current programs plus most of what's going on around town in a handy little weekly, *Victoria Guideline,* available in hotel lobbies. The *Guideline* not only keeps up with the food, drink, and entertainment scene, but features enlarged maps on where to locate the places mentioned—a practice more tourist publications should copy.

Nightclubs, Discos, Bars, Cabarets, etc.

The **Old Forge,** 919 Douglas St. (tel. 383-9913), is Victoria's largest nightclub, which isn't so very large at that. The Brothers Forbes and their band attract a wonderfully devoted clientele and there's a lot of dance floor and mike action from 9 p.m. to 2 a.m. Admission is $2.

Until about six years ago there was no such thing as a disco in the entire town. In fact, there was hardly any nightlife worth the title. Today Victoria is awash with discos of all shapes and sizes. The trouble is that they keep changing their names at a dazzling rate, and I can't guarantee that any of those mentioned below will still bear the same label by the time you get to read this.

A good proportion of them are housed in the remarkable entertainment complex centered by the **Strathcona Hotel** of which the Old Forge (above) forms a part. Above, below, beside, and across on the same premises you'll find three discos, **The Sting, Ivy's,** and **The Cuckoo's Nest.** All resemble each other, all generate mighty volumes of sound, pack in a remarkably relaxed crowd, stay open until 2 a.m., and charge $1 to $2 admission (tel. 383-7137). Still under the same hospitable roof is a jumping lounge bar called **Big Bad John's** and a restaurant known as **Barney's Hideaway,** although with the amount of traffic going through, it struck me as the unlikeliest spot to try to hide from anyone.

The Empress Hotel has **Tiffany's,** incongruously out of place in the lower lobby of the capital's grande dame. It does, however, enforce a dress code (no jeans, shorts, or sandals), the music is a few decibels lower, the decor considerably more elegant than the average. From 8:30 p.m. Monday to Saturday. Closed Sunday.

I found it quite impossible to distinguish between places calling themselves "cabarets," "nightclubs," or "discos." Lots of all three, but the labeling is so haphazard that I'll leave it to you to decide what tag belongs to which. (One reason for the confusion is that "cabaret," in Canada, refers to a certain type of liquor license and not to the brand of entertainment offered. Thus a so-called cabaret may consist of anything from a series of variety acts to one solitary combo without so much as a vocalist.)

Très Chic, 1325 Government St. (tel. 388-4114), which bills itself as an "adult discotheque," has a very smart interior, a pleasantly roomy dance floor, and possibly the best dressed crowd in town. Gentlemen *must* wear jackets. No generation gap here—the clientele reaches well into the prosperous 30s.

By contrast, the **Dancers Teen Disco,** 721 Fisgard St. (tel. 388-4432), tries to keep its patrons below the 19-year mark (you can't trust anyone over 21). It rocks Fridays and Saturdays till 12:30 a.m. and sells no liquor.

The **Forty Thieves,** 603 Pandora St., has the distinction of charging no admission, and features one Ladies Only night per week—until 9 p.m., that is, after which a masculine avalanche surges in. All age groups are represented, with plenty of elbow and toe space. A top favorite for mainland visitors, it frequently contains more Vancouverites than locals.

Two decidedly younger crowd hangouts are the **Hot City Disco,** 860 Yates St., and **Oly's,** 642 Johnson St., one a former cabaret, the other a "disco-lounge" (whatever that may be). Both offer mighty musical reverberations till 2 a.m.

Harpo's, Bastion Square, (tel. 385-5333), is currently a disco with live music. It uses both local and imported bands and their offerings switch from rock to jazz and back again. Open Monday to Saturday till 2 a.m.

SHOPPING: Downtown Victoria has several new shopping malls, all designed to blend beautifully with the old-world profile of the district. Latest on the scene is **Harbour Square,** at Government and Courtney Sts. On two levels and air-conditioned, the square houses 25 shops selling women's and men's fashions, jewelry, and a huge variety of imports.

Market Square, at the harbor end of Johnson and Pandora Sts., is a converted and rejuvenated cluster of old theaters, hotels, and residentials turned into retail stores without loss of charm. Spread over three levels around a courtyard garden—with popcorn vendor, balloons, and occasional music—the place has 40 stores, restaurants, lounges, snackeries, hairdressers, and news stands. This is summertime shopping at its nicest.

Victoria has department stores as well, but the accent here is on small, highly individualistic boutiques and specialty outlets, a large number of them dealing in imports—mostly from what used to be known as "Homeland & Empire."

One of the most unusual is **Alcheringa,** in Trounce Alley. The name is Australian Aboriginese for "Dream Time." A quiet little shop, pleasantly low pressure, it offers merchandise from Australia, New Zealand, and New Guinea: lambskin rugs and slippers, seashells from the Great Barrier Reef, Maori handicrafts, woolly toys. Plus, of course, opals of every size, boomerangs, and primitive Sepik art from New Guinea's headhunters territory.

Also in Trounce Alley is **Victoria Handloom Ltd.** This store sells a magnificent range of Canadian handicraft products, cloths from the cottage looms of New Brunswick being merely part of them. You'll find collectors' pieces in handmade vases, bowls, and plates, beautiful jade wildlife figures, jewelry crafted by some of Canada's masters in the field, and salespeople who really know what they're selling.

Sasquatch, 1233 Government St., specializes in the famous Cowichan Indian sweaters, bought directly from the homes of knitting Indian matrons on Vancouver Island. Their buyer, who tours the reservation thrice weekly, is so expert that he can tell which garment was made by whom by looking at the finished piece. The sweaters come only in white, black, or gray, and no two of them are alike.

OUT-OF-TOWN ATTRACTIONS: **Duncan** lies 38 miles north of Victoria up the Trans Canada Hwy. The little town is the center of the rural Cowichan Valley (an Indian word meaning "warmed by the sun"), the area where the famed Indian sweaters are knitted from naturally colored raw wool. The whole region is a forest, lake, and river playground, ideal for hiking, swimming, fishing, and camping. You can see the amazing **Glass Castle,** with a collection of 180,000 bottles, and **St. Francis Xavier Church,** an example of the community-built early pioneer churches.

Two miles north of Duncan is the **Forest Museum.** Extending over 100 acres, this out- and indoor showpiece tells the story of wood better than a library of books. You can ride in a logging handcar and a narrow-gauge steam train, tour an old logging camp, watch logging movies from the old days, and gaze at Douglas firs, five feet round and 180 feet tall, that were already a century old when Captain Cook landed on Vancouver Island in 1778. Open daily till 5:30 p.m. Admission (which includes the train ride) is $2 for adults, 50¢ for children.

Nanaimo, the "sun porch of Canada," basks 69 miles north of Victoria on the same highway. Small and friendly, Nanaimo is a major deep-sea fishing port, but used to be a Hudson's Bay Company outpost. In 1853 the company men built the **Bastion,** a small fort-tower designed to protect the settlers against Indian attacks—which never came. But the tower has become a historical landmark and is open to visitors. Another stop is the **Centennial Museum,** which shares a building with the tourist bureau.

Parksville, 92 miles north of Victoria, is the major beach resort area of Vancouver Island, and reputedly has the warmest ocean swimming in Canada. There are miles and miles of white sandy beaches, never overcrowded, superb camping in **Englishman River Park,** scenic forests with dark green pools on the road to **Port Alberni.** For overnight stays there's the charming **Beach Acres Lodge,** originally the manor house of a country estate, now a guest house offering bedrooms either with private or semiprivate baths. Open from June 23 to Labour Day, one mile south of Parksville on Island Hwy. 1. Rates from $17 for singles, $19 for doubles.

All the above places are serviced by **Pacific Coach Lines,** 710 Douglas St. (tel. 385-4411).

Tours and Excursions

Vancouver Island measures about 12,400 square miles and has 350,000 inhabitants, more than half of them clustered in the extreme southern tip within or around Greater Victoria. This leaves quite a chunk of island to explore beyond the area of the capital. The most pleasant, leisurely, and luxurious way of doing it is by boat. The **British Columbia Ferry Corp.** runs exploration cruises from Vancouver and from Victoria (tel. 669-1211 in Vancouver; tel. 386-3431 in Victoria).

The ship used for both ventures is the big and beautiful *Queen of Prince Rupert.* From Victoria the trip takes two days and one night, starting with a scenic drive to **Campbell River** (the world's Tyee salmon capital), where you stay overnight. Then you board the ship in Kelsey Bay and nose majestically through the Johnstone Strait, along the Gulf of Georgia to Tsawwassen (possibly the most misspelled spot in the atlas) during nine hours of panoramic cruising and wonderful views from the observation lounges. Tickets, at $61.15 per passenger, include the overnight hotel stay.

The **Grayline,** 912 Douglas St. (tel. 388-5248), runs a mixed fleet of sightseeing buses: authentic red double-deckers, imported from London, for the Victoria city jaunts, the customary parlor coaches for outside ventures. All tours depart from in front of the Empress Hotel.

The **Grand City Tour** departs daily at 11:30 a.m. and 1:30 p.m., takes in all the historic and scenic highlights of the capital (try to capture a seat on the top deck), and lasts 1½ hours. Tickets are $4.50. **Tour 2A,** leaving at 10 a.m. and 1 p.m. daily, visits Butchart Gardens and gives you a conducted tour through 30 acres of spectacular flowers, ponds, fountains, and waterfalls. The trip takes 2½ hours and costs $9. You can also take a twice-daily four-hour combination of both of the above tours for $12.

3. Elsewhere in British Columbia

THE BIG PEACE RIVER COUNTRY: The Far North of the province—twice the size of Ohio—is inhabited by barely 50,000 people. But also by moose, caribou, black bear, grizzlies, lynx, beavers, wolverines, and eagles. It offers the fantastic spectacle of the Northern Lights, shimmering across the sky in a Niagara of changing colors. The center is **Fort St. John,** dating from 1798. At **Dawson Creek** stands the world's most photographed milestone: the **Mile Zero Post,** marking the start of the famous Alaska Hwy.

KIMBERLEY: In the Rocky Mountains, 500 miles east of Vancouver, is the highest city in Canada—and one of the most amazing. The entire mining community of 8000 people has been turned into a Bavarian Alpine village! It's not terribly genuine, but there's enough likeness to make you believe you've stumbled into Central Europe by mistake. The core of the town is the "Platzl" (mall) with peasant-baroque storefronts, bubbling brook, flowers, and pedestrians wearing "lederhosen." In July the town celebrates its annual "Julyfest,"

with parades, folk dances, international entertainment, and tidal waves of beer. While you're there you can inspect the world's largest lead and zinc mine.

OSOYOOS: In complete and startling contrast to the above, this is a Spanish desert town that makes you rub your eyes in disbelief. The pocket desert in question lies 252 miles east of Vancouver, two miles from the U.S. border. But sparkling Lake Osoyoos lies right alongside, and the region grows the earliest fruit crop in the country, including magnificent peaches. The **Okanagan Valley,** of which this is the southern tip, was once the road to the eastern gold fields, and you can still pan for gold there—occasionally even find some.

KSAN: An authentic Indian village of the Gitskan tribe, reconstructed in every detail and similar to the one that stood there when the first explorers came to the Hazelton area, at the junction of the Skeena and Bulkley Rivers, the village consists of four communal houses, a House of the Arts and a Carving House, where you can see Indian craftsmen at work with leather, stone, wood, and cloth. The House of Treasures contains the tribal regalia of Gitksan chiefs. At the Frog House you can see the ingenious use the Indians made of bones, skins, feathers, fur, stones, and bark to produce implements they needed before the introduction of European tools. A modern campground and trailer park adjoins the village, complete with power hookups, showers, and toilets. Ksan is operated as a joint enterprise of the Indian association and the Canadian government.

KAMLOOPS: Located 267 miles northeast of Vancouver, this is a small community spread out over 140 square miles—with several ranches right within the city limits. Nestling in a scenic valley, Kamloops lies surrounded by 2000 lakes, offering some of the easiest and most rewarding fishing in all Canada. These are the homewaters of the famous Kamloops trout, and by a good rule of thumb the larger the lake the bigger the trout. Lake Shuswap produces the biggest of all—up to 20 pounds. The nearby Adams River spawns the world's largest sockeye salmon. There is no general closed season here. Kamloops has over 50 hotels and motels, while the entire region is peppered with dude ranches, chalets, motels, campsites, and trailer parks. It is serviced by Pacific Western Airlines, two railroads, and two bus lines on a regularly scheduled basis.

THE CARIBOO GOLD RUSH COUNTRY: Actually called Cariboo Chilcotin, this is a huge chunk of land north of Vancouver stretching from the Pacific Ocean almost to the Rockies. Parts of it are ranch country, with working cowboys and working guest ranches, including some of the biggest in North America. The Cariboo area abounds in gold-rush memorabilia—a historic museum in **Clinton,** the overland telegraph and a gigantic water wheel (used to pump out mine shafts) in **Quesnel.** This is the gateway to **Barkerville,** restored almost exactly as it was in the gold-rush days. The main street consists of false-fronted shops, looking like props from a Hollywood horse opera. You can visit the uproarious Royal Theatre Review, take a bumpy ride in a stage coach, or watch a reincarnation of Judge Begby (the notorious "hanging judge") presiding over his court. You can reach the area by train, bus, or plane from Vancouver, then take feeder buses to the various communities.

THE NORTHWEST TERRITORIES

HOWEVER YOU SLICE THEM, the Northwest Territories are a colossal chunk. Stretching from the 60th parallel to the North Pole, from Hudson Bay to the Arctic Ocean, they embrace 1.3 million square miles—more than twice the size of Alaska. The sheer stark loneliness of those landscapes of forests, lakes, mountains, Arctic tundra, and northern taiga is overwhelming when you see them from the air.

For the Territories have over a million lakes and barely 46,000 people—three national parks, but only 63 communities, some of them numbering 50 to 80 souls. There is no other inhabited part of the earth where you stand a better chance of casting a line in unfished waters or treading a path no white man has stepped on before.

Yet the land is changing before our eyes. Mineral, oil, and gas exploration is preparing the industrialization to come; you can already discern the first signs of it here and there. The changes are creating a paradox, or rather a whole pattern of paradoxes. Native hunters live in prefabs instead of igloos and drive trucks and snowmobiles out to their traplines. But the money they spend in supermarkets is earned by ancestral hunting skills and their lifestyle remains based on the pursuit of migrating game animals and marine creatures.

You'll find modern tourist lodges, supplied by air, dotting half-explored regions of wilderness; dog teams sharing an airstrip with cargo planes; roaming herds of caribou streaming across brand-new all-weather highways; families dining on French cuisine in one spot and on walrus blubber in another; Indian villages with rows of seaplanes moored alongside canoes.

The weather throws in a few paradoxes of its own. During the summer months the farther north you travel, the more daylight you get. Yellowknife, in the south, basks under 20 hours of sunshine a day, followed by four hours of milky twilight bright enough to read a newspaper by. But in northern Inuvik or Cambridge Bay the sun shines 24 hours around the clock. In winter, however, the northern sun doesn't rise above the horizon at all on certain days, while Yellowknifers have five hours of daylight.

The Northwest Territories are divided into two climatic zones: sub-Arctic and Arctic, and the division does not follow the Arctic Circle. And while there are permanent icecaps in the far northern islands, summer in the rest of the land gets considerably hotter than you might think. The average July and August temperatures run in the 60s and 70s, and the mercury has been known to climb into the 90s. You can go swimming in the lakes and rivers (although the water doesn't feel exactly Caribbean), but you can also get sudden cold snaps with freezing temperatures despite the almost constant daylight.

Even in summer you should bring a warm sweater or ski jacket—and don't forget a pair of really sturdy shoes or boots. In winter, with weather conditions truly Arctic, you need the heavily insulated clothing and footwear you'll see in every Territorian closet.

1. An Overall Look

THE PEOPLE: The earliest human inhabitants of the Northwest Territories were the ancestors of the American Indians, who entered Alaska from Siberia and moved into Canada about 10,000 years ago. Some 6000 or so years later came the Eskimos, also from Siberia via Alaska, and began wandering eastward across the Canadian Arctic.

Neither of them much like the names they are popularly known by. The Indians, of course, owe theirs to Columbus's miscalculation that made him believe he had reached India instead of a new continent. The Eskimos got their label from the Indians. It means "eater of raw flesh." Both prefer to be called "Dene" and "Inuit," respectively, words meaning "the people" in their own languages.

Together they make up the majority of the Northwest Territories' population, particularly when you add the Métis—offspring of white and Indian couples. All of them were originally nomadic, covering enormous distances in pursuit of migrating game animals. Today nearly all Dene and Inuit have permanent homes in their settlements, but many of them spend part of the year in remote tent camps, hunting, fishing, and trapping. And although nobody *lives* in igloos any more, these snow houses are still being built as temporary shelters when the occasion arises. Countless hunting groups owe their lives to their ability to construct snow dwellings, for the Arctic storms blow huts and tents to smithereens but leave igloos intact.

"Survival" is the key word for Dene and Inuit. They learned to survive in conditions unimaginably harsh for southern societies, by means of skills that become more wondrous the better you know them. The early white explorers soon learned that in order to stay alive they had to copy those skills as best they could. Those who refused to "go native" rarely made it back.

The first known white man to penetrate the region was Martin Frobisher. His account of meeting the Inuit, written 400 years ago, is the earliest on record. About the same time, European whalers, hunting whales for their oil, were occasionally forced ashore by storms or shipwreck and depended on Eskimo hospitality for survival. This almost legendary hospitality, extended to any stranger who came to them, remains the second outstanding characteristic of the Inuit.

Whites only began to move into the Canadian Arctic in any number during the great "fur rush" in the late 18th century. In the wake of the fur hunters and traders came the missionaries, Roman Catholic and Anglican, who built churches and opened schools where lessons were given in the native languages.

They also built hospitals, which became a desperate necessity because the Inuit—accustomed to a germ-free environment—were dying like flies from the measles, tuberculosis, scarlet fever, smallpox, and venereal diseases brought in by the whites. The same scourges were ravaging the Dene people.

For most of its recorded history, the far north was governed from afar, first by Great Britain, then by the Hudson's Bay Company, and from 1867 by the new Canadian government in Ottawa. At that time the Territories included all of the Yukon, Saskatchewan, Alberta, and huge parts of other provinces. The present boundaries were not drawn until 1920. Immense, isolated from the mainstream, administered by the Mounties on behalf of an absentee territorial council, the Northwest Territories were a textbook study of voiceless neglect.

Things began to change drastically when Territorians started electing their own council members. Today all 15 are chosen by local constituencies, and the commissioner resides in the Territorial capital, shifted from Fort Smith to Yellowknife in 1967. You only have to glance at the expanding highways, the new shopping centers, schools, hospitals, government offices, and tourist facilities to realize that the era of neglect is over. The Territories have joined Canada and the outside world in practice as well as in theory.

Tourism is one of the best barometers of this process, because the basis of a tourist industry is transportation and accommodation. Ten years ago the Territories had about 600 visitors per year and only eight communities with hotels. Today the annual figure is 25,000. They find accommodation in 29 communities, including formerly isolated places with exotic names like Tuktoyaktuk and Pangnirtung. Tourist lodges over the same period increased from 12 to 70.

ANIMALS: It's easy for outsiders to confuse caribou with reindeer because the two species look very much alike. Actually, caribou are wild and still travel in huge migrating herds stretching to the horizon, sometimes numbering 100,000 or more. They form the major food and clothing supply for many of the native people whose lives are cycled around the movements of caribou herds. Reindeer, on the other hand, are strictly domestic animals, and imported ones at that. They were first brought into the Northwest Territories early this century—contrary to the legend that had them helping Santa Claus on the North Pole since the invention of Christmas.

The mighty musk ox, on the other hand, is indigenous to the Arctic. About 12,000 of them live on the northern islands—immense and prehistoric looking, the bulls weighing up to 1300 pounds. They appear even larger than they are because they carry a mountain of the shaggiest fur in creation (they make the American buffalo look positively bald). This coat keeps them not only alive but comfortable in blizzard temperatures of 95° below zero. It is also the chief reason why Eskimos hunt them: there's no material quite like it. Underneath the shaggy outer coat musk oxen have a silky-soft layer of underwool, called "qiviut" in Eskimo. One pound of qiviut can be spun into a 40-strand thread 25 miles long! As light as it is soft, a sweater made from the stuff will keep its wearer warm in subzero weather. And it doesn't shrink when wet. Musk ox bulls may not be pretty, but they're true gentlemen of the wild. In the worst storms they will face the wind, shielding the cows and calves with their huge bodies, standing on their feet as long as the gale lasts, sometimes for days, like hairy bulwarks.

The monarch of the Arctic, *Ursus maritimus,* the great white bear (Nanook, as the Eskimos call him), has no such sentiments. Except for brief spring mating seasons he's a loner, constantly on the move and covering immense distances by ice and water in search of prey. Polar bears roam the Arctic coast and the shores of Hudson Bay, and you have to travel quite a ways over mighty tough country to see them in their habitat. Weighing up to 1450 pounds, they're the largest predators on the American continent, and probably the most dangerous.

Polar bears are almost entirely carniverous, but in an oddly selective fashion. Seals are their main diet, although the bears usually eat only the tough hide and the blubber underneath, leaving the meat and innards to foxes and other scavengers. They are surefooted on ice, fantastic swimmers, and aggressive enough to be given a very wide berth.

You can get a permit to hunt polar bears, but the total quota is 400 bears annually and only the local Eskimos can decide how many of these are to be shot by tourists. You must use an Eskimo hunter as a guide, and you can't use mechanical vehicles. Thus a bear hunt may mean two weeks or more of bone-jarring travel over huge ice ridges on a dog sled, facing winds that rip tents apart like wet paper. With these restrictions, the great white bears are maintaining their numbers in Canada and appear in no danger of joining the list of endangered species.

The Northwest Territories are full of animals much easier to observe than the bears. In the wooded regions you'll come across wolves and wolverines (harmless for men, despite the legends about them), mink, lynx, otters, and beavers. The sleek and beautiful white or brown Arctic foxes live in ice regions as well as beneath the tree line and near settlements.

From mid-July to the end of August, seals, walruses, and whales are in their breeding grounds off the coast of Baffin Island and in Hudson Bay. And in the endless skies above there are eagles, hawks, huge owls, razor-billed auks, and ivory gulls. Also a gourmet-renowned little partridge-like bird called the ptarmigan, as delicious to eat as imptossible—pardon me, impossible—to pronounce.

ARTS AND CRAFTS: These deserve a separate section here. The handiwork of the Dene and Inuit people is absolutely unique, regardless whether the materials used are indigenous or imported. Many of them have utility value—you won't get finer, more painstakingly stitched cold-weather clothing anywhere in the world. A genuine muskrat parka, for instance, is not only wonderfully warm but has a stylish originality that puts it above fashion trends.

The art objects—sculpture, prints, and tapestries—are connoisseurs' delights and acknowledged investment values. Quite apart from the aesthetic pleasure you may derive from an exquisitely shaped walrus tusk carving, it's also a means of beating inflation. And the Northwest Territories is one of the few places where you can buy these items without paying a sales tax.

Most arts and crafts articles are handled through community cooperatives that take care of the making as well as the marketing, thus avoiding the excess cut of the middlemen. This is an important business in the Territories, with sales averaging around $10 million a year. There are three official symbols stating clearly that a piece is a genuine Eskimo or Indian object. Watch for them when buying. Some stores make a habit of mixing the genuine stuff with second-rate imitations.

Don't hesitate to ask retailers where a particular object comes from, what it's made of, and how it was made. They'll be glad to tell you, and frequently can even let you know *who* made it.

2. Getting There and Getting Around

BY ROAD: In 1960 the Mackenzie Hwy. reached Yellowknife from Edmonton, establishing a 941-mile link between the capitals of Alberta and the Northwest Territories. The drive north is fascinating, either by private car or thrice-weekly bus service. You cross two major rivers, neither of them bridged. In summer the crossing (five to ten minutes) is by free car ferry. In winter you drive over a completely safe ice bridge four to six feet thick. In spring and fall, however, there are periods of up to six weeks when thaw or freezing puts both facilities out of service. For information on ferry schedules or ice bridge conditions, call 403/873-7799 in Yellowknife.

The Territories have a fairly extensive net of all-weather gravel-surfaced highways connecting the major attractions. But there are a few important points to consider before you go motoring in what was quite recently the Arctic wild:

Driving distances are vast. From Yellowknife, it's 1160 *air miles* to Cape Dorset, 1405 miles to Frobisher Bay, 1435 miles to Pangnirtung. Even the southerly old capital of Fort Smith is 190 miles off. There are long distances between service stops, gas prices average a dollar or more a gallon, spare parts are severely limited, and human settlements en route are very sparse indeed.

You should always carry a tow rope, spare tire, matches, tools, first-aid kit, extra gas, oil, and water, and some extra food. In summer you won't need a flashlight since you get about 22 hours of daylight driving. Don't bother to bring a compass either: near the Magnetic Pole they're not very reliable.

If you're unaccustomed to driving on gravel, remember to avoid sudden braking or abrupt steering movements—they can send you skidding. The great curse of gravel roads is dust, so don't accelerate too much when passing another motorist, and ease off the gas pedal when meeting another vehicle. A dumb or discourteous driver on a gravel road can enshroud you in a dust cloud as dense as a smoke screen and leave you virtually blinded for minutes.

BY AIR: The Northwest Territories are serviced by jets from Edmonton, Winnipeg, and Montréal, with scheduled flights as far north as Resolute in the high Arctic. In summer this means virtually all daylight flying. **Pacific Western** does the 1½-hour flight from Edmonton to Yellowknife 18 times weekly, to Inuvik eight times a week.

Within the Territories you have a large number of major and (very) minor airlines operating scheduled flights between communities. The bigger ones fly jets, the smaller outfits 4- to 50-passenger prop planes on wheels or on floats. Between them they serve virtually all populated centers in the Territories. You can also charter aircraft, ranging from 3-passenger Cessnas ($1 a mile) to 50-passenger Dashes ($4 a mile).

Here are some airline telephone numbers in Yellowknife: **Pacific Western** (tel. 403/873-2721), **Northward Airlines** (tel. 403/873-5311), **Northwest Territorial Airways** (tel. 403/873-4477), **Ptarmigan Airways** (tel. 403/873-4461), and **Latham Island Airways** (tel. 403/873-2891).

3. Yellowknife

The new capital of the Northwest Territories lies on the north shore of Great Slave Lake, 600 miles north of Edmonton and 272 miles south of the Arctic Circle. The site was originally occupied by the Dogrib Indians. The first white settlers didn't arrive until 1934, following the discovery of gold on the lake shores.

This first gold boom petered out in the 1940s, and Yellowknife dwindled nearly to a ghost town in its wake. But in 1945 came a second gold rush that put the place permanently on the map. Gold made this city, which lies 682 feet above sea level, and her landmarks are the two operating gold mines that flank her: **Cominco** and **Giant Yellowknife**, both open to visitors.

Most of the old gold boom marks have gone—the bordellos, gambling dens, log-cabin banks, and never-closing bars are merely memories now. But the original **Old Town** is there, a crazy tangle of wooden shacks hugging the lakeshore rocks, surrounded by bush-pilot operations that fly sturdy little planes—on floats in summer, on skis in winter.

The city's expanding urban center, **New Town,** spreads above the old section, a busy hub of modern hotels, shopping centers, office blocks, and government buildings. Together the two towns count about 12,000 inhabitants, by far the largest community in the Territories.

Looking at the rows of parking meters along **Franklin Ave.** it's hard to realize that the city's first two cars were only shipped in (by river barge) in 1944. They had one mile of road to use between them, yet somehow managed to collide head-on!

Yellowknife has one main street which begins out of town as **Old Airport Rd.,** becomes **Franklin Ave.** in midtown, and continues as **50th Ave.** for the remainder of its run (the avenues only go as low as 49th; I don't know what happened to the rest—maybe the gold prospectors carried them off). If you stand at the **post office,** Franklin Ave. and 49th St., you're at the geographical center, give or take a few blocks.

You are then facing northeast, the direction of **Old Town** and **Yellowknife Bay.** Behind you is Frame Lake with the magnificent Prince of Wales Northern Heritage Centre. Beyond the lake, up on a hillside, is the airport, a cozy little affair with a licensed restaurant, washrooms, vending machines, and waiting passengers who all know each other.

Northwest is the direction of the Giant Yellowknife Mine, half a mile away, and from the west the great **Mackenzie Hwy.** runs in all the way from Edmonton. Rat Lake and the Cominco Mine lie southwest from where you're standing. Just off 49th Ave. (the streets get a bit embryonic hereabouts) stand the Arena, City Hall, and the Royal Canadian Mounted Police post.

Kam Lake Rd. branches off Old Airport Rd. at the south end of town and leads to the Eskimo Dog Research Foundation, a colony of 100 canines whose job it is to preserve the indigenous kingmik breed, the world's original cold-weather pooch. 48th St. leads into the **Ingraham Trail,** a bush road heading out toward dozens of fishing, hiking, and camping spots.

For information concerning almost anything in the Northwest Territories, contact **TravelArctic,** Laing Building (tel. 403/873-7317). The absence of full addresses, with streets and numbers, is something you'll notice immediately in Yellowknife. Every local knows where certain offices are located and they're only too willing to let visitors in on the secret. So why bother printing addresses?

Yellowknife is still very much small town, and a frontier small town at that. This is changing rapidly as the population increases, but currently it gives the capital a distinctly rustic note. In Old Town, for instance, water is still delivered by truck—an advance from a few years ago when it was delivered by hand bucket, at 25¢ per pail.

But there is also a dramatic flavor about Yellowknife, one you don't usually encounter in little communities. It stems partly from the mushrooming high-rises, shopping malls, and public buildings, from the feeling of transformation and vitality that permeates the place. But mainly it comes from the sense of the endless boundless wilderness that starts at the town's doorstep and stretches all the way to the roof of the world.

ACCOMMODATIONS: Yellowknife now has over 450 hotel and motel rooms in a wide range of price brackets. Rates are generally somewhat higher than in the south, but this is eased by the fact that the Territories have no sales tax and therefore no surprise additions to your bill. Hotel standards are good, in parts excellent, although you mustn't expect room service in most establishments.

Explorer Hotel, 48th St. (tel. 403/873-3531), is a big, beautiful, snow-white structure overlooking the town like a guardian igloo. The Explorer is *the* hotel in the Territories, and lets you know it the moment you step inside. The lobby resembles the interior of a snowflake with some bright murals on the walls to supply color, subtly soft lighting arrangements on the ceiling, the elevator portion encased in glass, increasing the sparkling effect of the decor. The dining lounge is a local showpiece. The 106 guest rooms come furnished in dark wood, all equipped with air-conditioning, color TV, dial phone, and fluffy red carpets. You get a writing desk, large walk-in closet behind folding doors, chest of drawers, and a very handy closed cupboard for luggage. The small sparkling bathrooms have heat lamps with automatic timers. And the photomontages of Arctic scenery on the walls could enter for a camera award.

Singles cost $54; doubles, $64; with each additional person paying $10.

Yellowknife Inn, Franklin Ave. (tel. 403/873-2601), the largest and possibly friendliest hostelry in the Territories, was founded by a wooden-legged, two-fisted, big-hearted bootlegger, sailor, storekeeper, and character named Vic Ingraham. Part of the old hotel (built in 1938) still stands, but now there's a modern addition attached to it and the room prices depend on which portion you want to stay in.

The inn has a tavern, lounge, and dining room you'll find described in the appropriate section. It also produces a (highly) irregular newssheet (price: one wooden nickel) and some extraordinary cheerful ambience. Among its unusual features are the lobby inscriptions in Inuktitut (Eskimo) lettering. A big comfortably rambling place, the inn has 156 guest rooms, all with TV, dial telephone, bath or shower, and some with air conditioning. Most of the rooms are large and nicely, not stylishly, furnished: good beds, writing desks with lamps, lots of open hanging space. In the bathrooms, the basin with mirror is separated from the shower portion, a thoughtful arrangement for two persons. The walls are decorated with Eskimo art prints.

Rates come in three categories, regardless of whether the occupancy is single or double: economy, $31; standard, $42.50; deluxe, $47.50. After a stay of six successive days, the seventh is free.

Twin Pine Motor Inn, Franklin Ave. (tel. 403/873-8511), is an attractive two-story wood structure, painted a vivid green, at the bottom of the hill road leading to Old Town. It has 44 units, 30 of them with kitchenettes, and also a breakfast room where the continental breakfast is gratis and complimentary coffee is served all day! All units come equipped with bath and shower, color TV, and dial telephones. Furnishings are in elegant light wood: smart little writing desks with mirrors, two armchairs, a table, and excellent lighting fixtures. The kitchen dinettes are pleasantly spacious, and the kitchens stocked with electric ranges and all necessary utensils. Bathrooms come with electric ventilators. Altogether, a great value for your money.

You pay $38 for singles, $43 for doubles, and an extra $5 for kitchen facilities.

Gold Range Hotel, 50th St. and 50th Ave. (tel. 403/873-4441). A small, simple structure housing a lot of facilities, the Gold Range has a dining room, a coffeeshop, a tavern, and even a beauty parlor on the premises—also 50 bedrooms, half of them with bath or shower. Each room has a telephone, you can rent TV sets from the management, and the bathless habitats have hot- and cold-water basins. The furnishings are economy style (so are the rates), and the rooms fairly small. There are overhead lights only, no bedside or desk lamps.

Singles range from $14 to $35; doubles, $17 to $45.

The **YWCA,** Franklin Ave. at 54th St. (tel. 403/873-4767), a remarkably versatile establishment, not only accommodates male and female transients, but also provides permanent "cluster suites" for groups of bachelors of both sexes —an absolute blessing in a place as tight for living space as Yellowknife. It's a big, massively modern gravelstone building, with the *Y* almost hidden on the fifth floor and no sign to betray its presence. Being almost solely devoted to accommodations, the Y has none of the usual gym, pool, and athletic facilities. But the guest rooms are charming, and the management exceptionally amiable, even by Territorial standards. The bedrooms are bright and cheerful, the furniture modern, the bathroom facilities excellent.

You can get an "overnighter" in a small dormitory for $7. Or a private bedroom for $22.

MEALS: Yellowknife provides surprisingly good meals at prices that range 25% to 30% above most of Canada. This is *not* surprising in view of the fact that the supply of fresh meat and produce must be airlifted part of the way for 8 to 12 weeks of the year.

The capital is, let's face it, a hard-drinking town where most of the social life takes place in saloons—which, officially, don't exist at all. They're called lounge bars, cabarets, or what-have-you, but fulfill their purpose very gregariously until around 1 a.m. However, 11 communities in the Territories have voted themselves bone dry: you can neither possess nor consume liquor in their areas, so check it out before visiting.

The **Old Northwest Company** (tel. 873-3531), is the dining lounge of the Explorer Hotel, and quite a shock to those innocent visitors who expected log-cabin cuisine in the Territories. The logs are there alright, but on the ceiling and in the immense enclosed fireplace with copper chimney that forms the centerpiece. The vast and sumptuous room, heavily carpeted, functions on two levels, both overlooking the beautiful rock and tree landscape outside. The wooden chairs have leather upholstery and the walls are festooned with genuine pioneer kitchenware. The service is as smooth and silent as you'd find in top-ranking metropolitan dineries. For an appetizer, try the sauté shrimp in white wine ($5.60). Then pepper steak flambé ($11.75) or the delicious Arctic char filet, topped with lemon and butter ($9.50). For dessert, how about the Spanish coffee, a mixture of coffee, brandy, and Tia Maria ($3.75)? All meals include salad, potatoes, and a heaped bread basket. How's that for log-cabin fare?

Polar Bear Lounge, is a part of the Yellowknife Inn (tel. 873-2601), and by far the poshest. Queen Elizabeth and other visiting royalty have dined here and admired the superb polar bear skin that hangs near the entrance (worth about $2000). The place is bathed in dim chandelier and candle light, the wood-paneled walls decorated with Eskimo art prints. The service is excellent at all times, but the menu only occasionally features reindeer steaks—pity, because the special flavor of reindeer meat ranks among the culinary highlights of the north. The rolls come piping hot with your meal, and you help yourself from a small salad bar. The specialty is prime rib of beef, in three sizes (select according to your appetite), from $8.50 to $14.25. Irish coffee costs $3.50, and the desserts include incongruously good sherbets.

Cabin Fever (tel. 873-4441). Located next to the big bar of the Gold Range Hotel, this little dinery has the kind of atmosphere you'd have expected to find more of hereabouts: the interior is like a real log cabin, with red lanterns matching the scarlet napkins on the tables. It's a very relaxed place, with comfortable wooden stools and upholstered wall seats. The menu is a souvenir piece, covered with ironically captioned photographs from the bearded and bustled pioneer era. The house specialty is the barbecued ribs (with or without garlic) for $7.75. The charcoal-broiled filet mignon with mushrooms runs from $10 to $12, according to size. And you get Irish, Spanish, or other alcoholic coffees made to your specifications as meal-enders. Help-yourself salad bar portions and baked potato or french fries accompany each entree.

The **Lunchbox** (tel. 873-8242), is a basement cafeteria situated in the brand-new Yellowknife Mall complex. Fluorescently lit, streamlined, and plastic, this place provides fast, hygienic, cheap, and fairly good lunches for half the town's office workers. A solid breakfast of bacon, two eggs, and coffee costs $3.25; hamburgers come to $1.10.

Mike Mark's, on 51st St. (tel. 873-3309), despite the Western label, is a Chinese establishment, not exactly glamorous but tastefully decorated, with an extensive menu. The dining room has a bar on one side, steel chairs and yellow-draped tables on the other. The illumination comes from a multitude of tassled lanterns. The low ceiling is artistically hung with fish nets and marine creatures. Deep-fried shrimp and mushroom gai kine come for $4.85. The almond chicken is $5.15. Each diner gets one complimentary fortune cookie. There's a lengthy take-out menu in case you'd like to arrange a Chinese picnic. Open seven days a week till 2:30 a.m.

Northern Meats, next to the Gold Range Hotel, is a clean, bright, modern, and strictly utilitarian fast-food restaurant. Bare floors and fluorescent lighting, metal chairs, and plastic tabletops will give you the picture. The place, however, contains the only complete dairy bar in town, specializing in shakes, splits, and sundaes. The service is rapid and the management offers some neat bargains, such as: order a T-bone steak dinner (sauteed in wine sauce) for $6.50 and you get another of the same—free—for your dining companion. Open seven days a week, weekdays till 10 p.m., Sundays till 7 p.m.

Cantina, 50th Ave. (tel. 873-2772), is a small, romantically lit, and very intimate bar-restaurant. Candlelit tables, delightfully upholstered seats, and multicolored lanterns provide atmosphere. In the background is an open grill where you can watch your steaks sizzling. Apart from shrimp cocktails, the menu is an all-meat affair. A small salad bar provides the greens. There's a limited choice, but the tomato and lettuce salad is fine. Rib-eye steak is $8.95; New York steak, $9.95. Complimentary chocolate mints after dinner, and the steaks are served till 11 p.m.

Mr. Mike's (tel. 920-4744). Located downstairs in the shopping center, this attractive cafeteria is large, busy, fast, and popular. The color scheme is somewhat startling—purple ceiling and turquoise walls—but the effect is surprisingly harmonious. The hanging table lamps give you plenty of light to read a newspaper while munching. Most popular item here is the one-third-pound Mikeburger for $2.39. But you also get hefty char-broiled steaks with baked potato, garlic bread, and salad for $4.59. Open Monday to Saturday till 9:30 p.m., Sunday till 8:30 p.m.

DAYTIME ATTRACTIONS: The **Prince of Wales Northern Heritage Centre** was inaugurated in 1979, a museum in a class all its own. "Museum" is really the wrong term—it's a showcase, archive, traveling exhibition, and information service rolled in one, a living interpretation and presentation of the heritage of the north, its land, people, and animals. The architecture alone is worth a visit. All levels are accessible by ramps—no stairways to climb. It incorporates a lookout platform with a panoramic view, and a wonderful rest lounge with books and armchairs to read them in. Few museums have anything like it.

The exhibits are three dimensional. You learn the history, background, and characteristics of the Dene and Inuit peoples, of the Métis and pioneer whites, through dioramas, artifacts, talking, reciting, and singing slide presentations, and multimovie screens. The story begins some 400 million years ago and ends with the present age. It depicts the human struggle with an environment so incredibly harsh that survival alone seems a historical accomplishment. And you get an idea of how the natives of the north did it—not by struggling *against* their environment but by harmonizing with it. Admission is free.

Bush Pilot's Memorial is a massive stone pillar rising above Old Town that pays tribute to the little band of airmen who opened up the far north. The surrounding cluster of shacks and cottages is the original Yellowknife, built on the shores of a narrow peninsula jutting into Great Slave Lake. It's not exactly a pretty place, but definitely intriguing. Sprinkled along the inlets are half a dozen bush-pilot operations, minuscule airlines flying charter planes as well as scheduled routes to outlying areas. The little float planes shunt around like taxis, and you can watch one landing or taking off every hour of the day.

About 100 yards off the tip of the Old Town peninsula lies **Latham Island,** which you can reach by a causeway. The island has an Indian community and a new growing residential area.

Gold Mine Tours: In 1945 the Giant Yellowknife Mine began milling gold and thus inaugurated the rebirth of the town. **Frame and Perkins** offers a conducted tour of the mine, followed by a visit to the Bowspringer Kennels, where the true Eskimo dog is being bred. The tours last two hours and depart from your hotel six times weekly, on Tuesday, Thursday, and Saturday, at 9:30 a.m. and 1 p.m. Tickets cost $12 per person, including admission to the kennels. For bookings, call 873-4892.

Hiking, Boating, Rafting: The town is ringed by hiking trails, some gentle, some pretty rugged. The most popular branch out from the big **Ingraham Trail,** which starts at the Explorer Hotel and winds over 45 miles to **Tibbet Lake,** east of town. En route lie several territorial parks, two waterfalls, the Yellowknife Mine, and a bird habitat, plus lots of picnic sites, camping spots, boat rentals, and fishing spots.

You can rent canoes at **Sportsman,** on 50th St. in Yellowknife (tel. 873-2911) for $16 a day. **Prelude Lake,** 20 miles east of town, is a wonderful setting for scenic boating and trout, pike, and walleye fishing. At the lodge, motorboats rent from $6 to $7 an hour, rafts from $7 to $8 an hour, depending on size.

But before you take to the water, a few words of advice: You must take warm, waterproof clothing, regardless of the temperature. Summer storms can blow up very quickly and drench you to the skin. You'll also need some insect repellent—black flies and mosquitoes are the warm-weather curse of the north. Canoers are advised to bring mosquito headnets as well. If you camp on a water trip, pick an open island or sand bar where the lack of vegetation tends to discourage the winged pests.

Great Slave Lake Cruises: Organized by Fred and Helen Henne, these are two- to three-hour jaunts around Yellowknife Bay and the lake islands. They use comfortable 36-foot cabin cruisers and leave from the Old Town dock. For information about prices and departure times, call 873-4437.

While not strictly speaking an attraction, I think we ought to mention **Raymond,** Yellowknife's unofficial heraldic bird. Raymond is a raven—or rather swarms of them. Large, gleaming black, and fitted with brass nerve and vocal chords, these popular pests put on daily shows for spectators—snatching bones from outraged dogs, bullying seagulls, or knocking lids off garbage cans and arranging the contents in artistic patterns on the ground in a 50-foot radius. They'll also fly off with your golf ball while you're practicing on the (gravel and sand) course. Yet despite—or because of—his innumerable depredations, Raymond is the town mascot, his villainous features depicted on T-shirts, posters, and official brochures. Watch him sitting on a fence and squawking his own praises to heaven with all the leather-lunged smugness of a politician, and you'll understand why.

AFTER DARK: Yellowknife's nightlife revolves around a few bars and lounges in which most of the entertainment is self-generated. Several do employ professional vocalists or groups, but not on a regular basis. Sometimes the patrons put on turns of their own, usually uninvited. But the vibes are among the warmest you'll find anywhere, and the atmosphere pretty close to the fabled frontier spirit.

The deluxe spots in town are the **Explorer Cocktail Lounge** and **Snowshoe Lounge** of the Explorer Hotel (tel. 873-3531). The first is a sumptuously paneled and carpeted retreat centered around an open stone grill. The second has contemporary decor, an elegant bar, and a fully equipped games section.

The Yellowknife Inn (tel. 873-2601) has two imbibing spots with contrasting characteristics. The first is the **Mackenzie Lounge,** decked in tartan, sedate in atmosphere, handsomely paneled, and the birthplace of a superlative concoction called Mackenzie Masher for which I (vainly) tried to get the recipe. The **Miner's Mess** is the exact opposite of sedateness. Most nights it's a kind of Arctic U.N., with appropriate sound level. You can hear Dogrib or Slavey Indian spoken at one table, a couple of Inuktitut dialects at the next, Québecois French, English English, Alaska American, German, Italian, etc. It's a meeting and mingling place for miners and bush pilots, Eskimo council members and local Dene, tourists and Territorial oldtimers. You can learn more about the north while downing a drink—even coffee—here than in a week of concentrated book reading.

SHOPPING: Yellowknife is the main retail outlet for northern artwork and craft items, as well as the specialized clothing the climate demands. Some of it is so handsome and handy that sheer vanity will make you wear it in more southerly temperatures.

Northern Images, in the Yellowstone Mall, is a link in the cooperative chain of stores by that name that stretches across the entire Canadian north. The premises are as attractive as they are interesting, exhibitions as much as markets. They feature authentic Eskimo and Indian articles: apparel and carvings, graphic prints and ivory, jade and silver jewelry, ornamental moose hair tuftings and porcupine quill work. The items aren't cheap, but if you consider that they are handmade and have no sales tax on them, they have definite bargain value. Indian boots run from $50 to $150; mukluks, the wonderfully soft and warm Eskimo footwear, from $98 upward. Eskimo parkas, the finest cold-weather coats made anywhere, come at between $225 and $400.

Langlois Gallery, 50th St., is a beautiful showcase for native arts, crafts, and artifacts, and also for oil paintings, drawings, and photographs by other northern Canadian artists. You can admire—and purchase—macramé hangings, sealskin tapestries, native pottery, and an enormous range of silver, ivory, and soapstone jewelry. Browsing is encouraged, and there's definitely no subtle pressure to buy anything. Mukluks sell for $40 to $90, the moose hair tuftings at around $120.

INDIAN SETTLEMENT: Detah, a Dogrib Dene village of about 160 people, lies just across the bay from Yellowknife. In summer the connection is either by freighter canoe across the lake or by a 13-mile road around the bay. In winter an ice road cuts across the lake that can accommodate cars, trucks, and snowmobiles as well as dog teams. There's nothing in the least "touristy" about Detah. It's a quiet traditional community whose people shun city life, even the Yellowknife version of same. They're friendly, cheerful, and hospitable, but there's no tourist accommodation or meal service in the village.

SPECIAL EVENTS: The **Midnight Golf Tournament,** attended by visiting celebrities and local club swingers, is the only annual event of its kind that tees off at *midnight,* June 22. It's bright enough then to see individual sand grains on the "greens" (which are actually "browns"), but there are some unique handicaps. Thieving ravens, for instance, frequently hijack chip shots, and the entire course could be classified as one large sand trap.

Caribou Carnival, held from March 17 to 25 annually, is a burst of spring fever after a very long, very frigid winter (part of the fever symptoms consist of the delusion that winter is over). For a solid week Yellowknife is thronged with parades, local talent shows, and skit revues with imported celebrities. Some fascinating and specifically Arctic contests include igloo building, Indian wrestling, tea boiling, and the competition highlight: the **Canadian Championship Dog Derby.** A three-day, 150-mile dog sled race, with more than 200 huskies competing for the $20,000 prize, and their "mushers" running behind, yelling—well, maybe "porridge!" The carnival is kept "orderly" by swarms of helmeted Kariboo Kops, who swoop down on nonsmilers and other subversives, haul them off to kangaroo courts, and levy fines (which go to charity).

CABS AND CAR RENTALS: Yellow Cab (tel. 873-4444) charges $1.20 at flagfall, then $1.50 per mile. A ride to the airport costs about $6.30.

Tilden (Ted's U-Drives, tel. 403/873-2911) has a range of rental vehicles from full-size cars to half-ton four-speed vans. Rates for cars run between $24 and $27 per day plus 25¢ per kilometer, or $150 per week. The number of cars available during the summer season is rather limited and the demand very high. You may have to settle for what's to be had rather than what you want. Try to book ahead as far as possible.

4. Around the Territories

COMMUNITIES: Of the 63 communities spread across the Territories, here are 10 which offer some accommodation and/or are of interest to the tourist.

Fort Smith

Once the territorial capital, this town of 2360 people is located one mile from the Alberta border and close to the **Wood Buffalo National Park.** The settlement was founded as a Hudson's Bay Company fur-trading post in 1874. The adventurous history of the place is portrayed in the **Northern Life Museum.** Famous for a spectacular series of four rapids on the Slave River and the nesting site of a colony of white pelicans, it has several hotels and restaurants. Pacific Western provides scheduled air service to the town.

Hay River

This port on the southern shore of Great Slave Lake, opposite Yellowknife, with 5000 inhabitants and on the Mackenzie Hwy. route, is a busy fishing harbor and summer dockside for the stream of barges carrying cargos to the far-flung Arctic settlements in the north. Situated on a lake island facing the town is the only Indian reserve in the Territories. Some 33 miles to the south is the spectacular **Alexandra Falls,** where the Hay River plunges 106 feet and attracts camera bugs from all over Canada by the dramatic beauty of the spectacle. The town has tourist hotels and good restaurants, plus Pacific Western jet service from Edmonton and Yellowknife.

Fort Simpson

Originally a trapping outpost for beaver and marten skins, this is now the ideal springboard for excursions into **Nahanni National Park.** It lies 230 miles west of Yellowknife on the Mackenzie Hwy., and has a hotel and a lodge with restaurant facilities. Scheduled services are provided by four airlines.

Rae-Edzo

With about 1200 people, this is the largest Dene settlement in the Territories. The Indians belong to the Dogrib tribe, and have banned the sale or consumption of liquor in the township. But since Rae lies only 68 miles northwest of Yellowknife, the prohibition doesn't entail much hardship. There is an interesting native craftshop but no hotel facilities.

Inuvik

The name means "place of men," and this is the second-largest community in the Northwest Territories, with a population of 3200. Hewn out of the Arctic wilderness 680 miles northwest of Yellowknife, Inuvik was only founded in 1955 as the main supply base for the petro-chemical exploration of the area. It's a modern community with hotels, restaurants, and jet air service from Edmonton and Yellowknife.

Every July 21 to 25 the town becomes the site of the famous **Trans-Arctic Games,** biggest and most colorful of their kind. The games feature traditional Indian and Eskimo sports, competitions, drumming, dancing, craft displays, and the unique "Good Woman" contest. Inuit women show their amazing skill at seal and muskrat skinning, bannock baking, sewing, and other abilities that make a "good woman," Arctic edition.

Frobisher Bay

Another "young" settlement, established as a U.S. Air Force airstrip in 1942, it now boasts a population of more than 2500. Located on the east coast of the huge Baffin Island, 1405 miles northeast of Yellowknife, it's a bustling and expanding place with the excellent **Nunuuta Museum** for Arctic arts and crafts, three hotels, and several restaurants. A celebrated spring carnival is held every April, featuring igloo building, ice sculpture, and reputedly the toughest snowmobile race in the world.

Cape Dorset

On the south coast of Baffin Island, 1160 miles from Yellowknife, Cape Dorset has twice-weekly air service from Frobisher Bay. This is a world-renowned center of Eskimo art and seat of the **West Baffin Eskimo Co-Operative,** which handles the stone carvings, prints, and lithographs which have given the place international standing. About 700 people live in the village, some still by hunting, trapping, and sealing. Tourist accommodation is available at an inn.

Baker Lake

Another famous Inuit art center, located on the north shore of the huge lake at the approximate geographical center of Canada, this is the only inland Eskimo community in the Northwest Territories and has about 1000 people. The artisans here produce the highly regarded Baker Lake tapestries. Hotel accommodations are available, as well as scheduled air service. It's 585 miles northwest of Yellowknife.

Pangnirtung

Called "Pang" by Territorians and "Switzerland of the Arctic" by tour promoters, Pangnirtung lies at the entrance of **Auyuittuq National Park** on Baffin Island, 1435 miles from Yellowknife. In a beautiful scenic setting, surrounded by steeply rising mountains, "Pang" has about 900 people, living by fishing, sealing, walrus and caribou hunting and the sale of their art and craft products. Room and board are available at a local lodge, and there's scheduled air service from Frobisher Bay.

Tuktoyaktuk

On the shores of the Beaufort Sea, 100 miles south of the permanent polar ice cap in the Arctic Ocean, and popularly known as "Tuk," this is a famous base for fur trappers and has a reindeer herd of 10,000 head, which means the finest reindeer steaks in the Territories. There are three hotels, and scheduled air service is from Inuvik.

NATIONAL PARKS: There are three, all detailed below.

Wood Buffalo

The Northwest Territories share this park with Alberta, and the region is mentioned in the Alberta chapter. The main attraction is the roaming herd of 6000 wood bison—the last in Canada—which are actually hybrids, the result of a mixture with the slightly smaller plains buffalo brought in from Alberta in 1923.

The park has a campground and more than 30 miles of hiking trails. Park headquarters is in nearby Fort Smith, where you also have to buy whatever food you want on your excursion (none is available in the park—and you'd better not even *think* of buffalo stew).

Nahanni

A breathtaking, unspoiled wilderness of 1840 square miles in the southwest corner of the Territories, accessible only by motorboat, canoe, or charter aircraft (see "Organized Tours"), this is a region of scenic grandeur and mystery. The Nahanni River claws its path through the mountain ranges and at Virginia Falls plunges down in a 316-foot cataract that is over twice the height of Niagara Falls! The whole scene is a dramatic composition of sub-Arctic hot springs, white-water rapids, and cliffs soaring up vertically for 4000 feet.

The mystery stems from Indian lore, which makes this the region of the legendary Bigfoot, and from the white man's tales about a hidden tropical valley containing gold nuggets the size of marbles. One man, Albert Fallie, spent his entire life searching for this gold bonanza. The three McLeod brothers set out to find it in 1905. Their headless skeletons were discovered three years later. The canyon in which they were found is called Headless Valley.

Auyuittuq

Pronounced "ah-you-ee-tuk," which is Inuit for "the place that never melts," this is the world's first national park inside the Arctic Circle. But only about a quarter of the park's 8300 square miles is covered by the fringes of the immense Penny Ice Cap. Most of the park consists of wonderful hiking scenery in deep, glacier-carved valleys and along spectacular fjords with sheer cliffs rising to 4000 feet. From May through July this region has 24 hours of daylight —total darkness in midwinter.

On land you can spot an occasional polar bear. In the coastal waters there are thousands of harp seals, walruses, belugas (white whales), and narwhals, an odd little whale with a long ivory spear on its face. There is a campground on the Weasel River delta equipped with tentsites, drinking water, and firewood, and six emergency shelters are in strategic locations. The park administration office is located in Pangnirtung. Hikers and climbers must register there.

ORGANIZED TOURS: Tuliq Outfitting runs sightseeing, fishing, and camping trips to Auyuittuq National Park and the Penny Glacier, accompanied by highly experienced native guides. Guests are required to bring sleeping bags, fishing gear, and warm clothing. The trips operate from March till October, and can be extended to any length required. A canoe and guide costs $40 a day; camping trips (all meals provided) come to $75 per day per person. Contact A. Moss-Davies, Broughton Island, NT X0A 0B0 (tel. 403/819-8868).

Pacific Western Airlines offers a series of wilderness fishing packages in the remote lakes and streams of the Northwest Territories. They come in a wide variety and let you choose the kind of sport fishing and type of accommodation you prefer. ITF-Pwarl 7, for instance, is an eight-day deal at Rutledge Lake Lodge for $395. You pay for your flight to Hay River ($164 from Edmonton), then the package includes your stay at the lodge as well as the charter flight there and back, motorboats, gas, and landing nets. For a booklet listing all the ventures, contact Pacific Western at 310 W. Hastings St., Vancouver, BC V6E 2G5 (tel. 604/684-6161).

Nahanni River Trips in the national park are organized by **Deadman Valley Outfitters**, P.O. Box 406, Fort Simpson, N.W.T. Directed by expert native guides, these river journeys are made in sturdy flat-bottomed motorboats and go all the way through the dramatic wilderness to Virginia Falls, taking five days to complete. You bring your own food, tents, sleeping bags, etc. The total cost is $1200 for a maximum of five persons.

Arctic Safaris are run by CP Air in conjunction with Horizon Holidays, Horizon House, 37 Maitland St., Toronto, ON M4Y 2R9 (tel. 416/923-1144). As a sample, Tour 12 jets you to Frobisher Bay. You then get an extensive tour over and through Cape Dorset, Pangnirtung, Pond Inlet, Igloolik, The Arctic fjords and tundra, staying in lodges and inns en route. The entire safari takes nine days and costs $2582.

THE YUKON

There's a land where the mountains are nameless,
    And the rivers all run God knows where;
There are lives that are erring and aimless,
    And deaths that just hang by a hair;
There are hardships that nobody reckons;
    There are valleys unpeopled and still;
There's a land—oh, it beckons and beckons,
    And I want to go back—and I will.

These lines, written by Robert Service, the poet laureate of the north, paint the Yukon in the days of the Klondike gold rush that put it on the map. Well, the Yukon has grown considerably tamer since then, the mountains are no longer "nameless" and the hardships rather few and far between. But the land still "beckons," casting a peculiar spell over visitors that no other part of Canada can quite match. There's a tang of adventure lingering in the Yukon air, despite motor roads, jetports, and deluxe hotels.

Once part of the Northwest Territories, the Yukon is now a separate territory bordering on British Columbia in the south and Alaska in the west (when locals refer to the U.S., they nearly always mean Alaska). Compared to the Northwest Territories it's a mere midget in size, but with 200,000 square miles the Yukon is more than twice as big as Wyoming.

The entire territory has a population of only 23,000—two-thirds of them living in the capital of Whitehorse. But every year it attracts over 300,000 visitors, or 13 times the total number of residents. Tourism is the area's second-largest business, and hopefully, after reading this chapter you'll understand why.

Far from being a barren, frigid landscape, the Yukon has some of the most colorful scenery in Canada: rolling green hillsides blazing with wildflowers, sparkling lakes studded with wooded islands, broad rushing streams swirling against a backdrop of snow-capped mountain ranges.

Some of the biggest herds of caribou in North America populate the northern plains. Mountain sheep clamber around the slopes and timber wolves roam the forests. Eagles draw slow circles in the sky and the rare peregrine falcon is still breeding in the more remote valleys. The lake and river fishing is unsurpassed anywhere.

The climate, at least in summer, is much milder than you'd expect in a territory whose northern toe dips into the Arctic Ocean. First of all it's very dry, so you don't have to worry about chilling dampness. In Whitehorse the summer average hovers around 58° Fahrenheit, sometimes climbing into the 70s and 80s in July. And you hardly get any darkness during the summer months, only a few hours of gray dusk from 11 p.m. to 2 a.m. In winter the mercury may dip as low as −60°, but never longer than a few days at a stretch.

As the myth about the Yukon's "perpetual ice and snow" is dispelled, more and more visitors are coming during the "shoulder seasons" of spring and fall, and during the actual winter for superb snowmobiling, snowshoeing, and cross-country skiing. Among the attractions of fall and winter visits is the absence then of mosquitoes and blackflies. Communities have a continued spraying program to keep them scarce, but out in the bush they keep you slapping unless you venture forth equipped with insect repellent.

1. The Gold Rush

There are two things you won't get away from as long as you linger in the territory: the Klondike gold rush and the verses of Robert W. Service. One produced the other, and they combined to imprint the image of the Yukon on the outside world as well as the permanent inhabitants. Nobody is more gung-ho on gold rush lore and Service ballads than the locals, which is the highest compliment you can pay a bard.

Service may not have been a great poet in the literary sense, but he was a tremendously evocative one, depicting landscapes, characters, and emotions the way his contemporaries *felt* them, stirring echoes in their souls that an academically more brilliant wordsmith may never have aroused. I attended a local reading of "The Spell of the Yukon" and saw dozens of oldtimers nodding their heads in fervent agreement with the lines—

> I wanted the gold, and I got it—
> Came out with a fortune last fall,
> Yet somehow life's not what I thought it,
> And somehow the gold isn't all.

These, I promise, will be the last Service stanzas I'll quote. But the point about "the gold isn't all" could be the motto of the Territory today. The gold is gone, give or take a few ounces, and the "spell of the Yukon" now lies in scenic grandeur, in the overwhelming friendliness of its people, and in the pervasive feeling that this is one of the last genuine frontier regions left on earth.

Still, gold *made* the Yukon because few people even knew of its existence before the mad scramble that was the greatest gold rush in recorded history. It began with a wild war whoop from the throats of three men—two Indians and one white—that broke the silence of the Klondike Valley on the morning of August 17, 1896: "Gold!" they screamed, "gold—gold—gold . . ." and that cry rang through the Yukon, crossed to Alaska, and rippled down into the United States. Soon the whole world echoed with it, and people as far away as China and Australia began selling their household goods and homes to scrape together the fare to a place few of them had ever heard of before.

Some 100,000 men and women from every corner of the globe set out on the Klondike stampede, descending on a territory populated by a few hundred souls. Tens of thousands came by the Chilkoot Pass from Alaska, the shortest route but also the toughest. Canadian law required each stampeder to carry 2000 pounds of provisions up over the 3000-foot summit. Sometimes it took 30 or more trips up a 45-degree slope to get all the baggage over, and the entire trail—with only *one* pack—takes about 3½ days to hike.

You can see amazing silent movies today showing the endless human chain scrambling up the steep incline in an unbroken line of black dots against the white snow. And you can still pick up some of the items they discarded en route—rotting boots, rusted horse's bits, tin mugs, and broken bottles. Many collapsed on the way, but the rest slogged on—on to the Klondike and the untold riches to be found there.

The riches were real enough. The Klondike fields proved to be the richest ever found anywhere. Before the big strike on Bonanza Creek, the handful of prospectors in the Territory had considered 10¢ worth of glitter per gold pan a reasonably good find—and gold was then valued at around $15 an ounce. But the Klondike stampeders were netting $300 to $400 in a single pan! What's more, unlike some gold which lies embedded in veins of hard rock, the Klondike stuff came in dust or nugget forms buried in creek beds. This placer gold, as it's called, didn't have to be milled—it was already in an almost pure state!

The trouble was that most of the clerks who dropped their pens and butchers who shed their aprons to join the rush came too late. By the time they had completed the back-breaking trip, all the profitable claims along the Klondike creeks were staked out and defended by grim men with guns in their fists. Claim jumping was the quickest way to harvest lead instead of nuggets.

But the stream of humanity kept surging in and within a few years the Territory had changed utterly. By 1898 a railroad was running from Skagway in Alaska across 110 miles of clifted and gorged wilderness to the tiny hamlet of Whitehorse. It stopped there and hasn't progressed an inch since. From Whitehorse the "Trail of '98" led to Dawson city, springboard of the Klondike, 333 miles to the north.

Almost overnight Dawson boomed into a roaring, bustling, gambling, whoring metropolis of 30,000 people, thousands of them living in tents (today the place has a few hundred permanents, plus 100,000 annual tourists). And here gathered those who made fortunes from the rush without ever handling a pan: the supply merchants, the saloon keepers, dance-hall girls and card-sharps. Also some oddly peripheral characters like bar room janitors, who "panned" the shavings they swept from the floors every night for the gold dust that had spilled to the ground. And a stocky 21-year-old former sailor from San Francisco who adopted a big mongrel dog in Dawson, then went home and wrote a book about him that sold half a million copies. The book was *The Call of the Wild* and the sailor Jack London.

By 1903 over $500 million in gold had been shipped south from the Klondike and the rush petered out. A handful of millionaires bought mansions in Seattle, tens of thousands went home with empty pockets, thousands more lay dead in unmarked graves along the Yukon River. Dawson—"City" no longer—became a dreaming backwater haunted by 30,000 ghosts.

But the railroad still runs from Skagway to Whitehorse, and you can ride it. And on Bonanza Creek one free claim is left open for tourists—you can sluice a pan there and peer for tiny flakes of yellow in what was once the richest paydirt on earth. You might be able to buy a drink for what you find.

2. Transportation

Perhaps the most striking contrast between the Yukon of the gold rush and ours is the ease of getting there. You can fly in, drive in, or sail in (by the Alaska

Ferry to Port Chilkoot). Or, if you want a really picturesque journey, take the **White Pass & Yukon Railway** from Skagway that runs through infamous Dead Horse Gulch and lets you retrace the footsteps of the stampeders in cushioned comfort at $35 per trip.

But the vast majority of visitors choose the air or road routes. **CP Air** has daily jet flights to Whitehorse from Vancouver and Edmonton, both costing $130, and from Whitehorse on to Dawson for $84.25. **Air Alaska** links Whitehorse with Fairbanks, Juneau, and Anchorage.

Coachways has bus services to Whitehorse from Vancouver and Edmonton at $90.30 and $73.20, respectively. Over 90,000 private motorists every year choose to drive in on the **Alaska Hwy.**, which starts at Dawson Creek in British Columbia, taking you right into Whitehorse, some 918 miles north. It's a fairly good road through some very dramatic scenery, but in summer the dust is a nuisance and you have to watch the flying gravel that pits windshields and headlights.

3. Whitehorse

The capital of the Yukon is a late arrival on the scene. She was only established in the spring of 1900, fully two years after the stampeders had swarmed into Dawson City. But Whitehorse, located on the banks of the Yukon River, is the logical hub of the Territory and became the capital after Dawson fizzled out together with the gold.

The city has a curiously split personality. On the one hand she's a frontier outpost with a mere 15,000 residents living within a ridiculously large 162-square-mile area. On the other hand the tourist influx gives her an almost cosmopolitan tinge: a whiff of nightlife, some smart boutiques, gourmet restaurants, and international hotels.

The **airport,** placed on a rise above the city, is fair in size but short of facilities: no restaurant, only a primitive snackbar, and no drinks available. Which is rather odd since the smaller airport at Yellowknife has bar service. A limousine takes you to the downtown hotels for $2.

The main street of Whitehorse is, you guessed it, **Main St.,** with four blocks of stores and a lot of traffic. The city's layout generally can't be faulted: all *streets* run vertically, the *avenues*—first to eighth—bisecting them horizontally, all *roads* running around the periphery. Public transit is handled by bright-green mini-buses which touch the suburbs surrounding downtown.

Main St. runs into First Ave. at the site of the White Pass & Yukon railroad station. Beyond the railroad tracks flows the **Yukon River.** A bridge crosses the river at the end of Second Ave. and to right of the bridge lies S.S. *Klondike,* one of the 250 sternwheelers that once plied the river between Whitehorse and Dawson City.

On the left of Second Ave., heading toward the bridge, stands the big and massive stone complex of the **Territorial Government Building.** One of the newest and best equipped structures of its kind in Canada, it conveniently houses all territorial government departments, the legislature, public library, Territorial Archives, as well as the **Tourism Branch information office.** The Federal Building, housing the post office, stands at the corner of Third Ave. and Main St.

ACCOMMODATIONS: Whitehorse has more than 20 hotels, motels, and chalets in and around the downtown area, including a couple just opposite the airport. This is far more than you'd expect in a place her size, and the accommodation standards come up to big-city levels in every respect. Rates, however, are higher than in the south—the city has practically no budget accommodations except in hostels.

Travelodge, Second Ave. and Wood St. (tel. 403/667-4211). Medium-sized and cozy, this representative of a national chain has one of the busiest lobbies in town, nicely fitted with deep leather armchairs and settees. There's a "mini-mall" alongside, housing gift, barber, and flower shops, plus a travel agency. The lodge has a combination dining room and coffeeshop, the most complete conference facilities in the Territory, and a very handsomely decorated cocktail lounge.

The 117 guest rooms come with color TV, radio, and dial telephones. Each is handily divided into two parts, the front portion containing the bathroom and a dressing table with lights framing the mirror, theater fashion, plus hanging spaces; the rear has the beds, writing desk, table, and armchairs. One wall is wood-paneled and the decor kept in deep-brown and russet hues.

Singles cost $42; doubles, $50. Children under 12 stay free with their parents.

Regina Hotel, 102 Wood St. (tel. 403/667-7801). One of the oldest establishments in the Yukon, completely rebuilt in 1970, the Regina stands beside the Yukon River and breathes territorial tradition. The exterior is rather plain and has a frontier look, but the innards are charming as well as spacious and lofty. The lobby is crowded with Old Yukon memorabilia, from hand-cranked telephones to moose antlers—also two somewhat incongruous oil paintings of Yugoslavian scenery. There's a nicely intimate dining room open seven days a week.

The 52 bedrooms give you plenty of elbow room besides such facilities as color TV and dial phones. The decor is tastefully simple, hanging spaces large, and you get a neat writing desk, dressing table, plus bedside and desk lamps. The bathrooms are fitted with heat lamps and electric ventilators.

Singles cost $39; doubles, $46.

Klondike Inn, 2288 Second Ave. (tel. 403/677-6301). An entertainment center as much as hotel, this large and attractively new building stands framed against wooded mountain ranges that give it a picture-postcard backdrop. The beautifully carpeted foyer is a hive of action, the clocks on the wall indicating the different times around Canada (judging by the clientele, they should be showing the times around the globe). The inn has an outstanding coffeeshop decorated with absorbing old gold-rush photos, upholstered wooden chairs, and wood chandeliers. (For the cabaret and cocktail lounge attractions, see my nightlife recommendations.)

The 100 guest rooms, medium-sized, have a warm, soothing decor of burnt orange and deep reds, plus color TV and dial phones. A low table is flanked by armchairs beneath a hanging lamp, and there's a smartly rustic writing desk, plus a smaller desk, twin bedside lamps, an abundance of drawers, and ultramodern bathrooms with electric ventilators.

Singles cost $39; doubles, $45. Children up to 12 years stay free in their parents' room.

Yukon Inn, 4220 Fourth Ave. (tel. 403/667-2527). Another of the town's entertainment hives, this establishment features a disco and cabaret lounge that draws swarms of "Yukon belles," most of whom come from somewhere else. The hotel also has a dining room, coffeeshop, and 47 large and very pleasant bedrooms. Altogether it keeps a nice balance between catering to house guests and nightlife patrons.

The room decor is a delightful powder blue, and you get color TV/radio, and dial phones. Furnishings include a large dressing table with drawers and mirror, a standing lamp flanked by comfortable armchairs, a bedside lamp, and a very spacious closet with folding door. Bathrooms have heat lamps (with automatic timers) and electric ventilators.

Singles cost $36; doubles, $43. Additional occupants pay $5 each.

Airline Inn, 16 Burns Rd. (tel. 403/668-4400), just across the road from the airport and brand new (opened in 1979), is one of the most attractive hostelries in town. The entire place is paneled in light woods, which give it the appearance of a mountain cabin. The upstairs cocktail lounge has a good view of the airport (you can see your plane taking off if you don't watch the clock). There's a small, very trim lobby with adjoining coffeeshop-restaurant, deeply carpeted stairs, and a staff that acts like a welcoming committee.

The 30 rooms have color TV and dial phones, furniture that matches the paneling, and small settees. The mottled and beige decor blends in nicely, and the whole impression is ultramodern but devoid of stiffness: hanging bedlights, writing desks, bathrooms with heat lamps. The limousine to downtown stops at the door.

You pay $38 for singles, $41 for doubles (no charge for children).

Taku Hotel, 4109 Fourth Ave. (tel. 403/668-4545), a small and neat hotel at the busiest downtown corner, has a minute lobby but large rooms, a fast-service coffeeshop, and a gift store. The 53 guest rooms are fitted with fluffy red carpets and good, standard, comfortable furniture. There are handy wall mirrors (which many hotels lack), bedside tables with maps, leather-upholstered metal chairs, and large closets behind folding doors. The bathrooms are fair sized, and the units come in pleasing brown and red shades.

Singles pay $32; doubles, $35 to $39, with additional occupants costing $4 each. Children under 12 stay free with their parents.

Edgewater Hotel, Main St. (tel. 403/667-2573). At the end of Main St., overlooking the river, this miniature hotel with only a dozen rooms has a distinct rustic charm of its own, plus an intriguingly contrasting dining room, the Cellar, with downright sumptuous appointments. The lobby and bedrooms are small and cozy. The rooms all have color TV and dial phones, one wall is wood paneled, and furnishings include writing desks with hanging lamps, excellent beds with twin reading lights, all kept in soft brown and green colors. The bathrooms are small but modern, but hanging space is insufficient for two persons.

Singles go for $32; doubles, $35; additional occupants pay $3. Young children stay free in their parents' room.

Ben-Elle Hotel, 411 Main St. (tel. 403/668-4500). Smallish, modern with a chalet-like frontage, the Ben-Elle has 41 guest rooms, 10 of them kitchenette units, plus a very good dining room and a tavern. The lobby is rather cluttered with vending machines and potted plants, but the rooms—furnished in different styles—are all attractive (no assembly line decor here). Each has color TV and telephone, and a fluorescently lit bathroom with electric ventilator. The rooms are surprisingly spacious with excellent drapes and carpeting, large open hanging space, bedside lamps, and dressing tables with fluorescent lights. The kitchenettes come fully equipped.

Singles run $30 to $46; doubles, $36 to $54; additional occupants pay $3.

New North Motel, 2141 Second Ave. (tel. 403/668-4646). This is one of Whitehorse's entertainment spots and therefore very thronged. Apart from a popular cabaret, the New North also has a restaurant, tavern, and coffeeshop—but no lobby. Of the 30 units, 10 have kitchenettes. All come with color TV and dial phones. The furnishings are not stylish, but sufficient. The kitchen units have their own dinettes, electric cooking ranges, refrigerators, and all necessary utensils.

Singles pay $30; doubles, $36; additional persons, $4.

MEALS: Whitehorse has a much greater variety of restaurants than hotels—you can get meals in every price range and quality. The top establishments measure up to any cuisine served in the south, and occasionally outshine them in hospitality and tender loving care. Food generally is more expensive here than in the provinces, and this goes for wine as well. Be happy you didn't come during the gold rush, when eggs sold for 25¢ each.

Monte Carlo, 404 Wood St. (tel. 667-2116), is a deceptively simple dining room run by a gastronomic fanatic named Régent who is determined to turn every meal into a memorable occasion. The cuisine is French, of course, and the establishment resembles a rather posh wine cellar, with a low white ceiling supported by slender pillars, upstairs and downstairs portions holding about 80 diners, and absolutely beautiful wall murals to match the artistry of the chef.

Pâté of goose liver with truffles ($4.50) is the ideal starter. The summer specialty of the house is fresh poached salmon with hollandaise sauce for $10. In the spring it's rack of lamb, in fall Alaska king crab. But at no time will you go wrong with the fondue bourguignonne ($11), one of the finest I've had outside Switzerland. With the main course comes a salad and choice of two soups: lobster bisque or French onion. Open six days till 11 p.m. Closed Sundays.

Charlie's is the dining room of the Klondike Inn (tel. 677-6301), named and decorated in honor of the fabulous entrepreneur who founded the Palace Grand Theatre in Dawson City during the gold rush (from his wall portrait he looks a little as if he *might* have sold somebody the Brooklyn Bridge). The place is decked out like a gaslight-age "entertainment palace," with red plush curtains, "gas" chandeliers, and curlicued alcoves. The foyer is festooned with wonderfully pompous Palace Grand production photos, including the "Tableau representing Great Britain and her Colonies at a Concert given in Aid of the widows and orphans created by the War with the Transvaal, February 15th, 1900."

Charlie Meadows must have been quite a gourmand, judging by the fare dished up in his honor: genuine turtle soup ($2.50), superb tournedos Rossini ($13.50), and concluding with a ($1.95) peach Melba that actually blends with the setting. Open seven days a week till 11:30 p.m.

Prospector Lounge, Third Ave. and Jarvis St., is equipped like a miner's cabin, in wondrous contrast to the cuisine—stampeders got such grub, maybe, *after* they went home with a pile. It's lined with raw planks papered with antique advertisements lauding mustache developers and cough syrups. The walls are hung with genuine prospector's gear—drills, shovels, pickaxes, pans, chains, and hammers—enough to outfit a minor gold rush, and it's lit by softly shaded lamps, permeated with gentle background music. A bar and lounge adjoin the small dining room.

You get superb Cornish game hen here ($13.95), preceded perhaps by escargots or the fresh oyster cocktail (both $4.95). The "jar o' beef" is a house specialty and quite unique: spiced morsels of beef that had been sealed in the old-fashioned style—you open the seal yourself (served only for two persons, at $28). The salad bar here is easily the best in town—eight varieties, including absolutely outstanding potato salad. For dessert, try the ice cream parfait with liqueur. Open seven nights a week till 1 a.m.

The **Travelodge Dining Lounge** (tel. 667-4211), is small, quite simple, and handsomely paneled in dark wood, with whirring fans on the ceiling and revolving black leather armchairs to sit on. Very popular and usually packed (it doesn't hold many tables), the Travelodge dining portion serves excellent dinners, including succulent pork tenderloin for $8.95, followed by fresh strawberries Romanoff, soaked in Grand Marnier, for $2.95.

But the pièce de résistance here is the outstanding Sunday brunch: a grand and picturesque spread of barbecued chicken, smoked salmon, assorted cold cuts, salads, pancakes, eggs, bacon, hash browns, etc. Not to speak of cold ham, sardines, melon slices, fruit and super-rich German chocolate cake. The whole splendor is yours for $5.95—perhaps the greatest gluttony bargain in the Territory.

The **Casca Dining Room** of the Ben-Elle Hotel (tel. 668-4500), divided into the modern coffeeshop and the more stylish restaurant, is named after the famous flagship of the Yukon River fleet, with one wall devoted to a mural of the old sternwheeler. Green drapes at the street windows match the green table linen. Flower vases, attractively arranged, give the place a cheerful welcome look. The menu presents a difficult choice between the crab legs ($12.50) and the salmon steak ($8.50). Try the fine and rich Spanish coffee in conclusion ($3.10). And the management provides toothpicks and peppermints as an afterthought.

Eddy's, T & M Hotel, 401 Main St. (tel. 668-5191), is an American-Chinese establishment, the cuisine divided into roughly equal ethnic parts. The premises, in turn, are divided into a coffeeshop and restaurant. The latter portion is small, simple, and attractive: chestnut-colored walls, wooden chairs, glass candleholders on the tables, and amber lights on the walls. The windows are discreetly curtained against the street. Hearty onion soup and delicious hot rolls come with the meal. On the Oriental side, the spare ribs are excellent at $7. Alternatively, try the grilled salmon for $8.50. Open six nights a week till 11 p.m., Sundays till 10 p.m.

Mr. Mike's, 4114 Fourth Ave. (tel. 667-2242), a steak cafeteria several rungs above the norm, with black and red decor, is a low wooden enclosure gently lit by hanging lamps. It has good carpeting, and charming photo blow-ups on the wall showing loving couples, kittens, and suchlike. The counter service is exceptionally pleasant, even in rush hours. Mike's also boasts a surprisingly extensive wine list, including the house "special blend" at $2.75 per carafe. Canadian beer costs a dollar. You get a five-ounce char-broiled steak, baked potato, garlic bread, and salad for $3.79. Open seven days a week till 11 p.m.

Shangri-La, 309 Jarvis St. (tel. 668-4824), is a hut-like affair proclaiming "genuine Chinese cuisine by superb chef." It has a very simple interior, low roofed, with a smiling golden dragon taking up one wall and a kind of Chinese portal at the entrance. The premises are brightly lit and the service is charmingly personalized. The pineapple sweet-and-sour boneless pork comes for $4.50, egg roll for $1. Chinese tea is 25¢, and one fortune cookie per customer is on the house. The hours are liberal: open daily from 5 p.m. to 3 a.m.

The **Airline Inn** dining room (tel. 668-4400), opposite the airport, has a menu studded with aviation terminology, based (possibly) on the preferences of flying folk. There's a navigator's choice consisting of strips of beef, egg, baby shrimps, and cheese for $3.95. Or the pilot's preference of broiled filet mignon rolled in cheese omelet and served with french fries for $5.95. The 737 oyster burger is served on homemade bread with a special sauce and potato chips for $3.50. Monday to Friday from 11:30 a.m. to 2 p.m., the inn puts on a remarkable economy buffet—$4, including salad bar. And on weekends there's a pretty hefty Sunday brunch for $4.50.

The **Grill** at the Taku Hotel (tel. 668-4545) is characteristic of Whitehorse's fast-food operations—spotless, very busy, impeccably courteous. The soups are hearty, the coffee weak, the menu very American with only one or two alien touches. English fish and chips ($3.75) is among them, a relatively rare treat in Whitehorse. You should also try the other rarity on the menu: homemade meat pie for $3.25.

There are two spots in Whitehorse serving specialties not generally available in the Territory. One is **Annabelle,** 7225 Seventh Ave. (tel. 668-2868), which features European fare but also lists several vegetarian dishes. Open six days a week. Closed Sundays. The other is **Christie's Place,** 208 Main St. (tel. 667-7671), offering mostly Italian fare, including a small range of pizzas, which you can eat on the premises or take out. Open seven days a week.

DAYTIME ATTRACTIONS: The **S.S. Klondike,** one of the 250 riverboats that chuffed up and down the Klondike River between 1898 and 1952, is now a permanently drydocked museum piece, anchored at the south end of Second Ave. The still faintly majestic paddlewheeler is fully restored to almost her former glory, and open to visitors till 5:30 p.m. daily. Free.

The **MacBride Museum** is a log-cabin museum on First Ave. at the corner of Steele St. Within the museum compound you'll also find Sam McGee's Cabin (read Service's poem on the cremation of same) and the old Whitehorse Telegraph Office. The museum is crammed with relics from the gold-rush era, and has a large display of Yukon wildlife. It's interesting material, but the presentation isn't a patch on the Yellowknife museum in the Northwest Territories. Open daily till 9 p.m. Admission is $1.25 for adults, 50¢ for children.

When Whitehorse got its first resident priest in 1900, he lived and held services in a tent. By the next spring the **Old Log Church** and rectory were built, and both are currently the only buildings of that date in town still in use. The Old Log Church is now officially a cathedral—the only wooden cathedral in the world—and contains artifacts on the history of all churches in the Yukon. Service every Sunday evening, closed Sunday morning. Open to all, six days a week till 9 p.m. Admission is $1 for adults, half price for children. It's on Elliott St. at Third Ave.

Log Skyscrapers are log cabins, three stories high, used as apartment buildings, possibly the only species of their kind anywhere. They're on Lambert St. at Third Ave.

Yukon River Cruise

You can take an exciting two-hour trip following the route of the Klondike stampeders through the white waters of Miles Canyon—with the difference that they did it in small and often leaky boats while you relax in the comfort of a modern, partly enclosed motor vessel. As you cruise along, amid rugged scenery, you hear the history of the area and the perils of the original river trip. The cruise leaves daily at 2 p.m. from Schwatka Lake, June 1 to September 15. Transportation to the dock is available from the Whitehorse Travelodge, and the price is $8 per person. Contact **Atlas Travel,** 208 Steele St. (tel. 667-7824).

The same agency also features a **Whitehorse–Miles Canyon Tour.** This includes a sightseeing jaunt through the city, touching all the attractions, then takes you over the canyon water route. The part-bus, part-boat excursion lasts 2½ hours and costs $9 per passenger.

AFTER DARK: The top-of-the-bill attraction in Whitehorse is the **Frantic Follies** (tel. 633-2514), a singing, dancing, clowning, and declaiming gold-rush revue that has become famous throughout the north. The show is a very entertaining melange of skits, music-hall drollery, whooping, high-kicking, garter-flashing cancan girls, sentimental ballads, and dead-pan corn, interspersed with rolling recitations of Robert Service's poetry (I told you you couldn't get away from him). A sister company, the Gaslight Follies, performs in Dawson. Shows nightly except Mondays at the Travelodge. For reservations, call 667-7824. Tickets are $7.50 for adults, $3 for children.

A number of Whitehorse's hotels provide nightly entertainment in their cocktail lounges. The Yukon Inn features a cabaret on the premises and, next door, the **Supermarket Disco,** with fairly furious action every night except Monday. The Klondike Inn has a tavern and two cocktail bars. One of them, the **Strappers Lounge,** puts on singers, bands, and instrumentalists. The **New North Motel** offers a very lively lounge with a good dance floor, a high-decibel band, and attractive vocalist.

CABS AND RENTAL CARS: Yellow Cabs (tel. 668-4811) charge $1.45 at flagfall, then 10¢ for every one-ninth of a mile. A ride to the airport comes to $4.55.

Automobiles are for rent at: **Tilden** (tel. 667-2521), **Avis** (tel. 668-2136), and **Whitehorse Motors** (tel. 667-7866).

4. Dawson City

Dawson is more of a paradox than a community today. From the biggest Canadian city west of Winnipeg it withered to practically a ghost town after the stampeders stopped stampeding. In 1953 the seat of territorial government was shifted to Whitehorse, which might have spelled the end of Dawson—but didn't. For now, every summer, the influx of tourists more than matches the stream of gold rushers in its heyday. And while they don't scatter quite as much coin, their numbers grow larger instead of smaller each season.

The reason for this is the remarkable preservation and restoration work done by Parks Canada. Dawson today is the nearest thing to an authentic gold-rush town the world has to offer (with most of the seamy side dry-cleaned out). You can drop in for a drink at the Eldorado bar, ramble past ornately false-fronted buildings for a flutter at the tables in Diamond Tooth Gertie's Casino, head down to the banks of the Klondike River and take the highway southeast that leads to the claim sites at Bonanza Creek. It's a dream package, downtown nostalgia, for anyone who has ever fantasized about exchanging the feel of subway tokens for the weight of nuggets in his palm.

You reach Dawson from Whitehorse by various routes. Catch a **Northward Airline** plane, which costs $84.25 for the one-hour hop. Or a **Norline** bus for $35. Or drive to Carcross, then take the Klondike Hwy. north, following roughly the historic trail of the '98-ers.

There are ten or more hotels, motels, and inns in Dawson for any number of overnight stops. A few sample rates: **Downtown Hotel** (tel. 403/993-5346), $17 to $29; **Gold City Motor Inn** (tel. 403/993-5542), $30 to $45; and **Gold Nugget Motel** (tel. 403/993-5445), $20 to $28.

As for Dawson's prime attractions, there's first of all—

The **Palace Grand Theatre,** King St. Built at the height of the stampede by "Arizona Charlie" Meadows, this luxuriously flamboyantly tasteless opera house / dance hall had its slam-bang gala première in July 1899. Fitted with a Hollywood western-style false front incongruously at odds with the raftered roof and kitchen chairs, it now serves as showcase for the famous Gaslight Follies featuring assorted period "meller drammers" during which you are

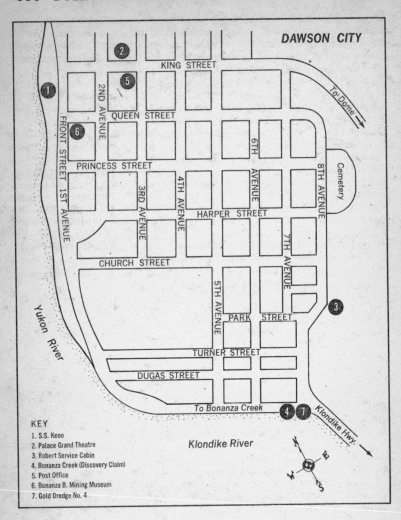

DAWSON CITY

KING STREET

2ND AVENUE

QUEEN STREET

FRONT STREET 1ST AVENUE

PRINCESS STREET

3RD AVENUE

4TH AVENUE

6TH AVENUE

8TH AVENUE

Cemetery

HARPER STREET

7TH AVENUE

CHURCH STREET

5TH AVENUE

Yukon River

PARK STREET

TURNER STREET

DUGAS STREET

To Bonanza Creek

Klondike Hwy.

To Dome

Klondike River

KEY
1. S.S. Keno
2. Palace Grand Theatre
3. Robert Service Cabin
4. Bonanza Creek (Discovery Claim)
5. Post Office
6. Bonanza B. Mining Museum
7. Gold Dredge No. 4

supposed to hiss the silk-cloaked villain and cheer the stalwart Mounted Police hero. Performances nightly except Monday.

Diamond Tooth Gertie's, Canada's only legal gambling casino (as distinct from charity operations), has an authentic gold-rush decor, from the shirt-sleeved honky-tonk pianist to the wooden floorboards. The games are black jack, roulette, crown and anchor; the minimum stakes are low, the ambience friendly rather than tense. There's a special high-stakes table for the bold and/or foolish. The establishment also puts on three floor shows nightly: a riotous row of cancan dancers with swishing skirts and lots of black-hosed leg work. Gertie's is in action five nights from 8 p.m., closed Sundays and Tuesdays.

The **Dawson City Museum** houses over 25,000 gold-rush artifacts, as well as displays of regional history and ethnology. Adjacent to the museum is **Minto Park,** where you can see an array of antique locomotives, including an old diamond stacker used in early mining operations. Open daily till 6 p.m. Admission for adults is $1, half price for children.

The **post office,** at the corner of King St. and Third Ave., has been completely restored to the way it was in 1900. Dawson originally had no post office, and in the early days of the rush, mail was handled by the North West Mounted Police in a tent. When the post office opened it was acclaimed a "miracle of the north" because mail usually arrived in one piece.

The **Robert Service Cabin,** Eighth Ave., is a two-room log cabin where the bard lived from 1909 to 1912. Set among trees on the lower slopes at the eastern end of town, the place today is the center of a permanent pilgrimage of Service admirers. They come to hear some of his most famous verses recited with suitable aplomb and in the right setting. In this cabin Service composed this third and final volume of *Songs of a Rolling Stone,* plus a middling awful novel entitled *The Trail of Ninety-Eight.* Oddly enough, the bard of the gold rush neither took part in nor even saw the actual stampede. Born in England, he didn't arrive in Dawson until 1908—as a bank teller—when the rush was well and truly over. He got most of his plots by listening to old prospectors in the saloons, but the atmosphere he soaked in at the same time was genuine enough—and his imagination did the rest.

S.S. Keno. Built in Whitehorse, now permanently berthed at the Dawson waterfront beside the Bank of Commerce, this high-structured riverboat dates from 1922. She was moved to her present site in 1960 and ran on a wood-burning boiler that supplied steam to the two engines that turned her stern wheel.

Klondike Era Films, St. Paul's Church and Front Sts., offers a cavalcade of wonderful antique films picturing the story of the gold rush and the history of gold mining, shown daily during the summer from 9 a.m. to 4:45 p.m.

Jack London's Cabin. Jack London lived in the Yukon less than a year—he left in June 1898 after a bout with scurvy—but his writings immortalized the north, particularly the animal stories like "White Fang," and "The Son of Wolf." Recitations from and about him are given daily at 11 a.m.

Discovery Claim, Bonanza Creek, is the spot, now marked by a National Historic Sites cairn, where George Carmack, Skookum Jim, and Tagish Charlie found the gold that unleashed the Klondike Stampede in 1896. They staked out the first four claims (the fourth partner, Bob Henderson, wasn't present). Within a week Bonanza and Eldorado Creeks had been staked out from end to end, but none of the later claims matched the wealth of the first. At Claim No. 17, just below Discovery, you can see one of the weird machines that ousted the hand-held pans. The huge ungainly elevator dredges were first used in New Zealand, and introduced in the Yukon in 1899. The one left in position is among the largest in North America and commenced operations in 1913. It could dig and sift 18,000 cubic yards in 24 hours, thus doing the work of an army of prospectors.

5. Kluane National Park

Tucked into the southwestern corner of the Yukon, two driving hours from Whitehorse, these 8500 square miles of glaciers, marches, mountains, and sand dunes are unsettled and virtually untouched wilderness. Bordering on Alaska in the west, Kluane contains Mt. Logan and Mt. St. Elias, respectively the second- and third-highest peaks in North America.

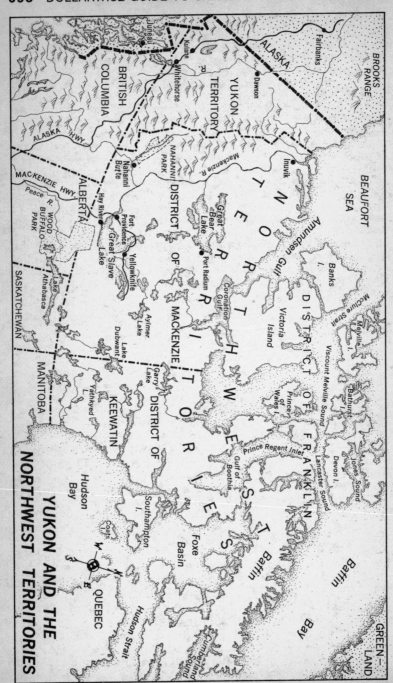

The park also contains an astonishing variety of wildlife. Large numbers of moose, wolves, red foxes, wolverines, lynx, otters, and beavers abound, plus black bears in the forested areas and lots of grizzlies in the major river valleys. The law makes it a serious offense to "feed or harass the bears," although personally I would love to see someone try to "harass" a grizzly.

6. Organized Tours and Excursions

Yukon Rafting, Dawson City (tel. 403/993-5391), offers a range of exciting river trips taking from 2½ hours to 14 days. The briefest excursion is an eight-mile jaunt in rubber rafts up the Klondike Valley to Bear Creek, costing $6 per rafter. The longest goes 570 miles on the Yukon River and costs $560 per person.

Goldrush River Tours, Whitehorse (tel. 403/667-7496), departs daily at 6 p.m. from the wharf at the foot of Strickland St. downtown. The 60-mile round trip on the Yukon includes a visit to historic Lake Laberge and a barbecued steak dinner at a river campsite. The entire tour takes 4½ hours. Adults pay $24.95; children under 12, $17.95.

Gateway Tours, Klondike Inn Hotel, Whitehorse (tel. 403/667-6115), has five "Adventure Tours" ranging from sightseeing trips around Whitehorse to excursions lasting four days and three nights, taking in Dawson City, Beaver Creek, parts of Kluane National Park, and the ghost town of Silver City at a cost of $247.50 per person.

Goldline Cruises, Dawson City (tel. 403/993-5331), has a Dawson City and gold field tour departing twice daily and costing $7.50 per person. Trips to the Midnight Dome, a famous lookout mountain affording a stunning view of Dawson, go twice daily and cost $3. Helicopter sightseeing jaunts that last 20 minutes can be arranged on request at $30 per passenger (minimum of four).

Atlas Travel, Travelodge, Whitehorse (tel. 403/667-7824), offers, among other choices, the "Gold Rush Air Excursion." You take a light aircraft to Dawson City, stop at Ft. Selkirk, sightsee, enjoy a river cruise and salmon bake, and drive to the top of the Midnight Dome, then return to Whitehorse. Accommodation is included in the price, from $199. The "Skagway Air-Rail Excursion" is a flight to Skagway, Alaska, by light aircraft over the Chilkoot Pass, overnight in Skagway, and return by the White Pass & Yukon Railway to Whitehorse. The tour takes two days and one night. Accommodations are included in the price of $188.90 (U.S.).

Appendix

PARLEZ-VOUS CANADIEN?

1. English-French Phrases
2. French-English Vocabulary

IN QUÉBEC, the French language is now the official language-of-state, and in other provinces of eastern Canada you'll encounter Canadians who speak French—perhaps they'll speak only French. Almost 40% of all New Brunswickers, for instance, look upon French as their mother tongue; Nova Scotia and Prince Edward Island have significant French-speaking populations, too. Sometimes the local dialect bears only a tenuous relationship to pure Parisian, and Québec French can even be different from the Acadian lingo in New Brunswick. But in any case, a few words of French will open doors and bring smiles in any situation. Here's a capsule vocabulary, including some words and phrases which are purely Canadian. For a more complete vade mecum of French phrases which can help you in virtually any situation, pick up *French for Travellers,* by Berlitz—the few dollars will be well spent.

1. English-French Phrases

		Pronunciation
Hello	**Bonjour**	bawn-zhoor
How are you?	**Comment allez-vous?**	kaw-maw tah-lay voo?
	Comment ça va?	kaw-maw sah vah?
Very well	**Très bien**	tray byen
Good-bye	**Bonjour, Au revoir**	bawn-zhure, oh ruh-voire
Yes, No	**Oui, Non**	wee, noh
Please	**S'il vous plaît**	seal voo play
Thank you	**Merci**	mare-see
Excuse me	**Pardon**	par-dohn
You're welcome	**De rien, Je vous en prie**	duh ree-en, zheh vooz ahn pree
What's this?	**Qu'est-ce que c'est?**	kess kah say?

English	French	Pronunciation
Where is . . .	Où se trouve . . .	oo suh troove . . .
the railroad station	la gare	lah gar
the bus station	la gare routière, la gare des autobuses	lah gar roo-tyere, lah gar days aw-toe-boos
an inexpensive restaurant	un restaurant bon marché	uh res-taw-rawn bawn mar-shay
the toilet	la toilette, la salle de bain	lah tawh-lette, lah sahl duh ban
Left, Right	Gauche, Droit	goh-sh, drwat
Straight ahead	Tout droit	too drwat
Here, There	Ici, Là (or là-bas)	ee-see, lah (or lah-bah)
Near, Far	Pres (or proche), loin	pray (or pow-sh), lwahn
North, South	Nord, Sud	nord, sewd
East, West	Est, Ouest	est, oo-est
Give me . . .	Donnez-moi . . .	duh-nay-mwah . . .
I would like . . .	Je voudrais . . .	zheh voo-dreh . . .
a menu	un menu	uh may-nyoo
breakfast	petit déjeuner	puh-tee day-zhuh-nay
lunch	déjeuner	day-zhuh-nay
dinner	dîner (souper)	dee-nay (soo-pay)
the check	l'addition	lah-dee-see-ohn
a receipt	un réçu	uh ray-soo
the price list	le tarif, la liste des prix	le tah-reef, lah leest day pree
a room	une chambre	oon shambruh
for one, two (persons)	pour une, deux (personnes)	poor oon, de (pair-son)
with . . . beds	avec . . . lits	ah-vek . . . lee
one double bed	un lit double	uh lee doo-bluh
a shower	avec douche	ah-vek doosh
a bathtub	avec salle de bain	ah-vek sahl duh ban
without bath	sans salle de bain	san sahl duh ban
for one night	pour une nuit	poor oon nwee
What does it cost?	Quel en est le prix?	kel ah nay le pree?
	Combien coûte-ça?	kom-byen koot-sah?
Do you have something cheaper?	Avez-vous quelque chose de meilleur marché?	ah-vay-voo kel-kuh shows duh may-ur marshay?
. . . something better?	. . . quelque chose de mieux?	. . . kel-kuh shows duh myuh?
Tax, Service charge	Taxe (or impôt), (frais de service	tax (or am-poh), (fray duh) sayr-veess
It's very expensive.	C'est très chère.	say tray share
How long?	Combien de temps?	kom-byen duh tah?
When, Which	Quand, Quel	kahn, kel
Now, later	Maintenant, apres	man-tuh-nah, ah-pray

	(or plus tard)	(or ploo tar)
Before, After	**Avant, Après**	ah-vahn, ah-pray
Yesterday, Today, Tomorrow	**Hier, Aujourd'hui, Demain**	ee-air, oh-zhoor-dwee, duh-man
Sunday	**Dimanche**	dee-mahnsh
Monday	**Lundi**	luhn-dee
Tuesday	**Mardi**	mar-dee
Wednesday	**Mercredi**	mare-kre-dee
Thursday	**Jeudi**	zhe-dee
Friday	**Vendredi**	vahn-dreh-dee
Saturday	**Samedi**	sam-dee

2. French–English Vocabulary

Ascenseur	Elevator
Autoroute	Expressway
À louer	For rent
À vendre	For sale
Bière à porter	Beer to go
Bière froide	Cold beer
Camion	Truck
Cantons de l'Est	Eastern Townships (Québec)
Caisse	Cashier
Car	Bus (sometimes car)
Casse-croûte	Snack
Chaud	Hot
Crème molle	Soft ice cream
Dames	Ladies
Dèfense de. . .	No. . .
entrer	Entry
fumer	Smoking
passer	Passing
stationner	Parking
toucher	Touching
Déjeuner (d'hommes d'affaires)	Businessman's lunch
Dépanneur	Convenience store
Dîner, souper	Dinner, supper
Entrée libre	Free entry ("Come on in!")
Epicerie	Grocery store
Escompte	Discount (sale)
Fermé	Closed
Gare	Railroad Station
Hôtel	Hotel, or hall (hôtel de ville—city hall)
Joual	Québec French dialect
Laurentides	Laurentians
Location de voitures	Car rentals
Messieurs	Gentlemen
Mets	Meals
Ouvert	Open
Pain de ménage	Homemade bread
Petit déjeuner	Breakfast
Poussez	Push
Remorquage à vos frais	(Cars) towed at your (owner's) expense
Soldes	Sale
Sortie	Exit
Stationnement (privé)	(Private) Parking
Terrain privé	Private property
Tirez	Pull
Zone de Remorquage	Tow-away Zone

1 un, une uh, oon
2 deux de
3 trois trwah
4 quatre katre
5 cinq sank
6 six seese
7 sept set
8 huit weet
9 neuf nuhf
10 dix deese
11 onze ohnze
12 douze dooz
13 treize trez
14 quatorze katorz

15 quinze kanz
16 seize sez
17 dix-sept deez-set
18 dix-huit deez-weet
19 dix-neuf deez-nuhf
20 vingt vant
21 vingt-et-un van-tay-uh
22 vingt-deux vant-de
30 trente trahnt
31 trente-un trahnt-uh
40 quarante karahnt
50 cinquante sankahnt
60 soixante swahsahnt
70 soixante-dix swahsahnt-

deese
71 soixante-onze
swahsahnt-ohnze
80 quatre-vingts katre-
vant
81 quatre-vingt-un katre-
vant-uh
90 quatre-vingt-dix katre-
vant-deese
91 quatre-vingt-onze
katre-vant-onze
100 cent sahnt
200 deux cents de sahnt

THE FROMMER/PASMANTIER PUBLISHING CORP.
380 MADISON AVE., NEW YORK, NY 10017   Date_____

Friends, please send me (postpaid) the books checked below:

$-A-DAY GUIDES
(In-depth guides to low-cost tourist accommodations and facilities.)

☐ Europe on $15 a Day	$6.95
☐ Australia on $20 a Day	$4.95
☐ England and Scotland on $20 a Day	$5.95
☐ Greece and Yugoslavia on $15 & $20 a Day	$4.95
☐ Hawaii on $25 a Day	$4.95
☐ Ireland on $15 a Day	$4.95
☐ Israel on $15 & $20 a Day	$4.95
☐ Mexico and Guatemala on $10 & $15 a Day	$5.95
☐ New Zealand on $15 and $20 a Day	$4.95
☐ New York on $20 a Day	$4.95
☐ Scandinavia on $20 a Day	$4.95
☐ South America on $15 a Day	$4.95
☐ Spain and Morocco (plus the Canary Is.) on $10 & $15 a Day	$4.95
☐ Turkey on $10 and $15 a Day	$4.50
☐ Washington, D.C. on $25 a Day	$4.95

DOLLARWISE GUIDES
(Guides to tourist accommodations and facilities from budget to deluxe, with emphasis on the medium-priced.)

☐ Egypt	$4.95	☐ Canada	$6.95
☐ England & Scotland	$5.95	☐ Caribbean (incl. Bermuda &	
☐ France	$5.95	the Bahamas)	$6.95
☐ Germany	$4.95	☐ California & Las Vegas	$4.95
☐ Italy	$4.95	☐ New England	$4.95
☐ Portugal (plus Madeira &		☐ Southeast & New Orleans	$4.95
the Azores)	$4.95		

THE ARTHUR FROMMER GUIDES
(Pocket-size guides to tourist accommodations and facilities in all price ranges.)

☐ Athens	$2.50	☐ Los Angeles	$2.50
☐ Boston	$2.50	☐ Mexico City/Acapulco	$2.50
☐ Honolulu	$2.50	☐ New York	$2.50
☐ Ireland/Dublin/Shannon	$2.50	☐ Paris	$2.50
☐ Las Vegas	$2.50	☐ Rome	$2.50
☐ Lisbon/Madrid/Costa del Sol	$2.50	☐ San Francisco	$2.50
☐ London	$2.50	☐ Washington, D.C.	$2.50

Special Editions

☐ The Caribbean Bargain Book $6.95

(Guide to "off-season" Caribbean—mid-April to mid-December—and the resorts that slash rates 20% to 60%; includes the Bahamas.)

☐ Where to Stay USA $4.95

(Guide to accommodations in all 50 states, from $3 to $20 per night.)

Include 60¢ for first book, 25¢ for each additional book for postage and handling.

Enclosed is my check or money order for $ _____

NAME _____

ADDRESS _____

CITY _____ STATE _____ ZIP _____